Dear West Customer:

West Academic Publishing has changed the look of its American Casebook Series®.

In keeping with our efforts to promote sustainability, we have replaced our former covers with book covers that are more environmentally friendly. Our casebooks will now be covered in a 100% renewable natural fiber. In addition, we have migrated to an ink supplier that favors vegetable-based materials, such as soy.

Using soy inks and natural fibers to print our textbooks reduces VOC emissions. Moreover, our primary paper supplier is certified by the Forest Stewardship Council, which is testament to our commitment to conservation and responsible business management.

The new cover design has migrated from the long-standing brown cover to a contemporary charcoal fabric cover with silver-stamped lettering and black accents. Please know that inside the cover, our books continue to provide the same trusted content that you've come to expect from West.

We've retained the ample margins that you have told us you appreciate in our texts while moving to a new, larger font, improving readability. We hope that you will find these books a pleasing addition to your bookshelf.

Another visible change is that you will no longer see the brand name Thomson West on our print products. With the recent merger of Thomson and Reuters, I am pleased to announce that books published under the West Academic Publishing imprint will once again display the West brand.

It will likely be several years before all of our casebooks are published with the new cover and interior design. We ask for your patience as the new covers are rolled out on new and revised books knowing that behind both the new and old covers, you will find the finest in legal education materials for teaching and learning.

Thank you for your continued patronage of the West brand, which is both rooted in history and forward looking towards future innovations in legal education. We invite you to be a part of our next evolution.

Best regards,

Louis H. Higgins
Editor in Chief, West Academic Publishing

CASES AND MATERIALS ON
THE DEATH PENALTY

Third Edition

■ ■ ■

By

Nina Rivkind

Lecturer, Berkeley Law (Boalt Hall)
University of California, Berkeley

Steven F. Shatz

Philip and Muriel Barnett Professor
University of San Francisco

AMERICAN CASEBOOK SERIES®

WEST®

A Thomson Reuters business

Mat #40776725

American Casebook Series is a trademark registered in the U.S. Patent and Trademark Office.

© West, a Thomson business, 2001, 2005
© 2009 Thomson Reuters
    610 Opperman Drive
    St. Paul, MN 55123
    1–800–313–9378
Printed in the United States of America

ISBN: 978–0–314–19956–0

This book is dedicated to our mothers

Marsha F. Rivkind
Fae C. Shatz

and to the memory of our fathers

Julius Rivkind
Gilbert F. Shatz

who, by their example, taught us to pursue justice.

*

PREFACE

The work on the first edition of this book began nineteen years ago when Nina first put together a set of materials to teach a new course in the death penalty at the University of San Francisco School of Law (U.S.F.). Those materials evolved in subsequent classes taught by Nina at U.S.F. and then at Berkeley Law (Boalt Hall) and by Steve at U.S.F. and eventually became a casebook, now in its third edition. This edition contains nine new cases and a number of updated notes and problems, incorporating changes in death penalty law over the last four years.

The book reflects our conviction that a successful casebook is one which presents students with a clear structure, a context within which to place the cases and cases that trace the development of legal principles and stimulate critical thinking. Each chapter begins with an introduction to give context to the cases and to outline the issues to be explored. Because we believe that the cases should be the main focus in a casebook, we present the principal cases in relatively full form. We have eschewed encyclopedic notes relating the holdings of other cases and quoting from secondary sources in favor of a limited number of notes and problems raising issues for discussion. We include several extended notes that synthesize the writings and empirical research of other scholars. We also have incorporated some articles from the popular press to connect the Supreme Court doctrines to the real world application of the death penalty. We have eliminated many citations and footnotes from the judicial opinions without so specifying, and we have simplified the citations we include by omitting pinpoint page cites. Numbered footnotes are from the original materials; lettered footnotes are ours.

The issue of the death penalty evokes strong opinions from academics as well as from the public at large. We are no exception. As our experience representing death row prisoners and our other writing in the field would suggest, we are strongly opposed to the use of the death penalty, certainly as it is administered in the United States today. Nonetheless, we believe that it is not appropriate, nor ultimately effective, to use our position as teachers and casebook authors to argue our personal views. Accordingly, we have made every effort to present the material in the book in a neutral fashion in the hope that the material itself will stimulate a broad and critical discussion of the issues.

We want to express our gratitude to those teachers who have used the previous editions in their classes and have given us encouraging feedback and helpful suggestions and to the students in our classes at Berkeley Law and

U.S.F., whose positive response to the course and the previous editions guided us in shaping this edition.

NINA RIVKIND
STEVEN F. SHATZ

August 2009

Summary of Contents

PART 5. THE DEATH PENALTY RECONSIDERED

TABLE OF CONTENTS

———————

TABLE OF CASES

The principal cases are in bold type. Cases cited or discussed in the text are in roman type. References are to pages. Cases cited in principal cases and within other quoted materials are not included.

CASES AND MATERIALS ON
THE DEATH
PENALTY

Third Edition

*

Part 1

Introduction to the Course

∎ ∎ ∎

The course in death penalty law is a course in the Supreme Court's interpretation and application of the Constitution, particularly the Eighth Amendment, to regulate the use of capital punishment in the United States. The Court's death penalty cases raise interrelated questions of substance and process. The Court has been asked to decide what elements constitutional death penalty schemes should contain and how they should operate. The Court also has had to address what role the courts (as opposed to the political branches), and particularly the Supreme Court (as opposed to the lower courts), should play in the administration of the death penalty.

The book is divided into five parts. Part 1 introduces the course with background information about the death penalty and with the Supreme Court's seminal cases on the death penalty. Part 2 contains the Supreme Court's elaboration of its seminal cases through consideration of challenges to various aspects of death penalty schemes. Part 3 considers the litigation of a capital case through an examination of the Supreme Court's constitutional decisions regarding the process as a whole—jury selection, the role of the defendant and defense counsel and the conduct of the prosecutor—and the penalty phase of the case in particular. Part 4 concerns issues arising after the death judgment, particularly, federal habeas corpus review and the execution itself. Part 5 reconsiders the role of the death penalty in the United States from the perspectives of international norms and critiques suggesting that the death penalty system is broken.

CHAPTER 1

INTRODUCTION

■ ■ ■

This chapter introduces the death penalty in the United States with material raising the question why the United States should or should not have a death penalty and to whom it should be applied (Section A) and with material on the history of the death penalty, including two death penalty decisions of the Supreme Court antedating the Court's landmark 1972 decision in *Furman v. Georgia* [Chapter 2] (Section B).

A.   WHY THE DEATH PENALTY?

This section introduces the death penalty, through consideration of the facts of an individual case in "The Crime, the Criminal and the Punishment: *People v. Manuel Babbitt*." Whether there should be a death penalty is then explicitly addressed in *An Outline of Arguments For and Against the Death Penalty*.

THE CRIME, THE CRIMINAL AND THE PUNISHMENT: *PEOPLE v. MANUEL BABBITT*

During the night of December 18/19, 1980, Leah Schendel, a 78–year–old woman, was assaulted and killed in her Sacramento, California apartment. The following evening, Mavis W. was assaulted and robbed in Sacramento. After reading about the attack on Schendel and discovering a lighter with the initials "LS" in his brother Manuel's possession, William Babbitt contacted the police and assisted them in arresting Manuel.[1]

---

1. At the time, the police promised William and Manuel that Manuel would get psychiatric help and would not be executed. ("You know you're not going to go to the gas chamber or anything like that." "[Y]ou're not gonna spend the rest of your life in jail. I'm sure. . . . I'm sure you realize that you don't have to worry about that. Definitely there's gonna be a few years ah . . . in your life that's going to have to be spent in an institution whether it's in a penal institution or a mental institution.")

The Crimes[2]

Defendant did not dispute that he committed the charged offenses, but in both the Schendel and the W. cases he asserted the defenses of diminished capacity and unconsciousness.

A. The Schendel Case.

Leah Schendel lived in the Sacramento Manor, a senior citizen's complex located on North Manor Drive in Sacramento. On the evening of December 18, 1980, she dined out with relatives and returned to her apartment about 11 p.m. That same evening, Vernon McMaster, her next door neighbor, went to bed at his usual time between 10:30 and 11 p.m. He awoke sometime between 2 and 4 a.m. While lying in bed he heard a noise like a "thud or a thump" in Ms. Schendel's apartment. After that he did not hear anything. He then heard the television go on. McMaster lay awake in response to the noises for about an hour.

The next morning, December 19, Edna Smith, Leah Schendel's neighbor on the other side, checked on Ms. Schendel at McMaster's urging. The screen door to Ms. Schendel's apartment had been cut or broken and the main door was open. The television was on, but the sound was turned down. Receiving no response when she called Ms. Schendel's name, Ms. Smith called John Balvin, the resident manager of the complex. Ms. Smith had been up until 2 a.m. the previous night and had heard nothing except Ms. Schendel arriving home from dinner about 11 p.m.

When Balvin entered Ms. Schendel's apartment, he found the furniture in disarray. Ms. Schendel's body was on the bedroom floor, covered from the waist up with a mattress or box springs. After determining that Ms. Schendel was dead, Balvin called the police.

The police arrived and secured the apartment. The apartment screen door had been ripped near the latch, apparently by a sharp instrument rather than a hand or finger. The apartment appeared to have been ransacked. The television set was turned on to channel 40, but there was no sound. Playing cards, broken dentures, and some pieces of glass were on the living room floor. A purse was on the floor. A knife was beside the television set. There was blood on the living room and kitchen floors, on the inside portion of the screen door, and on the doorway of the bedroom. Drawers and other items were scattered all over the bedroom.

When the mattress was removed from Ms. Schendel's body, it was noted that she was nude from the waist down. Her nightgown and pajama top were pulled above her breast area. A tea kettle was sitting on top of her pubic area, a leather strap was tied to her left ankle, an electrical cord lay across the lower part of her legs. A pillow by her head was heavily soaked with blood.

---

2. The description of the crimes is excerpted from the California Supreme Court's opinion in *People v. Babbitt*, 755 P.2d 253 (Cal. 1988).

According to the pathologist, Leah Schendel died from a heart attack brought on by a severe beating and possible suffocation. She also showed signs of possible rape. Her body had suffered numerous lacerations and abrasions. Had Ms. Schendel not suffered from coronary disease, and had she not experienced physical and psychological stress caused by fright, the struggle, and pain from her wounds, the physical blows she received would not of themselves have proved fatal.

Defendant's fingerprints and palmprints were found on the handle of the tea kettle and on other items strewn about the apartment. Articles missing from the apartment were subsequently found among defendant's belongings.

B.   The Mavis W. Assault.

About 10:30 or 11 p.m. on December 19, 1980, Mavis W. was returning to her home on 63d Avenue in Sacramento in her new Volkswagen Dasher automobile. As she approached her driveway she noticed defendant walking slowly by her house. When she turned into her driveway, defendant stopped, turned around, and looked at her.

As Mrs. W. alighted from her car, defendant grabbed her from behind. He demanded her car, but Mrs. W. threw the keys up the driveway. Defendant dragged Mrs. W. behind some bushes and struck her until she lost consciousness. When she regained consciousness, she was lying on her back and defendant was attempting to pull off her pants. Mrs. W. again lost consciousness.

Julie W., Mavis W.'s daughter, was visiting her mother's house the evening of December 19th, as was George Iwamura. When George left the house to go home he saw defendant running across the neighbors' lawn. He also saw Mrs. W. lying on the lawn near the neighbors' house. George ran back to Mrs. W.'s house, told Julie, and called the police.

Julie found her mother lying unconscious on the grass, blood on her face and her clothing. Mrs. W. was nude from the waist down. Her purse was on the ground, its contents strewn about the yard. Taken from Mrs. W. were a silver pendant, money, a silver ring, and a gold watch with a gold band.

The Criminal[3]

Manuel Babbitt was born on May 3, 1949, the sixth of eight children of poverty-stricken immigrants from Cape Verde, a possession of Portugal peopled by former slaves of mixed Portuguese and African descent. The family lived in the poorest part of a poor New England town, in a house without plumbing or central heating, and they depended heavily on welfare for their survival. As a child, Babbitt was discriminated against by other children because of his race, and he was ridiculed for his poverty. Babbitt's father was a brutal alcoholic who regularly beat his wife and

---

3. The facts are taken from the defendant's clemency petition. Not all of the facts set forth here were presented to the jury that sentenced him.

children when he was home but often abandoned them for long periods of time. There was also a pervasive strain of mental illness in the family. Four of the eight children were ultimately hospitalized for psychiatric disabilities, and others exhibited symptoms of mental illness. At least five other close relatives also were hospitalized for mental illness. Several of Babbitt's close relatives committed suicide, and Babbitt's mother attempted suicide on more than one occasion in front of the children. Babbitt's father and a number of close relatives were hospitalized for alcoholism.

On December 30, 1961, when Manuel Babbitt was 12 years old, he was hit by a car while riding a bicycle. He suffered a severe cerebral concussion. After a lengthy hospitalization he returned home, but he was noticeably slower mentally, unable to make decisions and fearful of making wrong decisions. At trial, the defense psychologist testified that Babbitt suffered from both functional and organic brain damage and psychomotor epilepsy, possibly caused by the head injuries he suffered in the accident. Babbitt struggled in school and, when he left school at 17 years old, he was only in the seventh grade and was functionally illiterate.

On June 1, 1967, Manuel Babbitt enlisted in the Marines Corps. Babbitt failed the intelligence test, but the Marine recruiter gave him a second chance, walking him through the test and answering those questions he could not. By all accounts Babbitt flourished in the Marines. His physical strength, his loyalty, his desire to do the right thing for others were positive attributes in the military. In a structured setting, he was part of a team with clearly defined goals and direction. He had clean clothing, a place to sleep, regular meals, and no decisions were required, just obedience. By the time he was sent to Vietnam, he had been promoted to Lance Corporal.

On December 2, 1967, Manuel Babbitt landed in Vietnam. He was immediately thrown into battle, and three weeks later he suffered a dissociative episode under the stress and was found wandering around aimlessly with complete amnesia for 20 hours. In January, he was sent to Khe Sanh, and there he suffered through a 77 day siege that marked one of the most intense ground battles of the war. The Marines were surrounded by North Vietnamese and endured round-the-clock shelling. They lived in a constant state of fear, waiting and watching for the next attack; one moment a group would be working, and the next moment several of them would be blown up. A chaplain described the conditions as follows:

> The base was overcrowded to begin with, and the constant shelling made it necessary for everyone to spend long hours inside a warren of bunkers and trenches. We went for two to three days at a stretch without any water and there was never water for washing. The heavy rains turned the landscape into oozing red mud that seemed to blend with the blood of the dead and wounded. * * * The trenches were filled with the stench of mold and urine, and the troops' clothes rotted off of them. But one of the worst things we had to contend with were

the rats. They were immense and they were everywhere * * * chewing on anything with food particles in it, including human hair.

On March 17, 1968, Babbitt was wounded, and he was evacuated. He was returned to Khe Sanh a week later. In the estimate of his fellow Marines, Babbitt did his job well. During a bombardment, Babbitt saved another Marine by getting him from the open road into a trench line just before artillery hit the spot where they had been. After the lifting of the siege at Khe Sanh, Babbitt fought in a number of other actions and even extended his tour of duty. In August, 1969, he returned on a permanent basis to the United States. He had served in five major campaigns and earned the rank of Corporal. He was awarded the National Defense Service Medal, Vietnam Service Medal, Vietnam Campaign Medal, Combat Action Ribbon, Presidential Unit Citation with palm, the Cross of Gallantry and the Purple Heart.

Shortly after his return to the United States, Manuel Babbitt began to deteriorate and to drink and take drugs. He could not hold a job, and he would either wander about aimlessly or withdraw in depression. In 1972, he was convicted of burglary, and, in 1973, he was convicted of the armed robbery of two gas stations and sent to the Bridgewater State Hospital for the Criminally Insane, where he was kept until his release in October 1975. The physician's Admission Note stated, in part:

> Patient is confused, irrational in his responses, somewhat confused, depressed, overactive, hostile, silly and inappropriate. Patient feels that he gets vibrations from the guards. Patient has a memory problem, he has a strange laugh and most probably hallucinating. He has a history of periods of depressions and drug use. Diagnosis: Schizophrenic Reaction, Paranoid Type. He shows tendencies toward self-destruction.

During this time he made several attempts at suicide. A petition for intensive psychiatric treatment was filed on Babbitt's behalf but was denied, and he was discharged. After his release, Babbitt fathered two children with a woman who became his common-law wife. In 1976, Babbitt's mental health again deteriorated. He was paranoid and unpredictable and roamed the streets at night talking to himself. In 1979, Babbitt was arrested for sexual assault on a 13–year–old girl, but the case was dismissed for insufficient evidence. In 1980, he was arrested for sexual assault of a prostitute, but he was acquitted. At the time, people in Babbitt's neighborhood considered him to be crazy. Dressed in military garb, Babbitt prowled the streets after midnight, babbling incoherently and at times taking cover as if in a war.

Manuel Babbitt then moved to Sacramento, California to live with his brother. His bizarre behavior continued, and he returned to using alcohol and drugs as a way of coping with his demons. He often spoke of suicide. At Babbitt's trial, the defense psychologist diagnosed Babbitt as suffering from Post Traumatic Stress Disorder. On the evening of December 18, 1980, the city of Sacramento was enveloped in a dense fog. Babbitt had been drinking and smoking marijuana. According to Babbitt, the last thing that he remembered was seeing headlights approaching him through the fog as he tried to cross a road near Leah Schendel's apartment. He said the headlights reminded him of aircraft approaching the airstrip at Khe Sanh for landing.

The Punishment

Manuel Babbitt was convicted by the jury of the first degree murder, robbery and attempted rape of Leah Schendel and the burglary of Ms. Schendel's apartment, and of the robbery and attempted rape of Mavis W. The jury also found the murder to have occurred in the course of burglary, robbery and rape. In a separate proceeding, the jury found that Babbitt was sane. At the penalty phase, the jury imposed the sentence of death. The California Supreme Court affirmed Babbitt's conviction and sentence and denied Babbitt's petition for habeas corpus (*People v. Babbitt*, 755 P.2d 253 (Cal.1988), *cert. den.* 488 U.S. 1034, 109 S.Ct. 849 (1989)), and the federal courts denied Babbitt's petition for federal habeas corpus. *Babbitt v. Calderon*, 151 F.3d 1170 (9th Cir.1998), *cert. den.* 525 U.S. 1159, 119 S.Ct. 1068 (1999).

Manuel Babbitt sought clemency from Governor Gray Davis. Veterans' organizations and marines who had served with him in Vietnam strongly supported Babbitt's clemency petition. The petition was opposed by members of Leah Schendel's family, who urged the governor to let the execution go forward. The victim's son said, "The guy's going to die—and I hope he suffers like my mother did." On April 30, 1999, Governor Davis, himself a Vietnam veteran, denied the clemency petition, saying, "countless people have suffered the ravages of war, [but] such experiences cannot justify or mitigate the savage beating and killing of defenseless, law-abiding citizens. * * * As difficult and unsettled as Mr. Babbitt's childhood, military service and return to civilian life may have been, such harsh life experience is not the type of mitigation sufficient to grant clemency for a brutal capital crime." On May 4, 1999, Babbitt was executed by lethal injection.

AN OUTLINE OF ARGUMENTS FOR AND AGAINST THE DEATH PENALTY

The literature on the death penalty in America is voluminous. Since the reintroduction of the death penalty after the Supreme Court's decision in *Furman v. Georgia*, 408 U.S. 238, 92 S.Ct. 2726 (1972), the debate over the use of the death penalty has been described and explored in dozens of books, hundreds of journal articles and thousands of articles in the popular press. The following is a necessarily brief outline of the principal arguments of death penalty supporters and opponents. The arguments fall into three broad categories: arguments about the morality of the death penalty and the appropriateness of retribution, arguments about the utility of the death penalty in terms of crime prevention, and arguments about reliability and fairness, *i.e.*, the practical consequences of employing the death penalty given the realities of the American criminal justice system.[1] Underlying all of these arguments is a fundamental question about how the death penalty compares to other punishments: Is the death penalty qualitatively different from other punishments and, therefore, required to meet a higher standard of justification?

Morality

Focusing on the question of the morality of the death penalty necessarily requires setting aside utilitarian claims and assuming, *arguendo*, that the penalty is reliably and fairly applied to punish "those offenders who commit 'a narrow category of the most serious crimes' and whose extreme culpability makes them 'the most deserving of execution.' "[2] The morality debate has both religious and non-religious dimensions. Those death penalty supporters who base their support on religious texts principally rely on the Old Testament, which prescribes the death penalty for a number of crimes[3] and endorses the principle of *lex talionis*, "an eye for an eye."[4] Christian death penalty supporters also find some support for the death penalty in the New Testament, generally in Romans 13:1–7 (injunction to obey rulers, who carry the sword and inflict avenging wrath on the wrongdoer) and in the writings of early and medieval church scholars.[5] Religious opponents of the death penalty argue that the Old Testament death penalty was drastically limited by oral traditions and the rabbinic writings of the First and Second Centuries which erected strin-

---

1. Although the arguments are presented as a binary choice, individuals' views about the death penalty fall on a continuum from support for the death penalty in its present form to opposition to the death penalty in any form. And, while the arguments are presented in three discrete categories, individuals may view the categories as interconnected, *e.g.*, that the morality of the death penalty may depend on its utility and the reliability and fairness of its administration.

2. *Roper v. Simmons*, 543 U.S. 551, 568, 125 S.Ct. 1183, 1194 (2005) quoting *Atkins v. Virginia*, 536 U.S. 304, 319, 122 S.Ct. 2242, 2251 (2002).

3. It has been estimated that there are at least 36 capital crimes, including, in addition to murder, adultery, working on the sabbath and being an unruly child. See S. Levine, *Capital Punishment in Jewish Law and its Application to the American Legal System: A Conceptual Overview*, 29 St. Mary's L.J. 1037, 1042 (1998) (citing Moses Maimonides).

4. Lev. 24:20; Exod. 21:24. "Whoever takes the life of any human being shall be put to death." Lev. 24:17. The debate in this country has taken place within the dominant Judeo–Christian tradition. For that reason, the views of minority religions in the United States, *e.g.*, Buddhism, Islam, are not explored here.

5. For example, Thomas Aquinas wrote:

"Now every individual person is compared to the whole community, as part to whole. Therefore if a man is dangerous and infectious to the [others], on account of some sin, it is praiseworthy and advantageous that he be killed in order to safeguard the common good, since a little leaven corrupted the whole lump.

"By sinning man departs from the order of reason, and consequently falls away from the dignity of his manhood, in so far as he is naturally free, and exists for himself, and he falls into the slavish state of the beasts, to be disposed of according as he is useful to others ... Hence, although it be evil in itself to kill a man so long as he preserve his dignity, yet it may be good to kill a man who has sinned, even as it is to kill a beast."

Summa Theologica II, reprinted in F. de Vitoria, Reflection on Homicide & Commentary on Summa Theologiae IIa–IIae q. 64, 240–241 (John P. Doyle trans., 1997).

gent procedural and evidentiary barriers to its use,[6] and Christian death penalty opponents argue that the New Testament message is inconsistent with a death penalty and particularly cite Jesus's explicit rejection of *lex talionis* (Matthew 5:38–42) and his intervention to prevent the execution of an adultress (John 8:4–11). At present, most of the major religious groups in the United States have taken a position against the death penalty.[7]

In its non-religious dimension, death penalty supporters draw on the arguments of philosophers, particularly Immanuel Kant, to argue that retribution, giving the criminal his or her "just deserts," justifies the death penalty for murderers. According to Kant, the only justification for punishment and the measure of punishment is the principle of equality:

> It is just the Principle of Equality, by which the pointer of the Scale of Justice is made to incline no more to the one side than the other. It may be rendered by saying that the undeserved evil which anyone commits on another, is to be regarded as perpetrated on himself. Hence it may be said: 'If you slander another, you slander yourself; if you steal from another, you steal from yourself; if you strike another, you strike yourself; if you kill another, you kill yourself.' This is the Right of RETALIATION (*jus talionis*); and properly understood, it is the only Principle which * * * can definitely assign both quality and quantity of a just penalty.[8]

In fact, as John Stuart Mill argued, imposing the death penalty on murderers is moral precisely because it demonstrates the state's regard for the value of life.

---

6. S. Levine, *Capital Punishment in Jewish Law and Its Application to the American Legal System: A Conceptual Overview*, 29 St. Mary's L.J. 1037, 1045 (1998). A similar process seems to have occurred in the Islamic tradition. Although the Qur'an absorbs the Old Testament into Islamic law and acknowledges the concept of *lex taliones* (5:44–45), "[w]orking with the micro-details and technicalities of the law, Muslim jurists challenged the discretion of the state and made it difficult for the state to carry out the death penalty." K. Abou El Fadl, *The Death Penalty, Mercy, and Islam: A Call for Retrospection*, in E. Owens, J. Carlson & E. Elshtain (eds), Religion and the Death Penalty (2004), 77–78.

7. In the encyclical, *Evangelium Vitae* (The Gospel of Life), Pope John Paul II set out the position of the Roman Catholic Church, stating that execution is only appropriate "in cases of absolute necessity, in other words, when it would not be possible otherwise to defend society. Today, however, as a result of steady improvement in the organization of the penal system, such cases are very rare, if not practically nonexistent." Representative of the Protestant position is this statement by the United Methodist Church:

"In spite of a common assumption to the contrary, an eye for an eye and a tooth for a tooth, does not give justification for the imposing of the penalty of death. Jesus explicitly repudiated the lex talionis (Matthew 5:38–39) and the Talmud denies its literal meaning, replacing it with financial indemnities.

"The United Methodist Church cannot accept retribution or social vengeance as a reason for taking human life. It violates our deepest belief in God as the creator and the redeemer of humankind. In this respect, there can be no assertion that human life can be taken humanely by the state. Indeed, in the long run, the use of the death penalty by the state will increase the acceptance of revenge in our society and will give official sanction to a climate of violence."

Among the major religious bodies that endorse the death penalty are: the Southern Baptist Convention, the Latter–Day Saints, the National Association of Evangelicals and Orthodox Judaism. E. Owens & E. Elshtain, *Religion and Capital Punishment: An Introduction*, in E. Owens, J. Carlson & E. Elshtain (eds), Religion and the Death Penalty (2004), 7 n.19.

8. I. Kant, The Philosophy of Law (W. Hastie, trans.) 196 (1887).

Much has been made of the sanctity of human life, and the absurdity of supposing that we can teach respect for life by ourselves destroying it. * * * Does fining a criminal show want of respect for property, or imprisoning him, for personal freedom? Just as unreasonable is it to think that to take the life of a man who has taken that of another is to show want of regard for human life. We show, on the contrary, most emphatically our regard for it, by the adoption of a rule that he who violates that right in another forfeits it for himself, and that while no other crime that he can commit deprives him of his right to live, this shall.[9]

In addition, death penalty supporters also justify the death penalty on the basis of its redemptive effects. Executing the murderer redeems society by restoring the balance that was lost through his or her act,[10] and it redeems the victim by reaffirming the victim's worth.[11]

Death penalty opponents make a number of responses to the retribution argument. Some argue that retribution is an altogether illegitimate basis for punishment.[12] Opponents also argue that death is not necessarily a proportionate punishment, even for murder. The death penalty cannot be justified on any general principle calling for imposition of the same harm on the criminal as was imposed on the victim: the state does not rape the rapist, rob the robber or beat the batterer. In fact, Albert Camus argued that the death penalty, as administered, imposes greater harm than the murder because an execution is not simply death:

It is just as different, in essence, from the privation of life as a concentration camp is from prison. It is a murder, to be sure, and one that arithmetically pays for the murder committed. But it adds to death a rule, a public premeditation known to the future victim, an organization, in short, which is itself a source of moral sufferings

---

9. J. Mill, *Capital Punishment* in J. Robson & B. Kinzer, (eds.), Collected Works 270–271 (1988). In the same vein, Ernest van den Haag has argued:

"The life of each man should be sacred to each other man," the ancients tell us. They unflinchingly executed murderers. They realized it is not enough to proclaim the sacredness and inviolability of human life. It must be secured as well, by threatening with the loss of their own life those who violate what has been proclaimed as inviolable—the right of innocents to live. Else, the inviolability of human life is neither credibly proclaimed nor actually protected. No society can profess that the lives of its members are secure if those who did not allow innocent others to continue living are themselves allowed to continue living—at the expense of the community. E. van den Haag, *In Defense of the Death Penalty: A Practical and Moral Analysis,* in H. Bedau (ed.), The Death Penalty in America (3rd Ed. 1982) (hereinafter "Bedau") 331.

10. Society has a "duty" to rectify the imbalance created by a crime, and the only way to rectify the balance is by punishing the offender and thus causing him to "pay back" his debt. M. Moore, *The Moral Worth of Retribution* in F. Schoeman (ed.), Responsibility, Character and Emotions 179 (1987). In the case of murder, the execution of the offender is required to restore the balance.

11. See J. Murphy & J. Hampton, *Forgiveness and Mercy* 125–143 (1988) (arguing that retributive punishment is the defeat of the wrongdoer by the victim or the victim's agent (the state) and is required to reaffirm a victim's equal worth after it has been diminished by the wrongdoer).

12. See, *e.g., Furman v. Georgia,* 408 U.S. 238, 343, 92 S.Ct. 2726 (1972) (Marshall, J., concurring) ("Retaliation, vengeance, and retribution have been roundly condemned as intolerable aspirations for a government in a free society.")

more terrible than death. Hence there is no equivalence. Many laws consider a premeditated crime more serious than a crime of pure violence. But what then is capital punishment but the most premeditated of murders, to which no criminal's deed, however calculated it may be can be compared? For there to be an equivalency, the death penalty would have to punish a criminal who had warned his victim of the date at which he would inflict a horrible death on him and who, from that moment onward, had confined him at his mercy for months. Such a monster is not encountered in private life.[13]

Opponents also argue that, given the length of time between the crime and the execution, the execution cannot serve any retributive purpose because the community outrage has dissipated and the prisoner has undoubtedly changed.[14] As to the supporters' arguments regarding the redemptive value of the death penalty, opponents would argue that, far from restoring a balance in the world, the murderer's execution simply expands the scope of the original harm by inflicting pain on the murderer's family and contributing to a general coarsening of society. Whether a murderer's execution serves any redemptive value for the victim's family also is open to question. The issue has not been carefully studied, but some suggest that the long process leading up to an execution may actually add to the pain experienced by family members and prevent them from resolving their grief and that the "closure" they may feel is simply relief that the death penalty process has come to an end.[15]

Utility

The principal utilitarian argument made for the death penalty is that it serves general deterrence: it deters potential murderers from killing.

> Our penal system rests on the proposition that more severe penalties are more deterrent than less severe penalties. We assume, rightly, I believe, that a $5 fine deters rape less than a $500 fine, and that the threat of five years in prison will deter more than either fine. This assumption of the penal system rests on the common experience that, once aware of them, people learn to avoid natural dangers the more likely these are to be injurious and the more severe the likely injuries. People endowed with ordinary common sense (a class which includes some sociologists) have found no reason why behavior with respect to legal dangers should differ from behavior with respect to natural dangers. Indeed, it does not. Hence, the legal system proportions threatened penalties to the gravity of crimes, both to do justice and to achieve deterrence in proportion to that gravity.

---

13. A. Camus, *Reflections on the Guillotine* in Resistance, Rebellion, and Death 199 (J. O'Brien trans., 1961).

14. See, *e.g.*, *Ceja v. Stewart*, 134 F.3d 1368, 1372–1374 (9th Cir. 1998) (Fletcher, J. dissenting).

15. F. Zimring, The Contradictions of American Capital Punishment 57–61 (2003). See generally H. Prejean, C.S.J., Dead Man Walking: An Eyewitness Account of the Death Penalty in the United States (1993).

Thus, if it is true that the more severe the penalty the greater the deterrent effect, then the most severe penalty—the death penalty— would have the greatest deterrent effect. Arguments to the contrary assume either that capital crimes never are deterrable (sometimes merely because not all capital crimes have been deterred), or that, beyond some point, the deterrent effect of added severity is necessarily zero. Perhaps. But the burden of proof must be borne by those who presume to have located the point of zero marginal returns before the death penalty.[16]

Death penalty opponents respond that there is no empirical evidence that the death penalty deters. Of the hundreds of studies done on deterrence and the death penalty, only a handful purport to find a deterrent effect.[17] Comparative studies—comparing homicide rates in contiguous states where one jurisdiction imposes capital punishment and the other does not; comparing homicide rates before and after the abolishment or reinstatement of the death penalty in a given state; comparing the homicide rate within a state before and after executions; comparing prison inmate killings in states with and without the death penalty—have never found a deterrent effect. For example, in 2000, the New York Times conducted a study examining homicide rates in death penalty and non-death penalty states over a twenty year period.[18] For each year of the period, the average homicide rate of the death penalty states was significantly higher than the average homicide rate of the non-death penalty states, from 48% to 101% higher. The report also compared homicide rates in three pairs of similar and contiguous states (South Dakota/North Dakota, Connecticut/Massachusetts, Virginia/West Virginia) and found that, with regard to each pair, the death penalty state had a higher homicide rate.[19]

The studies that have found a deterrent effect for the death penalty have been done by econometricians using sophisticated mathematical models.[20] One such study concluded that each execution saved eighteen

---

16. E. van den Haag, *In Defense of the Death Penalty: A Practical and Moral Analysis*, in Bedau 326–327.

17. M. Costanzo, Just Revenge 103 (1997).

18. R. Bonner & F. Fessenden, *Absence of Executions: A Special Report; States With No Death Penalty Share Lower Homicide Rates*, New York Times, September, 22, 2000 at p. A1.

19. Another recent example involved a study using state homicide and execution rates for the period 1983–84 to 2005–06. See M. Males, *Death Penalty and Deterrence: The Last Word* http:// www.cjcj.org/pdf/Death_Penalty_and_Deterrence.pdf. States were divided into three groups: the 13 "big death" states (states that conducted at least one execution per year); the 20 "little death" states (states that conducted at least one execution during the period); and the 17 "no death" states (states that conducted no executions during the period). The results were: the homicide rate declined by 34% in the "big death" states, by 24% in the "little death" states and by 36% in the "no death" states, suggesting that executing many people or nobody had the greatest deterrent effect and leading the author to conclude that the "death penalty is irrelevant to homicide."

20. See, *e.g.*, I. Ehrlich, *The Deterrent Effect of Capital Punishment: A Question of Life and Death*, 65 Am. Econ. Rev. 397–417 (1975); H. Mocan & K. Gittings, *Getting off Death Row: Commuted Sentences and the Deterrent Effect of Capital Punishment*, 46 J. Law & Econ. 453 (2003); J. Shepherd, *Murders of Passion, Execution Delays, and the Deterrence of Capital Punishment*, 33 J. Legal Studies 283 (2004).

lives.[21] However, those studies have been criticized as based on faulty assumptions and methodological errors.[22] The deterrence debate has been extended from scholarly journals to testimony before Congress,[23] and to the Supreme Court. In *Baze v. Rees*, ___ U.S. ___, 128 S.Ct. 1520 (2008) [Chapter 12], Justices Stevens and Scalia each relied on different studies to debate the deterrent effect of the death penalty.[24]

Some empirical research actually supports the opposite conclusion: that executions have a "brutalization effect," encouraging homicides. In one study reviewing executions and the homicide rate in New York over a more than 57 year period, the researchers concluded that there were, on average, two more homicides in the two months after an execution.[25] Other studies have yielded the same results and tend to show that the effect is greater when the execution is well publicized.[26] "Although the psychological process by which executions stimulate murders needs more exploration, the finding of brutalization is far more consistent with the evidence than is deterrence theory."[27]

Death penalty opponents point to the nature of murderers to explain the apparent failure of the deterrence theory.

Why is the death penalty not an effective deterrent? * * * [T]he vast majority of homicides occur between angry or drunk acquaintances. Very few killings involve rational calculation. Instead, they involve rage and/or intoxication and a lack of attention to consequences. Punishment cannot deter if killers do not consider it in advance. * * * Apparently those rare killers who think in advance about punishment find little meaningful difference between being put to death and spending the rest of their lives in prison. Both are very

21. H. Dezhbakhsh, et al., *Does Capital Punishment Have a Deterrent Effect? New Evidence from Postmoratorium Panel Data*, 5 Am. L. & Econ. Rev. 344 (2003).

22. See, *e.g.*, W. McManus, *Estimates of the Deterrent Effect of Capital Punishment: The Importance of the Researchers' Prior Beliefs*, 93 J. Polit. Econ. 417 (1985); R. Berk, *New Claims about Executions and General Deterrence: Deja Vu All Over Again?* 2 J. of Empirical Legal Studies 303 (2005); J. Donohue & J. Wolfers, *Uses and Abuses of Empirical Evidence in the Death Penalty Debate*, 58 Stan. L. Rev. 791 (2005).

23. Compare, *e.g.*, Testimony of Dr. Paul Rubin before the Senate Committee on the Judiciary (http://judiciary.senate.gov/testimony.cfm?id=1745 & wit_id=4991) with Testimony of Dr. Jeffrey Fagan before the Senate Committee on the Judiciary (http://judiciary.senate.gov/testimony.cfm?id=1745 & wit_id=4992).

24. See 128 S.Ct. at 1547 n.13 (Stevens, J. concurring) (relying, in part, on an article by Professors Donohue and Wolfers to argue against deterrence); 128 S.Ct. at 1553 (Scalia, J. concurring) (relying, in part, on an article by Professors Sunstein and Vermeule to argue in favor of deterrence). Professors Sunstein and Wolfers, authors of the competing articles, subsequently published an op-ed piece explaining that the justices had misread the evidence. C. Sunstein & J. Wolfers, *A Death Penalty Puzzle: The Murky Evidence for and Against Deterrence*, Washington Post, June 30, 2008 at A11. After summarizing the various studies, they concluded: "In short, the best reading of the accumulated data is that they do not establish a deterrent effect of the death penalty."

25. See W. Bowers and G. Pierce, *Deterrence or Brutalization: What is the Effect of Executions?* in V. Streib (Ed.), A Capital Punishment Anthology 86 (1993).

26. M. Costanzo, Just Revenge 109 (1997).

27. *Id.* at 110.

unattractive, and neither acts as a deterrent to a killing.[28]

As for the brutalization effect, they argue that executions may stimulate homicides in several ways:

> Media accounts of the execution and stories about the condemned man may bring violent images and ideas to the minds of a few susceptible and potentially violent people. Some of these people may become morbidly obsessed with a murder. For those people who are already primed and ready to act violently, fascination with a murder or an execution may be enough to push barely repressed impulses to the surface. Some sociologists and psychiatrists have suggested that persons haunted by self-loathing may even see execution as a means of escape rather than as a dreaded punishment. * * * "With the crime that leads to execution, the offender also strikes back at society or particular individuals. The execution will, of course, satisfy a guilt-inspired desire for punishment, and may also be seen as providing the opportunity to be seen and heard, an occasion to express resentment, alienation, and defiance."[29]

Death penalty supporters also argue a theory of specific deterrence: in the absence of a death penalty, murderers sentenced to a life sentence would be able to commit further murders inside prison with impunity since there would be no possibility of additional punishment. The empirical evidence, from studies of murders by prisoners in retentionist and abolitionist jurisdictions, does not support the argument.[30] Although imprisoned murderers are more likely to commit murders than are inmates imprisoned for other crimes, there is no difference in the rate of recidivism between states with and without the death penalty. "The threat of the death penalty in the retentionist jurisdiction does not even exert an *incremental* deterrent effect over the threat of a lesser punishment in the abolitionist state."[31]

---

28. R. Gerber, *Death is Not Worth It*, 28 Ariz. St. L.J. 335, 350–351 (1996). See also D. Von Drehle, Among the Lowest of the Dead: The Culture of Death Row 209 (1995):

"The problem with deterrence, as applied to aggravated murder, is that it assumes killers calculate risk and reward. The reality, with few exceptions is that murderers are not clear-thinking people. They are impulsive, self-centered, often warped; overwhelmingly they are products of violent homes; frequently they are addled by booze or drugs; and most of them are deeply anti-social. The values and sanctions of society don't concern them."

29. M. Costanzo, Just Revenge 109–110 (1997) quoting W. Bowers, *The Effect of Executions is Brutalization, Not Deterrence*, in K. Haas and J. Inciardi (eds.) Challenging Capital Punishment (1988).

30. See W. Wolfson, *The Deterrent Effect of the Death Penalty upon Prison Murder* in Bedau 167.

31. *Id.* A third utilitarian argument sometimes mentioned is that the death penalty may deter vigilantism. See *Furman v. Georgia*, 408 U.S. 238, 308, 92 S.Ct. 2726, 2761 (1972) (Stewart, J., concurring) ("When people begin to believe that organized society is unwilling or unable to impose upon criminal offenders the punishment they 'deserve' then there are sown the seeds of anarchy—of self-help, vigilante justice, lynch law.") Although it may well be that in the past a judicial death penalty may have served as a substitute for a lynching (see S. Bright, *Discrimination, Death and Denial: The Tolerance of Racial Discrimination in Infliction of the Death Penalty*, 35 Santa Clara L. Rev. 433, 439 (1995)), there is no empirical evidence to suggest that abolishing the death penalty would lead to a rise of vigilantism.

Death penalty opponents point to the cost of the death penalty as an argument against its utility. Studies of a number of different jurisdictions all establish that it is substantially more expensive to prosecute a capital case through to an execution than to prosecute an ordinary murder case and maintain the defendant in prison for life.[32] For example, in California, the death penalty costs the state $125 million more each year than if the maximum punishment were life imprisonment without parole.[33] Florida spends $51 million more each year.[34] Capital cases are more expensive to litigate than non-capital cases at the trial level because generally more resources are provided to the defense (*e.g.*, two counsel instead of one, a mitigation specialist, mental health experts), pre-trial proceedings are more extensive and trials are substantially longer (because of the need to "death-qualify" jurors and because of the penalty phase). Post-conviction proceedings also are more protracted than in non-capital cases and far more likely to result in a reversal, requiring a new round of spending in the trial court. Even the execution of the sentence is, in most jurisdictions, more expensive in capital cases because the cost of housing an inmate on death row for the length of time necessary for appellate and post-conviction review will exceed the cost of housing the inmate in the general prison population for life.

Reliability and Fairness

" '[T]o say that someone deserves to be executed is to make a godlike judgment with no assurance that it can be made with anything resembling godlike perspicacity.' "[35] Death penalty opponents argue that, even if the death penalty were thought to be moral and socially useful, it still should be abolished because it has not been, and cannot be, reliably and fairly imposed. This argument is supported by the most comprehensive study yet done on post-*Furman* death sentences: J. Liebman, J. Fagan & V. West, *A Broken System: Error Rates in Capital Cases, 1973–1995*, http:// justice.policy.net/jpreport/liebman2.pdf (2000) (hereinafter, *"Columbia Study I"*). The researchers studied all death sentences during the period 1973–95, and documented, *inter alia*, that 68% of all death sentences were reversed for prejudicial error and that 82% of those whose sentences were

32. J. Liebman, J. Fagan & V. West, *A Broken System: Error Rates in Capital Cases, 1973–1995*, http://justice.policy.net/jpreport/liebman2.pdf n.74 (2000) ("The trial, incarceration and execution of sentence in capital cases cost from $2.5 to $5 million dollars per inmate (in current dollars), compared to less than $1 million for each killer sentenced to life without parole."); E. Freedman, *Add Resources and Apply Them Systemically: Governments' Responsibilities Under the Revised ABA Capital Defense Representation Guidelines*, 31 Hofstra L. Rev. 1097, 1098 (2003) (citing numerous earlier studies). See also Death Penalty Information Center, http://www.death penaltyinfo.org/costs-death-penalty.

33. *Commission on the Fair Administration of Justice Report and Recommendations on the Administration of the Death Penalty in California* (2008), http://www.ccfaj.org/documents/reports/dp/official/FINAL% 20REPORT% 20DEATH% 20PENALTY.pdf. This is in part because it costs four times as much to maintain a prisoner on death row as in the general prison population. R. Tempest, *Death Penalty Hardly a Cost–Effective Measure*, Los Angeles Times, March 5, 2005.

34. S.V. Date, *The High Price of Killing Killers*, Palm Beach Post, January 4, 2000 at A1.

35. H. Bedau & M. Radelet, *Miscarriages of Justice in Potentially Capital Cases*, 40 Stanford L. Rev. 21, 96 (1987) quoting W. Berns, For Capital Punishment: Crime and the Morality of the Death Penalty 178 (1979).

reversed were not again sentenced to death. Thus, half the death sentences imposed during this period turned out to be "wrong."[36] Death penalty opponents point to three critical problems with a death penalty administered by persons without "godlike perspicacity."

The Execution of Innocent People

Death penalty opponents argue that the punishment is unacceptable because inevitably it results in the execution of innocent people. This contention, like the contention that the death penalty has a deterrent effect, is difficult to prove. Once a person is executed, there is little incentive to seek evidence to prove his or her innocence, nor is there any vehicle to develop the evidence. In the one comprehensive study attempting to determine the number of innocent people who have executed,[37] the authors described more than four hundred cases where persons were wrongfully convicted in capital or potentially capital cases. Nevertheless, as even the authors conceded, there is some element of subjectivity in the determination when the evidence actually proves someone innocent. Opponents point to the number of offenders released from death row after their innocence was proved as evidence that the system must have made fatal mistakes.

Death penalty supporters assert that the empirical data does not support the conclusion that any significant number of innocent people has been put to death and the release of innocent people from death rows is evidence that the system works to execute only the guilty. They also deny that the risk of an occasional execution of an innocent person is grounds for abolishing the death penalty.

> The execution of innocents believed guilty is a miscarriage of justice that must be opposed whenever detected. But such miscarriages of justice do not warrant abolition of the death penalty. Unless the moral drawbacks of an activity or practice, which include the possible death of innocent bystanders, outweigh the moral advantages, which include the innocent lives that might be saved by it, the activity is warranted. Most human activities—medicine, manufacturing, automobile and air traffic, sports, not to speak of wars and revolutions—cause the death of innocent bystanders. Nevertheless, if the advantages sufficiently outweigh the disadvantages, human activities, including those of the penal system with all its punishments, are morally justified.[38]

Racial Bias

A number of studies have shown that race is a significant factor in capital sentencing.[39] The most comprehensive study is that of David Baldus and others concerning 2,000 murder cases Georgia. The study

---

36. The number may be significantly higher. Given the politics of state courts [see Chapter 9] and the ever more stringent limitations on federal review [see Chapter 11], there is no reason to assume that all of the 32% of the cases that were not reversed were in fact rightly decided.

37. M. Radelet, H. Bedau & C. Putnam, In Spite of Innocence (1992).

38. E. van den Haag, *In Defense of the Death Penalty: A Practical and Moral Analysis*, in Bedau 325. See also L. Pojman, *Why the Death Penalty Is Morally Permissible* in H. Bedau & P. Cassell, Debating the Death Penalty (2004) 68.

39. See generally, S. Gross & R. Mauro, Death & Discrimination (1989).

found that, all factors being equal, black defendants were somewhat more likely than white defendants to receive a death sentence and defendants who killed whites were much more likely to receive the death penalty than those who killed blacks. Is racial bias in the administration of the death penalty a reason to abandon it? The arguments are set out in *McCleskey v. Kemp*, 481 U.S. 279, 107 S.Ct. 1756 (1987) [Chapter 3], where the Supreme Court considered the constitutionality of the Georgia death penalty in light of the Baldus study.

Arbitrariness

Opponents also contend that the imposition of the death penalty is entirely arbitrary, that it does not, in any rational fashion, single out the worst murderers for the most severe punishment. Three major factors are said to cause arbitrariness. First, prosecutors have virtually unlimited discretion as to when to seek the death penalty and may base their decisions on political and other considerations unrelated to the defendant's culpability, and death penalty cases are high-visibility cases tempting some prosecutors and police to cut corners to obtain a death sentence. [see Chapter 8] Second, virtually all capital case defendants are poor and receive appointed counsel, many of whom are not qualified to try a capital case. It is argued that the quality of defense counsel matters more than the defendant's conduct or character in determining whether the defendant receives the death penalty.[40] [see Chapter 7] Third, most of the death penalty states (30 out of 35) have elected judges, and it is argued that, in death penalty cases, those judges will incline to make political, rather than judicial decisions.[41] [see Chapter 9]

Death penalty supporters respond to the charge of arbitrariness with three arguments. First, they argue that misconduct by any of the participants in the process is corrected through the judicial process.[42] Second, if there is inconsistency in the imposition of the death penalty, it is justified because other important humanitarian and democratic values are being served, *e.g.*, by according broad discretion to prosecutors or by electing judges. Third, occasional unjust results are inevitable and unremarkable.

> Justice requires punishing the guilty—as many of the guilty as possible—even if only some can be punished, and sparing the innocent—as many of the innocent as possible, even if not all are spared. Morally, justice must always be preferred to equality. It would surely be wrong to treat everybody with equal injustice in preference to

---

40. See S. Bright, *Counsel for the Poor: The Death Sentence Not for the Worst Crime but for the Worst Lawyer*, 103 Yale L.J. 1835 (1994).

41. S. Bright & P. Keenan, *Judges and the Politics of Death: Deciding Between the Bill of Rights and the Next Election in Capital Cases*, 75 B.U. L. Rev. 759 (1995).

42. The *Columbia Study* found that the high reversal rate in capital cases was due primarily to "egregiously incompetent defense lawyering" and "prosecution suppression of evidence."

meting out justice to some. Justice cannot ever permit sparing some guilty persons, or punishing some innocent ones, for the sake of equality—because others have been unjustly spared or punished. In practice, penalties never could be applied if we insisted that they cannot be inflicted on any guilty persons unless we are able to make sure that they are equally applied to all other guilty persons. Anyone familiar with law enforcement knows that punishments can be inflicted only on an unavoidably capricious selection of the guilty.[43]

B. HISTORICAL BACKGROUND

The Supreme Court's effort to regulate the administration of the death penalty in the United States began with the landmark 1972 decision in *Furman v. Georgia*, 408 U.S. 238, 92 S.Ct. 2726 (1972) [Chapter 2]. This section provides an historical context for that effort, first through *A Short History of the American Death Penalty* and then by way of two Supreme Court cases that preceded *Furman*. The first, *Powell v. Alabama*, decided in 1932, is considered the Court's seminal decision on constitutional criminal procedure, the case that launched the Court's efforts to curb the most egregious abuses in the states' criminal justice systems. *Powell* had all the elements of classic Southern justice during the Jim Crow era: young black defendants facing dubious rape charges by white women, a hasty trial in a mob-dominated atmosphere and a conviction and death verdict by an all-white jury. For various reasons, the case became a *cause celebre* in the North and abroad, leading to demonstrations and other publicity calling for release of the "Scottsboro Boys." The Court reversed the conviction for denial of the right to counsel but raised no question concerning the constitutionality of the Alabama death penalty. In the succeeding forty years, the Court reversed or vacated convictions in 43 death penalty cases, but, as in *Powell*, the decisions were based on constitutional procedural errors—*e.g.*, denial of counsel,[a] race-based jury selection,[b] coerced confessions,[c] prosecutorial misconduct,[d]—rather than on any constitutional flaw in the death penalty itself.[e] Finally, in 1971, in *McGautha v. California*, the second case in this section, the Court addressed constitutional challenges to death penalty schemes themselves.

43. E. van den Haag, *In Defense of the Death Penalty: A Practical and Moral Analysis*, in Bedau 323.

a. See *Hamilton v. Alabama*, 368 U.S. 52, 82 S.Ct. 157 (1961); *White v. Maryland*, 373 U.S. 59, 83 S.Ct. 1050 (1963).

b. See *Patterson v. Alabama*, 294 U.S. 600, 55 S.Ct. 575 (1935); *Shepherd v. Florida*, 341 U.S. 50, 71 S.Ct. 549 (1951); *Avery v. Georgia*, 345 U.S. 559, 73 S.Ct. 891 (1953).

c. See *Brown v. Mississippi*, 297 U.S. 278, 56 S.Ct. 461 (1936); *Chambers v. Florida*, 309 U.S. 227, 60 S.Ct. 472 (1940); *Payne v. Arkansas*, 356 U.S. 560, 78 S.Ct. 844 (1958).

d. See *Alcorta v. Texas*, 355 U.S. 28, 78 S.Ct. 103 (1957); *Miller v. Pate*, 386 U.S. 1, 87 S.Ct. 785 (1967).

e. In two cases, the Court did reverse death sentences based on particular errors in the administration of the death penalty. See *Andres v. United States*, 333 U.S. 740, 68 S.Ct. 880 (1948) (ambiguous jury instructions as to penalty); *Witherspoon v. Illinois*, 391 U.S. 510, 88 S.Ct. 1770 (1968) (qualified jurors excluded because of views on death penalty) [Chapter 6].

The central debate in *McGautha* was over whether it is possible to administer the death penalty in a rational, non-arbitrary fashion, and that debate continues to this day. If the Court had required legislatures to establish standards for death-eligibility, should the standards have made either of the defendants in *McGautha* death-eligible?

A SHORT HISTORY OF THE AMERICAN DEATH PENALTY

The death penalty was employed from the earliest days of the British Colonies, and there now have been more than 15,000 confirmed executions—and perhaps as many as 22,500 authorized executions—in America.[1] These figures do not include the approximately 5,000 people lynched, many of them in the late 19th and early 20th centuries.[2] The first recorded execution in America was of Captain George Kendall, a councilor for the Virginia colony, who was executed in 1608 for spying for Spain.[3] The first woman executed in America was Jane Champion, who was put to death in the Virginia colony in 1632 for an unknown offense.[4] The first juvenile executed in America was Thomas Graunger, who was executed in Plymouth colony in 1642 for bestiality.[5] The American death penalty, which derives primarily from English law, is part of the long, worldwide history of capital punishment.

I. Antecedents of the American Death Penalty in Antiquity and in England.

Antiquity. Throughout history, societies have killed criminals as punishment for their transgressions. Death has long been the ultimate weapon against disorder. In ancient times, Phoenicians, Israelites, Egyptians, Persians, Chinese, Greeks and Romans imposed the death penalty. Murder historically has been a primary offense subject to the death penalty. But capital crimes varied greatly and covered more than crimes of violence. In ancient Egypt, the offense of magic was punished by death. Under Mosaic law, uttering blasphemy, gathering sticks on the Sabbath, and cursing a parent were capital crimes. And in the Roman Republic, capital punishment was imposed for a vestal virgin's violating her vow of chastity, publishing libels and insulting songs, and making disturbances in the city at night.[6] Executions were often gruesome and torturous. Flaying

---

1. B. Vila & C. Morris, Capital Punishment in the United States: A Documentary History (hereinafter, "Vila & Morris") Appendix B (1998); NAACP Legal Defense and Education Fund, Inc., *Death Row, U.S.A.* (2000); R. Bohm, Deathquest: An Introduction to the Theory and Practice of Capital Punishment in the United States (hereinafter, "Bohm") 2 (1999).

2. H. Bedau (Ed.), The Death Penalty in America (hereinafter "Bedau") 3 (3rd Ed. 1982).

3. Bohm 1.

4. K. O'Shea, Women and the Death Penalty in the United States, 1900–1998 4 (1999); V. Streib, *Death Penalty for Female Offenders*, 58 U. Cincinnati L.Rev. 845, 848 (1990).

5. V. Streib, *Imposing the Death Penalty on Children*, in K.C. Haas & J.A. Inciardi (Eds.), Challenging Capital Punishment: Legal and Social Science Approaches 251 (1988).

6. J. Laurence, A History of Capital Punishment 2–3 (1960).

alive, boiling in oil, hurling from a tower, sawing asunder, crucifying, drawing, quartering and disemboweling, burning at the stake, breaking on the wheel, and decapitating are only some of the modes of execution used around the world.[7]

England. The English common law, America's legal ancestor, recognized eight capital crimes: treason (including attempts and conspiracies), petty treason (the killing of a husband by a wife), murder, larceny, robbery, burglary, rape and arson.[8] The number of capital crimes in England increased dramatically between the 17th and 19th centuries. In 1688, there were 50 capital crimes. Coinciding with the widespread dislocations caused by the agricultural and industrial revolutions, nearly 100 new capital laws were enacted in the 18th century. By 1820, there were more than 200 capital crimes, many for property crimes, including such trivial offenses as forgery of a one pound note or theft of a pocket handkerchief.[9]

In the last quarter of the 17th century, murder accounted for a significant portion of executions, but by the last quarter of the 18th century, the death penalty was inflicted predominantly, and in some years almost exclusively, for economic crimes.[10] At the same time, there was considerable discrepancy between capital punishment laws and practice as seen in the declining execution rate over the 18th century. In the middle of the 18th century, more than two-thirds of those sentenced to death were executed, yet in the last decade of the century, the proportion dropped to less than one-third.[11]

The 19th century saw dramatic changes in English criminal law. By 1833, capital punishment was limited to relatively few serious offenses. After 1863, murder was essentially the only crime for which people were executed, although treason and piracy remained capital crimes until 1965, when England abolished the death penalty.

II. The Death Penalty in America.

The death penalty has been part of the American criminal justice system since the founding of the British colonies. Although capital punishment has endured, there have been recurring movements to abolish the death penalty throughout American history. The struggle between those who would abolish and those who would retain the death penalty has influenced important developments in American criminal law and procedure.

---

7. *Id.* at 220–230; G. Scott, The History of Capital Punishment 149–221 (1950).

8. L. Radzinowicz, A History of English Criminal Law And Its Administration From 1750 (hereinafter, "Radzinowicz") vol. 1, p. 4 (1948); Bedau 6.

9. Radzinowicz 3–5; G. Scott, The History of Capital Punishment 39–40 (1950).

10. Radzinowicz 150–151; W. Bowers, Legal Homicide: Death as Punishment in America, 1864–1982 (hereinafter, "Bowers") 136–139 (1984).

11. Radzinowicz 147–148.

A. From Colonial Times to the Civil War.

The Colonies. The English settlers carried the death penalty to America, but restricted its scope in the northern colonies. The crimes punished by death varied considerably among the colonies. The first capital laws of Massachusetts reflected the Pilgrims' strict religious beliefs. Twelve crimes, all derived from the Bible, were punished by death: idolatry, witchcraft, blasphemy, murder, manslaughter, poisoning, bestiality, sodomy, adultery, man stealing, bearing false witness in a capital trial, and rebellion (including attempts and conspiracies).[12] The hanging of convicted witches in Salem, Massachusetts in 1692 graphically illustrates the use of capital punishment to quell a challenge, real or perceived, to religious and political authority.[13] In 1700, rape, arson, treason and third offense of theft of goods over a certain value were added to the list of crimes punished by death. By 1780, the list of capital crimes had been reduced to seven secular crimes: murder, sodomy, burglary, buggery, arson, rape and treason.[14] In contrast to Massachusetts, the colonies of Pennsylvania and South Jersey, settled by Quakers as utopian communities, began with more lenient criminal codes. Pennsylvania's founding act limited the death penalty to murder and treason, while South Jersey's original charter did not authorize capital punishment at all.[15]

In the 18th century, the population of the colonies grew rapidly and, with continuing immigration, became more heterogenous. Without a general prison system, expanded capital punishment laws were one way to maintain public order amid increasing social and cultural diversity.[16] In addition, England required several colonies to adopt harsher criminal codes in its attempt to retain political control. Thus, by the time of the War of Independence, the northern colonies imposed the death penalty for murder, treason, piracy, rape, robbery, burglary, and sodomy. In some places, other offenses such as counterfeiting and horse theft were capital crimes.[17]

Penal reform. The ideas of the European Enlightenment of the 18th century, particularly the writings of Charles Montesquieu, inspired calls for legal and penal reforms. Theories of crime prevention through education, rehabilitation of criminals, and proportionality between crimes and punishments entered public discussion. The ideas of Italian jurist Cesare Beccaria, who argued that capital punishment was a barbarity, did not deter crime, and should be replaced with life imprisonment and servitude as the penalty for murder, gained currency in the United States after the War of Independence. Thomas Jefferson, although not in favor of total abolition of the death penalty, repeatedly introduced legislation in Virginia

---

12. Bedau 7; Vila & Morris 8–9.

13. Bowers 134.

14. Bedau 7.

15. *Id.*

16. Vila & Morris 3.

17. Bedau 7.

to substitute more proportionate sentences for some capital offenses. In 1787, Benjamin Rush, a physician and signer of the Declaration of Independence, launched the first movement to abolish the death penalty in the United States and to transform prisons into reform penitentiaries where solitary repentance was to lead to rehabilitation. However, in the early 19th century, the penal reform movement lost momentum without having realized its goals.[18]

Division of murder into degrees. At the end of the 18th century, a new definition of the crime of murder emerged. Until then, in Anglo–Saxon law any malicious homicide, *i.e.*, a killing that was not justified, excused, involuntary or provoked, was punished by death.[19] In 1794, Pennsylvania divided murder into first and second degrees. First degree murder consisted of killing by means of poison or lying in wait, or any other kind of wilful, deliberate and premeditated killing, or any killing committed during the perpetration or attempt to perpetrate arson, rape, robbery or burglary, and all other murders were second degree. Capital punishment, still a mandatory penalty, was limited to first degree murders. Over the next 40 years, most states adopted the distinction between first and second degree murder, despite criticisms that the distinction was vague and difficult to understand, and some states, but not all, limited the death penalty to first degree murders. The invention of degrees of murder essentially gave the jury the authority to decide that a defendant, although guilty of murder, had not acted with sufficient calculation to warrant execution.[20]

Southern states. In the South, capital punishment had a different history linked, in large part, to slavery. In contrast to capital punishment in the northern states, capital punishment in the South was not limited primarily to common law felonies. Rather, the death penalty was a powerful tool for keeping the slave population in submission.[21] Crimes that interfered with the ownership of slaves were punished by death. In 1837, North Carolina, which lacked a penitentiary, had about twenty-six capital crimes including slave-stealing, concealing a slave with intent to free him, second conviction of inciting slaves to insurrection, and second conviction of circulating seditious literature among slaves.[22] The death penalty also was imposed for taking a freed slave or mulatto out of the state with the intent to sell him or her into slavery. The harshness of the North Carolina code extended beyond slave-related crimes. The death penalty was mandated for stealing bank notes, crimes against nature

---

18. Bowers 6–8; L. Masur, Rites of Execution, Capital Punishment and the Transformation of American Culture, 1776–1865 (hereinafter, "Masur") 50–54, 88–89 (1989); Vila & Morris, 16–18, 25, 31–32.

19. Bedau 4.

20. *Id*. at 4–5; Vila & Morris 25; *McGautha v. California*, 402 U.S. 183, 197–199, 91 S.Ct. 1454, 1462–1463 (1971).

21. R. Paternoster, Capital Punishment in America 6–7 (1991); Bowers 140.

22. Bowers 139.

(buggery, sodomy, bestiality), burning a public building, second offense of forgery and statutory rape.[23]

In addition to punishing slave crimes with death, the Black Codes of many southern states differentiated between capital crimes for black slaves and white people. In the 1830's, Virginia had five capital crimes for whites, but an estimated seventy capital crimes for black slaves. In 1848, the Virginia Assembly passed a law requiring the death penalty for black slaves for any offense punishable by three or more years imprisonment for whites.[24] Racial discrimination also was codified in Georgia's rape statutes. In 1816, the death penalty was required for a slave or "freeman of colour" who raped or attempted to rape a white female, and, at the same time, the state reduced the minimum sentence from seven to two years and removed the hard labor requirement for a white man convicted of rape. A white man convicted of raping a slave woman or a free woman of color was punished by a fine and/or imprisonment at the court's discretion.[25]

Antebellum abolition movement. In the second quarter of the 19th century, the use of the death penalty increased significantly, public executions were replaced with executions inside prison walls, and anti-gallows societies were organized particularly in the Northeast.[26] This first wave of abolitionist activity occurred in the context of the reform movements for temperance, women's rights, the abolition of slavery, and better treatment of poor, imprisoned, and mentally ill people. Moral and religious arguments, rather than utilitarian philosophy, often dominated the public debate.[27] During this period, Michigan, Wisconsin, and Rhode Island abolished the death penalty, and there was *de facto* abolition in Maine. The campaign against capital punishment lost momentum as slavery grew to dominate the reform agenda, and the anti-gallows movement was halted by the Civil War.[28] Nevertheless, its impact was apparent: by the start of the Civil War, burglary and robbery were no longer capital crimes in three-fourths of the states.[29]

B. From the Civil War to World War I.

Discretionary sentencing. By the end of the 19th century, discretionary sentencing in capital cases emerged as an established feature of American criminal justice system. Under English and early American law, the death penalty was mandatory upon conviction of a capital crime.

---

23. Bedau 8.

24. Bowers 139–140.

25. *Id.* at 140.

26. S. Banner, The Death Penalty in American History 131–134 (2002).

27. H. Haines, Against Capital Punishment, The Anti–Death Penalty Movement in America, 1972–1994 (hereinafter, "Haines") 8–9 (1996); Vila & Morris 34–35; Masur 118–119, 139, 143, 159.

28. Haines 9; Vila & Morris 34–35.

29. Vila & Morris 35; M. Meltsner, Cruel and Unusual: The Supreme Court and Capital Punishment (hereinafter, "Meltsner") 50 (1973).

Faced with this prospect, juries would acquit a guilty but sympathetic defendant to spare him or her a death sentence. This problem of "jury nullification," which persisted even after states distinguished between degrees of murder, led states to abolish mandatory death penalties in favor of discretionary sentencing statutes that directly gave juries the option to impose the death penalty or a lesser punishment.[30] As early as 1642, Massachusetts had an alternative penalty for some capital crimes, but by 1780 had reverted to a mandatory death penalty. Tennessee, followed by Maryland, Alabama, and Louisiana, adopted discretionary capital punishment laws before the Civil War. Between 1860 and 1900, twenty other states and the federal government joined them. The trend continued into the 20th century.

Renewed abolition movement. After the brutality of the Civil War, the execution of convicted criminals probably seemed inconsequential to most Americans.[31] Abolitionist activity was sporadic in the first post-war decades. Maine and Iowa abolished and reinstated the death penalty in the 1870's and 1880's, and Maine finally abandoned capital punishment in 1887.[32] In the last years of 19th century, a progressive reform movement arose that carried a second wave of abolitionist activity. The arguments against capital punishment focused on utilitarian issues such as deterrence as well as on issues of religion and morality.[33] Capital punishment supporters argued that abolition of the death penalty would increase the already high number of lynchings.[34] By World War I, thirteen states—Arizona, Kansas, Maine, Michigan, Minnesota, Missouri, North Dakota, Oregon, Rhode Island, South Dakota, Tennessee, Washington, and Wisconsin—had abolished the death penalty, with some exceptions for murder of a police officer, murder by a prisoner, rape and treason.[35]

Southern Experience. The Black Codes were abolished with the Emancipation Proclamation. As a matter of law, all people were to be punished according to the laws for white freemen.[36] However, in reality, the sentiments underlying the Black Codes pervaded southern criminal justice systems. In some former slave states, such as Virginia, the number of capital statutes increased significantly after the Civil War and generally provided for discretionary, rather than mandatory, death sentences. Since black Americans were excluded from participating in the criminal justice system, except as defendants, these laws tended to be applied in a manner that echoed the old law.[37] Moreover, "lynching provided a *de facto* extralegal restoration of the antebellum Black Codes."[38] In the 1890's, lynchings,

---

30. Bedau, 9–11; *McGautha v. California*, 402 U.S. 183, 200, 91 S.Ct. 1454, 1463–1464.

31. Vila & Morris, 35.

32. Bowers, 9.

33. Vila & Morris, 35–37.

34. *Id.* at 37; Masur, 160–161.

35. Bowers, 9; *Furman v. Georgia*, 408 U.S. 238, 372, 92 S.Ct. 2726, 2794 (Marshall, J.).

36. Bowers 142.

37. Bedau 11.

38. Bowers 142.

at a record high, exceeded legal executions: there were 1,540 lynchings in the United States, the vast majority of victims being black men, and 1,215 legal executions. In the 20th century, lynchings declined steadily each decade through the 1930's, particularly after Congress threatened to enact an anti-lynching law, and disappeared in the 1950's.[39] In the South, perfunctory trials often followed by hasty executions replaced lynching and institutionalized racial violence against African–Americans.[40]

C. From World War I to 1972.

Status quo through the 1950's. The movement to abolish the death penalty was interrupted by World War I. For the next forty years, relatively little public attention was given to capital punishment. After World War I, public fears of immigrants and radicalism strengthened support for the death penalty. By 1920, five of the states that had abolished capital punishment before or during the war—Arizona, Oregon, Missouri, Tennessee and Washington—had reinstated the penalty. And no other state abolished the death penalty during this period.[41]

The Great Depression of the 1930's brought widespread and prolonged hardship to the United States, and reform movements focused on economic concerns, not capital punishment. More people were executed in the 1930's (1,667) than in the 17th and 18th centuries combined (1,553).[42] During this decade Kansas and South Dakota re-enacted the death penalty.[43] From 1918 to 1959, more than 4,700 people were executed in the United States.[44] Except for high-profile cases, such as the electrocutions of Nicola Sacco and Bartolomeo Vanzetti (1927) for murder and Ethel and Julius Rosenberg (1953) for conspiracy to commit espionage, executions took place without public debate.[45]

Revitalized abolition movement in the late 1950's and 1960's. During the late 1950's the issue of capital punishment re-entered public discourse. Nobel Laureate Albert Camus catalyzed an international debate with his fervent attack on the death penalty. In 1957, public opinion polls showed that 50% of Americans did not favor the death penalty for murder.[46] The civil rights movement began to focus the nation on the institutionalized inequality of African–Americans in all areas of society, including the criminal justice system. In 1960, the execution of Caryl Chessman in

---

39. *Id.* at 54. S. Bright, *Symposium: Discrimination, Death and Denial: The Tolerance of Racial Discrimination in Infliction of the Death Penalty,* 35 Santa Clara Law Review 433, 440 (1995) (hereinafter, "Bright").

40. Bright, 439–440.

41. P. Mackey, ed., Voices Against Death: American Opposition to Capital Punishment, 1787–1975, xxxvi–xxxvii (1976); Bowers, 9; F. Zimring and G. Hawkins, Capital Punishment and the American Agenda, 28–29 (1986).

42. Bohm, 2; Bowers, 25.

43. Bowers, 9.

44. *Id.* at 25–26, 50.

45. Vila & Morris, 75–76.

46. *Id.* at 102.

California for kidnaping sparked worldwide protests. In 1966, only 42% of Americans supported the death penalty.[47]

In the 1960's the NAACP Legal Defense and Education Fund ("the Fund") began to challenge the " 'legal lynchings' "[48] in the South, especially the execution of black men for the rape of white women.[49] The Fund found volunteer attorneys to represent death row prisoners in federal habeas corpus petitions. The immediate goal, a national moratorium on executions, was achieved by the end of 1967, and lasted until 1977.[50] Beginning in the late 1960's, the Fund litigated a series of challenges to the death penalty in the United States Supreme Court leading ultimately to *Furman v. Georgia*, 408 U.S. 238, 92 S.Ct. 2726 (1972).

D. From 1972 to the Present

In *Furman*, the Supreme Court held that the death penalty, as then administered in the United States, was unconstitutional. Legislation subsequently was passed by thirty-eight states and the federal government (for federal crimes and crimes in the military) restoring the death penalty, and thirty-four states and the federal government (but not the military) have carried out at least one execution since 1972.[51] Recently, three states—New York, New Jersey and New Mexico—have abandoned the death penalty. From 1973 through 2008, almost 8,000 defendants were sentenced to death, and 1,136 were executed. At the end of 2008, there were 3,297 inmates on death row. Among those who have been executed, 56% were white, and 99% were men; and, on death row, 55% of the inmates are non-white, and 98.5% are men.

The overall figures for the period 1973–2008 conceal at least two significant variations in executions and death sentences. First, executions and death sentences varied substantially over time. The number of executions rose fairly steadily after *Furman*, reaching a high of 98 in 1999 and declining to 37 in 2008. The number of death sentences rose dramatically in the three years after the *Furman* decision, and, during the 18–year period 1982–1999, there were never less than 250 death sentences in any one year. The peak for death sentences was 1996, and, during the 5–year period 1994–98, there was an average of 306 death sentences per year handed down. After 1999, the number of death sentences declined dramatically, and, in 2008, only 111 defendants were sentenced to death.

---

47. *Id.* at p. 110.

48. Bright, 439–440.

49. Meltsner, 73–78; Vila & Morris, 110, 130–131.

50. Meltsner, 107, 115; Bowers, 104; Vila & Morris, 131.

51. Death Penalty Information Center (http://www.deathpenaltyinfo.org). All subsequent figures in this section are taken from this website.

DEATH SENTENCES 1973-2008

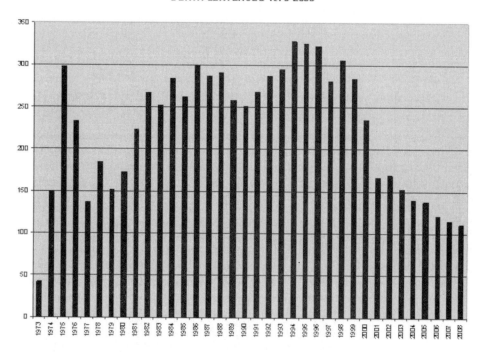

Executions 1977-2008

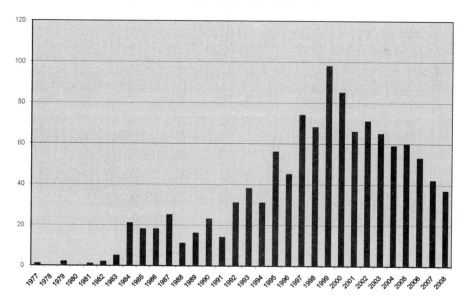

Second, executions have not been at all evenly distributed among the death penalty states. The eleven former Confederate States, all of which reenacted death penalty statutes after *Furman*, conducted over 70% of the executions during the period, and Texas and Virginia, alone, accounted for more than 46% of the executions in the country.[52]

POWELL v. ALABAMA

287 U.S. 45, 53 S.Ct. 55, 77 L.Ed. 158 (1932).

MR. JUSTICE SUTHERLAND delivered the opinion of the Court.

These cases were argued together and submitted for decision as one case.

The petitioners, hereinafter referred to as defendants, are negroes charged with the crime of rape, committed upon the persons of two white girls. The crime is said to have been committed on March 25, 1931. The indictment was returned in a state court of first instance on March 31, and the record recites that on the same day the defendants were arraigned and entered pleas of not guilty. There is a further recital to the effect that upon the arraignment they were represented by counsel. But no counsel had been employed, and aside from a statement made by the trial judge several days later during a colloquy immediately preceding the trial, the record does not disclose when, or under what circumstances, an appointment of counsel was made, or who was appointed. During the colloquy referred to, the trial judge, in response to a question, said that he had appointed all the members of the bar for the purpose of arraigning the defendants and then of course anticipated that the members of the bar would continue to help the defendants if no counsel appeared. Upon the argument here both sides accepted that as a correct statement of the facts concerning the matter.

There was a severance upon the request of the state, and the defendants were tried in three several groups * * *. As each of the three cases was called for trial, each defendant was arraigned, and, having the indictment read to him, entered a plea of not guilty. Whether the original arraignment and pleas were regarded as ineffective is not shown. Each of the three trials was completed within a single day. Under the Alabama statute the punishment for rape is to be fixed by the jury, and in its discretion may be from ten years imprisonment to death. The juries found defendants guilty and imposed the death penalty upon all. The trial court overruled motions for new trials and sentenced the defendants in accordance with the verdicts. The judgments were affirmed by the state supreme court. Chief Justice Anderson thought the defendants had not been accorded a fair trial and strongly dissented.

In this court the judgments are assailed upon the grounds that the defendants, and each of them, were denied due process of law and the

---

52. One study has suggested that this regional pattern of executions post-*Furman* tracks the regional pattern of lynchings during the period 1882–1968, the period for which records are available. See F. Zimring, The Contradictions of American Capital Punishment (2003), pp. 89–118. The 14 "high-lynching" states (states with more than 100 recorded lynchings)—the 11 former Confederate states plus the border states of Kentucky, Missouri and Oklahoma—all are death penalty states and include all of the top ten post-*Furman* execution states. By contrast, the 14 "low-lynching" states (states with less than 10 recorded lynchings) include seven states with no death penalty throughout the period and four other states with no post-*Furman* executions.

equal protection of the laws, in contravention of the Fourteenth Amendment, specifically as follows: (1) They were not given a fair, impartial, and deliberate trial; (2) they were denied the right of counsel, with the accustomed incidents of consultation and opportunity of preparation for trial; and (3) they were tried before juries from which qualified members of their own race were systematically excluded. These questions were properly raised and saved in the courts below.

The only one of the assignments which we shall consider is the second, in respect of the denial of counsel; and it becomes unnecessary to discuss the facts of the case or the circumstances surrounding the prosecution except in so far as they reflect light upon that question.

The record shows that on the day when the offense is said to have been committed, these defendants, together with a number of other negroes, were upon a freight train on its way through Alabama. On the same train were seven white boys and the two white girls. A fight took place between the negroes and the white boys, in the course of which the white boys, with the exception of one named Gilley, were thrown off the train. A message was sent ahead, reporting the fight and asking that every negro be gotten off the train. The participants in the fight, and the two girls, were in an open gondola car. The two girls testified that each of them was assaulted by six different negroes in turn, and they identified the seven defendants as having been among the number. None of the white boys was called to testify, with the exception of Gilley, who was called in rebuttal.

Before the train reached Scottsboro, Ala., a sheriff's posse seized the defendants and two other negroes. Both girls and the negroes then were taken to Scottsboro, the county seat. Word of their coming and of the alleged assault had preceded them, and they were met at Scottsboro by a large crowd. It does not sufficiently appear that the defendants were seriously threatened with, or that they were actually in danger of, mob violence; but it does appear that the attitude of the community was one of great hostility. The sheriff thought it necessary to call for the militia to assist in safeguarding the prisoners. Chief Justice Anderson pointed out in his opinion that every step taken from the arrest and arraignment to the sentence was accompanied by the military. Soldiers took the defendants to Gadsden for safe-keeping, brought them back to Scottsboro for arraignment, returned them to Gadsden for safe-keeping while awaiting trial, escorted them to Scottsboro for trial a few days later, and guarded the courthouse and grounds at every stage of the proceedings. It is perfectly apparent that the proceedings, from beginning to end, took place in an atmosphere of tense, hostile, and excited public sentiment. During the entire time, the defendants were closely confined or were under military guard. The record does not disclose their ages, except that one of them was nineteen; but the record clearly indicates that most, if not all, of them were youthful, and they are constantly referred to as "the boys." They were ignorant and illiterate. All of them were residents of other states, where alone members of their families or friends resided.

However guilty defendants, upon due inquiry, might prove to have been, they were, until convicted, presumed to be innocent. It was the duty of the court having their cases in charge to see that they were denied no necessary incident of a fair trial. With any error of the state court involving alleged contravention of the state statutes or Constitution we, of course, have nothing to do. The sole inquiry which we are permitted to make is whether the federal Constitution was contravened; and as to that, we confine ourselves, as already suggested, to the inquiry whether the defendants were in substance denied the right of counsel, and if so, whether such denial infringes the due process clause of the Fourteenth Amendment.

First. The record shows that immediately upon the return of the indictment defendants were arraigned and pleaded not guilty. Apparently they were not asked whether they had, or were able to employ, counsel, or wished to have counsel appointed; or whether they had friends or relatives who might assist in that regard if communicated with. That it would not have been an idle ceremony to have given the defendants reasonable opportunity to communicate with their families and endeavor to obtain counsel is demonstrated by the fact that very soon after conviction, able counsel appeared in their behalf. This was pointed out by Chief Justice Anderson in the course of his dissenting opinion. "They were nonresidents," he said, "and had little time or opportunity to get in touch with their families and friends who were scattered throughout two other states, and time has demonstrated that they could or would have been represented by able counsel had a better opportunity been given by a reasonable delay in the trial of the cases judging from the number and activity of counsel that appeared immediately or shortly after their conviction."

It is hardly necessary to say that the right to counsel being conceded, a defendant should be afforded a fair opportunity to secure counsel of his own choice. Not only was that not done here, but such designation of counsel as was attempted was either so indefinite or so close upon the trial as to amount to a denial of effective and substantial aid in that regard. This will be amply demonstrated by a brief review of the record.

April 6, six days after indictment, the trials began. When the first case was called, the court inquired whether the parties were ready for trial. The state's attorney replied that he was ready to proceed. No one answered for the defendants or appeared to represent or defend them. Mr. Roddy, a Tennessee lawyer not a member of the local bar, addressed the court, saying that he had not been employed, but that people who were interested had spoken to him about the case. He was asked by the court whether he intended to appear for the defendants, and answered that he would like to appear along with counsel that the court might appoint. The record then proceeds:

"The Court: If you appear for these defendants, then I will not appoint counsel; if local counsel are willing to appear and assist you under the circumstances all right, but I will not appoint them.

"Mr. Roddy: Your Honor has appointed counsel, is that correct?

"The Court: I appointed all the members of the bar for the purpose of arraigning the defendants and then of course I anticipated them to continue to help them if no counsel appears.

"Mr. Roddy: Then I don't appear then as counsel but I do want to stay in and not be ruled out in this case.

"The Court: Of course I would not do that—

"Mr. Roddy: I just appear here through the courtesy of Your Honor.

"The Court: Of course I give you that right * * *."

And then, apparently addressing all the lawyers present, the court inquired:

" * * * Well are you all willing to assist?

"Mr. Moody: Your Honor appointed us all and we have been proceeding along every line we know about it under Your Honor's appointment.

"The Court: The only thing I am trying to do is, if counsel appears for these defendants I don't want to impose on you all, but if you feel like counsel from Chattanooga—

"Mr. Moody: I see his situation of course and I have not run out of anything yet. Of course, if Your Honor purposes to appoint us, Mr. Parks, I am willing to go on with it. Most of the bar have been down and conferred with these defendants in this case; they did not know what else to do.

"The Court: The thing, I did not want to impose on the members of the bar if counsel unqualifiedly appears; if you all feel like Mr. Roddy is only interested in a limited way to assist, then I don't care to appoint—

"Mr. Parks: Your Honor, I don't feel like you ought to impose on any member of the local bar if the defendants are represented by counsel.

"The Court: That is what I was trying to ascertain, Mr. Parks.

"Mr. Parks: Of course if they have counsel, I don't see the necessity of the Court appointing anybody; if they haven't counsel, of course I think it is up to the Court to appoint counsel to represent them.

"The Court: I think you are right about it Mr. Parks and that is the reason I was trying to get an expression from Mr. Roddy.

"Mr. Roddy: I think Mr. Parks is entirely right about it, if I was paid down here and employed, it would be a different thing, but I have not prepared this case for trial and have only been called into it by people who are interested in these boys from Chattanooga. Now, they have not given me an opportunity to prepare the case and I am not familiar with the procedure in Alabama, but I merely came down here as a friend of the people who are interested and not as paid counsel, and certainly I haven't any money to pay them and nobody I am interested in had me to come down here has put up any fund of money to come down here and pay counsel. If they should do it I would be glad to turn it over—a counsel but

I am merely here at the solicitation of people who have become interested in this case without any payment of fee and without any preparation for trial and I think the boys would be better off if I step entirely out of the case according to my way of looking at it and according to my lack of preparation for it and not being familiar with the procedure in Alabama * * *.''

Mr. Roddy later observed:

"If there is anything I can do to be of help to them, I will be glad to do it; I am interested to that extent.

"The Court: Well gentlemen, if Mr. Roddy only appears as assistant that way, I think it is proper that I appoint members of this bar to represent them, I expect that is right. If Mr. Roddy will appear, I wouldn't of course, I would not appoint anybody. I don't see, Mr. Roddy, how I can make a qualified appointment or a limited appointment. Of course, I don't mean to cut off your assistance in any way—Well gentlemen, I think you understand it.

"Mr. Moody: I am willing to go ahead and help Mr. Roddy in anything I can do about it, under the circumstances.

"The Court: All right, all the lawyers that will, of course, I would not require a lawyer to appear if—

"Mr. Moody: I am willing to do that for him as a member of the bar; I will go ahead and help do anything I can do.

"The Court: All right."

And in this casual fashion the matter of counsel in a capital case was disposed of.

It thus will be seen that until the very morning of the trial no lawyer had been named or definitely designated to represent the defendants. Prior to that time, the trial judge had "appointed all the members of the bar" for the limited "purpose of arraigning the defendants." Whether they would represent the defendants thereafter, if no counsel appeared in their behalf, was a matter of speculation only, or, as the judge indicated, of mere anticipation on the part of the court. Such a designation, even if made for all purposes, would, in our opinion, have fallen far short of meeting, in any proper sense, a requirement for the appointment of counsel. How many lawyers were members of the bar does not appear; but, in the very nature of things, whether many or few, they would not, thus collectively named, have been given that clear appreciation of responsibility or impressed with that individual sense of duty which should and naturally would accompany the appointment of a selected member of the bar, specifically named and assigned.

That this action of the trial judge in respect of appointment of counsel was little more than an expansive gesture, imposing no substantial or definite obligation upon any one, is borne out by the fact that prior to the calling of the case for trial on April 6, a leading member of the local bar accepted employment on the side of the prosecution and actively participated in the trial. It is true that he said that before doing so he had understood Mr. Roddy would be employed as counsel for the defendants. This the lawyer in question, of his own accord, frankly stated to the court; and no doubt he acted with the utmost good faith. Probably other members of the bar had a like understanding. In any event, the circumstance lends emphasis to the conclusion that during perhaps the most critical period of the proceedings against these defendants, that is to say, from the time of their arraignment until the beginning of their trial, when consultation, thorough-going investigation and preparation were vitally important, the defendants did not have the aid of counsel in any real sense, although they were as much entitled to such aid during that period as at the trial itself.

Nor do we think the situation was helped by what occurred on the morning of the trial. At that time, as appears from the colloquy printed above, Mr. Roddy stated to the court that he did not appear as counsel, but that he would like to appear along with counsel that the court might appoint; that he had not been given an opportunity to prepare the case; that he was not familiar with the procedure in Alabama, but merely came down as a friend of the people who were interested; that he thought the boys would be better off if he should step entirely out of the case. Mr. Moody, a member of the local bar, expressed a willingness to help Mr. Roddy in anything he could do under the circumstances. To this the court responded: "All right, all the lawyers that will; of course I would not require a lawyer to appear if—." And Mr. Moody continued: "I am willing to do that for him as a member of the bar; I will go ahead and help do anything I can do." With this dubious understanding, the trials immediately proceeded. The defendants, young, ignorant, illiterate, surrounded by hostile sentiment, haled back and forth under guard of soldiers, charged with an atrocious crime regarded with especial horror in the community where they were to be tried, were thus put in peril of their lives within a few moments after counsel for the first time charged with any degree of responsibility began to represent them.

* * *

It never has been doubted by this court, or any other so far as we know, that notice and hearing are preliminary steps essential to the passing of an enforceable judgment, and that they, together with a legally competent tribunal having jurisdiction of the case, constitute basic elements of the constitutional requirement of due process of law. The words of Webster, so often quoted, that by "the law of the land" is intended "a law which hears before it condemns," have been repeated in varying forms of expression in a multitude of decisions. In *Holden v. Hardy*, 169 U.S. 366, 18 S.Ct. 383 (1898), the necessity of due notice and an opportunity of being heard is described as among the "immutable principles of justice which inhere in the very idea of free government which no member of the Union may disregard." And Mr. Justice Field, in an earlier case, *Galpin v. Page*, 85 U.S. 350 (1873), said that the rule that no one shall be personally bound until he has had his day in court was as old as the law, and it meant that he must be cited to appear and afforded an opportunity to be heard. "Judgment without such citation and opportunity wants all the attributes of a judicial determination; it is judicial usurpation and oppression, and never can be upheld where justice is justly administered." Citations to the same effect might be indefinitely multiplied, but there is no occasion for doing so.

What, then, does a hearing include? Historically and in practice, in our own country at least, it has always included the right to the aid of counsel when desired and provided by the party asserting the right. The right to be heard would be, in many cases, of little avail if it did not comprehend the right to be heard by counsel. Even the intelligent and educated layman has small and sometimes no skill in the science of law. If charged with crime, he is incapable, generally, of determining for himself whether the indictment is good or bad. He is unfamiliar with the rules of evidence. Left without the aid of counsel he may be put on trial without a proper charge, and convicted upon incompetent evidence, or evidence irrelevant to the issue or otherwise inadmissible. He lacks both the skill and knowledge adequately to prepare his defense, even though he have a perfect one. He requires the guiding hand of counsel at every step in the proceedings against him. Without it, though he be not guilty, he faces the danger of conviction because he does not know how to establish his innocence. If that be true of men of intelligence, how much more true is it of the ignorant and illiterate, or those of feeble intellect. If in any case, civil of criminal, a state or federal court were arbitrarily to refuse to hear a party by counsel, employed by and appearing for him, it reasonably may not be doubted that such a refusal would be a denial of a hearing, and, therefore, of due process in the constitutional sense.

       * * *

In the light of the facts outlined in the forepart of this opinion—the ignorance and illiteracy of the defendants, their youth, the circumstances of public hostility, the imprisonment and the close surveillance of the defendants by the military forces, the fact that their friends and families were all in other states and communication with them necessarily difficult, and above all that they stood in deadly peril of their lives—we think the failure of the trial court to give them reasonable time and opportunity to secure counsel was a clear denial of due process.

But passing that, and assuming their inability, even if opportunity had been given, to employ counsel, as the trial court evidently did assume, we are of opinion that, under the circumstances just stated, the necessity of counsel was so vital and imperative that the failure of the trial court to make an effective appointment of counsel was likewise a denial of due process within the meaning of the Fourteenth Amendment. Whether this would be so in other criminal prosecutions, or under other circumstances, we need not determine. All that it is necessary now to decide, as we do decide, is that in a capital case, where the defendant is unable to employ counsel, and is incapable adequately of making his own defense because of ignorance, feeble-mindedness, illiteracy, or the like, it is the duty of the court, whether requested or not, to assign counsel for him as a necessary requisite of due process of law; and that duty is not discharged by an assignment at such a time or under such circumstances as to preclude the giving of effective aid in the preparation and trial of the case. To hold otherwise would be to ignore the fundamental postulate, already adverted to, "that there are certain immutable principles of justice which inhere in the very idea of free government which no member of the Union may disregard." *Holden v. Hardy, supra.* In a case such as this, whatever may be the rule in other cases, the right to have counsel appointed, when necessary, is a logical corollary from the constitutional right to be heard by counsel.

> * * *

The United States by statute and every state in the Union by express provision of law, or by the determination of its courts, make it the duty of the trial judge, where the accused is unable to employ counsel, to appoint counsel for him. In most states the rule applies broadly to all criminal prosecutions, in others it is limited to the more serious crimes, and in a very limited number, to capital cases. A rule adopted with such unanimous accord reflects, if it does not establish the inherent right to have counsel appointed at least in cases like the present, and lends convincing support to the conclusion we have reached as to the fundamental nature of that right.

The judgments must be reversed and the causes remanded for further proceedings not inconsistent with this opinion.

[Dissenting opinion of Bᴜᴛʟᴇʀ, J. joined by McReʏɴoʟᴅs, J. omitted]

NOTE

1. *Subsequent developments.*

After the Supreme Court decision in *Powell*, venue for the retrials was changed to Decatur, Alabama, and the state decided to try the defendants one at a time. The second trial of Haywood Patterson began in March, 1933, and Patterson was represented by an experienced New York defense lawyer retained by the International Labor Defense. Unlike the first trial, the second trial received extensive publicity throughout the country and abroad. The state's principal witness, Victoria Price (one of the victims), was impeached on cross-examination, and the doctor who examined the two victims immediately after the incident admitted that he had observed no injuries and could find no motile sperm, but, most significantly, Ruby Bates (the other victim) recanted her previous testimony and testified for the defense that no rapes had occurred. Nevertheless, Patterson was again convicted and sentenced to death. Two months later, the trial judge set aside the verdict for lack of evidence. In November and December, Patterson was tried for the third time and Clarence Norris for the second time. Both were convicted and sentenced to death. In 1935, the United States Supreme Court reversed Norris's conviction in *Norris v. Alabama*, 294 U.S. 587, 55 S.Ct. 579 (1935) because of the long-standing exclusion of blacks from juries, and it vacated Patterson's conviction in *Patterson v. Alabama*, 294 U.S. 600, 55 S.Ct. 575 (1935) in light of its holding in *Norris*. In November, 1935, the reconstituted grand jury, with one black man on it, reindicted the defendants. In January, 1936, Patterson was tried for a fourth time, convicted and sentenced to seventy-five years. In July, 1937, Norris was tried for a third time, convicted and sentenced to death. Two other defendants, Andy Wright and Charlie Weems, were tried, convicted and sentenced to a terms of ninety-nine and seventy-five years, respectively. Ozzie Powell, who, a year and a half earlier, had gotten in a fight with a sheriff's deputy and had been shot in the head, was allowed to plead guilty to assault and was sentenced to 20 years. Charges against the other four defendants were dropped. A year later, the governor commuted Norris's sentence to life imprisonment. During the period 1943–1946, all the defendants but Patterson were paroled. In 1948, Patterson escaped from prison. When he was arrested in Detroit, the governor refused to extradite him to Alabama. In 1976, Clarence Norris, the last living defendant, was pardoned by the governor of Alabama. See J. Goodman, Stories of Scottsboro (1994).

McGAUTHA v. CALIFORNIA

402 U.S. 183, 91 S.Ct. 1454, 28 L.Ed.2d 711 (1971).

MR. JUSTICE HARLAN delivered the opinion of the Court.

Petitioners McGautha and Crampton were convicted of murder in the first degree in the courts of California and Ohio respectively and sentenced to death pursuant to the statutes of those States. In each case the decision whether the defendant should live or die was left to the absolute discretion of the jury. In McGautha's case the jury, in accordance with California law, determined punishment in a separate proceeding following the trial on the issue of guilt. In Crampton's case, in accordance with Ohio law, the jury determined guilt and punishment after a single trial and in a single verdict. We granted certiorari in the McGautha case limited to the question whether petitioner's constitutional rights were infringed by permitting the jury to impose the death penalty without any governing standards. We granted certiorari in the Crampton case limited to that same question and to the further question whether the jury's imposition of the death sentence in the same proceeding and verdict as determined the issue of guilt was constitutionally permissible. For the reasons that follow, we find no constitutional infirmity in the conviction of either petitioner, and we affirm in both cases.

I

It will put the constitutional issues in clearer focus to begin by setting out the course which each trial took.

A. McGautha's Guilt Trial

McGautha and his codefendant Wilkinson were charged with committing two armed robberies and a murder on February 14, 1967.[2] In accordance with California procedure in capital cases, the trial was in two stages, a guilt stage and a punishment stage. At the guilt trial the evidence tended to show that the defendants, armed with pistols, entered the market of Mrs. Pon Lock early in the afternoon of the murder. While Wilkinson kept a customer under guard, McGautha trained his gun on Mrs. Lock and took almost $300. Roughly three hours later, McGautha and Wilkinson held up another store, this one owned by Mrs. Benjamin Smetana and operated by her with her husband's assistance. While one defendant forcibly restrained a customer, the other struck Mrs. Smetana on the head. A shot was fired, fatally wounding Mr. Smetana. Wilkinson's former girl friend testified that shortly after the robbery McGautha told her he had shot a man and showed her an empty cartridge in the cylinder of his gun. Other evidence at the guilt stage was inconclusive on the issue as to who fired the fatal shot. The jury found both defendants guilty of two counts of armed robbery and one count of first-degree murder as charged.

B. McGautha's Penalty Trial

At the penalty trial, which took place on the following day but before the same jury, the State waived its opening, presented evidence of McGautha's prior felony convictions and sentences and then rested. Wilkinson testified in his own behalf, relating his unhappy childhood in Mississippi as the son of a white father and a Negro mother, his honorable discharge from the Army on the score of his low intelligence, his regular attendance at church, and his good record for holding jobs and supporting his mother and siblings up to the time he was shot in the back in an unprovoked assault by a street gang. Thereafter, he testified, he had difficulty obtaining or holding employment. About a year later he fell in with McGautha and his companions, and when they found themselves short of funds, one of the group suggested that they "knock over somebody." This was the first time, Wilkinson said, that he had ever had any thoughts of committing a robbery. He admitted participating in the two robberies but said he had not known that the stores were to be held up until McGautha drew his gun. He testified that it had been McGautha who struck Mrs. Smetana and shot Mr. Smetana.

Wilkinson called several witnesses in his behalf. An undercover narcotics agent testified that he had seen the murder weapon in McGautha's possession and had seen McGautha demonstrating his quick draw. A minister with whom Wilkinson had boarded testified to Wilkinson's church attendance and good reputation. He also stated that before trial Wilkinson had expressed his horror at what had happened and requested the minister's prayers on his behalf. A former fellow employee testified that Wilkinson had a good reputation and was honest and peaceable.

---

2. The information also alleged that McGautha had four prior felony convictions: felonious theft, robbery, murder without malice, and robbery by assault. The most recent of these convictions occurred in 1952. In a proceeding in chambers McGautha admitted the convictions, and the jury did not learn of them at the guilt stage of the trial.

McGautha also testified in his own behalf at the penalty hearing. He admitted that the murder weapon was his, but testified that he and Wilkinson had traded guns, and that it was Wilkinson who had struck Mrs. Smetana and killed her husband. McGautha testified that he came from a broken home and that he had been wounded during World War II. He related his employment record, medical condition, and remorse. He admitted his criminal record, but testified that he had been a mere accomplice in two of those robberies and that his prior conviction for murder had resulted from a slaying in self-defense. McGautha also admitted to a 1964 guilty plea to a charge of carrying a concealed weapon. He called no witnesses in his behalf.

The jury was instructed in the following language:

"in this part of the trial the law does not forbid you from being influenced by pity for the defendants and you may be governed by mere sentiment and sympathy for the defendants in arriving at a proper penalty in this case; however, the law does forbid you from being governed by mere conjecture, prejudice, public opinion or public feeling.

"The defendants in this case have been found guilty of the offense of murder in the first degree, and it is now your duty to determine which of the penalties provided by law should be imposed on each defendant for that offense. Now, in arriving at this determination you should consider all of the evidence received here in court presented by the People and defendants throughout the trial before this jury. You may also consider all of the evidence of the circumstances surrounding the crime, of each defendant's background and history, and of the facts in aggravation or mitigation of the penalty which have been received here in court. However, it is not essential to your decision that you find mitigating circumstances on the one hand or evidence in aggravation of the offense on the other hand.

" * * * Notwithstanding facts, if any, proved in mitigation or aggravation, in determining which punishment shall be inflicted, you are entirely free to act according to your own judgment, conscience, and absolute discretion. That verdict must express the individual opinion of each juror.

"Now, beyond prescribing the two alternative penalties, the law itself provides no standard for the guidance of the jury in the selection of the penalty, but, rather, commits the whole matter of determining which of the two penalties shall be fixed to the judgment, conscience, and absolute discretion of the jury. In the determination of that matter, if the jury does agree, it must be unanimous as to which of the two penalties is imposed."

Deliberations began in the early afternoon of August 24, 1967. * * * Late in the afternoon of August 25 the jury returned verdicts fixing Wilkinson's punishment at life imprisonment and McGautha's punishment at death.

[The trial judge pronounced a death judgment, and the judgment was affirmed by the California Supreme Court.]

C. Crampton's Trial

Petitioner Crampton was indicted for the murder of his wife, Wilma Jean, purposely and with premeditated malice. He pleaded not guilty and not guilty by reason of insanity. In accordance with the Ohio practice which he challenges, his guilt and punishment were determined in a single unitary proceeding.

At trial the State's case was as follows. The Cramptons had been married about four months at the time of the murder. Two months before the slaying Crampton was allowed to leave the state mental hospital, where he was undergoing observation and treatment for alcoholism and drug addiction, to attend the funeral of his wife's father. On this occasion he stole a knife from the house of his late father-in-law and ran away. He called the house several times and talked to his wife, greatly upsetting her. When she pleaded with him to return to the hospital and stated that she would have to call the police, he threatened to kill her if she did. Wilma and her brother nevertheless did notify the authorities, who picked Crampton up later the same evening. There was testimony of other threats Crampton had made on his wife's life, and it was revealed that about 10 days before the murder Mrs. Crampton's fear of her husband had caused her to request and receive police protection.

The State's main witness to the facts surrounding the murder was one William Collins, a convicted felon who had first met Crampton when they, along with Crampton's brother Jack, were in the State Prison in Michigan. On January 14, 1967, three days before the murder, Collins and Crampton met at Jack Crampton's house in Pontiac, Michigan. During those three days Collins and Crampton roamed the upper Midwest, committing a series of petty thefts and obtaining amphetamines, to which both were addicted, by theft and forged prescriptions.

About nine o'clock on the evening of January 16, Crampton called his wife from St. Joseph, Michigan; after the call he told Collins that he had to get back to Toledo, where his wife was, as fast as possible. They arrived in the early morning hours of January 17. After Crampton had stopped by his wife's home and sent Collins to the door with a purported message for her, the two went to the home of Crampton's mother-in-law, which Crampton knew to be empty, to obtain some guns. They broke in and stole a rifle, ammunition, and some handguns, including the .45 automatic which was later identified as the murder weapon. Crampton kept this gun with him. He indicated to Collins that he believed his wife was having an affair. He fired the .45 in the air with a remark to the effect that "a slug of that type would do quite a bit of damage," and said that if he found his wife with the man he suspected he would kill them both.

That evening Crampton called his wife's home and learned that she was present. He quickly drove out to the house, and told Collins, "Leave me off right here in front of the house and you take the car and go back to the parking lot and if I'm not there by six o'clock in the morning you're on your own."

About 11:20 that evening Crampton was arrested for driving a stolen car. The murder weapon was found between the seats of the car.

Mrs. Crampton's body was found the next morning. She had been shot in the face at close range while she was using the toilet. A .45–caliber shell casing was near the body. A jacket which Crampton had stolen a few days earlier was found in the living room. The coroner who examined the body at 11:30 p.m. on January 18, testified that in his opinion death had occurred 24 hours earlier, plus or minus four hours.

The defense called Crampton's mother as a witness. She testified about Crampton's background, including a serious concussion received at age nine, his good grades in junior high school, his stepfather's jealousy of him, his leaving home at age 14 to live with various relatives, his enlistment in the Navy at age 17, his marriage to a girl named Sandra, the birth of a son, a divorce, then a remarriage to Sandra and another divorce shortly after, and finally his marriage to Wilma. Mrs. Crampton also testified to Crampton's drug addiction, to his brushes with the law as a youth and as an adult, and to his undesirable discharge from the Navy.

Crampton's attorney also introduced into evidence a series of hospital reports which contained further information on Crampton's background, including his criminal record, which was substantial, his court-martial conviction and undesirable discharge from the Navy, and the absence of any significant employment record. They also contained his claim that the shooting was accidental; that he had been gathering up guns around the house and had just removed the clip from an automatic when his wife asked to see it; that as he handed it to her it went off accidentally and killed her. All the reports concluded that Crampton was sane in both the legal and the medical senses. He was diagnosed as having a sociopathic personality disorder, along with alcohol and drug addiction. Crampton himself did not testify.

The jury was instructed that:

> "If you find the defendant guilty of murder in the first degree, the punishment is death, unless you recommend mercy, in which event the punishment is imprisonment in the penitentiary during life."

The jury was given no other instructions specifically addressed to the decision whether to recommend mercy, but was told in connection with its verdict generally:

> "You must not be influenced by any consideration of sympathy or prejudice. It is your duty to carefully weigh the evidence, to decide all disputed questions of fact, to apply the instructions of the court to your findings and to render your verdict accordingly. In fulfilling your duty, your efforts must be to arrive at a just verdict.

"Consider all the evidence and make your finding with intelligence and impartiality, and without bias, sympathy, or prejudice, so that the State of Ohio and the defendant will feel that their case was fairly and impartially tried."

The jury deliberated for over four hours and returned a verdict of guilty, with no recommendation for mercy.

[The court imposed the death sentence, which was upheld by the Ohio courts.]

III

We consider first McGautha's and Crampton's common claim: that the absence of standards to guide the jury's discretion on the punishment issue is constitutionally intolerable. To fit their arguments within a constitutional frame of reference petitioners contend that to leave the jury completely at large to impose or withhold the death penalty as it see fit is fundamentally lawless and therefore violates the basic command of the Fourteenth Amendment that no State shall deprive a person of his life without due process of law. Despite the undeniable surface appeal of the proposition, we conclude that the courts below correctly rejected it.

A

In order to see petitioners' claim in perspective, it is useful to call to mind the salient features of the history of capital punishment for homicides under the common law in England, and subsequent statutory developments in this country. This history reveals continual efforts, uniformly unsuccessful, to identify before the fact those homicides for which the slayer should die. [Justice Harlan traced the development of the law of homicide, and in particular the development of "malice aforethought" as the distinguishing feature of capital murder.]

The growth of the law continued in this country, where there was rebellion against the common-law rule imposing a mandatory death sentence on all convicted murderers. Thus, in 1794, Pennsylvania attempted to reduce the rigors of the law by abolishing capital punishment except for "murder of the first degree," defined to include all "willful, deliberate and premeditated" killings, for which the death penalty remained mandatory. This reform was soon copied by Virginia and thereafter by many other States.

This new legislative criterion for isolating crimes appropriately punishable by death soon proved as unsuccessful as the concept of "malice aforethought." * * * At the same time, jurors on occasion took the law into their own hands in cases which were "willful, deliberate, and premeditated" in any view of that phrase, but which nevertheless were clearly inappropriate for the death penalty. In such cases they simply refused to convict of the capital offense.

In order to meet the problem of jury nullification, legislatures did not try, as before, to refine further the definition of capital homicides. Instead they adopted the method of forthrightly granting juries the discretion which they had been exercising in fact. Tennessee was the first State to give juries sentencing discretion in capital cases, but other States followed suit, as did the Federal Government in 1897.[11] Shortly thereafter, in *Winston v. United States*, 172 U.S. 303, 19 S.Ct. 212 (1899), this Court dealt with the federal statute for the first time. The Court reversed a murder conviction in which the trial judge instructed the jury that it should not return a recommendation of mercy unless it found the existence of mitigating circumstances. The Court found this instruction to interfere with the scheme of the Act to commit the whole question of capital punishment "to the judgment and the consciences of the jury."

> "How far considerations of age, sex, ignorance, illness or intoxication, of human passion or weakness, of sympathy or clemency, or the irrevocableness of an executed sentence of death, or an apprehension that explanatory facts may exist which have not been brought to light, or any other consideration whatever, should be allowed weight in deciding the question whether the accused should or should not be capitally punished, is committed by the act of congress to the sound discretion of the jury, and of the jury alone."

* * *

In recent years academic and professional sources have suggested that jury sentencing discretion should be controlled by standards of some sort. The American Law Institute first published such a recommendation in 1959. Several States have enacted new criminal codes in the intervening 12 years, some adopting features of the Model Penal Code. Other States have modified their laws with respect to murder and the death penalty in other ways. None of these States have followed the Model Penal Code and adopted statutory criteria for imposition of the death penalty. * * *

B

Petitioners seek to avoid the impact of this history by the observation that jury sentencing discretion in capital cases was introduced as a mechanism for dispensing mercy—a means for dealing with the rare case in which the death penalty was thought to be unjustified. Now, they assert, the death penalty is imposed on far fewer than half the defendants found guilty of capital crimes. The state and federal legislatures which provide for jury discretion in capital sentencing have, it is said, implicitly determined that some—indeed, the greater portion—of those guilty of capital crimes should be permitted to live. But having made that determination, petitioners argue, they have stopped short—the legislatures have not only failed to provide a rational basis for distinguishing the one group from the other, but they have failed even to suggest any basis at all.

---

11. California and Ohio, the two States involved in these cases, abolished mandatory death penalties in favor of jury discretion in 1874 and 1898. Except for four States that entirely abolished capital punishment in the middle of the last century, every American jurisdiction has at some time authorized jury sentencing in capital cases. None of these statutes have provided standards for the choice between death and life imprisonment.

Whatever the merits of providing such a mechanism to take account of the unforeseeable case calling for mercy, as was the original purpose, petitioners contend the mechanism is constitutionally intolerable as a means of selecting the extraordinary cases calling for the death penalty, which is its present-day function.

In our view, such force as this argument has derives largely from its generality. Those who have come to grips with the hard task of actually attempting to draft means of channeling capital sentencing discretion have confirmed the lesson taught by the history recounted above. To identify before the fact those characteristics of criminal homicides and their perpetrators which call for the death penalty, and to express these characteristics in language which can be fairly understood and applied by the sentencing authority, appear to be tasks which are beyond present human ability.

Thus the British Home Office, which before the recent abolition of capital punishment in that country had the responsibility for selecting the cases from England and Wales which should receive the benefit of the Royal Prerogative of Mercy, observed:

> "The difficulty of defining by any statutory provision the types of murder which ought or ought not to be punished by death may be illustrated by reference to the many diverse considerations to which the Home Secretary has regard in deciding whether to recommend clemency. No simple formula can take account of the innumerable degrees of culpability, and no formula which fails to do so can claim to be just or satisfy public opinion."

The Royal Commission accepted this view, and although it recommended a change in British practice to provide for discretionary power in the jury to find "extenuating circumstances," that term was to be left undefined; "[t]he decision of the jury would be within their unfettered discretion and in no sense governed by the principles of law." Report of the Royal Commission on Capital Punishment, 1949–1953. The Commission went on to say, in substantial confirmation of the views of the Home Office:

> "No formula is possible that would provide a reasonable criterion for the infinite variety of circumstances that may affect the gravity of the crime of murder. Discretionary judgment on the facts of each case is the only way in which they can be equitably distinguished. This conclusion is borne out by American experience: there the experiment of degrees of murder, introduced long ago, has had to be supplemented by giving to the courts a discretion that in effect supersedes it."

The draftsmen of the Model Penal Code expressly agreed with the conclusion of the Royal Commission that "the factors which determine whether the sentence of death is the appropriate penalty in particular cases are too complex to be compressed within the limits of a simple formula * * *." The draftsmen did think, however, "that it is within the realm of possibility to point to the main circumstances of aggravation and of mitigation that should be weighed and weighed against each other when they are presented in a concrete case." The circumstances the draftsmen selected * * * were not intended to be exclusive. The Code provides simply that the sentencing authority should "take into account the aggravating and mitigating circumstances enumerated * * * and any other facts that it deems relevant," and that the court should so instruct when the issue was submitted to the jury.[16] The Final Report of the National Commission on Reform of Federal Criminal Laws (1971) recommended entire abolition of the death penalty in federal cases. In a provisional chapter, prepared for the contingency that Congress might decide to retain the death penalty, the Report contains a set of criteria virtually identical with the aggravating and mitigating circumstances listed by the Model Penal Code. With respect to the use to be made of the criteria, the Report provides that: "[i]n deciding whether a sentence of death should be imposed, the court and the jury, if any, *may* consider the mitigating and aggravating circumstances set forth in the subsections below." (emphasis added).

It is apparent that such criteria do not purport to provide more than the most minimal control over the sentencing authority's exercise of discretion. They do not purport to give an exhaustive list of the relevant considerations or the way in which they may be affected by the presence or absence of other circumstances. They do not even undertake to exclude constitutionally impermissible considerations. And, of course, they provide no protection against the jury determined to decide on whimsy or caprice. In short, they do no more than suggest some subjects for the jury to consider during its deliberations, and they bear witness to the intractable nature of the problem of "standards" which the history of capital punishment has from the beginning reflected. Thus, they indeed caution against this Court's undertaking to establish such standards itself, or to pronounce at large that standards in this realm are constitutionally required.

In light of history, experience, and the present limitations of human knowledge, we find it quite impossible to say that committing to the untrammeled discretion of the jury the power to pronounce life or death in capital cases is offensive to anything in the Constitution. The States are entitled to assume that jurors confronted with the truly awesome responsibility of decreeing death for a fellow human will act with due regard for the consequences of their decision and will consider a variety of factors, many of which will have been suggested by the evidence or by the arguments of defense counsel. For a court to attempt to catalog the appropriate factors in this elusive area could inhibit rather than expand the scope of consideration, for no list of circumstances would ever be really

16. The Model Penal Code provides that the jury should not fix punishment at death unless it found at least one of the aggravating circumstances and no sufficiently substantial mitigating circumstances. As the reporter's comment recognized, there is no fundamental distinction between this procedure and a redefinition of the class of potentially capital murders. As we understand these petitioners' contentions, they seek standards for guiding the sentencing authority's discretion, not a greater strictness in the definition of the class of cases in which the discretion exists. If we are mistaken in this, and petitioners contend that Ohio's and California's definitions of first-degree murder are too broad, we consider their position constitutionally untenable.

complete. The infinite variety of cases and facets to each case would make general standards either meaningless "boiler-plate" or a statement of the obvious that no jury would need.

[The Court held that the unitary trial on guilt and penalty used by Ohio violated no constitutional right of Crampton, neither his right to remain silent nor his right to present evidence on the issue of penalty.]

V

Before we conclude this opinion, it is appropriate for us to make a broader observation than the issues raised by these cases strictly call for. It may well be, as the American Law Institute and the National Commission on Reform of Federal Criminal Laws have concluded, that bifurcated trials and criteria for jury sentencing discretion are superior means of dealing with capital cases if the death penalty is to be retained at all. But the Federal Constitution, which marks the limits of our authority in these cases, does not guarantee trial procedures that are the best of all worlds, or that accord with the most enlightened ideas of students of the infant science of criminology, or even those that measure up to the individual predilections of members of this Court. The Constitution requires no more than that trials be fairly conducted and that guaranteed rights of defendants be scrupulously respected. * * *

Certainly the facts of these gruesome murders bespeak no miscarriage of justice. The ability of juries, unassisted by standards, to distinguish between those defendants for whom the death penalty is appropriate punishment and those for whom imprisonment is sufficient is indeed illustrated by the discriminating verdict of the jury in McGautha's case, finding Wilkinson the less culpable of the two defendants and sparing his life.

The procedures which petitioners challenge are those by which most capital trials in this country are conducted, and by which all were conducted until a few years ago. We have determined that these procedures are consistent with the rights to which petitioners were constitutionally entitled, and that their trials were entirely fair. Having reached these conclusions we have performed our task of measuring the States' process by federal constitutional standards, and accordingly the judgment in each of these cases is affirmed.

[Separate opinion of BLACK, J. (concurring) and dissenting opinions of DOUGLAS, J. joined by BRENNAN and MARSHALL, JJ. and BRENNAN, J. joined by DOUGLAS and MARSHALL, JJ., omitted]

CHAPTER 2

THE SUPREME COURT'S SEMINAL CASES

■ ■ ■

Only a year and a half after its decision in *McGautha*, the Supreme Court dramatically reversed course in *Furman v. Georgia*, the first case in this chapter. Justices Stewart and White, who had been with the majority in *McGautha*, joined the *McGautha* dissenters to hold unconstitutional all existing death penalty statutes. The Justices in the majority rely for their decision on the Eighth Amendment, which provides: "Excessive bail shall not be required, nor excessive fines imposed, nor cruel and unusual punishments inflicted." Because there is no majority opinion in *Furman*, and each justice wrote an opinion, the implications of the *Furman* decision were far from clear.[a] However, the Court does decide that the Eighth Amendment imposes at least some limits on states' administration of the death penalty. In *Gregg v. Georgia* and its four companion cases, the plurality attempts to clarify or reinterpret *Furman* and to find a middle ground between holding the death penalty unconstitutional (as Justices Brennan and Marshall would do) and renouncing any attempt to subject the death penalty to constitutional constraints (as the *Furman* dissenters would have done). In *Gregg*, the plurality upholds the Georgia death penalty scheme as applied to the crime of murder, finding that the scheme limits the risk of arbitrary application. However, in *Woodson v. North Carolina*, the Court finds unconstitutional North Carolina's mandatory death penalty for murder. Finally, in *Jurek v. Texas*, the plurality upholds the very different scheme employed by Texas.

FURMAN v. GEORGIA
408 U.S. 238, 92 S.Ct. 2726, 33 L.Ed.2d 346 (1972).

PER CURIAM.

[Certiorari was granted in three capital cases. In *Furman v. Georgia*, the petitioner was convicted of murder in Georgia and was sentenced to death. In *Jackson v. Georgia*, the petitioner was convicted of rape in Georgia and was sentenced to death. In *Branch v. Texas*, the petitioner was convicted of rape in Texas and was sentenced to death.]

---

a. Because each justice wrote an opinion, the case occupies 233 pages in the official reports. A portion of each opinion is included here, but, of necessity, the opinions have been substantially edited.

Certiorari was granted limited to the following question: "Does the imposition and carrying out of the death penalty in [these cases] constitute cruel and unusual punishment in violation of the Eighth and Fourteenth Amendments?" The Court holds that the imposition and carrying out of the death penalty in these cases constitute cruel and unusual punishment in violation of the Eighth and Fourteenth Amendments. The judgment in each case is therefore reversed insofar as it leaves undisturbed the death sentence imposed, and the cases are remanded for further proceedings. So ordered.

Judgment in each case reversed in part and cases remanded.

MR. JUSTICE DOUGLAS, MR. JUSTICE BRENNAN, MR. JUSTICE STEWART, MR. JUSTICE WHITE, and MR. JUSTICE MARSHALL have filed separate opinions in support of the judgments.

THE CHIEF JUSTICE, MR. JUSTICE BLACKMUN, MR. JUSTICE POWELL, and MR. JUSTICE REHNQUIST have filed separate dissenting opinions.

MR. JUSTICE DOUGLAS, concurring.

* * *

The generality of a law inflicting capital punishment is one thing. What may be said of the validity of a law on the books and what may be done with the law in its application do, or may, lead to quite different conclusions.

It would seem to be incontestable that the death penalty inflicted on one defendant is "unusual" if it discriminates against him by reason of his race, religion, wealth, social position, or class, or if it is imposed under a procedure that gives room for the play of such prejudices.

* * *

The high service rendered by the "cruel and unusual" punishment clause of the Eighth Amendment is to require legislatures to write penal laws that are evenhanded, nonselective, and nonarbitrary, and to require judges to see to it that general laws are not applied sparsely, selectively, and spottily to unpopular groups.

A law that stated that anyone making more than $50,000 would be exempt from the death penalty would plainly fall, as would a law that in terms said that blacks, those who never went beyond the fifth grade in school, those who made less than $3,000 a year, or those who were unpopular or unstable should be the only people executed. A law which in the overall view reaches that result in practice has no more sanctity than a law which in terms provides the same.

Thus, these discretionary statutes are unconstitutional in their operation. They are pregnant with discrimination and discrimination is an ingredient not compatible with the idea of equal protection of the laws that is implicit in the ban on "cruel and unusual" punishments.

* * *

MR. JUSTICE BRENNAN, concurring.

* * *

Death is a unique punishment in the United States. In a society that so strongly affirms the sanctity of life, not surprisingly the common view is that death is the ultimate sanction. This natural human feeling appears all about us. There has been no national debate about punishment, in general or by imprisonment, comparable to the debate about the punishment of death. No other punishment has been so continuously restricted, nor has any State yet abolished prisons, as some have abolished this punishment. And those States that still inflict death reserve it for the most heinous crimes. Juries, of course, have always treated death cases differently, as have governors exercising their commutation powers. Criminal defendants are of the same view. "As all practicing lawyers know, who have defended persons charged with capital offenses, often the only goal possible is to avoid the death penalty." *Griffin v. Illinois*, 351 U.S. 12, 76 S.Ct. 585 (1956) (BURTON and MINTON, JJ., dissenting). Some legislatures have required particular procedures, such as two-stage trials and automatic appeals, applicable only in death cases. "It is the universal experience in the administration of criminal justice that those charged with capital offenses are granted special considerations." *Id.* This Court, too, almost always treats death cases as a class apart. And the unfortunate effect of this punishment upon the functioning of the judicial process is well known; no other punishment has a similar effect.

The only explanation for the uniqueness of death is its extreme severity. Death is today an unusually severe punishment, unusual in its pain, in its finality, and in its enormity. No other existing punishment is comparable to death in terms of physical and mental suffering. Although our information is not conclusive, it appears that there is no method available that guarantees an immediate and painless death. Since the discontinuance of flogging as a constitutionally permissible punishment, death remains as the only punishment that may involve the conscious infliction of physical pain. In addition, we know that mental pain is an inseparable part of our practice of punishing criminals by death, for the prospect of pending execution exacts a frightful toll during the inevitable long wait between the imposition of sentence and the actual infliction of death. As the California Supreme Court pointed out, "the process of carrying out a verdict of death is often so degrading and brutalizing to the human spirit as to constitute psychological torture." *People v. Anderson*, 493 P.2d 880 (Cal. 1972). Indeed, as Mr. Justice FRANKFURTER noted, "the onset of insanity while awaiting execution of a death sentence is not a rare phenomenon." *Solesbee v. Balkcom*, 339 U.S. 9, 70 S.Ct. 457 (1950) (dissenting opinion). The "fate of ever-increasing fear and distress" to which the expatriate is subjected, *Trop v. Dulles*, 356 U.S. 86, 78 S.Ct. 590 (1958) can only exist to a greater degree for a person confined in prison awaiting death.

The unusual severity of death is manifested most clearly in its finality and enormity. Death, in these respects, is in a class by itself. Expatriation, for example, is a punishment that "destroys for the individual the political existence that was centuries in the development[,]" that "strips the citizen of his status in the national and international political community[,]" and that puts "[h]is very existence" in jeopardy. Expatriation thus inherently entails "the total destruction of the individual's status in organized society." *Id.* "In short, the expatriate has lost the right to have rights." *Id.* Yet, demonstrably, expatriation is not "a fate worse than death." *Id.* (FRANKFURTER, J., dissenting). Although death, like expatriation, destroys the individual's "political existence" and his "status in organized society," it does more, for, unlike expatriation, death also destroys "[h]is very existence." There is, too, at least the possibility that the expatriate will in the future regain "the right to have rights." Death forecloses even that possibility.

Death is truly an awesome punishment. The calculated killing of a human being by the State involves, by its very nature, a denial of the executed person's humanity. The contrast with the plight of a person punished by imprisonment is evident. An individual in prison does not lose "the right to have rights." A prisoner retains, for example, the constitutional rights to the free exercise of religion, to be free of cruel and unusual punishments, and to treatment as a "person" for purposes of due process of law and the equal protection of the laws. A prisoner remains a member of the human family. Moreover, he retains the right of access to the courts. His punishment is not irrevocable. Apart from the common charge, grounded upon the recognition of human fallibility, that the punishment of death must inevitably be inflicted upon innocent men, we know that death has been the lot of men whose convictions were unconstitutionally secured in view of later, retroactively applied, holdings of this Court. The punishment itself may have been unconstitutionally inflicted, yet the finality of death precludes relief. An executed person has indeed "lost the right to have rights." As one 19th century proponent of punishing criminals by death declared, "When a man is hung, there is an end of our relations with him. His execution is a way of saying, 'You are not fit for this world, take your chance elsewhere.' "[39]

In comparison to all other punishments today, then, the deliberate extinguishment of human life by the State is uniquely degrading to human dignity. I would not hesitate to hold, on that ground alone, that death is today a "cruel and unusual" punishment, were it not that death is a punishment of longstanding usage and acceptance in this country. I therefore turn to the second principle—that the State may not arbitrarily inflict an unusually severe punishment.

The outstanding characteristic of our present practice of punishing criminals by death is the infrequency with which we resort to it. The

---

39. Stephen, *Capital Punishments*, 69 Fraser's Magazine 753 (1864).

evidence is conclusive that death is not the ordinary punishment for any crime.

There has been a steady decline in the infliction of this punishment in every decade since the 1930's, the earliest period for which accurate statistics are available. In the 1930's, executions averaged 167 per year; in the 1940's, the average was 128; in the 1950's, it was 72; and in the years 1960–1962, it was 48. There have been a total of 46 executions since then, 36 of them in 1963–1964. Yet our population and the number of capital crimes committed have increased greatly over the past four decades. The contemporary rarity of the infliction of this punishment is thus the end result of a long-continued decline. That rarity is plainly revealed by an examination of the years 1961–1970, the last 10–year period for which statistics are available. During that time, an average of 106 death sentences was imposed each year. Not nearly that number, however, could be carried out, for many were precluded by commutations to life or a term of years, transfers to mental institutions because of insanity, resentences to life or a term of years, grants of new trials and orders for resentencing, dismissals of indictments and reversals of convictions, and deaths by suicide and natural causes. * * *

                    * * *

When the punishment of death is inflicted in a trivial number of the cases in which it is legally available, the conclusion is virtually inescapable that it is being inflicted arbitrarily. Indeed, it smacks of little more than a lottery system. The States claim, however, that this rarity is evidence not of arbitrariness, but of informed selectivity: Death is inflicted, they say, only in "extreme" cases.

Informed selectivity, of course, is a value not to be denigrated. Yet presumably the States could make precisely the same claim if there were 10 executions per year, or five, or even if there were but one. That there may be as many as 50 per year does not strengthen the claim. When the rate of infliction is at this low level, it is highly implausible that only the worst criminals or the criminals who commit the worst crimes are selected for this punishment. No one has yet suggested a rational basis that could differentiate in those terms the few who die from the many who go to prison. Crimes and criminals simply do not admit of a distinction that can be drawn so finely as to explain, on that ground, the execution of such a tiny sample of those eligible. Certainly the laws that provide for this punishment do not attempt to draw that distinction; all cases to which the laws apply are necessarily "extreme." Nor is the distinction credible in fact. If, for example, petitioner Furman or his crime illustrates the "extreme," then nearly all murderers and their murders are also "extreme."[48] Furthermore, our procedures in death cases, rather than result-

---

48. The victim surprised Furman in the act of burglarizing the victim's home in the middle of the night. While escaping, Furman killed the victim with one pistol shot fired through the closed kitchen door from the outside. At the trial, Furman gave his version of the killing:

ing in the selection of "extreme" cases for this punishment, actually sanction an arbitrary selection. For this Court has held that juries may, as they do, make the decision whether to impose a death sentence wholly unguided by standards governing that decision. *McGautha v. California,* 402 U.S. 183, 91 S.Ct. 1454 (1971). In other words, our procedures are not constructed to guard against the totally capricious selection of criminals for the punishment of death.

Although it is difficult to imagine what further facts would be necessary in order to prove that death is, as my Brother STEWART puts it, "wantonly and ... freakishly" inflicted, I need not conclude that arbitrary infliction is patently obvious. I am not considering this punishment by the isolated light of one principle. The probability of arbitrariness is sufficiently substantial that it can be relied upon, in combination with the other principles, in reaching a judgment on the constitutionality of this punishment.

When there is a strong probability that an unusually severe and degrading punishment is being inflicted arbitrarily, we may well expect that society will disapprove of its infliction. I turn, therefore, to the third principle. An examination of the history and present operation of the American practice of punishing criminals by death reveals that this punishment has been almost totally rejected by contemporary society.

[Justice BRENNAN pointed out that over time older methods of execution had been replaced by supposedly more humane methods (electrocution and lethal gas), that public executions were rejected because they were "debasing and brutalizing," that capital punishment effectively had been restricted to murder and rape, and that nine states had abandoned the penalty and five others had restricted its use to extremely rare cases.]

The final principle to be considered is that an unusually severe and degrading punishment may not be excessive in view of the purposes for which it is inflicted. This principle, too, is related to the others. When there is a strong probability that the State is arbitrarily inflicting an unusually severe punishment that is subject to grave societal doubts, it is likely also that the punishment cannot be shown to be serving any penal

---

"They got me charged with murder and I admit, I admit going to these folks' home and they did caught me in there and I was coming back out, backing up and there was a wire down there on the floor. I was coming out backwards and fell back and I didn't intend to kill nobody. I didn't know they was behind the door. The gun went off and I didn't know nothing about no murder until they arrested me, and when the gun went off I was down on the floor and I got up and ran. That's all to it."

The Georgia Supreme Court accepted that version:

"The admission in open court by the accused ... that during the period in which he was involved in the commission of a criminal act at the home of the deceased, he accidentally tripped over a wire in leaving the premises causing the gun to go off, together with other facts and circumstances surrounding the death of the deceased by violent means, was sufficient to support the verdict of guilty of murder...."

About Furman himself, the jury knew only that he was black and that, according to his statement at trial, he was 26 years old and worked at "Superior Upholstery." It took the jury one hour and 35 minutes to return a verdict of guilt and a sentence of death.

purpose that could not be served equally well by some less severe punishment.

The States' primary claim is that death is a necessary punishment because it prevents the commission of capital crimes more effectively than any less severe punishment. The first part of this claim is that the infliction of death is necessary to stop the individuals executed from committing further crimes. The sufficient answer to this is that if a criminal convicted of a capital crime poses a danger to society, effective administration of the State's pardon and parole laws can delay or deny his release from prison, and techniques of isolation can eliminate or minimize the danger while he remains confined.

The more significant argument is that the threat of death prevents the commission of capital crimes because it deters potential criminals who would not be deterred by the threat of imprisonment. * * *

It is important to focus upon the precise import of this argument. It is not denied that many, and probably most, capital crimes cannot be deterred by the threat of punishment. Thus the argument can apply only to those who think rationally about the commission of capital crimes. Particularly is that true when the potential criminal, under this argument, must not only consider the risk of punishment, but also distinguish between two possible punishments. The concern, then, is with a particular type of potential criminal, the rational person who will commit a capital crime knowing that the punishment is long-term imprisonment, which may well be for the rest of his life, but will not commit the crime knowing that the punishment is death. On the face of it, the assumption that such persons exist is implausible.

In any event, this argument cannot be appraised in the abstract. We are not presented with the theoretical question whether under any imaginable circumstances the threat of death might be a greater deterrent to the commission of capital crimes than the threat of imprisonment. We are concerned with the practice of punishing criminals by death as it exists in the United States today. Proponents of this argument necessarily admit that its validity depends upon the existence of a system in which the punishment of death is invariably and swiftly imposed. Our system, of course, satisfies neither condition. A rational person contemplating a murder or rape is confronted, not with the certainty of a speedy death, but with the slightest possibility that he will be executed in the distant future. The risk of death is remote and improbable; in contrast, the risk of long-term imprisonment is near and great. In short, whatever the speculative validity of the assumption that the threat of death is a superior deterrent, there is no reason to believe that as currently administered the punishment of death is necessary to deter the commission of capital crimes. Whatever might be the case were all or substantially all eligible criminals quickly put to death, unverifiable possibilities are an insufficient basis upon which to conclude that the threat of death today has any greater deterrent efficacy than the threat of imprisonment.

* * *

In sum, the punishment of death is inconsistent with all four principles: Death is an unusually severe and degrading punishment; there is a strong probability that it is inflicted arbitrarily; its rejection by contemporary society is virtually total; and there is no reason to believe that it serves any penal purpose more effectively than the less severe punishment of imprisonment. The function of these principles is to enable a court to determine whether a punishment comports with human dignity. Death, quite simply, does not.

* * *

MR. JUSTICE STEWART, concurring.

The penalty of death differs from all other forms of criminal punishment, not in degree but in kind. It is unique in its total irrevocability. It is unique in its rejection of rehabilitation of the convict as a basic purpose of criminal justice. And it is unique, finally, in its absolute renunciation of all that is embodied in our concept of humanity.

* * *

Legislatures—state and federal—have sometimes specified that the penalty of death shall be the mandatory punishment for every person convicted of engaging in certain designated criminal conduct. Congress, for example, has provided that anyone convicted of acting as a spy for the enemy in time of war shall be put to death. The Rhode Island Legislature has ordained the death penalty for a life term prisoner who commits murder. Massachusetts has passed a law imposing the death penalty upon anyone convicted of murder in the commission of a forcible rape. An Ohio law imposes the mandatory penalty of death upon the assassin of the President of the United States or the Governor of a State.

If we were reviewing death sentences imposed under these or similar laws, we would be faced with the need to decide whether capital punishment is unconstitutional for all crimes and under all circumstances. We would need to decide whether a legislature—state or federal—could constitutionally determine that certain criminal conduct is so atrocious that society's interest in deterrence and retribution wholly outweighs any considerations of reform or rehabilitation of the perpetrator, and that, despite the inconclusive empirical evidence,[7] only the automatic penalty of death will provide maximum deterrence.

On that score I would say only that I cannot agree that retribution is a constitutionally impermissible ingredient in the imposition of punishment. The instinct for retribution is part of the nature of man, and

---

7. Many statistical studies—comparing crime rates in jurisdictions with and without capital punishment and in jurisdictions before and after abolition of capital punishment—have indicated that there is little, if any, measurable deterrent effect. There remains uncertainty, however, because of the difficulty of identifying and holding constant all other relevant variables.

channeling that instinct in the administration of criminal justice serves an important purpose in promoting the stability of a society governed by law. When people begin to believe that organized society is unwilling or unable to impose upon criminal offenders the punishment they "deserve," then there are sown the seeds of anarchy—of self-help, vigilante justice, and lynch law.

The constitutionality of capital punishment in the abstract is not, however, before us in these cases. For the Georgia and Texas Legislatures have not provided that the death penalty shall be imposed upon all those who are found guilty of forcible rape. And the Georgia Legislature has not ordained that death shall be the automatic punishment for murder. In a word, neither State has made a legislative determination that forcible rape and murder can be deterred only by imposing the penalty of death upon all who perpetrate those offenses. As Mr. Justice White so tellingly puts it, the "legislative will is not frustrated if the penalty is never imposed."

Instead, the death sentences now before us are the product of a legal system that brings them, I believe, within the very core of the Eighth Amendment's guarantee against cruel and unusual punishments, a guarantee applicable against the States through the Fourteenth Amendment. *Robinson v. California*, 370 U.S. 660, 82 S.Ct. 1417 (1962). In the first place, it is clear that these sentences are "cruel" in the sense that they excessively go beyond, not in degree but in kind, the punishments that the state legislatures have determined to be necessary. *Weems v. United States*, 217 U.S. 349, 30 S.Ct. 544 (1910). In the second place, it is equally clear that these sentences are "unusual" in the sense that the penalty of death is infrequently imposed for murder, and that its imposition for rape is extraordinarily rare. But I do not rest by conclusion upon these two propositions alone.

These death sentences are cruel and unusual in the same way that being struck by lightning is cruel and unusual. For, of all the people convicted of rapes and murders in 1967 and 1968, many just as reprehensible as these, the petitioners are among a capriciously selected random handful upon whom the sentence of death has in fact been imposed. My concurring Brothers have demonstrated that, if any basis can be discerned for the selection of these few to be sentenced to die, it is the constitutionally impermissible basis of race. But racial discrimination has not been proved, and I put it to one side. I simply conclude that the Eighth and Fourteenth Amendments cannot tolerate the infliction of a sentence of death under legal systems that permit this unique penalty to be so wantonly and so freakishly imposed.

Mr. Justice White, concurring.

The facial constitutionality of statutes requiring the imposition of the death penalty for first-degree murder, for more narrowly defined categories of murder, or for rape would present quite different issues under the Eighth Amendment than are posed by the cases before us. In joining the Court's judgments, therefore, I do not at all intimate that the death penalty is unconstitutional *per se* or that there is no system of capital punishment that would comport with the Eighth Amendment. That question, ably argued by several of my Brethren, is not presented by these cases and need not be decided.

The narrower question to which I address myself concerns the constitutionality of capital punishment statutes under which (1) the legislature authorizes the imposition of the death penalty for murder or rape; (2) the legislature does not itself mandate the penalty in any particular class or kind of case (that is, legislative will is not frustrated if the penalty is never imposed), but delegates to judges or juries the decisions as to those cases, if any, in which the penalty will be utilized; and (3) judges and juries have ordered the death penalty with such infrequency that the odds are now very much against imposition and execution of the penalty with respect to any convicted murderer or rapist. It is in this context that we must consider whether the execution of these petitioners would violate the Eighth Amendment.

I begin with what I consider a near truism: that the death penalty could so seldom be imposed that it would cease to be a credible deterrent or measurably to contribute to any other end of punishment in the criminal justice system. It is perhaps true that no matter how infrequently those convicted of rape or murder are executed, the penalty so imposed is not disproportionate to the crime and those executed may deserve exactly what they received. It would also be clear that executed defendants are finally and completely incapacitated from again committing rape or murder or any other crime. But when imposition of the penalty reaches a certain degree of infrequency, it would be very doubtful that any existing general need for retribution would be measurably satisfied. Nor could it be said with confidence that society's need for specific deterrence justifies death for so few when for so many in like circumstances life imprisonment or shorter prison terms are judged sufficient, or that community values are measurably reinforced by authorizing a penalty so rarely invoked.

Most important, a major goal of the criminal law—to deter others by punishing the convicted criminal—would not be substantially served where the penalty is so seldom invoked that it ceases to be the credible threat essential to influence the conduct of others. For present purposes I accept the morality and utility of punishing one person to influence another. I accept also the effectiveness of punishment generally and need not reject the death penalty as a more effective deterrent than a lesser punishment. But common sense and experience tell us that seldom-enforced laws become ineffective measures for controlling human conduct and that the death penalty, unless imposed with sufficient frequency, will make little contribution to deterring those crimes for which it may be exacted.

The imposition and execution of the death penalty are obviously cruel in the dictionary sense. But the penalty has not been considered cruel and unusual punishment in the constitutional sense because it was thought justified by the social ends it was deemed to serve. At the moment that it ceases realistically to further these purposes, however, the emerging question is whether its imposition in such circumstances would violate the Eighth Amendment. It is my view that it would, for its imposition would then be the pointless and needless extinction of life with only marginal contributions to any discernible social or public purposes. A penalty with such negligible returns to the State would be patently excessive and cruel and unusual punishment violative of the Eighth Amendment.

It is also my judgment that this point has been reached with respect to capital punishment as it is presently administered under the statutes involved in these cases. Concededly, it is difficult to prove as a general proposition that capital punishment, however administered, more effectively serves the ends of the criminal law than does imprisonment. But however that may be, I cannot avoid the conclusion that as the statutes before us are now administered, the penalty is so infrequently imposed that the threat of execution is too attenuated to be of substantial service to criminal justice.

I need not restate the facts and figures that appear in the opinions of my Brethren. Nor can I "prove" my conclusion from these data. But, like my Brethren, I must arrive at judgment; and I can do no more than state a conclusion based on 10 years of almost daily exposure to the facts and circumstances of hundreds and hundreds of federal and state criminal cases involving crimes for which death is the authorized penalty. That conclusion, as I have said, is that the death penalty is exacted with great infrequency even for the most atrocious crimes and that there is no meaningful basis for distinguishing the few cases in which it is imposed from the many cases in which it is not. The short of it is that the policy of vesting sentencing authority primarily in juries—a decision largely motivated by the desire to mitigate the harshness of the law and to bring community judgment to bear on the sentence as well as guilt or innocence—has so effectively achieved its aims that capital punishment within the confines of the statutes now before us has for all practical purposes run its course.

Judicial review, by definition, often involves a conflict between judicial and legislative judgment as to what the Constitution means or requires. In this respect, Eighth Amendment cases come to us in no different posture. It seems conceded by all that the Amendment imposes some obligations on the judiciary to judge the constitutionality of punishment and that there are punishments that the Amendment would bar whether legislatively approved or not. * * *

In this respect, I add only that past and present legislative judgment with respect to the death penalty loses much of its force when viewed in light of the recurring practice of delegating sentencing authority to the jury and the fact that a jury, in its own discretion and without violating its trust or any statutory policy, may refuse to impose the death penalty no matter what the circumstances of the crime. Legislative "policy" is thus necessarily defined not by what is legislatively authorized but by what juries and judges do in exercising the discretion so regularly conferred upon them. In my judgment what was done in these cases violated the Eighth Amendment.

I concur in the judgments of the Court.

MR. JUSTICE MARSHALL, concurring.

* * *

The criminal acts with which we are confronted are ugly, vicious, reprehensible acts. Their sheer brutality cannot and should not be minimized. But, we are not called upon to condone the penalized conduct; we are asked only to examine the penalty imposed on each of the petitioners and to determine whether or not it violates the Eighth Amendment. The question then is not whether we condone rape or murder, for surely we do not; it is whether capital punishment is "a punishment no longer consistent with our own self-respect" and, therefore, violative of the Eighth Amendment.

[Justice MARSHALL reviewed the origins of the cruel and unusual punishments clause in the English Declaration of Rights and the adoption of the same language by Virginia in its Declaration of Rights and by other states. He then reviewed the early cases in which the Supreme Court had interpreted the Eighth Amendment, particularly: *Wilkerson v. Utah*, 99 U.S. 130 (1878) (where the Court held constitutional execution by shooting after "examining the history of the Utah Territory and the then-current writings on capital punishment, and compar[ing] this Nation's practices with those of other countries"); *In re Kemmler*, 136 U.S. 436, 10 S.Ct. 930 (1890), (where Chief Justice FULLER wrote an opinion for a unanimous Court upholding electrocution as a permissible mode of punishment); and *O'Neil v. Vermont*, 144 U.S. 323, 12 S.Ct. 693 (1892) (where the Court reaffirmed that the Eighth Amendment was not applicable to the States, but where Mr. Justice FIELD, speaking for the three dissenters would have found the sentence unconstitutional: "That designation [cruel and unusual], it is true, is usually applied to punishments which inflict torture, such as the rack, the thumb-screw, the iron boot, the stretching of limbs, and the like, which are attended with acute pain and suffering. * * * The inhibition is directed, not only against punishments of the character mentioned, but against all punishments which by their excessive length or severity are greatly disproportioned to the offences charged. The whole inhibition is against that which is excessive * * * "). Justice MARSHALL argued that the dissenters' position in *O'Neil* became the opinion of the Court in *Weems v. United States*, 217 U.S. 349, 30 S.Ct. 544 (1910). There the Court, for the first time, invalidated a legislatively prescribed penalty and made it plain that "excessive punishments were as objectionable as those that were inherently cruel." The next important case was *Louisiana ex rel. Francis v. Resweber*, 329 U.S. 459, 67 S.Ct. 374 (1947), where the petitioner, whom the state had electrocuted but failed to kill, sought to bar a second attempt as a cruel and unusual punishment.

The petitioner lost in a 5–4 decision, but "[t]he Court was virtually unanimous in agreeing that '[t]he traditional humanity of modern Anglo–American law forbids the infliction of unnecessary pain ...' " In *Trop v. Dulles*, 356 U.S. 86, 78 S.Ct. 590 (1958), Chief Justice WARREN, writing for himself and three justices, applied the Eighth Amendment to the punishment of expatriation and wrote that "[t]he Amendment must draw its meaning from the evolving standards of decency that mark the progress of a maturing society." Finally, the Court, in *Robinson v. California*, 370 U.S. 660, 82 S.Ct. 1417 (1962), held that the Eighth Amendment barred a 90 day sentence for being "addicted to the use of narcotics," and Justice Stewart, writing for the Court, "reiterated what the Court had said in *Weems* and what Chief Justice WARREN wrote in *Trop*—that the cruel and unusual punishment clause was not a static concept, but one that must be continually re-examined 'in the light of contemporary human knowledge.' "]

III

Perhaps the most important principle in analyzing "cruel and unusual" punishment questions is one that is reiterated again and again in the prior opinions of the Court: *i.e.*, the cruel and unusual language "must draw its meaning from the evolving standards of decency that mark the progress of a maturing society." Thus, a penalty that was permissible at one time in our Nation's history is not necessarily permissible today.

The fact, therefore, that the Court, or individual Justices, may have in the past expressed an opinion that the death penalty is constitutional is not now binding on us. A fair reading of *Wilkerson v. Utah, supra*; *In re Kemmler, supra*; and *Louisiana ex rel. Francis v. Resweber, supra*, would certainly indicate an acceptance *sub silentio* of capital punishment as constitutionally permissible. Several Justices have also expressed their individual opinions that the death penalty is constitutional. Yet, some of these same Justices and others have at times expressed concern over capital punishment. There is no holding directly in point, and the very nature of the Eighth Amendment would dictate that unless a very recent decision existed, *stare decisis* would bow to changing values, and the question of the constitutionality of capital punishment at a given moment in history would remain open.

Faced with an open question, we must establish our standards for decision. The decisions discussed in the previous section imply that a punishment may be deemed cruel and unusual for any one of four distinct reasons.

First, there are certain punishments that inherently involve so much physical pain and suffering that civilized people cannot tolerate them—*e.g.*, use of the rack, the thumbscrew, or other modes of torture. * * *

Second, there are punishments that are unusual, signifying that they were previously unknown as penalties for a given offense. If these punishments are intended to serve a humane purpose, they may be constitutionally permissible. *In re Kemmler*; *Louisiana ex rel. Francis v. Resweber.* * * *

Third, a penalty may be cruel and unusual because it is excessive and serves no valid legislative purpose. *Weems v. United States, supra.* * * *

Fourth, where a punishment is not excessive and serves a valid legislative purpose, it still may be invalid if popular sentiment abhors it. * * * There are no prior cases in this Court striking down a penalty on this ground, but the very notion of changing values requires that we recognize its existence.

It is immediately obvious, then, that since capital punishment is not a recent phenomenon, if it violates the Constitution, it does so because it is excessive or unnecessary, or because it is abhorrent to currently existing moral values.

[Justice MARSHALL traced the history of capital punishment. A brief history of capital punishment is set out in Chapter 1.]

V

In order to assess whether or not death is an excessive or unnecessary penalty, it is necessary to consider the reasons why a legislature might select it as punishment for one or more offenses, and examine whether less severe penalties would satisfy the legitimate legislative wants as well as capital punishment. If they would, then the death penalty is unnecessary cruelty, and, therefore, unconstitutional.

There are six purposes conceivably served by capital punishment: retribution, deterrence, prevention of repetitive criminal acts, encouragement of guilty pleas and confessions, eugenics, and economy. These are considered *seriatim* below.

A.   The concept of retribution is one of the most misunderstood in all of our criminal jurisprudence. The principal source of confusion derives from the fact that, in dealing with the concept, most people confuse the question "why do men in fact punish?" with the question "what justifies men in punishing?" Men may punish for any number of reasons, but the one reason that punishment is morally good or morally justifiable is that someone has broken the law. Thus, it can correctly be said that breaking the law is the *sine qua non* of punishment, or, in other words, that we only tolerate punishment as it is imposed on one who deviates from the norm established by the criminal law.

The fact that the State may seek retribution against those who have broken its laws does not mean that retribution may then become the State's sole end in punishing. Our jurisprudence has always accepted deterrence in general, deterrence of individual recidivism, isolation of dangerous persons, and rehabilitation as proper goals of punishment. See *Trop v. Dulles* (BRENNAN, J., concurring). Retaliation, vengeance, and retribution have been roundly condemned as intolerable aspirations for a government in a free society.

Punishment as retribution has been condemned by scholars for centuries, and the Eighth Amendment itself was adopted to prevent punishment from becoming synonymous with vengeance.

* * *

To preserve the integrity of the Eighth Amendment, the Court has consistently denigrated retribution as a permissible goal of punishment. It is undoubtedly correct that there is a demand for vengeance on the part of many persons in a community against one who is convicted of a particularly offensive act. At times a cry is heard that morality requires vengeance to evidence society's abhorrence of the act. But the Eighth Amendment is our insulation from our baser selves. The "cruel and unusual" language limits the avenues through which vengeance can be channeled. Were this not so, the language would be empty and a return to the rack and other tortures would be possible in a given case.

* * *

B.   The most hotly contested issue regarding capital punishment is whether it is better than life imprisonment as a deterrent to crime.

While the contrary position has been argued, it is my firm opinion that the death penalty is a more severe sanction than life imprisonment. Admittedly, there are some persons who would rather die than languish in prison for a lifetime. But, whether or not they should be able to choose death as an alternative is a far different question from that presented here—*i.e.*, whether the State can impose death as a punishment. Death is irrevocable; life imprisonment is not. Death, of course, makes rehabilitation impossible; life imprisonment does not. In short, death has always been viewed as the ultimate sanction, and it seems perfectly reasonable to continue to view it as such.

It must be kept in mind, then, that the question to be considered is not simply whether capital punishment is a deterrent, but whether it is a better deterrent than life imprisonment.

There is no more complex problem than determining the deterrent efficacy of the death penalty. "Capital punishment has obviously failed as a deterrent when a murder is committed. We can number its failures. But we cannot number its successes. No one can ever know how many people have refrained from murder because of the fear of being hanged."[93] This is the nub of the problem, and it is exacerbated by the paucity of useful data. The United States is more fortunate than most countries, however, in that it has what are generally considered to be the world's most reliable statistics.

The two strongest arguments in favor of capital punishment as a deterrent are both logical hypotheses devoid of evidentiary support, but persuasive nonetheless. The first proposition was best stated by Sir James Stephen in 1864:

---

93.   Report of the Royal Commission on Capital Punishment, 1949–1953 (1953).

"No other punishment deters men so effectually from committing crimes as the punishment of death. This is one of those propositions which it is difficult to prove, simply because they are in themselves more obvious than any proof can make them. It is possible to display ingenuity in arguing against it, but that is all. The whole experience of mankind is in the other direction. The threat of instant death is the one to which resort has always been made when there was an absolute necessity for producing some result. ... No one goes to certain inevitable death except by compulsion. Put the matter the other way. Was there ever yet a criminal who, when sentenced to death and brought out to die, would refuse the offer of a commutation of his sentence for the severest secondary punishment? Surely not. Why is this? It can only be because 'All that a man has will he give for his life.' In any secondary punishment, however terrible, there is hope; but death is death; its terrors cannot be described more forcibly."[95]

This hypothesis relates to the use of capital punishment as a deterrent for any crime. The second proposition is that "if life imprisonment is the maximum penalty for a crime such as murder, an offender who is serving a life sentence cannot then be deterred from murdering a fellow inmate or a prison officer."[96] This hypothesis advocates a limited deterrent effect under particular circumstances.

Abolitionists attempt to disprove these hypotheses by amassing statistical evidence to demonstrate that there is no correlation between criminal activity and the existence or nonexistence of a capital sanction. Almost all of the evidence involves the crime of murder, since murder is punishable by death in more jurisdictions than are other offenses, and almost 90% of all executions since 1930 have been pursuant to murder convictions.

[Justice MARSHALL described the research of Thorsten Sellin concerning the deterrent effects of capital punishment.[99] Although Sellin used "homicide" rates rather than "murder" rates in his study, since the two are assumed to be proportionate, his conclusions were instructive. Sellin's statistics demonstrated that there was no correlation between the homicide rate and the presence or absence of the capital sanction. He compared states that had similar characteristics and found that irrespective of their position on capital punishment, they had similar homicide rates. He concluded that abolition and/or reintroduction of the death penalty had no effect on the homicide rates of the various states involved. He found that the deterrent effect of capital punishment was no greater in those communities where executions took place than in other communities. In fact, some evidence suggested that imposition of capital punishment might actually encourage crime, rather than deter it. Data also showed that the

---

95. Reprinted in Royal Commission, *supra*, n.93.

96. United Nations, Department of Economic and Social Affairs, Capital Punishment, Pt. II (1968).

99. T. Sellin, *The Death Penalty, A Report for the Model Penal Code Project of the American Law Institute* (1959).

existence of the death penalty has virtually no effect on the homicide rate in prisons.]

In sum, the only support for the theory that capital punishment is an effective deterrent is found in the hypotheses with which we began and the occasional stories about a specific individual being deterred from doing a contemplated criminal act. These claims of specific deterrence are often spurious, however, and may be more than counterbalanced by the tendency of capital punishment to incite certain crimes.

The United Nations Committee that studied capital punishment found that "[i]t is generally agreed between the retentionists and abolitionists, whatever their opinions about the validity of comparative studies of deterrence, that the data which now exist show no correlation between the existence of capital punishment and lower rates of capital crime."

  * * *

C. Much of what must be said about the death penalty as a device to prevent recidivism is obvious—if a murderer is executed, he cannot possibly commit another offense. The fact is, however, that murderers are extremely unlikely to commit other crimes either in prison or upon their release. For the most part, they are first offenders, and when released from prison they are known to become model citizens. Furthermore, most persons who commit capital crimes are not executed. With respect to those who are sentenced to die, it is critical to note that the jury is never asked to determine whether they are likely to be recidivists. In light of these facts, if capital punishment were justified purely on the basis of preventing recidivism, it would have to be considered to be excessive; no general need to obliterate all capital offenders could have been demonstrated, nor any specific need in individual cases.

D. The three final purposes which may underlie utilization of a capital sanction—encouraging guilty pleas and confessions, eugenics, and reducing state expenditures—may be dealt with quickly.

[Justice MARSHALL argued that: (1) if the death penalty were being used to coerce guilty pleas, such a practice would violate defendants' Sixth Amendment rights to a jury trial (*United States v. Jackson*, 390 U.S. 570, 88 S.Ct. 1209 (1968)); (2) eugenics would not justify the death penalty because there is no way to determine who would be a recidivist; and (3) it costs more to execute an offender than to imprison the offender for life.]

E. There is but one conclusion that can be drawn from all of this— *i.e.*, the death penalty is an excessive and unnecessary punishment that violates the Eighth Amendment. The statistical evidence is not convincing beyond all doubt, but it is persuasive. It is not improper at this point to take judicial notice of the fact that for more than 200 years men have labored to demonstrate that capital punishment serves no purpose that life imprisonment could not serve equally well. And they have done so with great success. Little, if any, evidence has been adduced to prove the contrary. The point has now been reached at which deference to the legislatures is tantamount to abdication of our judicial roles as factfinders, judges, and ultimate arbiters of the Constitution. We know that at some point the presumption of constitutionality accorded legislative acts gives way to a realistic assessment of those acts. This point comes when there is sufficient evidence available so that judges can determine, not whether the legislature acted wisely, but whether it had any rational basis whatsoever for acting. We have this evidence before us now. There is no rational basis for concluding that capital punishment is not excessive. It therefore violates the Eighth Amendment.

VI

In addition, even if capital punishment is not excessive, it nonetheless violates the Eighth Amendment because it is morally unacceptable to the people of the United States at this time in their history.

* * *

It has often been noted that American citizens know almost nothing about capital punishment. Some of the conclusions arrived at in the preceding section and the supporting evidence would be critical to an informed judgment on the morality of the death penalty: *e.g.*, that the death penalty is no more effective a deterrent than life imprisonment, that convicted murderers are rarely executed, but are usually sentenced to a term in prison; that convicted murderers usually are model prisoners, and that they almost always become lawabiding citizens upon their release from prison; that the costs of executing a capital offender exceed the costs of imprisoning him for life; that while in prison, a convict under sentence of death performs none of the useful functions that life prisoners perform; that no attempt is made in the sentencing process to ferret out likely recidivists for execution; and that the death penalty may actually stimulate criminal activity.

This information would almost surely convince the average citizen that the death penalty was unwise, but a problem arises as to whether it would convince him that the penalty was morally reprehensible. This problem arises from the fact that the public's desire for retribution, even though this is a goal that the legislature cannot constitutionally pursue as its sole justification for capital punishment, might influence the citizenry's view of the morality of capital punishment. The solution to the problem lies in the fact that no one has ever seriously advanced retribution as a legitimate goal of our society. Defenses of capital punishment are always mounted on deterrent or other similar theories. This should not be surprising. It is the people of this country who have urged in the past that prisons rehabilitate as well as isolate offenders, and it is the people who have injected a sense of purpose into our penology. I cannot believe that at this stage in our history, the American people would ever knowingly support purposeless vengeance. Thus, I believe that the great mass of citizens would conclude on the basis of the material already considered that the death penalty is immoral and therefore unconstitutional.

* * *

MR. CHIEF JUSTICE BURGER, with whom MR. JUSTICE BLACKMUN, MR. JUSTICE POWELL, and MR. JUSTICE REHNQUIST join, dissenting.

* * *

V

Today the Court has not ruled that capital punishment is *per se* violative of the Eighth Amendment; nor has it ruled that the punishment is barred for any particular class or classes of crimes. The substantially similar concurring opinions of Mr. Justice STEWART and Mr. Justice WHITE, which are necessary to support the judgment setting aside petitioners' sentences, stop short of reaching the ultimate question. The actual scope of the Court's ruling, which I take to be embodied in these concurring opinions, is not entirely clear. This much, however, seems apparent: if the legislatures are to continue to authorize capital punishment for some crimes, juries and judges can no longer be permitted to make the sentencing determination in the same manner they have in the past. This approach—not urged in oral arguments or briefs—misconceives the nature of the constitutional command against "cruel and unusual punishments," disregards controlling case law, and demands a rigidity in capital cases which, if possible of achievement, cannot be regarded as a welcome change. Indeed the contrary seems to be the case.

* * * [T]he Eighth Amendment forbids the imposition of punishments that are so cruel and inhumane as to violate society's standards of civilized conduct. The Amendment does not prohibit all punishments the States are unable to prove necessary to deter or control crime. The Amendment is not concerned with the process by which a State determines that a particular punishment is to be imposed in a particular case. And the Amendment most assuredly does not speak to the power of legislatures to confer sentencing discretion on juries, rather than to fix all sentences by statute.

The critical factor in the concurring opinions of both Mr. Justice STEWART and Mr. Justice WHITE is the infrequency with which the penalty is imposed. This factor is taken not as evidence of society's abhorrence of capital punishment—the inference that petitioners would have the Court draw—but as the earmark of a deteriorated system of sentencing. It is concluded that petitioners' sentences must be set aside, not because the punishment is impermissibly cruel, but because juries and judges have failed to exercise their sentencing discretion in acceptable fashion.

To be sure, there is a recitation cast in Eighth Amendment terms: petitioners' sentences are "cruel" because they exceed that which the legislatures have deemed necessary for all cases; petitioners' sentences are "unusual" because they exceed that which is imposed in most cases. This application of the words of the Eighth Amendment suggests that capital punishment can be made to satisfy Eighth Amendment values if its rate of imposition is somehow multiplied; it seemingly follows that the flexible sentencing system created by the legislatures, and carried out by juries and judges, has yielded more mercy than the Eighth Amendment can stand. The implications of this approach are mildly ironical. For example, by this measure of the Eighth Amendment, the elimination of death-qualified juries in *Witherspoon v. Illinois*, 391 U.S. 510, 88 S.Ct. 1770 (1968), can only be seen in retrospect as a setback to "the evolving standards of decency that mark the progress of a maturing society." *Trop v. Dulles*, 356 U.S. 86, 78 S.Ct. 590 (1958).

This novel formulation of Eighth Amendment principles—albeit necessary to satisfy the terms of our limited grant of certiorari—does not lie at the heart of these concurring opinions. The decisive grievance of the opinions—not translated into Eighth Amendment terms—is that the present system of discretionary sentencing in capital cases has failed to produce evenhanded justice; the problem is not that too few have been sentenced to die, but that the selection process has followed no rational pattern. This claim of arbitrariness is not only lacking in empirical support, but also it manifestly fails to establish that the death penalty is a "cruel and unusual" punishment. The Eighth Amendment was included in the Bill of Rights to assure that certain types of punishments would never be imposed, not to channelize the sentencing process. The approach of these concurring opinions has no antecedent in the Eighth Amendment cases. It is essentially and exclusively a procedural due process argument.

This ground of decision is plainly foreclosed as well as misplaced. Only one year ago, in *McGautha v. California*, 402 U.S. 183, 91 S.Ct. 1454 (1971), the Court upheld the prevailing system of sentencing in capital cases. The Court concluded:

> "In light of history, experience, and the present limitations of human knowledge, we find it quite impossible to say that committing to the untrammeled discretion of the jury the power to pronounce life or death in capital cases is offensive to anything in the Constitution."

In reaching this decision, the Court had the benefit of extensive briefing, full oral argument, and six months of careful deliberations. The Court's labors are documented by 130 pages of opinions in the United States Reports. All of the arguments and factual contentions accepted in the concurring opinions today were considered and rejected by the Court one year ago. *McGautha* was an exceedingly difficult case, and reasonable men could fairly disagree as to the result. But the Court entered its judgment, and if *stare decisis* means anything, that decision should be regarded as a controlling pronouncement of law.

Although the Court's decision in *McGautha* was technically confined to the dictates of the Due Process Clause of the Fourteenth Amendment, rather than the Eighth Amendment as made applicable to the States through the Due Process Clause of the Fourteenth Amendment, it would be disingenuous to suggest that today's ruling has done anything less than overrule *McGautha* in the guise of an Eighth Amendment adjudication. It may be thought appropriate to subordinate principles of *stare decisis* where the subject is as sensitive as capital punishment and the stakes are so high, but these external considerations were no less weighty last year. This pattern of decisionmaking will do little to inspire confidence in the stability of the law.

While I would not undertake to make a definitive statement as to the parameters of the Court's ruling, it is clear that if state legislatures and the Congress wish to maintain the availability of capital punishment, significant statutory changes will have to be made. Since the two pivotal concurring opinions turn on the assumption that the punishment of death is now meted out in a random and unpredictable manner, legislative bodies may seek to bring their laws into compliance with the Court's ruling by providing standards for juries and judges to follow in determining the sentence in capital cases or by more narrowly defining the crimes for which the penalty is to be imposed. If such standards can be devised or the crimes more meticulously defined, the result cannot be detrimental. However, Mr. Justice HARLAN's opinion for the Court in *McGautha* convincingly demonstrates that all past efforts "to identify before the fact" the cases in which the penalty is to be imposed have been "uniformly unsuccessful." * * *

Real change could clearly be brought about if legislatures provided mandatory death sentences in such a way as to deny juries the opportunity to bring in a verdict on a lesser charge; under such a system, the death sentence could only be avoided by a verdict of acquittal. If this is the only alternative that the legislatures can safely pursue under today's ruling, I would have preferred that the Court opt for total abolition.

It seems remarkable to me that with our basic trust in lay jurors as the keystone in our system of criminal justice, it should now be suggested that we take the most sensitive and important of all decisions away from them. I could more easily be persuaded that mandatory sentences of death, without the intervening and ameliorating impact of lay jurors, are so arbitrary and doctrinaire that they violate the Constitution. The very infrequency of death penalties imposed by jurors attests their cautious and discriminating reservation of that penalty for the most extreme cases. I had thought that nothing was clearer in history, as we noted in *McGautha* one year ago, than the American abhorrence of "the common-law rule imposing a mandatory death sentence on all convicted murderers." * * * [T]he 19th century movement away from mandatory death sentences marked an enlightened introduction of flexibility into the sentencing process. It recognized that individual culpability is not always measured by the category of the crime committed. This change in sentencing practice was greeted by the Court as a humanizing development. I do not see how this history can be ignored and how it can be suggested that the Eighth Amendment demands the elimination of the most sensitive feature of the sentencing system.

* * *

MR. JUSTICE BLACKMUN, dissenting.

I join the respective opinions of THE CHIEF JUSTICE, MR. JUSTICE POWELL, and MR. JUSTICE REHNQUIST, and add only the following, somewhat personal, comments.

1. Cases such as these provide for me an excruciating agony of the spirit. I yield to no one in the depth of my distaste, antipathy, and, indeed, abhorrence, for the death penalty, with all its aspects of physical distress and fear and of moral judgment exercised by finite minds. That distaste is buttressed by a belief that capital punishment serves no useful purpose that can be demonstrated. For me, it violates childhood's training and life's experiences, and is not compatible with the philosophical convictions I have been able to develop. It is antagonistic to any sense of "reverence for life." Were I a legislator, I would vote against the death penalty for the policy reasons argued by counsel for the respective petitioners and expressed and adopted in the several opinions filed by the Justices who vote to reverse these judgments.

* * *

4. The several concurring opinions acknowledge, as they must, that until today capital punishment was accepted and assumed as not unconstitutional *per se* under the Eighth Amendment or the Fourteenth Amendment. This is either the flat or the implicit holding of a unanimous Court in *Wilkerson v. Utah*, 99 U.S. 130, in 1879; of a unanimous Court in *In re Kemmler*, 136 U.S. 436, 10 S.Ct. 930, in 1890; of the Court in *Weems v. United States*, 217 U.S. 349, 30 S.Ct. 544, in 1910; of all those members of the Court, a majority, who addressed the issue in *Louisiana ex rel. Francis v. Resweber*, 329 U.S. 459, 67 S.Ct. 374, in 1947; of Mr. Chief Justice WARREN, speaking for himself and three others (Justices BLACK, DOUGLAS, and WHITTAKER) in *Trop v. Dulles*, 356 U.S. 86, 78 S.Ct. 590, in 1958; in the denial of certiorari in *Rudolph v. Alabama*, 375 U.S. 889, 84 S.Ct. 155, in 1963 (where, however, Justices DOUGLAS, BRENNAN, and GOLDBERG would have heard argument with respect to the imposition of the ultimate penalty on a convicted rapist who had "neither taken nor endangered human life"); and of Mr. Justice BLACK in *McGautha v. California*, 402 U.S. 183, 91 S.Ct. 1454, decided only last Term on May 3, 1971.

Suddenly, however, the course of decision is now the opposite way, with the Court evidently persuaded that somehow the passage of time has taken us to a place of greater maturity and outlook. The argument, plausible and high-sounding as it may be, is not persuasive, for it is only one year since *McGautha*, only eight and one-half years since *Rudolph*, 14 years since *Trop*, and 25 years since *Francis*, and we have been presented with nothing that demonstrates a significant movement of any kind in these brief periods. The Court has just decided that it is time to strike down the death penalty. There would have been as much reason to do this when any of the cited cases were decided. But the Court refrained from that action on each of those occasions.

The Court has recognized, and I certainly subscribe to the proposition, that the Cruel and Unusual Punishments Clause "may acquire meaning as public opinion becomes enlightened by a humane justice." *Weems v. United States.* And Mr. Chief Justice WARREN, for a plurality of the Court, referred to "the evolving standards of decency that mark the progress of a maturing society." *Trop v. Dulles.* * * *

My problem, however, as I have indicated, is the suddenness of the Court's perception of progress in the human attitude since decisions of only a short while ago.

5.   To reverse the judgments in these cases is, of course, the easy choice. It is easier to strike the balance in favor of life and against death. It is comforting to relax in the thoughts—perhaps the rationalizations— that this is the compassionate decision for a maturing society; that this is the moral and the "right" thing to do; that thereby we convince ourselves that we are moving down the road toward human decency; that we value life even though that life has taken another or others or has grievously scarred another or others and their families; and that we are less barbaric than we were in 1879, or in 1890, or in 1910, or in 1947, or in 1958, or in 1963, or a year ago, in 1971, when *Wilkerson, Kemmler, Weems, Francis, Trop, Rudolph,* and *McGautha* were respectively decided.

This, for me, is good argument, and it makes some sense. But it is good argument and it makes sense only in a legislative and executive way and not as a judicial expedient. * * *

> * * *

10.   It is not without interest, also, to note that, although the several concurring opinions acknowledge the heinous and atrocious character of the offenses committed by the petitioners, none of those opinions makes reference to the misery the petitioners' crimes occasioned to the victims, to the families of the victims, and to the communities where the offenses took place. The arguments for the respective petitioners, particularly the oral arguments, were similarly and curiously devoid of reference to the victims. There is risk, of course, in a comment such as this, for it opens one to the charge of emphasizing the retributive. But see *Williams v. New York*, 337 U.S. 241, 69 S.Ct. 1079 (1949). Nevertheless, these cases are here because offenses to innocent victims were perpetrated. This fact, and the terror that occasioned it, and the fear that stalks the streets of many of our cities today perhaps deserve not to be entirely overlooked. Let us hope that, with the Court's decision, the terror imposed will be forgotten by those upon whom it was visited, and that our society will reap the hoped-for benefits of magnanimity.

Although personally I may rejoice at the Court's result, I find it difficult to accept or to justify as a matter of history, of law, or of constitutional pronouncement. I fear the Court has overstepped. It has sought and has achieved an end.

MR. JUSTICE POWELL, with whom THE CHIEF JUSTICE, MR. JUSTICE BLACKMUN, and MR. JUSTICE REHNQUIST join, dissenting.

* * *

Whatever uncertainties may hereafter surface, several of the consequences of today's decision are unmistakably clear. The decision is plainly one of the greatest importance. The Court's judgment removes the death sentences previously imposed on some 600 persons awaiting punishment in state and federal prisons throughout the country. At least for the present, it also bars the States and the Federal Government from seeking sentences of death for defendants awaiting trial on charges for which capital punishment was heretofore a potential alternative. The happy event for these countable few constitutes, however, only the most visible consequence of this decision. Less measurable, but certainly of no less significance, is the shattering effect this collection of views has on the root principles of *stare decisis,* federalism, judicial restraint and—most importantly—separation of powers.

The Court rejects as not decisive the clearest evidence that the Framers of the Constitution and the authors of the Fourteenth Amendment believed that those documents posed no barrier to the death penalty. The Court also brushes aside an unbroken line of precedent reaffirming the heretofore virtually unquestioned constitutionality of capital punishment. Because of the pervasiveness of the constitutional ruling sought by petitioners, and accepted in varying degrees by five members of the Court, today's departure from established precedent invalidates a staggering number of state and federal laws. The capital punishment laws of no less than 39 States and the District of Columbia are nullified. In addition, numerous provisions of the Criminal Code of the United States and of the Uniform Code of Military Justice also are voided. The Court's judgment not only wipes out laws presently in existence, but denies to Congress and to the legislatures of the 50 States the power to adopt new policies contrary to the policy selected by the Court. Indeed, it is the view of two of my Brothers that the people of each State must be denied the prerogative to amend their constitutions to provide for capital punishment even selectively for the most heinous crime.

In terms of the constitutional role of this Court, the impact of the majority's ruling is all the greater because the decision encroaches upon an area squarely within the historic prerogative of the legislative branch—both state and federal—to protect the citizenry through the designation of penalties for prohibitable conduct. It is the very sort of judgment that the legislative branch is competent to make and for which the judiciary is ill-equipped. Throughout our history, Justices of this Court have emphasized the gravity of decisions invalidating legislative judgments, admonishing the nine men who sit on this bench of the duty of self-restraint, especially when called upon to apply the expansive due process and cruel and unusual punishment rubrics. I can recall no case in which, in the name of deciding constitutional questions, this Court has subordinated national and local democratic processes to such an extent. * * *

* * *

IV

* * *

Petitioners' contentions are premised * * * on the long-accepted view that concepts embodied in the Eighth and Fourteenth Amendments evolve. They present, with skill and persistence, a list of "objective indicators" which are said to demonstrate that prevailing standards of human decency have progressed to the final point of requiring the Court to hold, for all cases and for all time, that capital punishment is unconstitutional.

Briefly summarized, these proffered indicia of contemporary standards of decency include the following: (i) a worldwide trend toward the disuse of the death penalty; (ii) the reflection in the scholarly literature of a progressive rejection of capital punishment founded essentially on moral opposition to such treatment; (iii) the decreasing numbers of executions over the last 40 years and especially over the last decade;[18] (iv) the small number of death sentences rendered in relation to the number of cases in which they might have been imposed;[19] and (v) the indication of public abhorrence of the penalty reflected in the circumstance that executions are no longer public affairs. The foregoing is an incomplete summary but it touches the major bases of petitioners' presentation. Although they are not appropriate for consideration as objective evidence, petitioners strongly urge two additional propositions. They contend, first, that the penalty survives public condemnation only through the infrequency, arbitrariness, and discriminatory nature of its application, and, second, that there no longer exists any legitimate justification for the utilization of the ultimate penalty. These contentions, which have proved persuasive to several of the Justices constituting the majority, deserve separate consideration and will be considered in the ensuing sections. Before turning to those arguments, I first address the argument based on "objective" factors.

Any attempt to discern contemporary standards of decency through the review of objective factors must take into account several overriding considerations which petitioners choose to discount or ignore. In a democ-

---

18. * * * Petitioners concede, as they must, that little weight can be given to the lack of executions in recent years. A *de facto* moratorium has existed for five years now while cases challenging the procedures for implementing the capital sentence have been re-examined by this Court. *McGautha v. California*, 402 U.S. 183, 91 S.Ct. 1454 (1971); *Witherspoon v. Illinois*, 391 U.S. 510, 88 S.Ct. 1770 (1968). The infrequency of executions during the years before the moratorium became fully effective may be attributable in part to decisions of this Court giving expanded scope to the criminal procedural protections of the Bill of Rights, especially under the Fourth and Fifth Amendments. Additionally, decisions of the early 1960's amplifying the scope of the federal habeas corpus remedy also may help account for a reduction in the number of executions.

19. [While acknowledging that no "fully reliable" statistics were available, Justice POWELL cited various authorities for the estimate that there were death sentences in 20% of the cases where death was a statutorily permissible punishment.]

racy the first indicator of the public's attitude must always be found in the legislative judgments of the people's chosen representatives. * * * Forty States, the District of Columbia, and the Federal Government still authorize the death penalty for a wide variety of crimes. That number has remained relatively static since the end of World War I. That does not mean, however, that capital punishment has become a forgotten issue in the legislative arena. As recently as January, 1971, Congress approved the death penalty for congressional assassination. In 1965 Congress added the death penalty for presidential and vice presidential assassinations. Additionally, the aircraft piracy statute passed in 1961 also carries the death penalty. * * * On the converse side, a bill proposing the abolition of capital punishment for all federal crimes was introduced in 1967 but failed to reach the Senate floor.

[Justice POWELL reviewed the recent failures, in many states, to enact legislation repealing the death penalty and concluded that such failures refuted the abolitionist position.]

The second and even more direct source of information reflecting the public's attitude toward capital punishment is the jury. * * *

Any attempt to discern, * * * where the prevailing standards of decency lie must take careful account of the jury's response to the question of capital punishment. During the 1960's juries returned in excess of a thousand death sentences, a rate of approximately two per week. Whether it is true that death sentences were returned in less than 10% of the cases as petitioners estimate or whether some higher percentage is more accurate, these totals simply do not support petitioners' assertion at oral argument that "the death penalty is virtually unanimously repudiated and condemned by the conscience of contemporary society." It is also worthy of note that the annual rate of death sentences has remained relatively constant over the last 10 years and that the figure for 1970—127 sentences—is the highest annual total since 1961. It is true that the sentencing rate might be expected to rise, rather than remain constant, when the number of violent crimes increases as it has in this country. And it may be conceded that the constancy in these statistics indicates the unwillingness of juries to demand the ultimate penalty in many cases where it might be imposed. But these considerations fall short of indicating that juries are imposing the death penalty with such rarity as to justify this Court in reading into this circumstance a public rejection of capital punishment.

One must conclude, contrary to petitioners' submission, that the indicators most likely to reflect the public's view—legislative bodies, state referenda and the juries which have the actual responsibility—do not support the contention that evolving standards of decency require total abolition of capital punishment.[37] Indeed, the weight of the evidence

---

37. If, as petitioners suggest, the judicial branch itself reflects the prevailing standards of human decency in our society, it may be relevant to note the conclusion reached by state courts in recent years on the question of the acceptability of capital punishment. In the last five years

indicates that the public generally has not accepted either the morality or the social merit of the views so passionately advocated by the articulate spokesmen for abolition. But however one may assess the amorphous ebb and flow of public opinion generally on this volatile issue, this type of inquiry lies at the periphery—not the core—of the judicial process in constitutional cases. The assessment of popular opinion is essentially a legislative, not a judicial, function.

V

Petitioners seek to salvage their thesis by arguing that the infrequency and discriminatory nature of the actual resort to the ultimate penalty tend to diffuse public opposition. We are told that the penalty is imposed exclusively on uninfluential minorities—"the poor and powerless, personally ugly and socially unacceptable." It is urged that this pattern of application assures that large segments of the public will be either uninformed or unconcerned and will have no reason to measure the punishment against prevailing moral standards.

Implicitly, this argument concedes the unsoundness of petitioners' contention, examined above under Part IV, that objective evidence shows a present and widespread community rejection of the death penalty. It is now said, in effect, not that capital punishment presently offends our citizenry, but that the public would be offended if the penalty were enforced in a nondiscriminatory manner against a significant percentage of those charged with capital crimes, and if the public were thereby made aware of the moral issues surrounding capital punishment. Rather than merely registering the objective indicators on a judicial balance, we are asked ultimately to rest a far-reaching constitutional determination on a prediction regarding the subjective judgments of the mass of our people under hypothetical assumptions that may or may not be realistic.

Apart from the impermissibility of basing a constitutional judgment of this magnitude on such speculative assumptions, the argument suffers from other defects. If, as petitioners urge, we are to engage in speculation, it is not at all certain that the public would experience deep-felt revulsion if the States were to execute as many sentenced capital offenders this year as they executed in the mid–1930's. It seems more likely that public reaction, rather than being characterized by undifferentiated rejection, would depend upon the facts and circumstances surrounding each particular case.

* * *

But the discrimination argument does not rest alone on a projection of the assumed effect on public opinion of more frequent executions. Much also is made of the undeniable fact that the death penalty has a greater

---

alone, since the de facto "moratorium" on executions began (see n. 18, *supra*), the appellate courts of 26 States have passed on the constitutionality of the death penalty under the Eighth Amendment and under similar provisions of most state constitutions. Every court, except the California Supreme Court, has found the penalty to be constitutional. * * * Every federal court that has passed on the issue has ruled that the death penalty is not *per se* unconstitutional.

impact on the lower economic strata of society, which include a relatively higher percentage of persons of minority racial and ethnic group backgrounds. * * *

    * * *

    Certainly the claim is justified that this criminal sanction falls more heavily on the relatively impoverished and underprivileged elements of society. The "have-nots" in every society always have been subject to greater pressure to commit crimes and to fewer constraints than their more affluent fellow citizens. This is, indeed, a tragic byproduct of social and economic deprivation, but it is not an argument of constitutional proportions under the Eighth or Fourteenth Amendment. The same discriminatory impact argument could be made with equal force and logic with respect to those sentenced to prison terms. The Due Process Clause admits of no distinction between the deprivation of "life" and the deprivation of "liberty." If discriminatory impact renders capital punishment cruel and unusual, it likewise renders invalid most of the prescribed penalties for crimes of violence. The root causes of the higher incidence of criminal penalties on "minorities and the poor" will not be cured by abolishing the system of penalties. Nor, indeed, could any society have a viable system of criminal justice if sanctions were abolished or ameliorated because most of those who commit crimes happen to be underprivileged. The basic problem results not from the penalties imposed for criminal conduct but from social and economic factors that have plagued humanity since the beginning of recorded history, frustrating all efforts to create in any country at any time the perfect society in which there are no "poor," no "minorities" and no "underprivileged." The causes underlying this problem are unrelated to the constitutional issue before the Court.

    Finally, yet another theory for abolishing the death penalty—reflected in varying degrees in each of the concurring opinions today—is predicated on the discriminatory impact argument. Quite apart from measuring the public's acceptance or rejection of the death penalty under the "standards of decency" rationale, Mr. Justice DOUGLAS finds the punishment cruel and unusual because it is "arbitrarily" invoked. He finds that "the basic theme of equal protection is implicit" in the Eighth Amendment, and that the Amendment is violated when jury sentencing may be characterized as arbitrary or discriminatory. While Mr. Justice STEWART does not purport to rely on notions of equal protection, he also rests primarily on what he views to be a history of arbitrariness. Whatever may be the facts with respect to jury sentencing, this argument calls for a reconsideration of the "standards" aspects of the Court's decision in *McGautha v. California*. Although that is the unmistakable thrust of these opinions today, I see no reason to reassess the standards question considered so carefully in Mr. Justice HARLAN's opinion for the Court last Term. Having so recently reaffirmed our historic dedication to entrusting the sentencing function to the jury's "untrammeled discretion," it is difficult to see how the Court can now hold the entire process constitutionally defective under the Eighth Amendment. For all of these reasons I find little merit in the various discrimination arguments, at least in the several lights in which they have been cast in these cases.

Although not presented by any of the petitioners today, a different argument, premised on the Equal Protection Clause, might well be made. If a Negro defendant, for instance, could demonstrate that members of his race were being singled out for more severe punishment than others charged with the same offense, a constitutional violation might be established. * * *

    * * *

* * * The possibility of racial bias in the trial and sentencing process has diminished in recent years. The segregation of our society in decades past, which contributed substantially to the severity of punishment for interracial crimes, is now no longer prevalent in this country. Likewise, the day is past when juries do not represent the minority group elements of the community. The assurance of fair trials for all citizens is greater today than at any previous time in our history. Because standards of criminal justice have "evolved" in a manner favorable to the accused, discriminatory imposition of capital punishment is far less likely today than in the past.

    * * *

VIII

    * * *

With deference and respect for the views of the Justices who differ, it seems to me * * * that, as a matter of policy and precedent, this is a classic case for the exercise of our oft-announced allegiance to judicial restraint. I know of no case in which greater gravity and delicacy have attached to the duty that this Court is called on to perform whenever legislation—state or federal—is challenged on constitutional grounds. It seems to me that the sweeping judicial action undertaken today reflects a basic lack of faith and confidence in the democratic process. Many may regret, as I do, the failure of some legislative bodies to address the capital punishment issue with greater frankness or effectiveness. Many might decry their failure either to abolish the penalty entirely or selectively, or to establish standards for its enforcement. But impatience with the slowness, and even the unresponsiveness, of legislatures is no justification for judicial intrusion upon their historic powers. * * *

MR. JUSTICE REHNQUIST, with whom THE CHIEF JUSTICE, MR. JUSTICE BLACKMUN, and MR. JUSTICE POWELL join, dissenting.

The Court's judgments today strike down a penalty that our Nation's legislators have thought necessary since our country was founded. My Brothers DOUGLAS, BRENNAN, and MARSHALL would at one fell swoop invalidate laws enacted by Congress and 40 of the 50 state legislatures, and would consign to the limbo of unconstitutionality under a single rubric penalties for offenses as varied and unique as murder, piracy, mutiny, highjacking, and desertion in the face of the enemy. My Brothers STEWART and WHITE, asserting reliance on a more limited rationale—the reluctance of judges and juries actually to impose the death penalty in the majority of capital cases—join in the judgments in these cases. Whatever its precise rationale, today's holding necessarily brings into sharp relief the fundamental question of the role of judicial review in a democratic society. How can government by the elected representatives of the people co-exist with the power of the federal judiciary, whose members are constitutionally insulated from responsiveness to the popular will, to declare invalid laws duly enacted by the popular branches of government?

    * * *

If there can be said to be one dominant theme in the Constitution, perhaps more fully articulated in the Federalist Papers than in the instrument itself, it is the notion of checks and balances. * * *

This philosophy of the Framers is best described by one of the ablest and greatest of their number, James Madison, in Federalist No. 51:

> "In framing a government which is to be administered by men over men, the great difficulty lies in this: You must first enable the government to controul the governed; and in the next place, oblige it to controul itself."

Madison's observation applies to the Judicial Branch with at least as much force as to the Legislative and Executive Branches. While over-reaching by the Legislative and Executive Branches may result in the sacrifice of individual protections that the Constitution was designed to secure against action of the State, judicial overreaching may result in sacrifice of the equally important right of the people to govern themselves. The Due Process and Equal Protection Clauses of the Fourteenth Amendment were "never intended to destroy the States' power to govern themselves." Black, J., in *Oregon v. Mitchell*, 400 U.S. 112, 91 S.Ct. 260 (1970).

The very nature of judicial review * * * makes the courts the least subject to Madisonian check in the event that they shall, for the best of motives, expand judicial authority beyond the limits contemplated by the Framers. It is for this reason that judicial self-restraint is surely an implied, if not an expressed, condition of the grant of authority of judicial review. The Court's holding in these cases has been reached, I believe, in complete disregard of that implied condition.

NOTE

1. *The impact of Furman.*

As Justice Powell predicted, the *Furman* decision had an enormous effect, invalidating approximately 40 state death penalty statutes and overturning approximately 600 death sentences. The decision was front-page news with headlines of a size usually reserved for a declaration of war. The impact was rivaled only by the decision a year later in *Roe v. Wade*, 410 U.S. 113, 93 S.Ct. 705 (1973), and like *Roe*, *Furman* did not resolve the basic issue, but only galvanized the opposition, with political and judicial consequences continuing to this day. Whereas prior to the *Furman* decision, supporters of the death penalty were said to be "a distinct and dwindling minority" in the country (*Witherspoon v. Illinois*, 391 U.S. 510, 519, 88 S.Ct. 1770, 1775 (1968)), after the decision, a substantial majority of the states immediately passed new death penalty statutes, and juries began once more to impose death sentences.

GREGG v. GEORGIA

428 U.S. 153, 96 S.Ct. 2909, 49 L.Ed.2d 859 (1976).

Judgment of the Court, and opinion of MR. JUSTICE STEWART, MR. JUSTICE POWELL, and MR. JUSTICE STEVENS, announced by MR. JUSTICE STEWART.

The issue in this case is whether the imposition of the sentence of death for the crime of murder under the law of Georgia violates the Eighth and Fourteenth Amendments.

I

The petitioner, Troy Gregg, was charged with committing armed robbery and murder. In accordance with Georgia procedure in capital cases, the trial was in two stages, a guilt stage and a sentencing stage. [The evidence at the guilt trial established that Gregg and a traveling companion, Floyd Allen, while hitchhiking in Florida, were picked up by the two victims. The four stopped for a rest along the highway, and Gregg shot and killed the victims and took their car and valuables. The jury found Gregg guilty of two counts of armed robbery and two counts of murder.]

At the penalty stage, which took place before the same jury, neither the prosecutor nor the petitioner's lawyer offered any additional evidence. Both counsel, however, made lengthy arguments dealing generally with the propriety of capital punishment under the circumstances and with the weight of the evidence of guilt. The trial judge instructed the jury that it could recommend either a death sentence or a life prison sentence on each count. The judge further charged the jury that in determining what sentence was appropriate the jury was free to consider the facts and circumstances, if any, presented by the parties in mitigation or aggravation.

Finally, the judge instructed the jury that it "would not be authorized to consider [imposing] the penalty of death" unless it first found beyond a reasonable doubt one of these aggravating circumstances:

> "One—That the offense of murder was committed while the offender was engaged in the commission of two other capital felonies, to-wit the armed robbery of [Simmons and Moore].

"Two—That the offender committed the offense of murder for the purpose of receiving money and the automobile described in the indictment.

"Three—The offense of murder was outrageously and wantonly vile, horrible and inhuman, in that they [sic] involved the depravity of [the] mind of the defendant."

Finding the first and second of these circumstances, the jury returned verdicts of death on each count.

The Supreme Court of Georgia affirmed the convictions and the imposition of the death sentences for murder. After reviewing the trial transcript and the record, including the evidence, and comparing the evidence and sentence in similar cases in accordance with the requirements of Georgia law, the court concluded that, considering the nature of the crime and the defendant, the sentences of death had not resulted from prejudice or any other arbitrary factor and were not excessive or disproportionate to the penalty applied in similar cases. The death sentences imposed for armed robbery, however, were vacated on the grounds that the death penalty had rarely been imposed in Georgia for that offense and that the jury improperly considered the murders as aggravating circumstances for the robberies after having considered the armed robberies as aggravating circumstances for the murders.

We granted the petitioner's application for a writ of certiorari limited to his challenge to the imposition of the death sentences in this case as "cruel and unusual" punishment in violation of the Eighth and the Fourteenth Amendments.

II

Before considering the issues presented it is necessary to understand the Georgia statutory scheme for the imposition of the death penalty. The Georgia statute, as amended after our decision in *Furman v. Georgia*, 408 U.S. 238, 92 S.Ct. 2726 (1972), retains the death penalty for six categories of crime: murder, kidnaping for ransom or where the victim is harmed, armed robbery, rape, treason, and aircraft hijacking. The capital defendant's guilt or innocence is determined in the traditional manner, either by a trial judge or a jury, in the first stage of a bifurcated trial.

If trial is by jury, the trial judge is required to charge lesser included offenses when they are supported by any view of the evidence. After a verdict, finding, or plea of guilty to a capital crime, a presentence hearing is conducted before whoever made the determination of guilt. The sentencing procedures are essentially the same in both bench and jury trials. At the hearing:

"the judge [or jury] shall hear additional evidence in extenuation, mitigation, and aggravation of punishment, including the record of any prior criminal convictions and pleas of guilty or pleas of *nolo contendere* of the defendant, or the absence of any prior conviction and pleas: Provided, however, that only such evidence in aggravation as the State has made known to the defendant prior to his trial shall be admissible. The judge [or jury] shall also hear argument by the defendant or his counsel and the prosecuting attorney ... regarding the punishment to be imposed."

The defendant is accorded substantial latitude as to the types of evidence that he may introduce. Evidence considered during the guilt stage may be considered during the sentencing stage without being resubmitted.

In the assessment of the appropriate sentence to be imposed the judge is also required to consider or to include in his instructions to the jury "any mitigating circumstances or aggravating circumstances otherwise authorized by law and any of [10] statutory aggravating circumstances which may be supported by the evidence...." The scope of the nonstatutory aggravating or mitigating circumstances is not delineated in the statute. Before a convicted defendant may be sentenced to death, however, except in cases of treason or aircraft hijacking, the jury, or the trial judge in cases tried without a jury, must find beyond a reasonable doubt one of the 10 aggravating circumstances specified in the statute. The sentence of death may be imposed only if the jury (or judge) finds one of the statutory aggravating circumstances and then elects to impose that sentence. If the verdict is death, the jury or judge must specify the aggravating circumstance(s) found. In jury cases, the trial judge is bound by the jury's recommended sentence.

In addition to the conventional appellate process available in all criminal cases, provision is made for special expedited direct review by the Supreme Court of Georgia of the appropriateness of imposing the sentence of death in the particular case. The court is directed to consider "the punishment as well as any errors enumerated by way of appeal," and to determine:

"(1) Whether the sentence of death was imposed under the influence of passion, prejudice, or any other arbitrary factor, and

"(2) Whether, in cases other than treason or aircraft hijacking, the evidence supports the jury's or judge's finding of a statutory aggravating circumstance ..., and

"(3) Whether the sentence of death is excessive or disproportionate to the penalty imposed in similar cases, considering both the crime and the defendant."

If the court affirms a death sentence, it is required to include in its decision reference to similar cases that it has taken into consideration.

A transcript and complete record of the trial, as well as a separate report by the trial judge, are transmitted to the court for its use in reviewing the sentence. The report is in the form of a 6 1/2–page questionnaire, designed to elicit information about the defendant, the crime, and the circumstances of the trial. It requires the trial judge to characterize the trial in several ways designed to test for arbitrariness and disproportionality of sentence. Included in the report are responses to detailed questions concerning the quality of the defendant's representation, whether race played a role in the trial, and, whether, in the trial court's judgment, there was any doubt about the defendant's guilt or the appropriateness of the sentence. A copy of the report is served upon defense counsel. Under its special review authority, the court may either affirm the death sentence or remand the case for resentencing. In cases in which the death sentence is affirmed there remains the possibility of executive clemency.

III

We address initially the basic contention that the punishment of death for the crime of murder is, under all circumstances, "cruel and unusual" in violation of the Eighth and Fourteenth Amendments of the Constitution. In Part IV of this opinion, we will consider the sentence of death imposed under the Georgia statutes at issue in this case.

The Court on a number of occasions has both assumed and asserted the constitutionality of capital punishment. In several cases that assumption provided a necessary foundation for the decision, as the Court was asked to decide whether a particular method of carrying out a capital sentence would be allowed to stand under the Eighth Amendment. But until *Furman v. Georgia*, 408 U.S. 238, 92 S.Ct. 2726 (1972), the Court never confronted squarely the fundamental claim that the punishment of death always, regardless of the enormity of the offense or the procedure followed in imposing the sentence, is cruel and unusual punishment in violation of the Constitution. Although this issue was presented and addressed in *Furman*, it was not resolved by the Court. Four Justices would have held that capital punishment is not unconstitutional *per se* [Chief Justice BURGER and Justices BLACKMUN, POWELL and REHNQUIST]; two Justices would have reached the opposite conclusion [Justices BRENNAN and MARSHALL]; and three Justices, while agreeing that the statutes then before the Court were invalid as applied, left open the question whether such punishment may ever be imposed. [Justices DOUGLAS, STEWART and WHITE] We now hold that the punishment of death does not invariably violate the Constitution.

A

[Justice STEWART reviewed the history of the Eighth Amendment.]

It is clear from the foregoing precedents that the Eighth Amendment has not been regarded as a static concept. As Mr. Chief Justice Warren said, in an often-quoted phrase, "[t]he Amendment must draw its meaning from the evolving standards of decency that mark the progress of a maturing society." (*Trop v. Dulles*, 356 U.S. 86, 78 S.Ct. 590 (1958).) Thus, an assessment of contemporary values concerning the infliction of a challenged sanction is relevant to the application of the Eighth Amendment. As we develop below more fully, this assessment does not call for a subjective judgment. It requires, rather, that we look to objective indicia that reflect the public attitude toward a given sanction.

But our cases also make clear that public perceptions of standards of decency with respect to criminal sanctions are not conclusive. A penalty also must accord with "the dignity of man," which is the "basic concept underlying the Eighth Amendment." This means, at least, that the punishment not be "excessive." When a form of punishment in the abstract (in this case, whether capital punishment may ever be imposed as a sanction for murder) rather than in the particular (the propriety of death as a penalty to be applied to a specific defendant for a specific crime) is under consideration, the inquiry into "excessiveness" has two aspects. First, the punishment must not involve the unnecessary and wanton infliction of pain. Second, the punishment must not be grossly out of proportion to the severity of the crime.

B

Of course, the requirements of the Eighth Amendment must be applied with an awareness of the limited role to be played by the courts. This does not mean that judges have no role to play, for the Eighth Amendment is a restraint upon the exercise of legislative power. * * *[19]

But, while we have an obligation to insure that constitutional bounds are not overreached, we may not act as judges as we might as legislators.

> "Courts are not representative bodies. They are not designed to be a good reflex of a democratic society. Their judgment is best informed, and therefore most dependable, within narrow limits. Their essential quality is detachment, founded on independence. History teaches that the independence of the judiciary is jeopardized when courts become embroiled in the passions of the day and assume primary responsibility in choosing between competing political, economic and social pressures." *Dennis v. United States*, 341 U.S. 494, 71 S.Ct. 857 (1951) (FRANKFURTER, J., concurring in affirmance of judgment).

Therefore, in assessing a punishment selected by a democratically elected legislature against the constitutional measure, we presume its validity. We may not require the legislature to select the least severe penalty possible so long as the penalty selected is not cruelly inhumane or disproportionate to the crime involved. And a heavy burden rests on those who would attack the judgment of the representatives of the people.

---

19. Although legislative measures adopted by the people's chosen representatives provide one important means of ascertaining contemporary values, it is evident that legislative judgments alone cannot be determinative of Eighth Amendment standards since that Amendment was intended to safeguard individuals from the abuse of legislative power. See *Weems v. United States*, 217 U.S. 349, 30 S.Ct. 544 (1910); *Furman v. Georgia* (BRENNAN, J., concurring). *Robinson v. California*, 370 U.S. 660, 82 S.Ct. 1417 (1962), illustrates the proposition that penal laws enacted by state legislatures may violate the Eighth Amendment because "in the light of contemporary human knowledge" they "would doubtless be universally thought to be an infliction of cruel and unusual punishment." At the time of *Robinson* nine States in addition to California had criminal laws that punished addiction similar to the law declared unconstitutional in *Robinson*.

This is true in part because the constitutional test is intertwined with an assessment of contemporary standards and the legislative judgment weighs heavily in ascertaining such standards. "[I]n a democratic society legislatures, not courts, are constituted to respond to the will and consequently the moral values of the people." *Furman v. Georgia* (BURGER, C.J., dissenting). The deference we owe to the decisions of the state legislatures under our federal system (REHNQUIST, J., dissenting), is enhanced where the specification of punishments is concerned, for "these are peculiarly questions of legislative policy." *Gore v. United States*, 357 U.S. 386, 78 S.Ct. 1280 (1958). Caution is necessary lest this Court become, "under the aegis of the Cruel and Unusual Punishment Clause, the ultimate arbiter of the standards of criminal responsibility ... throughout the country." *Powell v. Texas*, 392 U.S. 514, 88 S.Ct. 2145 (1968) (plurality opinion). A decision that a given punishment is impermissible under the Eighth Amendment cannot be reversed short of a constitutional amendment. The ability of the people to express their preference through the normal democratic processes, as well as through ballot referenda, is shut off. Revisions cannot be made in the light of further experience.

C

In the discussion to this point we have sought to identify the principles and considerations that guide a court in addressing an Eighth Amendment claim. We now consider specifically whether the sentence of death for the crime of murder is a *per se* violation of the Eighth and Fourteenth Amendments to the Constitution. We note first that history and precedent strongly support a negative answer to this question.

The imposition of the death penalty for the crime of murder has a long history of acceptance both in the United States and in England. The common-law rule imposed a mandatory death sentence on all convicted murderers. And the penalty continued to be used into the 20th century by most American States, although the breadth of the common-law rule was diminished, initially by narrowing the class of murders to be punished by death and subsequently by widespread adoption of laws expressly granting juries the discretion to recommend mercy.

It is apparent from the text of the Constitution itself that the existence of capital punishment was accepted by the Framers. At the time the Eighth Amendment was ratified, capital punishment was a common sanction in every State. Indeed, the First Congress of the United States enacted legislation providing death as the penalty for specified crimes. The Fifth Amendment, adopted at the same time as the Eighth, contemplated the continued existence of the capital sanction by imposing certain limits on the prosecution of capital cases:

"No person shall be held to answer for a capital, or otherwise infamous crime, unless on a presentment or indictment of a Grand Jury ...; nor shall any person be subject for the same offense to be twice put in jeopardy of life or limb; . . . nor be deprived of life, liberty, or property, without due process of law. . . ."

And the Fourteenth Amendment, adopted over three-quarters of a century later, similarly contemplates the existence of the capital sanction in providing that no State shall deprive any person of "life, liberty, or property" without due process of law.

For nearly two centuries, this Court, repeatedly and often expressly, has recognized that capital punishment is not invalid *per se.* * * *

Four years ago, the petitioners in *Furman* and its companion cases predicated their argument primarily upon the asserted proposition that standards of decency had evolved to the point where capital punishment no longer could be tolerated. The petitioners in those cases said, in effect, that the evolutionary process had come to an end, and that standards of decency required that the Eighth Amendment be construed finally as prohibiting capital punishment for any crime regardless of its depravity and impact on society. This view was accepted by two Justices. Three other Justices were unwilling to go so far; focusing on the procedures by which convicted defendants were selected for the death penalty rather than on the actual punishment inflicted, they joined in the conclusion that the statutes before the Court were constitutionally invalid.

The petitioners in the capital cases before the Court today renew the "standards of decency" argument, but developments during the four years since *Furman* have undercut substantially the assumptions upon which their argument rested. Despite the continuing debate, dating back to the 19th century, over the morality and utility of capital punishment, it is now evident that a large proportion of American society continues to regard it as an appropriate and necessary criminal sanction.

The most marked indication of society's endorsement of the death penalty for murder is the legislative response to *Furman*. The legislatures of at least 35 States have enacted new statutes that provide for the death penalty for at least some crimes that result in the death of another person. And the Congress of the United States, in 1974, enacted a statute providing the death penalty for aircraft piracy that results in death. These recently adopted statutes have attempted to address the concerns expressed by the Court in *Furman* primarily (i) by specifying the factors to be weighed and the procedures to be followed in deciding when to impose a capital sentence, or (ii) by making the death penalty mandatory for specified crimes. But all of the post-*Furman* statutes make clear that capital punishment itself has not been rejected by the elected representatives of the people.

In the only statewide referendum occurring since *Furman* and brought to our attention, the people of California adopted a constitutional amendment that authorized capital punishment, in effect negating a prior ruling by the Supreme Court of California in *People v. Anderson*, 493 P.2d 880 (Cal.1972), that the death penalty violated the California Constitution.

The jury also is a significant and reliable objective index of contemporary values because it is so directly involved. The Court has said that "one of the most important functions any jury can perform in making ... a selection [between life imprisonment and death for a defendant convicted in a capital case] is to maintain a link between contemporary community values and the penal system." *Witherspoon v. Illinois*, 391 U.S. 510, 88 S.Ct. 1770 (1968). It may be true that evolving standards have influenced juries in recent decades to be more discriminating in imposing the sentence of death.[26] But the relative infrequency of jury verdicts imposing the death sentence does not indicate rejection of capital punishment *per se*. Rather, the reluctance of juries in many cases to impose the sentence may well reflect the humane feeling that this most irrevocable of sanctions should be reserved for a small number of extreme cases. Indeed, the actions of juries in many States since *Furman* are fully compatible with the legislative judgments, reflected in the new statutes, as to the continued utility and necessity of capital punishment in appropriate cases. At the close of 1974 at least 254 persons had been sentenced to death since *Furman*, and by the end of March 1976, more than 460 persons were subject to death sentences.

As we have seen, however, the Eighth Amendment demands more than that a challenged punishment be acceptable to contemporary society. The Court also must ask whether it comports with the basic concept of human dignity at the core of the Amendment. Although we cannot "invalidate a category of penalties because we deem less severe penalties adequate to serve the ends of penology," *Furman v. Georgia* (POWELL, J., dissenting), the sanction imposed cannot be so totally without penological justification that it results in the gratuitous infliction of suffering.

The death penalty is said to serve two principal social purposes: retribution and deterrence of capital crimes by prospective offenders.[28]

In part, capital punishment is an expression of society's moral outrage at particularly offensive conduct. This function may be unappealing to many, but it is essential in an ordered society that asks its citizens to rely on legal processes rather than self-help to vindicate their wrongs.

> "The instinct for retribution is part of the nature of man, and channeling that instinct in the administration of criminal justice serves an important purpose in promoting the stability of a society governed by law. When people begin to believe that organized society is unwilling or unable to impose upon criminal offenders the punishment they 'deserve,' then there are sown the seeds of anarchy—of

---

26. The number of prisoners who received death sentences in the years from 1961 to 1972 varied from a high of 140 in 1961 to a low of 75 in 1972, with wide fluctuations in the intervening years: 103 in 1962; 93 in 1963; 106 in 1964; 86 in 1965; 118 in 1966; 85 in 1967; 102 in 1968; 97 in 1969; 127 in 1970; and 104 in 1971. It has been estimated that before *Furman* less than 20% of those convicted of murder were sentenced to death in those States that authorized capital punishment.

28. Another purpose that has been discussed is the incapacitation of dangerous criminals and the consequent prevention of crimes that they may otherwise commit in the future.

self-help, vigilante justice, and lynch law." *Furman v. Georgia* (STEWART, J., concurring).

"Retribution is no longer the dominant objective of the criminal law," *Williams v. New York*, 337 U.S. 241, 69 S.Ct. 1079 (1949), but neither is it a forbidden objective nor one inconsistent with our respect for the dignity of men. Indeed, the decision that capital punishment may be the appropriate sanction in extreme cases is an expression of the community's belief that certain crimes are themselves so grievous an affront to humanity that the only adequate response may be the penalty of death.

Statistical attempts to evaluate the worth of the death penalty as a deterrent to crimes by potential offenders have occasioned a great deal of debate. The results simply have been inconclusive. As one opponent of capital punishment has said:

> "[A]fter all possible inquiry, including the probing of all possible methods of inquiry, we do not know, and for systematic and easily visible reasons cannot know, what the truth about this 'deterrent' effect may be. . . .
>
> "The inescapable flaw is . . . that social conditions in any state are not constant through time, and that social conditions are not the same in any two states. If an effect were observed (and the observed effects, one way or another, are not large) then one could not at all tell whether any of this effect is attributable to the presence or absence of capital punishment. A 'scientific'—that is to say, a soundly based— conclusion is simply impossible, and no methodological path out of this tangle suggests itself." Black, Capital Punishment: The Inevitability of Caprice and Mistake 25–26 (1974).

Although some of the studies suggest that the death penalty may not function as a significantly greater deterrent than lesser penalties, there is no convincing empirical evidence either supporting or refuting this view. We may nevertheless assume safely that there are murderers, such as those who act in passion, for whom the threat of death has little or no deterrent effect. But for many others, the death penalty undoubtedly is a significant deterrent. There are carefully contemplated murders, such as murder for hire, where the possible penalty of death may well enter into the cold calculus that precedes the decision to act.[33] And there are some categories of murder, such as murder by a life prisoner, where other sanctions may not be adequate.

The value of capital punishment as a deterrent of crime is a complex factual issue the resolution of which properly rests with the legislatures, which can evaluate the results of statistical studies in terms of their own local conditions and with a flexibility of approach that is not available to the courts. Indeed, many of the post-*Furman* statutes reflect just such a

---

33. Other types of calculated murders, apparently occurring with increasing frequency, include the use of bombs or other means of indiscriminate killings, the extortion murder of hostages or kidnap victims, and the execution-style killing of witnesses to a crime.

responsible effort to define those crimes and those criminals for which capital punishment is most probably an effective deterrent.

In sum, we cannot say that the judgment of the Georgia Legislature that capital punishment may be necessary in some cases is clearly wrong. Considerations of federalism, as well as respect for the ability of a legislature to evaluate, in terms of its particular State, the moral consensus concerning the death penalty and its social utility as a sanction, require us to conclude, in the absence of more convincing evidence, that the infliction of death as a punishment for murder is not without justification and thus is not unconstitutionally severe.

Finally, we must consider whether the punishment of death is disproportionate in relation to the crime for which it is imposed. There is no question that death as a punishment is unique in its severity and irrevocability. When a defendant's life is at stake, the Court has been particularly sensitive to insure that every safeguard is observed. *Powell v. Alabama*, 287 U.S. 45, 53 S.Ct. 55 (1932). But we are concerned here only with the imposition of capital punishment for the crime of murder, and when a life has been taken deliberately by the offender, we cannot say that the punishment is invariably disproportionate to the crime. It is an extreme sanction, suitable to the most extreme of crimes.

We hold that the death penalty is not a form of punishment that may never be imposed, regardless of the circumstances of the offense, regardless of the character of the offender, and regardless of the procedure followed in reaching the decision to impose it.

IV

We now consider whether Georgia may impose the death penalty on the petitioner in this case.

A

While *Furman* did not hold that the infliction of the death penalty *per se* violates the Constitution's ban on cruel and unusual punishments, it did recognize that the penalty of death is different in kind from any other punishment imposed under our system of criminal justice. Because of the uniqueness of the death penalty, *Furman* held that it could not be imposed under sentencing procedures that created a substantial risk that it would be inflicted in an arbitrary and capricious manner. MR. JUSTICE WHITE concluded that "the death penalty is exacted with great infrequency even for the most atrocious crimes and . . . there is no meaningful basis for distinguishing the few cases in which it is imposed from the many cases in which it is not." Indeed, the death sentences examined by the Court in *Furman* were "cruel and unusual in the same way that being struck by lightning is cruel and unusual. For, of all the people convicted of [capital crimes], many just as reprehensible as these, the petitioners [in *Furman* were] among a capriciously selected random handful upon whom the sentence of death has in fact been imposed. . . . [T]he Eighth and

Fourteenth Amendments cannot tolerate the infliction of a sentence of death under legal systems that permit this unique penalty to be so wantonly and so freakishly imposed." (STEWART, J., concurring).[35]

Furman mandates that where discretion is afforded a sentencing body on a matter so grave as the determination of whether a human life should be taken or spared, that discretion must be suitably directed and limited so as to minimize the risk of wholly arbitrary and capricious action.

* * *

Jury sentencing has been considered desirable in capital cases in order "to maintain a link between contemporary community values and the penal system—a link without which the determination of punishment could hardly reflect 'the evolving standards of decency that mark the progress of a maturing society.'" But it creates special problems. Much of the information that is relevant to the sentencing decision may have no relevance to the question of guilt, or may even be extremely prejudicial to a fair determination of that question. This problem, however, is scarcely insurmountable. Those who have studied the question suggest that a bifurcated procedure—one in which the question of sentence is not considered until the determination of guilt has been made—is the best answer. The drafters of the Model Penal Code concluded:

> "[if a unitary proceeding is used] the determination of the punishment must be based on less than all the evidence that has a bearing on that issue, such for example as a previous criminal record of the accused, or evidence must be admitted on the ground that it is relevant to sentence, though it would be excluded as irrelevant or prejudicial with respect to guilt or innocence alone. Trial lawyers understandably have little confidence in a solution that admits the evidence and trusts to an instruction to the jury that it should be considered only in determining the penalty and disregarded in assessing guilt.
>
> "... The obvious solution ... is to bifurcate the proceeding, abiding strictly by the rules of evidence until and unless there is a conviction, but once guilt has been determined opening the record to the further information that is relevant to sentence. This is the analogue of the procedure in the ordinary case when capital punishment is not in issue; the court conducts a separate inquiry before imposing sentence."

When a human life is at stake and when the jury must have information prejudicial to the question of guilt but relevant to the question of penalty in order to impose a rational sentence, a bifurcated system is more likely

---

35. This view was expressed by other Members of the Court who concurred in the judgments. [Justices Douglas and Brennan] The dissenters viewed this concern as the basis for the *Furman* decision: "The decisive grievance of the opinions ... is that the present system of discretionary sentencing in capital cases has failed to produce evenhanded justice; ... that the selection process has followed no rational pattern." [Chief Justice Burger]

to ensure elimination of the constitutional deficiencies identified in *Furman*.

But the provision of relevant information under fair procedural rules is not alone sufficient to guarantee that the information will be properly used in the imposition of punishment, especially if sentencing is performed by a jury. Since the members of a jury will have had little, if any, previous experience in sentencing, they are unlikely to be skilled in dealing with the information they are given. To the extent that this problem is inherent in jury sentencing, it may not be totally correctable. It seems clear, however, that the problem will be alleviated if the jury is given guidance regarding the factors about the crime and the defendant that the State, representing organized society, deems particularly relevant to the sentencing decision.

The idea that a jury should be given guidance in its decisionmaking is also hardly a novel proposition. Juries are invariably given careful instructions on the law and how to apply it before they are authorized to decide the merits of a lawsuit. It would be virtually unthinkable to follow any other course in a legal system that has traditionally operated by following prior precedents and fixed rules of law. When erroneous instructions are given, retrial is often required. It is quite simply a hallmark of our legal system that juries be carefully and adequately guided in their deliberations.

While some have suggested that standards to guide a capital jury's sentencing deliberations are impossible to formulate, the fact is that such standards have been developed. When the drafters of the Model Penal Code faced this problem, they concluded "that it is within the realm of possibility to point to the main circumstances of aggravation and of mitigation that should be weighed *and weighed against each other* when they are presented in a concrete case." (emphasis in original). While such standards are by necessity somewhat general, they do provide guidance to the sentencing authority and thereby reduce the likelihood that it will impose a sentence that fairly can be called capricious or arbitrary. Where the sentencing authority is required to specify the factors it relied upon in reaching its decision, the further safeguard of meaningful appellate review is available to ensure that death sentences are not imposed capriciously or in a freakish manner.

In summary, the concerns expressed in *Furman* that the penalty of death not be imposed in an arbitrary or capricious manner can be met by a carefully drafted statute that ensures that the sentencing authority is given adequate information and guidance. As a general proposition these concerns are best met by a system that provides for a bifurcated proceeding at which the sentencing authority is apprised of the information relevant to the imposition of sentence and provided with standards to guide its use of the information.

We do not intend to suggest that only the above described procedures would be permissible under *Furman* or that any sentencing system constructed along these general lines would inevitably satisfy the concerns of *Furman*, for each distinct system must be examined on an individual basis. Rather, we have embarked upon this general exposition to make clear that it is possible to construct capital-sentencing systems capable of meeting *Furman*'s constitutional concerns.

B

We now turn to consideration of the constitutionality of Georgia's capital-sentencing procedures. In the wake of *Furman*, Georgia amended its capital punishment statute, but chose not to narrow the scope of its murder provisions. Thus, now as before *Furman*, in Georgia "[a] person commits murder when he unlawfully and with malice aforethought, either express or implied, causes the death of another human being." All persons convicted of murder "shall be punished by death or by imprisonment for life."

Georgia did act, however, to narrow the class of murderers subject to capital punishment by specifying 10 statutory aggravating circumstances, one of which must be found by the jury to exist beyond a reasonable doubt before a death sentence can ever be imposed. In addition, the jury is authorized to consider any other appropriate aggravating or mitigating circumstances. The jury is not required to find any mitigating circumstance in order to make a recommendation of mercy that is binding on the trial court, but it must find a statutory aggravating circumstance before recommending a sentence of death.

These procedures require the jury to consider the circumstances of the crime and the criminal before it recommends sentence. No longer can a Georgia jury do as Furman's jury did: reach a finding of the defendant's guilt and then, without guidance or direction, decide whether he should live or die. Instead, the jury's attention is directed to the specific circumstances of the crime: Was it committed in the course of another capital felony? Was it committed for money? Was it committed upon a peace officer or judicial officer? Was it committed in a particularly heinous way or in a manner that endangered the lives of many persons? In addition, the jury's attention is focused on the characteristics of the person who committed the crime: Does he have a record of prior convictions for capital offenses? Are there any special facts about this defendant that mitigate against imposing capital punishment (*e.g.*, his youth, the extent of his cooperation with the police, his emotional state at the time of the crime). As a result, while some jury discretion still exists, "the discretion to be exercised is controlled by clear and objective standards so as to produce non-discriminatory application." *Coley v. State*, 204 S.E.2d 612 (Ga. 1974).

As an important additional safeguard against arbitrariness and caprice, the Georgia statutory scheme provides for automatic appeal of all death sentences to the State's Supreme Court. That court is required by statute to review each sentence of death and determine whether it was imposed under the influence of passion or prejudice, whether the evidence supports the jury's finding of a statutory aggravating circumstance, and whether the sentence is disproportionate compared to those sentences imposed in similar cases.

In short, Georgia's new sentencing procedures require as a prerequisite to the imposition of the death penalty, specific jury findings as to the circumstances of the crime or the character of the defendant. Moreover, to guard further against a situation comparable to that presented in *Furman*, the Supreme Court of Georgia compares each death sentence with the sentences imposed on similarly situated defendants to ensure that the sentence of death in a particular case is not disproportionate. On their face these procedures seem to satisfy the concerns of *Furman*. No longer should there be "no meaningful basis for distinguishing the few cases in which [the death penalty] is imposed from the many cases in which it is not." (WHITE, J., concurring).

The petitioner contends, however, that the changes in the Georgia sentencing procedures are only cosmetic, that the arbitrariness and capriciousness condemned by *Furman* continue to exist in Georgia both in traditional practices that still remain and in the new sentencing procedures adopted in response to *Furman*.

1

First, the petitioner focuses on the opportunities for discretionary action that are inherent in the processing of any murder case under Georgia law. He notes that the state prosecutor has unfettered authority to select those persons whom he wishes to prosecute for a capital offense and to plea bargain with them. Further, at the trial the jury may choose to convict a defendant of a lesser included offense rather than find him guilty of a crime punishable by death, even if the evidence would support a capital verdict. And finally, a defendant who is convicted and sentenced to die may have his sentence commuted by the Governor of the State and the Georgia Board of Pardons and Paroles.

The existence of these discretionary stages is not determinative of the issues before us. At each of these stages an actor in the criminal justice system makes a decision which may remove a defendant from consideration as a candidate for the death penalty. *Furman*, in contrast, dealt with the decision to impose the death sentence on a specific individual who had been convicted of a capital offense. Nothing in any of our cases suggests that the decision to afford an individual defendant mercy violates the Constitution. *Furman* held only that, in order to minimize the risk that the death penalty would be imposed on a capriciously selected group of offenders, the decision to impose it had to be guided by standards so that the sentencing authority would focus on the particularized circumstances of the crime and the defendant.[50]

---

50. The petitioner's argument is nothing more than a veiled contention that *Furman* indirectly outlawed capital punishment by placing totally unrealistic conditions on its use. In order to repair the alleged defects pointed to by the petitioner, it would be necessary to require that prosecuting authorities charge a capital offense whenever arguably there had been a capital murder and that they refuse to plea bargain with the defendant. If a jury refused to convict even

2

The petitioner further contends that the capital-sentencing procedures adopted by Georgia in response to *Furman* do not eliminate the
dangers of arbitrariness and caprice in jury sentencing that were held in
Furman to be violative of the Eighth and Fourteenth Amendments. He
claims that the statute is so broad and vague as to leave juries free to act
as arbitrarily and capriciously as they wish in deciding whether to impose
the death penalty. While there is no claim that the jury in this case relied
upon a vague or overbroad provision to establish the existence of a
statutory aggravating circumstance, the petitioner looks to the sentencing
system as a whole (as the Court did in *Furman* and we do today) and
argues that it fails to reduce sufficiently the risk of arbitrary infliction of
death sentences. Specifically, Gregg urges that the statutory aggravating
circumstances are too broad and too vague, that the sentencing procedure
allows for arbitrary grants of mercy, and that the scope of the evidence
and argument that can be considered at the presentence hearing is too
wide.

[The plurality held: that the Georgia Supreme Court might narrow
the scope of the aggravating circumstances by construction or, as in
Arnold v. State, 224 S.E.2d 386 (Ga. 1976), might find them too vague;
that, given the limits placed on a jury's discretion, grants of mercy would
not be arbitrary; and that the wide scope of evidence and argument was a
desirable feature of the scheme.]

3

Finally, the Georgia statute has an additional provision designed to
assure that the death penalty will not be imposed on a capriciously
selected group of convicted defendants. The new sentencing procedures
require that the State Supreme Court review every death sentence to
determine whether it was imposed under the influence of passion, prejudice, or any other arbitrary factor, whether the evidence supports the
findings of a statutory aggravating circumstance, and "[w]hether the
sentence of death is excessive or disproportionate to the penalty imposed
in similar cases, considering both the crime and the defendant." In
performing its sentence-review function, the Georgia court has held that
"if the death penalty is only rarely imposed for an act or it is substantially
out of line with sentences imposed for other acts it will be set aside as

---

though the evidence supported the charge, its verdict would have to be reversed and a verdict of
guilty entered or a new trial ordered, since the discretionary act of jury nullification would not be
permitted. Finally, acts of executive clemency would have to be prohibited. Such a system, of
course, would be totally alien to our notions of criminal justice.

Moreover, it would be unconstitutional. Such a system in many respects would have the vices of
the mandatory death penalty statutes we hold unconstitutional today in *Woodson v. North
Carolina*, 428 U.S. 280, 96 S.Ct. 2978 and *Roberts v. Louisiana*, 428 U.S. 325, 96 S.Ct. 3001. The
suggestion that a jury's verdict of acquittal could be overturned and a defendant retried would
run afoul of the Sixth Amendment jury-trial guarantee and the Double Jeopardy Clause of the
Fifth Amendment. In the federal system it also would be unconstitutional to prohibit a President
from deciding, as an act of executive clemency, to reprieve one sentenced to death. U.S.Const.,
Art. II, § 2.

excessive." *Coley v. State*, 204 S.E.2d 612 (1974). The court on another occasion stated that "we view it to be our duty under the similarity standard to assure that no death sentence is affirmed unless in similar cases throughout the state the death penalty has been imposed generally ..." *Moore v. State*, 213 S.E.2d 829 (1975).

It is apparent that the Supreme Court of Georgia has taken its review responsibilities seriously. In *Coley*, it held that "[t]he prior cases indicate that the past practice among juries faced with similar factual situations and like aggravating circumstances has been to impose only the sentence of life imprisonment for the offense of rape, rather than death." It thereupon reduced Coley's sentence from death to life imprisonment. Similarly, although armed robbery is a capital offense under Georgia law, the Georgia court concluded that the death sentences imposed in this case for that crime were "unusual in that they are rarely imposed for [armed robbery]. Thus, under the test provided by statute, ... they must be considered to be excessive or disproportionate to the penalties imposed in similar cases." The court therefore vacated Gregg's death sentences for armed robbery and has followed a similar course in every other armed robbery death penalty case to come before it.

The provision for appellate review in the Georgia capital-sentencing system serves as a check against the random or arbitrary imposition of the death penalty. In particular, the proportionality review substantially eliminates the possibility that a person will be sentenced to die by the action of an aberrant jury. If a time comes when juries generally do not impose the death sentence in a certain kind of murder case, the appellate review procedures assure that no defendant convicted under such circumstances will suffer a sentence of death.

V

The basic concern of *Furman* centered on those defendants who were being condemned to death capriciously and arbitrarily. Under the procedures before the Court in that case, sentencing authorities were not directed to give attention to the nature or circumstances of the crime committed or to the character or record of the defendant. Left unguided, juries imposed the death sentence in a way that could only be called freakish. The new Georgia sentencing procedures, by contrast, focus the jury's attention on the particularized nature of the crime and the particularized characteristics of the individual defendant. While the jury is permitted to consider any aggravating or mitigating circumstances, it must find and identify at least one statutory aggravating factor before it may impose a penalty of death. In this way the jury's discretion is channeled. No longer can a jury wantonly and freakishly impose the death sentence; it is always circumscribed by the legislative guidelines. In addition, the review function of the Supreme Court of Georgia affords additional assurance that the concerns that prompted our decision in *Furman* are not present to any significant degree in the Georgia procedure applied here.

For the reasons expressed in this opinion, we hold that the statutory system under which Gregg was sentenced to death does not violate the Constitution. Accordingly, the judgment of the Georgia Supreme Court is affirmed.

[Concurring opinion of WHITE, J., joined by BURGER, C.J. and REHNQUIST, J., omitted. Concurring statement of BURGER, C.J., joined by REHNQUIST, J., omitted. Concurring statement of BLACKMUN, J. omitted. Dissenting opinions of BRENNAN, J. and MARSHALL, J., omitted]

NOTE

1. *Proffitt v. Florida.*

In *Proffitt v. Florida*, 428 U.S. 242, 96 S.Ct. 2960 (1976), the Court upheld the Florida death penalty scheme, which like the Georgia scheme, provided for a separate evidentiary hearing on aggravating and mitigating circumstances after a defendant was convicted of capital murder (premeditated homicide or homicide committed during the perpetration or attempted perpetration of arson, involuntary sexual battery, robbery, burglary, kidnapping, aircraft piracy or homicide by destructive device or bomb or as the result of the distribution of heroin) and provided for automatic review in the state supreme court of any death sentence, but which differed in other respects. The Court described the scheme as follows:

> [I]f a defendant is found guilty of a capital offense, a separate evidentiary hearing is held before the trial judge and jury to determine his sentence. Evidence may be presented on any matter the judge deems relevant to sentencing and must include matters relating to certain legislatively specified aggravating and mitigating circumstances. Both the prosecution and the defense may present argument on whether the death penalty shall be imposed.
>
> At the conclusion of the hearing the jury is directed to consider "[w]hether sufficient mitigating circumstances exist ... which outweigh the aggravating circumstances found to exist; and ... [b]ased on these considerations, whether the defendant should be sentenced to life [imprisonment] or death."[6] The jury's verdict is determined by majority vote. It

---

6.   The aggravating circumstances are:

"(a) The capital felony was committed by a person under sentence of imprisonment.

"(b) The defendant was previously convicted of another capital felony or of a felony involving the use or threat of violence to the person.

"(c) The defendant knowingly created a great risk of death to many persons.

"(d) The capital felony was committed while the defendant was engaged, or was an accomplice, in the commission of, or an attempt to commit, or flight after committing or attempting to commit, any robbery, rape, arson, burglary, kidnapping, or aircraft piracy or the unlawful throwing, placing, or discharging of a destructive device or bomb.

"(e) The capital felony was committed for the purpose of avoiding or preventing a lawful arrest or effecting an escape from custody.

"(f) The capital felony was committed for pecuniary gain.

"(g) The capital felony was committed to disrupt or hinder the lawful exercise of any governmental function or the enforcement of laws.

"(h) The capital felony was especially heinous, atrocious, or cruel."

is only advisory; the actual sentence is determined by the trial judge. The Florida Supreme Court has stated, however, that "[i]n order to sustain a sentence of death following a jury recommendation of life, the facts suggesting a sentence of death should be so clear and convincing that virtually no reasonable person could differ."

The trial judge is also directed to weigh the statutory aggravating and mitigating circumstances when he determines the sentence to be imposed on a defendant. The statute requires that if the trial court imposes a sentence of death, "it shall set forth in writing its findings upon which the sentence of death is based as to the facts: (a) [t]hat sufficient [statutory] aggravating circumstances exist . . . and (b) [t]hat there are insufficient [statutory] mitigating circumstances . . . to out-weigh the aggravating circumstances."

The statute provides for automatic review by the Supreme Court of Florida of all cases in which a death sentence has been imposed. The law differs from that of Georgia in that it does not require the court to conduct any specific form of review. Since, however, the trial judge must justify the imposition of a death sentence with written findings, meaning-ful appellate review of each such sentence is made possible and the Supreme Court of Florida like its Georgia counterpart considers its function to be to "[guarantee] that the [aggravating and mitigating] reasons present in one case will reach a similar result to that reached under similar circumstances in another case."

How does the Florida scheme differ from the Georgia scheme discussed in *Gregg*? Do the aggravating and mitigating circumstances in the two schemes meet the concerns of the justices in *Furman*?

WOODSON v. NORTH CAROLINA

428 U.S. 280, 96 S.Ct. 2978, 49 L.Ed.2d 944 (1976).

Judgment of the Court, and opinion of MR. JUSTICE STEWART, MR. JUSTICE POWELL, and MR. JUSTICE STEVENS, announced by MR. JUSTICE STEWART.

The question in this case is whether the imposition of a death sentence for the crime of first-degree murder under the law of North Carolina violates the Eighth and Fourteenth Amendments.

The mitigating circumstances are:

"(a) The defendant has no significant history of prior criminal activity.

"(b) The capital felony was committed while the defendant was under the influence of extreme mental or emotional disturbance.

"(c) The victim was a participant in the defendant's conduct or consented to the act.

"(d) The defendant was an accomplice in the capital felony committed by another person and his participation was relatively minor.

"(e) The defendant acted under extreme duress or under the substantial domination of another person.

"(f) The capacity of the defendant to appreciate the criminality of his conduct or to conform his conduct to the requirements of law was substantially impaired.

"(g) The age of the defendant at the time of the crime."

I

The petitioners were convicted of first-degree murder as the result of their participation in an armed robbery of a convenience food store, in the course of which the cashier was killed and a customer was seriously wounded. There were four participants in the robbery: the petitioners James Tyrone Woodson and Luby Waxton and two others, Leonard Tucker and Johnnie Lee Carroll. At the petitioners' trial Tucker and Carroll testified for the prosecution after having been permitted to plead guilty to lesser offenses; the petitioners testified in their own defense.

The evidence for the prosecution established that the four men had been discussing a possible robbery for some time. On the fatal day Woodson had been drinking heavily. About 9:30 p.m., Waxton and Tucker came to the trailer where Woodson was staying. When Woodson came out of the trailer, Waxton struck him in the face and threatened to kill him in an effort to make him sober up and come along on the robbery. The three proceeded to Waxton's trailer where they met Carroll. Waxton armed himself with a nickel-plated derringer, and Tucker handed Woodson a rifle. The four then set out by automobile to rob the store. Upon arriving at their destination Tucker and Waxton went into the store while Carroll and Woodson remained in the car as lookouts. Once inside the store, Tucker purchased a package of cigarettes from the woman cashier. Waxton then also asked for a package of cigarettes, but as the cashier approached him he pulled the derringer out of his hip pocket and fatally shot her at point-blank range. Waxton then took the money tray from the cash register and gave it to Tucker, who carried it out of the store, pushing past an entering customer as he reached the door. After he was outside, Tucker heard a second shot from inside the store, and shortly thereafter Waxton emerged, carrying a handful of paper money. Tucker and Waxton got in the car and the four drove away.

The petitioners' testimony agreed in large part with this version of the circumstances of the robbery. It differed diametrically in one important respect: Waxton claimed that he never had a gun, and that Tucker had shot both the cashier and the customer.

During the trial Waxton asked to be allowed to plead guilty to the same lesser offenses to which Tucker had pleaded guilty,[1] but the solicitor refused to accept the pleas.[2] Woodson, by contrast, maintained throughout the trial that he had been coerced by Waxton, that he was therefore innocent, and that he would not consider pleading guilty to any offense.

---

1. Tucker had been allowed to plead guilty to charges of accessory after the fact to murder and to armed robbery. He was sentenced to 10 years' imprisonment on the first charge, and to not less than 20 years nor more than 30 years on the second, the sentences to run concurrently.

2. The solicitor gave no reason for refusing to accept Waxton's offer to plead guilty to a lesser offense. The Supreme Court of North Carolina, in finding that the solicitor had not abused his discretion, noted:

"The evidence that Waxton planned and directed the robbery and that he fired the shots which killed Mrs. Butler and wounded Mr. Stancil is overwhelming. No extenuating circumstances gave the solicitor any incentive to accept the plea he tendered at the close of the State's evidence."

The petitioners were found guilty on all charges,[3] and, as was required by statute, sentenced to death. The Supreme Court of North Carolina affirmed. We granted certiorari to consider whether the imposition of the death penalties in this case comports with the Eighth and Fourteenth Amendments to the United States Constitution.

* * *

III

At the time of this Court's decision in *Furman v. Georgia*, 408 U.S. 238, 92 S.Ct. 2726 (1972), North Carolina law provided that in cases of first-degree murder, the jury in its unbridled discretion could choose whether the convicted defendant should be sentenced to death or to life imprisonment. After the *Furman* decision the Supreme Court of North Carolina in *State v. Waddell*, 194 S.E.2d 19 (N.C. 1973), held unconstitutional the provision of the death penalty statute that gave the jury the option of returning a verdict of guilty without capital punishment, but held further that this provision was severable so that the statute survived as a mandatory death penalty law.

The North Carolina General Assembly in 1974 followed the court's lead and enacted a new statute that was essentially unchanged from the old one except that it made the death penalty mandatory. The statute now reads as follows:

> "*Murder in the first and second degree defined; punishment.*—A murder which shall be perpetrated by means of poison, lying in wait, imprisonment, starving, torture, or by any other kind of willful, deliberate and premeditated killing, or which shall be committed in the perpetration or attempt to perpetrate any arson, rape, robbery, kidnapping, burglary or other felony, shall be deemed to be murder in the first degree and shall be punished with death. All other kinds of murder shall be deemed murder in the second degree, and shall be punished by imprisonment for a term of not less than two years nor more than life imprisonment in the State's prison."

It was under this statute that the petitioners, who committed their crime on June 3, 1974, were tried, convicted, and sentenced to death.

North Carolina, unlike Florida, Georgia, and Texas, has thus responded to the *Furman* decision by making death the mandatory sentence for all persons convicted of first-degree murder.[6] In ruling on the constitutionality of the sentences imposed on the petitioners under this North Carolina statute, the Court now addresses for the first time the question whether a death sentence returned pursuant to a law imposing a manda-

---

3. In addition to first-degree murder, both petitioners were found guilty of armed robbery. Waxton was also found guilty of assault with a deadly weapon with intent to kill, a charge arising from the wounding of the customer.

6. North Carolina also has enacted a mandatory death sentence statute for the crime of first-degree rape.

tory death penalty for a broad category of homicidal offenses[7] constitutes cruel and unusual punishment within the meaning of the Eighth and Fourteenth Amendments. The issue, like that explored in *Furman*, involves the procedure employed by the State to select persons for the unique and irreversible penalty of death.

A

The Eighth Amendment stands to assure that the State's power to punish is "exercised within the limits of civilized standards." *Trop v. Dulles*, 356 U.S. 86, 78 S.Ct. 590 (1958) (plurality opinion). Central to the application of the Amendment is a determination of contemporary standards regarding the infliction of punishment. As discussed in *Gregg v. Georgia*, 428 U.S. 153, 96 S.Ct. 2909 (1976), indicia of societal values identified in prior opinions include history and traditional usage, legislative enactments, and jury determinations.

In order to provide a frame for assessing the relevancy of these factors in this case we begin by sketching the history of mandatory death penalty statutes in the United States. At the time the Eighth Amendment was adopted in 1791, the States uniformly followed the common-law practice of making death the exclusive and mandatory sentence for certain specified offenses. Although the range of capital offenses in the American Colonies was quite limited in comparison to the more than 200 offenses then punishable by death in England, the Colonies at the time of the Revolution imposed death sentences on all persons convicted of any of a considerable number of crimes, typically including at a minimum, murder, treason, piracy, arson, rape, robbery, burglary, and sodomy. As at common law, all homicides that were not involuntary, provoked, justified, or excused constituted murder and were automatically punished by death. Almost from the outset jurors reacted unfavorably to the harshness of mandatory death sentences. The States initially responded to this expression of public dissatisfaction with mandatory statutes by limiting the classes of capital offenses.

This reform, however, left unresolved the problem posed by the not infrequent refusal of juries to convict murderers rather than subject them to automatic death sentences. In 1794, Pennsylvania attempted to alleviate the undue severity of the law by confining the mandatory death penalty to "murder of the first degree" encompassing all "wilful, deliberate and premeditated" killings. Other jurisdictions, including Virginia and Ohio, soon enacted similar measures, and within a generation the practice spread to most of the States.

Despite the broad acceptance of the division of murder into degrees, the reform proved to be an unsatisfactory means of identifying persons appropriately punishable by death. Although its failure was due in part to

---

7. This case does not involve a mandatory death penalty statute limited to an extremely narrow category of homicide, such as murder by a prisoner serving a life sentence, defined in large part in terms of the character or record of the offender. We thus express no opinion regarding the constitutionality of such a statute.

the amorphous nature of the controlling concepts of willfulness, deliberateness, and premeditation, a more fundamental weakness of the reform
soon became apparent. Juries continued to find the death penalty inappropriate in a significant number of first-degree murder cases and refused to
return guilty verdicts for that crime.

The inadequacy of distinguishing between murderers solely on the
basis of legislative criteria narrowing the definition of the capital offense
led the States to grant juries sentencing discretion in capital cases.
Tennessee in 1838, followed by Alabama in 1841, and Louisiana in 1846,
were the first States to abandon mandatory death sentences in favor of
discretionary death penalty statutes. This flexibility remedied the harshness of mandatory statutes by permitting the jury to respond to mitigating
factors by withholding the death penalty. By the turn of the century, 23
States and the Federal Government had made death sentences discretionary for first-degree murder and other capital offenses. During the next two
decades 14 additional States replaced their mandatory death penalty
statutes. Thus, by the end of World War I, all but eight States, Hawaii,
and the District of Columbia either had adopted discretionary death
penalty schemes or abolished the death penalty altogether. By 1963, all of
these remaining jurisdictions had replaced their automatic death penalty
statutes with discretionary jury sentencing.[25]

The history of mandatory death penalty statutes in the United States
thus reveals that the practice of sentencing to death all persons convicted
of a particular offense has been rejected as unduly harsh and unworkably
rigid. The two crucial indicators of evolving standards of decency respecting the imposition of punishment in our society—jury determinations and
legislative enactments—both point conclusively to the repudiation of automatic death sentences. At least since the Revolution, American jurors
have, with some regularity, disregarded their oaths and refused to convict
defendants where a death sentence was the automatic consequence of a
guilty verdict. As we have seen, the initial movement to reduce the
number of capital offenses and to separate murder into degrees was
prompted in part by the reaction of jurors as well as by reformers who

---

25. Prior to this Court's 1972 decision in *Furman v. Georgia*, 408 U.S. 238, 92 S.Ct. 2726,
there remained a handful of obscure statutes scattered among the penal codes in various States
that required an automatic death sentence upon conviction of a specified offense. These statutes
applied to such esoteric crimes as trainwrecking resulting in death, perjury in a capital case
resulting in the execution of an innocent person, and treason against a state government. The
most prevalent of these statutes dealt with the crime of treason against state governments. It
appears that no one has ever been prosecuted under these or other state treason laws. Several
States retained mandatory death sentences for perjury in capital cases resulting in the execution
of an innocent person. Data covering the years from 1930 to 1961 indicate, however, that no State
employed its capital perjury statute during that period.

The only category of mandatory death sentence statutes that appears to have had any relevance
to the actual administration of the death penalty in the years preceding *Furman* concerned the
crimes of murder or assault with a deadly weapon by a life-term prisoner. Statutes of this type
apparently existed in five States in 1964. In 1970, only five of the more than 550 prisoners under
death sentence across the country had been sentenced under a mandatory death penalty statute.
Those prisoners had all been convicted under the California statute applicable to assaults by life-
term prisoners. We have no occasion in this case to examine the constitutionality of mandatory
death sentence statutes applicable to prisoners serving life sentences.

objected to the imposition of death as the penalty for any crime. Nineteenth century journalists, statesmen, and jurists repeatedly observed that jurors were often deterred from convicting palpably guilty men of first-degree murder under mandatory statutes. Thereafter, continuing evidence of jury reluctance to convict persons of capital offenses in mandatory death penalty jurisdictions resulted in legislative authorization of discretionary jury sentencing by Congress for federal crimes in 1897, by North Carolina in 1949, and by Congress for the District of Columbia in 1962.

As we have noted today in *Gregg v. Georgia*, legislative measures adopted by the people's chosen representatives weigh heavily in ascertaining contemporary standards of decency. The consistent course charted by the state legislatures and by Congress since the middle of the past century demonstrates that the aversion of jurors to mandatory death penalty statutes is shared by society at large.

Still further evidence of the incompatibility of mandatory death penalties with contemporary values is provided by the results of jury sentencing under discretionary statutes. In *Witherspoon v. Illinois*, 391 U.S. 510, 88 S.Ct. 1770, the Court observed that "one of the most important functions any jury can perform" in exercising its discretion to choose "between life imprisonment and capital punishment" is "to maintain a link between contemporary community values and the penal system." Various studies indicate that even in first-degree murder cases juries with sentencing discretion do not impose the death penalty "with any great frequency." H. Kalven & H. Zeisel, *The American Jury* (1966).[31] The actions of sentencing juries suggest that under contemporary standards of decency death is viewed as an inappropriate punishment for a substantial portion of convicted first-degree murderers.

Although the Court has never ruled on the constitutionality of mandatory death penalty statutes, on several occasions dating back to 1899 it has commented upon our society's aversion to automatic death sentences. In *Winston v. United States*, 172 U.S. 303, 19 S.Ct. 212 (1899), the Court noted that the "hardship of punishing with death every crime coming within the definition of murder at common law, and the reluctance of jurors to concur in a capital conviction, have induced American legislatures, in modern times, to allow some cases of murder to be punished by imprisonment, instead of by death." Fifty years after *Winston*, the Court underscored the marked transformation in our attitudes toward mandatory sentences: "The belief no longer prevails that every offense in a like legal category calls for an identical punishment without regard to the past life and habits of a particular offender. This whole country has traveled far from the period in which the death sentence was an automatic and

---

31. Data compiled on discretionary jury sentencing of persons convicted of capital murder reveal that the penalty of death is generally imposed in less than 20% of the cases. Statistics compiled by the Department of Justice show that only 66 convicted murderers were sentenced to death in 1972.

commonplace result of convictions ..." *Williams v. New York*, 337 U.S. 241, 69 S.Ct. 1079 (1949).

* * *

Although it seems beyond dispute that, at the time of the *Furman* decision in 1972, mandatory death penalty statutes had been renounced by American juries and legislatures, there remains the question whether the mandatory statutes adopted by North Carolina and a number of other States following *Furman* evince a sudden reversal of societal values regarding the imposition of capital punishment. In view of the persistent and unswerving legislative rejection of mandatory death penalty statutes beginning in 1838 and continuing for more than 130 years until *Furman*, it seems evident that the post-*Furman* enactments reflect attempts by the States to retain the death penalty in a form consistent with the Constitution, rather than a renewed societal acceptance of mandatory death sentencing.[34] The fact that some States have adopted mandatory measures following *Furman* while others have legislated standards to guide jury discretion appears attributable to diverse readings of this Court's multi-opinioned decision in that case.

A brief examination of the background of the current North Carolina statute serves to reaffirm our assessment of its limited utility as an indicator of contemporary values regarding mandatory death sentences. Before 1949, North Carolina imposed a mandatory death sentence on any person convicted of rape or first-degree murder. That year, a study commission created by the state legislature recommended that juries be granted discretion to recommend life sentences in all capital cases:

> "We propose that a recommendation of mercy by the jury in capital cases automatically carry with it a life sentence. Only three other states now have the mandatory death penalty and we believe its retention will be definitely harmful. Quite frequently, juries refuse to convict for rape or first degree murder because, from all the circumstances, they do not believe the defendant, although guilty, should suffer death. The result is that verdicts are returned hardly in harmony with evidence. Our proposal is already in effect in respect to the crimes of burglary and arson. There is much testimony that it has proved beneficial in such cases. We think the law can now be broadened to include all capital crimes."

The 1949 session of the General Assembly of North Carolina adopted the proposed modifications of its rape and murder statutes. Although in subsequent years numerous bills were introduced in the legislature to limit further or abolish the death penalty in North Carolina, they were

---

34. A study of public opinion polls on the death penalty concluded that "despite the increasing approval for the death penalty reflected in opinion polls during the last decade, there is evidence that many people supporting the general idea of capital punishment want its administration to depend on the circumstances of the case, the character of the defendant, or both." Vidmar & Ellsworth, *Public Opinion and the Death Penalty*, 26 Stan.L.Rev. 1245 (1974). One poll discussed by the authors revealed that a "substantial majority" of persons opposed mandatory capital punishment. Moreover, the public through the jury system has in recent years applied the death penalty in anything but a mandatory fashion.

rejected as were two 1969 proposals to return to mandatory death sentences for all capital offenses.

* * * The State's brief in this case relates that the legislature sought to remove "All sentencing discretion [so that] there could be no successful *Furman* based attack on the North Carolina statute."

It is now well established that the Eighth Amendment draws much of its meaning from "the evolving standards of decency that mark the progress of a maturing society." *Trop v. Dulles* (plurality opinion). As the above discussion makes clear, one of the most significant developments in our society's treatment of capital punishment has been the rejection of the common-law practice of inexorably imposing a death sentence upon every person convicted of a specified offense. North Carolina's mandatory death penalty statute for first-degree murder departs markedly from contemporary standards respecting the imposition of the punishment of death and thus cannot be applied consistently with the Eighth and Fourteenth Amendments' requirement that the State's power to punish "be exercised within the limits of civilized standards."

B

A separate deficiency of North Carolina's mandatory death sentence statute is its failure to provide a constitutionally tolerable response to *Furman*'s rejection of unbridled jury discretion in the imposition of capital sentences. Central to the limited holding in *Furman* was the conviction that the vesting of standardless sentencing power in the jury violated the Eighth and Fourteenth Amendments. It is argued that North Carolina has remedied the inadequacies of the death penalty statutes held unconstitutional in *Furman* by withdrawing all sentencing discretion from juries in capital cases. But when one considers the long and consistent American experience with the death penalty in first-degree murder cases, it becomes evident that mandatory statutes enacted in response to *Furman* have simply papered over the problem of unguided and unchecked jury discretion.

As we have noted in Part III–A, *supra*, there is general agreement that American juries have persistently refused to convict a significant portion of persons charged with first-degree murder of that offense under mandatory death penalty statutes. The North Carolina study commission reported that juries in that State "[q]uite frequently" were deterred from rendering guilty verdicts of first-degree murder because of the enormity of the sentence automatically imposed. Moreover, as a matter of historic fact, juries operating under discretionary sentencing statutes have consistently returned death sentences in only a minority of first-degree murder cases. In view of the historic record, it is only reasonable to assume that many juries under mandatory statutes will continue to consider the grave consequences of a conviction in reaching a verdict. North Carolina's mandatory death penalty statute provides no standards to guide the jury in its inevitable exercise of the power to determine which first-degree murderers shall live and which shall die. And there is no way under the

North Carolina law for the judiciary to check arbitrary and capricious exercise of that power through a review of death sentences. Instead of rationalizing the sentencing process, a mandatory scheme may well exacerbate the problem identified in *Furman* by resting the penalty determination on the particular jury's willingness to act lawlessly. While a mandatory death penalty statute may reasonably be expected to increase the number of persons sentenced to death, it does not fulfill *Furman*'s basic requirement by replacing arbitrary and wanton jury discretion with objective standards to guide, regularize, and make rationally reviewable the process for imposing a sentence of death.

C

A third constitutional shortcoming of the North Carolina statute is its failure to allow the particularized consideration of relevant aspects of the character and record of each convicted defendant before the imposition upon him of a sentence of death. In *Furman*, members of the Court acknowledge what cannot fairly be denied that death is a punishment different from all other sanctions in kind rather than degree. A process that accords no significance to relevant facets of the character and record of the individual offender or the circumstances of the particular offense excludes from consideration in fixing the ultimate punishment of death the possibility of compassionate or mitigating factors stemming from the diverse frailties of humankind. It treats all persons convicted of a designated offense not as uniquely individual human beings, but as members of a faceless, undifferentiated mass to be subjected to the blind infliction of the penalty of death.

This Court has previously recognized that "[f]or the determination of sentences, justice generally requires consideration of more than the particular acts by which the crime was committed and that there be taken into account the circumstances of the offense together with the character and propensities of the offender." *Pennsylvania ex rel. Sullivan v. Ashe*, 302 U.S. 51, 58 S.Ct. 59 (1937). Consideration of both the offender and the offense in order to arrive at a just and appropriate sentence has been viewed as a progressive and humanizing development. See *Williams v. New York*; *Furman v. Georgia* (Burger, C. J., dissenting). While the prevailing practice of individualizing sentencing determinations generally reflects simply enlightened policy rather than a constitutional imperative, we believe that in capital cases the fundamental respect for humanity underlying the Eighth Amendment requires consideration of the character and record of the individual offender and the circumstances of the particular offense as a constitutionally indispensable part of the process of inflicting the penalty of death.

This conclusion rests squarely on the predicate that the penalty of death is qualitatively different from a sentence of imprisonment, however long. Death, in its finality, differs more from life imprisonment than a 100–year prison term differs from one of only a year or two. Because of that qualitative difference, there is a corresponding difference in the need for reliability in the determination that death is the appropriate punishment in a specific case.

For the reasons stated, we conclude that the death sentences imposed upon the petitioners under North Carolina's mandatory death sentence statute violated the Eighth and Fourteenth Amendments and therefore must be set aside.[40] The judgment of the Supreme Court of North Carolina is reversed insofar as it upheld the death sentences imposed upon the petitioners, and the case is remanded for further proceedings not inconsistent with this opinion.

It is so ordered.

[Concurring statements of BRENNAN, J. and MARSHALL, J. and dissenting opinion of WHITE, joined by BURGER, C.J. and REHNQUIST, J., dissenting opinion of BLACKMUN, J. and dissenting opinion of REHNQUIST, J. omitted]

NOTES

1. *Roberts v. Louisiana.*

In *Roberts v. Louisiana*, 428 U.S. 325, 96 S.Ct. 3001 (1976), the Supreme Court addressed the constitutionality of Louisiana's mandatory death penalty statute which more narrowly defined first degree murder than did the North Carolina statute at issue in *Woodson*. The Louisiana statute limited first degree murder to killings where the killer had a specific intent to kill or to inflict great bodily harm and the killing fell within one of five categories: (1) the killing occurred in conjunction with the commission of the felonies of aggravated kidnapping, aggravated rape, or armed robbery; (2) the victim was a fireman or a policeman in the performance of his duties; (3) the killer had previously been convicted of murder or was serving a life sentence; (4) the killer had a specific intent to kill or to inflict great bodily harm on more than one person; and (5) the killer had been offered or had received anything of value for committing the murder. Nonetheless, the Court found that this narrower definition of capital murder was not "of controlling constitutional significance," and it held the statute unconstitutional.

2. *Sumner v. Shuman.*

The Court in *Woodson* left open the question whether a mandatory death penalty limited to "an extremely narrow category of homicide" would be constitutional. In *Sumner v. Shuman*, 483 U.S. 66, 107 S.Ct. 2716 (1987), Shuman, a prisoner serving a life sentence without possibility of parole as a result of a murder conviction, was convicted of murdering a fellow inmate. He was sentenced to death under a Louisiana statute making the death penalty mandatory for a murder by a prisoner serving a life sentence without possibility of parole. The Supreme Court held (6–3) that the requirement of

---

40. Our determination that the death sentences in this case were imposed under procedures that violated constitutional standards makes it unnecessary to reach the question whether imposition of the death penalty on petitioner Woodson would have been so disproportionate to the nature of his involvement in the capital offense as independently to violate the Eighth and Fourteenth Amendments.

an individualized penalty determination applied in all cases and that a mandatory death penalty, no matter how narrow, was unconstitutional.

JUREK v. TEXAS

428 U.S. 262, 96 S.Ct. 2950, 49 L.Ed.2d 929 (1976).

MR. JUSTICE STEWART, MR. JUSTICE POWELL, and MR. JUSTICE STEVENS announced the judgment of the Court and filed an opinion delivered by MR. JUSTICE STEVENS.

The issue in this case is whether the imposition of the sentence of death for the crime of murder under the law of Texas violates the Eighth and Fourteenth Amendments to the Constitution.

I

The petitioner in this case, Jerry Lane Jurek, was charged by indictment with the killing of Wendy Adams "by choking and strangling her with his hands, and by drowning her in water by throwing her into a river in the course of committing and attempting to commit kidnapping of and forcible rape upon the said Wendy Adams."[1]

The evidence at his trial consisted of incriminating statements made by the petitioner, the testimony of several people who saw the petitioner and the deceased during the day she was killed, and certain technical evidence. This evidence established that the petitioner, 22 years old at the time, had been drinking beer in the afternoon. He and two young friends later went driving together in his old pickup truck. The petitioner expressed a desire for sexual relations with some young girls they saw, but one of his companions said the girls were too young. The petitioner then dropped his two friends off at a pool hall. He was next seen talking to Wendy, who was 10 years old, at a public swimming pool where her grandmother had left her to swim. Other witnesses testified that they later observed a man resembling the petitioner driving an old pickup truck through town at a high rate of speed, with a young blond girl standing screaming in the bed of the truck. The last witness who saw them heard

---

1.   * * * Texas law prescribed the punishment for murder as follows:

"(a) Except as provided in subsection (b) of this Article, the punishment for murder shall be confinement in the penitentiary for life or for any term of years not less than two.

"(b) The punishment for murder with malice aforethought shall be death or imprisonment for life if:

"(1) the person murdered a peace officer or fireman who was acting in the lawful discharge of an official duty and who the defendant knew was a peace officer or fireman;

"(2) the person intentionally committed the murder in the course of committing or attempting to commit kidnapping, burglary, robbery, forcible rape, or arson;

"(3) the person committed the murder for remuneration or the promise of remuneration or employed another to commit the murder for remuneration or the promise of remuneration;

"(4) the person committed the murder while escaping or attempting to escape from a penal institution;

"(5) the person, while incarcerated in a penal institution, murdered another who was employed in the operation of the penal institution."

. . .

the girl crying "help me, help me." The witness tried to follow them, but lost them in traffic. According to the petitioner's statement, he took the girl to the river, choked her, and threw her unconscious body in the river. Her drowned body was found downriver two days later.

At the conclusion of the trial the jury returned a verdict of guilty.

Texas law requires that if a defendant has been convicted of a capital offense, the trial court must conduct a separate sentencing proceeding before the same jury that tried the issue of guilt. Any relevant evidence may be introduced at this proceeding, and both prosecution and defense may present argument for or against the sentence of death. The jury is then presented with two (sometimes three) questions, the answers to which determine whether a death sentence will be imposed.

During the punishment phase of the petitioner's trial, several witnesses for the State testified to the petitioner's bad reputation in the community. The petitioner's father countered with testimony that the petitioner had always been steadily employed since he had left school and that he contributed to his family's support.

The jury then considered the two statutory questions relevant to this case: (1) whether the evidence established beyond a reasonable doubt that the murder of the deceased was committed deliberately and with the reasonable expectation that the death of the deceased or another would result, and (2) whether the evidence established beyond a reasonable doubt that there was a probability that the defendant would commit criminal acts of violence that would constitute a continuing threat to society. The jury unanimously answered "yes" to both questions, and the judge, therefore, in accordance with the statute, sentenced the petitioner to death. The Court of Criminal Appeals of Texas affirmed the judgment.

        * * *

III

A

After this Court held Texas' system for imposing capital punishment unconstitutional in *Branch v. Texas*, decided *sub nom. Furman v. Georgia*, 408 U.S. 238, 92 S.Ct. 2726 (1972), the Texas Legislature narrowed the scope of its laws relating to capital punishment. The new Texas Penal Code limits capital homicides to intentional and knowing murders committed in five situations: murder of a peace officer or fireman; murder committed in the course of kidnaping, burglary, robbery, forcible rape, or arson; murder committed for remuneration; murder committed while escaping or attempting to escape from a penal institution; and murder committed by a prison inmate when the victim is a prison employee.

In addition, Texas adopted a new capital-sentencing procedure. That procedure requires the jury to answer three questions in a proceeding that takes place subsequent to the return of a verdict finding a person guilty of one of the above categories of murder. The questions the jury must answer are these:

"(1) whether the conduct of the defendant that caused the death of the deceased was committed deliberately and with the reasonable expectation that the death of the deceased or another would result;

"(2) whether there is a probability that the defendant would commit criminal acts of violence that would constitute a continuing threat to society; and

"(3) if raised by the evidence, whether the conduct of the defendant in killing the deceased was unreasonable in response to the provocation, if any, by the deceased."

If the jury finds that the State has proved beyond a reasonable doubt that the answer to each of the three questions is yes, then the death sentence is imposed. If the jury finds that the answer to any question is no, then a sentence of life imprisonment results.[5] The law also provides for an expedited review by the Texas Court of Criminal Appeals.

The Texas Court of Criminal Appeals has thus far affirmed only two judgments imposing death sentences under its post-*Furman* law in this case and in *Smith v. State* (rehearing pending). In the present case the state appellate court noted that its law "limits the circumstances under which the State may seek the death penalty to a small group of narrowly defined and particularly brutal offenses. This insures that the death penalty will only be imposed for the most serious crimes [and] . . . that [it] will only be imposed for the same type of offenses which occur under the same types of circumstances."

While Texas has not adopted a list of statutory aggravating circumstances the existence of which can justify the imposition of the death penalty as have Georgia and Florida, its action in narrowing the categories of murders for which a death sentence may ever be imposed serves much the same purpose. In fact, each of the five classes of murders made capital by the Texas statute is encompassed in Georgia and Florida by one or more of their statutory aggravating circumstances. For example, the Texas statute requires the jury at the guilt-determining stage to consider whether the crime was committed in the course of a particular felony, whether it was committed for hire, or whether the defendant was an inmate of a penal institution at the time of its commission. Thus, in essence, the Texas statute requires that the jury find the existence of a statutory aggravating circumstance before the death penalty may be imposed. So far as consideration of aggravating circumstances is concerned, therefore, the principal difference between Texas and the other two States is that the death penalty is an available sentencing option—even potentially—for a smaller class of murders in Texas. Otherwise the statutes are similar.

---

5. The jury can answer "yes" only if all members agree; it can answer "no" if 10 of 12 members agree. Texas law is unclear as to the procedure to be followed in the event that the jury is unable to answer the questions.

Each requires the sentencing authority to focus on the particularized nature of the crime.

But a sentencing system that allowed the jury to consider only aggravating circumstances would almost certainly fall short of providing the individualized sentencing determination that we today have held in *Woodson v. North Carolina*, 428 U.S. 280, 96 S.Ct. 2978, to be required by the Eighth and Fourteenth Amendments. For such a system would approach the mandatory laws that we today hold unconstitutional in *Woodson* and *Roberts v. Louisiana*, 428 U.S. 325, 96 S.Ct. 3001.[6] A jury must be allowed to consider on the basis of all relevant evidence not only why a death sentence should be imposed, but also why it should not be imposed.

Thus, in order to meet the requirement of the Eighth and Fourteenth Amendments, a capital-sentencing system must allow the sentencing authority to consider mitigating circumstances. In *Gregg v. Georgia*, we today hold constitutionally valid a capital-sentencing system that directs the jury to consider any mitigating factors, and in *Proffitt v. Florida* we likewise hold constitutional a system that directs the judge and advisory jury to consider certain enumerated mitigating circumstances. The Texas statute does not explicitly speak of mitigating circumstances; it directs only that the jury answer three questions. Thus, the constitutionality of the Texas procedures turns on whether the enumerated questions allow consideration of particularized mitigating factors.

The second Texas statutory question[7] asks the jury to determine "whether there is a probability that the defendant would commit criminal acts of violence that would constitute a continuing threat to society" if he were not sentenced to death. The Texas Court of Criminal Appeals has yet to define precisely the meanings of such terms as "criminal acts of violence" or "continuing threat to society." In the present case, however, it indicated that it will interpret this second question so as to allow a defendant to bring to the jury's attention whatever mitigating circumstances he may be able to show:

---

6. When the drafters of the Model Penal Code considered a proposal that would have simply listed aggravating factors as sufficient reasons for imposition of the death penalty, they found the proposal unsatisfactory:

"Such an approach has the disadvantage, however, of according disproportionate significance to the enumeration of aggravating circumstances when what is rationally necessary is ... the balancing of any aggravations against any mitigations that appear. The object sought is better attained, in our view, by requiring a finding that an aggravating circumstance has been established *and* a finding that there are no substantial mitigating circumstances." Model Penal Code § 201.6, Comment 3 (emphasis in original).

7. The Texas Court of Criminal Appeals has not yet construed the first and third questions; thus it is as yet undetermined whether or not the jury's consideration of those questions would properly include consideration of mitigating circumstances. In at least some situations the questions could, however, comprehend such an inquiry. For example, the third question asks whether the conduct of the defendant was unreasonable in response to any provocation by the deceased. This might be construed to allow the jury to consider circumstances which, though not sufficient as a defense to the crime itself, might nevertheless have enough mitigating force to avoid the death penalty a claim, for example, that a woman who hired an assassin to kill her husband was driven to it by his continued cruelty to her. We cannot, however, construe the statute; that power is reserved to the Texas courts.

"In determining the likelihood that the defendant would be a continuing threat to society, the jury could consider whether the defendant had a significant criminal record. It could consider the range and severity of his prior criminal conduct. It could further look to the age of the defendant and whether or not at the time of the commission of the offense he was acting under duress or under the domination of another. It could also consider whether the defendant was under an extreme form of mental or emotional pressure, something less, perhaps, than insanity, but more than the emotions of the average man, however inflamed, could withstand."

In the only other case in which the Texas Court of Criminal Appeals has upheld a death sentence, it focused on the question of whether any mitigating factors were present in the case. See *Smith v. State*. In that case the state appellate court examined the sufficiency of the evidence to see if a "yes" answer to question 2 should be sustained. In doing so it examined the defendant's prior conviction on narcotics charges, his subsequent failure to attempt to rehabilitate himself or obtain employment, the fact that he had not acted under duress or as a result of mental or emotional pressure, his apparent willingness to kill, his lack of remorse after the killing, and the conclusion of a psychiatrist that he had a sociopathic personality and that his patterns of conduct would be the same in the future as they had been in the past.

Thus, Texas law essentially requires that one of five aggravating circumstances be found before a defendant can be found guilty of capital murder, and that in considering whether to impose a death sentence the jury may be asked to consider whatever evidence of mitigating circumstances the defense can bring before it. It thus appears that, as in Georgia and Florida, the Texas capital-sentencing procedure guides and focuses the jury's objective consideration of the particularized circumstances of the individual offense and the individual offender before it can impose a sentence of death.

B

As in the Georgia and Florida cases, however, the petitioner contends that the substantial legislative changes that Texas made in response to this Court's *Furman* decision are no more than cosmetic in nature and have in fact not eliminated the arbitrariness and caprice of the system held in *Furman* to violate the Eighth and Fourteenth Amendments.

(1)

The petitioner first asserts that arbitrariness still pervades the entire criminal justice system of Texas from the prosecutor's decision whether to charge a capital offense in the first place and then whether to engage in plea bargaining, through the jury's consideration of lesser included offenses, to the Governor's ultimate power to commute death sentences.

This contention fundamentally misinterprets the *Furman* decision, and we reject it for the reasons set out in our opinion today in *Gregg v. Georgia.*

(2)

Focusing on the second statutory question that Texas requires a jury to answer in considering whether to impose a death sentence, the petitioner argues that it is impossible to predict future behavior and that the question is so vague as to be meaningless. It is, of course, not easy to predict future behavior. The fact that such a determination is difficult, however, does not mean that it cannot be made. Indeed, prediction of future criminal conduct is an essential element in many of the decisions rendered throughout our criminal justice system. The decision whether to admit a defendant to bail, for instance, must often turn on a judge's prediction of the defendant's future conduct. And any sentencing authority must predict a convicted person's probable future conduct when it engages in the process of determining what punishment to impose. For those sentenced to prison, these same predictions must be made by parole authorities. The task that a Texas jury must perform in answering the statutory question in issue is thus basically no different from the task performed countless times each day throughout the American system of criminal justice. What is essential is that the jury have before it all possible relevant information about the individual defendant whose fate it must determine. Texas law clearly assures that all such evidence will be adduced.

IV

We conclude that Texas' capital-sentencing procedures, like those of Georgia and Florida, do not violate the Eighth and Fourteenth Amendments. By narrowing its definition of capital murder, Texas has essentially said that there must be at least one statutory aggravating circumstance in a first-degree murder case before a death sentence may even be considered. By authorizing the defense to bring before the jury at the separate sentencing hearing whatever mitigating circumstances relating to the individual defendant can be adduced, Texas has ensured that the sentencing jury will have adequate guidance to enable it to perform its sentencing function. By providing prompt judicial review of the jury's decision in a court with statewide jurisdiction, Texas has provided a means to promote the evenhanded, rational, and consistent imposition of death sentences under law. Because this system serves to assure that sentences of death will not be "wantonly" or "freakishly" imposed, it does not violate the Constitution. Accordingly, the judgment of the Texas Court of Criminal Appeals affirmed.

It is so ordered.

[Concurring opinions of BURGER, C.J., WHITE, J., joined by BURGER, C.J. and REHNQUIST, J. and BLACKMUN, J. and dissenting opinions of BRENNAN, J. and MARSHALL, J. omitted]

LOOSE THE FATEFUL LIGHTNING[a]

By David Von Drehle

Florida State Prison.

Execution Day.

The Schedule:

> 4:30 a.m. The Food Service Director will personally prepare and serve last meal. Eating utensils will be a plate and spoon.

Spenkelink ordered nothing. A meal of steak and eggs was brought to his cell, in case he changed his mind. The steak was cut into bite-sized pieces because Spenkelink was not allowed to have a knife. But the chef, so that the prisoner wouldn't feel like a child, painstakingly reassembled the pieces into the shape of a steak.

> 5:00 a.m. The Administrative Assistant or designate will pick up executioner, proceed to the institution, enter through Sally Port and leave the executioner in the Waiting Room of the Death Chamber at 5:00 a.m. A security staff member will be posted in the chamber area.

The executioner, whose job was to trip the circuit breakers, had been chosen from several hundred applicants who had answered a classified ad. His identity was painstakingly concealed: He was picked up on a lonely road and driven to the prison by a circuitous back route; his $150–dollar fee was paid in cash so no record would appear on any checking account.

> 5:50 a.m. Authorized Media Witnesses will be picked up at the media onlooker area by two designated Department of Corrections staff escorts . . .

> 6:00 a.m. The Assistant Superintendent for Operations will supervise the shaving of the inmate's head and right leg. [The crown and the calf are the contact points for the electrodes; these points are shaved to reduce burning.]

> The Assistant Superintendent for Operations will supervise the showering of the condemned inmate. Immediately thereafter he will be returned to his cell and given a pair of shorts, a pair of trousers, a dress shirt, and socks. The Correctional Officer Chief IV will be responsible for the delivery of the clothes.

> Switchboard operator will be instructed by Superintendent to wire all calls to the Execution Chamber from governors's Office through switchboard.

---

a. From Among the Lowest of the Dead by David Von Drehle, copyright © 2005 by David Von Drehle. Used by permission of the University of Michigan Press. The excerpt describes the execution of John Spenkelink, the first non-"volunteer" to be executed since 1967, when the *de facto* moratorium on executions began. Gary Gilmore had been executed by the State of Utah two years earlier, but he had waived his right to appeal and had agreed to his own execution. See *Gilmore v. Utah*, 429 U.S. 1012, 97 S. Ct. 436 (1976).

The Administrative Assistant, or designate, three designated electricians, physician, and a physician's asst. will report to the execution chamber for preparation....

This schedule assumed a 7 a.m. execution. But the circuit court of appeals had delayed its order lifting [Circuit Judge] Tuttle's stay until 9:30 a.m., so the execution was running three hours late. Times were adjusted accordingly.

Ramsey Clark [former U.S. Attorney General and one of Spenkelink's attorneys] * * * met the defense papers at the U.S. Supreme Court clerk's office, read them through, and filed them shortly before 7 a.m. Then he settled in to wait. The execution was now three hours away. Periodically, Clark asked whether the papers had been delivered to any of the justices, but for more than an hour, no one would say whether any member of the Court was even in the building.

At the same time, in Tallahassee, the newly drafted defense team of Howell Ferguson and Steve Goldstein arrived at the home of Arthur England, chief justice of the Florida Supreme Court. Marky [Ray Marky, a deputy attorney general] was there with his boss, Jim Smith [Attorney General of Florida], and most of the court's justices had gathered. There were so many cars outside the England home that neighbors wondered if there might have been a tragedy. Inside, England was ready with rolls and orange juice, pencils and legal pads. He wore shirt sleeves, no tie, like a man welcoming guests to a weekend brunch. Ferguson and Goldstein kept their suit jackets on and declined the food. They wanted to impress the solemn nature of their mission on the justices.

This strange tribunal settled into England's sofas and chairs. Goldstein did most of the talking. The defense attorney's argument offered little that was new—just an overwhelming sense that events had gone badly wrong to put Spenkelink in this spot. Goldstein argued fervently, and the justices listened intently. But they were skeptical. "What about finality?" one justice asked. "When does it end?" Another justice, his mind apparently made up already, asked repeatedly whether Spenkelink was spelled with one *l* or two.

And the clock ticked down. At last, Marky interjected, "Look," he said, "I don't mind listening, but this man is being shaved and prepped as we speak. If the court is going to enter a stay, you better go ahead and do it now, out of consideration for him." That caught everyone's attention. Goldstein hastened to a close. Marky offered a brief rebuttal. England asked the lawyers to leave the room while the justices deliberated.

A few minutes later, Goldstein and Ferguson were summoned back inside and told that someone had called from Orlando claiming that the execution was covered by an obscure law requiring that all acts of government be published in advance through legal notices. The defense attorneys knew nothing about this claim, but what did they have to lose? They asked England to incorporate it into their brief.

The waiting resumed. "I remembered talking to Ray Marky," Goldstein recalled, "and him saying that he didn't want us to think he was a bad guy, that he was just doing his job."

Scores of protesters had spent the night outside the governor's mansion, chanting and singing and banging pipes against the iron fence. Bob Graham [Governor of Florida] passed the noisy night alone, except for his bodyguards. His wife and four daughters had been secretly moved to the home of a family friend. The strain was enormous: The younger girls were frightened by the clanging and shouting, and the older ones were angry at the things being said about their father. "My daddy's not a killer," one of them wailed. There were fears for the family's safety. Jim Smith's wife and children were in hiding, too, after a series of death threats.

That morning, the protesters from the mansion joined the protesters at Graham's office, and together they numbered over a hundred. When the doors to the governor's's suite were opened, the crowd surged into the reception area, where they began stomping on the floor and pounding on the walls and pressing against the locked double doors leading to the inner office. It happened so quickly that one receptionist was trapped and wound up cowering inside a closet. The protesters commandeered her telephone console and began shouting, "Murderer's office!" into the receiver each time a call came in. A television cameraman clambered onto the desk for a better angle. Another stepped up onto a newly upholstered chair. Soon people were swarming over all the furniture; when it was over, all the fabrics and finishes had to be redone.

Behind the locked doors, sheriff's deputies in riot helmets formed a human barricade, and everyone who could be moved upstairs was swiftly evacuated. The rest of the staff watched nervously as the doors heaved inward and the pictures rattled on the walls. Outside, police snipers watched from the rooftops of the capitol and the nearby supreme court building. An escape route from the governor's office had been plotted on old blueprints, and a helicopter sat on the lawn, ready to whisk Bob Graham away if the protest turned to an attack.

At the center of it all, Graham sat at his desk, flanked by his personal secretary and his chief of scheduling ... going through the morning's mail. If folks thought it weird, so be it: This was his way of coping with stress, to bury his emotions under a blanket of mundane detail. Graham had always done this. On the day of his wedding, he had irritated his bride by chattering vacuously about dairy cows. He was comforted by specifics, soothed by data; he wrote down every little thing that happened to him—each person he met, the price of every meal—in color-coded notebooks, a different color for each season of the year. Few people ever glimpsed beyond the wall of cool meticulousness that fronted Graham's personality.

Not that he was immune to the pressure that was squeezing him from every direction. The newspapers were almost unanimously opposed to the execution, and even some of his aides hoped he would reconsider. On the other hand, nearly everyone in the legislature was urging him on, and his phone rang constantly with unsolicited advice. The young governor of Arkansas, Bill Clinton, called with several picayune legal questions, concerned that Graham might make a mistake that would hamper the return of the death penalty in other states. Graham wrestled with the moral implications in conversations with George Bedell, a close friend and ordained minister. At one point, according to an ally, Graham had even considered reversing himself and commuting Spenkelink's sentence—an action his advisers believed would surely be political suicide. But if he had wavered, it was for only an instant, and by that Friday morning his resolve was granite.

Robin Gibson [Graham's advisor and counsel] stood behind Graham, keeping the phone line to the execution chamber open. Betty Steffens [Graham's clemency secretary] was on another phone, waiting for word from Arthur England's house. A third aide kept a line open to the attorney general's office, where lawyers were monitoring the federal courts. Everyone had to speak loudly so they could be hard over the din of the protest; Gibson, especially, grew more and more exasperated as the protest continued. Suddenly, he strode from the office toward the locked double doors. "Of course, we had direct lines to the courts and the prison, but the protesters didn't know that," Gibson recalled. "I figured I would go out and tell them that we were waiting for a call and that those phones they were disrupting were the only way to save John Spenkelink. So I opened the double doors.

"It was crazy. There were people up on top of the desk. Everyone was shouting and stomping. I tried to tell them that the best thing they could do for John Spenkelink was to quiet down and stop disrupting the office. Well, that didn't do any good. As soon as I said it, they immediately began chanting again like before."

Gibson's friends saw this as a display of incredible naivete. "He had read somewhere that if you could just find the leaders of a protest and reason with them, the rest of the crowd will disperse," Steffens said. But to the crowd in the reception area, Gibson's gambit was grossly cynical. Bob Graham had the power to save Spenkelink, and if he wanted to he could. They began chanting "Bloodsucker! Bloodsucker! Bloodsucker!" The renewed clamor further infuriated Gibson, and when he slammed the doors and turned to the armed deputies, he was trembling. "Nobody," he shouted, "gets past this line!"

Graham kept plodding through his mail. He looked up from one letter and asked his secretary to call upstairs for a speech writer named Bill Shade. When Shade answered his phone and heard that the governor needed him immediately, he thought, Oh, s——. He's gonna cancel it and he needs an instant speech. Shade hustled into Graham's office, where he found Gibson pacing, Steffens on a divan, and the governor plainly struggling with his nerves.

"You wanted to see me?" Shade asked.

Graham nodded, and handed him a letter from the stack. It was from a voter, complaining that her son was going to have to pay a fee to play in the school band. "Bill," the governor said above the racket from outside, "could you draft a response on this?"

Incongruous as it might seem, Dave Brierton [Warden of the state prison] wanted to make John Spenkelink as comfortable as possible before killing him. He thought about a tranquilizer but knew he'd catch hell if the press learned that the prisoner was drugged. Somewhere in his wide-ranging reading, though, Brierton had come across the fact that Anne Boleyn—just before she was beheaded on orders of her husband, Henry VIII—had been give a stiff drink to bolster her. If it was good enough for royalty, Brierton decided, it was good enough for Spenkelink.

He poured two generous shots from a Jack Daniel's bottle into a flask and gave the flask to his assistant, Richard Dugger. Dugger was headed down to the death-watch cell to supervise the shaving and showering.

"Would you like a drink?" Dugger asked when he reached the cell.

Spenkelink looked skeptically at the flask. "You first," he answered.

Dugger hadn't expected that—but he poured a mouthful into a paper cup and knocked it back. It burned, but the burn was welcome. Dugger was getting awfully nervous about strapping a man into a chair and watching him die.

"I'd like some of that," Spenkelink said, with a tight grin. He had himself one long bourbon, then another.

Arthur England called the lawyers back into his living room and announced that the request for a stay of execution had been denied. There was an awkward silence—no one knew what to do next. Then Justice Joe Boyd brightened. "Let's watch it on TV," he said.

Someone tuned the set to the local ABC affiliate, which was broadcasting live reports from outside the prison. Everyone huddled around. Ray Marky thought the whole scene was repulsive. Grown men glued to the set like they were watching the Super Bowl. He wandered into another room.

Justice Alan Sundberg followed him. The two men stood a moment, realizing they had nothing to say. So they, too, snapped on a television set, but they tuned it to cartoons, and tried to lose themselves in the cheerful noise.

Zero hour, 10 a.m., was approaching. At the U.S. Supreme Court, Ramsey Clark was handed a piece of paper. "The application for stay of execution, presented to Mr. Justice Powell and by him referred to the Court, is denied," he read. "Mr. Justice Brennan and Mr. Justice Marshall would grant the stay. Mr. Justice Blackmun took no part. . . ." At the bottom of the page were the initials "W.E.B.," hand-written by Chief Justice Warren E. Burger. Now every court had been heard from.

"The Lord is my shepherd, I shall not want," David Kendall [Spenkelink's lead attorney] intoned. He was standing next to Tom Feamster [minister] in the back of the windowless waiting room. Soon, a van would take them two hundred yards to the death house, to witness the execution. "What comes next?" he asked. Feamster said nothing.

"The Lord is my shepherd, I shall not want," Kendall repeated. "He leadeth me beside the still waters. He anointeth my head with oil, my cup runneth over. No, wait—He maketh me to lie down in green pastures. He, uh, He leadeth me beside still waters. Is that right?"

"Man, I don't know," Feamster answered.

"You're the preacher."

Kendall started again. "The Lord is my shepherd, I shall not want. He maketh me lie down in green pastures. He leadeth me beside still waters. Something, something. He restoreth my soul. He—Thou?—anointeth my head with oil, my cup runneth over. Help me out with this."

"I told you I don't know."

"You should know this. The Twenty-third Psalm. Pretty famous stuff. Don't you learn these things at seminary?"

Pause.

"You probably don't even know the word 'selah.' "

Feamster looked at him blankly.

" 'Selah.' It's Hebrew. They put it at the end of the psalms. It means 'right on!' Preachers should know that. C'mon," Kendall continued. "The Lord is my shepherd, I shall not want. He maketh me to lie down in green pastures. He leadeth me beside the still waters. What comes next?"

Feamster wanted to say, "Shut your mouth! What's your problem?" Yammering on at a time like this. For a priest, Tom Feamster—as he sometimes admitted—was not terribly religious, in the Bible-quoting sense. At a time of trouble, Scripture was not the first thing that sprang to his mind. He would get more solace, at this moment, from putting a big fist through the wall. Kendall, however, was at it again. "The Lord is my shepherd ..." Feamster tried to remember the psalm, if only to satisfy the lawyer. All he could think about, though, was that somewhere close by, John Spenkelink was being readied for death. Feamster felt stupid, he felt angry, and most of all, he felt helpless. But he held his tongue; apparently this was Kendall's way of dealing with it.

"The Lord is my shepherd ..." The room went dark.

Somewhere in the bowels of the prison, workers had switched off the feed from the local power company. About thirty seconds later, the prison's own generator kicked in, and the lights came back on. Utility executives had insisted on this; they were worried about bad public relations, or even sabotage, if their electricity was used to power the chair.

"Yea, though I walk through the valley of the shadow of death, I will fear no evil, for Thou art with me," Kendall intoned.

"Thy rod and Thy staff, they comfort me. Thou preparest a table before me in the presence of mine enemies. Something, something, something.

"Surely goodness and mercy shall follow me all the days of my life. And I will dwell in the House of the Lord forever."

He looked at Feamster. "Selah!"

Then the van came.

Joe Ingle [minister] had taken Lois Spenkelink [Spenkelink's mother] to a room at the ratty old Dixie Motel in Starke, where he hoped no reporters could find her. He pulled the drapes, asked the manager to hold any calls, and sat down beside the tired woman.

This ordeal had been unique and devilish torture for Lois Spenkelink. It's a hard thing for a mother to lose a child, bitterly hard, unnatural and out of time. But to have a child—so healthy looking in his tight T-shirts, so seemingly harmless in his letters dotted with smiley faces—separated out from all God's children as one unfit to live.... To think of that child being shaved, showered, and exterminated ... It was almost impossible to bear. She had tried her best, loved him and honored her every duty to him, and no doubt she once had dreamed that her investment would pay a dividend of pride. Instead, there was this insuperable shame, this shocking indictment that said her child was unlovable, irredeemable, incorrigible, and must die.

Perhaps a woman of a philosophical bent could find some meaning to it all, but Lois Spenkelink was not a philosopher. She was a simple school teacher, modest in her aspirations, noteworthy only in her sorrows. She was not a worldly woman, and was mystified by much of the frenzy around her. One night, earlier in the week, she had sat in a room full of lawyers and activists while they discussed their prospects in the U.S. Supreme Court. Ingle had recited the names of the justices, and the group had estimated their chances with each one. Lois had looked up and said, "I'll tell you one of them we don't need to worry about. One of them will do the right thing."

And Ingle asked, "Who's that, Lois?"

"Judge Wapner," she had said.

She had tried everything the Spenkelink team could think of to save her son. She had spoken at rallies and given television interviews and placed calls to anyone who might be in a position to help—Jerry Brown, the progressive governor of her home state of California; Ted Kennedy, the keeper of the liberal flame; even President Jimmy Carter. The president was not categorically opposed to capital punishment, but he was very public about his religious devotion. Lois Spenkelink hoped a "Christian appeal" to Carter would persuade him to call for mercy. Now, less than an hour from the scheduled execution, she sat on a worn bedspread and wondered what more she might have done. The ringing of the telephone startled her. Lois answered, listened for a moment, then passed the phone to Ingle. The White House was calling.

"Please tell Mrs. Spenkelink the president sympathizes with her deeply," a presidential aide said. "But as you probably know, this is a matter of state law, and he doesn't think it would be proper for him to intervene."

Ingle erupted; his voice was desperate. Didn't they understand? This wasn't about the law. "We called him for help because he claims to be a Christian," Ingle said. "We are pleading with him"—Ingle put his whole heart into the word pleading—"in the name of Jesus Christ, to call Governor Graham and stop this execution. Would you please give him that message?" The man at the White House promised he would.

What happened next would later strike Ingle as "the strangest, most wonderful thing, a miracle." At the hour of her greatest pain and fear, Lois Spenkelink, utterly drained, drifted off to sleep. Joe Ingle quietly turned on the television, leaving the volume off, and waited for a news bulletin.

A good-sized crowd was jammed into the Q-wing corridor when Dave Brierton reached Spenkelink's cell. Every prison staffer, it seemed, wanted to witness history being made. A list had been prepared of people who were allowed to be there, but a number of others had schemed or scammed their way in. A technician, for example, chose just that moment to replace an oxygen bottle in the first-aid station. He was turned away at the grille, but a staff psychologist took the bottle and the gambit worked for him. The prison chaplain arrived, a man whom Spenkelink deeply loathed as an unholy cog in the death machine. "Get him out of here," Spenkelink seethed, and when the chaplain did not immediately leave, he shouted: "Goddammit, get that piece of s___ out of here!" Afterward, the whole crowd would have stories to tell; a good number of those present would personally take credit for having said, "John, it's time to go."

Brierton recalled it this way: "The execution was scheduled for ten a.m., and I waited until five past ten before I went in there to get him. I was obsessed with the idea that we would get some last-minute calls after he was in the chair. I didn't want that. So I waited. Originally, I wanted to wait until ten-fifteen, but Richard Dugger convinced me that it would look too much like I was running my own show.

"I went back there figuring John would probably be at the acceptance stage. He'd spent the night with his priest, after all, and I kind of figured he would have worked it all through. But I got down there and, man, he was angry. And it hit me. You know, I don't think John ever really believed it was going to happen. There he was with his head shaved, and I don't think he believed it would happened until I walked up. I said, 'John, it's time.' And he stood up and he was really obviously angry. He shouted,

'You motherfuckers really think you're tough, don't you!' John had a temper on him.''

Others remember Spenkelink also said: ''You can't do this, this is America! This is murder!''

Brierton: ''And I said, 'John, I really don't think this is the time for this.' And after a minute, he came out. For a minute there, I wasn't sure what he was going to do, whether he was going to make us drag him out. But he got up and came out of the cell. There was no fighting at all.''

Spenkelink was handcuffed, and a thick white paste, called Electro-creme, was smeared on his head to enhance the flow of juice. It made him look comical, like a bald man having a shampoo. The strap squad walked him briskly down the corridor, through a heavy door and into the execution chamber. The prisoner saw the electric chair for the first time. It was a massive piece of furniture, scaled more like a throne than a chair. It was dark, shiny oak, heavy, angular, functional, with wide arms, a ladder back, two wooden pinions for a headrest, two stout legs in the rear and two more narrowly spaced legs in front. The brown chair completely dominated the tiny room, which had white walls, a white ceiling, and a white floor, like a piece of art dominating a bare gallery wall.

In one swift motion Spenkelink was thrust into the chair and the practiced hands began moving over him, cinching the leather straps tight. ''We came in and we strapped him into the chair and I remember John was looking all around the room, almost like he was curious,'' Brierton recalled. ''He turned his head and looked back at the executioner standing there in his black hood. He just stared at the guy. And then, I believe, his nerves started to go.'' The last strap was a wide band that went over Spenkelink's mouth and chin and anchored his head firmly against the pinions.

While this was going on, Venetian blinds remained closed over the window that separated the execution chamber from the witness room. During rehearsals, Brierton had concluded that the strapping-in was a spectacle potentially demeaning both to the prisoner and to the squad. ''Why do they have to see him coming in?'' he asked Dugger. ''Let's put in some blinds.''

''I don't think that would be a good idea,'' Dugger answered—and it turned out he was right. In the months that followed, people would charge that Spenkelink had been dragged to the chair, that he had been gagged under the head strap, even that he had been beaten to death or strangled before he ever got into the room. Investigations would be launched. Newspaper columnists would fulminate. A flaky Jacksonville evangelist would paper the state with letters claiming that Spenkelink had been murdered to prevent him from revealing, at the last moment, knowledge of a drug conspiracy reaching to the highest levels of Florida government. Eventually, Spenkelink's corpse would be exhumed by a big-name Los Angeles coroner in a gruesome publicity stunt.

All of this because of those Venetian blinds. The execution would become the circus Brierton had dreaded.

There were twenty-four white wooden chairs with heart-shaped backs crowded into the little witness room. They looked like overgrown pieces of a child's tea-party set. These were filled by twelve designated observers and twelve reporters. As many people from the prison staff as could fit crammed into the standing room.

Kendall carried in his coat pocket a copy of a 1947 U.S. Supreme Court decision, *Francis v. Resweber*, in which the court had agreed to consider whether it was cruel and unusual punishment to electrocute a man a second time if the chair malfunctioned and merely jolted him the first time. The case had not gone well for the man in question, because the justices concluded that what's acceptable punishment once should be acceptable twice. But to Kendall the question itself was grounds for an appeal, and he was ready to jump up and wave the opinion if the equipment malfunctioned this time.

There was nothing else he could do, so he put on a brave face. "We're still trying to get a Supreme Court justice to stop it," he informed a reporter in the witness room. "I can't tell you which one." Then he leaned toward Feamster and whispered, "Tom, he can see us from here."

"We sat there at least ten minutes, staring at the closed blinds," Feamster remembered. "I was thinking that I should do some kind of civil disobedience. I thought about throwing my chair through the window. Just standing up and slinging it through. It wouldn't stop the thing, but it would disrupt it. But then I realized that surely the window would be shatterproof, and the chair would bounce off, and they would take me out of there and I wouldn't be there for John.

"It seemed like years," Feamster said. "Then, *snap!* The blinds came up and John's eyes were staring right at me. There was a strap across his face pulling his head back and pressing his jaw down. His eyes were staring right at me. Then they rolled, they rolled around the room and . . . shut."

Inside the chamber, Brierton was stunned by how close the witnesses were. If not for the glass, he could reach over and touch the legislators in the front row. They hadn't rehearsed with witnesses, and the audience flustered the warden. Brierton caught sight of Kendall flashing a thumbs-up sign, and his heart raced faster. Did the lawyer know something was up?

There were three telephones on the rear wall, one beige, one green, one black. A squad member listened a moment at the first phone, which was connected to the attorney general's office, then announced quietly, "No stays."

Brierton turned to Spenkelink. "Do you have any last words?" He said hurriedly.

"I can't talk," Spenkelink gasped.

The man's nerve had failed. That was obvious to Brierton. Others present, including Richard Dugger, came to a different conclusion: the strap across his mouth was too tight. Spenkelink wanted to speak, but physically could not. There was no time to resolve the question, though, because Brierton had already stepped across the room to the black phone, and the electrician had begun fastening the electrodes.

Robin Gibson was on the other end of the line in the governor's office. "I was standing there with the phone, and I heard them enter the chamber. I could hear it over the phone. The feet shuffling. I heard a few syllables of what they were saying, Brierton asking Spenkelink if he had any last words. I don't know if he said anything. If he did, it was very short.

"Brierton came on the line, and I handed the phone to Bob. He was obviously very tense. He took the phone and said, 'This is Louis Pasteur.' The code. But he was supposed to just say, 'Louis Pasteur,' not 'This is Louis Pasteur.' He was nervous."

A press aide, who knew nothing of the password, was standing near Graham's desk, and when she heard the governor say "This is Louis Pasteur," she let out a burst of involuntary laughter. Had the man cracked? Graham ignored her. "There are no stays at this time," he said solemnly. "May God be with us." A nice touch, Gibson thought. "May God be with us." Clearly, his friend had been thinking about just the right words for the history books. It was a phrase to remember.

But actually, as it turned out, what Gibson himself would recall most vividly was "the feet shuffling. That's the strongest memory. I can still hear those shuffling feet."

Brierton gave the signal. There was a dull slap of sound, then another slap, with a harder edge to it, as the executioner opened the power to the control panel. Then, back to back, two loud metallic snaps, like gunshots, as the hooded man threw the switch.

Spenkelink stiffened in the chair. His right hand tightened slowly into a fist, like a wad of newspaper balling up in a fire. His left hand also made a fist, but then the thumb shot up and the forefinger distended grotesquely, pointing backward toward his stomach. The knuckles stood out like an arthritic's. The surge lasted perhaps a minute.

"Then the executioner turned off the power, and the doctor went over and opened one button of John's shirt and put the stethoscope to his chest. He listened, then he shook his head," Feamster recounted.

"Brierton signaled again, and the switch was thrown again. Now there was a little smoke curling up from John's leg. After a little while, the doctor listened at his chest, then shook his head. For the third time, they threw the switch," Feamster continued. "This time, his leg was burning. No flames, but a lot of smoke." The flesh under the electrode split open and turned black. Again, the power was cut off. "Then the doctor went to John and listened, and this time, he nodded his head, real slow," Feamster remembered. "Then, *slap!* Down came the blinds."

It was 10:18 a.m., Friday, May 25, 1979. The death penalty had returned to America.

*

PART 2

THE CONSTITUTION AND DEATH PENALTY SCHEMES

■ ■ ■

The next three chapters concern the Supreme Court's elaboration of its holdings in *Furman* and *Gregg* and its companion cases. At issue in each case is what constitutes a constitutional death penalty scheme. Chapter 3 addresses the basic requirement of *Furman* and *Gregg* that a constitutional scheme must limit the risk of arbitrariness in the imposition of the death penalty. Chapter 4 concerns the requirement expressed in *Woodson v. North Carolina* that a constitutional scheme must permit "the particularized consideration of relevant aspects of the character and record" of the defendant. In Chapter 5, the Supreme Court applies its proportionality analysis from *Gregg* in the context of particular crimes and particular defendants.

CHAPTER 3

LIMITING THE RISK OF ARBITRARINESS

■ ■ ■

The "holding" of the *Furman* case, as understood by the Court in *Gregg* and subsequent cases, was that, to satisfy the Eighth Amendment, a death penalty scheme had to limit the risk of arbitrary application. In *Gregg* and its companion cases, *Proffitt v. Florida* and *Jurek v. Texas*, the Court upheld, *on their face*, the Georgia, Florida and Texas schemes, respectively, but did not explicitly determine which aspects of each scheme satisfied the *Furman* principle. Thus, in subsequent cases, the Supreme Court, lower federal courts and state courts have attempted to define the limits placed by *Furman* on death penalty schemes.

The first two cases in the chapter involve the Supreme Court's rejection of *Furman* challenges to state schemes. In *Zant v. Stephens*, the Supreme Court again considers the Georgia scheme in light of a *Furman* challenge. Relying on an explanation from the Georgia Supreme Court as to how the scheme was supposed to work at each stage, the Court upholds the scheme, focusing particularly on the role of aggravating circumstances in narrowing the death-eligible class. In *Lowenfield v. Phelps*, the defendant challenges his death sentence under the Louisiana scheme on the ground that the sole aggravating factor found against him served no narrowing function since it merely duplicated an element of the crime itself. In the next two cases, the defendants challenge single aggravating circumstances as being so vague as to create a substantial risk of arbitrariness. In *Godfrey v. Georgia*, the defendant challenges Georgia's "outrageously or wantonly vile, horrible or inhuman" aggravating circumstance, while in *Arave v. Creech*, the defendant challenges Idaho's "utter disregard for human life" aggravating circumstance. The Court, in *Gregg* and *Zant*, referred to the importance of "meaningful appellate review" as a check on arbitrariness. In *Barclay v. Florida*, the Court considers how to judge whether the state supreme court provided the defendant with "meaningful appellate review." In *Pulley v. Harris*, the defendant challenges the California scheme on the ground that the California Supreme Court refused to engage in intercase proportionality review.

The intersection of race and capital punishment has posed the most profound challenge for the American criminal justice system. Studies going back to the turn of the century establish that minorities, particular-

ly African–Americans, have been sentenced to death in numbers disproportionate to their conviction of capital crimes. When the race of the
victim is taken into account, the disparities in sentencing have been
substantial. See W. Bowers & G. Pierce, *Racial Discrimination and
Criminal Homicide under Post–Furman Capital Statutes* in H. Bedau, The
Death Penalty in America (3rd. Ed.) 206–224. In *Furman v. Georgia* and
its two companion cases, the defendants were black, and Justices Douglas
(408 U.S. at 249–253, 92 S.Ct. 2732–2734) and Marshall (408 U.S. at 363–
365, 92 S.Ct. at 2790–2791) cited the incidence of racial discrimination as
support for finding the death penalty unconstitutional. Justice Powell, in
dissent, conceded that racial discrimination had been a factor in the past,
but he argued both that there was insufficient evidence that it continued
to affect capital sentencing and that, in any case, the issue should be
analyzed under the Equal Protection Clause rather than under the Eighth
Amendment (408 U.S. at 449–450, 92 S.Ct. at 2834). In *McCleskey v.
Kemp*, the last case in the chapter, the Court addresses the core question
of race and the death penalty when it considers a black defendant's Equal
Protection and Eighth Amendment challenge to his death sentence, a
challenge supported by an extensive empirical study of one state's administration of the death penalty.

ZANT v. STEPHENS

462 U.S. 862, 103 S.Ct. 2733, 77 L.Ed.2d 235 (1983).

Justice Stevens delivered the opinion of the Court.

The question presented is whether respondent's death penalty must
be vacated because one of the three statutory aggravating circumstances
found by the jury was subsequently held to be invalid by the Supreme
Court of Georgia, although the other two aggravating circumstances were
specifically upheld. The answer depends on the function of the jury's
finding of an aggravating circumstance under Georgia's capital sentencing
statute, and on the reasons that the aggravating circumstance at issue in
this particular case was found to be invalid.

In January 1975 a jury in Bleckley County, Georgia, convicted respondent of the murder of Roy Asbell and sentenced him to death. The
evidence received at the guilt phase of his trial, which included his
confessions and the testimony of a number of witnesses, described these
events: On August 19, 1974, while respondent was serving sentences for
several burglary convictions and was also awaiting trial for escape, he
again escaped from the Houston County jail. In the next two days he
committed three auto thefts, an armed robbery, and several burglaries. On
August 21st, Roy Asbell interrupted respondent and an accomplice in the
course of burglarizing the home of Asbell's son in Twiggs County. Respondent beat Asbell, robbed him, and, with the aid of the accomplice, drove
him in his own vehicle a short distance into Bleckley County. There they
killed Asbell by shooting him twice through the ear at point blank range.

At the sentencing phase of the trial the State relied on the evidence adduced at the guilt phase and also established that respondent's prior criminal record included convictions on two counts of armed robbery, five counts of burglary, and one count of murder. Respondent testified that he was "sorry" and knew he deserved to be punished, that his accomplice actually shot Asbell, and that they had both been "pretty high" on drugs. The State requested the jury to impose the death penalty and argued that the evidence established the aggravating circumstances identified in subparagraphs (b)(1), (b)(7), and (b)(9) of the Georgia capital sentencing statute.[1]

The trial judge instructed the jury that under the law of Georgia "every person found guilty of Murder shall be punished by death or by imprisonment for life, the sentence to be fixed by the jury trying the case." He explained that the jury was authorized to consider all of the evidence received during the trial as well as all facts and circumstances presented in extenuation, mitigation, or aggravation during the sentencing proceeding. He then stated: "You may consider any of the following statutory aggravating circumstances which you find are supported by the evidence. One, the offense of Murder was committed by a person with a prior record of conviction for a Capital felony, or the offense of Murder was committed by a person who has a substantial history of serious assaultive criminal convictions. Two, the offense of Murder was outrageously or wantonly vile, horrible or inhuman in that it involved torture, depravity of mind or an aggravated battery to the victim. Three, the offense of Murder was committed by a person who has escaped from the lawful custody of a peace officer or place of lawful confinement. These possible statutory circumstances are stated in writing and will be sent out with you during your deliberations on the sentencing phase of this case. They are in writing here, and I shall send this out with you. If the jury verdict on sentencing fixes punishment at death by electrocution you shall designate in writing, signed by the foreman, the aggravating circumstances or circumstance which you found to have been proven beyond a reasonable doubt. Unless one or more of these statutory aggravating circumstances are proved beyond a reasonable doubt you will not be authorized to fix punishment at death."

---

1. Section 27–2534.1(b) of the Georgia Code provided, in part: "In all cases of other offenses for which the death penalty may be authorized, the judge shall consider, or he shall include in his instructions to the jury for it to consider, any mitigating circumstances or aggravating circumstances otherwise authorized by law and any of the following statutory aggravating circumstances which may be supported by the evidence:

"(1) The offense of murder, rape, armed robbery, or kidnapping was committed by a person with a prior record of conviction for a capital felony, or the offense of murder was committed by a person who has a substantial history of serious assaultive criminal convictions.

* * *

"(7) The offense of murder, rape, armed robbery, or kidnapping was outrageously or wantonly vile, horrible or inhuman in that it involved torture, depravity of mind, or an aggravated battery to the victim.

* * *

"(9) The offense of murder was committed by a person in, or who has escaped from, the lawful custody of a peace officer or place of lawful confinement."

The jury followed the Court's instruction and imposed the death penalty. It designated in writing that it had found the aggravating circumstances described as "One" and "Three" in the judge's instruction. It made no such finding with respect to "Two". It should be noted that the jury's finding under "One" encompassed both alternatives identified in the judge's instructions and in subsection (b)(1) of the statute—that respondent had a prior conviction of a capital felony and that he had a substantial history of serious assaultive convictions. These two alternatives and the finding that the murder was committed by an escapee are described by the parties as the three aggravating circumstances found by the jury, but they may also be viewed as two statutory aggravating circumstances, one of which rested on two grounds.

In his direct appeal to the Supreme Court of Georgia respondent did not challenge the sufficiency of the evidence supporting the aggravating circumstances found by the jury. Nor did he argue that there was any infirmity in the statutory definition of those circumstances. While his appeal was pending, however, the Georgia Supreme Court held in *Arnold v. State*, 224 S.E.2d 386 (Ga.1976), that the aggravating circumstance described in the second clause of (b)(1)—"a substantial history of serious assaultive criminal convictions"—was unconstitutionally vague. Because such a finding had been made by the jury in this case, the Georgia Supreme Court, on its own motion, considered whether it impaired respondent's death sentence. It concluded that the two other aggravating circumstances adequately supported the sentence. The state court reaffirmed this conclusion in a subsequent appeal from the denial of state habeas corpus relief.

[Stephens' petition for federal habeas corpus relief was denied by the District Court, but the Court of Appeals granted relief on the ground that the instructions on the invalid circumstance "may have unduly directed the jury's attention to his prior convictions." The Supreme Court granted certiorari and, after briefing on the merits, deferred decision and certified the following question to the Georgia Supreme Court: "What are the premises of state law that support the conclusion that the death sentence in this case is not impaired by the invalidity of one of the statutory aggravating circumstances found by the jury?"]

In its response to our certified question, the Georgia Supreme Court * * * explained the state-law premises for its treatment of aggravating circumstances by analogizing the entire body of Georgia law governing homicides to a pyramid. It explained:

> "All cases of homicide of every category are contained within the pyramid. The consequences flowing to the perpetrator increase in severity as the cases proceed from the base to the apex, with the death penalty applying only to those few cases which are contained in the space just beneath the apex. To reach that category a case must pass through three planes of division between the base and the apex.

"The first plane of division above the base separates from all homicide cases those which fall into the category of murder. This plane is established by the legislature in statutes defining terms such as murder, voluntary manslaughter, involuntary manslaughter, and justifiable homicide. In deciding whether a given case falls above or below this plane, the function of the trier of facts is limited to finding facts. The plane remains fixed unless moved by legislative act.

"The second plane separates from all murder cases those in which the penalty of death is a possible punishment. This plane is established by statutory definitions of aggravating circumstances. The function of the factfinder is again limited to making a determination of whether certain facts have been established. Except where there is treason or aircraft hijacking, a given case may not move above this second plane unless at least one statutory aggravating circumstance exists.

"The third plane separates, from all cases in which a penalty of death may be imposed, those cases in which it shall be imposed. There is an absolute discretion in the factfinder to place any given case below the plane and not impose death. The plane itself is established by the factfinder. In establishing the plane, the factfinder considers all evidence in extenuation, mitigation and aggravation of punishment. There is a final limitation on the imposition of the death penalty resting in the automatic appeal procedure: This court determines whether the penalty of death was imposed under the influence of passion, prejudice, or any other arbitrary factor; whether the statutory aggravating circumstances are supported by the evidence; and whether the sentence of death is excessive or disproportionate to the penalty imposed in similar cases. Performance of this function may cause this court to remove a case from the death penalty category but can never have the opposite result.

"The purpose of the statutory aggravating circumstances is to limit to a large degree, but not completely, the factfinder's discretion. Unless at least one of the ten statutory aggravating circumstances exists, the death penalty may not be imposed in any event. If there exists at least one statutory aggravating circumstance, the death penalty may be imposed but the factfinder has a discretion to decline to do so without giving any reason. In making the decision as to the penalty, the factfinder takes into consideration all circumstances before it from both the guilt-innocence and the sentence phases of the trial. These circumstances relate both to the offense and the defendant.

"A case may not pass the second plane into that area in which the death penalty is authorized unless at least one statutory aggravating circumstance is found. However, this plane is passed regardless of the number of statutory aggravating circumstances found, so long as there is at least one. Once beyond this plane, the case enters the area of the factfinder's discretion, in which all the facts and circumstances of the case determine, in terms of our metaphor, whether or not the case passes the third plane and into the area in which the death penalty is imposed."

The Georgia Supreme Court then explained why the failure of the second ground of the (b)(1) statutory aggravating circumstance did not invalidate respondent's death sentence. It first noted that the evidence of respondent's prior convictions had been properly received and could properly have been considered by the jury. The court expressed the opinion that the mere fact that such evidence was improperly designated "statutory" had an "inconsequential impact" on the jury's death penalty decision. Finally, the court noted that a different result might be reached if the failed circumstance had been supported by evidence not otherwise admissible or if there was reason to believe that, because of the failure, the sentence was imposed under the influence of an arbitrary factor.

* * *

I

In Georgia, unlike some other States, the jury is not instructed to give any special weight to any aggravating circumstance, to consider multiple aggravating circumstances any more significant than a single such circumstance, or to balance aggravating against mitigating circumstances pursuant to any special standard. Thus, in Georgia, the finding of an aggravating circumstance does not play any role in guiding the sentencing body in the exercise of its discretion, apart from its function of narrowing the class of persons convicted of murder who are eligible for the death penalty. For this reason, respondent argues that Georgia's statutory scheme is invalid under the holding in *Furman v. Georgia*, 408 U.S. 238, 92 S.Ct. 2726 (1972).

A fair statement of the consensus expressed by the Court in *Furman* is "that where discretion is afforded a sentencing body on a matter so grave as the determination of whether a human life should be taken or spared, that discretion must be suitably directed and limited so as to minimize the risk of wholly arbitrary and capricious action." *Gregg v. Georgia*, 428 U.S. 153, 96 S.Ct. 2909 (1976) (opinion of STEWART, POWELL, and STEVENS, JJ.). After thus summarizing the central mandate of *Furman*, the plurality opinion in *Gregg* set forth a general exposition of sentencing procedures that would satisfy the concerns of *Furman*. But it expressly stated, "We do not intend to suggest that only the above-described procedures would be permissible under *Furman* or that any sentencing system constructed along these general lines would inevitably satisfy the concerns of *Furman*, for each distinct system must be examined on an individual basis." The opinion then turned to specific consideration of the constitutionality of Georgia's capital sentencing procedures.

Georgia's scheme includes two important features which the plurality described in its general discussion of sentencing procedures that would guide and channel the exercise of discretion. Georgia has a bifurcated procedure, and its statute also mandates meaningful appellate review of every death sentence. The statute does not, however, follow the Model Penal Code's recommendation that the jury's discretion in weighing aggravating and mitigating circumstances against each other should be governed by specific standards. Instead, as the Georgia Supreme Court has unambiguously advised us, the aggravating circumstance merely performs the function of narrowing the category of persons convicted of murder who are eligible for the death penalty.

Respondent argues that the mandate of *Furman* is violated by a scheme that permits the jury to exercise unbridled discretion in determining whether the death penalty should be imposed after it has found that the defendant is a member of the class made eligible for that penalty by statute. But that argument could not be accepted without overruling our specific holding in *Gregg*. For the Court approved Georgia's capital sentencing statute even though it clearly did not channel the jury's discretion by enunciating specific standards to guide the jury's consideration of aggravating and mitigating circumstances.

The plurality's approval of Georgia's capital sentencing procedure rested primarily on two features of the scheme: that the jury was required to find at least one valid statutory aggravating circumstance and to identify it in writing, and that the state supreme court reviewed the record of every death penalty proceeding to determine whether the sentence was arbitrary or disproportionate. These elements, the opinion concluded, adequately protected against the wanton and freakish imposition of the death penalty. This conclusion rested, of course, on the fundamental requirement that each statutory aggravating circumstance must satisfy a constitutional standard derived from the principles of *Furman* itself. For a system "could have standards so vague that they would fail adequately to channel the sentencing decision patterns of juries with the result that a pattern of arbitrary and capricious sentencing like that found unconstitutional in *Furman* could occur." To avoid this constitutional flaw, an aggravating circumstance must genuinely narrow the class of persons eligible for the death penalty and must reasonably justify the imposition of a more severe sentence on the defendant compared to others found guilty of murder.[15]

* * *

---

15. These standards for statutory aggravating circumstances address the concerns voiced by several of the opinions in *Furman v. Georgia, supra.* (DOUGLAS, J., concurring); (BRENNAN, J., concurring) ("it is highly implausible that only the worst criminals or the criminals who commit the worst crimes are selected for this punishment"); (STEWART, J., concurring) ("of all the people convicted of rapes and murders in 1967 and 1968, many just as reprehensible as these, the petitioners are among a capriciously selected random handful upon whom the sentence of death has in fact been imposed"); (WHITE, J., concurring) ("there is no meaningful basis for distinguishing the few cases in which it is imposed from the many cases in which it is not"). In *Gregg*, the plurality again recognized the need for legislative criteria to limit the death penalty to certain

Our cases indicate, then, that statutory aggravating circumstances play a constitutionally necessary function at the stage of legislative definition: they circumscribe the class of persons eligible for the death penalty. But the Constitution does not require the jury to ignore other possible aggravating factors in the process of selecting, from among that class, those defendants who will actually be sentenced to death. What is important at the selection stage is an individualized determination on the basis of the character of the individual and the circumstances of the crime.

The Georgia scheme provides for categorical narrowing at the definition stage, and for individualized determination and appellate review at the selection stage. We therefore remain convinced, as we were in 1976, that the structure of the statute is constitutional. Moreover, the narrowing function has been properly achieved in this case by the two valid aggravating circumstances upheld by the Georgia Supreme Court—that respondent had escaped from lawful confinement, and that he had a prior record of conviction for a capital felony. These two findings adequately differentiate this case in an objective, evenhanded, and substantively rational way from the many Georgia murder cases in which the death penalty may not be imposed. Moreover, the Georgia Supreme Court in this case reviewed the death sentence to determine whether it was arbitrary, excessive, or disproportionate. Thus the absence of legislative or court-imposed standards to govern the jury in weighing the significance of either or both of those aggravating circumstances does not render the Georgia capital sentencing statute invalid as applied in this case.

* * *

III

* * *

Respondent contends that the death sentence was impaired because the judge instructed the jury with regard to an invalid statutory aggravating circumstance, a "substantial history of serious assaultive criminal convictions," for these instructions may have affected the jury's deliberations. In analyzing this contention it is essential to keep in mind the sense in which that aggravating circumstance is "invalid." It is not invalid because it authorizes a jury to draw adverse inferences from conduct that is constitutionally protected. Georgia has not, for example, sought to characterize the display of a red flag, cf. *Stromberg v. California*, 283 U.S. 359, 51 S.Ct. 532 (1931), the expression of unpopular political views, cf. *Terminiello v. Chicago*, 337 U.S. 1, 69 S.Ct. 894 (1949), or the request for

---

crimes: "[T]he decision that capital punishment may be the appropriate sanction in extreme cases is an expression of the community's belief that certain crimes are themselves so grievous an affront to humanity that the only adequate response may be the penalty of death." The opinion also noted with approval the efforts of legislatures to "define those crimes and those criminals for which capital punishment is most probably an effective deterrent." The concurring opinion of Justice WHITE in *Gregg* asserted that, over time, as the aggravating circumstance requirement was applied, "the types of murders for which the death penalty may be imposed [would] become more narrowly defined and [would be] limited to those which are particularly serious or for which the death penalty is particularly appropriate."

trial by jury, cf. *United States v. Jackson*, 390 U.S. 570, 88 S.Ct. 1209 (1968), as an aggravating circumstance. Nor has Georgia attached the "aggravating" label to factors that are constitutionally impermissible or totally irrelevant to the sentencing process, such as for example the race, religion, or political affiliation of the defendant, cf. *Herndon v. Lowry*, 301 U.S. 242, 57 S.Ct. 732 (1937), or to conduct that actually should militate in favor of a lesser penalty, such as perhaps the defendant's mental illness. Cf. *Miller v. Florida*, 373 So.2d 882 (Fla.1979). If the aggravating circumstance at issue in this case had been invalid for reasons such as these, due process of law would require that the jury's decision to impose death be set aside.

But the invalid aggravating circumstance found by the jury in this case was struck down in *Arnold* because the Georgia Supreme Court concluded that it fails to provide an adequate basis for distinguishing a murder case in which the death penalty may be imposed from those cases in which such a penalty may not be imposed. The underlying evidence is nevertheless fully admissible at the sentencing phase. As we noted in *Gregg, supra,* the Georgia statute provides that, at the sentencing hearing, the judge or jury

> "shall hear additional evidence in extenuation, mitigation, and aggravation of punishment, *including the record of any prior criminal convictions and pleas of guilty or pleas of nolo contendere of the defendant,* or the absence of any prior conviction and pleas: Provided, however, that only such evidence in aggravation as the State has made known to the defendant prior to his trial shall be admissible." (emphasis supplied).

We expressly rejected petitioner's objection to the wide scope of evidence and argument allowed at presentence hearings.

> "We think that the Georgia court wisely has chosen not to impose unnecessary restrictions on the evidence that can be offered at such a hearing and to approve open and far-ranging argument. . . . So long as the evidence introduced and the arguments made at the presentence hearing do not prejudice a defendant, it is preferable not to impose restrictions. We think it desirable for the jury to have as much information before it as possible when it makes the sentencing decision."

Thus, any evidence on which the jury might have relied in this case to find that respondent had previously been convicted of a substantial number of serious assaultive offenses, as he concedes he had been, was properly adduced at the sentencing hearing and was fully subject to explanation by the defendant. This case involves a statutory aggravating circumstance, invalidated by the state Supreme Court on grounds of vagueness, whose terms plausibly described aspects of the defendant's background that were properly before the jury and whose accuracy was unchallenged. Hence the erroneous instruction does not implicate our repeated recognition that the "qualitative difference between death and other penalties calls for a greater degree of reliability when the death sentence is imposed." *Lockett v. Ohio*, 438 U.S. 586, 98 S.Ct. 2954 (1978) (opinion of BURGER, C.J.).

Although the Court of Appeals acknowledged on rehearing that the evidence was admissible, it expressed the concern that the trial court's instructions "may have unduly directed the jury's attention to his prior conviction." But, assuming that the instruction did induce the jury to place greater emphasis upon the respondent's prior criminal record than it would otherwise have done, the question remains whether that emphasis violated any constitutional right. In answering this question, it is appropriate to compare the instruction that was actually given, with an instruction on the same subject that would have been unobjectionable. Nothing in the United States Constitution prohibits a trial judge from instructing a jury that it would be appropriate to take account of a defendant's prior criminal record in making its sentencing determination, even though the defendant's prior history of noncapital convictions could not by itself provide sufficient justification for imposing the death sentence. There would have been no constitutional infirmity in an instruction stating, in substance: "If you find beyond a reasonable doubt that the defendant is a person who has previously been convicted of a capital felony, or that he has escaped from lawful confinement, you will be authorized to impose the death sentence, and in deciding whether or not that sentence is appropriate you may consider the remainder of his prior criminal record."

The effect the erroneous instruction may have had on the jury is therefore merely a consequence of the statutory label "aggravating circumstance." That label arguably might have caused the jury to give somewhat greater weight to respondent's prior criminal record than it otherwise would have given. But we do not think the Georgia Supreme Court erred in its conclusion that the "mere fact that some of the aggravating circumstances presented were improperly designated 'statutory' " had "an inconsequential impact on the jury's decision regarding the death penalty." The instructions did not place particular emphasis on the role of statutory aggravating circumstances in the jury's ultimate decision. Instead the trial court instructed the jury to "consider all of the evidence received in court throughout the trial before you" and to "consider all facts and circumstances presented in extinuation [sic], mitigation and aggravation of punishment as well as such arguments as have been presented for the State and for the Defense." More importantly, for the reasons discussed above, any possible impact cannot fairly be regarded as a constitutional defect in the sentencing process.

Our decision in this case depends in part on the existence of an important procedural safeguard, the mandatory appellate review of each death sentence by the Georgia Supreme Court to avoid arbitrariness and to assure proportionality. We accept that court's view that the subsequent invalidation of one of several statutory aggravating circumstances does not automatically require reversal of the death penalty, having been assured that a death sentence will be set aside if the invalidation of an aggravating circumstance makes the penalty arbitrary or capricious. The Georgia Supreme Court, in its response to our certified question, expressly stated, "A different result might be reached in a case where evidence was submitted in support of a statutory aggravating circumstance which was not otherwise admissible, and thereafter the circumstance failed." As we noted in *Gregg*, we have also been assured that a death sentence will be vacated if it is excessive or substantially disproportionate to the penalties that have been imposed under similar circumstances.

Finally, we note that in deciding this case we do not express any opinion concerning the possible significance of a holding that a particular aggravating circumstance is "invalid" under a statutory scheme in which the judge or jury is specifically instructed to weigh statutory aggravating and mitigating circumstances in exercising its discretion whether to impose the death penalty. As we have discussed, the Constitution does not require a State to adopt specific standards for instructing the jury in its consideration of aggravating and mitigating circumstances, and Georgia has not adopted such a system. Under Georgia's sentencing scheme, and under the trial judge's instructions in this case, no suggestion is made that the presence of more than one aggravating circumstance should be given special weight. Whether or not the jury had concluded that respondent's prior record of criminal convictions merited the label "substantial" or the label "assaultive," the jury was plainly entitled to consider that record, together with all of the other evidence before it, in making its sentencing determination.

> [Opinion of WHITE, J., concurring in part and concurring in the judgment, and opinion of REHNQUIST, J. concurring in the judgment omitted]

JUSTICE MARSHALL, with whom JUSTICE BRENNAN joins, dissenting.

* * *

II

Today the Court upholds a death sentence that was based in part on a statutory aggravating circumstance which the State concedes was so amorphous that it invited "subjective decision-making without . . . minimal, objective guidelines for its application." *Arnold v. State*, 224 S.E.2d 386 (Ga.1976). In order to reach this surprising result, the Court embraces the theory, which it infers from the Georgia Supreme Court response to this Court's certified question, that the only function of statutory aggravating circumstances in Georgia is to screen out at the threshold defendants to whom none of the 10 circumstances applies. According to this theory, once one of the 10 statutory factors has been found, they drop out of the picture entirely and play no part in the jury's decision whether to sentence the defendant to death. Relying on this "threshold" theory, the Court concludes that the submission of the unconstitutional statutory factor did not prejudice respondent.

If the jury instructions given some eight years ago were consistent with this new theory, we could assume that the jury did not focus on the vague statutory aggravating circumstance in making its actual sentencing decision. But if the jury had been so instructed, the instructions would have been constitutionally defective for a more basic reason, since they would have left the jury totally without guidance once it found a single statutory aggravating circumstance.

A

Until this Court's decision in *Furman v. Georgia*, 408 U.S. 238, 92 S.Ct. 2726 (1972) in 1972, the capital sentencing procedures in most States delegated to judges and juries plenary authority to decide when a death sentence should be imposed. The sentencer was given "practically untrammeled discretion to let an accused live or insist that he die." *Furman v. Georgia* (DOUGLAS, J., concurring).

In *Furman* this Court held that the system of capital punishment then in existence in this country was incompatible with the Eighth and Fourteenth Amendments. As was later recognized in *Gregg v. Georgia*, 428 U.S. 153, 96 S.Ct. 2909 (1976), *Furman* established one basic proposition if it established nothing else: "where the ultimate penalty of death is at issue a system of standardless jury discretion violates the Eighth and Fourteenth Amendments." (Opinion of STEWART, POWELL, and STEVENS, JJ.). The basic teaching of *Furman* is that a State may not leave the decision whether a defendant lives or dies to the unfettered discretion of the jury, since such a scheme is "pregnant with discrimination" (DOUGLAS, J., concurring), and inevitably results in death sentences which are "wantonly and . . . freakishly imposed" (STEWART, J., concurring), and for which "there is no meaningful basis for distinguishing the few cases in which [the death penalty] is imposed from the many cases in which it is not." (WHITE, J., concurring).

Four years after *Furman* was decided, this Court upheld the capital sentencing statutes of Georgia, Florida, and Texas against constitutional attack, concluding that those statutes contained safeguards that promised to eliminate the constitutional deficiencies found in *Furman*. See *Gregg v. Georgia*; *Proffitt v. Florida*, 428 U.S. 242, 96 S.Ct. 2960 (1976); *Jurek v. Texas*, 428 U.S. 262, 96 S.Ct. 2950 (1976). The Court's conclusion was based on the premise that the statutes ensured that sentencers would be "given guidance regarding the factors about the crime and the defendant that the State, representing organized society, deems particularly relevant to the sentencing decision." *Gregg v. Georgia* (Opinion of STEWART, POWELL, and STEVENS, JJ.). The Court assumed that the identification of specific statutory aggravating circumstances would put an end to standardless sentencing discretion:

"These procedures require the jury to consider the circumstances of the crime and the criminal before it recommends sentence. No longer can a Georgia jury do as Furman's jury did: reach a finding of the defendant's guilt and then, without guidance or direction, decide whether he should live or die. Instead, *the jury's attention is directed to the specific circumstances of the crime*: Was it committed in the course of another capital felony? Was it committed for money? Was it committed upon a peace officer or judicial officer? Was it committed in a particularly heinous way or in a manner that endangered the lives of many persons? In addition, *the jury's attention is focused on the characteristics of the person who committed the crime*: Does he have a record of prior convictions for capital offenses? Are there any special facts about this defendant that mitigate against imposing capital punishment. . . . As a result, while some jury discretion still exists, '*the discretion is to be exercised by clear and objective standards so as to produce nondiscriminatory application.*'" (Opinion of STEWART, POWELL, and STEVENS, JJ.) (emphasis added).

* * *

B

Today we learn for the first time that the Court did not mean what it said in *Gregg v. Georgia*. We now learn that the actual decision whether a defendant lives or dies may still be left to the unfettered discretion of the jury. Although we were assured in *Gregg* that sentencing discretion was "to be exercised by clear and objective standards," (Opinion of STEWART, POWELL, and STEVENS, JJ.), we are now told that the State need do nothing whatsoever to guide the jury's ultimate decision whether to sentence a defendant to death or spare his life.

Under today's decision all the State has to do is require the jury to make some threshold finding. Once that finding is made, the jurors can be left completely at large, with nothing to guide them but their whims and prejudices. They need not even consider any statutory aggravating circumstances that they have found to be applicable. Their sentencing decision is to be the product of their discretion and of nothing else.

If this is not a scheme based on "standardless jury discretion," *Gregg v. Georgia* (Opinion of STEWART, POWELL, and STEVENS, JJ.), I do not know what is. Today's decision makes an absolute mockery of this Court's precedents concerning capital sentencing procedures. There is no point in requiring State legislatures to identify specific aggravating circumstances if sentencers are to be left free to ignore them in deciding which defendants are to die. If this is all *Gregg v. Georgia* stands for, the States may as well be permitted to reenact the statutes that were on the books before *Furman*.

The system of discretionary sentencing that the Court approves today differs only in form from the capital sentencing procedures that this Court held unconstitutional more than a decade ago. The only difference between Georgia's pre-*Furman* capital sentencing scheme and the "threshold" theory that the Court embraces today is that the unchecked discretion previously conferred in all cases of murder is now conferred in cases of murder with one statutory aggravating circumstance. But merely circumscribing the category of cases eligible for the death penalty cannot remove from constitutional scrutiny the procedure by which those actually sentenced to death are selected.

More than a decade ago this Court struck down an Ohio statute that permitted a death sentence only if the jury found that the victim of the murder was a police officer, but gave the jury unbridled discretion once that aggravating factor was found. *Duling v. Ohio*, 408 U.S. 936, 92 S.Ct. 2861 (1972), summarily rev'g 254 N.E.2d 670 (Ohio 1970). There is no difference of any consequence between the Ohio scheme held impermissible in *Duling* and the "threshold" scheme that the Court endorses today. If, as *Duling* establishes, the Constitution prohibits a State from defining a crime (such as murder of a police officer) and then leaving the decision whether to impose the death sentence to the unchecked discretion of the jury, it must also prohibit a State from defining a lesser crime (such as murder) and then permitting the jury to make a standardless sentencing decision once it has found a single aggravating factor (such as that the victim was a police officer). In both cases the ultimate decision whether the defendant will be killed is left to the discretion of the sentencer, unguided by any legislative standards.[4] Whether a particular preliminary finding was made at the guilt phase of the trial or at the sentencing phase is irrelevant; a requirement that the finding be made at the sentencing phase in no way channels the sentencer's discretion once that finding has been made.[5] If the Constitution forbids one form of standardless discretion, it must forbid the other as well.

* * *

NOTES

1. *The Georgia scheme.*

Although the Georgia Supreme Court described its death penalty scheme as a pyramid with three planes, in fact, that court described a fourth narrowing plane created by the court's proportionality review of all death sentences. The Georgia scheme might be represented by the figure below:

---

4. This remains true whether or not the aggravating factor satisfies the Court's requirement that it "genuinely narrow the class of persons eligible for the death penalty and ... reasonably justify the imposition of a more severe sentence on the defendant compared to others found guilty of murder."

5. This Court has repeatedly recognized that a capital sentencing statute does not satisfy the Constitution simply because it requires a bifurcated trial and permits presentation at the penalty phase of evidence concerning the circumstances of the crime, the defendant's background and history, and other factors in aggravation and mitigation of punishment. Although the creation of a separate sentencing proceeding permits the exclusion from the guilt phase of information that is relevant only to sentencing and that might prejudice the determination of guilt, merely bifurcating the trial obviously does nothing to guide the discretion of the sentencer. See *Gregg v. Georgia* (Opinion of STEWART, POWELL, and STEVENS, JJ.). Nor is mandatory appellate review a substitute for legislatively defined criteria to guide the jury in imposing sentence. Although appellate review may serve to reduce arbitrariness and caprice "[w]here the sentencing authority is required to specify the factors it relied upon in reaching its decision," *Gregg v. Georgia* (Opinion of STEWART, POWELL, and STEVENS, JJ.), appellate review cannot serve this function where statutory aggravating circumstances play only a threshold role and an appellate court therefore has no means of ascertaining the factors underlying the jury's ultimate sentencing decision.

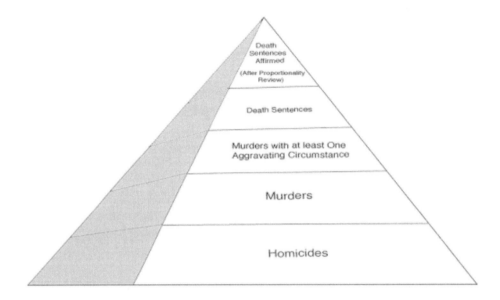

2. *"Weighing" and "non-weighing" states*

In *Zant*, the Court specifically left open the question whether the jury's consideration of an invalid aggravating circumstance would violate the Eighth Amendment in the case where "the judge or jury is specifically instructed to weigh statutory aggravating and mitigating circumstances," *i.e.*, in a "weighing" state. The Court addressed that issue in *Clemons v. Mississippi*, 494 U.S. 738, 110 S.Ct. 1441 (1990), where the jury was required to weigh the aggravating circumstances against any mitigating circumstances and one of the two aggravating circumstance found—the "especially heinous, atrocious or cruel" aggravating circumstance—was subsequently determined by the Mississippi Supreme Court to be invalid. Even though all of the facts of the crime could have been considered by the jury without the invalid circumstance, the Court found error in allowing the jury to consider the invalid circumstance. The Court held that nonetheless the Mississippi Supreme Court could uphold the death sentence if it were to reweigh the aggravating and mitigating circumstances and find that death was the appropriate sentence or if it were to find the error harmless beyond a reasonable doubt.

The Court revisited the question in *Brown v. Sanders*, 546 U.S. 212, 126 S.Ct. 884 (2006). At his guilt-phase trial, Sanders was convicted of murder, and the jury found true four special circumstances making Sanders death-eligible. The special circumstances found true are considered aggravating factors, as are the "circumstances of the crime," in deciding the sentence at the penalty phase. At Sanders's penalty phase, the jury was instructed as follows:

> If you conclude that the aggravating circumstances outweigh the mitigating circumstances, you shall impose a sentence of death. However, if you determine that the mitigating circumstances outweigh the aggravating

circumstances, you shall impose a sentence of confinement in the state prison for life without the possibility of parole.

The jury sentenced Sanders to death. On direct appeal, the California Supreme Court found two of the special circumstances were invalid, but the court nevertheless upheld the death sentence. On federal habeas corpus, the Ninth Circuit granted relief, but the Supreme Court (5–4) reversed, concluding that because the jury's consideration of the "circumstances of the crime" had the effect of rendering all the death-eligibility sentencing factors nonexclusive, California was a "non-weighing" state, and *Zant* controlled. The Court went on to state that the distinction between "weighing" and "non-weighing" states was "needlessly complex and incapable of providing for the full range of possible variations" in statutes and that "[a]n invalidated sentencing factor (whether an eligibility factor or not) will render the sentence unconstitutional by reason of its adding an improper element to the aggravation scale in the weighing process *unless* one of the other sentencing factors enables the sentencer to give aggravating weight to the same facts and circumstances." 546 U.S. at 220, 126 S.Ct. at 892 (footnote omitted). Although these statements might be read to call into question the "weighing"/"non-weighing" distinction, the lower courts have not understood *Sanders* in this way and have continued to apply *Clemons* in weighing states. See, *e.g., Styers v. Schriro,* 547 F.3d 1026 (9th Cir. 2008) (Arizona); *Wilson v. Mitchell,* 498 F.3d 491 (6th Cir. 2007) (Ohio).

3. *Alternative approaches to limiting arbitrariness.*

In theory, the Court might have required that the *Furman* concern—limiting the risk of arbitrariness in the administration of the death penalty—be addressed at one or more of four points in a state's criminal process: (1) the legislature's definition of capital offenses; (2) the prosecutor's decision whether to charge a capital offense; (3) the sentencer's determination to impose the death penalty; or (4) the appellate court's review of the sentencer's choice of a death sentence. In *Gregg,* the plurality rejected the second alternative—imposing any limits on the prosecutor's discretion to seek the death penalty. See *Gregg,* 428 U.S. at 199, 96 S.Ct. at 2937. Subsequently, the Court reaffirmed the prosecutor's "traditionally 'wide discretion' " to seek the death penalty. *McCleskey v. Kemp,* 481 U.S. 279, 296, 107 S.Ct. 1756, 1769 (1987). In *Zant,* the Court rejected the third alternative—limiting the sentencer's discretion to impose the death penalty—when it upheld the complete discretion afforded to the jury to impose the death penalty on any defendant as to whom an aggravating circumstance had been proved. This holding was reiterated in *Tuilaepa v. California,* 512 U.S. 967, 114 S.Ct. 2630 (1994) [Chapter 10], where the Court held that once the defendant is found to be a member of the narrowed death-eligible class at the "eligibility" stage, the Eighth Amendment imposes no further limits on jury discretion at the "selection" stage. Was the Court correct in deciding that the *Furman* principle should impose no limits on the prosecutor's decision to seek, or on the jury's decision to impose, the death penalty?

4. *The purpose of statutory narrowing.*

In *Zant,* at n. 15, Justice Stevens quotes briefly from Justice White's concurring opinion in *Gregg.* There Justice White, writing for himself, the

Chief Justice and Justice Rehnquist, articulated the rationale supporting the statutory narrowing requirement, as follows:

> As the types of murders for which the death penalty may be imposed become more narrowly defined and are limited to those which are particularly serious or for which the death penalty is particularly appropriate . . . it becomes reasonable to expect that juries . . . will impose the death penalty in a substantial portion of the cases so defined. If they do, it can no longer be said that the penalty is being imposed wantonly and freakishly or so infrequently that it loses its significance as a sentencing device.

428 U.S. at 222, 96 S.Ct. at 2948.[a] Justice White's unstated assumption was that the number of death sentences in a given jurisdiction will be relatively constant and reducing the size of the death-eligible class is the only way to make the imposition of the death penalty less "freakish." There is some empirical support for the proposition that the public within a given state desires a certain level of death penalty activity and that this level is relatively stable over time, irrespective of the particular death penalty scheme in effect. D. Baldus, *When Symbols Clash: Reflections on the Future of the Comparative Proportionality Review of Death Sentences*, 26 Seton Hall L. Rev. 1582, 1591 (1996).

In S. Shatz & N. Rivkind, *The California Death Penalty Scheme: Requiem for Furman?* 72 N.Y.U. L.Rev. 1283 (1997), the authors, citing the Court's opinion in *Zant* and Justice White's explanation in *Gregg*, argue that the central concern of *Furman* was the percentage of statutorily death-eligible murderers who are in fact sentenced to death. When that percentage is too low, there is too high a risk that the penalty is being imposed arbitrarily. Noting that at the time of the *Furman* decision, the justices understood that 15–20% of all murderers were being sentenced to death, the authors contend that any jurisdiction's death penalty scheme which produces a death sentence percentage of less than 20% is unconstitutional. Could a state satisfy the *Furman* principle without narrowing the death-eligible class, either by adopting other safeguards to limit the risk of arbitrariness or by seeking and obtaining a greater number of death sentences?

LOWENFIELD v. PHELPS

484 U.S. 231, 108 S.Ct. 546, 98 L.Ed.2d 568 (1988).

CHIEF JUSTICE REHNQUIST delivered the opinion of the Court.

[Lowenfield was sentenced to death in Louisiana for killing a woman with whom he had lived, three members of her family, and one of her male friends.]

* * *

III

Petitioner advances as a second ground for vacating his sentence of death that the sole aggravating circumstance found by the jury at the

---

a. Justice White's explanation subsequently was adopted by the majority in *Penry v. Lynaugh*, 492 U.S. 302, 327, 109 S.Ct. 2934, 2951 (1989).

sentencing phase was identical to an element of the capital crime of which he was convicted. Petitioner urges that this overlap left the jury at the sentencing phase free merely to repeat one of its findings in the guilt phase, and thus not to narrow further in the sentencing phase the class of death-eligible murderers. Upon consideration of the Louisiana capital punishment scheme in the light of the decisions of this Court we reject this argument.

Louisiana has established five grades of homicide: first-degree murder, second-degree murder, manslaughter, negligent homicide, and vehicular homicide. Second-degree murder includes intentional murder and felony murder, and provides for punishment of life imprisonment without the possibility of parole. Louisiana defines first-degree murder to include a narrower class of homicides:

"First degree murder is the killing of a human being:

"(1) When the offender has specific intent to kill or to inflict great bodily harm and is engaged in the perpetration or attempted perpetration of aggravated kidnapping, aggravated escape, aggravated arson, aggravated rape, aggravated burglary, armed robbery, or simple robbery;

"(2) When the offender has a specific intent to kill or to inflict great bodily harm upon a fireman or peace officer engaged in the performance of his lawful duties;

"(3) When the offender has a specific intent to kill or to inflict great bodily harm upon more than one person;

"(4) When the offender has specific intent to kill or inflict great bodily harm and has offered, has been offered, has given, or has received anything of value for the killing; or

"(5) When the offender has the specific intent to kill or to inflict great bodily harm upon a victim under the age of twelve years."

An individual found guilty of first-degree murder is sentenced by the same jury in a separate proceeding to either death or life imprisonment without benefit of parole, probation, or suspension of sentence. "A sentence of death shall not be imposed unless the jury finds beyond a reasonable doubt that at least one statutory aggravating circumstance exists and, after consideration of any mitigating circumstances, recommends that the sentence of death be imposed." Louisiana has established 10 statutory aggravating circumstances.[6] If the jury returns a sentence of

---

6. "The following shall be considered aggravating circumstances:

"(a) the offender was engaged in the perpetration or attempted perpetration of aggravated rape, aggravated kidnapping, aggravated burglary, aggravated arson, aggravated escape, armed robbery, or simple robbery;

"(b) the victim was a fireman or peace officer engaged in his lawful duties;

"(c) the offender was previously convicted of an unrelated murder, aggravated rape, or aggravated kidnapping or has a significant prior history of criminal activity;

"(d) the offender knowingly created a risk of death or great bodily harm to more than one person;

death, the sentence is automatically reviewable for excessiveness by the Supreme Court of Louisiana.

Petitioner was found guilty of three counts of first-degree murder: "[T]he offender has a specific intent to kill or to inflict great bodily harm upon more than one person." The sole aggravating circumstance both found by the jury and upheld by the Louisiana Supreme Court was that "the offender knowingly created a risk of death or great bodily harm to more than one person." In these circumstances, these two provisions are interpreted in a "parallel fashion" under Louisiana law. Petitioner's argument that the parallel nature of these provisions requires that his sentences be set aside rests on a mistaken premise as to the necessary role of aggravating circumstances.

To pass constitutional muster, a capital sentencing scheme must "genuinely narrow the class of persons eligible for the death penalty and must reasonably justify the imposition of a more severe sentence on the defendant compared to others found guilty of murder." *Zant v. Stephens*, 462 U.S. 862, 103 S.Ct. 2733 (1983). Under the capital sentencing laws of most States, the jury is required during the sentencing phase to find at least one aggravating circumstance before it may impose death. By doing so, the jury narrows the class of persons eligible for the death penalty according to an objective legislative definition. *Zant, supra* ("[S]tatutory aggravating circumstances play a constitutionally necessary function at the stage of legislative definition: they circumscribe the class of persons eligible for the death penalty").

In *Zant v. Stephens, supra*, we upheld a sentence of death imposed pursuant to the Georgia capital sentencing statute, under which "the finding of an aggravating circumstance does not play any role in guiding the sentencing body in the exercise of its discretion, apart from its function of narrowing the class of persons convicted of murder who are eligible for the death penalty." We found no constitutional deficiency in that scheme because the aggravating circumstances did all that the Constitution requires.

The use of "aggravating circumstances" is not an end in itself, but a means of genuinely narrowing the class of death-eligible persons and thereby channeling the jury's discretion. We see no reason why this

"(e) the offender offered or has been offered or has given or received anything of value for the commission of the offense;

"(f) the offender at the time of the commission of the offense was imprisoned after sentence for the commission of an unrelated forcible felony;

"(g) the offense was committed in an especially heinous, atrocious, or cruel manner;

"(h) the victim was a witness in a prosecution against the defendant, gave material assistance to the state in any investigation or prosecution of the defendant, or was an eyewitness to a crime alleged to have been committed by the defendant or possessed other material evidence against the defendant;

"(i) the victim was a correctional officer or any other employee of the Louisiana Department of Corrections who, in the normal course of his employment was required to come in close contact with persons incarcerated in a state prison facility, and the victim was engaged in his lawful duties at the time of the offense."

narrowing function may not be performed by jury findings at either the sentencing phase of the trial or the guilt phase. Our opinion in *Jurek v. Texas*, 428 U.S. 262, 96 S.Ct. 2950 (1976), establishes this point. The *Jurek* Court upheld the Texas death penalty statute, which, like the Louisiana statute, narrowly defined the categories of murders for which a death sentence could be imposed. If the jury found the defendant guilty of such a murder, it was required to impose death so long as it found beyond a reasonable doubt that the defendant's acts were deliberate, the defendant would probably constitute a continuing threat to society, and, if raised by the evidence, the defendant's acts were an unreasonable response to the victim's provocation. We concluded that the latter three elements allowed the jury to consider the mitigating aspects of the crime and the unique characteristics of the perpetrator, and therefore sufficiently provided for jury discretion. But the opinion announcing the judgment noted the difference between the Texas scheme, on the one hand, and the Georgia and Florida schemes discussed in the cases of *Gregg, supra*, and *Proffitt v. Florida*, 428 U.S. 242, 96 S.Ct. 2960 (1976):

> "While Texas has not adopted a list of statutory aggravating circumstances the existence of which can justify the imposition of the death penalty as have Georgia and Florida, its action in narrowing the categories of murders for which a death sentence may ever be imposed serves much the same purpose. . . . In fact, each of the five classes of murders made capital by the Texas statute is encompassed in Georgia and Florida by one or more of their statutory aggravating circumstances. . . . Thus, in essence, the Texas statute requires that the jury find the existence of a statutory aggravating circumstance before the death penalty may be imposed. So far as consideration of aggravating circumstances is concerned, therefore, the principal difference between Texas and the other two States is that the death penalty is an available sentencing option—even potentially—for a smaller class of murders in Texas."

It seems clear to us from this discussion that the narrowing function required for a regime of capital punishment may be provided in either of these two ways: The legislature may itself narrow the definition of capital offenses, as Texas and Louisiana have done, so that the jury finding of guilt responds to this concern, or the legislature may more broadly define capital offenses and provide for narrowing by jury findings of aggravating circumstances at the penalty phase.

Here, the "narrowing function" was performed by the jury at the guilt phase when it found defendant guilty of three counts of murder under the provision that "the offender has a specific intent to kill or to inflict great bodily harm upon more than one person." The fact that the sentencing jury is also required to find the existence of an aggravating circumstance in addition is no part of the constitutionally required narrowing process, and so the fact that the aggravating circumstance duplicated one of the elements of the crime does not make this sentence constitutionally infirm. There is no question but that the Louisiana scheme narrows the class of death-eligible murderers and then at the sentencing phase allows for the consideration of mitigating circumstances and the exercise of discretion. The Constitution requires no more.

The judgment of the Court of Appeals for the Fifth Circuit is accordingly affirmed.

JUSTICE MARSHALL, with whom JUSTICE BRENNAN joins, and JUSTICE STEVENS joins as to Part I, dissenting:

* * *

Since our decision in *Furman v. Georgia*, 408 U.S. 238, 92 S.Ct. 2726 (1972), we have required that there be a "meaningful basis for distinguishing the few cases in which [the death sentence] is imposed from the many cases in which it is not." Id., at 313 (WHITE, J., concurring). We have held consistently that statutory aggravating circumstances considered during the sentencing process provide one of the means by which the jury's discretion is guided in making such constitutionally mandated distinctions. See, e.g., *McCleskey v. Kemp*, 481 U.S. 279, 107 S.Ct. 1756 (1987) (describing "the role of the aggravating circumstance in guiding the sentencing jury's discretion"); *Zant v. Stephens*, 462 U.S. 862, 103 S.Ct. 2733 (1983) (holding that "an aggravating circumstance must genuinely narrow the class of persons eligible for the death penalty"); *Gregg v. Georgia*, 428 U.S. 153, 96 S.Ct. 2909 (opinion of STEWART, POWELL, and STEVENS, JJ.) (explaining that the finding of statutory aggravating circumstances helps the jury "to consider the circumstances of the crime and the criminal before it recommends sentence").

The Court today suggests that our emphasis on aggravating circumstances has been mere happenstance and holds that the critical narrowing function may be performed prior to and distinct from the sentencing process.[4] This holding misunderstands the significance of the narrowing requirement. The Court treats the narrowing function as a merely technical requirement that the number of those eligible for the death penalty be made smaller than the number of those convicted of murder. But narrowing the class of death eligible offenders is not "an end in itself" any more than aggravating circumstances are. Rather, as our cases have emphasized consistently, the narrowing requirement is meant to channel the discretion of the sentencer. It forces the capital sentencing jury to approach its

---

4. The Court argues that our opinion in *Jurek v. Texas*, 428 U.S. 262, 96 S.Ct. 2950 (1976), establishes that the narrowing requirement may constitutionally be met at the guilt phase rather than the sentencing phase. It focuses on dicta in the opinion announcing the judgment to the effect that the classes of capital murder established by the Texas Legislature serve " 'much the same purpose' " as a list of statutory aggravating circumstances. The Court ignores our later recognition that the three questions posed to the jury during the sentencing phase under the scheme approved in *Jurek* establish additional aggravating circumstances not already determined during the guilt phase. Hence, *Jurek* cannot establish our approval of a divorce of the narrowing requirement from the sentencing proceedings. Moreover, even if *Jurek* did stand for the proposition advanced by the Court, it would still be distinguishable from the instant case. Under the Texas capital sentencing statute evaluated in *Jurek*, jurors are explicitly instructed at the guilt phase that their findings would make the defendant eligible for the death penalty. In the instant case, the jurors were specifically instructed not to consider the penalty that might result from their findings during the guilt phase.

task in a structured, step-by-step way, first determining whether a defendant is eligible for the death penalty and then determining whether all of the circumstances justify its imposition. The only conceivable reason for making narrowing a constitutional requirement is its function in structuring sentencing deliberations. By permitting the removal of the narrowing function from the sentencing process altogether, the Court reduces it to a mechanical formality entirely unrelated to the choice between life and death.

* * *

In sum, the application of the Louisiana sentencing scheme in cases like this one, where there is a complete overlap between aggravating circumstances found at the sentencing phase and elements of the offense previously found at the guilt phase, violates constitutional principles in ways that will inevitably tilt the sentencing scales toward the imposition of the death penalty. The State will have an easier time convincing a jury beyond a reasonable doubt to find a necessary element of a capital offense at the guilt phase of a trial if the jury is unaware that such a finding will make the defendant eligible for the death penalty at the sentencing phase. Then the State will have an even easier time arguing for the imposition of the death penalty, because it can remind the jury at the sentencing phase, as it did in this case, that the necessary aggravating circumstances already have been established beyond a reasonable doubt. The State thus enters the sentencing hearing with the jury already across the threshold of death eligibility, without any awareness on the jury's part that it had crossed that line. By permitting such proceedings in a capital case, the Court ignores our early pronouncement that "a State may not entrust the determination of whether a man should live or die to a tribunal organized to return a verdict of death." *Witherspoon v. Illinois*, 391 U.S. 510, 88 S.Ct. 1770 (1968).

* * *

NOTES

1. *Problem 3–1.*

Defendant was convicted of murder and sentenced to prison. He made plans to kill Witness, who had testified against him. From his prison cell he directed two accomplices in the construction of a mail bomb, which they sent to Witness. Witness's father picked up the mail and was killed when the bomb went off. Defendant is charged in federal court with a violation of 18 U.S.C. § 844(d):

> Whoever transports or receives, or attempts to transport or receive, in interstate commerce or foreign commerce any explosive with the knowledge or intent that it will be used to kill, injure, or intimidate any individual or unlawfully to damage or destroy any building, vehicle, or other real or personal property, shall be imprisoned ...; and if ... death results to any person, including any public safety officer performing

duties as a direct or proximate result of conduct prohibited by this subsection, shall be subject to imprisonment for any term of years, or to the death penalty or life imprisonment . . .

What arguments should be made as to the constitutionality of the death penalty for this crime? See *United States v. Cheely*, 36 F.3d 1439 (9th Cir. 1994).

2. *"No-narrowing" challenges in the state courts.*

The leading state court no-narrowing challenge is *State v. Middlebrooks*, 840 S.W.2d 317 (Tenn. 1992). Under the Tennessee scheme in effect at the time of the murder, the commission of felony-murder *simpliciter* (*i.e.*, felony-murder without proof that the defendant had any *mens rea* as to the homicide) was sufficient to convict a defendant of first degree murder and, because felony-murder was an aggravating circumstance, to make the defendant death-eligible. The Tennessee Supreme Court held that the scheme failed to narrow sufficiently since the broad definition of felony-murder, coupled with the duplicating language of the aggravating circumstance, meant that an unacceptably large number of first degree murderers were automatically death-eligible. *Id.* at 346. The court also questioned whether the scheme met the qualitative prong of the *Furman* principle since the result of the felony-murder aggravating circumstance was to treat those who committed an unintentional felony-murder more harshly than those who killed with premeditation and deliberation. *Id.* at 345. The United States Supreme Court granted, but then dismissed, certiorari without deciding the case. *Tennessee v. Middlebrooks*, 510 U.S. 124, 114 S.Ct. 651 (1993).

Furman challenges to other state schemes have been uniformly unsuccessful, and the courts considering such challenges have usually rejected them without analysis. For example, in *State v. Young*, 853 P.2d 327 (Utah 1993), a no-narrowing challenge to the Utah death penalty scheme, Justice Durham, in dissent, argued at length that the statutes failed to narrow because the seventeen separate aggravating circumstances making a murderer death eligible "include[d] more categories of death-eligible murders than that of any other state, but also it *exclude[d]* almost no intentional killings at all." "In short, Utah's statutory definition of capital homicide * * * has in effect returned the state to where it was before *Furman* was decided; there is no meaningful narrowing of the class of death-eligible murders pursuant to objective, rational standards." *Id.* at 398–399. The majority rejected the claim without explanation, but Justice Zimmerman, in his concurring opinion, responded to Justice Durham by questioning whether *Furman* required quantitative narrowing at all. *Id.* at 412–413. In *State v. Wagner*, 752 P.2d 1136 (Or. 1988), the defendant's challenge to the Oregon death penalty scheme also was based on the number of aggravating circumstances—26 by the defendant's count. The Oregon Supreme Court rejected the challenge because the defendant had overcounted the circumstances by counting separately each form of felony-murder and each category of specially-identified victims. None of these challenges relied on empirical evidence about the narrowing effect of the state statutes.

3. *Problem 3–2.*

The statutes establishing the California death penalty scheme are set out in the Appendix. The statutory narrowing requirement is addressed by the special circumstances listed in Penal Code § 190.2(a). A defendant convicted of first degree murder is death-eligible if the fact-finder finds one of twenty-two enumerated special circumstances (encompassing thirty-three types of murder) true beyond a reasonable doubt. The special circumstances may be grouped as follows:

2 "other murder" circumstances: the defendant was convicted of more than one murder ((a)(3)) or was previously convicted of murder ((a)(2));

8 "victim" circumstances: the defendant intentionally killed a peace officer ((a)(7)), federal law enforcement officer or agent ((a)(8)), firefighter ((a)(9)), witness ((a)(10)), prosecutor or former prosecutor ((a)(11)), judge or former judge ((a)(12)), elected official or former elected official ((a)(13)) or juror ((a)(20));

7 "manner" circumstances: the murder was committed by a destructive device, bomb or explosive planted ((a)(4)) or mailed ((a)(6)) or was intentionally committed by lying in wait ((a)(15)), by the infliction of torture ((a)(18)), by poison ((a)(19)), by shooting from a motor vehicle ((a)(21)), or in furtherance of the activities of a criminal street gang ((a)(22)).

3 "motive" circumstances: the defendant committed the murder for financial gain ((a)(1)), to escape arrest ((a)(5)), or because of the victim's race, color, religion, national origin or country of origin ((a)(16));

12 felony circumstances: the murder was committed while the defendant was engaged in, or was the accomplice in, the commission of, attempted commission of, or the immediate flight after committing, or attempting to commit, robbery, kidnapping, rape, sodomy, child molestation, forcible oral copulation, burglary, arson, train wrecking, mayhem, rape by instrument or carjacking ((a)(17));

1 "catchall" circumstance: the murder was especially heinous, atrocious or cruel ((a)(14)).[a]

Defendant was found guilty of first degree murder during a burglary and robbery and sentenced to death. He has introduced evidence of an empirical study of California first degree murders showing: that 84% of convicted first degree murderers are statutorily death-eligible; that 9.6% of convicted first degree murderers are sentenced to death; and that the death sentence rate for death-eligible murderers is approximately 11.4%. What arguments should be made on his challenge to the constitutionality of the death sentence? See *People v. Musselwhite*, 954 P.2d 475 (Cal. 1998).

---

a. This circumstance was held unconstitutional on vagueness grounds. See *People v. Superior Court (Engert)*, 647 P.2d 76 (Cal. 1982). Nevertheless, it has been reenacted with each amendment to § 190.2 (see *e.g.*, 1995 Cal. Stat. ch. 478, enacted by Proposition 196 (approved March 26, 1996) § 2).

GODFREY v. GEORGIA

446 U.S. 420, 100 S.Ct. 1759, 64 L.Ed.2d 398 (1980).

MR. JUSTICE STEWART announced the judgment of the Court and delivered an opinion, in which MR. JUSTICE BLACKMUN, MR. JUSTICE POWELL, and MR. JUSTICE STEVENS joined.

Under Georgia law, a person convicted of murder[1] may be sentenced to death if it is found beyond a reasonable doubt that the offense "was outrageously or wantonly vile, horrible or inhuman in that it involved torture, depravity of mind, or an aggravated battery to the victim." In *Gregg v. Georgia*, 428 U.S. 153, 96 S.Ct. 2909 (1976), the Court held that this statutory aggravating circumstance (§ (b)(7)) is not unconstitutional on its face. Responding to the argument that the language of the provision is "so broad that capital punishment could be imposed in any murder case," the joint opinion said:

> "It is, of course, arguable that any murder involves depravity of mind or an aggravated battery. But this language need not be construed in this way, and there is no reason to assume that the Supreme Court of Georgia will adopt such an open-ended construction." (opinion of STEWART, POWELL, and STEVENS, JJ.).

Nearly four years have passed since the *Gregg* decision, and during that time many death sentences based in whole or in part on § (b)(7) have been affirmed by the Supreme Court of Georgia. The issue now before us is whether, in affirming the imposition of the sentences of death in the present case, the Georgia Supreme Court has adopted such a broad and vague construction of the § (b)(7) aggravating circumstance as to violate the Eighth and Fourteenth Amendments to the United States Constitution.

I

On a day in early September in 1977, the petitioner and his wife of 28 years had a heated argument in their home. During the course of this altercation, the petitioner, who had consumed several cans of beer, threatened his wife with a knife and damaged some of her clothing. At this point, the petitioner's wife declared that she was going to leave him, and departed to stay with relatives.[3] That afternoon she went to a Justice of the Peace and secured a warrant charging the petitioner with aggravated assault. A few days later, while still living away from home, she filed suit for divorce. Summons was served on the petitioner, and a court hearing

---

1. Georgia Code § 26–1101 (1978) defines "murder" as follows:

"(a) A person commits murder when he unlawfully and with malice aforethought, either express or implied, causes the death of another human being. Express malice is that deliberate intention unlawfully to take away the life of a fellow creature, which is manifested by external circumstances capable of proof. Malice shall be implied where no considerable provocation appears, and where all the circumstances of the killing show an abandoned and malignant heart.

"(b) A person also commits the crime of murder when in the commission of a felony he causes the death of another human being, irrespective of malice."

3. According to the petitioner, this was not the first time that he and his wife had been separated as a result of his violent behavior. On two or more previous occasions the petitioner had been hospitalized because of his drinking problem.

was set on a date some two weeks later. Before the date of the hearing, the petitioner on several occasions asked his wife to return to their home. Each time his efforts were rebuffed. At some point during this period, his wife moved in with her mother. The petitioner believed that his mother-in-law was actively instigating his wife's determination not to consider a possible reconciliation.

In the early evening of September 20, according to the petitioner, his wife telephoned him at home. Once again they argued. She asserted that reconciliation was impossible and allegedly demanded all the proceeds from the planned sale of their house. The conversation was terminated after she said that she would call back later. This she did in an hour or so. The ensuing conversation was, according to the petitioner's account, even more heated than the first. His wife reiterated her stand that reconciliation was out of the question, said that she still wanted all proceeds from the sale of their house, and mentioned that her mother was supporting her position. Stating that she saw no further use in talking or arguing, she hung up.

At this juncture, the petitioner got out his shotgun and walked with it down the hill from his home to the trailer where his mother-in-law lived. Peering through a window, he observed his wife, his mother-in-law, and his 11–year–old daughter playing a card game. He pointed the shotgun at his wife through the window and pulled the trigger. The charge from the gun struck his wife in the forehead and killed her instantly. He proceeded into the trailer, striking and injuring his fleeing daughter with the barrel of the gun. He then fired the gun at his mother-in-law, striking her in the head and killing her instantly.

The petitioner then called the local sheriff's office, identified himself, said where he was, explained that he had just killed his wife and mother-in-law, and asked that the sheriff come and pick him up. Upon arriving at the trailer, the law enforcement officers found the petitioner seated on a chair in open view near the driveway. He told one of the officers that "they're dead, I killed them" and directed the officer to the place where he had put the murder weapon. Later the petitioner told a police officer: "I've done a hideous crime, . . . but I have been thinking about it for eight years . . . I'd do it again."

The petitioner was subsequently indicted on two counts of murder and one count of aggravated assault. He pleaded not guilty and relied primarily on a defense of temporary insanity at his trial. The jury returned verdicts of guilty on all three counts.

The sentencing phase of the trial was held before the same jury. No further evidence was tendered, but counsel for each side made arguments to the jury. Three times during the course of his argument, the prosecutor stated that the case involved no allegation of "torture" or of an "aggravated battery." When counsel had completed their arguments, the trial judge instructed the jury orally and in writing on the standards that must guide them in imposing sentence. Both orally and in writing, the judge quoted to the jury the statutory language of the § (b)(7) aggravating circumstance in its entirety.

The jury imposed sentences of death on both of the murder convictions. As to each, the jury specified that the aggravating circumstance they had found beyond a reasonable doubt was "that the offense of murder was outrageously or wantonly vile, horrible and inhuman."

In accord with Georgia law in capital cases, the trial judge prepared a report in the form of answers to a questionnaire for use on appellate review. One question on the form asked whether or not the victim had been "physically harmed or tortured." The trial judge's response was "No, as to both victims, excluding the actual murdering of the two victims."[4]

The Georgia Supreme Court affirmed the judgments of the trial court in all respects. With regard to the imposition of the death sentence for each of the two murder convictions, the court rejected the petitioner's contention that § (b)(7) is unconstitutionally vague. The court noted that Georgia's death penalty legislation had been upheld in *Gregg v. Georgia*, and cited its prior decisions upholding § (b)(7) in the face of similar vagueness challenges. As to the petitioner's argument that the jury's phraseology was, as a matter of law, an inadequate statement of § (b)(7), the court responded by simply observing that the language "was not objectionable." The court found no evidence that the sentence had been "imposed under the influence of passion, prejudice, or any other arbitrary factor," held that the sentence was neither excessive nor disproportionate to the penalty imposed in similar cases, and stated that the evidence supported the jury's finding of the § (b)(7) statutory aggravating circumstance. Two justices dissented.

II

In *Furman v. Georgia*, 408 U.S. 238, 92 S.Ct. 2726 (1972) the Court held that the penalty of death may not be imposed under sentencing procedures that create a substantial risk that the punishment will be inflicted in an arbitrary and capricious manner. *Gregg v. Georgia, supra*, reaffirmed this holding:

> "[W]here discretion is afforded a sentencing body on a matter so grave as the determination of whether a human life should be taken or spared, that discretion must be suitably directed and limited so as to minimize the risk of wholly arbitrary and capricious action." (opinion of STEWART, POWELL, and STEVENS, JJ.).

A capital sentencing scheme must, in short, provide a " 'meaningful basis for distinguishing the few cases in which [the penalty] is imposed from the many cases in which it is not.' " quoting *Furman v. Georgia* (WHITE, J., concurring).

---

4. Another question on the form asked the trial judge to list the mitigating circumstances that were in evidence. The judge noted that the petitioner had no significant history of prior criminal activity.

This means that if a State wishes to authorize capital punishment it has a constitutional responsibility to tailor and apply its law in a manner that avoids the arbitrary and capricious infliction of the death penalty. Part of a State's responsibility in this regard is to define the crimes for which death may be the sentence in a way that obviates "standardless [sentencing] discretion." It must channel the sentencer's discretion by "clear and objective standards" that provide "specific and detailed guidance," and that "make rationally reviewable the process for imposing a sentence of death." As was made clear in *Gregg*, a death penalty "system could have standards so vague that they would fail adequately to channel the sentencing decision patterns of juries with the result that a pattern of arbitrary and capricious sentencing like that found unconstitutional in *Furman* could occur."

In the case before us the Georgia Supreme Court has affirmed a sentence of death based upon no more than a finding that the offense was "outrageously or wantonly vile, horrible and inhuman." There is nothing in these few words, standing alone, that implies any inherent restraint on the arbitrary and capricious infliction of the death sentence. A person of ordinary sensibility could fairly characterize almost every murder as "outrageously or wantonly vile, horrible and inhuman." Such a view may, in fact, have been one to which the members of the jury in this case subscribed. If so, their preconceptions were not dispelled by the trial judge's sentencing instructions. These gave the jury no guidance concerning the meaning of any of § (b)(7)'s terms. In fact, the jury's interpretation of § (b)(7) can only be the subject of sheer speculation.

The standardless and unchanneled imposition of death sentences in the uncontrolled discretion of a basically uninstructed jury in this case was in no way cured by the affirmance of those sentences by the Georgia Supreme Court. Under state law that court may not affirm a judgment of death until it has independently assessed the evidence of record and determined that such evidence supports the trial judge's or jury's finding of an aggravating circumstance.

In past cases the State Supreme Court has apparently understood this obligation as carrying with it the responsibility to keep § (b)(7) within constitutional bounds. Recognizing that "there is a possibility of abuse of [the § (b)(7)] statutory aggravating circumstance," the court has emphasized that it will not permit the language of that subsection simply to become a "catchall" for cases which do not fit within any other statutory aggravating circumstance. *Harris v. State*, 230 S.E.2d 1 (Ga.1976). Thus, in exercising its function of death sentence review, the court has said that it will restrict its "approval of the death penalty under this statutory aggravating circumstance to those cases that lie at the core."

When *Gregg* was decided by this Court in 1976, the Georgia Supreme Court had affirmed two death sentences based wholly on § (b)(7). See *McCorquodale v. State*, 211 S.E.2d 577 (Ga. 1974); *House v. State*, 205 S.E.2d 217 (Ga. 1974). The homicide in *McCorquodale* was "a horrifying torture-murder." There, the victim had been beaten, burned, raped, and otherwise severely abused before her death by strangulation. The homicide in *House* was of a similar ilk. In that case, the convicted murderer had choked two 7–year–old boys to death after having forced each of them to submit to anal sodomy.

Following our decision in *Gregg*, the Georgia Supreme Court for the first time articulated some of the conclusions it had reached with respect to § (b)(7):

> "This aggravating circumstance involves both the effect on the victim, viz., torture, or an aggravated battery; and the offender, viz., depravity of mind. As to both parties the test is that the acts (the offense) were outrageously or wantonly vile, horrible or inhuman.
>
>   * * *
>
> "We believe that each of [the cases decided to date that has relied exclusively on § (b)(7)] establishes beyond any reasonable doubt a depravity of mind and either involved torture or an aggravated battery to the victim as illustrating the crimes were outrageously or wantonly vile, horrible or inhuman. Each of the cases is at the core and not the periphery ..." *Harris v. State, supra.*

Subsequently, in *Blake v. State*, 236 S.E.2d 637 (Ga. 1977), the court elaborated on its understanding of § (b)(7). There, the contention was that a jury's finding of the aggravating circumstance could never be deemed unanimous without a polling of each member of the panel. The court said:

> "We find no significant dissimilarity between outrageously vile, wantonly vile, horrible or inhuman. Considering torture and aggravated battery on the one hand as substantially similar treatment of the victim and depravity of mind on the other hand as relating to the defendant, we find no room for nonunanimous verdicts for the reason that there is no prohibition upon measuring cause on the one hand by effect on the other hand. That is to say, the depravity of mind contemplated by the statute is that which results in torture or aggravated battery to the victim. ..."

The *Harris* and *Blake* opinions suggest that the Georgia Supreme Court had by 1977 reached three separate but consistent conclusions respecting the § (b)(7) aggravating circumstance. The first was that the evidence that the offense was "outrageously or wantonly vile, horrible or inhuman" had to demonstrate "torture, depravity of mind, or an aggravated battery to the victim." The second was that the phrase, "depravity of mind," comprehended only the kind of mental state that led the murderer to torture or to commit an aggravated battery before killing his victim. The third, derived from *Blake* alone, was that the word, "torture," must be construed in pari materia with "aggravated battery" so as to require evidence of serious physical abuse of the victim before death. Indeed, the circumstances proved in a number of the § (b)(7) death sentence cases affirmed by the Georgia Supreme Court have met all three of these criteria.

The Georgia courts did not, however, so limit § (b)(7) in the present case. No claim was made, and nothing in the record before us suggests, that the petitioner committed an aggravated battery upon his wife or mother-in-law or, in fact, caused either of them to suffer any physical injury preceding their deaths. Moreover, in the trial court, the prosecutor repeatedly told the jury—and the trial judge wrote in his sentencing report—that the murders did not involve "torture." Nothing said on appeal by the Georgia Supreme Court indicates that it took a different view of the evidence. The circumstances of this case, therefore, do not satisfy the criteria laid out by the Georgia Supreme Court itself in the *Harris* and *Blake* cases. In holding that the evidence supported the jury's § (b)(7) finding, the State Supreme Court simply asserted that the verdict was "factually substantiated."

Thus, the validity of the petitioner's death sentences turns on whether, in light of the facts and circumstances of the murders that he was convicted of committing, the Georgia Supreme Court can be said to have applied a constitutional construction of the phrase "outrageously or wantonly vile, horrible or inhuman in that [they] involved ... depravity of mind ..."[15] We conclude that the answer must be no. The petitioner's crimes cannot be said to have reflected a consciousness materially more "depraved" than that of any person guilty of murder. His victims were killed instantaneously.[16] They were members of his family who were causing him extreme emotional trauma. Shortly after the killings, he acknowledged his responsibility and the heinous nature of his crimes. These factors certainly did not remove the criminality from the petitioner's acts. But, as was said in *Gardner v. Florida*, 430 U.S. 349, 97 S.Ct. 1197 (1977), it "is of vital importance to the defendant and to the community that any decision to impose the death sentence be, and appear to be, based on reason rather than caprice or emotion."

That cannot be said here. There is no principled way to distinguish this case, in which the death penalty was imposed, from the many cases in which it was not. Accordingly, the judgment of the Georgia Supreme Court insofar as it leaves standing the petitioner's death sentences is reversed, and the case is remanded to that court for further proceedings.

> [Concurring opinion of MARSHALL, J. joined by BRENNAN, J. and dissenting opinions of BURGER, C.J. and WHITE, J., joined by REHNQUIST, J. omitted]

---

15. The sentences of death in this case rested exclusively on § (b)(7). Accordingly, we intimate no view as to whether or not the petitioner might constitutionally have received the same sentences on some other basis. Georgia does not, as do some States, make multiple murders an aggravating circumstance, as such.

16. In light of this fact, it is constitutionally irrelevant that the petitioner used a shotgun instead of a rifle as the murder weapon, resulting in a gruesome spectacle in his mother-in-law's trailer. An interpretation of § (b)(7) so as to include all murders resulting in gruesome scenes would be totally irrational.

NOTE

1. *Other versions of "vile, horrible or inhuman."*

Earlier, in *Proffitt v. Florida*, 428 U.S. 242, 96 S.Ct. 2960 (1976), the Supreme Court had upheld Florida's "especially heinous, atrocious or cruel" aggravating circumstance on the ground that the Florida Supreme Court had given the circumstance the following limiting construction: "the conscience-less or pitiless crime which is unnecessarily torturous to the victim." Later, in *Maynard v. Cartwright*, 486 U.S. 356, 108 S.Ct. 1853 (1988), the Court relied on *Godfrey* to invalidate Oklahoma's "especially heinous, atrocious, or cruel" aggravating circumstance, which had not been given a limiting construction by the Oklahoma Court of Criminal Appeals. In *Walton v. Arizona*, 497 U.S. 639, 110 S.Ct. 3047 (1990), the defendant challenged the aggravating factor that the murder was committed "in an 'especially heinous, cruel or depraved manner.'" The Arizona Supreme Court previously had given the factor a narrowing construction, holding that: (1) "a crime is committed in an especially cruel manner when the perpetrator inflicts mental anguish or physical abuse before the victim's death," and that "[m]ental anguish includes a victim's uncertainty as to his ultimate fate"; and (2) a crime is committed in an especially "depraved" manner when the perpetrator "relishes the murder, evidencing debasement or perversion," or "shows an indifference to the suffering of the victim and evidences a sense of pleasure" in the killing. The Court held (5–4) that the Arizona court's construction met constitutional standards.

ARAVE v. CREECH

507 U.S. 463, 113 S.Ct. 1534, 123 L.Ed.2d 188 (1993).

JUSTICE O'CONNOR delivered the opinion of the Court.

In 1981 Thomas Eugene Creech beat and kicked to death a fellow inmate at the Idaho State Penitentiary. He pleaded guilty to first-degree murder and was sentenced to death. The sentence was based in part on the statutory aggravating circumstance that "[b]y the murder, or circumstances surrounding its commission, the defendant exhibited utter disregard for human life." Idaho Code § 19–2515(g)(6) (1987). The sole question we must decide is whether the "utter disregard" circumstance, as interpreted by the Idaho Supreme Court, adequately channels sentencing discretion as required by the Eighth and Fourteenth Amendments.

I

The facts underlying this case could not be more chilling. Thomas Creech has admitted to killing or participating in the killing of at least 26 people. The bodies of 11 of his victims—who were shot, stabbed, beaten, or strangled to death—have been recovered in seven States. Creech has said repeatedly that, unless he is completely isolated from humanity, he likely will continue killing. And he has identified by name three people outside prison walls he intends to kill if given the opportunity.

Creech's most recent victim was David Dale Jensen, a fellow inmate in the maximum security unit of the Idaho State Penitentiary. When he killed Jensen, Creech was already serving life sentences for other first-degree murders. Jensen, about seven years Creech's junior, was a nonviolent car thief. He was also physically handicapped. Part of Jensen's brain had been removed prior to his incarceration, and he had a plastic plate in his skull.

The circumstances surrounding Jensen's death remain unclear, primarily because Creech has given conflicting accounts of them. In one version, Creech killed Jensen in self-defense. In another—the version that Creech gave at his sentencing hearing—other inmates offered to pay Creech or help him escape if he killed Jensen. Creech, through an intermediary, provided Jensen with makeshift weapons and then arranged for Jensen to attack him, in order to create an excuse for the killing. Whichever of these accounts (if either) is true, the Idaho Supreme Court found that the record supported the following facts:

> "Jensen approached Creech and swung a weapon at him which consisted of a sock containing batteries. Creech took the weapon away from Jensen, who returned to his cell but emerged with a toothbrush to which had been taped a razor blade. When the two men again met, Jensen made some movement toward Creech, who then struck Jensen between the eyes with the battery laden sock, knocking Jensen to the floor. The fight continued, according to Creech's version, with Jensen swinging the razor blade at Creech and Creech hitting Jensen with the battery filled sock. The plate imbedded in Jensen's skull shattered, and blood from Jensen's skull was splashed on the floor and walls. Finally, the sock broke and the batteries fell out, and by that time Jensen was helpless. Creech then commenced kicking Jensen about the throat and head. Sometime later a guard noticed blood, and Jensen was taken to the hospital, where he died the same day."

Creech pleaded guilty to first-degree murder. The trial judge held a sentencing hearing in accordance with Idaho Code § 19–2515(d) (1987). After the hearing, the judge issued written findings in the format prescribed by Rule 33.1 of the Idaho Criminal Rules. Under the heading "Facts and Argument Found in Mitigation," he listed that Creech "did not instigate the fight with the victim, but the victim, without provocation, attacked him. [Creech] was initially justified in protecting himself." Under the heading "Facts and Argumen[t] Found in Aggravation," the judge stated:

> "[T]he victim, once the attack commenced, was under the complete domination and control of the defendant. The murder itself was extremely gruesome evidencing an excessive violent rage. With the victim's attack as an excuse, the . . . murder then took on many of the aspects of an assassination. These violent actions . . . went well beyond self-defense.

* * *

> "... The murder, once commenced, appears to have been an intentional, calculated act."

The judge then found beyond a reasonable doubt five statutory aggravating circumstances, including that Creech, "[b]y the murder, or circumstances surrounding its commission, ... exhibited utter disregard for human life." He observed in this context that "[a]fter the victim was helpless [Creech] killed him." Next, the judge concluded that the mitigating circumstances did not outweigh the aggravating circumstances. Reiterating that Creech "intentionally destroyed another human being at a time when he was completely helpless," the judge sentenced Creech to death.

After temporarily remanding for the trial judge to impose sentence in open court in Creech's presence, the Idaho Supreme Court affirmed. The court rejected Creech's argument that the "utter disregard" circumstance is unconstitutionally vague, reaffirming the limiting construction it had placed on the statutory language in *State v. Osborn*, 631 P.2d 187 (Ida. 1981):

> " 'A ... limiting construction must be placed upon the aggravating circumstances in I.C. § 19–2515[g](6), that "[b]y the murder, or the circumstances surrounding its commission, the defendant exhibited utter disregard for human life." To properly define this circumstance, it is important to note the other aggravating circumstances with which this provision overlaps. The second aggravating circumstance, I.C. § 19–2515[g](2), that the defendant committed another murder at the time this murder was committed, obviously could show an utter disregard for human life, as could the third aggravating circumstance, I.C. § 19–2515[g](3), that the defendant knowingly created a great risk of death to many persons. The same can be said for the fourth aggravating circumstance, I.C. § 19–2515[g](4), that the murder was committed for remuneration. Since we will not presume that the legislative intent was to duplicate any already enumerated circumstance, thus making [the "utter disregard" circumstance] mere surplusage, we hold that the phrase "utter disregard" must be viewed in reference to acts other than those set forth in I.C. §§ 19–2515[g](2), (3), and (4). We conclude instead that the phrase is meant to be reflective of acts or circumstances surrounding the crime which exhibit the highest, the utmost, callous disregard for human life, *i.e.*, the cold-blooded, pitiless slayer.' " (quoting *Osborn, supra*).

[Creech petitioned for federal habeas corpus, and, after the District Court denied relief, the Court of Appeals reversed, holding that the "utter disregard" circumstance was unconstitutionally vague.]

Unlike the Court of Appeals, we do not believe it is necessary to decide whether the statutory phrase "utter disregard for human life" itself passes constitutional muster. The Idaho Supreme Court has adopted a limiting construction, and we believe that construction meets constitutional requirements.

Contrary to the dissent's assertions, the phrase "cold-blooded, pitiless slayer" is not without content. Webster's Dictionary defines "pitiless" to mean devoid of, or unmoved by, mercy or compassion. The lead entry for "cold-blooded" gives coordinate definitions. One, "marked by absence of warm feelings: without consideration, compunction, or clemency," mirrors the definition of "pitiless." The other defines "cold-blooded" to mean "matter of fact, emotionless." It is true that "cold-blooded" is sometimes also used to describe "premedita[tion]," Black's Law Dictionary 260 (6th ed. 1990)—a mental state that may coincide with, but is distinct from, a lack of feeling or compassion. But premeditation is clearly not the sense in which the Idaho Supreme Court used the word "cold-blooded" in *Osborn*. Other terms in the limiting construction—"callous" and "pitiless"— indicate that the court used the word "cold-blooded" in its first sense. "Premedita[tion]," moreover, is specifically addressed elsewhere in the Idaho homicide statutes; had the *Osborn* court meant premeditation, it likely would have used the statutory language.

In ordinary usage, then, the phrase "cold-blooded, pitiless slayer" refers to a killer who kills without feeling or sympathy. We assume that legislators use words in their ordinary, everyday senses, and there is no reason to suppose that judges do otherwise. The dissent questions our resort to dictionaries for the common meaning of the word "cold-blooded," but offers no persuasive authority to suggest that the word, in its present context, means anything else.

The Court of Appeals thought the *Osborn* limiting construction inadequate not because the phrase "cold-blooded, pitiless slayer" lacks meaning, but because it requires the sentencer to make a "subjective determination." We disagree. We are not faced with pejorative adjectives such as "especially heinous, atrocious, or cruel" or "outrageously or wantonly vile, horrible and inhuman"—terms that describe a crime as a whole and that this Court has held to be unconstitutionally vague. The terms "cold-blooded" and "pitiless" describe the defendant's state of mind: not his mens rea, but his attitude toward his conduct and his victim. The law has long recognized that a defendant's state of mind is not a "subjective" matter, but a fact to be inferred from the surrounding circumstances.

Determining whether a capital defendant killed without feeling or sympathy is undoubtedly more difficult than, for example, determining whether he "was previously convicted of another murder." But that does not mean that a State cannot, consistent with the Federal Constitution, authorize sentencing judges to make the inquiry and to take their findings into account when deciding whether capital punishment is warranted. This is the import of *Walton v. Arizona*, 497 U.S. 639, 110 S.Ct. 3047 (1990). In that case we considered Arizona's "especially heinous, cruel, or depraved" circumstance. The Arizona Supreme Court had held that a crime is committed in a "depraved" manner when the perpetrator " 'relishes the murder, evidencing debasement or perversion,' or 'shows an indifference to the suffering of the victim and evidences a sense of pleasure' in the killing." We concluded that this construction adequately guided sentencing discretion, even though "the proper degree of definition of an aggravating factor of this nature is not susceptible of mathematical precision."

The language at issue here is no less "clear and objective" than the language sustained in *Walton*. Whether a defendant "relishes" or derives "pleasure" from his crime arguably may be easier to determine than whether he acts without feeling or sympathy, since enjoyment is an affirmative mental state, whereas the cold-bloodedness inquiry in a sense requires the sentencer to find a negative. But we do not think so subtle a distinction has constitutional significance. The *Osborn* limiting construction, like the one upheld in *Walton*, defines a state of mind that is ascertainable from surrounding facts. Accordingly, we decline to invalidate the "utter disregard" circumstance on the ground that the Idaho Supreme Court's limiting construction is insufficiently "objective."

Of course, it is not enough for an aggravating circumstance, as construed by the state courts, to be determinate. Our precedents make clear that a State's capital sentencing scheme also must "genuinely narrow the class of persons eligible for the death penalty." *Zant v. Stephens*, 462 U.S. 862, 103 S.Ct. 2733 (1983). When the purpose of a statutory aggravating circumstance is to enable the sentencer to distinguish those who deserve capital punishment from those who do not, the circumstance must provide a principled basis for doing so. If the sentencer fairly could conclude that an aggravating circumstance applies to every defendant eligible for the death penalty, the circumstance is constitutionally infirm.

Although the question is close, we believe the *Osborn* construction satisfies this narrowing requirement. The class of murderers eligible for capital punishment under Idaho law is defined broadly to include all first-degree murderers. And the category of first-degree murderers is also broad. * * * In other words, a sizable class of even those murderers who kill with some provocation or without specific intent may receive the death penalty under Idaho law.

We acknowledge that, even within these broad categories, the word "pitiless," standing alone, might not narrow the class of defendants eligible for the death penalty. A sentencing judge might conclude that every first-degree murderer is "pitiless," because it is difficult to imagine how a person with any mercy or compassion could kill another human being without justification. Given the statutory scheme, however, we believe that a sentencing judge reasonably could find that not all Idaho capital defendants are "cold-blooded." That is because some within the broad class of first-degree murderers do exhibit feeling. Some, for example, kill with anger, jealousy, revenge, or a variety of other emotions. In *Walton* we held that Arizona could treat capital defendants who take pleasure in killing as more deserving of the death penalty than those who do not. Idaho similarly has identified the subclass of defendants who kill without feeling or sympathy as more deserving of death. By doing so, it has narrowed in a meaningful way the category of defendants upon whom capital punishment may be imposed.

Creech argues that the Idaho courts have not applied the "utter disregard" circumstance consistently. He points out that the courts have found defendants to exhibit "utter disregard" in a wide range of cases. This, he claims, demonstrates that the circumstance is nothing more than a catch-all. The dissent apparently agrees. The State, in turn, offers its own review of the cases and contends that they are consistent. In essence, the parties and the dissent would have us determine the facial constitutionality of the "utter disregard" circumstance, as construed in *Osborn*, by examining applications of the circumstance in cases not before us.

As an initial matter, we do not think the fact that "[a]ll kinds of ... factors," may demonstrate the requisite state of mind renders the *Osborn* construction facially invalid. That the Idaho courts may find first-degree murderers to be "cold-blooded" and "pitiless" in a wide range of circumstances is unsurprising. It also is irrelevant to the question before us. * * * To be sure, we previously have examined other state decisions when the construction of an aggravating circumstance has been unclear. * * * Under our precedents, a federal court may consider state court formulations of a limiting construction to ensure that they are consistent. But our decisions do not authorize review of state court cases to determine whether a limiting construction has been applied consistently.

A comparative analysis of state court cases, moreover, would be particularly inappropriate here. The Idaho Supreme Court upheld Creech's death sentence in 1983—before it had applied *Osborn* to any other set of facts. None of the decisions on which the dissent relies, or upon which Creech asks us to invalidate his death sentence, influenced either the trial judge who sentenced Creech or the appellate judges who upheld the sentence. And there is no question that Idaho's formulation of its limiting construction has been consistent. The Idaho Supreme Court has reaffirmed its original interpretation of "utter disregard" repeatedly, often reciting the definition given in *Osborn* verbatim. It also has explained that "utter disregard" differs from Idaho's "heinous, atrocious or cruel" aggravating circumstance because the *Osborn* construction focuses on the defendant's state of mind. *State v. Fain*, 774 P.2d 252 (Ida. 1989) ("[T]he 'utter disregard' factor refers not to the outrageousness of the acts constituting the murder, but to the defendant's lack of conscientious scruples against killing another human being"). In light of the consistent narrowing definition given the "utter disregard" circumstance by the Idaho Supreme Court, we are satisfied that the circumstance, on its face, meets constitutional standards.

* * *

* * * Accordingly, we hold today only that the "utter disregard" circumstance, as defined in *Osborn*, on its face meets constitutional requirements. The judgment of the Court of Appeals is therefore reversed

in part, and the case is remanded for proceedings consistent with this opinion.

JUSTICE BLACKMUN, with whom JUSTICE STEVENS joins, dissenting.

Confronted with an insupportable limiting construction of an unconstitutionally vague statute, the majority in turn concocts its own limiting construction of the state court's formulation. Like "nonsense upon stilts," however, the majority's reconstruction only highlights the deficient character of the nebulous formulation that it seeks to advance. Because the metaphor "cold-blooded" by which Idaho defines its "utter disregard" circumstance is both vague and unenlightening, and because the majority's recasting of that metaphor is not dictated by common usage, legal usage, or the usage of the Idaho courts, the statute fails to provide meaningful guidance to the sentencer as required by the Constitution. Accordingly, I dissent.

* * *

II

The Idaho Supreme Court has determined that under our cases Idaho's statutory phrase, "utter disregard for human life," requires a limiting construction, see *State v. Osborn*, 631 P.2d 187 (Ida. 1981), and petitioner does not challenge the Court of Appeals' conclusion that the phrase, unadorned, fails to meet constitutional standards. This is understandable. Every first-degree murder will demonstrate a lack of regard for human life, and there is no cause to believe that some murders somehow demonstrate only partial, rather than "utter" disregard. Nor is there any evidence that the phrase is intended to have a specialized meaning—other than that presented by the Idaho Supreme Court in its limiting constructions—that might successfully narrow the eligible class. The question is whether *Osborn*'s limiting construction saves the statute.[2]

Under *Osborn*, an offense demonstrates "utter disregard for human life" when the "acts or circumstances surrounding the crime ... exhibit the highest, the utmost, callous disregard for human life, *i.e.*, the cold-blooded, pitiless slayer." Jettisoning all but the term, "cold-blooded," the majority contends that this cumbersome construction clearly singles out the killing committed "without feeling or sympathy." As an initial matter, I fail to see how "without feeling or sympathy" is meaningfully different from "devoid of ... mercy or compassion"—the definition of "pitiless" that the majority concedes to be constitutionally inadequate.

---

2. Of course, even if the phrase "utter disregard" were narrowing and clear, a purported limiting construction from the State's high court that actually undid any narrowing or clarity would render the statute unconstitutional. For example, if the statute allowed the death sentence where the murder was committed for pay, but an authoritative construction from the State Supreme Court told trial courts that the statute covered every murder committed for "bad reasons," the state scheme would be unconstitutional. In the present case, any clarity that may be imparted, and any channeling that may be done by the phrase, "utter disregard for human life," is destroyed by the boundless and vague *Osborn* construction adopted as the authoritative interpretation of the statute.

Even if there is a distinction, however, the "without feeling or sympathy" test, which never has been articulated by any Idaho court, does not flow ineluctably from the phrase at issue in this case: "cold-blooded." I must stress in this regard the rather obvious point that a "facial" challenge of this nature—one alleging that a limiting construction provides inadequate guidance—cannot be defeated merely by a demonstration that there exists a narrowing way to apply the contested language. The entire point of the challenge is that the language's susceptibility to a variety of interpretations is what makes it (facially) unconstitutional. To save the statute, the State must provide a construction that, on its face, reasonably can be expected to be applied in a consistent and meaningful way so as to provide the sentencer with adequate guidance. The metaphor "cold-blooded" does not do this.

I begin with "ordinary usage." The majority points out that the first definition in Webster's Dictionary under the entry "cold-blooded" is " 'marked by absence of warm feelings: without consideration, compunction, or clemency.' " If Webster's rendition of the term's ordinary meaning is to be credited, then Idaho has singled out murderers who act without warm feelings: those who act without consideration, compunction, or clemency. Obviously that definition is no more illuminating than the adjective "pitiless" as defined by the majority. What murderer does act with consideration or compunction or clemency?[3]

In its eagerness to boil the phrase down to a serviceable core, the majority virtually ignores the very definition it cites. Instead, the majority comes up with a hybrid all its own—"without feeling or sympathy"—and then goes one step further, asserting that because the term "cold-blooded" so obviously means "without feeling," it cannot refer as ordinarily understood to murderers who "kill with anger, jealousy, revenge, or a variety of other emotions." That is incorrect. In everyday parlance, the term "cold-blooded" routinely is used to describe killings that fall outside the majority's definition. In the first nine weeks of this year alone, the label "cold-blooded" has been applied to a murder by an ex-spouse angry over visitation rights,[4] a killing by a jealous lover,[5] a revenge killing,[6] an ex-spouse "full of hatred,"[7] the close-range assassination of an enemy official

---

3. Cf. *State v. Charboneau*, 774 P.2d 299 (Ida. 1989) (Bistline, J., dissenting) ("What first degree murderer fails to show 'callous disregard for human life'? I suppose this would be the 'pitiful' slayer, who, prior to delivering the fatal blow, tells the victim, 'Excuse me, pardon me, I know it's inconvenient, but I must now take your life' ").

4. See Kuczka, Self–Defense Claimed in Murder Trial, Chicago Tribune, Feb. 3, 1993, p. 5 ("To prosecutors, Eric Moen is a cold-blooded killer who gunned down his wife's former boyfriend in a Streamwood restaurant parking [lot] during a quarrel over visitation rights to the ex-boyfriend's infant daughter").

5. See Caba, Friedman Prosecutor Rebuffed, Philadelphia Inquirer, Feb. 19, 1993, p. B3 ("The prosecution contends she killed Edwards in cold blood because he was leaving [her] to return to his wife in Texas").

6. See McMahon, Dad Does Everything Right, But Son Goes Wrong, Chicago Tribune, Mar. 7, 1993, p. 1 (youth who, according to charges, killed victim after saying "he was going to kill him in retaliation for something [the victim] had done" is, "the state reminds, a cold-blooded killer").

7. See Gorman, Millionaire Guilty of Killing Ex–Wife, Chicago Tribune, Feb. 3, 1993, p. 1 ("Assistant State's Atty. Robert Egan portrayed Davis as a 'manipulative,' cold-blooded killer.

by a foe in a bitter ethnic conflict,[8] a murder prompted by humiliation and hatred,[9] killings by fanatical cult members,[10] a murderer who enjoyed killing,[11] and, perhaps most appropriately, all murders.[12] All these killings occurred with "feelings" of one kind or another. All were described as cold-blooded. The majority's assertion that the Idaho construction narrows the class of capital defendants because it rules out those who "kill with anger, jealousy, revenge, or a variety of other emotions" clearly is erroneous, because in ordinary usage the nebulous description "cold-blooded" simply is not limited to defendants who kill without emotion.

In legal usage, the metaphor "cold blood" does have a specific meaning. "Cold blood" is used "to designate a willful, deliberate, and premeditated homicide." Black's Law Dictionary 260 (6th ed. 1990). As such, the term is used to differentiate between first-and second-degree murders. For example, in *United States v. Frady*, 456 U.S. 152 (1982), Justice O'CONNOR, writing for the Court, described the District of Columbia's homicide statute: " 'In homespun terminology, intentional murder is in the first degree if committed in cold blood, and is murder in the second degree if committed on impulse or in the sudden heat of passion.' " Murder in cold blood is, in this sense, the opposite of murder in "hot blood." Arguably, then, the *Osborn* formulation covers every intentional or first-degree murder. An aggravating circumstance so construed would clearly be unconstitutional under *Godfrey*.

Finally, I examine the construction's application by the Idaho courts. The majority acknowledges the appropriateness of examining "other state decisions when the construction of an aggravating circumstance has been unclear," such as where state courts have not adhered to a single limiting construction. Here, however, the majority believes such an inquiry is "irrelevant," because "there is no question that Idaho's formulation of its limiting construction has been consistent." The majority misses the point. Idaho's application of the *Osborn* formulation is relevant not because that formulation has been inconsistently invoked, but because the construction

---

. . . Egan depicted Davis as a man so filled with hatred that he killed Diane Davis two weeks after an Illinois Appellate Court had ruled . . . that he must turn over $1.4 million of his inherited money to his former spouse").

8. See Burns, U.N. to Ask NATO to Airdrop Supplies for Bosnians, N.Y. Times, Jan. 12, 1993, p. A10 (shooting of Bosnian Deputy Prime Minister by Serbian soldier was described by State Department spokesman Richard A. Boucher as "cold-blooded" murder).

9. See Man Gets Life For Double Murder, Toronto Star, Mar. 4, 1993, p. A12 (the prosecution "called it 'a cold-blooded killing' spurred by 'humiliation and hate of these people,' with whom he had squabbled during the 1991 mayoralty campaign").

10. See McKay, Koresh "Smiled Defiantly" Before Ambush, Agent Says, Houston Chronicle, Mar. 5, 1993, p. A1 (" 'These people aren't religious. These people are cold-blooded killers who were shooting at us from every window in that place' ").

11. See Milling, Man Charged in 2 Slayings, Crime Spree, Houston Chronicle, Mar. 5, 1993, p. A23 (" 'I'd describe him as a psychopath who gets his gratification by hurting other people,' Carroll said. 'He's not your typical serial killer. He just likes to pull the trigger and watch people die.' . . . 'We knew this guy was a cold-blooded killer,' Carroll said").

12. See Longenecker, Penalizing Convicts, Chicago Tribune, Mar. 4, 1993, p. 28 (letter) ("[L]egislation to expand the death penalty to include all convicted murderers is long needed. . . . [I]f an individual commits cold-blooded murder he should be removed from our society").

has never meant what the majority says it does. In other words, it is the majority's reconstruction of the (unconstitutional) construction that has not been applied consistently (or ever, for that matter). If, for example, a State declared that "jabberwocky" was an aggravating circumstance, and then carefully invoked "jabberwocky" in every one of its capital cases, this Court could not simply decide that "jabberwocky" means "killing a police officer" and then dispense with any inquiry into whether the term ever had been understood in that way by the State's courts, simply because the "jabberwocky" construction consistently had been reaffirmed.

An examination of the Idaho cases reveals that the *Osborn* formulation is not much better than "jabberwocky." As noted above, the Idaho courts never have articulated anything remotely approaching the majority's novel "those who kill without feeling or sympathy" interpretation. All kinds of other factors, however, have been invoked by Idaho courts applying the circumstance. For example, in *State v. Aragon*, 690 P.2d 293 (Ida. 1984), the killer's cold-bloodedness supposedly was demonstrated by his refusal to render aid to his victim and the fact that "[h]is only concern was to cover up his own participation in the incident." In *State v. Pizzuto* 810 P.2d 680 (Ida. 1991), a finding of "utter disregard" was held to be supported by evidence that the defendant "approached Mr. Herndon with a gun, then made him drop his pants and crawl into the cabin where he proceeded to bludgeon the skulls of both of his victims with a hammer. He then left them lying on the floor to die and Mr. Herndon was left lying on the floor of the cabin convulsing." And, in the present case, the trial judge's determination that Creech exhibited utter disregard for human life appears to have been based primarily on the fact that Creech had "intentionally destroyed another human being at a time when he was completely helpless." Each of these characteristics is frightfully deplorable, but what they have to do with a lack of emotion—or with each other, for that matter—eludes me. Without some rationalizing principle to connect them, the findings of "cold-bloodedness" stand as nothing more than fact-specific, "gut-reaction" conclusions that are unconstitutional under *Maynard v. Cartwright*, 486 U.S. 356, 108 S.Ct. 1853 (1988).

The futility of the Idaho courts' attempt to bring some rationality to the "utter disregard" circumstance is glaringly evident in the sole post-*Osborn* case that endeavors to explain the construction in any depth. In *State v. Fain* 774 P.2d 252 (Ida. 1989), the court declared that the "utter disregard" factor refers to "the defendant's lack of conscientious scruples against killing another human being." Thus, the latest statement from the Idaho Supreme Court on the issue says nothing about emotionless crimes, but, instead, sweepingly includes every murder committed that is without " 'conscientious scruples against killing.' " I can imagine no crime that would not fall within that construction.

Petitioner in his brief embraces *Fain*'s broad construction. "In every case in which the Idaho Supreme Court has upheld a death sentence based wholly or in part on a finding of utter disregard for human life, the defendant had acted without conscientious scruple against killing." Petitioner cites this reassuring fact as the "best evidence that Idaho's utter disregard factor is not so broad that it operates simply as a catch-all for murders not covered by other aggravating circumstances." This "best evidence" is not very good evidence, especially when viewed against the fact that the Idaho Supreme Court never has reversed a finding of utter disregard. Equally unsettling is petitioner's frank admission that the *Osborn* construction "does not make findings of the aggravating factors depend on the presence of particular facts. Instead Idaho has chosen to rely on the ability of the sentencing judge to make principled distinctions between capital and non-capital cases with guidance that is somewhat subjective. . . ." That kind of gestalt approach to capital sentencing is precisely what *Cartwright* and *Godfrey* forbid.

Ultimately, it hardly seems necessary to look beyond the record of this case to determine that either the majority's construction is inadequate, or that there was insufficient evidence to support the "utter disregard" factor here. The record, which the majority takes pains to assure us "could not be more chilling,"[15] includes an explicit finding by the trial judge that Creech was the subject of an unprovoked attack and that the killing took place in an "excessive violent rage." If Creech somehow is covered by the "utter disregard" factor as understood by the majority (one who kills not with anger, but indifference), then there can be no doubt that the factor is so broad as to cover any case. If Creech is not covered, then his sentence was wrongly imposed.

III

Let me be clear about what the majority would have to show in order to save the Idaho statute: that, on its face, the *Osborn* construction—"the highest, the utmost, callous disregard for human life, *i.e.*, the cold-blooded, pitiless slayer"—refers clearly and exclusively to crimes that occur "without feeling or sympathy," that is, to those that occur without "anger, jealousy, revenge, or a variety of other emotions." No such showing has been made.

There is, of course, something distasteful and absurd in the very project of parsing this lexicon of death. But as long as we are in the death business, we shall be in the parsing business as well. Today's majority stretches the bounds of permissible construction past the breaking point. " 'Vague terms do not suddenly become clear when they are defined by reference to other vague terms,' " *Walton v. Arizona* (dissenting opinion), nor do sweeping categories become narrow by mere restatement. The *Osborn* formulation is worthless, and neither common usage, nor legal

---

15. I note that much of the majority's discussion of the "facts underlying this case" centers on Creech's *other* crimes—which obviously do not bear on whether "[b]y the murder, or circumstances surrounding its commission, the defendant exhibited utter disregard for human life"—and on the argument, repeatedly rejected by the state courts, that Creech engineered the fight with Jensen in order to create a pretext for killing him. The Idaho Supreme Court explicitly noted that the trial court did not "find that the murder had been performed on contract or by plan." In fact, the trial court not only found that Jensen's attack was "unprovoked," but it went further and found that the unprovoked nature of the attack actually constituted a mitigating factor.

terminology, nor the Idaho cases support the majority's attempt to salvage it. The statute is simply unconstitutional and Idaho should be busy repairing it.

I would affirm the judgment of the Court of Appeals.

NOTES

1. *Problem 3–3.*

Defendant was convicted of the murder of Wife, who had been shot twice in the head with a .22 caliber pistol. There was evidence that the killing took place because of Defendant's desire to collect Wife's life insurance. Defendant was charged with the aggravating circumstance that the murder was "outrageously or wantonly vile, horrible or inhuman in that it involved ... depravity of mind." State's supreme court had previously articulated a limiting construction for the term "depravity of mind," requiring consideration of the following factors: the "mental state of the defendant, infliction of physical or psychological torture upon the victim as when the victim has a substantial period of time before death to anticipate and reflect upon it; brutality of defendant's conduct; mutilation of the body after death; absence of any substantive motive; absence of defendant's remorse and the nature of the crime." The judge instructed the jury as follows:

> In determining the punishment to be assessed against the defendant for the murder of Wife, you must first unanimously determine whether the murder of Wife involved depravity of mind and whether, as a result thereof, the murder was outrageously and wantonly vile, horrible, and inhuman. You can make a determination of depravity of mind only if you find: That the defendant committed repeated and excessive acts of physical abuse upon Wife and the killing was therefore unreasonably brutal.

The jury returned a death sentence. On appeal, what arguments should be made on the constitutionality of the death sentence? See *State v. Butler*, 951 S.W.2d 600 (Mo. 1997).

2. *The effects of broad death eligibility.*

The principal concern with broad death-eligibility statutes is that they lead to arbitrary imposition of the death penalty, *i.e.*, that, under such schemes, there is no rational distinction between the few who are sent to death row and the many who are not. However, commentators have argued that there are other unacceptable consequences of such schemes. It has been argued that the existence of an overly broad death penalty statute greatly affects those murder defendants who are not ultimately sentenced to death because the threat of the death penalty inevitably works to encourage guilty pleas.

> "[T]here can be little question that the prospect of a death sentence exerts a powerful influence once the defendant has been apprehended and must decide how to plead. Death can be the price for a refusal to plead or otherwise cooperate. Indeed, an examination of the system as it actually operates suggests that in fact the most important function of the death penalty may be to facilitate prosecutors' efforts to induce guilty pleas."

D. Givelber, *The New Law of Murder*, 69 Ind. L.J. 375, 410–11 (1994), quoting Welsh S. White, *The Death Penalty in the Eighties* 46–47 (1987). It has also been argued that overly broad statutes deceive capital juries as to their role in the process by suggesting to them that certain decisions have already been made by the legislature.

> Under the pre-*Furman* scheme in California, juries had complete discretion whether to sentence a convicted first degree murderer to death, and they were aware of that fact. They knew that the responsibility was theirs to act as the voice of the community in choosing the "worst of the worst." Under the present scheme, juries have the same discretion, but they are deceived as to their role. When jurors learn that their finding on a charged special circumstance determines whether the defendant is death-eligible, they necessarily assume, *and are entitled to assume*, that the legislature, on behalf of the community, has already determined that the defendant before them is among the 'worst of the worst.' There is no way for the jurors to know otherwise . . .

S. Shatz & N. Rivkind, *The California Death Penalty Scheme: Requiem for Furman?* 72 N.Y.U. L.Rev. 1283, 1341 (1997) (emphasis added). Finally, it has been argued that the illusion that the Supreme Court is regulating the administration of the death penalty by enforcement of *Furman*, without the reality of regulation, tends to legitimate the death penalty in its present form, thus muting any concerns that otherwise might be felt by the participants in its administration and by the public in general.

> We are left with the worst of all possible worlds: the Supreme Court's detailed attention to death penalty law has generated negligible improvements over the pre-*Furman* era, but has helped people to accept without second thoughts . . . our profoundly failed system of capital punishment.

C. Steiker and J. Steiker, *Sober Second Thoughts: Reflections on Two Decades of Constitutional Regulation of Capital Punishment*, 109 Harv. L. Rev. 355, 438 (1995).

BARCLAY v. FLORIDA
463 U.S. 939, 103 S.Ct. 3418, 77 L.Ed.2d 1134 (1983).

JUSTICE REHNQUIST announced the judgment of the Court and delivered an opinion in which THE CHIEF JUSTICE, JUSTICE WHITE, and JUSTICE O'CONNOR joined.

The central question in this case is whether Florida may constitutionally impose the death penalty on petitioner Elwood Barclay when one of the "aggravating circumstances" relied upon by the trial judge to support the sentence was not among those established by the Florida death penalty statute.

[Barclay, Dougan, Crittendon, Evans and Hearn were members of a group known as the "Black Liberation Army," whose apparent purpose was to start a race war. They set out by car on the evening of June 17, 1974 to find and kill a white person. They drove around Jacksonville making several stops and considering various white people as possible victims. Eventually, they picked up Stephen Anthony Orlando, who was hitch-hiking. They took Orlando to an isolated spot, ordered him out and threw him down. Barclay repeatedly stabbed him, and then Dougan shot him twice in the head, killing him. Dougan then stuck a note (which he had previously written) on Orlando's body. The note consisted of inflammatory political rhetoric combined with a detailed and gloating description of how the victim was killed.]

Barclay and Dougan were convicted by a jury of first degree murder.[1] As required by the Florida death penalty statute, Fla.Stat. § 921.141(1), a separate sentencing hearing was held before the same jury. The jury rendered advisory sentences under § 921.141(2), recommending that Dougan be sentenced to death and, by a 7 to 5 vote, that Barclay be sentenced to life imprisonment. The trial judge, after receiving a presentence report, decided to sentence both men to death. He made written findings of fact concerning aggravating and mitigating circumstances as required by § 921.141(3). The trial judge found that several of the aggravating circumstances set out in the statute were present. He found that Barclay had knowingly created a great risk of death to many persons, § 921.141(5)(c), had committed the murder while engaged in a kidnapping, § 921.141(5)(d), had endeavored to disrupt governmental functions and law enforcement, § 921.141(5)(g), and had been especially heinous, atrocious and cruel. § 921.141(5)(h).

The trial judge did not find any mitigating circumstances. He noted in particular that Barclay had an extensive criminal record, and therefore did not qualify for the mitigating circumstance of having no significant history of prior criminal activity. § 921.141(6)(a). He found that Barclay's record constituted an aggravating, rather than a mitigating circumstance. The trial judge also noted that the aggravating circumstance of § 921.141(5)(a) ("The capital felony was committed by a convict under sentence of imprisonment") was not present, but restated Barclay's criminal record and again found it to be an aggravating circumstance. He made a similar finding as to the aggravating circumstance of § 921.141(5)(b) ("The defendant was previously convicted of another capital felony or of a felony involving the use or threat of violence to the person"). Barclay had been convicted of breaking and entering with intent to commit the felony of grand larceny, but the trial judge did not know whether it involved the use or threat of violence. He pointed out that crimes such as this often involve the use or threat of violence, and stated that "there are more aggravating than mitigating circumstances."

The trial judge concluded that "[t]here are sufficient and great aggravating circumstances which exist to justify the sentence of death as to both defendants." He therefore rejected part of the jury's recommendation, and sentenced Barclay as well as Dougan to death.[a]

---

1. Evans and Crittendon, who did not actually kill Orlando, were convicted of second degree murder and sentenced to 199 years in prison. Hearns pleaded guilty to second degree murder and testified for the prosecution.

a. At the end of his opinion, the trial judge described his twenty-eight years legal experience almost exclusively in criminal law, and his experience in the infantry in World War II and concluded:

On the automatic appeal provided by Fla.Stat. § 921.141(4), the Florida Supreme Court affirmed. It approved the findings of the trial judge and his decision to reject the jury's recommendation that Barclay be sentenced to death. It concluded that "[t]his is a case ... where the jury did not act reasonably in the imposition of sentence, and the trial judge properly rejected one of their recommendations."

* * *

A

Barclay argues that the trial judge improperly found that his criminal record was an "aggravating circumstance." The state concedes that this is correct: Florida law plainly provides that a defendant's prior criminal record is not a proper "aggravating circumstance."

B

Barclay also argues that the trial judge improperly found the "under sentence of imprisonment" and "previously been convicted of a [violent] felony" aggravating circumstances. The Florida Supreme Court, however, construed the trial judge's opinion as finding that these aggravating circumstances "essentially had no relevance here." We see no reason to disturb that conclusion. The trial judge plainly stated that Barclay "was not under sentence of imprisonment." The trial judge also stated in the same paragraph that Barclay's criminal record "is an aggravating circumstance," but this is simply a repetition of the error noted above.

Barclay also challenges the findings on several other aggravating circumstances. He claims that the trial court improperly found that he caused a great risk of death to many people,[2] that the murder was committed during a kidnapping, that the murder was committed to disrupt the lawful exercise of a governmental function or the enforcement of the laws,[3] and that the murder was especially heinous, atrocious or cruel.[4] All of these findings were made by the trial court and approved by

---

"To attempt to initiate such a race war in this country is too horrible to contemplate for both our black and white citizens. Such an attempt must be dealt with by just and swift legal process and when justified by a Jury verdict of guilty—then to terminate and remove permanently from society those who would choose to initiate this diabolical course.

"HAD THE DEFENDANT BEEN EXPOSED TO THE CARNAGE OF THE BATTLE-FIELDS AND THE HORRORS OF THE CONCENTRATION CAMPS INSTEAD OF MOVIES, TELEVISION PROGRAMS AND REVOLUTIONARY TRACTS GLORIFYING VIOLENCE AND RACIAL STRIFE—THEN PERHAPS HIS THOUGHTS AND ACTIONS WOULD HAVE TAKEN A LESS VIOLENT COURSE.

"Having set forth my personal experiences above, it is understandable that I am not easily shocked or moved by tragedy—but this present murder and call for racial war is especially shocking and meets every definition of heinous, atrocious and cruel. The perpetrator thereby forfeits further right to life—for certainly his life is no more sacred than that of the innocent eighteen year old victim, Stephen Anthony Orlando."

2. The Florida Supreme Court stated: "The trial judge noted five aborted attempts to select a victim from the streets of Jacksonville before Stephen Orlando was chosen, plus the taped threat made to white Jacksonville citizens that a race war had begun and none would be safe."

3. The Florida Supreme Court stated: "The basis for this finding was the judge's observation that the notion of a race war essentially threatened the foundations of American society."

4. The Florida Supreme Court noted that the tape recordings petitioner and Dougan made "explained how Stephen Orlando had begged for his life while being beaten and stabbed before Dougan 'executed' him with two pistol shots in the head."

the Florida Supreme Court under Florida law. Our review of these findings is limited to the question whether they are so unprincipled or arbitrary as to somehow violate the United States Constitution. We think they were not. It was not irrational or arbitrary to apply these aggravating circumstances to the facts of this case.

    * * *

II

A

    * * *

* * * One question that has arisen is whether defendants must be resentenced when trial courts erroneously consider improper aggravating factors. If the trial court found that some mitigating circumstances exist, the case will generally be remanded for resentencing. *Elledge v. State*, 346 So.2d 998 (Fla. 1977). If the trial court properly found that there are no mitigating circumstances, the Florida Supreme Court applies a harmless error analysis. *Elledge, supra.* * * *

The Florida Supreme Court has not always found that consideration of improper aggravating factors is harmless, even when no mitigating circumstances exist. In *Lewis v. State*, 398 So.2d 432 (Fla.1981), for example, the defendant shot the victim once in the head through his bedroom window, killing him instantly. The jury recommended life imprisonment, but the trial judge sentenced Lewis to death, finding four aggravating circumstances and no mitigating circumstances. The Florida Supreme Court found that the evidence did not support three of the aggravating circumstances. It did find that the "under sentence of imprisonment" aggravating circumstance was properly applied because Lewis was on parole from a prison sentence when he committed the crime. On these facts, and with only this one relatively weak aggravating circumstance left standing, the Florida Supreme Court did not find harmless error, but rather remanded for resentencing.

The Florida Supreme Court has placed another check on the harmless error analysis permitted by *Elledge*. When the jury has recommended life imprisonment, the trial judge may not impose a death sentence unless "the facts suggesting a sentence of death [are] so clear and convincing that virtually no reasonable person could differ." *Tedder v. State*, 322 So.2d 908 (Fla. 1975). In *Williams v. State*, 386 So.2d 538 (Fla. 1980), and *Dobbert v. State*, 375 So.2d 1069 (Fla. 1979), the Florida Supreme Court reversed the trial judges' findings of several aggravating circumstances. In each case at least one valid aggravating circumstance remained, and there were no mitigating circumstances. In each case, however, the Florida Supreme Court concluded that in the absence of the improperly found aggravating circumstances the *Tedder* test could not be met. Therefore it reduced the sentences to life imprisonment.

B

The trial judge's consideration of Barclay's criminal record as an aggravating circumstance was improper as a matter of state law: that record did not fall within the definition of any statutory aggravating circumstance, and Florida law prohibits consideration of nonstatutory aggravating circumstances. In this case, like in *Zant v. Stephens*, 462 U.S. 862, 103 S.Ct. 2733 (1983), nothing in the United States Constitution prohibited the trial court from considering Barclay's criminal record. The trial judge did not consider any constitutionally protected behavior to be an aggravating circumstance. And, again like in *Zant*, nothing in the Eighth Amendment or in Florida law prohibits the admission of the evidence of Barclay's criminal record. On the contrary, this evidence was properly introduced to prove that the mitigating circumstance of absence of a criminal record did not exist. This statutory aggravating circumstance "plausibly described aspects of the defendant's background that were properly before the [trial judge] and whose accuracy was unchallenged."

C

The crux of the issue, then, is whether the trial judge's consideration of this improper aggravating circumstance so infects the balancing process created by the Florida statute that it is constitutionally impermissible for the Florida Supreme Court to let the sentence stand. * * *

Barclay's brief is interlarded with rhetorical references to "lawless findings of statutory aggravating circumstances," "protective pronouncements which ... seem to be turned on and off from case to case without notice or explanation," and others in a similar vein. These varied assertions seem to suggest that the Florida Supreme Court failed to properly apply its own cases in upholding petitioner's death sentence. The obvious answer to this question, as indicated in the previous discussion, is that mere errors of state law are not the concern of this Court, *Gryger v. Burke*, 334 U.S. 728, 68 S.Ct. 1256 (1948), unless they rise for some other reason to the level of a denial of rights protected by the United States Constitution.

In any event, we do not accept Barclay's premise. Cases such as *Lewis, supra, Williams, supra,* and *Dobbert, supra,* indicate that the Florida Supreme Court does not apply its harmless error analysis in an automatic or mechanical fashion, but rather upholds death sentences on the basis of this analysis only when it actually finds that the error is harmless. There is no reason why the Florida Supreme Court cannot examine the balance struck by the trial judge and decide that the elimination of improperly considered aggravating circumstances could not possibly affect the balance. "What is important ... is an *individualized* determination on the basis of the character of the individual and the circumstances of the crime." *Zant, supra* (emphasis in original).

In this case, as in *Zant, supra,* our decision is buttressed by the Florida Supreme Court's practice of reviewing each death sentence to compare it with other Florida capital cases and to determine whether "the punishment is too great." It is further buttressed by the rule prohibiting the trial judge from overriding a jury recommendation of life imprisonment unless "virtually no reasonable person could differ."

The judgment of the Supreme Court of Florida is affirmed.

JUSTICE STEVENS, with whom JUSTICE POWELL joins, concurring in the judgment.

* * *

II

In this case the Florida Supreme Court held that the trial judge had properly determined that at least four statutory aggravating circumstances were present. Petitioner alleges that none of those four aggravating circumstances withstands scrutiny under Florida law * * * But it is not necessary to agree with the Florida Supreme Court's appraisal of all four findings. Under Florida law, if there are no statutory mitigating circumstances,[13] one valid statutory aggravating circumstance will generally suffice to uphold a death sentence on appeal even if other aggravating circumstances are not valid. The federal Constitution requires no more, at least as long as none of the invalid aggravating circumstances is supported by erroneous or misleading information. See *Zant v. Stephens*, 462 U.S. 862, 103 S.Ct. 2733 (1983).

I do not accept petitioner's contention that none of the statutory aggravating circumstances found by the trial court may be sustained under Florida law and the federal Constitution. The trial court found that the murder was "especially heinous, atrocious, and cruel" because the victim "was knocked to the ground and repeatedly stabbed by Barclay as he writhed in pain begging for mercy." The court also found that the crime took place in the commission of a kidnapping, because "the defendants picked up the hitch-hiking victim with intent to murder him. They refused to take him to the place requested and by force and/or threats kept him in their car until they found an appropriate place for the murder." It is not our role to reexamine the trial court's findings of fact, which have been affirmed by the Florida Supreme Court. Assuming those facts to be true, there is no federal constitutional infirmity in these two findings of statutory aggravating circumstances.

* * *

---

13. Petitioner argues that the jury must have found nonstatutory mitigating circumstances because when it recommended life imprisonment, it stated that "sufficient mitigating circumstances do exist which outweigh any aggravating circumstances." But at the time of Barclay's trial, nonstatutory mitigating circumstances did not play any role under Florida law in determining whether the legal threshold had been crossed. Nor does the possible existence of nonstatutory mitigating circumstances require that the death sentence automatically be set aside if one or more statutory aggravating circumstances are invalid under state law, or if nonstatutory aggravating factors have improperly been considered. As long as the federal Constitution did not bar introduction of the evidence underlying those aggravating factors, it does not require that the death sentence be set aside. See *Zant v. Stephens*, 462 U.S. 862, 103 S.Ct. 2733 (1983).

* * * [P]etitioner contends that the Florida Supreme Court has abdicated its constitutionally-mandated responsibility to perform meaningful appellate review. This contention cannot stand or fall on a single case, particularly since the rather unusual circumstances in this case help to explain the limited analysis provided by the Florida Supreme Court. On direct appeal from the initial imposition of the death sentence in 1975, it appears that petitioner did not challenge the validity of any of the statutory aggravating circumstances. The sentence was affirmed. Most of the Florida case law on which petitioner now relies was developed after the initial decision in his case. Barclay did not receive the benefit of this case law because of the limited nature of the Florida Supreme Court's remand in light of this Court's decision in *Gardner v. Florida*, 430 U.S. 349, 97 S.Ct. 1197 (1977). When that court vacated the death sentence and ordered the trial court to hold a hearing to permit petitioner to rebut undisclosed information in the presentence report, it applied a uniform procedure which expressly limited the scope of the trial court's proceedings and the scope of appellate review to "matters related to compliance with this order." The court's subsequent opinion accordingly dealt only with the presentence report and treated the previous affirmance of the death sentence as "law of the case" with regard to the aggravating circumstances.

More generally, the question is whether, in its regular practice, the Florida Supreme Court has become a rubber stamp for lower court death-penalty determinations. It has not. On 212 occasions since 1972 the Florida Supreme Court has reviewed death sentences; it has affirmed only 120 of them. The remainder have been set aside, with instructions either to hold a new sentencing proceeding or to impose a life sentence. In making these judgments the court has the benefit of specific written findings by the trial court, setting forth the facts underlying each aggravating and mitigating circumstance. Although no appellate court's written decisions, including those of the Florida Supreme Court, are always a model of clarity and analysis, the actual decisions by that court have confirmed one of the premises supporting our decision in *Proffitt v. Florida*, 428 U.S. 242, 96 S.Ct. 2960 (1976)—

> "The Florida capital-sentencing procedures thus seek to assure that the death penalty will not be imposed in an arbitrary or capricious manner. Moreover, to the extent that any risk to the contrary exists, it is minimized by Florida's appellate review system, under which the evidence of the aggravating and mitigating circumstances is reviewed and reweighed by the Supreme Court of Florida 'to determine independently whether the imposition of the ultimate penalty is warranted.' *Songer v. State*, 322 So.2d 481 (Fla. 1975)."

The cursory analysis in the two opinions upholding petitioner's death sentence—which admittedly I do not applaud—does not require us to set aside the sentence when we have determined that the sentence itself does not suffer from any constitutional flaw.

I therefore concur in the judgment.

JUSTICE MARSHALL, with whom JUSTICE BRENNAN joins, dissenting.

Based on a sentencing order rife with errors, the trial judge condemned petitioner Elwood Barclay to death. The Florida Supreme Court then conducted a perfunctory review and affirmed the sentence. Today the plurality approves this miscarriage of justice. In doing so it is utterly faithless to the safeguards established by the Court's prior decisions. I dissent.

[Although the state had relied on only one statutory aggravating circumstance during the sentencing hearing, the trial judge had found that six were relevant. Justice Marshall analyzed the evidence in support of each of the six circumstances and concluded that all six findings were unsupportable under Florida law. He also pointed out that the judge, in finding no mitigating circumstances, had failed even to mention various non-statutory mitigating circumstances, for example, that petitioner was the father of five children and was gainfully employed, that petitioner was a follower and not a leader among the murderers and that three of the other participants faced punishment for only second degree murder.]

* * *

C

In reviewing the hopelessly flawed sentencing order, the Florida Supreme Court did not identify a single error in the trial judge's explanation. Instead, it praised Judge Olliff's performance:

"The trial judge here painstakingly and with reasoned judgment detailed the factors which caused his departure from the jury's recommendation. *His thorough analysis is precisely the type we would expect* from mature, deliberative judges in this state. It suggests why the Legislature put the trial judges of Florida in the middle of the sentencing process for capital cases." (emphasis added).

The Florida Supreme Court's perfunctory analysis focused on the death sentence imposed on petitioner's codefendant, Jacob Dougan. The Court subsequently indicated that "virtually the same considerations" applied to Barclay. As a result, it never discussed the trial judge's specific findings concerning Barclay. With respect to the aggravating circumstances applicable to Dougan, the Florida Supreme Court stated that "the trial judge recited that four factors essentially had no relevance here." However, two of the factors referred to in this sentence were aggravating circumstances that the trial judge had explicitly discussed. In short, the Florida Supreme Court mischaracterized the trial judge's opinion as to these aggravating circumstances. The Florida Supreme Court then listed the four other aggravating circumstances that had been relied upon and stated in conclusory fashion that the trial judge's findings were "well documented in the record before us."

The Florida Supreme Court recognized that the jury had recommended a life sentence for Barclay. But the court stated that this recommendation was properly rejected so that there would be no disparity of treatment between Dougan and Barclay: " 'Equal Justice Under Law' is carved over the doorway to the United States Supreme Court building in Washington. It would have a hollow ring in the halls of that building if the sentences in these cases were not equalized." The court ignored the differences between Barclay and Dougan which the jury had apparently found decisive. In addition to obscuring the proper focus on the individual offender, the court's invocation of principles of equal justice is particularly inappropriate in this case in light of the treatment of two of petitioner's codefendants, Evans and Crittendon. Both of these individuals participated in the murder of Stephen Orlando; indeed, Evans was the first to stab Orlando. Moreover, after Orlando was murdered, Evans and Crittendon committed a second murder in the name of the Black Liberation Army in which petitioner Barclay played absolutely no part. Yet, these two received prison sentences while Barclay was condemned to death.

III

* * *

B

To avoid the arbitrary and capricious imposition of the death penalty, this Court has * * * stressed "the further safeguard of meaningful appellate review." *Gregg v. Georgia*, 428 U.S. 153, 96 S.Ct. 2909 (1976) (Opinion of STEWART, POWELL, and STEVENS, JJ.). In his opinion concurring in the judgment, Justice STEVENS notes the importance of this safeguard. In my view, the failure of the Florida Supreme Court to conduct any considered appellate review in this case requires that petitioner's death sentence be vacated.

If appellate review is to be meaningful, it must fulfill its basic historic function of correcting error in the trial court proceedings. A review for correctness reinforces the authority and acceptability of the trial court's decision and controls the adverse effects of any personal shortcomings in the initial decisionmaker. The Florida Supreme Court's review of Barclay's sentence utterly failed to fulfill this function. The Court glossed over all of the errors in the sentencing order. Instead, it lauded the trial judge's performance, stating that Judge Olliff's "thorough analysis is precisely the type we would expect." Given such encouragement, it is hardly surprising that in subsequent cases Judge Olliff has persisted in misapplying the Florida death penalty statute.[b]

---

b. Justice Marshall had earlier referred to the three other cases where the same trial judge had sentenced defendants to death: *Lewis v. State*, 398 So.2d 432 (Fla.1981); *Dobbert v. State*, 375 So.2d 1069 (Fla.1979); *Carnes v. State*, No. 74–2024, 74–2131, Cir.Ct. 4th Jud.Cir., Duval County, Florida (Nov. 19, 1964).

"In each of these cases, as in petitioner's case, Judge Olliff ignored a jury's advisory sentence of life imprisonment. In each of the cases, as in petitioner's case, the judge failed to find a single mitigating circumstance. The judge has repeatedly found that the felony was committed by a

The trial judge in this case plainly misapplied aggravating circumstances enumerated in Florida law. For example, he relied upon a conviction for breaking and entering to establish that petitioner had previously been convicted of a violent felony, even though the Florida Supreme Court has expressly held that such a crime does not satisfy the statutory factor. Similarly, the judge concluded that petitioner had created a great risk of death to many persons even though the homicidal act itself created no such risk. Faced with such findings, the Florida Supreme Court simply failed to consider whether they were consistent with Florida law. Conceivably it would have been possible to reconcile the findings in this case with other decisions which the Florida Supreme Court has rendered, although I doubt it. But if the process of appellate review means anything, it requires that the legal principles applied in one case be harmonized with settled law.

The plurality proceeds on the unfounded assumption that, although errors may have been made by the trial judge, the Florida Supreme Court nonetheless concluded that the errors were harmless. * * *

The plurality's reliance on the harmless-error doctrine has no relation to the Florida Supreme Court's decision in this case. As one might surmise from the terminology, a "harmless error" inquiry refers to a process by which an appellate court identifies legal errors and then determines whether they could have affected the judgment being reviewed. Here, the Florida Supreme Court did not identify *any* legal errors in the trial judge's sentencing order; it extolled the merits of the sentencing order. It therefore never reached the question whether the error was harmless. The Florida Supreme Court's decision in this case can readily be contrasted with those decisions in which it actually conducted a harmless error analysis. For example, in *White v. State*, 403 So.2d 331 (Fla. 1981), the court examined each of the aggravating circumstances upon which the sentencer had relied, explained the errors that the sentencer had committed, and then assessed the significance of the errors.

The plurality's reliance on the harmless-error review conducted by the Florida Supreme Court in *other* cases is entirely misplaced. When a defendant's life is at stake, it hardly suffices to tell him that some of the time the state's highest court does its job. Every defendant sentenced to death is entitled to meaningful appellate review, and where it is clear that the Florida Supreme Court has not provided such review, the death sentence should be vacated.

IV

This case illustrates the capital sentencing process gone awry. Relying on factors not mentioned in Florida law and statutory factors distorted

---

person under a sentence of imprisonment, that the defendant had previously been convicted of a violent felony, and that the defendant created a great risk of death to many persons, *even though virtually all of these findings had no foundation in Florida law.* And each time, Judge Olliff has recounted his experiences during World War II and recited boiler-plate language to the effect that he was not easily shocked but that the offense involved shocked him."

As noted by the plurality, the Florida Supreme Court vacated the death sentences in *Lewis* and *Dobbert*.

beyond recognition, Judge Olliff overrode the jury's recommendation of life and sentenced petitioner to death. The Florida Supreme Court failed to conduct any meaningful review and instead showered the trial judge with praise for his performance. "Justice of this kind is obviously no less shocking than the crime itself, and the new 'official' murder, far from offering redress for the offense committed against society, adds instead a second defilement to the first." A. Camus, Reflections on the Guillotine 5–6 (Fridtjof–Karla Pub. 1960). I therefore dissent.

[Dissenting opinion of BLACKMUN, J. omitted]

NOTES

1. *The requirement of "meaningful appellate review."*

The Supreme Court on several occasions has suggested that "meaningful appellate review" is a necessary element of a constitutional death penalty scheme. For example, in *Murray v. Giarratano*, 492 U.S. 1, 23, 109 S.Ct. 2765, 2777 (1989), the Court said:

> "[M]eaningful appellate review" in capital cases, however, "serves as a check against the random or arbitrary imposition of the death penalty." *Gregg v. Georgia*, 428 U.S. 153, 195, 206, 96 S.Ct. 2909, 2935, 2940 (1976) (opinion of STEWART, POWELL, and STEVENS, JJ.). It is therefore an integral component of a State's "constitutional responsibility to tailor and apply its law in a manner that avoids the arbitrary and capricious infliction of the death penalty." *Godfrey v. Georgia*, 446 U.S. 420, 428, 100 S.Ct. 1759, 1764 (1980).

By what standard can the Court determine whether a state supreme court generally fails, or failed in the particular case, to afford meaningful appellate review?

Parker v. Dugger, 498 U.S. 308, 111 S.Ct. 731 (1991), a Florida jury override case, is the only case where the Court appears to have relied on a lack of meaningful appellate review to overturn a sentence. Parker was one of four people who participated in a triple killing, and he was convicted of two first degree murders and a third degree murder. At his trial and penalty hearing Parker presented substantial non-statutory mitigating evidence. The jury found statutory aggravating circumstances as to both murders, but recommended a life sentence as to both murders. The trial judge overrode the jury recommendation and sentenced Parker to death on one of the murders. He explained that he had found six aggravating circumstances and no statutory mitigating circumstances and that "[t]here are no mitigating circumstances that outweigh the aggravating circumstances." The Florida Supreme Court found insufficient evidence as to two of the aggravating circumstances, but affirmed the death judgment, writing:

> The trial court found no mitigating circumstances to balance against the aggravating factors, of which four were properly applied. In light of these findings the facts suggesting the sentence of death are so clear and convincing that virtually no reasonable person could differ.

On federal habeas corpus, the United States Supreme Court overturned the death sentence because the state court's affirmance deprived Parker of the individualized treatment to which he was entitled under the Eighth Amendment. The Court reasoned that, in light of the evidence and the trial judge's rulings, he must have found that there were non-statutory mitigating circumstances which were outweighed by the aggravating circumstances. The normal practice of the Florida Supreme Court when it strikes one or more aggravating circumstances and mitigating circumstances are present is to remand to the trial court for resentencing. The Florida Supreme Court's failure to remand indicated that it did not even consider Parker's mitigating evidence and it thereby violated Parker's Eighth Amendment rights. Justice White, writing for the four dissenters, took issue with the majority's whole approach. According to Justice White, the Eighth Amendment does not regulate the procedures of sentencing, beyond assuring that the defendant can present mitigating evidence, and, therefore, "the procedural elements of a sentencing scheme come within the prohibition, if at all, only when they are of such a nature as *systematically* to render the infliction of a cruel punishment 'unusual.'" 498 U.S. at 328, 111 S.Ct. at 743. Who is right?

2.   *State courts' application of state law.*

In *Barclay*, the Supreme Court ruled that the state court findings on matters of state law were not so "unprincipled or arbitrary" as to violate the federal constitution. As a general rule, a state court's interpretation of its own law or its denial of state-created rights, does not raise a federal question. However, the Court has recognized two situations arising in criminal cases where such state court action may violate the Fourteenth Amendment Due Process Clause. First, if a state appellate court interprets state criminal law in a novel manner, thus denying the defendant fair notice of the elements of the crime of which he was convicted or the terms of the punishment to which he was sentenced, due process will be violated. See *Bouie v. City of Columbia*, 378 U.S. 347, 84 S.Ct. 1697 (1964) (due process violation from unforeseeable and retroactive expansion of trespass law to encompass defendant's conduct); but see *Rogers v. Tennessee*, 532 U.S. 451, 121 S.Ct. 1693 (2001) (no due process violation from retroactive abrogation of "year-and-a-day rule" for murder because rule was not well-established and change was not unexpected).

Second, state laws which guarantee criminal defendants certain rights beyond those required by the federal constitution may give rise to liberty interests that are protected against arbitrary deprivation under the due process clause. See *Hicks v. Oklahoma*, 447 U.S. 343, 100 S.Ct. 2227 (1980); *Kentucky Dept. of Corrections v. Thompson*, 490 U.S. 454, 109 S.Ct. 1904 (1989) partially abrogated by *Sandin v. Conner*, 515 U.S. 472, 115 S.Ct. 2293 (1995). This principle has been applied in capital and potentially capital cases. See, *e.g.*, *Carter v. Bowersox*, 265 F.3d 705 (8th Cir. 2001) (failure to instruct, as required by state law, that jury had to find unanimously that the aggravating circumstances warranted death); *Rojem v. Gibson*, 245 F.3d 1130 (10th Cir. 2001) (failure to give state-required "weighing" instruction); *Vansickel v. White*, 166 F.3d 953 (9th Cir. 1999) (failure to accord the defendant state-authorized twenty peremptory challenges).

PULLEY v. HARRIS

465 U.S. 37, 104 S.Ct. 871, 79 L.Ed.2d 29 (1984).

JUSTICE WHITE delivered the opinion of the Court.

Respondent Harris was convicted of a capital crime in a California court and was sentenced to death. Along with many other challenges to the conviction and sentence, Harris claimed on appeal that the California capital punishment statute was invalid under the United States Constitution because it failed to require the California Supreme Court to compare Harris's sentence with the sentences imposed in similar capital cases and thereby to determine whether they were proportionate. Rejecting the constitutional claims by citation to earlier cases, the California Supreme Court affirmed. *People v. Harris*, 623 P.2d 240 (Cal. 1981). We denied certiorari. 454 U.S. 882 (1981).

[After denial of state habeas corpus relief, Harris sought habeas corpus in federal court. The District Court denied relief, but the Court of Appeals ordered that the writ issue vacating Harris's death sentence unless within 120 days the California Supreme Court undertook to determine whether the penalty imposed on Harris was proportionate to sentences imposed for similar crimes.]

* * *

II

At the outset, we should more clearly identify the issue before us. Traditionally, "proportionality" has been used with reference to an abstract evaluation of the appropriateness of a sentence for a particular crime. Looking to the gravity of the offense and the severity of the penalty, to sentences imposed for other crimes, and to sentencing practices in other jurisdictions, this Court has occasionally struck down punishments as inherently disproportionate, and therefore cruel and unusual, when imposed for a particular crime or category of crime. See, e.g., *Solem v. Helm*, 463 U.S. 277, 103 S.Ct. 3001 (1983); *Enmund v. Florida*, 458 U.S. 782, 102 S.Ct. 3368 (1982); *Coker v. Georgia*, 433 U.S. 584, 97 S.Ct. 2861 (1977). The death penalty is not in all cases a disproportionate penalty in this sense. *Gregg v. Georgia*, 428 U.S. 153, 96 S.Ct. 2909 (1976).

The proportionality review sought by Harris, required by the Court of Appeals,[6] and provided for in numerous state statutes[7] is of a different

---

6. The Court of Appeals noted a distinction between the proportionality of the death penalty to the crime for which it was imposed, and the proportionality of a given defendant's sentence to other sentences imposed for similar crimes. "This latter proportionality review . . . is what concerns us here."

7. Under the much-copied Georgia scheme, for example, the Supreme Court is required in every case to determine "[w]hether the sentence of death is excessive or disproportionate to the penalty imposed in similar cases, considering both the crime and the defendant." If the court affirms the death sentence, it is to include in its decision reference to similar cases that it has taken into consideration. The court is required to maintain records of all capital felony cases in which the death penalty was imposed since 1970.

sort. This sort of proportionality review presumes that the death sentence is not disproportionate to the crime in the traditional sense. It purports to inquire instead whether the penalty is nonetheless unacceptable in a particular case because disproportionate to the punishment imposed on others convicted of the same crime. The issue in this case, therefore, is whether the Eighth Amendment, applicable to the States through the Fourteenth Amendment, requires a state appellate court, before it affirms a death sentence, to compare the sentence in the case before it with the penalties imposed in similar cases if requested to do so by the prisoner. Harris insists that it does and that this is the invariable rule in every case. Apparently, the Court of Appeals was of the same view. We do not agree.

III

Harris's submission is rooted in *Furman v. Georgia*, 408 U.S. 238, 92 S.Ct. 2726 (1972). In *Furman*, the Court concluded that capital punishment, as then administered under statutes vesting unguided sentencing discretion in juries and trial judges, had become unconstitutionally cruel and unusual punishment. The death penalty was being imposed so discriminatorily (DOUGLAS, J., concurring), so wantonly and freakishly, (STEWART, J., concurring), and so infrequently (WHITE, J., concurring), that any given death sentence was cruel and unusual. In response to that decision, roughly two-thirds of the States promptly redrafted their capital sentencing statutes in an effort to limit jury discretion and avoid arbitrary and inconsistent results. All of the new statutes provide for automatic appeal of death sentences. Most, such as Georgia's, require the reviewing court, to some extent at least, to determine whether, considering both the crime and the defendant, the sentence is disproportionate to that imposed in similar cases. Not every State has adopted such a procedure. In some States, such as Florida, the appellate court performs proportionality review despite the absence of a statutory requirement; in others, such as California and Texas, it does not.

Four years after *Furman*, this Court examined several of the new state statutes. We upheld one of each of the three sorts mentioned above. See *Gregg v. Georgia, supra*; *Proffitt v. Florida*, 428 U.S. 242, 96 S.Ct. 2960 (1976); *Jurek v. Texas*, 428 U.S. 262, 96 S.Ct. 2950 (1976). Needless to say, that some schemes providing proportionality review are constitutional does not mean that such review is indispensable. We take statutes as we find them. To endorse the statute as a whole is not to say that anything different is unacceptable. As was said in *Gregg*, "[w]e do not intend to suggest that only the above-described procedures would be permissible under *Furman* or that any sentencing system constructed along these general lines would inevitably satisfy the concerns of *Furman*, for each distinct system must be examined on an individual basis." Examination of our 1976 cases makes clear that they do not establish proportionality review as a constitutional requirement.

In *Gregg*, six Justices concluded that the Georgia system adequately directed and limited the jury's discretion. The bifurcated proceedings, the limited number of capital crimes, the requirement that at least one aggravating circumstance be present, and the consideration of mitigating circumstances minimized the risk of wholly arbitrary, capricious, or freakish sentences. In the opinion announcing the judgment of the Court, three Justices concluded that sentencing discretion under the statute was sufficiently controlled by clear and objective standards. In a separate concurrence, three other Justices found sufficient reason to expect that the death penalty would not be imposed so wantonly, freakishly, or infrequently as to be invalid under *Furman*.

Both opinions made much of the statutorily-required comparative proportionality review. This was considered an additional safeguard against arbitrary or capricious sentencing. While the opinion of Justices STEWART, POWELL and STEVENS suggested that some form of meaningful appellate review is required, those Justices did not declare that comparative review was so critical that without it the Georgia statute would not have passed constitutional muster. Indeed, in summarizing the components of an adequate capital sentencing scheme, Justices STEWART, POWELL, and STEVENS did not mention comparative review:

> "[T]he concerns expressed in *Furman* ... can be met by a carefully drafted statute that ensures that the sentencing authority be given adequate information and guidance. As a general proposition, these concerns are best met by a system that provides for a bifurcated proceeding at which the sentencing authority is apprised of the information relevant to the imposition of sentence and provided with standards to guide its use of the information."

In short, the Court of Appeals erred in concluding that *Gregg* required proportionality review.

[The Court found even less support for Harris's position in *Proffitt* and *Jurek*, noting that the Texas scheme upheld in *Jurek* did not provide for proportionality review. Thus, according to the Court, at the time of the decisions in the three cases, the Court had not found proportionality review to be constitutionally required.]

Harris also relies on *Zant v. Stephens*, 462 U.S. 862, 103 S.Ct. 2733 (1983), which was announced after the Court of Appeals' decision in this case. *Zant* did not depart from *Gregg* and did not question *Jurek*. Indeed, *Jurek* was cited in support of the decision. While emphasizing the importance of mandatory appellate review under the Georgia statute, we did not hold that without comparative proportionality review the statute would be unconstitutional. To the contrary, we relied on the jury's finding of aggravating circumstances, not the State Supreme Court's finding of proportionality, as rationalizing the sentence.[12] Thus, the emphasis was on the constitutionally necessary narrowing function of statutory aggrava-

---

12. We upheld the death sentence even though the State Supreme Court had invalidated, as unconstitutionally vague, one of the three aggravating circumstances relied on by the jury. The two remaining circumstances "adequately differentiated this case in an objective, evenhanded, and substantively rational way from the many Georgia murder cases in which the death penalty may not be imposed."

ting circumstances. Proportionality review was considered to be an additional safeguard against arbitrarily imposed death sentences, but we certainly did not hold that comparative review was constitutionally required.

There is thus no basis in our cases for holding that comparative proportionality review by an appellate court is required in every case in which the death penalty is imposed and the defendant requests it. Indeed, to so hold would effectively overrule *Jurek* and would substantially depart from the sense of *Gregg* and *Proffitt*. We are not persuaded that the Eighth Amendment requires us to take that course.

IV

Assuming that there could be a capital sentencing system so lacking in other checks on arbitrariness that it would not pass constitutional muster without comparative proportionality review, the 1977 California statute is not of that sort. Under this scheme, a person convicted of first degree murder is sentenced to life imprisonment unless one or more "special circumstances" are found, in which case the punishment is either death or life imprisonment without parole.[13] Special circumstances are alleged in the charging paper and tried with the issue of guilt at the initial phase of the trial. At the close of evidence, the jury decides guilt or innocence and determines whether the special circumstances alleged are present. Each special circumstance must be proved beyond a reasonable doubt. If the jury finds the defendant guilty of first degree murder and finds at least one special circumstance, the trial proceeds to a second phase to determine the appropriate penalty. Additional evidence may be offered and the jury is given a list of relevant factors. "After having heard all the evidence, the trier of fact shall consider, take into account and be guided by the aggravating and mitigating circumstances referred to in this section, and shall determine whether the penalty shall be death or life imprisonment without the possibility of parole." If the jury returns a verdict of death, the defendant is deemed to move to modify the verdict. The trial judge then reviews the evidence and, in light of the statutory factors, makes an "independent determination as to whether the weight of the evidence supports the jury's findings and verdicts." The judge is required to state on the record the reasons for his findings. If the trial judge denies the motion for modification, there is an automatic appeal. The statute does not require comparative proportionality review or otherwise describe the nature of the appeal. It does state that the trial judge's refusal to modify the sentence "shall be reviewed." This would seem to include review of the evidence relied on by the judge. As the California

---

13. Briefly, the statutory special circumstances are: 1) the murder was for profit; 2) the murder was perpetrated by an explosive; 3) the victim was a police officer killed in the line of duty; 4) the victim was a witness to a crime, killed to prevent his testifying in a criminal proceeding; 5) the murder was committed during the commission of robbery, kidnapping, rape, performance of a lewd or lascivious act on someone under 14, or burglary; 6) the murder involved torture; 7) the defendant had been previously convicted of first or second degree murder, or was convicted of more than one murder in the first or second degree in this proceeding. Cal. Penal Code Ann. § 190.2 (West 1977). These are greatly expanded in the current statute.

Supreme Court has said, "the statutory requirements that the jury specify the special circumstances which permit imposition of the death penalty, and that the trial judge specify his reasons for denying modification of the death penalty, serve to assure thoughtful and effective appellate review, focusing upon the circumstances present in each particular case." *People v. Frierson*, 599 P.2d 587 (Cal. 1979). That court has reduced a death sentence to life imprisonment because the evidence did not support the findings of special circumstances. *People v. Thompson*, 611 P.2d 883 (Cal. 1980).

By requiring the jury to find at least one special circumstance beyond a reasonable doubt, the statute limits the death sentence to a small sub-class of capital-eligible cases. The statutory list of relevant factors, applied to defendants within this sub-class, "provide[s] jury guidance and lessen[s] the chance of arbitrary application of the death penalty," *Harris v. Pulley*, 692 F.2d 1189 (9th Cir.1982), "guarantee[ing] that the jury's discretion will be guided and its consideration deliberate." The jury's "discretion is suitably directed and limited so as to minimize the risk of wholly arbitrary and capricious action." Its decision is reviewed by the trial judge and the State Supreme Court. On its face, this system, without any requirement or practice of comparative proportionality review, cannot be successfully challenged under *Furman* and our subsequent cases.

Any capital sentencing scheme may occasionally produce aberrational outcomes. Such inconsistencies are a far cry from the major systemic defects identified in *Furman*. As we have acknowledged in the past, "there can be 'no perfect procedure for deciding in which cases governmental authority should be used to impose death.'" *Zant v. Stephens* quoting *Lockett v. Ohio*, 438 U.S. 586, 98 S.Ct. 2954 (1978) (plurality opinion). As we are presently informed, we cannot say that the California procedures provided Harris inadequate protection against the evil identified in *Furman*. The Court of Appeals therefore erred in ordering the writ of habeas corpus to issue. Its judgment is reversed and the case remanded for further proceedings consistent with this opinion.

> [Opinion of STEVENS, J., concurring in part and concurring in the judgment and dissenting opinion of BRENNAN, J. joined by MARSHALL, J. omitted]

McCLESKEY v. KEMP

481 U.S. 279, 107 S.Ct. 1756, 95 L.Ed.2d 262 (1987).

JUSTICE POWELL delivered the opinion of the Court.

This case presents the question whether a complex statistical study that indicates a risk that racial considerations enter into capital sentencing determinations proves that petitioner McCleskey's capital sentence is unconstitutional under the Eighth or Fourteenth Amendment.

I

McCleskey, a black man, was convicted of two counts of armed robbery and one count of murder in the Superior Court of Fulton County,

Georgia, on October 12, 1978. McCleskey's convictions arose out of the robbery of a furniture store and the killing of a white police officer during the course of the robbery. The evidence at trial indicated that McCleskey and three accomplices planned and carried out the robbery. All four were armed. McCleskey entered the front of the store while the other three entered the rear. McCleskey secured the front of the store by rounding up the customers and forcing them to lie face down on the floor. The other three rounded up the employees in the rear and tied them up with tape. The manager was forced at gunpoint to turn over the store receipts, his watch, and $6. During the course of the robbery, a police officer, answering a silent alarm, entered the store through the front door. As he was walking down the center aisle of the store, two shots were fired. Both struck the officer. One hit him in the face and killed him.

Several weeks later, McCleskey was arrested in connection with an unrelated offense. He confessed that he had participated in the furniture store robbery, but denied that he had shot the police officer. At trial, the State introduced evidence that at least one of the bullets that struck the officer was fired from a .38 caliber Rossi revolver. This description matched the description of the gun that McCleskey had carried during the robbery. The State also introduced the testimony of two witnesses who had heard McCleskey admit to the shooting.

The jury convicted McCleskey of murder. At the penalty hearing, the jury heard arguments as to the appropriate sentence. Under Georgia law, the jury could not consider imposing the death penalty unless it found beyond a reasonable doubt that the murder was accompanied by one of the statutory aggravating circumstances. The jury in this case found two aggravating circumstances to exist beyond a reasonable doubt: the murder was committed during the course of an armed robbery; and the murder was committed upon a peace officer engaged in the performance of his duties. In making its decision whether to impose the death sentence, the jury considered the mitigating and aggravating circumstances of McCleskey's conduct. McCleskey offered no mitigating evidence. The jury recommended that he be sentenced to death on the murder charge and to consecutive life sentences on the armed robbery charges. The court followed the jury's recommendation and sentenced McCleskey to death.

On appeal, the Supreme Court of Georgia affirmed the convictions and the sentences. This Court denied a petition for a writ of certiorari. The Superior Court of Fulton County denied McCleskey's extraordinary motion for a new trial. McCleskey then filed a petition for a writ of habeas corpus in the Superior Court of Butts County. After holding an evidentiary hearing, the Superior Court denied relief. The Supreme Court of Georgia denied McCleskey's application for a certificate of probable cause to appeal the Superior Court's denial of his petition, and this Court again denied certiorari.

McCleskey next filed a petition for a writ of habeas corpus in the Federal District Court for the Northern District of Georgia. His petition raised 18 claims, one of which was that the Georgia capital sentencing process is administered in a racially discriminatory manner in violation of the Eighth and Fourteenth Amendments to the United States Constitution. In support of his claim, McCleskey proffered a statistical study performed by Professors David C. Baldus, Charles Pulaski, and George Woodworth (the Baldus study) that purports to show a disparity in the imposition of the death sentence in Georgia based on the race of the murder victim and, to a lesser extent, the race of the defendant. The Baldus study is actually two sophisticated statistical studies that examine over 2,000 murder cases that occurred in Georgia during the 1970's. The raw numbers collected by Professor Baldus indicate that defendants charged with killing white persons received the death penalty in 11% of the cases, but defendants charged with killing blacks received the death penalty in only 1% of the cases. The raw numbers also indicate a reverse racial disparity according to the race of the defendant: 4% of the black defendants received the death penalty, as opposed to 7% of the white defendants.

Baldus also divided the cases according to the combination of the race of the defendant and the race of the victim. He found that the death penalty was assessed in 22% of the cases involving black defendants and white victims; 8% of the cases involving white defendants and white victims; 1% of the cases involving black defendants and black victims; and 3% of the cases involving white defendants and black victims. Similarly, Baldus found that prosecutors sought the death penalty in 70% of the cases involving black defendants and white victims; 32% of the cases involving white defendants and white victims; 15% of the cases involving black defendants and black victims; and 19% of the cases involving white defendants and black victims.

Baldus subjected his data to an extensive analysis, taking account of 230 variables that could have explained the disparities on nonracial grounds. One of his models concludes that, even after taking account of 39 nonracial variables, defendants charged with killing white victims were 4.3 times as likely to receive a death sentence as defendants charged with killing blacks. According to this model, black defendants were 1.1 times as likely to receive a death sentence as other defendants. Thus, the Baldus study indicates that black defendants, such as McCleskey, who kill white victims have the greatest likelihood of receiving the death penalty.[5]

The District Court held an extensive evidentiary hearing on McCleskey's petition. ... It concluded that McCleskey's "statistics do not demonstrate a prima facie case in support of the contention that the death penalty was imposed upon him because of his race, because of the race of

5. Baldus' 230–variable model divided cases into eight different ranges, according to the estimated aggravation level of the offense. Baldus argued in his testimony to the District Court that the effects of racial bias were most striking in the midrange cases. "When the cases become tremendously aggravated so that everybody would agree that if we're going to have a death sentence,these are the cases that should get it, the race effects go away. It's only in the mid-range of cases where the decision-makers have a real choice as to what to do. If there's room for the exercise of discretion, then the [racial] factors begin to play a role." Under this model, Baldus found that 14.4% of the black-victim midrange cases received the death penalty, and 34.4% of the white-victim cases received the death penalty.

the victim, or because of any Eighth Amendment concern." As to McCleskey's Fourteenth Amendment claim, the court found that the methodology of the Baldus study was flawed in several respects. Because of these defects, the court held that the Baldus study "fail[ed] to contribute anything of value" to McCleskey's claim. Accordingly, the court denied the petition insofar as it was based upon the Baldus study.

* * *

II

McCleskey's first claim is that the Georgia capital punishment statute violates the Equal Protection Clause of the Fourteenth Amendment.[7] He argues that race has infected the administration of Georgia's statute in two ways: persons who murder whites are more likely to be sentenced to death than persons who murder blacks, and black murderers are more likely to be sentenced to death than white murderers.[8] As a black defendant who killed a white victim, McCleskey claims that the Baldus study demonstrates that he was discriminated against because of his race and because of the race of his victim. In its broadest form, McCleskey's claim of discrimination extends to every actor in the Georgia capital sentencing process, from the prosecutor who sought the death penalty and the jury that imposed the sentence, to the State itself that enacted the capital punishment statute and allows it to remain in effect despite its allegedly discriminatory application.

[The Court rejected McCleskey's Equal Protection claim because his statistical showing failed to establish that the prosecutor in seeking the death penalty, the jury, in deciding his case, or the legislature, in enacting or retaining the state's death penalty scheme, was acting with a "discriminatory purpose."]

III

McCleskey also argues that the Baldus study demonstrates that the Georgia capital sentencing system violates the Eighth Amendment.

* * *

---

7. Although the District Court rejected the findings of the Baldus study as flawed, the Court of Appeals assumed that the study is valid and reached the constitutional issues. Accordingly, those issues are before us. As did the Court of Appeals, we assume the study is valid statistically without reviewing the factual findings of the District Court. Our assumption that the Baldus study is statistically valid does not include the assumption that the study shows that racial considerations actually enter into any sentencing decisions in Georgia. Even a sophisticated multiple-regression analysis such as the Baldus study can only demonstrate a risk that the factor of race entered into some capital sentencing decisions and a necessarily lesser risk that race entered into any particular sentencing decision.

8. Although McCleskey has standing to claim that he suffers discrimination because of his own race, the State argues that he has no standing to contend that he was discriminated against on the basis of his victim's race. While it is true that we are reluctant to recognize "standing to assert the rights of third persons," this does not appear to be the nature of McCleskey's claim. He does not seek to assert some right of his victim, or the rights of black murder victims in general. Rather, McCleskey argues that application of the State's statute has created a classification that is "an irrational exercise of governmental power," because it is not "necessary to the accomplishment of some permissible state objective." It would violate the Equal Protection Clause for a State to base enforcement of its criminal laws on "an unjustifiable standard such as race, religion, or other arbitrary classification." Because McCleskey raises such a claim, he has standing.

IV

* * *

B

Although our decision in *Gregg v. Georgia*, 428 U.S. 153, 96 S.Ct. 2909 (1976) as to the facial validity of the Georgia capital punishment statute appears to foreclose McCleskey's disproportionality argument, he further contends that the Georgia capital punishment system is arbitrary and capricious in application, and therefore his sentence is excessive, because racial considerations may influence capital sentencing decisions in Georgia. We now address this claim.

To evaluate McCleskey's challenge, we must examine exactly what the Baldus study may show. Even Professor Baldus does not contend that his statistics prove that race enters into any capital sentencing decisions or that race was a factor in McCleskey's particular case.[29] Statistics at most may show only a likelihood that a particular factor entered into some decisions. There is, of course, some risk of racial prejudice influencing a jury's decision in a criminal case. There are similar risks that other kinds of prejudice will influence other criminal trials. The question "is at what point that risk becomes constitutionally unacceptable," *Turner v. Murray*, 476 U.S. 28, 106 S.Ct. 1683 (1986), McCleskey asks us to accept the likelihood allegedly shown by the Baldus study as the constitutional measure of an unacceptable risk of racial prejudice influencing capital sentencing decisions. This we decline to do.

Because of the risk that the factor of race may enter the criminal justice process, we have engaged in "unceasing efforts" to eradicate racial prejudice from our criminal justice system. *Batson v. Kentucky*, 476 U.S. 79, 106 S.Ct. 1712 (1986).[30] Our efforts have been guided by our recognition that "the inestimable privilege of trial by jury . . . is a vital principle, underlying the whole administration of criminal justice." *Ex parte Milligan*, 4 Wall. 2 (1866). Thus, it is the jury that is a criminal defendant's fundamental "protection of life and liberty against race or color prejudice." *Strauder v. West Virginia*, 100 U.S. 303 (1880). Specifically, a capital sentencing jury representative of a criminal defendant's community assures a " 'diffused impartiality' " in the jury's task of "express[ing]

---

29.   According to Professor Baldus:

"McCleskey's case falls in [a] grey area where . . . you would find the greatest likelihood that some inappropriate consideration may have come to bear on the decision.

"In an analysis of this type, obviously one cannot say that we can say to a moral certainty what it was that influenced the decision. We can't do that."

30.   This Court has repeatedly stated that prosecutorial discretion cannot be exercised on the basis of race. Nor can a prosecutor exercise peremptory challenges on the basis of race. More generally, this Court has condemned state efforts to exclude blacks from grand and petit juries.

Other protections apply to the trial and jury deliberation process. Widespread bias in the community can make a change of venue constitutionally required. The Constitution prohibits racially biased prosecutorial arguments. If the circumstances of a particular case indicate a significant likelihood that racial bias may influence a jury, the Constitution requires questioning as to such bias. Finally, in a capital sentencing hearing, a defendant convicted of an interracial murder is entitled to such questioning without regard to the circumstances of the particular case.

the conscience of the community on the ultimate question of life or death," *Witherspoon v. Illinois*, 391 U.S. 510, 88 S.Ct. 1770 (1968).

Individual jurors bring to their deliberations "qualities of human nature and varieties of human experience, the range of which is unknown and perhaps unknowable." *Peters v. Kiff*, 407 U.S. 493, 92 S.Ct. 2163 (1972). The capital sentencing decision requires the individual jurors to focus their collective judgment on the unique characteristics of a particular criminal defendant. It is not surprising that such collective judgments often are difficult to explain. But the inherent lack of predictability of jury decisions does not justify their condemnation. On the contrary, it is the jury's function to make the difficult and uniquely human judgments that defy codification and that "buil[d] discretion, equity, and flexibility into a legal system." H. Kalven & H. Zeisel, The American Jury (1966).

McCleskey's argument that the Constitution condemns the discretion allowed decisionmakers in the Georgia capital sentencing system is antithetical to the fundamental role of discretion in our criminal justice system. Discretion in the criminal justice system offers substantial benefits to the criminal defendant. Not only can a jury decline to impose the death sentence, it can decline to convict or choose to convict of a lesser offense. Whereas decisions against a defendant's interest may be reversed by the trial judge or on appeal, these discretionary exercises of leniency are final and unreviewable. Similarly, the capacity of prosecutorial discretion to provide individualized justice is "firmly entrenched in American law." 2 W. LaFave & D. Israel, Criminal Procedure § 13.2(a) (1984). As we have noted, a prosecutor can decline to charge, offer a plea bargain, or decline to seek a death sentence in any particular case. Of course, "the power to be lenient [also] is the power to discriminate," but a capital punishment system that did not allow for discretionary acts of leniency "would be totally alien to our notions of criminal justice." *Gregg v. Georgia.*

C

At most, the Baldus study indicates a discrepancy that appears to correlate with race. Apparent disparities in sentencing are an inevitable part of our criminal justice system. The discrepancy indicated by the Baldus study is "a far cry from the major systemic defects identified in *Furman.*"[36] As this Court has recognized, any mode for determining guilt or punishment "has its weaknesses and the potential for misuse." Specifically, "there can be 'no perfect procedure for deciding in which cases governmental authority should be used to impose death.' " *Zant v. Stephens*, 462 U.S. 862, 103 S.Ct. 2733 (1983) (quoting *Lockett v. Ohio*, 438 U.S. 586, 98 S.Ct. 2954 (1978) (plurality opinion of Burger, C. J.)). Despite these imperfections, our consistent rule has been that constitutional

---

36. The Baldus study in fact confirms that the Georgia system results in a reasonable level of proportionality among the class of murderers eligible for the death penalty. As Professor Baldus confirmed, the system sorts out cases where the sentence of death is highly likely and highly unlikely, leaving a midrange of cases where the imposition of the death penalty in any particular case is less predictable.

guarantees are met when "the mode [for determining guilt or punishment] itself has been surrounded with safeguards to make it as fair as possible." *Singer v. United States*, 380 U.S. 24, 85 S.Ct. 783 (1965). Where the discretion that is fundamental to our criminal process is involved, we decline to assume that what is unexplained is invidious. In light of the safeguards designed to minimize racial bias in the process, the fundamental value of jury trial in our criminal justice system, and the benefits that discretion provides to criminal defendants, we hold that the Baldus study does not demonstrate a constitutionally significant risk of racial bias affecting the Georgia capital sentencing process.[37]

V

Two additional concerns inform our decision in this case. First, McCleskey's claim, taken to its logical conclusion, throws into serious question the principles that underlie our entire criminal justice system. The Eighth Amendment is not limited in application to capital punishment, but applies to all penalties. Thus, if we accepted McCleskey's claim that racial bias has impermissibly tainted the capital sentencing decision, we could soon be faced with similar claims as to other types of penalty. Moreover, the claim that his sentence rests on the irrelevant factor of race easily could be extended to apply to claims based on unexplained discrepancies that correlate to membership in other minority groups, and even to gender. Similarly, since McCleskey's claim relates to the race of his victim, other claims could apply with equally logical force to statistical disparities that correlate with the race or sex of other actors in the criminal justice system, such as defense attorneys or judges. Also, there is no logical reason that such a claim need be limited to racial or sexual bias. If arbitrary and capricious punishment is the touchstone under the Eighth Amendment, such a claim could—at least in theory—be based upon any arbitrary variable, such as the defendant's facial characteristics, or the physical attractiveness of the defendant or the victim, that some statistical study indicates may be influential in jury decisionmaking. As these examples illustrate, there is no limiting principle to the type of challenge brought by McCleskey. The Constitution does not require that a State eliminate any demonstrable disparity that correlates with a potentially irrelevant factor in order to operate a criminal justice system that includes

---

37. * * *

The dissent repeatedly emphasizes the need for "a uniquely high degree of rationality in imposing the death penalty." Again, no suggestion is made as to how greater "rationality" could be achieved under any type of statute that authorizes capital punishment. The *Gregg*-type statute imposes unprecedented safeguards in the special context of capital punishment. These include: (i) a bifurcated sentencing proceeding; (ii) the threshold requirement of one or more aggravating circumstances; and (iii) mandatory State Supreme Court review. All of these are administered pursuant to this Court's decisions interpreting the limits of the Eighth Amendment on the imposition of the death penalty, and all are subject to ultimate review by this Court. These ensure a degree of care in the imposition of the sentence of death that can be described only as unique. Given these safeguards already inherent in the imposition and review of capital sentences, the dissent's call for greater rationality is no less than a claim that a capital punishment system cannot be administered in accord with the Constitution. As we reiterate, *infra*, the requirement of heightened rationality in the imposition of capital punishment does not "plac[e] totally unrealistic conditions on its use."

capital punishment. As we have stated specifically in the context of capital punishment, the Constitution does not "plac[e] totally unrealistic conditions on its use." *Gregg v. Georgia.*

Second, McCleskey's arguments are best presented to the legislative bodies. It is not the responsibility—or indeed even the right—of this Court to determine the appropriate punishment for particular crimes. It is the legislatures, the elected representatives of the people, that are "constituted to respond to the will and consequently the moral values of the people." *Furman v. Georgia* (BURGER, C. J., dissenting). Legislatures also are better qualified to weigh and "evaluate the results of statistical studies in terms of their own local conditions and with a flexibility of approach that is not available to the courts," *Gregg v. Georgia.* Capital punishment is now the law in more than two-thirds of our States. It is the ultimate duty of courts to determine on a case-by-case basis whether these laws are applied consistently with the Constitution. Despite McCleskey's wide-ranging arguments that basically challenge the validity of capital punishment in our multiracial society, the only question before us is whether in his case the law of Georgia was properly applied. We agree with the District Court and the Court of Appeals for the Eleventh Circuit that this was carefully and correctly done in this case.

VI

Accordingly, we affirm the judgment of the Court of Appeals for the Eleventh Circuit.

It is so ordered.

JUSTICE BRENNAN, with whom JUSTICE MARSHALL joins, and with whom JUSTICE BLACKMUN and JUSTICE STEVENS join in all but Part I, dissenting.

* * *

II

At some point in this case, Warren McCleskey doubtless asked his lawyer whether a jury was likely to sentence him to die. A candid reply to this question would have been disturbing. First, counsel would have to tell McCleskey that few of the details of the crime or of McCleskey's past criminal conduct were more important than the fact that his victim was white. Furthermore, counsel would feel bound to tell McCleskey that defendants charged with killing white victims in Georgia are 4.3 times as likely to be sentenced to death as defendants charged with killing blacks. In addition, frankness would compel the disclosure that it was more likely than not that the race of McCleskey's victim would determine whether he received a death sentence: 6 of every 11 defendants convicted of killing a white person would not have received the death penalty if their victims had been black, while, among defendants with aggravating and mitigating factors comparable to McCleskey's, 20 of every 34 would not have been sentenced to die if their victims had been black. Finally, the assessment would not be complete without the information that cases involving black defendants and white victims are more likely to result in a death sentence than cases featuring any other racial combination of defendant and victim. The story could be told in a variety of ways, but McCleskey could not fail to grasp its essential narrative line: there was a significant chance that race would play a prominent role in determining if he lived or died.

The Court today holds that Warren McCleskey's sentence was constitutionally imposed. It finds no fault in a system in which lawyers must tell their clients that race casts a large shadow on the capital sentencing process. The Court arrives at this conclusion by stating that the Baldus study cannot "prove that race enters into any capital sentencing decisions or that race was a factor in McCleskey's particular case." Since, according to Professor Baldus, we cannot say "to a moral certainty" that race influenced a decision, we can identify only "a likelihood that a particular factor entered into some decisions," and "a discrepancy that appears to correlate with race." This "likelihood" and "discrepancy," holds the Court, is insufficient to establish a constitutional violation. The Court reaches this conclusion by placing four factors on the scales opposite McCleskey's evidence: the desire to encourage sentencing discretion, the existence of "statutory safeguards" in the Georgia scheme, the fear of encouraging widespread challenges to other sentencing decisions, and the limits of the judicial role. The Court's evaluation of the significance of petitioner's evidence is fundamentally at odds with our consistent concern for rationality in capital sentencing, and the considerations that the majority invokes to discount that evidence cannot justify ignoring its force.

III

A

It is important to emphasize at the outset that the Court's observation that McCleskey cannot prove the influence of race on any particular sentencing decision is irrelevant in evaluating his Eighth Amendment claim. Since *Furman v. Georgia*, 408 U.S. 238, 92 S.Ct. 2726 (1972), the Court has been concerned with the risk of the imposition of an arbitrary sentence, rather than the proven fact of one. *Furman* held that the death penalty "may not be imposed under sentencing procedures that create a substantial risk that the punishment will be inflicted in an arbitrary and capricious manner." *Godfrey v. Georgia*, 446 U.S. 420, 100 S.Ct. 1759 (1980). As JUSTICE O'CONNOR observed in *Caldwell v. Mississippi*, 472 U.S. 320, 105 S.Ct. 2633 (1985), a death sentence must be struck down when the circumstances under which it has been imposed "creat[e] an unacceptable *risk* that 'the death penalty [may have been] meted out arbitrarily or capriciously' or through 'whim or mistake' " (emphasis added)). This emphasis on risk acknowledges the difficulty of divining the jury's motivation in an individual case. In addition, it reflects the fact that concern for arbitrariness focuses on the rationality of the system as a whole, and that a system that features a significant probability that sentencing decisions are influenced by impermissible considerations cannot be regarded as rational. As we said in *Gregg v. Georgia*, "the petitioner looks to the sentencing system as a whole (as the Court did in *Furman* and we do today)": a constitutional violation is established if a plaintiff demonstrates a "*pattern* of arbitrary and capricious sentencing." (emphasis added) (joint opinion of STEWART, POWELL, and STEVENS, JJ.).

* * *

B

The Baldus study indicates that, after taking into account some 230 nonracial factors that might legitimately influence a sentencer, the jury more likely than not would have spared McCleskey's life had his victim been black. The study distinguishes between those cases in which (1) the jury exercises virtually no discretion because the strength or weakness of aggravating factors usually suggests that only one outcome is appropriate;[2] and (2) cases reflecting an "intermediate" level of aggravation, in which the jury has considerable discretion in choosing a sentence.[3] McCleskey's case falls into the intermediate range. In such cases, death is imposed in 34% of white-victim crimes and 14% of black-victim crimes, a difference of 139% in the rate of imposition of the death penalty. In other words, just under 59%—almost 6 in 10—defendants comparable to McCleskey would not have received the death penalty if their victims had been black.

Furthermore, even examination of the sentencing system as a whole, factoring in those cases in which the jury exercises little discretion, indicates the influence of race on capital sentencing. For the Georgia system as a whole, race accounts for a six percentage point difference in the rate at which capital punishment is imposed. Since death is imposed in 11% of all white-victim cases, the rate in comparably aggravated black-victim cases is 5%. The rate of capital sentencing in a white-victim case is thus 120% greater than the rate in a black-victim case. Put another way, over half—55%—of defendants in white-victim crimes in Georgia would not have been sentenced to die if their victims had been black. Of the more than 200 variables potentially relevant to a sentencing decision, race of the victim is a powerful explanation for variation in death sentence rates—as powerful as nonracial aggravating factors such as a prior murder conviction or acting as the principal planner of the homicide.

These adjusted figures are only the most conservative indication of the risk that race will influence the death sentences of defendants in

---

2. The first two and the last of the study's eight case categories represent those cases in which the jury typically sees little leeway in deciding on a sentence. Cases in the first two categories are those that feature aggravating factors so minimal that juries imposed no death sentences in the 88 cases with these factors during the period of the study. Cases in the eighth category feature aggravating factors so extreme that the jury imposed the death penalty in 88% of the 58 cases with these factors in the same period.

3. In the five categories characterized as intermediate, the rate at which the death penalty was imposed ranged from 8% to 41%. The overall rate for the 326 cases in these categories was 20%.

Georgia. Data unadjusted for the mitigating or aggravating effect of other factors show an even more pronounced disparity by race. The capital sentencing rate for all white-victim cases was almost 11 times greater than the rate for black-victim cases. Furthermore, blacks who kill whites are sentenced to death at nearly 22 times the rate of blacks who kill blacks, and more than 7 times the rate of whites who kill blacks. In addition, prosecutors seek the death penalty for 70% of black defendants with white victims, but for only 15% of black defendants with black victims, and only 19% of white defendants with black victims. Since our decision upholding the Georgia capital sentencing system in *Gregg*, the State has executed seven persons. All of the seven were convicted of killing whites, and six of the seven executed were black. Such execution figures are especially striking in light of the fact that, during the period encompassed by the Baldus study, only 9.2% of Georgia homicides involved black defendants and white victims, while 60.7% involved black victims.

* * *

IV

The Court cites four reasons for shrinking from the implications of McCleskey's evidence: the desirability of discretion for actors in the criminal justice system, the existence of statutory safeguards against abuse of that discretion, the potential consequences for broader challenges to criminal sentencing, and an understanding of the contours of the judicial role. While these concerns underscore the need for sober deliberation, they do not justify rejecting evidence as convincing as McCleskey has presented.

The Court maintains that petitioner's claim "is antithetical to the fundamental role of discretion in our criminal justice system." It states that "where the discretion that is fundamental to our criminal process is involved, we decline to assume that what is unexplained is invidious." Reliance on race in imposing capital punishment, however, is antithetical to the very rationale for granting sentencing discretion. Discretion is a means, not an end. It is bestowed in order to permit the sentencer to "trea[t] each defendant in a capital case with that degree of respect due the uniqueness of the individual." *Lockett v. Ohio*, 438 U.S. 586, 98 S.Ct. 2954 (1978). The decision to impose the punishment of death must be based on a "particularized consideration of relevant aspects of the character and record of each convicted defendant." *Woodson v. North Carolina*. Failure to conduct such an individualized moral inquiry "treats all persons convicted of a designated offense not as unique individual human beings, but as members of a faceless, undifferentiated mass to be subjected to the blind infliction of the penalty of death."

Considering the race of a defendant or victim in deciding if the death penalty should be imposed is completely at odds with this concern that an individual be evaluated as a unique human being. Decisions influenced by race rest in part on a categorical assessment of the worth of human beings according to color, insensitive to whatever qualities the individuals in question may possess. Enhanced willingness to impose the death sentence on black defendants, or diminished willingness to render such a sentence when blacks are victims, reflects a devaluation of the lives of black persons. When confronted with evidence that race more likely than not plays such a role in a capital sentencing system, it is plainly insufficient to say that the importance of discretion demands that the risk be higher before we will act—for in such a case the very end that discretion is designed to serve is being undermined.

Our desire for individualized moral judgments may lead us to accept some inconsistencies in sentencing outcomes. Since such decisions are not reducible to mathematical formulae, we are willing to assume that a certain degree of variation reflects the fact that no two defendants are completely alike. There is thus a presumption that actors in the criminal justice system exercise their discretion in responsible fashion, and we do not automatically infer that sentencing patterns that do not comport with ideal rationality are suspect.

As we made clear in *Batson v. Kentucky*, 476 U.S. 79, 106 S.Ct. 1712 (1986), however, that presumption is rebuttable. *Batson* dealt with another arena in which considerable discretion traditionally has been afforded, the exercise of peremptory challenges. Those challenges are normally exercised without any indication whatsoever of the grounds for doing so. The rationale for this deference has been a belief that the unique characteristics of particular prospective jurors may raise concern on the part of the prosecution or defense, despite the fact that counsel may not be able to articulate that concern in a manner sufficient to support exclusion for cause. As with sentencing, therefore, peremptory challenges are justified as an occasion for particularized determinations related to specific individuals, and, as with sentencing, we presume that such challenges normally are not made on the basis of a factor such as race. As we said in *Batson*, however, such features do not justify imposing a "crippling burden of proof," in order to rebut that presumption. The Court in this case apparently seeks to do just that. On the basis of the need for individualized decisions, it rejects evidence, drawn from the most sophisticated capital sentencing analysis ever performed, that reveals that race more likely than not infects capital sentencing decisions. The Court's position converts a rebuttable presumption into a virtually conclusive one.

The Court also declines to find McCleskey's evidence sufficient in view of "the safeguards designed to minimize racial bias in the [capital sentencing] process." *Gregg v. Georgia* upheld the Georgia capital sentencing statute against a facial challenge which JUSTICE WHITE described in his concurring opinion as based on "simply an assertion of lack of faith" that the system could operate in a fair manner (opinion concurring in judgment). JUSTICE WHITE observed that the claim that prosecutors might act in an arbitrary fashion was "unsupported by any facts," and that prosecutors must be assumed to exercise their charging duties properly "absent facts to the contrary." It is clear that *Gregg* bestowed no permanent approval on the Georgia system. It simply held that the State's statutory safeguards were assumed sufficient to channel discretion without evidence otherwise.

It has now been over 13 years since Georgia adopted the provisions upheld in *Gregg*. Professor Baldus and his colleagues have compiled data on almost 2,500 homicides committed during the period 1973–1979. They have taken into account the influence of 230 nonracial variables, using a multitude of data from the State itself, and have produced striking evidence that the odds of being sentenced to death are significantly greater than average if a defendant is black or his or her victim is white. The challenge to the Georgia system is not speculative or theoretical; it is empirical. As a result, the Court cannot rely on the statutory safeguards in discounting McCleskey's evidence, for it is the very effectiveness of those safeguards that such evidence calls into question. While we may hope that a model of procedural fairness will curb the influence of race on sentencing, "we cannot simply assume that the model works as intended; we must critique its performance in terms of its results." Hubbard, *"Reasonable Levels of Arbitrariness" in Death Sentencing Patterns: A Tragic Perspective on Capital Punishment*, 18 U.C.Davis L.Rev. 1113 (1985).

The Court next states that its unwillingness to regard petitioner's evidence as sufficient is based in part on the fear that recognition of McCleskey's claim would open the door to widespread challenges to all aspects of criminal sentencing. Taken on its face, such a statement seems to suggest a fear of too much justice. Yet surely the majority would acknowledge that if striking evidence indicated that other minority groups, or women, or even persons with blond hair, were disproportionately sentenced to death, such a state of affairs would be repugnant to deeply rooted conceptions of fairness. The prospect that there may be more widespread abuse than McCleskey documents may be dismaying, but it does not justify complete abdication of our judicial role. The Constitution was framed fundamentally as a bulwark against governmental power, and preventing the arbitrary administration of punishment is a basic ideal of any society that purports to be governed by the rule of law.

In fairness, the Court's fear that McCleskey's claim is an invitation to descend a slippery slope also rests on the realization that any humanly imposed system of penalties will exhibit some imperfection. Yet to reject McCleskey's powerful evidence on this basis is to ignore both the qualitatively different character of the death penalty and the particular repugnance of racial discrimination, considerations which may properly be taken into account in determining whether various punishments are "cruel and unusual." Furthermore, it fails to take account of the unprecedented refinement and strength of the Baldus study.

It hardly needs reiteration that this Court has consistently acknowledged the uniqueness of the punishment of death. "Death, in its finality, differs more from life imprisonment than a 100-year prison term differs from one of only a year or two. Because of that qualitative difference, there is a corresponding difference in the need for reliability in the determination that death is the appropriate punishment." *Woodson v. North Carolina*. Furthermore, the relative interests of the state and the defendant differ dramatically in the death penalty context. The marginal benefits accruing to the state from obtaining the death penalty rather than life imprisonment are considerably less than the marginal difference to the defendant between death and life in prison. Such a disparity is an additional reason for tolerating scant arbitrariness in capital sentencing. Even those who believe that society can impose the death penalty in a manner sufficiently rational to justify its continuation must acknowledge that the level of rationality that is considered satisfactory must be uniquely high. As a result, the degree of arbitrariness that may be adequate to render the death penalty "cruel and unusual" punishment may not be adequate to invalidate lesser penalties. What these relative degrees of arbitrariness might be in other cases need not concern us here; the point is that the majority's fear of wholesale invalidation of criminal sentences is unfounded.

The Court also maintains that accepting McCleskey's claim would pose a threat to all sentencing because of the prospect that a correlation might be demonstrated between sentencing outcomes and other personal characteristics. Again, such a view is indifferent to the considerations that enter into a determination whether punishment is "cruel and unusual." Race is a consideration whose influence is expressly constitutionally proscribed. We have expressed a moral commitment, as embodied in our fundamental law, that this specific characteristic should not be the basis for allotting burdens and benefits. Three constitutional amendments, and numerous statutes, have been prompted specifically by the desire to address the effects of racism. "Over the years, this Court has consistently repudiated 'distinctions between citizens solely because of their ancestry' as being 'odious to a free people whose institutions are founded upon the doctrine of equality.' " *Loving v. Virginia*, 388 U.S. 1, 87 S.Ct. 1817 (1967) (quoting *Hirabayashi v. United States*, 320 U.S. 81, 63 S.Ct. 1375 (1943)). Furthermore, we have explicitly acknowledged the illegitimacy of race as a consideration in capital sentencing, *Zant v. Stephens*, 462 U.S. 862, 103 S.Ct. 2733 (1983). That a decision to impose the death penalty could be influenced by race is thus a particularly repugnant prospect, and evidence that race may play even a modest role in levying a death sentence should be enough to characterize that sentence as "cruel and unusual."

* * *

Finally, the Court justifies its rejection of McCleskey's claim by cautioning against usurpation of the legislatures' role in devising and monitoring criminal punishment. The Court is, of course, correct to emphasize the gravity of constitutional intervention and the importance that it be sparingly employed. The fact that "capital punishment is now the law in more than two thirds of our States," however, does not diminish the fact that capital punishment is the most awesome act that a State can perform. The judiciary's role in this society counts for little if the use of governmental power to extinguish life does not elicit close scrutiny. It is true that society has a legitimate interest in punishment. Yet, as Alexander Bickel wrote:

> "It is a premise we deduce not merely from the fact of a written constitution but from the history of the race, and ultimately as a moral judgment of the good society, that government should serve not only what we conceive from time to time to be our immediate material needs but also certain enduring values. This in part is what is meant by government under law." The Least Dangerous Branch (1962).

Our commitment to these values requires fidelity to them even when there is temptation to ignore them. Such temptation is especially apt to arise in criminal matters, for those granted constitutional protection in this context are those whom society finds most menacing and opprobrious. Even less sympathetic are those we consider for the sentence of death, for execution "is a way of saying, 'You are not fit for this world, take your chance elsewhere.' " *Furman v. Georgia* (BRENNAN, J., concurring) (quoting Stephen, *Capital Punishment*, 69 Fraser's Magazine 753 (1864)).

For these reasons, "the methods we employ in the enforcement of our criminal law have aptly been called the measures by which the quality of our civilization may be judged." *Coppedge v. United States*, 369 U.S. 438, 82 S.Ct. 917 (1962). Those whom we would banish from society or from the human community itself often speak in too faint a voice to be heard above society's demand for punishment. It is the particular role of courts to hear these voices, for the Constitution declares that the majoritarian chorus may not alone dictate the conditions of social life. The Court thus fulfills, rather than disrupts, the scheme of separation of powers by closely scrutinizing the imposition of the death penalty, for no decision of a society is more deserving of "sober second thought." Stone, *The Common Law in the United States*, 50 Harv.L.Rev. 4 (1936).

V

At the time our Constitution was framed 200 years ago this year, blacks "had for more than a century before been regarded as beings of an inferior order, and altogether unfit to associate with the white race, either in social or political relations; and so far inferior, that they had no rights which the white man was bound to respect." *Dred Scott v. Sandford*, 60 U.S. 393, 19 How. 393 (1856). Only 130 years ago, this Court relied on these observations to deny American citizenship to blacks. A mere three generations ago, this Court sanctioned racial segregation, stating that "if one race be inferior to the other socially, the Constitution of the United States cannot put them upon the same plane." *Plessy v. Ferguson*, 163 U.S. 537, 16 S.Ct. 1138 (1896).

In more recent times, we have sought to free ourselves from the burden of this history. Yet it has been scarcely a generation since this Court's first decision striking down racial segregation, and barely two decades since the legislative prohibition of racial discrimination in major domains of national life. These have been honorable steps, but we cannot pretend that in three decades we have completely escaped the grip of a historical legacy spanning centuries. Warren McCleskey's evidence confronts us with the subtle and persistent influence of the past. His message is a disturbing one to a society that has formally repudiated racism, and a frustrating one to a Nation accustomed to regarding its destiny as the product of its own will. Nonetheless, we ignore him at our peril, for we remain imprisoned by the past as long as we deny its influence in the present.

It is tempting to pretend that minorities on death row share a fate in no way connected to our own, that our treatment of them sounds no echoes beyond the chambers in which they die. Such an illusion is ultimately corrosive, for the reverberations of injustice are not so easily confined. "The destinies of the two races in this country are indissolubly linked together" *Plessy v. Ferguson* (HARLAN, J., dissenting), and the way in which we choose those who will die reveals the depth of moral commitment among the living.

The Court's decision today will not change what attorneys in Georgia tell other Warren McCleskeys about their chances of execution. Nothing will soften the harsh message they must convey, nor alter the prospect that race undoubtedly will continue to be a topic of discussion. McCleskey's evidence will not have obtained judicial acceptance, but that will not affect what is said on death row. However many criticisms of today's decision may be rendered, these painful conversations will serve as the most eloquent dissents of all.

* * *

[Dissenting opinion of BLACKMUN, J., joined by MARSHALL and STEVENS, J.J. and, in part, by BRENNAN, J., and dissenting opinion of STEVENS, J., joined by BLACKMUN, J., omitted.]

NOTES

1. *"Underprotection" of the African–American community.*

McCleskey's statistics established that, in the application of the death penalty in Georgia, although there was some "overenforcement" against African–American defendants, there was far more "underprotection" of African–American victims. Professor Randall Kennedy has argued that, historically, the consistent failure of criminal justice officials to treat crimes against African–Americans as seriously as crimes against white people has had more insidious consequences than the discriminatory treatment of African–American suspects and defendants:

> Deliberately withholding protection against criminality (or conduct that should be deemed criminal) is one of the most destructive forms of oppression that has been visited upon African–Americans. The specter of the wrongly convicted black defendant rushed to punishment by a racially biased process is haunting ... even worse is racially selective underpro-

tection. This form of discrimination is worse because it has directly and adversely affected more people than have episodic misjudgments of guilt. Racially selective underprotection is also worse in the sense that society is not as well equipped to combat it. Even before the abolition of slavery, officials everywhere acknowledged, at least in principle, that government is obliged to punish for crimes only duly convicted persons, regardless of race. Much more difficult to establish has been the idea that government is obliged to protect blacks from crime on the same terms as it protects whites.

R. Kennedy, Race, Crime and the Law 28 (1997). Can the criminal justice system address this problem?

2. *Findings in other states*

Racial disparities similar to those found in the administration of Georgia's death penalty have been found in a number of other death penalty states. In 2004–07, the American Bar Association Death Penalty Moratorium Implementation Project conducted studies in eight states—Alabama, Arizona, Florida, Georgia, Indiana, Ohio, Pennsylvania and Tennessee—to assess the extent to which the capital punishment systems had implemented ABA policies designed to promote fairness. One of the findings of the studies was: "Every state studied appears to have significant racial disparities in its capital system, particularly those associated with the race of the victim."[a] Recent studies also have documented racial disparities in California,[b] Connecticut,[c] Maryland[d] and South Carolina.[e] Does the pervasiveness of racial disparities validate Justice Powell's concern that McCleskey's challenge was not just to the administration of the death penalty in Georgia, but to the constitutionality of the death penalty itself?

3. *The "inevitability" of racial disparities.*

The Court's suggestion that apparent racial disparities in sentencing are "inevitable" has been challenged by the authors of the Georgia study. See D. Baldus, G. Woodworth & C. Pulaski, Jr., *Reflections on the "Inevitability" of Racial Discrimination in Capital Sentencing and the "Impossibility" of its Prevention, Detection, and Correction*, 51 Wash. & Lee L. Rev. 359 (1994). They identify at least four possible approaches to dealing with racial discrimination in capital punishment: "(a) narrowing the class of death-eligible cases, (b) requiring standards to limit the exercise of prosecutorial discretion, (c) recognizing claims of racial discrimination in individual cases and evaluating those claims under burdens of proof comparable to those applied in other areas of the law, or (d) abolishing the death penalty." *Id.* at 362, n.7. They conclude that, "[w]hat some may describe as the inevitability of such sen-

---

a. American Bar Association, *State Death Penalty Assessments: Key Findings* (2008) (http://www.abanet.org/moratorium/assessmentproject/keyfindings.doc)

b. G. Pierce & M. Radelet, *The Impact of Legally Inappropriate Factors on Death Sentencing for California Homicides, 1990–1999*, 46 Santa Clara L. Rev. 1 (2005).

c. J. Donohue, III, *Capital Punishment in Connecticut, 1973–2007: a Comprehensive Evaluation from 4600 Murders to One Execution* (2008) (http://works.bepress.com/john_donohue/55).

d. R. Paternoster, et al., *Justice by Geography and Race: The Administration of the Death Penalty in Maryland, 1978–1999*, 4 Margins: Md. L.J. Race, Religion, Gender & Class 1 (2004).

e. M. Songer and I. Unah, *The Effect of Race, Gender, and Location on Prosecutorial Decision to Seek the Death Penalty in South Carolina*, 58 S. Carolina Law Rev. 161 (2006).

tences or the impossibility of preventing, detecting and correcting them reflects, in our judgment, only an unwillingness to make the effort." *Id.* at 419.

4. *The Racial Justice Act.*

Shortly after the *McCleskey* decision, the Racial Justice Act (RJA) was introduced in Congress. H.R. 4442, 100th Cong., 2d Sess. (1988) The RJA would have established as *prima facie* evidence of racial discrimination the type of statistical evidence presented in the Baldus study. The first version of the RJA failed in the House. In succeeding years, different versions of the RJA were introduced in Congress, and all were rejected. As of 2009, only two states, Kentucky and North Carolina, had enacted a Racial Justice Act.

5. *Non-racial arbitrariness.*

In *McCleskey*, the Court voiced the concern that if McCleskey's claim were recognized, the same claim could be made regarding statistical disparities that correlate with "other minority groups and even . . . gender" or "the race or sex of other actors in the criminal justice system" or "any arbitrary variable." Post–*McCleskey* empirical studies suggest that there are non-racial arbitrary variables—gender, geography and politics—which correlate with sentencing results. First, there is evidence that application of the death penalty does depend on gender and that it is a penalty generally reserved for men. During the period 1973–2007, women accounted for about 10% of the murder arrests in the United States, but only 2% of the death sentences and only 1% of the executions.[f] It is also a penalty that is imposed disproportionally on those who kill women.[g] Second, a number of studies have established that, within a particular state, there are substantial disparities in the use of the death penalty among the various counties.[h] Third, one study found that, in a gubernatorial election year, the probability of an execution increases more than 25%, suggesting that electoral politics may also inject an arbitrary variable into the administration of the death penalty.[i] Does *McCleskey* fore-

---

f. V. Streib, *Death Penalty for Female Offenders, January 1, 1973 through December 31, 2007* (2008) (http://www.deathpenaltyinfo.org/FemDeathDec2007.pdf)

g. S. Hindson, H. Potter & M. Radelet, *Race, Gender, Region and Death Sentencing in Colorado, 1980–1999*, 77 U. Colo. L. Rev. 549 (2006); M. Songer and I. Unah, *The Effect of Race, Gender, and Location on Prosecutorial Decision to Seek the Death Penalty in South Carolina*, 58 S. Carolina Law Rev. 161 (2006).

h. See, *e.g.*, G. Pierce & M. Radelet, *The Impact of Legally Inappropriate Factors on Death Sentencing for California Homicides, 1990–1999*, 46 Santa Clara L. Rev. 1 (2005); R. Paternoster & R. Brame, *An Empirical Analysis of Maryland's Death Sentencing System with Respect to the Influence of Race and Legal Jurisdiction*, (http://www.newsdesk.umd.edu/pdf/finalrep.pdf) ("There is a statistically significant variation across the different jurisdictions in the probability of a death sentence for all death-eligible cases due primarily to the way charging decisions are handled."); G. Pierce & M. Radelet, *Race, Region and Death Sentencing in Illinois, 1988–1997*, 81 Ore. L. Rev. 39 (2002) ("[T]he odds of receiving a death sentence for killing a victim(s) in Cook County are on average 83.6% lower than for killing a victim(s) in the rural county region of Illinois controlling for the other twenty-six variables in the analysis.").

A Department of Justice study of the first twelve years of the federal death penalty also revealed significant geographical disparities. See *Federal Death Penalty System: A Statistical Survey (1988–2000)* (2000) (http://www.usdoj.gov/dag/pubdoc/dpsurvey.html). Five of the 94 judicial districts had produced 42% of the death penalty recommendations to the Attorney General; 40 districts had never recommended a death penalty prosecution.

i. See J. Kubik & J. Moran, *Lethal Elections: Gubernatorial Politics and the Timing of Executions*, 46 J. Law & Econ. 1 (2003).

close challenges based on the empirical evidence of arbitrariness adduced by these studies?

6. *Reconsideration by Justice Powell.*

In 1991, after his retirement from the Court, Justice Powell, the author of *McCleskey v. Kemp*, was asked whether he would change his vote in any case:

A. Yes, *McCleskey v. Kemp*.

Q. Do you mean you would now accept the argument from statistics?

A. No, I would vote the other way in any capital case.

Q. In *any* capital case?

A. Yes.

Q. Even in *Furman v. Georgia*?

A. Yes. I have come to think that capital punishment should be abolished.

J. Jefferies, Jr., Justice Lewis F. Powell, Jr. 451 (1994).

CHAPTER 4

THE REQUIREMENT OF AN INDIVIDUALIZED PENALTY DETERMINATION

■ ■ ■

In *Woodson v. North Carolina* and *Roberts v. Louisiana* [Chapter 2], the Court held unconstitutional mandatory death penalty statutes because they failed "to allow the particularized consideration of relevant aspects of the character and record of each convicted defendant." Thus, the defendant must be permitted to present mitigation evidence, but the question presented in each of the cases in this chapter is to what extent the state may guide or limit the sentencer's consideration of such evidence. In *Lockett v. Ohio*, the state statute required the imposition of a death sentence unless the judge found one of three listed mitigating factors. In *Eddings v. Oklahoma*, the trial judge refused to consider certain mitigation evidence under the apparent assumption that, as a matter of law, he could only consider evidence to be mitigating if it would tend to support a legal excuse from criminal liability. *Smith v. Texas* is the seventh case in which the Court has addressed whether the former Texas capital sentencing scheme, upheld in *Jurek v. Texas* [Chapter 2], sufficiently allowed for the consideration of the defendant's mitigation evidence. In *Kansas v. Marsh*, the Court considers whether putting the burden of persuasion as to whether mitigating circumstances outweigh aggravating circumstances on the defendant interferes "in a constitutionally significant way" with the jury's consideration of the mitigation evidence. The final case in the chapter, *Walton v. Arizona*, does not involve a challenge to limitations on mitigation evidence, but Justice Scalia, in his concurring opinion, takes the occasion to attack the *Woodson–Lockett* line of cases as fundamentally inconsistent with *Furman*. Justice Stevens, in his dissenting opinion, responds with a defense of the Court's constitutional analysis.

LOCKETT v. OHIO

438 U.S. 586, 98 S.Ct. 2954, 57 L.Ed.2d 973 (1978).

MR. CHIEF JUSTICE BURGER delivered the opinion of the Court with respect to the constitutionality of petitioner's conviction (Parts I and II), together with an opinion (Part III), in which MR. JUSTICE STEWART, MR. JUSTICE POWELL, and MR. JUSTICE STEVENS, joined, on the constitutionality of the statute under which petitioner was sentenced to death and announced the judgment of the Court.

We granted certiorari in this case to consider, among other questions, whether Ohio violated the Eighth and Fourteenth amendments by sentencing Sandra Lockett to death pursuant to a statute that narrowly limits the sentencer's discretion to consider the circumstances of the crime and the record and character of the offender as mitigating factors.

I

Lockett was charged with aggravated murder with the aggravating specifications (1) that the murder was "committed for the purpose of escaping detection, apprehension, trial, or punishment" for aggravated robbery, and (2) that the murder was "committed while ... committing, attempting to commit, or fleeing immediately after committing or attempting to commit ... aggravated robbery." That offense was punishable by death in Ohio. She was also charged with aggravated robbery. The State's case against her depended largely upon the testimony of a coparticipant, one Al Parker, who gave the following account of her participation in the robbery and murder.

Lockett became acquainted with Parker and Nathan Earl Dew while she and a friend, Joanne Baxter, were in New Jersey. Parker and Dew then accompanied Lockett, Baxter, and Lockett's brother back to Akron, Ohio, Lockett's home town. After they arrived in Akron, Parker and Dew needed money for the trip back to New Jersey. Dew suggested that he pawn his ring. Lockett overheard his suggestion, but felt that the ring was too beautiful to pawn, and suggested instead that they could get some money by robbing a grocery store and a furniture store in the area. She warned that the grocery store's operator was a "big guy" who carried a "45" and that they would have "to get him real quick." She also volunteered to get a gun from her father's basement to aid in carrying out the robberies, but by that time, the two stores had closed and it was too late to proceed with the plan to rob them.

Someone, apparently Lockett's brother, suggested a plan for robbing a pawnshop. He and Dew would enter the shop and pretend to pawn a ring. Next Parker, who had some bullets, would enter the shop, ask to see a gun, load it, and use it to rob the shop. No one planned to kill the pawnshop operator in the course of the robbery. Because she knew the owner, Lockett was not to be among those entering the pawnshop, though she did guide the others to the shop that night.

The next day Parker, Dew, Lockett, and her brother gathered at Baxter's apartment. Lockett's brother asked if they were "still going to do it," and everyone, including Lockett, agreed to proceed. The four then drove by the pawnshop several times and parked the car. Lockett's brother and Dew entered the shop. Parker then left the car and told Lockett to start it again in two minutes. The robbery proceeded according to plan until the pawnbroker grabbed the gun when Parker announced the "stickup." The gun went off with Parker's finger on the trigger firing a fatal shot into the pawnbroker.

Parker went back to the car where Lockett waited with the engine running. While driving away from the pawnshop, Parker told Lockett what had happened. She took the gun from the pawnshop and put it into her purse. Lockett and Parker drove to Lockett's aunt's house and called a taxicab. Shortly thereafter, while riding away in a taxicab, they were stopped by the police, but by this time Lockett had placed the gun under the front seat. Lockett told the police that Parker rented a room from her mother and lived with her family. After verifying this story with Lockett's parents, the police released Lockett and Parker. Lockett hid Dew and Parker in the attic when the police arrived at the Lockett household later that evening.

Parker was subsequently apprehended and charged with aggravated murder with specifications, an offense punishable by death, and aggravated robbery. Prior to trial, he pleaded guilty to the murder charge and agreed to testify against Lockett, her brother, and Dew. In return, the prosecutor dropped the aggravated robbery charge and the specifications to the murder charge, thereby eliminating the possibility that Parker could receive the death penalty.

Lockett's brother and Dew were later convicted of aggravated murder with specifications. Lockett's brother was sentenced to death, but Dew received a lesser penalty because it was determined that his offense was "primarily the product of mental deficiency," one of the three mitigating circumstances specified in the Ohio death penalty statute.

Two weeks before Lockett's separate trial, the prosecutor offered to permit her to plead guilty to voluntary manslaughter and aggravated robbery (offenses which each carried a maximum penalty of 25 years' imprisonment and a maximum fine of $10,000) * * * if she would cooperate with the State, but she rejected the offer. Just prior to her trial, the prosecutor offered to permit her to plead guilty to aggravated murder without specifications, an offense carrying a mandatory life penalty, with the understanding that the aggravated robbery charge and an outstanding forgery charge would be dismissed. Again she rejected the offer.

[At trial, during the prosecution's case, the prosecutor again offered to allow Lockett to plead to a lesser charge, and Lockett again refused. Because Lockett decided not to testify, the defense presented no evidence.]

The jury found Lockett guilty as charged.

Once a verdict of aggravated murder with specifications had been returned, the Ohio death penalty statute required the trial judge to impose a death sentence unless, after "considering the nature and circumstances of the offense" and Lockett's "history, character, and condition," he found by a preponderance of the evidence that (1) the victim had induced or facilitated the offense, (2) it was unlikely that Lockett would have committed the offense but for the fact that she "was under duress, coercion, or strong provocation," or (3) the offense was "primarily the product of [Lockett's] psychosis or mental deficiency."

In accord with the Ohio statute, the trial judge requested a presentence report as well as psychiatric and psychological reports. The reports contained detailed information about Lockett's intelligence, character, and background. The psychiatric and psychological reports described her as a 21–year–old with low-average or average intelligence, and not suffering from a mental deficiency. One of the psychologists reported that "her prognosis for rehabilitation" if returned to society was favorable. The presentence report showed that Lockett had committed no major offenses although she had a record of several minor ones as a juvenile and two minor offenses as an adult. It also showed that she had once used heroin but was receiving treatment at a drug abuse clinic and seemed to be "on the road to success" as far as her drug problem was concerned. It concluded that Lockett suffered no psychosis and was not mentally deficient.

After considering the reports and hearing argument on the penalty issue, the trial judge concluded that the offense had not been primarily the product of psychosis or mental deficiency. Without specifically addressing the other two statutory mitigating factors, the judge said that he had "no alternative, whether [he] like[d] the law or not" but to impose the death penalty. He then sentenced Lockett to death.

* * *

III

Lockett challenges the constitutionality of Ohio's death penalty statute on a number of grounds. We find it necessary to consider only her contention that her death sentence is invalid because the statute under which it was imposed did not permit the sentencing judge to consider, as mitigating factors, her character, prior record, age, lack of specific intent to cause death, and her relatively minor part in the crime. To address her contention from the proper perspective, it is helpful to review the developments in our recent cases where we have applied the Eighth and Fourteenth Amendments to death penalty statutes. We do not write on a "clean slate."

A

Prior to *Furman v. Georgia*, 408 U.S. 238, 92 S.Ct. 2726 (1972), every State that authorized capital punishment had abandoned mandatory death penalties, and instead permitted the jury unguided and unrestrained discretion regarding the imposition of the death penalty in a particular capital case. Mandatory death penalties had proved unsatisfactory, as the plurality noted in *Woodson v. North Carolina*, 428 U.S. 280, 96 S.Ct. 2978 (1976), in part because juries, "with some regularity, disregarded their oaths and refused to convict defendants where a death sentence was the automatic consequence of a guilty verdict."

This Court had never intimated prior to *Furman* that discretion in sentencing offended the Constitution. * * * As recently as *McGautha v. California*, 402 U.S. 183, 91 S.Ct. 1454 (1971), the Court had specifically rejected the contention that discretion in imposing the death penalty violated the fundamental standards of fairness embodied in Fourteenth Amendment due process and had asserted that States were entitled to assume that "jurors confronted with the truly awesome responsibility of decreeing death for a fellow human [would] act with due regard for the consequences of their decision."

The constitutional status of discretionary sentencing in capital cases changed abruptly, however, as a result of the separate opinions supporting the judgment in *Furman*. * * *

Predictably, the variety of opinions supporting the judgment in *Furman* engendered confusion as to what was required in order to impose the death penalty in accord with the Eighth Amendment. Some States responded to what was thought to be the command of *Furman* by adopting mandatory death penalties for a limited category of specific crimes thus eliminating all discretion from the sentencing process in capital cases. Other States attempted to continue the practice of individually assessing the culpability of each individual defendant convicted of a capital offense and, at the same time, to comply with *Furman*, by providing standards to guide the sentencing decision.

Four years after *Furman*, we considered Eighth Amendment issues posed by five of the post-*Furman* death penalty statutes. Four Justices took the position that all five statutes complied with the Constitution; two Justices took the position that none of them complied. Hence, the disposition of each case varied according to the votes of three Justices who delivered a joint opinion in each of the five cases. * * *

The joint opinion reasoned that, to comply with *Furman*, sentencing procedures should not create "a substantial risk that the death penalty [will] be inflicted in an arbitrary and capricious manner." *Gregg v. Georgia*, 428 U.S. 153, 96 S.Ct. 2909 (1976). In the view of the three Justices, however, *Furman* did not require that all sentencing discretion be eliminated, but only that it be "directed and limited," so that the death penalty would be imposed in a more consistent and rational manner and so that there would be a "meaningful basis for distinguishing the ... cases in which it is imposed from ... the many cases in which it is not." The plurality concluded, in the course of invalidating North Carolina's mandatory death penalty statute, that the sentencing process must permit consideration of the "character and record of the individual offender and the circumstances of the particular offense as a constitutionally indispensable part of the process of inflicting the penalty of death," *Woodson v. North Carolina*, in order to ensure the reliability, under Eighth Amendment standards, of the determination that "death is the appropriate punishment in a specific case."

In the last decade, many of the States have been obliged to revise their death penalty statutes in response to the various opinions supporting the judgments in *Furman* and *Gregg* and its companion cases. The signals from this Court have not, however, always been easy to decipher. The States now deserve the clearest guidance that the Court can provide; we have an obligation to reconcile previously differing views in order to provide that guidance.

B

With that obligation in mind we turn to Lockett's attack on the Ohio statute. Essentially she contends that the Eighth and Fourteenth Amendments require that the sentencer be given a full opportunity to consider mitigating circumstances in capital cases and that the Ohio statute does not comply with that requirement. * * *

We begin by recognizing that the concept of individualized sentencing in criminal cases generally, although not constitutionally required, has long been accepted in this country. See *Williams v. New York*, 337 U.S. 241, 69 S.Ct. 1079 (1949). Consistent with that concept, sentencing judges traditionally have taken a wide range of factors into account. That States have authority to make aiders and abettors equally responsible, as a matter of law, with principals, or to enact felony-murder statutes is beyond constitutional challenge. But the definition of crimes generally has not been thought automatically to dictate what should be the proper penalty. And where sentencing discretion is granted, it generally has been agreed that the sentencing judge's "possession of the fullest information possible concerning the defendant's life and characteristics" is "[h]ighly relevant—*if not essential*—[to the] selection of an appropriate sentence . . ." *Williams v. New York* (emphasis added).

The opinions of this Court going back many years in dealing with sentencing in capital cases have noted the strength of the basis for individualized sentencing. For example, Mr. Justice Black, writing for the Court in *Williams v. New York*—a capital case—observed that the

> "whole country has traveled far from the period in which the death sentence was an automatic and commonplace result of convictions— even for offenses today deemed trivial."

Ten years later, in *Williams v. Oklahoma*, 358 U.S. 576, 79 S.Ct. 421 (1959), another capital case, the Court echoed Mr. Justice Black, stating that

> "[i]n discharging his duty of imposing a proper sentence, the sentencing judge is authorized, *if not required*, to consider all of the mitigating and aggravating circumstances involved in the crime." (Emphasis added.)

Most would agree that "the 19th century movement away from mandatory death sentences marked an enlightened introduction of flexibility into the sentencing process." *Furman v. Georgia* (BURGER, C. J., dissenting).

Although legislatures remain free to decide how much discretion in sentencing should be reposed in the judge or jury in noncapital cases, the plurality opinion in *Woodson*, after reviewing the historical repudiation of mandatory sentencing in capital cases, concluded that "in capital cases the fundamental respect for humanity underlying the Eighth Amendment . . . requires consideration of the character and record of the individual offender and the circumstances of the particular offense as a constitutionally indispensable part of the process of inflicting the penalty of death." That declaration rested "on the predicate that the penalty of death is qualitatively different" from any other sentence. We are satisfied that this qualitative difference between death and other penalties calls for a greater degree of reliability when the death sentence is imposed. The mandatory death penalty statute in *Woodson* was held invalid because it permitted no consideration of "relevant facets of the character and record of the individual offender or the circumstances of the particular offense." The plurality did not attempt to indicate, however, which facets of an offender or his offense it deemed "relevant" in capital sentencing or what degree of consideration of "relevant facets" it would require.

We are now faced with those questions and we conclude that the Eighth and Fourteenth Amendments require that the sentencer, in all but the rarest kind of capital case, not be precluded from considering, as a mitigating factor, any aspect of a defendant's character or record and any of the circumstances of the offense that the defendant proffers as a basis for a sentence less than death.[12] We recognize that, in noncapital cases, the established practice of individualized sentences rests not on constitutional commands, but on public policy enacted into statutes. The considerations that account for the wide acceptance of individualization of sentences in noncapital cases surely cannot be thought less important in capital cases. Given that the imposition of death by public authority is so profoundly different from all other penalties, we cannot avoid the conclusion that an individualized decision is essential in capital cases. The need for treating each defendant in a capital case with that degree of respect due the uniqueness of the individual is far more important than in noncapital cases. A variety of flexible techniques—probation, parole, work furloughs, to name a few—and various postconviction remedies may be available to modify an initial sentence of confinement in noncapital cases. The nonavailability of corrective or modifying mechanisms with respect to an executed capital sentence underscores the need for individualized consideration as a constitutional requirement in imposing the death sentence.

There is no perfect procedure for deciding in which cases governmental authority should be used to impose death. But a statute that prevents the sentencer in all capital cases from giving independent mitigating weight to aspects of the defendant's character and record and to circum-

---

12.   Nothing in this opinion limits the traditional authority of a court to exclude, as irrelevant, evidence not bearing on the defendant's character, prior record, or the circumstances of his offense.

stances of the offense proffered in mitigation creates the risk that the death penalty will be imposed in spite of factors which may call for a less severe penalty. When the choice is between life and death, that risk is unacceptable and incompatible with the commands of the Eighth and Fourteenth Amendments.

C

The Ohio death penalty statute does not permit the type of individualized consideration of mitigating factors we now hold to be required by the Eighth and Fourteenth Amendments in capital cases. * * *

     * * *

[Under the Ohio statute,] once a defendant is found guilty of aggravated murder with at least one of seven specified aggravating circumstances, the death penalty must be imposed unless, considering "the nature and circumstances of the offense and the history, character, and condition of the offender," the sentencing judge determines that at least one of the following mitigating circumstances is established by a preponderance of the evidence:

"(1) The victim of the offense induced or facilitated it.

"(2) It is unlikely that the offense would have been committed, but for the fact that the offender was under duress, coercion, or strong provocation.

"(3) The offense was primarily the product of the offender's psychosis or mental deficiency, though such condition is insufficient to establish the defense of insanity."

* * * We see, therefore, that once it is determined that the victim did not induce or facilitate the offense, that the defendant did not act under duress or coercion, and that the offense was not primarily the product of the defendant's mental deficiency, the Ohio statute mandates the sentence of death. The absence of direct proof that the defendant intended to cause the death of the victim is relevant for mitigating purposes only if it is determined that it sheds some light on one of the three statutory mitigating factors. Similarly, consideration of a defendant's comparatively minor role in the offense, or age, would generally not be permitted, as such, to affect the sentencing decision.

The limited range of mitigating circumstances which may be considered by the sentencer under the Ohio statute is incompatible with the Eighth and Fourteenth Amendments. To meet constitutional requirements, a death penalty statute must not preclude consideration of relevant mitigating factors.

Accordingly, the judgment under review is reversed to the extent that it sustains the imposition of the death penalty, and the case is remanded for further proceedings.

MR. JUSTICE BRENNAN took no part in the consideration or decision of this case.

[Concurring opinions of BLACKMUN, J. and MARSHALL, J. and opinions of WHITE, J., dissenting in part and concurring, and REHNQUIST, J., concurring in part and dissenting, omitted]

EDDINGS v. OKLAHOMA

455 U.S. 104, 102 S.Ct. 869, 71 L.Ed.2d 1 (1982).

JUSTICE POWELL delivered the opinion of the Court.

Petitioner Monty Lee Eddings was convicted of first-degree murder and sentenced to death. Because this sentence was imposed without "the type of individualized consideration of mitigating factors ... required by the Eighth and Fourteenth Amendments in capital cases," *Lockett v. Ohio*, 438 U.S. 586, 98 S.Ct. 2954 (1978) (opinion of BURGER, C. J.), we reverse.

I

On April 4, 1977, Eddings, a 16–year–old youth, and several younger companions ran away from their Missouri homes. They traveled in a car owned by Eddings' brother, and drove without destination or purpose in a southwesterly direction eventually reaching the Oklahoma Turnpike. Eddings had in the car a shotgun and several rifles he had taken from his father. After he momentarily lost control of the car, he was signalled to pull over by Officer Crabtree of the Oklahoma Highway Patrol. Eddings did so, and when the officer approached the car, Eddings stuck a loaded shotgun out of the window and fired, killing the officer.

Because Eddings was a juvenile, the State moved to have him certified to stand trial as an adult. Finding that there was prosecutive merit to the complaint and that Eddings was not amenable to rehabilitation within the juvenile system, the trial court granted the motion. The ruling was affirmed on appeal. Eddings was then charged with murder in the first degree, and the District Court of Creek County found him guilty upon his plea of nolo contendere.

The Oklahoma death penalty statute provides in pertinent part:

"Upon conviction ... of guilt of a defendant of murder in the first degree, the court shall conduct a separate sentencing proceeding to determine whether the defendant should be sentenced to death or life imprisonment. ... In the sentencing proceeding, evidence may be presented as to *any mitigating circumstances* or as to any of the aggravating circumstances enumerated in this act." (emphasis added).

Section 701.12 lists seven separate aggravating circumstances; the statute nowhere defines what is meant by "any mitigating circumstances."

At the sentencing hearing, the State alleged three of the aggravating circumstances enumerated in the statute: that the murder was especially heinous, atrocious, or cruel, that the crime was committed for the purpose of avoiding or preventing a lawful arrest, and that there was a probability that the defendant would commit criminal acts of violence that would constitute a continuing threat to society.

In mitigation, Eddings presented substantial evidence at the hearing of his troubled youth. The testimony of his supervising Juvenile Officer indicated that Eddings had been raised without proper guidance. His parents were divorced when he was 5 years old, and until he was 14 Eddings lived with his mother without rules or supervision. There is the suggestion that Eddings' mother was an alcoholic and possibly a prostitute. By the time Eddings was 14 he no longer could be controlled, and his mother sent him to live with his father. But neither could the father control the boy. Attempts to reason and talk gave way to physical punishment. The Juvenile Officer testified that Eddings was frightened and bitter, that his father overreacted and used excessive physical punishment: "Mr. Eddings found the only thing that he thought was effectful with the boy was actual punishment, or physical violence—hitting with a strap or something like this."[1]

Testimony from other witnesses indicated that Eddings was emotionally disturbed in general and at the time of the crime, and that his mental and emotional development were at a level several years below his age. A state psychologist stated that Eddings had a sociopathic or antisocial personality and that approximately 30% of youths suffering from such a disorder grew out of it as they aged. A sociologist specializing in juvenile offenders testified that Eddings was treatable. A psychiatrist testified that Eddings could be rehabilitated by intensive therapy over a 15–to 20–year period. He testified further that Eddings "did pull the trigger, he did kill someone, but I don't even think he knew that he was doing it."[2] The psychiatrist suggested that, if treated, Eddings would no longer pose a serious threat to society.

At the conclusion of all the evidence, the trial judge weighed the evidence of aggravating and mitigating circumstances. He found that the State had proved each of the three alleged aggravating circumstances beyond a reasonable doubt.[3] Turning to the evidence of mitigating circum-

---

1. There was evidence that immediately after the shooting Eddings said: "I would rather have shot an Officer than go back to where I live."

2. The psychiatrist suggested that, at the time of the murder, Eddings was in his own mind shooting his stepfather—a policeman who had been married to his mother for a brief period when Eddings was seven. The psychiatrist stated: "I think that given the circumstances and the facts of his life, and the facts of his arrested development, he acted as a seven year old seeking revenge and rebellion; and the act—he did pull the trigger, he did kill someone, but I don't even think he knew that he was doing it."

3. The trial judge found first that the crime was "heinous, atrocious, and cruel" because "designed to inflict a high degree of pain ... in utter indifference to the rights of Patrolman Crabtree." Second, the judge found that the crime was "committed for the purpose of avoiding or preventing a lawful arrest or prosecution." The evidence was sufficient to indicate that at the time of the offense Eddings did not wish to be returned to Missouri and that in stopping the car the officer's intent was to make a lawful arrest. Finally, the trial judge found that Eddings posed a continuing threat of violence to society. There was evidence that at one point on the day of the murder, after Eddings had been taken to the county jail, he told two officers that "if he was loose ... he would shoot" them all. There was also evidence that at another time, when an officer refused to turn off the light in Eddings' cell, Eddings became angry and threatened the officer:

stances, the judge found that Eddings' youth was a mitigating factor of great weight: "I have given very serious consideration to the youth of the Defendant when this particular crime was committed. Should I fail to do this, I think I would not be carrying out my duty." But he would not consider in mitigation the circumstances of Eddings' unhappy upbringing and emotional disturbance: ". . . the Court cannot be persuaded entirely by the . . . fact that the youth was sixteen years old when this heinous crime was committed. *Nor can the Court in following the law, in my opinion, consider the fact of this young man's violent background.*" (emphasis added). Finding that the only mitigating circumstance was Eddings' youth and finding further that this circumstance could not outweigh the aggravating circumstances present, the judge sentenced Eddings to death.

The Court of Criminal Appeals affirmed the sentence of death. It found that each of the aggravating circumstances alleged by the State had been present. It recited the mitigating evidence presented by Eddings in some detail, but in the end it agreed with the trial court that only the fact of Eddings' youth was properly considered as a mitigating circumstance:

> "[Eddings] also argues his mental state at the time of the murder. He stresses his family history in saying he was suffering from severe psychological and emotional disorders, and that the killing was in actuality an inevitable product of the way he was raised. There is no doubt that the petitioner has a personality disorder. But all the evidence tends to show that he knew the difference between right and wrong at the time he pulled the trigger, and that is the test of criminal responsibility in this State. For the same reason, the petitioner's family history is useful in explaining why he behaved the way he did, but it does not excuse his behavior."

II

In *Lockett v. Ohio*, 438 U.S. 586, 98 S.Ct. 2954 (1978), Chief Justice BURGER, writing for the plurality, stated the rule that we apply today:

> "[W]e conclude that the Eighth and Fourteenth Amendments require that the sentencer . . . not be precluded from considering, *as a mitigating factor*, any aspect of a defendant's character or record and any of the circumstances of the offense that the defendant proffers as a basis for a sentence less than death." (emphasis in original).

Recognizing "that the imposition of death by public authority is . . . profoundly different from all other penalties," the plurality held that the sentencer must be free to give "independent mitigating weight to aspects of the defendant's character and record and to circumstances of the offense proffered in mitigation. . . ." Because the Ohio death penalty statute only permitted consideration of three mitigating circumstances, the Court found the statute to be invalid.

"Now I have shot one of you people, and I'll get you too if you don't turn this light out." Based on these two "spontaneous utterances," the trial judge found a strong likelihood that Eddings would again commit a criminal act of violence if released.

As THE CHIEF JUSTICE explained, the rule in *Lockett* is the product of a considerable history reflecting the law's effort to develop a system of capital punishment at once consistent and principled but also humane and sensible to the uniqueness of the individual. Since the early days of the common law, the legal system has struggled to accommodate these twin objectives. Thus, the common law began by treating all criminal homicides as capital offenses, with a mandatory sentence of death. Later it allowed exceptions, first through an exclusion for those entitled to claim benefit of clergy and then by limiting capital punishment to murders upon "malice prepensed." In this country we attempted to soften the rigor of the system of mandatory death sentences we inherited from England, first by grading murder into different degrees of which only murder of the first degree was a capital offense and then by committing use of the death penalty to the absolute discretion of the jury. By the time of our decision in *Furman v. Georgia*, 408 U.S. 238, 92 S.Ct. 2726 (1972), the country had moved so far from a mandatory system that the imposition of capital punishment frequently had become arbitrary and capricious.

Beginning with *Furman*, the Court has attempted to provide standards for a constitutional death penalty that would serve both goals of measured, consistent application and fairness to the accused. [Justice Powell reviewed the Court's holdings in *Gregg v. Georgia*, 428 U.S. 153, 96 S.Ct. 2909 (1976) and *Woodson v. North Carolina*, 428 U.S. 280, 96 S.Ct. 2978 (1976)]

Thus, the rule in *Lockett* followed from the earlier decisions of the Court and from the Court's insistence that capital punishment be imposed fairly, and with reasonable consistency, or not at all. By requiring that the sentencer be permitted to focus "on the characteristics of the person who committed the crime," *Gregg v. Georgia, supra*, the rule in *Lockett* recognizes that "justice ... requires ... that there be taken into account the circumstances of the offense together with the character and propensities of the offender." *Pennsylvania v. Ashe*, 302 U.S. 51, 58 S.Ct. 59 (1937). By holding that the sentencer in capital cases must be permitted to consider any relevant mitigating factor, the rule in *Lockett* recognizes that a consistency produced by ignoring individual differences is a false consistency.

III

We now apply the rule in *Lockett* to the circumstances of this case. The trial judge stated that "in following the law," he could not "consider the fact of this young man's violent background." There is no dispute that by "violent background" the trial judge was referring to the mitigating evidence of Eddings' family history. From this statement it is clear that the trial judge did not evaluate the evidence in mitigation and find it wanting as a matter of fact; rather he found that as a matter of law he was unable even to consider the evidence.

The Court of Criminal Appeals took the same approach. It found that the evidence in mitigation was not relevant because it did not tend to provide a legal excuse from criminal responsibility. Thus the court conceded that Eddings had a "personality disorder," but cast this evidence aside on the basis that "he knew the difference between right and wrong . . . and that is the test of criminal responsibility." Similarly, the evidence of Eddings' family history was "useful in explaining" his behavior, but it did not "excuse" the behavior. From these statements it appears that the Court of Criminal Appeals also considered only that evidence to be mitigating which would tend to support a legal excuse from criminal liability.

We find that the limitations placed by these courts upon the mitigating evidence they would consider violated the rule in *Lockett*. Just as the State may not by statute preclude the sentencer from considering any mitigating factor, neither may the sentencer refuse to consider, as a matter of law, any relevant mitigating evidence. In this instance, it was as if the trial judge had instructed a jury to disregard the mitigating evidence Eddings proffered on his behalf. The sentencer, and the Court of Criminal Appeals on review, may determine the weight to be given relevant mitigating evidence. But they may not give it no weight by excluding such evidence from their consideration.[10]

Nor do we doubt that the evidence Eddings offered was relevant mitigating evidence. Eddings was a youth of 16 years at the time of the murder. Evidence of a difficult family history and of emotional disturbance is typically introduced by defendants in mitigation. See *McGautha v. California*, 402 U.S. 183, 91 S.Ct. 1454 (1971). In some cases, such evidence properly may be given little weight. But when the defendant was 16 years old at the time of the offense there can be no doubt that evidence of a turbulent family history, of beatings by a harsh father, and of severe emotional disturbance is particularly relevant.

The trial judge recognized that youth must be considered a relevant mitigating factor. But youth is more than a chronological fact. It is a time and condition of life when a person may be most susceptible to influence and to psychological damage. Our history is replete with laws and judicial recognition that minors, especially in their earlier years, generally are less mature and responsible than adults. Particularly "during the formative years of childhood and adolescence, minors often lack the experience, perspective, and judgment" expected of adults. *Bellotti v. Baird*, 443 U.S. 622, 99 S.Ct. 3035 (1979).

Even the normal 16–year–old customarily lacks the maturity of an adult. In this case, Eddings was not a normal 16–year–old; he had been deprived of the care, concern, and paternal attention that children deserve. On the contrary, it is not disputed that he was a juvenile with serious emotional problems, and had been raised in a neglectful, sometimes even violent, family background. In addition, there was testimony that Eddings' mental and emotional development were at a level several

---

10. We note that the Oklahoma death penalty statute permits the defendant to present evidence "as to any mitigating circumstances." *Lockett* requires the sentencer to listen.

years below his chronological age. All of this does not suggest an absence of responsibility for the crime of murder, deliberately committed in this case. Rather, it is to say that just as the chronological age of a minor is itself a relevant mitigating factor of great weight, so must the background and mental and emotional development of a youthful defendant be duly considered in sentencing.

We are not unaware of the extent to which minors engage increasingly in violent crime. Nor do we suggest an absence of legal responsibility where crime is committed by a minor. We are concerned here only with the manner of the imposition of the ultimate penalty: the death sentence imposed for the crime of murder upon an emotionally disturbed youth with a disturbed child's immaturity.

On remand, the state courts must consider all relevant mitigating evidence and weigh it against the evidence of the aggravating circumstances. We do not weigh the evidence for them. Accordingly, the judgment is reversed to the extent that it sustains the imposition of the death penalty, and the case is remanded for further proceedings not inconsistent with this opinion.

> [Concurring opinions of BRENNAN, J. and O'CONNOR, J. omitted. CHIEF JUSTICE BURGER, with whom JUSTICES WHITE, BLACKMUN and REHNQUIST joined, dissented on the grounds that (1) *certiorari* was granted only to consider whether the Eighth and Fourteenth Amendments prohibit imposition of a death sentence on an offender who was 16 years old at the time of the crime; (2) the Oklahoma statute, in contrast to the Ohio statute at issue in *Lockett*, expressly permitted the consideration of *any* mitigating circumstance; and (3) the record did not show that the trial court or the appellate court failed to consider Eddings' mitigating evidence but suggested that both courts may have concluded that the mitigating evidence did not offset the aggravating circumstances.]

NOTE

1. *Subsequent cases in the Supreme Court.*

In *Skipper v. South Carolina*, 476 U.S. 1, 106 S.Ct. 1669 (1986), the defendant challenged his death sentence on the grounds that the trial court had erroneously excluded testimony of two jailers and a regular visitor that the defendant had adjusted well during his pre-trial detention. The Court ruled that although the testimony would not relate to the defendant's culpability for the crime he had committed, the evidence would be mitigating in the sense that it might serve as a basis for a sentence less than death. Similarly, in *Hitchcock v. Dugger*, 481 U.S. 393, 107 S.Ct. 1821 (1987), a unanimous Court held that Florida's limitation of mitigation to statutory factors and the trial judge's refusal to consider nonstatutory mitigating factors (such a possible damage to the defendant from his habit as a child of inhaling gas fumes, his upbringing as one of seven children in a poor family, and his fond and affectionate relationship with his brother's children) ran afoul of *Lockett* and *Eddings.*

SMITH v. TEXAS

543 U.S. 37, 125 S.Ct. 400, 160 L.Ed.2d 303 (2004).

PER CURIAM.

Petitioner LaRoyce Lathair Smith was convicted of capital murder and sentenced to death by a jury in Dallas County, Texas. Before the jury reached its sentence, the trial judge issued a supplemental "nullification instruction." That instruction directed the jury to give effect to mitigation evidence, but allowed the jury to do so only by negating what would otherwise be affirmative responses to two special issues relating to deliberateness and future dangerousness. In *Penry v. Johnson,* 532 U.S. 782, 121 S.Ct. 1910 (2001) *(Penry II),* we held a similar "nullification instruction" constitutionally inadequate because it did not allow the jury to give " *'full* consideration and *full* effect to mitigating circumstances' " in choosing the defendant's appropriate sentence. (quoting *Johnson v. Texas,* 509 U.S. 350, 113 S.Ct. 2658 (1993) (O'CONNOR, J., dissenting)). Despite our holding in *Penry II,* the Texas Court of Criminal Appeals rejected petitioner's request for postconviction relief. The court reasoned that the instruction either was irrelevant because petitioner did not proffer "constitutionally significant" mitigation evidence, or was sufficiently distinguishable from the instruction in *Penry II* to survive constitutional scrutiny. We grant the petition for certiorari and petitioner's motion for leave to proceed *in forma pauperis,* and reverse.

I

In 1991, petitioner was convicted of brutally murdering one of his former co-workers at a Taco Bell in Dallas County. The victim and one of her co-workers were closing down the restaurant when petitioner and several friends asked to be let in to use the telephone. The two employees recognized petitioner and let him in. Petitioner then told his former co-workers to leave because he wanted to rob the restaurant. When they did not leave, petitioner killed one co-worker by pistol-whipping her and shooting her in the back. Petitioner also threatened, but did not harm, his other former co-worker before exiting with his friends. The jury found petitioner guilty of capital murder beyond a reasonable doubt.

At the punishment phase, the jury was instructed on two special issues: first, whether the killing was deliberate; and second, whether the defendant posed a continuing danger to others.[1] Approximately two years prior to the trial, we had held that presenting only these two special issues, without additional instructions regarding the jury's duty to consid-

---

1. The text of the special issues given to the jury was as follows: "(1) Was the conduct of the defendant that caused the death of the deceased committed deliberately, and with the reasonable expectation that the death of the deceased or another would result? (2) Is there a probability that the defendant would commit criminal acts of violence that would constitute a continuing threat to society?"

er mitigation evidence, violated the Eighth Amendment. *Penry v. Lynaugh,* 492 U.S. 302, 109 S.Ct. 2934 (1989) *(Penry I).* Shortly after petitioner's trial, the Texas Legislature amended its capital sentencing scheme to require juries to take "into consideration all of the evidence, including the circumstances of the offense, the defendant's character and background, and the personal moral culpability of the defendant" in deciding whether there are sufficient mitigating circumstances to warrant a sentence of life imprisonment rather than a death sentence. Petitioner, however, did not receive the benefit of the new statutory instruction at his trial. Instead, just as in *Penry II,* petitioner was sentenced pursuant to a supplemental instruction provided to the jury by the trial judge. That instruction read:

> " 'You are instructed that you shall consider any evidence which, in your opinion, is mitigating. Mitigating evidence is evidence that reduces the Defendant's personal or moral culpability or blameworthiness, and may include, but is not limited to, any aspect of the Defendant's character, record, background, or circumstances of the offense for which you have found him guilty. Our law does not specify what may or may not be considered as mitigating evidence. Neither does our law provide a formula for determining how much weight, if any, a mitigating circumstance deserves. You may hear evidence which, in your judgment, has no relationship to any of the Special Issues, but if you find such evidence is mitigating under these instructions, you shall consider it in the following instructions of the Court. You, and each of you, are the sole judges of what evidence, if any, is mitigating and how much weight, if any, the mitigating circumstances, if any, including those which have no relationship to any of the Special Issues, deserves.

> " 'In answering the Special Issues submitted to you herein, if you believe that the State has proved beyond a reasonable doubt that the answers to the Special Issues are "Yes," and you also believe from the mitigating evidence, if any, that the Defendant should not be sentenced to death, then you shall answer at least one of the Special Issues "No" in order to give effect to your belief that the death penalty should not be imposed due to the mitigating evidence presented to you. In this regard, you are further instructed that the State of Texas must prove beyond a reasonable doubt that the death sentence should be imposed despite the mitigating evidence, if any, admitted before you.

> " 'You are instructed that you may deliberate as a body about mitigating circumstances, but you are not required to reach a unanimous verdict as to their existence or weight. When you vote about the Special Issues, each of you must decide for yourself whether mitigating circumstances exist and, if so, how much weight they deserve.' "

Employing the framework of special issues modified by the supplemental nullification instruction, the jury considered a variety of mitigation evidence. Petitioner presented evidence that (1) he had been diagnosed with potentially organic learning disabilities and speech handicaps at an early age; (2) he had a verbal IQ score of 75 and a full IQ of 78 and, as a result, had been in special education classes throughout most of his time in school; (3) despite his low IQ and learning disabilities, his behavior at school was often exemplary; (4) his father was a drug addict who was involved with gang violence and other criminal activities, and regularly stole money from family members to support a drug addiction; and (5) he was only 19 when he committed the crime.

In response, the prosecution submitted evidence demonstrating that petitioner acted deliberately and cruelly. The prosecution emphasized that petitioner knew his victim, yet stabbed her repeatedly in numerous places on her body. With respect to petitioner's future dangerousness, the prosecution stressed that petitioner had previously been convicted of misdemeanor assault and proffered evidence suggesting that he had violated several drug laws.

During closing arguments at the punishment phase, the prosecution reminded the jury of its duty to answer truthfully the two special issues of deliberateness and future dangerousness.

"Now, when we talked to you on voir dire, we talked to you about— and we spent a lot of time talking to you to determine whether or not you could follow the law. You told us two very important things when we talked to you. First of all, you told us that in the appropriate case that you could give the death penalty. Second, you said, 'Mr. Nancarrow, Ms. McDaniel, if you prove to me that the answers to those special issues should be yes, then I can answer them yes.' If you wavered, if you hesitated one minute on that, then I guarantee you, you weren't going to be on this jury. We believed you then, and we believe you now."

The jury verdict form tracked the final reminders the prosecution gave the jury. The form made no mention of nullification. Nor did it say anything about mitigation evidence. Instead, the verdict form asked whether petitioner committed the act deliberately and whether there was a probability that he would commit criminal acts of violence that would constitute a continuing threat to society. The jury was allowed to give "Yes" or "No" answers only. The jury answered both questions "Yes" and sentenced petitioner to death.

* * *

II

The Texas Court of Criminal Appeals issued its opinion [denying Smith's petition for habeas corpus] just prior to our decision in *Tennard v. Dretke*, 542 U.S. 274, 124 S.Ct. 2562 (2004). In *Tennard*, we reversed the Fifth Circuit's refusal to grant a certificate of appealability (COA)[a] to a

a. Under the Antiterrorism and Effective Death Penalty Act, a defendant may not appeal from the denial of a habeas corpus petition in the federal district court unless the defendant first obtains a Certificate of Appealability from the district court or the court of appeals. [See Chapter 11]

defendant who was sentenced under the Texas capital sentencing scheme prior to the legislative revisions which took place in the aftermath of *Penry I.* Tennard, relying upon *Penry I,* argued that Texas' two special issues—deliberateness and future dangerousness—did not allow the jury to give effect to his mitigation evidence and that the trial court's failure to issue a supplemental mitigation instruction that would allow the jury to give full effect to his evidence rendered his death sentence unconstitutional. The state court and the Fifth Circuit both held that the lack of an adequate mitigation instruction was irrelevant. The courts both determined that Tennard had failed to satisfy the Fifth Circuit's threshold standard for " 'constitutionally relevant' mitigating evidence, that is, evidence of a 'uniquely severe permanent handicap with which the defendant was burdened through no fault of his own,' and evidence that 'the criminal act was attributable to this severe permanent condition.' "

Our rejection of that threshold test was central to our decision to reverse in *Tennard.* We held that "[t]he Fifth Circuit's test has no foundation in the decisions of this Court. Neither *Penry I* nor its progeny screened mitigating evidence for 'constitutional relevance' before considering whether the jury instructions comported with the Eighth Amendment." Rather, we held that the jury must be given an effective vehicle with which to weigh mitigating evidence so long as the defendant has met a "low threshold for relevance," which is satisfied by " 'evidence which tends logically to prove or disprove some fact or circumstance which a fact-finder could reasonably deem to have mitigating value.' " (quoting *McKoy v. North Carolina,* 494 U.S. 433, 110 S.Ct. 1227 (1990)).

The Texas Court of Criminal Appeals relied on precisely the same "screening test" we held constitutionally inadequate in *Tennard.* Employing this test, the court concluded that petitioner's low IQ and placement in special-education classes were irrelevant because they did not demonstrate that he suffered from a "severe disability." But, as we explained in *Tennard,* "[e]vidence of significantly impaired intellectual functioning is obviously evidence that 'might serve as a basis for a sentence less than death.' " (quoting *Skipper v. South Carolina,* 476 U.S. 1, 106 S.Ct. 1669 (1986)). There is no question that a jury might well have considered petitioner's IQ scores and history of participation in special-education classes as a reason to impose a sentence more lenient than death. Indeed, we have held that a defendant's IQ score of 79, a score slightly higher than petitioner's, constitutes relevant mitigation evidence. See *Wiggins v. Smith,* 539 U.S. 510, 123 S.Ct. 2527 (2003) [Chapter 7].

The state court also held that petitioner had offered "no evidence of any link or nexus between his troubled childhood or his limited mental abilities and this capital murder." We rejected the Fifth Circuit's "nexus" requirement in *Tennard* (noting that none of our prior opinions "suggested that a mentally retarded individual must establish a nexus between her mental capacity and her crime before the Eighth Amendment prohibition on executing her is triggered" and holding that the jury must be allowed the opportunity to consider *Penry* evidence even if the defendant cannot establish "a nexus to the crime").

That petitioner's evidence was relevant for mitigation purposes is plain * * * We therefore hold that the state court "assessed [petitioner's legal] claim under an improper legal standard." Because petitioner's proffered evidence was relevant, the Eighth Amendment required the trial court to empower the jury with a vehicle capable of giving effect to that evidence. Whether the "nullification instruction" satisfied that charge is the question to which we now turn.

III

The Texas Court of Criminal Appeals held that even if petitioner did proffer relevant mitigation evidence, the supplemental "nullification instruction" provided to the jury adequately allowed the jury to give effect to that evidence. The court found it significant that the supplemental instruction in this case "told the jury that it 'shall' consider all mitigating evidence, even evidence unrelated to the special issues, [and] it also told the jury how to answer the special issues to give effect to that mitigation evidence." The court also concluded that the nullification instruction made it clear to the jury that a "No" answer was required if it "believed that the death penalty was not warranted because of the mitigating circumstances."

In *Penry II,* we held that "the key under *Penry I* is that the jury be able to 'consider and *give effect to* [a defendant's mitigation] evidence in imposing sentence.'" (quoting *Penry I, supra*). We explained at length why the supplemental instruction employed by the Texas courts did not provide the jury with an adequate vehicle for expressing a "reasoned moral response" to *all* of the evidence relevant to the defendant's culpability. Although there are some distinctions between the *Penry II* supplemental instruction and the instruction petitioner's jury received, those distinctions are constitutionally insignificant.

Penry II identified a broad and intractable problem—a problem that the state court ignored here—inherent in any requirement that the jury nullify special issues contained within a verdict form.

> "We generally presume that jurors follow their instructions. Here, however, it would have been both logically and ethically impossible for a juror to follow both sets of instructions. Because Penry's mitigating evidence did not fit within the scope of the special issues, answering those issues in the manner prescribed on the verdict form necessarily meant ignoring the command of the supplemental instruction. And answering the special issues in the mode prescribed by the supplemental instruction necessarily meant ignoring the verdict form instructions. Indeed, jurors who wanted to answer one of the special

issues falsely to give effect to the mitigating evidence would have had to violate their oath to render a " 'true verdict.' "

"The mechanism created by the supplemental instruction thus inserted 'an element of capriciousness' into the sentencing decision, 'making the jurors' power to avoid the death penalty dependent on their willingness' to elevate the supplemental instruction over the verdict form instructions. There is, at the very least, 'a reasonable likelihood that the jury ... applied the challenged instruction in a way that prevent[ed] the consideration' of Penry's mental retardation and childhood abuse. The supplemental instruction therefore provided an inadequate vehicle for the jury to make a reasoned moral response to Penry's mitigating evidence."

It is certainly true that the mandatory aspect of the nullification instruction made petitioner's instruction distinct from Penry's. Indeed, the "shall" command in the nullification instruction resolved the ambiguity inherent in the *Penry II* instruction, which we held was *either* a nullification instruction or an instruction that "shackled and confined" Penry's mitigating evidence within the scope of the impermissibly narrow special issues. That being said, the clearer instruction given to petitioner's jury did not resolve the ethical problem described *supra*. To the contrary, the mandatory language in the charge could possibly have intensified the dilemma faced by ethical jurors. Just as in *Penry II*, petitioner's jury was required by law to answer a verdict form that made no mention whatsoever of mitigation evidence. And just as in *Penry II*, the burden of proof on the State was tied by law to findings of deliberateness and future dangerousness that had little, if anything, to do with the mitigation evidence petitioner presented. Even if we were to assume that the jurors could easily and effectively have comprehended an orally delivered instruction directing them to disregard, in certain limited circumstances, a mandatory written instruction given at a later occasion, that would not change the fact that the "jury was essentially instructed to return a false answer to a special issue in order to avoid a death sentence." *Penry II, supra.*

There is no principled distinction, for Eighth Amendment purposes, between the instruction given to petitioner's jury and the instruction in *Penry II*. Petitioner's evidence was relevant mitigation evidence for the jury under *Tennard* and *Penry I*. We therefore hold that the nullification instruction was constitutionally inadequate under *Penry II*. The judgment of the Texas Court of Criminal Appeals is reversed, and the case is remanded for further proceedings not inconsistent with this opinion.

It is so ordered.

[Dissenting statement of SCALIA, J., joined by THOMAS, J. omitted]

NOTES

1. *Changes in the Texas statute.*

As noted by the Court, in 1991 the Texas Legislature revised the capital sentencing statute to eliminate the issue addressed in *Smith*. Under the amended law, after the presentation of evidence, the jury must decide two special issues:

(1) whether there is a probability that the defendant would commit criminal acts of violence that would constitute a continuing threat to society; and

(2) in cases in which the jury charge at the guilt or innocence stage permitted the jury to find the defendant guilty [as a principal or an accomplice], whether the defendant actually caused the death of the deceased or did not actually cause the death of the deceased but intended to kill the deceased or another or anticipated that a human life would be taken.

The court must inform the jury that in deliberating these special issues, "it shall consider all evidence admitted at the guilt or innocence stage and the punishment stage, including evidence of the defendant's background or character or the circumstances of the offense that militates for or mitigates against the imposition of the death penalty." If the jury returns a unanimous affirmative finding as to each of the special issues, then the jury is instructed to answer the following issue:

Whether, taking into consideration all of the evidence, including the circumstances of the offense, the defendant's character and background, and the personal moral culpability of the defendant, there is a sufficient mitigating circumstance or circumstances to warrant that a sentence of life imprisonment rather than a death sentence be imposed.

Article 37.071, sec. 2(b)–(c) and (i) of the Texas Code of Criminal Procedure.

2. *Problem 4–1.*

At his capital murder trial under the pre–1991 version of the Texas capital sentencing scheme, Defendant's defense was one of mistaken identity. He also presented evidence to the effect that Victim's death was not attributable to the stabbing she suffered, but to incompetent treatment at the hospital. Defendant was convicted of capital murder. At the sentencing hearing, pursuant to Texas law, the trial judge submitted two "Special Issues" to the jury, asking whether it found beyond a reasonable doubt, (1) that the murder was committed deliberately and with the reasonable expectation that death would result, and (2) that there was a probability that petitioner would constitute a continuing threat to society. The court instructed the jury that if their answer was "Yes" to both questions, Defendant would be sentenced to death. The court refused Defendant's request to instruct the jury that it could consider any "lingering doubt" as to his guilt in deciding the penalty. Defendant was sentenced to death. On appeal, what arguments should be made as to whether the court was constitutionally required to give the requested instruction? See *Franklin v. Lynaugh*, 487 U.S. 164, 108 S.Ct. 2320 (1988).

3. *Problem 4–2.*

Defendant was convicted of first degree murder, and, at the penalty phase of his trial, he presented mitigation evidence concerning his background and character. Pursuant to State's statute, the jury was read a list of "sentencing factors," was told to consider all aggravating and mitigating circumstances and was then instructed: "If you conclude that the aggravating circumstances outweigh the mitigating circumstances, you shall impose a sentence of death. However, if you determine that the mitigating circumstances outweigh the aggravating circumstances, you shall impose a sentence of confinement in the state prison for life without the possibility of parole." Defendant was sentenced to death. What arguments should be made on appeal? How should the court rule? See *Boyde v. California*, 494 U.S. 370, 110 S.Ct. 1190 (1990); *Blystone v. Pennsylvania*, 494 U.S. 299, 110 S.Ct. 1078 (1990).

4.   *Problem 4–3.*

State's death penalty statute provides that in deciding whether to impose the death penalty or a life sentence, a jury can consider only mitigating factors that it unanimously finds to exist. What are the arguments as to whether the statute is constitutional? See *McKoy v. North Carolina*, 494 U.S. 433, 110 S.Ct. 1227 (1990) and *Mills v. Maryland*, 486 U.S. 367, 108 S.Ct. 1860 (1988).

KANSAS v. MARSH
548 U.S. 163, 126 S.Ct. 2516, 165 L.Ed.2d 429 (2006).

JUSTICE THOMAS delivered the opinion of the Court.

Kansas law provides that if a unanimous jury finds that aggravating circumstances are not outweighed by mitigating circumstances, the death penalty shall be imposed. Kan. Stat. Ann. § 21–4624(e) (1995). We must decide whether this statute, which requires the imposition of the death penalty when the sentencing jury determines that aggravating evidence and mitigating evidence are in equipoise, violates the Constitution. We hold that it does not.

I

Respondent Michael Lee Marsh II broke into the home of Marry Ane Pusch and lay in wait for her to return. When Marry Ane entered her home with her 19–month–old daughter, M. P., Marsh repeatedly shot Marry Ane, stabbed her, and slashed her throat. The home was set on fire with the toddler inside, and M.P. burned to death.

The jury convicted Marsh of the capital murder of M. P., the first-degree premeditated murder of Marry Ane, aggravated arson, and aggravated burglary. The jury found beyond a reasonable doubt the existence of three aggravating circumstances, and that those circumstances were not outweighed by any mitigating circumstances. On the basis of those findings, the jury sentenced Marsh to death for the capital murder of M.P. The jury also sentenced Marsh to life imprisonment without possibility of parole for 40 years for the first-degree murder of Marry Ane, and consecutive sentences of 51 months' imprisonment for aggravated arson and 34 months' imprisonment for aggravated burglary.

On direct appeal, Marsh challenged § 21–4624(e), which reads:

"If, by unanimous vote, the jury finds beyond a reasonable doubt that one or more of the aggravating circumstances enumerated in K.S.A. 21–4625 . . . exist and, further, that the existence of such aggravating circumstances is not outweighed by any mitigating circumstances which are found to exist, the defendant shall be sentenced to death; otherwise the defendant shall be sentenced as provided by law."

Focusing on the phrase "shall be sentenced to death," Marsh argued that § 21–4624(e) establishes an unconstitutional presumption in favor of death because it directs imposition of the death penalty when aggravating and mitigating circumstances are in equipoise.

The Kansas Supreme Court agreed, and held that the Kansas death penalty statute, § 21–4624(e), is facially unconstitutional. The court concluded that the statute's weighing equation violated the Eighth and Fourteenth Amendments of the United States Constitution because, "[i]n the event of equipoise, i.e., the jury's determination that the balance of any aggravating circumstances and any mitigating circumstances weighed equal, the death penalty would be required." The Kansas Supreme Court affirmed Marsh's conviction and sentence for aggravated burglary and premeditated murder of Marry Ane, and reversed and remanded for new trial Marsh's convictions for capital murder of M.P. and aggravated arson.[2] We granted certiorari and now reverse the Kansas Supreme Court's judgment that Kansas' capital sentencing statute, Kan. Stat. Ann. § 21–4624(e), is facially unconstitutional.

[The Court held that it had jurisdiction to review the judgment even though the state proceedings were not complete and that the state court's judgment did not rest on adequate and independent state grounds.]

III

This case is controlled by *Walton v. Arizona,* 497 U.S. 639, 110 S.Ct. 3047 (1990), overruled on other grounds, *Ring v. Arizona,* 536 U.S. 584, 122 S.Ct. 2428 (2002). In that case, a jury had convicted Walton of a capital offense. At sentencing, the trial judge found the existence of two aggravating circumstances and that the mitigating circumstances did not call for leniency, and sentenced Walton to death. The Arizona Supreme Court affirmed, and this Court granted certiorari to resolve the conflict between the Arizona Supreme Court's decision in *State v. Walton,* 769 P.2d 1017 (Ariz. 1989) (en banc) (holding the Arizona death penalty statute constitutional), and the Ninth Circuit's decision in *Adamson v. Ricketts,* 865 F.2d 1011 (1988) (en banc) (finding the Arizona death penalty statute unconstitutional because, "in situations where the mitigating and aggravating circumstances are in balance, or, where the mitigating circumstances give the court reservation but still fall below the weight of the aggravating circumstances, the statute bars the court from imposing a sentence less than death").

---

2. The Kansas Supreme Court found that the trial court committed reversible error by excluding circumstantial evidence of third-party guilt connecting Eric Pusch, Marry Ane's husband, to the crimes, and, accordingly ordered a new trial on this ground.

Consistent with the Ninth Circuit's conclusion in *Adamson,* Walton argued to this Court that the Arizona capital sentencing system created an unconstitutional presumption in favor of death because it "tells an Arizona sentencing judge who finds even a single aggravating factor, that death must be imposed, unless—as the Arizona Supreme Court put it in Petitioner's case—there are 'outweighing mitigating factors.' " Rejecting Walton's argument, this Court stated:

> "So long as a State's method of allocating the burdens of proof does not lessen the State's burden to prove every element of the offense charged, or in this case to prove the existence of aggravating circumstances, a defendant's constitutional rights are not violated by placing on him the burden of proving mitigating circumstances sufficiently substantial to call for leniency."

This Court noted that, as a requirement of individualized sentencing, a jury must have the opportunity to consider all evidence relevant to mitigation, and that a state statute that permits a jury to consider any mitigating evidence comports with that requirement. (citing *Blystone v. Pennsylvania,* 494 U.S. 299, 110 S.Ct. 1078 (1990)). The Court also pointedly observed that while the Constitution requires that a sentencing jury have discretion, it does not mandate that discretion be unfettered; the States are free to determine the manner in which a jury may consider mitigating evidence. (citing *Boyde v. California,* 494 U.S. 370, 110 S.Ct. 1190 (1990)). So long as the sentencer is not precluded from considering relevant mitigating evidence, a capital sentencing statute cannot be said to impermissibly, much less automatically, impose death. Indeed, *Walton* suggested that the only capital sentencing systems that would be impermissibly mandatory were those that would "automatically impose death upon conviction for certain types of murder."

[The Court concluded that, even though the *Walton* opinion did not discuss the equipoise issue directly, the issue was before the Court in *Walton* and the Arizona and Kansas statutes are so comparable that *Walton* necessarily controls.]

IV

A

Even if, as Marsh contends, *Walton* does not directly control, the general principles set forth in our death penalty jurisprudence would lead us to conclude that the Kansas capital sentencing system is constitutionally permissible. Together, our decisions in *Furman v. Georgia,* 408 U.S. 238, 92 S.Ct. 2726 (1972) (*per curiam*) and *Gregg v. Georgia,* 428 U.S. 153, 96 S.Ct. 2909 (1976) (joint opinion of Stewart, Powell, and Stevens, JJ.), establish that a state capital sentencing system must: (1) rationally narrow the class of death-eligible defendants; and (2) permit a jury to render a reasoned, individualized sentencing determination based on a death-eligible defendant's record, personal characteristics, and the circumstances of his crime. So long as a state system satisfies these requirements, our precedents establish that a State enjoys a range of discretion in imposing the death penalty, including the manner in which aggravating and mitigating circumstances are to be weighed.

The use of mitigation evidence is a product of the requirement of individualized sentencing. In *Lockett v. Ohio,* 438 U.S. 586, 98 S.Ct. 2954 (1978), a plurality of this Court held that "the Eighth and Fourteenth Amendments require that the sentencer ... not be precluded from considering, *as a mitigating factor,* any aspect of a defendant's character or record and any of the circumstances of the offense that the defendant proffers as a basis for a sentence less than death." (Emphasis in original.) The Court has held that the sentencer must have full access to this " 'highly relevant' " information. *Id.* (quoting *Williams v. New York,* 337 U.S. 241, 69 S.Ct. 1079 (1949)). Thus, in *Lockett,* the Court struck down the Ohio death penalty statute as unconstitutional because, by limiting a jury's consideration of mitigation to three factors specified in the statute, it prevented sentencers in capital cases from giving independent weight to mitigating evidence militating in favor of a sentence other than death. Following *Lockett,* in *Eddings v. Oklahoma,* 455 U.S. 104, 102 S.Ct. 869 (1982), a majority of the Court held that a sentencer may not categorically refuse to consider any relevant mitigating evidence.

In aggregate, our precedents confer upon defendants the right to present sentencers with information relevant to the sentencing decision and oblige sentencers to consider that information in determining the appropriate sentence. The thrust of our mitigation jurisprudence ends here. "[W]e have never held that a specific method for balancing mitigating and aggravating factors in a capital sentencing proceeding is constitutionally required." *Franklin v. Lynaugh,* 487 U.S. 164, 108 S.Ct. 2320 (1988). Rather, this Court has held that the States enjoy " 'a constitutionally permissible range of discretion in imposing the death penalty.' " *Blystone* (quoting *McCleskey v. Kemp,* 481 U.S. 279, 305–306, 107 S.Ct. 1756 (1987)).

B

The Kansas death penalty statute satisfies the constitutional mandates of *Furman* and its progeny because it rationally narrows the class of death-eligible defendants and permits a jury to consider any mitigating evidence relevant to its sentencing determination. It does not interfere, in a constitutionally significant way, with a jury's ability to give independent weight to evidence offered in mitigation.

Kansas' procedure narrows the universe of death-eligible defendants consistent with Eighth Amendment requirements. Under Kansas law, imposition of the death penalty is an *option* only after a defendant is convicted of capital murder, which requires that one or more specific elements beyond intentional premeditated murder be found. Once convicted of capital murder, a defendant becomes *eligible* for the death penalty only if the State seeks a separate sentencing hearing and proves beyond a reasonable doubt the existence of one or more statutorily enumerated aggravating circumstances.

Consonant with the individualized sentencing requirement, a Kansas jury is permitted to consider *any* evidence relating to *any* mitigating circumstance in determining the appropriate sentence for a capital defendant, so long as that evidence is relevant. § 21–4624(c). Specifically, jurors are instructed:

> "A mitigating circumstance is that which in fairness or mercy may be considered as extenuating or reducing the degree of moral culpability or blame or which justify a sentence of less than death, although it does not justify or excuse the offense. The determination of what are mitigating circumstances is for you as jurors to resolve under the facts and circumstances of this case.

> "The appropriateness of the exercise of mercy can itself be a mitigating factor you may consider in determining whether the State has proved beyond a reasonable doubt that the death penalty is warranted."[3]

Jurors are then apprised of, but not limited to, the factors that the defendant contends are mitigating. They are then instructed that "[e]ach juror must consider every mitigating factor that he or she individually finds to exist."

Kansas' weighing equation merely channels a jury's discretion by providing it with criteria by which it may determine whether a sentence of life or death is appropriate. The system in Kansas provides the type of "guided discretion" we have sanctioned in *Walton, Boyde,* and *Blystone.*

* * *

Contrary to Marsh's argument, § 21–4624(e) does not create a general presumption in favor of the death penalty in the State of Kansas. Rather, the Kansas capital sentencing system is dominated by the presumption that life imprisonment is the appropriate sentence for a capital conviction. If the State fails to meet its burden to demonstrate the existence of an aggravating circumstance(s) beyond a reasonable doubt, a sentence of life imprisonment must be imposed. If the State overcomes this hurdle, then it bears the additional burden of proving beyond a reasonable doubt that aggravating circumstances are not outweighed by mitigating circumstances. Significantly, although the defendant appropriately bears the burden of proffering mitigating circumstances—a burden of production—he never bears the burden of demonstrating that mitigating circumstances outweigh aggravating circumstances. Instead, the State always has the burden of demonstrating that mitigating evidence does not outweigh aggravating evidence. Absent the State's ability to meet that burden, the default is life imprisonment. Moreover, if the jury is unable to

---

3. The "mercy" jury instruction alone forecloses the possibility of *Furman*-type error as it "eliminate[s] the risk that a death sentence will be imposed in spite of facts calling for a lesser penalty."

reach a unanimous decision—in any respect—a sentence of life must be imposed. This system does not create a presumption that death is the appropriate sentence for capital murder.

Nor is there any force behind Marsh's contention that an equipoise determination reflects juror confusion or inability to decide between life and death, or that a jury may use equipoise as a loophole to shirk its constitutional duty to render a reasoned, moral decision regarding whether death is an appropriate sentence for a particular defendant. Such an argument rests on an implausible characterization of the Kansas statute— that a jury's determination that aggravators and mitigators are in equipoise is not a *decision,* much less a decision *for death*—and thus misses the mark. Weighing is not an end; it is merely a means to reaching a decision. The decision the jury must reach is whether life or death is the appropriate punishment. The Kansas jury instructions clearly inform the jury that a determination that the evidence is in equipoise is a decision for—not a presumption in favor of—death. Kansas jurors, presumed to follow their instructions, are made aware that: a determination that mitigators outweigh aggravators is a decision that a life sentence is appropriate; a determination that aggravators outweigh mitigators *or* a determination that mitigators do not outweigh aggravators—including a finding that aggravators and mitigators are in balance—is a decision that death is the appropriate sentence; and an inability to reach a unanimous decision will result in a sentence of life imprisonment. So informed, far from the abdication of duty or the inability to select an appropriate sentence depicted by Marsh and Justice SOUTER, a jury's conclusion that aggravating evidence and mitigating evidence are in equipoise is a *decision for death* and is indicative of the type of measured, normative process in which a jury is constitutionally tasked to engage when deciding the appropriate sentence for a capital defendant.

V

Justice SOUTER argues (hereinafter the dissent) that the advent of DNA testing has resulted in the "exoneratio[n]" of "innocent" persons "in numbers never imagined before the development of DNA tests." Based upon this "new empirical demonstration of how 'death is different,'" the dissent concludes that Kansas' sentencing system permits the imposition of the death penalty in the absence of reasoned moral judgment.

But the availability of DNA testing, and the questions it might raise about the accuracy of guilt-phase determinations in capital cases, is simply irrelevant to the question before the Court today, namely, the constitutionality of Kansas' capital *sentencing* system. Accordingly, the accuracy of the dissent's factual claim that DNA testing has established the "innocence" of numerous convicted persons under death sentences—and the incendiary debate it invokes—is beyond the scope of this opinion.

The dissent's general criticisms against the death penalty are ultimately a call for resolving all legal disputes in capital cases by adopting the outcome that makes the death penalty more difficult to impose. While such a bright-line rule may be easily applied, it has no basis in law. Indeed, the logical consequence of the dissent's argument is that the death penalty can only be just in a system that does not permit error. Because the criminal justice system does not operate perfectly, abolition of the death penalty is the only answer to the moral dilemma the dissent poses. This Court, however, does not sit as a moral authority. Our precedents do not prohibit the States from authorizing the death penalty, even in our imperfect system. And those precedents do not empower this Court to chip away at the States' prerogatives to do so on the grounds the dissent invokes today.

* * *

We hold that the Kansas capital sentencing system, which directs imposition of the death penalty when a jury finds that aggravating and mitigating circumstances are in equipoise, is constitutional. Accordingly, we reverse the judgment of the Kansas Supreme Court, and remand the case for further proceedings not inconsistent with this opinion.

It is so ordered.

[JUSTICE SCALIA concurred, responding "first to JUSTICE STEVENS' contention that this case, and cases like it, do not merit our attention, and second to JUSTICE SOUTER's claims about risks inherent in capital punishment."]

[JUSTICE STEVENS dissented, distinguishing *Walton* and also arguing that there was no reason for the Court to have taken the case since "no rule of law commanded the Court to grant certiorari" and "[n]o other State would have been required to follow the [Kansas] precedent if it had been permitted to stand."]

JUSTICE SOUTER, with whom JUSTICE STEVENS, JUSTICE GINSBURG, and JUSTICE BREYER join, dissenting.

I

Kansas's capital sentencing statute provides that a defendant "shall be sentenced to death" if, by unanimous vote, "the jury finds beyond a reasonable doubt that one or more aggravating circumstances ... exist and ... that the existence of such aggravating circumstances is not outweighed by any mitigating circumstances which are found to exist." Kan. Stat. Ann. § 21–4624(e) (1995). The Supreme Court of Kansas has read this provision to require imposition of the death penalty "[i]n the event of equipoise, [that is,] the jury's determination that the balance of any aggravating circumstances and any mitigating circumstances weighed equal." Given this construction, the state court held the law unconstitutional on the ground that the Eighth Amendment requires that a " 'tie g[o] to the defendant' " when life or death is at issue." Because I agree with the Kansas judges that the Constitution forbids a mandatory death penalty in what they describe as "doubtful cases," when aggravating and mitigating factors are of equal weight, I respectfully dissent.[1]

II

More than 30 years ago, this Court explained that the Eighth Amendment's guarantee against cruel and unusual punishment barred imposition of the death penalty under statutory schemes so inarticulate that sentencing discretion produced wanton and freakish results. See *Furman v. Georgia,* 408 U.S. 238, 92 S.Ct. 2726 (1972) *(per curiam)* (Stewart, J., concurring) ("[T]he Eighth and Fourteenth Amendments cannot tolerate the infliction of a sentence of death under legal systems that permit this unique penalty to be ... wantonly and ... freakishly imposed" on a "capriciously selected random handful" of individuals). The Constitution was held to require, instead, a system structured to produce reliable, rational and rationally reviewable determinations of sentence.

Decades of back-and-forth between legislative experiment and judicial review have made it plain that the constitutional demand for rationality goes beyond the minimal requirement to replace unbounded discretion with a sentencing structure; a State has much leeway in devising such a structure and in selecting the terms for measuring relative culpability, but a system must meet an ultimate test of constitutional reliability in producing " 'a reasoned moral response to the defendant's background, character, and crime,' " *Penry v. Lynaugh,* 492 U.S. 302, 109 S.Ct. 2934 (1989) (quoting *California v. Brown,* 479 U.S. 538, 107 S.Ct. 837 (1987) (O'Connor, J., concurring); emphasis deleted). The Eighth Amendment, that is, demands both form and substance, both a system for decision and one geared to produce morally justifiable results.

The State thinks its scheme is beyond questioning, whether as to form or substance, for it sees the tie-breaker law as equivalent to the provisions examined in *Blystone v. Pennsylvania,* 494 U.S. 299, 110 S.Ct. 1078 (1990), and *Boyde v. California,* 494 U.S. 370, 110 S.Ct. 1190 (1990), where we approved statutes that required a death sentence upon a jury finding that aggravating circumstances outweighed mitigating ones. But the crucial fact in those systems was the predominance of the aggravators, and our recognition of the moral rationality of a mandatory capital sentence based on that finding is no authority for giving States free rein to select a different conclusion that will dictate death.

Instead, the constitutional demand for a reasoned moral response requires the state statute to satisfy two criteria that speak to the issue before us now, one governing the character of sentencing evidence, and one going to the substantive justification needed for a death sentence. As to the first, there is an obligation in each case to inform the jury's choice

---

1. The majority views *Walton v. Arizona,* 497 U.S. 639, 110 S.Ct. 3047 (1990), as having decided this issue. But *Walton* is ambiguous on this point; while the Court there approved Arizona's practice of placing the burden on capital defendants to prove, "by a preponderance of the evidence, the existence of mitigating circumstances sufficiently substantial to call for leniency," it did not quantify the phrase "sufficiently substantial." * * *

of sentence with evidence about the crime as actually committed and about the specific individual who committed it. Since the sentencing choice is, by definition, the attribution of particular culpability to a criminal act and defendant, as distinct from the general culpability necessarily implicated by committing a given offense, the sentencing decision must turn on the uniqueness of the individual defendant and on the details of the crime, to which any resulting choice of death must be "directly" related. *Penry, supra.*

Second, there is the point to which the particulars of crime and criminal are relevant: within the category of capital crimes, the death penalty must be reserved for "the worst of the worst." One object of the structured sentencing proceeding required in the aftermath of *Furman* is to eliminate the risk that a death sentence will be imposed in spite of facts calling for a lesser penalty, and the essence of the sentencing authority's responsibility is to determine whether the response to the crime and defendant "must be death," *Spaziano v. Florida*, 468 U.S. 447, 104 S.Ct. 3154 (1984). Of course, in the moral world of those who reject capital punishment in principle, a death sentence can never be a moral imperative. The point, however, is that within our legal and moral system, which allows a place for the death penalty, "must be death" does not mean "may be death."

Since a valid capital sentence thus requires a choice based upon unique particulars identifying the crime and its perpetrator as heinous to the point of demanding death even within the class of potentially capital offenses, the State's provision for a tie breaker in favor of death fails on both counts. The dispositive fact under the tie breaker is not the details of the crime or the unique identity of the individual defendant. The determining fact is not directly linked to a particular crime or particular criminal at all; the law operates merely on a jury's finding of equipoise in the State's own selected considerations for and against death. Nor does the tie breaker identify the worst of the worst, or even purport to reflect any evidentiary showing that death must be the reasoned moral response; it does the opposite. The statute produces a death sentence exactly when a sentencing impasse demonstrates as a matter of law that the jury does not see the evidence as showing the worst sort of crime committed by the worst sort of criminal, in a combination heinous enough to demand death. It operates, that is, when a jury has applied the State's chosen standards of culpability and mitigation and reached nothing more than what the Supreme Court of Kansas calls a "tie." It mandates death in what that court identifies as "doubtful cases." The statute thus addresses the risk of a morally unjustifiable death sentence, not by minimizing it as precedent unmistakably requires, but by guaranteeing that in equipoise cases the risk will be realized, by "placing a 'thumb [on] death's side of the scale,'" *Sochor v. Florida*, 504 U.S. 527, 112 S.Ct. 2114 (1992) (quoting *Stringer v. Black*, 503 U.S. 222, 112 S.Ct. 1130 (1992); alteration in original).

In Kansas, when a jury applies the State's own standards of relative culpability and cannot decide that a defendant is among the most culpable, the state law says that equivocal evidence is good enough and the defendant must die. A law that requires execution when the case for aggravation has failed to convince the sentencing jury is morally absurd, and the Court's holding that the Constitution tolerates this moral irrationality defies decades of precedent aimed at eliminating freakish capital sentencing in the United States.

[Justice SOUTER argued that the substantial number of exonerations in recent years, particularly as a result to the use of DNA evidence, further establishes that "death is different" and, "[i]n the face of evidence of the hazards of capital prosecution, maintaining a sentencing system mandating death when the sentencer finds the evidence pro and con to be in equipoise is obtuse by any moral or social measure" and renders the Kansas law unconstitutional.]

WALTON v. ARIZONA

497 U.S. 639, 110 S.Ct. 3047, 111 L.Ed.2d 511 (1990).

[In a 5–4 decision, the Court upheld Arizona's capital sentencing scheme, which leaves to the judge the determination of the existence of aggravating or mitigating circumstances and the decision as to penalty, and the Court rejected the defendant's challenge to the "especially heinous, cruel or depraved" aggravating circumstance. In their separate opinions, Justices SCALIA and STEVENS set forth their different views as to the relationship between the *Furman* and *Lockett* principles.]

JUSTICE SCALIA, concurring in part and concurring in the judgment.

Today a petitioner before this Court says that a state sentencing court (1) had unconstitutionally *broad* discretion to sentence him to death instead of imprisonment, *and* (2) had unconstitutionally *narrow* discretion to sentence him to imprisonment instead of death. An observer unacquainted with our death penalty jurisprudence (and in the habit of thinking logically) would probably say these positions cannot both be right. The ultimate choice in capital sentencing, he would point out, is a unitary one—the choice between death and imprisonment. One cannot have discretion whether to select the one yet lack discretion whether to select the other. Our imaginary observer would then be surprised to discover that, under this Court's Eighth Amendment jurisprudence of the past 15 years, petitioner would have a strong chance of winning on *both* of these antagonistic claims, simultaneously—as evidenced by the fact that four Members of this Court think he should win on both (BLACKMUN, J., dissenting) * * * But that just shows that our jurisprudence and logic have long since parted ways. I write separately to say that, and explain why, I will no longer seek to apply one of the two incompatible branches of that jurisprudence. * * *

I

A

Over the course of the past 15 years, this Court has assumed the role of rulemaking body for the States' administration of capital sentencing—

effectively requiring capital sentencing proceedings separate from the adjudication of guilt, see, *e.g.*, *Woodson v. North Carolina*, 428 U.S. 280, 96 S.Ct. 2978 (1976) (plurality opinion); *Gregg v. Georgia*, 428 U.S. 153, 96 S.Ct. 2909 (1976) (opinion announcing judgment), dictating the type and extent of discretion the sentencer must and must not have, see, *e.g.*, *Lockett v. Ohio*, 438 U.S. 586, 98 S.Ct. 2954 (1978) (plurality opinion); *Godfrey v. Georgia*, 446 U.S. 420, 100 S.Ct. 1759 (1980), requiring that certain categories of evidence must and must not be admitted, see, *e.g.*, *Skipper v. South Carolina*, 476 U.S. 1, 106 S.Ct. 1669 (1986), undertaking minute inquiries into the wording of jury instructions to ensure that jurors understand their duties under our labyrinthine code of rules, see, *e.g.*, *Caldwell v. Mississippi*, 472 U.S. 320, 105 S.Ct. 2633 (1985), and prescribing the procedural forms that sentencing decisions must follow, see, *e.g.*, *McKoy v. North Carolina*, 494 U.S. 433, 110 S.Ct. 1227 (1990). The case that began the development of this Eighth Amendment jurisprudence was *Furman v. Georgia*, 408 U.S. 238, 92 S.Ct. 2726 (1972) (*per curiam*), which has come to stand for the principle that a sentencer's discretion to return a death sentence must be constrained by specific standards, so that the death penalty is not inflicted in a random and capricious fashion.

     * * *

B

Shortly after introducing our doctrine *requiring* constraints on the sentencer's discretion to "impose" the death penalty, the Court began developing a doctrine *forbidding* constraints on the sentencer's discretion to "*decline* to impose" it. *McCleskey v. Kemp*, 481 U.S. 279, 107 S.Ct. 1756 (1987). This second doctrine—counterdoctrine would be a better word—has completely exploded whatever coherence the notion of "guided discretion" once had.

Some States responded to *Furman* by making death the mandatory punishment for certain categories of murder. We invalidated these statutes in *Woodson v. North Carolina*, 428 U.S. 280, 96 S.Ct. 2978 (1976), and *Roberts v. Louisiana*, 428 U.S. 325, 96 S.Ct. 3001 (1976), a plurality of the Court concluding that the sentencing process must accord at least some consideration to the "character and record of the individual offender." *Woodson, supra* (plurality opinion). Other States responded to *Furman* by leaving the sentencer some discretion to spare capital defendants, but limiting the kinds of mitigating circumstances the sentencer could consider. We invalidated these statutes in *Lockett v. Ohio*, 438 U.S. 586, 98 S.Ct. 2954 (1978), a plurality saying the Eighth Amendment requires that the sentencer "not be precluded from considering, as a mitigating factor, *any aspect* of a defendant's character or record and any of the circumstances of the offense that the defendant proffers as a basis for a sentence less than death," (opinion of BURGER, C.J., joined by STEWART, POWELL, and STEVENS, JJ.) (emphasis omitted and added). The reasoning of the pluralities in these cases was later adopted by a majority of the Court.

See *Sumner v. Shuman*, 483 U.S. 66, 107 S.Ct. 2716 (1987) (embracing *Woodson*); *Eddings v. Oklahoma, supra* (embracing *Lockett*).

These decisions, of course, had no basis in *Furman*. One might have supposed that curtailing or eliminating discretion in the sentencing of capital defendants was not only consistent with *Furman*, but positively required by it—as many of the States, of course, *did* suppose. But in *Woodson* and *Lockett*, it emerged that uniform treatment of offenders guilty of the same capital crime was not only not *required* by the Eighth Amendment, but was all but *prohibited*. Announcing the proposition that "[c]entral to the application of the [Eighth] Amendment is a determination of contemporary standards regarding the infliction of punishment," *Woodson, supra,* and pointing to the steady growth of discretionary sentencing systems over the previous 150 years (those very systems we had found unconstitutional in *Furman*), the pluralities in those cases determined that a defendant could not be sentenced to death unless the sentencer was convinced, by an unconstrained and unguided evaluation of offender and offense, that death was the appropriate punishment. In short, the practice which in *Furman* had been described as the discretion to sentence to death and pronounced constitutionally prohibited, was in *Woodson* and *Lockett* renamed the discretion not to sentence to death and pronounced constitutionally required.

As elaborated in the years since, the *Woodson–Lockett* principle has prevented States from imposing all but the most minimal constraints on the sentencer's discretion to decide that an offender eligible for the death penalty should nonetheless not receive it. We have, in the first place, repeatedly rebuffed States' efforts to channel that discretion by specifying objective factors on which its exercise should rest. It would misdescribe the sweep of this principle to say that "all mitigating evidence" must be considered by the sentencer. That would assume some objective criterion of what is mitigating, which is precisely what we have forbidden. Our cases proudly announce that the Constitution effectively prohibits the States from excluding from the sentencing decision *any* aspect of a defendant's character or record, or any circumstance surrounding the crime: that the defendant had a poor and deprived childhood, or that he had a rich and spoiled childhood; that he had a great love for the victim's race, or that he had a pathological hatred for the victim's race; that he has limited mental capacity, or that he has a brilliant mind which can make a great contribution to society; that he was kind to his mother, or that he despised his mother. Whatever evidence bearing on the crime or the criminal the defense wishes to introduce as rendering the defendant less deserving of the death penalty must be admitted into evidence and considered by the sentencer. See, *e.g., Lockett, supra* ("character, prior record, age, lack of specific intent to cause death, and . . . relatively minor part in the crime"); *Eddings v. Oklahoma, supra* (*inter alia*, that the defendant's "parents were divorced when he was 5 years old, and until he was 14 [he] lived with his mother without rules or supervision"); *Hitchcock v. Dugger*, 481 U.S. 393, 107 S.Ct. 1821 (1987) (*inter alia*, that "petitioner had been one of seven children in a poor family that earned its living by picking cotton; that his father had died of cancer; and that petitioner had been a fond and affectionate uncle"); *Skipper v. South Carolina* (that "petitioner had been a well-behaved and well-adjusted prisoner" while awaiting trial). Nor may States channel the sentencer's consideration of this evidence by defining the weight or significance it is to receive—for example, by making evidence of mental retardation relevant only insofar as it bears on the question whether the crime was committed deliberately. See *Penry v. Lynaugh*, 492 U.S. 302, 109 S.Ct. 2934 (1989). Rather, they must let the sentencer "give effect," *McKoy v. North Carolina*, to mitigating evidence in whatever manner it pleases. Nor, when a jury is assigned the sentencing task, may the State attempt to impose structural rationality on the sentencing decision by requiring that mitigating circumstances be found unanimously, see *McKoy*; each juror must be allowed to determine and "give effect" to his perception of what evidence favors leniency, regardless of whether those perceptions command the assent of (or are even comprehensible to) other jurors.

To acknowledge that "there perhaps is an inherent tension" between this line of cases and the line stemming from *Furman*, *McCleskey v. Kemp* (BLACKMUN, J., dissenting), is rather like saying that there was perhaps an inherent tension between the Allies and the Axis Powers in World War II. And to refer to the two lines as pursuing "twin objectives," *Spaziano v. Florida*, 468 U.S. 447, 104 S.Ct. 3154 (1984), is rather like referring to the twin objectives of good and evil. They cannot be reconciled. Pursuant to *Furman*, and in order "to achieve a more rational and equitable administration of the death penalty," *Franklin v. Lynaugh*, 487 U.S. 164, 108 S.Ct. 2320 (1988), we require that States "channel the sentencer's discretion by 'clear and objective standards' that provide 'specific and detailed guidance,'" *Godfrey v. Georgia*. In the next breath, however, we say that "the State *cannot* channel the sentencer's discretion ... to consider any relevant [mitigating] information offered by the defendant," *McCleskey v. Kemp* (emphasis added), and that the sentencer must enjoy unconstrained discretion to decide whether any sympathetic factors bearing on the defendant or the crime indicate that he does not "deserve to be sentenced to death," *Penry v. Lynaugh*, *supra*. The latter requirement quite obviously destroys whatever rationality and predictability the former requirement was designed to achieve.*

---

* Justice STEVENS contends that the purpose of *Furman* is merely to narrow the group of crimes (to which the sentencer's unconstrained discretion is then applied) to some undefined point near the "tip of the pyramid" or murder—the base of that pyramid consisting of all murders, and the apex consisting of a particular type crime of murder defined in minute detail. There is, however, no hint in our *Furman* jurisprudence of an attempt to determine what constitutes the critical line below the "tip of the pyramid," and to assess whether *either* the elements of the crime are alone sufficient to bring the statute above that line (in which case no aggravating factors whatever need be specified) *or* whether the aggravating factors are sufficient for that purpose. I read the cases (and the States, in enacting their post-*Furman* statutes, have certainly read them) as requiring aggravating factors to be specified *whenever* the sentencer is given discretion. It is a means of confining the sentencers' discretion—giving them something specific to look for rather than leaving them to wander at large among all aggravating circumstances. That produces a consistency of result which is unachievable—no matter how narrowly

The Court has attempted to explain the contradiction by saying that the two requirements serve different functions: the first serves to "narrow" according to rational criteria the class of offenders eligible for the death penalty, while the second guarantees that each offender who is death eligible is not actually sentenced to death without "an individualized assessment of the appropriateness of the death penalty." *Penry v. Lynaugh, supra.* But it is not "individualized assessment" that is the issue here. No one asserts that the Constitution permits condemnation *en masse.* The issue is whether, in the process of the individualized sentencing determination, the society may specify which factors are relevant, and which are not—whether it may insist upon a rational scheme in which all sentencers making the individualized determinations apply the same standard. That is precisely the issue that was involved in *Furman,* no more and no less. Having held, in *Furman,* that the aggravating factors to be sought in the individualized determination must be specified in advance, we are able to refer to the defendants who will qualify under those factors as a "class of death eligibles"—from among whom those actually to receive death will be selected on the basis of unspecified mitigating factors. But if we had held in *Lockett* that the *mitigating* factors to be sought in the individualized determination must be specified in advance, we would equally have been able to refer to the defendants who will qualify under those factors as a "class of mercy eligibles"—from among whom those actually to receive mercy will be selected on the basis of unspecified aggravating factors. In other words, classification *versus* individuation does not *explain* the opposite treatment of aggravating and mitigating factors; it is merely one way of *describing the result* of that opposite treatment. What is involved here is merely setting standards for individualized determinations, and the question remains why the Constitution demands that the aggravating standards and mitigating standards be accorded opposite treatment. It is impossible to understand why. Since the individualized determination is a unitary one (does this defendant deserve death for this crime?) once one says each sentencer must be able to answer "no" for whatever reason it deems morally sufficient (and indeed, for whatever reason any one of 12 jurors deems morally sufficient), it becomes impossible to claim that the Constitution requires consistency and rationality among sentencing determinations to be preserved by strictly limiting the reasons for which each sentencer can say "yes." In fact, randomness and "freakishness" are even more evident in a system that requires aggravating factors to be found in great detail, since it permits sentencers to accord different treatment, for whatever mitigating

---

the crime is defined—if they are left to take into account any aggravating factor at all. We have, to be sure, held that the discretion-limiting aggravating factor can duplicate a factor already required by the definition of the crime, see *Lowenfield v. Phelps,* 484 U.S. 231, 108 S.Ct. 546 (1988), but in those circumstances the sentencer's discretion is *still* focused and confined. We have never allowed sentencers to be given complete discretion without a requisite finding of aggravating factors. If and when the Court redefines *Furman* to permit the latter, and to require an assessment (I cannot imagine on what basis) that a sufficiently narrow level of the "pyramid" of murder has been reached, I shall be prepared to reconsider my evaluation of *Woodson* and *Lockett.*

reasons they wish, not only to two different murderers, but to two murderers whose crimes have been found to be of similar gravity. It is difficult enough to justify the *Furman* requirement so long as the States are *permitted* to allow random mitigation; but to impose it while simultaneously requiring random mitigation is absurd. I agree with Justice WHITE's observation that the *Lockett* rule represents a sheer "about-face" from *Furman*, an outright negation of the principle of guided discretion that brought us down the path of regulating capital sentencing procedure in the first place. *Lockett v. Ohio*, (opinion of WHITE, J.).

C

The simultaneous pursuit of contradictory objectives necessarily produces confusion. As THE CHIEF JUSTICE has pointed out, in elaborating our doctrine "the Court has gone from pillar to post, with the result that the sort of reasonable predictability upon which legislatures, trial courts, and appellate courts must of necessity rely has been all but completely sacrificed." *Lockett v. Ohio* (REHNQUIST, J., dissenting). Repeatedly over the past 20 years state legislatures and courts have adopted discretion-reducing procedures to satisfy the *Furman* principle, only to be told years later that their measures have run afoul of the *Lockett* principle. * * *

In a jurisprudence containing the contradictory commands that discretion to impose the death penalty must be limited but discretion not to impose the death penalty must be virtually unconstrained, a vast number of procedures support a plausible claim in one direction or the other. Conscientious counsel are obliged to make those claims, and conscientious judges to consider them. There has thus arisen, in capital cases, a permanent floodtide of stay applications and petitions for certiorari to review adverse judgments at each round of direct and collateral review, alleging novel defects in sentencing procedure arising out of some permutation of either *Furman* or *Lockett*. State courts, attempting to give effect to the contradictory principles in our jurisprudence and reluctant to condemn an offender without virtual certainty that no error has been committed, often suspend the normal rules of procedural bar to give ear to each new claim that the sentencer's discretion was overconstrained or underconstrained. An adverse ruling typically gives rise to yet another round of federal habeas review—and by the time that is concluded we may well have announced yet another new rule that will justify yet another appeal to the state courts. The effects of the uncertainty and unpredictability are evident in this Court alone, even though we see only the tip of a mountainous iceberg. Since granting certiorari in *McKoy v. North Carolina, supra,* on February 21, 1989 (the first of this Term's capital cases to have certiorari granted), we have received over 350 petitions for certiorari in capital cases; 8 were granted, and 84 were held for the 9 cases granted for this Term; 37 were held for this case alone. Small wonder, then, that the statistics show a capital punishment system that has been approved, in many States, by the democratic vote of the people, that has theoretically been approved as constitutional by this Court, but that seems unable to function except as a parody of swift or even timely justice. As of May 1990 there were 2,327 convicted murderers on death row; only 123 have been executed since our 1972 *Furman* decision. Those executions that have been carried out have occurred an average of eight years after the commission of the capital crime.

In my view, it is time for us to reexamine our efforts in this area and to measure them against the text of the constitutional provision on which they are purportedly based.

II

The Eighth Amendment, made applicable to the States by the Fourteenth Amendment, provides:

> "Excessive bail shall not be required, nor excessive fines imposed, nor cruel and unusual punishments inflicted."

The requirement as to punishments stands in stark contrast to the requirement for bail and fines, which are invalid if they are "excessive." When punishments other than fines are involved, the Amendment explicitly requires a court to consider not only whether the penalty is severe or harsh, but also whether it is "unusual." If it is not, then the Eighth Amendment does not prohibit it, no matter how cruel a judge might think it to be. Moreover, the Eighth Amendment's prohibition is directed against cruel and unusual punishments. It does not, by its terms, regulate the procedures of sentencing as opposed to the substance of punishment. As THE CHIEF JUSTICE has observed, "[t]he prohibition of the Eighth Amendment relates to the character of the punishment, and not to the process by which it is imposed." *Gardner v. Florida*, 430 U.S. 349, 97 S.Ct. 1197 (1977) (REHNQUIST, J., dissenting). Thus, the procedural elements of a sentencing scheme come within the prohibition, if at all, only when they are of such a nature as systematically to render the infliction of a cruel punishment "unusual."

Our decision in *Furman v. Georgia*, 408 U.S. 238, 92 S.Ct. 2726 (1972), was arguably supported by this text. As I have already described, see Part I–A, *supra*, the critical opinions of Justice STEWART and Justice WHITE in that case rested on the ground that discretionary capital sentencing had made the death sentence such a random and infrequent event among capital offenders ("wanto[n] and freakis[h]," as Justice STEWART colorfully put it) that its imposition had become cruel and unusual. As far as I can discern (this is not the occasion to explore the subject), that is probably not what was meant by an "unusual punishment" in the Eighth Amendment—that is to say, the text did not originally prohibit a traditional form of punishment that is rarely imposed, as opposed to a form of punishment that is not traditional. But the phrase can bear the former meaning. Moreover, since in most States, until the beginning of this century, the death penalty was mandatory for the convictions for which it was prescribed, it cannot be said that the *Furman* interpretation of the phrase is contradicted by the clear references to a permissible death penalty in the Constitution. I am therefore willing to adhere to the precedent established by our *Furman* line of cases, and to hold that when a State adopts capital punishment for a given crime but does not make it mandatory, the Eighth Amendment bars it from giving the sentencer unfettered discretion to select the recipients, but requires it to establish in advance, and convey to the sentencer, a governing standard.

The *Woodson–Lockett* line of cases, however, is another matter. As far as I can discern, that bears no relation whatever to the text of the Eighth Amendment. The mandatory imposition of death—without sentencing discretion—for a crime which States have traditionally punished with death cannot possibly violate the Eighth Amendment, because it will not be "cruel" (neither absolutely nor for the particular crime) and it will not be "unusual" (neither in the sense of being a type of penalty that is not traditional nor in the sense of being rarely or "freakishly" imposed). It is quite immaterial that most States have abandoned the practice of automatically sentencing to death all offenders guilty of a capital crime, in favor of a separate procedure in which the sentencer is given the opportunity to consider the appropriateness of death in the individual case; still less is it relevant that mandatory capital sentencing is (or is alleged to be) out of touch with " 'contemporary community values' " regarding the administration of justice.

I am aware of the argument that mandatory capital sentencing schemes may suffer from the same defects that characterize absolutely discretionary schemes. In mandatory systems, the argument goes, juries frequently acquit offenders whom they find guilty but believe do not deserve the death penalty for their crime; and because this "jury nullification" occurs without the benefit of any guidance or standards from the State, the result is the same "arbitrary and capricious imposition of death sentences" struck down in *Furman*. One obvious problem with this argument is that it proves too much, invalidating *Furman* at the same time that it validates *Woodson*. If juries will ignore their instructions in determining guilt in a mandatory capital sentencing scheme, there is no reason to think they will not similarly chafe at the " 'clear and objective standards' ... provid[ing] 'specific and detailed guidance,' " *Godfrey v. Georgia, supra*, that *Furman* requires. The *Furman* approach must be preferred, since it is facially implausible that the risk of arbitrariness arising from juries' ignoring their instructions is greater than the risk of arbitrariness from giving them no instructions at all. The theory of "unusualness" adopted in *Furman* is tenuous enough when used to invalidate explicitly conferred standardless sentencing discretion; I am unwilling to extend that theory to situations in which the sentencer is *denied* that discretion, on the basis of a conjecture (found nowhere else in the law) that juries systematically disregard their oaths.

Despite the fact that I think *Woodson* and *Lockett* find no proper basis in the Constitution, they have some claim to my adherence because of the doctrine of *stare decisis*. I do not reject that claim lightly, but I must reject it here. My initial and my fundamental problem, as I have described it in detail above, is not that *Woodson* and *Lockett* are wrong, but that *Woodson* and *Lockett* are rationally irreconcilable with *Furman*. It is that which led me into the inquiry whether either they or *Furman* was wrong. I would not know how to apply them—or, more precisely, how to apply both them and *Furman*—if I wanted to. I cannot continue to say, in case after case, what degree of "narrowing" is sufficient to achieve the constitutional objective enunciated in *Furman* when I know that that objective is in any case impossible of achievement because of *Woodson–Lockett*. And I cannot continue to say, in case after case, what sort of restraints upon sentencer discretion are unconstitutional under *Woodson–Lockett* when I know that the Constitution positively favors constraints under *Furman*. *Stare decisis* cannot command the impossible. Since I cannot possibly be guided by what seem to me incompatible principles, I must reject the one that is plainly in error.

The objectives of the doctrine of *stare decisis* are not furthered by adhering to *Woodson–Lockett* in any event. The doctrine exists for the purpose of introducing certainty and stability into the law and protecting the expectations of individuals and institutions that have acted in reliance on existing rules. As I have described, the *Woodson–Lockett* principle has frustrated this very purpose from the outset—contradicting the basic thrust of much of our death penalty jurisprudence, laying traps for unwary States, and generating a fundamental uncertainty in the law that shows no signs of ending or even diminishing.

I cannot adhere to a principle so lacking in support in constitutional text and so plainly unworthy of respect under *stare decisis*. Accordingly, I will not, in this case or in the future, vote to uphold an Eighth Amendment claim that the sentencer's discretion has been unlawfully restricted.

JUSTICE STEVENS, dissenting.

* * *

II

Justice SCALIA announces in a separate opinion that henceforth he will not regard *Woodson v. North Carolina*, 428 U.S. 280, 96 S.Ct. 2978 (1976), *Roberts v. Louisiana*, 428 U.S. 325, 96 S.Ct. 3001 (1976), *Lockett v. Ohio*, 438 U.S. 586, 98 S.Ct. 2954 (1978), *Godfrey v. Georgia*, 446 U.S. 420, 100 S.Ct. 1759 (1980), and other cases adopting their reasoning as binding precedent. The major premise for this rejection of our capital sentencing jurisprudence is his professed inability to reconcile those cases with the central holding in *Furman v. Georgia*, 408 U.S. 238, 92 S.Ct. 2726 (1972). Although there are other flaws in Justice SCALIA's opinion, it is at least appropriate to explain why his major premise is simply wrong.

The cases that Justice SCALIA categorically rejects today rest on the theory that the risk of arbitrariness condemned in *Furman* is a function of the size of the class of convicted persons who are eligible for the death penalty. When *Furman* was decided, Georgia included virtually all defendants convicted of forcible rape, armed robbery, kidnaping, and first-degree murder in that class. As the opinions in *Furman* observed, in that large class of cases race and other irrelevant factors unquestionably played an unacceptable role in determining which defendants would die and which would live. However, the size of the class may be narrowed to reduce sufficiently that risk of arbitrariness, even if a jury is then given complete discretion to show mercy when evaluating the individual characteristics of the few individuals who have been found death eligible.

The elaborate empirical study of the administration of Georgia's capital sentencing statute that the Court considered in *McCleskey v. Kemp*, 481 U.S. 279, 107 S.Ct. 1756 (1987), further illustrates the validity of this theory. In my opinion in that case I observed:

> "One of the lessons of the Baldus study is that there exist certain categories of extremely serious crimes for which prosecutors consistently seek, and juries consistently impose, the death penalty without regard to the race of the victim or the race of the offender. If Georgia were to narrow the class of death-eligible defendants to those categories, the danger of arbitrary and discriminatory imposition of the death penalty would be significantly decreased, if not eradicated."

The Georgia Supreme Court itself understood the concept that Justice SCALIA apparently has missed. [Justice STEVENS quoted from the Court's decision in *Zant v. Stephens* [Chapter 3] the Georgia Supreme Court's analogy of the law governing homicides in Georgia to a pyramid.] Justice SCALIA ignores the difference between the base of the pyramid and its apex. A rule that forbids unguided discretion at the base is completely consistent with one that requires discretion at the apex. After narrowing the class of cases to those at the tip of the pyramid, it is then appropriate to allow the sentencer discretion to show mercy based on individual mitigating circumstances in the cases that remain.

Perhaps a rule that allows the specific facts of particular cases to make the difference between life and death—a rule that is consistent with the common-law tradition of case-by-case adjudication—provides less certainty than legislative guidelines that mandate the death penalty whenever specified conditions are met. Such guidelines would fit nicely in a Napoleonic Code drafted in accord with the continental approach to the formulation of legal rules. However, this Nation's long experience with mandatory death sentences—a history recounted at length in our opinion in *Woodson* and entirely ignored by Justice SCALIA today—has led us to reject such rules. I remain convinced that the approach adopted by this Court in *Weems v. United States*, 217 U.S. 349, 30 S.Ct. 544 (1910), and in *Trop v. Dulles*, 356 U.S. 86, 78 S.Ct. 590 (1958), followed by Justice STEWART, Justice POWELL, and myself in 1976, and thereafter repeatedly endorsed by this Court, is not only wiser, but far more just, than the reactionary position espoused by Justice SCALIA today.

NOTE

1. *Justice Stevens's understanding confirmed.*

In *Tuilaepa v. California*, 512 U.S. 967, 114 S.Ct. 2630 (1994) [Chapter 10], the majority of the Court confirmed Justice Stevens's understanding that there are two steps involved in the penalty determination—the eligibility determination and the selection decision—and that each serves a different constitutional purpose. The eligibility determination, where the prosecution typically must prove an aggravating circumstance, satisfies the *Furman* concern by narrowing the eligible class. The selection decision, where the sentencer may be given "unbridled discretion" in making its penalty choice, satisfies the *Woodson/Lockett* concern for an individualized determination.

CHAPTER 5

THE REQUIREMENT OF PROPORTIONALITY

■ ■ ■

The two companion cases decided with *Furman v. Georgia* both involved petitioners who had been sentenced to death for rape rather than murder. They had argued that the death penalty was a disproportionate punishment for rape and it therefore violated the Eighth Amendment. Because the Court decided all three cases on "risk of arbitrariness" grounds, the Court never reached the proportionality issue. However, after holding in *Gregg v. Georgia* that the death penalty was not, in all cases, a disproportionate punishment for murder, the Court has addressed a number of proportionality challenges to particular applications of the death penalty. The defendants in the first two cases in this chapter challenge the death penalty as disproportionate to their offenses. In *Coker v. Georgia*, the Court decides that the death penalty for rape of an adult woman violates the Eighth Amendment. In *Enmund v. Florida*, 458 U.S. 782, 102 S.Ct. 3368 (1982) (described in *Tison v. Arizona*), the Court held that execution of a "getaway driver" who had no direct involvement in the killing but was only guilty of murder on a felony-murder theory violated the Eighth Amendment. In *Tison v. Arizona*, the Court delineates when the death penalty constitutionally may be applied to a felon who has not intended to kill. The next two cases concern challenges to the death penalty by defendants who have objective traits arguably making them less culpable. Although youth and mental retardation may be considered as mitigating circumstances in determining whether to sentence a defendant to death [see Chapter 4], does the fact that a defendant is mentally retarded or a juvenile at the time of the offense make application of the death penalty disproportionate and therefore unconstitutional? In 1989, the Supreme Court held, in *Penry v. Lynaugh*, 492 U.S. 302, 109 S.Ct. 2934 (1989), that the Eighth Amendment did not prohibit the execution of a mentally retarded defendant and, in *Stanford v. Kentucky*, 492 U.S. 361, 109 S.Ct. 2969 (1989), that the Eighth Amendment did not prohibit the execution of a defendant who was a juvenile at the time of the offense. In *Atkins v. Virginia*, the Court revisits the *Penry* decision. In *Roper v. Simmons*, the Court revisits the *Stanford* decision. The final case in the chapter, *Kennedy v. Louisiana*, concerns a defendant sentenced to death for rape of a child under 12 years old and is the Court's most recent proportionality case.

COKER v. GEORGIA

433 U.S. 584, 97 S.Ct. 2861, 53 L.Ed.2d 982 (1977).

MR. JUSTICE WHITE announced the judgment of the Court and filed an opinion in which MR. JUSTICE STEWART, MR. JUSTICE BLACKMUN, and MR. JUSTICE STEVENS, joined.

Georgia Code Ann. § 26–2001 (1972) provides that "[a] person convicted of rape shall be punished by death or by imprisonment for life, or by imprisonment for not less than one nor more than 20 years." Punishment is determined by a jury in a separate sentencing proceeding in which at least one of the statutory aggravating circumstances must be found before the death penalty may be imposed. Petitioner Coker was convicted of rape and sentenced to death. Both the conviction and the sentence were affirmed by the Georgia Supreme Court. Coker was granted a writ of certiorari limited to the single claim, rejected by the Georgia court, that the punishment of death for rape violates the Eighth Amendment, which proscribes "cruel and unusual punishments" and which must be observed by the States as well as the Federal Government. *Robinson v. California*, 370 U.S. 660, 82 S.Ct. 1417 (1962).

I

While serving various sentences for murder, rape, kidnaping, and aggravated assault, petitioner escaped from the Ware Correctional Institution near Waycross, Ga., on September 2, 1974. At approximately 11 o'clock that night, petitioner entered the house of Allen and Elnita Carver through an unlocked kitchen door. Threatening the couple with a "board," he tied up Mr. Carver in the bathroom, obtained a knife from the kitchen, and took Mr. Carver's money and the keys to the family car. Brandishing the knife and saying "you know what's going to happen to you if you try anything, don't you," Coker then raped Mrs. Carver. Soon thereafter, petitioner drove away in the Carver car, taking Mrs. Carver with him. Mr. Carver, freeing himself, notified the police; and not long thereafter petitioner was apprehended. Mrs. Carver was unharmed.

Petitioner was charged with escape, armed robbery, motor vehicle theft, kidnaping, and rape. Counsel was appointed to represent him. Having been found competent to stand trial, he was tried. The jury returned a verdict of guilty, rejecting his general plea of insanity. A sentencing hearing was then conducted in accordance with the procedures dealt with at length in *Gregg v. Georgia*, 428 U.S. 153, 96 S.Ct. 2909 (1976), where this Court sustained the death penalty for murder when imposed pursuant to the statutory procedures. The jury was instructed that it could consider as aggravating circumstances whether the rape had been committed by a person with a prior record of conviction for a capital felony and whether the rape had been committed in the course of committing another capital felony, namely, the armed robbery of Allen Carver. The court also instructed, pursuant to statute, that even if aggravating circumstances were present, the death penalty need not be imposed if the jury found they were outweighed by mitigating circumstances, that is, circumstances not constituting justification or excuse for the offense in question, "but which, in fairness and mercy, may be considered as extenuating or reducing the degree" of moral culpability or punishment. The jury's verdict on the rape count was death by electrocution. Both aggravating circumstances on which the court instructed were found to be present by the jury.

* * *

We have concluded that a sentence of death is grossly disproportionate and excessive punishment for the crime of rape and is therefore forbidden by the Eighth Amendment as cruel and unusual punishment.[4]

A

As advised by recent cases, we seek guidance in history and from the objective evidence of the country's present judgment concerning the acceptability of death as a penalty for rape of an adult woman. At no time in the last 50 years have a majority of the States authorized death as a punishment for rape. In 1925, 18 States, the District of Columbia, and the Federal Government authorized capital punishment for the rape of an adult female. By 1971, just prior to the decision in *Furman v. Georgia*, 408 U.S. 238, 92 S.Ct. 2726 (1972), that number had declined, but not substantially, to 16 States plus the Federal Government. *Furman* then invalidated most of the capital punishment statutes in this country, including the rape statutes, because, among other reasons, of the manner in which the death penalty was imposed and utilized under those laws.

With their death penalty statutes for the most part invalidated, the States were faced with the choice of enacting modified capital punishment laws in an attempt to satisfy the requirements of *Furman* or of being satisfied with life imprisonment as the ultimate punishment for any offense. Thirty-five States immediately reinstituted the death penalty for at least limited kinds of crime. This public judgment as to the acceptability of capital punishment, evidenced by the immediate, post-*Furman* legislative reaction in a large majority of the States, heavily influenced the Court to sustain the death penalty for murder in *Gregg v. Georgia*.

But if the "most marked indication of society's endorsement of the death penalty for murder is the legislative response to *Furman*," it should also be a telling datum that the public judgment with respect to rape, as reflected in the statutes providing the punishment for that crime, has been dramatically different. In reviving death penalty laws to satisfy *Furman*'s mandate, none of the States that had not previously authorized death for rape chose to include rape among capital felonies. Of the 16

---

4. Because the death sentence is a disproportionate punishment for rape, it is cruel and unusual punishment within the meaning of the Eighth Amendment even though it may measurably serve the legitimate ends of punishment and therefore is not invalid for its failure to do so. We observe that in the light of the legislative decisions in almost all of the States and in most of the countries around the world, it would be difficult to support a claim that the death penalty for rape is an indispensable part of the States' criminal justice system.

States in which rape had been a capital offense, only three provided the death penalty for rape of an adult woman in their revised statutes— Georgia, North Carolina, and Louisiana. In the latter two States, the death penalty was mandatory for those found guilty, and those laws were invalidated by *Woodson v. North Carolina*, 428 U.S. 280, 96 S.Ct. 2978 (1976) and *Roberts v. Louisiana*, 428 U.S. 325, 96 S.Ct. 3001 (1976). When Louisiana and North Carolina, responding to those decisions, again revised their capital punishment laws, they re-enacted the death penalty for murder but not for rape; none of the seven other legislatures that to our knowledge have amended or replaced their death penalty statutes since July 2, 1976, including four States (in addition to Louisiana and North Carolina) that had authorized the death sentence for rape prior to 1972 and had reacted to *Furman* with mandatory statutes, included rape among the crimes for which death was an authorized punishment.

Georgia argues that 11 of the 16 States that authorized death for rape in 1972 attempted to comply with *Furman* by enacting arguably mandatory death penalty legislation and that it is very likely that, aside from Louisiana and North Carolina, these States simply chose to eliminate rape as a capital offense rather than to require death for each and every instance of rape. The argument is not without force; but 4 of the 16 States did not take the mandatory course and also did not continue rape of an adult woman as a capital offense. Further, as we have indicated, the legislatures of 6 of the 11 arguably mandatory States have revised their death penalty laws since *Woodson* and *Roberts* without enacting a new death penalty for rape. And this is to say nothing of 19 other States that enacted nonmandatory, post-*Furman* statutes and chose not to sentence rapists to death.

It should be noted that Florida, Mississippi, and Tennessee also authorized the death penalty in some rape cases, but only where the victim was a child and the rapist an adult. The Tennessee statute has since been invalidated because the death sentence was mandatory. The upshot is that Georgia is the sole jurisdiction in the United States at the present time that authorizes a sentence of death when the rape victim is an adult woman, and only two other jurisdictions provide capital punishment when the victim is a child.

The current judgment with respect to the death penalty for rape is not wholly unanimous among state legislatures, but it obviously weighs very heavily on the side of rejecting capital punishment as a suitable penalty for raping an adult woman.[10]

B

It was also observed in *Gregg* that "[t]he jury ... is a significant and reliable objective index of contemporary values because it is so directly

---

10. In *Trop v. Dulles*, 356 U.S. 86, 78 S.Ct. 590 (1958), the plurality took pains to note the climate of international opinion concerning the acceptability of a particular punishment. It is thus not irrelevant here that out of 60 major nations in the world surveyed in 1965, only 3 retained the death penalty for rape where death did not ensue. United Nations, Department of Economic and Social Affairs, Capital Punishment 40, 86 (1968).

involved,'' and that it is thus important to look to the sentencing decisions that juries have made in the course of assessing whether capital punishment is an appropriate penalty for the crime being tried. Of course, the jury's judgment is meaningful only where the jury has an appropriate measure of choice as to whether the death penalty is to be imposed. As far as execution for rape is concerned, this is now true only in Georgia and in Florida; and in the latter State, capital punishment is authorized only for the rape of children.

According to the factual submissions in this Court, out of all rape convictions in Georgia since 1973—and that total number has not been tendered—63 cases had been reviewed by the Georgia Supreme Court as of the time of oral argument; and of these, 6 involved a death sentence, 1 of which was set aside, leaving 5 convicted rapists now under sentence of death in the State of Georgia. Georgia juries have thus sentenced rapists to death six times since 1973. This obviously is not a negligible number; and the State argues that as a practical matter juries simply reserve the extreme sanction for extreme cases of rape and that recent experience surely does not prove that jurors consider the death penalty to be a disproportionate punishment for every conceivable instance of rape, no matter how aggravated. Nevertheless, it is true that in the vast majority of cases, at least 9 out of 10, juries have not imposed the death sentence.

IV

These recent events evidencing the attitude of state legislatures and sentencing juries do not wholly determine this controversy, for the Constitution contemplates that in the end our own judgment will be brought to bear on the question of the acceptability of the death penalty under the Eighth Amendment. Nevertheless, the legislative rejection of capital punishment for rape strongly confirms our own judgment, which is that death is indeed a disproportionate penalty for the crime of raping an adult woman.

We do not discount the seriousness of rape as a crime. It is highly reprehensible, both in a moral sense and in its almost total contempt for the personal integrity and autonomy of the female victim and for the latter's privilege of choosing those with whom intimate relationships are to be established. Short of homicide, it is the "ultimate violation of self." It is also a violent crime because it normally involves force, or the threat of force or intimidation, to overcome the will and the capacity of the victim to resist. Rape is very often accompanied by physical injury to the female and can also inflict mental and psychological damage. Because it undermines the community's sense of security, there is public injury as well.

Rape is without doubt deserving of serious punishment; but in terms of moral depravity and of the injury to the person and to the public, it does not compare with murder, which does involve the unjustified taking of human life. Although it may be accompanied by another crime, rape by definition does not include the death of or even the serious injury to another person. The murderer kills; the rapist, if no more than that, does not. Life is over for the victim of the murderer; for the rape victim, life may not be nearly so happy as it was, but it is not over and normally is not beyond repair. We have the abiding conviction that the death penalty, which "is unique in its severity and irrevocability," is an excessive penalty for the rapist who, as such, does not take human life.

This does not end the matter; for under Georgia law, death may not be imposed for any capital offense, including rape, unless the jury or judge finds one of the statutory aggravating circumstances and then elects to impose that sentence. For the rapist to be executed in Georgia, it must therefore be found not only that he committed rape but also that one or more of the following aggravating circumstances were present: (1) that the rape was committed by a person with a prior record of conviction for a capital felony; (2) that the rape was committed while the offender was engaged in the commission of another capital felony, or aggravated battery; or (3) the rape "was outrageously or wantonly vile, horrible or inhuman in that it involved torture, depravity of mind, or aggravated battery to the victim." Here, the first two of these aggravating circumstances were alleged and found by the jury.

Neither of these circumstances, nor both of them together, change our conclusion that the death sentence imposed on Coker is a disproportionate punishment for rape. Coker had prior convictions for capital felonies—rape, murder, and kidnaping—but these prior convictions do not change the fact that the instant crime being punished is a rape not involving the taking of life.

It is also true that the present rape occurred while Coker was committing armed robbery, a felony for which the Georgia statutes authorize the death penalty. But Coker was tried for the robbery offense as well as for rape and received a separate life sentence for this crime; the jury did not deem the robbery itself deserving of the death penalty, even though accompanied by the aggravating circumstance, which was stipulated, that Coker had been convicted of a prior capital crime.

We note finally that in Georgia a person commits murder when he unlawfully and with malice aforethought, either express or implied, causes the death of another human being. He also commits that crime when in the commission of a felony he causes the death of another human being, irrespective of malice. But even where the killing is deliberate, it is not punishable by death absent proof of aggravating circumstances. It is difficult to accept the notion, and we do not, that the rapist, with or without aggravating circumstances, should be punished more heavily than the deliberate killer as long as the rapist does not himself take the life of his victim. The judgment of the Georgia Supreme Court upholding the death sentence is reversed, and the case is remanded to that court for further proceedings not inconsistent with this opinion.

So ordered.

[Concurring opinions of BRENNAN, J. and MARSHALL, J., concurring and dissenting opinion of POWELL, J., and dissenting opinion of BURGER, C.J. joined by REHNQUIST, J. omitted.]

NOTE

1. *Rape and the death penalty.*

The Supreme Court's decision in *Coker* does not mention race, yet the decision was issued against a background of extreme racial discrimination in the use of the death penalty in rape cases. From 1930 until the decision in *Furman*, 455 men were executed for rape in the United States, and almost 90% of them were black. U.S. Law Enforcement Assistance Administration Reports (1930–1976).

TISON v. ARIZONA

481 U.S. 137, 107 S.Ct. 1676, 95 L.Ed.2d 127 (1987).

JUSTICE O'CONNOR delivered the opinion of the Court.

The question presented is whether the petitioners' participation in the events leading up to and following the murder of four members of a family makes the sentences of death imposed by the Arizona courts constitutionally permissible although neither petitioner specifically intended to kill the victims and neither inflicted the fatal gunshot wounds. We hold that the Arizona Supreme Court applied an erroneous standard in making the findings required by *Enmund v. Florida*, 458 U.S. 782, 102 S.Ct. 3368 (1982), and, therefore, vacate the judgments below and remand the case for further proceedings not inconsistent with this opinion.

I

Gary Tison was sentenced to life imprisonment as the result of a prison escape during the course of which he had killed a guard. After he had been in prison a number of years, Gary Tison's wife, their three sons Donald, Ricky, and Raymond, Gary's brother Joseph, and other relatives made plans to help Gary Tison escape again. The Tison family assembled a large arsenal of weapons for this purpose. Plans for escape were discussed with Gary Tison, who insisted that his cellmate, Randy Greenawalt, also a convicted murderer, be included in the prison break. The following facts are largely evidenced by petitioners' detailed confessions given as part of a plea bargain according to the terms of which the State agreed not to seek the death sentence. The Arizona courts interpreted the plea agreement to require that petitioners testify to the planning stages of the breakout. When they refused to do so, the bargain was rescinded and they were tried, convicted, and sentenced to death.

On July 30, 1978, the three Tison brothers entered the Arizona State Prison at Florence carrying a large ice chest filled with guns. The Tisons armed Greenawalt and their father, and the group, brandishing their weapons, locked the prison guards and visitors present in a storage closet.

The five men fled the prison grounds in the Tisons' Ford Galaxy automobile. No shots were fired at the prison.

After leaving the prison, the men abandoned the Ford automobile and proceeded on to an isolated house in a white Lincoln automobile that the brothers had parked at a hospital near the prison. At the house, the Lincoln automobile had a flat tire; the only spare tire was pressed into service. After two nights at the house, the group drove toward Flagstaff. As the group traveled on back roads and secondary highways through the desert, another tire blew out. The group decided to flag down a passing motorist and steal a car. Raymond stood out in front of the Lincoln; the other four armed themselves and lay in wait by the side of the road. One car passed by without stopping, but a second car, a Mazda occupied by John Lyons, his wife Donnelda, his 2–year–old son Christopher, and his 15–year–old niece, Theresa Tyson, pulled over to render aid.

As Raymond showed John Lyons the flat tire on the Lincoln, the other Tisons and Greenawalt emerged. The Lyons family was forced into the backseat of the Lincoln. Raymond and Donald drove the Lincoln down a dirt road off the highway and then down a gas line service road farther into the desert; Gary Tison, Ricky Tison, and Randy Greenawalt followed in the Lyons' Mazda. The two cars were parked trunk to trunk and the Lyons family was ordered to stand in front of the Lincoln's headlights. The Tisons transferred their belongings from the Lincoln into the Mazda. They discovered guns and money in the Mazda which they kept, and they put the rest of the Lyons' possessions in the Lincoln.

Gary Tison then told Raymond to drive the Lincoln still farther into the desert. Raymond did so, and, while the others guarded the Lyons and Theresa Tyson, Gary fired his shotgun into the radiator, presumably to completely disable the vehicle. The Lyons and Theresa Tyson were then escorted to the Lincoln and again ordered to stand in its headlights. Ricky Tison reported that John Lyons begged, in comments "more or less directed at everybody," "Jesus, don't kill me." Gary Tison said he was "thinking about it." John Lyons asked the Tisons and Greenawalt to "give us some water . . . just leave us out here, and you all go home." Gary Tison then told his sons to go back to the Mazda and get some water. Raymond later explained that his father "was like in conflict with himself . . . What it was, I think it was the baby being there and all this, and he wasn't sure about what to do."

The petitioners' statements diverge to some extent, but it appears that both of them went back towards the Mazda, along with Donald, while Randy Greenawalt and Gary Tison stayed at the Lincoln guarding the victims. Raymond recalled being at the Mazda filling the water jug "when we started hearing the shots." Ricky said that the brothers gave the water jug to Gary Tison who then, with Randy Greenawalt went behind the Lincoln, where they spoke briefly, then raised the shotguns and started firing. In any event, petitioners agree they saw Greenawalt and their father brutally murder their four captives with repeated blasts from their shotguns. Neither made an effort to help the victims, though both later stated they were surprised by the shooting. The Tisons got into the Mazda and drove away, continuing their flight. Physical evidence suggested that Theresa Tyson managed to crawl away from the bloodbath, severely injured. She died in the desert after the Tisons left.

Several days later the Tisons and Greenawalt were apprehended after a shootout at a police roadblock. Donald Tison was killed. Gary Tison escaped into the desert where he subsequently died of exposure. Raymond and Ricky Tison and Randy Greenawalt were captured and tried jointly for the crimes associated with the prison break itself and the shootout at the roadblock; each was convicted and sentenced.

The State then individually tried each of the petitioners for capital murder of the four victims as well as for the associated crimes of armed robbery, kidnaping, and car theft. The capital murder charges were based on Arizona felony-murder law providing that a killing occurring during the perpetration of robbery or kidnaping is capital murder and that each participant in the kidnaping or robbery is legally responsible for the acts of his accomplices. Each of the petitioners was convicted of the four murders under these accomplice liability and felony-murder statutes.

Arizona law also provided for a capital sentencing proceeding, to be conducted without a jury, to determine whether the crime was sufficiently aggravated to warrant the death sentence. The statute set out six aggravating and four mitigating factors. The judge found three statutory aggravating factors:

> (1) the Tisons had created a grave risk of death to others (not the victims);

> (2) the murders had been committed for pecuniary gain;

> (3) the murders were especially heinous.

The judge found no statutory mitigating factor. Importantly, the judge specifically found that the crime was not mitigated by the fact that each of the petitioners' "participation was relatively minor." Rather, he found that the "participation of each [petitioner] in the crimes giving rise to the application of the felony murder rule in this case was very substantial." The trial judge also specifically found that each "could reasonably have foreseen that his conduct . . . would cause or create a grave risk of . . . death." He did find, however, three nonstatutory mitigating factors:

> (1) the petitioners' youth—Ricky was 20 and Raymond was 19;

> (2) neither had prior felony records;

> (3) each had been convicted of the murders under the felony-murder rule.

Nevertheless, the judge sentenced both petitioners to death.

* * *

II

In *Enmund v. Florida*, this Court reversed the death sentence of a defendant convicted under Florida's felony-murder rule. Enmund was the driver of the "getaway" car in an armed robbery of a dwelling. The occupants of the house, an elderly couple, resisted and Enmund's accomplices killed them. The Florida Supreme Court found the inference that Enmund was the person in the car by the side of the road waiting to help his accomplices escape sufficient to support his sentence of death. * * *

This Court, citing the weight of legislative and community opinion, found a broad societal consensus, with which it agreed, that the death penalty was disproportional to the crime of robbery-felony murder "in these circumstances." The Court noted that although 32 American jurisdictions permitted the imposition of the death penalty for felony murders under a variety of circumstances, Florida was 1 of only 8 jurisdictions that authorized the death penalty "solely for participation in a robbery in which another robber takes life." Enmund was, therefore, sentenced under a distinct minority regime, a regime that permitted the imposition of the death penalty for felony murder *simpliciter*. At the other end of the spectrum, eight States required a finding of intent to kill before death could be imposed in a felony-murder case and one State required actual participation in the killing. The remaining States authorizing capital punishment for felony murders fell into two somewhat overlapping middle categories: three authorized the death penalty when the defendant acted with recklessness or extreme indifference to human life, and nine others, including Arizona, required a finding of some aggravating factor beyond the fact that the killing had occurred during the course of a felony before a capital sentence might be imposed. Arizona fell into a subcategory of six States which made "minimal participation in a capital felony committed by another person a [statutory] mitigating circumstance." Two more jurisdictions required a finding that the defendant's participation in the felony was not "relatively minor" before authorizing a capital sentence.[3]

After surveying the States' felony-murder statutes, the *Enmund* Court next examined the behavior of juries in cases like Enmund's in its attempt to assess American attitudes toward capital punishment in felony-murder cases. Of 739 death row inmates, only 41 did not participate in the fatal assault. All but 16 of these were physically present at the scene of the murder and of these only 3, including Enmund, were sentenced to death in the absence of a finding that they had collaborated in a scheme designed to kill. The Court found the fact that only 3 of 739 death row inmates had been sentenced to death absent an intent to kill, physical presence, or direct participation in the fatal assault persuasive evidence that American juries considered the death sentence disproportional to felony murder *simpliciter*.

---

3. Vermont fell into none of these categories. Vermont limited the death penalty to defendants who commit a second unrelated murder or murder a correctional officer.

Against this background, the Court undertook its own proportionality analysis. Armed robbery is a serious offense, but one for which the penalty of death is plainly excessive; the imposition of the death penalty for robbery, therefore, violates the Eighth and Fourteenth Amendments' proscription " 'against all punishments which by their excessive length or severity are greatly disproportioned to the offenses charged.' " *Weems v. United States*, 217 U.S. 349, 30 S.Ct. 544 (1910) (quoting *O'Neil v. Vermont*, 144 U.S. 323, 12 S.Ct. 693 (1892)); *cf. Coker v. Georgia*, 433 U.S. 584, 97 S.Ct. 2861 (1977) (holding the death penalty disproportional to the crime of rape). Furthermore, the Court found that Enmund's degree of participation in the murders was so tangential that it could not be said to justify a sentence of death. It found that neither the deterrent nor the retributive purposes of the death penalty were advanced by imposing the death penalty upon Enmund. The *Enmund* Court was unconvinced "that the threat that the death penalty will be imposed for murder will measurably deter one who does not kill and has no intention or purpose that life will be taken." In reaching this conclusion, the Court relied upon the fact that killing only rarely occurred during the course of robberies, and such killing as did occur even more rarely resulted in death sentences if the evidence did not support an inference that the defendant intended to kill. The Court acknowledged, however, that "it would be very different if the likelihood of a killing in the course of a robbery were so substantial that one should share the blame for the killing if he somehow participated in the felony."

That difference was also related to the second purpose of capital punishment, retribution. The heart of the retribution rationale is that a criminal sentence must be directly related to the personal culpability of the criminal offender. While the States generally have wide discretion in deciding how much retribution to exact in a given case, the death penalty, "unique in its severity and irrevocability," requires the State to inquire into the relevant facets of "the character and record of the individual offender." *Woodson v. North Carolina*, 428 U.S. 280, 96 S.Ct. 2978 (1976). Thus, in Enmund's case, "the focus [had to] be on *his* culpability, not on that of those who committed the robbery and shot the victims, for we insist on 'individualized consideration as a constitutional requirement in imposing the death sentence.' " *Enmund v. Florida* (quoting *Lockett v. Ohio*, 438 U.S. 586, 98 S.Ct. 2954 (1978)) (emphasis in original). Since Enmund's own participation in the felony murder was so attenuated and since there was no proof that Enmund had any culpable mental state, the death penalty was excessive retribution for his crimes.

* * *

* * * [I]t is * * * clear that petitioners * * * fall outside the category of felony murderers for whom *Enmund* explicitly held the death penalty disproportional: their degree of participation in the crimes was major rather than minor, and the record would support a finding of the culpable mental state of reckless indifference to human life. We take the facts as the Arizona Supreme Court has given them to us.

Raymond Tison brought an arsenal of lethal weapons into the Arizona State Prison which he then handed over to two convicted murderers, one of whom he knew had killed a prison guard in the course of a previous escape attempt. By his own admission he was prepared to kill in furtherance of the prison break. He performed the crucial role of flagging down a passing car occupied by an innocent family whose fate was then entrusted to the known killers he had previously armed. He robbed these people at their direction and then guarded the victims at gunpoint while they considered what next to do. He stood by and watched the killing, making no effort to assist the victims before, during, or after the shooting. Instead, he chose to assist the killers in their continuing criminal endeavors, ending in a gun battle with the police in the final showdown.

Ricky Tison's behavior differs in slight details only. Like Raymond, he intentionally brought the guns into the prison to arm the murderers. He could have foreseen that lethal force might be used, particularly since he knew that his father's previous escape attempt had resulted in murder. He, too, participated fully in the kidnaping and robbery and watched the killing after which he chose to aid those whom he had placed in the position to kill rather than their victims.

These facts not only indicate that the Tison brothers' participation in the crime was anything but minor; they also would clearly support a finding that they both subjectively appreciated that their acts were likely to result in the taking of innocent life. The issue raised by this case is whether the Eighth Amendment prohibits the death penalty in the intermediate case of the defendant whose participation is major and whose mental state is one of reckless indifference to the value of human life. *Enmund* does not specifically address this point. We now take up the task of determining whether the Eighth Amendment proportionality requirement bars the death penalty under these circumstances.

Like the *Enmund* Court, we find the state legislatures' judgment as to proportionality in these circumstances relevant to this constitutional inquiry. The largest number of States still fall into the two intermediate categories discussed in *Enmund*. Four States authorize the death penalty in felony-murder cases upon a showing of culpable mental state such as recklessness or extreme indifference to human life. Two jurisdictions require that the defendant's participation be substantial and the statutes of at least six more, including Arizona, take minor participation in the felony expressly into account in mitigation of the murder. These requirements significantly overlap both in this case and in general, for the greater the defendant's participation in the felony murder, the more likely that he acted with reckless indifference to human life. At a minimum, however, it can be said that all these jurisdictions, as well as six States which *Enmund* classified along with Florida as permitting capital punishment for felony murder *simpliciter*, and the three States which simply require some additional aggravation before imposing the death penalty upon a felony murderer, specifically authorize the death penalty in a felony-murder case where, though the defendant's mental state fell short of intent to kill, the defendant was a major actor in a felony in which he knew death was highly likely to occur. On the other hand, even after *Enmund*, only 11 States authorizing capital punishment forbid imposition of the death penalty even though the defendant's participation in the felony murder is major and the likelihood of killing is so substantial as to raise an inference of extreme recklessness. This substantial and recent legislative authorization of the death penalty for the crime of felony murder regardless of the absence of a finding of an intent to kill powerfully suggests that our society does not reject the death penalty as grossly excessive under these circumstances.

Moreover, a number of state courts have interpreted *Enmund* to permit the imposition of the death penalty in such aggravated felony murders. We do not approve or disapprove the judgments as to proportionality reached on the particular facts of these cases, but we note the apparent consensus that substantial participation in a violent felony under circumstances likely to result in the loss of innocent human life may justify the death penalty even absent an "intent to kill." * * *

Against this backdrop, we now consider the proportionality of the death penalty in these midrange felony-murder cases for which the majority of American jurisdictions clearly authorize capital punishment and for which American courts have not been nearly so reluctant to impose death as they are in the case of felony murder *simpliciter*.

A critical facet of the individualized determination of culpability required in capital cases is the mental state with which the defendant commits the crime. Deeply ingrained in our legal tradition is the idea that the more purposeful is the criminal conduct, the more serious is the offense, and, therefore, the more severely it ought to be punished. The ancient concept of malice aforethought was an early attempt to focus on mental state in order to distinguish those who deserved death from those who through "Benefit of ... Clergy" would be spared. Over time, malice aforethought came to be inferred from the mere act of killing in a variety of circumstances; in reaction, Pennsylvania became the first American jurisdiction to distinguish between degrees of murder, reserving capital punishment to "wilful, deliberate and premeditated" killings and felony murders. 3 Pa. Laws 1794, ch. 1766, pp. 186–187 (1810). More recently, in *Lockett v. Ohio*, 438 U.S. 586, 98 S.Ct. 2954 (1978), the plurality opinion made clear that the defendant's mental state was critical to weighing a defendant's culpability under a system of guided discretion, vacating a death sentence imposed under an Ohio statute that did not permit the sentencing authority to take into account "the absence of direct proof that the defendant intended to cause the death of the victim." In *Enmund v. Florida*, the Court recognized again the importance of mental state, explicitly permitting the death penalty in at least those cases where the felony murderer intended to kill and forbidding it in the case of a minor actor not shown to have had any culpable mental state.

A narrow focus on the question of whether or not a given defendant "intended to kill," however, is a highly unsatisfactory means of definitively distinguishing the most culpable and dangerous of murderers. Many who intend to, and do, kill are not criminally liable at all—those who act in self-defense or with other justification or excuse. Other intentional homicides, though criminal, are often felt undeserving of the death penalty—those that are the result of provocation. On the other hand, some nonintentional murderers may be among the most dangerous and inhumane of all—the person who tortures another not caring whether the victim lives or dies, or the robber who shoots someone in the course of the robbery, utterly indifferent to the fact that the desire to rob may have the unintended consequence of killing the victim as well as taking the victim's property. This reckless indifference to the value of human life may be every bit as shocking to the moral sense as an "intent to kill." Indeed it is for this very reason that the common law and modern criminal codes alike have classified behavior such as occurred in this case along with intentional murders. *Enmund* held that when "intent to kill" results in its logical though not inevitable consequence—the taking of human life—the Eighth Amendment permits the State to exact the death penalty after a careful weighing of the aggravating and mitigating circumstances. Similarly, we hold that the reckless disregard for human life implicit in knowingly engaging in criminal activities known to carry a grave risk of death represents a highly culpable mental state, a mental state that may be taken into account in making a capital sentencing judgment when that conduct causes its natural, though also not inevitable, lethal result.

The petitioners' own personal involvement in the crimes was not minor, but rather, as specifically found by the trial court, "substantial." Far from merely sitting in a car away from the actual scene of the murders acting as the getaway driver to a robbery, each petitioner was actively involved in every element of the kidnaping-robbery and was physically present during the entire sequence of criminal activity culminating in the murder of the Lyons family and the subsequent flight. The Tisons' high level of participation in these crimes further implicates them in the resulting deaths. Accordingly, they fall well within the overlapping second intermediate position which focuses on the defendant's degree of participation in the felony.

Only a small minority of those jurisdictions imposing capital punishment for felony murder have rejected the possibility of a capital sentence absent an intent to kill, and we do not find this minority position constitutionally required. We will not attempt to precisely delineate the particular types of conduct and states of mind warranting imposition of the death penalty here. Rather, we simply hold that major participation in the felony committed, combined with reckless indifference to human life, is sufficient to satisfy the *Enmund* culpability requirement.[12] The Arizona

---

12. Although we state these two requirements separately, they often overlap. For example, we do not doubt that there are some felonies as to which one could properly conclude that any major participant necessarily exhibits reckless indifference to the value of human life. Moreover, even in

courts have clearly found that the former exists; we now vacate the judgments below and remand for determination of the latter in further proceedings not inconsistent with this opinion.

It is so ordered.

JUSTICE BRENNAN, with whom JUSTICE MARSHALL joins, and with whom JUSTICE BLACKMUN and JUSTICE STEVENS join as to Parts I through IV–A, dissenting.

[The dissenters argued that the facts were not sufficient to support the Court's conclusion that petitioners acted with reckless disregard for human life. Petitioners were young, had no prior felony record and had no role in planning the escape. Their "presence at the scene of the murders, and their participation in flagging down the vehicle, and robbing and guarding the family, indicate nothing whatsoever about their subjective appreciation that their father and his friend would suddenly decide to kill the family." Petitioners were getting a jug of water for the victims when the shootings occurred, and they were surprised by the shootings because, as Raymond testified, "Well, I just think you should know when we first came into this we had an agreement with my dad that nobody would get hurt because we [the brothers] wanted no one hurt."]

III

Notwithstanding the Court's unwarranted observations on the applicability of its new standard to this case, the basic flaw in today's decision is the Court's failure to conduct the sort of proportionality analysis that the Constitution and past cases require. Creation of a new category of culpability is not enough to distinguish this case from *Enmund v. Florida*, 458 U.S. 782, 102 S.Ct. 3368 (1982). The Court must also establish that death is a proportionate punishment for individuals in this category. In other words, the Court must demonstrate that major participation in a felony with a state of mind of reckless indifference to human life deserves the same punishment as intending to commit a murder or actually committing a murder. The Court does not attempt to conduct a proportionality review of the kind performed in past cases raising a proportionality question, but instead offers two reasons in support of its view.

A

One reason the Court offers for its conclusion that death is proportionate punishment for persons falling within its new category is that limiting the death penalty to those who intend to kill "is a highly unsatisfactory means of definitively distinguishing the most culpable and dangerous of murderers." To illustrate that intention cannot be dispositive, the Court offers as examples "the person who tortures another not caring whether the victim lives or dies, or the robber who shoots someone in the course of the robbery, utterly indifferent to the fact that the desire

---

cases where the fact that the defendant was a major participant in a felony did not suffice to establish reckless indifference, that fact would still often provide significant support for such a finding.

to rob may have the unintended consequence of killing the victim as well as taking the victim's property." Influential commentators and some States have approved the use of the death penalty for persons, like those given in the Court's examples, who kill others in circumstances manifesting an extreme indifference to the value of human life. Thus an exception to the requirement that only intentional murders be punished with death might be made for persons who actually commit an act of homicide; *Enmund*, by distinguishing from the accomplice case "those who kill," clearly reserved that question. But the constitutionality of the death penalty for those individuals is no more relevant to this case than it was to *Enmund*, because this case, like *Enmund*, involves accomplices who did not kill. Thus, although some of the "most culpable and dangerous of murderers" may be those who killed without specifically intending to kill, it is considerably more difficult to apply that rubric convincingly to those who not only did not intend to kill, but who also have not killed.

It is precisely in this context—where the defendant has not killed—that a finding that he or she nevertheless intended to kill seems indispensable to establishing capital culpability. It is important first to note that such a defendant has not committed an act for which he or she could be sentenced to death. The applicability of the death penalty therefore turns entirely on the defendant's mental state with regard to an act committed by another. Factors such as the defendant's major participation in the events surrounding the killing or the defendant's presence at the scene are relevant insofar as they illuminate the defendant's mental state with regard to the killings. They cannot serve, however, as independent grounds for imposing the death penalty.

Second, when evaluating such a defendant's mental state, a determination that the defendant acted with intent is qualitatively different from a determination that the defendant acted with reckless indifference to human life. The difference lies in the nature of the choice each has made. The reckless actor has not chosen to bring about the killing in the way the intentional actor has. The person who chooses to act recklessly and is indifferent to the possibility of fatal consequences often deserves serious punishment. But because that person has not chosen to kill, his or her moral and criminal culpability is of a different degree than that of one who killed or intended to kill.

　　* * *

In *Enmund*, the Court explained at length the reasons a finding of intent is a necessary prerequisite to the imposition of the death penalty. In any given case, the Court said, the death penalty must "measurably contribut[e]" to one or both of the two "social purposes"—deterrence and retribution—which this Court has accepted as justifications for the death penalty. *Enmund*, citing *Gregg v. Georgia*, 428 U.S. 153, 96 S.Ct. 2909 (1976). If it does not so contribute, it " 'is nothing more than the purposeless and needless imposition of pain and suffering' and hence an unconstitutional punishment." *Enmund*, quoting *Coker v. Georgia*. Enmund's lack of intent to commit the murder—rather than the lack of evidence as to his mental state—was the decisive factor in the Court's decision that the death penalty served neither of the two purposes. With regard to deterrence, the Court was

> "quite unconvinced ... that the threat that the death penalty will be imposed for murder will measurably deter one who does not kill and has no intention or purpose that life will be taken. Instead, it seems likely that capital punishment can serve as a deterrent only when murder is the result of premeditation and deliberation ..."[11]

As for retribution, the Court again found that Enmund's lack of intent, together with the fact that he did not kill the victims, was decisive. "American criminal law has long considered a defendant's intention—and therefore his moral guilt—to be critical to the degree of [his] criminal culpability." The Court concluded that "putting Enmund to death to avenge two killings that he did not commit and had no intention of committing or causing does not measurably contribute to the retributive end of ensuring that the criminal gets his just deserts." Thus, in *Enmund* the Court established that a finding of an intent to kill was a constitutional prerequisite for the imposition of the death penalty on an accomplice who did not kill. The Court has since reiterated that "*Enmund* ... imposes a categorical rule: a person who has not in fact killed, attempted to kill, or intended that a killing take place or that lethal force be used may not be sentenced to death." *Cabana v. Bullock*, 474 U.S. 376, 106 S.Ct. 689 (1986). The Court's decision today to approve the death penalty for accomplices who lack this mental state is inconsistent with *Enmund* and with the only justifications this Court has put forth for imposing the death penalty in any case.

B

The Court's second reason for abandoning the intent requirement is based on its survey of state statutes authorizing the death penalty for felony murder, and on a handful of state cases. On this basis, the Court concludes that only "a small minority *of those jurisdictions imposing capital punishment for felony murder* have rejected the possibility of a capital sentence absent an intent to kill, and we do not find this minority position constitutionally required." (emphasis added). The Court would thus have us believe that "the majority of American jurisdictions clearly authorize capital punishment" in cases such as this. This is not the case. First, the Court excludes from its survey those jurisdictions that have abolished the death penalty and those that have authorized it only in

---

11. The Court acknowledged that "it would be very different if the likelihood of a killing in the course of a robbery were so substantial that one should share the blame for the killing if he somehow participated in the felony." Nevertheless, the Court saw no reason to depart from its conclusion that the death penalty could not be justified as a deterrent in that case, because "competent observers have concluded that there is no basis in experience for the notion that death so frequently occurs in the course of a felony for which killing is not an essential ingredient that the death penalty should be considered as a justifiable deterrent to the felony itself." The trial court found that the killings in the case were not an essential ingredient of the felony. Thus the goal of deterrence is no more served in this case than it was in *Enmund*.

circumstances different from those presented here. When these jurisdictions are included, and are considered with those jurisdictions that require a finding of intent to kill in order to impose the death sentence for felony murder, one discovers that approximately three-fifths of American jurisdictions do not authorize the death penalty for a nontriggerman absent a finding that he intended to kill. Thus, contrary to the Court's implication that its view is consonant with that of "the majority of American jurisdictions," the Court's view is itself distinctly the minority position.

Second, it is critical to examine not simply those jurisdictions that authorize the death penalty in a given circumstance, but those that actually *impose* it. Evidence that a penalty is imposed only infrequently suggests not only that jurisdictions are reluctant to apply it but also that, when it is applied, its imposition is arbitrary and therefore unconstitutional. *Furman v. Georgia*, 408 U.S. 238, 92 S.Ct. 2726 (1972). Thus, the Court in *Enmund* examined the relevant statistics on the imposition of the death penalty for accomplices in a felony murder. The Court found that of all executions between 1954 and 1982, there were "*only 6 cases out of 362 where a nontriggerman felony murderer was executed. All six executions took place in 1955.*" (emphasis added). This evidence obviously militates against imposing the death penalty on petitioners as powerfully as it did against imposing it on Enmund.

The Court in *Enmund* also looked at the imposition of the death penalty for felony murder within Florida, the State that had sentenced Enmund. Of the 45 murderers then on death row, 36 had been found to have "intended" to take life, and 8 of the 9 for which there was no finding of intent had been the triggerman. Thus in only one case—*Enmund*—had someone (such as the Tisons) who had neither killed nor intended to kill received the death sentence. Finally, the Court noted that in no Commonwealth or European country could Enmund have been executed, since all have either abolished or never employed a felony-murder doctrine.

The Court today neither reviews nor updates this evidence. Had it done so, it would have discovered that, even including the 65 executions since *Enmund*, "the fact remains that we are not aware of a single person convicted of felony murder over the past quarter century who did not kill or attempt to kill, and did not intend the death of the victim, who has been executed...." Of the 64 persons on death row in Arizona, all of those who have raised and lost an *Enmund* challenge in the Arizona Supreme Court have been found either to have killed or to have specifically intended to kill. Thus, like *Enmund*, the Tisons' sentence appears to be an aberration within Arizona itself as well as nationally and internationally. The Court's objective evidence that the statutes of roughly 20 States appear to authorize the death penalty for defendants in the Court's new category is therefore an inadequate substitute for a proper proportionality analysis, and is not persuasive evidence that the punishment that was unconstitutional for Enmund is constitutional for the Tisons.

* * *

NOTES

1. *Problem 5–1.*

A, B and C, all carrying guns, entered a convenience store late at night, and one of them yelled "Everybody freeze." C remained by the door, and A and B approached Clerk. A demanded money and then shot Clerk, killing him. A and B emptied the cash register, and the three fled. A, B and C have been convicted of first degree murder, and the prosecutor is seeking the death penalty against each of them. What are the arguments as to whether imposition of the death penalty on B and C would be constitutional?

2. *Problem 5–2.*

Defendant was burglarizing Victim's house when he was surprised by Victim. Defendant attempted to escape and was backing away from the house with his gun drawn when he tripped on a wire causing the gun to go off. The bullet passed through the closed kitchen door and killed Victim. Defendant has been convicted of first degree murder, and the prosecutor is seeking the death penalty. What are the arguments as to whether imposition of the death penalty on Defendant would be constitutional? Cf. *Hopkins v. Reeves*, 524 U.S. 88, 118 S.Ct. 1895 (1998).

ATKINS v. VIRGINIA

536 U.S. 304, 122 S.Ct. 2242, 153 L.Ed.2d 335 (2002).

JUSTICE STEVENS delivered the opinion of the Court.

Those mentally retarded persons who meet the law's requirements for criminal responsibility should be tried and punished when they commit crimes. Because of their disabilities in areas of reasoning, judgment, and control of their impulses, however, they do not act with the level of moral culpability that characterizes the most serious adult criminal conduct. Moreover, their impairments can jeopardize the reliability and fairness of capital proceedings against mentally retarded defendants. Presumably for these reasons, in the 13 years since we decided *Penry* v. *Lynaugh,* 492 U.S. 302, 109 S.Ct. 2934 (1989), the American public, legislators, scholars, and judges have deliberated over the question whether the death penalty should ever be imposed on a mentally retarded criminal. The consensus reflected in those deliberations informs our answer to the question presented by this case: whether such executions are "cruel and unusual punishments" prohibited by the Eighth Amendment to the Federal Constitution.

I

Petitioner, Daryl Renard Atkins, was convicted of abduction, armed robbery, and capital murder, and sentenced to death. At approximately midnight on August 16, 1996, Atkins and William Jones, armed with a semiautomatic handgun, abducted Eric Nesbitt, robbed him of the money on his person, drove him to an automated teller machine in his pickup truck where cameras recorded their withdrawal of additional cash, then took him to an isolated location where he was shot eight times and killed.

Jones and Atkins both testified in the guilt phase of Atkins' trial.[1] Each confirmed most of the details in the other's account of the incident, with the important exception that each stated that the other had actually shot and killed Nesbitt. Jones' testimony, which was both more coherent and credible than Atkins', was obviously credited by the jury and was sufficient to establish Atkins' guilt.[2] At the penalty phase of the trial, the State introduced victim impact evidence and proved two aggravating circumstances: future dangerousness and "vileness of the offense." To prove future dangerousness, the State relied on Atkins' prior felony convictions as well as the testimony of four victims of earlier robberies and assaults. To prove the second aggravator, the prosecution relied upon the trial record, including pictures of the deceased's body and the autopsy report.

In the penalty phase, the defense relied on one witness, Dr. Evan Nelson, a forensic psychologist who had evaluated Atkins before trial and concluded that he was "mildly mentally retarded."[3] His conclusion was based on interviews with people who knew Atkins, a review of school and court records, and the administration of a standard intelligence test which indicated that Atkins had a full scale IQ of 59.[5]

---

1. Initially, both Jones and Atkins were indicted for capital murder. The prosecution ultimately permitted Jones to plead guilty to first-degree murder in exchange for his testimony against Atkins. As a result of the plea, Jones became ineligible to receive the death penalty.

2. Highly damaging to the credibility of Atkins' testimony was its substantial inconsistency with the statement he gave to the police upon his arrest. Jones, in contrast, had declined to make an initial statement to the authorities.

3. The American Association of Mental Retardation (AAMR) defines mental retardation as follows: "*Mental retardation* refers to substantial limitations in present functioning. It is characterized by significantly subaverage intellectual functioning, existing concurrently with related limitations in two or more of the following applicable adaptive skill areas: communication, self-care, home living, social skills, community use, self-direction, health and safety, functional academics, leisure, and work. Mental retardation manifests before age 18." Mental Retardation: Definition, Classification, and Systems of Supports (9th ed.1992).

The American Psychiatric Association's definition is similar: "The essential feature of Mental Retardation is significantly subaverage general intellectual functioning (Criterion A) that is accompanied by significant limitations in adaptive functioning in at least two of the following skill areas: communication, self-care, home living, social/interpersonal skills, use of community resources, self-direction, functional academic skills, work, leisure, health, and safety (Criterion B). The onset must occur before age 18 years (Criterion C). Mental Retardation has many different etiologies and may be seen as a final common pathway of various pathological processes that affect the functioning of the central nervous system." American Psychiatric Association, Diagnostic and Statistical Manual of Mental Disorders (4th ed. 2000). "Mild" mental retardation is typically used to describe people with an IQ level of 50–55 to approximately 70.

5. Dr. Nelson administered the Wechsler Adult Intelligence Scales test (WAIS–III), the standard instrument in the United States for assessing intellectual functioning. The WAIS–III is scored by adding together the number of points earned on different subtests, and using a mathematical formula to convert this raw score into a scaled score. The test measures an intelligence range from 45 to 155. The mean score of the test is 100, which means that a person receiving a score of 100 is considered to have an average level of cognitive functioning. It is estimated that between 1 and 3 percent of the population has an IQ between 70 and 75 or lower, which is typically considered the cutoff IQ score for the intellectual function prong of the mental retardation definition.

At the sentencing phase, Dr. Nelson testified: "[Atkins'] full scale IQ is 59. Compared to the population at large, that means less than one percentile.... Mental retardation is a relatively

The jury sentenced Atkins to death, but the Virginia Supreme Court ordered a second sentencing hearing because the trial court had used a misleading verdict form. At the resentencing, Dr. Nelson again testified. The State presented an expert rebuttal witness, Dr. Stanton Samenow, who expressed the opinion that Atkins was not mentally retarded, but rather was of "average intelligence, at least," and diagnosable as having antisocial personality disorder.[6] The jury again sentenced Atkins to death.

The Supreme Court of Virginia affirmed the imposition of the death penalty. Atkins did not argue before the Virginia Supreme Court that his sentence was disproportionate to penalties imposed for similar crimes in Virginia, but he did contend "that he is mentally retarded and thus cannot be sentenced to death." The majority of the state court rejected this contention, relying on our holding in *Penry*. The Court was "not willing to commute Atkins' sentence of death to life imprisonment merely because of his IQ score."

Justice Hassell and Justice Koontz dissented. They rejected Dr. Samenow's opinion that Atkins possesses average intelligence as "incredulous as a matter of law," and concluded that "the imposition of the sentence of death upon a criminal defendant who has the mental age of a child between the ages of 9 and 12 is excessive." In their opinion, "it is indefensible to conclude that individuals who are mentally retarded are not to some degree less culpable for their criminal acts. By definition, such individuals have substantial limitations not shared by the general population. A moral and civilized society diminishes itself if its system of justice does not afford recognition and consideration of those limitations in a meaningful way."

Because of the gravity of the concerns expressed by the dissenters, and in light of the dramatic shift in the state legislative landscape that has occurred in the past 13 years, we granted certiorari to revisit the issue that we first addressed in the *Penry* case.

II

[The Court's review of claims that a punishment is excessive under the Eighth Amendment, has been based on the following principles. "The Amendment must draw its meaning from the evolving standards of decency that mark the progress of a maturing society." *Trop v. Dulles,* 356 U.S. 86, 78 S.Ct. 590 (1958) (plurality opinion). Determination of those

---

rare thing. It's about one percent of the population." According to Dr. Nelson, Atkins' IQ score "would automatically qualify for Social Security disability income." Dr. Nelson also indicated that of the over 40 capital defendants that he had evaluated, Atkins was only the second individual who met the criteria for mental retardation. He testified that, in his opinion, Atkins' limited intellect had been a consistent feature throughout his life, and that his IQ score of 59 is not an "aberration, malingered result, or invalid test score."

6. Dr. Samenow's testimony was based upon two interviews with Atkins, a review of his school records, and interviews with correctional staff. He did not administer an intelligence test, but did ask Atkins questions taken from the 1972 version of the Wechsler Memory Scale. Dr. Samenow attributed Atkins' "academic performance [that was] by and large terrible" to the fact that he "is a person who chose to pay attention sometimes, not to pay attention others, and did poorly because he did not want to do what he was required to do."

evolving standards should be informed by " 'objective factors to the maximum possible extent' " (*Harmelin v. Michigan,* 501 U.S. 957, 111 S.Ct. 2680 (1991) (quoting *Rummel v. Estelle,* 445 U.S. 263, 100 S.Ct. 1133 (1980))), and the "clearest and most reliable objective evidence of contemporary values is the legislation enacted by the country's legislatures." *Penry.* However, objective evidence does not "wholly determine" the controversy, "for the Constitution contemplates that in the end our own judgment will be brought to bear on the question of the acceptability of the death penalty under the Eighth Amendment." *Coker v. Georgia,* 433 U.S. 584, 97 S.Ct. 2861 (1977).]

Guided by our approach in these cases, we shall first review the judgment of legislatures that have addressed the suitability of imposing the death penalty on the mentally retarded and then consider reasons for agreeing or disagreeing with their judgment.

III

The parties have not called our attention to any state legislative consideration of the suitability of imposing the death penalty on mentally retarded offenders prior to 1986. In that year, the public reaction to the execution of a mentally retarded murderer in Georgia [Jerome Bowden] apparently led to the enactment of the first state statute prohibiting such executions. In 1988, when Congress enacted legislation reinstating the federal death penalty, it expressly provided that a "sentence of death shall not be carried out upon a person who is mentally retarded." In 1989, Maryland enacted a similar prohibition. It was in that year that we decided *Penry,* and concluded that those two state enactments, "even when added to the 14 States that have rejected capital punishment completely, do not provide sufficient evidence at present of a national consensus."

Much has changed since then. Responding to the national attention received by the Bowden execution and our decision in *Penry,* state legislatures across the country began to address the issue. In 1990 Kentucky and Tennessee enacted statutes similar to those in Georgia and Maryland, as did New Mexico in 1991, and Arkansas, Colorado, Washington, Indiana, and Kansas in 1993 and 1994. In 1995, when New York reinstated its death penalty, it emulated the Federal Government by expressly exempting the mentally retarded. Nebraska followed suit in 1998. There appear to have been no similar enactments during the next two years, but in 2000 and 2001 six more States—South Dakota, Arizona, Connecticut, Florida, Missouri, and North Carolina—joined the procession. The Texas Legislature unanimously adopted a similar bill, and bills have passed at least one house in other States, including Virginia and Nevada.

It is not so much the number of these States that is significant, but the consistency of the direction of change.[18] Given the well-known fact

---

18. A comparison to *Stanford v. Kentucky,* 492 U.S. 361, 109 S.Ct. 2969 (1989), in which we held that there was no national consensus prohibiting the execution of juvenile offenders over age

that anticrime legislation is far more popular than legislation providing protections for persons guilty of violent crime, the large number of States prohibiting the execution of mentally retarded persons (and the complete absence of States passing legislation reinstating the power to conduct such executions) provides powerful evidence that today our society views mentally retarded offenders as categorically less culpable than the average criminal. The evidence carries even greater force when it is noted that the legislatures that have addressed the issue have voted overwhelmingly in favor of the prohibition. Moreover, even in those States that allow the execution of mentally retarded offenders, the practice is uncommon. Some States, for example New Hampshire and New Jersey, continue to authorize executions, but none have been carried out in decades. Thus there is little need to pursue legislation barring the execution of the mentally retarded in those States. And it appears that even among those States that regularly execute offenders and that have no prohibition with regard to the mentally retarded, only five have executed offenders possessing a known IQ less than 70 since we decided *Penry*.[20] The practice, therefore, has become truly unusual, and it is fair to say that a national consensus has developed against it.[21]

To the extent there is serious disagreement about the execution of mentally retarded offenders, it is in determining which offenders are in fact retarded. In this case, for instance, the Commonwealth of Virginia disputes that Atkins suffers from mental retardation. Not all people who claim to be mentally retarded will be so impaired as to fall within the range of mentally retarded offenders about whom there is a national consensus. As was our approach in *Ford v. Wainwright,* with regard to insanity, "we leave to the State[s] the task of developing appropriate ways to enforce the constitutional restriction upon its execution of sentences." 477 U.S. 399, 106 S.Ct. 2595 (1986).

IV

This consensus unquestionably reflects widespread judgment about the relative culpability of mentally retarded offenders, and the relation-

---

15, is telling. Although we decided *Stanford* on the same day as *Penry*, apparently only two state legislatures have raised the threshold age for imposition of the death penalty.

20. Those States are Alabama, Texas, Louisiana, South Carolina and Virginia.

21. Additional evidence makes it clear that this legislative judgment reflects a much broader social and professional consensus. For example, several organizations with germane expertise [including the American Psychological Association and AAMR] have adopted official positions opposing the imposition of the death penalty upon a mentally retarded offender. In addition, representatives of widely diverse religious communities in the United States, reflecting Christian, Jewish, Muslim, and Buddhist traditions, have filed an *amicus curiae* brief explaining that even though their views about the death penalty differ, they all "share a conviction that the execution of persons with mental retardation cannot be morally justified." Moreover, within the world community, the imposition of the death penalty for crimes committed by mentally retarded offenders is overwhelmingly disapproved. Finally, polling data shows a widespread consensus among Americans, even those who support the death penalty, that executing the mentally retarded is wrong. Although these factors are by no means dispositive, their consistency with the legislative evidence lends further support to our conclusion that there is a consensus among those who have addressed the issue. See *Thompson v. Oklahoma*, 487 U.S. 815, 108 S.Ct. 2687 (1988) (considering the views of "respected professional organizations, by other nations that share our Anglo–American heritage, and by the leading members of the Western European community").

ship between mental retardation and the penological purposes served by the death penalty. Additionally, it suggests that some characteristics of mental retardation undermine the strength of the procedural protections that our capital jurisprudence steadfastly guards.

As discussed above, clinical definitions of mental retardation require not only subaverage intellectual functioning, but also significant limitations in adaptive skills such as communication, self-care, and self-direction that became manifest before age 18. Mentally retarded persons frequently know the difference between right and wrong and are competent to stand trial. Because of their impairments, however, by definition they have diminished capacities to understand and process information, to communicate, to abstract from mistakes and learn from experience, to engage in logical reasoning, to control impulses, and to understand the reactions of others. There is no evidence that they are more likely to engage in criminal conduct than others, but there is abundant evidence that they often act on impulse rather than pursuant to a premeditated plan, and that in group settings they are followers rather than leaders. Their deficiencies do not warrant an exemption from criminal sanctions, but they do diminish their personal culpability.

In light of these deficiencies, our death penalty jurisprudence provides two reasons consistent with the legislative consensus that the mentally retarded should be categorically excluded from execution. First, there is a serious question as to whether either justification that we have recognized as a basis for the death penalty applies to mentally retarded offenders. *Gregg v. Georgia*, 428 U.S. 153, 96 S.Ct. 2909 (1976), identified "retribution and deterrence of capital crimes by prospective offenders" as the social purposes served by the death penalty. Unless the imposition of the death penalty on a mentally retarded person "measurably contributes to one or both of these goals, it 'is nothing more than the purposeless and needless imposition of pain and suffering,' and hence an unconstitutional punishment." *Enmund v. Florida,* 458 U.S. 782, 102 S.Ct. 3368 (1982).

With respect to retribution—the interest in seeing that the offender gets his "just deserts"—the severity of the appropriate punishment necessarily depends on the culpability of the offender. Since *Gregg,* our jurisprudence has consistently confined the imposition of the death penalty to a narrow category of the most serious crimes. For example, in *Godfrey v. Georgia*, 446 U.S. 420, 100 S.Ct. 1759 (1980), we set aside a death sentence because the petitioner's crimes did not reflect "a consciousness materially more 'depraved' than that of any person guilty of murder." If the culpability of the average murderer is insufficient to justify the most extreme sanction available to the State, the lesser culpability of the mentally retarded offender surely does not merit that form of retribution. Thus, pursuant to our narrowing jurisprudence, which seeks to ensure that only the most deserving of execution are put to death, an exclusion for the mentally retarded is appropriate.

With respect to deterrence—the interest in preventing capital crimes by prospective offenders—"it seems likely that capital punishment can serve as a deterrent only when murder is the result of premeditation and deliberation," *Enmund*. Exempting the mentally retarded from that punishment will not affect the "cold calculus that precedes the decision" of other potential murderers. *Gregg*. Indeed, that sort of calculus is at the opposite end of the spectrum from behavior of mentally retarded offenders. The theory of deterrence in capital sentencing is predicated upon the notion that the increased severity of the punishment will inhibit criminal actors from carrying out murderous conduct. Yet it is the same cognitive and behavioral impairments that make these defendants less morally culpable—for example, the diminished ability to understand and process information, to learn from experience, to engage in logical reasoning, or to control impulses—that also make it less likely that they can process the information of the possibility of execution as a penalty and, as a result, control their conduct based upon that information. Nor will exempting the mentally retarded from execution lessen the deterrent effect of the death penalty with respect to offenders who are not mentally retarded. Such individuals are unprotected by the exemption and will continue to face the threat of execution. Thus, executing the mentally retarded will not measurably further the goal of deterrence.

The reduced capacity of mentally retarded offenders provides a second justification for a categorical rule making such offenders ineligible for the death penalty. The risk "that the death penalty will be imposed in spite of factors which may call for a less severe penalty," *Lockett v. Ohio*, 438 U.S. 586, 98 S.Ct. 2954 (1978), is enhanced, not only by the possibility of false confessions, but also by the lesser ability of mentally retarded defendants to make a persuasive showing of mitigation in the face of prosecutorial evidence of one or more aggravating factors. Mentally retarded defendants may be less able to give meaningful assistance to their counsel and are typically poor witnesses, and their demeanor may create an unwarranted impression of lack of remorse for their crimes. As *Penry* demonstrated, moreover, reliance on mental retardation as a mitigating factor can be a two-edged sword that may enhance the likelihood that the aggravating factor of future dangerousness will be found by the jury. Mentally retarded defendants in the aggregate face a special risk of wrongful execution.

Our independent evaluation of the issue reveals no reason to disagree with the judgment of "the legislatures that have recently addressed the matter" and concluded that death is not a suitable punishment for a mentally retarded criminal. We are not persuaded that the execution of mentally retarded criminals will measurably advance the deterrent or the retributive purpose of the death penalty. Construing and applying the Eighth Amendment in the light of our "evolving standards of decency," we therefore conclude that such punishment is excessive and that the Constitution "places a substantive restriction on the State's power to take the life" of a mentally retarded offender. *Ford*.

The judgment of the Virginia Supreme Court is reversed and the case is remanded for further proceedings not inconsistent with this opinion.

It is so ordered.

[CHIEF JUSTICE REHNQUIST, dissenting in an opinion joined by JUSTICES SCALIA and THOMAS, rejected the majority's reliance on "on foreign laws, the views of professional and religious organizations, and opinion polls" to determine "contemporary values." In his view, "the work product of legislatures and sentencing jury determinations" ought to be "the sole indicators by which courts ascertain the contemporary American conceptions of decency for purposes of the Eighth Amendment."]

JUSTICE SCALIA, with whom THE CHIEF JUSTICE and JUSTICE THOMAS join, dissenting.

Today's decision is the pinnacle of our Eighth Amendment death-is-different jurisprudence. Not only does it, like all of that jurisprudence, find no support in the text or history of the Eighth Amendment; it does not even have support in current social attitudes regarding the conditions that render an otherwise just death penalty inappropriate. Seldom has an opinion of this Court rested so obviously upon nothing but the personal views of its members.

I

I begin with a brief restatement of facts that are abridged by the Court but important to understanding this case. After spending the day drinking alcohol and smoking marijuana, petitioner Daryl Renard Atkins and a partner in crime drove to a convenience store, intending to rob a customer. Their victim was Eric Nesbitt, an airman from Langley Air Force Base, whom they abducted, drove to a nearby automated teller machine, and forced to withdraw $200. They then drove him to a deserted area, ignoring his pleas to leave him unharmed. According to the co-conspirator, whose testimony the jury evidently credited, Atkins ordered Nesbitt out of the vehicle and, after he had taken only a few steps, shot him one, two, three, four, five, six, seven, eight times in the thorax, chest, abdomen, arms, and legs.

The jury convicted Atkins of capital murder. At resentencing (the Virginia Supreme Court affirmed his conviction but remanded for resentencing because the trial court had used an improper verdict form), the jury heard extensive evidence of petitioner's alleged mental retardation. A psychologist testified that petitioner was mildly mentally retarded with an IQ of 59, that he was a "slow learne[r]," who showed a "lack of success in pretty much every domain of his life," and that he had an "impaired" capacity to appreciate the criminality of his conduct and to conform his conduct to the law. Petitioner's family members offered additional evidence in support of his mental retardation claim (*e.g.,* that petitioner is a "follower"). The State contested the evidence of retardation and presented testimony of a psychologist who found "absolutely no evidence other than the IQ score ... indicating that [petitioner] was in the least bit mentally retarded" and concluded that petitioner was "of average intelligence, at least."

The jury also heard testimony about petitioner's 16 prior felony convictions for robbery, attempted robbery, abduction, use of a firearm, and maiming. The victims of these offenses provided graphic depictions of petitioner's violent tendencies: He hit one over the head with a beer bottle; he slapped a gun across another victim's face, clubbed her in the head with it, knocked her to the ground, and then helped her up, only to shoot her in the stomach. The jury sentenced petitioner to death. The Supreme Court of Virginia affirmed petitioner's sentence.

II

As the foregoing history demonstrates, petitioner's mental retardation was a *central issue* at sentencing. The jury concluded, however, that his alleged retardation was not a compelling reason to exempt him from the death penalty in light of the brutality of his crime and his long demonstrated propensity for violence. "In upsetting this particularized judgment on the basis of a constitutional absolute," the Court concludes that no one who is even slightly mentally retarded can have sufficient "moral responsibility to be subjected to capital punishment for any crime. As a sociological and moral conclusion that is implausible; and it is doubly implausible as an interpretation of the United States Constitution." *Thompson v. Oklahoma,* 487 U.S. 815, 108 S.Ct. 2687 (1988) (SCALIA, J., dissenting).

Under our Eighth Amendment jurisprudence, a punishment is "cruel and unusual" if it falls within one of two categories: "those modes or acts of punishment that had been considered cruel and unusual at the time that the Bill of Rights was adopted," *Ford v. Wainwright,* 477 U.S. 399, 106 S.Ct. 2595 (1986), and modes of punishment that are inconsistent with modern "standards of decency," as evinced by objective indicia, the most important of which is "legislation enacted by the country's legislatures," *Penry v. Lynaugh,* 492 U.S. 302, 109 S.Ct. 2934 (1989).

The Court makes no pretense that execution of the mildly mentally retarded would have been considered "cruel and unusual" in 1791. Only the *severely* or *profoundly* mentally retarded, commonly known as "idiots," enjoyed any special status under the law at that time. They, like lunatics, suffered a "deficiency in will" rendering them unable to tell right from wrong. 4 W. Blackstone, Commentaries on the Laws of England (1769) (hereinafter Blackstone); see also *Penry* (citing sources indicating that idiots generally had an IQ of 25 or below, which would place them within the "profound" or "severe" range of mental retardation under modern standards); A. Fitz–Herbert, *Natura Brevium* (9th ed. 1794) (originally published 1534) (An idiot is "such a person who cannot account or number twenty pence, nor can tell who was his father or mother, nor how old he is, etc., so as it may appear that he hath no understanding of reason what shall be for his profit, or what for his loss"). Due to their incompetence, idiots were "excuse[d] from the guilt, and of course from the punishment, of any criminal action committed under such deprivation of the senses." Blackstone. Instead, they were often committed to civil confinement or made wards of the State, thereby preventing them from "go[ing] loose, to the terror of the king's subjects." Blackstone. Mentally retarded offenders with less severe impairments—those who were not "idiots"—suffered criminal prosecution and punishment, including capital punishment. See, *e.g.,* I. Ray, Medical Jurisprudence of Insanity (W. Overholser ed.1962) (recounting the 1834 trial and execution in Concord, New Hampshire, of an apparent "imbecile"—imbecility being a less severe form of retardation which "differs from idiocy in the circumstance that while in [the idiot] there is an utter destitution of every thing like reason, [imbeciles] possess some intellectual capacity, though infinitely less than is possessed by the great mass of mankind").

The Court is left to argue, therefore, that execution of the mildly retarded is inconsistent with the "evolving standards of decency that mark the progress of a maturing society." *Trop v. Dulles,* 356 U.S. 86, 78 S.Ct. 590 (1958) (plurality opinion) (Warren, C. J.). Before today, our opinions consistently emphasized that Eighth Amendment judgments regarding the existence of social "standards" "should be informed by objective factors to the maximum possible extent" and "should not be, or appear to be, merely the subjective views of individual Justices." *Coker v. Georgia,* 433 U.S. 584, 97 S.Ct. 2861 (1977) (plurality opinion); because it "will rarely if ever be the case that the Members of this Court will have a better sense of the evolution in views of the American people than do their elected representatives," *Thompson* (SCALIA, J., dissenting).

The Court pays lipservice to these precedents as it miraculously extracts a "national consensus" forbidding execution of the mentally retarded, from the fact that 18 States—less than *half* (47%) of the 38 States that permit capital punishment (for whom the issue exists)—have very recently enacted legislation barring execution of the mentally retarded. Even that 47% figure is a distorted one. If one is to say, as the Court does today, that *all* executions of the mentally retarded are so morally repugnant as to violate our national "standards of decency," surely the "consensus" it points to must be one that has set its righteous face against *all* such executions. Not 18 States, but only seven—18% of death penalty jurisdictions—have legislation of that scope. Eleven of those that the Court counts enacted statutes prohibiting execution of mentally retarded defendants *convicted after, or convicted of crimes committed after, the effective date* of the legislation; those already on death row, or consigned there before the statute's effective date, or even (in those States using the date of the crime as the criterion of retroactivity) tried in the future for murders committed many years ago, could be put to death. That is not a statement of absolute moral repugnance, but one of current preference between two tolerable approaches. Two of these States permit execution of the mentally retarded in other situations as well: Kansas apparently permits execution of all except the *severely* mentally retarded;

New York permits execution of the mentally retarded who commit murder in a correctional facility.

But let us accept, for the sake of argument, the Court's faulty count. That bare number of States alone—*18*—should be enough to convince any reasonable person that no "national consensus" exists. How is it possible that agreement among 47% of the death penalty jurisdictions amounts to "consensus"? Our prior cases have generally required a much higher degree of agreement before finding a punishment cruel and unusual on "evolving standards" grounds. In *Coker*, we proscribed the death penalty for rape of an adult woman after finding that only one jurisdiction, Georgia, authorized such a punishment. In *Enmund*, we invalidated the death penalty for mere participation in a robbery in which an accomplice took a life, a punishment not permitted in 28 of the death penalty States (78%). In *Ford*, we supported the common-law prohibition of execution of the insane with the observation that "[t]his ancestral legacy has not outlived its time," since not a single State authorizes such punishment. In *Solem v. Helm,* 463 U.S. 277, 103 S.Ct. 3001 (1983), we invalidated a life sentence without parole under a recidivist statute by which the criminal "was treated more severely than he would have been in any other State." What the Court calls evidence of "consensus" in the present case (a fudged 47%) more closely resembles evidence that we found *inadequate* to establish consensus in earlier cases. *Tison v. Arizona*, 481 U.S. 137, 107 S.Ct. 1676 (1987), upheld a state law authorizing capital punishment for major participation in a felony with reckless indifference to life where only 11 of the 37 death penalty States (30%) prohibited such punishment. *Stanford*, upheld a state law permitting execution of defendants who committed a capital crime at age 16 where only 15 of the 36 death penalty States (42%) prohibited death for such offenders.

Moreover, a major factor that the Court entirely disregards is that the legislation of all 18 States it relies on is still in its infancy. The oldest of the statutes is only 14 years old; five were enacted last year; over half were enacted within the past eight years. Few, if any, of the States have had sufficient experience with these laws to know whether they are sensible in the long term. It is "myopic to base sweeping constitutional principles upon the narrow experience of [a few] years." *Coker* (Burger, C. J., dissenting).

The Court attempts to bolster its embarrassingly feeble evidence of "consensus" with the following: "It is not so much the number of these States that is significant, but the *consistency* of the direction of change." (emphasis added). But in what *other* direction *could we possibly* see change? Given that 14 years ago *all* the death penalty statutes included the mentally retarded, *any* change (except precipitate undoing of what had just been done) was *bound to be* in the one direction the Court finds significant enough to overcome the lack of real consensus. That is to say, to be accurate the Court's "*consistency*-of-the-direction-of-change" point should be recast into the following unimpressive observation: "No State has yet undone its exemption of the mentally retarded, one for as long as

14 whole years." In any event, reliance upon "trends," even those of much longer duration than a mere 14 years, is a perilous basis for constitutional adjudication, as Justice O'CONNOR eloquently explained in *Thompson:*

> "In 1846, Michigan became the first State to abolish the death penalty.... In succeeding decades, other American States continued the trend towards abolition.... Later, and particularly after World War II, there ensued a steady and dramatic decline in executions.... In the 1950's and 1960's, more States abolished or radically restricted capital punishment, and executions ceased completely for several years beginning in 1968....

> "In 1972, when this Court heard arguments on the constitutionality of the death penalty, such statistics might have suggested that the practice had become a relic, implicitly rejected by a new societal consensus.... We now know that any inference of a societal consensus rejecting the death penalty would have been mistaken. But had this Court then declared the existence of such a consensus, and outlawed capital punishment, legislatures would very likely not have been able to revive it. The mistaken premise of the decision would have been frozen into constitutional law, making it difficult to refute and even more difficult to reject."

Her words demonstrate, of course, not merely the peril of riding a trend, but also the peril of discerning a consensus where there is none.

The Court's thrashing about for evidence of "consensus" includes reliance upon the *margins* by which state legislatures have enacted bans on execution of the retarded. Presumably, in applying our Eighth Amendment "evolving-standards-of-decency" jurisprudence, we will henceforth weigh not only how many States have agreed, but how many States have agreed *by how much*. Of course if the percentage of legislators voting for the bill is significant, surely the number of people *represented* by the legislators voting for the bill is also significant: the fact that 49% of the legislators in a State with a population of 60 million voted *against* the bill should be more impressive than the fact that 90% of the legislators in a state with a population of 2 million voted *for* it. (By the way, the population of the death penalty States that exclude the mentally retarded is only 44% of the population of all death penalty States.) This is quite absurd. What we have looked for in the past to "evolve" the Eighth Amendment is a consensus of the same sort as the consensus that *adopted* the Eighth Amendment: a consensus of the sovereign States that form the Union, not a nose count of Americans for and against.

Even less compelling (if possible) is the Court's argument, that evidence of "national consensus" is to be found in the infrequency with which retarded persons are executed in States that do not bar their execution. To begin with, what the Court takes as true is in fact quite doubtful. It is not at all clear that execution of the mentally retarded is "uncommon," as even the sources cited by the Court suggest (citing D. Keyes, W. Edwards, & R. Perske, People with Mental Retardation are

Dying Legally, 35 Mental Retardation (Feb.1997) (updated by Death Penalty Information Center; available at http://www.advocacyone.org/deathpenalty.html) (June 12, 2002) (showing that 12 States executed 35 allegedly mentally retarded offenders during the period 1984–2000)). See also Bonner & Rimer, Executing the Mentally Retarded Even as Laws Begin to Shift, N.Y. Times, Aug. 7, 2000 p. A1 (reporting that 10% of death row inmates are retarded). *If,* however, execution of the mentally retarded *is* "uncommon"; and if it is not a sufficient explanation of this that the retarded comprise a tiny fraction of society (1% to 3%); then surely the explanation is that mental retardation is a constitutionally mandated mitigating factor at sentencing. For that reason, even if there were uniform national sentiment in *favor* of executing the retarded in appropriate cases, one would still expect execution of the mentally retarded to be "uncommon." To adapt to the present case what the Court itself said in *Stanford*: "[I]t is not only possible, but overwhelmingly probable, that the very considerations which induce [today's majority] to believe that death should *never* be imposed on [mentally retarded] offenders . . . cause prosecutors and juries to believe that it should *rarely* be imposed."

But the Prize for the Court's Most Feeble Effort to fabricate "national consensus" must go to its appeal (deservedly relegated to a footnote) to the views of assorted professional and religious organizations, members of the so-called "world community," and respondents to opinion polls. I agree with the Chief Justice, that the views of professional and religious organizations and the results of opinion polls are irrelevant. Equally irrelevant are the practices of the "world community," whose notions of justice are (thankfully) not always those of our people. "We must never forget that it is a Constitution for the United States of America that we are expounding. . . . [W]here there is not first a settled consensus among our own people, the views of other nations, however enlightened the Justices of this Court may think them to be, cannot be imposed upon Americans through the Constitution." *Thompson* (SCALIA, J., dissenting).

III

Beyond the empty talk of a "national consensus," the Court gives us a brief glimpse of what really underlies today's decision: pretension to a power confined *neither* by the moral sentiments originally enshrined in the Eighth Amendment (its original meaning) *nor even* by the current moral sentiments of the American people. " '[T]he Constitution,' the Court says, 'contemplates that in the end *our own judgment* will be brought to bear on the question of the acceptability of the death penalty under the Eighth Amendment.' " (quoting *Coker*) (emphasis added). (The unexpressed reason for this unexpressed "contemplation" of the Constitution is presumably that really good lawyers have moral sentiments superior to those of the common herd, whether in 1791 or today.) The arrogance of this assumption of power takes one's breath away. And it explains, of course, why the Court can be so cavalier about the evidence of consensus. It is just a game, after all. "[I]n the end," it is the *feelings* and *intuition* of a majority of the Justices that count—"the perceptions of decency, or of penology, or of mercy, entertained . . . by a majority of the small and unrepresentative segment of our society that sits on this Court." *Thompson* (SCALIA, J., dissenting).

The genuinely operative portion of the opinion, then, is the Court's statement of the reasons why it agrees with the contrived consensus it has found, that the "diminished capacities" of the mentally retarded render the death penalty excessive. The Court's analysis rests on two fundamental assumptions: (1) that the Eighth Amendment prohibits excessive punishments, and (2) that sentencing juries or judges are unable to account properly for the "diminished capacities" of the retarded. The first assumption is wrong, as I explained at length in *Harmelin v. Michigan,* 501 U.S. 957, 111 S.Ct. 2680 (1991) (opinion of SCALIA, J.). The Eighth Amendment is addressed to always-and-everywhere "cruel" punishments, such as the rack and the thumbscrew. But where the punishment is in itself permissible, "[t]he Eighth Amendment is not a ratchet, whereby a temporary consensus on leniency for a particular crime fixes a permanent constitutional maximum, disabling the States from giving effect to altered beliefs and responding to changed social conditions." The second assumption—inability of judges or juries to take proper account of mental retardation—is not only unsubstantiated, but contradicts the immemorial belief, here and in England, that they play an *indispensable* role in such matters:

> "[I]t is very difficult to define the indivisible line that divides perfect and partial insanity; but it must rest upon circumstances duly to be weighed and considered both by the judge and jury, lest on the one side there be a kind of inhumanity towards the defects of human nature, or on the other side too great an indulgence given to great crimes. . . ." 1 Hale, Pleas of the Crown.

Proceeding from these faulty assumptions, the Court gives two reasons why the death penalty is an excessive punishment for all mentally retarded offenders. First, the "diminished capacities" of the mentally retarded raise a "serious question" whether their execution contributes to the "social purposes" of the death penalty, viz., retribution and deterrence. (The Court conveniently ignores a third "social purpose" of the death penalty—"incapacitation of dangerous criminals and the consequent prevention of crimes that they may otherwise commit in the future," *Gregg v. Georgia*, 428 U.S. 153, 96 S.Ct. 2909 (1976) (joint opinion of STEWART, POWELL, and STEVENS, JJ.). But never mind; its discussion of even the other two does not bear analysis.) Retribution is not advanced, the argument goes, because the mentally retarded are *no more culpable* than the average murderer, whom we have already held lacks sufficient culpability to warrant the death penalty. Who says so? Is there an established correlation between mental acuity and the ability to conform one's conduct to the law in such a rudimentary matter as murder? Are the mentally retarded really more disposed (and hence more likely) to commit willfully cruel and serious crime than others? In my experience, the opposite is true: being childlike generally suggests innocence rather than brutality.

Assuming, however, that there is a direct connection between diminished intelligence and the inability to refrain from murder, what scientific analysis can possibly show that a mildly retarded individual who commits an exquisite torture-killing is "no more culpable" than the "average" murderer in a holdup-gone-wrong or a domestic dispute? Or a moderately retarded individual who commits a series of 20 exquisite torture-killings? Surely culpability, and deservedness of the most severe retribution, depends not merely (if at all) upon the mental capacity of the criminal (above the level where he is able to distinguish right from wrong) but also upon the depravity of the crime—which is precisely why this sort of question has traditionally been thought answerable not by a categorical rule of the sort the Court today imposes upon all trials, but rather by the sentencer's weighing of the circumstances (both degree of retardation and depravity of crime) in the particular case. The fact that juries continue to sentence mentally retarded offenders to death for extreme crimes shows that society's moral outrage sometimes demands execution of retarded offenders. By what principle of law, science, or logic can the Court pronounce that this is wrong? There is none. Once the Court admits (as it does) that mental retardation does not render the offender morally *blameless*, there is no basis for saying that the death penalty is *never* appropriate retribution, no matter *how* heinous the crime. As long as a mentally retarded offender knows "the difference between right and wrong," only the sentencer can assess whether his retardation reduces his culpability enough to exempt him from the death penalty for the particular murder in question.

As for the other social purpose of the death penalty that the Court discusses, deterrence: That is not advanced, the Court tells us, because the mentally retarded are "less likely" than their non-retarded counterparts to "process the information of the possibility of execution as a penalty and . . . control their conduct based upon that information." Of course this leads to the same conclusion discussed earlier—that the mentally retarded (because they are less deterred) are more likely to kill—which neither I nor the society at large believes. In any event, even the Court does not say that *all* mentally retarded individuals cannot "process the information of the possibility of execution as a penalty and . . . control their conduct based upon that information"; it merely asserts that they are "less likely" to be able to do so. But surely the deterrent effect of a penalty is adequately vindicated if it successfully deters many, but not all, of the target class. Virginia's death penalty, for example, does not fail of its deterrent effect simply because *some* criminals are unaware that Virginia *has* the death penalty. In other words, the supposed fact that *some* retarded criminals cannot fully appreciate the death penalty has nothing to do with the deterrence rationale, but is simply an echo of the arguments denying a retribution rationale, discussed and rejected above. I am not sure that a murderer is somehow less blameworthy if (though he knew his act was wrong) he did not fully appreciate that he could die for it; but if so, we should treat a mentally retarded murderer the way we treat an offender who may be "less likely" to respond to the death penalty because he was abused as a child. We do not hold him immune from capital punishment, but require his background to be considered by the sentencer as a mitigating factor. *Eddings v. Oklahoma,* 455 U.S. 104, 102 S.Ct. 869 (1982).

The Court throws one last factor into its grab bag of reasons why execution of the retarded is "excessive" in all cases: Mentally retarded offenders "face a special risk of wrongful execution" because they are less able "to make a persuasive showing of mitigation," "to give meaningful assistance to their counsel," and to be effective witnesses. "Special risk" is pretty flabby language (even flabbier than "less likely")—and I suppose a similar "special risk" could be said to exist for just plain stupid people, inarticulate people, even ugly people. If this unsupported claim has any substance to it (which I doubt) it might support a due process claim in all criminal prosecutions of the mentally retarded; but it is hard to see how it has anything to do with an *Eighth Amendment* claim that execution of the mentally retarded is cruel and unusual. We have never before held it to be cruel and unusual punishment to impose a sentence in violation of some *other* constitutional imperative.

* * *

Today's opinion adds one more to the long list of substantive and procedural requirements impeding imposition of the death penalty imposed under this Court's assumed power to invent a death-is-different jurisprudence. None of those requirements existed when the Eighth Amendment was adopted, and some of them were not even supported by current moral consensus. They include prohibition of the death penalty for "ordinary" murder, *Godfrey,* for rape of an adult woman, *Coker,* and for felony murder absent a showing that the defendant possessed a sufficiently culpable state of mind, *Enmund*; prohibition of the death penalty for any person under the age of 16 at the time of the crime, *Thompson* (plurality opinion); prohibition of the death penalty as the mandatory punishment for any crime, *Woodson v. North Carolina,* 428 U.S. 280, 96 S.Ct. 2978 (1976) (plurality opinion), *Sumner v. Shuman,* 483 U.S. 66, 107 S.Ct. 2716 (1987); a requirement that the sentencer not be given unguided discretion, *Furman v. Georgia,* 408 U.S. 238, 92 S.Ct. 2726 (1972) (*per curiam*), a requirement that the sentencer be empowered to take into account all mitigating circumstances, *Lockett v. Ohio*, 438 U.S. 586, 98 S.Ct. 2954 (1978) (plurality opinion), *Eddings v. Oklahoma*; and a requirement that the accused receive a judicial evaluation of his claim of insanity before the sentence can be executed, *Ford* (plurality opinion). There is something to be said for popular abolition of the death penalty; there is nothing to be said for its incremental abolition by this Court.

This newest invention promises to be more effective than any of the others in turning the process of capital trial into a game. One need only read the definitions of mental retardation adopted by the American Association of Mental Retardation and the American Psychiatric Association to realize that the symptoms of this condition can readily be feigned. And whereas the capital defendant who feigns insanity risks commitment to a mental institution until he can be cured (and then tried and executed), *Jones v. United States,* 463 U.S. 354, 103 S.Ct. 3043 (1983), the capital defendant who feigns mental retardation risks nothing at all. The mere pendency of the present case has brought us petitions by death row inmates claiming for the first time, after multiple habeas petitions, that they are retarded.

Perhaps these practical difficulties will not be experienced by the minority of capital-punishment States that have very recently changed mental retardation from a mitigating factor (to be accepted or rejected by the sentencer) to an absolute immunity. Time will tell—and the brief time those States have had the new disposition in place (an average of 6.8 years) is surely not enough. But if the practical difficulties do not appear, and if the other States share the Court's perceived moral consensus that *all* mental retardation renders the death penalty inappropriate for *all* crimes, then that majority will presumably follow suit. But there is no justification for this Court's pushing them into the experiment—and turning the experiment into a permanent practice—on constitutional pretext. Nothing has changed the accuracy of Matthew Hale's endorsement of the common law's traditional method for taking account of guilt-reducing factors, written over three centuries ago:

> "[Determination of a person's incapacity] is a matter of great difficulty, partly from the easiness of counterfeiting this disability ... and partly from the variety of the degrees of this infirmity, whereof some are sufficient, and some are insufficient to excuse persons in capital offenses. ...

> "Yet the law of England hath afforded the best method of trial, that is possible, of this and all other matters of fact, namely, by a jury of twelve men all concurring in the same judgment, by the testimony of witnesses ..., and by the inspection and direction of the judge." 1 Hale, Pleas of the Crown.

I respectfully dissent.

NOTES

1. *Problem 5–3.*

The Court in *Atkins* leaves to the states "the task of developing appropriate ways to enforce the constitutional restriction upon its execution of sentences." State is now in the process of drafting legislation to implement *Atkins*. What should that legislation provide as to: (a) the definition of mental retardation; and (b) the procedure by which the mental retardation decision will be made, *i.e.*, who will decide the issue, when a hearing will be held, what burdens of proof and evidentiary rules will apply?

2. *The risk of false confessions.*

Justice Stevens cites the risk of false confessions as one justification for a categorical rule barring application of the death penalty to mentally retarded defendants. Until recently, relatively little attention was given to the tendency of mildly retarded suspects to make false confessions. Although people without mental retardation also are known to have falsely confessed (see W. White, *False Confessions and the Constitution: Safeguards Against Untrustworthy Confessions*, 32 Harv. Civ. R. & Civ. Lib. L. Rev. 105, 124 (1997)), mentally retarded people are more likely than suspects without mental deficits to give a false confession. Often confused, easily intimidated, susceptible to suggestion, and eager to please, suspects with mental retardation may readily agree with the accusations made by police investigators during an interrogation. With impaired cognitive skills, a mentally retarded suspect may not understand the thrust of police questioning or appreciate the consequences of a confession. In addition, mentally retarded people commonly overrate their own skills, either from a genuine misreading of their own abilities or in an attempt to avoid the stigma of mental retardation. J. Ellis and R. Luckasson, *Mentally Retarded Criminal Defendants*, 53 Geo. Wash. L. Rev. 414, 430–431 (1985). A common way to hide an inability to understand is to rely on, and agree with, an authority figure such as a police officer. Compounding the problem, few law enforcement officers (or defense attorneys) are trained to identify mental retardation.

The case of Earl Washington illustrates the issue. Washington, a mildly retarded man with an IQ of 69, was arrested in 1983 in Virginia for burglary and assault. While in custody he was interrogated about five different crimes, and he confessed to all of them. With regard to four of the crimes, his confession was rejected as too inconsistent with the crime it purported to describe. His confession to the fifth crime, the 1982 rape and murder of Rebecca Williams in a nearby town, consisted of a series of leading questions about the crime to which Washington gave affirmative answers. This confession led to his conviction and death sentence, despite the fact that, when asked non-leading questions, Washington gave erroneous answers to questions about the victim's race and height, the number of stab wounds, and whether anyone else was present during the crime. After obtaining his confession, police officers took Washington to identify the apartment where the killing took place. Washington repeatedly identified the wrong residence until a police officer pointed to Rebecca Williams's apartment and asked Washington if it was the right one. Washington responded affirmatively. At trial the defense attorney failed to show that Washington confessed in response to suggestive questioning, that Washington was incapable of understanding *Miranda* warnings, and that his adaptive strategy for living in the "normal" world consisted of trying to please people, including his police interlocutors, by telling them what they wanted to hear. Washington was a week away from being executed when a fellow inmate, Joseph Giarratano, the plaintiff in *Murray v. Giarratano*, 492 U.S. 1, 109 S.Ct. 2765 (1989) [Chapter 7], begged a visiting attorney to help Washington. In 1993, DNA testing showed that the sperm found in Rebecca Williams's body did not belong to Washington. In 1994, then-Governor Wilder commuted Washington's death sentence to a sentence of life with the possibility of parole. In 2000, additional

DNA testing again confirmed that Washington was not the killer, and Governor James Gilmore granted Washington a complete pardon. M. Edds, *Earl Washington Jr.—Dissecting A Murder Confession,* The Virginian–Pilot, September 17, 2000, at J5; F. Clines, *Virginia Man Is Pardoned in a Murder; DNA Is Cited,* New York Times, October 3, 2000 at A1.

ROPER v. SIMMONS

543 U.S. 551, 125 S.Ct. 1183, 161 L.Ed.2d 1 (2005).

JUSTICE KENNEDY delivered the opinion of the Court.

This case requires us to address, for the second time in a decade and a half, whether it is permissible under the Eighth and Fourteenth Amendments to the Constitution of the United States to execute a juvenile offender who was older than 15 but younger than 18 when he committed a capital crime. In *Stanford v. Kentucky,* 492 U.S. 361, 109 S.Ct. 2969 (1989), a divided Court rejected the proposition that the Constitution bars capital punishment for juvenile offenders in this age group. We reconsider the question.

I

At the age of 17, when he was still a junior in high school, Christopher Simmons, the respondent here, committed murder. About nine months later, after he had turned 18, he was tried and sentenced to death.

[Simmons planned the murder, proposing to two younger friends that they tie up a victim and throw the victim off a bridge, and he assured the friends they could "get away with it" because they were minors. With one of the friends, Simmons broke into a house occupied by Shirley Crook in the middle of the night, drove her to a bridge, bound her hands and feet with electrical wire, wrapped her face in duct tape and threw her off the bridge into a river where she drowned. Simmons later bragged about the killing to friends and, after his arrest, confessed to the police.]

The State charged Simmons with burglary, kidnaping, stealing, and murder in the first degree. As Simmons was 17 at the time of the crime, he was outside the criminal jurisdiction of Missouri's juvenile court system. He was tried as an adult. At trial the State introduced Simmons' confession and the videotaped reenactment of the crime, along with testimony that Simmons discussed the crime in advance and bragged about it later. The defense called no witnesses in the guilt phase. The jury having returned a verdict of murder, the trial proceeded to the penalty phase.

The State sought the death penalty. As aggravating factors, the State submitted that the murder was committed for the purpose of receiving money; was committed for the purpose of avoiding, interfering with, or preventing lawful arrest of the defendant; and involved depravity of mind and was outrageously and wantonly vile, horrible, and inhuman. The State called Shirley Crook's husband, daughter, and two sisters, who presented moving evidence of the devastation her death had brought to their lives.

In mitigation Simmons' attorneys first called an officer of the Missouri juvenile justice system, who testified that Simmons had no prior convictions and that no previous charges had been filed against him. Simmons' mother, father, two younger half brothers, a neighbor, and a friend took the stand to tell the jurors of the close relationships they had formed with Simmons and to plead for mercy on his behalf. Simmons' mother, in particular, testified to the responsibility Simmons demonstrated in taking care of his two younger half brothers and of his grandmother and to his capacity to show love for them.

During closing arguments, both the prosecutor and defense counsel addressed Simmons' age, which the trial judge had instructed the jurors they could consider as a mitigating factor. Defense counsel reminded the jurors that juveniles of Simmons' age cannot drink, serve on juries, or even see certain movies, because "the legislatures have wisely decided that individuals of a certain age aren't responsible enough." Defense counsel argued that Simmons' age should make "a huge difference to [the jurors] in deciding just exactly what sort of punishment to make." In rebuttal, the prosecutor gave the following response: "Age, he says. Think about age. Seventeen years old. Isn't that scary? Doesn't that scare you? Mitigating? Quite the contrary I submit. Quite the contrary."

The jury recommended the death penalty after finding the State had proved each of the three aggravating factors submitted to it. Accepting the jury's recommendation, the trial judge imposed the death penalty.

[Simmons obtained new counsel, who moved in the trial court to set aside the conviction and sentence. To support the contention that Simmons had received ineffective assistance of counsel at trial, numerous witnesses were called to establish that Simmons was "very immature," "very impulsive," and "very susceptible to being manipulated or influenced." The motion was denied; the Missouri Supreme Court affirmed the conviction and sentence, and the federal courts denied Simmons' petition for a writ of habeas corpus.]

After these proceedings in Simmons' case had run their course, this Court held that the Eighth and Fourteenth Amendments prohibit the execution of a mentally retarded person. *Atkins v. Virginia,* 536 U.S. 304, 122 S.Ct. 2242 (2002). Simmons filed a new petition for state postconviction relief, arguing that the reasoning of *Atkins* established that the Constitution prohibits the execution of a juvenile who was under 18 when the crime was committed.

The Missouri Supreme Court agreed. ... [I]t set aside Simmons' death sentence and resentenced him to "life imprisonment without eligibility for probation, parole, or release except by act of the Governor."

We granted certiorari and now affirm.

II

[Justice KENNEDY reviewed the Court's Eighth Amendment jurisprudence and its cases addressing whether certain categories of defendants should be ineligible for the death penalty: *Thompson v. Oklahoma,* 487 U.S. 815, 108 S.Ct. 2687 (1988) (plurality holds Eighth Amendment does not permit execution of offender under the age of 16 at the time of the crime); *Stanford v. Kentucky, supra* (Eighth Amendment does not proscribe execution of juvenile offenders over 15 but under 18); *Penry v. Lynaugh,* 492 U.S. 302, 109 S.Ct. 2934 (1989) (Eighth Amendment does not proscribe execution of mentally retarded persons); *Atkins v. Virginia, supra* (Eighth Amendment prohibits execution of mentally retarded persons).]

III

A

The evidence of national consensus against the death penalty for juveniles is similar, and in some respects parallel, to the evidence *Atkins* held sufficient to demonstrate a national consensus against the death penalty for the mentally retarded. When *Atkins* was decided, 30 States prohibited the death penalty for the mentally retarded. This number comprised 12 that had abandoned the death penalty altogether, and 18 that maintained it but excluded the mentally retarded from its reach. By a similar calculation in this case, 30 States prohibit the juvenile death penalty, comprising 12 that have rejected the death penalty altogether and 18 that maintain it but, by express provision or judicial interpretation, exclude juveniles from its reach. *Atkins* emphasized that even in the 20 States without formal prohibition, the practice of executing the mentally retarded was infrequent. Since *Penry,* only five States had executed offenders known to have an IQ under 70. In the present case, too, even in the 20 States without a formal prohibition on executing juveniles, the practice is infrequent. Since *Stanford,* six States have executed prisoners for crimes committed as juveniles. In the past 10 years, only three have done so: Oklahoma, Texas, and Virginia. In December 2003 the Governor of Kentucky decided to spare the life of Kevin Stanford, and commuted his sentence to one of life imprisonment without parole, with the declaration that " '[w]e ought not be executing people who, legally, were children.' " By this act the Governor ensured Kentucky would not add itself to the list of States that have executed juveniles within the last 10 years even by the execution of the very defendant whose death sentence the Court had upheld in *Stanford v. Kentucky.*

There is, to be sure, at least one difference between the evidence of consensus in *Atkins* and in this case. Impressive in *Atkins* was the rate of abolition of the death penalty for the mentally retarded. Sixteen States that permitted the execution of the mentally retarded at the time of *Penry* had prohibited the practice by the time we heard *Atkins.* By contrast, the rate of change in reducing the incidence of the juvenile death penalty, or in taking specific steps to abolish it, has been slower. Five States that allowed the juvenile death penalty at the time of *Stanford* have abandoned it in the intervening 15 years—four through legislative enactments and one through judicial decision.

Though less dramatic than the change from *Penry* to *Atkins* ..., we still consider the change from *Stanford* to this case to be significant. As noted in *Atkins,* with respect to the States that had abandoned the death penalty for the mentally retarded since *Penry,* "[i]t is not so much the number of these States that is significant, but the consistency of the direction of change." In particular we found it significant that, in the wake of *Penry,* no State that had already prohibited the execution of the mentally retarded had passed legislation to reinstate the penalty. The number of States that have abandoned capital punishment for juvenile offenders since *Stanford* is smaller than the number of States that abandoned capital punishment for the mentally retarded after *Penry;* yet we think the same consistency of direction of change has been demonstrated. Since *Stanford,* no State that previously prohibited capital punishment for juveniles has reinstated it. This fact, coupled with the trend toward abolition of the juvenile death penalty, carries special force in light of the general popularity of anticrime legislation, and in light of the particular trend in recent years toward cracking down on juvenile crime in other respects. Any difference between this case and *Atkins* with respect to the pace of abolition is thus counterbalanced by the consistent direction of the change.

The slower pace of abolition of the juvenile death penalty over the past 15 years, moreover, may have a simple explanation. When we heard *Penry,* only two death penalty States had already prohibited the execution of the mentally retarded. When we heard *Stanford,* by contrast, 12 death penalty States had already prohibited the execution of any juvenile under 18, and 15 had prohibited the execution of any juvenile under 17. If anything, this shows that the impropriety of executing juveniles between 16 and 18 years of age gained wide recognition earlier than the impropriety of executing the mentally retarded. In the words of the Missouri Supreme Court: "It would be the ultimate in irony if the very fact that the inappropriateness of the death penalty for juveniles was broadly recognized sooner than it was recognized for the mentally retarded were to become a reason to continue the execution of juveniles now that the execution of the mentally retarded has been barred."

Petitioner cannot show national consensus in favor of capital punishment for juveniles but still resists the conclusion that any consensus exists against it. Petitioner supports this position with, in particular, the observation that when the Senate ratified the International Covenant on Civil and Political Rights (ICCPR), it did so subject to the President's proposed reservation regarding Article 6(5) of that treaty, which prohibits capital punishment for juveniles. This reservation at best provides only faint support for petitioner's argument. First, the reservation was passed in 1992; since then, five States have abandoned capital punishment for juveniles. Second, Congress considered the issue when enacting the Federal Death Penalty Act in 1994, and determined that the death penalty should not extend to juveniles. The reservation to Article 6(5) of the ICCPR provides minimal evidence that there is not now a national consensus against juvenile executions.

As in *Atkins,* the objective indicia of consensus in this case—the rejection of the juvenile death penalty in the majority of States; the infrequency of its use even where it remains on the books; and the consistency in the trend toward abolition of the practice—provide sufficient evidence that today our society views juveniles, in the words *Atkins* used respecting the mentally retarded, as "categorically less culpable than the average criminal."

B

A majority of States have rejected the imposition of the death penalty on juvenile offenders under 18, and we now hold this is required by the Eighth Amendment.

Because the death penalty is the most severe punishment, the Eighth Amendment applies to it with special force. Capital punishment must be limited to those offenders who commit "a narrow category of the most serious crimes" and whose extreme culpability makes them "the most deserving of execution." *Atkins, supra.* * * *

Three general differences between juveniles under 18 and adults demonstrate that juvenile offenders cannot with reliability be classified among the worst offenders. First, as any parent knows and as the scientific and sociological studies respondent and his *amici* cite tend to confirm, "[a] lack of maturity and an underdeveloped sense of responsibility are found in youth more often than in adults and are more understandable among the young. These qualities often result in impetuous and ill-considered actions and decisions." *Johnson v. Texas*, 509 U.S. 350, 113 S.Ct. 2658 (1993). It has been noted that "adolescents are overrepresented statistically in virtually every category of reckless behavior." Arnett, Reckless Behavior in Adolescence: A Developmental Perspective, 12 Developmental Review 339 (1992). In recognition of the comparative immaturity and irresponsibility of juveniles, almost every State prohibits those under 18 years of age from voting, serving on juries, or marrying without parental consent.

The second area of difference is that juveniles are more vulnerable or susceptible to negative influences and outside pressures, including peer pressure. *Eddings, supra* ("[Y]outh is more than a chronological fact. It is a time and condition of life when a person may be most susceptible to influence and to psychological damage"). This is explained in part by the prevailing circumstance that juveniles have less control, or less experience with control, over their own environment.

The third broad difference is that the character of a juvenile is not as well formed as that of an adult. The personality traits of juveniles are more transitory, less fixed.

These differences render suspect any conclusion that a juvenile falls among the worst offenders. The susceptibility of juveniles to immature and irresponsible behavior means "their irresponsible conduct is not as morally reprehensible as that of an adult." *Thompson, supra.* Their own vulnerability and comparative lack of control over their immediate surroundings mean juveniles have a greater claim than adults to be forgiven for failing to escape negative influences in their whole environment. The reality that juveniles still struggle to define their identity means it is less supportable to conclude that even a heinous crime committed by a juvenile is evidence of irretrievably depraved character. From a moral standpoint it would be misguided to equate the failings of a minor with those of an adult, for a greater possibility exists that a minor's character deficiencies will be reformed. Indeed, "[t]he relevance of youth as a mitigating factor derives from the fact that the signature qualities of youth are transient; as individuals mature, the impetuousness and recklessness that may dominate in younger years can subside." *Johnson, supra.*

In *Thompson,* a plurality of the Court recognized the import of these characteristics with respect to juveniles under 16, and relied on them to hold that the Eighth Amendment prohibited the imposition of the death penalty on juveniles below that age. We conclude the same reasoning applies to all juvenile offenders under 18.

Once the diminished culpability of juveniles is recognized, it is evident that the penological justifications for the death penalty apply to them with lesser force than to adults. We have held there are two distinct social purposes served by the death penalty: " 'retribution and deterrence of capital crimes by prospective offenders.' " *Atkins* (quoting *Gregg v. Georgia,* 428 U.S. 153, 96 S.Ct. 2909 (1976) (joint opinion of STEWART, POWELL, and STEVENS, JJ.)). As for retribution, we remarked in *Atkins* that "[i]f the culpability of the average murderer is insufficient to justify the most extreme sanction available to the State, the lesser culpability of the mentally retarded offender surely does not merit that form of retribution." The same conclusions follow from the lesser culpability of the juvenile offender. Whether viewed as an attempt to express the community's moral outrage or as an attempt to right the balance for the wrong to the victim, the case for retribution is not as strong with a minor as with an adult. Retribution is not proportional if the law's most severe penalty is imposed on one whose culpability or blameworthiness is diminished, to a substantial degree, by reason of youth and immaturity.

As for deterrence, it is unclear whether the death penalty has a significant or even measurable deterrent effect on juveniles, as counsel for the petitioner acknowledged at oral argument. In general we leave to legislatures the assessment of the efficacy of various criminal penalty schemes. Here, however, the absence of evidence of deterrent effect is of special concern because the same characteristics that render juveniles less culpable than adults suggest as well that juveniles will be less susceptible to deterrence. In particular, as the plurality observed in *Thompson,* "[t]he likelihood that the teenage offender has made the kind of cost-benefit analysis that attaches any weight to the possibility of execution is so remote as to be virtually nonexistent.'' To the extent the juvenile death penalty might have residual deterrent effect, it is worth noting that the punishment of life imprisonment without the possibility of parole is itself a severe sanction, in particular for a young person.

In concluding that neither retribution nor deterrence provides adequate justification for imposing the death penalty on juvenile offenders, we cannot deny or overlook the brutal crimes too many juvenile offenders have committed. Certainly it can be argued, although we by no means concede the point, that a rare case might arise in which a juvenile offender has sufficient psychological maturity, and at the same time demonstrates sufficient depravity, to merit a sentence of death. Indeed, this possibility is the linchpin of one contention pressed by petitioner and his *amici*. They assert that even assuming the truth of the observations we have made about juveniles' diminished culpability in general, jurors nonetheless should be allowed to consider mitigating arguments related to youth on a case-by-case basis, and in some cases to impose the death penalty if justified. A central feature of death penalty sentencing is a particular assessment of the circumstances of the crime and the characteristics of the offender. The system is designed to consider both aggravating and mitigating circumstances, including youth, in every case. Given this Court's own insistence on individualized consideration, petitioner maintains that it is both arbitrary and unnecessary to adopt a categorical rule barring imposition of the death penalty on any offender under 18 years of age.

We disagree. The differences between juvenile and adult offenders are too marked and well understood to risk allowing a youthful person to receive the death penalty despite insufficient culpability. An unacceptable likelihood exists that the brutality or cold-blooded nature of any particular crime would overpower mitigating arguments based on youth as a matter of course, even where the juvenile offender's objective immaturity, vulnerability, and lack of true depravity should require a sentence less severe than death. In some cases a defendant's youth may even be counted against him. In this very case, as we noted above, the prosecutor argued Simmons' youth was aggravating rather than mitigating. While this sort of overreaching could be corrected by a particular rule to ensure that the mitigating force of youth is not overlooked, that would not address our larger concerns.

It is difficult even for expert psychologists to differentiate between the juvenile offender whose crime reflects unfortunate yet transient immaturity, and the rare juvenile offender whose crime reflects irreparable corruption. As we understand it, this difficulty underlies the rule forbidding psychiatrists from diagnosing any patient under 18 as having antisocial personality disorder, a disorder also referred to as psychopathy or sociopathy, and which is characterized by callousness, cynicism, and contempt for the feelings, rights, and suffering of others. If trained psychiatrists with the advantage of clinical testing and observation refrain, despite diagnostic expertise, from assessing any juvenile under 18 as having antisocial personality disorder, we conclude that States should refrain from asking jurors to issue a far graver condemnation—that a juvenile offender merits the death penalty. When a juvenile offender commits a heinous crime, the State can exact forfeiture of some of the most basic liberties, but the State cannot extinguish his life and his potential to attain a mature understanding of his own humanity.

Drawing the line at 18 years of age is subject, of course, to the objections always raised against categorical rules. The qualities that distinguish juveniles from adults do not disappear when an individual turns 18. By the same token, some under 18 have already attained a level of maturity some adults will never reach. For the reasons we have discussed, however, a line must be drawn. The plurality opinion in *Thompson* drew the line at 16. In the intervening years the *Thompson* plurality's conclusion that offenders under 16 may not be executed has not been challenged. The logic of *Thompson* extends to those who are under 18. The age of 18 is the point where society draws the line for many purposes between childhood and adulthood. It is, we conclude, the age at which the line for death eligibility ought to rest.

These considerations mean *Stanford v. Kentucky* should be deemed no longer controlling on this issue. To the extent *Stanford* was based on review of the objective indicia of consensus that obtained in 1989, it suffices to note that those indicia have changed. It should be observed, furthermore, that the *Stanford* Court should have considered those States that had abandoned the death penalty altogether as part of the consensus against the juvenile death penalty; a State's decision to bar the death penalty altogether of necessity demonstrates a judgment that the death penalty is inappropriate for all offenders, including juveniles. Last, to the extent *Stanford* was based on a rejection of the idea that this Court is required to bring its independent judgment to bear on the proportionality of the death penalty for a particular class of crimes or offenders, it suffices to note that this rejection was inconsistent with prior Eighth Amendment decisions. It is also inconsistent with the premises of our recent decision in *Atkins*.

* * *

IV

Our determination that the death penalty is disproportionate punishment for offenders under 18 finds confirmation in the stark reality that the United States is the only country in the world that continues to give official sanction to the juvenile death penalty. This reality does not become controlling, for the task of interpreting the Eighth Amendment remains our responsibility. Yet at least from the time of the Court's decision in *Trop*, the Court has referred to the laws of other countries and to international authorities as instructive for its interpretation of the Eighth Amendment's prohibition of "cruel and unusual punishments." (plurality opinion) [citing *Atkins, Thompson, Enmund v. Florida*, 458 U.S.

782, 102 S.Ct. 3368 (1982) and *Coker v. Georgia*, 433 U.S. 594, 97 S.Ct. 2861 (1977)].

As respondent and a number of *amici* emphasize, Article 37 of the United Nations Convention on the Rights of the Child, which every country in the world has ratified save for the United States and Somalia, contains an express prohibition on capital punishment for crimes committed by juveniles under 18. No ratifying country has entered a reservation to the provision prohibiting the execution of juvenile offenders. Parallel prohibitions are contained in other significant international covenants. See ICCPR, Art. 6(5); American Convention on Human Rights (prohibiting capital punishment for anyone under 18 at the time of offense): Pact of San Jose, Costa Rica, Art. 4(5) (same); African Charter on the Rights and Welfare of the Child, Art. 5(3) (same).

Respondent and his *amici* have submitted, and petitioner does not contest, that only seven countries other than the United States have executed juvenile offenders since 1990: Iran, Pakistan, Saudi Arabia, Yemen, Nigeria, the Democratic Republic of Congo, and China. Since then each of these countries has either abolished capital punishment for juveniles or made public disavowal of the practice. In sum, it is fair to say that the United States now stands alone in a world that has turned its face against the juvenile death penalty.

* * *

It is proper that we acknowledge the overwhelming weight of international opinion against the juvenile death penalty, resting in large part on the understanding that the instability and emotional imbalance of young people may often be a factor in the crime. The opinion of the world community, while not controlling our outcome, does provide respected and significant confirmation for our own conclusions.

Over time, from one generation to the next, the Constitution has come to earn the high respect and even, as Madison dared to hope, the veneration of the American people. The document sets forth, and rests upon, innovative principles original to the American experience, such as federalism; a proven balance in political mechanisms through separation of powers; specific guarantees for the accused in criminal cases; and broad provisions to secure individual freedom and preserve human dignity. These doctrines and guarantees are central to the American experience and remain essential to our present-day self-definition and national identity. Not the least of the reasons we honor the Constitution, then, is because we know it to be our own. It does not lessen our fidelity to the Constitution or our pride in its origins to acknowledge that the express affirmation of certain fundamental rights by other nations and peoples simply underscores the centrality of those same rights within our own heritage of freedom.

* * *

The Eighth and Fourteenth Amendments forbid imposition of the death penalty on offenders who were under the age of 18 when their crimes were committed. The judgment of the Missouri Supreme Court setting aside the sentence of death imposed upon Christopher Simmons is affirmed.

It is so ordered.

JUSTICE STEVENS, with whom JUSTICE GINSBURG joins, concurring.

Perhaps even more important than our specific holding today is our reaffirmation of the basic principle that informs the Court's interpretation of the Eighth Amendment. If the meaning of that Amendment had been frozen when it was originally drafted, it would impose no impediment to the execution of 7–year–old children today. See *Stanford v. Kentucky,* 492 U.S. 361, 109 S.Ct. 2969 (1989) (describing the common law at the time of the Amendment's adoption). The evolving standards of decency that have driven our construction of this critically important part of the Bill of Rights foreclose any such reading of the Amendment. In the best tradition of the common law, the pace of that evolution is a matter for continuing debate; but that our understanding of the Constitution does change from time to time has been settled since John Marshall breathed life into its text. If great lawyers of his day—Alexander Hamilton, for example—were sitting with us today, I would expect them to join Justice KENNEDY's opinion for the Court. In all events, I do so without hesitation.

JUSTICE O'CONNOR, dissenting.

The Court's decision today establishes a categorical rule forbidding the execution of any offender for any crime committed before his 18th birthday, no matter how deliberate, wanton, or cruel the offense. Neither the objective evidence of contemporary societal values, nor the Court's moral proportionality analysis, nor the two in tandem suffice to justify this ruling.

* * *

I

[Agreeing with much of the Court's description of the general principles guiding the Court's Eighth Amendment jurisprudence, Justice O'CONNOR reiterated that: the Amendment bars punishments that are excessive in relationship to the crime committed; that the prohibition of cruel and unusual punishments is not a static concept, but rather draws its meaning from the evolving standards of decency as measured by "[l]aws enacted by the Nation's legislatures" and the "actions of sentencing juries"; and that the Court has a duty to bring its own judgment to bear on the question. She then reviewed the Court's decisions in *Thompson v. Oklahoma,* 487 U.S. 815, 108 S.Ct. 2687 (1988), *Stanford v. Kentucky,* 492 U.S. 361, 109 S.Ct. 2969 (1989), *Penry v. Lynaugh,* 492 U.S. 302, 109 S.Ct. 2934 (1989) and *Atkins v. Virginia,* 536 U.S. 304, 122 S.Ct. 2242 (2002).]

II

* * *

B

In determining whether the juvenile death penalty comports with contemporary standards of decency, our inquiry begins with the "clearest and most reliable objective evidence of contemporary values"—the actions of the Nation's legislatures. *Penry, supra.* As the Court emphasizes, the overall number of jurisdictions that currently disallow the execution of under–18 offenders is the same as the number that forbade the execution of mentally retarded offenders when *Atkins* was decided. At present, 12 States and the District of Columbia do not have the death penalty, while an additional 18 States and the Federal Government authorize capital punishment but prohibit the execution of under–18 offenders. And here, as in *Atkins,* only a very small fraction of the States that permit capital punishment of offenders within the relevant class has actually carried out such an execution in recent history: six States have executed under–18 offenders in the 16 years since *Stanford,* while five States had executed mentally retarded offenders in the 13 years prior to *Atkins.* In these respects, the objective evidence in this case is, indeed, "similar, and in some respects parallel to" the evidence upon which we relied in *Atkins.*

While the similarities between the two cases are undeniable, the objective evidence of national consensus is marginally weaker here. Most importantly, in *Atkins* there was significant evidence of *opposition* to the execution of the mentally retarded, but there was virtually no countervailing evidence of affirmative legislative *support* for this practice. The States that permitted such executions did so only because they had not enacted any prohibitory legislation. Here, by contrast, at least eight States have current statutes that specifically set 16 or 17 as the minimum age at which commission of a capital crime can expose the offender to the death penalty. Five of these eight States presently have one or more juvenile offenders on death row (six if respondent is included in the count), and four of them have executed at least one under–18 offender in the past 15 years. In all, there are currently over 70 juvenile offenders on death row in 12 different States (13 including respondent). This evidence suggests some measure of continuing public support for the availability of the death penalty for 17–year–old capital murderers.

Moreover, the Court in *Atkins* made clear that it was "not so much the number of [States forbidding execution of the mentally retarded] that [was] significant, but the consistency of the direction of change." In contrast to the trend in *Atkins,* the States have not moved uniformly towards abolishing the juvenile death penalty. Instead, since our decision in *Stanford,* two States have expressly reaffirmed their support for this practice by enacting statutes setting 16 as the minimum age for capital punishment. Furthermore, as the Court emphasized in *Atkins* itself, the pace of legislative action in this context has been considerably slower than it was with regard to capital punishment of the mentally retarded. In the

13 years between our decisions in *Penry* and *Atkins,* no fewer than 16 States banned the execution of mentally retarded offenders. By comparison, since our decision 16 years ago in *Stanford,* only four States that previously permitted the execution of under–18 offenders, plus the Federal Government, have legislatively reversed course, and one additional State's high court has construed the State's death penalty statute not to apply to under–18 offenders. The slower pace of change is no doubt partially attributable, as the Court says, to the fact that 11 States had already imposed a minimum age of 18 when *Stanford* was decided. Nevertheless, the extraordinary wave of legislative action leading up to our decision in *Atkins* provided strong evidence that the country truly had set itself against capital punishment of the mentally retarded. Here, by contrast, the halting pace of change gives reason for pause.

To the extent that the objective evidence supporting today's decision is similar to that in *Atkins,* this merely highlights the fact that such evidence is not dispositive in either of the two cases. After all, as the Court today confirms, the Constitution requires that " 'in the end our own judgment ... be brought to bear' " in deciding whether the Eighth Amendment forbids a particular punishment. *Atkins, supra* (quoting *Coker* (plurality opinion)). This judgment is not merely a rubber stamp on the tally of legislative and jury actions. Rather, it is an integral part of the Eighth Amendment inquiry—and one that is entitled to independent weight in reaching our ultimate decision.

Here, as in *Atkins,* the objective evidence of a national consensus is weaker than in most prior cases in which the Court has struck down a particular punishment under the Eighth Amendment. See Coker (striking down death penalty for rape of an adult woman, where only one jurisdiction authorized such punishment); *Enmund* (striking down death penalty for certain crimes of aiding and abetting felony-murder, where only eight jurisdictions authorized such punishment); *Ford v. Wainwright,* 477 U.S. 399, 106 S.Ct. 2595 (1986) (striking down capital punishment of the insane, where no jurisdiction permitted this practice). In my view, the objective evidence of national consensus, standing alone, was insufficient to dictate the Court's holding in *Atkins.* Rather, the compelling moral proportionality argument against capital punishment of mentally retarded offenders played a *decisive* role in persuading the Court that the practice was inconsistent with the Eighth Amendment. Indeed, the force of the proportionality argument in *Atkins* significantly bolstered the Court's confidence that the objective evidence in that case did, in fact, herald the emergence of a genuine national consensus. Here, by contrast, the proportionality argument against the juvenile death penalty is so flawed that it can be given little, if any, analytical weight—it proves too weak to resolve the lingering ambiguities in the objective evidence of legislative consensus or to justify the Court's categorical rule.

C

Seventeen-year-old murderers must be categorically exempted from capital punishment, the Court says, because they "cannot with reliability be classified among the worst offenders." That conclusion is premised on three perceived differences between "adults," who have already reached their 18th birthdays, and "juveniles," who have not. First, juveniles lack maturity and responsibility and are more reckless than adults. Second, juveniles are more vulnerable to outside influences because they have less control over their surroundings. And third, a juvenile's character is not as fully formed as that of an adult. Based on these characteristics, the Court determines that 17–year–old capital murderers are not as blameworthy as adults guilty of similar crimes; that 17–year–olds are less likely than adults to be deterred by the prospect of a death sentence; and that it is difficult to conclude that a 17–year–old who commits even the most heinous of crimes is "irretrievably depraved." The Court suggests that "a rare case might arise in which a juvenile offender has sufficient psychological maturity, and at the same time demonstrates sufficient depravity, to merit a sentence of death." However, the Court argues that a categorical age-based prohibition is justified as a prophylactic rule because "[t]he differences between juvenile and adult offenders are too marked and well understood to risk allowing a youthful person to receive the death penalty despite insufficient culpability."

It is beyond cavil that juveniles as a class are generally less mature, less responsible, and less fully formed than adults, and that these differences bear on juveniles' comparative moral culpability. But even accepting this premise, the Court's proportionality argument fails to support its categorical rule.

First, the Court adduces no evidence whatsoever in support of its sweeping conclusion that it is only in "rare" cases, if ever, that 17–year–old murderers are sufficiently mature and act with sufficient depravity to warrant the death penalty. The fact that juveniles are generally *less* culpable for their misconduct than adults does not necessarily mean that a 17–year–old murderer cannot be *sufficiently* culpable to merit the death penalty. At most, the Court's argument suggests that the average 17–year–old murderer is not as culpable as the average adult murderer. But an especially depraved juvenile offender may nevertheless be just as culpable as many adult offenders considered bad enough to deserve the death penalty. Similarly, the fact that the availability of the death penalty may be *less* likely to deter a juvenile from committing a capital crime does not imply that this threat cannot *effectively* deter some 17–year–olds from such an act. Surely there is an age below which no offender, no matter what his crime, can be deemed to have the cognitive or emotional maturity necessary to warrant the death penalty. But at least at the margins between adolescence and adulthood—and especially for 17–year–olds such as respondent—the relevant differences between "adults" and "juveniles" appear to be a matter of degree, rather than of kind. It follows that a legislature may reasonably conclude that at least *some* 17–year–olds can act with sufficient moral culpability, and can be sufficiently deterred by the threat of execution, that capital punishment may be warranted in an appropriate case.

Indeed, this appears to be just such a case. Christopher Simmons' murder of Shirley Crook was premeditated, wanton, and cruel in the extreme. Well before he committed this crime, Simmons declared that he wanted to kill someone. On several occasions, he discussed with two friends (ages 15 and 16) his plan to burglarize a house and to murder the victim by tying the victim up and pushing him from a bridge. Simmons said they could "get away with it" because they were minors. In accord with this plan, Simmons and his 15–year–old accomplice broke into Mrs. Crook's home in the middle of the night, forced her from her bed, bound her, and drove her to a state park. There, they walked her to a railroad trestle spanning a river, "hog-tied" her with electrical cable, bound her face completely with duct tape, and pushed her, still alive, from the trestle. She drowned in the water below. One can scarcely imagine the terror that this woman must have suffered throughout the ordeal leading to her death. Whatever can be said about the comparative moral culpability of 17–year–olds as a general matter, Simmons' actions unquestionably reflect "a consciousness materially more 'depraved' than that of . . . the average murderer." And Simmons' prediction that he could murder with impunity because he had not yet turned 18—though inaccurate—suggests that he *did* take into account the perceived risk of punishment in deciding whether to commit the crime. Based on this evidence, the sentencing jury certainly had reasonable grounds for concluding that, despite Simmons' youth, he "ha[d] sufficient psychological maturity" when he committed this horrific murder, and "at the same time demonstrate[d] sufficient depravity, to merit a sentence of death."

The Court's proportionality argument suffers from a second and closely related defect: It fails to establish that the differences in maturity between 17–year–olds and young "adults" are both universal enough and significant enough to justify a bright-line prophylactic rule against capital punishment of the former. The Court's analysis is premised on differences *in the aggregate* between juveniles and adults, which frequently do not hold true when comparing individuals. Although it may be that many 17–year–old murderers lack sufficient maturity to deserve the death penalty, some juvenile murderers may be quite mature. Chronological age is not an unfailing measure of psychological development, and common experience suggests that many 17–year–olds are more mature than the average young "adult." In short, the class of offenders exempted from capital punishment by today's decision is too broad and too diverse to warrant a categorical prohibition. Indeed, the age-based line drawn by the Court is indefensibly arbitrary—it quite likely will protect a number of offenders who are mature enough to deserve the death penalty and may well leave vulnerable many who are not.

For purposes of proportionality analysis, 17–year–olds as a class are qualitatively and materially different from the mentally retarded. "Mentally retarded" offenders, as we understood that category in *Atkins*, are *defined* by precisely the characteristics which render death an excessive punishment. A mentally retarded person is, "by definition," one whose cognitive and behavioral capacities have been proven to fall below a certain minimum. Accordingly, for purposes of our decision in *Atkins,* the mentally retarded are not merely *less* blameworthy for their misconduct or *less* likely to be deterred by the death penalty than others. Rather, a mentally retarded offender is one whose demonstrated impairments make it so highly unlikely that he is culpable enough to deserve the death penalty or that he could have been deterred by the threat of death, that execution is not a defensible punishment. There is no such inherent or accurate fit between an offender's chronological age and the personal limitations which the Court believes make capital punishment excessive for 17–year–old murderers. Moreover, it defies common sense to suggest that 17–year–olds as a class are somehow equivalent to mentally retarded persons with regard to culpability or susceptibility to deterrence. Seventeen-year-olds may, on average, be less mature than adults, but that lesser maturity simply cannot be equated with the major, lifelong impairments suffered by the mentally retarded.

The proportionality issues raised by the Court clearly implicate Eighth Amendment concerns. But these concerns may properly be addressed not by means of an arbitrary, categorical age-based rule, but rather through individualized sentencing in which juries are required to give appropriate mitigating weight to the defendant's immaturity, his susceptibility to outside pressures, his cognizance of the consequences of his actions, and so forth. In that way the constitutional response can be tailored to the specific problem it is meant to remedy. The Eighth Amendment guards against the execution of those who are "insufficiently culpable" by requiring sentencing that "reflect[s] a reasoned *moral* response to the defendant's background, character, and crime." *California v. Brown,* 479 U.S. 538, 107 S.Ct. 837 (1987) (O'CONNOR, J., concurring). Accordingly, the sentencer in a capital case must be permitted to give full effect to all constitutionally relevant mitigating evidence. A defendant's youth or immaturity is, of course, a paradigmatic example of such evidence.

Although the prosecutor's apparent attempt to use respondent's youth as an aggravating circumstance in this case is troubling, that conduct was never challenged with specificity in the lower courts and is not directly at issue here. As the Court itself suggests, such "overreaching" would best be addressed, if at all, through a more narrowly tailored remedy. The Court argues that sentencing juries cannot accurately evaluate a youthful offender's maturity or give appropriate weight to the mitigating characteristics related to youth. But, again, the Court presents no real evidence—and the record appears to contain none—supporting this claim. Perhaps more importantly, the Court fails to explain why this duty should be so different from, or so much more difficult than, that of assessing and giving proper effect to any other qualitative capital sentencing factor. I would not be so quick to conclude that the constitutional safeguards, the sentencing juries, and the trial judges upon which we place so much reliance in all capital cases are inadequate in this narrow context.

D

* * *

Reasonable minds can differ as to the minimum age at which commission of a serious crime should expose the defendant to the death penalty, if at all. Many jurisdictions have abolished capital punishment altogether, while many others have determined that even the most heinous crime, if committed before the age of 18, should not be punishable by death. Indeed, were my office that of a legislator, rather than a judge, then I, too, would be inclined to support legislation setting a minimum age of 18 in this context. But a significant number of States, including Missouri, have decided to make the death penalty potentially available for 17–year–old capital murderers such as respondent. Without a clearer showing that a genuine national consensus forbids the execution of such offenders, this Court should not substitute its own "inevitably subjective judgment" on how best to resolve this difficult moral question for the judgments of the Nation's democratically elected legislatures. I respectfully dissent.

> [JUSTICE SCALIA, joined by THE CHIEF JUSTICE and JUSTICE THOMAS, dissented, reiterating arguments made in his *Atkins* dissent regarding the majority's Eighth Amendment analysis and its finding of a "national consensus" and disparaging the majority's reliance on scientific and sociological studies and the opinions of the international community to bolster its own judgment as to the acceptability of the death penalty.]

KENNEDY v. LOUISIANA[a]
— U.S. —, 128 S.Ct. 2641, 171 L.Ed.2d 525 (2008).

JUSTICE KENNEDY delivered the opinion of the Court.

The National Government and, beyond it, the separate States are bound by the proscriptive mandates of the Eighth Amendment to the Constitution of the United States, and all persons within those respective jurisdictions may invoke its protection. Patrick Kennedy, the petitioner here, seeks to set aside his death sentence under the Eighth Amendment. He was charged by the respondent, the State of Louisiana, with the aggravated rape of his then–8–year–old stepdaughter. After a jury trial petitioner was convicted and sentenced to death under a state statute authorizing capital punishment for the rape of a child under 12 years of age. This case presents the question whether the Constitution bars respondent from imposing the death penalty for the rape of a child where the crime did not result, and was not intended to result, in death of the victim. We hold the Eighth Amendment prohibits the death penalty for this offense. The Louisiana statute is unconstitutional.

___

a. As amended on denial of rehearing. See — U.S. —, 129 S.Ct. 1 (2008).

I

Petitioner's crime was one that cannot be recounted in these pages in a way sufficient to capture in full the hurt and horror inflicted on his victim or to convey the revulsion society, and the jury that represents it, sought to express by sentencing petitioner to death. At 9:18 a.m. on March 2, 1998, petitioner called 911 to report that his stepdaughter, referred to here as L. H., had been raped. He told the 911 operator that L.H. had been in the garage while he readied his son for school. Upon hearing loud screaming, petitioner said, he ran outside and found L.H. in the side yard. Two neighborhood boys, petitioner told the operator, had dragged L.H. from the garage to the yard, pushed her down, and raped her. Petitioner claimed he saw one of the boys riding away on a blue 10–speed bicycle.

[When police arrived, they found L.H. bleeding profusely from the vaginal area. She had been very seriously injured and required emergency surgery. In the weeks following the rape, both petitioner and L.H. reiterated the story petitioner had first told to the police. Nevertheless, eight days after the rape, on the basis of substantial evidence contradicting petitioner's story—including a call he made between 6:30 and 7:30 a.m. to ask a colleague how to get blood out of a white carpet because his daughter had "just become a young lady"—police arrested him. On June 22, 1998, L.H., for the first time, told her mother that petitioner had raped her.]

The State charged petitioner with aggravated rape of a child under La. Stat. Ann. § 14:42 and sought the death penalty. [The statute defined aggravated rape of a child as "anal or vaginal sexual intercourse" with a victim under the age of twelve years and, in combination with La. Code Crim.Proc. Art. 905.4 (aggravating circumstances), made one convicted of the crime death-eligible.]

The trial began in August 2003. L.H. was then 13 years old. She testified that she " 'woke up one morning and Patrick was on top of [her].' " She remembered petitioner bringing her "[a] cup of orange juice and pills chopped up in it" after the rape and overhearing him on the telephone saying she had become a "young lady." L.H. acknowledged that she had accused two neighborhood boys but testified petitioner told her to say this and that it was untrue.

The jury having found petitioner guilty of aggravated rape, the penalty phase ensued. The State presented the testimony of S. L., who is the cousin and goddaughter of petitioner's ex-wife. S.L. testified that petitioner sexually abused her three times when she was eight years old and that the last time involved sexual intercourse. She did not tell anyone until two years later and did not pursue legal action.

The jury unanimously determined that petitioner should be sentenced to death. The Supreme Court of Louisiana [distinguishing *Coker v. Georgia,* 433 U.S. 584, 97 S.Ct. 2861 (1977)] affirmed.

* * *

We granted certiorari.

II

The Eighth Amendment, applicable to the States through the Fourteenth Amendment, provides that "[e]xcessive bail shall not be required, nor excessive fines imposed, nor cruel and unusual punishments inflicted." The Amendment proscribes "all excessive punishments, as well as cruel and unusual punishments that may or may not be excessive." *Atkins v. Virginia*, 536 U.S. 304, 122 S.Ct. 2242 (2002). The Court explained in *Atkins* and *Roper v. Simmons*, 543 U.S. 551, 125 S.Ct. 1183 (2005), that the Eighth Amendment's protection against excessive or cruel and unusual punishments flows from the basic "precept of justice that punishment for [a] crime should be graduated and proportioned to [the] offense." *Weems v. United States,* 217 U.S. 349, 30 S.Ct. 544 (1910). Whether this requirement has been fulfilled is determined not by the standards that prevailed when the Eighth Amendment was adopted in 1791 but by the norms that "currently prevail." *Atkins.* The Amendment "draw[s] its meaning from the evolving standards of decency that mark the progress of a maturing society." *Trop v. Dulles,* 356 U.S. 86, 78 S.Ct. 590 (1958) (plurality opinion). This is because "[t]he standard of extreme cruelty is not merely descriptive, but necessarily embodies a moral judgment. The standard itself remains the same, but its applicability must change as the basic mores of society change." *Furman v. Georgia,* 408 U.S. 238, 92 S.Ct. 2726 (1972) (Burger, C. J., dissenting).

Evolving standards of decency must embrace and express respect for the dignity of the person, and the punishment of criminals must conform to that rule. As we shall discuss, punishment is justified under one or more of three principal rationales: rehabilitation, deterrence, and retribution. It is the last of these, retribution, that most often can contradict the law's own ends. This is of particular concern when the Court interprets the meaning of the Eighth Amendment in capital cases. When the law punishes by death, it risks its own sudden descent into brutality, transgressing the constitutional commitment to decency and restraint.

For these reasons we have explained that capital punishment must "be limited to those offenders who commit 'a narrow category of the most serious crimes' and whose extreme culpability makes them 'the most deserving of execution.'" *Roper* (quoting *Atkins*). Though the death penalty is not invariably unconstitutional, see *Gregg v. Georgia,* 428 U.S. 153, 96 S.Ct. 2909 (1976), the Court insists upon confining the instances in which the punishment can be imposed.

Applying this principle, we held in *Roper* and *Atkins* that the execution of juveniles and mentally retarded persons are punishments violative of the Eighth Amendment because the offender had a diminished personal responsibility for the crime. The Court further has held that the death penalty can be disproportionate to the crime itself where the crime did not result, or was not intended to result, in death of the victim. In *Coker*, for instance, the Court held it would be unconstitutional to execute an offender who had raped an adult woman. And in *Enmund v. Florida,* 458

U.S. 782, 102 S.Ct. 3368 (1982), the Court overturned the capital sentence of a defendant who aided and abetted a robbery during which a murder was committed but did not himself kill, attempt to kill, or intend that a killing would take place. On the other hand, in *Tison v. Arizona,* 481 U.S. 137, 107 S.Ct. 1676 (1987), the Court allowed the defendants' death sentences to stand where they did not themselves kill the victims but their involvement in the events leading up to the murders was active, recklessly indifferent, and substantial.

In these cases the Court has been guided by "objective indicia of society's standards, as expressed in legislative enactments and state practice with respect to executions." *Roper*; see also *Coker* (plurality opinion) (finding that both legislatures and juries had firmly rejected the penalty of death for the rape of an adult woman); *Enmund* (looking to "historical development of the punishment at issue, legislative judgments, international opinion, and the sentencing decisions juries have made"). The inquiry does not end there, however. Consensus is not dispositive. Whether the death penalty is disproportionate to the crime committed depends as well upon the standards elaborated by controlling precedents and by the Court's own understanding and interpretation of the Eighth Amendment's text, history, meaning, and purpose.

Based both on consensus and our own independent judgment, our holding is that a death sentence for one who raped but did not kill a child, and who did not intend to assist another in killing the child, is unconstitutional under the Eighth and Fourteenth Amendments.

III

A

The existence of objective indicia of consensus against making a crime punishable by death was a relevant concern in *Roper, Atkins, Coker,* and *Enmund,* and we follow the approach of those cases here. The history of the death penalty for the crime of rape is an instructive beginning point.

In 1925, 18 States, the District of Columbia, and the Federal Government had statutes that authorized the death penalty for the rape of a child or an adult. Between 1930 and 1964, 455 people were executed for those crimes. To our knowledge the last individual executed for the rape of a child was Ronald Wolfe in 1964.

In 1972, *Furman* invalidated most of the state statutes authorizing the death penalty for the crime of rape; and in *Furman*'s aftermath only six States reenacted their capital rape provisions. Three States—Georgia, North Carolina, and Louisiana—did so with respect to all rape offenses. Three States—Florida, Mississippi, and Tennessee—did so with respect only to child rape. All six statutes were later invalidated under state or federal law.

Louisiana reintroduced the death penalty for rape of a child in 1995. Under the current statute, any anal, vaginal, or oral intercourse with a child under the age of 13 constitutes aggravated rape and is punishable by death. Mistake of age is not a defense, so the statute imposes strict liability in this regard. Five States have since followed Louisiana's lead: Georgia (1999); Montana (1997); Oklahoma (2006); South Carolina (2006); and Texas (2007). Four of these States' statutes [those of Montana, Oklahoma, South Carolina, Texas] are more narrow than Louisiana's in that only offenders with a previous rape conviction are death eligible. Georgia's statute makes child rape a capital offense only when aggravating circumstances are present, including but not limited to a prior conviction.

By contrast, 44 States have not made child rape a capital offense. As for federal law, Congress in the Federal Death Penalty Act of 1994 expanded the number of federal crimes for which the death penalty is a permissible sentence, including certain nonhomicide offenses; but it did not do the same for child rape or abuse. * * *

[Whether Georgia should be included in the list of states authorizing the death penalty for rape of a child and whether Florida should be excluded from the list is subject to dispute.]

Definitive resolution of state-law issues is for the States' own courts, and there may be disagreement over the statistics. It is further true that some States, including States that have addressed the issue in just the last few years, have made child rape a capital offense. The summary recited here, however, does allow us to make certain comparisons with the data cited in the *Atkins, Roper,* and *Enmund* cases.

When *Atkins* was decided in 2002, 30 States, including 12 noncapital jurisdictions, prohibited the death penalty for mentally retarded offenders; 20 permitted it. When *Roper* was decided in 2005, the numbers disclosed a similar division among the States: 30 States prohibited the death penalty for juveniles, 18 of which permitted the death penalty for other offenders; and 20 States authorized it. Both in *Atkins* and in *Roper,* we noted that the practice of executing mentally retarded and juvenile offenders was infrequent. Only five States had executed an offender known to have an IQ below 70 between 1989 and 2002; and only three States had executed a juvenile offender between 1995 and 2005.

The statistics in *Enmund* bear an even greater similarity to the instant case. There eight jurisdictions had authorized imposition of the death penalty solely for participation in a robbery during which an accomplice committed murder, and six defendants between 1954 and 1982 had been sentenced to death for felony murder where the defendant did not personally commit the homicidal assault. These facts, the Court concluded, "weigh[ed] on the side of rejecting capital punishment for the crime."

The evidence of a national consensus with respect to the death penalty for child rapists, as with respect to juveniles, mentally retarded offenders, and vicarious felony murderers, shows divided opinion but, on balance, an opinion against it. Thirty-seven jurisdictions—36 States plus the Federal Government—have the death penalty. As mentioned above, only six of those jurisdictions authorize the death penalty for rape of a child. Though our review of national consensus is not confined to tallying the number of States with applicable death penalty legislation, it is of significance that, in 45 jurisdictions, petitioner could not be executed for child rape of any kind. That number surpasses the 30 States in *Atkins* and *Roper* and the 42 States in *Enmund* that prohibited the death penalty under the circumstances those cases considered.*

B

[Justice Kennedy rejected the argument that the failure of more states to make child rape a capital crime stemmed from the legislatures' misreading of *Coker* as barring the death penalty for all non-homicide crimes. He pointed out that the *Coker* plurality several times described the issue and the Court's holding as concerning only the constitutionality of the death penalty for rape of "an adult woman" or "adult female," and he argued that there was no evidence that state legislatures were confused by the holding and that, had the legislatures looked for guidance to the courts, they would have found that "[t]he state courts that have confronted the precise question before us have been uniform in concluding that *Coker* did not address the constitutionality of the death penalty for the crime of child rape."]

We conclude on the basis of this review that there is no clear indication that state legislatures have misinterpreted *Coker* to hold that the death penalty for child rape is unconstitutional. The small number of States that have enacted this penalty, then, is relevant to determining whether there is a consensus against capital punishment for this crime.

C

Respondent insists that the six States where child rape is a capital offense, along with the States that have proposed but not yet enacted applicable death penalty legislation, reflect a consistent direction of change in support of the death penalty for child rape. Consistent change might counterbalance an otherwise weak demonstration of consensus. But whatever the significance of consistent change where it is cited to show emerging support for expanding the scope of the death penalty, no showing of consistent change has been made in this case.

Respondent and its *amici* identify five States where, in their view, legislation authorizing capital punishment for child rape is pending. It is not our practice, nor is it sound, to find contemporary norms based upon state legislation that has been proposed but not yet enacted. There are compelling reasons not to do so here. Since the briefs were submitted by the parties, legislation in two of the five States [Colorado and Mississippi] has failed. In Tennessee, the house bills were rejected almost a year ago,

---

*When issued and announced on June 25, 2008, the Court's decision neither noted nor discussed the military penalty for rape under the Uniform Code of Military Justice. In a petition for rehearing respondent argues that the military penalty bears on our consideration of the question in this case. For the reasons set forth in the statement respecting the denial of rehearing, we find that the military penalty does not affect our reasoning or conclusions.

and the senate bills appear to have died in committee. In Alabama, the recent legislation is similar to a bill that failed in 2007. And in Missouri, the 2008 legislative session has ended, tabling the pending legislation.

Aside from pending legislation, it is true that in the last 13 years there has been change towards making child rape a capital offense. This is evidenced by six new death penalty statutes, three enacted in the last two years. But this showing is not as significant as the data in *Atkins,* where 18 States between 1986 and 2001 had enacted legislation prohibiting the execution of mentally retarded persons. Respondent argues the instant case is like *Roper* because, there, only five States had shifted their positions between 1989 and 2005, one less State than here. But in *Roper,* we emphasized that, though the pace of abolition was not as great as in *Atkins,* it was counterbalanced by the total number of States that had recognized the impropriety of executing juvenile offenders. When we decided *Stanford v. Kentucky,* 492 U.S. 361, 109 S.Ct. 2969 (1989), 12 death penalty States already prohibited the execution of any juvenile under 18, and 15 prohibited the execution of any juvenile under 17. Here, the total number of States to have made child rape a capital offense after *Furman* is six. This is not an indication of a trend or change in direction comparable to the one supported by data in *Roper.* The evidence here bears a closer resemblance to the evidence of state activity in *Enmund,* where we found a national consensus against the death penalty for vicarious felony murder despite eight jurisdictions having authorized the practice.

D

There are measures of consensus other than legislation. Statistics about the number of executions may inform the consideration whether capital punishment for the crime of child rape is regarded as unacceptable in our society. These statistics confirm our determination from our review of state statutes that there is a social consensus against the death penalty for the crime of child rape.

Nine States—Florida, Georgia, Louisiana, Mississippi, Montana, Oklahoma, South Carolina, Tennessee, and Texas—have permitted capital punishment for adult or child rape for some length of time between the Court's 1972 decision in *Furman* and today. Yet no individual has been executed for the rape of an adult or child since 1964, and no execution for any other nonhomicide offense has been conducted since 1963.

Louisiana is the only State since 1964 that has sentenced an individual to death for the crime of child rape; and petitioner and Richard Davis, who was convicted and sentenced to death for the aggravated rape of a 5–year–old child by a Louisiana jury in December 2007, are the only two individuals now on death row in the United States for a nonhomicide offense.

After reviewing the authorities informed by contemporary norms, including the history of the death penalty for this and other nonhomicide crimes, current state statutes and new enactments, and the number of executions since 1964, we conclude there is a national consensus against capital punishment for the crime of child rape.

IV

A

As we have said in other Eighth Amendment cases, objective evidence of contemporary values as it relates to punishment for child rape is entitled to great weight, but it does not end our inquiry. "[T]he Constitution contemplates that in the end our own judgment will be brought to bear on the question of the acceptability of the death penalty under the Eighth Amendment." *Coker* (plurality opinion). We turn, then, to the resolution of the question before us, which is informed by our precedents and our own understanding of the Constitution and the rights it secures.

It must be acknowledged that there are moral grounds to question a rule barring capital punishment for a crime against an individual that did not result in death. These facts illustrate the point. Here the victim's fright, the sense of betrayal, and the nature of her injuries caused more prolonged physical and mental suffering than, say, a sudden killing by an unseen assassin. The attack was not just on her but on her childhood. For this reason, we should be most reluctant to rely upon the language of the plurality in *Coker,* which posited that, for the victim of rape, "life may not be nearly so happy as it was" but it is not beyond repair. We cannot dismiss the years of long anguish that must be endured by the victim of child rape.

It does not follow, though, that capital punishment is a proportionate penalty for the crime. The constitutional prohibition against excessive or cruel and unusual punishments mandates that the State's power to "punish be exercised within the limits of civilized standards." *Trop* (plurality opinion). Evolving standards of decency that mark the progress of a maturing society counsel us to be most hesitant before interpreting the Eighth Amendment to allow the extension of the death penalty, a hesitation that has special force where no life was taken in the commission of the crime. It is an established principle that decency, in its essence, presumes respect for the individual and thus moderation or restraint in the application of capital punishment.

To date the Court has sought to define and implement this principle, for the most part, in cases involving capital murder. One approach has been to insist upon general rules that ensure consistency in determining who receives a death sentence. See *California v. Brown,* 479 U.S. 538, 107 S.Ct. 837 (1987) ("[D]eath penalty statutes [must] be structured so as to prevent the penalty from being administered in an arbitrary and unpredictable fashion.") At the same time the Court has insisted, to ensure restraint and moderation in use of capital punishment, on judging the "character and record of the individual offender and the circumstances of the particular offense as a constitutionally indispensable part of the process of inflicting the penalty of death." *Woodson v. North Carolina,* 428 U.S. 280, 96 S.Ct. 2978 (1976) (plurality opinion).

The tension between general rules and case-specific circumstances has produced results not all together satisfactory. See *Tuilaepa v. California,* 512 U.S. 967, 114 S.Ct. 2630 (1994) ("The objectives of these two inquiries can be in some tension, at least when the inquiries occur at the same time"); *Walton v. Arizona,* 497 U.S. 639, 110 S.Ct. 3047 (1990) (SCALIA, J., concurring in part and concurring in judgment) ("The latter requirement quite obviously destroys whatever rationality and predictability the former requirement was designed to achieve"). This has led some Members of the Court to say we should cease efforts to resolve the tension and simply allow legislatures, prosecutors, courts, and juries greater latitude. See *id.* (advocating that the Court adhere to the *Furman* line of cases and abandon the *Woodson–Lockett* line of cases). For others the failure to limit these same imprecisions by stricter enforcement of narrowing rules has raised doubts concerning the constitutionality of capital punishment itself. See *Baze v. Rees,* ___ U.S. ___, 128 S.Ct. 1520 (2008) (STEVENS, J., concurring in judgment); *Furman,* (White, J., concurring); *Callins v. Collins,* 510 U.S. 1141, 114 S.Ct. 1127 (1994) (Blackmun, J., dissenting from denial of certiorari).

Our response to this case law, which is still in search of a unifying principle, has been to insist upon confining the instances in which capital punishment may be imposed. See *Gregg* (joint opinion of Stewart, Powell, and Stevens, JJ.) (because "death as a punishment is unique in its severity and irrevocability," capital punishment must be reserved for those crimes that are "so grievous an affront to humanity that the only adequate response may be the penalty of death" (citing in part *Furman* (Brennan, J., concurring); *id.* (Stewart, J., concurring)).

Our concern here is limited to crimes against individual persons. We do not address, for example, crimes defining and punishing treason, espionage, terrorism, and drug kingpin activity, which are offenses against the State. As it relates to crimes against individuals, though, the death penalty should not be expanded to instances where the victim's life was not taken. We said in *Coker* of adult rape:

> "We do not discount the seriousness of rape as a crime. It is highly reprehensible, both in a moral sense and in its almost total contempt for the personal integrity and autonomy of the female victim.... Short of homicide, it is the 'ultimate violation of self.' ... [But] [t]he murderer kills; the rapist, if no more than that, does not.... We have the abiding conviction that the death penalty, which is unique in its severity and irrevocability, is an excessive penalty for the rapist who, as such, does not take human life." (plurality opinion).

The same distinction between homicide and other serious violent offenses against the individual informed the Court's analysis in *Enmund,* where the Court held that the death penalty for the crime of vicarious felony murder is disproportionate to the offense. The Court repeated there the fundamental, moral distinction between a "murderer" and a "robber," noting that while "robbery is a serious crime deserving serious punishment," it is not like death in its "severity and irrevocability."

Consistent with evolving standards of decency and the teachings of our precedents we conclude that, in determining whether the death penalty is excessive, there is a distinction between intentional first-degree murder on the one hand and nonhomicide crimes against individual persons, even including child rape, on the other. The latter crimes may be devastating in their harm, as here, but "in terms of moral depravity and of the injury to the person and to the public," *Coker*, they cannot be compared to murder in their "severity and irrevocability."

In reaching our conclusion we find significant the number of executions that would be allowed under respondent's approach. The crime of child rape, considering its reported incidents, occurs more often than first-degree murder. Approximately 5,702 incidents of vaginal, anal, or oral rape of a child under the age of 12 were reported nationwide in 2005; this is almost twice the total incidents of intentional murder for victims of all ages (3,405) reported during the same period. Although we have no reliable statistics on convictions for child rape, we can surmise that, each year, there are hundreds, or more, of these convictions just in jurisdictions that permit capital punishment. Cf. Brief for Louisiana Association of Criminal Defense Lawyers et al. as *Amici Curiae* 1–2, and n. 2 (noting that there are now at least 70 capital rape indictments pending in Louisiana and estimating the actual number to be over 100). As a result of existing rules, only 2.2% of convicted first-degree murderers are sentenced to death. But under respondent's approach, the 36 States that permit the death penalty could sentence to death all persons convicted of raping a child less than 12 years of age. This could not be reconciled with our evolving standards of decency and the necessity to constrain the use of the death penalty.

It might be said that narrowing aggravators could be used in this context, as with murder offenses, to ensure the death penalty's restrained application. We find it difficult to identify standards that would guide the decisionmaker so the penalty is reserved for the most severe cases of child rape and yet not imposed in an arbitrary way. Even were we to forbid, say, the execution of first-time child rapists, or require as an aggravating factor a finding that the perpetrator's instant rape offense involved multiple victims, the jury still must balance, in its discretion, those aggravating factors against mitigating circumstances. In this context, which involves a crime that in many cases will overwhelm a decent person's judgment, we have no confidence that the imposition of the death penalty would not be so arbitrary as to be "freakis[h]," *Furman* (Stewart, J., concurring). We cannot sanction this result when the harm to the victim, though grave, cannot be quantified in the same way as death of the victim.

It is not a solution simply to apply to this context the aggravating factors developed for capital murder. The Court has said that a State may carry out its obligation to ensure individualized sentencing in capital murder cases by adopting sentencing processes that rely upon the jury to exercise wide discretion so long as there are narrowing factors that have some "common-sense core of meaning ... that criminal juries should be capable of understanding." *Tuilaepa, supra.* The Court, accordingly, has upheld the constitutionality of aggravating factors ranging from whether the defendant was a "cold-blooded, pitiless slayer," *Arave v. Creech,* 507 U.S. 463, 113 S.Ct. 1534 (1993), to whether the "perpetrator inflict[ed] mental anguish or physical abuse before the victim's death," *Walton,* to whether the defendant "would commit criminal acts of violence that would constitute a continuing threat to society," *Jurek v. Texas,* 428 U.S. 262, 96 S.Ct. 2950 (1976) (joint opinion of Stewart, Powell, and Stevens, JJ.). All of these standards have the potential to result in some inconsistency of application.

As noted above, the resulting imprecision and the tension between evaluating the individual circumstances and consistency of treatment have been tolerated where the victim dies. It should not be introduced into our justice system, though, where death has not occurred.

Our concerns are all the more pronounced where, as here, the death penalty for this crime has been most infrequent. We have developed a foundational jurisprudence in the case of capital murder to guide the States and juries in imposing the death penalty. Starting with *Gregg,*we have spent more than 32 years articulating limiting factors that channel the jury's discretion to avoid the death penalty's arbitrary imposition in the case of capital murder. Though that practice remains sound, beginning the same process for crimes for which no one has been executed in more than 40 years would require experimentation in an area where a failed experiment would result in the execution of individuals undeserving of the death penalty. Evolving standards of decency are difficult to reconcile with a regime that seeks to expand the death penalty to an area where standards to confine its use are indefinite and obscure.

B

Our decision is consistent with the justifications offered for the death penalty. *Gregg* instructs that capital punishment is excessive when it is grossly out of proportion to the crime or it does not fulfill the two distinct social purposes served by the death penalty: retribution and deterrence of capital crimes.

As in *Coker,* here it cannot be said with any certainty that the death penalty for child rape serves no deterrent or retributive function. This argument does not overcome other objections, however. The incongruity between the crime of child rape and the harshness of the death penalty poses risks of overpunishment and counsels against a constitutional ruling that the death penalty can be expanded to include this offense.

The goal of retribution, which reflects society's and the victim's interests in seeing that the offender is repaid for the hurt he caused, does not justify the harshness of the death penalty here. In measuring retribution, as well as other objectives of criminal law, it is appropriate to distinguish between a particularly depraved murder that merits death as a form of retribution and the crime of child rape.

There is an additional reason for our conclusion that imposing the death penalty for child rape would not further retributive purposes. In considering whether retribution is served, among other factors we have looked to whether capital punishment "has the potential ... to allow the community as a whole, including the surviving family and friends of the victim, to affirm its own judgment that the culpability of the prisoner is so serious that the ultimate penalty must be sought and imposed." *Panetti v. Quarterman*, 551 U.S. 930, 127 S.Ct. 2842 (2007). In considering the death penalty for nonhomicide offenses this inquiry necessarily also must include the question whether the death penalty balances the wrong to the victim.

It is not at all evident that the child rape victim's hurt is lessened when the law permits the death of the perpetrator. Capital cases require a long-term commitment by those who testify for the prosecution, especially when guilt and sentencing determinations are in multiple proceedings. In cases like this the key testimony is not just from the family but from the victim herself. During formative years of her adolescence, made all the more daunting for having to come to terms with the brutality of her experience, L.H. was required to discuss the case at length with law enforcement personnel. In a public trial she was required to recount once more all the details of the crime to a jury as the State pursued the death of her stepfather. And in the end the State made L.H. a central figure in its decision to seek the death penalty, telling the jury in closing statements: "[L.H.] is asking you, asking you to set up a time and place when he dies."

Society's desire to inflict the death penalty for child rape by enlisting the child victim to assist it over the course of years in asking for capital punishment forces a moral choice on the child, who is not of mature age to make that choice. The way the death penalty here involves the child victim in its enforcement can compromise a decent legal system; and this is but a subset of fundamental difficulties capital punishment can cause in the administration and enforcement of laws proscribing child rape.

There are, moreover, serious systemic concerns in prosecuting the crime of child rape that are relevant to the constitutionality of making it a capital offense. The problem of unreliable, induced, and even imagined child testimony means there is a "special risk of wrongful execution" in some child rape cases. *Atkins.* This undermines, at least to some degree, the meaningful contribution of the death penalty to legitimate goals of punishment. Studies conclude that children are highly susceptible to suggestive questioning techniques like repetition, guided imagery, and selective reinforcement.

Similar criticisms pertain to other cases involving child witnesses; but child rape cases present heightened concerns because the central narrative and account of the crime often comes from the child herself. She and the accused are, in most instances, the only ones present when the crime was committed. And the question in a capital case is not just the fact of the crime, including, say, proof of rape as distinct from abuse short of rape, but details bearing upon brutality in its commission. Although capital punishment does bring retribution, and the legislature here has chosen to use it for this end, its judgment must be weighed, in deciding the constitutional question, against the special risks of unreliable testimony with respect to this crime.

With respect to deterrence, if the death penalty adds to the risk of non-reporting, that, too, diminishes the penalty's objectives. Underreporting is a common problem with respect to child sexual abuse. [Citing studies showing that 88% of minor female rape victims did not report the rape to authorities] Although we know little about what differentiates those who report from those who do not report, one of the most commonly cited reasons for nondisclosure is fear of negative consequences for the perpetrator, a concern that has special force where the abuser is a family member. The experience of the *amici* who work with child victims indicates that, when the punishment is death, both the victim and the victim's family members may be more likely to shield the perpetrator from discovery, thus increasing underreporting. As a result, punishment by death may not result in more deterrence or more effective enforcement.

In addition, by in effect making the punishment for child rape and murder equivalent, a State that punishes child rape by death may remove a strong incentive for the rapist not to kill the victim. Assuming the offender behaves in a rational way, as one must to justify the penalty on grounds of deterrence, the penalty in some respects gives less protection, not more, to the victim, who is often the sole witness to the crime. It might be argued that, even if the death penalty results in a marginal increase in the incentive to kill, this is counterbalanced by a marginally increased deterrent to commit the crime at all. Whatever balance the legislature strikes, however, uncertainty on the point makes the argument for the penalty less compelling than for homicide crimes.

Each of these propositions, standing alone, might not establish the unconstitutionality of the death penalty for the crime of child rape. Taken in sum, however, they demonstrate the serious negative consequences of making child rape a capital offense. These considerations lead us to conclude, in our independent judgment, that the death penalty is not a proportional punishment for the rape of a child.

V

Our determination that there is a consensus against the death penalty for child rape raises the question whether the Court's own institutional position and its holding will have the effect of blocking further or later consensus in favor of the penalty from developing. The Court, it will be argued, by the act of addressing the constitutionality of the death penalty, intrudes upon the consensus-making process. By imposing a negative restraint, the argument runs, the Court makes it more difficult for consensus to change or emerge. The Court, according to the criticism, itself becomes enmeshed in the process, part judge and part the maker of that which it judges.

These concerns overlook the meaning and full substance of the established proposition that the Eighth Amendment is defined by "the evolving standards of decency that mark the progress of a maturing society." *Trop* (plurality opinion). Confirmed by repeated, consistent rulings of this Court, this principle requires that use of the death penalty be restrained. The rule of evolving standards of decency with specific marks on the way to full progress and mature judgment means that resort to the penalty must be reserved for the worst of crimes and limited in its instances of application. In most cases justice is not better served by terminating the life of the perpetrator rather than confining him and preserving the possibility that he and the system will find ways to allow him to understand the enormity of his offense. Difficulties in administering the penalty to ensure against its arbitrary and capricious application require adherence to a rule reserving its use, at this stage of evolving standards and in cases of crimes against individuals, for crimes that take the life of the victim.

The judgment of the Supreme Court of Louisiana upholding the capital sentence is reversed. This case is remanded for further proceedings not inconsistent with this opinion.

It is so ordered.

JUSTICE ALITO, with whom THE CHIEF JUSTICE, JUSTICE SCALIA, and JUSTICE THOMAS join, dissenting.

The Court today holds that the Eighth Amendment categorically prohibits the imposition of the death penalty for the crime of raping a child. This is so, according to the Court, no matter how young the child, no matter how many times the child is raped, no matter how many children the perpetrator rapes, no matter how sadistic the crime, no matter how much physical or psychological trauma is inflicted, and no matter how heinous the perpetrator's prior criminal record may be. The Court provides two reasons for this sweeping conclusion: First, the Court claims to have identified "a national consensus" that the death penalty is never acceptable for the rape of a child; second, the Court concludes, based on its "independent judgment," that imposing the death penalty for child rape is inconsistent with " 'the evolving standards of decency that mark the progress of a maturing society.' " Because neither of these justifications is sound, I respectfully dissent.

I

A

I turn first to the Court's claim that there is a "national consensus" that it is never acceptable to impose the death penalty for the rape of a child. The Eighth Amendment's requirements, the Court writes, are "determined not by the standards that prevailed" when the Amendment was adopted but "by the norms that 'currently prevail.' " (quoting *Atkins v. Virginia,* 536 U.S. 304, 122 S.Ct. 2242 (2002)). In assessing current norms, the Court relies primarily on the fact that only 6 of the 50 States now have statutes that permit the death penalty for this offense. But this statistic is a highly unreliable indicator of the views of state lawmakers and their constituents. As I will explain, dicta in this Court's decision in *Coker v. Georgia,* 433 U.S. 584, 97 S.Ct. 2861 (1977), has stunted legislative consideration of the question whether the death penalty for the targeted offense of raping a young child is consistent with prevailing standards of decency. The *Coker* dicta gave state legislators and others good reason to fear that any law permitting the imposition of the death penalty for this crime would meet precisely the fate that has now befallen the Louisiana statute that is currently before us, and this threat strongly discouraged state legislators—regardless of their own values and those of their constituents—from supporting the enactment of such legislation.

[Justice Alito argued that the *Coker* plurality's summary—"We have the abiding conviction that the death penalty . . . is an excessive penalty for the rapist who, as such, does not take human life"—although dicta, implied that the death penalty for *any* rape would have been unconstitutional. He cited to state court opinions and commentators who, while recognizing the limits of the *Coker* holding, assumed that the logic of the decision would bar imposition of the death penalty for any non-homicide crime. He concluded that "the *Coker* dicta gave state legislators a strong incentive not to push for the enactment of new capital child-rape laws even though these legislators and their constituents may have believed that the laws would be appropriate and desirable," and, in support of that point, he cited to opponents' contentions that the recent Oklahoma and Texas child-rape bills were unconstitutional under *Coker*.]

C

Because of the effect of the *Coker* dicta, the Court is plainly wrong in comparing the situation here to that in *Atkins* or *Roper v. Simmons,* 543 U.S. 551, 125 S.Ct. 1183 (2005). *Atkins* concerned the constitutionality of imposing the death penalty on a mentally retarded defendant. Thirteen years earlier, in *Penry v. Lynaugh,* 492 U.S. 302, 109 S.Ct. 2934 (1989), the Court had held that this was permitted by the Eighth Amendment, and therefore, during the time between *Penry* and *Atkins,* state legislators had reason to believe that this Court would follow its prior precedent and uphold statutes allowing such punishment.

The situation in *Roper* was similar. *Roper* concerned a challenge to the constitutionality of imposing the death penalty on a defendant who had not reached the age of 18 at the time of the crime. Sixteen years earlier in *Stanford v. Kentucky,* 492 U.S. 361, 109 S.Ct. 2969 (1989), the Court had rejected a similar challenge, and therefore state lawmakers had cause to believe that laws allowing such punishment would be sustained.

When state lawmakers believe that their decision will prevail on the question whether to permit the death penalty for a particular crime or class of offender, the legislators' resolution of the issue can be interpreted as an expression of their own judgment, informed by whatever weight they attach to the values of their constituents. But when state legislators think that the enactment of a new death penalty law is likely to be futile, inaction cannot reasonably be interpreted as an expression of their under-standing of prevailing societal values. In that atmosphere, legislative inaction is more likely to evidence acquiescence.

D

If anything can be inferred from state legislative developments, the message is very different from the one that the Court perceives. In just the past few years, despite the shadow cast by the *Coker* dicta, five States have enacted targeted capital child-rape laws. If, as the Court seems to think, our society is "[e]volving" toward ever higher "standards of decen-cy," these enactments might represent the beginning of a new evolution-ary line.

Such a development would not be out of step with changes in our society's thinking since *Coker* was decided. During that time, reported instances of child abuse have increased dramatically;[2] and there are many indications of growing alarm about the sexual abuse of children. In 1994, Congress enacted the Jacob Wetterling Crimes Against Children and Sexually Violent Offender Registration Program, 42 U.S.C. § 14071, which requires States receiving certain federal funds to establish registration systems for convicted sex offenders and to notify the public about persons convicted of the sexual abuse of minors. All 50 States have now enacted such statutes. In addition, at least 21 States and the District of Columbia now have statutes permitting the involuntary commitment of sexual predators, and at least 12 States have enacted residency restrictions for sex offenders.

Seeking to counter the significance of the new capital child-rape laws enacted during the past two years, the Court points out that in recent months efforts to enact similar laws in five other States have stalled. These developments, however, all took place after our decision to grant

---

2. From 1976 to 1986, the number of reported cases of child sexual abuse grew from 6,000 to 132,000, an increase of 2,100%. By 1991, the number of cases totaled 432,000, an increase of another 227%. In 1995, local child protection services agencies identified 126,000 children who were victims of either substantiated or indicated sexual abuse. Nearly 30% of those child victims were between the age of four and seven. There were an estimated 90,000 substantiated cases of child sexual abuse in 2003.

certiorari in this case, which gave state legislators reason to delay the enactment of new legislation until the constitutionality of such laws was clarified. And there is no evidence of which I am aware that these legislative initiatives failed because the proposed laws were viewed as inconsistent with our society's standards of decency.

On the contrary, the available evidence suggests otherwise. For example, in Colorado, the Senate Appropriations Committee in April voted 6 to 4 against Senate Bill 195, reportedly because it "would have cost about $616,000 next year for trials, appeals, public defenders, and prison costs." Likewise, in Tennessee, the capital child-rape bill was withdrawn in committee "because of the high associated costs." * * * Thus, the failure to enact capital child-rape laws cannot be viewed as evidence of a moral consensus against such punishment.

E

Aside from its misleading tally of current state laws, the Court points to two additional "objective indicia" of a "national consensus," but these arguments are patent makeweights. The Court notes that Congress has not enacted a law permitting a federal district court to impose the death penalty for the rape of a child, but due to the territorial limits of the relevant federal statutes, very few rape cases, not to mention child-rape cases, are prosecuted in federal court. Congress' failure to enact a death penalty statute for this tiny set of cases is hardly evidence of Congress' assessment of our society's values.[6]

Finally, the Court argues that statistics about the number of executions in rape cases support its perception of a "national consensus," but here too the statistics do not support the Court's position. The Court notes that the last execution for the rape of a child occurred in 1964, but the Court fails to mention that litigation regarding the constitutionality of the death penalty brought executions to a halt across the board in the late 1960's. In 1965 and 1966, there were a total of eight executions for all offenses, and from 1968 until 1977, the year when *Coker* was decided, there were no executions for any crimes. The Court also fails to mention that in Louisiana, since the state law was amended in 1995 to make child rape a capital offense, prosecutors have asked juries to return death verdicts in four cases. In two of those cases, Louisiana juries imposed the death penalty. This 50% record is hardly evidence that juries share the Court's view that the death penalty for the rape of a young child is unacceptable under even the most aggravated circumstances.[8]

F

In light of the points discussed above, I believe that the "objective indicia" of our society's "evolving standards of decency" can be fairly

6. Moreover, as noted in the petition for rehearing, the Uniform Code of Military Justice permits such a sentence.

8. Of course, the other five capital child rape statutes are too recent for any individual to have been sentenced to death under them.

summarized as follows. Neither Congress nor juries have done anything that can plausibly be interpreted as evidencing the "national consensus" that the Court perceives. State legislatures, for more than 30 years, have operated under the ominous shadow of the *Coker* dicta and thus have not been free to express their own understanding of our society's standards of decency. And in the months following our grant of certiorari in this case, state legislatures have had an additional reason to pause. Yet despite the inhibiting legal atmosphere that has prevailed since 1977, six States have recently enacted new, targeted child-rape laws.

I do not suggest that six new state laws necessarily establish a "national consensus" or even that they are sure evidence of an ineluctable trend. In terms of the Court's metaphor of moral evolution, these enactments might have turned out to be an evolutionary dead end. But they might also have been the beginning of a strong new evolutionary line. We will never know, because the Court today snuffs out the line in its incipient stage.

II

A

The Court is willing to block the potential emergence of a national consensus in favor of permitting the death penalty for child rape because, in the end, what matters is the Court's "own judgment" regarding the "acceptability of the death penalty." Although the Court has much to say on this issue, most of the Court's discussion is not pertinent to the Eighth Amendment question at hand. And once all of the Court's irrelevant arguments are put aside, it is apparent that the Court has provided no coherent explanation for today's decision.

In the next section of this opinion, I will attempt to weed out the arguments that are not germane to the Eighth Amendment inquiry, and in the final section, I will address what remains.

B

A major theme of the Court's opinion is that permitting the death penalty in child-rape cases is not in the best interests of the victims of these crimes and society at large. In this vein, the Court suggests that it is more painful for child-rape victims to testify when the prosecution is seeking the death penalty. The Court also argues that "a State that punishes child rape by death may remove a strong incentive for the rapist not to kill the victim," and may discourage the reporting of child rape.

These policy arguments, whatever their merits, are simply not pertinent to the question whether the death penalty is "cruel and unusual" punishment. The Eighth Amendment protects the right of an accused. It does not authorize this Court to strike down federal or state criminal laws on the ground that they are not in the best interests of crime victims or the broader society. The Court's policy arguments concern matters that legislators should—and presumably do—take into account in deciding whether to enact a capital child-rape statute, but these arguments are irrelevant to the question that is before us in this case. Our cases have cautioned against using the " 'aegis of the Cruel and Unusual Punishment Clause' to cut off the normal democratic processes," *Atkins* (Rehnquist, C. J., dissenting), in turn quoting *Gregg v. Georgia,* 428 U.S. 153, 96 S.Ct. 2909 (1976), (joint opinion of Stewart, Powell, and Stevens, JJ.), but the Court forgets that warning here.

The Court also contends that laws permitting the death penalty for the rape of a child create serious procedural problems. Specifically, the Court maintains that it is not feasible to channel the exercise of sentencing discretion in child-rape cases, and that the unreliability of the testimony of child victims creates a danger that innocent defendants will be convicted and executed. Neither of these contentions provides a basis for striking down all capital child-rape laws no matter how carefully and narrowly they are crafted.

The Court's argument regarding the structuring of sentencing discretion is hard to comprehend. The Court finds it "difficult to identify standards that would guide the decisionmaker so the penalty is reserved for the most severe cases of child rape and yet not imposed in an arbitrary way." Even assuming that the age of a child is not alone a sufficient factor for limiting sentencing discretion, the Court need only examine the child-rape laws recently enacted in Texas, Oklahoma, Montana, and South Carolina, all of which use a concrete factor to limit quite drastically the number of cases in which the death penalty may be imposed. In those States, a defendant convicted of the rape of a child may be sentenced to death only if the defendant has a prior conviction for a specified felony sex offense.

Moreover, it takes little imagination to envision other limiting factors that a State could use to structure sentencing discretion in child rape cases. Some of these might be: whether the victim was kidnapped, whether the defendant inflicted severe physical injury on the victim, whether the victim was raped multiple times, whether the rapes occurred over a specified extended period, and whether there were multiple victims.

The Court refers to limiting standards that are "indefinite and obscure," but there is nothing indefinite or obscure about any of the above-listed aggravating factors. Indeed, they are far more definite and clear-cut than aggravating factors that we have found to be adequate in murder cases. See, *e.g., Arave v. Creech,* 507 U.S. 463, 113 S.Ct. 1534 (1993) (whether the defendant was a " 'cold-blooded, pitiless slayer' "); *Walton v. Arizona,* 497 U.S. 639, 110 S.Ct. 3047 (1990) (whether the " 'perpetrator inflict[ed] mental anguish or physical abuse before the victim's death' "); *Jurek v. Texas,* 428 U.S. 262, 269, 96 S.Ct. 2950 (1976) (joint opinion of Stewart, Powell, and Stevens, JJ.) (whether the " 'defendant would commit criminal acts of violence that would constitute a continuing threat to society' "). For these reasons, concerns about limiting sentencing discretion provide no support for the Court's blanket condemnation of all capital child-rape statutes.

That sweeping holding is also not justified by the Court's concerns about the reliability of the testimony of child victims. First, the Eighth Amendment provides a poor vehicle for addressing problems regarding the admissibility or reliability of evidence, and problems presented by the testimony of child victims are not unique to capital cases. Second, concerns about the reliability of the testimony of child witnesses are not present in every child-rape case. In the case before us, for example, there was undisputed medical evidence that the victim was brutally raped, as well as strong independent evidence that petitioner was the perpetrator. Third, if the Court's evidentiary concerns have Eighth Amendment relevance, they could be addressed by allowing the death penalty in only those child-rape cases in which the independent evidence is sufficient to prove all the elements needed for conviction and imposition of a death sentence. There is precedent for requiring special corroboration in certain criminal cases. For example, some jurisdictions do not allow a conviction based on the uncorroborated testimony of an accomplice. A State wishing to permit the death penalty in child-rape cases could impose an analogous corroboration requirement.

C

After all the arguments noted above are put aside, what is left? What remaining grounds does the Court provide to justify its independent judgment that the death penalty for child rape is categorically unacceptable? I see two.

1

The first is the proposition that we should be "most hesitant before interpreting the Eighth Amendment to allow the *extension* of the death penalty." (emphasis added). But holding that the Eighth Amendment does not categorically prohibit the death penalty for the rape of a young child would not "extend" or "expand" the death penalty. Laws enacted by the state legislatures are presumptively constitutional, and until today, this Court has not held that capital child rape laws are unconstitutional. Consequently, upholding the constitutionality of such a law would not "extend" or "expand" the death penalty; rather, it would confirm the status of presumptive constitutionality that such laws have enjoyed up to this point. And in any event, this Court has previously made it clear that "[t]he Eighth Amendment is not a ratchet, whereby a temporary consensus on leniency for a particular crime fixes a permanent constitutional maximum, disabling States from giving effect to altered beliefs and responding to changed social conditions." *Harmelin v. Michigan*, 501 U.S. 957, 111 S.Ct. 2680 (1991) (principal opinion).

2

The Court's final—and, it appears, principal—justification for its holding is that murder, the only crime for which defendants have been executed since this Court's 1976 death penalty decisions, is unique in its moral depravity and in the severity of the injury that it inflicts on the victim and the public. But the Court makes little attempt to defend these conclusions.

With respect to the question of moral depravity, is it really true that every person who is convicted of capital murder and sentenced to death is more morally depraved than every child rapist? Consider the following two cases. In the first, a defendant robs a convenience store and watches as his accomplice shoots the store owner. The defendant acts recklessly, but was not the triggerman and did not intend the killing. See, *e.g., Tison v. Arizona,* 481 U.S. 137, 107 S.Ct. 1676 (1987). In the second case, a previously convicted child rapist kidnaps, repeatedly rapes, and tortures multiple child victims. Is it clear that the first defendant is more morally depraved than the second?

The Court's decision here stands in stark contrast to *Atkins* and *Roper,* in which the Court concluded that characteristics of the affected defendants—mental retardation in *Atkins* and youth in *Roper*—diminished their culpability. Nor is this case comparable to *Enmund v. Florida,* 458 U.S. 782, 102 S.Ct. 3368 (1982), in which the Court held that the Eighth Amendment prohibits the death penalty where the defendant participated in a robbery during which a murder was committed but did not personally intend for lethal force to be used. I have no doubt that, under the prevailing standards of our society, robbery, the crime that the petitioner in *Enmund* intended to commit, does not evidence the same degree of moral depravity as the brutal rape of a young child. Indeed, I have little doubt that, in the eyes of ordinary Americans, the very worst child rapists—predators who seek out and inflict serious physical and emotional injury on defenseless young children—are the epitome of moral depravity.

With respect to the question of the harm caused by the rape of child in relation to the harm caused by murder, it is certainly true that the loss of human life represents a unique harm, but that does not explain why other grievous harms are insufficient to permit a death sentence. And the Court does not take the position that no harm other than the loss of life is sufficient. The Court takes pains to limit its holding to "crimes against individual persons" and to exclude "offenses against the State," a category that the Court stretches—without explanation—to include "drug kingpin activity." But the Court makes no effort to explain why the harm caused by such crimes is necessarily greater than the harm caused by the rape of young children. This is puzzling in light of the Court's acknowledgment that "[r]ape has a permanent psychological, emotional, and sometimes physical impact on the child." As the Court aptly recognizes, "[w]e cannot dismiss the years of long anguish that must be endured by the victim of child rape."

The rape of any victim inflicts great injury, and "[s]ome victims are so grievously injured physically or psychologically that life *is* beyond repair." *Coker* (opinion of Powell, J.). "The immaturity and vulnerability of a child, both physically and psychologically, adds a devastating dimension to rape that is not present when an adult is raped." Meister, *Murdering Innocence: The Constitutionality of Capital Child Rape Statutes*, 45 Ariz. L.Rev. 197 (2003). Long-term studies show that sexual abuse is "grossly intrusive in the lives of children and is harmful to their normal psychological, emotional and sexual development in ways which no just or humane society can tolerate." C. Bagley & K. King, Child Sexual Abuse: The Search for Healing (1990).

It has been estimated that as many as 40% of 7–to 13–year–old sexual assault victims are considered "seriously disturbed." A. Lurigio, M. Jones, & B. Smith, *Child Sexual Abuse: Its Causes, Consequences, and Implications for Probation Practice*, 59 Sep Fed. Probation 69 (1995). Psychological problems include sudden school failure, unprovoked crying, dissociation, depression, insomnia, sleep disturbances, nightmares, feelings of guilt and inferiority, and self-destructive behavior, including an increased incidence of suicide.

The deep problems that afflict child-rape victims often become society's problems as well. Commentators have noted correlations between childhood sexual abuse and later problems such as substance abuse, dangerous sexual behaviors or dysfunction, inability to relate to others on an interpersonal level, and psychiatric illness. Victims of child rape are nearly 5 times more likely than nonvictims to be arrested for sex crimes and nearly 30 times more likely to be arrested for prostitution.

The harm that is caused to the victims and to society at large by the worst child rapists is grave. It is the judgment of the Louisiana lawmakers and those in an increasing number of other States that these harms justify the death penalty. The Court provides no cogent explanation why this legislative judgment should be overridden. Conclusory references to "decency," "moderation," "restraint," "full progress," and "moral judgment" are not enough.

III

In summary, the Court holds that the Eighth Amendment categorically rules out the death penalty in even the most extreme cases of child rape even though: (1) This holding is not supported by the original meaning of the Eighth Amendment; (2) neither *Coker* nor any other prior precedent commands this result; (3) there are no reliable "objective indicia" of a "national consensus" in support of the Court's position; (4) sustaining the constitutionality of the state law before us would not "extend" or "expand" the death penalty; (5) this Court has previously rejected the proposition that the Eighth Amendment is a one-way ratchet that prohibits legislatures from adopting new capital punishment statutes to meet new problems; (6) the worst child rapists exhibit the epitome of moral depravity; and (7) child rape inflicts grievous injury on victims and on society in general.

The party attacking the constitutionality of a state statute bears the "heavy burden" of establishing that the law is unconstitutional. That burden has not been discharged here, and I would therefore affirm the decision of the Louisiana Supreme Court.

NOTE

1. *The federal death penalty.*

The federal death penalty was restored post-*Furman* with the enactment of the Anti–Drug Abuse Act of 1988 (see 21 U.S.C. § 848 (e)–(r)) and the Violent Crime Control and Law Enforcement Act of 1994 (see 18 U.S.C. §§ 3591–3597). Federal law now authorizes the death penalty for a wide range of homicides, including a number of categories of unintentional killings. In addition, federal law authorizes the death penalty for four categories of non-homicidal crimes: treason (18 U.S.C. § 2381); espionage (18 U.S.C. § 794); drug trafficking in large amounts (18 U.S.C. § 3591(b)(1)); and attempted murder of a public officer, juror or witness by a major drug trafficker (18 U.S.C. § 3591(b)(2)). Would the death penalty be constitutional for any of these non-homicidal crimes?

*

PART 3

LITIGATING THE CAPITAL CASE

■ ■ ■

Part 3 considers a number of constitutional issues that arise in the litigation of a capital case. The article, *The Death Squad*, introduces the topic by describing the attorneys involved in capital case litigation. The first three chapters largely concern issues that are not peculiar to capital cases, but might arise in any criminal case. However, does the fact that "death is different" and there is a need for "heightened reliability" in capital cases call for different treatment of these issues in capital cases than in ordinary criminal cases? In many of the cases, the application of the legal standards established by the Supreme Court requires a close examination of facts. Should the Supreme Court, in particular, and the federal courts, in general, be reviewing the highly fact-specific determinations of the state courts? Chapter 6 looks at the issue of jury selection in a capital case. Chapter 7 considers the respective roles of the defendant and the defense counsel and, as to the defense counsel, the issue of adequacy of representation. Chapter 8 addresses the role of the prosecutor and the issue of prosecutorial misconduct.

The last two chapters address the penalty phase of the capital case. Although the Supreme Court has never expressly so held, it has been assumed, since the Court's decisions in *Gregg v. Georgia* and its companion cases, that the Constitution requires capital case penalty determinations to be made in bifurcated proceedings. Consequently, all states provide for a separate penalty hearing after the defendant is found guilty at trial. In some states (*e.g.*, California, Texas), death eligibility is determined at the guilt phase, leaving only the penalty to be determined in the penalty hearing, while in other states (*e.g.*, Georgia, Tennessee), both death eligibility and the penalty are determined in the penalty hearing. In most states the defendant is entitled to a jury determination of penalty, but, in some states (*e.g.*, Alabama, Florida), the judge determines the penalty after receiving a recommendation from an advisory jury. Chapter 9 examines the nature and requisites of the penalty hearing. Chapter 10 addresses the issue of how the sentencer is to be guided in making the penalty decision.

THE DEATH SQUAD[a]

By Dashka Slater.

For most of us, capital punishment is an issue, a position to take, for or against. But for the people who try these cases, the death penalty is a way of life.

Senior District Attorney Jim Anderson keeps the framed photographs of seven men on the wall of his office. They are not handsome men. Their expressions are grim or fierce, sullen or startled. Six are black, one is white. Only the men's heads are shown in the photographs. Mounted on Anderson's office wall, they look like trophy heads hanging over the mantel of a big-game hunter.

Those are the seven men that Jim Anderson has convinced a jury to sentence to death. The photographs are pasted over the death verdicts, simple typewritten sheets each signed by the jury foreman. "It's nice to think of these people on death row," Anderson says, looking at the photographs. "Each death penalty case costs you a significant part of your life. It's nice thinking maybe they're getting their just desserts."

Anderson has been a district attorney in Alameda County since 1969. In 1980, he prosecuted the county's first capital case after the death penalty was reinstated in California. In the intervening years he has made prosecuting death penalty cases his life's work. So far he's had a total of nine capital cases, and he shows no signs of tiring. "I always said I'd leave this job when it stopped being fun," he says. "So far it's still fun."

Anderson is a tall, balding man with twinkling blue eyes, fair, ruddy skin, and a chuckle that communicates immense self-confidence. He has two passions—death penalty cases and golf, although six-and-a-half years of nearly constant trials have taken their toll on his golf game. Pictures of the seventh, eighth and fourteenth holes at Pebble Beach hang on the wall opposite the seven death verdicts.

"I'm a naturally competitive person," he says. "When I was growing up, I didn't like my twin brother to walk in front of me going down the street—that meant he was winning. Now that I'm old and gray, death penalty work is my competition and I view it as such. This is my game, my arena."

If there's a common thread among people who do death penalty trials, it's this love of competition. A capital trial is the legal equivalent of gladiatorial combat—a literal fight to the death—and it's not surprising that the work attracts adrenaline junkies. There's little to recommend it besides the thrill of battle—the pay, when computed on an hourly basis, is

---

a. © 1992 by Dashka Slater. This article originally appeared in the East Bay Express. Reprinted by permission of the author. The article describes death penalty litigation in Alameda County, California (Oakland and surrounding cities), where both sides are represented by experienced attorneys, and the cases are handled with some care. This situation may not be representative of other jurisdictions.

paltry, and the stress is almost beyond comprehension. The trials are grueling, lasting four to six months on average and requiring another four to six months of preparation. But there's something addicting about an arena in which the consequences are so profound, the emotions are so feverish, and the moral questions so immediate. The death penalty creates a world in which mercy and compassion grapple with outrage and vengeance, in which the ultimate moral choice is not hypothetical. For most of us the death penalty is an issue, a position to take, for or against. But for the people who try these cases, the death penalty is a way of life.

Anderson refers to the seven faces on his office wall as "my boys." He can recite the crimes of each one, recalling the chilling particulars he pounded into the minds of jurors, the details he used to convince them that life imprisonment would not be punishment enough. "This guy," he says, gesturing toward the meaty, dread locked head of Ralph "International" Thomas, "tried to rape a girl, a Grateful Dead follower, and she resisted and her boyfriend resisted and he blew their heads off. This guy, Moochie Welch, took an Uzi and killed a house full of six people, two of them were babies, everyone shot right between the eyes." And so on, down the row of photos. "That's what the death penalty is for," he concludes. "These kind of guys."

Anderson himself seems made for these fights to the death. From the time he was a student at St. Ignatius High School in San Francisco, his identification with law enforcement was so strong that he says it bothered him that Hamilton Burger, the DA on *Perry Mason*, used to lose all the time. He's a staunch conservative who opposes any kind of gun control, thinks executions should be public, and considers himself a Catholic. He describes the men he prosecutes as "sub-humans," and seems comfortable with neatly cleaving humanity into two categories: those who do wrong, and those who do right. Nor does he have any doubt about which group he belongs to. "I think we're doing good," he says. "I really do. I think people like to see bad guys get it. That's just human nature."

Under the California death penalty statute, there are nineteen different "special circumstances" which, when combined with a first-degree murder, mean that a defendant can be sentenced to death. "Special circumstances" are an attempt to codify horror, to write into law the kinds of circumstances that make people cringe and cry out for vengeance. They include murder for financial gain, murder of more than one person, torture murder, murder committed in connection with rape, robbery, burglary, or kidnaping, and murder motivated by racial or religious hatred. The DA's office doesn't add the special circumstances charge every time the crime fits into one of these categories; instead, a committee, on which Anderson sits, decides which cases are best suited for the death penalty. "Do we have a reasonable shot at getting a death penalty is probably the main concern," Anderson says. "And then of course the atrocity of the crime itself."

Capital cases are tried in two phases. First, the jury decides whether the defendant is guilty of the charges. If the defendant is convicted of first-degree murder with special circumstances, the trial moves into the penalty phase, the sole purpose of which is to decide whether the defendant will get "life"—life imprisonment without possibility of parole—or death.

To be accepted as a juror in a death penalty case, you must believe in the death penalty, but Anderson says that even pro-death penalty jurors will hesitate to condemn a person to death without a kick in the pants from the prosecutor. "You've got to believe in the death penalty. 'Cause if you don't believe in it, and really think the guy deserves it, then you're not going to sell it to the jury," he says. "If you don't ram it down their throats, I know what the result's going to be. 'Life without,' no question. I've seen it happen."

Even though he wants them dead, Anderson insists he doesn't hate the men he prosecutes, he just hates what they do. "I guess you just get this inner rage," he says. "Where you think, 'You miserable SOB, you had your day in the sun and now I'm going to have mine.' I don't look at myself as any great savior of the peace of the world, but he's not going to get away with it from my point of view."

Victory, if it comes, is sweet. Anderson says he spends about a week after a death verdict "walking on a cloud." None of his "boys" have been executed yet, but it's not hard to imagine how Anderson will react when they are. "Would I watch an execution?" He asks, echoing my question. "You bet. In fact, we get to go. If one of our persons gets executed, the prosecutor has every right to be there under the law to view his handi-work, so to speak. And I would go—hell, I wouldn't mind going to the next one. 'Cause I saw what happened with a lot of the witnesses there and a lot of them were saying how gross it was that we could take another life. Well, look at the carnage that the defendant left behind if you want to see gross. He was judge, jury, and executioner and now he's had a fair trial. No question I'd go. I'd love it. I would."

He swivels in his chair to cast a glance at the flat, angry faces on the wall, and smiles. It's a smile of a man who is absolutely certain of being right.[b]

Bill Tingle's office is down the hall from Anderson's. It has neither the space nor the view that his colleague's has; he shares it with another deputy district attorney and neither one has put much thought into the decor. The room is bare except for two desks and a tall, overflowing file cabinet. A few cardboard boxes crammed with files are stacked against one wall.

Though Tingle supports capital punishment, he isn't a member of the elite death penalty team. In fact, for most of his fifteen years in the

---

b. In 2004, Anderson retired from the District Attorney's office, having sent 10 defendants to death row, the most by any prosecutor in California history. G. Chapman, *A Passionate Foe of Killers Cedes Stage After 34 Years*, Oakland Tribune, October 7, 2004 at B1.

Alameda County DA's office he wanted nothing to do with death penalty cases. "I'm a black man in America, okay? I know that there are proportionately many more black men in prison than there are in this society. There are reasons for that that have to do with the things these people have done, and there are reasons that have to do with circumstances that they're caught in. Which aren't justifications to maim, murder, and kill, but they give you a context within which to view the conduct of a person and I think that's real important." He pauses, choosing his words carefully. "So many people incarcerated—I can't help but be somewhat moved by that. So coming into this office with that kind of attitude, the idea of participating in a process that might ultimately take any individual's life was very, very scary to me. And I didn't know if I was responsible enough to undertake that."

In June, Tingle finished trying his first death penalty case. He attributes his change of heart more to the conservatism that comes with age than to any sudden shift in point of view. "I'm really, really put off by the kind of inhumane things people do to each other," he says. "And I've come to believe now that some of them are only answerable by the imposition of the ultimate punishment."

The trial was emotionally and physically exhausting. Now sitting at his desk in front of the paperwork for an upcoming four-defendant murder case, Tingle still looks tired. A mustached man with a wary smile, his gaze has a certain weariness to it at the best of times, a weariness that maybe comes from a lifetime of almost fierce self-reliance. One of the first black students to attend Oakland's Crocker Highlands Elementary School, a resident of Castro Valley, a suburb where young rednecks in pickup trucks occasionally find it amusing to yell "nigger" at a black attorney taking an early morning jog, a man for whom becoming a district attorney has meant distancing himself from most of his friends he grew up with in Oakland, Tingle is someone who thrives in the solitary, adversarial arena of the courtroom.

Tingle recalls his first capital case quite clearly: "I remember times when I'd make my first appearances on the case and I couldn't talk. Because I was just locked up inside. As I got into it, my instincts took over, but it took four months to prepare it. And five months to try it. And that's quite a bit of time to live with a case."

The defendant was a man named Cedric Harrison. Harrison had given ten dollars to a woman he knew to buy a rock of crack. When the rock she came back with what turned out to be bunk and a trip to the dealer's house didn't produce a refund, Harrison led the woman and her husband into an alley and killed them. Later, he told the story of what happened to his best friend, even displaying a newspaper clipping about the murder. But after a week, Harrison began to regret the confidence, so he took the friend into the Oakland hills and tried to kill as well, succeeding in blowing off half his face. It was not a case likely to make Tingle reconsider his position on the death penalty.

"This man threatened two witnesses while in custody," Tingle says, ticking off the defendant's crimes on his fingers. "He had a prior conviction for a robbery and while he was on probation for that, he participated in a gang rape of a teenager. We had him in possession of deadly weapons in prison—shanks, stabbing devices. This man is completely without redemption and there was nothing left for him. I believe, and will always believe, that he's what the death penalty is here for."

Tingle usually goes running every morning at 5:30. During the trial, he was too exhausted. Often he worked through lunch, going back to the office during the noon recess. The only break he took was in the early evening, after court was finished for the day. "I'd go home, say hi to my kids, kiss my wife, and then I'd go out in the yard," he says. "I grow vegetables and that stabilized me during the trial. I would work for a couple of hours in the garden, come in and eat dinner and work until one, two, or three o'clock in the morning. Whatever it took. I hate coffee and I was drinking a pot a night. I had to do it, though. For what you're asking a jury to do, you damn well better be prepared."

It wasn't just the time commitment that made the trial different from any other case he'd tried. The relationships he formed with the victims and their families were deeper, more complicated, and ultimately longer-lasting. He grew particularly close to the defendant's erstwhile best friend, the man who was shot in the face so he wouldn't be able to implicate his buddy. "I'll have a life-long relationship with him," Tingle says. "Because I have a lot of respect for his ability to get out of the lifestyle he was in. You see, he had to testify about the kind of house he used to live in and how he ruined his family because of his use of cocaine. How it got him involved with this nut who tried to kill him. He's a strong man, a good man. I don't know anybody who's had a perfect life. So you see, I can't judge. There but for the grace of God go I."

"There but for the grace of God" is a phrase uttered more often by defense attorneys than by DAs. But Tingle points out that in lots of crimes the victims are not so very different from the defendants. "Flip a coin," he says. "Many times, the defendant is the one who got off the first shot. To me, it's all a circle. We're all potential victims."

The jury convicted Cedric Harrison of all charges, but hung on the question of punishment, with ten jurors voting for death, two for life without possibility of parole. Tingle will be retrying the penalty phase of the case early next year. He says he'll be ready for it, if he can only get a little rest beforehand.

"But I'll tell you something that I believe in my heart," he says quietly. "When I walked into the courtroom and started that case, that was one thing. But when I finished it and walked out of that courtroom for the last time, I left something behind that I'll never find again inside myself. I don't know how to put it into words. I'm still trying to come to grips with it."

"What was it you left behind?" I ask.

Tingle sighs and considers the question carefully. "I don't know," he says at last. "I'm a lot more serious now. I had to do that case with a raised consciousness to deal with the personal and professional issues, and once I did that I found that I had aged. It just made me more sensitized to life. And death."

Alex Selvin was an Alameda County prosecutor for fifteen years. Now he's a defense lawyer, one of about twenty private lawyers who handle death penalty cases for the county when the public defender's office is unable to do so. He's defended seven capital cases in the last seven years; he also prosecuted two as a DA. There was no change of philosophy behind the crossover, Selvin says—he just wanted to go into private practice. "I've always thought of myself as a trial lawyer," he says. "If you're a trial lawyer it's my philosophy that you can try a case for the people or for the defendant."

Selvin shares a suite of offices with four other "special circumstances attorneys" in an elegant old building in a down-at-the-heels section of downtown Oakland. Tall—he went to Cal on a basketball scholarship—and gray-haired, he speaks in quiet measured tones except when making a point, when he leans across his desk and spears me with a pair of intent brown eyes. He says he does death penalty work because it's the most interesting and complex wing of criminal law, and has the highest stakes in the game. He laughs when I ask about the pay. "I could make more money doing driving-under-the-influence cases," he says. "If money were my only interest, I'd do white-collar crime. I enjoy this kind of thing."

Selvin is a philosophical man. His parents were Orthodox Jews, but he is not religious. "I believe in good, bad, right, wrong," he says. Still having worked the death penalty from both sides, he's never been able to decide how he feels about it. "I guess my feeling is something like this," he says, swiveling to reach the can of Diet Coke near the edge of his mammoth desk. "If there were not a death penalty, that would be fine with me. But there is a death penalty and perhaps, perhaps in certain cases, it may be valid."

Having done both, Selvin says it's harder to defend a death penalty case than it is to prosecute one. The difference, he says, is in the interpersonal relationships. By the time a death penalty case goes to trial, Selvin and the defendant have known each other for years. Selvin has learned everything he can about the other man's life, sometimes more than the defendant wants him to know. "I've had clients just tell me to stop," he says, and pauses, almost whispering the next word. "Stop. You're going too far." He breaks off, searching for a way to describe the discomfiture these men feel as he relentlessly digs through their pasts, trying to convince a jury to spare their lives. "Like most people, their real lives are not as projected. Our real lives have a lot of failings." In a death penalty case everything must be exposed, the childhood sexual abuse, the alcoholic mother, the bad grades, the failed love affairs, everything.

People facing the death penalty go through enormous emotional changes, huge rushes of optimism, long periods of impatience and gloom as they wait for their trial date to come, and then spurts of panic as the verdict approaches. They may mistrust their lawyer, argue over strategy. Selvin visits his clients once a week and talks to them on the phone in between, sometimes about the case, sometimes just listening to complaints about life in prison. "It's important for you to know what's going on because there are things that can come back to haunt you. If they get into altercations with other prisoners, or with guards, that can be used as evidence against them in the penalty phase," he says.

When he's in trial, Selvin usually wakes up at 3:30 or 4:00 a.m., his mind already sifting through the case. It's useless to try to sleep, so he goes into his kitchen, makes himself a cup of tea, and works until sunrise, when he gets dressed and goes to the office. Court starts at 9 and goes until around 4:30. Afterwards it's back to the office to catch up on paperwork and talk over the case with his co-counsel until 6 or 6:30. Sleep, not surprisingly, comes early. "You have a love-hate relationship with this kind of work," he says. "You love the high, the enjoyment, all the things that you can get. You hate what it takes away from the rest of your life, the effect it has on your family, your children."

Then, at last, the trial is over. Waiting for the verdict, Selvin says he fidgets and drinks even more Cokes than usual. Work is impossible. He says the few minutes between the time the clerk calls to say the jury has a verdict and the time the verdict is read are the worst. "Inside you feel like you're going to break, just tear apart," he says. "I don't think I've had more anxiety over anything than in those minutes."

Anytime you don't get a death verdict, it's a miracle, Selvin says, because the DA's office only charges special circumstances in cases where the evidence is strong and the crimes are horrifying. Complete acquittals are rare—Selvin has never had one. Usually what it comes down to is "life" or death.

If the verdict is life without possibility of parole, often the client keeps in touch for a while and then fades away. Selvin frequently likes his clients and says that often, if you took the man out of the setting he was in, the crime would never have happened. But once the intensity of the trial relationship is over, things change. "You can look at these people like your high school friends," he says. "You have some high school friends and then life goes on, your life changes, their life changes and you lose contact."

And what if the verdict is death? "It's upsetting. This person isn't just the person named in the complaint. You've known them sometimes four or five years. This is a person who you've interacted with—him and his life. It's impossible not to feel bad, regardless about how you feel philosophically about the death penalty or the case."

So how do you convince a jury to save a life? Selvin shakes his head. "If I knew that," he says, "I'd be the one they all wanted." It's the million-dollar question, the mystery that lawyers who defend capital crimes debate the way alchemists once debated the secret of transmuting base metals into gold. The jurors, by definition, all believe in the death penalty. By the time the jury reaches the trial's penalty phase, they've been convinced that the defendant has committed a terrible, shocking crime. How do you convince them that he or she should be spared? "It's a difficult thing," Selvin says, gaze intent. "It's a very difficult type of thing."

Each defense lawyer gets asked the same question. Barry Morris figures he gets asked it by maybe 95 percent of the people he meets. "How can you represent someone who's guilty?" they ask.

"If they're guilty it's easy," he replies. "It's when they're innocent that it's difficult. Because if they're guilty, whatever you do for them is wonderful. But if they're innocent, s___, you've got to get them off."

Like Selvin, Morris is a private attorney who takes on capital cases that are farmed out by the public defender's office. He also does death penalty appeals. A brawny amateur bodybuilder with longish brown hair and an earring in one ear, Morris is not exactly your tasseled-loafer type of lawyer. But listening to him tell stories about the cases he's tried, it's easy to see how bewitching he must be to a jury. It was TV shows like *The Defenders* and *Perry Mason* and movies like *Inherit the Wind* that drew him to criminal law, and he has never allowed the work to degenerate into a dry recitation of facts.

It's the details that he enjoys telling. Not just that his first death penalty client, one Freddie Lee White, murdered four drug dealers in the course of a summer-long crime spree in 1978, but that he did so while he and his girlfriend Nelise Coleman were living in the London Lodge motel, across the street from the Oakland police station. Not just that one of the murders took place in a West Oakland shooting gallery, but that the owner of the shooting gallery was a forty-year-old woman who looked ninety and that she, Freddie, Nelise, and the victim were sharing a syringe of methamphetamines with two six-foot-tall black transvestites when the murder took place. "It's really unclear what the motivating thing was," Morris recalls. "But Freddie apparently decided that this guy wasn't passing the needle along quick enough and shot him in both arms. That didn't kill him, but Freddie hogtied him, and the guy kept struggling and Nelise kept saying, 'He's making noise.' So Freddie took a five-pound dumbbell weight and smashed him over the head a bunch of times. Then he wrapped the body in a carpet and put it in a car trunk in July or August to rot until somebody passing noticed liquid dripping out of the car and an awful stench. The pictures are terrible, I mean the guy was unrecognizable as a human being."

It was not an easy case to try. Not only was Freddie White arrested with the gun in hand, but Nelise Coleman also pled guilty to second-degree murder and became a witness against him. "This is what's known as a *very* dead case," Morris says with a small laugh. The defense was that

White had been lead astray by Coleman and by drugs; before the summer of '78 he had never been arrested for anything more violent than passing bad checks. The jury ended up convicting White of three of the four murders but stopped short of imposing the death penalty. "I knew I had some impact in my closing argument when the judge went into instructions and his voice cracked," Morris says. "He was a gruff old guy, so I knew I'd reached somebody." Still, it took the jury three torturous days to make its decision. Every time the jurors came into the courtroom to ask a question or have testimony read back to them, one juror, a teamster who had said during the jury selection that he watched PBS would look at Morris and wink. It was maddening. Was that the wink of a friend or an executioner? It turned out that it was the winking teamster who led the charge for letting Freddie Lee White live.

Morris tries to make his closing argument in the penalty phase of the death penalty trial as emotional as possible. He likes to quote from Portia's speech in *The Merchant of Venice*:

> The quality of mercy is not strain'd It droppeth as the gentle rain from heaven Upon the place beneath: it is twice bless'd It blesseth him that gives and him that takes...

He brings the technical arguments in, too, rebuttals of the prosecutor's arguments, mitigating evidence, but Morris says that all of that is just to give the juries an intellectual justification for a decision they've reached for emotional reasons. "So it sort of has to be a seamless web," he explains. "It can't be too long, and the way I have it structured there's sort of like a coda at the end where I bring it all together and plead for mercy."

It's the kind of performance that has more than an Oscar riding on it. The penalty phase of every death penalty trial is like a scene from *The Perils of Pauline*—the defendant is tied to the railroad tracks, the train is bearing down on him, and somehow the lawyer has to pluck him from the jaws of death using only words and the power of persuasion. So you can imagine Morris's reaction when, just as he reached the coda of his closing argument in the penalty phase of one particularly long and complicated death penalty case, his client passed a note to the judge that caused the whole speech to be interrupted. The judged asked the jury to leave the room and then presented Morris with the note. It said that the defendant wanted him fired.

The judge denied the motion, the jury was called back in, and Morris managed to swallow his fury and finish the argument, although with perhaps a little less enthusiasm than he'd had previously. "The jury came back in an hour and a half and I figured, well, I've heard everything, I guess I can listen to a death sentence," Morris says and then pauses: "You know, when you do trials the longest five seconds in the whole world is, 'We the jury, in the above entitled case find the defendant ...' "

The verdict was life without possibility of parole. "I was totally amazed," Morris says. "It turned out that the jury basically liked him, and they had a certain lingering doubt about the conviction and so they gave him life."

Death penalty appeals don't allow for this kind of inadvertent theatrics, but they have a drama of their own. An appeal is a puzzle, a gargantuan maze made out of paper. Appellate lawyers sleuth through the transcript of the original trial, sniffing out legal errors. Morris's most recent appeal brief was 350 pages long; the trial transcript he worked from was 10,000 pages. "See that?" he says, pointing to a four-drawer filing cabinet in one corner of his office. "That's the record for one capital appeal."

A lengthy discussion of judicial errors doesn't have quite the emotional impact of Portia's speech from *The Merchant of Venice*. On the other hand, every level of appeal brings the client one step closer to the gas chamber, and that adds about as much drama to the process as any admirer of the theater could possibly want. "There's an immediacy that trial lawyers don't deal with, namely, *I may be the guy*. I ran across a guy in Mississippi who was literally walking with his client to the gas chamber." Morris shakes his head, "I don't want to do that."

One afternoon when I was sitting in on a death penalty trial, and an investigator from the DA's office commented to me that you don't know how you feel about the death penalty until you have to make the decision yourself. I ask Morris if his feelings have changed over twelve years of death penalty trials and eleven years of appeals. "I still think the death penalty is unnecessary," he says. "I mean, I think that putting people in prison for the rest of their lives without parole is not only a worse punishment, it's certainly adequate to protect society." But he admits that his opposition has moderated a little over time. "Sometimes when I read death penalty opinions and I read the statement of the facts," he says, "the crime is so awful that even though I myself am opposed to the death penalty, if the jury gave the person the death penalty I can't say I'm angry about it. But that hasn't changed my feeling that we don't need a death penalty and we could get along just fine without one."

      * * *

The penalty phase of a death penalty trial is an odd sort of moral battleground in which the worth of the defendant is debated by the two attorneys. The prosecutor presents evidence that shows that the defendant is violent and heartless—evidence of previous crimes, for example, or testimony about fights he may have had in prison. The defense lawyers try to show the defendant's good side, using the testimony of teachers, friends, and family, or they may bring in experts to explain to the jury how he became the way he is. Once, when I was sitting in on the penalty phase of the trial of a man convicted of several brutal drug-related murders, I had an investigator from the DA's office turn to me and scoff, "They've had the guy's high school football coach and his fourth grade teacher in here. Who are we going to have next, his mother's Lamaze coach?"

Susan Sawyer is the penalty phase coordinator for the Alameda County public defender's office. It is her job to prepare the evidence that will be used in the penalty phase of every capital case handled by the PD's office. "I think of myself as kind of a biographer," she says. "Ideally I'd like to be able to do a time line from birth to the present day in as much detail as I can."

Sawyer reconstructs her client's histories by interviewing people who have known them—teachers, family members, friends—and by pouring over medical, school, prison, and military records—anything that will help her understand how the defendant got to the edge of the precipice he stands on now. After working on some thirty capital cases, she's found that certain common threads run through the lives of these men. "We jokingly call this unit the dysfunctional family unit," she says. "Some of these families read like soap operas. And this is just anecdotal, but we see a lot of brain damage—from fetal alcohol syndrome, from drugs, from head traumas."

Sawyer has thick brown hair and a voice that tends to get softer rather than louder with emotion. She's been a public defender since 1976 and was the first woman in Alameda County to defend a death penalty case. We talk the day before she leaves for Belgium, where she and her husband are going to watch the Grand Prix. She looks ready for vacation, although you probably wouldn't peg her for a Formula One racing fan. Life in the office has been rough lately; two death verdicts have come in, and both were men she thought could be saved. One, a man named Thomas Walker, was awaiting a trial for his second murder when he tried to commit suicide. He was brought to Highland Hospital and managed to escape, eventually making his way to Arizona, where he joined a drug and alcohol rehabilitation program. "He'd been there for some time when he was put on *America's Most Wanted*, and they recognized who he was and he was arrested," Sawyer explains. "But all the people in the program liked him and felt he was sincere in his attempts to turn his life around. While he was in custody awaiting trial he was very involved in doing things in the jail through various Christian ministries. He seemed to be someone who had something to offer in prison and really felt very remorseful, did those things that you'd want someone to do who has done something wrong—try to clear up his life and change direction. And he did that when he didn't need to—I mean when he was escaping; he could have gone anywhere. So that was a hard one."

Most of the people think of the people who commit capital crimes as the worst of the worst, the absolute rock bottom of society. But Sawyer doesn't see it that way. "When I think of my death penalty clients in comparison to a lot of the people I've represented who are just your run-of-the-mill felons, I don't see them as being the worst of the worst," she says. "Many of the cases—I'd say most of them—are not cold-blooded situations. A lot of them just seem to be situations of panic by people who are very unsophisticated and who happen to have a gun. If you asked me,

'Are these people any more evil than other people who commit crimes?' I would have to say no."

Sawyer is against the death penalty, not out of the absolutist feeling that vengeance is wrong, but because she feels that it is impossible to administer the death penalty fairly. Innocent people do get executed. People who kill whites are given the death penalty more often than people who kill blacks. Her voice drifts down to a whisper when I ask how she thinks she'll feel when one of her clients is executed. "I'd rather not think about it," she says.

Of course, not every client wants to live. Sawyer says that often when she goes to meet with clients right after they've been charged, they aren't particularly interested in talking about their past. They want to focus on the future—on not getting convicted. "If it ends up being a choice between dying and spending the rest of my life in prison," they say, "I'd rather die anyway." But death penalty cases take years to go to trial, and defendants have plenty of time to get used to prison life. By the time the question gets put to the jury, they usually want to live.

So what will convince the jury to spare the defendant's life? "You can't do too much," Sawyer says. "You need to examine every single thing about a client's life and present it to the jury. Sometimes you think, 'Will the grandmother who raised him be too hokey?' Maybe eleven jurors will find it hokey, but it might persuade one. Do I put on an artist to say that my guy's paintings in jail are pretty good or will they think that's too hokey? Nothing should be left out, because maybe one juror will think, 'Okay, this guy's an artist, he deserves to live.' "

But often, the jury isn't moved by the artist or the grandmother or the expert who testified about the long-term effects of childhood abuse. * * * Too often, outrage overwhelms compassion.

Even after it's all over, Sawyer says, these cases don't go away. Sometimes she wakes up in the middle of the night thinking about a case she tried, and lost years ago. "I have to say that I'm giving some thought to maybe taking a break from this job," she says quietly. "Because it is hard. It's very anxiety producing work. And it's very emotionally hard to have been involved in a case and have a jury decide death."

CHAPTER 6

SELECTING THE JURY

■ ■ ■

The Supreme Court has held that constitutional rights are implicated at four different stages of the jury selection process: (1) at the selection of the jury venire, where the Sixth Amendment requires that the venire represent a "fair cross section" of the community (see, *e.g., Taylor v. Louisiana*, 419 U.S. 522, 95 S.Ct. 692 (1975)); (2) at the *voir dire* of the potential jurors, where the Sixth Amendment right to an impartial jury may require that the defense be permitted to question on certain subjects (see, *e.g., Turner v. Murray*, set out below); (3) when jurors are challenged for cause and the right to an impartial jury may be implicated (see, *e.g., Witherspoon v. Illinois*, set out below); and (4) when jurors are peremptorily challenged and their equal protection rights may be violated (see, *e.g., Miller–El v. Dretke*, set out below). The cases in Section A involve "death-qualification" of the jury, *i.e.*, challenging jurors for cause based on their death penalty views. The cases in Section B concern the issue of race in the jury selection process.

A. "DEATH QUALIFICATION"

The three cases in this section all concern the question whether the defendant's constitutional rights are violated when the court excuses for cause potential jurors who have expressed feelings against the death penalty. Although the defendants made "fair cross section" challenges to the jury selection, the Court finds that right inapplicable and instead addresses the defendants' main argument—that excluding potential jurors with feelings against the death penalty denied the defendants an impartial jury. In *Witherspoon v. Illinois*, the state excluded jurors with "conscientious scruples" against the death penalty, and the Court has to decide whether that exclusion violated the defendant's rights, and, if so, whether the exclusion affected only the penalty determination, or the guilt determination as well. *Uttecht v. Brown* is the Court's most recent case elaborating on *Witherspoon*. In *Lockhart v. McCree*, the Court addresses the defendant's argument that excusing jurors who cannot be impartial on the issue of the death penalty inevitably creates a jury that is biased on the issue of guilt.

WITHERSPOON v. ILLINOIS

391 U.S. 510, 88 S.Ct. 1770, 20 L.Ed.2d 776 (1968).

MR. JUSTICE STEWART delivered the opinion of the Court.

The petitioner was brought to trial in 1960 in Cook County, Illinois, upon a charge of murder. The jury found him guilty and fixed his penalty at death. At the time of his trial an Illinois statute provided:

> "In trials for murder it shall be a cause for challenge of any juror who shall, on being examined, state that he has conscientious scruples against capital punishment, or that he is opposed to the same."

Through this provision the State of Illinois armed the prosecution with unlimited challenges for cause in order to exclude those jurors who, in the words of the State's highest court, "might hesitate to return a verdict inflicting [death]."[2] At the petitioner's trial, the prosecution eliminated nearly half the venire of prospective jurors by challenging, under the authority of this statute, any venireman who expressed qualms about capital punishment. From those who remained were chosen the jurors who ultimately found the petitioner guilty and sentenced him to death. The Supreme Court of Illinois denied post-conviction relief, and we granted certiorari to decide whether the Constitution permits a State to execute a man pursuant to the verdict of a jury so composed.

I

The issue before us is a narrow one. It does not involve the right of the prosecution to challenge for cause those prospective jurors who state that their reservations about capital punishment would prevent them from making an impartial decision as to the defendant's guilt.[5] Nor does it involve the State's assertion of a right to exclude from the jury in a capital case those who say that they could never vote to impose the death penalty or that they would refuse even to consider its imposition in the case before them. For the State of Illinois did not stop there, but authorized the prosecution to exclude as well all who said that they were opposed to capital punishment and all who indicated that they had conscientious scruples against inflicting it.

In the present case the tone was set when the trial judge said early in the *voir dire*, "Let's get these conscientious objectors out of the way,

---

2. "In the trial of the case where capital punishment may be inflicted a juror who has religious or conscientious scruples against capital punishment *might hesitate to return a verdict inflicting such punishment*, and in the present proceedings (a post-sentence sanity hearing) a juror having such scruples might like-wise hesitate in returning a verdict finding [the defendant] sane, which in effect confirms the death sentence." *People v. Carpenter*, 150 N.E.2d 100 (Ill.1958). (Emphasis added.)

5. Unlike the statutory provision in this case, statutes and rules disqualifying jurors with scruples against capital punishment are often couched in terms of reservations against finding a man guilty when the penalty might be death. Yet, despite such language, courts in other States have sometimes permitted the exclusion for cause of jurors opposed to the death penalty even in the absence of a showing that their scruples would have interfered with their ability to determine guilt in accordance with the evidence and the law.

without wasting any time on them." In rapid succession, 47 veniremen were successfully challenged for cause on the basis of their attitudes toward the death penalty. Only five of the 47 explicitly stated that under no circumstances would they vote to impose capital punishment.[6] Six said that they did not "believe in the death penalty" and were excused without any attempt to determine whether they could nonetheless return a verdict of death.[7] Thirty-nine veniremen, including four of the six who indicated that they did not believe in capital punishment, acknowledged having "conscientious or religious scruples against the infliction of the death penalty" or against its infliction "in a proper case" and were excluded without any effort to find out whether their scruples would invariably compel them to vote against capital punishment.

Only one venireman who admitted to a religious or conscientious scruple against the infliction of the death penalty in a proper case was examined at any length. She was asked: "You don't believe in the death penalty?" She replied: "No. It's just I wouldn't want to be responsible." The judge admonished her not to forget her "duty as a citizen" and again asked her whether she had "a religious or conscientious scruple" against capital punishment. This time, she replied in the negative. Moments later, however, she repeated that she would not "like to be responsible for * * * deciding somebody should be put to death." Evidently satisfied that this elaboration of the prospective juror's views disqualified her under the Illinois statute, the judge told her to "step aside."[9]

II

The petitioner contends that a State cannot confer upon a jury selected in this matter the power to determine guilt. He maintains that such a jury, unlike one chosen at random from a cross section of the community, must necessarily be biased in favor of conviction, for the kind of juror who would be unperturbed by the prospect of sending a man to his death, he contends, is the kind of juror who would too readily ignore the presumption of the defendant's innocence, accept the prosecution's version of the facts, and return a verdict of guilt. To support this view, the

6. The State stresses the fact that the judge who presided during the *voir dire* implied several times that only those jurors who could never agree to a verdict of death should deem themselves disqualified because of their scruples against capital punishment. The record shows, however, that the remarks relied upon by the State were not made within the hearing of every venireman ultimately excused for cause under the statute. On the contrary, three separate venires were called into the courtroom, and it appears that at least 30 of the 47 veniremen eliminated in this case were not even present when the statements in question were made.

7. It is entirely possible, of course, that even a juror who believes that capital punishment should never be inflicted and who is irrevocably committed to its abolition could nonetheless subordinate his personal views to what he perceived to be his duty to abide by his oath as a juror and to obey the law of the State.

9. As the *voir dire* examination of this venireman illustrates, it cannot be assumed that a juror who describes himself as having "conscientious or religious scruples" against the infliction of the death penalty or against its infliction "in a proper case" thereby affirmed that he could never vote in favor of it or that he would not consider doing so in the case before him. * * *

* * * Unless a venireman states unambiguously that he would automatically vote against the imposition of capital punishment no matter what the trial might reveal, it simply cannot be assumed that that is his position.

petitioner refers to what he describes as "competent scientific evidence that death-qualified jurors are partial to the prosecution on the issue of guilt or innocence."[10]

The data adduced by the petitioner, however, are too tentative and fragmentary to establish that jurors not opposed to the death penalty tend to favor the prosecution in the determination of guilt. We simply cannot conclude, either on the basis of the record now before us or as a matter of judicial notice, that the exclusion of jurors opposed to capital punishment results in an unrepresentative jury on the issue of guilt or substantially increases the risk of conviction. In light of the presently available information, we are not prepared to announce a *per se* constitutional rule requiring the reversal of every conviction returned by a jury selected as this one was.

III

It does not follow, however, that the petitioner is entitled to no relief. For in this case the jury was entrusted with two distinct responsibilities: first, to determine whether the petitioner was innocent or guilty; and second, if guilty, to determine whether his sentence should be imprisonment or death. It has not been shown that this jury was biased with respect to the petitioner's guilt. But it is self-evident that, in its role as arbiter of the punishment to be imposed, this jury fell woefully short of that impartiality to which the petitioner was entitled under the Sixth and Fourteenth Amendments.

The only justification the State has offered for the jury-selection technique it employed here is that individuals who express serious reservations about capital punishment cannot be relied upon to vote for it even when the laws of the State and the instructions of the trial judge would make death the proper penalty. But in Illinois, as in other States, the jury is given broad discretion to decide whether or not death is "the proper penalty" in a given case, and a juror's general views about capital punishment play an inevitable role in any such decision.

A man who opposes the death penalty, no less than one who favors it, can make the discretionary judgment entrusted to him by the State and can thus obey the oath he takes as a juror. But a jury from which all such men have been excluded cannot perform the task demanded of it. Guided by neither rule nor standard, "free to select or reject as it [sees] fit," a jury that must choose between life imprisonment and capital punishment can do little more—and must do nothing less—than express the conscience of the community on the ultimate question of life or death.[15] Yet, in a

---

10. In his brief, the petitioner cites two surveys, one involving 187 college students and the other involving 200 college students. In his petition for certiorari, he cited a study based upon interviews with 1,248 jurors in New York and Chicago. A preliminary, unpublished summary of the results of that study stated that "a jury consisting only of jurors who have no scruples against the death penalty is likely to be more prosecution prone than a jury on which objectors to the death penalty sit," and that "the defendant's chances of acquittal are somewhat reduced if the objectors are excluded from the jury."

15. It is suggested in a dissenting opinion today that the State of Illinois might "impose a particular penalty, including death, on all persons convicted of certain crimes." But Illinois has

nation less than half of whose people believe in the death penalty,[16] a jury composed exclusively of such people cannot speak for the community. Culled of all who harbor doubts about the wisdom of capital punishment—of all who would be reluctant to pronounce the extreme penalty—such a jury can speak only for a distinct and dwindling minority.

If the State had excluded only those prospective jurors who stated in advance of trial that they would not even consider returning a verdict of death, it could argue that the resulting jury was simply "neutral" with respect to penalty.[18] But when it swept from the jury all who expressed conscientious or religious scruples against capital punishment and all who opposed it in principle, the State crossed the line of neutrality. In its quest for a jury capable of imposing the death penalty, the State produced a jury uncommonly willing to condemn a man to die.

It is, of course, settled that a State may not entrust the determination of whether a man is innocent or guilty to a tribunal "organized to convict." *Fay v. People of State of New York*, 332 U.S. 261, 67 S.Ct. 1613 (1947). It requires but a short step from that principle to hold, as we do today, that a State may not entrust the determination of whether a man should live or die to a tribunal organized to return a verdict of death. Specifically, we hold that a sentence of death cannot be carried out if the jury that imposed or recommended it was chosen by excluding veniremen for cause simply because they voiced general objections to the death penalty or expressed conscientious or religious scruples against its infliction.[21] No defendant can constitutionally be put to death at the hands of a tribunal so selected.

---

attempted no such thing. Nor has it defined a category of capital cases in which "death [is] the *preferred* penalty." *People v. Bernette*, 197 N.E.2d 436 (Ill. 1964). Instead, it has deliberately "made * * * the death penalty * * * an optional form of punishment which 'the jury remains' free to select or reject as it [sees] fit." And one of the most important functions any jury can perform in making such a selection is to maintain a link between contemporary community values and the penal system—a link without which the determination of punishment would hardly reflect "the evolving standards of decency that mark the progress of a maturing society." *Trop v. Dulles*, 356 U.S. 86, 78 S.Ct. 590 (opinion of THE CHIEF JUSTICE, joined by MR. JUSTICE BLACK, MR. JUSTICE DOUGLAS, and MR. JUSTICE WHITTAKER).

16. It appears that, in 1966, approximately 42% of the American public favored capital punishment for convicted murderers, while 47% opposed it and 11% were undecided. In 1960, the comparable figures were 51% in favor, 36% opposed, and 13% undecided.

18. Even so, a defendant convicted by such a jury in some future case might still attempt to establish that the jury was less than neutral with respect to guilt. If he were to succeed in that effort, the question would then arise whether the State's interest in submitting the penalty issue to a jury capable of imposing capital punishment may be vindicated at the expense of the defendant's interest in a completely fair determination of guilt or innocence—given the possibility of accommodating both interests by means of a bifurcated trial, using one jury to decide guilt and another to fix punishment. That problem is not presented here, however, and we intimate no view as to its proper resolution.

21. Just as veniremen cannot be excluded for cause on the ground that they hold such views, so too they cannot be excluded for cause simply because they indicate that there are some kinds of cases in which they would refuse to recommend capital punishment. And a prospective juror cannot be expected to say in advance of trial whether he would in fact vote for the extreme penalty in the case before him. The most that can be demanded of a venireman in this regard is that he be willing to consider all of the penalties provided by state law, and that he not be irrevocably committed, before the trial has begun, to vote against the penalty of death regardless of the facts and circumstances that might emerge in the course of the proceedings. If the *voir dire*

Whatever else might be said of capital punishment, it is at least clear that its imposition by a hanging jury cannot be squared with the Constitution. The State of Illinois has stacked the deck against the petitioner. To execute this death sentence would deprive him of his life without due process of law.

[JUSTICE DOUGLAS wrote separately to state his opinion that the right to a jury drawn from a fair cross section of the community requires the inclusion of people who are so opposed to capital punishment that they would never inflict it on a defendant. JUSTICE BLACK, joined by JUSTICES HARLAN and WHITE, dissented on the grounds that the statute was designed to insure an impartial jury by excluding people who are biased as to one of the critical issues in the case.]

UTTECHT v. BROWN

551 U.S. 1, 127 S.Ct. 2218, 167 L.Ed.2d 1014 (2007).

JUSTICE KENNEDY delivered the opinion of the Court.

Respondent Cal Coburn Brown robbed, raped, tortured, and murdered one woman in Washington. Two days later, he robbed, raped, tortured, and attempted to murder a second woman in California. Apprehended, Brown confessed to these crimes and pleaded guilty to the California offenses, for which he received a sentence of life imprisonment. The State of Washington, however, sought the death penalty and brought Brown to trial. Based on the jury's verdicts in the guilt and sentencing phases of the trial, Brown was sentenced to death. His conviction and sentence were affirmed by the Supreme Court of the State of Washington.

[Brown filed a petition for habeas corpus in the United States District Court. The District Court denied relief, but the Court of Appeals reversed finding that the exclusion for cause of Juror Z was unconstitutional under *Witherspoon v. Illinois,* 391 U.S. 510, 88 S.Ct. 1770 (1968).]

I

When considering the controlling precedents, *Witherspoon* is not the final word, but it is a necessary starting point. During the *voir dire* that preceded William Witherspoon's capital trial, the prosecution succeeded in removing a substantial number of jurors based on their general scruples against inflicting the death penalty. The State challenged, and the trial court excused for cause, 47 members of the 96–person venire, without

---

testimony in a given case indicates that veniremen were excluded on any broader basis than this, the death sentence cannot be carried out even if applicable statutory or case law in the relevant jurisdiction would appear to support only a narrower ground of exclusion. See nn. 5 and 9, *supra.* We repeat, however, that nothing we say today bears upon the power of a State to execute a defendant sentenced to death by a jury from which the only veniremen who were in fact excluded for cause were those who made unmistakably clear (1) that they would automatically vote against the imposition of capital punishment without regard to any evidence that might be developed at the trial of the case before them, or (2) that their attitude toward the death penalty would prevent them from making an impartial decision as to the defendant's guilt. Nor does the decision in this case affect the validity of any sentence other than one of death. Nor, finally, does today's holding render invalid the conviction, as opposed to the sentence, in this or any other case.

significant examination of the individual prospective jurors. The Court held that the systematic removal of those in the venire opposed to the death penalty had led to a jury "uncommonly willing to condemn a man to die" and thus "woefully short of that impartiality to which the petitioner was entitled under the Sixth and Fourteenth Amendments." Because "[a] man who opposes the death penalty, no less than one who favors it, can make the discretionary judgment entrusted to him by the State," the Court held that "a sentence of death cannot be carried out if the jury that imposed or recommended it was chosen by excluding veniremen for cause simply because they voiced general objections to the death penalty." The Court also set forth, in dicta in a footnote [n.21], a strict standard for when an individual member of the venire may be removed for cause on account of his or her views on the death penalty.

In *Wainwright v. Witt,* 469 U.S. 412, 105 S.Ct. 844 (1985), the Court explained that "*Witherspoon* is best understood in the context of its facts." The Court noted that in *Witherspoon* the trial court had excused half the venire—every juror with conscientious objections to capital punishments. Furthermore, the state sentencing scheme under which Witherspoon's sentence was imposed permitted the jury "unlimited discretion in choice of sentence." When a juror is given unlimited discretion, the Court explained, all he or she must do to follow instructions is consider the death penalty, even if in the end he or she would not be able to impose it. Rejecting the strict standard found in *Witherspoon's* footnote 21, the Court recognized that the diminished discretion now given to capital jurors and the State's interest in administering its capital punishment scheme called for a different standard. The Court relied on *Adams v. Texas,* 448 U.S. 38, 100 S.Ct. 2521 (1980), which provided the following standard: "[W]hether the juror's views would prevent or substantially impair the performance of his duties as a juror in accordance with his instructions and his oath."

The Court in *Witt* instructed that, in applying this standard, reviewing courts are to accord deference to the trial court. Deference is owed regardless of whether the trial court engages in explicit analysis regarding substantial impairment; even the granting of a motion to excuse for cause constitutes an implicit finding of bias. The judgment as to "whether a veniremen is biased ... is based upon determinations of demeanor and credibility that are peculiarly within a trial judge's province. Such determinations [are] entitled to deference even on direct review; the respect paid such findings in a habeas proceeding certainly should be no less." And the finding may be upheld even in the absence of clear statements from the juror that he or she is impaired because "many veniremen simply cannot be asked enough questions to reach the point where their bias has been made 'unmistakably clear'; these veniremen may not know how they will react when faced with imposing the death sentence, or may be unable to articulate, or may wish to hide their true feelings." Thus, when there is ambiguity in the prospective juror's statements, "the trial court, aided as it undoubtedly [is] by its assessment of [the venireman's] demeanor, [is] entitled to resolve it in favor of the State."

[In *Darden v. Wainwright,* 477 U.S. 168, 106 S.Ct. 2464 (1986), the Court, reinforcing the rule of deference, found no error in the exclusion of a juror, who gave an ambiguous answer to one question and was not questioned further, because the defense did not object and the trial judge had the benefit of being able to judge the juror's demeanor. In *Gray v. Mississippi,* 481 U.S. 648, 107 S.Ct. 2045 (1987), the Court found reversible error in the exclusion of a single juror where the prosecution was engaged in a "systematic" attempt to eliminate "every juror who expressed any degree of uncertainty in the ability to cast ... a vote for the death penalty" and, on appeal, the state court justices agreed that the juror could not be excused for cause.]

These precedents establish at least four principles of relevance here. First, a criminal defendant has the right to an impartial jury drawn from a venire that has not been tilted in favor of capital punishment by selective prosecutorial challenges for cause. Second, the State has a strong interest in having jurors who are able to apply capital punishment within the framework state law prescribes. Third, to balance these interests, a juror who is substantially impaired in his or her ability to impose the death penalty under the state-law framework can be excused for cause; but if the juror is not substantially impaired, removal for cause is impermissible. Fourth, in determining whether the removal of a potential juror would vindicate the State's interest without violating the defendant's right, the trial court makes a judgment based in part on the demeanor of the juror, a judgment owed deference by reviewing courts.

Deference to the trial court is appropriate because it is in a position to assess the demeanor of the venire, and of the individuals who compose it, a factor of critical importance in assessing the attitude and qualifications of potential jurors. Leading treatises in the area make much of nonverbal communication.

The requirements of the Antiterrorism and Effective Death Penalty Act of 1996 (AEDPA), of course, provide additional, and binding, directions to accord deference. The provisions of that statute create an independent, high standard to be met before a federal court may issue a writ of habeas corpus to set aside state-court rulings.

By not according the required deference, the Court of Appeals failed to respect the limited role of federal habeas relief in this area prescribed by Congress and by our cases.

II

A

In applying the principles of *Witherspoon* and *Witt,* it is instructive to consider the entire *voir dire* in Brown's case. [Eleven days of the *voir dire* were devoted to death qualifying the jury. Prior to questioning the jurors, the court instructed the jurors on two separate occasions that the only two possible penalties were death or life without the possibility of release or parole. During the questioning, the defense counsel challenged 18 members of the venire for cause, and, 11 of those prospective jurors were excused over the State's objection. The State made 12 challenges for cause; defense counsel objected seven times; and only twice did the court excuse the juror over a defense objection. Before deciding a contested challenge, the trial court permitted each side to explain its position and to recall the potential juror for additional questioning, and gave "careful and measured explanations" for its decisions.]

With this background, we turn to Juror Z's examination.

B

Juror Z was examined on the seventh day of the *voir dire* and the fifth day of the death-qualification phase. The State argues that Juror Z was impaired not by his general outlook on the death penalty, but rather by his position regarding the specific circumstances in which the death penalty would be appropriate. The transcript of Juror Z's questioning reveals that, despite the preceding instructions and information, he had both serious misunderstandings about his responsibility as a juror and an attitude toward capital punishment that could have prevented him from returning a death sentence under the facts of this case.

Under the *voir dire* procedures, the prosecution and defense alternated in commencing the examination. For Juror Z, the defense went first. When questioned, Juror Z demonstrated no general opposition to the death penalty or scruples against its infliction. In fact, he soon explained that he "believe [d] in the death penalty in severe situations." He elaborated, "I don't think it should never happen, and I don't think it should happen 10 times a week either." "[T]here [are] times when it would be appropriate."

The questioning soon turned to when that would be so. Juror Z's first example was one in which "the defendant actually came out and said that he actually wanted to die." Defense set this aside and sought another example. Despite having been told at least twice by the trial court that if convicted of first-degree murder, Brown could not be released from prison, the only example Juror Z could provide was when "a person is . . . incorrigible and would reviolate if released." The defense counsel replied that there would be no possibility of Brown's release and asked whether the lack of arguments about recidivism during the penalty phase would frustrate Juror Z. He answered, "I'm not sure."

The State began its examination of Juror Z by noting that his questionnaire indicated he was "in favor of the death penalty if it is proved beyond a shadow of a doubt if a person has killed and would kill again." The State explained that the burden of proof was beyond a reasonable doubt, not beyond a shadow of a doubt, and asked whether Juror Z understood. He answered, "[I]t would have to be in my mind very obvious that the person would reoffend." In response the State once more explained to Juror Z, now for at least the fourth time, that there was no possibility of Brown's being released to reoffend. Juror Z explained, "[I]t wasn't until today that I became aware that we had a life without parole in the state of Washington," although in fact a week earlier the trial judge had explained to Juror Z's group that there was no possibility of parole when a defendant was convicted of aggravated first-degree murder. The prosecution then asked, "And now that you know there is such a thing . . . can you think of a time when you would be willing to impose a death penalty . . .?" Juror Z answered, "I would have to give that some thought." He supplied no further answer to the question.

The State sought to probe Juror Z's position further by asking whether he could "consider" the death penalty; Juror Z said he could, including under the general facts of Brown's crimes. When asked whether he no longer felt it was necessary for the State to show that Brown would reoffend, Juror Z gave this confusing answer: "I do feel that way if parole is an option, without parole as an option. I believe in the death penalty." Finally, when asked whether he could impose the death penalty when there was no possibility of parole, Juror Z answered, "[I]f I was convinced that was the appropriate measure." Over the course of his questioning, he stated six times that he could consider the death penalty or follow the law, but these responses were interspersed with more equivocal statements.

The State challenged Juror Z, explaining that he was confused about the conditions under which death could be imposed and seemed to believe it only appropriate when there was a risk of release and recidivism. Before the trial court could ask Brown for a response, the defense volunteered, "We have no objection." The court then excused Juror Z.

III

* * *

B

From our own review of the state trial court's ruling, we conclude the trial court acted well within its discretion in granting the State's motion to excuse Juror Z.

Juror Z's answers, on their face, could have led the trial court to believe that Juror Z would be substantially impaired in his ability to impose the death penalty in the absence of the possibility that Brown would be released and would reoffend. And the trial court, furthermore, is entitled to deference because it had an opportunity to observe the demeanor of Juror Z. We do not know anything about his demeanor, in part because a transcript cannot fully reflect that information but also because the defense did not object to Juror Z's removal. Nevertheless, the State's challenge, Brown's waiver of an objection, and the trial court's excusal of Juror Z support the conclusion that the interested parties present in the courtroom all felt that removing Juror Z was appropriate under the *Witherspoon–Witt* rule.

Juror Z's assurances that he would consider imposing the death penalty and would follow the law do not overcome the reasonable inference from his other statements that in fact he would be substantially impaired in this case because there was no possibility of release. His assurances did not require the trial court to deny the State's motion to excuse Juror Z. The defense itself had told the trial court that any juror would make similar guarantees and that they were worth little; instead, defense counsel explained, the court should listen to arguments concerning the substance of the juror's answers. The trial court in part relied, as diligent judges often must, upon both parties' counsel to explain why a challenged juror's problematic beliefs about the death penalty would not rise to the level of substantial impairment. Brown's counsel offered no defense of Juror Z. In light of the deference owed to the trial court the position Brown now maintains does not convince us the decision to excuse Juror Z was unreasonable.

It is true that in order to preserve a *Witherspoon* claim for federal habeas review there is no independent federal requirement that a defendant in state court object to the prosecution's challenge; state procedural rules govern. We nevertheless take into account voluntary acquiescence to, or confirmation of, a juror's removal. By failing to object, the defense did not just deny the conscientious trial judge an opportunity to explain his judgment or correct any error. It also deprived reviewing courts of further factual findings that would have helped to explain the trial court's decision. * * *

The defense's volunteered comment that there was no objection is especially significant because of frequent defense objections to the excusal of other jurors and the trial court's request that if both parties wanted a juror removed, saying so would expedite the process. In that context the statement was not only a failure to object but also an invitation to remove Juror Z.

We reject the conclusion of the Court of Appeals that the excusal of Juror Z entitles Brown to federal habeas relief. The need to defer to the trial court's ability to perceive jurors' demeanor does not foreclose the possibility that a reviewing court may reverse the trial court's decision where the record discloses no basis for a finding of substantial impairment. But where, as here, there is lengthy questioning of a prospective juror and the trial court has supervised a diligent and thoughtful *voir dire,* the trial court has broad discretion. The record does not show the trial court exceeded this discretion in excusing Juror Z; indeed the transcript shows considerable confusion on the part of the juror, amounting to substantial impairment. The Supreme Court of Washington recognized the deference owed to the trial court and, contrary to the Court of Appeals' misreading of the state court's opinion, identified the correct standard required by federal law and found it satisfied. That decision, like the trial court's, was not contrary to, or an unreasonable application of, clearly established federal law.

* * *

APPENDIX TO OPINION OF THE COURT

Excerpts of Verbatim Report of Proceedings *(Voir Dire)* (Nov. 3, 1993) in *State v. Brown,* Cause No. 91–1–03233–1 (Super. Ct. King Cty., Wash.), App. 57–75:

THE COURT: All right. [Juror Z]. (Prospective Juror, [Juror Z], entered the courtroom.)

THE COURT: That's fine, [Juror Z]. Good afternoon.

[JUROR Z]: Good afternoon.

THE COURT: Do you have any questions at all about any of the preliminary instructions that you got this afternoon and the format that we were talking about or the reasons why the attorneys have to discuss the penalty phase when there may never really be a penalty phase.

[JUROR Z]: No, I think I understand the situation.

THE COURT: Did you answer or nod your head about remembering something about having heard this crime before?

[JUROR Z]: No, I did not.

THE COURT: Okay. We'll start with the defense.

MS. HUPP: Thank you, your Honor.

VOIR DIRE EXAMINATION BY MS. HUPP:

Q Good afternoon. My name is Lin–Marie Hupp, and I'm one of Cal Brown's attorneys.

I would like to start off asking you some questions about your feelings about the death penalty. I want to reinforce what the Judge has already told you, which is there are no right or wrong answers. We just need to get information about your feelings so we can do our job.

A Okay.

Q Can you tell me when it was you first realized this was a potential death penalty case?

A Not until last Monday when I was here in the initial jury information session.

Q Okay. Can you tell me when the Judge read that long thing to you and basically told you that this was a potential in the case, can you tell me what you were thinking when you heard that?

A I guess I wasn't surprised when I got the announcement for jury duty. And it was more than the standard two weeks that most everybody else goes to. I thought it must be a pretty substantial case. In my mind I tried to guess what it might be, so this is one of the things that entered into it.

Q Can you give me an idea of what your general feelings about the death penalty are?

A I do believe in the death penalty in severe situations. A good example might be the young man from, I believe he was from Renton that killed a couple of boys down in the Vancouver area and was sentenced to the death penalty, and wanted the death penalty. And I think it is appropriate in severe cases.

Q And that case you're talking about, that is the one where he actually came out, the defendant actually came out and said that he actually wanted to die?

A I believe that was the case.

Q Does that have any kind of bearing on your idea that the death penalty was appropriate in his case?

A I believe that it was in that case.

Q If you removed that factor completely from it, is that again the type of case that you think the death penalty would be appropriate?

A It would have to be a severe case. I guess I can't put a real line where that might be, but there are a lot of cases that I don't think it's where people would—

Q Okay. And let me kind of fill in the blanks for myself here by just asking you a couple of questions about that. I'm assuming that there would not be any case other than murder that you would think the death penalty would be appropriate?

A I think that is correct.

Q Okay. And the way the law is in Washington anyway, in order to get to the point where you would even consider the death penalty, the State would first have to prove that you had committed a premeditate murder and one that had been thought about beforehand. Do you have any kind of feeling that something other than a premeditated murder, in other words, one that would have been planned that would be appropriate for the death penalty?

A No. I think it would have to be premeditated.

Q In addition to that in Washington even premeditated murders are not eligible for a potential death penalty unless the State also proves aggravating circumstances. In this case the State is alleging or is going to try and prove a number of aggravating circumstances, four of them. Okay. And the ones that they are going to try and prove are that the murder was committed, a premeditated murder was committed during a rape, a robbery, a kidnapping and that it was done in order to conceal a witness or eliminate a witness. Does that fall within the class of cases that you think the death penalty is appropriate?

A I think that would be.

Q Okay. Now, how about other sentencing options in a case like that, do you think that something other than the death penalty might be an appropriate sentence?

A I think that if a person is temporarily insane or things of that that lead a person to do things that they would not normally do, I think that would enter into it.

Q All right. Other than—well, maybe what we should do—the way that the law is in Washington, if the jury finds beyond a reasonable doubt that somebody has committed a premeditated murder with at least one aggravating circumstance, and in this case you have a potential for the four, then the jury reconvenes to consider whether or not the death penalty should be imposed or whether or not a life sentence without parole should be imposed. One sort of aside here, life without parole is exactly what it sounds like. It is a life sentence. You're not ever eligible for parole. You hear about it in the papers sometimes where somebody has got a life sentence and they're going to be eligible for parole in 10 years or 20 years.

A I understand.

Q Were you aware before that Washington has got this kind of sentence where it's life without parole where you are not ever eligible for parole?

A I did not until this afternoon.

Q That is the two options that the jury has if they found the person guilty of premeditated murder beyond a reasonable doubt plus aggravating circumstances beyond a reasonable doubt. Do you think that you could consider both options?

A Yes, I could.

Q Could you give me an idea sort of have you thought about sort of the underlying reason why you think the death penalty is appropriate, what purpose it serves, that kind of thing?

A I think if a person is, would be incorrigible and would reviolate if released, I think that's the type of situation that would be appropriate.

Q Okay. Now, knowing that you didn't know before when you were coming to those opinions about the two options that we have here obviously somebody who is not going to get out of jail no matter which sentence you give them if you got to that point of making a decision about the sentence, does that mean what I'm hearing you say is that you could consider either alternative?

A I believe so, yes.

Q Now, in your, I think in your questionnaire you sort of referred to that also, what you kind of thought about was if somebody had been killed and it had been proven to you that they would kill again. Understanding that the two options there are life without parole or the death penalty, there is not a lot of likelihood that people are going to spend a lot of time talking about whether or not they're going to kill again in the sentencing phase of this case. Is that going to make you frustrated? Are you going to want to hear about things like that, about people's opinions in the penalty phase?

A I'm not sure.

Q Okay. That's very fair. Do you have any kind of feelings about the frequency of the use of the death penalty in the United States today? Do you think it's used too frequently or not often enough?

A It seemed like there were several years when it wasn't used at all and just recently it has become more prevalent in the news anyway. I don't think it should never happen, and I don't think it should happen 10 times a week either. I'm not sure what the appropriate number is but I think in severe situations, it is appropriate.

Q It sounds like you're a little more comfortable that it is being used some of the time?

A Yes.

Q You weren't happy with the time when it wasn't being used at all?

A I can't say I was happy or unhappy, I just felt that there were times when it would be appropriate.

Q Let me ask you, and we may have covered this already, but let me ask you just to make sure I understand. If the State were to prove beyond a reasonable doubt that the defendant had committed a premeditated murder with aggravating circumstances that I have laid out for you, rape, robbery, kidnapping, to conceal or eliminate a witness, at least one of those, in addition another thing you might hear in this trial is some evidence that the defendant deliberately inflicted pain upon the victim before she died for some period of time. If that was the crime that you heard about and came to a decision about guilty about, do you think you consider a life sentence?

A I could consider it but I don't know if I really have enough information to make a determination.

Q Right. And it's real tough to be asking you these questions and even tougher for you to have to answer them without any evidence before you. But you understand that this is our only time to do that before you have heard all the evidence?

A I understand, yes.

Q As a matter of fact, the law in this state after, even after you have found somebody guilty of really hideous crime like that presumes that the sentence, the appropriate sentence is life without parole. The State has the burden of proof, again, in the penalty phase. And they would have to prove beyond a reasonable doubt that there are not sufficient mitigating circumstances to merit a life sentence. Are you comfortable with that idea that you start off presuming that, as a matter of fact, even for a hideous crime that a life sentence is the appropriate sentence?

A It is or is not?

Q That it is an appropriate sentence.

A I guess I'm a little confused by the question. So, you go into it with a life sentence is the appropriate sentence?

Q Right. If you look at the chart here, there's almost a mirror image to start off a trial presuming that somebody is innocent and you start off a sentencing presuming that a life sentence is appropriate?

A I see.

Q Okay.

A Yes.

Q Okay. Now, as far as mitigating circumstances, you had mentioned the idea that maybe somebody was temporarily insane. The Judge is going to give you an instruction on mitigating circumstances, and I will defines it for you, but the definition is real broad. The definition basically is, any reason, not a justification, not an excuse for the crime and not a defense to the crime, but a reason for imposing something other than death. That's pretty broad.

MR. MATTHEWS: I object to that question. I don't believe that is a question. I believe that's a statement.

THE COURT: The objection will be sustained.

Q (BY MS. HUPP) The judge will instruct you about what a mitigating circumstance is.

But what I want to be real clear about is that it's not a defense to the crime. Okay. In other words, if you believe that somebody was really temporarily insane at the time he committed the offense, well, then it wouldn't be premeditated. It would be an insanity defense, and that would all get dealt with—

MR. MATTHEWS: Your Honor, again, I am going to object to the nature of the question.

THE COURT: [Juror Z], you were the one that actually brought it up in terms of the mental status of the person. You are the one who said temporarily insane when they committed this kind of crime. You realize that there are particular defenses that may be available in the actual criminal case itself, the guilt phase. But once you get to the penalty phase, we're not talking about the crime in any way, and you're simply trying to determine what the appropriate punishment or sanction should be for a crime that a person has been found guilty of. At that point in time, something like all sorts of mitigating circumstances come into it, and mental status can come into it. But it would only be evaluated in the light of the mitigating circumstances, not a defense. Do you understand that?

A Understand.

Q (BY MS. HUPP) To just sort of follow up on that, if mental status came into play and you were presented with some sort of evidence about mental status, is that the sort of evidence you would consider?

A Yes, I could.

Q How about things like somebody's childhood or their emotional development?

A I could consider it. I don't have strong feelings one way or the other.

Q Okay. All right. And, also, when we talk about mitigating circumstances, what might be mitigating to you might not matter much to the person sitting next to you in juror's box. Do you think you could discuss your feelings about those things?

A Yes.

Q Could you, say the person next to you says something is mitigating and you don't think it's very mitigating at all, could you also discuss it in this situation?

A (Nodding head).

Q Could you respect that other person's opinion?

A Everybody is entitled to an opinion, yes.

Q Another thing that happens at the sentencing phase of the trial is that the jury would have to be unanimous, in other words, everybody would have to agree if they were going to impose a death sentence. If one person, four people, five people, how ever many people don't agree with that, then the sentence is life. Okay. So, it kind of strips away that sort of comfort in numbers that some people get from the idea of having a unanimous decision. Do you think you can accept the responsibility for such an important decision for yourself?

A I do.

Q Okay. Thank you.

MS. HUPP: I have no further questions.

THE COURT: The State.

VOIR DIRE EXAMINATION BY MR. MATTHEWS:

Q [Juror Z], I'm Al Matthews. I'm one of two prosecutors in the case. I have got some very specific questions, and perhaps we can clear them up real rapidly. I see your step-brother is a policeman and you see him about four times a year.

A (Nodding head).

Q Do you ever have any discussions about the death penalty, is this a subject that ever comes up?

A No.

Q Have you ever had occasion to discuss it at all within the family circle?

A I don't believe so.

Q You mentioned on your questionnaire, and we do read them, that you're in favor of the death penalty if it is proved beyond a shadow of a doubt if a person has killed and would kill again. Do you remember making that statement?

A Yes.

Q First of all, have you ever been on a jury trial before?

A I have not.

Q Now, you made this statement before you read your juror's handbook I imagine?

A Yes.

Q So, I want to ask you, the thing that bothers me, of course, is the idea beyond a shadow of a doubt. The law says beyond a reasonable doubt, and it will be explained to you what it actually means. But I want to assure you it doesn't mean, I don't believe the Court would instruct would you it means beyond all doubt or beyond any shadow of a doubt. Knowing that, would you still require the State to prove beyond a shadow of a doubt that the crime occurred knowing that the law doesn't require that much of us?

A I would have to know the, I'm at a loss for the words here.

Q You can ask me any questions, too, if you need some clarification.

A I guess it would have to be in my mind very obvious that the person would reoffend.

Q Well, we're not talking about that, sir.

A Or was guilty, yes.

Q So, we're talking about that?

A Yes.

Q So, you would be satisfied with a reasonable doubt standard? You would be willing to follow the law?

A Yes.

Q In other words, nothing, there is very few things in life absolutely certain?

A I understand.

Q And that is basically what we're saying to you, and that is what the term reasonable doubt means—

A (Nodding head).

Q—that we don't have to prove it beyond all doubt. Now, we get to the penalty phase and the question becomes slightly different. It presumes life as a person is presumed innocent in the guilt phase, it is presumed that the proper penalty for the beginning point in the penalty phase is life in prison without parole. Now, you mentioned that you would have to be satisfied that the person would not kill again. Now, you know that the

possible, that the only two penalties are life in prison without parole or death. The person, if he is committed, if he is convicted of aggravated murder, is not going to be out on the streets again, not going to come in contact with the people that he had a chance to run into before. So, the likelihood of him killing someone out in the street is nil or practically nil at that point. I guess the reverse side of what you're saying is, if you could be convinced that he wouldn't kill again, would you find it difficult to vote for the death penalty given a situation where he couldn't kill again?

A I think I made that statement more under assumption that a person could be paroled. And it wasn't until today that I became aware that we had a life without parole in the state of Washington.

Q And now that you know there is such a thing and they do mean what they say, can you think of a time when you would be willing to impose a death penalty since the person would be locked up for the rest of his life?

A I would have to give that some thought. I really, like I said, up until an hour ago did not realize that there was an option of life without parole.

Q And I realize this is put on you rather suddenly, but you also recognize as someone who is representing the State in this case, we have made the election to ask that the jury if he is found guilty, ask that the jury vote for the death penalty. And I'm asking you a very important thing and to everyone in here, whether you, knowing that the person would never get out for the rest of his life, two things. And they're slightly different. One, whether you could consider the death penalty and the second thing I would ask you is whether you could impose the death penalty. I'm not asking a promise or anything. But I'm asking you, first, could you consider it, and if you could consider it, do you think under the conditions where the man would never get out again you could impose it?

A Yes, sir.

Q So, this idea of him having to kill again to deserve the death penalty is something that you are not firm on, you don't feel that now?

A I do feel that way if parole is an option, without parole as an option. I believe in the death penalty. Like I said, I'm not sure that there should be a waiting line of people happening every day or every week even, but I think in severe situations it's an appropriate measure.

Q But in the situation where a person is locked up for the rest of his life and there is no chance of him ever getting out again, which would be the situation in this case, do you think you could also consider and vote for the death penalty under those circumstances?

A I could consider it, yes.

Q Then could you impose it?

A I could if I was convinced that was the appropriate measure.

MR. MATTHEWS: I have no further questions.

THE COURT: All right. [Juror Z], there is something that I want to clarify in response to some of the questions that were asked of you.

VOIR DIRE EXAMINATION BY THE COURT:

Q In your questionnaire it talks about beyond a shadow of a doubt, and the prosecutor here went into that a little further. You realize that that is the standard that the law imposes on the State to prove a case beyond a reasonable doubt. And, obviously, that is a question of interpretation.

You officiate basketball games. That's in your questionnaire. You, even at the college level, knowing how fast that game is, you have to make a call on some of those calls and you have to decide whether to blow that whistle and make that particular call. Do you think you understand the difference between a reasonable call and beyond a shadow of a doubt type call?

A I guess I do. The terminology beyond a shadow of a doubt, when I wrote that I wasn't even sure whether, I mean, it's just terminology that I have heard probably watching Perry Mason or something over the years. But I guess the point I was making that it has to be—

Q You would have to be positive?

A I would have to be positive, that's correct.

Q The State has to convince you?

A Yes.

Q As they would have to convince any reasonable person?

A Yes.

THE COURT: [Juror Z], let me have you step back into the juryroom. The bailiff will excuse you from there in just a few minutes. Thank you. Counsel, any challenge to this particular juror?

MR. MATTHEWS: I would, your Honor, not on the term beyond a shadow of a doubt, I think he would certainly stick with the reasonable doubt standard. But I think he is very confused about the statements where he said that if a person can't kill again, in other words, he's locked up for the rest of his life, he said, basically, he could vote for the death penalty if it was proved beyond a shadow of. And I am certainly going to concede that he means beyond a reasonable doubt. And if a person kills and will kill again. And I think he has some real problems with that. He said he hadn't really thought about it. And I don't think at this period of time he's had an opportunity to think about it, and I don't think he said anything that overcame this idea of he must kill again before he imposed the death penalty or be in a position to kill again. So, that is my only challenge.

MR. MULLIGAN: We have no objection.

THE COURT: Counsel, the request of the prosecutor's office, we will go ahead and excuse [Juror Z].

[Dissenting opinions of STEVENS, J., joined by SOUTER, J., GINSBURG, J. and BREYER, J. and BREYER J. joined by SOUTER, J. omitted]

NOTES

1. *The effect of improper exclusion.*

The Supreme Court has reaffirmed the principle that the improper exclusion of a prospective juror under *Witherspoon–Witt* is reversible *per se* even if the prosecutor had unused peremptory challenges. See *Gray v. Mississippi,* 481 U.S. 648, 107 S.Ct. 2045 (1987).

2. *"Reverse" Witherspoon.*

In *Morgan v. Illinois*, 504 U.S. 719, 112 S.Ct. 2222 (1992), the Supreme Court decided whether, during *voir dire* for a capital offense, a state trial court may refuse inquiry into whether a potential juror would automatically impose the death penalty upon conviction of the defendant. After reviewing the teaching of *Witt* and other cases that a juror who will vote against capital punishment in all cases, regardless of the instructions, is not an impartial juror, the majority held that "[a] juror who will automatically vote for the death penalty in every case will fail in good faith to consider the evidence of aggravating and mitigating circumstances as the instructions require him to do. Indeed, because such a juror has already formed an opinion on the merits, the presence or absence of either aggravating or mitigating circumstances is entirely irrelevant to such a juror. Therefore, based on the requirement of impartiality embodied in the Due Process Clause of the Fourteenth Amendment, a capital defendant may challenge for cause any prospective juror who maintains such views. If even one such juror is empaneled and the death sentence is imposed, the State is disentitled to execute the sentence."

Justice Scalia, with Chief Justice Rehnquist and Justice Thomas, dissented. He argued, among other things, that Illinois law requires that the jury "consider all the aggravating factors supported by the evidence and all the mitigating factors supported by the evidence" but does not define what is aggravating and what is mitigating. That task rests with each juror. Therefore, a juror who would never find mitigating factors "sufficient to preclude imposition of the death sentence" (as the Illinois law instructs) does not fail to consider the evidence but "simply fails to give it the effect the defendant desires." Justice Scalia emphasized that the Eighth Amendment requires that a juror "not be precluded from considering" mitigating evidence but does not require that the sentencer must give effect to, or even that he must consider, the defendant's mitigating evidence.

LOCKHART v. McCREE

476 U.S. 162, 106 S.Ct. 1758, 90 L.Ed.2d 137 (1986).

JUSTICE REHNQUIST delivered the opinion of the Court.

In this case we address the question left open by our decision nearly 18 years ago in *Witherspoon v. Illinois*, 391 U.S. 510, 88 S.Ct. 1770 (1968): Does the Constitution prohibit the removal for cause, prior to the guilt phase of a bifurcated capital trial, of prospective jurors whose opposition to the death penalty is so strong that it would prevent or substantially impair the performance of their duties as jurors at the sentencing phase of the trial? We hold that it does not.

[Ardia McCree was charged with capital felony murder based on evidence that he shot and killed Evelyn Boughton during a service station robbery. During *voir dire* at McCree's trial, the trial judge (over McCree's objections) removed for cause those prospective jurors who stated that they could not under any circumstances vote for the imposition of the death penalty. Eight prospective jurors were excluded for this reason. McCree was convicted of murder and was sentenced by the jury to life imprisonment without possibility of parole. On appeal, the conviction was affirmed, and McCree's petition for post-conviction relief was denied.]

McCree then filed a federal habeas corpus petition raising, *inter alia*, the claim that "death qualification," or the removal for cause of the so-called "*Witherspoon*-excludable" prospective jurors, violated his right under the Sixth and Fourteenth Amendments to have his guilt or innocence determined by an impartial jury selected from a representative cross section of the community. * * *

The District Court held a hearing on the "death qualification" issue in July 1981, receiving in evidence numerous social science studies concerning the attitudes and beliefs of "*Witherspoon*-excludables," along with the potential effects of excluding them from the jury prior to the guilt phase of a bifurcated capital trial. In August 1983, the court concluded, based on the social science evidence, that "death qualification" produced juries that "were more prone to convict" capital defendants than "non-death-qualified" juries. The court ruled that "death qualification" thus violated both the fair-cross-section and impartiality requirements of the Sixth and Fourteenth Amendments, and granted McCree habeas relief.

The Eighth Circuit found "substantial evidentiary support" for the District Court's conclusion that the removal for cause of "*Witherspoon*-excludables" resulted in "conviction-prone" juries, and affirmed the grant of habeas relief on the ground that such removal for cause violated McCree's constitutional right to a jury selected from a fair cross section of the community. The Eighth Circuit did not address McCree's impartiality claim. The Eighth Circuit left it up to the discretion of the State "to construct a fair process" for future capital trials that would comply with the Sixth Amendment. Four judges dissented.

[Justice REHNQUIST discussed the "serious flaws" in the 15 social science studies McCree introduced. Nine studies were not relevant to the effect on the guilt-innocence determination of removing "*Witherspoon*-excludables": 8 studies dealt solely with generalized attitudes and beliefs about the death penalty, and 1 study dealt with the effect of *voir dire* questioning about the death penalty. Of the 6 studies relevant to the issue before the Court, 3 were before the Court when it decided *Witherspoon* and 3 "new" studies did not involve actual jurors sworn in an actual case.]

Having identified some of the more serious problems with McCree's studies, however, we will assume for purposes of this opinion that the studies are both methodologically valid and adequate to establish that "death qualification" in fact produces juries somewhat more "conviction-prone" than "non-death-qualified" juries. We hold, nonetheless, that the Constitution does not prohibit the States from "death qualifying" juries in capital cases.

The Eighth Circuit ruled that "death qualification" violated McCree's right under the Sixth Amendment, as applied to the States via incorporation through the Fourteenth Amendment to a jury selected from a representative cross section of the community. But we do not believe that the fair-cross-section requirement can, or should, be applied as broadly as that court attempted to apply it. We have never invoked the fair-cross-section principle to invalidate the use of either for-cause or peremptory challenges to prospective jurors, or to require petit juries, as opposed to jury panels or venires, to reflect the composition of the community at large. See *Duren v. Missouri*, 439 U.S. 357, 99 S.Ct. 664 (1979); *Taylor v. Louisiana*, 419 U.S. 522, 95 S.Ct. 692 (1975) ("[W]e impose no requirement that petit juries actually chosen must mirror the community and reflect the various distinctive groups in the population"). The limited scope of the fair-cross-section requirement is a direct and inevitable consequence of the practical impossibility of providing each criminal defendant with a truly "representative" petit jury, a basic truth that the Court of Appeals itself acknowledged for many years prior to its decision in the instant case. We remain convinced that an extension of the fair-cross-section requirement to petit juries would be unworkable and unsound, and we decline McCree's invitation to adopt such an extension.

[Justice REHNQUIST added that exclusion of "*Witherspoon*-excludables" would not constitute exclusion of a "distinctive group" for fair-cross-section purposes. Unlike blacks, women or Mexican–Americans, whose exclusion the Court had found violated the fair cross-section requirement, "*Witherspoon*-excludables" constituted a group defined solely by shared attitudes, attitudes which were directly related to the state's legitimate interest in seeking the jurors' exclusion.]

McCree argues that, even if we reject the Eighth Circuit's fair-cross-section holding, we should affirm the judgment below on the alternative ground, adopted by the District Court, that "death qualification" violated his constitutional right to an impartial jury. McCree concedes that the individual jurors who served at his trial were impartial, as that term was defined by this Court * * * McCree does not claim that his conviction was tainted by any of the kinds of jury bias or partiality that we have previously recognized as violative of the Constitution. Instead, McCree argues that his jury lacked impartiality because the absence of "*Witherspoon*-excludables" "slanted" the jury in favor of conviction.

We do not agree. McCree's "impartiality" argument apparently is based on the theory that, because all individual jurors are to some extent predisposed towards one result or another, a constitutionally impartial *jury* can be constructed only by "balancing" the various predispositions of the individual *jurors*. Thus, according to McCree, when the State "tips the scales" by excluding prospective jurors with a particular viewpoint, an impermissibly partial jury results. We have consistently rejected this view of jury impartiality, including as recently as last Term when we squarely held that an impartial jury consists of nothing more than "*jurors* who will conscientiously apply the law and find the facts." *Wainwright v. Witt*, 469 U.S. 412, 105 S.Ct. 844 (1985) (emphasis added).

The view of jury impartiality urged upon us by McCree is both illogical and hopelessly impractical. McCree characterizes the jury that convicted him as "slanted" by the process of "death qualification." But McCree admits that exactly the same 12 individuals could have ended up on his jury through the "luck of the draw," without in any way violating the constitutional guarantee of impartiality. Even accepting McCree's position that we should focus on the jury rather than the individual jurors, it is hard for us to understand the logic of the argument that a given jury is unconstitutionally partial when it results from a state-ordained process, yet impartial when exactly the same jury results from mere chance. On a more practical level, if it were true that the Constitution required a certain mix of individual viewpoints on the jury, then trial judges would be required to undertake the Sisyphean task of "balancing" juries, making sure that each contains the proper number of Democrats and Republicans, young persons and old persons, white-collar executives and blue-collar laborers, and so on. Adopting McCree's concept of jury impartiality would also likely require the elimination of peremptory challenges, which are commonly used by both the State and the defendant to attempt to produce a jury favorable to the challenger.

McCree argues, however, that this Court's decisions in *Witherspoon* and *Adams v. Texas*, 448 U.S. 38, 100 S.Ct. 2521 (1980), stand for the proposition that a State violates the Constitution whenever it "slants" the jury by excluding a group of individuals more likely than the population at large to favor the criminal defendant. We think McCree overlooks two fundamental differences between *Witherspoon* and *Adams* and the instant case, and therefore misconceives the import and scope of those two decisions.

First, the Court in *Witherspoon* viewed the Illinois system as having been deliberately slanted for the purpose of making the imposition of the death penalty more likely. * * * *Adams*, in turn, involved a fairly straight-forward application of the *Witherspoon* rule to the Texas capital punishment scheme. See *Adams, supra* (Texas exclusion statute "focuses the inquiry directly on the prospective juror's beliefs about the death penalty, and hence clearly falls within the scope of the *Witherspoon* doctrine").

Here, on the other hand, the removal for cause of "*Witherspoon*-excludables" serves the State's entirely proper interest in obtaining a single jury that could impartially decide all of the issues in McCree's case.

Arkansas by legislative enactment and judicial decision provides for the use of a unitary jury in capital cases. We have upheld against constitutional attack the Georgia capital sentencing plan which provided that the same jury must sit in both phases of a bifurcated capital murder trial, *Gregg v. Georgia*, 428 U.S. 153, 96 S.Ct. 2909 (1976) (opinion of STEWART, POWELL, and STEVENS, JJ.), and since then have observed that we are "unwilling to say that there is any one right way for a State to set up its capital sentencing scheme." *Spaziano v. Florida*, 468 U.S. 447, 104 S.Ct. 3154 (1984).

* * * Another interest identified by the State in support of its system of unitary juries is the possibility that, in at least some capital cases, the defendant might benefit at the sentencing phase of the trial from the jury's "residual doubts" about the evidence presented at the guilt phase. The dissenting opinion in the Court of Appeals also adverted to this interest: "[A]s several courts have observed, jurors who decide both guilt and penalty are likely to form residual doubts or 'whimsical' doubts . . . about the evidence so as to bend them to decide against the death penalty. Such residual doubt has been recognized as an extremely effective argument for defendants in capital cases. To divide the responsibility . . . to some degree would eliminate the influence of such doubts." Justice MARSHALL's dissent points out that some States which adhere to the unitary jury system do not allow the defendant to argue "residual doubts" to the jury at sentencing. But while this may justify skepticism as to the extent to which such States are willing to go to allow defendants to capitalize on "residual doubts," it does not wholly vitiate the claimed interest. Finally, it seems obvious to us that in most, if not all, capital cases much of the evidence adduced at the guilt phase of the trial will also have a bearing on the penalty phase; if two different juries were to be required, such testimony would have to be presented twice, once to each jury. * * *

Unlike the Illinois system criticized by the Court in *Witherspoon*, and the Texas system at issue in *Adams*, the Arkansas system excludes from the jury only those who may properly be excluded from the penalty phase of the deliberations under *Witherspoon*, *Adams* and *Wainwright v. Witt*, 469 U.S. 412, 105 S.Ct. 844 (1985). That State's reasons for adhering to its preference for a single jury to decide both the guilt and penalty phases of a capital trial are sufficient to negate the inference which the Court drew in *Witherspoon* concerning the lack of any neutral justification for the Illinois rule on jury challenges.

Second, and more importantly, both *Witherspoon* and *Adams* dealt with the special context of capital sentencing, where the range of jury discretion necessarily gave rise to far greater concern over the possible effects of an "imbalanced" jury. * * * [In *Witherspoon*] [b]ecause capital sentencing under the Illinois statute involved such an exercise of essentially unfettered discretion, we held that the State violated the Constitution when it "crossed the line of neutrality" and "produced a jury uncommonly willing to condemn a man to die."

In *Adams*, we applied the same basic reasoning to the Texas capital sentencing scheme, which, although purporting to limit the jury's role to answering several "factual" questions, in reality vested the jury with considerable discretion over the punishment to be imposed on the defendant. * * * Again, as in *Witherspoon*, the discretionary nature of the jury's task led us to conclude that the State could not "exclude all jurors who would be in the slightest way affected by the prospect of the death penalty or by their views about such a penalty."

In the case at bar, by contrast, we deal not with capital sentencing, but with the jury's more traditional role of finding the facts and determining the guilt or innocence of a criminal defendant, where jury discretion is more channeled. We reject McCree's suggestion that *Witherspoon* and *Adams* have broad applicability outside the special context of capital sentencing, and conclude that those two decisions do not support the result reached by the Eighth Circuit here.

In our view, it is simply not possible to define jury impartiality, for constitutional purposes, by reference to some hypothetical mix of individual viewpoints. Prospective jurors come from many different backgrounds, and have many different attitudes and predispositions. But the Constitution presupposes that a jury selected from a fair cross section of the community is impartial, regardless of the mix of individual viewpoints actually represented on the jury, so long as the jurors can conscientiously and properly carry out their sworn duty to apply the law to the facts of the particular case. We hold that McCree's jury satisfied both aspects of this constitutional standard. The judgment of the Court of Appeals is therefore reversed.

Justice Blackmun concurs in the result.

Justice Marshall, with whom Justice Brennan and Justice Stevens join, dissenting.

Eighteen years ago, this Court vacated the sentence of a defendant from whose jury the State had excluded all venirepersons expressing any scruples against capital punishment. Such a practice, the Court held, violated the Constitution by creating a "tribunal organized to return a verdict of death." *Witherspoon v. Illinois*, 391 U.S. 510, 88 S.Ct. 1770 (1968). The only venirepersons who could be constitutionally excluded from service in capital cases were those who "made unmistakably clear . . . that they would automatically vote against the imposition of capital punishment" or that they could not assess the defendant's guilt impartially.

Respondent contends here that the "death-qualified" jury that convicted him, from which the State, as authorized by *Witherspoon*, had excluded all venirepersons unwilling to consider imposing the death penalty, was in effect "organized to return a verdict" of guilty. In support of this claim, he has presented overwhelming evidence that death-qualified juries are substantially more likely to convict or to convict on more serious charges than juries on which unalterable opponents of capital punishment are permitted to serve. Respondent does not challenge the application of *Witherspoon* to the jury in the sentencing stage of bifurcated capital cases. Neither does he demand that individuals unable to assess culpability impartially ("nullifiers") be permitted to sit on capital juries. All he asks is the chance to have his guilt or innocence determined by a jury like those that sit in noncapital cases—one whose composition has not been tilted in favor of the prosecution by the exclusion of a group of prospective jurors uncommonly aware of an accused's constitutional rights but quite capable of determining his culpability without favor or bias.

With a glib nonchalance ill suited to the gravity of the issue presented and the power of respondent's claims, the Court upholds a practice that allows the State a special advantage in those prosecutions where the charges are the most serious and the possible punishments, the most severe. The State's mere announcement that it intends to seek the death penalty if the defendant is found guilty of a capital offense will, under today's decision, give the prosecution license to empanel a jury especially likely to return that very verdict. Because I believe that such a blatant disregard for the rights of a capital defendant offends logic, fairness, and the Constitution, I dissent.

[Justice MARSHALL responded to the Court's criticism of the evidence on several grounds: (1) the data strongly suggests that death qualification excludes from 11% to 17% of potential jurors who could be impartial at the guilt phase; (2) the jurors who survive death qualification show a pro-prosecution bias; (3) data showing prejudicial effects of death qualification upon actual trials will be impossible to obtain until a state permits two separate juries to deliberate on the same capital case and return simultaneous verdicts; (4) McCree's studies, despite diverse subjects and varied methodologies, were unanimous in their results; and (5) there was no evidence which contradicted McCree's evidence.]

III

In *Witherspoon, supra,* the Court observed that a defendant convicted by a jury from which those unalterably opposed to the death penalty had been excluded "might still attempt to establish that the jury was less than neutral with respect to guilt." Respondent has done just that. And I believe he has succeeded in proving that his trial by a jury so constituted violated his right to an impartial jury, guaranteed by both the Sixth Amendment and principles of due process. We therefore need not rely on respondent's alternative argument that death qualification deprived him of a jury representing a fair cross section of the community.

A

Respondent does not claim that any individual on the jury that convicted him fell short of the constitutional standard for impartiality. Rather, he contends that, by systematically excluding a class of potential jurors less prone than the population at large to vote for conviction, the State gave itself an unconstitutional advantage at his trial. Thus, according to respondent, even though a nonbiased selection procedure might have left him with a jury composed of the very same individuals that actually sat on his panel, the process by which those 12 individuals were chosen violated the Constitution.

I am puzzled by the difficulty that the majority has in understanding the "logic of the argument." For the logic is precisely that which carried the day in *Witherspoon*, and which has never been repudiated by this Court—not even today, if the majority is to be taken at its word. There was no question in *Witherspoon* that if the defendant's jury had been chosen by the "luck of the draw," the same 12 jurors who actually sat on his case might have been selected. Nonetheless, because the State had removed from the pool of possible jurors all those expressing general opposition to the death penalty, the Court overturned the defendant's conviction, declaring "that a State may not entrust the determination of whether a man should live or die to a tribunal organized to return a verdict of death." *Witherspoon* had been denied a fair sentencing determination, the Court reasoned, not because any member of his jury lacked the requisite constitutional impartiality, but because the manner in which that jury had been selected "stacked the deck" against him. Here, respondent adopts the approach of the *Witherspoon* Court and argues simply that the State entrusted the determination of his guilt and the level of his culpability to a tribunal organized to convict.

The Court offers but two arguments to rebut respondent's constitutional claim. First, it asserts that the "State's reasons for adhering to its preference for a single jury to decide both the guilt and penalty phases of a capital trial are sufficient to negate the inference which the Court drew in *Witherspoon* concerning the lack of any neutral justification for the Illinois rule on jury challenges." This argument, however, does not address the question whether death qualification infringes a defendant's constitutional interest in "a completely fair determination of guilt or innocence," *Witherspoon*. It merely indicates the state interest that must be considered once an infringement of that constitutional interest is found.

The Court's second reason for rejecting respondent's challenge to the process that produced his jury is that the notion of "neutrality" adumbrated in *Witherspoon* must be confined to "the special context of capital sentencing, where the range of jury discretion necessarily gave rise to far greater concern over the possible effects of an 'imbalanced' jury." But in the wake of this Court's decision in *Adams v. Texas*, 448 U.S. 38, 100 S.Ct. 2521 (1980), this distinction is simply untenable.

B

In *Adams*, this Court applied the principles of *Witherspoon* to the Texas death-penalty scheme [under which the jury decides the penalty by answering three statutory questions]. * * * The "process" of answering the statutory questions, the Court observed, "is not an exact science, and the jurors under the Texas bifurcated procedure unavoidably exercise a range of judgment and discretion while remaining true to their instructions and their oaths." Consequently, while Texas could constitutionally exclude jurors whose scruples against the death penalty left them unable "to answer the statutory questions without conscious distortion or bias," it could not exclude those "[who] aver that they will honestly find the facts and answer the questions in the affirmative if they are convinced beyond reasonable doubt, but not otherwise, yet who frankly concede that the prospects of the death penalty may affect what their honest judgment of the facts will be or what they may deem to be a reasonable doubt. Such assessments and judgments by jurors are inherent in the jury system, and to exclude all jurors who would be in the slightest way affected by the prospect of the death penalty or by their views about such a penalty would be to deprive the defendant of the impartial jury to which he or she is entitled under the law."

The message of *Adams* is thus that even where the role of the jury at the penalty stage of a capital trial is limited to what is essentially a factfinding role, the right to an impartial jury established in *Witherspoon* bars the State from skewing the composition of its capital juries by excluding scrupled jurors who are nonetheless able to find those facts without distortion or bias. This proposition cannot be limited to the penalty stage of a capital trial, for the services that *Adams'* jury was called upon to perform at his penalty stage "are nearly indistinguishable" from those required of juries at the culpability phase of capital trials. * * *

     * * *

V

As the *Witherspoon* Court recognized, "the State's interest in submitting the penalty issue to a jury capable of imposing capital punishment" may be accommodated without infringing a capital defendant's interest in a fair determination of his guilt if the State uses "one jury to decide guilt and another to fix punishment." Any exclusion of death-penalty opponents, the Court reasoned, could await the penalty phase of a trial. The question here is thus whether the State has other interests that require the use of a single jury and demand the subordination of a capital defendant's Sixth and Fourteenth Amendment rights.

The only two reasons that the Court invokes to justify the State's use of a single jury are efficient trial management and concern that a defendant at his sentencing proceedings may be able to profit from "residual doubts" troubling jurors who have sat through the guilt phase of his trial. The first of these purported justifications is merely unconvincing. The second is offensive.

In *Ballew v. Georgia*, 435 U.S. 223, 98 S.Ct. 1029 (1978) [which held unconstitutional 5–person juries in criminal cases], the Court found that the State's interest in saving "court time and ... financial costs" was insufficient to justify further reductions in jury size. The same is true here. The additional costs that would be imposed by a system of separate juries are not particularly high. * * *

In a system using separate juries for guilt and penalty phases, time and resources would be saved every time a capital case did not require a penalty phase. The *voir dire* needed to identify nullifiers before the guilt phase is less extensive than the questioning that under the current scheme is conducted before every capital trial. The State could, of course, choose to empanel a death-qualified jury at the start of every trial, to be used only if a penalty stage is required. However, if it opted for the cheaper alternative of empaneling a death-qualified jury only in the event that a defendant were convicted of capital charges, the State frequently would be able to avoid retrying the entire guilt phase for the benefit of the penalty jury. Stipulated summaries of prior evidence might, for example, save considerable time. Thus, it cannot fairly be said that the costs of accommodating a defendant's constitutional rights under these circumstances are prohibitive, or even significant.

Even less convincing is the Court's concern that a defendant be able to appeal at sentencing to the "residual doubts" of the jurors who found him guilty. Any suggestion that the current system of death qualification "may be in the defendant's best interests, seems specious unless the state is willing to grant the defendant the option to waive this paternalistic protection in exchange for better odds against conviction." Finch & Ferraro, *The Empirical Challenge to Death Qualified Juries: On Further Examination*, 65 Neb.L.Rev. 21 (1986). Furthermore, this case will stand as one of the few times in which any legitimacy has been given to the power of a convicted capital defendant facing the possibility of a death sentence to argue as a mitigating factor the chance that he might be innocent. Where a defendant's sentence but not his conviction has been set aside on appeal, States have routinely empaneled juries whose only duty is to assess punishment, thereby depriving defendants of the chance to profit from the "residual doubts" that jurors who had already sat through a guilt phase might bring to the sentencing proceeding. * * *

But most importantly, it ill-behooves the majority to allude to a defendant's power to appeal to "residual doubts" at his sentencing when this Court has consistently refused to grant certiorari in state cases holding that these doubts cannot properly be considered during capital sentencing proceedings. Any suggestion that capital defendants will benefit from a single jury thus is more than disingenuous. It is cruel.

VI

On occasion, this Court has declared what I believe should be obvious—that when a State seeks to convict a defendant of the most serious and severely punished offenses in its criminal code, any procedure that "diminish[es] the reliability of the guilt determination" must be struck down. *Beck v. Alabama*, 447 U.S. 625, 100 S.Ct. 2382 (1980). But in spite of such declarations, I cannot help thinking that respondent here would have stood a far better chance of prevailing on his constitutional claims had he not been challenging a procedure peculiar to the administration of the death penalty. For in no other context would a majority of this Court refuse to find any constitutional violation in a state practice that systematically operates to render juries more likely to convict, and to convict on the more serious charges. I dissent.

B. RACE AND JURY SELECTION

The two cases in this section are capital cases in which the Supreme Court addresses the issue of racial discrimination. In *Turner v. Murray*, the Court considers the problem of race and the death penalty in the context of the *voir dire* of the capital jury. Is the plurality's decision granting relief as to penalty, but not as to guilt, defensible? In *Miller–El v. Dretke*, the Court addresses the defendant's claim that the prosecutors engaged in racial discrimination in their use of peremptory challenges.

TURNER v. MURRAY
476 U.S. 28, 106 S.Ct. 1683, 90 L.Ed.2d 27 (1986).

JUSTICE WHITE announced the judgment of the Court and delivered the opinion of the Court with respect to Parts I and III, and an opinion with respect to Parts II and IV, in which JUSTICE BLACKMUN, JUSTICE STEVENS, and JUSTICE O'CONNOR join.

Petitioner is a black man sentenced to death for the murder of a white storekeeper. The question presented is whether the trial judge committed reversible error at *voir dire* by refusing petitioner's request to question prospective jurors on racial prejudice.

[Petitioner was engaged in the robbery of a jewelry store in Virginia when a police officer responded to a silent alarm. Petitioner disarmed the officer, but, when he heard a police siren, he became angry and shot and killed the victim. He was indicted for capital murder and other crimes.]

Prior to the commencement of *voir dire*, petitioner's counsel submitted to the trial judge a list of proposed questions, including the following:

> "The defendant, Willie Lloyd Turner, is a member of the Negro race. The victim, W. Jack Smith, Jr., was a white Caucasian. Will these facts prejudice you against Willie Lloyd Turner or affect your ability to render a fair and impartial verdict based solely on the evidence?"

The judge declined to ask this question, stating that it "has been ruled on by the Supreme Court." The judge did ask the venire, who were questioned in groups of five in petitioner's presence, whether any person was aware of any reason why he could not render a fair and impartial verdict, to which all answered "no." At the time the question was asked, the prospective jurors had no way of knowing that the murder victim was white.

The jury that was empaneled, which consisted of eight whites and four blacks, convicted petitioner on all of the charges against him. After a separate sentencing hearing on the capital charge, the jury recommended that petitioner be sentenced to death, a recommendation the trial judge accepted.

Petitioner appealed his death sentence to the Virginia Supreme Court. Among other points, he argued that the trial judge deprived him of his constitutional right to a fair and impartial jury by refusing to question prospective jurors on racial prejudice. The Virginia Supreme Court rejected this argument. Relying on our decision in *Ristaino v. Ross*, 424 U.S. 589, 96 S.Ct. 1017 (1976), the court stated that a trial judge's refusal to ask prospective jurors about their racial attitudes, while perhaps not the wisest decision as a matter of policy, is not constitutionally objectionable in the absence of factors akin to those in *Ham v. South Carolina*, 409 U.S. 524, 93 S.Ct. 848 (1973).[3] The court held that "[t]he mere fact that a defendant is black and that a victim is white does not constitutionally mandate ... an inquiry [into racial prejudice].[4]

[Petitioner sought habeas corpus relief in federal court. The District Court denied relief, and the Court of Appeals affirmed.]

II

The Fourth Circuit's opinion correctly states the analytical framework for evaluating petitioner's argument: "The broad inquiry in each case must be ... whether under all of the circumstances presented there was a constitutionally significant likelihood that, absent questioning about racial prejudice, the jurors would not be indifferent as [they stand] unsworn." The Fourth Circuit was correct, too, in holding that under *Ristaino* the mere fact that petitioner is black and his victim white does not constitute a "special circumstance" of constitutional proportions. What sets this case apart from *Ristaino*, however, is that in addition to petitioner's being accused of a crime against a white victim, the crime charged was a capital offense.

In a capital sentencing proceeding before a jury, the jury is called upon to make a "highly subjective, unique, individualized judgment regarding the punishment that a particular person deserves." *Caldwell v. Mississippi*, 472 U.S. 320, 105 S.Ct. 2633 (1985). The Virginia statute under which petitioner was sentenced is instructive of the kinds of

---

3. In *Ham*, a young black man known in his small South Carolina hometown as a civil rights activist was arrested and charged with possession of marijuana. We held that the trial judge committed reversible error in refusing to honor Ham's request to question prospective jurors on racial prejudice. In *Ristaino, supra*, we specified the factors which mandated an inquiry into racial prejudice in *Ham*:

"Ham's defense was that he had been framed because of his civil rights activities. His prominence in the community as a civil rights activist, if not already known to veniremen, inevitably would have been revealed to the members of the jury in the course of his presentation of that defense. Racial issues therefore were inextricably bound up with the conduct of the trial. Further, Ham's reputation as a civil rights activist and the defense he interposed were likely to intensify any prejudice that individual members of the jury might harbor."

4. The court also rejected petitioner's reliance on a statistical study showing that black defendants who kill white victims are sentenced to death with disproportionate frequency. The court stated that the study, which is based on statistics compiled in other States, has little utility in establishing the potential for racial prejudice in Virginia.

judgments a capital sentencing jury must make. First, in order to consider the death penalty, a Virginia jury must find either that the defendant is likely to commit future violent crimes or that his crime was "outrageously or wantonly vile, horrible or inhuman in that it involved torture, depravity of mind or an aggravated battery to the victim." Second, the jury must consider any mitigating evidence offered by the defendant. Mitigating evidence may include, but is not limited to, facts tending to show that the defendant acted under the influence of extreme emotional or mental disturbance, or that at the time of the crime the defendant's capacity "to appreciate the criminality of his conduct or to conform his conduct to the requirements of law was significantly impaired." Finally, even if the jury has found an aggravating factor, and irrespective of whether mitigating evidence has been offered, the jury has discretion not to recommend the death sentence, in which case it may not be imposed.

Virginia's death-penalty statute gives the jury greater discretion than other systems which we have upheld against constitutional challenge. However, our cases establish that every capital sentencer must be free to weigh relevant mitigating evidence before deciding whether to impose the death penalty, and that in the end it is the jury that must make the difficult, individualized judgment as to whether the defendant deserves the sentence of death.

Because of the range of discretion entrusted to a jury in a capital sentencing hearing, there is a unique opportunity for racial prejudice to operate but remain undetected. On the facts of this case, a juror who believes that blacks are violence prone or morally inferior might well be influenced by that belief in deciding whether petitioner's crime involved the aggravating factors specified under Virginia law. Such a juror might also be less favorably inclined toward petitioner's evidence of mental disturbance as a mitigating circumstance. More subtle, less consciously held racial attitudes could also influence a juror's decision in this case. Fear of blacks, which could easily be stirred up by the violent facts of petitioner's crime, might incline a juror to favor the death penalty.[7]

The risk of racial prejudice infecting a capital sentencing proceeding is especially serious in light of the complete finality of the death sentence. "The Court, as well as the separate opinions of a majority of the individual Justices, has recognized that the qualitative difference of death from all other punishments requires a correspondingly greater degree of scrutiny of the capital sentencing determination." *California v. Ramos*, 463 U.S. 992, 103 S.Ct. 3446 (1983). We have struck down capital sentences when

---

7. In referring to the facts of petitioner's crime, we do not retreat from our holding in *Ristaino*. The fact of interracial violence alone is not a "special circumstance" entitling the defendant to have prospective jurors questioned about racial prejudice. It should be clear, though, that our holding in *Ristaino* was not based on a blind belief that the facts presented in that case could not evoke racial prejudice. As we stated in *Rosales–Lopez v. United States*, 451 U.S. 182, 101 S.Ct. 1629 (1981): "It remains an unfortunate fact in our society that violent crimes perpetrated against members of other racial or ethnic groups often raise [a reasonable possibility that racial prejudice would influence the jury]." *Ristaino* does not condone this possibility, but simply leaves it to the trial judge's discretion to decide what measures to take in screening out racial prejudice, absent a showing of "significant likelihood that racial prejudice might infect [the] trial."

we found that the circumstances under which they were imposed "created an unacceptable risk that the death penalty [may have been] meted out arbitrarily or capriciously or through whim ... or mistake." *Caldwell, supra* (O'CONNOR, J., concurring in part and concurring in judgment). In the present case, we find the risk that racial prejudice may have infected petitioner's capital sentencing unacceptable in light of the ease with which that risk could have been minimized. By refusing to question prospective jurors on racial prejudice, the trial judge failed to adequately protect petitioner's constitutional right to an impartial jury.

III

We hold that a capital defendant accused of an interracial crime is entitled to have prospective jurors informed of the race of the victim and questioned on the issue of racial bias.[10] The rule we propose is minimally intrusive; as in other cases involving "special circumstances," the trial judge retains discretion as to the form and number of questions on the subject, including the decision whether to question the venire individually or collectively. Also, a defendant cannot complain of a judge's failure to question the venire on racial prejudice unless the defendant has specifically requested such an inquiry.

IV

The inadequacy of *voir dire* in this case requires that petitioner's death sentence be vacated. It is not necessary, however, that he be retried on the issue of guilt. Our judgment in this case is that there was an unacceptable risk of racial prejudice infecting the *capital sentencing proceeding*. This judgment is based on a conjunction of three factors: the fact that the crime charged involved interracial violence, the broad discretion given the jury at the death-penalty hearing, and the special seriousness of the risk of improper sentencing in a capital case.[11] At the guilt phase of petitioner's trial, the jury had no greater discretion than it would have had if the crime charged had been noncapital murder. Thus, with respect to the guilt phase of petitioner's trial, we find this case to be indistinguishable from *Ristaino*, to which we continue to adhere.

The judgment of the Court of Appeals is reversed, and the case is remanded for further proceedings consistent with this opinion.

THE CHIEF JUSTICE concurs in the judgment.

JUSTICE BRENNAN, concurring in part and dissenting in part.

* * *

---

10. Justice POWELL contends that inquiry into racial prejudice "in the absence of circumstances that make clear a need for it could well have the negative effect of suggesting to the jurors that race somehow is relevant to the case." Whether such a concern is purely chimerical or not is a decision we leave up to a capital defendant's counsel. Should defendant's counsel decline to request *voir dire* on the subject of racial prejudice, we in no way require or suggest that the judge broach the topic *sua sponte*.

11. We find it unnecessary to evaluate the statistical studies which petitioner has introduced in support of the proposition that black defendants who kill whites are executed with disproportionate frequency.

* * * I cannot fully join either the Court's judgment or opinion. For in my view, the decision in this case, although clearly half right, is even more clearly half wrong. After recognizing that the constitutional guarantee of an impartial jury entitles a defendant in a capital case involving interracial violence to have prospective jurors questioned on the issue of racial bias—a holding which requires that this case be reversed and remanded for new sentencing—the Court disavows the logic of its own reasoning in denying petitioner Turner a new trial on the issue of his guilt. It accomplishes this by postulating a jury role at the sentencing phase of a capital trial fundamentally different from the jury function at the guilt phase and by concluding that the former gives rise to a significantly greater risk of a verdict tainted by racism. Because I believe that the Court's analysis improperly intertwines the significance of the *risk* of bias with the *consequences* of bias, and because in my view the distinction between the jury's role at a guilt trial and its role at a sentencing hearing is a distinction without substance in so far as juror bias is concerned, I join only that portion of the Court's judgment granting petitioner a new sentencing proceeding, but dissent from that portion of the judgment refusing to vacate the conviction.

* * *

The Court identifies three factors, the "conjunction" of which in its view entitled petitioner Turner as a matter of constitutional right to have the jury questioned on racial bias. These are (1) the fact that the crime committed involved interracial violence; (2) the broad discretion given the jury at the death penalty hearing; and (3) the "special seriousness of the risk of improper sentencing in a capital case." I agree with the Court that when these three factors are present, as they were at petitioner's sentencing hearing, the trial court commits constitutional error in refusing a defense request to ask the jurors if the race of either the victim or the accused will bear on their ability to render a decision based solely on the evidence. What I cannot accept is that the judge is released from this obligation to insure an impartial jury—or, to put it another way, that the defendant is stripped of this constitutional safeguard—when a capital jury is hearing evidence concerning a crime involving interracial violence but passing "only" on the issue of guilt/innocence, rather than on the appropriate sentence.

The Court's argument is simply untenable on its face. As best I can understand it, the thesis is that since there is greater discretion entrusted to a capital jury in the sentencing phase than in the guilt phase, "there is [in the sentencing hearing] a unique opportunity for racial prejudice to operate but remain undetected." However, the Court's own discussion of the issues demonstrates that the opportunity for racial bias to taint the jury process is not "uniquely" present at a sentencing hearing, but is equally a factor at the guilt phase of a bifurcated capital trial.

According to the Court, a prejudiced juror sitting at a sentencing hearing might be influenced by his racial bias in deciding whether the crime committed involved aggravating factors specified under state law; the Court notes that racial prejudice might similarly cause that juror to be less favorably inclined toward an accused's evidence of mitigating circumstances. Moreover, the Court informs us:

> "More subtle, less consciously held racial attitudes could also influence a juror's decision.... Fear of blacks, which could easily be stirred up by the violent facts of [a] crime, might incline a juror to favor the death penalty."

The flaw in this "analysis" is that there is simply no connection between the proposition advanced, the support proffered for that thesis, and the conclusion drawn. In other words, it is certainly true, as the Court maintains, that racial bias inclines one to disbelieve and disfavor the object of the prejudice, and it is similarly incontestable that subconscious, as well as express, racial fears and hatreds operate to deny fairness to the person despised; that is why we seek to insure that the right to an impartial jury is a meaningful right by providing the defense with the opportunity to ask prospective jurors questions designed to expose even hidden prejudices. But the Court never explains why these biases should be of less concern at the guilt phase than at the sentencing phase. The majority asserts that "a juror who believes that blacks are violence prone or morally inferior might well be influenced by that belief in deciding whether petitioner's crime involved the aggravating factors specified under Virginia law." But might not that same juror be influenced by those same prejudices in deciding whether, for example, to credit or discredit white witnesses as opposed to black witnesses at the guilt phase? Might not those same racial fears that would incline a juror to favor death not also incline a juror to favor conviction?

A trial to determine guilt or innocence is, at bottom, nothing more than the sum total of a countless number of small discretionary decisions made by each individual who sits in the jury box. The difference between conviction and acquittal turns on whether key testimony is believed or rejected; on whether an alibi sounds plausible or dubious; on whether a character witness appears trustworthy or unsavory; and on whether the jury concludes that the defendant had a motive, the inclination, or the means available to commit the crime charged. A racially biased juror sits with blurred vision and impaired sensibilities and is incapable of fairly making the myriad decisions that each juror is called upon to make in the course of a trial. To put it simply, he cannot judge because he has prejudged. This is equally true at the trial on guilt as at the hearing on sentencing.

To sentence an individual to death on the basis of a proceeding tainted by racial bias would violate the most basic values of our criminal justice system. This the Court understands. But what it seems not to comprehend is that to permit an individual to be *convicted* by a prejudiced jury violates those same values in precisely the same way. The incongruity of the Court's split judgment is made apparent after it is appreciated that the opportunity for bias to poison decisionmaking operates at a guilt trial in the same way as it does at a sentencing hearing and after one returns to the context of the case before us. Implicit in the Court's judgment is the acknowledgment that there was a likelihood that the jury that pronounced the death sentence acted, in part, on the basis of racial prejudice. But the exact same jury convicted Turner. Does the Court really mean to suggest that the constitutional entitlement to an impartial jury attaches only at the sentencing phase? Does the Court really believe that racial biases are turned on and off in the course of one criminal prosecution?

* * *

The Court may believe that it is being Solomonic in "splitting the difference" in this case and granting petitioner a new sentencing hearing while denying him the other "half" of the relief demanded. Starkly put, petitioner "wins" in that he gets to be resentenced, while the State "wins" in that it does not lose its conviction. But King Solomon did not, in fact, split the baby in two, and had he done so, I suspect that he would be remembered less for his wisdom than for his hardheartedness. Justice is not served by compromising principles in this way. I would reverse the conviction as well as the sentence in this case to insure compliance with the constitutional guarantee of an impartial jury.

[Opinion of MARSHALL, J., joined by BRENNAN, J., concurring in the judgment in part and dissenting in part omitted]

JUSTICE POWELL, with whom JUSTICE REHNQUIST joins, dissenting.

The Court today adopts a *per se* rule applicable in capital cases, under which "a capital defendant accused of an interracial crime is entitled to have prospective jurors informed of the race of the victim and questioned on the issue of racial bias." This rule is certain to add to the already heavy burden of habeas petitions filed by prisoners under sentence of death without affording any real protection beyond that provided by our decisions in *Ham v. South Carolina*, 409 U.S. 524, 93 S.Ct. 848 (1973), and *Ristaino v. Ross*, 424 U.S. 589, 96 S.Ct. 1017 (1976).

* * *

The trial judge declined to ask the proposed [*voir dire*] question, but he did ask general questions designed to uncover bias. For example, the prospective jurors were asked, "Do any of you know any reason whatsoever why you cannot render a fair and impartial verdict in this case, either for the defendant or for the Commonwealth of Virginia?" Each juror responded negatively.[6] The jury of 12 persons ultimately empaneled included 4 black citizens, and a black juror was selected to act as foreman.

There is nothing in the record of this trial that reflects racial overtones of any kind. From *voir dire* through the close of trial, no

---

6. As the facts of *Ristaino v. Ross* demonstrate, such a general question can prompt a juror who is aware of the defendant's race, as the jurors were in this case, to admit to racial bias. This general inquiry into bias does not have the undesirable result of suggesting to the jurors that race is relevant to the issues in the case.

circumstance suggests that the trial judge's refusal to inquire particularly into racial bias posed "an impermissible threat to the fair trial guaranteed by due process." *Ristaino v. Ross*. The Court does not purport to identify any such circumstance, or to explain why the facts that a capital defendant is of one race and his victim of another now create a significant likelihood that racial issues will distort the jurors' consideration of the issues in the trial. This case illustrates that it is unnecessary for the Court to adopt a *per se* rule that constitutionalizes the unjustifiable presumption that jurors are racially biased.

II

Until today a trial judge committed an unconstitutional abuse of discretion by refusing to inquire into racial prejudice only when the defendant showed that racial issues "were inextricably bound up with the conduct of the trial." *Ristaino v. Ross*. When a defendant makes such a showing, there is an unacceptable risk that racial prejudice will "distort the trial." Under such circumstances, therefore, due process requires "a *voir dire* that include[s] questioning specifically directed to racial prejudice." In *Ristaino*, however, the Court expressly declined to adopt a *per se* rule requiring *voir dire* inquiry into racial bias in every trial for an interracial crime. Neither the Constitution nor sound policy considerations supported such a *per se* approach. But today the Court decides that the Constitution does require a *per se* rule in capital cases because the capital jury exercises discretion at the sentencing phase. The Court's reasoning ignores the many procedural and substantive safeguards, similar to those governing the jury's decision on guilt or innocence, that circumscribe the capital jury's sentencing decision.

Under Virginia law, murder is a capital offense only if it is "willful, deliberate and premeditated" and is committed while the perpetrator is engaged in another crime or under specified aggravating circumstances. As in any criminal prosecution, of course, the State carries the burden of proving all elements of the capital offense beyond a reasonable doubt. Following a sentencing hearing, the death sentence may not be imposed unless the State proves beyond a reasonable doubt statutorily defined aggravating factors. Virginia law recognizes only two aggravating factors: whether, based on the defendant's criminal record, there is a probability that he would commit future crimes of violence, and whether the defendant's crime was "outrageously or wantonly vile, horrible or inhuman, in that it involved torture, depravity of mind or aggravated battery to the victim." The jury also is required to consider any relevant mitigating evidence offered by the defendant.

The existence of these significant limitations on the jury's exercise of sentencing discretion illustrates why the Court's *per se* rule is wholly unfounded. Just as the trial judge's charge at the guilt phase instructs the jurors that they may consider only the evidence in the case and that they must determine if the prosecution has established each element of the crime beyond a reasonable doubt, the charge at the penalty phase directs the jurors to focus solely on considerations relevant to determination of appropriate punishment and to decide if the prosecution has established beyond a reasonable doubt factors warranting imposition of death. Accordingly, just as there is no reason to presume racial bias on the part of jurors who determine the guilt of a defendant who has committed a violent crime against a person of another race, there is no reason to constitutionalize such a presumption with respect to the jurors who sit to recommend the penalty in a capital case.

* * *

MILLER–EL v. DRETKE

545 U.S. 231, 125 S.Ct. 2317, 162 L.E.2d 196 (2005).

JUSTICE SOUTER delivered the opinion of the Court.

Two years ago, we ordered that a certificate of appealability, under 28 U.S.C. § 2253(c), be issued to habeas petitioner Miller–El, affording review of the District Court's rejection of the claim that prosecutors in his capital murder trial made peremptory strikes of potential jurors based on race. Today we find Miller–El entitled to prevail on that claim and order relief under § 2254.

I

In the course of robbing a Holiday Inn in Dallas, Texas in late 1985, Miller–El and his accomplices bound and gagged two hotel employees, whom Miller–El then shot, killing one and severely injuring the other. During jury selection in Miller–El's trial for capital murder, prosecutors used peremptory strikes against 10 qualified black venire members. Miller–El objected that the strikes were based on race and could not be presumed legitimate, given a history of excluding black members from criminal juries by the Dallas County District Attorney's Office. The trial court received evidence of the practice alleged but found no "systematic exclusion of blacks as a matter of policy" by that office, and therefore no entitlement to relief under *Swain v. Alabama,* 380 U.S. 202, 85 S.Ct. 824 (1965), the case then defining and marking the limits of relief from racially biased jury selection. The court denied Miller–El's request to pick a new jury, and the trial ended with his death sentence for capital murder.

While an appeal was pending, this Court decided *Batson v. Kentucky,* 476 U.S. 79, 106 S.Ct. 1712 (1986), which replaced *Swain*'s threshold requirement to prove systemic discrimination under a Fourteenth Amendment jury claim, with the rule that discrimination by the prosecutor in selecting the defendant's jury sufficed to establish the constitutional violation. The Texas Court of Criminal Appeals then remanded the matter to the trial court to determine whether Miller–El could show that prosecutors in his case peremptorily struck prospective black jurors because of race.

The trial court found no such demonstration. After reviewing the *voir dire* record of the explanations given for some of the challenged strikes, and after hearing one of the prosecutors, Paul Macaluso, give his justification for those previously unexplained, the trial court accepted the stated race-neutral reasons for the strikes, which the judge called "completely credible [and] sufficient" as the grounds for a finding of "no purposeful discrimination." [After the Court of Criminal Appeals affirmed, Miller–El sought habeas relief in federal court. The District Court denied relief, and the Court of Appeals for the Fifth Circuit precluded appeal by denying a certificate of appealability. The Supreme Court granted certiorari and reversed. *Miller–El v. Cockrell,* 534 U.S. 1122, 122 S.Ct. 981 (2002). On remand, the Fifth Circuit, granted a Certificate of Appealability but rejected Miller–El's *Batson* claim on the merits. The Supreme Court again granted certiorari.]

II

A

"It is well known that prejudices often exist against particular classes in the community, which sway the judgment of jurors, and which, therefore, operate in some cases to deny to persons of those classes the full enjoyment of that protection which others enjoy." *Strauder v. West Virginia,* 100 U.S. 303 (1880). Defendants are harmed, of course, when racial discrimination in jury selection compromises the right of trial by impartial jury, but racial minorities are harmed more generally, for prosecutors drawing racial lines in picking juries establish "state-sponsored group stereotypes rooted in, and reflective of, historical prejudice," *J.E.B. v. Alabama ex rel. T. B.,* 511 U.S. 127, 114 S.Ct. 1419 (1994).

Nor is the harm confined to minorities. When the government's choice of jurors is tainted with racial bias, that "overt wrong ... casts doubt over the obligation of the parties, the jury, and indeed the court to adhere to the law throughout the trial...." *Powers v. Ohio,* 499 U.S. 400, 111 S.Ct. 1364 (1991). That is, the very integrity of the courts is jeopardized when a prosecutor's discrimination "invites cynicism respecting the jury's neutrality," *id.,* and undermines public confidence in adjudication. So, "[f]or more than a century, this Court consistently and repeatedly has reaffirmed that racial discrimination by the State in jury selection offends the Equal Protection Clause." *Georgia v. McCollum,* 505 U.S. 42, 112 S.Ct. 2348 (1992).

The rub has been the practical difficulty of ferreting out discrimination in selections discretionary by nature, and choices subject to myriad legitimate influences, whatever the race of the individuals on the panel from which jurors are selected. In *Swain v. Alabama,* we tackled the problem of "the quantum of proof necessary" to show purposeful discrimination with an eye to preserving each side's historical prerogative to make a peremptory strike or challenge, the very nature of which is traditionally "without a reason stated." The *Swain* Court tried to relate peremptory challenge to equal protection by presuming the legitimacy of prosecutors' strikes except in the face of a longstanding pattern of discrimination: when "in case after case, whatever the circumstances," no blacks served on juries, then "giving even the widest leeway to the operation of irrational but trial-related suspicions and antagonisms, it would appear that the purposes of the peremptory challenge [were] being perverted."

Swain's demand to make out a continuity of discrimination over time, however, turned out to be difficult to the point of unworkable, and in *Batson v. Kentucky,* we recognized that this requirement to show an extended pattern imposed a "crippling burden of proof" that left prosecutors' use of peremptories "largely immune from constitutional scrutiny." By *Batson*'s day, the law implementing equal protection elsewhere had evolved into less discouraging standards for assessing a claim of purposeful discrimination, and we accordingly held that a defendant could make out a prima facie case of discriminatory jury selection by "the totality of the relevant facts" about a prosecutor's conduct during the defendant's own trial. "Once the defendant makes a prima facie showing, the burden shifts to the State to come forward with a neutral explanation for challenging . . . jurors" within an arguably targeted class. Although there may be "any number of bases on which a prosecutor reasonably [might] believe that it is desirable to strike a juror who is not excusable for cause . . ., the prosecutor must give a clear and reasonably specific explanation of his legitimate reasons for exercising the challeng[e]." "The trial court then will have the duty to determine if the defendant has established purposeful discrimination."

Although the move from *Swain* to *Batson* left a defendant free to challenge the prosecution without having to cast *Swain*'s wide net, the net was not entirely consigned to history, for *Batson*'s individualized focus came with a weakness of its own owing to its very emphasis on the particular reasons a prosecutor might give. If any facially neutral reason sufficed to answer a *Batson* challenge, then *Batson* would not amount to much more than *Swain*. Some stated reasons are false, and although some false reasons are shown up within the four corners of a given case, sometimes a court may not be sure unless it looks beyond the case at hand. Hence *Batson*'s explanation that a defendant may rely on "all relevant circumstances" to raise an inference of purposeful discrimination.

B

This case comes to us on review of a denial of habeas relief sought under 28 U.S.C. § 2254, following the Texas trial court's prior determination of fact that the State's race-neutral explanations were true.

Under the Antiterrorism and Effective Death Penalty Act of 1996, Miller–El may obtain relief only by showing the Texas conclusion to be "an unreasonable determination of the facts in light of the evidence presented in the State court proceeding." Thus we presume the Texas court's factual findings to be sound unless Miller–El rebuts the "presumption of correctness by clear and convincing evidence." The standard is demanding but not insatiable; as we said the last time this case was here, "[d]eference does not by definition preclude relief." *Miller–El v. Cockrell, supra.*

III

A

The numbers describing the prosecution's use of peremptories are remarkable. Out of 20 black members of the 108–person venire panel for Miller–El's trial, only 1 served. Although 9 were excused for cause or by agreement, 10 were peremptorily struck by the prosecution. "The prosecutors used their peremptory strikes to exclude 91% of the eligible African–American venire members.... Happenstance is unlikely to produce this disparity." *Id.*

More powerful than these bare statistics, however, are side-by-side comparisons of some black venire panelists who were struck and white panelists allowed to serve. If a prosecutor's proffered reason for striking a black panelist applies just as well to an otherwise-similar nonblack who is permitted to serve, that is evidence tending to prove purposeful discrimination to be considered at *Batson*'s third step. * * * The details of two panel member comparisons bear this out.

The prosecution used its second peremptory strike to exclude Billy Jean Fields, a black man who expressed unwavering support for the death penalty. On the questionnaire filled out by all panel members before individual examination on the stand, Fields said that he believed in capital punishment, and during questioning he disclosed his belief that the State acts on God's behalf when it imposes the death penalty. "Therefore, if the State exacts death, then that's what it should be." He testified that he had no religious or philosophical reservations about the death penalty and that the death penalty deterred crime. He twice averred, without apparent hesitation, that he could sit on Miller–El's jury and make a decision to impose this penalty.

Although at one point in the questioning, Fields indicated that the possibility of rehabilitation might be relevant to the likelihood that a defendant would commit future acts of violence, he responded to ensuing questions by saying that although he believed anyone could be rehabilitated, this belief would not stand in the way of a decision to impose the death penalty:

> "[B]ased on what you [the prosecutor] said as far as the crime goes, there are only two things that could be rendered, death or life in prison. If for some reason the testimony didn't warrant death, then life imprisonment would give an individual an opportunity to rehabilitate. But, you know, you said that the jurors didn't have the opportunity to make a personal decision in the matter with reference to what I thought or felt, but it was just based on the questions according to the way the law has been handed down."

Fields also noted on his questionnaire that his brother had a criminal history. During questioning, the prosecution went into this, too:

"Q Could you tell me a little bit about that?

"A He was arrested and convicted on [a] number of occasions for possession of a controlled substance.

"Q Was that here in Dallas?

"A Yes.

"Q Was he involved in any trials or anything like that?

"A I suppose of sorts. I don't really know too much about it.

"Q Was he ever convicted?

"A Yeah, he served time.

"Q Do you feel that that would in any way interfere with your service on this jury at all?

"A No."

Fields was struck peremptorily by the prosecution, with prosecutor James Nelson offering a race-neutral reason:

"[W]e ... have concern with reference to some of his statements as to the death penalty in that he said that he could only give death if he thought a person could not be rehabilitated and he later made the comment that any person could be rehabilitated if they find God or are introduced to God and the fact that we have a concern that his religious feelings may affect his jury service in this case."

Thus, Nelson simply mischaracterized Fields's testimony. He represented that Fields said he would not vote for death if rehabilitation was possible, whereas Fields unequivocally stated that he could impose the death penalty regardless of the possibility of rehabilitation. Perhaps Nelson misunderstood, but unless he had an ulterior reason for keeping Fields off the jury we think he would have proceeded differently. In light of Fields's outspoken support for the death penalty, we expect the prosecutor would have cleared up any misunderstanding by asking further questions before getting to the point of exercising a strike.

If, indeed, Fields's thoughts on rehabilitation did make the prosecutor uneasy, he should have worried about a number of white panel members he accepted with no evident reservations. Sandra Hearn said that she believed in the death penalty "if a criminal cannot be rehabilitated and continues to commit the same type of crime." Hearn went so far as to express doubt that at the penalty phase of a capital case she could conclude that a convicted murderer "would probably commit some criminal acts of violence in the future." "People change," she said, making it hard to assess the risk of someone's future dangerousness. "[T]he evidence would have to be awful strong." But the prosecution did not respond to Hearn the way it did to Fields, and without delving into her views about rehabilitation with any further question, it raised no objection to her serving on the jury. White panelist Mary Witt said she would take the possibility of rehabilitation into account in deciding at the penalty phase of the trial about a defendant's probability of future dangerousness, but the prosecutors asked her no further question about her views on reformation, and they accepted her as a juror. Latino venireman Fernando Gutierrez, who served on the jury, said that he would consider the death penalty for someone who could not be rehabilitated, but the prosecutors did not question him further about this view. In sum, nonblack jurors whose remarks on rehabilitation could well have signaled a limit on their willingness to impose a death sentence were not questioned further and drew no objection, but the prosecution expressed apprehension about a black juror's belief in the possibility of reformation even though he repeatedly stated his approval of the death penalty and testified that he could impose it according to state legal standards even when the alternative sentence of life imprisonment would give a defendant (like everyone else in the world) the opportunity to reform.[5]

The unlikelihood that his position on rehabilitation had anything to do with the peremptory strike of Fields is underscored by the prosecution's response after Miller–El's lawyer pointed out that the prosecutor had misrepresented Fields's responses on the subject. A moment earlier the prosecutor had finished his misdescription of Fields's views on potential rehabilitation with the words, "Those are our reasons for exercising our ... strike at this time." When defense counsel called him on his misstatement, he neither defended what he said nor withdrew the strike. Instead, he suddenly came up with Fields's brother's prior conviction as another reason for the strike.

It would be difficult to credit the State's new explanation, which reeks of afterthought. While the Court of Appeals tried to bolster it with the observation that no seated juror was in Fields's position with respect to his brother, the court's readiness to accept the State's substitute reason ignores not only its pretextual timing but the other reasons rendering it implausible. Fields's testimony indicated he was not close to his brother ("I don't really know too much about it"), and the prosecution asked nothing further about the influence his brother's history might have had on Fields, as it probably would have done if the family history had actually mattered. There is no good reason to doubt that the State's afterthought about Fields's brother was anything but makeweight.

* * *

In sum, when we look for nonblack jurors similarly situated to Fields, we find strong similarities as well as some differences.[6] But the differences

---

5. Prosecutors did exercise peremptory strikes on Penny Crowson and Charlotte Whaley, who expressed views about rehabilitation similar to those of Witt and Gutierrez.

6. The dissent contends that there are no white panelists similarly situated to Fields and to panel member Joe Warren because " '[s]imilarly situated' does not mean matching any one of several reasons the prosecution gave for striking a potential juror—it means matching *all* of them." (quoting *Miller–El v. Cockrell* (THOMAS, J., dissenting)). None of our cases announces a rule that no comparison is probative unless the situation of the individuals compared is identical in all respects, and there is no reason to accept one. Nothing in the combination of Fields's statements about rehabilitation and his brother's history discredits our grounds for inferring that these purported reasons were pretextual. A *per se* rule that a defendant cannot win a *Batson*

seem far from significant, particularly when we read Fields's *voir dire* testimony in its entirety. Upon that reading, Fields should have been an ideal juror in the eyes of a prosecutor seeking a death sentence, and the prosecutors' explanations for the strike cannot reasonably be accepted.

The prosecution's proffered reasons for striking Joe Warren, another black venireman, are comparably unlikely. Warren gave this answer when he was asked what the death penalty accomplished:

"I don't know. It's really hard to say because I know sometimes you feel that it might help to deter crime and then you feel that the person is not really suffering. You're taking the suffering away from him. So it's like I said, sometimes you have mixed feelings about whether or not this is punishment or, you know, you're relieving personal punishment."

The prosecution said nothing about these remarks when it struck Warren from the panel, but prosecutor Paul Macaluso referred to this answer as the first of his reasons when he testified at the later *Batson* hearing:

"I thought [Warren's statements on *voir dire*] were inconsistent responses. At one point he says, you know, on a case-by-case basis and at another point he said, well, I think—I got the impression, at least, that he suggested that the death penalty was an easy way out, that they should be made to suffer more."

On the face of it, the explanation is reasonable from the State's point of view, but its plausibility is severely undercut by the prosecution's failure to object to other panel members who expressed views much like Warren's. Kevin Duke, who served on the jury, said, "sometimes death would be better to me than—being in prison would be like dying every day and, if you were in prison for life with no hope of parole, I['d] just as soon have it over with than be in prison for the rest of your life." Troy Woods, the one black panelist to serve as juror, said that capital punishment "is too easy. I think that's a quick relief.... I feel like [hard labor is] more of a punishment than putting them to sleep." Sandra Jenkins, whom the State accepted (but who was then struck by the defense) testified that she thought "a harsher treatment is life imprisonment with no parole." Leta Girard, accepted by the State (but also struck by the defense) gave her opinion that "living sometimes is a worse—is worse to me than dying would be." The fact that Macaluso's reason also applied to these other panel members, most of them white, none of them struck, is evidence of pretext.

The suggestion of pretext is not, moreover, mitigated much by Macaluso's explanation that Warren was struck when the State had 10 peremptory challenges left and could afford to be liberal in using them. If that were the explanation for striking Warren and later accepting panel members who thought death would be too easy, the prosecutors should have struck Sandra Jenkins, whom they examined and accepted before Warren.

claim unless there is an exactly identical white juror would leave *Batson* inoperable; potential jurors are not products of a set of cookie cutters.

Indeed, the disparate treatment is the more remarkable for the fact that the prosecutors repeatedly questioned Warren on his capacity and willingness to impose a sentence of death and elicited statements of his ability to do so if the evidence supported that result and the answer to each special question was yes, whereas the record before us discloses no attempt to determine whether Jenkins would be able to vote for death in spite of her view that it was easy on the convict. Yet the prosecutors accepted the white panel member Jenkins and struck the black venireman Warren.

Macaluso's explanation that the prosecutors grew more sparing with peremptory challenges as the jury selection wore on does, however, weaken any suggestion that the State's acceptance of Woods, the one black juror, shows that race was not in play. Woods was the eighth juror, qualified in the fifth week of jury selection. When the State accepted him, 11 of its 15 peremptory strikes were gone, 7 of them used to strike black panel members. The juror questionnaires show that at least three members of the venire panel yet to be questioned on the stand were opposed to capital punishment.[7] With at least three remaining panel members highly undesirable to the State, the prosecutors had to exercise prudent restraint in using strikes. This late-stage decision to accept a black panel member willing to impose a death sentence does not, therefore, neutralize the early-stage decision to challenge a comparable venireman, Warren. In fact, if the prosecutors were going to accept any black juror to obscure the otherwise consistent pattern of opposition to seating one, the time to do so was getting late.[8]

The Court of Appeals pretermitted these difficulties by stating that the prosecution's reason for striking Warren was a more general ambivalence about the penalty and his ability to impose it. But this rationalization was erroneous as a matter of fact and as a matter of law.

As to fact, Macaluso said nothing about any general ambivalence. He simply alluded to the possibility that Warren might think the death penalty too easy on some defendants, saying nothing about Warren's ability to impose the penalty when it appeared to be warranted.[9] On the

---

7. Each of them was black and each was peremptorily struck by the State after Woods's acceptance. It is unclear whether the prosecutors knew they were black prior to the *voir dire* questioning on the stand, though there is some indication that they did: prosecutors noted the race of each panelist on all of the juror cards, even for those panelists who were never questioned individually because the week ended before it was their turn.

8. Nor is pretextual indication mitigated by Macaluso's further reason that Warren had a brother-in-law convicted of a crime having to do with food stamps for which he had to make restitution. Macaluso never questioned Warren about his errant relative at all; as with Fields's brother, the failure to ask undermines the persuasiveness of the claimed concern. And Warren's brother's criminal history was comparable to those of relatives of other panel members not struck by prosecutors. Cheryl Davis's husband had been convicted of theft and received seven years' probation. Chatta Nix's brother was involved in white-collar fraud. Noad Vickery's sister served time in a penitentiary several decades ago.

9. But even if Macaluso actually had explained that he exercised the strike because Warren was diffident about imposing death, it would have been hard to square that explanation with the prosecution's tolerance for a number of ambivalent white panel members. Juror Marie Mazza, for example, admitted some concern about what her associates might think of her if she sat on a jury that called for the death penalty. Ronald Salsini, accepted by the prosecution but then struck by

contrary, though Warren had indeed questioned the extent to which the death penalty served a purpose in society, he explained his position in response to the very next question: it was not any qualm about imposing what society generally deems its harshest punishment, but his concern that the death penalty might not be severe enough. When Warren was asked whether he could impose the death penalty he said he thought he could; when told that answering yes to the special issue questions would be tantamount to voting for death he said he could give yes answers if the evidence supported them.

As for law, the rule in *Batson* provides an opportunity to the prosecutor to give the reason for striking the juror, and it requires the judge to assess the plausibility of that reason in light of all evidence with a bearing on it. It is true that peremptories are often the subjects of instinct, and it can sometimes be hard to say what the reason is. But when illegitimate grounds like race are in issue, a prosecutor simply has got to state his reasons as best he can and stand or fall on the plausibility of the reasons he gives. A *Batson* challenge does not call for a mere exercise in thinking up any rational basis. If the stated reason does not hold up, its pretextual significance does not fade because a trial judge, or an appeals court, can imagine a reason that might not have been shown up as false. The Court of Appeals's and the dissent's substitution of a reason for eliminating Warren does nothing to satisfy the prosecutors' burden of stating a racially neutral explanation for their own actions.

The whole of the *voir dire* testimony subject to consideration casts the prosecution's reasons for striking Warren in an implausible light. Comparing his strike with the treatment of panel members who expressed similar views supports a conclusion that race was significant in determining who was challenged and who was not.

B

The case for discrimination goes beyond these comparisons to include broader patterns of practice during the jury selection. The prosecution's shuffling of the venire panel, its enquiry into views on the death penalty, its questioning about minimum acceptable sentences: all indicate decisions probably based on race. Finally, the appearance of discrimination is confirmed by widely known evidence of the general policy of the Dallas County District Attorney's Office to exclude black venire members from juries at the time Miller–El's jury was selected.

The first clue to the prosecutors' intentions, distinct from the peremptory challenges themselves, is their resort during *voir dire* to a procedure known in Texas as the jury shuffle. In the State's criminal practice, either side may literally reshuffle the cards bearing panel members' names, thus rearranging the order in which members of a venire panel are seated and reached for questioning. Once the order is established, the panel members

---

the defense, worried that if he gave the death penalty he might have a "problem" in the future with having done so. Witt, another panel member accepted by the State but struck by the defense, said she did not know if she could give that sentence.

seated at the back are likely to escape *voir dire* altogether, for those not questioned by the end of the week are dismissed. * * *

In this case, the prosecution and then the defense shuffled the cards at the beginning of the first week of *voir dire;* the record does not reflect the changes in order. At the beginning of the second week, when a number of black members were seated at the front of the panel, the prosecution shuffled. At the beginning of the third week, the first four panel members were black. The prosecution shuffled, and these black panel members ended up at the back. Then the defense shuffled, and the black panel members again appeared at the front. The prosecution requested another shuffle, but the trial court refused. Finally, the defense shuffled at the beginning of the fourth and fifth weeks of *voir dire;* the record does not reflect the panel's racial composition before or after those shuffles.

The State notes in its brief that there might be racially neutral reasons for shuffling the jury, and we suppose there might be. But no racially neutral reason has ever been offered in this case, and nothing stops the suspicion of discriminatory intent from rising to an inference.

The next body of evidence that the State was trying to avoid black jurors is the contrasting *voir dire* questions posed respectively to black and nonblack panel members, on two different subjects. First, there were the prosecutors' statements preceding questions about a potential juror's thoughts on capital punishment. Some of these prefatory statements were cast in general terms, but some followed the so-called graphic script, describing the method of execution in rhetorical and clinical detail. It is intended, Miller–El contends, to prompt some expression of hesitation to consider the death penalty and thus to elicit plausibly neutral grounds for a peremptory strike of a potential juror subjected to it, if not a strike for cause. If the graphic script is given to a higher proportion of blacks than whites, this is evidence that prosecutors more often wanted blacks off the jury, absent some neutral and extenuating explanation.

As we pointed out last time, for 94% of white venire panel members, prosecutors gave a bland description of the death penalty before asking about the individual's feelings on the subject. The abstract account went something like this:

> "I feel like it [is] only fair that we tell you our position in this case. The State of Texas ... is actively seeking the death penalty in this case for Thomas Joe Miller–El. We anticipate that we will be able to present to a jury the quantity and type of evidence necessary to convict him of capital murder and the quantity and type of evidence sufficient to allow a jury to answer these three questions over here in the affirmative. A yes answer to each of those questions results in an automatic death penalty from Judge McDowell."

Only 6% of white venire panelists, but 53% of those who were black, heard a different description of the death penalty before being asked their feelings about it. This is an example of the graphic script:

"I feel like you have a right to know right up front what our position is. Mr. Kinne, Mr. Macaluso and myself, representing the people of Dallas County and the state of Texas, are actively seeking the death penalty for Thomas Joe Miller–El. . . .

"We do that with the anticipation that, when the death penalty is assessed, at some point Mr. Thomas Joe Miller–El—the man sitting right down there—will be taken to Huntsville and will be put on death row and at some point taken to the death house and placed on a gurney and injected with a lethal substance until he is dead as a result of the proceedings that we have in this court on this case. So that's basically our position going into this thing."

The State concedes that this disparate questioning did occur but argues that use of the graphic script turned not on a panelist's race but on expressed ambivalence about the death penalty in the preliminary questionnaire. Prosecutors were trying, the argument goes, to weed out noncommittal or uncertain jurors, not black jurors. And while some white venire members expressed opposition to the death penalty on their questionnaires, they were not read the graphic script because their feelings were already clear. The State says that giving the graphic script to these panel members would only have antagonized them.

This argument, however, first advanced in dissent when the case was last here, *Miller–El v. Cockrell, supra* (opinion of THOMAS, J.), and later adopted by the State and the Court of Appeals, simply does not fit the facts. Looking at the answers on the questionnaires, and at *voir dire* testimony expressly discussing answers on the questionnaires, we find that black venire members were more likely than nonblacks to receive the graphic script regardless of their expressions of certainty or ambivalence about the death penalty, and the State's chosen explanation for the graphic script fails in the cases of four out of the eight black panel members who received it. Two of them, Janice Mackey and Anna Keaton, clearly stated opposition to the death penalty but they received the graphic script, while the black panel members Wayman Kennedy and Jeannette Butler were unambiguously in favor but got the graphic description anyway. The State's explanation does even worse in the instances of the five nonblacks who received the graphic script, missing the mark four times out of five: Vivian Sztybel and Filemon Zablan received it, although each was unambiguously in favor of the death penalty, while Dominick Desinise and Clara Evans unambiguously opposed it but were given the graphic version.

The State's purported rationale fails again if we look only to the treatment of ambivalent panel members, ambivalent black individuals having been more likely to receive the graphic description than ambivalent nonblacks. Three nonblack members of the venire indicated ambivalence to the death penalty on their questionnaires; only one of them, Fernando Gutierrez, received the graphic script. But of the four black panel members who expressed ambivalence, all got the graphic treatment.

The State's attempt at a race-neutral rationalization thus simply fails to explain what the prosecutors did. But if we posit instead that the prosecutors' first object was to use the graphic script to make a case for excluding black panel members opposed to or ambivalent about the death penalty, there is a much tighter fit of fact and explanation. Of the 10 nonblacks whose questionnaires expressed ambivalence or opposition, only 30% received the graphic treatment. But of the seven blacks who expressed ambivalence or opposition, 86% heard the graphic script. As between the State's ambivalence explanation and Miller–El's racial one, race is much the better, and the reasonable inference is that race was the major consideration when the prosecution chose to follow the graphic script.

The same is true for another kind of disparate questioning, which might fairly be called trickery. The prosecutors asked members of the panel how low a sentence they would consider imposing for murder. Most potential jurors were first told that Texas law provided for a minimum term of five years, but some members of the panel were not, and if a panel member then insisted on a minimum above five years, the prosecutor would suppress his normal preference for tough jurors and claim cause to strike. Two Terms ago, we described how this disparate questioning was correlated with race:

> "Ninety-four percent of whites were informed of the statutory minimum sentence, compared [with] only twelve and a half percent of African–Americans. No explanation is proffered for the statistical disparity. Indeed, while petitioner's appeal was pending before the Texas Court of Criminal Appeals, that court found a *Batson* violation where this precise line of disparate questioning on mandatory minimums was employed by one of the same prosecutors who tried the instant case." *Miller–El v. Cockrell, supra.*

The State concedes that the manipulative minimum punishment questioning was used to create cause to strike, but now it offers the extenuation that prosecutors omitted the 5–year information not on the basis of race, but on stated opposition to the death penalty, or ambivalence about it, on the questionnaires and in the *voir dire* testimony. On the State's identification of black panel members opposed or ambivalent, all were asked the trick question. But the State's rationale flatly fails to explain why most white panel members who expressed similar opposition or ambivalence were not subjected to it. It is entirely true, as the State argues, that prosecutors struck a number of nonblack members of the panel (as well as black members) for cause or by agreement before they reached the point in the standard *voir dire* sequence to question about minimum punishment. But this is no answer; 8 of the 11 nonblack individuals who voiced opposition or ambivalence were asked about the acceptable minimum only after being told what state law required. Hence, only 27% of nonblacks questioned on the subject who expressed these views were subjected to the trick question, as against 100% of black members. Once again, the implication of race in the prosecutors' choice of questioning cannot be explained away.

There is a final body of evidence that confirms this conclusion. We know that for decades leading up to the time this case was tried prosecutors in the Dallas County office had followed a specific policy of systematically excluding blacks from juries, as we explained the last time the case was here.

> "Although most of the witnesses [presented at the *Swain* hearing in 1986] denied the existence of a systematic policy to exclude African–Americans, others disagreed. A Dallas County district judge testified that, when he had served in the District Attorney's Office from the late–1950's to early–1960's, his superior warned him that he would be fired if he permitted any African–Americans to serve on a jury. Similarly, another Dallas County district judge and former assistant district attorney from 1976 to 1978 testified that he believed the office had a systematic policy of excluding African–Americans from juries.

> "Of more importance, the defense presented evidence that the District Attorney's Office had adopted a formal policy to exclude minorities from jury service.... A manual entitled 'Jury Selection in a Criminal Case' [sometimes known as the Sparling Manual] was distributed to prosecutors. It contained an article authored by a former prosecutor (and later a judge) under the direction of his superiors in the District Attorney's Office, outlining the reasoning for excluding minorities from jury service. Although the manual was written in 1968, it remained in circulation until 1976, if not later, and was available at least to one of the prosecutors in Miller–El's trial." *Miller–El v. Cockrell, supra.*

     * * *

In the course of drawing a jury to try a black defendant, 10 of the 11 qualified black venire panel members were peremptorily struck. At least two of them, Fields and Warren, were ostensibly acceptable to prosecutors seeking a death verdict, and Fields was ideal. The prosecutors' chosen race-neutral reasons for the strikes do not hold up and are so far at odds with the evidence that pretext is the fair conclusion, indicating the very discrimination the explanations were meant to deny.

The strikes that drew these incredible explanations occurred in a selection process replete with evidence that the prosecutors were selecting and rejecting potential jurors because of race. At least two of the jury shuffles conducted by the State make no sense except as efforts to delay consideration of black jury panelists to the end of the week, when they might not even be reached. The State has in fact never offered any other explanation. Nor has the State denied that disparate lines of questioning were pursued: 53% of black panelists but only 3% of nonblacks were questioned with a graphic script meant to induce qualms about applying the death penalty (and thus explain a strike), and 100% of blacks but only 27% of nonblacks were subjected to a trick question about the minimum acceptable penalty for murder, meant to induce a disqualifying answer. The State's attempts to explain the prosecutors' questioning of particular witnesses on nonracial grounds fit the evidence less well than the racially discriminatory hypothesis.

If anything more is needed for an undeniable explanation of what was going on, history supplies it. The prosecutors took their cues from a 20–year old manual of tips on jury selection, as shown by their notes of the race of each potential juror. By the time a jury was chosen, the State had peremptorily challenged 12% of qualified nonblack panel members, but eliminated 91% of the black ones.

It blinks reality to deny that the State struck Fields and Warren, included in that 91%, because they were black. The strikes correlate with no fact as well as they correlate with race, and they occurred during a selection infected by shuffling and disparate questioning that race explains better than any race-neutral reason advanced by the State. The State's pretextual positions confirm Miller–El's claim, and the prosecutors' own notes proclaim that the Sparling Manual's emphasis on race was on their minds when they considered every potential juror.

The state court's conclusion that the prosecutors' strikes of Fields and Warren were not racially determined is shown up as wrong to a clear and convincing degree; the state court's conclusion was unreasonable as well as erroneous. The judgment of the Court of Appeals is reversed, and the case is remanded for entry of judgment for petitioner together with orders of appropriate relief.

It is so ordered.

Justice Breyer, concurring.

In *Batson v. Kentucky,* 476 U.S. 79, 106 S.Ct. 1712 (1986), the Court adopted a burden-shifting rule designed to ferret out the unconstitutional use of race in jury selection. In his separate opinion, Justice Thurgood Marshall predicted that the Court's rule would not achieve its goal. The only way to "end the racial discrimination that peremptories inject into the jury-selection process," he concluded, was to "eliminat[e] peremptory challenges entirely." (concurring opinion). Today's case reinforces Justice Marshall's concerns.

I

To begin with, this case illustrates the practical problems of proof that Justice Marshall described. As the Court's opinion makes clear, Miller–El marshaled extensive evidence of racial bias. But despite the strength of his claim, Miller–El's challenge has resulted in 17 years of largely unsuccessful and protracted litigation—including 8 different judicial proceedings and 8 different judicial opinions, and involving 23 judges, of whom 6 found the *Batson* standard violated and 16 the contrary.

The complexity of this process reflects the difficulty of finding a legal test that will objectively measure the inherently subjective reasons that underlie use of a peremptory challenge. *Batson* seeks to square this circle by (1) requiring defendants to establish a prima facie case of discrimination, (2) asking prosecutors then to offer a race-neutral explanation for their use of the peremptory, and then (3) requiring defendants to prove that the neutral reason offered is pretextual. But *Batson* embodies defects intrinsic to the task.

At *Batson's* first step, litigants remain free to misuse peremptory challenges as long as the strikes fall *below* the prima facie threshold level. At *Batson's* second step, prosecutors need only tender a neutral reason, not a "persuasive, or even plausible" one. *Purkett v. Elem,* 514 U.S. 765, 115 S.Ct. 1769 (1995) *(per curiam)* ("mustaches and the beards look suspicious"). And most importantly, at step three, *Batson* asks judges to engage in the awkward, sometime hopeless, task of second-guessing a prosecutor's instinctive judgment—the underlying basis for which may be invisible even to the prosecutor exercising the challenge. See *Batson* (Marshall, J., concurring) (noting that the unconscious internalization of racial stereotypes may lead litigants more easily to conclude "that a prospective black juror is 'sullen,' or 'distant,'" even though that characterization would not have sprung to mind had the prospective juror been white). In such circumstances, it may be impossible for trial courts to discern if a " 'seat-of-the-pants' " peremptory challenge reflects a " 'seat-of-the-pants' " racial stereotype. *Batson* (Marshall, J., concurring) (quoting *id.* (REHNQUIST, J., dissenting)).

* * *

II

Practical problems of proof to the side, peremptory challenges seem increasingly anomalous in our judicial system. On the one hand, the Court has widened and deepened *Batson's* basic constitutional rule. It has applied *Batson's* antidiscrimination test to the use of peremptories by criminal defendants, *Georgia v. McCollum,* 505 U.S. 42, 112 S.Ct. 2348 (1992), by private litigants in civil cases, *Edmonson v. Leesville Concrete Co.,* 500 U.S. 614, 111 S.Ct. 2077 (1991), and by prosecutors where the defendant and the excluded juror are of different races, *Powers v. Ohio,* 499 U.S. 400, 111 S.Ct. 1364 (1991). It has recognized that the Constitution protects not just defendants, but the jurors themselves. *Id..* And it has held that equal protection principles prohibit excusing jurors on account of gender. See *J.E.B. v. Alabama ex rel. T. B.,* 511 U.S. 127, 114 S.Ct. 1419 (1994). Some lower courts have extended *Batson's* rule to religious affiliation as well.

On the other hand, the use of race- and gender-based stereotypes in the jury-selection process seems better organized and more systematized than ever before. [Justice Breyer cited several practice guides and advertisements from jury-selection consultants which recommended that attorneys perform sophisticated demographic analyses, based on a number of factors, including race and gender, in selecting juries.]

These examples reflect a professional effort to fulfill the lawyer's obligation to help his or her client. Nevertheless, the outcome in terms of jury selection is the same as it would be were the motive less benign. And as long as that is so, the law's antidiscrimination command and a peremptory jury-selection system that permits or encourages the use of stereotypes work at cross-purposes.

Finally, a jury system without peremptories is no longer unthinkable. * * * And England, a common-law jurisdiction that has eliminated peremptory challenges, continues to administer fair trials based largely on random jury selection.

III

I recognize that peremptory challenges have a long historical pedigree. They may help to reassure a party of the fairness of the jury. But long ago, Blackstone recognized the peremptory challenge as an "arbitrary and capricious species of [a] challenge." 4 W. Blackstone, Commentaries on the Laws of England 346 (1769). If used to express stereotypical judgments about race, gender, religion, or national origin, peremptory challenges betray the jury's democratic origins and undermine its representative function. The "scientific" use of peremptory challenges may also contribute to public cynicism about the fairness of the jury system and its role in American government. And, of course, the right to a jury free of discriminatory taint is constitutionally protected—the right to use peremptory challenges is not.

Justice Goldberg, dissenting in *Swain v. Alabama,* 380 U.S. 202, 85 S.Ct. 824 (1965), wrote, "Were it necessary to make an absolute choice between the right of a defendant to have a jury chosen in conformity with the requirements of the Fourteenth Amendment and the right to challenge peremptorily, the Constitution compels a choice of the former." This case suggests the need to confront that choice. In light of the considerations I have mentioned, I believe it necessary to reconsider *Batson*'s test and the peremptory challenge system as a whole. With that qualification, I join the Court's opinion.

[Dissenting opinion of THOMAS, J., joined by REHNQUIST, C.J. and SCALIA, J. omitted]

NOTES

1. *Snyder v. Louisiana*

In *Snyder v. Louisiana,* ___ U.S. ___, 128 S.Ct. 1203 (2008), the Supreme Court again reviewed the state courts' denial of a *Batson* challenge. At Snyder's trial for capital murder, 85 prospective jurors were questioned as members of a panel. Thirty-six survived challenges for cause; 5 of the 36 were black; and all 5 of the black prospective jurors were eliminated by the prosecution through the use of peremptory strikes. Defense counsel challenged the strikes under *Batson*. With regard to one juror, Brooks, the prosecutor offered two reasons for the strike: (1) "he looked very nervous during the questioning" and (2) Brooks was in college and in the process of doing his student teaching and therefore might be anxious to get the case over quickly with a lesser verdict in order not to miss so much class time. This second reason was explored on *voir dire*. Brooks testified that he was obliged to be at school every day and that he had to teach for 300 hours during the semester, but the judge contacted Brooks' dean and was told that Brooks would have no problem making up the five days the trial was anticipated to last. Brooks voiced no further concern about missing class, and the prosecution did not question him more deeply about the matter. The judge denied the *Batson* challenge, and Snyder was convicted and sentenced to death. The conviction and sentence were upheld by the Louisiana Supreme Court.

The Supreme Court reversed (7–2). As to the prosecutor's first justification for the strike—that Brooks appeared nervous—the Court reaffirmed that a reviewing court is required to give a trial judge's evaluation of a juror great deference but held that, since the trial judge made no finding as to Brooks' nervousness, the Court could not presume that any such finding was made. As to the prosecutor's second justification—his alleged concern that Brooks would want to shorten the trial by finding Snyder guilty of a lesser included offense—the Court cited to three reasons for finding it to be a pretext: (1) the concern was "highly speculative" because whether Brooks' voting for a lesser included offense would shorten the trial would depend entirely on the position of the other jurors—if the majority favored a first-degree murder verdict, voting with them would be the way to speed deliberations; (2) the concern was "suspicious," given the anticipated shortness of the trial and the dean's assurances that Brooks could make up the hours; and (3) the prosecutor accepted at least two white jurors who claimed conflicting obligations at least as serious as those of Brooks and who had, in fact, asked to be excused for cause.

2. *Establishing a prima facie case.*

Miller–El concerned whether the defendant had satisfied his burden of proof of discriminatory purpose at the third stage of his *Batson* challenge. In *Johnson v. California*, 545 U.S. 162, 125 S.Ct. 2410 (2005), decided the same day as *Miller–El*, the Supreme Court addressed the burden of proof at the first stage of a *Batson* challenge. In *Johnson*, the defendant, a black man, was charged with second degree murder and assault on a child resulting in death in the killing of a 19–month–old white child. During jury selection, he objected after the prosecutor struck all three blacks in the jury pool. The trial judge rejected the challenge, without requiring the prosecutor to explain his strikes, finding that the defendant had not made out a *prima facie* case of discriminatory purpose. On appeal after the defendant's conviction, the California Supreme Court upheld the trial court's ruling on the ground that the defendant had failed to produce "strong evidence that makes discriminatory intent *more likely than not* if the challenges are not explained." The Supreme Court reversed, finding no support in *Batson* for a "more likely than not" standard for the defendant's *prima facie* case and holding that the defendant need do no more than proffer facts giving rise to an inference of discrimination.

3. *Does jurors' race matter?*

Empirical studies of decision-making by mock jurors and actual capital jurors have attempted to determine whether, and how, jurors' race affects penalty decisions in capital cases. The most recent and substantial study of actual capital jurors used data collected on 340 capital cases in 14 states by the Capital Jury Project. See W. Bowers, B. Steiner & M. Sandys, *Death Sentencing in Black and White: An Empirical Analysis of the Role of Jurors' Race and Jury Racial Composition*, 3 U. Pa. J. Const. L. 171 (2001). The researchers focused on cases involving three defendant/victim racial combinations, together accounting for 88% of the cases in the sample: white defendant/white victim (W/W); black defendant/white victim (B/W); and black defendant/black victim (B/B).[a] Juror interviews revealed differences in perspective between black and white jurors on three significant factors in the penalty decision: (1) lingering doubt as to the defendant's guilt; (2) the defendant's remorse; and (3) the defendant's future dangerousness. Black jurors, more than white jurors, were likely to have a lingering doubt and were likely to feel the defendant was remorseful. With regard to future dangerousness, white jurors tended to believe that black defendants were more dangerous than white defendants, and black jurors tended to believe those who killed blacks were more dangerous than those who killed whites. In W/W and B/B cases, the same-race jurors tended to reach their penalty decision at an earlier stage and to be more pro-death than jurors of the other race, but outcomes were not significantly affected by jury composition. In B/W cases, the jurors diverged dramatically.

> Compared to the decision patterns of black and white jurors in the W/W and B/B cases, the progressive polarization of jurors' punishment stands in B/W cases is unique. By the time of the jury's first vote on punishment, two out of three whites believe the punishment should be death and two out of three blacks believe it should be life imprisonment.

Id. at 259–260. Because of this polarization, the racial composition of the jury in B/W cases, and, in particular the race of the men on the jury, had a critical effect on the outcome. The researchers found:

> [T]hese data indicate that the race and gender composition of juries had a decisive effect on capital sentencing in B/W cases. The presence of five or more white male jurors dramatically increased the likelihood of a death sentence in B/W cases, but not in W/W or B/B cases. Having a black male on the jury substantially reduced the likelihood of a death sentence in B/W cases, less so in B/B cases, and not at all in W/W cases. By contrast, the number of black or white female jurors was largely unrelated to sentencing outcomes. Only in the fourteen W/W cases with three or more black female jurors was death sentencing reduced. The number of white female jurors was unrelated to sentencing outcomes in all three defendant-victim categories of cases.

Id. at 195.

---

a. The remaining cases involved white defendants and black victims, Hispanic defendants or victims, or cases where the race or ethnicity of the defendant or victim could not be determined.

CHAPTER 7

THE DEFENDANT AND DEFENSE COUNSEL

■ ■ ■

The cases in this chapter consider the respective roles of the defendant and defense counsel in a capital case. The first case, *Godinez v. Moran*, involves a defendant who decided not to resist execution. (Such defendants are known among death penalty litigators as "volunteers.") The defendant, prior to trial, was permitted to discharge his attorneys and plead guilty, and he was thereafter sentenced to death. The Supreme Court delineates the standards for determining the defendant's competency to make such decisions.

The next five cases in the chapter concern claims of ineffective assistance of counsel at trial. The Sixth Amendment right to counsel at trial encompasses a right to effective assistance of counsel. The Supreme Court has recognized four species of ineffective assistance claims. One kind of claim is based on official interference with counsel's performance. See *Geders v. United States*, 425 U.S. 80, 96 S.Ct. 1330 (1976) (trial court order that defendant, who was on the witness stand, and defense counsel not consult during 17–hour overnight recess). A second kind of claim is that the circumstances of counsel's appointment rendered effective assistance so unlikely as to create "presumed ineffectiveness." See *Powell v. Alabama* [Chapter 1] (general appointment of the local bar made shortly before trial). A third kind of claim is that the counsel's performance was affected by a conflict of interest. See *Cuyler v. Sullivan*, 446 U.S. 335, 100 S.Ct. 1708 (1980). Finally, the most common claim is of "actual ineffectiveness" based on counsel's performance in the defendant's case. See *Strickland v. Washington*, below. *Strickland* and the succeeding three cases all involve actual ineffectiveness claims based on the failure of the defendant's attorney to investigate and present evidence at the penalty phase. In *Strickland*, the Court sets out and applies the test for "actual ineffectiveness" claims, rejecting defendant's claim of penalty phase ineffectiveness. In *Wiggins v. Smith*, the Court, as in *Strickland*, considers a claim that counsel was ineffective for failure to investigate mitigating evidence and finds ineffectiveness. In *Rompilla v. Beard*, the Court again applies the *Strickland* test to find penalty phase ineffectiveness, this time for failure to investigate aggravating evidence. *Schriro v. Landrigan* addresses a situation in which the defendant directed his attorney not to present mitigating evidence. *Mickens v. Taylor*, unlike the four preceding

384

cases, concerns a "conflict of interest," rather than an "actual ineffectiveness" claim. The Sixth Amendment right to counsel at trial does not does not apply on appeal. However, the Supreme Court has held that an indigent convicted defendant has a Fourteenth Amendment right to counsel on a first appeal as of right (*Douglas v. California*, 372 U.S. 353, 83 S.Ct. 814 (1963)) and, consequently, that ineffective assistance by an appellate attorney violates the defendant's constitutional rights. *Evitts v. Lucey*, 469 U.S. 387, 105 S.Ct. 830 (1985). In *Murray v. Giarratano*, the last case in the chapter, the Court considers whether an indigent defendant has a constitutional right to appointed counsel for the purpose of filing a state habeas corpus petition. Finally, *The ABA Guidelines* summarizes the American Bar Association's revised guidelines for defense representation in capital cases.

GODINEZ v. MORAN

509 U.S. 389, 113 S.Ct. 2680, 125 L.Ed.2d 321 (1993).

JUSTICE THOMAS delivered the opinion of the Court.

This case presents the question whether the competency standard for pleading guilty or waiving the right to counsel is higher than the competency standard for standing trial. We hold that it is not.

I

On August 2, 1984, in the early hours of the morning, respondent entered the Red Pearl Saloon in Las Vegas, Nevada, and shot the bartender and a patron four times each with an automatic pistol. He then walked behind the bar and removed the cash register. Nine days later, respondent arrived at the apartment of his former wife and opened fire on her; five of his seven shots hit their target. Respondent then shot himself in the abdomen and attempted, without success, to slit his wrists. Of the four victims of respondent's gunshots, only respondent himself survived. On August 13, respondent summoned police to his hospital bed and confessed to the killings.

After respondent pleaded not guilty to three counts of first-degree murder, the trial court ordered that he be examined by a pair of psychiatrists, both of whom concluded that he was competent to stand trial. The State thereafter announced its intention to seek the death penalty. On November 28, 1984, 2 1/2 months after the psychiatric evaluations, respondent again appeared before the trial court. At this time respondent informed the court that he wished to discharge his attorneys and change his pleas to guilty. The reason for the request, according to respondent, was to prevent the presentation of mitigating evidence at his sentencing.

On the basis of the psychiatric reports, the trial court found that respondent

"is competent in that he knew the nature and quality of his acts, had the capacity to determine right from wrong; that he understands the nature of the criminal charges against him and is able to assist in his defense of such charges, or against the pronouncement of the judgment thereafter; that he knows the consequences of entering a plea of guilty to the charges; and that he can intelligently and knowingly waive his constitutional right to assistance of an attorney."

The court advised respondent that he had a right both to the assistance of counsel and to self-representation, warned him of the "dangers and disadvantages" of self-representation, inquired into his understanding of the proceedings and his awareness of his rights, and asked why he had chosen to represent himself. It then accepted respondent's waiver of counsel. The court also accepted respondent's guilty pleas, but not before it had determined that respondent was not pleading guilty in response to threats or promises, that he understood the nature of the charges against him and the consequences of pleading guilty, that he was aware of the rights he was giving up, and that there was a factual basis for the pleas. The trial court explicitly found that respondent was "knowingly and intelligently" waiving his right to the assistance of counsel, and that his guilty pleas were "freely and voluntarily" given.

On January 21, 1985, a three-judge court sentenced respondent to death for each of the murders. The Supreme Court of Nevada affirmed respondent's sentences for the Red Pearl Saloon murders, but reversed his sentence for the murder of his ex-wife and remanded for imposition of a life sentence without the possibility of parole.

On July 30, 1987, respondent filed a petition for post-conviction relief in state court. Following an evidentiary hearing, the trial court rejected respondent's claim that he was "mentally incompetent to represent himself," concluding that "the record clearly shows that he was examined by two psychiatrists both of whom declared [him] competent." The Supreme Court of Nevada dismissed respondent's appeal.

Respondent then filed a habeas petition in the United States District Court for the District of Nevada. The District Court denied the petition, but the Ninth Circuit reversed. The Court of Appeals concluded that the "record in this case" should have led the trial court to "entertai[n] a good faith doubt about [respondent's] competency to make a voluntary, knowing, and intelligent waiver of constitutional rights,"[3] and that the Due Process Clause therefore "required the court to hold a hearing to evaluate and determine [respondent's] competency ... before it accepted his decision to discharge counsel and change his pleas." Rejecting petitioner's argument that the trial court's error was "cured by the postconviction hearing," * * * the Court of Appeals held that "the state court's postconviction ruling was premised on the wrong legal standard of competency." "Competency to waive constitutional rights," according to the Court of

---

3. The specific features of the record upon which the Court of Appeals relied were respondent's suicide attempt; his desire to discharge his attorneys so as to prevent the presentation of mitigating evidence at sentencing; his "monosyllabic" responses to the trial court's questions; and the fact that he was on medication at the time he sought to waive his right to counsel and plead guilty.

Appeals, "requires a higher level of mental functioning than that required to stand trial"; while a defendant is competent to stand trial if he has "a rational and factual understanding of the proceedings and is capable of assisting his counsel," a defendant is competent to waive counsel or plead guilty only if he has "the capacity for 'reasoned choice' among the alternatives available to him." The Court of Appeals determined that the trial court had "erroneously applied the standard for evaluating competency to stand trial, instead of the correct 'reasoned choice' standard," and further concluded that when examined "in light of the correct legal standard," the record did not support a finding that respondent was "mentally capable of the reasoned choice required for a valid waiver of constitutional rights." * * *

Whether the competency standard for pleading guilty or waiving the right to counsel is higher than the competency standard for standing trial is a question that has divided the Federal Courts of Appeals and state courts of last resort. We granted certiorari to resolve the conflict.

II

A criminal defendant may not be tried unless he is competent. *Pate v. Robinson*, 383 U.S. 375, 86 S.Ct. 836 (1966), and he may not waive his right to counsel or plead guilty unless he does so "competently and intelligently," *Johnson v. Zerbst*, 304 U.S. 458, 58 S.Ct. 1019 (1938). In *Dusky v. United States*, 362 U.S. 402, 80 S.Ct. 788 (1960) (per curiam), we held that the standard for competence to stand trial is whether the defendant has "sufficient present ability to consult with his lawyer with a reasonable degree of rational understanding" and has "a rational as well as factual understanding of the proceedings against him." While we have described the standard for competence to stand trial, however, we have never expressly articulated a standard for competence to plead guilty or to waive the right to the assistance of counsel.

Relying in large part upon our decision in *Westbrook v. Arizona*, 384 U.S. 150, 86 S.Ct. 1320 (1966) (per curiam), the Ninth Circuit adheres to the view that the competency standard for pleading guilty or waiving the right to counsel is higher than the competency standard for standing trial. In *Westbrook*, a two-paragraph per curiam opinion, we vacated the lower court's judgment affirming the petitioner's conviction, because there had been "a hearing on the issue of [the petitioner's] competence to stand trial," but "no hearing or inquiry into the issue of his competence to waive his constitutional right to the assistance of counsel." The Ninth Circuit has reasoned that the "clear implication" of *Westbrook* is that the *Dusky* formulation is not "a high enough standard" for determining whether a defendant is competent to waive a constitutional right.[7] We think the Ninth Circuit has read too much into *Westbrook*, and we think it errs in applying two different competency standards.

---

7. A criminal defendant waives three constitutional rights when he pleads guilty: the privilege against self-incrimination, the right to a jury trial, and the right to confront one's accusers.

A

The standard adopted by the Ninth Circuit is whether a defendant who seeks to plead guilty or waive counsel has the capacity for "reasoned choice" among the alternatives available to him. How this standard is different from (much less higher than) the *Dusky* standard—whether the defendant has a "rational understanding" of the proceedings—is not readily apparent to us. * * * But even assuming that there is some meaningful distinction between the capacity for "reasoned choice" and a "rational understanding" of the proceedings, we reject the notion that competence to plead guilty or to waive the right to counsel must be measured by a standard that is higher than (or even different from) the *Dusky* standard.

We begin with the guilty plea. A defendant who stands trial is likely to be presented with choices that entail relinquishment of the same rights that are relinquished by a defendant who pleads guilty: He will ordinarily have to decide whether to waive his "privilege against compulsory self-incrimination" by taking the witness stand; if the option is available, he may have to decide whether to waive his "right to trial by jury"; and, in consultation with counsel, he may have to decide whether to waive his "right to confront [his] accusers" by declining to cross-examine witnesses for the prosecution. A defendant who pleads not guilty, moreover, faces still other strategic choices: In consultation with his attorney, he may be called upon to decide, among other things, whether (and how) to put on a defense and whether to raise one or more affirmative defenses. In sum, all criminal defendants—not merely those who plead guilty—may be required to make important decisions once criminal proceedings have been initiated. And while the decision to plead guilty is undeniably a profound one, it is no more complicated than the sum total of decisions that a defendant may be called upon to make during the course of a trial. (The decision to plead guilty is also made over a shorter period of time, without the distraction and burden of a trial.) This being so, we can conceive of no basis for demanding a higher level of competence for those defendants who choose to plead guilty. If the *Dusky* standard is adequate for defendants who plead not guilty, it is necessarily adequate for those who plead guilty.

Nor do we think that a defendant who waives his right to the assistance of counsel must be more competent than a defendant who does not, since there is no reason to believe that the decision to waive counsel requires an appreciably higher level of mental functioning than the decision to waive other constitutional rights. Respondent suggests that a higher competency standard is necessary because a defendant who represents himself " 'must have greater powers of comprehension, judgment, and reason than would be necessary to stand trial with the aid of an attorney.' " But this argument has a flawed premise; the competence that is required of a defendant seeking to waive his right to counsel is the competence to waive the right, not the competence to represent himself. In *Faretta v. California*, 422 U.S. 806, 95 S.Ct. 2525 (1975), we held that a defendant choosing self-representation must do so "competently and intelligently," but we made it clear that the defendant's "technical legal knowledge" is "not relevant" to the determination whether he is competent to waive his right to counsel, and we emphasized that although the defendant "may conduct his own defense ultimately to his own detriment, his choice must be honored." Thus, while "[i]t is undeniable that in most criminal prosecutions defendants could better defend with counsel's guidance than by their own unskilled efforts," a criminal defendant's ability to represent himself has no bearing upon his competence to choose self-representation.

B

A finding that a defendant is competent to stand trial, however, is not all that is necessary before he may be permitted to plead guilty or waive his right to counsel. In addition to determining that a defendant who seeks to plead guilty or waive counsel is competent, a trial court must satisfy itself that the waiver of his constitutional rights is knowing and voluntary. In this sense there is a "heightened" standard for pleading guilty and for waiving the right to counsel, but it is not a heightened standard of competence.[12]

This two-part inquiry is what we had in mind in *Westbrook*. When we distinguished between "competence to stand trial" and "competence to waive [the] constitutional right to the assistance of counsel," we were using "competence to waive" as a shorthand for the "intelligent and competent waiver" requirement of *Johnson v. Zerbst*. * * *

III

Requiring that a criminal defendant be competent has a modest aim: It seeks to ensure that he has the capacity to understand the proceedings and to assist counsel. While psychiatrists and scholars may find it useful to classify the various kinds and degrees of competence, and while States are free to adopt competency standards that are more elaborate than the *Dusky* formulation, the Due Process Clause does not impose these additional requirements. The judgment of the Court of Appeals is reversed, and the case is remanded for further proceedings consistent with this opinion.

So ordered.

[Opinion of KENNEDY, J., joined by SCALIA, J., concurring in part and concurring in the judgment omitted]

---

12. The focus of a competency inquiry is the defendant's mental capacity; the question is whether he has the ability to understand the proceedings. The purpose of the "knowing and voluntary" inquiry, by contrast, is to determine whether the defendant actually does understand the significance and consequences of a particular decision and whether the decision is uncoerced. See *Faretta v. California*, *supra* (defendant waiving counsel must be "made aware of the dangers and disadvantages of self-representation, so that the record will establish that he knows what he is doing and his choice is made with eyes open"); *Boykin v. Alabama*, 395 U.S. 238, 89 S.Ct. 1709 (1969) (defendant pleading guilty must have "a full understanding of what the plea connotes and of its consequence").

J<small>USTICE</small> B<small>LACKMUN</small>, with whom J<small>USTICE</small> S<small>TEVENS</small> joins, dissenting.

Today, the majority holds that a standard of competence designed to measure a defendant's ability to consult with counsel and to assist in preparing his defense is constitutionally adequate to assess a defendant's competence to waive the right to counsel and represent himself. In so doing, the majority upholds the death sentence for a person whose decision to discharge counsel, plead guilty, and present no defense well may have been the product of medication or mental illness. I believe the majority's analysis is contrary to both common sense and longstanding case law. Therefore, I dissent.

I

As a preliminary matter, the circumstances under which respondent Richard Allan Moran waived his right to an attorney and pleaded guilty to capital murder bear elaboration. For, although the majority's exposition of the events is accurate, the most significant facts are omitted or relegated to footnotes.

In August 1984, after killing three people and wounding himself in an attempt to commit suicide, Moran was charged in a Nevada state court with three counts of capital murder. He pleaded not guilty to all charges, and the trial court ordered a psychiatric evaluation. At this stage, Moran's competence to represent himself was not at issue.

The two psychiatrists who examined him therefore focused solely upon his capacity to stand trial with the assistance of counsel. Dr. Jack A. Jurasky found Moran to be "in full control of his faculties insofar as his ability to aid counsel, assist in his own defense, recall evidence and to give testimony if called upon to do so." Dr. Jurasky, however, did express some reservations, observing: "Psychologically, and perhaps legally speaking, this man, because he is expressing and feeling considerable remorse and guilt, may be inclined to exert less effort towards his own defense." Nevertheless, under the circumstances, Dr. Jurasky felt that Moran's depressed state of mind was not "necessarily a major consideration." Dr. William D. O'Gorman also characterized Moran as "very depressed," remarking that he "showed much tearing in talking about the episodes that led up to his present incarceration, particularly in talking about his ex-wife." But Dr. O'Gorman ultimately concluded that Moran "is knowledgeable of the charges being made against him" and "can assist his attorney, in his own defense, if he so desires."

In November 1984, just three months after his suicide attempt, Moran appeared in court seeking to discharge his public defender, waive his right to counsel, and plead guilty to all three charges of capital murder. When asked to explain the dramatic change in his chosen course of action, Moran responded that he wished to represent himself because he opposed all efforts to mount a defense. His purpose, specifically, was to prevent the presentation of any mitigating evidence on his behalf at the sentencing phase of the proceeding. The trial judge inquired whether

Moran was "presently under the influence of any drug or alcohol," and Moran replied: "Just what they give me in, you know, medications." Despite Moran's affirmative answer, the trial judge failed to question him further regarding the type, dosage, or effect of the "medications" to which he referred. Had the trial judge done so, he would have discovered that Moran was being administered simultaneously four different prescription drugs—phenobarbital, dilantin, inderal, and vistaril. Moran later testified to the numbing effect of these drugs, stating: "I guess I really didn't care about anything.... I wasn't very concerned about anything that was going on ... as far as the proceedings and everything were going."[1]

Disregarding the mounting evidence of Moran's disturbed mental state, the trial judge accepted Moran's waiver of counsel and guilty pleas after posing a series of routine questions regarding his understanding of his legal rights and the offenses, to which Moran gave largely monosyllabic answers. In a string of affirmative responses, Moran purported to acknowledge that he knew the import of waiving his constitutional rights, that he understood the charges against him, and that he was, in fact, guilty of those charges. One part of this exchange, however, highlights the mechanical character of Moran's answers to the questions. When the trial judge asked him whether he killed his ex-wife "deliberately, with premeditation and malice aforethought," Moran unexpectedly responded: "No. I didn't do it—I mean, I wasn't looking to kill her, but she ended up dead." Instead of probing further, the trial judge simply repeated the question, inquiring again whether Moran had acted deliberately. Once again, Moran replied: "I don't know. I mean, I don't know what you mean by deliberately. I mean, I pulled the trigger on purpose, but I didn't plan on doing it; you know what I mean?" Ignoring the ambiguity of Moran's responses, the trial judge reframed the question to elicit an affirmative answer, stating: "Well, I've previously explained to you what is meant by deliberation and premeditation. Deliberate means that you arrived at or determined as a result of careful thought and weighing the consideration for and against the proposed action. Did you do that?" This time, Moran responded: "Yes."

It was only after prodding Moran through the plea colloquy in this manner that the trial judge concluded that he was competent to stand trial and that he voluntarily and intelligently had waived his right to counsel. Accordingly, Moran was allowed to plead guilty and appear without counsel at his sentencing hearing. Moran presented no defense, called no witness, and offered no mitigating evidence on his own behalf. Not surprisingly, he was sentenced to death.

---

1. Moran's medical records, read in conjunction with the Physician's Desk Reference (46 ed. 1992), corroborate his testimony concerning the medications he received and their impact upon him. The records show that Moran was administered dilantin, an antiepileptic medication that may cause confusion; inderal, a beta-blocker antiarrhythmic that may cause light-headedness, mental depression, hallucinations, disorientation, and short-term memory loss; and vistaril, a depressant that may cause drowsiness, tremors, and convulsions.

II

It is axiomatic by now that criminal prosecution of an incompetent defendant offends the Due Process Clause of the Fourteenth Amendment. The majority does not deny this principle, nor does it dispute the standard that has been set for competence to stand trial with the assistance of counsel: whether the accused possesses "the capacity to understand the nature and object of the proceedings against him, to consult with counsel, and to assist in preparing his defense." *Drope v. Missouri*, 420 U.S. 162, 95 S.Ct. 896 (1975). My disagreement with the majority turns, then, upon another standard—the one for assessing a defendant's competence to waive counsel and represent himself.

The majority "reject[s] the notion that competence to plead guilty or to waive the right to counsel must be measured by a standard that is higher than (or even different from)" the standard for competence to stand trial articulated in *Dusky* and *Drope*. But the standard for competence to stand trial is specifically designed to measure a defendant's ability to "consult with counsel" and to "assist in preparing his defense." A finding that a defendant is competent to stand trial establishes only that he is capable of aiding his attorney in making the critical decisions required at trial or in plea negotiations. The reliability or even relevance of such a finding vanishes when its basic premise—that counsel will be present—ceases to exist. The question is no longer whether the defendant can proceed with an attorney, but whether he can proceed alone and uncounseled. I do not believe we place an excessive burden upon a trial court by requiring it to conduct a specific inquiry into that question at the juncture when a defendant whose competency already has been questioned seeks to waive counsel and represent himself.

The majority concludes that there is no need for such a hearing because a defendant who is found competent to stand trial with the assistance of counsel is, *ipso facto*, competent to discharge counsel and represent himself. But the majority cannot isolate the term "competent" and apply it in a vacuum, divorced from its specific context. A person who is "competent" to play basketball is not thereby "competent" to play the violin. The majority's monolithic approach to competency is true to neither life nor the law. Competency for one purpose does not necessarily translate to competency for another purpose. Consistent with this commonsense notion, our cases always have recognized that "a defendant's mental condition may be relevant to more than one legal issue, each governed by distinct rules reflecting quite different policies." *Drope*. To this end, this Court has required competency evaluations to be specifically tailored to the context and purpose of a proceeding.

In *Massey v. Moore*, 348 U.S. 105, 75 S.Ct. 145 (1954), for example, the Court ruled that a defendant who had been found competent to stand trial with the assistance of counsel should have been given a hearing as to his competency to represent himself because "[o]ne might not be insane in the sense of being incapable of standing trial and yet lack the capacity to stand trial without benefit of counsel." And in *Westbrook v. Arizona*, 384 U.S. 150, 86 S.Ct. 1320 (1966), the Court reiterated the requirement that the determination of a defendant's competency be tailored to the particular capacity in question, observing: "Although petitioner received a hearing on the issue of his competence to stand trial, there appears to have been no hearing or inquiry into the issue of his competence to waive his constitutional right to the assistance of counsel and proceed, as he did, to conduct his own defense."

    * * *

The record in this case gives rise to grave doubts regarding respondent Moran's ability to discharge counsel and represent himself. Just a few months after he attempted to commit suicide, Moran essentially volunteered himself for execution: He sought to waive the right to counsel, to plead guilty to capital murder, and to prevent the presentation of any mitigating evidence on his behalf. The psychiatrists' reports supplied one explanation for Moran's self-destructive behavior: his deep depression. And Moran's own testimony suggested another: the fact that he was being administered simultaneously four different prescription medications. It has been recognized that such drugs often possess side effects that may "compromise the right of a medicated criminal defendant to receive a fair trial ... by rendering him unable or unwilling to assist counsel." *Riggins v. Nevada*, 504 U.S. 127, 112 S.Ct. 1810 (1992) (KENNEDY, J., concurring). Moran's plea colloquy only augments the manifold causes for concern by suggesting that his waivers and his assent to the charges against him were not rendered in a truly voluntary and intelligent fashion. Upon this evidence, there can be no doubt that the trial judge should have conducted another competency evaluation to determine Moran's capacity to waive the right to counsel and represent himself, instead of relying upon the psychiatrists' reports that he was able to stand trial with the assistance of counsel.

To try, convict, and punish one so helpless to defend himself contravenes fundamental principles of fairness and impugns the integrity of our criminal justice system. I cannot condone the decision to accept, without further inquiry, the self-destructive "choice" of a person who was so deeply medicated and who might well have been severely mentally ill. I dissent.

NOTES

1. *Competence to represent oneself.*

In *Indiana v. Edwards*, ___ U.S. ___, 128 S.Ct. 2379 (2008), the Court considered whether a defendant found competent to stand trial could be found incompetent to represent himself. The trial court, in a non-capital case, after holding several hearings on the subject, held that the defendant was competent to stand trial, but denied his request to represent himself on the ground that he was not competent to defend himself. The state supreme court reversed, holding that the defendant had been denied his Sixth Amendment right to represent himself. The United States Supreme Court found that there was no constitutional violation, distinguishing *Godinez* on two grounds: (1) *Godinez* concerned the competence of a defendant who wanted to plead guilty, not, as in the case at bar, a defendant who wanted to go to trial; and (2) *Godinez* held only that a state may *permit* a mentally ill defendant to plead guilty, but did not decide the converse, *i.e.*, whether a state may *deny* a mentally ill defendant the right to represent himself.

2.   *Burden of proof on incompetence.*

In two cases, the Supreme Court has set forth constitutional rules regarding the burden of proof of incompetence. The burden of proof often is of paramount importance since the party bearing the burden of proof bears the risk of an erroneous decision. In *Medina v. California*, 505 U.S. 437, 112 S.Ct. 2572 (1992), the Court held that a state may presume that the defendant is competent and require him to shoulder the burden of proving his incompetence by a preponderance of the evidence. In *Cooper v. Oklahoma*, 517 U.S. 348, 116 S.Ct. 1373 (1996), the Court held that although a state may presume that the defendant is competent, it may not require that the defendant prove his incompetence by clear and convincing evidence. In *Cooper*, the trial judge under Oklahoma's "clear and convincing evidence" test found the defendant competent before and during his capital trial for first-degree murder, despite his bizarre behavior and the conflicting expert testimony on the issue. Oklahoma's heightened standard conflicted with the traditional and prevailing rule for proving incompetence. The Court held that because the rule allowed the state to try a defendant who was more likely than not incompetent, it threatened the basic fairness of the trial itself in violation of the due process clause of the Fourteenth Amendment.

3.   *Medicating a defendant for competency.*

In *Sell v. United States*, 539 U.S. 166, 123 S.Ct. 2174 (2003), the Supreme Court considered whether the government may forcibly medicate a defendant solely to render the defendant competent to stand trial. The Court held that, although the instances where the government could forcibly medicate a defendant for that purpose would be rare:

> "the Constitution permits the Government involuntarily to administer antipsychotic drugs to a mentally ill defendant facing serious criminal charges in order to render that defendant competent to stand trial, but only if the treatment is medically appropriate, is substantially unlikely to have side effects that may undermine the fairness of the trial, and, taking account of less intrusive alternatives, is necessary significantly to further important governmental trial-related interests."

539 U.S. at 179. The issue whether *Sell* applies to forcibly medicating a defendant for execution is discussed below in conjunction with *Ford v. Wainwright* [Chapter 12].

4.   *Problem 7–1.*

Defendant was an inmate in state prison, and he participated with another inmate in stabbing to death Victim, who was serving a sentence for murder of a child. Defendant was charged with murder, and Prosecutor sought the death penalty. Attorney was appointed to represent Defendant. At a pretrial hearing, Defendant, over the adamant objection of Attorney, offered to plead guilty if he could receive the death penalty. The following colloquy took place:

> THE COURT: Defendant, this is highly unusual. You've been charged, sir, with Murder . . .
>
> DEFENDANT: I understand that.
>
> THE COURT: and Conspiracy to Commit Murder, sir, and the State at a later date has filed what is known as the death penalty. Your request is very unusual, sir.
>
> DEFENDANT: Well, if they don't give me my request the next time I butcher somebody it won't be a, I won't be as selected in my butchering.
>
> THE COURT: Defendant, I need to advise you that you understand . . .
>
> DEFENDANT: Well, he filed a death penalty on me. He feels the case merits it. I feel it merits the death penalty, you know. I'm asking the Court to grant that, you know.
>
> THE COURT: But you understand, Defendant, that you have the right to a speedy and public trial by a Jury?
>
> DEFENDANT: I haven't had a fast and speedy . . . I've been seven eight, nine months waiting on a fast and speedy trial, you know.
>
> THE COURT: Do you also understand that you also have the right to require the State to bring forward all witnesses against you and to see, hear, question and cross-examine those persons?
>
> DEFENDANT: I understand the case completely. I've read everything that Prosecutor has got, every piece of paper that he's had access to I've had access to, and I'm just asking the Court and Prosecutor and he feels it merits the death penalty, I feel it merits the death penalty, draw a contract up and I will sign it and we can get on about our business and quit "p_____" around with this. If he doesn't do it I'm telling the Court that the next person that I go at won't be a baby killer, it will be a state employee and I will butcher him. It will be a massacre. I'll butcher the son-of-bitch.

A written agreement was subsequently signed between Prosecutor and Defendant providing that Defendant would plead guilty and would be sentenced to death. Attorney refused to sign.

The court thoroughly questioned Defendant about his signature on the agreement, his mental capacity and the understanding of the rights he would waive by pleading guilty and determined that the plea agreement was knowing and voluntary. Subsequently, a further competency hearing was held. Psychologist, who had been examining Defendant over several months, testified that Defendant was severely depressed and incapable of making rational decisions about his defense and that the cause of his depression was the fact that he had been in solitary confinement during the nine months since the killing. Defendant then spoke, denying that he was incompetent and again asking for the death penalty:

I know what I'm doing, you know. I'm fully aware, you know. This is one of the tests they gave me here. I want to read it to the court here, some of the questions on here, and this is how they say I'm extremely depressed, you know, I mean, I'm in prison. Everybody in prison is depressed, you know. I mean, if I was happy, I mean, ... I wouldn't want to die if I was happy where I was at. I mean, it's no secret, you know. Prison isn't a nice place, you know. I've been in prison for the last 13 years, you know. I'm tired of being in prison, you know, and I'm at the point now where life doesn't have a whole lot of meaning for me and—you know, these are some of the questions that they—Question One, "I feel downhearted, blue, and sad." It says "none or little of the time, some of the time, a good part of the time, more or all of the time." I mean, how would anybody in prison answer that question? "All of the time." I mean, you know, I'm not living at the Hilton Hotel, you know. The second question is, "Morning is when I feel the best." You know, I don't feel good any of the time, you know. I'm miserable. You know, my life is miserable. It's a miserable existence. I don't blame anybody for it, you know. I put myself in prison, you, and I'm dealing with what I've got to do, you know. ... Any normal man that's in prison, you know, is, you know, going to feel downhearted, blue, or sad, you know. I mean, I don't see anybody running around the prison smiling and laughing, you know. I mean, it don't happen. ... "My mind is as clear as it used to be." My mind is probably more clear now than it's ever been. ... "I feel hopeful about the future." I don't have a future, you know. I mean, if I don't get the death sentence, I still don't have a future. What I've got is a slow death. I'm asking the court to give me justice, give me—let me die, you know. I mean, I've got a slow death right now, you know. I'm never getting out of prison. You know, I killed somebody. You know, I'm asking the court to give me what I've got coming, you know.

Defendant was examined by two more experts, who testified at a further hearing that he was depressed, but competent. The court then found that Defendant was competent, accepted the plea agreement and found Defendant guilty of murder. At the sentencing hearing, Defendant declined to offer any mitigating evidence. What arguments should be made as to whether the court may sentence Defendant to death? See *Smith v. State*, 686 N.E.2d 1264 (Ind. 1997).

STRICKLAND v. WASHINGTON

466 U.S. 668, 104 S.Ct. 2052, 80 L.Ed.2d 674 (1984).

JUSTICE O'CONNOR delivered the opinion of the Court.

This case requires us to consider the proper standards for judging a criminal defendant's contention that the Constitution requires a conviction or death sentence to be set aside because counsel's assistance at the trial or sentencing was ineffective.

I

A

During a 10–day period in September 1976, respondent planned and committed three groups of crimes, which included three brutal stabbing murders, torture, kidnaping, severe assaults, attempted murders, attempted extortion, and theft. After his two accomplices were arrested, respondent surrendered to police and voluntarily gave a lengthy statement confessing to the third of the criminal episodes. The State of Florida indicted respondent for kidnaping and murder and appointed an experienced criminal lawyer to represent him.

Counsel actively pursued pretrial motions and discovery. He cut his efforts short, however, and he experienced a sense of hopelessness about the case, when he learned that, against his specific advice, respondent had also confessed to the first two murders. By the date set for trial, respondent was subject to indictment for three counts of first-degree murder and multiple counts of robbery, kidnaping for ransom, breaking and entering and assault, attempted murder, and conspiracy to commit robbery. Respondent waived his right to a jury trial, again acting against counsel's advice, and pleaded guilty to all charges, including the three capital murder charges.

In the plea colloquy, respondent told the trial judge that, although he had committed a string of burglaries, he had no significant prior criminal record and that at the time of his criminal spree he was under extreme stress caused by his inability to support his family. He also stated, however, that he accepted responsibility for the crimes. The trial judge told respondent that he had "a great deal of respect for people who are willing to step forward and admit their responsibility" but that he was making no statement at all about his likely sentencing decision.

Counsel advised respondent to invoke his right under Florida law to an advisory jury at his capital sentencing hearing. Respondent rejected the advice and waived the right. He chose instead to be sentenced by the trial judge without a jury recommendation.

In preparing for the sentencing hearing, counsel spoke with respondent about his background. He also spoke on the telephone with respondent's wife and mother, though he did not follow up on the one unsuccessful effort to meet with them. He did not otherwise seek out character witnesses for respondent. Nor did he request a psychiatric examination, since his conversations with his client gave no indication that respondent had psychological problems.

Counsel decided not to present and hence not to look further for evidence concerning respondent's character and emotional state. That decision reflected trial counsel's sense of hopelessness about overcoming the evidentiary effect of respondent's confessions to the gruesome crimes. It also reflected the judgment that it was advisable to rely on the plea colloquy for evidence about respondent's background and about his claim of emotional stress: the plea colloquy communicated sufficient information about these subjects, and by forgoing the opportunity to present new evidence on these subjects, counsel prevented the State from cross-examining respondent on his claim and from putting on psychiatric evidence of its own.

Counsel also excluded from the sentencing hearing other evidence he thought was potentially damaging. He successfully moved to exclude respondent's "rap sheet." Because he judged that a presentence report might prove more detrimental than helpful, as it would have included respondent's criminal history and thereby would have undermined the claim of no significant history of criminal activity, he did not request that one be prepared.

At the sentencing hearing, counsel's strategy was based primarily on the trial judge's remarks at the plea colloquy as well as on his reputation as a sentencing judge who thought it important for a convicted defendant to own up to his crime. Counsel argued that respondent's remorse and acceptance of responsibility justified sparing him from the death penalty. Counsel also argued that respondent had no history of criminal activity and that respondent committed the crimes under extreme mental or emotional disturbance, thus coming within the statutory list of mitigating circumstances. He further argued that respondent should be spared death because he had surrendered, confessed, and offered to testify against a codefendant and because respondent was fundamentally a good person who had briefly gone badly wrong in extremely stressful circumstances. The State put on evidence and witnesses largely for the purpose of describing the details of the crimes. Counsel did not cross-examine the medical experts who testified about the manner of death of respondent's victims.

The trial judge found several aggravating circumstances with respect to each of the three murders. He found that all three murders were especially heinous, atrocious, and cruel, all involving repeated stabbings. All three murders were committed in the course of at least one other dangerous and violent felony, and since all involved robbery, the murders were for pecuniary gain. All three murders were committed to avoid arrest for the accompanying crimes and to hinder law enforcement. In the course of one of the murders, respondent knowingly subjected numerous persons to a grave risk of death by deliberately stabbing and shooting the murder victim's sisters-in-law, who sustained severe—in one case, ultimately fatal—injuries.

With respect to mitigating circumstances, the trial judge made the same findings for all three capital murders. First, although there was no admitted evidence of prior convictions, respondent had stated that he had engaged in a course of stealing. In any case, even if respondent had no significant history of criminal activity, the aggravating circumstances "would still clearly far outweigh" that mitigating factor. Second, the judge found that, during all three crimes, respondent was not suffering from extreme mental or emotional disturbance and could appreciate the criminality of his acts. Third, none of the victims was a participant in, or consented to, respondent's conduct. Fourth, respondent's participation in the crimes was neither minor nor the result of duress or domination by an accomplice. Finally, respondent's age (26) could not be considered a factor in mitigation, especially when viewed in light of respondent's planning of the crimes and disposition of the proceeds of the various accompanying thefts.

In short, the trial judge found numerous aggravating circumstances and no (or a single comparatively insignificant) mitigating circumstance. With respect to each of the three convictions for capital murder, the trial judge concluded: "A careful consideration of all matters presented to the court impels the conclusion that there are insufficient mitigating circumstances ... to outweigh the aggravating circumstances." He therefore sentenced respondent to death on each of the three counts of murder and to prison terms for the other crimes. The Florida Supreme Court upheld the convictions and sentences on direct appeal.

B

Respondent subsequently sought collateral relief in state court on numerous grounds, among them that counsel had rendered ineffective assistance at the sentencing proceeding. Respondent challenged counsel's assistance in six respects. He asserted that counsel was ineffective because he failed to move for a continuance to prepare for sentencing, to request a psychiatric report, to investigate and present character witnesses, to seek a presentence investigation report, to present meaningful arguments to the sentencing judge, and to investigate the medical examiner's reports or cross-examine the medical experts. In support of the claim, respondent submitted 14 affidavits from friends, neighbors, and relatives stating that they would have testified if asked to do so. He also submitted one psychiatric report and one psychological report stating that respondent, though not under the influence of extreme mental or emotional disturbance, was "chronically frustrated and depressed because of his economic dilemma" at the time of his crimes.

The trial court denied relief without an evidentiary hearing, finding that the record evidence conclusively showed that the ineffectiveness claim was meritless. * * *

     * * *

Applying the standard for ineffectiveness claims articulated by the Florida Supreme Court, the trial court concluded that respondent had not shown that counsel's assistance reflected any substantial and serious deficiency measurably below that of competent counsel that was likely to have affected the outcome of the sentencing proceeding. The court specifically found: "[A]s a matter of law, the record affirmatively demonstrates beyond any doubt that even if [counsel] had done each of the ... things [that respondent alleged counsel had failed to do] at the time of sentencing, there is not even the remotest chance that the outcome would have been any different. The plain fact is that the aggravating circumstances proved in this case were completely overwhelming. . . . ''

The Florida Supreme Court affirmed the denial of relief. * * *

[Respondent filed a petition for a writ of habeas corpus in the United States District Court claiming, *inter alia*, that he had received ineffective assistance of counsel. The District Court held an evidentiary hearing and found that, although trial counsel made errors in judgment in failing to investigate nonstatutory mitigating evidence further than he did, no prejudice to respondent's sentence resulted. The Court of Appeals reversed.]

II

In a long line of cases that includes *Powell v. Alabama*, 287 U.S. 45, 53 S.Ct. 55 (1932), *Johnson v. Zerbst*, 304 U.S. 458, 58 S.Ct. 1019 (1938), and *Gideon v. Wainwright*, 372 U.S. 335, 83 S.Ct. 792 (1963), this Court has recognized that the Sixth Amendment right to counsel exists, and is needed, in order to protect the fundamental right to a fair trial. The Constitution guarantees a fair trial through the Due Process Clauses, but it defines the basic elements of a fair trial largely through the several provisions of the Sixth Amendment, including the Counsel Clause * * *. Thus, a fair trial is one in which evidence subject to adversarial testing is presented to an impartial tribunal for resolution of issues defined in advance of the proceeding. The right to counsel plays a crucial role in the adversarial system embodied in the Sixth Amendment, since access to counsel's skill and knowledge is necessary to accord defendants the "ample opportunity to meet the case of the prosecution" to which they are entitled.

Because of the vital importance of counsel's assistance, this Court has held that, with certain exceptions, a person accused of a federal or state crime has the right to have counsel appointed if retained counsel cannot be obtained. That a person who happens to be a lawyer is present at trial alongside the accused, however, is not enough to satisfy the constitutional command. The Sixth Amendment recognizes the right to the assistance of counsel because it envisions counsel's playing a role that is critical to the ability of the adversarial system to produce just results. An accused is entitled to be assisted by an attorney, whether retained or appointed, who plays the role necessary to ensure that the trial is fair.

For that reason, the Court has recognized that "the right to counsel is the right to the effective assistance of counsel." *McMann v. Richardson*, 397 U.S. 759, 90 S.Ct. 1441 (1970). Government violates the right to effective assistance when it interferes in certain ways with the ability of counsel to make independent decisions about how to conduct the defense. Counsel, however, can also deprive a defendant of the right to effective assistance, simply by failing to render "adequate legal assistance," *Cuyler v. Sullivan*, 446 U.S. 335, 100 S.Ct. 1708 (1980) (actual conflict of interest adversely affecting lawyer's performance renders assistance ineffective).

The Court has not elaborated on the meaning of the constitutional requirement of effective assistance in the latter class of cases—that is, those presenting claims of "actual ineffectiveness." In giving meaning to the requirement, however, we must take its purpose—to ensure a fair trial—as the guide. The benchmark for judging any claim of ineffectiveness must be whether counsel's conduct so undermined the proper functioning of the adversarial process that the trial cannot be relied on as having produced a just result.

The same principle applies to a capital sentencing proceeding such as that provided by Florida law. We need not consider the role of counsel in an ordinary sentencing, which may involve informal proceedings and standardless discretion in the sentencer, and hence may require a different approach to the definition of constitutionally effective assistance. A capital sentencing proceeding like the one involved in this case, however, is sufficiently like a trial in its adversarial format and in the existence of standards for decision, that counsel's role in the proceeding is comparable to counsel's role at trial—to ensure that the adversarial testing process works to produce a just result under the standards governing decision. For purposes of describing counsel's duties, therefore, Florida's capital sentencing proceeding need not be distinguished from an ordinary trial.

III

A convicted defendant's claim that counsel's assistance was so defective as to require reversal of a conviction or death sentence has two components. First, the defendant must show that counsel's performance was deficient. This requires showing that counsel made errors so serious that counsel was not functioning as the "counsel" guaranteed the defendant by the Sixth Amendment. Second, the defendant must show that the deficient performance prejudiced the defense. This requires showing that counsel's errors were so serious as to deprive the defendant of a fair trial, a trial whose result is reliable. Unless a defendant makes both showings, it cannot be said that the conviction or death sentence resulted from a breakdown in the adversary process that renders the result unreliable.

A

As all the Federal Courts of Appeals have now held, the proper standard for attorney performance is that of reasonably effective assistance. The Court indirectly recognized as much when it stated in *McMann v. Richardson*, that a guilty plea cannot be attacked as based on inadequate legal advice unless counsel was not "a reasonably competent attorney" and the advice was not "within the range of competence demanded of attorneys in criminal cases." When a convicted defendant complains of the ineffectiveness of counsel's assistance, the defendant must show that counsel's representation fell below an objective standard of reasonableness.

More specific guidelines are not appropriate. The Sixth Amendment refers simply to "counsel," not specifying particular requirements of effective assistance. It relies instead on the legal profession's maintenance of standards sufficient to justify the law's presumption that counsel will fulfill the role in the adversary process that the Amendment envisions. The proper measure of attorney performance remains simply reasonableness under prevailing professional norms.

Representation of a criminal defendant entails certain basic duties. Counsel's function is to assist the defendant, and hence counsel owes the client a duty of loyalty, a duty to avoid conflicts of interest. See *Cuyler v. Sullivan, supra.* From counsel's function as assistant to the defendant derive the overarching duty to advocate the defendant's cause and the more particular duties to consult with the defendant on important decisions and to keep the defendant informed of important developments in the course of the prosecution. Counsel also has a duty to bring to bear such skill and knowledge as will render the trial a reliable adversarial testing process.

These basic duties neither exhaustively define the obligations of counsel nor form a checklist for judicial evaluation of attorney performance. In any case presenting an ineffectiveness claim, the performance inquiry must be whether counsel's assistance was reasonable considering all the circumstances. Prevailing norms of practice as reflected in American Bar Association standards and the like, *e.g.,* ABA Standards for Criminal Justice 4–1.1 to 4–8.6 (2d ed. 1980) ("The Defense Function"), are guides to determining what is reasonable, but they are only guides. No particular set of detailed rules for counsel's conduct can satisfactorily take account of the variety of circumstances faced by defense counsel or the range of legitimate decisions regarding how best to represent a criminal defendant. Any such set of rules would interfere with the constitutionally protected independence of counsel and restrict the wide latitude counsel must have in making tactical decisions. Indeed, the existence of detailed guidelines for representation could distract counsel from the overriding mission of vigorous advocacy of the defendant's cause. Moreover, the purpose of the effective assistance guarantee of the Sixth Amendment is not to improve the quality of legal representation, although that is a goal of considerable importance to the legal system. The purpose is simply to ensure that criminal defendants receive a fair trial.

Judicial scrutiny of counsel's performance must be highly deferential. It is all too tempting for a defendant to second-guess counsel's assistance after conviction or adverse sentence, and it is all too easy for a court, examining counsel's defense after it has proved unsuccessful, to conclude that a particular act or omission of counsel was unreasonable. A fair assessment of attorney performance requires that every effort be made to eliminate the distorting effects of hindsight, to reconstruct the circumstances of counsel's challenged conduct, and to evaluate the conduct from counsel's perspective at the time. Because of the difficulties inherent in making the evaluation, a court must indulge a strong presumption that counsel's conduct falls within the wide range of reasonable professional assistance; that is, the defendant must overcome the presumption that, under the circumstances, the challenged action "might be considered sound trial strategy." There are countless ways to provide effective assistance in any given case. Even the best criminal defense attorneys would not defend a particular client in the same way.

The availability of intrusive post-trial inquiry into attorney performance or of detailed guidelines for its evaluation would encourage the proliferation of ineffectiveness challenges. Criminal trials resolved unfavorably to the defendant would increasingly come to be followed by a second trial, this one of counsel's unsuccessful defense. Counsel's performance and even willingness to serve could be adversely affected. Intensive scrutiny of counsel and rigid requirements for acceptable assistance could dampen the ardor and impair the independence of defense counsel, discourage the acceptance of assigned cases, and undermine the trust between attorney and client.

Thus, a court deciding an actual ineffectiveness claim must judge the reasonableness of counsel's challenged conduct on the facts of the particular case, viewed as of the time of counsel's conduct. A convicted defendant making a claim of ineffective assistance must identify the acts or omissions of counsel that are alleged not to have been the result of reasonable professional judgment. The court must then determine whether, in light of all the circumstances, the identified acts or omissions were outside the wide range of professionally competent assistance. In making that determination, the court should keep in mind that counsel's function, as elaborated in prevailing professional norms, is to make the adversarial testing process work in the particular case. At the same time, the court should recognize that counsel is strongly presumed to have rendered adequate assistance and made all significant decisions in the exercise of reasonable professional judgment.

These standards require no special amplification in order to define counsel's duty to investigate, the duty at issue in this case. As the Court of Appeals concluded, strategic choices made after thorough investigation of law and facts relevant to plausible options are virtually unchallengeable; and strategic choices made after less than complete investigation are reasonable precisely to the extent that reasonable professional judgments support the limitations on investigation. In other words, counsel has a duty to make reasonable investigations or to make a reasonable decision that makes particular investigations unnecessary. In any ineffectiveness case, a particular decision not to investigate must be directly assessed for reasonableness in all the circumstances, applying a heavy measure of deference to counsel's judgments.

The reasonableness of counsel's actions may be determined or substantially influenced by the defendant's own statements or actions. Counsel's actions are usually based, quite properly, on informed strategic choices made by the defendant and on information supplied by the defendant. In particular, what investigation decisions are reasonable depends critically on such information. For example, when the facts that support a certain potential line of defense are generally known to counsel because of what the defendant has said, the need for further investigation may be considerably diminished or eliminated altogether. And when a defendant has given counsel reason to believe that pursuing certain investigations would be fruitless or even harmful, counsel's failure to pursue those investigations may not later be challenged as unreasonable. * * *

B

An error by counsel, even if professionally unreasonable, does not warrant setting aside the judgment of a criminal proceeding if the error had no effect on the judgment. The purpose of the Sixth Amendment guarantee of counsel is to ensure that a defendant has the assistance necessary to justify reliance on the outcome of the proceeding. Accordingly, any deficiencies in counsel's performance must be prejudicial to the defense in order to constitute ineffective assistance under the Constitution.

In certain Sixth Amendment contexts, prejudice is presumed. Actual or constructive denial of the assistance of counsel altogether is legally presumed to result in prejudice. So are various kinds of state interference with counsel's assistance. Prejudice in these circumstances is so likely that case-by-case inquiry into prejudice is not worth the cost. Moreover, such circumstances involve impairments of the Sixth Amendment right that are easy to identify and, for that reason and because the prosecution is directly responsible, easy for the government to prevent.

One type of actual ineffectiveness claim warrants a similar, though more limited, presumption of prejudice. In *Cuyler v. Sullivan*, the Court held that prejudice is presumed when counsel is burdened by an actual conflict of interest. In those circumstances, counsel breaches the duty of loyalty, perhaps the most basic of counsel's duties. Moreover, it is difficult to measure the precise effect on the defense of representation corrupted by conflicting interests. Given the obligation of counsel to avoid conflicts of interest and the ability of trial courts to make early inquiry in certain situations likely to give rise to conflicts, see, *e.g.*, Fed.Rule Crim.Proc. 44(c), it is reasonable for the criminal justice system to maintain a fairly rigid rule of presumed prejudice for conflicts of interest. Even so, the rule is not quite the *per se* rule of prejudice that exists for the Sixth Amendment claims mentioned above. Prejudice is presumed only if the defendant demonstrates that counsel "actively represented conflicting interests" and that "an actual conflict of interest adversely affected his lawyer's performance." *Cuyler v. Sullivan*.

Conflict of interest claims aside, actual ineffectiveness claims alleging a deficiency in attorney performance are subject to a general requirement that the defendant affirmatively prove prejudice. The government is not responsible for, and hence not able to prevent, attorney errors that will result in reversal of a conviction or sentence. Attorney errors come in an infinite variety and are as likely to be utterly harmless in a particular case as they are to be prejudicial. They cannot be classified according to likelihood of causing prejudice. Nor can they be defined with sufficient precision to inform defense attorneys correctly just what conduct to avoid. Representation is an art, and an act or omission that is unprofessional in one case may be sound or even brilliant in another. Even if a defendant shows that particular errors of counsel were unreasonable, therefore, the defendant must show that they actually had an adverse effect on the defense.

* * *

* * * [T]he appropriate test for prejudice finds its roots in the test for materiality of exculpatory information not disclosed to the defense by the prosecution, *United States v. Agurs*, 427 U.S. 97, 96 S.Ct. 2392 (1976), and in the test for materiality of testimony made unavailable to the defense by Government deportation of a witness, *United States v. Valenzuela–Bernal*, 458 U.S. 858, 102 S.Ct. 3440 (1982). The defendant must show that there is a reasonable probability that, but for counsel's unprofessional errors, the result of the proceeding would have been different. A reasonable probability is a probability sufficient to undermine confidence in the outcome.

In making the determination whether the specified errors resulted in the required prejudice, a court should presume, absent challenge to the judgment on grounds of evidentiary insufficiency, that the judge or jury acted according to law. An assessment of the likelihood of a result more favorable to the defendant must exclude the possibility of arbitrariness, whimsy, caprice, "nullification," and the like. A defendant has no entitlement to the luck of a lawless decisionmaker, even if a lawless decision cannot be reviewed. The assessment of prejudice should proceed on the assumption that the decisionmaker is reasonably, conscientiously, and impartially applying the standards that govern the decision. It should not depend on the idiosyncracies of the particular decisionmaker, such as unusual propensities toward harshness or leniency. Although these factors may actually have entered into counsel's selection of strategies and, to that limited extent, may thus affect the performance inquiry, they are irrelevant to the prejudice inquiry. Thus, evidence about the actual process of decision, if not part of the record of the proceeding under review, and evidence about, for example, a particular judge's sentencing practices, should not be considered in the prejudice determination.

The governing legal standard plays a critical role in defining the question to be asked in assessing the prejudice from counsel's errors. When a defendant challenges a conviction, the question is whether there is a reasonable probability that, absent the errors, the factfinder would have had a reasonable doubt respecting guilt. When a defendant challenges a death sentence such as the one at issue in this case, the question is whether there is a reasonable probability that, absent the errors, the sentencer—including an appellate court, to the extent it independently reweighs the evidence—would have concluded that the balance of aggravating and mitigating circumstances did not warrant death.

In making this determination, a court hearing an ineffectiveness claim must consider the totality of the evidence before the judge or jury. Some of the factual findings will have been unaffected by the errors, and factual findings that were affected will have been affected in different ways. Some errors will have had a pervasive effect on the inferences to be drawn from the evidence, altering the entire evidentiary picture, and some will have had an isolated, trivial effect. Moreover, a verdict or conclusion only weakly supported by the record is more likely to have been affected by errors than one with overwhelming record support. Taking the unaffected findings as a given, and taking due account of the effect of the errors on the remaining findings, a court making the prejudice inquiry must ask if the defendant has met the burden of showing that the decision reached would reasonably likely have been different absent the errors.

* * *

IV

A number of practical considerations are important for the application of the standards we have outlined. Most important, in adjudicating a claim of actual ineffectiveness of counsel, a court should keep in mind that the principles we have stated do not establish mechanical rules. Although those principles should guide the process of decision, the ultimate focus of inquiry must be on the fundamental fairness of the proceeding whose result is being challenged. In every case the court should be concerned with whether, despite the strong presumption of reliability, the result of the particular proceeding is unreliable because of a breakdown in the adversarial process that our system counts on to produce just results.

* * *

V

Having articulated general standards for judging ineffectiveness claims, we think it useful to apply those standards to the facts of this case in order to illustrate the meaning of the general principles. * * *

Application of the governing principles is not difficult in this case. The facts as described above make clear that the conduct of respondent's counsel at and before respondent's sentencing proceeding cannot be found unreasonable. They also make clear that, even assuming the challenged conduct of counsel was unreasonable, respondent suffered insufficient prejudice to warrant setting aside his death sentence.

With respect to the performance component, the record shows that respondent's counsel made a strategic choice to argue for the extreme emotional distress mitigating circumstance and to rely as fully as possible on respondent's acceptance of responsibility for his crimes. Although counsel understandably felt hopeless about respondent's prospects, nothing in the record indicates, as one possible reading of the District Court's opinion suggests that counsel's sense of hopelessness distorted his professional judgment. Counsel's strategy choice was well within the range of professionally reasonable judgments, and the decision not to seek more character or psychological evidence than was already in hand was likewise reasonable.

The trial judge's views on the importance of owning up to one's crimes were well known to counsel. The aggravating circumstances were utterly overwhelming. Trial counsel could reasonably surmise from his conversations with respondent that character and psychological evidence would be of little help. Respondent had already been able to mention at the plea colloquy the substance of what there was to know about his financial and emotional troubles. Restricting testimony on respondent's character to what had come in at the plea colloquy ensured that contrary character and psychological evidence and respondent's criminal history, which counsel had successfully moved to exclude, would not come in. On these facts, there can be little question, even without application of the presumption of adequate performance, that trial counsel's defense, though unsuccessful, was the result of reasonable professional judgment.

With respect to the prejudice component, the lack of merit of respondent's claim is even more stark. The evidence that respondent says his trial counsel should have offered at the sentencing hearing would barely have altered the sentencing profile presented to the sentencing judge. As the state courts and District Court found, at most this evidence shows that numerous people who knew respondent thought he was generally a good person and that a psychiatrist and a psychologist believed he was under considerable emotional stress that did not rise to the level of extreme disturbance. Given the overwhelming aggravating factors, there is no reasonable probability that the omitted evidence would have changed the conclusion that the aggravating circumstances outweighed the mitigating circumstances and, hence, the sentence imposed. Indeed, admission of the evidence respondent now offers might even have been harmful to his case: his "rap sheet" would probably have been admitted into evidence, and the psychological reports would have directly contradicted respondent's claim that the mitigating circumstance of extreme emotional disturbance applied to his case.

* * *

Failure to make the required showing of either deficient performance or sufficient prejudice defeats the ineffectiveness claim. Here there is a double failure. More generally, respondent has made no showing that the justice of his sentence was rendered unreliable by a breakdown in the adversary process caused by deficiencies in counsel's assistance. Respondent's sentencing proceeding was not fundamentally unfair.

We conclude, therefore, that the District Court properly declined to issue a writ of habeas corpus. The judgment of the Court of Appeals is accordingly reversed.

[Opinion of Brennan, J., concurring in part and dissenting in part, and dissenting opinion of Marshall, J., omitted]

WIGGINS v. SMITH

539 U.S. 510, 123 S.Ct. 2527, 156 L.Ed.2d 471 (2003).

Justice O'Connor delivered the opinion of the Court.

Petitioner, Kevin Wiggins, argues that his attorneys' failure to investigate his background and present mitigating evidence of his unfortunate life history at his capital sentencing proceedings violated his Sixth Amendment right to counsel. In this case, we consider whether the United States Court of Appeals for the Fourth Circuit erred in upholding the Maryland Court of Appeals' rejection of this claim.

I

A

On September 17, 1988, police discovered 77–year–old Florence Lacs drowned in the bathtub of her ransacked apartment in Woodlawn, Maryland. The State indicted petitioner for the crime on October 20, 1988, and later filed a notice of intention to seek the death penalty. Two Baltimore County public defenders, Carl Schlaich and Michelle Nethercott, assumed responsibility for Wiggins' case. In July 1989, petitioner elected to be tried before a judge in Baltimore County Circuit Court. On August 4, after a 4–day trial, the court found petitioner guilty of first-degree murder, robbery, and two counts of theft.

After his conviction, Wiggins elected to be sentenced by a jury, and the trial court scheduled the proceedings to begin on October 11, 1989. On September 11, counsel filed a motion for bifurcation of sentencing in hopes of presenting Wiggins' case in two phases. Counsel intended first to prove that Wiggins did not act as a "principal in the first degree,"—*i.e.,* that he did not kill the victim by his own hand.[a] Counsel then intended, if necessary, to present a mitigation case. In the memorandum in support of their motion, counsel argued that bifurcation would enable them to present each case in its best light; separating the two cases would prevent the introduction of mitigating evidence from diluting their claim that Wiggins was not directly responsible for the murder.

On October 12, the court denied the bifurcation motion, and sentencing proceedings commenced immediately thereafter. In her opening statement, Nethercott told the jurors they would hear evidence suggesting that someone other than Wiggins actually killed Lacs. Counsel then explained that the judge would instruct them to weigh Wiggins' clean record as a factor against a death sentence. She concluded: "You're going to hear that Kevin Wiggins has had a difficult life. It has not been easy for him. But he's worked. He's tried to be a productive citizen, and he's reached the age

---

a. Under former Md. Code Ann. § 413, Wiggins would not have been death-eligible unless he was found to have been a principal in the first degree.

of 27 with no convictions for prior crimes of violence and no convictions, period. . . . I think that's an important thing for you to consider." During the proceedings themselves, however, counsel introduced no evidence of Wiggins' life history.

Before closing arguments, Schlaich made a proffer to the court, outside the presence of the jury, to preserve bifurcation as an issue for appeal. He detailed the mitigation case counsel would have presented had the court granted their bifurcation motion. He explained that they would have introduced psychological reports and expert testimony demonstrating Wiggins' limited intellectual capacities and childlike emotional state on the one hand, and the absence of aggressive patterns in his behavior, his capacity for empathy, and his desire to function in the world on the other. At no point did Schlaich proffer any evidence of petitioner's life history or family background. On October 18, the court instructed the jury on the sentencing task before it, and later that afternoon, the jury returned with a sentence of death. A divided Maryland Court of Appeals affirmed.

B

In 1993, Wiggins sought postconviction relief in Baltimore County Circuit Court. With new counsel, he challenged the adequacy of his representation at sentencing, arguing that his attorneys had rendered constitutionally defective assistance by failing to investigate and present mitigating evidence of his dysfunctional background. To support his claim, petitioner presented testimony by Hans Selvog, a licensed social worker certified as an expert by the court. Selvog testified concerning an elaborate social history report he had prepared containing evidence of the severe physical and sexual abuse petitioner suffered at the hands of his mother and while in the care of a series of foster parents. Relying on state social services, medical, and school records, as well as interviews with petitioner and numerous family members, Selvog chronicled petitioner's bleak life history.

According to Selvog's report, petitioner's mother, a chronic alcoholic, frequently left Wiggins and his siblings home alone for days, forcing them to beg for food and to eat paint chips and garbage. Mrs. Wiggins' abusive behavior included beating the children for breaking into the kitchen, which she often kept locked. She had sex with men while her children slept in the same bed and, on one occasion, forced petitioner's hand against a hot stove burner—an incident that led to petitioner's hospitalization. At the age of six, the State placed Wiggins in foster care. Petitioner's first and second foster mothers abused him physically, and, as petitioner explained to Selvog, the father in his second foster home repeatedly molested and raped him. At age 16, petitioner ran away from his foster home and began living on the streets. He returned intermittently to additional foster homes, including one in which the foster mother's sons allegedly gang-raped him on more than one occasion. After leaving the foster care system, Wiggins entered a Job Corps program and was allegedly sexually abused by his supervisor.

During the postconviction proceedings, Schlaich testified that he did not remember retaining a forensic social worker to prepare a social history, even though the State made funds available for that purpose. He explained that he and Nethercott, well in advance of trial, decided to focus their efforts on "retry[ing] the factual case" and disputing Wiggins' direct responsibility for the murder. In April 1994, at the close of the proceedings, the judge observed from the bench that he could not remember a capital case in which counsel had not compiled a social history of the defendant, explaining, "[n]ot to do a social history, at least to see what you have got, to me is absolute error. I just—I would be flabbergasted if the Court of Appeals said anything else." In October 1997, however, the trial court denied Wiggins' petition for postconviction relief. The court concluded that "when the decision not to investigate ... is a matter of trial tactics, there is no ineffective assistance of counsel."

The Maryland Court of Appeals affirmed the denial of relief, concluding that trial counsel had made "a deliberate, tactical decision to concentrate their effort at convincing the jury" that appellant was not directly responsible for the murder. The court observed that counsel knew of Wiggins' unfortunate childhood. They had available to them both the presentence investigation (PSI) report prepared by the Division of Parole and Probation, as required by Maryland law, as well as "more detailed social service records that recorded incidences of physical and sexual abuse, an alcoholic mother, placements in foster care, and borderline retardation." The court acknowledged that this evidence was neither as detailed nor as graphic as the history elaborated in the Selvog report but emphasized that "counsel *did* investigate and *were* aware of appellant's background." Counsel knew that at least one uncontested mitigating factor—Wiggins' lack of prior convictions—would be before the jury should their attempt to disprove Wiggins' direct responsibility for the murder fail. As a result, the court concluded, Schlaich and Nethercott "made a reasoned choice to proceed with what they thought was their best defense."

[Wiggins filed a petition for habeas corpus in federal court. The district court granted relief, finding that the Maryland courts' rejection of his ineffective assistance claim "involved an unreasonable application of clearly established federal law." The Fourth Circuit reversed, and the Supreme Court granted certiorari.]

II

A

[Under the Antiterrorism and Effective Death Penalty Act of 1996 (AEDPA),[b] Wiggins would be entitled to relief only if he showed that the state court decision was "contrary to, or involved an unreasonable application of," *Strickland v. Washington,* 466 U.S. 668, 104 S.Ct. 2052 (1984) or "was based on an unreasonable determination of the facts." Under

---

b. AEDPA is examined in Chapter 11.

Strickland, a petitioner must show that counsel's performance was deficient, and that the deficiency prejudiced the defense. To establish deficient performance, a petitioner must demonstrate that counsel's representation "fell below an objective standard of reasonableness." As in *Strickland*, Wiggins claimed that his attorneys' decision to limit the scope of their investigation into potential mitigating evidence constituted deficient performance. And, as in *Strickland,* the attorneys attempted to justify their limited investigation as reflecting a tactical judgment to present no mitigating evidence at sentencing and to pursue an alternate strategy.]

In light of these standards, our principal concern in deciding whether Schlaich and Nethercott exercised "reasonable professional judgmen[t]," is not whether counsel should have presented a mitigation case. Rather, we focus on whether the investigation supporting counsel's decision not to introduce mitigating evidence of Wiggins' background *was itself reasonable.* * * *

B

1

The record demonstrates that counsel's investigation drew from three sources. Counsel arranged for William Stejskal, a psychologist, to conduct a number of tests on petitioner. Stejskal concluded that petitioner had an IQ of 79, had difficulty coping with demanding situations, and exhibited features of a personality disorder. These reports revealed nothing, however, of petitioner's life history.

With respect to that history, counsel had available to them the written PSI, which included a one-page account of Wiggins' "personal history" noting his "misery as a youth," quoting his description of his own background as " 'disgusting,' " and observing that he spent most of his life in foster care. Counsel also "tracked down" records kept by the Baltimore City Department of Social Services (DSS) documenting petitioner's various placements in the State's foster care system. In describing the scope of counsel's investigation into petitioner's life history, both the Fourth Circuit and the Maryland Court of Appeals referred only to these two sources of information.

Counsel's decision not to expand their investigation beyond the PSI and the DSS records fell short of the professional standards that prevailed in Maryland in 1989. As Schlaich acknowledged, standard practice in Maryland in capital cases at the time of Wiggins' trial included the preparation of a social history report. Despite the fact that the Public Defender's office made funds available for the retention of a forensic social worker, counsel chose not to commission such a report. Counsel's conduct similarly fell short of the standards for capital defense work articulated by the American Bar Association (ABA)—standards to which we long have referred as "guides to determining what is reasonable." *Strickland, supra.* The ABA Guidelines provide that investigations into mitigating evidence "should comprise efforts to discover *all reasonably available* mitigating evidence and evidence to rebut any aggravating evidence that may be introduced by the prosecutor." ABA Guidelines for the Appointment and Performance of Counsel in Death Penalty Cases 11.4.1(C), p. 93 (1989) (emphasis added). Despite these well-defined norms, however, counsel abandoned their investigation of petitioner's background after having acquired only rudimentary knowledge of his history from a narrow set of sources.

The scope of their investigation was also unreasonable in light of what counsel actually discovered in the DSS records. The records revealed several facts: Petitioner's mother was a chronic alcoholic; Wiggins was shuttled from foster home to foster home and displayed some emotional difficulties while there; he had frequent, lengthy absences from school; and, on at least one occasion, his mother left him and his siblings alone for days without food. As the Federal District Court emphasized, any reasonably competent attorney would have realized that pursuing these leads was necessary to making an informed choice among possible defenses, particularly given the apparent absence of any aggravating factors in petitioner's background. Indeed, counsel uncovered no evidence in their investigation to suggest that a mitigation case, in its own right, would have been counterproductive, or that further investigation would have been fruitless; this case is therefore distinguishable from our precedents in which we have found limited investigations into mitigating evidence to be reasonable. See, *e.g.*, *Strickland* (concluding that counsel could "reasonably surmise ... that character and psychological evidence would be of little help") Had counsel investigated further, they may well have discovered the sexual abuse later revealed during state postconviction proceedings.

The record of the actual sentencing proceedings underscores the unreasonableness of counsel's conduct by suggesting that their failure to investigate thoroughly resulted from inattention, not reasoned strategic judgment. Counsel sought, until the day before sentencing, to have the proceedings bifurcated into a retrial of guilt and a mitigation stage. On the eve of sentencing, counsel represented to the court that they were prepared to come forward with mitigating evidence and that they intended to present such evidence in the event the court granted their motion to bifurcate. In other words, prior to sentencing, counsel never actually abandoned the possibility that they would present a mitigation defense. Until the court denied their motion, then, they had every reason to develop the most powerful mitigation case possible.

What is more, during the sentencing proceeding itself, counsel did not focus exclusively on Wiggins' direct responsibility for the murder. After introducing that issue in her opening statement, Nethercott entreated the jury to consider not just what Wiggins "is found to have done," but also "who [he] is." Though she told the jury it would "hear that Kevin Wiggins has had a difficult life," counsel never followed up on that suggestion with details of Wiggins' history. At the same time, counsel called a criminologist to testify that inmates serving life sentences tend to adjust well and refrain from further violence in prison—testimony with no bearing on whether petitioner committed the murder by his own hand. Far from focusing exclusively on petitioner's direct responsibility, then, counsel put on a halfhearted mitigation case, taking precisely the type of "shotgun" approach the Maryland Court of Appeals concluded counsel sought to avoid. When viewed in this light, the "strategic decision" the state courts and respondents all invoke to justify counsel's limited pursuit of mitigating evidence resembles more a *post-hoc* rationalization of counsel's conduct than an accurate description of their deliberations prior to sentencing.

In rejecting petitioner's ineffective assistance claim, the Maryland Court of Appeals appears to have assumed that because counsel had *some* information with respect to petitioner's background—the information in the PSI and the DSS records—they were in a position to make a tactical choice not to present a mitigation defense. In assessing the reasonableness of an attorney's investigation, however, a court must consider not only the quantum of evidence already known to counsel, but also whether the known evidence would lead a reasonable attorney to investigate further. Even assuming Schlaich and Nethercott limited the scope of their investigation for strategic reasons, *Strickland* does not establish that a cursory investigation automatically justifies a tactical decision with respect to sentencing strategy. Rather, a reviewing court must consider the reasonableness of the investigation said to support that strategy.

The Maryland Court of Appeals' application of *Strickland*'s governing legal principles was objectively unreasonable. Though the state court acknowledged petitioner's claim that counsel's failure to prepare a social history "did not meet the minimum standards of the profession," the court did not conduct an assessment of whether the decision to cease all investigation upon obtaining the PSI and the DSS records actually demonstrated reasonable professional judgment. The state court merely assumed that the investigation was adequate. In light of what the PSI and the DSS records actually revealed, however, counsel chose to abandon their investigation at an unreasonable juncture, making a fully informed decision with respect to sentencing strategy impossible. The Court of Appeals' assumption that the investigation was adequate, thus reflected an unreasonable application of *Strickland*. As a result, the court's subsequent deference to counsel's strategic decision not "to present every conceivable mitigation defense," despite the fact that counsel based this alleged choice on what we have made clear was an unreasonable investigation, was also objectively unreasonable. As we established in *Strickland,* "strategic choices made after less than complete investigation are reasonable precisely to the extent that reasonable professional judgments support the limitations on investigation."

Additionally, the court based its conclusion, in part, on a clear factual error—that the "social service records ... recorded incidences of ... sexual abuse." As the State and the United States [as *amicus curiae*] now concede, the records contain no mention of sexual abuse, much less of the repeated molestations and rapes of petitioner detailed in the Selvog report. The state court's assumption that the records documented instances of this abuse has been shown to be incorrect by "clear and convincing evidence," and reflects "an unreasonable determination of the facts in light of the evidence presented in the State court proceeding." This partial reliance on an erroneous factual finding further highlights the unreasonableness of the state court's decision.

* * *

2

* * *

In its assessment of the Maryland Court of Appeals' opinion, the dissent apparently does not dispute that if counsel's investigation in this case had consisted exclusively of the PSI and the DSS records, the court's decision would have constituted an unreasonable application of *Strickland*. Of necessity, then, the dissent's primary contention is that the Maryland Court of Appeals *did* decide that Wiggins' counsel looked beyond the PSI and the DSS records and that we must therefore defer to that finding. *Had* the court found that counsel's investigation extended beyond the PSI and the DSS records, the dissent, of course, would be correct that [AEDPA] would require that we defer to that finding. But the state court made no such finding.

The dissent bases its conclusion on the Maryland Court of Appeals' statements that "[c]ounsel were aware that appellant had a most unfortunate childhood," and that "counsel *did* investigate and *were* aware of appellant's background." But the state court's description of how counsel learned of petitioner's childhood speaks for itself. The court explained: "Counsel were aware that appellant had a most unfortunate childhood. Mr. Schlaich had available to him not only the pre-sentence investigation report . . . but also more detailed social service records." This construction reflects the state court's understanding that the investigation consisted of the two sources the court mentions. Indeed, when describing counsel's investigation into petitioner's background, the court never so much as implies that counsel uncovered any source other than the PSI and the DSS records. The court's conclusion that counsel were aware of "incidences . . . of sexual abuse" does not suggest otherwise because the court assumed that counsel learned of such incidents from the social services records.

The court's subsequent statement that, "as noted, counsel *did* investigate and *were* aware of appellant's background," underscores our conclusion that the Maryland Court of Appeals assumed counsel's investigation into Wiggins' childhood consisted of the PSI and the DSS records. The court's use of the phrase "as noted," which the dissent ignores, further confirms that counsel's investigation consisted of the sources previously described, *i.e.,* the PSI and the DSS records. It is the dissent, therefore, that "rests upon a fundamental fallacy"—that the Maryland Court of

Appeals determined that Schlaich's investigation extended beyond the PSI and the DSS records.

We therefore must determine, *de novo,* whether counsel reached beyond the PSI and the DSS records in their investigation of petitioner's background. The record as a whole does not support the conclusion that counsel conducted a more thorough investigation than the one we have described. The dissent, like the State and the United States, relies primarily on Schlaich's postconviction testimony to establish that counsel investigated more extensively. But the questions put to Schlaich during his postconviction testimony all referred to what he knew from the social services records; the line of questioning, after all, first directed him to his discovery of those documents. His subsequent reference to "other people's reports," made in direct response to a question concerning petitioner's mental retardation, appears to be an acknowledgement of the psychologist's reports we know counsel commissioned—reports that also revealed nothing of the sexual abuse Wiggins experienced. As the state trial judge who heard this testimony concluded at the close of the proceedings, there is *"no reason to believe* that [counsel] did have all of this information." (emphasis added).

The State maintained at oral argument that Schlaich's reference to "other people's reports" indicated that counsel learned of the sexual abuse from sources other than the PSI and the DSS records. But when pressed repeatedly to identify the sources counsel might have consulted, the State acknowledged that no written reports documented the sexual abuse and speculated that counsel must have learned of it through "[o]ral reports" from Wiggins himself. Not only would the phrase "other people's reports" have been an unusual way for counsel to refer to conversations with his client, but the record contains no evidence that counsel ever pursued this line of questioning with Wiggins. For its part, the United States emphasized counsel's retention of the psychologist. But again, counsel's decision to hire a psychologist sheds no light on the extent of their investigation into petitioner's social background. Though Stejskal based his conclusions on clinical interviews with Wiggins, as well as meetings with Wiggins' family members, his final report discussed only petitioner's mental capacities and attributed nothing of what he learned to Wiggins' social history.

To further underscore that counsel did not know, prior to sentencing, of the sexual abuse, as well as of the other incidents not recorded in the DSS records, petitioner directs us to the content of counsel's October 17, 1989, proffer. Before closing statements and outside the presence of the jury, Schlaich proffered to the court the mitigation case counsel would have introduced had the court granted their motion to bifurcate. In his statement, Schlaich referred only to the results of the psychologist's test and mentioned nothing of Wiggins' troubled background. Given that the purpose of the proffer was to preserve their pursuit of bifurcation as an issue for appeal, they had every incentive to make their mitigation case seem as strong as possible. Counsel's failure to include in the proffer the powerful evidence of repeated sexual abuse is therefore explicable only if we assume that counsel had no knowledge of the abuse.

Contrary to the dissent's claim, we are not accusing Schlaich of lying. His statements at the postconviction proceedings that he knew of this abuse, as well as of the hand-burning incident, may simply reflect a mistaken memory shaped by the passage of time. After all, the state postconviction proceedings took place over four years after Wiggins' sentencing. Ultimately, given counsel's likely ignorance of the history of sexual abuse at the time of sentencing, we cannot infer from Schlaich's postconviction testimony that counsel looked further than the PSI and the DSS records in investigating petitioner's background. Indeed, the record contains no mention of sources other than those it is undisputed counsel possessed. We therefore conclude that counsel's investigation of petitioner's background was limited to the PSI and the DSS records.

3

In finding that Schlaich and Nethercott's investigation did not meet *Strickland*'s performance standards, we emphasize that *Strickland* does not require counsel to investigate every conceivable line of mitigating evidence no matter how unlikely the effort would be to assist the defendant at sentencing. Nor does *Strickland* require defense counsel to present mitigating evidence at sentencing in every case. Both conclusions would interfere with the "constitutionally protected independence of counsel" at the heart of *Strickland*. We base our conclusion on the much more limited principle that "strategic choices made after less than complete investigation are reasonable" only to the extent that "reasonable professional judgments support the limitations on investigation." A decision not to investigate thus "must be directly assessed for reasonableness in all the circumstances."

Counsel's investigation into Wiggins' background did not reflect reasonable professional judgment. Their decision to end their investigation when they did was neither consistent with the professional standards that prevailed in 1989, nor reasonable in light of the evidence counsel uncovered in the social services records—evidence that would have led a reasonably competent attorney to investigate further. Counsel's pursuit of bifurcation until the eve of sentencing and their partial presentation of a mitigation case suggest that their incomplete investigation was the result of inattention, not reasoned strategic judgment. In deferring to counsel's decision not to pursue a mitigation case despite their unreasonable investigation, the Maryland Court of Appeals unreasonably applied *Strickland*. Furthermore, the court partially relied on an erroneous factual assumption. The requirements for habeas relief established by [AEDPA] are thus satisfied.

III

In order for counsel's inadequate performance to constitute a Sixth Amendment violation, petitioner must show that counsel's failures prejudiced his defense. In *Strickland,* we made clear that, to establish prejudice, a "defendant must show that there is a reasonable probability that, but for counsel's unprofessional errors, the result of the proceeding would have been different. A reasonable probability is a probability sufficient to undermine confidence in the outcome." In assessing prejudice, we reweigh the evidence in aggravation against the totality of available mitigating evidence. In this case, our review is not circumscribed by a state court conclusion with respect to prejudice, as neither of the state courts below reached this prong of the *Strickland* analysis.

The mitigating evidence counsel failed to discover and present in this case is powerful. As Selvog reported based on his conversations with Wiggins and members of his family, Wiggins experienced severe privation and abuse in the first six years of his life while in the custody of his alcoholic, absentee mother. He suffered physical torment, sexual molestation, and repeated rape during his subsequent years in foster care. The time Wiggins spent homeless, along with his diminished mental capacities, further augment his mitigation case. Petitioner thus has the kind of troubled history we have declared relevant to assessing a defendant's moral culpability. *Penry v. Lynaugh,* 492 U.S. 302, 109 S.Ct. 2934 (1989) ("[E]vidence about the defendant's background and character is relevant because of the belief, long held by this society, that defendants who commit criminal acts that are attributable to a disadvantaged background . . . may be less culpable than defendants who have no such excuse").

Given both the nature and the extent of the abuse petitioner suffered, we find there to be a reasonable probability that a competent attorney, aware of this history, would have introduced it at sentencing in an admissible form. While it may well have been strategically defensible upon a reasonably thorough investigation to focus on Wiggins' direct responsibility for the murder, the two sentencing strategies are not necessarily mutually exclusive. Moreover, given the strength of the available evidence, a reasonable attorney may well have chosen to prioritize the mitigation case over the direct responsibility challenge, particularly given that Wiggins' history contained little of the double edge we have found to justify limited investigations in other cases.

* * *

Wiggins' sentencing jury heard only one significant mitigating factor—that Wiggins had no prior convictions. Had the jury been able to place petitioner's excruciating life history on the mitigating side of the scale, there is a reasonable probability that at least one juror would have struck a different balance. Cf. *Borchardt v. Maryland,* 786 A.2d 631 (Md. 2001) (noting that as long as a single juror concludes that mitigating evidence outweighs aggravating evidence, the death penalty cannot be imposed).

Moreover, in contrast to the petitioner in *Williams v. Taylor,* 529 U.S. 362 (2000) [Chapter 11], Wiggins does not have a record of violent conduct that could have been introduced by the State to offset this powerful mitigating narrative. As the Federal District Court found, the mitigating evidence in this case is stronger, and the State's evidence in support of the death penalty far weaker, than in *Williams,* where we found prejudice as the result of counsel's failure to investigate and present mitigating evidence. We thus conclude that the available mitigating evidence, taken as a whole, "might well have influenced the jury's appraisal" of Wiggins' moral culpability. Accordingly, the judgment of the United States Court of Appeals for the Fourth Circuit is reversed, and the case is remanded for further proceedings consistent with this opinion.

It is so ordered.

JUSTICE SCALIA, with whom JUSTICE THOMAS joins, dissenting.

The Court today vacates Kevin Wiggins' death sentence on the ground that his trial counsel's investigation of potential mitigating evidence was "incomplete." Wiggins' trial counsel testified under oath, however, that he was aware of the basic features of Wiggins' troubled childhood that the Court claims he overlooked. The Court chooses to disbelieve this testimony for reasons that do not withstand analysis. Moreover, even if this disbelief could plausibly be entertained, that would certainly not establish (as [AEDPA] requires) that the Maryland Court of Appeals was *unreasonable* in believing it, and in therefore concluding that counsel adequately investigated Wiggins' background. The Court also fails to observe [AEDPA's] requirement that federal habeas courts respect state-court factual determinations not rebutted by "clear and convincing evidence." * * *

I

Wiggins claims that his death sentence violates *Strickland v. Washington,* 466 U.S. 668, 104 S.Ct. 2052 (1984), because his trial attorneys, had they further investigated his background, would have learned—and could have presented to the jury—the following evidence: (1) according to family members, Wiggins' mother was an alcoholic who neglected her children and failed to feed them properly; (2) according to Wiggins and his sister India, Wiggins' mother intentionally burned 5–year–old Wiggins' hands on a kitchen stove as punishment for playing with matches; (3) Wiggins was placed in foster care at age six because of his mother's neglect, and was moved in and out of various foster families; (4) according to Wiggins, one of his foster parents sexually abused him "two or three times a week, sometimes every day," when he was eight years old; (5) according to Wiggins, at age 16 he was knocked unconscious and raped by two of his foster mother's teenage children; (6) according to Wiggins, when he joined the Job Corps at age 18 a Job Corps administrator "made sexual advances ... and they became sexually involved" (later, according to Wiggins, the Job Corps supervisor drugged him and when Wiggins woke up, he "knew he had been anally penetrated"); and (7) Wiggins is "borderline" mentally retarded. All this information is contained in a "social history" report prepared by social worker Hans Selvog for use in the state postconviction proceedings.

In those proceedings, Carl Schlaich (one of Wiggins' two trial attorneys) testified that, although he did not retain a social worker to assemble a "social history" report, he nevertheless had detailed knowledge of Wiggins' background[.] * * * In light of this testimony, the Maryland Court of Appeals found that "counsel *did* investigate and *were* aware of [Wiggins'] background," (emphasis in original), and, specifically, that "[c]ounsel were aware that [Wiggins] had a most unfortunate childhood." These state-court determinations of factual issues are binding on federal habeas courts, including this Court, unless rebutted by clear and convincing evidence. Relying on these factual findings, the Maryland Court of Appeals rejected Wiggins' claim that his trial attorneys failed adequately to investigate potential mitigating evidence. Wiggins' trial counsel, it said, "did not have as detailed or graphic a history as was prepared by Mr. Selvog, but that is not a Constitutional deficiency."

[Justice SCALIA argued that the majority's contention that the Maryland Court of Appeals "clearly assumed that counsel's investigation began and ended with the PSI and the DSS records" was demonstrably false.]

Once one eliminates the Court's mischaracterization of the state-court opinion—which did not and could not have "assumed" that Wiggins' counsel knew only what was contained in the DSS and PSI reports—there is no basis for finding it "unreasonable" to believe that counsel's investigation was adequate. As noted earlier, Schlaich testified in the state postconviction proceedings that he was aware of the essential items contained in the later-prepared "social history" report. He knew that Wiggins was subjected to neglect and abuse from his mother, that there were reports of sexual abuse at one of his foster homes, that his mother had burned his hands as a child, that a Job Corps supervisor had made homosexual overtures towards him, and that Wiggins was " 'borderline' " mentally retarded.[2] Schlaich explained that, although he was aware of all this potential mitigating evidence, he chose not to present it to the jury for a strategic reason—namely, that it would conflict with his efforts to persuade the jury that Wiggins was not a "principal" in Mrs. Lacs' murder (*i.e.* that he did not kill Lacs by his own hand).

There are only two possible responses to this testimony that might salvage Wiggins' ineffective-assistance claim. The first would be to declare that Schlaich had an inescapable *duty* to hire a social worker to construct a so-called "social history" report, *regardless* of Schlaich's pre-existing knowledge of Wiggins' background. * * * To think that the requirement of a "social history" was part of "clearly established Federal law" * * * when the events here occurred would be absurd. Nothing in our clearly

---

2. The only incident contained in the "social history" report about which Schlaich did not confirm knowledge was the occurrence of sexual abuse in *more than one* of Wiggins' foster homes. And *that* knowledge remained unconfirmed only because the question posed asked him whether he knew of reports of abuse at "one" of the foster homes. The record does not show that Schlaich knew of all these incidents in the degree of detail contained in the "social history" report—but it does not show that he did *not,* either. In short, given Schlaich's testimony there is *no basis* for finding that he was without knowledge of *anything* in the "social history" report.

established precedents requires counsel to retain a social worker when he is already largely aware of his client's background. * * *

The second possible response to Schlaich's testimony about his extensive awareness of Wiggins' background is to assert that Schlaich lied. The Court assumes *sub silentio* throughout its opinion that Schlaich was not telling the truth when he testified that he knew of reports of sexual abuse in one of Wiggins' foster homes and eventually declares straight-out that it disbelieves Schlaich. This conclusion rests upon a blatant mischaracterization of the record, and an improper shifting of the burden of proof to the State to demonstrate Schlaich's awareness of Wiggins' background, rather than requiring Wiggins to prove Schlaich's ignorance of it. But, more importantly, it is simply not enough for the Court to conclude that it "cannot infer from Schlaich's postconviction testimony that counsel looked further than the PSI and DSS reports in investigating petitioner's background." If it is at least *reasonable* to believe Schlaich told the truth, then it could not have been *unreasonable* for the Maryland Court of Appeals to conclude that Wiggins' trial attorneys conducted an adequate investigation into his background.

[Justice SCALIA argued that the record was silent as to the source of Schlaich's information about Wiggins' claimed sexual abuse, and that the likely source was Wiggins, himself.]

The Court's final reason for disbelieving Schlaich's sworn testimony is his failure to mention the alleged sexual abuse in the proffer of mitigating evidence he would introduce if the trial court granted his motion to bifurcate. "Counsel's failure to include in the proffer the powerful evidence of repeated sexual abuse is ... explicable only if we assume that counsel had no knowledge of the abuse." But because the *only* evidence of sexual abuse consisted of Wiggins' own assertions (evidence not exactly worthy of the Court's flattering description as "powerful"), *there was nothing to proffer unless Schlaich declared an intent to put Wiggins on the stand.* Given counsel's chosen trial strategy to prevent Wiggins from testifying during the sentencing proceedings, the decision not to mention sexual abuse in the proffer is perfectly consistent with counsel's claimed knowledge of the alleged abuse.

[Justice SCALIA conceded that the Maryland Court of Appeals' statement that Wiggins' social service records "recorded incidences of ... sexual abuse" was unreasonable in light of the evidence presented in the state court but argued that the state court's decision was not based on that error.]

II

The Court's indefensible holding [on the issue of deficient performance] is not alone enough to entitle Wiggins to habeas relief on his Sixth Amendment claim. Wiggins *still* must establish that he was "prejudiced" by his counsel's alleged "error." Specifically, Wiggins must demonstrate that, if his trial attorneys had retained a licensed social worker to assemble a "social history" of their client, there is a "reasonable probability" that (1) his attorneys would have chosen to present the social history evidence to the jury, *and* (2) upon hearing that evidence, the jury would have spared his life. The Court's analysis on these points continues its disregard for the record in a determined procession towards a seemingly preordained result.

There is no "reasonable probability" that a social-history investigation would have altered the chosen strategy of Wiggins' trial counsel. As noted earlier, Schlaich was well aware—without the benefit of a "social history" report—that Wiggins had a troubled childhood and background. * * * Wiggins' trial attorneys chose, however, not to present evidence of Wiggins' background to the jury because of their "deliberate, tactical decision to concentrate their effort at convincing the jury that appellant was not a principal in the killing of Ms. Lacs."

Wiggins has not shown that the incremental information in Hans Selvog's social-history report would have induced counsel to change this course. Schlaich testified under oath that presenting the type of evidence in Selvog's report would have conflicted with his chosen defense strategy to raise doubts as to Wiggins' role as a principal, and that he wanted to avoid a "shotgun approach" with the jury.[4] (This testimony is entirely unrefuted by the Court's statement that *at the time of trial* counsel "were not in a position to make a reasonable strategic choice," because of their alleged inadequate investigation. Schlaich presented this testimony in state postconviction proceedings, when *there was no doubt* he was fully aware of the details of Wiggins' background.) It is irrelevant whether a hypothetical "reasonable attorney" might have introduced evidence of alleged sexual abuse; *Wiggins'* attorneys would *not* have done so, and therefore Wiggins was not prejudiced by their allegedly inadequate investigation. There is simply *nothing* to show (and the Court does not even dare to *assert*) that there is a "reasonable probability" this evidence would have been introduced *in this case.*

[Justice SCALIA argued that, in any event, "almost all of Selvog's social-history evidence was *inadmissible*" because it was not reliable since Wiggins, himself, who was never sworn as a witness or examined, was the only source for most of the information and anecdotes related by Selvog.[5]]

* * *

---

4. Introducing evidence that Wiggins suffered semiweekly (or perhaps daily) sexual abuse as a child, for example, could have led the jury to conclude that this horrible experience made Wiggins precisely the type of person who could perpetrate this bizarre crime—in which a 77–year–old woman was found drowned in the bathtub of her apartment, clothed but missing her underwear, and sprayed with Black Flag Ant and Roach Killer.

5. Wiggins' postconviction lawyers could have increased the credibility of these anecdotes, and assisted this Court's prejudice determination, by at least having Wiggins testify under oath in the state postconviction proceedings as to his allegedly abusive childhood. They did not do that— perhaps anticipating, correctly alas, that they could succeed in getting this Court to vacate a jury verdict of death on the basis of rumor and innuendo in a "social history" report that would never be admissible in a court of law.

Today's decision is extraordinary—even for our "death is different" jurisprudence. It fails to give effect to [the] requirement that state court factual determinations be presumed correct, and disbelieves the sworn testimony of a member of the bar while treating hearsay accounts of statements of a convicted murderer as established fact. I dissent.

ROMPILLA v. BEARD

545 U.S. 374, 125 S.Ct. 2456, 162 L.Ed.2d 360 (2005).

JUSTICE SOUTER delivered the opinion of the Court.

This case calls for specific application of the standard of reasonable competence required on the part of defense counsel by the Sixth Amendment. We hold that even when a capital defendant's family members and the defendant himself have suggested that no mitigating evidence is available, his lawyer is bound to make reasonable efforts to obtain and review material that counsel knows the prosecution will probably rely on as evidence of aggravation at the sentencing phase of trial.

I

On the morning of January 14, 1988, James Scanlon was discovered dead in a bar he ran in Allentown, Pennsylvania, his body having been stabbed repeatedly and set on fire. Ronald Rompilla was indicted for the murder and related offenses, and the Commonwealth gave notice of intent to ask for the death penalty. Two public defenders were assigned to the case.

The jury at the guilt phase of trial found Rompilla guilty on all counts, and during the ensuing penalty phase, the prosecutor sought to prove three aggravating factors to justify a death sentence: that the murder was committed in the course of another felony; that the murder was committed by torture; and that Rompilla had a significant history of felony convictions indicating the use or threat of violence. The Commonwealth presented evidence on all three aggravators, and the jury found all proven. Rompilla's evidence in mitigation consisted of relatively brief testimony: five of his family members argued in effect for residual doubt, and beseeched the jury for mercy, saying that they believed Rompilla was innocent and a good man. Rompilla's 14–year–old son testified that he loved his father and would visit him in prison. The jury acknowledged this evidence to the point of finding, as two factors in mitigation, that Rompilla's son had testified on his behalf and that rehabilitation was possible. But the jurors assigned the greater weight to the aggravating factors, and sentenced Rompilla to death. The Supreme Court of Pennsylvania affirmed both conviction and sentence.

[Rompilla unsuccessfully sought post-conviction relief in the state courts and then petitioned for a writ of habeas corpus in Federal District Court, raising claims that included inadequate representation. The District granted relief, but the Third Circuit reversed, and the Supreme Court granted certiorari.]

II

Under 28 U.S.C. § 2254, Rompilla's entitlement to federal habeas relief turns on showing that the state court's resolution of his claim of ineffective assistance of counsel under *Strickland v. Washington*, 466 U.S. 668, 104 S.Ct. 2052 (1984), "resulted in a decision that was contrary to, or involved an unreasonable application of, clearly established Federal law, as determined by the Supreme Court of the United States," § 2254(d)(1). * * *

Ineffective assistance under *Strickland* is deficient performance by counsel resulting in prejudice, with performance being measured against an "objective standard of reasonableness" "under prevailing professional norms." This case, like some others recently, looks to norms of adequate investigation in preparing for the sentencing phase of a capital trial, when defense counsel's job is to counter the State's evidence of aggravated culpability with evidence in mitigation. In judging the defense's investigation, as in applying *Strickland* generally, hindsight is discounted by pegging adequacy to "counsel's perspective at the time" investigative decisions are made, and by giving a "heavy measure of deference to counsel's judgments."

A

A standard of reasonableness applied as if one stood in counsel's shoes spawns few hard-edged rules, and the merits of a number of counsel's choices in this case are subject to fair debate. This is not a case in which defense counsel simply ignored their obligation to find mitigating evidence, and their workload as busy public defenders did not keep them from making a number of efforts, including interviews with Rompilla and some members of his family, and examinations of reports by three mental health experts who gave opinions at the guilt phase. None of the sources proved particularly helpful.

Rompilla's own contributions to any mitigation case were minimal. Counsel found him uninterested in helping, as on their visit to his prison to go over a proposed mitigation strategy, when Rompilla told them he was "bored being here listening" and returned to his cell. To questions about childhood and schooling, his answers indicated they had been normal, save for quitting school in the ninth grade. There were times when Rompilla was even actively obstructive by sending counsel off on false leads.

The lawyers also spoke with five members of Rompilla's family (his former wife, two brothers, a sister-in-law, and his son), and counsel testified that they developed a good relationship with the family in the course of their representation. The state postconviction court found that counsel spoke to the relatives in a "detailed manner", attempting to unearth mitigating information, although the weight of this finding is qualified by the lawyers' concession that "the overwhelming response from the family was that they didn't really feel as though they knew him all that well since he had spent the majority of his adult years and some of his childhood years in custody." Defense counsel also said that because the family was "coming from the position that [Rompilla] was innocent ... they weren't looking for reasons for why he might have done this."

The third and final source tapped for mitigating material was the cadre of three mental health witnesses who were asked to look into Rompilla's mental state as of the time of the offense and his competency to stand trial. But their reports revealed "nothing useful" to Rompilla's case, and the lawyers consequently did not go to any other historical source that might have cast light on Rompilla's mental condition.

When new counsel entered the case to raise Rompilla's postconviction claims, however, they identified a number of likely avenues the trial lawyers could fruitfully have followed in building a mitigation case. School records are one example, which trial counsel never examined in spite of the professed unfamiliarity of the several family members with Rompilla's childhood, and despite counsel's knowledge that Rompilla left school after the ninth grade. Other examples are records of Rompilla's juvenile and adult incarcerations, which counsel did not consult, although they were aware of their client's criminal record. And while counsel knew from police reports provided in pretrial discovery that Rompilla had been drinking heavily at the time of his offense, and although one of the mental health experts reported that Rompilla's troubles with alcohol merited further investigation, counsel did not look for evidence of a history of dependence on alcohol that might have extenuating significance.

Before us, trial counsel and the Commonwealth respond to these unexplored possibilities by emphasizing this Court's recognition that the duty to investigate does not force defense lawyers to scour the globe on the off chance something will turn up; reasonably diligent counsel may draw a line when they have good reason to think further investigation would be a waste. The Commonwealth argues that the information trial counsel gathered from Rompilla and the other sources gave them sound reason to think it would have been pointless to spend time and money on the additional investigation espoused by postconviction counsel, and we can say that there is room for debate about trial counsel's obligation to follow at least some of those potential lines of enquiry. There is no need to say more, however, for a further point is clear and dispositive: the lawyers were deficient in failing to examine the court file on Rompilla's prior conviction.

B

There is an obvious reason that the failure to examine Rompilla's prior conviction file fell below the level of reasonable performance. Counsel knew that the Commonwealth intended to seek the death penalty by proving Rompilla had a significant history of felony convictions indicating the use or threat of violence, an aggravator under state law. Counsel further knew that the Commonwealth would attempt to establish this history by proving Rompilla's prior conviction for rape and assault, and would emphasize his violent character by introducing a transcript of the rape victim's testimony given in that earlier trial. There is no question that defense counsel were on notice, since they acknowledge that a "plea letter", written by one of them four days prior to trial, mentioned the prosecutor's plans. It is also undisputed that the prior conviction file was a public document, readily available for the asking at the very courthouse where Rompilla was to be tried.

It is clear, however, that defense counsel did not look at any part of that file, including the transcript, until warned by the prosecution a second time, [in] a colloquy the day before the evidentiary sentencing phase began, [that] the prosecutor * * * would present the transcript of the victim's testimony to establish the prior conviction. * * * [C]rucially, even after obtaining the transcript of the victim's testimony on the eve of the sentencing hearing, counsel apparently examined none of the other material in the file.[3]

With every effort to view the facts as a defense lawyer would have done at the time, it is difficult to see how counsel could have failed to realize that without examining the readily available file they were seriously compromising their opportunity to respond to a case for aggravation. The prosecution was going to use the dramatic facts of a similar prior offense, and Rompilla's counsel had a duty to make all reasonable efforts to learn what they could about the offense. Reasonable efforts certainly included obtaining the Commonwealth's own readily available file on the prior conviction to learn what the Commonwealth knew about the crime, to discover any mitigating evidence the Commonwealth would downplay, and to anticipate the details of the aggravating evidence the Commonwealth would emphasize. Without making reasonable efforts to review the file, defense counsel could have had no hope of knowing whether the prosecution was quoting selectively from the transcript, or whether there were circumstances extenuating the behavior described by the victim. The obligation to get the file was particularly pressing here owing to the similarity of the violent prior offense to the crime charged and Rompilla's sentencing strategy stressing residual doubt. Without making efforts to learn the details and rebut the relevance of the earlier crime, a convincing argument for residual doubt was certainly beyond any hope.[5]

---

3. Defense counsel also stated at the postconviction hearing that she believed at some point she had looked at some files regarding that prior conviction and that she was familiar with the particulars of the case. But she could not recall what the files were or how she obtained them. In addition, counsel apparently obtained Rompilla's rap sheet, which showed that he had prior convictions, including the one for rape. At oral argument, the United States, arguing as an *amicus* in support of Pennsylvania, maintained that counsel had fulfilled their obligations to investigate the prior conviction by obtaining the rap sheet. But this cannot be so. The rap sheet would reveal only the charges and dispositions, being no reasonable substitute for the prior conviction file. The dissent nonetheless concludes on this evidence that counsel knew all they needed to know about the prior conviction. Given counsel's limited investigation into the prior conviction, the dissent's parsing of the record seems generous to a fault.

5. This requirement answers the dissent's and the United States's contention that defense counsel provided effective assistance with regard to the prior conviction file because it argued that it would be prejudicial to allow the introduction of the transcript. Counsel's obligation to rebut aggravating evidence extended beyond arguing it ought to be kept out. As noted above, counsel

The notion that defense counsel must obtain information that the State has and will use against the defendant is not simply a matter of common sense. As the District Court points out, the American Bar Association Standards for Criminal Justice in circulation at the time of Rompilla's trial describes the obligation in terms no one could misunderstand in the circumstances of a case like this one:

> "It is the duty of the lawyer to conduct a prompt investigation of the circumstances of the case and to explore all avenues leading to facts relevant to the merits of the case and the penalty in the event of conviction. The investigation should always include efforts to secure information in the possession of the prosecution and law enforcement authorities. The duty to investigate exists regardless of the accused's admissions or statements to the lawyer of facts constituting guilt or the accused's stated desire to plead guilty."

"[W]e long have referred [to these ABA Standards] as 'guides to determining what is reasonable.' " *Wiggins v. Smith,* 539 U.S. 510, 123 S.Ct. 2527 (quoting *Strickland*), and the Commonwealth has come up with no reason to think the quoted standard impertinent here.

At argument the most that Pennsylvania (and the United States as *amicus*) could say was that defense counsel's efforts to find mitigating evidence by other means excused them from looking at the prior conviction file. And that, of course, is the position taken by the state postconviction courts. Without specifically discussing the prior case file, they too found that defense counsel's efforts were enough to free them from any obligation to enquire further.

We think this conclusion of the state court fails to answer the considerations we have set out, to the point of being an objectively unreasonable conclusion. It flouts prudence to deny that a defense lawyer should try to look at a file he knows the prosecution will cull for aggravating evidence, let alone when the file is sitting in the trial courthouse, open for the asking. No reasonable lawyer would forgo examination of the file thinking he could do as well by asking the defendant or family relations whether they recalled anything helpful or damaging in the prior victim's testimony. Nor would a reasonable lawyer compare possible searches for school reports, juvenile records, and evidence of drinking

---

had no way of knowing the context of the transcript and the details of the prior conviction without looking at the file as a whole. Counsel could not effectively rebut the aggravation case or build their own case in mitigation.

Nor is there any merit to the United States's contention that further enquiry into the prior conviction file would have been fruitless because the sole reason the transcript was being introduced was to establish the aggravator that Rompilla had committed prior violent felonies. The Government maintains that because the transcript would incontrovertibly establish the fact that Rompilla had committed a violent felony, the defense could not have expected to rebut that aggravator through further investigation of the file. That analysis ignores the fact that the sentencing jury was required to weigh aggravating factors against mitigating factors. We may reasonably assume that the jury could give more relative weight to a prior violent felony aggravator where defense counsel missed an opportunity to argue that circumstances of the prior conviction were less damning than the prosecution's characterization of the conviction would suggest.

habits to the opportunity to take a look at a file disclosing what the prosecutor knows and even plans to read from in his case. Questioning a few more family members and searching for old records can promise less than looking for a needle in a haystack, when a lawyer truly has reason to doubt there is any needle there. But looking at a file the prosecution says it will use is a sure bet: whatever may be in that file is going to tell defense counsel something about what the prosecution can produce.

The dissent thinks this analysis creates a "rigid, *per se*" rule that requires defense counsel to do a complete review of the file on any prior conviction introduced, but that is a mistake. Counsel fell short here because they failed to make reasonable efforts to review the prior conviction file, despite knowing that the prosecution intended to introduce Rompilla's prior conviction not merely by entering a notice of conviction into evidence but by quoting damaging testimony of the rape victim in that case. The unreasonableness of attempting no more than they did was heightened by the easy availability of the file at the trial courthouse, and the great risk that testimony about a similar violent crime would hamstring counsel's chosen defense of residual doubt. It is owing to these circumstances that the state courts were objectively unreasonable in concluding that counsel could reasonably decline to make any effort to review the file. Other situations, where a defense lawyer is not charged with knowledge that the prosecutor intends to use a prior conviction in this way, might well warrant a different assessment.

C

Since counsel's failure to look at the file fell below the line of reasonable practice, there is a further question about prejudice, that is, whether "there is a reasonable probability that, but for counsel's unprofessional errors, the result of the proceeding would have been different." Because the state courts found the representation adequate, they never reached the issue of prejudice, and so we examine this element of the *Strickland* claim *de novo* and agree with the dissent in the Court of Appeals. We think Rompilla has shown beyond any doubt that counsel's lapse was prejudicial; Pennsylvania, indeed, does not even contest the claim of prejudice.

If the defense lawyers had looked in the file on Rompilla's prior conviction, it is uncontested they would have found a range of mitigation leads that no other source had opened up. In the same file with the transcript of the prior trial were the records of Rompilla's imprisonment on the earlier conviction, which defense counsel testified she had never seen. The prison files pictured Rompilla's childhood and mental health very differently from anything defense counsel had seen or heard. An evaluation by a corrections counselor states that Rompilla was "reared in the slum environment of Allentown, Pa. vicinity. He early came to [the] attention of juvenile authorities, quit school at 16, [and] started a series of incarcerations in and out Penna. often of assaultive nature and commonly related to over-indulgence in alcoholic beverages." The same file discloses test results that the defense's mental health experts would have viewed as pointing to schizophrenia and other disorders, and test scores showing a third grade level of cognition after nine years of schooling.[8]

The accumulated entries would have destroyed the benign conception of Rompilla's upbringing and mental capacity defense counsel had formed from talking with Rompilla himself and some of his family members, and from the reports of the mental health experts. With this information, counsel would have become skeptical of the impression given by the five family members and would unquestionably have gone further to build a mitigation case. Further effort would presumably have unearthed much of the material postconviction counsel found, including testimony from several members of Rompilla's family, whom trial counsel did not interview. Judge Sloviter summarized this evidence:

> "Rompilla's parents were both severe alcoholics who drank constantly. His mother drank during her pregnancy with Rompilla, and he and his brothers eventually developed serious drinking problems. His father, who had a vicious temper, frequently beat Rompilla's mother, leaving her bruised and black-eyed, and bragged about his cheating on her. His parents fought violently, and on at least one occasion his mother stabbed his father. He was abused by his father who beat him when he was young with his hands, fists, leather straps, belts and sticks. All of the children lived in terror. There were no expressions of parental love, affection or approval. Instead, he was subjected to yelling and verbal abuse. His father locked Rompilla and his brother Richard in a small wire mesh dog pen that was filthy and excrement filled. He had an isolated background, and was not allowed to visit other children or to speak to anyone on the phone. They had no indoor plumbing in the house, he slept in the attic with no heat, and the children were not given clothes and attended school in rags." (dissenting opinion)

The jury never heard any of this and neither did the mental health experts who examined Rompilla before trial. While they found "nothing helpful to [Rompilla's] case," their postconviction counterparts, alerted by information from school, medical, and prison records that trial counsel never saw, found plenty of "red flags" pointing up a need to test further. When they tested, they found that Rompilla "suffers from organic brain damage, an extreme mental disturbance significantly impairing several of

---

8. The dissent would ignore the opportunity to find this evidence on the ground that its discovery (and the consequent analysis of prejudice) "rests on serendipity." But once counsel had an obligation to examine the file, counsel had to make reasonable efforts to learn its contents; and once having done so, they could not reasonably have ignored mitigation evidence or red flags simply because they were unexpected. The dissent, however, assumes that counsel could reasonably decline even to read what was in the file (if counsel had reviewed the case file for mitigating evidence, "[t]here would have been no reason for counsel to read, or even to skim, this obscure document"). While that could well have been true if counsel had been faced with a large amount of possible evidence, there is no indication that examining the case file in question here would have required significant labor. Indeed, Pennsylvania has conspicuously failed to contest Rompilla's claim that because the information was located in the prior conviction file, reasonable efforts would have led counsel to this information.

his cognitive functions." They also said that "Rompilla's problems relate back to his childhood, and were likely caused by fetal alcohol syndrome [and that] Rompilla's capacity to appreciate the criminality of his conduct or to conform his conduct to the law was substantially impaired at the time of the offense." (Sloviter, J., dissenting).

These findings in turn would probably have prompted a look at school and juvenile records, all of them easy to get, showing, for example, that when Rompilla was 16 his mother "was missing from home frequently for a period of one or several weeks at a time." The same report noted that his mother "has been reported . . . frequently under the influence of alcoholic beverages, with the result that the children have always been poorly kept and on the filthy side which was also the condition of the home at all times." School records showed Rompilla's IQ was in the mentally retarded range.

This evidence adds up to a mitigation case that bears no relation to the few naked pleas for mercy actually put before the jury, and although we suppose it is possible that a jury could have heard it all and still have decided on the death penalty, that is not the test. It goes without saying that the undiscovered "mitigating evidence, taken as a whole, 'might well have influenced the jury's appraisal' of [Rompilla's] culpability," *Wiggins v. Smith*, and the likelihood of a different result if the evidence had gone in is "sufficient to undermine confidence in the outcome" actually reached at sentencing.

JUSTICE O'CONNOR, concurring.

I write separately to put to rest one concern. The dissent worries that the Court's opinion "imposes on defense counsel a rigid requirement to review all documents in what it calls the 'case file' of any prior conviction that the prosecution might rely on at trial." But the Court's opinion imposes no such rule. Rather, today's decision simply applies our long-standing case-by-case approach to determining whether an attorney's performance was unconstitutionally deficient under *Strickland v. Washington,* 466 U.S. 668, 104 S.Ct. 2052 (1984). Trial counsel's performance in Rompilla's case falls short under that standard, because the attorneys' behavior was not "reasonable considering all the circumstances." In particular, there were three circumstances which made the attorneys' failure to examine Rompilla's prior conviction file unreasonable.

First, Rompilla's attorneys knew that their client's prior conviction would be at the very heart of the *prosecution's* case. The prior conviction went not to a collateral matter, but rather to one of the aggravating circumstances making Rompilla eligible for the death penalty. The prosecutors intended not merely to mention the fact of prior conviction, but to read testimony about the details of the crime. * * *

Second, the prosecutor's planned use of the prior conviction threatened to eviscerate one of the *defense's* primary mitigation arguments. Rompilla was convicted on the basis of strong circumstantial evidence. His lawyers structured the entire mitigation argument around the hope of convincing the jury that residual doubt about Rompilla's guilt made it inappropriate to impose the death penalty. In announcing an intention to introduce testimony about Rompilla's similar prior offense, the prosecutor put Rompilla's attorneys on notice that the prospective defense on mitigation likely would be ineffective and counterproductive. The similarities between the two crimes, combined with the timing and the already strong circumstantial evidence, raised a strong likelihood that the jury would reject Rompilla's residual doubt argument. * * *

Third, the attorneys' decision not to obtain Rompilla's prior conviction file was not the result of an informed tactical decision about how the lawyers' time would best be spent. Although Rompilla's attorneys had ample warning that the details of Rompilla's prior conviction would be critical to their case, their failure to obtain that file would not necessarily have been deficient if it had resulted from the lawyers' careful exercise of judgment about how best to marshal their time and serve their client. But Rompilla's attorneys did not ignore the prior case file in order to spend their time on other crucial leads. They did not determine that the file was so inaccessible or so large that examining it would necessarily divert them from other trial-preparation tasks they thought more promising. They did not learn at the 11th hour about the prosecution's intent to use the prior conviction, when it was too late for them to change plans. Rather, their failure to obtain the crucial file "was the result of inattention, not reasoned strategic judgment." *Wiggins v. Smith,* 539 U.S. 510, 123 S.Ct. 2527 (2003). As a result, their conduct fell below constitutionally required standards. * * *

> [Dissenting opinion of KENNEDY, J., joined by THE CHIEF JUSTICE and SCALIA and THOMAS, JJ., omitted]

NOTES

1. *Ake v. Oklahoma.*

What resources must the government provide to the indigent defendant in addition to counsel? In *Ake v. Oklahoma,* 470 U.S. 68, 105 S.Ct. 1087 (1985), after the defendant's arraignment, the trial court ordered a psychiatric examination to determine his competency to stand trial. Although the defendant initially was found to be incompetent, he was subsequently found to be competent. His attorney informed the court that the defendant would present an insanity defense, and the attorney requested a psychiatric evaluation at state expense to determine the defendant's mental state at the time of the offense. The court denied the request, and the defendant was convicted and sentenced to death after the psychiatrists who had examined the defendant regarding competency to stand trial testified as to his future dangerousness. The Supreme Court held that the denial of a psychiatric evaluation violated the defendant's due process rights in two respects: he was deprived of his opportunity to present an insanity defense at the guilt phase, and he was prevented from rebutting the state psychiatrists' testimony at the penalty phase.

2. *Presumed ineffectiveness.*

In *Bell v. Cone*, 535 U.S. 685, 122 S.Ct. 1843 (2002), the Supreme Court addressed a "presumed" ineffectiveness claim (see *United States v. Cronic*, 466 U.S. 648, 104 S.Ct. 2039 (1984)) in addition to an "actual" ineffectiveness claim under *Strickland*. Cone was tried for the double murder of an elderly couple following a robbery and two other shootings, and defense counsel presented an insanity defense based on testimony from a clinical psychologist, a neuropharmacologist and Cone's mother. The defense was rejected, and Cone was found guilty on all charges. At the penalty hearing, defense counsel made an opening statement and cross-examined the prosecution witnesses, but he called no witnesses and waived closing statement. After Cone was convicted and sentenced to death and had exhausted his state remedies, he contended, on federal habeas corpus, that his counsel's failure to call witnesses or argue the case entitled him to a presumption of ineffectiveness because "counsel entirely fail[ed] to subject the prosecution's case to meaningful adversarial testing." *Cronic*. The Supreme Court rejected the contention, holding that counsel had taken some actions during the penalty hearing and that the presumption only applied when the attorney's failure was "complete." The Court then held that, in light of the defense counsel's stated reasons for his defense (he was able to introduce mitigation evidence at the guilt phase; any additional mitigation witnesses might have revealed additional negative evidence about Cone; and waiver of closing argument deprived the prosecution of the opportunity to make an emotional rebuttal), the state court's rejection of Cone's actual ineffectiveness claim was not an "unreasonable application" of *Strickland*.

3. *Problem 7–2.*

Defendant was convicted of capital murder in Arkansas for a killing during the course of a robbery. At the penalty phase, the prosecution sought the death penalty on the basis of a "pecuniary gain" aggravating factor. Six months prior to Defendant's trial the Court of Appeals for the Eighth Circuit had held that a death sentence is unconstitutional if it is based on an aggravating factor that duplicates an element of the underlying felony. Nonetheless, although the pecuniary gain aggravator duplicated an element of the robbery-murder, Defendant's counsel raised no objection to the aggravator, and the jury found the aggravator and sentenced Defendant to death. The Arkansas Supreme Court affirmed the conviction and death sentence and denied habeas corpus relief. Defendant sought federal habeas corpus on the ground, *inter alia*, that trial counsel had been ineffective for failing to challenge the pecuniary gain aggravator. In the meantime, however, the Supreme Court had decided *Lowenfield v. Phelps* [Chapter 3], and the Eighth Circuit had overturned its previous precedent regarding duplicate aggravators in reliance on *Lowenfield*. What arguments should be made on whether Defendant is entitled to relief? See *Lockhart v. Fretwell*, 506 U.S. 364, 113 S.Ct. 838 (1993).

4. *Problem 7–3.*

Defendant committed a kidnap-murder. After his arrest, he confessed in detail to the crime, and the police also developed substantial corroborating evidence of Defendant's guilt. Attorney, representing Defendant, deposed the prosecution's witnesses and determined that it would be better to concede guilt, thereby preserving credibility for a penalty phase plea to spare Defendant. Attorney explained this strategy to Defendant, but Defendant neither consented to, nor protested, the strategy. At trial, Attorney conceded Defendant's guilt in his opening statement, participated in the trial to the extent of objecting to the introduction of crime scene photographs, cross-examining certain witnesses for clarification and contesting aspects of the jury instructions, and he again conceded Defendant's guilt in his closing argument. Defendant was convicted and sentenced to death. What arguments should be made on Defendant's ineffective assistance of counsel claim? See *Florida v. Nixon*, 543 U.S. 175, 125 S.Ct. 551 (2004).

SCHRIRO v. LANDRIGAN

550 U.S. 465, 127 S.Ct. 1933, 167 L.Ed.2d 836 (2007).

JUSTICE THOMAS delivered the opinion of the Court.

In cases where an applicant for federal habeas relief is not barred from obtaining an evidentiary hearing by 28 U.S.C. § 2254(e)(2), the decision to grant such a hearing rests in the discretion of the district court. Here, the District Court determined that respondent could not make out a colorable claim of ineffective assistance of counsel and therefore was not entitled to an evidentiary hearing. It did so after reviewing the state-court record and expanding the record to include additional evidence offered by the respondent. The Court of Appeals held that the District Court abused its discretion in refusing to grant the hearing. We hold that it did not.

I

Respondent Jeffrey Landrigan was convicted in Oklahoma of second-degree murder in 1982. In 1986, while in custody for that murder, Landrigan repeatedly stabbed another inmate and was subsequently convicted of assault and battery with a deadly weapon. Three years later, Landrigan escaped from prison and murdered Chester Dean Dyer in Arizona.

An Arizona jury found Landrigan guilty of theft, second-degree burglary, and felony murder for having caused the victim's death in the course of a burglary. At sentencing, Landrigan's counsel attempted to present the testimony of Landrigan's ex-wife and birth mother as mitigating evidence. But at Landrigan's request, both women refused to testify. When the trial judge asked why the witnesses refused, Landrigan's counsel responded that "it's at my client's wishes." Counsel explained that he had "advised [Landrigan] very strongly that I think it's very much against his interests to take that particular position." The court then questioned Landrigan:

> "THE COURT: Mr. Landrigan, have you instructed your lawyer that you do not wish for him to bring any mitigating circumstances to my attention?

"THE DEFENDANT: Yeah.

"THE COURT: Do you know what that means?

"THE DEFENDANT: Yeah.

"THE COURT: Mr. Landrigan, are there mitigating circumstances I should be aware of?

"THE DEFENDANT: Not as far as I'm concerned."

Still not satisfied, the trial judge directly asked the witnesses to testify. Both refused. The judge then asked counsel to make a proffer of the witnesses' testimony. Counsel attempted to explain that the witnesses would testify that Landrigan's birth mother used drugs and alcohol (including while she was pregnant with Landrigan), that Landrigan abused drugs and alcohol, and that Landrigan had been a good father.

But Landrigan would have none of it. When counsel tried to explain that Landrigan had worked in a legitimate job to provide for his family, Landrigan interrupted and stated "[i]f I wanted this to be heard, I'd have my wife say it." Landrigan then explained that he was not only working but also "doing robberies supporting my family." When counsel characterized Landrigan's first murder as having elements of self-defense, Landrigan interrupted and clarified: "He didn't grab me. I stabbed him." Responding to counsel's statement implying that the prison stabbing involved self-defense because the assaulted inmate knew Landrigan's first murder victim, Landrigan interrupted to clarify that the inmate was not acquainted with his first victim, but just "a guy I got in an argument with. I stabbed him 14 times. It was lucky he lived."

At the conclusion of the sentencing hearing, the judge asked Landrigan if he had anything to say. Landrigan made a brief statement that concluded, "I think if you want to give me the death penalty, just bring it right on. I'm ready for it."

The trial judge found two statutory aggravating circumstances: that Landrigan murdered Dyer in expectation of pecuniary gain and that Landrigan was previously convicted of two felonies involving the use or threat of violence on another person. In addition, the judge found two nonstatutory mitigating circumstances: that Landrigan's family loved him and an absence of premeditation. Finally, the trial judge stated that she considered Landrigan "a person who has no scruples and no regard for human life and human beings." Based on these findings, the court sentenced Landrigan to death. On direct appeal, the Arizona Supreme Court unanimously affirmed Landrigan's sentence and conviction. In addressing an ineffective-assistance-of-counsel claim not relevant here, the court noted that Landrigan had stated his "desire not to have mitigating evidence presented in his behalf."

On January 31, 1995, Landrigan filed a petition for state postconviction relief and alleged his counsel's "fail[ure] to explore additional grounds for arguing mitigation evidence." Specifically, Landrigan maintained that his counsel should have investigated the "biological component" of his violent behavior by interviewing his biological father and other relatives. In addition, Landrigan stated that his biological father could confirm that his biological mother used drugs and alcohol while pregnant with Landrigan.

The Arizona postconviction court, presided over by the same judge who tried and sentenced Landrigan, rejected Landrigan's claim. The court found that "[Landrigan] instructed his attorney not to present any evidence at the sentencing hearing, [so] it is difficult to comprehend how [Landrigan] can claim counsel should have presented other evidence at sentencing." Noting Landrigan's contention that he " 'would have cooperated' " had other mitigating evidence been presented, the court concluded that Landrigan's "statements at sentencing belie his new-found sense of cooperation." Describing Landrigan's claim as "frivolous," the court declined to hold an evidentiary hearing and dismissed Landrigan's petition. The Arizona Supreme Court denied Landrigan's petition for review on June 19, 1996.

[On federal habeas corpus, the District Court denied relief finding that Landrigan could not demonstrate any prejudice from any error counsel may have made. The Ninth Circuit panel affirmed, but, on rehearing en banc, the court reversed and ordered an evidentiary hearing on the claim, finding that Landrigan had raised a colorable claim that his counsel's lack of investigation constituted deficient performance and that there was a reasonable probability that, with the additional mitigation evidence, the sentencing judge would have reached a different conclusion.]

We granted certiorari and now reverse.

II

[Under the Antiterrorism and Effective Death Penalty Act of 1996 (AEDPA), the District Court has the discretion to grant an evidentiary hearing if, giving deference to the state court decision, the petitioner has alleged a colorable claim, *i.e.*, if an evidentiary hearing could enable the petitioner to prove "factual allegations, which, if true, would entitle the [petitioner] to federal habeas relief."]

III

For several reasons, the Court of Appeals believed that Landrigan might be entitled to federal habeas relief and that the District Court, therefore, abused its discretion by denying Landrigan an evidentiary hearing. To the contrary, the District Court was well within its discretion to determine that, even with the benefit of an evidentiary hearing, Landrigan could not develop a factual record that would entitle him to habeas relief.

A

The Court of Appeals first addressed the State's contention that Landrigan instructed his counsel not to offer any mitigating evidence. If

Landrigan issued such an instruction, counsel's failure to investigate further could not have been prejudicial under *Strickland*. The Court of Appeals rejected the findings of "the Arizona Supreme Court (on direct appeal) and the Arizona Superior Court (on habeas review)" that Landrigan instructed his counsel not to introduce any mitigating evidence. According to the Ninth Circuit, those findings took Landrigan's colloquy with the sentencing court out of context in a manner that "amounts to an 'unreasonable determination of the facts.'"

Upon review of record material and the transcripts from the state courts, we disagree. As a threshold matter, the language of the colloquy plainly indicates that Landrigan informed his counsel not to present any mitigating evidence. When the Arizona trial judge asked Landrigan if he had instructed his lawyer not to present mitigating evidence, Landrigan responded affirmatively. Likewise, when asked if there was any relevant mitigating evidence, Landrigan answered, "Not as far as I'm concerned." These statements establish that the Arizona postconviction court's determination of the facts was reasonable. And it is worth noting, again, that the judge presiding on postconviction review was ideally situated to make this assessment because she is the same judge that sentenced Landrigan and discussed these issues with him.

Notwithstanding the plainness of these statements, the Court of Appeals concluded that they referred to only the specific testimony that counsel planned to offer—that of Landrigan's ex-wife and birth mother. The Court of Appeals further concluded that Landrigan, due to counsel's failure to investigate, could not have known about the mitigating evidence he now wants to explore. The record conclusively dispels that interpretation. First, Landrigan's birth mother would have offered testimony that overlaps with the evidence Landrigan now wants to present. For example, Landrigan wants to present evidence from his biological father that would "confirm [his biological mother's] alcohol and drug use during her pregnancy." But the record shows that counsel planned to call Landrigan's birth mother to testify about her "drug us[e] during her pregnancy" and the possible effects of such drug use. Second, Landrigan interrupted repeatedly when counsel tried to proffer anything that could have been considered mitigating. He even refused to allow his attorney to proffer that he had worked a regular job at one point. This behavior confirms what is plain from the transcript of the colloquy: that Landrigan would have undermined the presentation of any mitigating evidence that his attorney might have uncovered.

On the record before us, the Arizona court's determination that Landrigan refused to allow the presentation of any mitigating evidence was a reasonable determination of the facts. In this regard, we agree with the initial Court of Appeals panel that reviewed this case:

> "In the constellation of refusals to have mitigating evidence presented ... this case is surely a bright star. No other case could illuminate the state of the client's mind and the nature of counsel's dilemma quite as

brightly as this one. No flashes of insight could be more fulgurous than those which this record supplies."

Because the Arizona postconviction court reasonably determined that Landrigan "instructed his attorney not to bring any mitigation to the attention of the [sentencing] court," it was not an abuse of discretion for the District Court to conclude that Landrigan could not overcome § 2254(d)(2)'s bar to granting federal habeas relief. The District Court was entitled to conclude that regardless of what information counsel might have uncovered in his investigation, Landrigan would have interrupted and refused to allow his counsel to present any such evidence. Accordingly, the District Court could conclude that because of his established recalcitrance, Landrigan could not demonstrate prejudice under *Strickland* even if granted an evidentiary hearing.

B

The Court of Appeals offered two alternative reasons for holding that Landrigan's inability to make a showing of prejudice under *Strickland* did not bar any potential habeas relief and, thus, an evidentiary hearing.

1

The Court of Appeals held that, even if Landrigan did not want any mitigating evidence presented, the Arizona courts' determination that Landrigan's claims were " 'frivolous' and 'meritless' was an unreasonable application of United States Supreme Court precedent." This holding was founded on the belief, derived from *Wiggins v. Smith,* 539 U.S. 510, 123 S.Ct. 2527 (2003), that "Landrigan's apparently last-minute decision cannot excuse his counsel's failure to conduct an adequate investigation *prior* to the sentencing."

Neither *Wiggins* nor *Strickland* addresses a situation in which a client interferes with counsel's efforts to present mitigating evidence to a sentencing court. Indeed, we have never addressed a situation like this. In *Rompilla v. Beard,* 545 U.S. 374, 125 S.Ct. 2456 (2005), on which the Court of Appeals also relied, the defendant refused to assist in the development of a mitigation case, but did not inform the court that he did not want mitigating evidence presented. In short, at the time of the Arizona postconviction court's decision, it was not objectively unreasonable for that court to conclude that a defendant who refused to allow the presentation of any mitigating evidence could not establish *Strickland* prejudice based on his counsel's failure to investigate further possible mitigating evidence.

2

The Court of Appeals also stated that the record does not indicate that Landrigan's decision not to present mitigating evidence was "informed and knowing" and that "[t]he trial court's dialogue with Landrigan tells us little about his understanding of the consequences of his decision." We have never imposed an "informed and knowing" requirement upon a defendant's decision not to introduce evidence. Even assuming, however, that an "informed and knowing" requirement exists in this case, Landrigan cannot benefit from it, for three reasons.

First, Landrigan never presented this claim to the Arizona courts. Rather, he argued that he would have complied had other evidence been offered. Thus, Landrigan failed to develop this claim properly before the Arizona courts, and § 2254(e)(2) therefore barred the District Court from granting an evidentiary hearing on that basis.

Second, in Landrigan's presence, his counsel told the sentencing court that he had carefully explained to Landrigan the importance of mitigating evidence, "especially concerning the fact that the State is seeking the death penalty." Counsel also told the court that he had explained to Landrigan that as counsel, he had a duty to disclose "any and all mitigating factors ... to th[e] [c]ourt for consideration regarding the sentencing." In light of Landrigan's demonstrated propensity for interjecting himself into the proceedings, it is doubtful that Landrigan would have sat idly by while his counsel lied about having previously discussed these issues with him. And as Landrigan's counsel conceded at oral argument before this Court, we have never required a specific colloquy to ensure that a defendant knowingly and intelligently refused to present mitigating evidence.

Third, the Court of Appeals overlooked Landrigan's final statement to the sentencing court: "I think if you want to give me the death penalty, just bring it right on. I'm ready for it." It is apparent from this statement that Landrigan clearly understood the consequences of telling the judge that, "as far as [he was] concerned," there were no mitigating circumstances of which she should be aware.

IV

Finally, the Court of Appeals erred in rejecting the District Court's finding that the poor quality of Landrigan's alleged mitigating evidence prevented him from making "a colorable claim" of prejudice. As summarized by the Court of Appeals, Landrigan wanted to introduce as mitigation evidence:

> "[that] he was exposed to alcohol and drugs *in utero,* which may have resulted in cognitive and behavioral deficiencies consistent with fetal alcohol syndrome. He was abandoned by his birth mother and suffered abandonment and attachment issues, as well as other behavioral problems throughout his childhood.
>
> His adoptive mother was also an alcoholic, and Landrigan's own alcohol and substance abuse began at an early age. Based on his biological family's history of violence, Landrigan claims he may also have been genetically predisposed to violence."

As explained above, all but the last sentence refer to information that Landrigan's birth mother and ex-wife could have offered if Landrigan had allowed them to testify. Indeed, the state postconviction court had much of this evidence before it by way of counsel's proffer. The District Court could reasonably conclude that any additional evidence would have made no difference in the sentencing.

In sum, the District Court did not abuse its discretion in finding that Landrigan could not establish prejudice based on his counsel's failure to present the evidence he now wishes to offer. Landrigan's mitigation evidence was weak, and the postconviction court was well acquainted with Landrigan's exceedingly violent past and had seen first hand his belligerent behavior. Again, it is difficult to improve upon the initial Court of Appeals panel's conclusion:

> "The prospect was chilling; before he was 30 years of age, Landrigan had murdered one man, repeatedly stabbed another one, escaped from prison, and within two months murdered still another man. As the Arizona Supreme Court so aptly put it when dealing with one of Landrigan's other claims, '[i]n his comments [to the sentencing judge], defendant not only failed to show remorse or offer mitigating evidence, but he flaunted his menacing behavior.' On this record, assuring the court that genetics made him the way he is could not have been very helpful. There was no prejudice." (citations and footnote omitted).

* * *

JUSTICE STEVENS, with whom JUSTICE SOUTER, JUSTICE GINSBURG, and JUSTICE BREYER join, dissenting.

Significant mitigating evidence—evidence that may well have explained respondent's criminal conduct and unruly behavior at his capital sentencing hearing—was unknown at the time of sentencing. Only years later did respondent learn that he suffers from a serious psychological condition that sheds important light on his earlier actions. The reason why this and other mitigating evidence was unavailable is that respondent's counsel failed to conduct a constitutionally adequate investigation. In spite of this, the Court holds that respondent is not entitled to an evidentiary hearing to explore the prejudicial impact of his counsel's inadequate representation. It reasons that respondent "would have" waived his right to introduce any mitigating evidence that counsel might have uncovered and that such evidence "would have" made no difference in the sentencing anyway. Without the benefit of an evidentiary hearing, this is pure guesswork.

The Court's decision rests on a parsimonious appraisal of a capital defendant's constitutional right to have the sentencing decision reflect meaningful consideration of all relevant mitigating evidence, a begrudging appreciation of the need for a knowing and intelligent waiver of constitutionally protected trial rights and a cramped reading of the record. Unlike this Court, the en banc Court of Appeals properly accounted for these important constitutional and factual considerations. Its narrow holding that the District Court abused its discretion in denying respondent an evidentiary hearing should be affirmed.

I

No one, not even the Court, seriously contends that counsel's investigation of possible mitigating evidence was constitutionally sufficient. Indeed, both the majority and dissenting judges on the en banc Court of Appeals agreed that "counsel's limited investigation of Landrigan's background fell below the standards of professional representation prevailing" at the time of his sentencing hearing. The list of evidence that counsel failed to investigate is long. For instance, counsel did not complete a psychological evaluation of respondent, which we now know would have uncovered a serious organic brain disorder. He failed to consult an expert to explore the effects of respondent's birth mother's drinking and drug use during pregnancy. And he never developed a history of respondent's troubled childhood with his adoptive family—a childhood marked by physical and emotional abuse, neglect by his adoptive parents, his own serious substance abuse problems (including an overdose in his eighth or ninth grade classroom), a stunted education, and recurrent placement in substance abuse rehabilitation facilities, a psychiatric ward, and police custody. Counsel's failure to develop this background evidence was so glaring that even the sentencing judge noted that she had "received very little information concerning the defendant's difficult family history." At the time of sentencing, counsel was only prepared to put on the testimony by respondent's ex-wife and birth mother. By any measure, and especially for a capital case, this meager investigation "fell below an objective standard of reasonableness." *Strickland v. Washington,* 466 U.S. 668, 104 S.Ct. 2052 (1984).

Given this deficient performance, the only issue is whether counsel's inadequate investigation prejudiced the outcome of sentencing. The bulk of the Court's opinion argues that the District Court reasonably found that respondent waived his right to present any and all mitigating evidence. As I shall explain, this argument finds no support in the Constitution or the record of this case.

II

It is well established that a citizen's waiver of a constitutional right must be knowing, intelligent, and voluntary. As far back as *Johnson v. Zerbst,* 304 U.S. 458, 58 S.Ct. 1019 (1938), we held that courts must " 'indulge every reasonable presumption against waiver' of fundamental constitutional rights." Since then, "[w]e have been unyielding in our insistence that a defendant's waiver of his trial rights cannot be given effect unless it is 'knowing' and 'intelligent.' " *Illinois v. Rodriguez,* 497 U.S. 177, 110 S.Ct. 2793 (1990) (citing *Zerbst*).

[Justice STEVENS reviewed cases applying the *Zerbst* rule to the waiver of various trial rights.]

Given this unmistakable focus on trial rights, it makes little difference that we have not specifically "imposed an 'informed and knowing' requirement upon a defendant's decision not to introduce evidence." A capital defendant's right to present mitigating evidence is firmly established and can only be exercised at a sentencing *trial*. For a capital defendant, the right to have the sentencing authority give full consideration to mitigating evidence that might support a sentence other than death is of paramount importance—in some cases just as important as the right to representation by counsel protected in *Zerbst* or any of the trial rights discussed in *Schneckloth v. Bustamonte*, 412 U.S. 218, 93 S.Ct. 2041 (1973). Our longstanding precedent—from *Zerbst* to *Schneckloth* to the only waiver case that the majority cites, *Iowa v. Tovar*, 541 U.S. 77, 124 S.Ct. 1379 (2004)—requires that any waiver of the right to adduce such evidence be knowing, intelligent, and voluntary. As such, the state post-conviction court's conclusion that respondent completely waived his right to present mitigating evidence involved an unreasonable application of clearly established federal law as determined by this Court.

[Respondent's statements did not constitute a knowing and intelligent waiver under the Court's precedents, and the Court's conclusion that respondent never raised a "knowing-and-intelligent-waiver argument" in the state courts is misguided because respondent never thought he had made a waiver—that was the state's response to respondent's ineffective assistance claim. In any case, the purported waiver is itself arguably a product of counsel's deficient investigation because a more thorough psychological investigation would have revealed respondent's organic brain disorder, calling into question respondent's capacity to make such decisions.]

On the day of the sentencing hearing, the only mitigating evidence that respondent's counsel had investigated was the testimony of respondent's birth mother and ex-wife. None of this neuropsychological information was available to respondent at the time of his purported waiver. Yet the Court conspicuously avoids any mention of respondent's organic brain disorder. It instead provides an incomplete list of other mitigating evidence that respondent would have presented and incorrectly assumes that respondent's birth mother and ex-wife would have covered it all. Unless I missed the portion of the record indicating that respondent's ex-wife and birth mother were trained psychologists, neither could have offered expert testimony about respondent's organic brain disorder.

It is of course true that respondent was aware of many of the individual pieces of mitigating evidence that contributed to Dr. Thompson's subsequent diagnosis. He knew that his birth mother abandoned him at the age of six months; that his biological family had an extensive criminal history; that his adoptive mother had "affective disturbances and chronic alcoholism"; that she routinely drank vodka until she passed out; that she would frequently strike him, once even "hit[ting him] with a frying pan hard enough to leave a dent"; that his childhood was difficult and he exhibited abandonment and attachment problems at an early age; that he had a bad temper and often threw violent tantrums as a child; and that he "began getting into trouble and using alcohol and drugs at an early age and, by adolescence, he had begun a series of placements in juvenile detention facilities, a psychiatric ward, and twice in drug abuse rehabilitation programs." Perhaps respondent also knew that his biological mother abused alcohol and amphetamines during her pregnancy, and that *in utero* exposure to drugs and alcohol has deleterious effects on the child.

But even if respondent knew all these things, we cannot assume that he could understand their consequences the way an expert psychologist could. Without years of advanced education and a battery of complicated testing, respondent could not know that these experiences resulted in a serious organic brain disorder or what effect such a disorder might have on his behavior. And precisely because his counsel failed to conduct a proper investigation, he did not know that this important evidence was available to him when he purportedly waived the right to present mitigating evidence. It is hard to see how respondent's claim of *Strickland* prejudice can be prejudiced by counsel's *Strickland* error.

Without ever acknowledging that respondent lacked this information, the Court clings to counsel's discussion with respondent about "the importance of mitigating evidence." The majority also places great weight on the fact that counsel explained to respondent that, as counsel, he had a "duty to disclose 'any and all mitigating factors . . . to th[e] [c]ourt for consideration regarding the sentencing.'" Leaving aside the fact that counsel's deficient performance did not demonstrate an understanding of the "importance of mitigating evidence"—let alone knowledge of "'any and all'" such evidence—counsel's abstract explanation cannot satisfy the demands of *Zerbst* and *Schneckloth*. Unless respondent knew of the most significant mitigation evidence available to him, he could not have made a knowing and intelligent waiver of his constitutional rights.

III

Even if the putative waiver had been fully informed, the Arizona postconviction court's determination that respondent "instructed his attorney not to bring any mitigation to the attention of the [sentencing] court" is plainly contradicted by the record. The Court nevertheless defers to this finding, concluding that it was not an "unreasonable determination of the facts" under 28 U.S.C. § 2254(d)(2). "[I]n the context of federal habeas," however, "deference does not imply abandonment or abdication of judicial review." *Miller–El v. Cockrell,* 537 U.S. 322, 123 S.Ct. 1029 (2003). A careful examination of the "record material and the transcripts from the state courts" does not indicate that respondent intended to make a waiver that went beyond the testimony of his birth mother and ex-wife.

The Court reads the following exchange as definitive proof that respondent "informed his counsel not to present any mitigating evidence":

> "THE COURT: Mr. Landrigan, have you instructed your lawyer that you do not wish for him to bring any mitigating circumstances to my attention?

"THE DEFENDANT: Yeah.

"THE COURT: Do you know what that means?

"THE DEFENDANT: Yeah.

"THE COURT: Mr. Landrigan, are there mitigating circumstances I should be aware of?

"THE DEFENDANT: Not as far as I'm concerned."

The Court also infers from respondent's disruptive behavior at the sentencing hearing that he "would have undermined the presentation of any mitigating evidence that his attorney might have uncovered." But this record material does not conclusively establish that respondent would have waived his right to present other mitigating evidence if his counsel had made it available to him.

The brief exchange between respondent and the trial court must be considered in the context of the *entire* sentencing proceeding. The above-quoted dialogue came immediately after a lengthy colloquy between the trial court and respondent's counsel:

"MR. FARRELL: Your Honor, at this time ... I have two witnesses that I wished to testify before this Court, one I had brought in from out of state and is my client's ex-wife, Ms. Sandy Landrigan. The second witness is my client's natural mother, Virginia Gipson. I believe both of those people had some important evidence that I believed the Court should take into mitigation concerning my client. *However, Mr. Landrigan has made it clear to me ... that he does not wish anyone from his family to testify on his behalf today.*

"I have talked with Sandra Landrigan, his ex-wife. I have talked a number of times with her and confirmed what I thought was important evidence that she should present for the Court. And I have also talked with Ms. Gipson, and her evidence I think is very important and should have been brought to this Court's attention. Both of them, after talking with Jeff today, have agreed with their, in one case son and the other ex-husband, they will not testify in his behalf.

"THE COURT: Why not?

"MR. FARRELL: Basically it's at my client's wishes, Your Honor. I told him that in order to effectively represent him, especially concerning the fact that the State is seeking the death penalty, any and all mitigating factors, I was under a duty to disclose those factors to this Court for consideration regarding the sentencing. *He is adamant he does not want any testimony from his family, specifically these two people that I have here, his mother, under subpoena, and as well as having flown in his ex-wife.*" (emphasis added).

Respondent's answers to the trial judge's questions must be read in light of this discussion. When the judge immediately turned from counsel to respondent and asked about "any mitigating circumstances," the entire proceeding to that point had been about the possible testimony of his birth mother or ex-wife. Counsel had only informed the court that respondent did not want any testimony "from his family." Neither counsel nor respondent said anything about other mitigating evidence. A fair reading of the full sentencing transcript makes clear that respondent's answers referred only to the testimony of his ex-wife and birth mother.[9]

What is more, respondent's answers were necessarily infected by his counsel's failure to investigate. Respondent does not dispute that he instructed his counsel not to present his family's testimony. But his limited waiver cannot change the fact that he was unaware that the words "any mitigating circumstances" could include his organic brain disorder, the medical consequences of his mother's drinking and drug use during pregnancy, and his abusive upbringing with his adoptive family. In respondent's mind, the words "any mitigating circumstances" just meant the incomplete evidence that counsel offered to present. As the en banc Court of Appeals explained, "[h]ad his lawyer conducted an investigation and uncovered other types of mitigating evidence, Landrigan might well have been able to direct the court to other mitigating circumstances." It is therefore error to read respondent's simple "Yeah" and "Not as far as I'm concerned" as waiving anything other than the little he knew was available to him.

Accordingly, the state postconviction court's finding that petitioner waived his right to present any mitigating evidence was an unreasonable determination of the facts under § 2254(d)(2). While the Court is correct that the postconviction judge was the same judge who sentenced respondent, we must remember that her postconviction opinion was written in 1995—*five years* after the sentencing proceeding. Although the judge's memory deserves some deference, her opinion reflects many of the same flaws as does the Court's opinion. Instead of reexamining the entire trial transcript, she only quoted the same two-question exchange with respondent. And unlike this Court's repeated reference to respondent's behavior at sentencing, she did not mention it at all. Her analysis consists of an incomplete review of the transcript and an unsupported summary conclusion that respondent told his attorney not to present any mitigating evidence.

While I believe that neither the Constitution nor the record supports the Court's waiver holding, respondent is at least entitled to an evidentiary hearing on this question as well as his broader claim of ineffective assistance of counsel. Respondent insists that he never instructed his counsel not to investigate other mitigating evidence. Even the State concedes that there has been no finding on this issue. He has long

---

9. The Court disregards another important contextual clue–that respondent's counsel requested three 30–day continuances to investigate and prepare a mitigation case, and that respondent consented on the record to each one. If respondent had instructed his counsel not to develop any mitigating evidence, his consent would be difficult to explain. Similarly, there is clear evidence that respondent cooperated with counsel's minimal investigation. He allowed counsel to interview his birth mother and ex-wife, he assisted in counsel's gathering of his medical records, and he freely met with Dr. McMahon. These are not the actions of a man who wanted to present no mitigating evidence.

maintained that he would have permitted the presentation of mitigating evidence if only counsel was prepared to introduce evidence other than testimony from his birth mother and ex-wife. Respondent planned to call his counsel at an evidentiary hearing to testify about these very assertions. Because counsel is in the best position to clarify whether respondent gave any blanket instructions not to investigate or present mitigating evidence, the Court is wrong to decide this case before any evidence regarding respondent's instructions can be developed.

IV

Almost as an afterthought, the Court holds in the alternative that "the District Court did not abuse its discretion in finding that Landrigan could not establish prejudice based on his counsel's failure to present the evidence he now wishes to offer." It of course does this on a cold and incomplete factual record. Describing respondent's mitigation case as "weak," and emphasizing his "exceedingly violent past" and "belligerent behavior" at sentencing, the Court concludes that there is no way that respondent can establish prejudice with the evidence he seeks to introduce. This reasoning is flawed in several respects.

First, as has been discussed above but bears repeating, the Court thoroughly misrepresents respondent's mitigating evidence. It is all too easy to view respondent's mitigation case as "weak" when you assume away his most powerful evidence. The Court ignores respondent's organic brain disorder, which would have explained not only his criminal history but also the repeated outbursts at sentencing. It mistakenly assumes that respondent's birth mother and ex-wife could have testified about the medical consequences of fetal alcohol syndrome. And it inaccurately states that these women could have described his turbulent childhood with his adoptive family. We have repeatedly said that evidence of this kind can influence a sentencer's decision as to whether death is the proper punishment. The evidence here might well have convinced a sentencer that a death sentence was not appropriate.

Second, the aggravating circumstances relied on by the sentencing judge are not as strong as the Court makes them out to be.[12] To be sure, respondent had already committed two violent offenses. But so had Terry Williams, and this Court still concluded that he suffered prejudice when his attorney failed to investigate and present mitigating evidence. See *Williams v. Taylor,* 529 U.S. 362, 120 S.Ct. 1495 (2000) (noting that Williams confessed to "two separate violent assaults on elderly victims," including one that left an elderly woman in a "vegetative state"). The only other aggravating factor was that Landrigan committed his crime for pecuniary gain—but there are serious doubts about that. As the en banc Court of Appeals explained, "[t]here was limited evidence regarding the

---

12. In fact, while the Court's terse prejudice analysis relies heavily on a colorful quote from the original Ninth Circuit panel, it declines to mention that one judge on that panel switched her vote and joined the en banc majority after further consideration of respondent's mitigating evidence.

pecuniary gain aggravator. The judge noted that the victim's apartment had been ransacked as if the perpetrator were looking for something, and that this demonstrated an expectation of pecuniary gain, *even though Landrigan did not actually steal anything of value.*" (emphasis added). Thus, while we should not ignore respondent's violent past, it is certainly possible—even likely—that evidence of his neurological disorder, fetal alcohol syndrome, and abusive upbringing would have influenced the sentencing judge's assessment of his moral blameworthiness and altered the outcome of his sentencing. As such, respondent has plainly alleged facts that, if substantiated at an evidentiary hearing, would entitle him to relief.

V

In the end, the Court's decision can only be explained by its increasingly familiar effort to guard the floodgates of litigation. Immediately before turning to the facts of this case, it states that "[i]f district courts were required to allow federal habeas applicants to develop even the most insubstantial factual allegations in evidentiary hearings, district courts would be forced to reopen factual disputes that were conclusively resolved in the state courts." However, habeas cases requiring evidentiary hearings have been "few in number," and "there is no clear evidence that this particular classification of habeas proceedings has burdened the dockets of the federal courts." *Keeney v. Tamayo–Reyes,* 504 U.S.1, 112 S.Ct. 1715 (KENNEDY, J., dissenting). Even prior to the passage of the Antiterrorism and Effective Death Act of 1996, district courts held evidentiary hearings in only *1.17%* of all federal habeas cases. This figure makes it abundantly clear that doing justice does not always cause the heavens to fall. The Court would therefore do well to heed Justice KENNEDY's just reminder that "[w]e ought not take steps which diminish the likelihood that [federal] courts will base their legal decision on an accurate assessment of the facts."

It may well be true that respondent would have completely waived his right to present mitigating evidence if that evidence had been adequately investigated at the time of sentencing. It may also be true that respondent's mitigating evidence could not outweigh his violent past. What is certainly true, however, is that an evidentiary hearing would provide answers to these questions. I emphatically agree with the majority of judges on the en banc Court of Appeals that it was an abuse of discretion to refuse to conduct such a hearing in this capital case.

Accordingly, I respectfully dissent.

MICKENS v. TAYLOR

535 U.S. 162, 122 S.Ct. 1237, 152 L.Ed.2d 291 (2002).

JUSTICE SCALIA delivered the opinion of the Court.

The question presented in this case is what a defendant must show in order to demonstrate a Sixth Amendment violation where the trial court fails to inquire into a potential conflict of interest about which it knew or reasonably should have known.

I

In 1993, a Virginia jury convicted petitioner Mickens of the premeditated murder of Timothy Hall during or following the commission of an attempted forcible sodomy. Finding the murder outrageously and wantonly vile, it sentenced petitioner to death. In June 1998, Mickens filed a petition for writ of habeas corpus, in the United States District Court for the Eastern District of Virginia, alleging, *inter alia,* that he was denied effective assistance of counsel because one of his court-appointed attorneys had a conflict of interest at trial. Federal habeas counsel had discovered that petitioner's lead trial attorney, Bryan Saunders, was representing Hall (the victim) on assault and concealed-weapons charges at the time of the murder. Saunders had been appointed to represent Hall, a juvenile, on March 20, 1992, and had met with him once for 15 to 30 minutes some time the following week. Hall's body was discovered on March 30, 1992, and four days later a juvenile court judge dismissed the charges against him, noting on the docket sheet that Hall was deceased. The one-page docket sheet also listed Saunders as Hall's counsel. On April 6, 1992, the same judge appointed Saunders to represent petitioner. Saunders did not disclose to the court, his co-counsel, or petitioner that he had previously represented Hall. Under Virginia law, juvenile case files are confidential and may not generally be disclosed without a court order, see Va.Code Ann. § 16.1–305 (1999), but petitioner learned about Saunders' prior representation when a clerk mistakenly produced Hall's file to federal habeas counsel.

The District Court held an evidentiary hearing and denied petitioner's habeas petition. A divided panel of the Court of Appeals for the Fourth Circuit reversed, and the Court of Appeals granted rehearing en banc. * * * On the merits, the Court of Appeals assumed that the juvenile court judge had neglected a duty to inquire into a potential conflict, but rejected petitioner's argument that this failure either mandated automatic reversal of his conviction or relieved him of the burden of showing that a conflict of interest adversely affected his representation. Relying on *Cuyler v. Sullivan,* 446 U.S. 335, 100 S.Ct. 1708 (1980), the court held that a defendant must show "both an actual conflict of interest and an adverse effect even if the trial court failed to inquire into a potential conflict about which it reasonably should have known." Concluding that petitioner had not demonstrated adverse effect, it affirmed the District Court's denial of habeas relief. We granted a stay of execution of petitioner's sentence and granted certiorari.

II

The Sixth Amendment provides that a criminal defendant shall have the right to "the assistance of counsel for his defence." This right has been accorded, we have said, "not for its own sake, but because of the effect it has on the ability of the accused to receive a fair trial." *United States v. Cronic*, 466 U.S. 648, 104 S.Ct. 2039 (1984). It follows from this that assistance which is ineffective in preserving fairness does not meet the constitutional mandate, see *Strickland v. Washington*, 466 U.S. 668, 104 S.Ct. 2052 (1984); and it also follows that defects in assistance that have no probable effect upon the trial's outcome do not establish a constitutional violation. As a general matter, a defendant alleging a Sixth Amendment violation must demonstrate "a reasonable probability that, but for counsel's unprofessional errors, the result of the proceeding would have been different."

There is an exception to this general rule. We have spared the defendant the need of showing probable effect upon the outcome, and have simply presumed such effect, where assistance of counsel has been denied entirely or during a critical stage of the proceeding. When that has occurred, the likelihood that the verdict is unreliable is so high that a case-by-case inquiry is unnecessary. See *Cronic*. But only in "circumstances of that magnitude" do we forgo individual inquiry into whether counsel's inadequate performance undermined the reliability of the verdict. *Cronic*.

We have held in several cases that "circumstances of that magnitude" may also arise when the defendant's attorney actively represented conflicting interests. The nub of the question before us is whether the principle established by these cases provides an exception to the general rule of *Strickland* under the circumstances of the present case. To answer that question, we must examine those cases in some detail.

In *Holloway v. Arkansas,* 435 U.S. 475, 98 S.Ct. 1173 (1978), defense counsel had objected that he could not adequately represent the divergent interests of three codefendants. Without inquiry, the trial court had denied counsel's motions for the appointment of separate counsel and had refused to allow counsel to cross-examine any of the defendants on behalf of the other two. The *Holloway* Court deferred to the judgment of counsel regarding the existence of a disabling conflict, recognizing that a defense attorney is in the best position to determine when a conflict exists, that he has an ethical obligation to advise the court of any problem, and that his declarations to the court are "virtually made under oath." *Holloway* presumed, moreover, that the conflict, "which [the defendant] and his counsel tried to avoid by timely objections to the joint representation" undermined the adversarial process. The presumption was justified because joint representation of conflicting interests is inherently suspect, and because counsel's conflicting obligations to multiple defendants "effectively sea[l] his lips on crucial matters" and make it difficult to measure the precise harm arising from counsel's errors. *Holloway* thus creates an automatic reversal rule only where defense counsel is forced to represent codefendants over his timely objection, unless the trial court has determined that there is no conflict. ("[W]henever a trial court improperly requires joint representation over timely objection reversal is automatic").

In *Cuyler v. Sullivan,* 446 U.S. 335, 100 S.Ct. 1708 (1980), the respondent was one of three defendants accused of murder who were tried separately, represented by the same counsel. Neither counsel nor anyone else objected to the multiple representation, and counsel's opening argument at Sullivan's trial suggested that the interests of the defendants were aligned. We declined to extend *Holloway*'s automatic reversal rule to this situation and held that, absent objection, a defendant must demonstrate that "a conflict of interest actually affected the adequacy of his representation." In addition to describing the defendant's burden of proof, *Sullivan* addressed separately a trial court's duty to inquire into the propriety of a multiple representation, construing *Holloway* to require inquiry only when "the trial court knows or reasonably should know that a particular conflict exists"—which is not to be confused with when the trial court is aware of a vague, unspecified possibility of conflict, such as that which "inheres in almost every instance of multiple representation." In *Sullivan,* no "special circumstances" triggered the trial court's duty to inquire.

Finally, in *Wood v. Georgia,* 450 U.S. 261, 101 S.Ct. 1097 (1981), three indigent defendants convicted of distributing obscene materials had their probation revoked for failure to make the requisite $500 monthly payments on their $5,000 fines. We granted certiorari to consider whether this violated the Equal Protection Clause, but during the course of our consideration certain disturbing circumstances came to our attention: At the probation-revocation hearing (as at all times since their arrest) the defendants had been represented by the lawyer for their employer (the owner of the business that purveyed the obscenity), and their employer paid the attorney's fees. The employer had promised his employees he would pay their fines, and had generally kept that promise but had not done so in these defendants' case. This record suggested that the employer's interest in establishing a favorable equal-protection precedent (reducing the fines he would have to pay for his indigent employees in the future) diverged from the defendants' interest in obtaining leniency or paying lesser fines to avoid imprisonment. Moreover, the possibility that counsel was actively representing the conflicting interests of employer and defendants "was sufficiently apparent at the time of the revocation hearing to impose upon the court a duty to inquire further." Because "[o]n the record before us, we [could not] be sure whether counsel was influenced in his basic strategic decisions by the interests of the employer who hired him," we remanded for the trial court "to determine whether the conflict of interest that this record strongly suggests actually existed."

Petitioner argues that the remand instruction in *Wood* established an "unambiguous rule" that where the trial judge neglects a duty to inquire into a potential conflict, the defendant, to obtain reversal of the judgment, need only show that his lawyer was subject to a conflict of interest, and need not show that the conflict adversely affected counsel's performance. He relies upon the language in the remand instruction directing the trial court to grant a new revocation hearing if it determines that "an actual conflict of interest existed," *Wood*, without requiring a further determination that the conflict adversely affected counsel's performance. As used in the remand instruction, however, we think "an actual conflict of interest" meant precisely a conflict *that affected counsel's performance*—as opposed to a mere theoretical division of loyalties. It was shorthand for the statement in *Sullivan* that "a defendant who shows that a conflict of interest *actually affected the adequacy of his representation* need not demonstrate prejudice in order to obtain relief."(emphasis added). This is the only interpretation consistent with the *Wood* Court's earlier description of why it could not decide the case without a remand: "On the record before us, we cannot be sure whether counsel *was influenced in his basic strategic decisions* by the interests of the employer who hired him. *If this was the case,* the due process rights of petitioners were not respected...." (emphasis added). The notion that *Wood* created a new rule *sub silentio*— and in a case where certiorari had been granted on an entirely different question, and the parties had neither briefed nor argued the conflict-of-interest issue—is implausible.

Petitioner's proposed rule of automatic reversal when there existed a conflict that did not affect counsel's performance, but the trial judge failed to make the *Sullivan*-mandated inquiry, makes little policy sense. As discussed, the rule applied when the trial judge is not aware of the conflict (and thus not obligated to inquire) is that prejudice will be presumed only if the conflict has significantly affected counsel's performance—thereby rendering the verdict unreliable, even though *Strickland* prejudice cannot be shown. The trial court's awareness of a potential conflict neither renders it more likely that counsel's performance was significantly affected nor in any other way renders the verdict unreliable. Nor does the trial judge's failure to make the *Sullivan*-mandated inquiry often make it harder for reviewing courts to determine conflict and effect, particularly since those courts may rely on evidence and testimony whose importance only becomes established at the trial.

Nor, finally, is automatic reversal simply an appropriate means of enforcing *Sullivan*'s mandate of inquiry. Despite Justice SOUTER's belief that there must be a threat of sanction (to-wit, the risk of conferring a windfall upon the defendant) in order to induce "resolutely obdurate" trial judges to follow the law, we do not presume that judges are as careless or as partial as those police officers who need the incentive of the exclusionary rule, see *United States v. Leon,* 468 U.S. 897, 104 S.Ct. 3405 (1984). And in any event, the *Sullivan* standard, which requires proof of effect upon representation but (once such effect is shown) presumes prejudice, already creates an "incentive" to inquire into a potential conflict. In those cases where the potential conflict is in fact an actual one, only inquiry will enable the judge to avoid all possibility of reversal by either seeking waiver or replacing a conflicted attorney. We doubt that the deterrence of "judicial dereliction" that would be achieved by an automatic reversal rule is significantly greater.

Since this was not a case in which (as in *Holloway*) counsel protested his inability simultaneously to represent multiple defendants; and since the trial court's failure to make the *Sullivan*-mandated inquiry does not reduce the petitioner's burden of proof; it was at least necessary, to void the conviction, for petitioner to establish that the conflict of interest adversely affected his counsel's performance. The Court of Appeals having found no such effect, the denial of habeas relief must be affirmed.

III

Lest today's holding be misconstrued, we note that the only question presented was the effect of a trial court's failure to inquire into a potential conflict upon the *Sullivan* rule that deficient performance of counsel must be shown. The case was presented and argued on the assumption that (absent some exception for failure to inquire) *Sullivan* would be applicable—requiring a showing of defective performance, but *not* requiring in addition (as *Strickland* does in other ineffectiveness-of-counsel cases), a showing of probable effect upon the outcome of trial. That assumption was not unreasonable in light of the holdings of Courts of Appeals, which have applied *Sullivan* "unblinkingly" to "all kinds of alleged attorney ethical conflicts," *Beets v. Scott*, 65 F.3d 1258 (5th Cir. 1995) (en banc). They have invoked the *Sullivan* standard not only when (as here) there is a conflict rooted in counsel's obligations to *former* clients, but even when representation of the defendant somehow implicates counsel's personal or financial interests, including a book deal, a job with the prosecutor's office, the teaching of classes to Internal Revenue Service agents, a romantic "entanglement" with the prosecutor, or fear of antagonizing the trial judge.

It must be said, however, that the language of *Sullivan* itself does not clearly establish, or indeed even support, such expansive application. "[U]ntil," it said, "a defendant shows that his counsel *actively represented* conflicting interests, he has not established the constitutional predicate for his claim of ineffective assistance." (emphasis added). Both *Sullivan* itself, and *Holloway*, stressed the high probability of prejudice arising from multiple concurrent representation, and the difficulty of proving that prejudice. Not all attorney conflicts present comparable difficulties. Thus, the Federal Rules of Criminal Procedure treat concurrent representation and prior representation differently, requiring a trial court to inquire into the likelihood of conflict whenever jointly charged defendants are represented by a single attorney (Rule 44(c)), but not when counsel previously represented another defendant in a substantially related matter, even where the trial court is aware of the prior representation.

This is not to suggest that one ethical duty is more or less important than another. The purpose of our *Holloway* and *Sullivan* exceptions from the ordinary requirements of *Strickland,* however, is not to enforce the Canons of Legal Ethics, but to apply needed prophylaxis in situations where *Strickland* itself is evidently inadequate to assure vindication of the defendant's Sixth Amendment right to counsel. See *Nix v. Whiteside,* 475

U.S. 157, 106 S.Ct. 988 (1986) ("[B]reach of an ethical standard does not necessarily make out a denial of the Sixth Amendment guarantee of assistance of counsel"). In resolving this case on the grounds on which it was presented to us, we do not rule upon the need for the *Sullivan* prophylaxis in cases of successive representation. Whether *Sullivan* should be extended to such cases remains, as far as the jurisprudence of this Court is concerned, an open question.

* * *

For the reasons stated, the judgment of the Court of Appeals is *Affirmed*.

[Concurring opinion of KENNEDY, J., joined by O'CONNOR, J. omitted]

JUSTICE STEVENS, dissenting.

This case raises three uniquely important questions about a fundamental component of our criminal justice system—the constitutional right of a person accused of a capital offense to have the effective assistance of counsel for his defense. The first is whether a capital defendant's attorney has a duty to disclose that he was representing the defendant's alleged victim at the time of the murder. Second, is whether, assuming disclosure of the prior representation, the capital defendant has a right to refuse the appointment of the conflicted attorney. Third, is whether the trial judge, who knows or should know of such prior representation, has a duty to obtain the defendant's consent before appointing that lawyer to represent him. Ultimately, the question presented by this case is whether, if these duties exist and if all of them are violated, there exist "circumstances that are so likely to prejudice the accused that the cost of litigating their effect in a particular case is unjustified." *United States v. Cronic*, 466 U.S. 648, 104 S.Ct. 2039 (1984).

I

The first critical stage in the defense of a capital case is the series of pretrial meetings between the accused and his counsel when they decide how the case should be defended. A lawyer cannot possibly determine how best to represent a new client unless that client is willing to provide the lawyer with a truthful account of the relevant facts. When an indigent defendant first meets his newly appointed counsel, he will often falsely maintain his complete innocence. Truthful disclosures of embarrassing or incriminating facts are contingent on the development of the client's confidence in the undivided loyalty of the lawyer. Quite obviously, knowledge that the lawyer represented the victim would be a substantial obstacle to the development of such confidence.

It is equally true that a lawyer's decision to conceal such an important fact from his new client would have comparable ramifications. The suppression of communication and truncated investigation that would unavoidably follow from such a decision would also make it difficult, if not altogether impossible, to establish the necessary level of trust that should characterize the "delicacy of relation" between attorney and client.

In this very case, it is likely that Mickens misled his counsel, Bryan Saunders, given the fact that Mickens gave false testimony at his trial denying any involvement in the crime despite the overwhelming evidence that he had killed Timothy Hall after a sexual encounter. In retrospect, it seems obvious that the death penalty might have been avoided by acknowledging Mickens' involvement, but emphasizing the evidence suggesting that their sexual encounter was consensual. Mickens' habeas counsel garnered evidence suggesting that Hall was a male prostitute; that the area where Hall was killed was known for prostitution; and that there was no evidence that Hall was forced to the secluded area where he was ultimately murdered. An unconflicted attorney could have put forward a defense tending to show that Mickens killed Hall only after the two engaged in consensual sex, but Saunders offered no such defense. This was a crucial omission—a finding of forcible sodomy was an absolute prerequisite to Mickens' eligibility for the death penalty. Of course, since that strategy would have led to conviction of a noncapital offense, counsel would have been unable to persuade the defendant to divulge the information necessary to support such a defense and then ultimately to endorse the strategy unless he had earned the complete confidence of his client.

Saunders' concealment of essential information about his prior representation of the victim was a severe lapse in his professional duty. The lawyer's duty to disclose his representation of a client related to the instant charge is not only intuitively obvious, it is as old as the profession. * * * Mickens' lawyer's violation of this fundamental obligation of disclosure is indefensible. The relevance of Saunders' prior representation of Hall to the new appointment was far too important to be concealed.

II

If the defendant is found guilty of a capital offense, the ensuing proceedings that determine whether he will be put to death are critical in every sense of the word. At those proceedings, testimony about the impact of the crime on the victim, including testimony about the character of the victim, may have a critical effect on the jury's decision. *Payne v. Tennessee,* 501 U.S. 808, 111 S.Ct. 2597 (1991). Because a lawyer's fiduciary relationship with his deceased client survives the client's death, Saunders necessarily labored under conflicting obligations that were irreconcilable. He had a duty to protect the reputation and confidences of his deceased client, and a duty to impeach the impact evidence presented by the prosecutor.[4]

---

4. For example, at the time of Hall's death, Saunders was representing Hall in juvenile court for charges arising out of an incident involving Hall's mother. She had sworn out a warrant for Hall's arrest charging him with assault and battery. Despite knowledge of this, Mickens' lawyer offered no rebuttal to the victim-impact statement submitted by Hall's mother that " 'all [she] lived for was that boy.' "

Saunders' conflicting obligations to his deceased client, on the one hand, and to his living client, on the other, were unquestionably sufficient to give Mickens the right to insist on different representation. For the "right to counsel guaranteed by the Constitution contemplates the services of an attorney devoted solely to the interests of his client," *Von Moltke v. Gillies,* 332 U.S. 708, 68 S.Ct. 316 (1948). * * *

III

When an indigent defendant is unable to retain his own lawyer, the trial judge's appointment of counsel is itself a critical stage of a criminal trial. At that point in the proceeding, by definition, the defendant has no lawyer to protect his interests and must rely entirely on the judge. For that reason it is "the solemn duty of a ... judge before whom a defendant appears without counsel to make a thorough inquiry and to take all steps necessary to insure the fullest protection of this constitutional right at every stage of the proceedings." *Von Moltke.*

This duty with respect to indigent defendants is far more imperative than the judge's duty to investigate the possibility of a conflict that arises when retained counsel represents either multiple or successive defendants. It is true that in a situation of retained counsel, "[u]nless the trial court knows or reasonably should know that a particular conflict exists, the court need not initiate an inquiry." *Cuyler v. Sullivan,* 446 U.S. 335, 100 S.Ct. 1708 (1980).[8] But when, as was true in this case, the judge is not merely reviewing the permissibility of the defendants' choice of counsel, but is responsible for making the choice herself, and when she knows or should know that a conflict does exist, the duty to make a thorough inquiry is manifest and unqualified.[9] Indeed, under far less compelling circumstances, we squarely held that when a record discloses the "possibility of a conflict" between the interests of the defendants and the interests of the party paying their counsel's fees, the Constitution imposes a duty of inquiry on the state court judge even when no objection was made. *Wood v. Georgia,* 450 U.S. 261, 101 S.Ct. 1097 (1981).

---

8. Part III of the Court's opinion is a foray into an issue that is not implicated by the question presented. In dicta, the Court states that *Sullivan* may not even apply in the first place to *successive* representations. Most Courts of Appeals, however, have applied *Sullivan* to claims of successive representation as well as to some insidious conflicts arising from a lawyer's self-interest. We have done the same. See *Wood v. Georgia,* 450 U.S. 261, 101 S.Ct. 1097 (1981) (applying *Sullivan* to a conflict stemming from a third-party payment arrangement). Neither we nor the Courts of Appeals have applied this standard "unblinkingly," as the Court accuses, but rather have relied upon principled reason. When a conflict of interest, whether multiple, successive, or otherwise, poses so substantial a risk that a lawyer's representation would be materially and adversely affected by diverging interests or loyalties and the trial court judge knows of this and yet fails to inquire, it is a "[c]ircumstanc[e] of [such] magnitude" that "the likelihood that any lawyer, even a fully competent one, could provide effective assistance is so small that a presumption of prejudice is appropriate without inquiry into the actual conduct of the trial." *Cronic.*

9. There is no dispute before us as to the appointing judge's knowledge. The court below assumed, *arguendo,* that the judge who, upon Hall's death, dismissed Saunders from his representation of Hall and who then three days later appointed Saunders to represent Mickens in the killing of Hall "reasonably should have known that Saunders labored under a potential conflict of interest arising from his previous representation of Hall." This assumption has not been challenged.

IV

Mickens had a constitutional right to the services of an attorney devoted solely to his interests. That right was violated. The lawyer who did represent him had a duty to disclose his prior representation of the victim to Mickens and to the trial judge. That duty was violated. When Mickens had no counsel, the trial judge had a duty to "make a thorough inquiry and to take all steps necessary to insure the fullest protection of" his right to counsel. *Von Moltke.* Despite knowledge of the lawyer's prior representation, she violated that duty.

We will never know whether Mickens would have received the death penalty if those violations had not occurred nor precisely what effect they had on Saunders' representation of Mickens. We do know that he did not receive the kind of representation that the Constitution guarantees. If Mickens had been represented by an attorney-impostor who never passed a bar examination, we might also be unable to determine whether the impostor's educational shortcomings "actually affected the adequacy of his representation." We would, however, surely set aside his conviction if the person who had represented him was not a real lawyer. Four compelling reasons make setting aside the conviction the proper remedy in this case.

First, it is the remedy dictated by our holdings in *Holloway v. Arkansas,* 435 U.S. 475, 98 S.Ct. 1173 (1978), *Cuyler v. Sullivan,* and *Wood v. Georgia.* In this line of precedent, our focus was properly upon the duty of the trial court judge to inquire into a potential conflict. This duty was triggered either via defense counsel's objection, as was the case in *Holloway,* or some other "special circumstances" whereby the serious potential for conflict was brought to the attention of the trial court judge. *Sullivan.* As we unambiguously stated in *Wood,* "*Sullivan* mandates a reversal when the trial court has failed to make an inquiry even though it 'knows or reasonably should know that a particular conflict exists.'"
* * *12

Second, it is the only remedy that responds to the real possibility that Mickens would not have received the death penalty if he had been represented by conflict-free counsel during the critical stage of the proceeding in which he first met with his lawyer. We should presume that the lawyer for the victim of a brutal homicide is incapable of establishing the

---

12. Because the appointing judge knew of the conflict, there is no need in this case to decide what should be done when the judge neither knows, nor should know, about the existence of an intolerable conflict. Nevertheless the Court argues that it makes little sense to reverse automatically upon a showing of actual conflict when the trial court judge knows (or reasonably should know) of a potential conflict and yet has failed to inquire, but *not* to do so when the trial court judge does not know of the conflict. Although it is true that the defendant faces the same potential for harm as a result of a conflict in either instance, in the former case the court committed the error and in the latter the harm is entirely attributable to the misconduct of defense counsel. A requirement that the defendant show adverse effect when the court committed no error surely does not justify such a requirement when the court did err. It is the Court's rule that leads to an anomalous result. Under the Court's analysis, if defense counsel objects to the appointment, reversal without inquiry into adverse effect is required. But counsel's failure to object posed a greater—not a lesser—threat to Mickens' Sixth Amendment right. Had Saunders objected to the appointment, Mickens would at least have been apprised of the conflict.

kind of relationship with the defendant that is essential to effective representation.

Third, it is the only remedy that is consistent with the legal profession's historic and universal condemnation of the representation of conflicting interests without the full disclosure and consent of all interested parties. The Court's novel and naive assumption that a lawyer's divided loyalties are acceptable unless it can be proved that they actually affected counsel's performance is demeaning to the profession.

Finally, "justice must satisfy the appearance of justice." *Offutt v. United States,* 348 U.S. 11, 75 S.Ct. 11 (1954). Setting aside Mickens' conviction is the only remedy that can maintain public confidence in the fairness of the procedures employed in capital cases. Death is a different kind of punishment from any other that may be imposed in this country. "From the point of view of the defendant, it is different in both its severity and its finality. From the point of view of society, the action of the sovereign in taking the life of one of its citizens also differs dramatically from any other legitimate state action. It is of vital importance to the defendant and to the community that any decision to impose the death sentence be, and appear to be, based on reason rather than caprice or emotion." *Gardner v. Florida,* 430 U.S. 349, 97 S.Ct. 1197 (1977). A rule that allows the State to foist a murder victim's lawyer onto his accused is not only capricious; it poisons the integrity of our adversary system of justice.

I respectfully dissent.

[Dissenting opinion of SOUTER, J. omitted]

JUSTICE BREYER, with whom JUSTICE GINSBURG joins, dissenting.

The Commonwealth of Virginia seeks to put the petitioner, Walter Mickens, Jr., to death after having appointed to represent him as his counsel a lawyer who, at the time of the murder, was representing the very person Mickens was accused of killing. I believe that, in a case such as this one, a categorical approach is warranted and automatic reversal is required. To put the matter in language this Court has previously used: By appointing this lawyer to represent Mickens, the Commonwealth created a "structural defect affecting the framework within which the trial [and sentencing] proceeds, rather than simply an error in the trial process itself." *Arizona v. Fulminante,* 499 U.S. 279, 111 S.Ct. 1246 (1991).

The parties spend a great deal of time disputing how this Court's precedents of *Holloway v. Arkansas,* 435 U.S. 475, 98 S.Ct. 1173 (1978), *Cuyler v. Sullivan,* 446 U.S. 335, 100 S.Ct. 1708 (1980), and *Wood v. Georgia,* 450 U.S. 261, 101 S.Ct. 1097 (1981), resolve the case. Those precedents involve the significance of a trial judge's "failure to inquire" if that judge "knew or should have known" of a "potential" conflict. The majority and dissenting opinions dispute the meaning of these cases as well. Although I express no view at this time about how our precedents should treat *most* ineffective-assistance-of-counsel claims involving an alleged conflict of interest (or, for that matter, whether *Holloway*, *Sullivan*, and *Wood* provide a sensible or coherent framework for dealing with those cases at all), I am convinced that *this* case is not governed by those precedents, for the following reasons.

First, this is the kind of representational incompatibility that is egregious on its face. Mickens was represented by the murder victim's lawyer; that lawyer had represented the victim on a criminal matter; and that lawyer's representation of the victim had continued until one business day before the lawyer was appointed to represent the defendant.

Second, the conflict is exacerbated by the fact that it occurred in a capital murder case. In a capital case, the evidence submitted by both sides regarding the victim's character may easily tip the scale of the jury's choice between life or death. Yet even with extensive investigation in post-trial proceedings, it will often prove difficult, if not impossible, to determine whether the prior representation affected defense counsel's decisions regarding, for example: which avenues to take when investigating the victim's background; which witnesses to call; what type of impeachment to undertake; which arguments to make to the jury; what language to use to characterize the victim; and, as a general matter, what basic strategy to adopt at the sentencing stage. Given the subtle forms that prejudice might take, the consequent difficulty of proving actual prejudice, and the significant likelihood that it will nonetheless occur when the same lawyer represents both accused killer and victim, the cost of litigating the existence of actual prejudice in a particular case cannot be easily justified.

Third, the Commonwealth itself *created* the conflict in the first place. Indeed, it was the *same judge* who dismissed the case against the victim who then appointed the victim's lawyer to represent Mickens one business day later. In light of the judge's active role in bringing about the incompatible representation, I am not sure why the concept of a judge's "duty to inquire" is thought to be central to this case. No "inquiry" by the trial judge could have shed more light on the conflict than was obvious on the face of the matter, namely, that the lawyer who would represent Mickens today is the same lawyer who yesterday represented Mickens' alleged victim in a criminal case.

This kind of breakdown in the criminal justice system creates, at a minimum, the appearance that the proceeding will not "reliably serve its function as a vehicle for determination of guilt or innocence," and the resulting "criminal punishment" will not "be regarded as fundamentally fair." *Fulminante*. This appearance, together with the likelihood of prejudice in the typical case, are serious enough to warrant a categorical rule— a rule that does not require proof of prejudice in the individual case. The Commonwealth complains that this argument "relies heavily on the immediate visceral impact of learning that a lawyer previously represented the victim of his current client." And that is so. The "visceral impact," however, arises out of the obvious, unusual nature of the conflict. It arises from the fact that the Commonwealth seeks to execute a defendant, having provided that defendant with a lawyer who, only yesterday, represented the victim. In my view, to carry out a death sentence so obtained would invariably "diminis[h] faith" in the fairness and integrity of our criminal justice system. That is to say, it would diminish that public confidence in the criminal justice system upon which the successful functioning of that system continues to depend.

I therefore dissent.

NOTE

1. *Problem 7–4.*

Defendant and Co-defendant were charged with capital murder in the small town in Georgia under the following undisputed facts. The two were soldiers stationed at a nearby army base. Defendant was a teenager, two years younger than Co-defendant, and Defendant had an IQ of 82. The two got a ride from Victim, a cab driver, and, threatening him with weapons, they kidnapped Victim in his cab. With Defendant driving, Co-defendant tied and blindfolded Victim and sodomized him. The two then put Victim in the trunk of the cab and drove the cab to the edge of a lake. Defendant put the car in gear and jumped as the cab went into the lake. Victim drowned.

Attorney, who had tried dozens of capital cases, was appointed to represent Defendant. Attorney's law partner, Co-counsel, was appointed to represent Co-defendant in a separate proceeding. The two law partners interviewed both defendants and assisted in the preparation of both cases. Co-counsel sat in on Defendant's trial and helped Attorney. At his first trial, Defendant was convicted and sentenced to death, but the death sentence was overturned on appeal. At his penalty retrial, Defendant was again sentenced to death. Meanwhile, Attorney assisted Co-counsel with Co-defendant's trial, although he did not attend the proceedings. Co-defendant was also convicted and sentenced to death. Attorney prepared the briefs for both defendants on appeal and did not make a "lesser culpability" argument for either defendant. Both convictions and sentences were affirmed. On habeas corpus, what arguments should be made on Defendant's claim that he received ineffective assistance of counsel? See *Burger v. Kemp*, 483 U.S. 776, 107 S.Ct. 3114 (1987).

MURRAY v. GIARRATANO

492 U.S. 1, 109 S.Ct. 2765, 106 L.Ed.2d 1 (1989).

CHIEF JUSTICE REHNQUIST announced the judgment of the Court and delivered an opinion, in which JUSTICE WHITE, JUSTICE O'CONNOR, and JUSTICE SCALIA join.

Virginia death row inmates brought a civil rights suit against various officials of the Commonwealth of Virginia. The prisoners claimed, based on several theories, that the Constitution required that they be provided with counsel at the Commonwealth's expense for the purpose of pursuing collateral proceedings related to their convictions and sentences. The courts below ruled that appointment of counsel upon request was necessary for the prisoners to enjoy their constitutional right to access to the courts in pursuit of state habeas corpus relief. We think this holding is inconsistent with our decision two Terms ago in *Pennsylvania v. Finley*, 481 U.S. 551, 107 S.Ct. 1990 (1987), and rests on a misreading of our decision in *Bounds v. Smith*, 430 U.S. 817, 97 S.Ct. 1491 (1977).

Joseph M. Giarratano is a Virginia prisoner under a sentence of death. He initiated this action under 42 U.S.C. § 1983, by *pro se* complaint in Federal District Court, against various state officials including Edward W. Murray who is the Director of the Virginia Department of Corrections. Some months later, the District Court certified a class comprising all current and future Virginia inmates awaiting execution who do not have and cannot afford counsel to pursue postconviction proceedings. The inmates asserted a number of constitutional theories for an entitlement to appointed counsel and the case was tried to the court.

After the evidence, post-trial briefs, and other memoranda, the District Court expressed "serious doubts as to the viability of many of th[e] theories." It was, however, "satisfied that the United States Supreme Court's decision in *Bounds* dictates that the plaintiffs here be granted some form of relief." The District Court noted three special "considerations" relating to death row inmates that it believed required that these inmates receive greater assistance than *Bounds* had outlined. It found that death row inmates had a limited amount of time to prepare their petitions, that their cases were unusually complex, and that the shadow of impending execution would interfere with their ability to do legal work. These "considerations" led the court to believe that the "plaintiffs are incapable of effectively using lawbooks to raise their claims." As a result, it found that Virginia's policy of either allowing death row inmates time in the prison law library or permitting them to have lawbooks sent to their cells did "little to satisfy Virginia's obligation." "Virginia must fulfill its duty by providing these inmates trained legal assistance."

     * * *

On appeal to the United States Court of Appeals for the Fourth Circuit, a divided panel reversed the District Court's judgment that the Commonwealth was constitutionally required to provide personal attorneys to represent death row inmates in state collateral proceedings. But that court, en banc, subsequently reheard the case and affirmed the District Court. The en banc court viewed as findings of fact the special "considerations" relating to death row inmates which had led the District Court to conclude that Virginia was not in compliance with the constitutional rights of access. It accepted these findings as not clearly erroneous and so affirmed the District Court's remedial order. The en banc court did not believe the case to be controlled by *Pennsylvania v. Finley*, 481 U.S. 551, 107 S.Ct. 1990 (1987), which held that the Constitution did not require States to provide counsel in postconviction proceedings. "*Finley* was not a meaningful access case, nor did it address the rule enunciated in *Bounds v. Smith.*" "Most significantly," thought the Fourth Circuit, "*Finley* did not involve the death penalty." Four judges dissented. We granted certiorari and now reverse.

In *Finley* we ruled that neither the Due Process Clause of the Fourteenth Amendment nor the equal protection guarantee of "meaningful access" required the State to appoint counsel for indigent prisoners seeking state postconviction relief. The Sixth and Fourteenth Amendments to the Constitution assure the right of an indigent defendant to counsel at the trial stage of a criminal proceeding, *Gideon v. Wainwright*, 372 U.S. 335, 83 S.Ct. 792 (1963), and an indigent defendant is similarly entitled as a matter of right to counsel for an initial appeal from the judgment and sentence of the trial court. *Douglas v. California*, 372 U.S. 353, 83 S.Ct. 814 (1963). But we held in *Ross v. Moffitt*, 417 U.S. 600, 94 S.Ct. 2437 (1974), that the right to counsel at these earlier stages of a criminal procedure did not carry over to a discretionary appeal provided by North Carolina law from the intermediate appellate court to the Supreme Court of North Carolina. We contrasted the trial stage of a criminal proceeding, where the State by presenting witnesses and arguing to a jury attempts to strip from the defendant the presumption of innocence and convict him of a crime, with the appellate stage of such a proceeding, where the defendant needs an attorney "not as a shield to protect him against being 'haled into court' by the State and stripped of his presumption of innocence, but rather as a sword to upset the prior determination of guilt."

We held in *Finley* that the logic of *Ross v. Moffitt* required the conclusion that there was no federal constitutional right to counsel for indigent prisoners seeking state postconviction relief:

> "Postconviction relief is even further removed from the criminal trial than is discretionary direct review. It is not part of the criminal proceeding itself, and it is in fact considered to be civil in nature. ... States have no obligation to provide this avenue of relief, and when they do, the fundamental fairness mandated by the Due Process Clause does not require that the state supply a lawyer as well."

Respondents, like the courts below, believe that *Finley* does not dispose of respondents' constitutional claim to appointed counsel in habeas proceedings because *Finley* did not involve the death penalty. They argue that, under the Eighth Amendment, "evolving standards of decency" do not permit a death sentence to be carried out while a prisoner is unrepresented. In the same vein, they contend that due process requires appointed counsel in postconviction proceedings, because of the nature of the punishment and the need for accuracy.

We have recognized on more than one occasion that the Constitution places special constraints on the procedures used to convict an accused of a capital offense and sentence him to death. The finality of the death penalty requires "a greater degree of reliability" when it is imposed. *Lockett v. Ohio*, 438 U.S. 586, 98 S.Ct. 2954 (1978).

These holdings, however, have dealt with the trial stage of capital offense adjudication, where the court and jury hear testimony, receive evidence, and decide the questions of guilt and punishment. In *Pulley v. Harris*, 465 U.S. 37, 104 S.Ct. 871 (1984), we declined to hold that the Eighth Amendment required appellate courts to perform proportionality review of death sentences. And in *Satterwhite v. Texas*, 486 U.S. 249, 108 S.Ct. 1792 (1988), we applied the traditional appellate standard of harmless-error review set out in *Chapman v. California*, 386 U.S. 18, 87 S.Ct. 824 (1967), when reviewing a claim of constitutional error in a capital case.

We have similarly refused to hold that the fact that a death sentence has been imposed requires a different standard of review on federal habeas corpus. In *Smith v. Murray*, 477 U.S. 527, 106 S.Ct. 2661 (1986), a case involving federal habeas corpus, this Court unequivocally rejected "the suggestion that the principles [governing procedural fault] of *Wainwright v. Sykes*, 433 U.S. 72, 97 S.Ct. 2497 (1977), apply differently depending on the nature of the penalty a State imposes for the violation of its criminal laws" and similarly discarded the idea that "there is anything 'fundamentally unfair' about enforcing procedural default rules...." And, in *Barefoot v. Estelle*, 463 U.S. 880, 103 S.Ct. 3383 (1983), we observed that "direct appeal is the primary avenue for review of a conviction or sentence, and death penalty cases are no exception."

Finally, in *Ford v. Wainwright*, 477 U.S. 399, 106 S.Ct. 2595 (1986), we held that the Eighth Amendment prohibited the State from executing a validly convicted and sentenced prisoner who was insane at the time of his scheduled execution. Five Justices of this Court, however, rejected the proposition that "the ascertainment of a prisoner's sanity as a predicate to lawful execution calls for no less stringent standards than those demanded in any other aspect of a capital proceeding." Justice Powell recognized that the prisoner's sanity at the time of execution was "not comparable to the antecedent question of whether the petitioner should be executed at all." "It follows that this Court's decisions imposing heightened procedural requirements on capital trials and sentencing proceedings do not apply in this context."

We think that these cases require the conclusion that the rule of *Pennsylvania v. Finley* should apply no differently in capital cases than in noncapital cases. State collateral proceedings are not constitutionally required as an adjunct to the state criminal proceedings and serve a different and more limited purpose than either the trial or appeal.[5] The

---

5. The dissent offers surveys to show that Virginia is one of a handful of States without a "system for appointing counsel for condemned prisoners before a postconviction petition is filed." But even these surveys indicate that only 18 of the 37 States make such appointment automatic. These 18 States overlap to a significant extent with the 13 States that have created "resource centers to assist counsel in litigating capital cases," which, in any event, is not the same thing as requiring automatic appointment of counsel before the filing of a petition. Consequently, a

additional safeguards imposed by the Eighth Amendment at the trial stage of a capital case are, we think, sufficient to assure the reliability of the process by which the death penalty is imposed. We therefore decline to read either the Eighth Amendment or the Due Process Clause to require yet another distinction between the rights of capital case defendants and those in noncapital cases.

The dissent opines that the rule that it would constitutionally mandate "would result in a net benefit to Virginia." But this "mother knows best" approach should play no part in traditional constitutional adjudication. Even as a matter of policy, the correctness of the dissent's view is by no means self-evident. If, as we said in *Barefoot v. Estelle, supra*, direct appeal is the primary avenue for review of capital cases as well as other sentences, Virginia may quite sensibly decide to concentrate the resources it devotes to providing attorneys for capital defendants at the trial and appellate stages of a capital proceeding. Capable lawyering there would mean fewer colorable claims of ineffective assistance of counsel to be litigated on collateral attack.

The Court of Appeals, as an additional basis for its holding, relied on what it perceived as a tension between the rule in *Finley* and the implication of our decision in *Bounds v. Smith*, 430 U.S. 817, 97 S.Ct. 1491 (1977); we find no such tension. Whether the right of access at issue in *Bounds* is primarily one of due process or equal protection, in either case it rests on a constitutional theory considered in *Finley*. The Court held in *Bounds* that a prisoner's "right of access" to the courts required a State to furnish access to adequate law libraries in order that the prisoners might prepare petitions for judicial relief. *Bounds*. But it would be a strange jurisprudence that permitted the extension of that holding to partially overrule a subsequently decided case such as *Finley* which held that prisoners seeking judicial relief from their sentence in state proceedings were not entitled to counsel.

* * *

There is no inconsistency whatever between the holding of *Bounds* and the holding in *Finley*; the holding of neither case squarely decides the question presented in this case. For the reasons previously stated in this opinion, we now hold that *Finley* applies to those inmates under sentence of death as well as to other inmates, and that holding necessarily imposes limits on *Bounds*.

* * *

[Concurring opinion of O'CONNOR, J. omitted]

---

substantial balance of States do not accord the right that the dissent would require Virginia to grant as a matter of constitutional law. Virginia courts presently have the authority to appoint counsel to represent any inmate in state habeas proceedings, and the attorney general represents that such appointments have been made, upon request, before the filing of any petition.

JUSTICE KENNEDY, with whom JUSTICE O'CONNOR joins, concurring in the judgment.

It cannot be denied that collateral relief proceedings are a central part of the review process for prisoners sentenced to death. As Justice STEVENS observes, a substantial proportion of these prisoners succeed in having their death sentences vacated in habeas corpus proceedings. The complexity of our jurisprudence in this area, moreover, makes it unlikely that capital defendants will be able to file successful petitions for collateral relief without the assistance of persons learned in the law.

The requirement of meaningful access can be satisfied in various ways, however. This was made explicit in our decision in *Bounds v. Smith*, 430 U.S. 817, 97 S.Ct. 1491 (1977). The intricacies and range of options are of sufficient complexity that state legislatures and prison administrators must be given "wide discretion" to select appropriate solutions. Indeed, judicial imposition of a categorical remedy such as that adopted by the court below might pretermit other responsible solutions being considered in Congress and state legislatures. Assessments of the difficulties presented by collateral litigation in capital cases are now being conducted by committees of the American Bar Association and the Judicial Conference of the United States, and Congress has stated its intention to give the matter serious consideration.

Unlike Congress, this Court lacks the capacity to undertake the searching and comprehensive review called for in this area, for we can decide only the case before us. While Virginia has not adopted procedures for securing representation that are as far reaching and effective as those available in other States, no prisoner on death row in Virginia has been unable to obtain counsel to represent him in postconviction proceedings, and Virginia's prison system is staffed with institutional lawyers to assist in preparing petitions for postconviction relief. I am not prepared to say that this scheme violates the Constitution.

On the facts and record of this case, I concur in the judgment of the Court.

JUSTICE STEVENS, with whom JUSTICE BRENNAN, JUSTICE MARSHALL, and JUSTICE BLACKMUN join, dissenting.

Two Terms ago this Court reaffirmed that the Fourteenth Amendment to the Federal Constitution obligates a State " 'to assure the indigent defendant an adequate opportunity to present his claims fairly in the context of the State's appellate process.' " *Pennsylvania v. Finley*, 481 U.S. 551, 107 S.Ct. 1990 (1987) (quoting *Ross v. Moffitt*, 417 U.S. 600, 94 S.Ct. 2437 (1974)). The narrow question presented is whether that obligation includes appointment of counsel for indigent death row inmates who wish to pursue state postconviction relief. Viewing the facts in light of our precedents, we should answer that question in the affirmative.

I

The parties before us, like the Court of Appeals en banc and the District Court below, have accorded controlling importance to our decision in *Bounds v. Smith*, 430 U.S. 817, 97 S.Ct. 1491 (1977). In that case, inmates had alleged that North Carolina violated the Fourteenth Amendment by failing to provide research facilities to help them prepare habeas corpus petitions and federal civil rights complaints. Stressing "meaningful" access to the courts as a "touchstone," we held:

> "[T]he fundamental constitutional right of access to the courts requires prison authorities to assist inmates in the preparation and filing of meaningful legal papers by providing prisoners with adequate law libraries or adequate assistance from persons trained in the law."

Far from creating a discrete constitutional right, *Bounds* constitutes one part of a jurisprudence that encompasses "right-to-counsel" as well as "access-to-courts" cases. Although each case is shaped by its facts, all share a concern, based upon the Fourteenth Amendment, that accused and convicted persons be permitted to seek legal remedies without arbitrary governmental interference.

[Justice STEVENS reviewed the Court's precedents, including *Powell v. Alabama*, 287 U.S. 45, 53 S.Ct. 55 (1932) (indigent defendant's right to appointed counsel at trial in a capital case) [Chapter 1], *Griffin v. Illinois*, 351 U.S. 12, 76 S.Ct. 585 (1956) (indigent defendant's right to free transcript on appeal), *Gideon v. Wainwright*, 372 U.S. 335, 83 S.Ct. 792 (1963) (indigent defendant's right to appointed counsel at trial in a felony case) and *Douglas v. California*, 372 U.S. 353, 83 S.Ct. 814 (1963) (indigent defendant's right to counsel on a first appeal as of right).]

In two subsequent opinions the Court rejected inmates' attempts to secure legal assistance. In *Ross v. Moffitt*, 417 U.S. 600, 94 S.Ct. 2437 (1974), the Court held there was no right to appointment of counsel for discretionary state appeals or certiorari petitions to this Court. It later announced for the first time that a State has no obligation to provide defendants with any collateral review of their convictions, and that if it does, "the fundamental fairness mandated by the Due Process Clause does not require that the State supply a lawyer as well." *Pennsylvania v. Finley*. Although one might distinguish these opinions as having a different legal basis than the present case, it is preferable to consider them, like *Powell*, *Griffin*, *Douglas*, and *Bounds*, as applications of the Fourteenth Amendment's guarantees to particular situations. Indeed the Court reaffirmed in *Ross*:

> "The Fourteenth Amendment ... does require that the state appellate system be 'free of unreasoned distinctions,' and that indigents have an adequate opportunity to present their claims fairly within the adversary system. The State cannot adopt procedures which leave an indigent defendant 'entirely cut off from any appeal at all,' by virtue of his indigency, or extend to such indigents merely a 'meaningless ritual' while others in better economic circumstances have a 'meaningful appeal.' The question is not one of absolutes, but one of degrees."

II

These precedents demonstrate that the appropriate question in this case is not whether there is an absolute "right to counsel" in collateral proceedings, but whether due process requires that these respondents be appointed counsel in order to pursue legal remedies. Three critical differences between *Finley* and this case demonstrate that even if it is permissible to leave an ordinary prisoner to his own resources in collateral proceedings, it is fundamentally unfair to require an indigent death row inmate to initiate collateral review without counsel's guiding hand. I shall address each of these differences in turn.

First. These respondents, like petitioners in *Powell* but unlike respondent in *Finley*, have been condemned to die. Legislatures conferred greater access to counsel on capital defendants than on persons facing lesser punishment even in colonial times. Our First Congress required assignment of up to two attorneys to a capital defendant at the same time it initiated capital punishment; nearly a century passed before Congress provided for appointment of counsel in other contexts. Similarly, Congress at first limited the federal right of appeal to capital cases. Just last year, it enacted a statute requiring provision of counsel for state and federal prisoners seeking federal postconviction relief—but only if they are under sentence of death.

This Court also expanded capital defendants' ability to secure counsel and other legal assistance long before bestowing similar privileges on persons accused of less serious crimes. Both before and after *Furman v. Georgia*, 408 U.S. 238, 92 S.Ct. 2726 (1972), established that the Constitution requires channeling of the death-sentencing decision, various Members of this Court have recognized that "the penalty of death is qualitatively different from a sentence of imprisonment, however long." *Woodson v. North Carolina*, 428 U.S. 280, 96 S.Ct. 2978 (1976) (plurality opinion).

The unique nature of the death penalty not only necessitates additional protections during pretrial, guilt, and sentencing phases, but also enhances the importance of the appellate process. Generally there is no constitutional right to appeal a conviction. "[M]eaningful appellate review" in capital cases, however, "serves as a check against the random or arbitrary imposition of the death penalty." *Gregg v. Georgia*, 428 U.S. 153, 96 S.Ct. 2909 (1976) (opinion of STEWART, POWELL, and STEVENS, JJ.). It is therefore an integral component of a State's "constitutional responsibility to tailor and apply its law in a manner that avoids the arbitrary and capricious infliction of the death penalty." *Godfrey v. Georgia*, 446 U.S. 420, 100 S.Ct. 1759 (1980).

Ideally, "direct appeal is the primary avenue for review of a conviction or sentence, and death penalty cases are no exception. When the process of direct review . . . comes to an end, a presumption of finality and legality attaches to the conviction and sentence." *Barefoot v. Estelle*, 463 U.S. 880, 103 S.Ct. 3383 (1983). There is, however, significant evidence that in capital cases what is ordinarily considered direct review does not sufficiently safeguard against miscarriages of justice to warrant this presumption of finality. Federal habeas courts granted relief in only 0.25% to 7% of noncapital cases in recent years; in striking contrast, the success rate in capital cases ranged from 60% to 70%. Such a high incidence of uncorrected error demonstrates that the meaningful appellate review necessary in a capital case extends beyond the direct appellate process.

Second. In contrast to the collateral process discussed in *Finley*, Virginia law contemplates that some claims ordinarily heard on direct review will be relegated to postconviction proceedings. Claims that trial or appellate counsel provided constitutionally ineffective assistance, for instance, usually cannot be raised until this stage. Furthermore, some irregularities, such as prosecutorial misconduct, may not surface until after the direct review is complete. Occasionally, new evidence even may suggest that the defendant is innocent. Given the irreversibility of capital punishment, such information deserves searching, adversarial scrutiny even if it is discovered after the close of direct review.

* * *

Third. As the District Court's findings reflect, the plight of the death row inmate constrains his ability to wage collateral attacks far more than does the lot of the ordinary inmate considered in *Finley*. The District Court found that the death row inmate has an extremely limited period to prepare and present his postconviction petition and any necessary applications for stays of execution. Unlike the ordinary inmate, who presumably has ample time to use and reuse the prison library and to seek guidance from other prisoners experienced in preparing *pro se* petitions, a grim deadline imposes a finite limit on the condemned person's capacity for useful research.

Capital litigation, the District Court observed, is extremely complex. Without regard to the special characteristics of Virginia's statutory procedures, this Court's death penalty jurisprudence unquestionably is difficult even for a trained lawyer to master.[22] A judgment that it is not unfair to require an ordinary inmate to rely on his own resources to prepare a petition for postconviction relief, does not justify the same conclusion for the death row inmate who must acquire an understanding of this specialized area of the law and prepare an application for stay of execution as well as a petition for collateral relief.[23] This is especially true, the District Court concluded, because the "evidence gives rise to a fair inference that an inmate preparing himself and his family for impending death is incapable of performing the mental functions necessary to adequately

---

22. In apparent recognition of this fact, Congress has required that when a court appoints counsel in capital postconviction proceedings, at least one attorney must have been a member of the bar for at least five years and have at least three years felony litigation experience.

23. Compounding matters is the typically low educational attainment of prisoners. In 1982 more than half of Florida's general inmate population was found to be functionally illiterate, while in 1979 the State's death row inmates possessed a ninth-grade mean educational level. Virginia's death row inmates apparently have similar educational backgrounds.

pursue his claims.''[24]

These three critical factors demonstrate that there is a profound difference between capital postconviction litigation and ordinary postconviction litigation in Virginia. The District Court's findings unequivocally support the conclusion that to obtain an adequate opportunity to present their postconviction claims fairly, death row inmates need greater assistance of counsel than Virginia affords them. Meaningful access, and meaningful judicial review, would be effected in this case only if counsel were appointed, on request, in time to enable examination of the case record, factual investigation, and preparation of a petition containing all meritorious claims, which the same attorney then could litigate to its conclusion.

* * *

IV

The basic question in this case is whether Virginia's procedure for collateral review of capital convictions and sentences assures its indigent death row inmates an adequate opportunity to present their claims fairly. The District Court and Court of Appeals en banc found that it did not, and neither the State nor this Court's majority provides any reasoned basis for disagreeing with their conclusion. Simple fairness requires that this judgment be affirmed.

NOTES

1. *Access to counsel in state post-conviction proceedings.*

Without a federal constitutional right to appointed counsel in state post-conviction proceedings, the right to counsel is determined by state law. There is wide divergence among death penalty states on the provision of counsel in capital post-conviction cases. A few states, such as Georgia and Wyoming, preclude appointment of post-conviction counsel, and, as a result, counsel are not compensated for their work representing indigent death-row petitioners. See, *e.g., Gibson v. Turpin*, 513 S.E.2d 186 (Ga. 1999); Wyo.Stat. § 7–14–104. In a minority of states, the court has discretion to appoint to counsel for indigent petitioners. See, *e.g.* Ala.Code § 15–12–23 (Alabama); Neb.Rev.Stat. 29–3004 (Nebraska). In most death penalty states, there is a right to appointment of counsel, see, *e.g.* Mo.Rev.Stat. § 547.370 (Missouri); R.C.W. 10.73.150(3) (Washington), although some states permit a court to deny counsel if the proceeding is not one a reasonable person with adequate means would bring at his or her own expense. See Ky.Rev.Stat.Ann. § 31.110(2)(c) (Kentucky).

---

24. For example, one lawyer testified:

"I have had lots of clients in those last 60 day time periods, and what they are forced to do is to prepare themselves mentally and spiritually and emotionally to deal with their family and their children, all of whom see them as about to die. And that is a full time job.

"And very few of them, I think, even have the emotional resources to talk with you meaningfully at that point about their case. Much less to take it over." * * *

Even a state right to counsel does not guarantee timely appointment of counsel or effective representation. There is a shortage of qualified attorneys, resulting in part from the failure of most states to provide adequate compensation and reasonable expenses in capital post-conviction cases. A 1987 study commissioned by the American Bar Association Death Penalty Representation Project found that on average counsel devoted 2,000 hours to a capital post-conviction case. The Spangenberg Group, *Time and Expense Analysis in Post–Conviction Death Penalty Cases*, February 1987, 11, 20. According to a more recent study, experienced lawyers estimated that, on average, over 3,300 lawyer hours are required to take a case through the state post-conviction process in Florida, where evidentiary hearings are routine in capital post-conviction proceedings. The Spangenberg Group, *Amended Time and Expense Analysis of Post–Conviction Capital Cases in Florida,* April 1998, at 16. Despite these estimates, many states set unrealistically low statutory limits on compensation and expenses. Thus, in Alabama, where the court in its discretion may appoint counsel, there is a $1,000 statutory limit on attorney fees in capital post-conviction proceedings. Ala. Code § 15–12–23(d). Nevada, which provides a right to post-conviction counsel, generally limits counsels' compensation to $750 and limits expenses to $500. NRS §§ 7.125, 7.135. Other states compensate attorneys for many more hours, but still less time than a case requires. Since 1996, South Carolina has provided a right to post-conviction counsel in capital cases and has authorized compensation at the rate of $50 per hour for out-of-court work and $75 per hour for in-court work with a $25,000 statutory maximum that may be exceeded if the court certifies that payment in excess of the statutory rate is necessary to ensure effective assistance of counsel. S.C. Code §§ 16–3–26 and 17–27–160. In contrast, private firms that have handled capital post-conviction cases in Florida on a *pro bono* basis report having spent, on average, $200,000 in litigation expenses. *Amended Time and Expense Analysis of Post–Conviction Capital Cases in Florida* at 13.

Even states that provide a right to counsel and more generous funding have experienced a crisis in post-conviction representation. Two states illustrate the problem. In 1985, Florida became the first state to provide post-conviction counsel for death-row inmates when it established the Office of Capital Collateral Representative (CCR). However, the Florida Legislature failed to adequately fund CCR. In 1995, CCR informed the Florida Supreme Court that it lacked the staff and resources to assign counsel to the high number of capital cases entering the collateral review process. In 1993 and 1997, two commissions created by the Florida Supreme Court concluded that CCR was underfunded. In 1997, CCR ran out of money. In the same year, the Florida Legislature, dissatisfied with the slow pace of executions, abolished CCR and created regional offices as the Capital Collateral Regional Counsel (CCRC). The turmoil resulted in an exodus of experienced defense attorneys from the capital post-conviction system. The new offices, understaffed by inexperienced attorneys and underfunded, were unable to meet filing deadlines or conduct hearings. *Amended Time and Expense Analysis of Post–Conviction Capital Cases in Florida* at 5–7; *Death Row Lawyers Ask for More Time: Regional Offices Understaffed, Causing Delays*, Florida Today, October 1, 1997, at B6; *Amendments To Florida Rules of Criminal Procedure—Capital*

Postconviction Public Records Production, 708 So.2d 913, 914 (Fla.1998). Meanwhile, Florida established a state-wide registry of private attorneys for appointment in capital post-conviction cases and then closed one of the three regional offices (for the Northern region) on a "trial basis" and transferred its responsibilities to registry attorneys. By statute, compensation for registry attorneys is capped at $84,000 and expenses at $15,000 (Fla.Stat.Ann. § 27.711; 27.7002(5)), although the Florida Supreme Court has held that the statute cannot be construed to bar compensation above the cap in "extraordinary circumstances." *Maas v. Olive*, 992 So.2d 196, 204 (2008). The American Bar Association, in its 2006 assessment, was critical of the qualifications and performance of post-conviction counsel and of the cap on fees and expenses. *Evaluating Fairness and Accuracy in State Death Penalty Systems: The Florida Death Penalty Assessment Report*, pp. 235–239.

Similarly, there is a shortage of attorneys in California, which also provides a state right to counsel in capital post-conviction cases. Cal. Govt.Code § 68662; Internal Operating Practice and Procedures of the California Supreme Court, parts XV A–D; California Supreme Court Policies Regarding Cases Arising From Judgments of Death, policy 3. California now pays appointed attorneys at the rate of $145 per hour for the time it takes to review the record and for 180–500 hours to investigate and prepare a capital habeas corpus petition. Payment Guidelines For Appointed Counsel Representing Indigent Criminal Appellants in the California Supreme Court (as amended 2007). The state provides additional compensation in the exceptional case where an evidentiary hearing is held, and in all capital habeas cases guarantees $50,000 in expenses. Alternatively, California compensates counsel on a flat-fee basis for state habeas corpus and clemency representation which, depending on the length of the trial record and complexity of the case, ranges from $85,000 to $127,000 plus compensation for reading the record. Guidelines for Fixed Fee Appointments, On Optional Basis, To Automatic Appeals and Related Habeas Corpus Proceedings in the California Supreme Court, Guideline 1.2 (as amended 2007). Nevertheless, a dearth of available, qualified attorneys has forced condemned inmates to wait four years or more for appointment of appellate counsel and often another four or more years for appointment of habeas counsel. In 2008, almost 300 inmates on California's death row had no habeas counsel. In 1998, the California Legislature established a new state agency, the Habeas Corpus Resource Center, in an effort to remedy the lack of post-conviction counsel, but even with a staff of around thirty attorneys, the center is not able to fill the ever-growing need for post-conviction counsel.

2. *AEDPA and counsel.*

Some of the recent state efforts to provide post-conviction counsel were spurred by the enactment of the Antiterrorism and Effective Death Penalty Act of 1996, 110 Stat. 1214, 1217–1226 (April 24, 1996) ("AEDPA"). AEDPA [discussed in more detail in Chapter 11] creates certain incentives for states to provide counsel to prisoners subject to a death sentence who seek state court collateral review. States can "opt in" and take advantage of special rules designed to reduce delay and enhance the finality of death judgments by providing: (1) a "post-conviction" procedure that provides, among other things, competent habeas counsel following final state conviction, or (2) a "unitary review procedure" for states that provide competent counsel for an integrated or simultaneous collateral and direct appeal. 28 U.S.C. §§ 2261, 2265. To qualify, the state must establish a mechanism for the appointment, compensation, and payment of reasonable litigation expenses of competent counsel in state post-conviction proceedings. Unless expressly requested by the prisoner, no counsel who represented the prisoner at trial or on direct appeal may be appointed for the habeas representation.

THE ABA GUIDELINES

In 2003, the American Bar Association issued a revised edition of the *Guidelines for the Appointment and Performance of Defense Counsel in Death Penalty Cases.*[1] The Guidelines are an attempt to address problems with the quality of defense representation in death penalty cases that are "profound and pervasive."[2] As one commentator has described the situation:

> The ABA, ... and others[a] have documented the abysmally ineffectual lawyers—chronically under-remunerated; often young and inexperienced, patently unqualified and incompetent, unethical, or bar-disciplined; sometimes drug-impaired, drunken, comatose, psychotic, or senile; very often grossly negligent; and nearly always out-gunned—who represent capital defendants in most death penalty states around the country. This counsel situation is worse in capital than in noncapital cases in two important respects. First, capital trials are much harder to litigate well than noncapital trials. Built into them are a hugely complicated body of specialized law, a second, sentencing trial that almost always is more far-ranging, expert-dependent, and factually complex than the guilt phase, and a host of peculiar tactical and strategic decisions caused by the need to "unify" one's defense strategy at two individually daunting and jointly contradictory proceedings (the defendant didn't commit capital murder; even though the defendant committed capital murder, it wasn't (or he isn't) so bad that he deserves a death sentence). Second, although most criminal defense lawyers are overworked and (even more so than in noncapital cases) underpaid, what they do for a living in the main is settle cases for lower sentences than would be imposed after a trial. To use Vivian Berger's metaphor, what they do most of the time is hardly brain surgery.[b] But capital cases settle much less frequently,

---

1. Published at 31 Hofstra L. Rev. 913 (2003). Citations to the various guidelines appear as numbers in parentheses.

2. *Id.* at 928.

a. [See, *e.g.*, Spec. Comm. on Capital Representation & Comm. on Civ. Rts., Ass'n of the Bar of the City of N.Y., The Crisis in Capital Representation, 51 Rec. of Ass'n of the Bar of City of N.Y. 169, 185–87 (1996); J. Kirchmeier, *Drink, Drugs, and Drowsiness: The Constitutional Right to Effective Assistance of Counsel and the Strickland Prejudice Requirement*, 75 Neb. L. Rev. 425, 428–34 (1996); S. Bright, *Counsel for the Poor: The Death Sentence Not for the Worst Crime but for the Worst Lawyer*, 103 Yale L.J. 1835 (1994); Notes, The Eighth Amendment and Ineffective Assistance of Counsel in Capital Trials, 107 Harv. L. Rev. 1923 (1994).—Eds.]

b. [citing V. Berger, *Chiropractor as Brain Surgeon: Defense Lawyering in Capital Cases*, 18 N.Y.U. Rev. L. & Soc. Change 245 (1990–1991)] and when they do, the bargaining is far harder and more sophisticated than in other kinds of cases—hence the many depredations (in Professor Berger's full phrase) of "the chiropractor as brain surgeon." Indeed, because a case in which a death sentence was imposed is virtually certain to have gone to trial—not many lawyers are reckless enough to advise clients to plead guilty to capital murder without an agreement or understanding that doing so will avoid the death penalty—it is highly likely that any capitally sentenced defendant who finds himself in that fix got there after a settlement-specializing chiropractor attempted to open up that capital defendant's cranium at trial.[3]

The guidelines are intended to establish a "national standard of practice for the defense of capital cases," and they are applicable from the moment the client is taken into custody through any clemency proceedings. (1.1) As the Guidelines' title indicates, the Guidelines address two distinct elements of the provision of effective assistance: appointment and performance.

Appointment

The Guidelines require that each death penalty jurisdiction develop a plan to provide "high quality legal representation in death penalty cases." (2.1) The plan would provide for a "Responsible Agency," independent of the judiciary and elected officials, to control the appointment of counsel. (3.1) The Guidelines require that in every potential capital case, the defendant would be represented by a defense team, consisting of no less than four professionals: two lawyers, an investigator and a mitigation specialist. (4.1.A.1) At least one member of the team must be qualified "to screen individuals for the presence of mental or psychological disorders or impairments." (4.1.A.2) Counsel should also have the right to reasonably necessary "expert, investigative, and other ancillary professional services" and to protect the confidentiality of communications with the persons providing such services. (4.1.B) The Guidelines require the Agency to select attorneys based on the demonstrated knowledge and skills (rather than simply their experience) (5.1.B), to implement workload controls for those attorneys (6.1), to monitor attorneys' performance and, where necessary, remove attorneys from appointment lists (7.1) and to create, and require attorneys to complete, a comprehensive training program. (8.1)

Perhaps the most ambitious element of the Guidelines is their requirement that capital defense be adequately funded. (9.1) The Guidelines forbid limiting the compensation of capital defense attorneys by means of flat fees, caps on compensation and lump-sum contracts. (9.1.B.1) They require that salaried attorneys be compensated according a salary scale commensurate with the prosecutor's office salary scale (9.1.B.2), and that appointed counsel be compensated at an hourly rate commensurate with

---

3.   J. Liebman, *The Overproduction of Death*, 100 Colum. L. Rev. 2030, 2102–2108 (2000).

the prevailing rates for similar services charged by retained counsel. (9.1.B.3). Non-attorney members of the defense team must be compensated similarly. (9.1.C) Members of the defense team should be fully reimbursed for reasonable incidental expenses. (9.1.E)

Performance

The performance standards established by the Guidelines, although they refer on occasion to the role of the Responsible Agency, apply directly to defense counsel. For example, the performance standards repeat the requirements that defense counsel establish a defense teams (10.4) and that counsel limit their caseload if necessary to provide high quality representation. (10.3) The standards require prompt and regular consultations with clients about all aspects of the case. (10.5) They require that defense counsel conduct "thorough and independent investigations relating to the issues of both guilt and penalty" regardless of the client's admission of the crime or overwhelming evidence of guilt and *regardless* of the client's desire *not* to have such investigation take place. (10.7.A) Counsel has a duty to consider and thoroughly investigate all legal claims and to evaluate such claims in light of, *inter alia*, "the near certainty that all available avenues of post-conviction relief will be pursued in the event of conviction and imposition of a death sentence" and "the importance of protecting the client's rights against later contentions by the government that the claim has been waived, defaulted, not exhausted, or otherwise forfeited." (10.8.A)

The Guidelines also require that defense counsel, at every stage of the case, explore the possibility of a negotiated settlement irrespective of initial refusals by the prosecutor to negotiate or initial opposition to a settlement by the client. (10.9.E) The Guidelines detail the types of pleas that might be entered and the various concessions and benefits that might be incorporated in a plea agreement. (10.9.B) In similar vein, the Guidelines detail the categories of evidence defense counsel should consider presenting at the penalty phase, including witnesses who can testify about the applicable alternative sentence and witnesses who can testify about "the adverse impact of the client's execution on the client's family and loved ones."[4] (10.11.F) Defense counsel also must be familiar with the techniques of jury selection in a capital case (10.10.2), must take care that jury instructions and verdict forms ensure jurors will able to give effect to mitigating evidence (10.11.K) and must provide information for, and monitor the information in, any pre-sentence report. (10.12) Each defense counsel has a continuing duty to cooperate fully with any successor counsel by maintaining records, providing files, sharing research and cooperating fully with "professionally appropriate legal strategies as may be chosen by successor counsel." (10.13)

---

4. Whether evidence such as this would be admissible is addressed in Chapter 9.

CHAPTER 8

THE PROSECUTOR

■ ■ ■

The three cases in this chapter involve claims of denial of due process because of prosecutorial misconduct. Most prosecutorial misconduct claims concern either the prosecutor's failure to disclose evidence to the defense prior to trial or the prosecutor's conduct during the trial. *Brady v. Maryland*, 373 U.S. 83, 83 S.Ct. 1194 (1963) is the leading case in the former category. The defendant and a companion were charged with murder, and the defendant's attorney had requested to see all of the companion's statements made to the police. At his separate trial, the defendant conceded involvement in the murder, but claimed that he was not the actual killer. He was convicted of murder and sentenced to death. Later it was discovered that the prosecutor had failed to disclose a statement by the companion admitting he was the killer. The Supreme Court found a due process violation and affirmed the Court of Appeals' grant of penalty relief. *Miller v. Pate*, 386 U.S. 1, 87 S.Ct. 785 (1967) is an extreme example from the latter category. The defendant was charged with the sexual attack and murder of a little girl. There were no eyewitnesses to the crime, and a key piece of evidence against the defendant was a pair of men's underwear shorts covered with large, dark, reddish-brown stains. The shorts had been found about a mile from the scene of the crime. Throughout the trial, the prosecutor and his witnesses, including his expert witness, described the shorts as "blood-stained." The defendant was convicted and sentenced to death, and the sentence was upheld on appeal. In the course of federal habeas corpus proceedings, the shorts were analyzed, and the stains were determined to be paint. The Supreme Court found a due process violation and ordered the writ granted.

Kyles v. Whitley is a case in the first category. The defendant's claim is that the prosecutor violated his obligation to disclose favorable evidence, and the Court has to decide whether the withheld evidence was material to the case. *Darden v. Wainwright* is a case in the second category. The defendant claims that the prosecutors engaged in misconduct in their arguments to the jury, and the Court has to determine whether the concededly improper arguments deprived the defendant of a fair trial. *Jacobs v. Scott* involves another claim of prosecutorial misconduct in the second category. The defendant claims misconduct because, in separate trials against the defendant and a co-defendant, the prosecutor argued inconsistent factual theories to obtain a conviction against each. The Court denies the defendant's petition for certiorari, but Justices Stevens and Ginsburg dissent.

KYLES v. WHITLEY

514 U.S. 419, 115 S.Ct. 1555, 131 L.Ed.2d 490 (1995).

Justice Souter delivered the opinion of the Court.

After his first trial in 1984 ended in a hung jury, petitioner Curtis Lee Kyles was tried again, convicted of first-degree murder, and sentenced to death. On habeas review, we follow the established rule that the state's obligation under *Brady v. Maryland*, 373 U.S. 83, 83 S.Ct. 1194 (1963), to disclose evidence favorable to the defense, turns on the cumulative effect of all such evidence suppressed by the government, and we hold that the prosecutor remains responsible for gauging that effect regardless of any failure by the police to bring favorable evidence to the prosecutor's attention. Because the net effect of the evidence withheld by the State in this case raises a reasonable probability that its disclosure would have produced a different result, Kyles is entitled to a new trial.

* * *

II

A

The record indicates that, at about 2:20 p.m. on Thursday, September 20, 1984, 60–year–old Dolores Dye left the Schwegmann Brothers' store (Schwegmann's) on Old Gentilly Road in New Orleans after doing some food shopping. As she put her grocery bags into the trunk of her red Ford LTD, a man accosted her and after a short struggle drew a revolver, fired into her left temple, and killed her. The gunman took Dye's keys and drove away in the LTD.

New Orleans police took statements from six eyewitnesses, who offered various descriptions of the gunman. They agreed that he was a black man, and four of them said that he had braided hair. The witnesses differed significantly, however, in their descriptions of height, age, weight, build, and hair length. Two reported seeing a man of 17 or 18, while another described the gunman as looking as old as 28. One witness described him as 5'4" or 5'5", medium build, 140–150 pounds; another described the man as slim and close to six feet. One witness said he had a mustache; none of the others spoke of any facial hair at all. One witness said the murderer had shoulder-length hair; another described the hair as "short."

Since the police believed the killer might have driven his own car to Schwegmann's and left it there when he drove off in Dye's LTD, they recorded the license numbers of the cars remaining in the parking lots around the store at 9:15 p.m. on the evening of the murder. Matching these numbers with registration records produced the names and addresses of the owners of the cars, with a notation of any owner's police record. Despite this list and the eyewitness descriptions, the police had no lead to the gunman until the Saturday evening after the shooting.

At 5:30 p.m., on September 22, a man identifying himself as James Joseph called the police and reported that on the day of the murder he had bought a red Thunderbird from a friend named Curtis, whom he later identified as petitioner, Curtis Kyles. He said that he had subsequently read about Dye's murder in the newspapers and feared that the car he purchased was the victim's. He agreed to meet with the police.

A few hours later, the informant met New Orleans Detective John Miller, who was wired with a hidden body microphone, through which the ensuing conversation was recorded. The informant now said his name was Joseph Banks and that he was called Beanie. His actual name was Joseph Wallace.[3]

His story, as well as his name, had changed since his earlier call. In place of his original account of buying a Thunderbird from Kyles on Thursday, Beanie told Miller that he had not seen Kyles at all on Thursday and had bought a red LTD the previous day, Friday. Beanie led Miller to the parking lot of a nearby bar, where he had left the red LTD, later identified as Dye's.

Beanie told Miller that he lived with Kyles's brother-in-law (later identified as Johnny Burns),[4] whom Beanie repeatedly called his "partner." Beanie described Kyles as slim, about 6–feet tall, 24 or 25 years old, with a "bush" hairstyle. When asked if Kyles ever wore his hair in plaits, Beanie said that he did but that he "had a bush" when Beanie bought the car.

During the conversation, Beanie repeatedly expressed concern that he might himself be a suspect in the murder. He explained that he had been seen driving Dye's car on Friday evening in the French Quarter, admitted that he had changed its license plates, and worried that he "could have been charged" with the murder on the basis of his possession of the LTD. He asked if he would be put in jail. Miller acknowledged that Beanie's possession of the car would have looked suspicious, but reassured him that he "didn't do anything wrong."

Beanie seemed eager to cast suspicion on Kyles, who allegedly made his living by "robbing people," and had tried to kill Beanie at some prior time. Beanie said that Kyles regularly carried two pistols, a .38 and a .32, and that if the police could "set him up good," they could "get that same gun" used to kill Dye. Beanie rode with Miller and Miller's supervisor, Sgt. James Eaton, in an unmarked squad car to Desire Street, where he pointed out the building containing Kyles's apartment.

---

3. Because the informant had so many aliases, we will follow the convention of the court below and refer to him throughout this opinion as Beanie.

4. Johnny Burns is the brother of a woman known as Pinky Burns. A number of trial witnesses referred to the relationship between Kyles and Pinky Burns as a common-law marriage (Louisiana's civil law notwithstanding). Kyles is the father of several of Pinky Burns's children.

Beanie told the officers that after he bought the car, he and his "partner" (Burns) drove Kyles to Schwegmann's about 9 p.m. on Friday evening to pick up Kyles's car, described as an orange four-door Ford.[5] When asked where Kyles's car had been parked, Beanie replied that it had been "[o]n the same side [of the lot] where the woman was killed at." The officers later drove Beanie to Schwegmann's, where he indicated the space where he claimed Kyles's car had been parked. Beanie went on to say that when he and Burns had brought Kyles to pick up the car, Kyles had gone to some nearby bushes to retrieve a brown purse, which Kyles subsequently hid in a wardrobe at his apartment. Beanie said that Kyles had "a lot of groceries" in Schwegmann's bags and a new baby's potty "in the car." Beanie told Eaton that Kyles's garbage would go out the next day and that if Kyles was "smart" he would "put [the purse] in [the] garbage." Beanie made it clear that he expected some reward for his help, saying at one point that he was not "doing all of this for nothing." The police repeatedly assured Beanie that he would not lose the $400 he paid for the car.

After the visit to Schwegmann's, Eaton and Miller took Beanie to a police station where Miller interviewed him again on the record, which was transcribed and signed by Beanie, using his alias "Joseph Banks." This statement, Beanie's third (the telephone call being the first, then the recorded conversation), repeats some of the essentials of the second one: that Beanie had purchased a red Ford LTD from Kyles for $400 on Friday evening; that Kyles had his hair "combed out" at the time of the sale; and that Kyles carried a .32 and a .38 with him "all the time."

Portions of the third statement, however, embellished or contradicted Beanie's preceding story and were even internally inconsistent. Beanie reported that after the sale, he and Kyles unloaded Schwegmann's grocery bags from the trunk and back seat of the LTD and placed them in Kyles's own car. Beanie said that Kyles took a brown purse from the front seat of the LTD and that they then drove in separate cars to Kyles's apartment, where they unloaded the groceries. Beanie also claimed that, a few hours later, he and his "partner" Burns went with Kyles to Schwegmann's, where they recovered Kyles's car and a "big brown pocket book" from "next to a building." Beanie did not explain how Kyles could have picked up his car and recovered the purse at Schwegmann's, after Beanie had seen Kyles with both just a few hours earlier. The police neither noted the inconsistencies nor questioned Beanie about them.

Although the police did not thereafter put Kyles under surveillance, they learned about events at his apartment from Beanie, who went there twice on Sunday. According to a fourth statement by Beanie, this one given to the chief prosecutor in November (between the first and second trials), he first went to the apartment about 2 p.m., after a telephone conversation with a police officer who asked whether Kyles had the gun that was used to kill Dye. Beanie stayed in Kyles's apartment until about

---

5. According to photographs later introduced at trial, Kyles's car was actually a Mercury and, according to trial testimony, a two-door model.

5 p.m., when he left to call Detective John Miller. Then he returned about 7 p.m. and stayed until about 9:30 p.m., when he left to meet Miller, who also asked about the gun. According to this fourth statement, Beanie "rode around" with Miller until 3 a.m. on Monday, September 24. Sometime during those same early morning hours, detectives were sent at Sgt. Eaton's behest to pick up the rubbish outside Kyles's building. As Sgt. Eaton wrote in an interoffice memorandum, he had "reason to believe the victims [sic] personal papers and the Schwegmann's bags will be in the trash."

At 10:40 a.m., Kyles was arrested as he left the apartment, which was then searched under a warrant. Behind the kitchen stove, the police found a .32–caliber revolver containing five live rounds and one spent cartridge. Ballistics tests later showed that this pistol was used to murder Dye. In a wardrobe in a hallway leading to the kitchen, the officers found a homemade shoulder holster that fit the murder weapon. In a bedroom dresser drawer, they discovered two boxes of ammunition, one containing several .32–caliber rounds of the same brand as those found in the pistol. Back in the kitchen, various cans of cat and dog food, some of them of the brands Dye typically purchased, were found in Schwegmann's sacks. No other groceries were identified as possibly being Dye's, and no potty was found. Later that afternoon at the police station, police opened the rubbish bags and found the victim's purse, identification, and other personal belongings wrapped in a Schwegmann's sack.

The gun, the LTD, the purse, and the cans of pet food were dusted for fingerprints. The gun had been wiped clean. Several prints were found on the purse and on the LTD, but none was identified as Kyles's. Dye's prints were not found on any of the cans of pet food. Kyles's prints were found, however, on a small piece of paper taken from the front passenger-side floorboard of the LTD. The crime laboratory recorded the paper as a Schwegmann's sales slip, but without noting what had been printed on it, which was obliterated in the chemical process of lifting the fingerprints. A second Schwegmann's receipt was found in the trunk of the LTD, but Kyles's prints were not found on it. Beanie's fingerprints were not compared to any of the fingerprints found.

The lead detective on the case, John Dillman, put together a photo lineup that included a photograph of Kyles (but not of Beanie) and showed the array to five of the six eyewitnesses who had given statements. Three of them picked the photograph of Kyles; the other two could not confidently identify Kyles as Dye's assailant.

B

Kyles was indicted for first-degree murder. Before trial, his counsel filed a lengthy motion for disclosure by the State of any exculpatory or impeachment evidence. The prosecution responded that there was "no exculpatory evidence of any nature," despite the government's knowledge of the following evidentiary items: (1) the six contemporaneous eyewitness statements taken by police following the murder; (2) records of Beanie's initial call to the police; (3) the tape recording of the Saturday conversation between Beanie and officers Eaton and Miller; (4) the typed and signed statement given by Beanie on Sunday morning; (5) the computer print-out of license numbers of cars parked at Schwegmann's on the night of the murder, which did not list the number of Kyles's car; (6) the internal police memorandum calling for the seizure of the rubbish after Beanie had suggested that the purse might be found there; and (7) evidence linking Beanie to other crimes at Schwegmann's and to the unrelated murder of one Patricia Leidenheimer, committed in January before the Dye murder.

At the first trial, in November, the heart of the State's case was eyewitness testimony from four people who were at the scene of the crime (three of whom had previously picked Kyles from the photo lineup). Kyles maintained his innocence, offered supporting witnesses, and supplied an alibi that he had been picking up his children from school at the time of the murder. The theory of the defense was that Kyles had been framed by Beanie, who had planted evidence in Kyles's apartment and his rubbish for the purposes of shifting suspicion away from himself, removing an impediment to romance with Pinky Burns, and obtaining reward money. Beanie did not testify as a witness for either the defense or the prosecution.

Because the State withheld evidence, its case was much stronger, and the defense case much weaker, than the full facts would have suggested. Even so, after four hours of deliberation, the jury became deadlocked on the issue of guilt, and a mistrial was declared.

[After the mistrial, the chief trial prosecutor interviewed Beanie and made notes indicating that Beanie again changed important elements of his story.] Notwithstanding the many inconsistencies and variations among Beanie's statements, neither [these] notes nor any of the other notes and transcripts were given to the defense.

In December 1984, Kyles was tried a second time. Again, the heart of the State's case was the testimony of four eyewitnesses who positively identified Kyles in front of the jury. The prosecution also offered a blown-up photograph taken at the crime scene soon after the murder, on the basis of which the prosecutors argued that a seemingly two-toned car in the background of the photograph was Kyles's. They repeatedly suggested during cross-examination of defense witnesses that Kyles had left his own car at Schwegmann's on the day of the murder and had retrieved it later, a theory for which they offered no evidence beyond the blown-up photograph. Once again, Beanie did not testify.

As in the first trial, the defense contended that the eyewitnesses were mistaken. Kyles's counsel called several individuals, including Kevin Black, who testified to seeing Beanie, with his hair in plaits, driving a red car similar to the victim's about an hour after the killing. Another witness testified that Beanie, with his hair in braids, had tried to sell him the car on Thursday evening, shortly after the murder. Another witness testified that Beanie, with his hair in a "Jheri curl," had attempted to sell him the car on Friday. One witness, Beanie's "partner," Burns, testified that he had seen Beanie on Sunday at Kyles's apartment, stooping down near the stove where the gun was eventually found, and the defense presented testimony that Beanie was romantically interested in Pinky Burns. To explain the pet food found in Kyles's apartment, there was testimony that Kyles's family kept a dog and cat and often fed stray animals in the neighborhood.

Finally, Kyles again took the stand. Denying any involvement in the shooting, he explained his fingerprints on the cash register receipt found in Dye's car by saying that Beanie had picked him up in a red car on Friday, September 21, and had taken him to Schwegmann's, where he purchased transmission fluid and a pack of cigarettes. He suggested that the receipt may have fallen from the bag when he removed the cigarettes.

On rebuttal, the prosecutor had Beanie brought into the courtroom. All of the testifying eyewitnesses, after viewing Beanie standing next to Kyles, reaffirmed their previous identifications of Kyles as the murderer. Kyles was convicted of first-degree murder and sentenced to death. Beanie received a total of $1,600 in reward money.

Following direct appeal, it was revealed in the course of state collateral review that the State had failed to disclose evidence favorable to the defense. After exhausting state remedies, Kyles sought relief on federal habeas, claiming, among other things, that the evidence withheld was material to his defense and that his conviction was thus obtained in violation of *Brady*. [The District Court denied relief and the Fifth Circuit affirmed.][6]

III

The prosecution's affirmative duty to disclose evidence favorable to a defendant can trace its origins to early 20th-century strictures against misrepresentation and is of course most prominently associated with this Court's decision in *Brady v. Maryland*, 373 U.S. 83, 83 S.Ct. 1194 (1963). *Brady* held "that the suppression by the prosecution of evidence favorable to an accused upon request violates due process where the evidence is material either to guilt or to punishment, irrespective of the good faith or bad faith of the prosecution." [In *United States v. Agurs*, 427 U.S. 97, 96 S.Ct. 2392 (1976) and *United States v. Bagley*, 473 U.S. 667, 105 S.Ct. 3375 (1985), the Court elaborated on the *Brady* rule. Distinguishing the situation where the prosecution presents perjured testimony,[7] the Court

---

6. [While his federal appeal was pending, Kyles obtained an affidavit from Darlene Kersh, one of the eyewitnesses, to the effect that she had committed perjury when she identified Kyles at trial. On the basis of the affidavit, the Supreme Court of Louisiana granted discretionary review and ordered that an evidentiary hearing be held. State proceedings were then stayed pending determination of the federal appeal.]

7. The Court [in *Agurs*] noted that "a conviction obtained by the knowing use of perjured testimony is fundamentally unfair, and must be set aside if there is any reasonable likelihood that the false testimony could have affected the judgment of the jury." As the ruling pertaining to Kersh's affidavit is not before us, we do not consider the question whether Kyles's conviction was

held that a defendant's due process rights are violated where the prosecution fails to disclose favorable evidence which is material and that evidence is material "if there is a reasonable probability that, had the evidence been disclosed to the defense, the result of the proceeding would have been different."]

Four aspects of materiality under *Bagley* bear emphasis. Although the constitutional duty is triggered by the potential impact of favorable but undisclosed evidence, a showing of materiality does not require demonstration by a preponderance that disclosure of the suppressed evidence would have resulted ultimately in the defendant's acquittal (whether based on the presence of reasonable doubt or acceptance of an explanation for the crime that does not inculpate the defendant). *Bagley*'s touchstone of materiality is a "reasonable probability" of a different result, and the adjective is important. The question is not whether the defendant would more likely than not have received a different verdict with the evidence, but whether in its absence he received a fair trial, understood as a trial resulting in a verdict worthy of confidence. A "reasonable probability" of a different result is accordingly shown when the government's evidentiary suppression "undermines confidence in the outcome of the trial."

The second aspect of *Bagley* materiality bearing emphasis here is that it is not a sufficiency of evidence test. A defendant need not demonstrate that after discounting the inculpatory evidence in light of the undisclosed evidence, there would not have been enough left to convict. The possibility of an acquittal on a criminal charge does not imply an insufficient evidentiary basis to convict. One does not show a *Brady* violation by demonstrating that some of the inculpatory evidence should have been excluded, but by showing that the favorable evidence could reasonably be taken to put the whole case in such a different light as to undermine confidence in the verdict.

Third, we note that once a reviewing court applying *Bagley* has found constitutional error there is no need for further harmless-error review. Assuming, arguendo, that a harmless-error enquiry were to apply, a *Bagley* error could not be treated as harmless, since "a reasonable probability that, had the evidence been disclosed to the defense, the result of the proceeding would have been different," necessarily entails the conclusion that the suppression must have had " 'substantial and injurious effect or influence in determining the jury's verdict,' " *Brecht v. Abrahamson*, 507 U.S. 619, 113 S.Ct. 1710 (1993), quoting *Kotteakos v. United States*, 328 U.S. 750, 66 S.Ct. 1239 (1946). * * *

The fourth and final aspect of *Bagley* materiality to be stressed here is its definition in terms of suppressed evidence considered collectively, not item by item. As Justice Blackmun emphasized in the portion of his opinion written for the Court, the Constitution is not violated every time the government fails or chooses not to disclose evidence that might prove

obtained by the knowing use of perjured testimony and our decision today does not address any claim under the first *Agurs* category. See n. 6, *supra.*

helpful to the defense. We have never held that the Constitution demands an open file policy (however such a policy might work out in practice), and the rule in *Bagley* (and, hence, in *Brady*) requires less of the prosecution than the ABA Standards for Criminal Justice, which call generally for prosecutorial disclosures of any evidence tending to exculpate or mitigate.

While the definition of *Bagley* materiality in terms of the cumulative effect of suppression must accordingly be seen as leaving the government with a degree of discretion, it must also be understood as imposing a corresponding burden. On the one side, showing that the prosecution knew of an item of favorable evidence unknown to the defense does not amount to a *Brady* violation, without more. But the prosecution, which alone can know what is undisclosed, must be assigned the consequent responsibility to gauge the likely net effect of all such evidence and make disclosure when the point of "reasonable probability" is reached. This in turn means that the individual prosecutor has a duty to learn of any favorable evidence known to the others acting on the government's behalf in the case, including the police. But whether the prosecutor succeeds or fails in meeting this obligation (whether, that is, a failure to disclose is in good faith or bad faith), the prosecution's responsibility for failing to disclose known, favorable evidence rising to a material level of importance is inescapable.

* * *

IV

In this case, disclosure of the suppressed evidence to competent counsel would have made a different result reasonably probable.

A

As the District Court put it, "the essence of the State's case" was the testimony of eyewitnesses, who identified Kyles as Dye's killer. Disclosure of their statements would have resulted in a markedly weaker case for the prosecution and a markedly stronger one for the defense. To begin with, the value of two of those witnesses would have been substantially reduced or destroyed.

The State rated Henry Williams as its best witness, who testified that he had seen the struggle and the actual shooting by Kyles. The jury would have found it helpful to probe this conclusion in the light of Williams's contemporaneous statement, in which he told the police that the assailant was "a black male, about 19 or 20 years old, about 5'4" or 5'5", 140 to 150 pounds, medium build" and that "his hair looked like it was platted." If cross-examined on this description, Williams would have had trouble explaining how he could have described Kyles, 6–feet tall and thin, as a man more than half a foot shorter with a medium build. Indeed, since Beanie was 22 years old, 5'5" tall, and 159 pounds, the defense would have had a compelling argument that Williams's description pointed to Beanie but not to Kyles.[13]

The trial testimony of a second eyewitness, Isaac Smallwood, was equally damning to Kyles. He testified that Kyles was the assailant, and that he saw him struggle with Dye. He said he saw Kyles take a ".32, a small black gun" out of his right pocket, shoot Dye in the head, and drive off in her LTD. When the prosecutor asked him whether he actually saw Kyles shoot Dye, Smallwood answered "Yeah."

Smallwood's statement taken at the parking lot, however, was vastly different. Immediately after the crime, Smallwood claimed that he had not seen the actual murder and had not seen the assailant outside the vehicle. "I heard a lound [sic] pop," he said. "When I looked around I saw a lady laying on the ground, and there was a red car coming toward me." Smallwood said that he got a look at the culprit, a black teenage male with a mustache and shoulder-length braided hair, as the victim's red Thunderbird passed where he was standing. When a police investigator specifically asked him whether he had seen the assailant outside the car, Smallwood answered that he had not; the gunman "was already in the car and coming toward me."

A jury would reasonably have been troubled by the adjustments to Smallwood's original story by the time of the second trial. The struggle and shooting, which earlier he had not seen, he was able to describe with such detailed clarity as to identify the murder weapon as a small black .32–caliber pistol, which, of course, was the type of weapon used. His description of the victim's car had gone from a "Thunderbird" to an "LTD"; and he saw fit to say nothing about the assailant's shoulder-length hair and moustache, details noted by no other eyewitness. These developments would have fueled a withering cross-examination, destroying confidence in Smallwood's story and raising a substantial implication that the prosecutor had coached him to give it.

Since the evolution over time of a given eyewitness's description can be fatal to its reliability, the Smallwood and Williams identifications would

---

13. The defense could have further underscored the possibility that Beanie was Dye's killer through cross-examination of the police on their failure to direct any investigation against Beanie. If the police had disclosed Beanie's statements, they would have been forced to admit that their informant Beanie described Kyles as generally wearing his hair in a "bush" style (and so wearing it when he sold the car to Beanie), whereas Beanie wore his in plaits. There was a considerable amount of such *Brady* evidence on which the defense could have attacked the investigation as shoddy. The police failed to disclose that Beanie had charges pending against him for a theft at the same Schwegmann's store and was a primary suspect in the January 1984 murder of Patricia Leidenheimer, who, like Dye, was an older woman shot once in the head during an armed robbery. (Even though Beanie was a primary suspect in the Leidenheimer murder as early as September, he was not interviewed by the police about it until after Kyles's second trial in December. Beanie confessed his involvement in the murder, but was never charged in connection with it.) These were additional reasons for Beanie to ingratiate himself with the police and for the police to treat him with a suspicion they did not show. Indeed, notwithstanding Justice SCALIA's suggestion that Beanie would have been "stupid" to inject himself into the investigation, the *Brady* evidence would have revealed at least two motives for Beanie to come forward: he was interested in reward money and he was worried that he was already a suspect in Dye's murder (indeed, he had been seen driving the victim's car, which had been the subject of newspaper and television reports). * * *

have been severely undermined by use of their suppressed statements. The likely damage is best understood by taking the word of the prosecutor, who contended during closing arguments that Smallwood and Williams were the State's two best witnesses. (After discussing Territo's and Kersh's testimony: "Isaac Smallwood, have you ever seen a better witness[?] ... What's better than that is Henry Williams.... Henry Williams was the closest of them all right here"). Nor, of course, would the harm to the State's case on identity have been confined to their testimony alone. The fact that neither Williams nor Smallwood could have provided a consistent eyewitness description pointing to Kyles would have undercut the prosecution all the more because the remaining eyewitnesses called to testify (Territo and Kersh) had their best views of the gunman only as he fled the scene with his body partly concealed in Dye's car. And even aside from such important details, the effective impeachment of one eyewitness can call for a new trial even though the attack does not extend directly to others, as we have said before.

B

Damage to the prosecution's case would not have been confined to evidence of the eyewitnesses, for Beanie's various statements would have raised opportunities to attack not only the probative value of crucial physical evidence and the circumstances in which it was found, but the thoroughness and even the good faith of the investigation, as well. * * *

[Justice SOUTER argued that Beanie, who the prosecution admitted "made the case" against Kyles, could have been thoroughly discredited (either by calling him as a witness or by questioning the police investigators about him) by his many inconsistent statements and his obvious attempt to shift suspicion away from himself. With the *Brady* material, the defense could have called into question the entire investigation, suggesting that it was Beanie who was in fact determining the investigation's direction and success. The *Brady* material would have supported the testimony of defense witnesses, *e.g.*, Burns's testimony that he had seen Beanie change the license plate on the LTD, that he walked in on Beanie stooping near the stove in Kyles's kitchen, that he had seen Beanie with handguns of various calibers, including a .32, and that he was testifying for the defense even though Beanie was his "best friend." Discovery of the list of cars in the Schwegmann's parking lot at mid-evening after the murder would have tended to contradict Beanie's reports and the prosecution's theory of the crime. Nor was the physical evidence so incriminating as to negate any likelihood of a defense verdict. The jury might have suspected Beanie of planting the gun and holster; the dog food in the defendant's apartment was common; and the Schwegmann's receipt was too small to have been the receipt for the weeks' worth of groceries Dye had gone to Schwegmann's to purchase.]

* * * "[F]airness" cannot be stretched to the point of calling this a fair trial. Perhaps, confidence that the verdict would have been the same could survive the evidence impeaching even two eyewitnesses if the

discoveries of gun and purse were above suspicion. Perhaps those suspicious circumstances would not defeat confidence in the verdict if the eyewitnesses had generally agreed on a description and were free of impeachment. But confidence that the verdict would have been unaffected cannot survive when suppressed evidence would have entitled a jury to find that the eyewitnesses were not consistent in describing the killer, that two out of the four eyewitnesses testifying were unreliable, that the most damning physical evidence was subject to suspicion, that the investigation that produced it was insufficiently probing, and that the principal police witness was insufficiently informed or candid. This is not the "massive" case envisioned by the dissent; it is a significantly weaker case than the one heard by the first jury, which could not even reach a verdict.

[Concurring opinion of STEVENS, J., joined by GINSBURG and BREYER, JJ. omitted]

JUSTICE SCALIA, with whom the CHIEF JUSTICE, JUSTICE KENNEDY, and JUSTICE THOMAS join, dissenting.

In a sensible system of criminal justice, wrongful conviction is avoided by establishing, at the trial level, lines of procedural legality that leave ample margins of safety (for example, the requirement that guilt be proved beyond a reasonable doubt)—not by providing recurrent and repetitive appellate review of whether the facts in the record show those lines to have been narrowly crossed. The defect of the latter system was described, with characteristic candor, by Justice Jackson:

"Whenever decisions of one court are reviewed by another, a percentage of them are reversed. That reflects a difference in outlook normally found between personnel comprising different courts. However, reversal by a higher court is not proof that justice is thereby better done." *Brown v. Allen*, 344 U.S. 443, 73 S.Ct. 397 (1953) (opinion concurring in result).

Since this Court has long shared Justice Jackson's view, today's opinion—which considers a fact-bound claim of error rejected by every court, state and federal, that previously heard it—is, so far as I can tell, wholly unprecedented. The Court has adhered to the policy that, when the petitioner claims only that a concededly correct view of the law was incorrectly applied to the facts, certiorari should generally (*i.e.*, except in cases of the plainest error) be denied. That policy has been observed even when the fact-bound assessment of the federal court of appeals has differed from that of the district court, *Sumner v. Mata*, 449 U.S. 539, 101 S.Ct. 764 (1981); and under what we have called the "two-court rule," the policy has been applied with particular rigor when district court and court of appeals are in agreement as to what conclusion the record requires. How much the more should the policy be honored in this case, a federal habeas proceeding where not only both lower federal courts but also the state courts on postconviction review have all reviewed and rejected precisely the fact-specific claim before us. Instead, however, the Court not only grants certiorari to consider whether the Court of Appeals (and all the previous courts that agreed with it) was correct as to what the facts showed in a case where the answer is far from clear, but in the process of such consideration renders new findings of fact and judgments of credibility appropriate to a trial court of original jurisdiction.

The Court says that we granted certiorari "[b]ecause '[o]ur duty to search for constitutional error with painstaking care is never more exacting than it is in a capital case,' *Burger v. Kemp*, 483 U.S. 776, 107 S.Ct. 3114 (1987)." The citation is perverse, for the reader who looks up the quoted opinion will discover that the very next sentence confirms the traditional practice from which the Court today glaringly departs: "Nevertheless, when the lower courts have found that [no constitutional error occurred], . . . deference to the shared conclusion of two reviewing courts prevent[s] us from substituting speculation for their considered opinions."

The greatest puzzle of today's decision is what could have caused this capital case to be singled out for favored treatment. Perhaps it has been randomly selected as a symbol, to reassure America that the United States Supreme Court is reviewing capital convictions to make sure no factual error has been made. If so, it is a false symbol, for we assuredly do not do that. At, and during the week preceding, our February 24 Conference, for example, we considered and disposed of 10 petitions in capital cases, from seven States. We carefully considered whether the convictions and sentences in those cases had been obtained in reliance upon correct principles of federal law; but if we had tried to consider, in addition, whether those correct principles had been applied, not merely plausibly, but accurately, to the particular facts of each case, we would have done nothing else for the week. The reality is that responsibility for factual accuracy, in capital cases as in other cases, rests elsewhere—with trial judges and juries, state appellate courts, and the lower federal courts; we do nothing but encourage foolish reliance to pretend otherwise.

* * *

I

* * *

In any analysis of this case, the desperate implausibility of the theory that petitioner put before the jury must be kept firmly in mind. The first half of that theory—designed to neutralize the physical evidence (Mrs. Dye's purse in his garbage, the murder weapon behind his stove)—was that petitioner was the victim of a "frame-up" by the police informer and evil genius, Beanie. Now it is not unusual for a guilty person who knows that he is suspected of a crime to try to shift blame to someone else; and it is less common, but not unheard of, for a guilty person who is neither suspected nor subject to suspicion (because he has established a perfect alibi), to call attention to himself by coming forward to point the finger at an innocent person. But petitioner's theory is that the guilty Beanie, who could plausibly be accused of the crime (as petitioner's brief amply demonstrates), but who was not a suspect any more than Kyles was (the police as yet had no leads), injected both Kyles and himself into the investigation in order to get the innocent Kyles convicted. If this were not stupid enough, the wicked Beanie is supposed to have suggested that the police search his victim's premises a full day before he got around to planting the incriminating evidence on the premises.

The second half of petitioner's theory was that he was the victim of a quadruple coincidence, in which four eyewitnesses to the crime mistakenly identified him as the murderer—three picking him out of a photo array without hesitation, and all four affirming their identification in open court after comparing him with Beanie. The extraordinary mistake petitioner had to persuade the jury these four witnesses made was not simply to mistake the real killer, Beanie, for the very same innocent third party (hard enough to believe), but in addition to mistake him for the very man Beanie had chosen to frame—the last and most incredible level of coincidence. However small the chance that the jury would believe any one of those improbable scenarios, the likelihood that it would believe them all together is far smaller. The Court concludes that it is "reasonably probable" the undisclosed witness interviews would have persuaded the jury of petitioner's implausible theory of mistaken eyewitness testimony, and then argues that it is "reasonably probable" the undisclosed information regarding Beanie would have persuaded the jury of petitioner's implausible theory regarding the incriminating physical evidence. I think neither of those conclusions is remotely true, but even if they were the Court would still be guilty of a fallacy in declaring victory on each implausibility in turn, and thus victory on the whole, without considering the infinitesimal probability of the jury's swallowing the entire concoction of implausibility squared.

* * *

II

The undisclosed evidence does not create a " 'reasonable probability' of a different result." To begin with the eyewitness testimony: Petitioner's basic theory at trial was that the State's four eyewitnesses happened to mistake Beanie, the real killer, for petitioner, the man whom Beanie was simultaneously trying to frame. Police officers testified to the jury, and petitioner has never disputed, that three of the four eyewitnesses (Territo, Smallwood, and Williams) were shown a photo lineup of six young men four days after the shooting and, without aid or duress, identified petitioner as the murderer; and that all of them, plus the fourth eyewitness, Kersh, reaffirmed their identifications at trial after petitioner and Beanie were made to stand side by side.

Territo, the first eyewitness called by the State, was waiting at a red light in a truck 30 or 40 yards from the Schwegmann's parking lot. He saw petitioner shoot Mrs. Dye, start her car, drive out onto the road, and pull up just behind Territo's truck. When the light turned green petitioner pulled beside Territo and stopped while waiting to make a turn. Petitioner looked Territo full in the face. Territo testified, "I got a good look at him.

If I had been in the passenger seat of the little truck, I could have reached out and not even stretched my arm out, I could have grabbed hold of him.'' Territo also testified that a detective had shown him a picture of Beanie and asked him if the picture "could have been the guy that did it. I told him no.'' The second eyewitness, Kersh, also saw petitioner shoot Mrs. Dye. When asked whether she got "a good look'' at him as he drove away, she answered "yes.'' She also answered "yes'' to the question whether she "got to see the side of his face'' and said that while petitioner was stopped she had driven to within reaching distance of the driver's-side door of Mrs. Dye's car and stopped there. The third eyewitness, Small-wood, testified that he saw petitioner shoot Mrs. Dye, walk to the car, and drive away. Petitioner drove slowly by, within a distance of 15 or 25 feet, and Smallwood saw his face from the side. The fourth eyewitness, Williams, who had been working outside the parking lot, testified that "the gentleman came up the side of the car,'' struggled with Mrs. Dye, shot her, walked around to the driver's side of the car, and drove away. Williams not only "saw him before he shot her,'' but watched petitioner drive slowly by "within less than ten feet.'' When asked "[d]id you get an opportunity to look at him good?'', Williams said, "I did.''

The Court attempts to dispose of this direct, unqualified, and consistent eyewitness testimony in two ways. First, by relying on a theory so implausible that it was apparently not suggested by petitioner's counsel until the oral-argument-cum-evidentiary-hearing held before us, perhaps because it is a theory that only the most removed appellate court could love. This theory is that there is a reasonable probability that the jury would have changed its mind about the eyewitness identification because the *Brady* material would have permitted the defense to argue that the eyewitnesses only got a good look at the killer when he was sitting in Mrs. Dye's car, and thus could identify him, not by his height and build, but only by his face. Never mind, for the moment, that this is factually false, since the *Brady* material showed that only one of the four eyewitnesses, Smallwood, did not see the killer outside the car. And never mind, also, the dubious premise that the build of a man 6-feet tall (like petitioner) is indistinguishable, when seated behind the wheel, from that of a man less than 5 1/2-feet tall (like Beanie). To assert that unhesitant and categorical identification by four witnesses who viewed the killer, close-up and with the sun high in the sky, would not eliminate reasonable doubt if it were based only on facial characteristics, and not on height and build, is quite simply absurd. Facial features are the primary means by which human beings recognize one another. That is why police departments distribute "mug'' shots of wanted felons, rather than Ivy-League-type posture pictures; it is why bank robbers wear stockings over their faces instead of floor-length capes over their shoulders; it is why the Lone Ranger wears a mask instead of a poncho; and it is why a criminal defense lawyer who seeks to destroy an identifying witness by asking "You admit that you saw only the killer's face?'' will be laughed out of the courtroom.

It would be different, of course, if there were evidence that Kyles's and Beanie's faces looked like twins, or at least bore an unusual degree of resemblance. That facial resemblance would explain why, if Beanie committed the crime, all four witnesses picked out Kyles at first (though not why they continued to pick him out when he and Beanie stood side-by-side in court), and would render their failure to observe the height and build of the killer relevant. But without evidence of facial similarity, the question "You admit that you saw only the killer's face?" draws no blood; it does not explain any witness's identification of petitioner as the killer. While the assumption of facial resemblance between Kyles and Beanie underlies all of the Court's repeated references to the partial concealment of the killer's body from view, the Court never actually says that such resemblance exists. That is because there is not the slightest basis for such a statement in the record. No court has found that Kyles and Beanie bear any facial resemblance. In fact, quite the opposite: every federal and state court that has reviewed the record photographs, or seen the two men, has found that they do not resemble each other in any respect.

* * *

* * * In sum, the undisclosed statements, credited with everything they could possibly have provided to the defense, leave two prosecution witnesses (Territo and Kersh) totally untouched; one prosecution witness (Smallwood) barely affected (he saw "only" the killer's face); and one prosecution witness (Williams) somewhat impaired (his description of the killer's height and weight did not match Kyles). We must keep all this in due perspective, remembering that the relevant question in the materiality inquiry is not how many points the defense could have scored off the prosecution witnesses, but whether it is reasonably probable that the new evidence would have caused the jury to accept the basic thesis that all four witnesses were mistaken. I think it plainly is not. No witness involved in the case ever identified anyone but petitioner as the murderer. Their views of the crime and the escaping criminal were obtained in bright daylight from close at hand; and their identifications were reaffirmed before the jury. After the side-by-side comparison between Beanie and Kyles, the jury heard Territo say that there was "[n]o doubt in my mind" that petitioner was the murderer; heard Kersh say "I know it was him. . . . I seen his face and I know the color of his skin. I know it. I know it's him"; heard Smallwood say "I'm positive . . . [b]ecause that's the man who I seen kill that woman"; and heard Williams say "[n]o doubt in my mind." With or without the *Brady* evidence, there could be no doubt in the mind of the jury either.

[Justice SCALIA argued that the physical evidence—the purse and belongings in the garbage bag, the murder weapon and ammunition in the apartment, the shoulder holster, Schwegmann's bags and the pet food—confirmed the immateriality of the nondisclosures.]

The State presented to the jury a massive core of evidence (including four eyewitnesses) showing that petitioner was guilty of murder, and that he lied about his guilt. The effect that the *Brady* materials would have had in chipping away at the edges of the State's case can only be called immaterial. For the same reasons I reject petitioner's claim that the *Brady* materials would have created a "residual doubt" sufficient to cause the sentencing jury to withhold capital punishment.

I respectfully dissent.

NOTES

1. *Subsequent developments.*

After the Supreme Court decision, Kyles was tried three more times, each trial resulting in a hung jury and a mistrial. In early 1998, the prosecution finally gave up and decided not to try Kyles for a sixth time. See J. Gill, *Murder Trial's Inglorious End*, The New Orleans Times–Picayune, February 20, 1998, p. B7.

2. *Problem 8–1.*

Defendant was convicted of the murder of Victim and was sentenced to death under the following circumstances. After the discovery of Victim's body, Deputy learned that Defendant and Victim had been together three days earlier, and he was told by a paid informant that Defendant was driving to Dallas to obtain a weapon. Deputy followed Defendant to a house in Dallas, stopped Defendant's car after he left the house, found a handgun and arrested Defendant and the car's other occupants, Farr and Jefferson. Deputy then returned to the house, encountered Cook and recovered a second gun, which Cook said Defendant had left there. The second gun was the murder weapon. Prior to trial, Prosecutor assured defense counsel that he would provide the defense with all discovery to which the defense was entitled. At the guilt phase of the trial, Cook testified that Defendant had arrived at his house the morning after the murder and admitted "killing a white boy," and, on cross-examination, Cook repeatedly denied having talked to anyone about his testimony. Farr testified that he had traveled to Dallas with Defendant in attempt to retrieve Defendant's gun, and, on cross-examination, Farr asserted that he had never taken money from the police and that he had not been promised anything for his testimony. In his guilt phase summation, Prosecutor argued that "Cook brought you absolute truth." At the penalty phase, the state called two witnesses on the issue of future dangerousness. Jefferson testified that, around the time of the murder, Defendant had struck him with a gun and threatened to kill him. Farr testified that they had traveled to Dallas to retrieve the gun because the two intended to "pull some robberies" and that Defendant had said, "he would take care of it" if there was any trouble. On cross-examination, Farr denied telling Deputy about the Dallas trip and denied that he was facing drug charges that might influence his testimony. Defendant had no prior criminal record, and he called a number of mitigation witnesses, who testified to his good character. Defendant testified and admitted hitting Jefferson and traveling to Dallas to obtain a gun for Farr, but he denied that he had planned to participate in the robberies that Farr intended to commit. In his penalty phase summation, Prosecutor highlighted Farr's testimony (saying it was "of the utmost significance") and urged his credibility (stating that he was "open and honest ... in every way").

Subsequent to his conviction, Defendant learned that both Cook and Farr had perjured themselves, and, on his petition for habeas corpus, Defendant produced affidavits from the two of them and other evidence which established the following: (1) Prosecutor and Deputy had intensively coached Cook about his testimony during three or four practice sessions where they had told him to testify as they wanted him to or he would spend the rest of his life in prison; (2) Prosecutor had, in his files, a transcript of one of those sessions; (3) Farr was the informant who had notified Deputy about the trip to Dallas, and he was paid $200 for the case; (4) Farr had proposed the trip to Dallas to Defendant to "set him up"; and (5) Farr helped Deputy because he assumed that if he did not help Deputy, Deputy would have him arrested for drug charges.

What arguments should be made on Defendant's petition for habeas corpus based on his *Brady* claim? See *Banks v. Dretke*, 540 U.S. 668, 124 S.Ct. 1256 (2004).

3. *Problem 8–2.*

Defendant and Co-defendant were convicted at separate trials of the kidnapping, robbery and murder of Victim, an African–American woman. Defendant was sentenced to death; Co-defendant was not. The evidence at Defendant's trial established that, on the evening in question, Victim was kidnapped in her own car from a shopping mall. Her body was later discovered in a field, and a 69–pound rock spotted with blood lay nearby. Victim had died from multiple blunt-force blows. The evidence was overwhelming that both Defendant and Co-defendant had participated in the crimes. The night of the murder, both men were seen driving Victim's car. They went to a bar, where Co-defendant gave Victim's watch to a woman he met. The two left the bar with another woman, and Defendant subsequently gave her Victim's pearl earrings. While the three were together, the two men alluded to having killed a black person with a "rock crusher." There was testimony that both men had blood on their pants. Co-defendant's wallet was found in the field near Victim's body, and a witness testified to having seen Defendant driving Victim's car with a white woman in front and another man in back near the field at approximately the time of Victim's death.

The key witness against Defendant was Student, who testified that she had witnessed the abduction of Victim. Student did not report the incident to the police, and she only came to the attention of the police when a friend of Student's called the police a week and a half after the murder and reported that Student had mentioned seeing the incident. According to Student, she was shopping in the mall when she first saw Defendant (whom she referred to as "Mountain Man," Co-defendant (whom she called "Shy Guy") and a blonde woman shopping. She described them in detail, including their clothing. Mountain Man's loud behavior in the store frightened her. She ran into the three later, and, because of Mountain Man's odd behavior, she tried to follow the three, but lost them. When she was leaving the mall in her car, she saw Victim in her car stopped at a stop sign behind a van. She described Victim, including a description of her clothing and her appearance as a college kid who was "singing" and "happy." Mountain Man suddenly ran up to the van and began banging on it. He left off and returned to where Shy Guy and Blonde Girl were standing, but he immediately returned, pounded on Victim's car door, yanked it open and jumped in. Then he motioned for Shy Guy and Blonde Girl to jump in also. Victim could not go anywhere because there were people all around the car, so she honked her horn. Mountain Man began hitting Victim, and, as the car drove slowly away, Student and her daughter took down the license number, West Virginia NKA243. Student identified Victim from a picture as the driver of the car and identified Defendant as "Mountain Man." When asked if pretrial publicity about the murder had influenced her identification, Student replied "absolutely not." "[F]irst of all, I have an exceptionally good memory. I had very close contact with [Defendant] and he made an emotional impression with me because of his behavior and I, he caught my attention and I paid attention. So I have absolutely no doubt of my identification."

After his conviction, Defendant discovered that Prosecutor had failed to disclose certain documents concerning Student's contacts with the police, as follows:

1. A handwritten note prepared by Detective after his first interview with Student just two weeks after the crime. The note indicates that she could not identify the black female victim. The only person Student apparently could identify at this time was the white female.

2. A report prepared by Detective summarizing his first two interviews with Student, stating, *inter alia*, "she was not sure whether she could identify the white males but felt sure she could identify the white female."

3. A document entitled "Observations" and including a summary of the abduction.

4. A letter from Student to Detective three days after their first interview "to clarify some of my confusion for you." The letter states that she had not remembered being at the mall, but that her daughter had helped jog her memory. Her description of the abduction includes the comment: "I have a very vague memory that I'm not sure of. It seems as if the wild guy that I saw had come running through the door and up to a bus as the bus was pulling off. . . . Then the guy I saw came running up to the black girl's window? Were those 2 memories the same person?" In a postscript she noted that her daughter "doesn't remember seeing the 3 people get into the black girl's car. . . ."

5. A note to Detective captioned "My Impressions of 'The Car,'" which contains three paragraphs describing the size of the car and comparing it with Student's Volkswagen Rabbit, but not mentioning the license plate number that she vividly recalled at the trial.

6. A brief note from Student to Detective dated six days after the first interview stating that, after spending several hours with Boyfriend (Victim's boyfriend) "looking at current photos," she had identified Victim "beyond a shadow of a doubt." (Her trial testimony made no mention of her meeting with Boyfriend.)

7. A letter from Student to Detective dated the day of their first meeting, in which she thanks him for his "patience with my sometimes muddled memories." She states that if the student at school had not called the police, "I never would have made any of the associations that you helped me make."

8. An undated document describing the events in Student's trial testimony, including a comment by Student: "So where is the 3x4 card? . . . It would have been very nice if I could have remembered all this at the time and had simply gone to the police with the information. But I totally wrote this off as a trivial episode of college kids carrying on and proceeded with my own full-time college load . . . Monday, [the day before being contacted by Detective] I was cleaning out my car and found the 3x4 card. I tore it into little pieces and put it in the bottom of a trash bag."

What are the arguments as to whether Defendant's due process rights were violated? See *Strickler v. Greene*, 527 U.S. 263, 119 S.Ct. 1936 (1999).

DARDEN v. WAINWRIGHT

477 U.S. 168, 106 S.Ct. 2464, 91 L.Ed.2d 144 (1986).

JUSTICE POWELL delivered the opinion of the Court.

* * *

I

Petitioner was tried and found guilty of murder, robbery, and assault with intent to kill in the Circuit Court for Citrus County, Florida, in January 1974. Pursuant to Florida's capital sentencing statute, the same jury that convicted petitioner heard further testimony and argument in order to make a nonbinding recommendation as to whether a death sentence should be imposed. The jury recommended a death sentence, and the trial judge followed that recommendation. On direct appeal, the Florida Supreme Court affirmed the conviction and the sentence. Petitioner made several of the same arguments in that appeal that he makes here. With respect to the prosecutorial misconduct claim, the court disapproved of the closing argument, but reasoned that the law required a new trial "only in those cases in which it is reasonably evident that the remarks might have influenced the jury to reach a more severe verdict of guilt . . . or in which the comment is unfair." It concluded that the comments had not rendered petitioner's trial unfair. * * *

Petitioner then sought federal habeas corpus relief, raising the same claims he raises here. * * *

II

Because of the nature of petitioner's claims, the facts of this case will be stated in more detail than is normally necessary in this Court. On September 8, 1973, at about 5:30 p.m., a black adult male entered Carl's Furniture Store near Lakeland, Florida. The only other person in the store was the proprietor, Mrs. Turman, who lived with her husband in a house behind the store. Mr. Turman, who worked nights at a juvenile home, had awakened at about 5 p.m., had a cup of coffee at the store with his wife, and returned home to let their dogs out for a run. Mrs. Turman showed the man around the store. He stated that he was interested in purchasing about $600 worth of furniture for a rental unit, and asked to see several different items. He left the store briefly, stating that his wife would be back to look at some of the items.

The same man returned just a few minutes later asking to see some stoves, and inquiring about the price. When Mrs. Turman turned toward the adding machine, he grabbed her and pressed a gun to her back, saying "Do as I say and you won't get hurt." He took her to the rear of the store and told her to open the cash register. He took the money, then ordered her to the part of the store where some box springs and mattresses were stacked against the wall. At that time Mr. Turman appeared at the back door. Mrs. Turman screamed while the man reached across her right shoulder and shot Mr. Turman between the eyes. Mr. Turman fell backwards, with one foot partially in the building. Ordering Mrs. Turman not to move, the man tried to pull Mr. Turman into the building and close the door, but could not do so because one of Mr. Turman's feet was caught in the door. The man left Mr. Turman faceup in the rain, and told Mrs. Turman to get down on the floor approximately five feet from where her husband lay dying. While she begged to go to her husband, he told her to remove her false teeth. He unzipped his pants, unbuckled his belt, and demanded that Mrs. Turman perform oral sex on him. She began to cry "Lord, have mercy." He told her to get up and go towards the front of the store.

Meanwhile, a neighbor family, the Arnolds, became aware that something had happened to Mr. Turman. The mother sent her 16–year–old son Phillip, a part-time employee at the furniture store, to help. When Phillip reached the back door he saw Mr. Turman lying partially in the building. When Phillip opened the door to take Turman's body inside, Mrs. Turman shouted "Phillip, no, go back." Phillip did not know what she meant and asked the man to help get Turman inside. He replied, "Sure, buddy, I will help you." As Phillip looked up, the man was pointing a gun in his face. He pulled the trigger and the gun misfired; he pulled the trigger again and shot Phillip in the mouth. Phillip started to run away, and was shot in the neck. While he was still running, he was shot a third time in the side. Despite these wounds, Phillip managed to stumble to the home of a neighbor, Mrs. Edith Hill. She had her husband call an ambulance while she tried to stop Phillip's bleeding. While she was helping Phillip, she saw a late model green Chevrolet leave the store and head towards Tampa on State Highway 92. Phillip survived the incident; Mr. Turman, who never regained consciousness, died later that night.

Minutes after the murder petitioner was driving towards Tampa on Highway 92, just a few miles away from the furniture store. He was out on furlough from a Florida prison, and was driving a car borrowed from his girl friend in Tampa. He was driving fast on a wet road. Petitioner testified that as he came up on a line of cars in his lane, he was unable to slow down. He attempted to pass, but was forced off the road to avoid a head-on collision with an oncoming car. Petitioner crashed into a telephone pole. The driver of the oncoming car, John Stone, stopped his car and went to petitioner to see if he could help. Stone testified that as he approached the car, petitioner was zipping up his pants and buckling his belt. Police at the crash site later identified petitioner's car as a 1969 Chevrolet Impala of greenish golden brown color. Petitioner paid a bystander to give him a ride to Tampa. Petitioner later returned with a wrecker, only to find that the car had been towed away by the police.

By the time the police arrived at the scene of the accident, petitioner had left. The fact that the car matched the description of the car leaving the scene of the murder, and that the accident had occurred within three and one-half miles of the furniture store and within minutes of the murder, led police to suspect that the car was driven by the murderer. They searched the area. An officer found a pistol—a revolver—about 40 feet from the crash site. The arrangement of shells within the chambers exactly matched the pattern that should have been found in the murder weapon: one shot, one misfire, followed by three shots, with a live shell remaining in the next chamber to be fired. A specialist for the Federal Bureau of Investigation examined the pistol and testified that it was a Smith & Wesson .38 special revolver. It had been manufactured as a standard .38; it later was sent to England to be rebored, making it a much rarer type of gun than the standard .38. An examination of the bullet that killed Mr. Turman revealed that it came from a .38 Smith & Wesson special.

On the day following the murder petitioner was arrested at his girl friend's house in Tampa. A few days later Mrs. Turman identified him at a preliminary hearing as her husband's murderer. Phillip Arnold selected petitioner's picture out of a spread of six photographs as the man who had shot him.[1] * * *

* * *

---

1. There are some minor discrepancies in the eyewitness identification. Mrs. Turman first described her assailant immediately after the murder while her husband was being taken to the emergency room. She told the investigating officer that the attacker was a heavy set-man. When asked if he was "neat in his appearance, clean-looking, clean-shaven," she responded "[a]s far as I can remember, yes, sir." She also stated to the officer that she thought that the attacker was about her height, 5'6" tall, and that he was wearing a pullover shirt with a stripe around the neck. The first time she saw petitioner after the attack was when she identified him at the preliminary hearing. She had not read any newspaper accounts of the crime, nor had she seen any picture of petitioner. When she was asked if petitioner was the man who had committed the crimes, she said yes. She also repeatedly identified him at trial.

Phillip Arnold first identified petitioner in a photo lineup while in the hospital. He could not speak at the time, and in response to the written question whether petitioner had a mustache, Phillip wrote back "I don't think so." Phillip also testified at trial that the attacker was a heavy-set man wearing a dull, light color knit shirt with a ring around the neck. He testified that the man was almost his height, about 6'2" tall.

A motorist who stopped at the scene of the accident testified that petitioner was wearing a white or off-grey button-down shirt and that he had a slight mustache. In fact, the witness stated

IV

Petitioner * * * contends that the prosecution's closing argument at the guilt-innocence stage of the trial rendered his conviction fundamentally unfair and deprived the sentencing determination of the reliability that the Eighth Amendment requires.

It is helpful as an initial matter to place these remarks in context. Closing argument came at the end of several days of trial. Because of a state procedural rule petitioner's counsel had the opportunity to present the initial summation as well as a rebuttal to the prosecutors' closing arguments. The prosecutors' comments must be evaluated in light of the defense argument that preceded it, which blamed the Polk County Sheriff's Office for a lack of evidence,[5] alluded to the death penalty,[6] characterized the perpetrator of the crimes as an "animal,"[7] and contained counsel's personal opinion of the strength of the State's evidence.[8]

The prosecutors then made their closing argument. That argument deserves the condemnation it has received from every court to review it, although no court has held that the argument rendered the trial unfair. Several comments attempted to place some of the blame for the crime on the Division of Corrections, because Darden was on weekend furlough from a prison sentence when the crime occurred.[9] Some comments implied that the death penalty would be the only guarantee against a future similar act.[10] Others incorporated the defense's use of the word "animal."[11] Prosecutor McDaniel made several offensive comments reflecting

that he "didn't know it was that [the mustache] or the raindrops on him or not. I couldn't really tell that much to it, it was real thin, that's all." Petitioner is about 5'10" tall, and at the time of trial testified that he weighed about 175 pounds.

5. "The Judge is going to tell you to consider the evidence or the lack of evidence. We have a lack of evidence, almost criminally negligent on the part of the Polk County Sheriff's Office in this case. You could go on and on about it."

6. "They took a coincidence and magnified that into a capital case. And they are asking you to kill a man on coincidence."

7. "The first witness you saw was Mrs. Turman, who was a pathetic figure; who worked and struggled all of her life to build what little she had, the little furniture store; and a woman who was robbed, sexually assaulted, and then had her husband slaughtered before her eyes, by what would have to be a vicious animal." "And this murderer ran after him, aimed again, and this poor kid with half his brains blown away.... It's the work of an animal, there's no doubt about it."

8. "So they come on up here and ask Citrus County people to kill the man. You will be instructed on lesser included offenses.... The question is, do they have enough evidence to kill that man, enough evidence? And I honestly do not think they do."

9. "As far as I am concerned, there should be another Defendant in this courtroom, one more, and that is the division of corrections, the prisons.... Can't we expect him to stay in a prison when they go there? Can we expect them to stay locked up once they go there? Do we know that they're going to be out on the public with guns, drinking?" "Yes, there is another Defendant, but I regret that I know of no charges to place upon him, except the public condemnation of them, condemn them."

10. "I will ask you to advise the Court to give him death. That's the only way that I know that he is not going to get out on the public. It's the only way I know. It's the only way I can be sure of it. It's the only way that anybody can be sure of it now, because the people that turned him loose.—"

11. "As far as I am concerned, and as Mr. Maloney said as he identified this man this person, as an animal, this animal was on the public for one reason."

an emotional reaction to the case.[12] These comments undoubtedly were improper. But as both the District Court and the original panel of the Court of Appeals (whose opinion on this issue still stands) recognized, it "is not enough that the prosecutors' remarks were undesirable or even universally condemned." The relevant question is whether the prosecutors' comments "so infected the trial with unfairness as to make the resulting conviction a denial of due process." *Donnelly v. DeChristoforo*, 416 U.S. 637, 94 S.Ct. 1868 (1974). Moreover, the appropriate standard of review for such a claim on writ of habeas corpus is "the narrow one of due process, and not the broad exercise of supervisory power." *DeChristoforo.*

Under this standard of review, we agree with the reasoning of every court to consider these comments that they did not deprive petitioner of a fair trial. The prosecutors' argument did not manipulate or misstate the evidence, nor did it implicate other specific rights of the accused such as the right to counsel or the right to remain silent. Much of the objectionable content was invited by or was responsive to the opening summation of the defense. As we explained in *United States v. Young*, 470 U.S. 1, 105 S.Ct. 1038 (1985), the idea of "invited response" is used not to excuse improper comments, but to determine their effect on the trial as a whole. The trial court instructed the jurors several times that their decision was to be made on the basis of the evidence alone, and that the arguments of counsel were not evidence. The weight of the evidence against petitioner was heavy; the "overwhelming eyewitness and circumstantial evidence to support a finding of guilt on all charges," reduced the likelihood that the jury's decision was influenced by argument. Finally, defense counsel made the tactical decision not to present any witness other than petitioner. This decision not only permitted them to give their summation prior to the prosecution's closing argument, but also gave them the opportunity to make a final rebuttal argument. Defense counsel were able to use the opportunity for rebuttal very effectively, turning much of the prosecutors' closing argument against them by placing many of the prosecutors' comments and actions in a light that was more likely to engender strong disapproval than result in inflamed passions against petitioner.[14] For

12. "He shouldn't be out of his cell unless he has a leash on him and a prison guard at the other end of that leash." "I wish [Mr. Turman] had had a shotgun in his hand when he walked in the back door and blown his [Darden's] face off. I wish that I could see him sitting here with no face, blown away by a shotgun." "I wish someone had walked in the back door and blown his head off at that point." "He fired in the boy's back, number five, saving one. Didn't get a chance to use it. I wish he had used it on himself." "I wish he had been killed in the accident, but he wasn't. Again, we are unlucky that time." "[D]on't forget what he has done according to those witnesses, to make every attempt to change his appearance from September the 8th, 1973. The hair, the goatee, even the moustache and the weight. The only thing he hasn't done that I know of is cut his throat." After this, the last in a series of such comments, defense counsel objected for the first time.

14. "Mr. McDaniel made an impassioned plea ... how many times did he repeat [it]? I wish you had been shot, I wish they had blown his face away. My God, I get the impression he would like to be the man that stands there and pulls the switch on him."

One of Darden's counsel testified at the habeas corpus hearing that he made the tactical decision not to object to the improper comments. Based on his long experience with prosecutor McDaniel, he knew McDaniel would "get much more vehement in his remarks if you allowed him

these reasons, we agree with the District Court below that "Darden's trial was not perfect—few are—but neither was it fundamentally unfair."

* * *

[Concurring opinion of BURGER, C.J. and dissenting statement of BRENNAN, J. omitted]

JUSTICE BLACKMUN, with whom JUSTICE BRENNAN, JUSTICE MARSHALL, and JUSTICE STEVENS join, dissenting.

Although the Constitution guarantees a criminal defendant only "a fair trial [and] not a perfect one," *Lutwak v. United States*, 344 U.S. 604, 73 S.Ct. 481 (1953); *Bruton v. United States*, 391 U.S. 123, 88 S.Ct. 1620 (1968), this Court has stressed repeatedly in the decade since *Gregg v. Georgia*, 428 U.S. 153, 96 S.Ct. 2909 (1976), that the Eighth Amendment requires a heightened degree of reliability in any case where a State seeks to take the defendant's life. Today's opinion, however, reveals a Court willing to tolerate not only imperfection but a level of fairness and reliability so low it should make conscientious prosecutors cringe.

I

A

The Court's discussion of Darden's claim of prosecutorial misconduct is noteworthy for its omissions. Despite the fact that earlier this Term the Court relied heavily on standards governing the professional responsibility of defense counsel in ruling that an attorney's actions did not deprive his client of any constitutional right, see *Nix v. Whiteside*, 475 U.S. 157, 106 S.Ct. 988 (1986), today it entirely ignores standards governing the professional responsibility of prosecutors in reaching the conclusion that the summations of Darden's prosecutors did not deprive him of a fair trial.

The prosecutors' remarks in this case reflect behavior as to which "virtually all the sources speak with one voice," *Nix v. Whiteside*, that is, a voice of strong condemnation. The following brief comparison of established standards of prosecutorial conduct with the prosecutors' behavior in this case merely illustrates, but hardly exhausts, the scope of the misconduct involved:

1. "A lawyer shall not ... state a personal opinion as to ... the credibility of a witness ... or the guilt or innocence of an accused." Model Rules of Professional Conduct, Rule 3.4(e) (1984). Yet one prosecutor, White, stated: "I am convinced, as convinced as I know I am standing before you today, that Willie Jasper Darden is a murderer, that he murdered Mr. Turman, that he robbed Mrs. Turman and that he shot to kill Phillip Arnold. I will be convinced of that the rest of my life." And the other prosecutor, McDaniel, stated, with respect to Darden's testimony: "Well, let me tell you something: If I am ever over in that chair over

_____

to go on." By not immediately objecting, he hoped to encourage the prosecution to commit reversible error.

there, facing life or death, life imprisonment or death, I guarantee you I will lie until my teeth fall out."

2.   "The prosecutor should refrain from argument which would divert the jury from its duty to decide the case on the evidence, by injecting issues broader than the guilt or innocence of the accused under the controlling law, or by making predictions of the consequences of the jury's verdict." ABA Standards for Criminal Justice 3–5.8(d) (2d ed. 1980). Yet McDaniel's argument was filled with references to Darden's status as a prisoner on furlough who "shouldn't be out of his cell unless he has a leash on him." Again and again, he sought to put on trial an absent "defendant," the State Department of Corrections that had furloughed Darden. He also implied that defense counsel would use improper tricks to deflect the jury from the real issue. Darden's status as a furloughed prisoner, the release policies of the Department of Corrections, and his counsel's anticipated tactics obviously had no legal relevance to the question the jury was being asked to decide: whether he had committed the robbery and murder at the Turmans' furniture store. Indeed, the State argued before this Court that McDaniel's remarks were harmless precisely because he "failed to discuss the issues, the weight of the evidence, or the credibility of the witnesses."

3.   "The prosecutor should not use arguments calculated to inflame the passions or prejudices of the jury." ABA Standards for Criminal Justice 3–5.8(c) (2d ed. 1980). Yet McDaniel repeatedly expressed a wish "that I could see [Darden] sitting here with no face, blown away by a shotgun." Indeed, I do not think McDaniel's summation, taken as a whole, can accurately be described as anything but a relentless and single-minded attempt to inflame the jury.

　　* * *

C

The Court presents what is, for me, an entirely unpersuasive one-page laundry list of reasons for ignoring this blatant misconduct. First, the Court says that the summations "did not manipulate or misstate the evidence [or] . . . implicate other specific rights of the accused such as the right to counsel or the right to remain silent." With all respect, that observation is quite beside the point. The "solemn purpose of endeavoring to ascertain the truth . . . is the *sine qua non* of a fair trial," *Estes v. Texas*, 381 U.S. 532, 85 S.Ct. 1628 (1965), and the summations cut to the very heart of the Due Process Clause by diverting the jury's attention "from the ultimate question of guilt or innocence that should be the central concern in a criminal proceeding." *Stone v. Powell*, 428 U.S. 465, 96 S.Ct. 3037 (1976).

Second, the Court says that "[m]uch of the objectionable content was invited by or was responsive to the opening summation of the defense." The Court identifies four portions of the defense summation that it thinks somehow "invited" McDaniel's sustained barrage. The State, however, did not object to any of these statements, and, to my mind, none of them is so objectionable that it would have justified a tactical decision to interrupt the defense summation and perhaps irritate the jury.

[Justice BLACKMUN argued that defense counsel's single statement "blaming" the Sheriff's Office for lack of evidence, his allusion to the death penalty, his reference to the perpetrator as an "animal" and his single expression of his belief in the weakness of the case could not possibly justify McDaniel's tirade to "right the scale."]

The third reason the Court gives for discounting the effects of the improper summations is the supposed curative effect of the trial judge's instructions: the judge had instructed the jury that it was to decide the case on the evidence and that the arguments of counsel were not evidence. But the trial court overruled Darden's objection to McDaniel's repeated expressions of his wish that Darden had been killed, thus perhaps leaving the jury with the impression that McDaniel's comments were somehow relevant to the question before them. The trial judge's instruction that the attorneys were "trained in the law," and thus that their "analysis of the issues" could be "extremely helpful," might also have suggested to the jury that the substance of McDaniel's tirade was pertinent to their deliberations.

Fourth, the Court suggests that because Darden enjoyed the tactical advantage of having the last summation, he was able to "tur[n] much of the prosecutors' closing argument against them." But the issue before the jury was whether Darden was guilty, not whether McDaniel's summation was proper. And the question before this Court is not whether we agree with defense counsel's criticism of the summation but whether the jury was affected by it. Since Darden was ultimately convicted, it is hard to see what basis the Court has for its naked assertion that "[d]efense counsel were able to use the opportunity for rebuttal very effectively."

Fifth, the Court finds, in essence, that any error was harmless: "The weight of the evidence against petitioner was heavy; the 'overwhelming eyewitness and circumstantial evidence to support a finding of guilt on all charges,' reduced the likelihood that the jury's decision was influenced by argument." * * *

* * *

* * * I simply do not believe the evidence in this case was so overwhelming that this Court can conclude, on the basis of the written record before it, that the jury's verdict was not the product of the prosecutors' misconduct. The three most damaging pieces of evidence—the identifications of Darden by Phillip Arnold and Helen Turman and the ballistics evidence—are all sufficiently problematic that they leave me unconvinced that a jury not exposed to McDaniel's egregious summation would necessarily have convicted Darden.

Arnold first identified Darden in a photo array shown to him in the hospital. The trial court suppressed that out-of-court identification following a long argument concerning the reliability and constitutionality of the procedures by which it was obtained.

Mrs. Turman's initial identification was made under even more suggestive circumstances. She testified at trial that she was taken to a preliminary hearing at which Darden appeared in order "[t]o identify him." Instead of being asked to view Darden in a lineup, Mrs. Turman was brought into the courtroom, where Darden apparently was the only black man present. Over defense counsel's objection, after the prosecutor asked her whether "this man sitting here" was "the man that shot your husband," she identified Darden.

* * * While the question whether the various in-and out-of-court identifications ought to have been suppressed is not now before the Court, my confidence in their reliability is nonetheless undermined by the suggestiveness of the procedures by which they were obtained, particularly in light of Mrs. Turman's earlier difficulties in describing the criminal.

Finally, the ballistics evidence is hardly overwhelming. The purported murder weapon was tied conclusively neither to the crime nor to Darden. Special Agent Cunningham of the Federal Bureau of Investigation's Firearms Identification Unit testified that the bullets recovered at the scene of the crime "could have been fired" from the gun, but he was unwilling to say that they in fact had come from that weapon. He also testified, contrary to the Court's assertion, that rebored Smith & Wessons were fairly common. Deputy Sheriff Weatherford testified that the gun was discovered in a roadside ditch adjacent to where Darden had wrecked his car on the evening of the crime. But the gun was discovered the next day, and the ditch was also next to a bar's parking lot.

Darden testified at trial on his own behalf and denied any involvement in the robbery and murder. His account of his actions on the day of the crime was contradicted only by Mrs. Turman's and Arnold's identifications. Indeed, a number of the State's witnesses corroborated parts of Darden's account. The trial judge who had seen and heard Darden testify found that he "emotionally and with what appeared on its face to be sincerity, proclaimed his innocence." In setting sentence, he viewed the fact that Darden "repeatedly professed his complete innocence of the charges" as a mitigating factor.

Thus, at bottom, this case rests on the jury's determination of the credibility of three witnesses—Helen Turman and Phillip Arnold, on the one side, and Willie Darden, on the other. I cannot conclude that McDaniel's sustained assault on Darden's very humanity did not affect the jury's ability to judge the credibility question on the real evidence before it. Because I believe that he did not have a trial that was fair, I would reverse Darden's conviction; I would not allow him to go to his death until he has been convicted at a fair trial.

* * *

NOTE

1. *Problem 8–3.*

While awaiting trial on felony charges, Defendant escaped and, two days later, broke into a house and stole a shotgun, which he later sawed off. He then used the shotgun to confront Victim as she was jogging and later to kill her. After the killing, Defendant returned to Victim's hotel room, showered, ate some fruit and departed in Victim's rental car, taking her money and travelers' checks. He was subsequently arrested on unrelated charges and confessed to the murder. Defendant was charged with first degree murder, and, after denial of his motion to suppress the confession, Defendant pled guilty. Prosecutor then sought the death penalty based on three aggravating circumstances: prior conviction of a violent felony; murder to avoid arrest; and murder in the course of robbery. At the penalty hearing, Defendant called two mitigation witnesses, Mother and Psychiatrist. Mother testified as to Defendant's medical and psychological problems as a child and the physical abuse he suffered at the hands of Father. He rarely attended school and was in and out of juvenile institutions. Psychiatrist testified that Defendant had serious health, behavior and substance abuse problems as a child, and there was evidence of organic brain damage.

During his closing argument, Prosecutor made a number of inflammatory remarks. He repeatedly told the jury that they would "become an accomplice" to Defendant's crime by "permitting this man to live" and argued that the jury would be responsible for the future deaths of others if they sentenced him to life. He argued, for example:

> This man is going to kill again as he deems it necessary in his own framework of what he thinks is right. Where is fundamental fairness in that, to let this man live and, in essence, to sentence someone else to die? If he goes to the state penitentiary under a life sentence and he is permitted to be among the general population in the facility where he is going to be housed, by your actions of voting for life for him, you are voting for death for someone else.

> If you are going to find life imprisonment for Defendant because he is depressed, then take him, give him back his gun that he stole, and let him take it to the penitentiary with him. . . . It might solve the overcrowding problem in prison if you put Defendant down there with his gun, but it is sure not the right thing to do. . . .

Prosecutor compared Defendant to a rabid dog:

> Ladies and gentlemen, there is an old saying out in the country that there is no cure for a rabid dog. Defendant is a rabid dog. There are dogs that become rabid that might be your favorite pet, and you might love them to death; but once they do become rabid, it's a fact that if they bite someone, the other animal or person is going to die.

On at least nine occasions, even after objections had been sustained, Prosecutor expressed his personal opinion as to the credibility of the witnesses or the ultimate issue in the hearing, arguing, *inter alia*, as to Defendant's mitigating evidence:

> You don't believe that, and I don't believe it; and I don't even believe Defendant's lawyers believe that.

> Do you think, as you look over the facts in this case, there is anything, ladies and gentlemen, that will ever inhibit him from killing again if he escapes? I think not, and I believe that you share that feeling also.

When Defendant's lawyers objected to Prosecutor's summation, Prosecutor several times, and even after being admonished by the court, accused them of objecting as a diversionary tactic.

Defendant was sentenced to death. What are the arguments as to Defendant's due process claim of prosecutorial misconduct? See *Bates v. Bell*, 402 F.3d 635 (6th Cir. 2005).

JACOBS v. SCOTT

513 U.S. 1067, 115 S.Ct. 711, 130 L.Ed.2d 618 (1995).

The application for stay of execution of sentence of death presented to Justice SCALIA and by him referred to the Court is denied. The petition for writ of certiorari is denied.

JUSTICE STEVENS, with whom JUSTICE GINSBURG joins, dissenting.

In my opinion, it is fundamentally unfair for the State of Texas to go forward with the execution of Jesse Dewayne Jacobs. The principal evidence supporting his conviction was a confession that was expressly and unequivocally disavowed, at a subsequent trial, by the same prosecutor who presented the case against Jacobs. That same prosecutor's office now insists that the State may constitutionally go forward and execute Jacobs. The injustice, in my view, is self-evident.

Jacobs was convicted of murdering a woman named Etta Urdiales. After his arrest, he gave a videotaped confession stating that he abducted the victim and fatally shot her in a wooded area. He led investigators to her body. At his trial, the State introduced this confession and relied heavily on it.

Jacobs, however, testified at trial that the confession was false. He claimed to have given the false confession because he believed it would lead to a death sentence, which he perceived to be preferable to the alternative of spending the rest of his life in jail. In his trial testimony, Jacobs admitted kidnaping Urdiales, and taking her to an abandoned house where his sister, Bobbie Hogan, was waiting. But he denied shooting the victim. According to Jacobs' testimony, he left Urdiales in the house with his sister and then went outside and sat on the porch. He did not know Hogan was armed, or that she planned to kill Urdiales. Rather, he believed Hogan, who was romantically involved with Urdiales' estranged husband, wanted to scare the victim into giving up custody of her children. Jacobs testified that while he was waiting outside, Hogan shot

Urdiales. When Jacobs entered the house, Hogan said that she did not mean to kill Urdiales. Jacobs then told Hogan to go home, said he would take care of things, and buried the victim's body.

The prosecution disputed Jacobs' trial testimony, arguing that " '[t]he simple fact of the matter is that Jesse Jacobs and Jesse Jacobs alone killed Etta Ann Urdiales.' " The jury convicted Jacobs of capital murder and sentenced him to death.

Several months later, Hogan was tried in connection with the Urdiales killing. At this trial, the State abandoned its theory that Jacobs had shot Urdiales. It called Jacobs as a witness, vouched for his veracity, and, according to the Court of Appeals for the Fifth Circuit, "told the jury that the evidence revealed [through further] investigation cast doubt on Jacobs's conviction." As described by the Court of Appeals:

> "[T]he prosecutor said that the state had been wrong in taking the position in Jacobs's trial that Jacobs had done the actual killing. The prosecutor stated that, after further investigation, he had determined that Hogan, not Jacobs, had killed the victim. The prosecution maintained that Jacobs did not know that Hogan had a gun. The state called Jacobs as a witness to testify that Hogan shot the victim."

The prosecutor told the jury that he had " 'changed my mind about what actually happened. . . . And I'm convinced that Jesse Jacobs is telling the truth when he says that Bobbie Hogan is the one that pulled the trigger.' " He also "claimed that Jacobs was telling the truth when he testified that he did not in any way anticipate that the victim would be shot." Several police officers testified at the sister's trial that portions of Jacobs' confession were untrue.

Despite these post-trial developments, the State of Texas now insists that it may constitutionally carry out Jacobs' death sentence. I find this course of events deeply troubling. If the prosecutor's statements at the Hogan trial were correct, then Jacobs is innocent of capital murder. Moreover, for a sovereign State represented by the same lawyer to take flatly inconsistent positions in two different cases—and to insist on the imposition of the death penalty after repudiating the factual basis for that sentence—surely raises a serious question of prosecutorial misconduct. In my opinion, it would be fundamentally unfair to execute a person on the basis of a factual determination that the State has formally disavowed.

Almost 60 years ago, we recognized that a prosecutor's knowing presentation of false testimony is "inconsistent with the rudimentary demands of justice." *Mooney v. Holohan*, 294 U.S. 103, 55 S.Ct. 340 (1935). We have refined this principle over the years, finding a due process violation when a prosecutor fails to correct testimony he knows to be false, *Alcorta v. Texas*, 355 U.S. 28, 78 S.Ct. 103 (1957), even when the falsehood in the testimony goes only to the witness' credibility, *Napue v. Illinois*, 360 U.S. 264, 79 S.Ct. 1173 (1959).

In *Durley v. Mayo*, 351 U.S. 277, 76 S.Ct. 806 (1956), we granted certiorari to consider whether due process was offended by a conviction which was later alleged to rest upon perjured testimony, despite the fact that the prosecutor did not know of the testimony's falsity at trial. Although the Court ultimately held that jurisdiction was lacking, and disposed of the case on that basis, four Justices would have reached the merits. Writing for the dissenters, Justice Douglas would have found a "clear" due process violation:

> "It is well settled that to obtain a conviction by the use of testimony known by the prosecution to be perjured offends due process. While the petition did not allege that the prosecution knew that petitioner's codefendants were lying when they implicated petitioner, the State now knows that the testimony of the only witnesses against petitioner was false. No competent evidence remains to support the conviction. Deprivation of a hearing under these circumstances amounts in my opinion to a denial of due process of law."

Here, the facts are far stronger than in *Durley*, as the State itself has formally vouched for the credibility of Jacobs' recantation of his confession and police officers have testified, under oath, that parts of Jacobs' confession were false.

I have long believed that serious questions are raised "when the sovereign itself takes inconsistent positions in two separate criminal proceedings against two of its citizens." *United States v. Powers*, 467 F.2d 1089 (7th Cir.1972), cert. denied, 410 U.S. 983, 93 S.Ct. 1499 (1973). The "heightened need for reliability" in capital cases only underscores the gravity of those questions in the circumstances of this case. At a minimum, Jacobs' execution should be stayed so that we may carefully consider his claims by way of our ordinary procedure respecting petitions for certiorari.

I respectfully dissent from the order denying the application for a stay of execution.

JUSTICE BREYER would grant the application for stay of execution.

NOTES

1. *Prosecutors' use of inconsistent theories.*

Prosecutors' use of inconsistent factual theories in the separate trials of co-defendants is not uncommon in capital cases. Since *Jacobs*, a number of death-sentenced defendants have sought to set aside their sentences on that basis, with mixed results. See *Stumpf v. Mitchell*, 367 F.3d 594 (6th Cir. 2004) *vac. and rem. sub nom. Bradshaw v. Stumpf*, 545 U.S. 175, 125 S.Ct. 2398 (2005) (due process violation because prosecutor's "flip-flopping" inherently unfair); *Smith v. Groose*, 205 F.3d 1045, 1051–1052 (8th Cir. 2000) (due process violation because prosecutor presented inconsistent evidence and inconsistency went to "the core of the prosecutor's cases"); *Beathard v. Johnson*, 177 F.3d 340, 348 (5th Cir. 1999) (no due process violation because "a prosecutor can make inconsistent arguments at the separate trials of co-defendants without violating the due process clause"); *In re Sakarias*, 25 Cal.Rptr.3d 265, 106 P.3d 931 (Cal. 2005) (due process violation as to one defendant, but no prejudice, and therefore no violation, as to the other). See also S. Shatz & L. Whitt, *The California Death Penalty: Prosecutors' Use of Inconsistent Theories Plays Fast and Loose with the Courts and the Defendants*, 36 U.S.F. L. Rev. 853 (2002) (reviewing six pairs of California capital cases where prosecutors used inconsistent factual theories against separately tried co-defendants). What factors should a reviewing court consider in deciding whether a defendant's constitutional rights were violated?

2. *Deterring prosecutorial misconduct.*

Does the prosecutor who engages in serious misconduct suffer any consequences? Generally, the prosecutor is immune from civil suits for his or her misconduct. In holding that prosecutors were absolutely immune from federal civil rights actions, the Supreme Court stated:

> We emphasize that the immunity of prosecutors from liability in suits under § 1983 does not leave the public powerless to deter misconduct or to punish that which occurs. This Court has never suggested that the policy considerations which compel civil immunity for certain governmental officials also place them beyond the reach of the criminal law. Even judges, cloaked with absolute civil immunity for centuries, could be punished criminally for willful deprivations of constitutional rights * * * The prosecutor would fare no better for his willful acts. Moreover, a prosecutor stands perhaps unique, among officials whose acts could deprive persons of constitutional rights, in his amenability to professional discipline by an association of his peers.

Imbler v. Pachtman, 424 U.S. 409, 428–429, 96 S.Ct. 984, 994 (1976). In 1999, the Chicago Tribune reported on a survey of 381 murder conviction cases, including 67 death cases, where convictions were thrown out because of prosecutorial misconduct in concealing evidence suggesting innocence or presenting evidence known to be false. See K. Armstrong & M. Possley, *The Verdict*, Chicago Tribune, Jan. 10, 1999, p.1. In many of the cases, the misconduct was extreme: "They have prosecuted black men, hiding evidence the real killers were white. They have prosecuted a wife, hiding evidence her husband committed suicide. They have prosecuted parents, hiding evidence their daughter was killed by wild dogs." The survey found only one instance where the prosecutors were prosecuted and actually tried for serious misconduct leading to a wrongful conviction, and, in that case, they were acquitted. See M. Possley & T. Gregory, *Dupage 5 Win Acquittal*, Chicago Tribune, June 5, 1999, p.1. Although appellate courts in the cases studied denounced prosecutors' actions with words like "unforgivable," "intolerable," "beyond reprehension," and "illegal, improper and dishonest," and some of the prosecutors were investigated, the sanctions imposed on prosecutors in the 381 cases were minimal: "One was fired, but appealed and was reinstated with back pay. Another received an in-house suspension of 30 days. A third prosecutor's law license was suspended for 59 days, but because of other misconduct in the case." None of the prosecutors received any kind of public sanction from a state lawyer disciplinary agency.

If, as appears from the survey, there are no consequences for a prosecutor who engages in serious misconduct, what incentives can be created to encourage prosecutors to play by the rules?

CHAPTER 9

THE PENALTY HEARING

■ ■ ■

The cases in this chapter concern the nature and requisites of the penalty hearing. Section A addresses the constitutional procedural rights guaranteed to the defendant at the penalty hearing. To what extent do the rights applicable at the guilt phase apply in the penalty hearing? Section B considers whether there are any constitutional limits on the application of state evidence rules at the penalty hearing.

A.   PROCEDURAL REQUISITES

In the four cases in this section, the Justices debate the nature of the penalty hearing. Is the hearing analogous to the trial on guilt, or is it analogous to non-capital case sentencing? In *Bullington v. Missouri*, the specific issue is whether double jeopardy principles apply to the penalty determination. In *Spaziano v. Florida*, the trial judge imposed a death sentence after the jury had recommended a life sentence, and the issue is whether the defendant had a right to a jury determination as to penalty. In *Ring v. Arizona*, the Court must decide whether the defendant has a right to a jury determination of the facts making him death-eligible. In *Gardner v. Florida*, the Court considers a due process (fair notice) challenge to the penalty determination.

BULLINGTON v. MISSOURI
451 U.S. 430, 101 S.Ct. 1852, 68 L.Ed.2d 270 (1981).

JUSTICE BLACKMUN delivered the opinion of the Court.

Stroud v. United States, 251 U.S. 15, 40 S.Ct. 50 (1919), concerned a defendant who was convicted of first-degree murder and sentenced to life imprisonment, and who then obtained, upon confession of error by the Solicitor General, a reversal of his conviction and a new trial. This Court, by a unanimous vote in that case, held that the Double Jeopardy Clause of the Fifth Amendment did not bar the imposition of the death penalty when Stroud at his new trial was again convicted.

The issue in the present case is whether the reasoning of *Stroud* is also to apply under a system where a jury's sentencing decision is made at a bifurcated proceeding's second stage at which the prosecution has the burden of proving certain elements beyond a reasonable doubt before the death penalty may be imposed.

I

Missouri law provides two, and only two, possible sentences for a defendant convicted of capital murder: (a) death, or (b) life imprisonment without eligibility for probation or parole for 50 years. Mo.Rev.Stat. § 565.008.1 (1978).

Like most death penalty legislation enacted after this Court's decision in *Furman v. Georgia*, 408 U.S. 238, 92 S.Ct. 2726 (1972), the Missouri statutes contain substantive standards to guide the discretion of the sentencer. The statutes also afford procedural safeguards to the convicted defendant. Section 565.006 provides that the trial court shall conduct a separate presentence hearing for the defendant who is convicted by a jury of capital murder. The hearing must be held before the same jury that found the defendant guilty, and "additional evidence in extenuation, mitigation, and aggravation of punishment" shall be heard. "Only such evidence in aggravation as the prosecution has made known to the defendant prior to his trial shall be admissible." The jury must consider whether the evidence shows that there exist any of the 10 aggravating circumstances or the 7 mitigating circumstances specified by the statute; whether any other mitigating or aggravating circumstances authorized by law exist; whether any aggravating circumstances that do exist are sufficient to warrant the imposition of the death penalty; and whether any mitigating circumstances that exist outweigh the aggravating circumstances. A jury that imposes the death penalty must designate in writing the aggravating circumstance or circumstances that it finds beyond a reasonable doubt. It also must be convinced beyond a reasonable doubt that any aggravating circumstance or circumstances that it finds to exist are sufficient to warrant the imposition of the death penalty. A Missouri jury is instructed that it is not compelled to impose the death penalty even if it decides that a sufficient aggravating circumstance or circumstances exist and that it or they are not outweighed by any mitigating circumstance or circumstances. A jury's decision to impose the death penalty must be unanimous. If the jury is unable to agree, the defendant receives the alternative sentence of life imprisonment described above.

II

In December 1977, petitioner Robert Bullington was indicted in St. Louis County, Mo., for capital murder and other crimes arising out of the abduction of a young woman and her subsequent death by drowning.

The Circuit Court of St. Louis County granted petitioner's pretrial motion for a change of venue to Jackson County in the western part of the State. The prosecution, by letter, informed the defense that the State would seek the death penalty if the jury convicted the defendant of capital murder. The letter-notice stated that the prosecution would present evidence of two aggravating circumstances specified by the statute: that "[t]he offense was committed by a person ... who has a substantial history of serious assaultive criminal convictions" and that "[t]he offense was outrageously or wantonly vile, horrible or inhuman in that it involved torture, or depravity of mind."

At the guilt-or-innocence phase of petitioner's trial, the jury returned a verdict of guilty of capital murder. On the following day, the trial court proceeded to hold the presentence hearing required by § 565.006.2. Evidence submitted by the prosecution was received. None was offered by the defense. After argument by counsel, instructions from the judge and deliberation, the jury returned its additional verdict fixing petitioner's punishment not at death, but at imprisonment for life without eligibility for probation or parole for 50 years.

[While petitioner's post-trial motions were pending, the Supreme Court decided *Duren v. Missouri*, 439 U.S. 357, 99 S.Ct. 664 (1979), holding unconstitutional aspects of Missouri's jury selection system. Based on *Duren*, the trial judge granted petitioner a new trial. The prosecution again filed a formal "Notice of Evidence in Aggravation," stating that it intended again to seek the death penalty and that it would rely on the same aggravating circumstances sought to be proved at the first trial. Petitioner moved, on double jeopardy grounds, to bar the prosecution from seeking the death penalty, and the trial court granted the motion. The Missouri Supreme Court reversed.]

III

It is well established that the Double Jeopardy Clause forbids the retrial of a defendant who has been acquitted of the crime charged. *United States v. DiFrancesco*, 449 U.S. 117, 101 S.Ct. 426 (1980). This Court, however, has resisted attempts to extend that principle to sentencing. The imposition of a particular sentence usually is not regarded as an "acquittal" of any more severe sentence that could have been imposed. The Court generally has concluded, therefore, that the Double Jeopardy Clause imposes no absolute prohibition against the imposition of a harsher sentence at retrial after a defendant has succeeded in having his original conviction set aside.

The procedure that resulted in the imposition of the sentence of life imprisonment upon petitioner Bullington at his first trial, however, differs significantly from those employed in any of the Court's cases where the Double Jeopardy Clause has been held inapplicable to sentencing. The jury in this case was not given unbounded discretion to select an appropriate punishment from a wide range authorized by statute. Rather, a separate hearing was required and was held, and the jury was presented both a choice between two alternatives and standards to guide the making of that choice. Nor did the prosecution simply recommend what it felt to be an appropriate punishment. It undertook the burden of establishing certain facts beyond a reasonable doubt in its quest to obtain the harsher of the two alternative verdicts. The presentence hearing resembled and, indeed, in all relevant respects was like the immediately preceding trial on the issue of guilt or innocence. It was itself a trial on the issue of punishment so precisely defined by the Missouri statutes.[10]

    * * *

In only one prior case, *United States v. DiFrancesco*, 449 U.S. 117, 101 S.Ct. 426 (1980), has this Court considered a separate or bifurcated sentencing procedure at which it was necessary for the prosecution to prove additional facts. The federal statute under consideration there, the "dangerous special offender" provision of the Organized Crime Control Act of 1970, 18 U.S.C. §§ 3575 and 3576, requires a separate presentence hearing. The Government must prove the additional fact that the defendant is a "dangerous special offender," as defined in the statute, in order for the court to impose an enhanced sentence. But there are highly pertinent differences between the Missouri procedures controlling the present case and those found constitutional in *DiFrancesco*. The federal procedures at issue in *DiFrancesco* include appellate review of a sentence "on the record of the sentencing court," § 3576, not a *de novo* proceeding that gives the Government the opportunity to convince a second factfinder of its view of the facts. Moreover, the choice presented to the federal judge under § 3575 is far broader than that faced by the state jury at the present petitioner's trial. Bullington's Missouri jury was given—and under the State's statutes could be given—only two choices, death or life imprisonment. On the other hand, if the Federal Government proves that a person convicted of a felony is a dangerous special offender, the judge may sentence that person to "an appropriate term not to exceed twenty-five years and not disproportionate in severity to the maximum term otherwise authorized by law for such felony." § 3575(b). Finally, although the statute requires the Government to prove the additional fact that the defendant is a "dangerous special offender," it need do so only by a preponderance of the evidence. This stands in contrast to the reasonable-doubt standard of the Missouri statute, the same standard required to be used at the trial on the issue of guilt or innocence. * * *

IV

These procedural differences become important when the underlying rationale of the cases is considered. The State here relies principally upon *North Carolina v. Pearce*, 395 U.S. 711, 89 S.Ct. 2072 (1969). The Court's starting point in that case was the established rule that there is no double jeopardy bar to retrying a defendant who has succeeded in overturning his conviction. The Court stated that this rule rests on the premise that the

---

10. At the statutorily prescribed presentence hearing, counsel make opening statements, testimony is taken, evidence is introduced, the jury is instructed, and final arguments are made. The jury then deliberates and returns its formal punishment verdict. All these steps were taken at petitioner's presentence hearing following his first trial.

We think it not without some significance that the pertinent Missouri statute itself speaks specifically of the presentence hearing in terms of a continuing "trial." Section 565.006.2 states that after the verdict of guilty of capital murder is returned, "the court shall *resume the trial* and conduct a presentence hearing." (Emphasis added.)

original conviction has been nullified and "the slate wiped clean." Therefore, if the defendant is convicted again, he constitutionally may be subjected to whatever punishment is lawful, subject only to the limitation that he receive credit for time served.

There is an important exception, however, to the rule recognized in *Pearce*. A defendant may not be retried if he obtains a reversal of his conviction on the ground that the evidence was insufficient to convict. *Burks v. United States*, 437 U.S. 1, 98 S.Ct. 2141 (1978). The reasons for this exception are relevant here:

> "[R]eversal for trial error, as distinguished from evidentiary insufficiency, does not constitute a decision to the effect that the government has failed to prove its cases. As such, it implies nothing with respect to the guilt or innocence of the defendant. . . .
>
> "The same cannot be said when a defendant's conviction has been overturned due to a failure of proof at trial, in which case the prosecution cannot complain of prejudice, for it has been given one fair opportunity to offer whatever proof it can assemble. . . . Since we necessarily accord absolute finality to a jury's *verdict* of acquittal—no matter how erroneous its decision—it is difficult to conceive how society has any greater interest in retrying a defendant when, on review, it is decided as a matter of law that the jury could not properly have returned a verdict of guilty." (emphasis in original).

The decision in *Burks* was foreshadowed by *Green v. United States*, 355 U.S. 184, 78 S.Ct. 221 (1957). In that case, the defendant had been indicted for first-degree murder, and the trial court instructed the jury that it could convict him either of that crime or of the lesser included offense of second-degree murder. The jury convicted him of second-degree murder, but the conviction was reversed on appeal. The Court held that a retrial on the first-degree murder charge was barred by the Double Jeopardy Clause, because the defendant "was forced to run the gantlet once on that charge and the jury refused to convict him."

Thus, the "clean slate" rationale recognized in *Pearce* is inapplicable whenever a jury agrees or an appellate court decides that the prosecution has not proved its case.

In the usual sentencing proceeding, however, it is impossible to conclude that a sentence less than the statutory maximum "constitute[s] a decision to the effect that the government has failed to prove its case." In the normal process of sentencing, "there are virtually no rules or tests or standards—and thus no issues to resolve. . . ." M. Frankel, Criminal Sentences: Law Without Order (1973). * * *

     * * *

By enacting a capital sentencing procedure that resembles a trial on the issue of guilt or innocence, however, Missouri explicitly requires the jury to determine whether the prosecution has "proved its case." Both *Burks* and *Green*, as has been noted, state an exception to the general rule relied upon in *North Carolina v. Pearce*. That exception is applicable here, and we therefore refrain from extending the rationale of *Pearce* to the very different facts of the present case. Chief Justice Bardgett, in his dissent from the ruling of the Missouri Supreme Court majority, observed that the sentence of life imprisonment which petitioner received at his first trial meant that "the jury has already acquitted the defendant of whatever was necessary to impose the death sentence." We agree.

A verdict of acquittal on the issue of guilt or innocence is, of course, absolutely final. The values that underlie this principle, stated for the Court by Justice Black, are equally applicable when a jury has rejected the State's claim that the defendant deserves to die:

> "The underlying idea, one that is deeply ingrained in at least the Anglo–American system of jurisprudence, is that the State with all its resources and power should not be allowed to make repeated attempts to convict an individual for an alleged offense, thereby subjecting him to embarrassment, expense and ordeal and compelling him to live in a continuing state of anxiety and insecurity, as well as enhancing the possibility that even though innocent he may be found guilty." *Green v. United States*.

The "embarrassment, expense and ordeal" and the "anxiety and insecurity" faced by a defendant at the penalty phase of a Missouri capital murder trial surely are at least equivalent to that faced by any defendant at the guilt phase of a criminal trial. The "unacceptably high risk that the [prosecution], with its superior resources, would wear down a defendant," thereby leading to an erroneously imposed death sentence, would exist if the State were to have a further opportunity to convince a jury to impose the ultimate punishment. Missouri's use of the reasonable-doubt standard indicates that in a capital sentencing proceeding, it is the State, not the defendant, that should bear "almost the entire risk of error." *Addington v. Texas*, 441 U.S. 418, 99 S.Ct. 1804 (1979). Given these considerations, our decision today does not at all depend upon the State's announced intention to rely only upon the same aggravating circumstances it sought to prove at petitioner's first trial or upon its statement that it would introduce no new evidence in support of its contention that petitioner deserves the death penalty. Having received "one fair opportunity to offer whatever proof it could assemble," *Burks v. United States*, the State is not entitled to another.

V

* * *

The judgment of the Supreme Court of Missouri is reversed, and the case is remanded to that court for further proceedings not inconsistent with this opinion.

JUSTICE POWELL, with whom THE CHIEF JUSTICE, JUSTICE WHITE, and JUSTICE REHNQUIST join, dissenting.

This case concerns the force of the Double Jeopardy Clause after a defendant convicted of a crime and sentenced has succeeded in having his conviction reversed. The Court holds that the jury's decision at petitioner's first trial to sentence him to life imprisonment precludes Missouri from asking the jury at petitioner's second trial to sentence him to death. I consider the Court's opinion irreconcilable in principle with the precedents of this Court.

I

It is well-established law that the Double Jeopardy Clause does not apply to sentencing decisions after retrial with the same force that it applies to redeterminations of guilt or innocence. Since *Stroud v. United States*, 251 U.S. 15, 40 S.Ct. 50 (1919), it has been settled that a defendant whose conviction is reversed may receive a more severe sentence upon retrial than he received at his first trial. The Court followed this principle in *North Carolina v. Pearce*, 395 U.S. 711, 89 S.Ct. 2072 (1969), where it held that a "corollary of the power to retry a defendant is the power, upon the defendant's reconviction, to impose whatever sentence may be legally authorized, whether or not it is greater than the sentence imposed after the first conviction." In contrast, where the question was whether a defendant could be retried for first-degree murder after the jury at his first trial had found him guilty only of second-degree murder, the Court "regarded the jury's verdict as an implicit acquittal on the charge of first degree murder" and held that the Double Jeopardy Clause therefore barred retrial on that charge. *Green v. United States*, 355 U.S. 184, 78 S.Ct. 221 (1957).

Although there is some tension between the *Green* and *Pearce* opinions, their holdings are not inconsistent. Both have become landmarks in the law of the Double Jeopardy Clause. The Court has cited each opinion time and time again, and more than once the court has declined to reexamine *Pearce*. Indeed, its rationale has been reaffirmed in recent cases. *United States v. DiFrancesco*, 449 U.S. 117, 101 S.Ct. 426 (1980). Earlier this Term, the Court stated without qualification that "the difference in result reached in *Green* and *Pearce* can be explained only on the grounds that the imposition of sentence does not operate as an implied acquittal of any greater sentence." *United States v. DiFrancesco, supra* ("The imposition of a particular sentence *usually* is not regarded as an 'acquittal' of any more severe sentence ..." (emphasis added)). But today the Court applies *Green*'s principle of "implicit acquittal" to sentencing, despite *Pearce* and the unqualified statement in *DiFrancesco*.

II

* * *

This is the first time the Court has held that the Double Jeopardy Clause applies equally to sentencing and to determinations of guilt or innocence. It heretofore has been thought that there is a fundamental difference between the two. I would adhere to these precedents, and think they control this case.

Underlying the question of guilt or innocence is an objective truth: the defendant, in fact, did or did not commit the acts constituting the crime charged. From the time an accused is first suspected to the time the decision on guilt or innocence is made, our criminal justice system is designed to enable the trier of fact to discover that truth according to law. But triers of fact can err, and an innocent person can be pronounced guilty. In contrast, the law provides only limited standards for assessing the validity of a sentencing decision. The sentencer's function is not to discover a fact, but to mete out just deserts as he sees them. Absent a mandatory sentence, there is no objective measure by which the sentencer's decision can be deemed correct or erroneous if it is duly made within the authority conferred by the legislature.

In light of this difference in the nature of the decisions, the question in this case is not—as the Court would frame it—whether the procedures by which a sentencing decision is made are similar to the procedures by which a decision on guilt or innocence is made. Rather, the question is whether the reasons for considering an acquittal on guilt or innocence as absolutely final apply equally to a sentencing decision imposing less than the most severe sentence authorized by law. I would have thought that the pertinence of this question was clear, and that the answer consistently given in the past could not have escaped the Court. Earlier this Term, in *United States v. DiFrancesco*, we stated that "[t]here are ... fundamental distinctions between a sentence and an acquittal, and to fail to recognize them is to ignore the particular significance of an acquittal."

The reasons for considering an acquittal on guilt or innocence as absolutely final do not apply equally to a sentencing decision for less than the most severe sentence authorized by law. A retrial of a defendant once found to have been innocent "enhanc[es] the possibility that even though innocent he may be found guilty." *Green v. United States.* * * * The possibility of a higher sentence is acceptable under the Double Jeopardy Clause, whereas the possibility of error as to guilt or innocence is not, because the second jury's sentencing decision is as "correct" as the first jury's. Similarly, a defendant once found to have been innocent cannot be forced a second time through the ordeal of trial. But when a defendant is found guilty, he must bear the ordeal of being sentenced just as he does the ordeal of serving sentence.

In sum, I find wholly unpersuasive the Court's justification for applying the implicit-acquittal principle to sentencing. * * *[4]

     * * *

---

4. I would have trouble concurring in the Court's judgment even if I agreed with the Court that the procedures of the Missouri death penalty statute distinguish this case from [earlier double jeopardy cases]. In the Court's view, the first jury's decision to sentence petitioner to life imprisonment rather than death reveals that the State failed to "prove its case" that petitioner deserved capital punishment. On this premise the Court concludes that the principle of *Green* and

Note

1. *Problem 9–1.*

At his initial trial, Defendant was convicted of first degree murder, and the case proceeded to a penalty phase. Under State's law, the jury is instructed that the verdict must be death if the jury unanimously finds at least one aggravating circumstance and no mitigating circumstance or one or more aggravating circumstances outweighing any mitigating circumstances, but it must be life imprisonment in all other instances. In the event the jury is unable to reach a unanimous agreement on sentence, the trial judge may discharge the jury, in which case the court must then enter a life sentence. At the penalty phase, the jury reported to the trial judge that it was hopelessly deadlocked 9–to–3 for life imprisonment, and the court discharged the jury and entered a life sentence. On appeal, Defendant's conviction was reversed, and the case was remanded for a new trial. Over Defendant's objection, Prosecutor again sought the death penalty, and Defendant was again convicted of first degree murder and, this time, sentenced to death. On appeal, what arguments should be made as to whether the sentence is a violation of Double Jeopardy? See *Sattazahn v. Pennsylvania,* 537 U.S. 101, 123 S.Ct. 732 (2003).

SPAZIANO v. FLORIDA

468 U.S. 447, 104 S.Ct. 3154, 82 L.Ed.2d 340 (1984).

Justice Blackmun delivered the opinion of the Court.

[Petitioner Joseph Robert Spaziano was indicted and tried for first-degree murder. The primary evidence against him was given by a witness who testified that petitioner had taken him to a garbage dump, where petitioner had pointed out the remains of two women he claimed to have tortured and murdered. Petitioner challenged the sufficiency of the witness's recall and perception because the witness had a substantial drug habit. The jury returned a verdict of first degree murder. Under Florida procedure, the sentencing hearing was before the same jury, but their decision, made by majority vote, was only advisory. The trial judge was permitted to override the jury's recommendation of a life sentence where "the facts suggesting a sentence of death [are] so clear and convincing that virtually no reasonable person could differ." See *Tedder v. State,* 322

Burks v. United States, 437 U.S. 1, 98 S.Ct. 2141 (1978), bars a second attempt by the State to secure a death sentence.

Under the Missouri statute, the "case" that the State had to prove was that petitioner committed the murder under circumstances defined as "aggravating" and that these circumstances warranted the imposition of the death penalty. But the trial court expressly instructed the jury that it could choose life imprisonment rather than death even if it found beyond a reasonable doubt that the State had proved the existence and gravity of such circumstances. Thus, the jury's decision for life imprisonment rather than death does not necessarily mean that the State adduced insufficient evidence. To be sure, an acquittal on the question of guilt or innocence does not necessarily mean that the State adduced insufficient evidence, and yet such acquittals are final. But juries instructed on the question of guilt or innocence are not told that they can ignore the State's evidence. Where the jury is so instructed, as in this case, there is significantly less reason to assume that the State failed to prove its case. Accordingly, there is less reason to consider a second attempt to obtain the death penalty an unfair " 'second bite at the apple.' " *Burks v. United States, supra.*

So.2d 908 (Fla.1975). At the sentencing hearing, both sides presented evidence and arguments, and a majority of the jury recommended life imprisonment. However, the trial judge found that two aggravating circumstances—that the homicide was especially heinous and atrocious and that the defendant had been convicted previously of felonies involving the use or threat of violence to the person—outweighed the mitigating circumstances, and he sentenced petitioner to death. On appeal, the Supreme Court of Florida affirmed the conviction but reversed the death sentence because the trial judge had considered a confidential portion of the presentence investigation report.]

On remand, the trial court ordered a new presentence investigation report and scheduled a hearing to allow petitioner to present evidence in response to the report. At the hearing, petitioner offered no evidence. The State presented evidence that petitioner had been convicted previously of forcible carnal knowledge and aggravated battery. Although the State had attempted to introduce evidence of the prior conviction in petitioner's initial sentencing hearing before the jury, the trial judge had excluded the evidence on the ground that the conviction was then on appeal. By the time of the * * * rehearing, the conviction was final and the trial judge agreed that it was a proper consideration. Accordingly, he relied on that conviction in finding the aggravating circumstance that the defendant had been convicted previously of a felony involving the use of violence to the person. The judge also reaffirmed his conclusion that the crime was especially heinous, atrocious, and cruel. He sentenced petitioner to death.

The Supreme Court of Florida affirmed. * * *

* * *

III

Petitioner's second challenge concerns the trial judge's imposition of a sentence of death after the jury had recommended life imprisonment. Petitioner urges that allowing a judge to override a jury's recommendation of life violates the Eighth Amendment's proscription against "cruel and unusual punishments." Because the jury's verdict of life should be final, petitioner argues, the practice also violates the Fifth Amendment's Double Jeopardy Clause made applicable to the States through the Fourteenth Amendment. Finally, drawing on this Court's recognition of the value of the jury's role, particularly in a capital proceeding, petitioner urges that the practice violates the Sixth Amendment and the Due Process Clause of the Fourteenth Amendment.

Petitioner points out that we need not decide whether jury sentencing in all capital cases is required; this case presents only the question whether, given a jury verdict of life, the judge may override that verdict and impose death. As counsel acknowledged at oral argument, however, his fundamental premise is that the capital sentencing decision is one that, in all cases, should be made by a jury. We therefore address that fundamental premise. Before doing so, however, it is useful to clarify what is not at issue here.

Petitioner does not urge that capital sentencing is so much like a trial on guilt or innocence that it is controlled by the Court's decision in *Duncan v. Louisiana*, 391 U.S. 145, 88 S.Ct. 1444 (1968). In *Duncan*, the Court found that the right to jury trial guaranteed by the Sixth Amendment is so " 'basic in our system of jurisprudence,' " quoting *In re Oliver*, 333 U.S. 257, 68 S.Ct. 499 (1948), that it is also protected against state action by the Fourteenth Amendment.

This Court, of course, has recognized that a capital proceeding in many respects resembles a trial on the issue of guilt or innocence. See *Bullington v. Missouri*, 451 U.S. 430, 101 S.Ct. 1852 (1981). Because the "embarrassment, expense and ordeal ... faced by a defendant at the penalty phase of a ... capital murder trial ... are at least equivalent to that faced by any defendant at the guilt phase of a criminal trial," the Court has concluded that the Double Jeopardy Clause bars the State from making repeated efforts to persuade a sentencer to impose the death penalty. The fact that a capital sentencing is like a trial in the respects significant to the Double Jeopardy Clause, however, does not mean that it is like a trial in respects significant to the Sixth Amendment's guarantee of a jury trial. The Court's concern in *Bullington* was with the risk that the State, with all its resources, would wear a defendant down, thereby leading to an erroneously imposed death penalty. There is no similar danger involved in denying a defendant a jury trial on the sentencing issue of life or death. The sentencer, whether judge or jury, has a constitutional obligation to evaluate the unique circumstances of the individual defendant and the sentencer's decision for life is final. More important, despite its unique aspects, a capital sentencing proceeding involves the same fundamental issue involved in any other sentencing proceeding—a determination of the appropriate punishment to be imposed on an individual. The Sixth Amendment never has been thought to guarantee a right to a jury determination of that issue.

Nor does petitioner urge that this Court's recognition of the "qualitative difference" of the death penalty requires the benefit of a jury. In *Furman v. Georgia*, 408 U.S. 238, 92 S.Ct. 2726 (1972), the Court struck down the then-existing capital sentencing statutes of Georgia and Texas, in large part because of its conclusion that, under those statutes, the penalty was applied arbitrarily and discriminatorily. Since then, the Court has emphasized its pursuit of the "twin objectives" of "measured, consistent application and fairness to the accused." *Eddings v. Oklahoma*, 455 U.S. 104, 102 S.Ct. 869 (1982). If a State has determined that death should be an available penalty for certain crimes, then it must administer that penalty in a way that can rationally distinguish between those individuals for whom death is an appropriate sanction and those for whom it is not. *Zant v. Stephens*, 462 U.S. 862, 103 S.Ct. 2733 (1983). It must also allow the sentencer to consider the individual circumstances of the defendant, his background, and his crime. *Lockett v. Ohio*, 438 U.S. 586, 98 S.Ct. 2954 (1978).

Nothing in those twin objectives suggests that the sentence must or should be imposed by a jury. While it is to be hoped that current procedures have greatly reduced the risk that jury sentencing will result in arbitrary or discriminatory application of the death penalty, there certainly is nothing in the safeguards necessitated by the Court's recognition of the qualitative difference of the death penalty that requires that the sentence be imposed by a jury.

Petitioner's primary argument is that the laws and practice in most of the States indicate a nearly unanimous recognition that juries, not judges, are better equipped to make reliable capital-sentencing decisions and that a jury's decision for life should be inviolate. The reason for that recognition, petitioner urges, is that the nature of the decision whether a defendant should live or die sets capital sentencing apart and requires that a jury have the ultimate word. Noncapital sentences are imposed for various reasons, including rehabilitation, incapacitation, and deterrence. In contrast, the primary justification for the death penalty is retribution. As has been recognized, "the decision that capital punishment may be the appropriate sanction in extreme cases is an expression of the community's belief that certain crimes are themselves so grievous an affront to humanity that the only adequate response may be the penalty of death." *Gregg v. Georgia*, 428 U.S. 153, 96 S.Ct. 2909 (1976) (joint opinion). The imposition of the death penalty, in other words, is an expression of community outrage. Since the jury serves as the voice of the community, the jury is in the best position to decide whether a particular crime is so heinous that the community's response must be death. If the answer is no, that decision should be final.

Petitioner's argument obviously has some appeal. But it has two fundamental flaws. First, the distinctions between capital and noncapital sentences are not so clear as petitioner suggests. Petitioner acknowledges, for example, that deterrence may be a justification for capital as well as for noncapital sentences. He suggests only that deterrence is not a proper consideration for particular sentencers who are deciding whether the penalty should be imposed in a given case. The same is true, however, in noncapital cases. Whatever the sentence, its deterrent function is primarily a consideration for the legislature. Similar points can be made about the other purposes of capital and noncapital punishment. Although incapacitation has never been embraced as a sufficient justification for the death penalty, it is a legitimate consideration in a capital sentencing proceeding. While retribution clearly plays a more prominent role in a capital case, retribution is an element of all punishments society imposes, and there is no suggestion as to any of these that the sentence may not be imposed by a judge.

Second, even accepting petitioner's premise that the retributive purpose behind the death penalty is the element that sets the penalty apart, it does not follow that the sentence must be imposed by a jury. Imposing the sentence in individual cases is not the sole or even the primary vehicle through which the community's voice can be expressed. This Court's decisions indicate that the discretion of the sentencing authority, whether judge or jury, must be limited and reviewable. The sentencer is responsible for weighing the specific aggravating and mitigating circumstances the legislature has determined are necessary touchstones in determining whether death is the appropriate penalty. Thus, even if it is a jury that imposes the sentence, the "community's voice" is not given free rein. The community's voice is heard at least as clearly in the legislature when the death penalty is authorized and the particular circumstances in which death is appropriate are defined.

We do not denigrate the significance of the jury's role as a link between the community and the penal system and as a bulwark between the accused and the State. The point is simply that the purpose of the death penalty is not frustrated by, or inconsistent with, a scheme in which the imposition of the penalty in individual cases is determined by a judge.

We also acknowledge the presence of the majority view that capital sentencing, unlike other sentencing, should be performed by a jury. As petitioner points out, 30 out of 37 jurisdictions with a capital sentencing statute give the life-or-death decision to the jury, with only 3 of the remaining 7 allowing a judge to override a jury's recommendation of life. The fact that a majority of jurisdictions have adopted a different practice, however, does not establish that contemporary standards of decency are offended by the jury override. The Eighth Amendment is not violated every time a State reaches a conclusion different from a majority of its sisters over how best to administer its criminal laws. "Although the judgments of legislatures, juries, and prosecutors weigh heavily in the balance, it is for us ultimately to judge whether the Eighth Amendment" is violated by a challenged practice. See *Enmund v. Florida*, 458 U.S. 782, 102 S.Ct. 3368 (1982); *Coker v. Georgia*, 433 U.S. 584, 97 S.Ct. 2861 (1977) (plurality opinion). In light of the facts that the Sixth Amendment does not require jury sentencing, that the demands of fairness and reliability in capital cases do not require it, and that neither the nature of, nor the purpose behind, the death penalty requires jury sentencing, we cannot conclude that placing responsibility on the trial judge to impose the sentence in a capital case is unconstitutional.

As the Court several times has made clear, we are unwilling to say that there is any one right way for a State to set up its capital sentencing scheme. The Court twice has concluded that Florida has struck a reasonable balance between sensitivity to the individual and his circumstances and ensuring that the penalty is not imposed arbitrarily or discriminatorily. *Barclay v. Florida*, 463 U.S. 939, 103 S.Ct. 3418 (1983); *Proffitt v. Florida*, 428 U.S. 242, 96 S.Ct. 2960 (1976) (joint opinion of STEWART, POWELL, and STEVENS, JJ.). We are not persuaded that placing the responsibility on a trial judge to impose the sentence in a capital case is so fundamentally at odds with contemporary standards of fairness and decency that Florida must be required to alter its scheme and give final authority to the jury to make the life-or-death decision.

IV

Our determination that there is no constitutional imperative that a jury have the responsibility of deciding whether the death penalty should be imposed also disposes of petitioner's double jeopardy challenge to the jury-override procedure. If a judge may be vested with sole responsibility for imposing the penalty, then there is nothing constitutionally wrong with the judge's exercising that responsibility after receiving the advice of the jury. The advice does not become a judgment simply because it comes from the jury.

V

Petitioner's final challenge is to the application of the standard the Florida Supreme Court has announced for allowing a trial court to override a jury's recommendation of life. See *Tedder v. State*, 322 So.2d 908 (Fla. 1975). * * *

We see nothing that suggests that the application of the jury-override procedure has resulted in arbitrary or discriminatory application of the death penalty, either in general or in this particular case. Regardless of the jury's recommendation, the trial judge is required to conduct an independent review of the evidence and to make his own findings regarding aggravating and mitigating circumstances. If the judge imposes a sentence of death, he must set forth in writing the findings on which the sentence is based. The Florida Supreme Court must review every capital sentence to ensure that the penalty has not been imposed arbitrarily or capriciously. As Justice STEVENS noted in *Barclay*, there is no evidence that the Florida Supreme Court has failed in its responsibility to perform meaningful appellate review of each death sentence, either in cases in which both the jury and the trial court have concluded that death is the appropriate penalty or in cases when the jury has recommended life and the trial court has overridden the jury's recommendation and sentenced the defendant to death.

In this case, the trial judge based his decision on the presence of two statutory aggravating circumstances. The first, that the defendant had previously been convicted of another capital felony or of a felony involving the use or threat of violence to the person, was based on evidence not available to the advisory jury but, under Florida law, was properly considered by the trial judge. Petitioner's prior conviction was for rape and aggravated battery. The trial judge also found that the murder in this case was heinous, atrocious, and cruel. The witness who accompanied petitioner to the dump site where the victim's body was found testified that the body was covered with blood and that there were cuts on the breasts, stomach, and chest. The witness also testified that petitioner had recounted his torture of the victim while she was still living. The trial judge found no mitigating circumstances.

The Florida Supreme Court reviewed petitioner's sentence and concluded that the death penalty was properly imposed under state law. It is not our function to decide whether we agree with the majority of the advisory jury or with the trial judge and the Florida Supreme Court. Whether or not "reasonable people" could differ over the result here, we see nothing irrational or arbitrary about the imposition of the death penalty in this case.

The judgment of the Supreme Court of Florida is affirmed.

[Opinion of WHITE, J., joined by REHNQUIST, J., concurring in part and concurring in the judgment, omitted]

JUSTICE STEVENS, with whom JUSTICE BRENNAN and JUSTICE MARSHALL join, concurring in part and dissenting in part.

In this case, as in 82 others arising under the capital punishment statute enacted by Florida in 1972, the trial judge sentenced the defendant to death after a jury had recommended a sentence of life imprisonment. The question presented is whether the Constitution of the United States permits petitioner's execution when the prosecution has been unable to persuade a jury of his peers that the death penalty is the appropriate punishment for his crime.

* * *

In the 12 years since *Furman v. Georgia*, 408 U.S. 238, 92 S.Ct. 2726 (1972), every Member of this Court has written or joined at least one opinion endorsing the proposition that because of its severity and irrevocability, the death penalty is qualitatively different from any other punishment, and hence must be accompanied by unique safeguards to ensure that it is a justified response to a given offense. Because it is the one punishment that cannot be prescribed by a rule of law as judges normally understand such rules, but rather is ultimately understood only as an expression of the community's outrage—its sense that an individual has lost his moral entitlement to live—I am convinced that the danger of an excessive response can only be avoided if the decision to impose the death penalty is made by a jury rather than by a single governmental official. This conviction is consistent with the judgment of history and the current consensus of opinion that juries are better equipped than judges to make capital sentencing decisions. The basic explanation for that consensus lies in the fact that the question whether a sentence of death is excessive in the particular circumstances of any case is one that must be answered by the decisionmaker that is best able to "express the conscience of the community on the ultimate question of life or death." *Witherspoon v. Illinois*, 391 U.S. 510, 88 S.Ct. 1770 (1968).

* * *

III

Florida is one of only a few States that permits the imposition of a sentence of death without the consent of a jury. Examination of the reasons for Florida's decision illuminates the extent to which this statute can be considered consistent with contemporary standards of fairness and decency.

During the century between 1872 and 1972 Florida law required the jury to make the capital sentencing decision. The change in the decision-making process that occurred in 1972 was not motivated by any identifiable change in the legislature's assessment of community values; rather, it was a response to this Court's decision in *Furman*. In *Furman* a plurality of the Court had condemned the arbitrary pattern of results under the then-existing capital punishment statutes. A number of States responded to *Furman* by reducing the discretion granted to juries not because of some deeply rooted communal value, but rather in an attempt to comply with the several opinions in that case. In *Dobbert v. Florida*, 432 U.S. 282, 97 S.Ct. 2290 (1977), we specifically noted that the Florida jury override now under challenge was adopted in an attempt to comply with *Furman*. We have subsequently made it clear that jury sentencing is not inconsistent with *Furman*, thereby undermining the basis for the legislative judgment challenged here. A legislative choice that is predicated on this sort of misunderstanding is not entitled to the same presumption of validity as one that rests wholly on a legislative assessment of sound policy and community sentiment.[14]

Even apart from its history, there is reason to question whether the Florida statute can be viewed as representing a judgment that judicial sentencing is consistent with contemporary standards. The administration of the statute actually reflects a deeply rooted impulse to legitimate the process through involvement of the jury. That is made evident not only through the use of an advisory jury, but also by the fact that the statute has been construed to forbid a trial judge to reject the jury's decision unless he finds that the evidence favoring a sentence of death is so clear and convincing that virtually no reasonable person could impose a lesser sentence. Thus, the Florida experience actually lends support to the conclusion that American jurisprudence has considered the use of the jury to be important to the fairness and legitimacy of capital punishment.

IV

The Court correctly notes that sentencing has traditionally been a question with which the jury is not concerned. Deciding upon the appro-

---

14. A separate reason for discounting the normal presumption of validity is that the statute has not worked as intended to protect the rights of the defendant. Although technically only the judge may impose a death sentence, in a practical sense the accused confronts the jeopardy of a death sentence twice. If the jury recommends death, an elected Florida judge sensitive to community sentiment would have an additional reason to follow that recommendation. If there are any cases in which the jury override procedure has worked to the defendant's advantage because the trial judge rejected a jury's recommendation of death, they have not been brought to our attention by the Attorney General of Florida, who would presumably be aware of any such cases. On the other hand, the fact that more persons identify with victims of crime than with capital defendants inevitably encourages judges who must face election to reject a recommendation of leniency. The fact that 83 defendants persuaded juries to recommend mercy but were thereafter sentenced to death under the Florida statute lends support to the thesis that as a practical matter the prosecution is given two chances to obtain a death sentence under the statute.

priate sentence for a person who has been convicted of a crime is the routine work of judges. By reason of this experience, as well as their training, judges presumably perform this function well. But, precisely because the death penalty is unique, the normal presumption that a judge is the appropriate sentencing authority does not apply in the capital context. The decision whether or not an individual must die is not one that has traditionally been entrusted to judges. This tradition, which has marked a sharp distinction between the usual evaluations of judicial competence with respect to capital and noncapital sentencing, not only eliminates the general presumption that judicial sentencing is appropriate in the capital context, but also in itself provides reason to question whether assigning this role to governmental officials and not juries is consistent with the community's moral sense.[17]

* * *

VI

The authors of our federal and state constitutional guarantees uniformly recognized the special function of the jury in any exercise of plenary power over the life and liberty of the citizen. In our jurisprudence, the jury has always played an essential role in legitimating the system of criminal justice.

"The guarantees of jury trial in the Federal and State Constitutions reflect a profound judgment about the way in which law should be enforced and justice administered. A right to jury trial is granted to criminal defendants in order to prevent oppression by the Government. Those who wrote our constitutions knew from history and experience that it was necessary to protect against unfounded criminal charges brought to eliminate enemies and against judges too responsive to the voice of higher authority. The framers of the constitutions strove to create an independent judiciary but insisted upon further protection against arbitrary action. Providing an accused with the right to be tried by a jury of his peers gave him an inestimable safeguard against the corrupt or overzealous prosecutor and against the compliant, biased, or eccentric judge. If the defendant preferred the common-sense judgment of a jury to the more tutored but perhaps less sympathetic reaction of the single judge, he was to

---

17. In *Proffitt*, the joint opinion stated: "[I]t would appear that judicial sentencing should lead, if anything, to even greater consistency in the imposition at the trial court level of capital punishment, since a trial judge is more experienced in sentencing than a jury, and is therefore better able to impose sentences similar to those imposed in analogous cases." Of course, since Proffitt was not challenging judicial sentencing in that case, this statement was directed only at the risk of arbitrariness that had been identified by the plurality in *Furman*, and was not concerned with the claim made here that jury sentencing is more consistent with community values. Moreover, experience under the Florida statute indicates that this prediction concerning judicial sentencing has not been borne out. Not only has the Florida Supreme Court proved much more likely to reverse in a jury override case than in any other type of capital case, but also the clear majority of override cases ultimately result in sentences of life imprisonment rather than death. Thus, it is doubtful that judicial sentencing has worked to reduce the level of capital sentencing disparity; if anything, the evidence in override cases suggests that the jury reaches the appropriate result more often than does the judge.

have it. Beyond this, the jury trial provisions in the Federal and State Constitutions reflect a fundamental decision about the exercise of official power—a reluctance to entrust plenary powers over the life and liberty of the citizen to one judge or to a group of judges. Fear of unchecked power, so typical of our State and Federal Governments in other respects, found expression in the criminal law in this insistence upon community participation in the determination of guilt or innocence." *Duncan v. Louisiana*, 391 U.S. 145, 88 S.Ct. 1444 (1968).

Thus, the jury serves to ensure that the criminal process is not subject to the unchecked assertion of arbitrary governmental power; community participation is "critical to public confidence in the fairness of the criminal justice system." *Taylor v. Louisiana*, 419 U.S. 522, 95 S.Ct. 692 (1975).

The same consideration that supports a constitutional entitlement to a trial by a jury rather than a judge at the guilt or innocence stage—the right to have an authentic representative of the community apply its lay perspective to the determination that must precede a deprivation of liberty—applies with special force to the determination that must precede a deprivation of life. In many respects capital sentencing resembles a trial on the question of guilt, involving as it does a prescribed burden of proof of given elements through the adversarial process. But more important than its procedural aspects, the life-or-death decision in capital cases depends upon its link to community values for its moral and constitutional legitimacy. In *Witherspoon v. Illinois*, 391 U.S. 510, 88 S.Ct. 1770 (1968), after observing that "a jury that must choose between life imprisonment and capital punishment can do little more—and must do nothing less—than express the conscience of the community on the ultimate question of life or death," the Court added:

"[O]ne of the most important functions any jury can perform in making such a selection is to maintain a link between contemporary community values and the penal system—a line without which the determination of punishment could hardly reflect 'the evolving standards of decency that mark the progress of a maturing society.'" (quoting *Trop v. Dulles*, 356 U.S. 86, 78 S.Ct. 590 (1958) (plurality opinion)).

* * *

That the jury provides a better link to community values than does a single judge is supported not only by our cases, but also by common sense. Juries—comprised as they are of a fair cross section of the community—are more representative institutions than is the judiciary; they reflect more accurately the composition and experiences of the community as a whole, and inevitably make decisions based on community values more reliably, than can that segment of the community that is selected for service on the bench. Indeed, as the preceding discussion demonstrates, the belief that juries more accurately reflect the conscience of the community than can a single judge is the central reason that the jury right has been recognized at the guilt stage in our jurisprudence. This same belief firmly supports the use of juries in capital sentencing, in order to address the Eighth Amendment's concern that capital punishment be administered consistently with community values. In fact, the available empirical evidence indicates that judges and juries do make sentencing decisions in capital cases in significantly different ways,[34] thus supporting the conclusion that entrusting the capital decision to a single judge creates an unacceptable risk that the decision will not be consistent with community values.

* * *

VIII

History, tradition, and the basic structure and purpose of the jury system persuade me that jury sentencing is essential if the administration of capital punishment is to be governed by the community's evolving standards of decency. The constitutional legitimacy of capital punishment depends upon the extent to which the process is able to produce results which reflect the community's moral sensibilities. Judges simply cannot acceptably mirror those sensibilities—the very notion of a right to jury trial is premised on that realization. Judicial sentencing in capital cases cannot provide the type of community participation in the process upon which its legitimacy depends.

If the State wishes to execute a citizen, it must persuade a jury of his peers that death is an appropriate punishment for his offense. If it cannot do so, then I do not believe it can be said with an acceptable degree of assurance that imposition of the death penalty would be consistent with the community's sense of proportionality. Thus, in this case Florida has authorized the imposition of disproportionate punishment in violation of the Eighth and Fourteenth Amendments. * * *

---

34. A respected study of the matter found that judges and juries disagree as to the imposition of the death penalty in 59 percent of the cases, with juries being much more likely to show mercy than judges. See H. Zeisel, Some Data on Juror Attitudes Toward Capital Punishment (1968). This study must be viewed with some caution, because it was based on pre-*Furman* sentencing, when juries were given no guidance concerning the standards for decision. But then there were no standards for judges to follow either, and the wide disparity between judge and jury sentencing in an era in which all the sentencer could do was express its sense of proportionality suggests that judicial sentencing does not reflect the same moral sensibility as does jury sentencing. That there has been such a large number of jury overrides under the Florida statute tends to indicate that the disparity between judge and jury has continued in the post-*Furman* era. Indeed, the facts of this very case illustrate the point. While the crime for which petitioner was convicted was quite horrible, the case against him was rather weak, resting as it did on the largely uncorroborated testimony of a drug addict who said that petitioner had bragged to him of having killed a number of women, and had led him to the victim's body. It may well be that the jury was sufficiently convinced of petitioner's guilt to convict him, but nevertheless also sufficiently troubled by the possibility that an irrevocable mistake might be made, coupled with evidence indicating that petitioner had suffered serious head injuries when he was 20 years old which had induced a personality change, that the jury concluded that a sentence of death could not be morally justified in this case. A judge trained to distinguish proof of guilt from questions concerning sentencing might react quite differently to this case than would a jury.

NOTES

1. *Subsequent developments.*

In 1995, nineteen years after Spaziano was first sentenced to death and eleven years after the Supreme Court's decision upholding his death sentence, Spaziano was saved from his fifth death warrant when the key witness against him recanted his story. After a six-day hearing to consider this new evidence, the state court judge accepted the recantation and overturned Spaziano's conviction. Rather than retry the case, the prosecutor entered into a plea bargain whereby Spaziano was permitted to change his plea to *nolo contendere* to a charge of second degree murder and was sentenced to 23 years in prison, the amount of time he had already served. Since Spaziano was serving a life sentence for another crime, he remained in prison, but he was released from solitary confinement and allowed to join the general prison population.

2. *Problem 9–2.*

Alabama law vests capital sentencing authority in the trial judge, but requires (without additional explanation) that the judge "consider" an advisory jury verdict. The state must prove statutory aggravating factors beyond a reasonable doubt and must disprove, by a preponderance of the evidence, any mitigating circumstance the defendant may proffer. At least 10 jurors must agree for an advisory verdict of death, while an advisory verdict of life imprisonment requires only a simple majority. Defendant was convicted of capital murder on evidence that she had conspired with her paramour to kill her husband for his $250,000 insurance policy and that the paramour had hired others who had killed the husband. At her sentencing hearing, Defendant called a number of witnesses who attested to her good background and strong character. She was rearing seven children, held three jobs simultaneously and participated actively in her church. The jury recommended (7–5) that she be imprisoned for life without parole. The trial judge sentenced Defendant to death, finding that the one aggravating circumstance (murder for pecuniary gain) far outweighed the statutory mitigating circumstance (no prior criminal record) and non-statutory mitigating circumstances (Defendant was a hard-working, respected member of her church and community).

In light of *Spaziano*, what arguments should be made on Defendant's appeal concerning the Alabama procedure? See *Harris v. Alabama*, 513 U.S. 504, 115 S.Ct. 1031 (1995).

3. *Elected judges and the death penalty.*

Thirty-nine states provide that some or all of their judges must be voted on, in competitive or retention elections, at some time in their careers.[a] In 30 of the 35 death penalty states, trial court judges must stand for election, and, in all but four of those states, the same is true of appellate judges.[b] In his dissent in *Harris v. Alabama*, 513 U.S. 504, 521, 115 S.Ct. 1031, 1040 (1995)

---

a. S. Zeidman, *To Elect or Not to Elect: A Case Study of Judicial Selection in New York City, 1977–2002*, 37 U.Mich. J. L. Reform 791 (2004). Judges are elected on a similar scale in no other constitutional democracy. S. Croley, *The Majoritarian Difficulty: Elective Judiciaries and the Rule of Law*, 62 U.Chi. L.Rev. 689, 690–691 (1995).

b. S. Bright & P. Keenan, *Judges and the Politics of Death: Deciding Between the Bill of Rights and the Next Election in Capital Cases*, 75 B.U. L. Rev. 759, 776–780 (1995).

[see Problem 9–2], Justice Stevens noted that there were substantially different results when judges, rather than juries, made the penalty decision in a capital case. He noted that Alabama judges vetoed only five jury recommendations of death, but overrode jury recommendations of life in order to impose the death penalty on 47 defendants. In Florida, judges overrode jury recommendations 134 times in order to impose the death penalty, but only 51 times to impose a life sentence. In Indiana, judges used overrides to impose eight death sentences, but only four life sentences. Justice Stevens attributed the difference to the fact that jurors, even those who support candidates who are "tough on crime," are not subject to the same political pressures as elected judges:

> I am convinced that our jury system provides reliable insulation against the passions of the polity. Voting for a political candidate who vows to be "tough on crime" differs vastly from voting at the conclusion of an actual trial to condemn a specific individual to death. Jurors' responsibilities terminate when their case ends; they answer only to their own consciences; they rarely have any concern about possible reprisals after their work is done. More importantly, they focus their attention on a particular case involving the fate of one fellow citizen, rather than on a generalized remedy for a global category of faceless violent criminals who, in the abstract, may appear unworthy of life.

513 U.S. at 518, 115 S.Ct. at 1039. He decried the "political climate in which judges who covet higher office—or who merely wish to remain judges—must constantly profess their fealty to the death penalty.... The danger that they will bend to political pressures when pronouncing sentence in highly publicized capital cases is the same danger confronted by judges beholden to King George III." 513 U.S. at 519–520, 115 S.Ct. at 1039 (1995).

The political pressures which concerned Justice Stevens have been manifested in a number of death penalty states. Perhaps the most dramatic example occurred in California, the state with the largest death row in the country. In 1986, in the retention election for four justices of the Supreme Court, the governor spearheaded a successful campaign to remove Chief Justice Rose Bird and two associate justices because of their votes in capital cases.[c] The Bird court had affirmed death sentences in fewer than 10% of the cases to come before the court. The newly reconstituted court, in its first five years, had an affirmance rate of nearly 97%.[d] Similar successful campaigns to remove appellate judges based on their votes in death penalty cases have been waged in Mississippi, Texas and other states.[e] A judge's actions in death penalty cases and views on the death penalty are staples of election campaigns at the trial court level.

RING v. ARIZONA
536 U.S. 584, 122 S.Ct. 2428, 153 L.Ed.2d 556 (2002).

JUSTICE GINSBURG delivered the opinion of the Court.

This case concerns the Sixth Amendment right to a jury trial in capital prosecutions. In Arizona, following a jury adjudication of a defen-

---
c. *Id.* at 760–761.
d. *Id.* at 761.
e. *Id.* at 761–763.

dant's guilt of first-degree murder, the trial judge, sitting alone, determines the presence or absence of the aggravating factors required by Arizona law for imposition of the death penalty.

In *Walton v. Arizona*, 497 U.S. 639, 110 S.Ct. 3047 (1990), this Court held that Arizona's sentencing scheme was compatible with the Sixth Amendment because the additional facts found by the judge qualified as sentencing considerations, not as "element[s] of the offense of capital murder." Ten years later, however, we decided *Apprendi v. New Jersey*, 530 U.S. 466, 120 S.Ct. 2348 (2000), which held that the Sixth Amendment does not permit a defendant to be "expose[d] ... to a penalty *exceeding* the maximum he would receive if punished according to the facts reflected in the jury verdict alone." This prescription governs, *Apprendi* determined, even if the State characterizes the additional findings made by the judge as "sentencing factor[s]."

Apprendi's reasoning is irreconcilable with *Walton*'s holding in this regard, and today we overrule *Walton* in relevant part. Capital defendants, no less than non-capital defendants, we conclude, are entitled to a jury determination of any fact on which the legislature conditions an increase in their maximum punishment.

I

[The evidence at trial established that Timothy Ring was involved with James Greenham and William Ferguson in the armed robbery and murder of an armored van driver, John Magoch. On the murder charge, the trial judge instructed the jury on the alternate theories of premeditated murder and felony-murder occurring in the course of an armed robbery. Under Arizona law, a person is guilty of felony-murder if "the person commits or attempts to commit ... [one of several enumerated felonies] ... and in the course of and in furtherance of the offense or immediate flight from the offense, the person or another person causes the death of any person." Felony-murder "requires no specific mental state other than what is required for the commission of any of the enumerated felonies." The jury deadlocked on premeditated murder, but convicted Ring of felony-murder. In the view of the Arizona Supreme Court, "the evidence admitted at trial failed to prove, beyond a reasonable doubt, that [Ring] was a major participant in the armed robbery" or even that he was on the scene of the robbery.]

Under Arizona law, Ring could not be sentenced to death, the statutory maximum penalty for first-degree murder, unless further findings were made. The State's first-degree murder statute prescribes that the offense "is punishable by death or life imprisonment as provided by § 13–703." The cross-referenced section, § 13–703, directs the judge who presided at trial to "conduct a separate sentencing hearing to determine the existence or nonexistence of [certain enumerated] circumstances ... for the purpose of determining the sentence to be imposed." The statute further instructs:

"The hearing shall be conducted before the court alone. The court alone shall make all factual determinations required by this section or the constitution of the United States or this state."

At the conclusion of the sentencing hearing, the judge is to determine the presence or absence of the enumerated "aggravating circumstances" and any "mitigating circumstances." The State's law authorizes the judge to sentence the defendant to death only if there is at least one aggravating circumstance and "there are no mitigating circumstances sufficiently substantial to call for leniency."

[At the sentencing hearing, Greenham, who had entered into a plea agreement whereby he was permitted to plead guilty to second-degree murder and armed robbery in return for his cooperation with the prosecution in the cases against Ring and Ferguson, testified that Ring had been the leader in planning the robbery and that Ring had been the one to kill the Magoch. On cross-examination, Greenham admitted that he had "previously told Ring's counsel that Ring had nothing to do with the planning or execution of the robbery" and that his testimony against Ring was "pay back" for threats made by Ring and for Ring's interference in Greenham's relationship with Greenham's ex-wife. Relying on Greenham's testimony, the trial judge found that Ring's role in the killing satisfied the *Enmund/Tison* requirements for imposition of the death penalty because he was " 'the one who shot and killed Mr. Magoch' " and because "Ring was a major participant in the robbery."]

The judge then turned to the determination of aggravating and mitigating circumstances. He found two aggravating factors. First, the judge determined that Ring committed the offense in expectation of receiving something of "pecuniary value," as described in § 13–703; "[t]aking the cash from the armored car was the motive and reason for Mr. Magoch's murder and not just the result." Second, the judge found that the offense was committed "in an especially heinous, cruel or depraved manner." In support of this finding, he cited Ring's comment, as reported by Greenham at the sentencing hearing, expressing pride in his marksmanship. The judge found one nonstatutory mitigating factor: Ring's "minimal" criminal record. In his judgment, that mitigating circumstance did not "call for leniency"; he therefore sentenced Ring to death.

On appeal, Ring argued that Arizona's capital sentencing scheme violates the Sixth and Fourteenth Amendments to the U.S. Constitution because it entrusts to a judge the finding of a fact raising the defendant's maximum penalty. See *Jones v. United States*, 526 U.S. 227, 119 S.Ct. 1215 (1999); *Apprendi v. New Jersey*, 530 U.S. 466, 120 S.Ct. 2348 (2000). The State, in response, noted that this Court had upheld Arizona's system in *Walton v. Arizona*, 497 U.S. 639, 110 S.Ct. 3047 (1990), and had stated in *Apprendi* that *Walton* remained good law.

[The Arizona Supreme Court acknowledged that *Apprendi* and *Jones* "raise some question about the continued viability of *Walton*," particularly since the *Apprendi* majority, in attempting to distinguish *Walton*, had misdescribed the Arizona scheme as one where the judge determined and weighed aggravating circumstances "after a jury verdict holding a defendant guilty of a capital crime." Nevertheless, finding itself bound to follow *Walton*, the court rejected Ring's challenge to the Arizona scheme. Although the court found insufficient evidence to support the "depravity" aggravating circumstance, it upheld Ring's death sentence on the basis of the "pecuniary gain" aggravating circumstance.]

We granted Ring's petition for a writ of certiorari, to allay uncertainty in the lower courts caused by the manifest tension between *Walton* and the reasoning of *Apprendi*. We now reverse the judgment of the Arizona Supreme Court.

II

Based solely on the jury's verdict finding Ring guilty of first-degree felony murder, the maximum punishment he could have received was life imprisonment. This was so because, in Arizona, a "death sentence may not legally be imposed . . . unless at least one aggravating factor is found to exist beyond a reasonable doubt." The question presented is whether that aggravating factor may be found by the judge, as Arizona law specifies, or whether the Sixth Amendment's jury trial guarantee, made applicable to the States by the Fourteenth Amendment, requires that the aggravating factor determination be entrusted to the jury.[4]

As earlier indicated, this is not the first time we have considered the constitutionality of Arizona's capital sentencing system. In *Walton v. Arizona*, 497 U.S. 639, 110 S.Ct. 3047 (1990), we upheld Arizona's scheme against a charge that it violated the Sixth Amendment. The Court had previously denied a Sixth Amendment challenge to Florida's capital sentencing system, in which the jury recommends a sentence but makes no explicit findings on aggravating circumstances; we so ruled, *Walton* noted, on the ground that "the Sixth Amendment does not require that the specific findings authorizing the imposition of the sentence of death be made by the jury." *Walton* found unavailing the attempts by the defendant-petitioner in that case to distinguish Florida's capital sentencing

---

4. Ring's claim is tightly delineated: He contends only that the Sixth Amendment required jury findings on the aggravating circumstances asserted against him. No aggravating circumstance related to past convictions in his case; Ring therefore does not challenge *Almendarez–Torres v. United States*, 523 U.S. 224, 118 S.Ct. 1219 (1998), which held that the fact of prior conviction may be found by the judge even if it increases the statutory maximum sentence. He makes no Sixth Amendment claim with respect to mitigating circumstances. See *Apprendi v. New Jersey*, 530 U.S. 466, 120 S.Ct. 2348 (2000) (noting "the distinction the Court has often recognized between facts in aggravation of punishment and facts in mitigation" (citation omitted)). Nor does he argue that the Sixth Amendment required the jury to make the ultimate determination whether to impose the death penalty. See *Proffitt v. Florida*, 428 U.S. 242, 96 S.Ct. 2960 (1976) (plurality opinion) ("[I]t has never [been] suggested that jury sentencing is constitutionally required."). He does not question the Arizona Supreme Court's authority to reweigh the aggravating and mitigating circumstances after that court struck one aggravator. See *Clemons v. Mississippi*, 494 U.S. 738, 110 S.Ct. 1441 (1990). Finally, Ring does not contend that his indictment was constitutionally defective. See *Apprendi* (Fourteenth Amendment "has not . . . been construed to include the Fifth Amendment right to 'presentment or indictment of a Grand Jury' ").

system from Arizona's. In neither State, according to *Walton*, were the aggravating factors "elements of the offense"; in both States, they ranked as "sentencing considerations" guiding the choice between life and death.

Walton drew support from *Cabana v. Bullock*, 474 U.S. 376, 106 S.Ct. 689 (1986), in which the Court held there was no constitutional bar to an appellate court's finding that a defendant killed, attempted to kill, or intended to kill, as *Enmund v. Florida,* 458 U.S. 782, 102 S.Ct. 3368 (1982), required for imposition of the death penalty in felony-murder cases. The *Enmund* finding could be made by a court, *Walton* maintained, because it entailed no "element of the crime of capital murder"; it "only place[d] a substantive limitation on sentencing." "If the Constitution does not require that the *Enmund* finding be proved as an element of the offense of capital murder, and does not require a jury to make that finding," *Walton* stated, "we cannot conclude that a State is required to denominate aggravating circumstances 'elements' of the offense or permit only a jury to determine the existence of such circumstances."

In dissent in *Walton*, Justice STEVENS urged that the Sixth Amendment requires "a jury determination of facts that must be established before the death penalty may be imposed." Aggravators "operate as statutory 'elements' of capital murder under Arizona law," he reasoned, "because in their absence, [the death] sentence is unavailable." "If th[e] question had been posed in 1791, when the Sixth Amendment became law," Justice STEVENS said, "the answer would have been clear," for "[b]y that time, the English jury's role in determining critical facts in homicide cases was entrenched. As fact-finder, the jury had the power to determine not only whether the defendant was guilty of homicide but also the degree of the offense. Moreover, *the jury's role in finding facts that would determine a homicide defendant's eligibility for capital punishment was particularly well established.* Throughout its history, the jury determined which homicide defendants would be subject to capital punishment by making factual determinations, many of which related to difficult assessments of the defendant's state of mind. By the time the Bill of Rights was adopted, the jury's right to make these determinations was unquestioned."

[In *Jones v. United States*, 526 U.S. 227, 119 S.Ct. 1215 (1999), the Court construed the federal carjacking statute, which provided for three different maximum penalties depending on whether the crime resulted in (1) no serious bodily injury; (2) serious bodily injury; or (3) death. The Court held that the defendant was entitled to a jury trial on "the facts— causation of serious bodily injury or death—necessary to trigger the escalating maximum penalties." The Court distinguished *Walton* by characterizing the finding of aggravating facts "as a choice between a greater and a lesser penalty, not as a process of raising the ceiling of the sentencing range available." A year later, in *Apprendi v. New Jersey,* 530 U.S. 466, 120 S.Ct. 2348 (2000), the Court considered the defendant's challenge to a "hate crime enhancement" to his possession of a firearm conviction. The enhancement was found by a judge under a preponderance of the evidence standard and resulted in the defendant receiving a sentence two years longer than the maximum possible sentence under the firearm conviction. The Court held Apprendi's right to a jury trial was violated. "If a State makes an increase in a defendant's authorized punishment contingent on the finding of a fact, that fact—no matter how the State labels it—must be found by a jury beyond a reasonable doubt. A defendant may not be expose[d] ... to a penalty *exceeding* the maximum he would receive if punished according to the facts reflected in the jury verdict alone." The Court again distinguished *Walton*, finding that "[O]nce a jury has found the defendant guilty of all the elements of an offense which carries as its maximum penalty the sentence of death, it may be left to the judge to decide whether that maximum penalty, rather than a lesser one, ought to be imposed."]

In an effort to reconcile its capital sentencing system with the Sixth Amendment as interpreted by *Apprendi*, Arizona first restates the *Apprendi* majority's portrayal of Arizona's system: Ring was convicted of first-degree murder, for which Arizona law specifies "death or life imprisonment" as the only sentencing options; Ring was therefore sentenced within the range of punishment authorized by the jury verdict. This argument overlooks *Apprendi*'s instruction that "the relevant inquiry is one not of form, but of effect." In effect, "the required finding [of an aggravated circumstance] expose[d] [Ring] to a greater punishment than that authorized by the jury's guilty verdict." The Arizona first-degree murder statute "authorizes a maximum penalty of death only in a formal sense," *Apprendi* (O'CONNOR, J., dissenting), for it explicitly cross-references the statutory provision requiring the finding of an aggravating circumstance before imposition of the death penalty. If Arizona prevailed on its opening argument, *Apprendi* would be reduced to a "meaningless and formalistic" rule of statutory drafting. (O'CONNOR, J., dissenting).

Arizona also supports the distinction relied upon in *Walton* between elements of an offense and sentencing factors. As to elevation of the maximum punishment, however, *Apprendi* renders the argument untenable;[5] *Apprendi* repeatedly instructs in that context that the characterization of a fact or circumstance as an "element" or a "sentencing factor" is not determinative of the question "who decides," judge or jury.

Even if facts increasing punishment beyond the maximum authorized by a guilty verdict standing alone ordinarily must be found by a jury, Arizona further urges, aggravating circumstances necessary to trigger a death sentence may nonetheless be reserved for judicial determination. As Arizona's counsel maintained at oral argument, there is no doubt that "[d]eath is different." States have constructed elaborate sentencing procedures in death cases, Arizona emphasizes, because of constraints we have said the Eighth Amendment places on capital sentencing.

---

5. In *Harris v. United States*, 536 U.S. 545, 122 S.Ct. 2406 (2002), a majority of the Court concludes that the distinction between elements and sentencing factors continues to be meaningful as to facts increasing the minimum sentence.

Apart from the Eighth Amendment provenance of aggravating factors, Arizona presents "no specific reason for excepting capital defendants from the constitutional protections ... extend[ed] to defendants generally, and none is readily apparent." *Apprendi* (O'CONNOR, J., dissenting). The notion "that the Eighth Amendment's restriction on a state legislature's ability to define capital crimes should be compensated for by permitting States more leeway under the Fifth and Sixth Amendments in proving an aggravating fact necessary to a capital sentence ... is without precedent in our constitutional jurisprudence." *Ibid.*

* * *

Arizona suggests that judicial authority over the finding of aggravating factors "may ... be a better way to guarantee against the arbitrary imposition of the death penalty." The Sixth Amendment jury trial right, however, does not turn on the relative rationality, fairness, or efficiency of potential factfinders. Entrusting to a judge the finding of facts necessary to support a death sentence might be "an admirably fair and efficient scheme of criminal justice designed for a society that is prepared to leave criminal justice to the State.... The founders of the American Republic were not prepared to leave it to the State, which is why the jury-trial guarantee was one of the least controversial provisions of the Bill of Rights. It has never been efficient; but it has always been free." *Apprendi* (SCALIA, J., concurring).

In any event, the superiority of judicial factfinding in capital cases is far from evident. Unlike Arizona, the great majority of States responded to this Court's Eighth Amendment decisions requiring the presence of aggravating circumstances in capital cases by entrusting those determinations to the jury.[6]

Although " 'the doctrine of *stare decisis* is of fundamental importance to the rule of law[,]' ... [o]ur precedents are not sacrosanct." *Patterson v. McLean Credit Union,* 491 U.S. 164, 109 S.Ct. 2363 (1989). "[W]e have overruled prior decisions where the necessity and propriety of doing so has been established." We are satisfied that this is such a case.

For the reasons stated, we hold that *Walton* and *Apprendi* are irreconcilable; our Sixth Amendment jurisprudence cannot be home to both. Accordingly, we overrule *Walton* to the extent that it allows a sentencing judge, sitting without a jury, to find an aggravating circumstance necessary for imposition of the death penalty. Because Arizona's enumerated aggravating factors operate as "the functional equivalent of an element of a greater offense," *Apprendi*, the Sixth Amendment requires that they be found by a jury.

* * *

---

6. Of the 38 States with capital punishment, 29 generally commit sentencing decisions to juries. Other than Arizona, only four States [Colorado, Idaho, Montana, Nebraska] commit both capital sentencing factfinding and the ultimate sentencing decision entirely to judges. Four States [Alabama, Delaware, Florida, Indiana] have hybrid systems, in which the jury renders an advisory verdict but the judge makes the ultimate sentencing determinations.

"The guarantees of jury trial in the Federal and State Constitutions reflect a profound judgment about the way in which law should be enforced and justice administered.... If the defendant preferred the common-sense judgment of a jury to the more tutored but perhaps less sympathetic reaction of the single judge, he was to have it." *Duncan v. Louisiana,* 391 U.S. 145, 155–156, 88 S.Ct. 1444 (1968).

The right to trial by jury guaranteed by the Sixth Amendment would be senselessly diminished if it encompassed the factfinding necessary to increase a defendant's sentence by two years, but not the factfinding necessary to put him to death. We hold that the Sixth Amendment applies to both. The judgment of the Arizona Supreme Court is therefore reversed, and the case is remanded for further proceedings not inconsistent with this opinion.[7]

JUSTICE SCALIA, with whom JUSTICE THOMAS joins, concurring.

The question whether *Walton v. Arizona,* 497 U.S. 639, 110 S.Ct. 3047 (1990), survives our decision in *Apprendi v. New Jersey,* 530 U.S. 466, 120 S.Ct. 2348 (2000), confronts me with a difficult choice. What compelled Arizona (and many other States) to specify particular "aggravating factors" that must be found before the death penalty can be imposed was the line of this Court's cases beginning with *Furman v. Georgia,* 408 U.S. 238, 92 S.Ct. 2726 (1972) (*per curiam*). In my view, that line of decisions had no proper foundation in the Constitution. *Walton* ("'[T]he prohibition of the Eighth Amendment relates to the character of the punishment, and not to the process by which it is imposed'" (quoting *Gardner v. Florida,* 430 U.S. 349, 97 S.Ct. 1197 (1977) (REHNQUIST, J., dissenting))). I am therefore reluctant to magnify the burdens that our *Furman* jurisprudence imposes on the States. Better for the Court to have invented an evidentiary requirement that a judge can find by a preponderance of the evidence, than to invent one that a unanimous jury must find beyond a reasonable doubt.

On the other hand, as I wrote in my dissent in *Almendarez–Torres v. United States,* 523 U.S. 224, 118 S.Ct. 1219 (1998), and as I reaffirmed by joining the opinion for the Court in *Apprendi,* I believe that the fundamental meaning of the jury-trial guarantee of the Sixth Amendment is that all facts essential to imposition of the level of punishment that the defendant receives—whether the statute calls them elements of the offense, sentencing factors, or Mary Jane—must be found by the jury beyond a reasonable doubt.

The quandary is apparent: Should I continue to apply the last-stated principle when I know that the only reason the fact *is* essential is that this Court has mistakenly said that the Constitution *requires* state law to impose such "aggravating factors"? In *Walton,* to tell the truth, the Sixth Amendment claim was not put with the clarity it obtained in *Almendarez–Torres* and *Apprendi.* There what the appellant argued had to be found by

---

7. We do not reach the State's assertion that any error was harmless because a pecuniary gain finding was implicit in the jury's guilty verdict.

the jury was not all facts essential to imposition of the death penalty, but rather "*every* finding of fact underlying the sentencing decision," including not only the aggravating factors without which the penalty could not be imposed, but also the *mitigating* factors that might induce a sentencer to give a lesser punishment. (emphasis added). But even if the point had been put with greater clarity in *Walton*, I think I still would have approved the Arizona scheme—I would have favored the States' freedom to develop their own capital sentencing procedures (already erroneously abridged by *Furman*) over the logic of the *Apprendi* principle.

Since *Walton*, I have acquired new wisdom that consists of two realizations—or, to put it more critically, have discarded old ignorance that consisted of the failure to realize two things: First, that it is impossible to identify with certainty those aggravating factors whose adoption has been wrongfully coerced by *Furman,* as opposed to those that the State would have adopted in any event. Some States, for example, already had aggravating-factor requirements for capital murder when *Furman* was decided. When such a State has added aggravating factors, are the new ones the *Apprendi*-exempt product of *Furman*, and the old ones not? And even as to those States that did not previously have aggravating-factor requirements, who is to say that their adoption of a new one today—or, for that matter, even their retention of old ones adopted immediately post-*Furman*—is still the product of that case, and not of a changed social belief that murder *simpliciter* does not deserve death?

Second, and more important, my observing over the past 12 years the accelerating propensity of both state and federal legislatures to adopt "sentencing factors" determined by judges that increase punishment beyond what is authorized by the jury's verdict, and my witnessing the belief of a near majority of my colleagues that this novel practice is perfectly OK, see *Apprendi* (O'CONNOR, J., dissenting), cause me to believe that our people's traditional belief in the right of trial by jury is in perilous decline. That decline is bound to be confirmed, and indeed accelerated, by the repeated spectacle of a man's going to his death because *a judge* found that an aggravating factor existed. We cannot preserve our veneration for the protection of the jury in criminal cases if we render ourselves callous to the need for that protection by regularly imposing the death penalty without it.

Accordingly, *whether or not* the States have been erroneously coerced into the adoption of "aggravating factors," wherever those factors exist they must be subject to the usual requirements of the common law, and to the requirement enshrined in our Constitution, in criminal cases: they must be found by the jury beyond a reasonable doubt.

I add one further point, lest the holding of today's decision be confused by the separate concurrence. Justice BREYER, who refuses to accept *Apprendi* (BREYER, J., dissenting), nonetheless concurs in today's judgment because he "believe[s] that jury sentencing in capital cases is mandated by the Eighth Amendment." While I am, as always, pleased to travel in Justice BREYER's company, the unfortunate fact is that today's judgment has nothing to do with jury sentencing. What today's decision says is that the jury must find the existence of the *fact* that an aggravating factor existed. Those States that leave the ultimate life-or-death decision to the judge may continue to do so—by requiring a prior jury finding of aggravating factor in the sentencing phase or, more simply, by placing the aggravating-factor determination (where it logically belongs anyway) in the guilt phase. There is really no way in which Justice BREYER can travel with the happy band that reaches today's result unless he says yes to *Apprendi*. Concisely put, Justice BREYER is on the wrong flight; he should either get off before the doors close, or buy a ticket to *Apprendi*-land.

JUSTICE KENNEDY, concurring.

Though it is still my view that *Apprendi v. New Jersey*, 530 U.S. 466, 120 S.Ct. 2348 (2000), was wrongly decided, *Apprendi* is now the law, and its holding must be implemented in a principled way. As the Court suggests, no principled reading of *Apprendi* would allow *Walton v. Arizona*, 497 U.S. 639, 110 S.Ct. 3047 (1990), to stand. It is beyond question that during the penalty phase of a first-degree murder prosecution in Arizona, the finding of an aggravating circumstance exposes "the defendant to a greater punishment than that authorized by the jury's guilty verdict." *Apprendi*. When a finding has this effect, *Apprendi* makes clear, it cannot be reserved for the judge.

This is not to say *Apprendi* should be extended without caution, for the States' settled expectations deserve our respect. A sound understanding of the Sixth Amendment will allow States to respond to the needs and realities of criminal justice administration, and *Apprendi* can be read as leaving in place many reforms designed to reduce unfairness in sentencing. I agree with the Court, however, that *Apprendi* and *Walton* cannot stand together as the law.

With these observations I join the opinion of the Court.

JUSTICE BREYER, concurring in the judgment.

I

Given my views in *Apprendi v. New Jersey*, 530 U.S. 466, 555, 120 S.Ct. 2348 (2000) (dissenting opinion), and *Harris v. United States*, 536 U.S. 545, 122 S.Ct. 2406 (2002) (BREYER, J., concurring in part and concurring in judgment), I cannot join the Court's opinion. I concur in the judgment, however, because I believe that jury sentencing in capital cases is mandated by the Eighth Amendment.

II

This Court has held that the Eighth Amendment requires States to apply special procedural safeguards when they seek the death penalty. *Gregg v. Georgia*, 428 U.S. 153, 96 S.Ct. 2909 (1976). Otherwise, the constitutional prohibition against "cruel and unusual punishments" would forbid its use. *Furman v. Georgia,* 408 U.S. 238, 92 S.Ct. 2726 (1972) (*per curiam*). Justice STEVENS has written that those safeguards include a requirement that a *jury* impose any sentence of death. *Harris v. Alabama,* 513 U.S. 504, 115 S.Ct. 1031 (1995) (dissenting opinion); *Spaziano v. Florida,* 468 U.S. 447, 104 S.Ct. 3154 (1984) (STEVENS, J., joined by BRENNAN and MARSHALL, JJ., concurring in part and dissenting in part). Although I joined the majority in *Harris v. Alabama,* I have come to agree with the dissenting view, and with the related views of others upon which it in part relies. Cf. *Henslee v. Union Planters Nat. Bank & Trust Co.,* 335 U.S. 595, 69 S.Ct. 290 (1949) (Frankfurter, J., dissenting) ("Wisdom too often never comes, and so one ought not to reject it merely because it comes late"). I therefore conclude that the Eighth Amendment requires that a jury, not a judge, make the decision to sentence a defendant to death.

I am convinced by the reasons that Justice STEVENS has given. These include (1) his belief that retribution provides the main justification for capital punishment, and (2) his assessment of the jury's comparative advantage in determining, in a particular case, whether capital punishment will serve that end.

As to the first, I note the continued difficulty of justifying capital punishment in terms of its ability to deter crime, to incapacitate offenders, or to rehabilitate criminals. Studies of deterrence are, at most, inconclusive. See, *e.g.,* Sorenson, Wrinkle, Brewer, & Marquart, Capital Punishment and Deterrence: Examining the Effect of Executions on Murder in Texas, 45 Crime & Delinquency 481 (1999) (no evidence of a deterrent effect); Bonner & Fessenden, Absence of Executions: A special report, States With No Death Penalty Share Lower Homicide Rates, N.Y. Times, Sept. 22, 2000, p. A1 (during last 20 years, homicide rate in death penalty States has been 48% to 101% higher than in non-death-penalty States); see also Radelet & Akers, Deterrence and the Death Penalty: The Views of the Experts, 87 J.Crim. L. & C. 1, 8 (1996) (over 80% of criminologists believe existing research fails to support deterrence justification).

As to incapacitation, few offenders sentenced to life without parole (as an alternative to death) commit further crimes. See, *e.g.,* Sorensen & Pilgrim, An Actuarial Risk Assessment of Violence Posed by Capital Murder Defendants, 90 J.Crim. L. & C. 1251 (2000) (studies find average repeat murder rate of .002% among murderers whose death sentences were commuted); Marquart & Sorensen, A National Study of the *Furman*–Commuted Inmates: Assessing the Threat to Society from Capital Offenders, 23 Loyola (LA) L.Rev. 5 (1989) (98% did not kill again either in prison or in free society). But see *Roberts v. Louisiana,* 428 U.S. 325, 96 S.Ct. 3001 (1976) (White, J., dissenting) ("[D]eath finally forecloses the possibility that a prisoner will commit further crimes, whereas life imprisonment does not"). And rehabilitation, obviously, is beside the point.

In respect to retribution, jurors possess an important comparative advantage over judges. In principle, they are more attuned to "the community's moral sensibility," *Spaziano* (STEVENS, J., concurring in part and dissenting in part), because they "reflect more accurately the composition and experiences of the community as a whole." Hence they are more likely to "express the conscience of the community on the ultimate question of life or death," *Witherspoon v. Illinois*, 391 U.S. 510, 88 S.Ct. 1770 (1968), and better able to determine in the particular case the need for retribution, namely, "an expression of the community's belief that certain crimes are themselves so grievous an affront to humanity that the only adequate response may be the penalty of death." *Gregg* (joint opinion of STEWART, POWELL, and STEVENS, JJ.).

* * *

JUSTICE O'CONNOR, with whom THE CHIEF JUSTICE joins, dissenting.

I understand why the Court holds that the reasoning of *Apprendi v. New Jersey*, 530 U.S. 466, 120 S.Ct. 2348 (2000), is irreconcilable with *Walton v. Arizona*, 497 U.S. 639, 110 S.Ct. 3047 (1990). Yet in choosing which to overrule, I would choose *Apprendi*, not *Walton*.

I continue to believe, for the reasons I articulated in my dissent in *Apprendi*, that the decision in *Apprendi* was a serious mistake. As I argued in that dissent, *Apprendi*'s rule that any fact that increases the maximum penalty must be treated as an element of the crime is not required by the Constitution, by history, or by our prior cases. Indeed, the rule directly contradicts several of our prior cases. And it ignores the "significant history in this country of ... discretionary sentencing by judges." *Id.* (O'CONNOR, J., dissenting). The Court has failed, both in *Apprendi* and in the decision announced today, to "offer any meaningful justification for deviating from years of cases both suggesting and holding that application of the 'increase in the maximum penalty' rule is not required by the Constitution."

Not only was the decision in *Apprendi* unjustified in my view, but it has also had a severely destabilizing effect on our criminal justice system. I predicted in my dissent that the decision would "unleash a flood of petitions by convicted defendants seeking to invalidate their sentences in whole or in part on the authority of [*Apprendi*]." As of May 31, 2002, less than two years after *Apprendi* was announced, the United States Courts of Appeals had decided approximately 1,802 criminal appeals in which defendants challenged their sentences, and in some cases even their convictions, under *Apprendi*. These federal appeals are likely only the tip of the iceberg, as federal criminal prosecutions represent a tiny fraction of the total number of criminal prosecutions nationwide. The number of second or successive habeas corpus petitions filed in the federal courts also increased by 77% in 2001, a phenomenon the Administrative Office of the United States Courts attributes to prisoners bringing *Apprendi* claims. This Court has been similarly overwhelmed by the aftershocks of *Apprendi*. A survey of the petitions for certiorari we received in the past year indicates that 18% raised *Apprendi*-related claims. It is simply beyond dispute that *Apprendi* threw countless criminal sentences into doubt and thereby caused an enormous increase in the workload of an already overburdened judiciary.

The decision today is only going to add to these already serious effects. The Court effectively declares five States' capital sentencing schemes unconstitutional. There are 168 prisoners on death row in these States, each of whom is now likely to challenge his or her death sentence. I believe many of these challenges will ultimately be unsuccessful, either because the prisoners will be unable to satisfy the standards of harmless error or plain error review, or because, having completed their direct appeals, they will be barred from taking advantage of today's holding on federal collateral review. Nonetheless, the need to evaluate these claims will greatly burden the courts in these five States. In addition, I fear that the prisoners on death row in Alabama, Delaware, Florida, and Indiana, which the Court identifies as having hybrid sentencing schemes in which the jury renders an advisory verdict but the judge makes the ultimate sentencing determination, may also seize on today's decision to challenge their sentences. There are 529 prisoners on death row in these States.

By expanding on *Apprendi.* the Court today exacerbates the harm done in that case. Consistent with my dissent, I would overrule *Apprendi* rather than *Walton*.

NOTES

1. *Problem 9–3.*

Under State's death penalty scheme, the jury, at the penalty phase, after hearing evidence regarding statutory aggravating and mitigating circumstances, is instructed as follows: (1) that they must first determine, whether one or more of the aggravating circumstances exists beyond a reasonable doubt; (2) that, if they find, beyond a reasonable doubt, that an aggravating circumstance exists, they must determine, by a preponderance of the evidence, whether one or more of the mitigating circumstances exists; and (3) that, if they find that one or more mitigating circumstances exists, they must determine, by a preponderance of the evidence, whether the aggravating circumstances outweigh the mitigating circumstances. All of the findings have to be unanimous and in writing. If the jury finds that the aggravating circumstances outweigh the mitigating circumstances, the sentence is death. Defendant was convicted of first degree murder and sentenced to death. What arguments should be made as to the constitutionality of the sentence? See *Oken v. State*, 835 A.2d 1105 (Md. 2003).

2. *Problem 9–4.*

Defendant was charged with capital murder based on his participation in a robbery during which his accomplice killed the victim. At trial, Defendant testified that he neither intended the killing, nor was aware that his accomplice intended the killing. Defendant was convicted and sentenced to death without any finding having been made by the jury that he acted with reckless indifference to human life. [See *Tison v. Arizona*, Chapter 5.] What are the arguments as to whether the state supreme court can affirm the sentence by itself making the requisite finding? See *Cabana v. Bullock*, 474 U.S. 376, 106 S.Ct. 689 (1986).

3. *Judge sentencing in capital cases.*

In his concurring opinion in *Ring v. Arizona*, Justice Breyer revived the argument, made by the dissenters in *Spaziano v. Florida*, that the Eighth Amendment requires that the defendant be afforded the right to jury sentencing in a capital case. In *Schriro v. Summerlin*, 542 U.S. 348, 124 S.Ct. 2519 (2004) [Chapter 11], he reiterated the argument, this time in an opinion joined by Justices Stevens, Souter and Ginsburg. Meanwhile, in the wake of *Ring*, four states that had employed judge sentencing in capital cases enacted legislation authorizing jury sentencing, leaving only five states (Alabama, Delaware, Florida, Montana and Nebraska) still requiring judge sentencing. Do these developments raise the possibility that the Court might at some point overrule *Spaziano*?

GARDNER v. FLORIDA

430 U.S. 349, 97 S.Ct. 1197, 51 L.Ed.2d 393 (1977).

MR. JUSTICE STEVENS announced the judgment of the Court and delivered an opinion, in which MR. JUSTICE STEWART and MR. JUSTICE POWELL joined.

Petitioner was convicted of first-degree murder and sentenced to death. When the trial judge imposed the death sentence he stated that he was relying in part on information in a presentence investigation report. Portions of the report were not disclosed to counsel for the parties. Without reviewing the confidential portion of the presentence report, the Supreme Court of Florida, over the dissent of two justices, affirmed the death sentence. We conclude that this procedure does not satisfy the constitutional command that no person shall be deprived of life without due process of law.

I

On June 30, 1973, the petitioner assaulted his wife with a blunt instrument, causing her death. On January 10, 1974, after a trial in the Circuit Court of Citrus County, Fla., a jury found him guilty of first-degree murder.

The separate sentencing hearing required by Florida law in capital cases was held later on the same day. The State merely introduced two photographs of the decedent, otherwise relying on the trial testimony. That testimony, if credited, was sufficient to support a finding of one of the statutory aggravating circumstances, that the felony committed by petitioner "was especially heinous, atrocious, or cruel."

In mitigation petitioner testified that he had consumed a vast quantity of alcohol during a day-long drinking spree which preceded the crime, and professed to have almost no recollection of the assault itself. His testimony, if credited, was sufficient to support a finding of at least one of the statutory mitigating circumstances.[3]

After hearing this evidence the jury was instructed to determine by a majority vote (1) whether the State had proved one of the aggravating circumstances defined by statute, (2) whether mitigating circumstances outweighed any such aggravating circumstance, and (3) based on that determination, whether the defendant should be sentenced to life or death.

After the jury retired to deliberate, the judge announced that he was going to order a presentence investigation of petitioner. Twenty-five minutes later the jury returned its advisory verdict. It expressly found that the mitigating circumstances outweighed the aggravating circumstances and advised the court to impose a life sentence.

The presentence investigation report was completed by the Florida Parole and Probation Commission on January 28, 1974. On January 30, 1974, the trial judge entered findings of fact and judgment sentencing petitioner to death. His ultimate finding was that the felony "was especially heinous, atrocious or cruel; and that such aggravating circumstances outweighs the mitigating circumstance, to-wit: none." As a preface to that ultimate finding, he recited that his conclusion was based on the evidence presented at both stages of the bifurcated proceeding, the arguments of counsel, and his review of "the factual information contained in said presentence investigation."

There is no dispute about the fact that the presentence investigation report contained a confidential portion which was not disclosed to defense counsel. Although the judge noted in his findings of fact that the State and petitioner's counsel had been given "a copy of that portion [of the report] to which they are entitled," counsel made no request to examine the full report or to be apprised of the contents of the confidential portion. The trial judge did not comment on the contents of the confidential portion. His findings do not indicate that there was anything of special importance in the undisclosed portion, or that there was any reason other than customary practice for not disclosing the entire report to the parties.

On appeal to the Florida Supreme Court, petitioner argued that the sentencing court had erred in considering the presentence investigation report, including the confidential portion, in making the decision to impose the death penalty. The per curiam opinion of the Supreme Court did not specifically discuss this contention, but merely recited the trial judge's finding, stated that the record had been carefully reviewed, and concluded that the conviction and sentence should be affirmed. The record

---

3. The statute provides, in part:

"(6) Mitigating circumstances.—Mitigating circumstances shall be the following:

"(b) The capital felony was committed while the defendant was under the influence of extreme mental or emotional disturbance.

"(f) The capacity of the defendant to appreciate the criminality of his conduct or to conform his conduct to the requirements of law was substantially impaired."

on appeal, however, did not include the confidential portion of the presentence report.

* * *

II

The State places its primary reliance on this Court's landmark decision in *Williams v. New York*, 337 U.S. 241, 69 S.Ct. 1079 (1949). In that case, as in this, the trial judge rejected the jury's commendation of mercy and imposed the death sentence in reliance, at least in part, on material contained in a report prepared by the court's probation department. The New York Court of Appeals had affirmed the sentence, rejecting the contention that it was a denial of due process to rely on information supplied by witnesses whom the accused could neither confront nor cross-examine.

This Court referred to appellant's claim as a "narrow contention" and characterized the case as one which

"presents a serious and difficult question ... relat[ing] to the rules of evidence applicable to the manner in which a judge may obtain information to guide him in the imposition of sentence upon an already convicted defendant."

The conviction and sentence were affirmed, over the dissent of two Justices.

* * *

III

In 1949, when the *Williams* case was decided, no significant constitutional difference between the death penalty and lesser punishments for crime had been expressly recognized by this Court. At that time the Court assumed that after a defendant was convicted of a capital offense, like any other offense, a trial judge had complete discretion to impose any sentence within the limits prescribed by the legislature. As long as the judge stayed within those limits, his sentencing discretion was essentially unreviewable and the possibility of error was remote, if, indeed, it existed at all. In the intervening years there have been two constitutional developments which require us to scrutinize a State's capital-sentencing procedures more closely than was necessary in 1949.

First, five Members of the Court have now expressly recognized that death is a different kind of punishment from any other which may be imposed in this country. *Gregg v. Georgia*, 428 U.S. 153, 96 S.Ct. 2909 (1976) (opinion of STEWART, POWELL, and STEVENS, JJ.); (MARSHALL, J., dissenting); *Furman v. Georgia*, 408 U.S. 238, 92 S.Ct. 2726 (1972) (BRENNAN, J., concurring), (STEWART, J., concurring); (MARSHALL, J., concurring). From the point of view of the defendant, it is different in both its severity and its finality. From the point of view of society, the action of the sovereign in taking the life of one of its citizens also differs dramatically from any other legitimate state action. It is of vital importance to the defendant and to the community that any decision to impose the death sentence be, and appear to be, based on reason rather than caprice or emotion.

Second, it is now clear that the sentencing process, as well as the trial itself, must satisfy the requirements of the Due Process Clause. Even though the defendant has no substantive right to a particular sentence within the range authorized by statute, the sentencing is a critical stage of the criminal proceeding at which he is entitled to the effective assistance of counsel. *Mempa v. Rhay*, 389 U.S. 128, 88 S.Ct. 254 (1967). The defendant has a legitimate interest in the character of the procedure which leads to the imposition of sentence even if he may have no right to object to a particular result of the sentencing process. See *Witherspoon v. Illinois*, 391 U.S. 510, 88 S.Ct. 1770 (1968).

In the light of these developments we consider the justifications offered by the State for a capital-sentencing procedure which permits a trial judge to impose the death sentence on the basis of confidential information which is not disclosed to the defendant or his counsel.

The State first argues that an assurance of confidentiality to potential sources of information is essential to enable investigators to obtain relevant but sensitive disclosures from persons unwilling to comment publicly about a defendant's background or character. The availability of such information, it is argued, provides the person who prepares the report with greater detail on which to base a sentencing recommendation and, in turn, provides the judge with a better basis for his sentencing decision. But consideration must be given to the quality, as well as the quantity, of the information on which the sentencing judge may rely. Assurances of secrecy are conducive to the transmission of confidences which may bear no closer relation to fact than the average rumor or item of gossip, and may imply a pledge not to attempt independent verification of the information received. The risk that some of the information accepted in confidence may be erroneous, or may be misinterpreted, by the investigator or by the sentencing judge, is manifest.

If, as the State argues, it is important to use such information in the sentencing process, we must assume that in some cases it will be decisive in the judge's choice between a life sentence and a death sentence. If it tends to tip the scales in favor of life, presumably the information would be favorable and there would be no reason why it should not be disclosed. On the other hand, if it is the basis for a death sentence, the interest in reliability plainly outweighs the State's interest in preserving the availability of comparable information in other cases.

The State also suggests that full disclosure of the presentence report will unnecessarily delay the proceeding. We think the likelihood of significant delay is overstated because we must presume that reports prepared by professional probation officers, as the Florida procedure requires, are generally reliable. In those cases in which the accuracy of a report is contested, the trial judge can avoid delay by disregarding the disputed material. Or if the disputed matter is of critical importance, the time invested in ascertaining the truth would surely be well spent if it makes the difference between life and death.

The State further urges that full disclosure of presentence reports, which often include psychiatric and psychological evaluations, will occasionally disrupt the process of rehabilitation. The argument, if valid, would hardly justify withholding the report from defense counsel. Moreover, whatever force that argument may have in noncapital cases, it has absolutely no merit in a case in which the judge has decided to sentence the defendant to death. Indeed, the extinction of all possibility of rehabilitation is one of the aspects of the death sentence that makes it different in kind from any other sentence a State may legitimately impose.

Finally, Florida argues that trial judges can be trusted to exercise their discretion in a responsible manner, even though they may base their decisions on secret information. However acceptable that argument might have been before *Furman v. Georgia*, it is now clearly foreclosed. Moreover, the argument rests on the erroneous premise that the participation of counsel is superfluous to the process of evaluating the relevance and significance of aggravating and mitigating facts. Our belief that debate between adversaries is often essential to the truth-seeking function of trials requires us also to recognize the importance of giving counsel an opportunity to comment on facts which may influence the sentencing decision in capital cases.

Even if it were permissible to withhold a portion of the report from a defendant, and even from defense counsel, pursuant to an express finding of good cause for nondisclosure, it would nevertheless be necessary to make the full report a part of the record to be reviewed on appeal. Since the State must administer its capital-sentencing procedures with an even hand, it is important that the record on appeal disclose to the reviewing court the considerations which motivated the death sentence in every case in which it is imposed. Without full disclosure of the basis for the death sentence, the Florida capital-sentencing procedure would be subject to the defects which resulted in the holding of unconstitutionality in *Furman v. Georgia*. In this particular case, the only explanation for the lack of disclosure is the failure of defense counsel to request access to the full report. That failure cannot justify the submission of a less complete record to the reviewing court than the record on which the trial judge based his decision to sentence petitioner to death.

* * *

We conclude that petitioner was denied due process of law when the death sentence was imposed, at least in part, on the basis of information which he had no opportunity to deny or explain.

IV

There remains only the question of what disposition is now proper. Petitioner's conviction, of course, is not tainted by the error in the sentencing procedure. The State argues that we should merely remand the case to the Florida, Supreme Court with directions to have the entire presentence report made a part of the record to enable that court to complete its reviewing function. That procedure, however, could not fully correct the error. For it is possible that full disclosure, followed by explanation or argument by defense counsel, would have caused the trial judge to accept the jury's advisory verdict. Accordingly, the death sentence is vacated, and the case is remanded to the Florida Supreme Court with directions to order further proceedings at the trial court level not inconsistent with this opinion.

THE CHIEF JUSTICE concurs in the judgment.

[JUSTICE WHITE, concurred in the judgment, relying solely on the Eighth Amendment rather than the due process clause.]

[Opinions of BLACKMUN, J., concurring, BRENNAN, J., concurring in part and dissenting in part, and MARSHALL, J., dissenting, omitted]

[JUSTICE REHNQUIST dissented, arguing that sentencing procedures of the kind used by Florida had never been found to violate due process and "[t]he prohibition of the Eighth Amendment relates to the character of the punishment, and not to the process by which it is imposed."]

NOTES

1. *Problem 9–5.*

Defendant was convicted of capital murder for aiding in the murder of a police officer who was killed by one of Defendant's companions during a traffic stop. At the sentencing hearing Prosecutor alleged three aggravating circumstances, including that Defendant had been "previously convicted of a felony involving the use or threat of violence to [a] person" (a circumstance proved by introduction of an authenticated copy of the order committing him to prison in another state for assault with intent to commit rape). During argument, Prosecutor repeatedly urged the jury to give weight to the prior conviction. The jury found all three aggravating circumstances and sentenced Defendant to death. While Defendant's appeal was pending, he obtained a new appeal and a reversal with regard to his assault conviction. What arguments should be made in his present appeal as to the validity of his death sentence? See *Johnson v. Mississippi*, 486 U.S. 578, 108 S.Ct. 1981 (1988).

2. *Problem 9–6.*

Defendant and Brother (Defendant's older brother) were charged with a double murder in connection with a robbery. At the arraignment, Judge informed Defendant that the punishment, if he was convicted, would be life imprisonment or death. Defendant's counsel entered into plea negotiations with Prosecutor, pursuant to which Defendant took two lie detector tests that convinced Prosecutor that Brother was primarily responsible for the crimes and was the actual killer of both victims. An agreement was reached whereby Defendant would plead guilty in return for an indeterminate sentence with a

10–year minimum. Judge refused to accept the plea, and Defendant was convicted at trial on both murder counts. Under state law, the convictions established at least one aggravating circumstance (multiple murder) and possibly others (*e.g.*, "heinous, atrocious or cruel" aggravating circumstance), and, therefore, Judge was required to sentence Defendant to death unless he found that mitigating circumstances outweighed the aggravating circumstances. The sentencing hearing was put off for six months until after the trial of Brother. In the interim, at Defendant's request, Judge entered an order requiring Prosecutor to notify Defendant whether he would seek the death penalty and, if so, on what aggravating circumstances he intended to rely. Prosecutor filed a response stating he would not be recommending the death penalty on either count. At the sentencing hearing, there was no discussion of the death penalty as a possible sentence. Prosecutor offered no evidence and recommended an indeterminate life sentence with a minimum of "somewhere between ten and 20 years." Defense counsel put on a number of witnesses who testified to Defendant's nonviolent character and his domination by Brother, and she asked the court to impose concurrent indeterminate life sentences, making him eligible for parole in ten years. At the conclusion of the hearing Judge found two aggravating circumstances and sentenced Defendant to death.

What arguments should be made as to the constitutionality of the sentence? See *Lankford v. Idaho*, 500 U.S. 110, 111 S.Ct. 1723 (1991).

B. EVIDENTIARY LIMITS

The three cases in this section concern the constitutionality of various state evidentiary rules applied at the penalty hearings. In *Green v. Georgia*, the defendant challenges the state's hearsay rule that barred him from introducing evidence that he was only an accomplice rather than the actual killer. In *Barefoot v. Estelle*, the defendant challenges the prosecution's use of psychiatric testimony to prove "future dangerousness." The subject of *Travels with Dr. Death* is Dr. James Grigson, one of the psychiatrists whose testimony was challenged in *Barefoot*, and the article describes Dr. Grigson's penalty phase testimony in three subsequent cases resulting in death verdicts. In *Payne v. Tennessee*, the defendant challenges the introduction of "victim impact" evidence. *Capital Jurors' Assessment of the Evidence* reports on empirical studies examining what evidence influences jurors' penalty decisions.

GREEN v. GEORGIA
442 U.S. 95, 99 S.Ct. 2150, 60 L.Ed.2d 738 (1979).

PER CURIAM.

Petitioner and Carzell Moore were indicted together for the rape and murder of Teresa Carol Allen. Moore was tried separately, was convicted of both crimes, and has been sentenced to death. Petitioner subsequently was convicted of murder, and also received a capital sentence. The Supreme Court of Georgia upheld the conviction and sentence, and petitioner has sought review of so much of the judgment as affirmed the capital sentence. We grant the motion for leave to proceed in forma pauperis and the petition for certiorari and vacate the sentence.

The evidence at trial tended to show that petitioner and Moore abducted Allen from the store where she was working alone and, acting either in concert or separately, raped and murdered her. After the jury determined that petitioner was guilty of murder, a second trial was held to decide whether capital punishment would be imposed. At this second proceeding, petitioner sought to prove he was not present when Allen was killed and had not participated in her death. He attempted to introduce the testimony of Thomas Pasby, who had testified for the State at Moore's trial. According to Pasby, Moore had confided to him that he had killed Allen, shooting her twice after ordering petitioner to run an errand. The trial court refused to allow introduction of this evidence, ruling that Pasby's testimony constituted hearsay that was inadmissible under Ga. Code § 38–301 (1978).[4] The State then argued to the jury that in the absence of direct evidence as to the circumstances of the crime, it could infer that petitioner participated directly in Allen's murder from the fact that more than one bullet was fired into her body.[5]

Regardless of whether the proffered testimony comes within Georgia's hearsay rule, under the facts of this case its exclusion constituted a violation of the Due Process Clause of the Fourteenth Amendment. The excluded testimony was highly relevant to a critical issue in the punishment phase of the trial, and substantial reasons existed to assume its reliability. Moore made his statement spontaneously to a close friend. The evidence corroborating the confession was ample, and indeed sufficient to procure a conviction of Moore and a capital sentence. The statement was against interest, and there was no reason to believe that Moore had any ulterior motive in making it. Perhaps most important, the State considered the testimony sufficiently reliable to use it against Moore, and to base a sentence of death upon it.[6] In these unique circumstances, "the hearsay rule may not be applied mechanistically to defeat the ends of justice." *Chambers v. Mississippi*, 410 U.S. 284, 93 S.Ct. 1038 (1973). Because the exclusion of Pasby's testimony denied petitioner a fair trial on the issue of

4. Georgia recognizes an exception to the hearsay rule for declarations against pecuniary interest, but not for declarations against penal interest.

5. The District Attorney stated to the jury:

"We couldn't possibly bring any evidence other than the circumstantial evidence and the direct evidence that we had pointing to who did it, and I think it's especially significant for you to remember what Dr. Dawson said in this case. When the first shot, in his medical opinion, he stated that Miss Allen had positive blood pressure when both shots were fired but I don't know whether Carzell Moore fired the first shot and handed the gun to Roosevelt Green and he fired the second shot or whether it was vice versa or whether Roosevelt Green had the gun and fired the shot or Carzell Moore had the gun and fired the first shot or the second, but I think it can be reasonably stated that you Ladies and Gentlemen can believe that each one of them fired the shots so that they would be as equally involved and one did not exceed the other's part in the commission of this crime."

6. A confession to a crime is not considered hearsay under Georgia law when admitted against a declarant.

punishment, the sentence is vacated and the case is remanded for further proceedings not inconsistent with this opinion.

MR. JUSTICE BRENNAN and MR. JUSTICE MARSHALL would vacate the death sentence without remanding for further proceedings.

MR. JUSTICE REHNQUIST, dissenting.

The Court today takes another step toward embalming the law of evidence in the Due Process Clause of the Fourteenth Amendment to the United States Constitution. I think it impossible to find any justification in the Constitution for today's ruling, and take comfort only from the fact that since this is a capital case, it is perhaps an example of the maxim that "hard cases make bad law."

　　　＊　＊　＊

Nothing in the United States Constitution gives this Court any authority to supersede a State's code of evidence because its application in a particular situation would defeat what this Court conceives to be "the ends of justice." The Court does not disagree that the testimony at issue is hearsay or that it fails to come within any of the exceptions to the hearsay rule provided by Georgia's rules of evidence. The Court obviously is troubled by the fact that the same testimony was admissible at the separate trial of petitioner's codefendant at the behest of the State. But this fact by no means demonstrates that the Georgia courts have not evenhandedly applied their code of evidence, with its various hearsay exceptions, so as to deny petitioner a fair trial. No practicing lawyer can have failed to note that Georgia's evidentiary rules, like those of every other State and of the United States, are such that certain items of evidence may be introduced by one party, but not by another. This is a fact of trial life, embodied throughout the hearsay rule and its exceptions. This being the case, the United States Constitution must be strained to or beyond the breaking point to conclude that all capital defendants who are unable to introduce all of the evidence which they seek to admit are denied a fair trial. I therefore dissent from the vacation of petitioner's sentence.

BAREFOOT v. ESTELLE

463 U.S. 880, 103 S.Ct. 3383, 77 L.Ed.2d 1090 (1983).

JUSTICE WHITE delivered the opinion of the Court.

　　　＊　＊　＊

On November 14, 1978, petitioner was convicted of the capital murder of a police officer in Bell County, Texas. A separate sentencing hearing before the same jury was then held to determine whether the death penalty should be imposed. Under Tex.Code Crim.Proc.Ann. § 37.071, two special questions were to be submitted to the jury: whether the conduct causing death was "committed deliberately and with reasonable expectation that the death of the deceased or another would result"; and whether "there is a probability that the defendant would commit criminal acts of violence that would constitute a continuing threat to society." The State introduced into evidence petitioner's prior convictions and his reputation for lawlessness. The State also called two psychiatrists, John Holbrook and James Grigson, who, in response to hypothetical questions, testified that petitioner would probably commit further acts of violence and represent a continuing threat to society. The jury answered both of the questions put to them in the affirmative, a result which required the imposition of the death penalty.

* * *

III

Petitioner's merits submission is that his death sentence must be set aside because the Constitution of the United States barred the testimony of the two psychiatrists who testified against him at the punishment hearing. There are several aspects to this claim. First, it is urged that psychiatrists, individually and as a group, are incompetent to predict with an acceptable degree of reliability that a particular criminal will commit other crimes in the future and so represent a danger to the community. Second, it is said that in any event, psychiatrists should not be permitted to testify about future dangerousness in response to hypothetical questions and without having examined the defendant personally. Third, it is argued that in the particular circumstances of this case, the testimony of the psychiatrists was so unreliable that the sentence should be set aside. As indicated below, we reject each of these arguments.

A

The suggestion that no psychiatrist's testimony may be presented with respect to a defendant's future dangerousness is somewhat like asking us to disinvent the wheel. In the first place, it is contrary to our cases. If the likelihood of a defendant committing further crimes is a constitutionally acceptable criterion for imposing the death penalty, which it is, *Jurek v. Texas*, 428 U.S. 262, 96 S.Ct. 2950 (1976), and if it is not impossible for even a lay person sensibly to arrive at that conclusion, it makes little sense, if any, to submit that psychiatrists, out of the entire universe of persons who might have an opinion on the issue, would know so little about the subject that they should not be permitted to testify. In *Jurek*, seven Justices rejected the claim that it was impossible to predict future behavior and that dangerousness was therefore an invalid consideration in imposing the death penalty. Justice STEVENS responded directly to the argument:

> "It is, of course, not easy to predict future behavior. The fact that such a determination is difficult, however, does not mean that it cannot be made. Indeed, prediction of future criminal conduct is an essential element in many of the decisions rendered throughout our criminal justice system. The decision whether to admit a defendant to bail, for instance, must often turn on a judge's prediction of the

defendant's future conduct. Any sentencing authority must predict a convicted person's probable future conduct when it engages in the process of determining what punishment to impose. For those sentenced to prison, these same predictions must be made by parole authorities. The task that a Texas jury must perform in answering the statutory question in issue is thus basically no different from the task performed countless times each day throughout the American system of criminal justice. What is essential is that the jury have before it all possible relevant information about the individual defendant whose fate it must determine. Texas law clearly assures that all such evidence will be adduced.''

Although there was only lay testimony with respect to dangerousness in *Jurek*, there was no suggestion by the Court that the testimony of doctors would be inadmissible. To the contrary, the Court said that the jury should be presented with all of the relevant information. Furthermore, in *Estelle v. Smith*, 451 U.S. 454, 101 S.Ct. 1866 (1981), in the face of a submission very similar to that presented in this case with respect to psychiatric testimony, we approvingly repeated the above quotation from *Jurek* and went on to say that we were in "no sense disapproving the use of psychiatric testimony bearing on future dangerousness."

Acceptance of petitioner's position that expert testimony about future dangerousness is far too unreliable to be admissable would immediately call into question those other contexts in which predictions of future behavior are constantly made. For example, in *O'Connor v. Donaldson*, 422 U.S. 563, 95 S.Ct. 2486 (1975), we held that a non-dangerous civil committee could not be held in confinement against his will. Later, speaking about the requirements for civil commitments, we said:

> "There may be factual issues in a commitment proceeding, but the factual aspects represent only the beginning of the inquiry. Whether the individual is mentally ill and dangerous to either himself or others and is in need of confined therapy turns on the meaning of the facts which must be interpreted by expert psychiatrists and psychologists." *Addington v. Texas*, 441 U.S. 418, 99 S.Ct. 1804 (1979).

In the second place, the rules of evidence generally extant at the federal and state levels anticipate that relevant, unprivileged evidence should be admitted and its weight left to the fact finder, who would have the benefit of cross examination and contrary evidence by the opposing party. Psychiatric testimony predicting dangerousness may be countered not only as erroneous in a particular case but as generally so unreliable that it should be ignored. If the jury may make up its mind about future dangerousness unaided by psychiatric testimony, jurors should not be barred from hearing the views of the State's psychiatrists along with opposing views of the defendant's doctors.[5]

---

5. In this case, no evidence was offered by petitioner at trial to contradict the testimony of Doctors Holbrook and Grigson. Nor is there a contention that, despite petitioner's claim of indigence, the court refused to provide an expert for petitioner. In cases of indigency, Texas law

Third, petitioner's view mirrors the position expressed in the amicus brief of the American Psychiatric Association (APA). As indicated above, however, the same view was presented and rejected in *Estelle v. Smith.* We are no more convinced now that the view of the APA should be converted into a constitutional rule barring an entire category of expert testimony. We are not persuaded that such testimony is almost entirely unreliable and that the factfinder and the adversary system will not be competent to uncover, recognize, and take due account of its shortcomings.

The *amicus* does not suggest that there are not other views held by members of the Association or of the profession generally. Indeed, as this case and others indicate, there are those doctors who are quite willing to testify at the sentencing hearing, who think, and will say, that they know what they are talking about, and who expressly disagree with the Association's point of view.[7] Furthermore, their qualifications as experts are regularly accepted by the courts. If they are so obviously wrong and should be discredited, there should be no insuperable problem in doing so by calling members of the Association who are of that view and who

---

provides for the payment of $500 for "expenses incurred for purposes of investigation and expert testimony."

7. At trial, Dr. Holbrook testified without contradiction that a psychiatrist could predict the future dangerousness of an individual, if given enough background information about the individual. Dr. Grigson obviously held a similar view. At the District Court hearing on the habeas petition, the State called two expert witnesses, Dr. George Parker, a psychologist, and Dr. Richard Koons, a psychiatrist. Both of these doctors agreed that accurate predictions of future dangerousness can be made if enough information is provided; furthermore, they both deemed it highly likely that an individual fitting the characteristics of the one in the Barefoot hypothetical would commit future acts of violence.

Although Barefoot did not present any expert testimony at his trial, at the habeas hearing he called Dr. Fred Fason, a psychiatrist, and Dr. Wendell Dickerson, a psychologist. Dr. Fason did not dwell on the general ability of mental health professionals to predict future dangerousness. Instead, for the most part, he merely criticized the giving of a diagnosis based upon a hypothetical question, without an actual examination. He conceded that, if a medical student described a patient in the terms of the Barefoot hypothetical, his "highest order of suspicion," to the degree of 90%, would be that the patient had a sociopathic personality. He insisted, however, that this was only an "initial impression," and that no doctor should give a firm "diagnosis" without a full examination and testing. Dr. Dickerson, petitioner's other expert, was the only person to testify who suggested that no reliable psychiatric predictions of dangerousness could ever be made.

We are aware that many mental health professionals have questioned the usefulness of psychiatric predictions of future dangerousness in light of studies indicating that such predictions are often inaccurate. For example, at the habeas hearing, Dr. Dickerson, one of petitioner's expert witnesses, testified that psychiatric predictions of future dangerousness were wrong two out of three times. He conceded, however, that, despite the high error rate, one "excellently done" study had shown "some predictive validity for predicting violence." Dr. John Monahan, upon whom one of the State's experts relied as "the leading thinker on this issue," concluded that "the 'best' clinical research currently in existence indicates that *psychiatrists and psychologists are accurate in no more than one out of three predictions of violent behavior over a several-year period among institutionalized populations that had both committed violence in the past . . . and who were diagnosed as mentally ill.*" Monahan, *The Clinical Prediction of Violent Behavior* (1981) (emphasis in original). However, although Dr. Monahan originally believed that it was impossible to predict violent behavior, by the time he had completed his monograph, he felt that "there may be circumstances in which prediction is both empirically possible and ethically appropriate," and he hoped that his work would improve the appropriateness and accuracy of clinical predictions.

All of these professional doubts about the usefulness of psychiatric predictions can be called to the attention of the jury. Petitioner's entire argument, as well as that of Justice BLACKMUN's dissent, is founded on the premise that a jury will not be able to separate the wheat from the chaff. We do not share in this low evaluation of the adversary process.

confidently assert that opinion in their *amicus* brief. Neither petitioner nor the Association suggests that psychiatrists are always wrong with respect to future dangerousness, only most of the time. Yet the submission is that this category of testimony should be excised entirely from all trials. We are unconvinced, however, at least as of now, that the adversary process cannot be trusted to sort out the reliable from the unreliable evidence and opinion about future dangerousness, particularly when the convicted felon has the opportunity to present his own side of the case.

* * *

B

Whatever the decision may be about the use of psychiatric testimony, in general, on the issue of future dangerousness, petitioner urges that such testimony must be based on personal examination of the defendant and may not be given in response to hypothetical questions. We disagree. Expert testimony, whether in the form of an opinion based on hypothetical questions or otherwise, is commonly admitted as evidence where it might help the factfinder do its assigned job. As the Court said long ago, *Spring Co. v. Edgar*, 99 U.S. 645 (1878):

> "Men who have made questions of skill or science the object of their particular study, says Phillips, are competent to give their opinions in evidence. Such opinions ought, in general, to be deduced from facts that are not disputed, or from facts given in evidence; but the author proceeds to say that they need not be founded upon their own personal knowledge of such facts, but may be founded upon the statement of facts proved in the case. Medical men, for example, may give their opinions not only to the state of a patient they may have visited, or as to cause of the death of a person whose body they have examined or as to the nature of the instruments which caused the wounds they have examined, but also in cases where they have not themselves seen the patient, and have only heard the symptoms and particulars of his state detailed by other witnesses at the trial. Judicial tribunals have in many instances held that medical works are not admissible, but they everywhere hold that men skilled in science, art, or particular trades may give their opinions as witnesses in matters pertaining to their professional calling."

* * *

Like the Court of Criminal Appeals, the District Court, and the Court of Appeals, we reject petitioner's constitutional arguments against the use of hypothetical questions. Although cases such as this involve the death penalty, we perceive no constitutional barrier to applying the ordinary rules of evidence governing the use of expert testimony.

C

As we understand petitioner, he contends that even if the use of hypothetical questions in predicting future dangerousness is acceptable as a general rule, the use made of them in his case violated his right to due process of law. For example, petitioner insists that the doctors should not have been permitted to give an opinion on the ultimate issue before the jury, particularly when the hypothetical questions were phrased in terms of petitioner's own conduct; that the hypothetical questions referred to controverted facts;[10] and that the answers to the questions were so positive as to be assertions of fact and not opinion.[11] These claims of misuse of the hypothetical questions, as well as others, were rejected by the Texas courts, and neither the District Court nor the Court of Appeals found any constitutional infirmity in the application of the Texas Rules of Evidence in this particular case. We agree.

IV

In sum, we affirm the judgment of the District Court. There is no doubt that the psychiatric testimony increased the likelihood that petitioner would be sentenced to death, but this fact does not make that evidence inadmissible, any more than it would with respect to other relevant evidence against any defendant in a criminal case. At bottom, to agree with petitioner's basic position would seriously undermine and in effect overrule *Jurek v. Texas*. Petitioner conceded as much at oral argument. We are not inclined, however, to overturn the decision in that case.

The judgment of the District Court is affirmed.

[Opinion of STEVENS, J., concurring in the judgment, and dissenting opinion of MARSHALL, J., joined by BRENNAN, J., omitted]

JUSTICE BLACKMUN, with whom JUSTICE BRENNAN and JUSTICE MARSHALL join in Parts I–IV, dissenting.

* * * The Court holds that psychiatric testimony about a defendant's future dangerousness is admissible, despite the fact that such testimony is wrong two times out of three. The Court reaches this result—even in a capital case—because, it is said, the testimony is subject to cross-examination and impeachment. In the present state of psychiatric knowledge, this is too much for me. One may accept this in a routine lawsuit for money damages, but when a person's life is at stake—no matter how heinous his offense—a requirement of greater reliability should prevail. In a capital case, the specious testimony of a psychiatrist, colored in the eyes of an impressionable jury by the inevitable untouchability of a medical specialist's words, equates with death itself.

---

10. Nothing prevented petitioner from propounding a hypothetical to the doctors based on his own version of the facts. On cross-examination, both Drs. Holbrook and Grigson readily admitted that their opinions might change if some of the assumptions in the State's hypothetical were not true.

11. The more certain a State expert is about his prediction, the easier it is for the defendant to impeach him. For example, in response to Dr. Grigson's assertion that he was "100% sure" that an individual with the characteristics of the one in the hypothetical would commit acts of violence in the future, Dr. Fason testified at the habeas hearing that if a doctor claimed to be 100% sure of something without examining the patient, "we would kick him off the staff of the hospital for his arrogance." Similar testimony could have been presented at Barefoot's trial, but was not.

I

To obtain a death sentence in Texas, the State is required to prove beyond a reasonable doubt that "there is a probability that the defendant would commit criminal acts of violence that would constitute a continuing threat to society." As a practical matter, this prediction of future dangerousness was the only issue to be decided by Barefoot's sentencing jury.[1]

At the sentencing hearing, the State established that Barefoot had two prior convictions for drug offenses and two prior convictions for unlawful possession of firearms. None of these convictions involved acts of violence. At the guilt stage of the trial, for the limited purpose of establishing that the crime was committed in order to evade police custody, the State had presented evidence that Barefoot had escaped from jail in New Mexico where he was being held on charges of statutory rape and unlawful restraint of a minor child with intent to commit sexual penetration against the child's will. The prosecution also called several character witnesses at the sentencing hearing, from towns in five States. Without mentioning particular examples of Barefoot's conduct, these witnesses testified that Barefoot's reputation for being a peaceable and law abiding citizen was bad in their respective communities.

Last, the prosecution called Doctors Holbrook and Grigson, whose testimony extended over more than half the hearing. Neither had examined Barefoot or requested the opportunity to examine him. In the presence of the jury, and over defense counsel's objection, each was qualified as an expert psychiatrist witness. Doctor Holbrook detailed at length his training and experience as a psychiatrist, which included a position as chief of psychiatric services at the Texas Department of Corrections. He explained that he had previously performed many "criminal evaluations" and that he subsequently took the post at the Department of Corrections to observe the subjects of these evaluations so that he could "be certain those opinions that [he] had were accurate at the time of trial and pretrial." He then informed the jury that it was "within [his] *capacity as a doctor of psychiatry* to predict the future dangerousness of an individual within a *reasonable medical certainty*" (emphasis supplied), and that he could give "*an expert medical opinion* that would be *within reasonable psychiatric certainty* as to whether or not that individual would be dangerous to the degree that there would be a probability that that person would commit criminal acts of violence in the future that would constitute a continuing threat to society" (emphasis supplied).

Doctor Grigson also detailed his training and medical experience, which, he said, included examination of "between thirty and forty thousand individuals," including eight thousand charged with felonies, and at least three hundred charged with murder. He testified that with enough

---

1. It appears that every person convicted of capital murder in Texas will satisfy the other requirement relevant to Barefoot's sentence, that "the conduct of the defendant that caused the death of the deceased was committed deliberately and with the reasonable expectation that the death of the deceased or another would result," because a capital murder conviction requires a finding that the defendant "intentionally or knowingly cause[d] the death of an individual."

information he would be able to "give *a medical opinion within reasonable psychiatric certainty* as to [the] psychological or psychiatric makeup of an individual" (emphasis supplied), and that this skill was "particular to the field of psychiatr[y] and not to the average layman."

Each psychiatrist then was given an extended hypothetical question asking him to assume as true about Barefoot the four prior convictions for nonviolent offenses, the bad reputation for being law abiding in various communities, the New Mexico escape, the events surrounding the murder for which he was on trial and, in Doctor Grigson's case, the New Mexico arrest. On the basis of the hypothetical question, Doctor Holbrook diagnosed Barefoot "within a reasonable psychiatr[ic] certainty," as a "criminal sociopath." He testified that he knew of no treatment that could change this condition, and that the condition would not change for the better but "may become accelerated" in the next few years. Finally, Doctor Holbrook testified that, "within reasonable psychiatric certainty," there was "a probability that the Thomas A. Barefoot in that hypothetical will commit criminal acts of violence in the future that would constitute a continuing threat to society," and that his opinion would not change if the "society" at issue was that within Texas prisons rather than society outside prison.

Doctor Grigson then testified that, on the basis of the hypothetical question, he could diagnose Barefoot "within reasonable psychiatric certainty" as an individual with "a fairly classical, typical, sociopathic personality disorder." He placed Barefoot in the "most severe category" of sociopaths (on a scale of one to ten, Barefoot was "above ten"), and stated that there was no known cure for the condition. Finally, Doctor Grigson testified that whether Barefoot was in society at large or in a prison society there was a *"one hundred percent and absolute"* chance that Barefoot would commit future acts of criminal violence that would constitute a continuing threat to society. (Emphasis supplied).

On cross-examination, defense counsel questioned the psychiatrists about studies demonstrating that psychiatrists' predictions of future dangerousness are inherently unreliable. Doctor Holbrook indicated his familiarity with many of these studies but stated that he disagreed with their conclusions. Doctor Grigson stated that he was not familiar with most of these studies, and that their conclusions were accepted by only a "small minority group" of psychiatrists—"[i]t's not the American Psychiatric Association that believes that."

After an hour of deliberation, the jury answered "yes" to the two statutory questions, and Thomas Barefoot was sentenced to death.

II

A

The American Psychiatric Association (APA), participating in this case as *amicus curiae*, informs us that "[t]he unreliability of psychiatric predictions of long-term future dangerousness is by now an established fact within the profession." Brief for American Psychiatric Association, as Amicus Curiae, 12 (APA Brief). The APA's best estimate is that *two out of three* predictions of long-term future violence made by psychiatrists are wrong. The Court does not dispute this proposition, and indeed it could not do so; the evidence is overwhelming. For example, the APA's Draft Report of the Task Force on the Role of Psychiatry in the Sentencing Process (Draft Report) states that "[c]onsiderable evidence has been accumulated by now to demonstrate that long-term prediction by psychiatrists of future violence is an extremely inaccurate process." John Monahan, recognized as "the leading thinker on this issue" even by the State's expert witness at Barefoot's federal habeas corpus hearing, concludes that "the 'best' clinical research currently in existence indicates that psychiatrists and psychologists are accurate in no more than one out of three predictions of violent behavior," even among populations of individuals who are mentally ill and have committed violence in the past. J. Monahan, The Clinical Prediction of Violent Behavior (1981) (emphasis deleted) (J. Monahan, Clinical Prediction). Another study has found it impossible to identify any subclass of offenders "whose members have a greater-than-even chance of engaging again in an assaultive act." Wenk, Robison & Smith, *Can Violence Be Predicted?*, 18 Crime & Delinquency 393 (1972). Yet another commentator observes that "[i]n general, mental health professionals . . . are more likely to be wrong than right when they predict legally relevant behavior. When predicting violence, dangerousness, and suicide, they are far more likely to be wrong than right." Morse, *Crazy Behavior, Morals, and Science: An Analysis of Mental Health Law*, 51 S.Cal.L.Rev. 527 (1978) (Morse, *Analysis of Mental Health Law*). Neither the Court nor the State of Texas has cited a single reputable scientific source contradicting the unanimous conclusion of professionals in this field that psychiatric predictions of long-term future violence are wrong more often than they are right [citing to 11 studies to the contrary].

The APA also concludes, as do researchers that have studied the issue, that psychiatrists simply have no expertise in predicting long-term future dangerousness. A layman with access to relevant statistics can do at least as well and possibly better; psychiatric training is not relevant to the factors that validly can be employed to make such predictions, and psychiatrists consistently err on the side of overpredicting violence. Thus, while Doctors Grigson and Holbrook were presented by the State and by self-proclamation as experts at predicting future dangerousness, the scientific literature makes crystal clear that they had no expertise whatever. Despite their claims that they were able to predict Barefoot's future behavior "within reasonable psychiatric certainty," or to a "one hundred percent and absolute" certainty, there was in fact no more than a one in three chance that they were correct.[5]

---

5. Like the District Court and the Court of Appeals, the Court seeks to justify the admission of psychiatric testimony on the ground that " '[t]he majority of psychiatric experts agree that where there is a pattern of repetitive assault and violent conduct, the accuracy of psychiatric predictions of future dangerousness dramatically rises.' " The District Court correctly found that there is empirical evidence supporting the common-sense correlation between repetitive past

B

It is impossible to square admission of this purportedly scientific but actually baseless testimony with the Constitution's paramount concern for reliability in capital sentencing.[6] Death is a permissible punishment in Texas only if the jury finds beyond a reasonable doubt that there is a probability the defendant will commit future acts of criminal violence. The admission of unreliable psychiatric predictions of future violence, offered with unabashed claims of "reasonable medical certainty" or "absolute" professional reliability, creates an intolerable danger that death sentences will be imposed erroneously.

* * *

* * * [U]nreliable scientific evidence is widely acknowledged to be prejudicial. The reasons for this are manifest. "The major danger of scientific evidence is its potential to mislead the jury; an aura of scientific infallibility may shroud the evidence and thus lead the jury to accept it without critical scrutiny." Giannelli, *The Admissibility of Novel Scientific Evidence: Frye v. United States, a Half–Century Later*, 80 Colum.L.Rev. 1197 (1980). Where the public holds an exaggerated opinion of the accuracy of scientific testimony, the prejudice is likely to be indelible. There is little question that psychiatrists are perceived by the public as

---

violence and future violence; the APA states that "[t]he *most* that can be said about any individual is that a history of past violence increases the probability that future violence will occur." Draft Report (emphasis supplied). But psychiatrists have no special insights to add to this actuarial fact, and a single violent crime cannot provide a basis for a reliable prediction of future violence. The lower courts and this Court have sought solace in this statistical correlation without acknowledging its obvious irrelevance to the facts of this case. The District Court did not find that the State demonstrated any pattern of repetitive assault and violent conduct by Barefoot. Recognizing the importance of giving some credibility to its experts' specious prognostications, the State now claims that the "reputation" testimony adduced at the sentencing hearing "can only evince repeated, widespread acts of criminal violence." This is simply absurd. There was no testimony worthy of credence that Barefoot had committed acts of violence apart from the crime for which he was being tried; there was testimony only of a bad reputation for peaceable and law abiding conduct. In light of the fact that each of Barefoot's prior convictions was for a nonviolent offense, such testimony obviously could have been based on antisocial but nonviolent behavior. Neither psychiatrist informed the jury that he considered this reputation testimony to show a history of repeated acts of violence. Moreover, if the psychiatrists or the jury were to rely on such vague hearsay testimony in order to show a "pattern of repetitive assault and violent conduct," Barefoot's death sentence would rest on information that might "bear no closer relation to fact than the average rumor or item of gossip," *Gardner v. Florida*, 430 U.S. 349, 97 S.Ct. 1197 (1977), and should be invalid for that reason alone. A death sentence cannot rest on highly dubious predictions secretly based on a factual foundation of hearsay and pure conjecture.

6. Although I believe that the misleading nature of any psychiatric prediction of future violence violates due process when introduced in a capital sentencing hearing, admitting the predictions in this case—which were made without even examining the defendant—was particularly indefensible. In the APA's words, if prediction following even an in-depth examination is inherently unreliable, "there is all the more reason to shun the practice of testifying without having examined the defendant at all. . . . Needless to say, responding to hypotheticals is just as fraught with the possibility of error as testifying in any other way about an individual whom one has not personally examined. Although the courts have not yet rejected the practice, psychiatrists should." Draft Report. Such testimony is offensive not only to legal standards; the APA has declared that "it is unethical for a psychiatrist to offer a professional opinion unless he/she has conducted an examination." *The Principles of Medical Ethics, With Annotations Especially Applicable to Psychiatry* § 7(3) (1981). The Court today sanctions admission in a capital sentencing hearing of "expert" medical testimony so unreliable and unprofessional that it violates the canons of medical ethics.

having a special expertise to predict dangerousness, a perception based on psychiatrists' study of mental disease. It is this perception that the State in Barefoot's case sought to exploit. Yet mental disease is not correlated with violence, see J. Monahan, *Clinical Prediction*; Steadman & Cocozza, *Psychiatry, Dangerousness and the Repetitively Violent Offender*, 69 J.Crim.L. & Criminology 226 (1978), and the stark fact is that no such expertise exists. Moreover, psychiatrists, it is said, sometimes attempt to perpetuate this illusion of expertise, and Doctors Grigson and Holbrook—who purported to be able to predict future dangerousness "within reasonable psychiatric certainty," or absolutely—present extremely disturbing examples of this tendency. The problem is not uncommon.

Furthermore, as is only reasonable, the Court's concern in encouraging the introduction of a wide scope of evidence has been to ensure that *accurate* information is provided to the sentencing authority without restriction. The plurality in *Gregg* explained the jury's need for relevant evidence in these terms:

> "If an experienced trial judge, who daily faces the difficult task of imposing sentences, has a vital need for *accurate* information ... to be able to impose a rational sentence in the typical criminal case, then *accurate* sentencing information is an indispensable prerequisite to a reasoned determination of whether a defendant shall live or die by a jury of people who may never before have made a sentencing decision." (emphasis supplied).

So far as I am aware, the Court never has suggested that there is any interest in providing deceptive and inaccurate testimony to the jury.

Psychiatric predictions of future dangerousness *are not accurate*; wrong two times out of three, their probative value, and therefore any possible contribution they might make to the ascertainment of truth, is virtually nonexistent. Indeed, given a psychiatrist's prediction that an individual will be dangerous, it is more likely than not that the defendant will *not* commit further violence. It is difficult to understand how the admission of such predictions can be justified as advancing the search for truth, particularly in light of their clearly prejudicial effect.

Thus, the Court's remarkable observation that "[n]either petitioner nor the [APA] suggests that psychiatrists are *always wrong* with respect to future dangerousness, *only most of the time*" (emphasis supplied), misses the point completely, and its claim that this testimony was no more problematic than "other relevant evidence against any defendant in a criminal case" is simply incredible. Surely, this Court's commitment to ensuring that death sentences are imposed reliably and reasonably requires that nonprobative and highly prejudicial testimony on the ultimate question of life or death be excluded from a capital sentencing hearing.

III

A

Despite its recognition that the testimony at issue was probably wrong and certainly prejudicial, the Court holds this testimony admissible because the Court is "unconvinced . . . that the adversary process cannot be trusted to sort out the reliable from the unreliable evidence and opinion about future dangerousness." One can only wonder how juries are to separate valid from invalid expert opinions when the "experts" themselves are so obviously unable to do so. Indeed, the evidence suggests that juries are not effective at assessing the validity of scientific evidence.

There can be no question that psychiatric predictions of future violence will have an undue effect on the ultimate verdict. Even judges tend to accept psychiatrists' recommendations about a defendant's dangerousness with little regard for cross-examination or other testimony. Cocozza & Steadman, *Prediction in Psychiatry: An Example of Misplaced Confidence in Experts*, 25 Soc.Probs. 265 (in making involuntary commitment decisions, psychiatric predictions of future dangerousness accepted in 86.7% of cases). There is every reason to believe that inexperienced jurors will be still less capable of "separat[ing] the wheat from the chaff," despite the Court's blithe assumption to the contrary. The American Bar Association has warned repeatedly that sentencing juries are particularly incapable of dealing with information relating to "the likelihood that the defendant will commit other crimes," and similar predictive judgments. American Bar Association Project on Standards for Criminal Justice, *Sentencing Alternatives and Procedures* § 1.1(b), Commentary (Approved Draft 1968). Relying on the ABA's conclusion, the plurality in *Gregg v. Georgia*, recognized that "[s]ince the members of a jury will have had little, if any, previous experience in sentencing, they are unlikely to be skilled in dealing with the information they are given." But the Court in this case, in its haste to praise the jury's ability to find the truth, apparently forgets this well-known and worrisome shortcoming.

As if to suggest that petitioner's position that unreliable expert testimony should be excluded is unheard of in the law, the Court relies on the proposition that the rules of evidence generally "anticipate that relevant, unprivileged evidence should be admitted and its weight left to the factfinder, who would have the benefit of cross-examination and contrary evidence by the opposing party." But the Court simply ignores hornbook law that, despite the availability of cross-examination and rebuttal witnesses, "opinion evidence is not admissible if the court believes that the state of the pertinent art or scientific knowledge does not permit a reasonable opinion to be asserted." McCormick, Evidence (1972). Because it is feared that the jury will overestimate its probative value, polygraph evidence, for example, almost invariably is excluded from trials despite the fact that, at a conservative estimate, an experienced polygraph examiner can detect truth or deception correctly about 80 to 90 percent of the time. Ennis & Litwak, *Psychiatry and the Presumption of Expertise: Flipping Coins in the Courtroom*, 62 Calif.L.Rev. 693 (1974).[9] In no area is

---

9. Other purportedly scientific proof has met a similar fate. See, *e.g.*, *United States v. Kilgus*, 571 F.2d 508 (9th Cir. 1978) (expert testimony identifying aircraft through "forward looking infrared system" inadmissible because unreliable and not generally accepted in scientific field to which it belongs); *United States v. Brown*, 557 F.2d 541 (6th Cir. 1977) (expert identification

purportedly "expert" testimony admitted for the jury's consideration where it cannot be demonstrated that it is correct more often than not. "It is inconceivable that a judgment could be considered an 'expert' judgment when it is less accurate than the flip of a coin." The risk that a jury will be incapable of separating "scientific" myth from reality is deemed unacceptably high.[10]

B

The Constitution's mandate of reliability, with the stakes at life or death, precludes reliance on cross-examination and the opportunity to present rebuttal witnesses as an antidote for this distortion of the truth-finding process. Cross examination is unlikely to reveal the fatuousness of psychiatric predictions because such predictions often rest, as was the case here, on psychiatric categories and intuitive clinical judgments not suscep-tible to cross-examination and rebuttal. Psychiatric categories have little or no demonstrated relationship to violence, and their use often obscures the unimpressive statistical or intuitive bases for prediction. The APA particularly condemns the use of the diagnosis employed by Doctors Grigson and Holbrook in this case, that of sociopathy:

> "In this area confusion reigns. The psychiatrist who is not careful can mislead the judge or jury into believing that a person has a major mental disease simply on the basis of a description of prior criminal behavior. Or a psychiatrist can mislead the court into believing that an individual is devoid of conscience on the basis of a description of criminal acts alone.... The profession of psychiatry has a responsibil-ity to avoid inflicting this confusion upon the courts and to spare the defendant the harm that may result.... Given our uncertainty about the implications of the finding, the diagnosis of sociopathy ... should not be used to justify or to support predictions of future conduct. There is no certainty in this area."

* * *

Nor is the presentation of psychiatric witnesses on behalf of the defense likely to remove the prejudicial taint of misleading testimony by prosecution psychiatrists.[12] No reputable expert would be able to predict

---

based on "ion microprobic analysis of human hair" not admissible because insufficiently reliable and accurate, and not accepted in its field); *United States v. Addison*, 498 F.2d 741 (D.C.Cir. 1974) (expert identification based on voice spectrogram inadmissible because not shown reliable); *United States v. Hearst*, 412 F.Supp. 893 (N.D.Cal. 1976) (identification testimony of expert in "psycholinguistics" inadmissible because not demonstrably reliable).

10. The Court observes that this well established rule is a matter of evidence law, not constitutional law. But the principle requiring that capital sentencing procedures ensure reliable verdicts, which the Court ignores, and the principle that due process is violated by the introduction of certain types of seemingly conclusive, but actually unreliable, evidence, which the Court ignores, are constitutional doctrines of long standing. The teaching of the evidence doctrine is that unreliable scientific testimony creates a serious and unjustifiable risk of an erroneous verdict, and that the adversary process at its best does not remove this risk. We should not dismiss this lesson merely by labeling the doctrine nonconstitutional; its relevance to the constitutional question before the Court could not be more certain.

12. For one thing, although most members of the mental health professions believe that such predictions cannot be made, defense lawyers may experience significant difficulties in locating

with confidence that the defendant will not be violent; at best, the witness will be able to give his opinion that all predictions of dangerousness are unreliable. Consequently, the jury will not be presented with the traditional battle of experts with opposing views on the ultimate question. Given a choice between an expert who says that he can predict with certainty that the defendant, whether confined in prison or free in society, will kill again, and an expert who says merely that no such prediction can be made, members of the jury charged by law with making the prediction surely will be tempted to opt for the expert who claims he can help them in performing their duty, and who predicts dire consequences if the defendant is not put to death.

Moreover, even at best, the presentation of defense psychiatrists will convert the death sentence hearing into a battle of experts, with the Eighth Amendment's well established requirement of individually focused sentencing a certain loser. The jury's attention inevitably will turn from an assessment of the propriety of sentencing to death the defendant before it to resolving a scientific dispute about the capabilities of psychiatrists to predict future violence. In such an atmosphere, there is every reason to believe that the jury may be distracted from its constitutional responsibility to consider "particularized mitigating factors" in passing on the defendant's future dangerousness.

One searches the Court's opinion in vain for a plausible justification for tolerating the State's creation of this risk of an erroneous death verdict. As one Court of Appeals has observed: "A courtroom is not a research laboratory. The fate of a defendant ... should not hang on his ability to successfully rebut scientific evidence which bears an 'aura of special reliability and trustworthiness,' although, in reality the witness is testifying on the basis of an unproved hypothesis ... which has yet to gain general acceptance in its field." *United States v. Brown*, 557 F.2d 541 (6th Cir.1977). Ultimately, when the Court knows full well that psychiatrists' predictions of dangerousness are specious, there can be no excuse for imposing on the defendant, on pain of his life, the heavy burden of convincing a jury of laymen of the fraud.[14]

---

effective rebuttal witnesses. I presume that the Court's reasoning suggests that, were a defendant to show that he was unable, for financial or other reasons, to obtain an adequate rebuttal expert, a constitutional violation might be found.

14. The Court is far wide of the mark in asserting that excluding psychiatric predictions of future dangerousness from capital sentencing proceedings "would immediately call into question those other contexts in which predictions of future behavior are constantly made." Short-term predictions of future violence, for the purpose of emergency commitment or treatment, are considerably more accurate than long-term predictions. In other contexts where psychiatric predictions of future dangerousness are made, moreover, the subject will not be criminally convicted, much less put to death, as a result of predictive error. The risk of error therefore may be shifted to the defendant to some extent. The APA, discussing civil commitment proceedings based on determinations of dangerousness, states that in light of the unreliability of psychiatric predictions, "[c]lose monitoring, frequent follow-up, and a willingness to change one's mind about treatment recommendations and dispositions for violent persons, whether within the legal system or without, is the *only* acceptable practice if the psychiatrist is to play a helpful role in these assessments of dangerousness." APA, *Clinical Aspects* (emphasis supplied). In a capital case there will be no chance for "follow-up" or "monitoring." A subsequent change of mind brings not justice delayed, but the despair of irreversible error.

NOTES

1. *Estelle v. Smith.*

In *Estelle v. Smith*, 451 U.S. 454, 101 S.Ct. 1866 (1981), the Supreme Court found that Smith's constitutional rights were violated by the introduction of Dr. Grigson's testimony at the penalty phase of Smith's trial, and it affirmed the grant of habeas corpus relief. After Smith was indicted for murder and the State announced its intention to seek the death penalty, the trial court ordered Smith to be examined by Dr. Grigson to determine his competency to stand trial. Dr. Grigson determined that Smith was competent. At trial, Smith was convicted of murder. At Smith's sentencing hearing, Dr. Grigson testified, over defense objection, that Smith would be a danger to society. Dr. Grigson based his conclusion on what he had learned in the competency examination. The Supreme Court held that Smith's Fifth Amendment rights had been violated because he had not been warned before the competency examination that his statements could be used against him. See *Miranda v. Arizona*, 384 U.S. 436, 86 S.Ct. 1602 (1966). The Court also found that Smith's Sixth Amendment rights had been violated since the competency examination was a "critical stage" of the prosecution and Smith's counsel had not been notified in advance that the examination would encompass the issue of future dangerousness. See *United States v. Wade,* 388 U.S. 218, 87 S.Ct. 1926 (1967).

2. *Statutory challenges to the reliability of psychiatric testimony.*

In rejecting Barefoot's Eighth Amendment challenge to expert predictions of future violence, the Supreme Court noted that "the rules of evidence generally extant at the federal and state levels anticipate that relevant, unprivileged evidence should be admitted and its weight left to the fact finder * * *." However, a decade later in *Daubert v. Merrell Dow Pharmaceuticals, Inc.,* 509 U.S. 579, 113 S.Ct. 2786 (1993), the Supreme Court held that, to be admissible under Federal Rule of Evidence 702, scientific, technical or specialized evidence must be shown to be both relevant and reliable. Many states have adopted the *Daubert* rule as a matter of state evidentiary law. For example, in Texas, the state rule on expert testimony, Rule 702 of the Rules of Criminal Evidence, is identical to Rule 702 of the Federal Rules of Evidence. *E.I. du Pont de Nemours & Co. v. Robinson*, 923 S.W.2d 549, 554 (Tex. 1995). In 1992, the year before *Daubert* was decided, the Texas Court of Criminal Appeals ruled that the proponent of scientific evidence has the burden of proving, by clear and convincing evidence, that the expert's testimony is relevant to the issues in the case and is based upon a reliable foundation. *Kelly v. State*, 824 S.W.2d 568 (Tex.Crim.App. 1992). The Texas court set forth the factors to be considered in assessing the reliability of the proposed evidence:

> As a matter of common sense, evidence derived from a scientific theory, to be considered reliable, must satisfy three criteria in any particular case: (a) the underlying scientific theory must be valid; (b) the technique applying the theory must be valid; and (c) the technique must have been properly applied on the occasion in question. * * * [A]ll three criteria

must be proven to the trial court, outside the presence of the jury, before the evidence may be admitted. Factors that could affect a trial court's determination of reliability include, but are not limited to, the following: (1) the extent to which the underlying scientific theory and technique are accepted as valid by the relevant scientific community, if such a community can be ascertained; (2) the qualifications of the expert(s) testifying; (3) the existence of literature supporting or rejecting the underlying scientific theory and technique; (4) the potential rate of error of the technique; (5) the availability of other experts to test and evaluate the technique; (6) the clarity with which the underlying scientific theory and technique can be explained to the court; and (7) the experience and skill of the person(s) who applied the technique on the occasion in question.

Id. at 573. Is there any reason that this evidentiary rule should not be applied in a capital sentencing hearing to an expert's testimony about a defendant's future dangerousness? What effect would it have on such testimony? In *Nenno v. State*, 970 S.W.2d 549 (Tex.Crim.App.1998), the Texas Court of Criminal Appeals held that *Daubert* does apply to experts offering testimony on future dangerousness but held that experts in "non-hard" scientific areas did not have to meet the same reliability test applied to experts in the hard sciences. In the social sciences, reliability is to be judged primarily on the expert's experience and training, rather than on whether the expert's technique or conclusions are subject to validation or peer review. So saying, the court held that a veteran F.B.I. agent who had studied numerous cases involving offenders who had sexually victimized children could testify as to the defendant's future dangerousness.

3. *Problem 9–7.*

At the punishment phase of his capital trial in Texas, Defendant sought to introduce evidence by Expert, a professor of criminal justice, that predictions about future dangerousness of capital murder defendants, including predictions made by juries in answers to special issues under the Texas statute, had proven to be generally inaccurate. Expert did not intend to rebut any of the prosecution's aggravating evidence about Defendant or to testify specifically about Defendant. The trial court excluded Expert's testimony as irrelevant under Rule 401 of the Texas Rules of Criminal Evidence, which defines relevant evidence "as evidence having any tendency to make the existence of any fact that is of consequence to the determination of the action more probable or less probable than it would be without the evidence." On appeal, what arguments should be made as to whether the trial court's ruling was erroneous? See *Rachal v. State*, 917 S.W.2d 799 (Tex.Crim.App. 1996).

4. *"Future dangerousness" as an aggravator.*

Texas is one of a handful of death penalty states that makes future dangerousness an aggravating factor for purposes of death eligibility. Although jurors in other states are likely to consider future dangerousness in making the penalty decision,[a] critics have raised at least two arguments

---

a. The Supreme Court assumed as much in *California v. Ramos*, 463 U.S. 992, 108, 103 S.Ct. 3446, 3457 (1983) [Chapter 10].

against using a future dangerousness to determine death eligibility. First, as studies since *Barefoot* have confirmed, even using newer methodologies for predicting future violence, the error rate in such predictions is extraordinarily high, around 50%.[b] To permit the state to exact the most extreme penalty on the basis of such dubious evidence is inevitably arbitrary. Second, the purpose served by imposing the death penalty on a defendant based on a finding of future dangerousness is incapacitation, but the death penalty is clearly excessive for that purpose since life imprisonment, especially without the possibility of parole and perhaps with isolation, would do as well. In fact, the rate of violence among capital murderers in prison is quite low; one study found the rate to be lower than that of other prison populations.[c] The three states that have conducted the most executions post-*Furman*–Texas, Virginia and Oklahoma (together accounting for the majority of post-*Furman* executions in the country)—make future dangerousness an explicit aggravating factor. Is there a relationship between the use of this aggravator and a high execution rate, and, if so, what might explain it?

5. *Race and dangerousness.*

Victor Saldano, an Argentinean, was convicted of murder in Collin County, Texas. At the penalty hearing, Walter Quijano, former chief psychologist for the Texas Department of Criminal Justice, testified that Saldano would be a future danger to society in part because he was Hispanic and Hispanics have a higher crime rate than other people. Saldano was sentenced to death, and his sentence was affirmed by the Texas Court of Criminal Appeals on the ground that he had waived his challenge to Quijano's testimony by not objecting at trial. In response to Saldano's petition for certiorari, the Attorney General of Texas confessed error in the sentencing and refused to raise a procedural default defense, and, as a result, the Supreme Court vacated the judgment and remanded the case. *Saldano v. Texas*, 530 U.S. 1212, 120 S.Ct. 2214 (2000). On remand to the Texas Court of Criminal Appeals, with the state represented by the State Prosecutor and John Roach, the Collin County District Attorney, the court again affirmed Saldano's death sentence on the ground of procedural default. *Saldano v. State*, 70 S.W.3d 873 (Tex.Crim.App. 2002). Saldano petitioned for federal habeas corpus, and the Attorney General, representing the respondent warden, again confessed error in the sentencing and refused to raise the issue of procedural default. Roach moved to intervene to argue the procedural default issue, but the District Court denied the motion and then granted the writ, finding that the introduction of Quijano's testimony violated the Eighth Amendment. *Saldano v. Cockrell*, 267 F.Supp.2d 635 (E.D.Tex. 2003). The Fifth Circuit dismissed Roach's appeal. *Saldano v. Roach*, 363 F.3d 545 (2004).

---

b. C. Slobogin, *Capital Punishment and Dangerousness*, in Mental Disorder and Criminal Law: Responsibility, Punishment and Competence (2008), available at http://ssrn.com/abstract= 1135647 at n.3.

c. M. Dorland & D. Krauss, *The Danger of Dangerousness in Capital Sentencing: Exacerbating the Problem of Arbitrary and Capricious Decision-making*, 29 Law & Psychol. Rev. 63, 71 (2005).

TRAVELS WITH DR. DEATH[a]

By Ron Rosenbaum.

Dr. James Grigson, a.k.a. "the hanging shrink," is a traveling sales-man for the Texas death penalty. His lethal court testimony has sent 118 convicted murderers to death row. RON ROSENBAUM crosses the prairie with Dr. Death as he notches up three death sentences—two in one day.

Three lives hang in the balance this morning as Dr. James Grigson pulls up in a gleaming white Cadillac, ready to make his rounds. The tall Texan with one hand on the wheel and one hand on his flamboyant golden cigarette holder, the legendary forensic psychiatrist known as "Dr. Death," is about to head out for the West Texas prairie to do some testifying. Indeed, for the Doctor—the traveling expert witness for hire, the courtroom terror of death-penalty foes—this is going to be the most extraordinarily concentrated stretch of testifying he's ever done. Three death-penalty trials in three Texas towns in two days.

If things go according to plan, if jurors follow his advice and vote for death—as they usually do when the Doctor takes the stand and, in effect, prescribes it—three convicted murderers will be sent to death row to face the Big Needle, execution by lethal injection.

In fact, if the Doctor can adhere to his demanding schedule of appearances, he'll succeed in doing something even he has never done before: dispatch two lives in a single day.

Dr. Grigson's lopsided record over the past twenty years favors his chances: going into these three trials he has testified against 124 murder-ers, and acting on his advice, juries have sentenced 115 of them to death. He is the death penalty's cutting edge in Texas, its circuit rider. Oppo-nents call him "the hanging shrink." But even he has never done so many so fast.

This morning in Dallas, the Doctor swings open the door of the Sedan de Ville to admit me into the chocolate leather interior. We're off to Love Field, where we'll catch a flight to Lubbock, four hundred miles west. He's agreed to allow me to accompany him on these hectic, history-making-rounds, to observe him game-planning his testimony with prosecutors, plotting against defense witnesses. And blasting defense attorneys out of the water: the Doctor has a reputation as a lethal weapon on the witness stand in Texas, which has sent more defendants to death row than any other state. Indeed, one defense attorney calls him "a killing machine."

Grigson, a perpetually grinning, relentlessly gregarious type, gives me a vigorous handshake and puts the Caddy into gear. We begin a journey that will take us deep into the heart of Texas, deep into the minds of three murderers, and deeper into that poorly charted borderline realm between

---

a. © May 1990 by Ron Rosenbaum. This article originally appeared in Vanity Fair. Reprinted by permission of the author.

evil and madness that is the Doctor's special turf. Because, despite his controversial methods (the American Psychiatric Association has denounced his practice of telling juries he can "guarantee" that a defendant "will kill again"), despite his embarrassing setback in the Randall Dale Adams *Thin Blue Line* case (the Doctor, who had predicted Adams would "kill again," *still* believes the now absolved defendant is guilty and "will kill again"), it cannot be denied that the Doctor has looked longer and deeper into the minds and hearts of more murderers (1,400 so far) than just about anyone else. One may disagree with where he draws the boundary lines between evil and madness, criminality and sickness. But one can't deny he knows the territory.

On the evening of March 17. 1989, a twenty-one-year-old white kid named Aaron Lee Fuller was drinking beer over at a girlfriend's apartment in Lamesa, Texas, when he had an idea. Which was that the easiest way to make quick money was to roll old ladies. Some of Aaron Lee Fuller's previous ideas, about how to commit burglaries, for instance, had not turned out well, and he'd ended up spending a couple of stretches in the state pen in Huntsville. This was his worst idea of all.

Before long Aaron Lee Fuller found himself at Loretta Stephens's house, staring through her screen door at the sixty-eight-year-old widow, who was sound asleep on a recliner in her living room. Word on the street had it that Loretta Stephen kept large amounts of cash at home. Fuller used a house key to rip a hole in the screen door and let himself in. Tiptoed past the sleeping figure, proceeded to her bedroom, where, sure enough, he found more than $500 in small bills stuffed into various envelopes.

When he emerged with the money, Loretta Stephens was still sound asleep. All Fuller had to do was make a quick exit and he'd be home free with the cash. The perfect petty crime.

But he didn't make that quick easy, exit. Something drew him to the sleeping woman on the recliner. According to a videotaped confession he later made, he stopped in front of her. Stood over her. Stared at her for a full ten minutes. And then began smashing her face in with his fists, shattering her jaw, causing massive hemorrhages and multiple blunt-force traumas to the brain.

He went into the bathroom, washed the blood spatter off his face, and returned to Loretta Stephens's side. Noticed her stirring, still breathing through her broken face. Which caused him to go back to the bedroom, get a pillow, and use it to smother the remaining life out of her. She was dead, but he still wasn't through with her. According to his original confession, he proceeded to sexually assault her dead body. When he took the stand at his trial, Fuller retracted parts of his confession. Claimed that although he punched Loretta Stephens's face it was not he, but a friend who'd accompanied him, who smothered her to death. And that it was his friend who'd committed the sexual assault.

The jury, didn't believe him and convicted him of committing the murder himself. But what may have sealed Aaron Lee Fuller's fate—what made him a prime candidate for the Doctor's death-penalty diagnosis of "future dangerousness" was Fuller's behavior immediately following the crime. Because it is the Doctor's belief that the special subspecies of murderers who are likely to kill again (unless the state kills them first) betray their "severe sociopath" nature by their emotional reaction—or lack of it—in the aftermath of the killing.

To severe sociopaths "killing someone is less emotional than eating a plate of scrambled eggs," the Doctor maintains. To them "it's not much different from having a meal at a good restaurant. If you like it, you'll come back again."

What Aaron Lee Fuller did in the immediate aftermath of Loretta Stephens's murder was, essentially, *party hearty*. With the body tied up in a bundle in the back of her car, he and a friend tore off for the bright lights of Lubbock to spend the woman's cash.

They drove to a convenience store, flirted with the cashier, flashed her the roll of bills, and headed off for Lubbock. Almost as an afterthought they dumped the body in a patch of tall weeds by the roadside. When they got to Lubbock they bought a keg, checked into a motel called the Koko Inn. There, Aaron Lee Fuller commenced the last best party of his life.

It took a jury in the tiny West Texas county-seat town of Lamesa (pronounced La-meese-ah) all of twenty-seven minutes to convict Aaron Lee Fuller of "capital murder"—a murder done in the course of committing another felony—the most severe degree of the crime, the one that carries only two possible sentences in Texas: life imprisonment or death.

But the real trial only began with the guilty verdict. On Thursday, February 1, 1990, the Lamesa jury reconvened to begin hearing arguments on the question of whether to put Aaron Lee Fuller to death. U.S. Supreme Court decisions and death-penalty law in Texas require this separate "penalty phase" trial for all candidates for capital punishment. A pure trial on the life-or-death issue.

* * *

How do you decide who really deserves to die? In Texas, a jury never actually votes life or death up or down. Instead, it is called upon to decide three questions about the murder and the murderer, three "Special Issues."

The jurors must agree unanimously, first, that the murderer "deliberately" sought the death of his victim; second, that there is "a probability that the defendant would commit criminal acts of violence" in the future, acts which would "constitute a continuing threat to society"; and, third, that there was no reasonable "provocation" for the defendant's murderous conduct.

In practice, it's Special Issue No. 2—the question of future dangerousness—that has become the battleground on which the life-or-death struggle of Texas death-penalty trials is fought.

What makes Special Issue No. 2 so thorny and contentious—what makes Dr. Grigson's testimony so controversial within the psychiatric profession and among death-penalty foes—is that it asks jurors to make a life-or-death decision based on a prediction of the future. It allows the jurors to punish the defendant with the extra, ultimate sanction of death, not only for the crime he's been convicted of but for crimes he might commit later. (It's a novel but not unique requirement. One other state of the thirty-six that have a death penalty requires a finding of future dangerousness.) In doing so, Special Issue No. 2 asks a lot more of jurors than merely looking into a criminal's record. It asks them to look into his soul—indeed, into the evolution of his soul in the future, into the life he *might* get to live, if they don't give him death.

This is where the Doctor comes in. He'll take the stand, listen to a recitation of facts about the killing and the killer and then—usually without examining the defendant, without ever setting eyes on him until the day of the trial—tell the jury that, *as a matter of medical science*, he can assure that the defendant *will* pose a continuing danger to society as defined by Special Issue No. 2. That's all it takes.

But the Doctor's impact on a jury is more profound than the mere content of what he says. A death-penalty decision is far more emotionally unsettling to jurors than a mere guilt-or-innocence vote. It's a grave and even terrifying decision to make, in which the desire to exact collective vengeance upon a killer may conflict with the reluctance to pull the trigger personally—which, in effect, death-penalty jurors must do for us all. What makes the Doctor so effective—both prosecution and defense lawyers will tell you this—is his bedside manner with the jury. His kindly, gregarious, country-doctor manner, his reassuring, beautifully modulated East Texas drawl, help jurors get over the hump, and do the deed.

Says one bitter defense lawyer, "He's kind of like a Marcus Welby who tells you it's O.K. to kill."

And as a bonus for the prosecutors who hire him, the Doctor also does his lethal best to destroy defense attorneys and defense witnesses who challenge him.

Which is why, as soon as Lamesa County prosecutor Ricky Smith got a trial date for Aaron Lee Fuller, he put in a call to the Doctor. He knew a conviction would be easy. But death-penalty deliberations can be trickier, even in the conservative West Texas countryside in which Lamesa is situated. There is always a danger of a holdout juror. And the Doctor has a way with holdouts.

On our flight from Dallas to Lubbock, the Doctor tells me about how, in a recent trial, he worked on one stubborn holdout who, he was convinced, had her mind set against voting for death.

"I was watching her and I could tell she didn't believe what the first [prosecution] psychiatrist told her, and she wasn't gonna believe what I'd say. She just had her legs crossed, wasn't gonna hear what we had to say. So we took a coffee break after the first psychiatrist, and I told the prosecutor, 'You got trouble. You got one woman who's gonna hang up this jury, because she's not buying it.' "

The prosecutor then dug up some biographical information on the reluctant woman from the jury questionnaire.

"We discovered she had a fourteen-year-old daughter. And I got back on the stand and had the prosecutor ask me [about the defendant], 'Is this the kind of man that would rape and kill fourteen-year-old girls?' And we went into that. And she uncrossed her legs." The jury voted unanimously for death.

The Doctor repeatedly contends under oath that he testifies neither *for* nor *against* the prosecution or defense, that he testifies only as to what his scientific objectivity tells him. (Indeed, the Doctor points out, he's diagnosed future dangerousness in only 60 percent of the potential death-penalty defendants he's examined. Many other defendants owe their lives to him because the Doctor was willing to predict they wouldn't be dangerous.) Nonetheless, what makes him popular with prosecutors is that he will go the extra mile; he will go for the jugular to score points to win. He's so popular, in fact, that as his plane touches down in Lubbock he's the subject of a tug-of-war between two prosecutors: Ricky Smith in Lamesa, seventy miles south of Lubbock, wants him on the stand to testify against Aaron Lee Fuller tomorrow, Wednesday. But prosecutor Travis Ware in Lubbock wants him to take the stand in *his* death-penalty trial on Wednesday, too.

Travis Ware has tried a half-dozen death-penalty cases—four of them with the Doctor—and never lost one.

"Defense lawyers *fear* Dr. Grigson," Travis Ware explained to me. "They fear his effect on juries. He knows more about the criminal mind than anyone else in America, and he can put it in layman's terms. His demeanor. his sincerity. his charisma is absolutely uncontrollable by the defense. It drives them crazy."

Indeed, the Doctor's scheduled testimony drives them so crazy that during this particular week in February it has created a remarkable, unprecedented phenomenon on the West Texas prairie. Total shrink gridlock! Defense teams in both Lubbock and Lamesa are flying psychiatrists, psychologists, sociologists, and penologists in from all over America to do battle with the Doctor. They're shuttling back and forth between Lubbock and Lamesa, causing scheduling nightmares.

Finally, after two days of shuffling and shuttling and reshuffling, the order of battle has sorted itself out: the Doctor will take the stand in Lamesa first, in the Aaron Lee Fuller trial. Which means leaving Lubbock before dawn Friday morning, driving the seventy miles to Lamesa, facing

Aaron Lee Fuller for the first time and pronouncing on his life, then racing back to Lubbock to take the stand and pronounce on the life of defendant Adolfo Hemandez in the afternoon. It will be the Doctor's first-ever doubleheader. And if all goes well, we'll be back in Dallas Monday morning in time for the Doctor to take the stand in a *third* murder trial— which will make it three in two working days.

Dawn on the road from Lubbock to Lemesa. The sunrises are spectacular on this part of the West Texas prairie, spanning a horizon line virtually unobstructed by tree, barn, or settlement. One lonely sign advertises one lonely tourist attraction on this stretch of road, the Dan Blocker Memorial. The sign is in the shape of the big hat Hoss wore on *Bonanza*. The chief treasure of the museum in the Big Guy's tiny hometown of O'Donnell is a pair of size 44 trousers Hoss wore at age eleven.

It was about the time we passed the Dan Blocker Memorial sign that the Doctor made his Rock of Ages revelation. He was talking about growing up in the thirties in Texarkana, five hundred miles away in East Texas.

"The Grigsons had the Rock of Ages franchise," he said, "for the four-state area, of Arkansas—"

"Rock of Ages is what?" I asked, not comprehending at first.

"It's a particular—Rock of Ages is a trademark or name of a thicker type of marble. During the Depression and after, you would only bury your loved ones under Rock of Ages marble."

The amazing fact slowly began to dawn on me: Dr. Death's family was in the tombstone business. You could say that the Doctor is still traveling in the family business. Not Death's traveling salesman exactly, but surely his jurisprudential franchisee.

Indeed, there's a bit of the old-fashioned Willy Lomanesque commercial traveler you can't help but notice in the Doctor. None of the downbeat, defeated Loman stuff, but the salesman's relentlessly cheerful glad-handing style. Nothing phony about it—it appears to be his natural temperament, the nonstop pepster with a cheery word for strangers in elevators and airports. * * *

But the Doctor's corn-pone Dale Carnegie sweetness and light can be extremely deceptive, as I would discover later that morning in Lamesa. Beneath the good-ol'-boy guise there's a steel-trap mind. The Doctor may be an East Texas country boy on the surface, but he's a country boy like L.B.J. was a country boy. A country boy with a killer instinct.

It's an instinct he began to develop in his youth when he and his brother would come home from work and lock themselves into epic fratricidal chess matches, hour after hour, night after night. The Doctor's brother went on to become a professional pool shark and gambler. And while the Doctor chose a more conventional career path, graduating from Southwestern Medical School in Dallas and doing a psychiatric residency at Parkland Hospital, his restless competitive nature, the pool shark in him, was not satisfied by the passive, couch-centered life of a private practitioner of psychoanalytically-based psychiatry. He sought out something that satisfied his appetite for competition. He found it in forensic psychiatry, in the high-intensity combat of criminal-trial testimony and cross-examination. He found it in the duel of wits with dangerous criminals. He began to specialize in examining killers.

At first they were mainly competency exams—judging whether a killer was sane enough to stand trial or not. And at first, he says, he got fooled a lot.

"At first I got the s___ conned out of me. In medical school I was as liberal as any psychiatrist you'll ever meet. You know, most psychiatrists will say if you commit a crime there's something *wrong* with you." But after thousands of hours in jail cells with killers, he came to believe that most of them were not suffering from mental diseases or disorders. "They were just mean, I often think there ought to be a diagnosis, you know: *'mean son of a bitch.'* "

He became less easily conned, fell less often for tears of remorse or faked madness, he says.

"These days when they'll have tears failing down from their eyes, I've learned to give this response: *'You can knock that s___ off; you're not fooling me a bit.'* And you can't believe—tears will dry up just like that."

As for fakers of insanity, well, to illustrate just how hard it is to get him to believe somebody's really crazy these days, the Doctor tells me what is clearly one of his favorite stories, the one about the fellow in jail who sliced off his penis and one testicle.

"Judge called me up and he said, 'Jim boy, have we got a crazy one.' And I go examine him, and even one of the jailers there said, 'Boy, Dr. Grigson, that guy is crazy.' Anyway, I went back and examined him. And I didn't think he was crazy. I called the judge up and said, 'Judge, he's faking [insanity].' And the judge said, 'Jim, *nobody's faking who cuts their d___ off!*' And I said, 'Judge, I promise you he's faking.' And they insisted on having a competency hearing. And I got up and told the jury, which was made up of six men and six women, that he cut off his penis and one testicle and that he was faking. They looked at me like 'Man, you know, not only is *he* crazy, but you're crazy. too.' " But then the Doctor explained to the jury what he'd gotten the prisoner to confide to him in his exam. "I explained to them that every time he had been caught—and he'd been in the pen four or five times—each time he'd cut his wrist, cut his finger, cut his throat. This time he was up for a habitual [a life sentence for repeated felonies] and he said, 'I knew I had to cut something serious!' He said, 'God Almighty! Damn! I wished I hadn't done it.' Well, the jury just laughed and they voted with me and found he was faking."

The Doctor thinks this is an extremely funny story. In any case it certainly illustrates the extreme lengths to which he takes the notion of personal moral responsibility for conduct, his reluctance to ever excuse or forgive criminal conduct on the ground of mental debility.

* * *

Lamesa is an old-fashioned Texas town out of *The Last Picture Show*. It even features one of those classics from the James Dean/Buddy Holly era, a Sonic drive-in, the kind with loudspeakers that look like parking meters for you to call in your orders to the carhops. Our directions were to take a left at the Sonic and look for D.A. Ricky Smith's blue pickup in front of his office on a side street.

When we arrived for the Doctor's pre-trial conference with Smith, the D.A. had a word of warning for the Doctor: the hotshot defense attorney brought in from Lubbock, Floyd Holder, "has done his homework on you. He's read all the propaganda, probably gonna bring up that Dr. Death stuff."

The courtroom was packed. The jury was seated. The defendant looked shockingly young. Cleaned up and clean-cut for his trial, Aaron Lee Fuller looked less like a killer facing death than one of the Brady Bunch facing after-school detention.

Photos taken at the time of his arrest show Aaron Lee Fuller with a greaser pompadour—the Texas version of the white-trash low-life look he affected back then. Today, seated straight up, hands folded formally and politely in front of him at the defense table, Aaron Lee Fuller was wearing a crew cut and a crew-neck sweater, and looking more like an all-American college sophomore than a granny murdering necrophiliac.

The image, of course, was more than a fashion statement. It was Aaron Lee Fuller's plea, his last resort, a petition to the jury for his life. One that said he'd done bad, he'd gone wrong, but he wasn't beyond hope of redemption. If he could clean up his image, at least there was a chance he could cleanse his soul.

It was an appeal on an emotional, not a legal, level, but death penalty decisions, despite all the multistage decision-making processes, are made on an emotional as well as legal level. And so the Doctor was there to combat that image, to help the jury get past it, beneath it, to see Aaron Lee Fuller the way he did: as the moral and medical equivalent of a rabid dog who must be destroyed.

What troubles his critics in the psychiatric profession most is that the Doctor would take the stand today and make his diagnosis of future dangerousness with complete certainty, yet without even having examined Aaron Lee Fuller. Indeed, without even seeing him, barely thinking about him before taking the stand. In fact, in the two days I spent with him waiting around to testify, the Doctor talked more about the lambada than he did about Aaron Lee Fuller.

In the first half of his career as a forensic-psychiatric expert witness, in the sixties and seventies, the Doctor would almost always examine the murderers he'd testify against. Frequently when they were first brought in, he'd be called upon by a court to give them a competency exam—to see if they were rational enough to stand trial. Then, fairly often prosecutors would call him to take the stand at the death penalty trial of the same defendant, and the Doctor would use information and insights he obtained in the pre-trail competency exam against the defendant in the death-penalty phase.

The Supreme Court rejected that practice in 1981 in *Estelle v. Smith* (and dozens of death sentences obtained on the basis of the Doctor's testimony were subsequently invalidated as a result) because, the Court said, it violated the defendant's Miranda rights against self-incrimination.

After that the Doctor continued to testify in murder trials, but rarely performed any personal examinations. What replaced them was a curious, carefully choreographed ritual built around him, something known as the Hypothetical. The purpose of the Hypothetical is to allow the Doctor to diagnose the defendant without having seen him or heard the details of his crime until the very moment of Judgement.

The Hypothetical in the Aaron Lee Fuller case was a single question that took no less than *forty minutes* to ask. A vast Moby Dick of a question that swallowed up all the ugly details of Aaron Lee Fuller's crime, everything bad he'd done before in his life, all the bad things he'd been overheard saying to others in jail after, and then regurgitated them, laid them before the Doctor for his inspection, and finally asked him—hypothetically—if he, as a scientist, came across such a sorry specimen, would this sorry specimen present a continuing danger to society?

And so the epic Hypothetical began. *Assume, Doctor*, the D.A. began, that in the early hours of March 18, 1989, Aaron Lee Fuller ripped open Loretta Stephen's screen door, and *assume, Doctor*, that he proceeded to steal her money, and *assume, Doctor*, that he beat her, smothered her, sexually assaulted her dead body—all of these "assumptions" repeated for the jury in clinical detail and all of them reflecting the prosecution's version of events—and *assume, Doctor*, that he dumped the body and partied all night long at the Koko Inn, and *assume, Doctor*, that his prior criminal record consists of such and such crimes and arrests, and *assume, Doctor*, that he told so-and-so he wasn't sorry about killing Loretta Stephens, "that he felt he'd done her a favor," and *assume, Doctor*, that he bragged about his plans to go after other victims ...

The forty-minute question was coming to a close now. The Doctor leaned forward in the witness stand, smiling broadly. *Assuming* all that, Doctor, do you have an opinion about such an—

Objection!

A booming voice from the defense table interrupted the impending climax of the ritual. Floyd Holder, the big, burly, white-bearded defense attorney from Texas Tech law school in Lubbock, rose to speak.

"Your Honor, I would like to take the witness on voir dire [preliminary examination]."

The judge granted the request. And suddenly big Floyd Holder launched a furious attack on the Doctor.

"Doctor," he boomed out, "I understand that it is your opinion that the board of trustees of the American Psychiatric Association are a bunch of liberals who think queers are normal?"

Whew. Everyone in the jammed courtroom sucked in a little air as it became clear that a real courtroom mano-a-mano had begun.

The Doctor demurred mildly to that liberal/queers charge, but before he could finish, Holder demanded, "The board of trustees of the American Psychiatric Association has reprimanded you for your expression of an opinion as to predictions of future dangerousness, have they not?"

Seemingly unperturbed, the Doctor replied, "They sent me a letter saying that this will serve as a reprimand."

"And the American Psychiatric Association has labeled your predictions as quackery, haven't they?"

"No, sir, they have not," the Doctor said, still smiling. A majority of the profession is "in agreement with me, that you have to predict dangerousness every day" in commitment proceedings and the like.

"And isn't it true that the A.P.A. filed an amicus brief in which they labeled your opinions as quackery?"

"The Supreme Court disagreed with them," said the Doctor, "and thought that my testimony was appropriate."

"I would object, Your Honor, to any testimony, as not being recognized within the field in which he practices."

"I will overrule the objection," said the judge. And at last prosecutor Smith was able to ask the Doctor for an answer to the killer question.

"Doctor, based upon that hypothetical, those facts that I explained to you, do you have an opinion within reasonable medical probability as to whether the defendant, Aaron Lee Fuller, will commit criminal acts of violence that will constitute a continuing threat to society?"

"Yes, sir, I most certainly do have an opinion with regard to that."

"What is your opinion, please, sir?"

"That absolutely there is no question, no doubt whatsoever, that the individual you described, that has been involved in repeated escalating behavior of violence, will commit acts of violence in the future, and represents a very serious threat to any society in which he finds himself in."

"Do you mean that he will be a threat in any society, even the prison society?"

"Absolutely, yes, sir. He will do the same thing there that he will do outside."

And that was it. All the "medical," "scientific" testimony the jury needed—in any case all they'd *get*—to justify a judgement that Aaron Lee Fuller was too dangerous to live, beyond hope of redemption, and ought to be put to death.

But Floyd Holder wasn't quite finished with his assault on the Doctor. He still had cross-examination. He still had one more shot at saving Aaron Lee Fuller's life.

Do you recall the Randall Dale Adams case? Holder began.

The Doctor nodded warily and said, "I recall it well, yes, sir."

Are you as sure about this defendant as you were when you declared Randall Dale Adams was guilty and would kill again? Holder asked.

Again the courtroom tensed up. Even out on the prairie the papers had reported on the Adams case. How Adams, a convicted cop killer, was sentenced to death with the help of the Doctor's testimony; how the New York film maker Errol Morris came down to Dallas (originally to do a film about the Doctor) and began digging into the Adams case, eventually getting Adams' chief accuser—on death row for another murder—to claim that he, not Adams, had fired the fatal bullet at the cop. How this, and holes in purported eyewitness testimony uncovered in *The Thin Blue Line*, resulted in Adams's conviction being thrown out and Adams being freed last year after twelve years in prison.

Looking totally unperturbed, the Doctor said dramatically, "Those people that were involved with the case know that he is guilty. I examined Mr. Adams ... there is no question in my mind as well as [the mind of] the jury who convicted him that he is guilty."

And did you say of Randall Dale Adams that he will continue his previous behavior? Holder asked.

"I most certainly said that," the Doctor said defiantly. "And he will."

     * * *

For a brief moment there in Lamesa, it looked as if Floyd Holder might have some momentum going in his assault on the Doctor. But then Holder made a fatal mistake. He fell into a Doctor death trap, one of the patented devastating counter-punches that have earned the Doctor a reputation as a killing machine on cross-examination. Many lawyers told me the best thing to do is not to cross the Doctor at all, to minimize the damage he can do.

The Doctor had told me of the particular relish he has for doing damage on cross-examination. "I always hold something back for cross," he said one evening in Lubbock.

But Holder had done a lot of homework he didn't want to go to waste. He began as he had with the Adams question, a bit smugly. "In the case of *Rodriguez v. Texas*, 1978, [did you say of Rodriguez], 'No matter where he is he will kill again'? ... Do you remember that?"

Now, this might have been a good question because it was clear the Doctor couldn't recall who the hell Rodriguez was. But the Doctor—a poker player as well as a chess player—shrewdly calculated that Holder didn't know the details either. And so he felt free to spring a trap of his own.

The Doctor replied as if searching his memory and then coming upon a grim recollection. "Is Rodriguez the one that killed four women and raped thirty-eight?"

Of course, he had no idea what Rodriguez had done. But what the jury heard was: killed four, raped thirty-eight. In the silence that followed it became embarrassingly clear that Floyd Holder had no idea whether the Rodriguez he was citing had killed one or a hundred.

Holder tried to conceal how taken aback he was, but he didn't conceal it well. He looked down and shuffled some papers. He said something huffy about "I have no idea" who Rodriguez is, as if that wasn't the point.

But the point had been made, indelibly. And it wasn't his point. The point the jury got was that the Doctor was trying to protect society, protect them, from multiple rapist-murderers, and that Holder hadn't troubled to find out how many women Rodriguez had raped and murdered (five of the twelve jurors were women); that he was only interested in some kind of legal loophole that let a monster like that loose on the streets again.

It was all over then, Holder had lost not only the moment but his composure, and he never did get it back. He continued briefly; he even brought up the nickname "Dr. Death." ("The jury may not appreciate how famous you are, sir ... They call you Dr. Death, don't they?") But he never recovered from the deadly land mine the Doctor had detonated under his feet with his Rodriguez reply.

A day later the Lamesa jury took two hours to agree unanimously on a death sentence for twenty-one-year-old Aaron Lee Fuller.

One down, two to go.

* * *

Back when his practice of predicting future dangerousness in death-penalty trials first became controversial, the Doctor says, "a Dallas judge named Zimmermann decided to see how I'd done in my record of predictions in his courtroom. So they went back and looked at the people I'd examined in court. And there were only two people I said would kill again: Terry Turner and Jesse Eugene Woods. Because it's rare for me to say someone will kill again. Most murderers aren't going to—a majority of them will never kill again. Spouse-passion-type killing, you know, after going through all that they'd do almost anything in the world to avoid trouble. Passion killers often make model prisoners. That's one of the things that's misleading. Most murderers on the whole make model prisoners. But that is not true of these sociopaths."

Like, for instance, Terry Turner and Jesse Eugene Woods.

"Terry Turner was a little sociopath—he was, oh, nineteen, twenty, years old and a forty-five-year-old woman took him in. She felt sorry for him. Gave him a place to stay, got him a little job. He raped and killed her. They didn't find him guilty of capital murder—something got screwed up, I can't remember. Anyway, Terry got out of the pen in three years. *On the way home* from the pen he raped a women. Within thirty days he'd taken a fourteen-year-old girl and raped and killed her. And took a tree branch and shoved it all the way up in her vagina.

"Then there was the other one, Jesse Eugene Woods. I'm trying to think what Jesse did the first time. I believe he killed somebody in a fight. [Actually, the charge was aggravated assault and sexual assault, not murder.] Anyway, I examined Jesse and I said, 'I guarantee this guy is going to kill again.' Anyway, Woods got out and beat, I think it was, an old woman to death. And after Judge Zimmermann looked at those cases he said, 'Well, I can testify that Dr. Grigson has been 100 percent accurate in this court.' "

The Doctor does not offer the two-case Zimmerman story as serious statistical vindication. What he's saying is that he's got to be aggressive, persuasive, he's got to sell his testimony to juries, so they won't let people like Terry Turner and Jesse Eugene Woods loose to kill again. That's why, he says, he feels compelled to go the extra mile. Not just to testify, but to win—in order to protect potential victims from horrific fates like that suffered by the fourteen-year-old girl.

The problems the psychiatric profession has with the Doctor concern not so much his motives as his claims to be testifying as a *scientist*. In a blistering attack on the Doctor's testimonial practice in its 1983 brief to the Supreme Court in *Barefoot v. Estelle*, the American Psychiatric Association, the governing body of the profession, flatly states:

> Psychiatrists should not be permitted to offer a prediction concerning the long-term future dangerousness of a defendant in a capital case, at least ... where the psychiatrist purports to testify *as a medical expert* possessing a predictive expertise.... The large body of research in this area indicates that, even under the best of conditions, *psychiatric predictions of long-term future dangerousness are wrong in at least two out of every three cases*. The forecast of future violent conduct ... is, at bottom, a lay determination ... made on the basis of essentially actuarial data to which *psychiatrists qua psychiatrists can bring no special interpretive skills*.... The use of psychiatric testimony on this issue causes serious prejudice to the defendant. By dressing up the actuarial data with an "expert" opinion the psychiatrist's testimony is likely to receive undue weight.... [It] provides a false aura of certainty ... impermissibly distorts the fact-finding process of capital cases. [My italics.]

Equally objectionable, the A.P.A. brief charges, it is the Doctor's practice of diagnosing a defendant as a severe sociopath on the basis of a prosecutor's hypothetical question, without examining him—and then telling the jury that the sociopath "diagnosis" is scientific basis for guaranteeing future dangerousness.

"Such a diagnosis simply cannot be made on the basis of a hypothetical question.... The psychiatrist cannot exclude alternative diagnoses [such as] illnesses that plainly do not indicate a general propensity to commit criminal acts.

"These deficiencies," the A.P.A. told the Supreme Court, "strip the psychiatric testimony of all value in the present context."

In a six-three decision in that case the Supreme Court majority held that—even granting the truth of the A.P.A.'s objections—the Doctor's testimony should not be barred as constitutionally impermissible because the adversary process of the trial would permit other psychiatrists to challenge his conclusions in court, allowing the jurors as fact finders to decide the merits.

But Justice Harry Blackmun, ordinarily a middle-of-the-roader in death-penalty cases, wrote a furious dissent declaring, "In capital cases the specious testimony, colored, in the eyes of an impressionable jury, by the inevitable untouchability of a medical specialist's words, *equates with death itself*." (My italics.)

The doctor disagrees. The Doctor believes the A.P.A. condemnation is based not on science but on the emotional animus of liberal psychiatrists against the death penalty—and against *him* for being the death penalty's cutting edge in Texas.

The Doctor says he's better qualified than any American Psychiatric Association Committee to pronounce upon the science involved because of his unmatchable database—the examinations he's done of 12,000 criminals, 1,400 murderers, 391 capital murder defendants.

The Doctor has a hyperbolic counter-argument for those who criticize future-dangerousness predictions. "It's ridiculous to say you can't predict future dangerousness. After Hitler killed the first Jew, would you say he was dangerous? After the second? After a million? How many do you need to know for sure?"

True enough, perhaps, but what if instead of Hitler we look at twenty-one-year-old Aaron Lee Fuller. Is he incorrigibly evil? His defense attorney introduced evidence that Fuller had been physically abused as a child. Is he beyond rehabilitation? Should a jury be told there's a "medical certainty" he's too dangerous to live?

Curiously enough, considering the Doctor's Hitler analogy, the next defendant, the one the Doctor is racing back to Lubbock to pronounce upon this afternoon, is sometimes called "Adolf." The defendant usually refers to himself as *Adolfo* Hernandez, but on his rap sheet, his list of a.k.a.'s included "aka *Adolf* Hernandez." And Lubbock prosecutor Travis Ware invariably refers to him as Adolf Hernandez.

Adolfo Hernandez was a thirty-eight year old ex-con with a long history of glue sniffing and house burglaries when he committed his first murder—beating an elderly woman to death with a baseball bat, a big, heavyweight Louisville Slugger type. Just so the jury wouldn't forget, throughout the Lubbock trial, or at least during the death-penalty portion of it I saw, D.A. Travis Ware stalked around the courtroom questioning witnesses with the menacing bloodstained Louisville Slugger resting on his shoulder.

* * *

This time, Brian Murray, an aggressive young lawyer on the Hernandez defense team, led the direct assault against the Doctor. He began confidently because he was building on two days of testimony by defense experts who had recited studies all saying you couldn't do it—you couldn't scientifically, medically, accurately predict the dangerousness of any given killer.

"Did you follow up on [your predications]," Murray asked the Doctor, "to see whether your analysis was correct?"

The Doctor smiled almost beatifically at the question as it came floating up to the plate, stepped into it, smashed it out of the park.

"The only study I know," he said mildly, "was done by Judge James Zimmermann in Dallas, who conducted a study of all those [times] where I'd predicted a person would kill again in his court. And I had only predicted two of them. And both of them did again." He didn't go into the tree branch. He didn't need to. It would have been overkill.

What he said, in the mildest of tones, was: "Both of them *unfortunately* had been released from the pen after committing murder. [Only one was in for murder.] And both of them within a very short period of time committed murder again."

He might as well have given Adolfo Hernandez a lethal injection right then and there. He was throwing the bodies left for dead by Turner and Woods in the jury's lap and telling each juror: Twice before I told juries these men would kill, and both times those juries ignored me and both times innocent people were murdered because those juries didn't listen to me. If you let Adolfo Hernandez live and if—*when*—he kills again, don't say I didn't warn you.

In the mildest friendliest, courtliest, country-doctor, Marcus Welby way he was telling them: *The blood will be on your hands.*

Once again the poor defense attorney who'd stepped into this trap found himself demoralized, disoriented, the wind knocked out of him, stumbling through the remainder of his examination of the Doctor. Stumbling eventually into a final, extra-cruel trap the Doctor sprang on him at the end.

Defender Murray was asking the Doctor about the absence of any neurological or mental-test evidence on the defendant.

Isn't it true, he asked the Doctor, that in the absence of any neurological studies you can't rule out that organic brain damage or retardation might be at the bottom of Adolfo Hernandez's problem, not your diagnosis of sociopathy?

"An attorney representing a client in a capital murder case *not knowing* a possibility that would be a defense?" the Doctor replied. "That would be absurd."

Bad enough. But the doomed defense attorney wouldn't withdraw from this disaster area soon enough.

"The question was, what if that [testing for retardation, etc.] was not done? Would that affect the result?"

"Are we talking about a mentally retarded *attorney*?" the Doctor asked.

The whole courtroom rocked with laughter. Attorney Murray was left standing there glaring, humiliated, paralyzed.

The Doctor smiled benignly. Murray sat down defeated. A day later the jury voted unanimously for death. It took them two hours.

Two down, one to go.

By the time we got back to Dallas for the final trial of the Doctor's triple header I'd begun to believe that he was invulnerable, unstoppable on the stand. That the death-penalty process in Texas was fatally skewed whenever the Doctor took the stand to testify—his skills as a witness unbalanced the scales of justice.

The problem is, the Supreme Court decision in *Barefoot v. Estelle* (which permitted the Doctor's hypothetical future-dangerousness testimony) envisioned a vigorous adversarial process in which defense psychiatrists and lawyers could present their case to the jury, dispute, refute his "science." In reality, the Doctor's charisma and deadliness as a witness just overwhelm the process and create an intrinsic unfairness.

But finally, in Dallas, I saw the Doctor take a hit. Not a fatal one, but one that threw him off his stride for a moment—something that nobody's ever seen before. For that one moment, the Doctor's mask of utter confidence and geniality, of Marcus Welby-like disinterested benevolence, slipped.

It happened in the death penalty trial of Gayland Bradford, a twenty-one-year-old black man accused of murdering a twenty-nine-year-old security guard in a Dallas grocery store.

There was little doubt about the nature of Gayland Bradford's deed. It's all in there in the sickly-gray cinema verite of the security-camera videotape they played at his trial.

The tape was particularly devastating because in its opening moments it captured something about the security-guard victim's life as well as his death. It showed him, moments before he was blown away, horsing around with the cashiers, doing a bit of an Oliver Hardy imitation, arms akimbo, saying, with mock outrage, *"I hate this tie."*

Enter Gayland Bradford. A black-clad figure cuts purposefully through the gray static of the videotape, swiftly reaches the security guard. Sticks a gun into his spine and, before he knows what's happened, blows a hole in him.

There's a sickening POP on the sound track.

The guard sprawls backward beneath a checkout counter, bleeding but alive. "O.K., O.K., *O.K.!"* he pleads, holding up his hand, as if to fend of the gun Gayland Bradford is pointing at him. *"O.K.!"* he says one last time.

It's not O.K. with Gayland Bradford. He pumps three more shots into the guy, quieting him forever.

An open-and-shut case. To nobody's surprise, the jury took twenty minutes to bring in a guilty verdict.

But the death-penalty phase of the trial brought two surprises. First, the doctor would get to do something he rarely does these days. He'd get to go in and examine the murderer before testifying against him. (The judge had granted a prosecution motion that would have barred defense shrinks from introducing mitigating evidence from their exams unless the prosecution shrink—the Doctor—got to examine Bradford, too.)

That was the first surprise. The other surprise in this case was the Doctor's attitude toward Gayland Bradford. It seemed to me from the moment he showed up at the trial and got a look at Bradford that the Doctor brought more than his usual competitive zeal to this case—he brought something extra, an almost personal animus, to the crusade to get Gayland Bradford executed.

I'm not sure why. Perhaps in part because we were back in Dallas, the Doctor's home turf, but also a place where widespread publicity about his role in the Randall Dale Adams case had revived the Dr. Death image, challenged his reputation for invincibility and certitude. Perhaps also because he would be facing a particularly wily and experienced opponent on the defense team—Paul Brauchle—who'd tangled with the Doctor before and knew his tricks.

Or maybe it was just cultural, maybe it *did* all come down to Gayland Bradford's lightning bolt haircut, which, as we shall see, was certainly the flash point at the climax of the trial.

Whatever the source, I first noticed the Doctor's extra-aggressiveness in this case on the Monday afternoon following the big Friday doubleheader. He was sitting in court furiously scribbling notes about the defense psychiatrist's testimony, urgently passing notes up to Dallas D.A. Dan Hagood to use in his cross-examination of the defense shrink. It was as if the Doctor wanted not merely to refute the defense psychiatrist's testimony, he wanted to destroy him.

And, oddly enough, for different reasons I was feeling outrage about the defense psychiatrist, whose ineffectual performance on the stand typified what seemed to me the bankruptcy of conventional psychiatry in dealing with the life-or-death urgency of death-penalty trials.

Because this case had a real, arguable psychiatric issue. Unlike the Aaron Lee Fuller case, unlike the Adolfo Hernandez case, in which there was very little the defense could find to mitigate the horror and cold-bloodedness of the killings (Fuller was very young, Hernandez was very drunk—that was the best they could do), here there was a quantifiable mitigating issue: the possibility that Gayland Bradford was retarded. The defense psychologist who examined him had tested Bradford at an I.Q. of 75, borderline retarded; the Texas penitentiary had tested him at 68.

* * *

What Gayland Bradford needed was a powerful advocate to make the case that his lack of mental capacity diminished the degree of cold-blooded deliberation he brought to his crime.

What he got instead was a shrinking violet of an academic psychiatrist who clung to jargon-encrusted textbook cliches, who cowered behind his pose as an objective scientist and refused to contend for the life at stake, the way the Doctor contended for Gayland Bradford's death.

When this defense shrink came under furious attack on cross-examination by D.A. Hagood, he acted petulant, insulted, and irritated that a scientist of his stature and dignity should have to defend himself in the sweaty arena of the courtroom.

Even the defense team was dismayed by its witness's performance.

"This f_____ is so stupid," Paul Brauchle confided to me after the slaughter was over, "that he doesn't even know how stupid he really is."

I asked the Doctor what he might have said if he'd been hired to testify in Gayland Bradford's defense. And he said in effect that he could probably have saved Gayland Bradford's life.

How?

"What you do," he said offhandedly, "is tell the jury, 'Look, it's an awful crime, a tragedy, but this is a scared retarded kid.' Sure the prosecution objects to your injecting this, but you've reached out and planted something the jury can hold on to, not all that bull____ about the *Diagnostic Manual*."

Of course. Suddenly it seemed obvious. But in none of the three death-penalty trials I'd observed had any of the supposedly liberal psychiatrists had the will or the skill to reach out to the jury's heart the way the Doctor does. I began to think the only way a death-penalty trial in which he testifies can be fair is if the Doctor is forced to make the case for both sides.

That was not the case in the Gayland Bradford trial. After demonstrating how he might have saved Bradford's life, the Doctor proceeded, over the next forty-eight hours, to throw himself with redoubled vigor into the effort to ensure his death.

To this end he focused his sights on the unusual one-on-one, head-to-head "examination" of Gayland Bradford the court's ruling had mandated.

Before the exam, he had two objectives. First, he wanted to refute the notion that Bradford was retarded. He didn't buy the 75 I.Q. figure.

"That's bull____," he told me. "I know it's higher than that."

"Based on what?" I asked him.

"Based on what I've heard," he said vaguely.

He didn't disclose the other objective to me right away, but it became the main objective of his exam. He wanted to pin another murder on Gayland Bradford. He wanted to prove he'd killed more than once—all the more reason to guarantee he'd kill again.

He's played investigative shrink before with great success, he told me. A number of times he has examined killers arrested for the first time for murder and—acting on a hunch, on experience, on his data base—he's not only tumbled to the fact these people have killed before, he's gotten them to confess it. He can smell a repeat killer when he sees one, he says. He thought he saw one in Gayland Bradford.

And so it came to pass that at 4:35 p.m. on February 7, 1990, the Doctor was ushered into a conference room in the Dallas county jail. He introduced himself to Gayland Bradford, who was advised of his Fifth Amendment rights against self-incrimination. The Doctor gave Gayland Bradford cigarettes: he gave him coffee; he gave him a ninety-minute "psychiatric examination" that was less like a medical procedure than a third degree in a precinct detective tank.

"He's killed before. I know it." Those were the Doctor's first words when he and his wife joined me for a previously scheduled dinner—right after leaving Gayland Bradford.

* * *

I'd never seen the Doctor so animated, so thrilled with the chase, the hunt, as he was that night in his dramatic fresh-from-the-jail account of going head-to-head with Gayland Bradford.

He came on strong, he said. Forgetting about the conventional psychiatric procedure, which usually begins with a history and leads up to the crime, the Doctor early on got Gayland Bradford to take him through the murder step-by-step.

It was so fresh in the Doctor's mind—and he still had his notes with him—that he recounted whole chunks of dialogue verbatim.

"Gayland goes through the whole killing bit," the Doctor began. "How the guard is saying '*O.K.,* O.K.' and he's shooting him a few more times. At this point I say, 'Gayland, where did you get the gun?'"

" 'Well, I had it.'

" 'How long have you had it?'

" 'Well, I don't know.'

"Finally I say, 'What did you *do* with your gun?'

" 'Well, I ditched it.'

" 'Well, *why*? Why did you do that? You didn't ditch the security guard's gun?'

" 'I wanted to get rid of it.'

" 'Look, something doesn't make sense here. You've made your confession, but you didn't tell them where the gun is. How come?'

" 'I just wanted *me* to know.'

"You hear that?" the Doctor asked us. "He says, 'I just wanted *me* to know.' It had already dawned on me that he's killed somebody else with it. Ballistics would show that. So because he doesn't want to be connected with the other killings, he won't say where the gun is. I don't say that to him. My mind's turning like mad. I said, 'Gayland, how come you won't tell them where the gun is? It doesn't make any sense. *Why, Gayland? Why?'*

Of course, I'm giving him cigarettes and coffee and we almost smoked the defense psychiatrist [there observing] out of the room.

"And by the way," the Doctor added, "this kid's not retarded. This kid's vocabulary—I told him 'I've heard doctors say that you have a 75 I.Q., that you are mentally retarded, but I want you to know whoever made that stupid statement is 100 per cent wrong.' This with the defense psychiatrist who made the statement sitting right there," the Doctor chortled.

But the Doctor hadn't finished with the missing gun question, and things soon built to an angry climax. "I kept going, 'Why, Gayland? Why won't you tell me where the gun is?' Well, after the fourth or fifth time he said the reason he wouldn't say where the gun was is 'I don't know what the man who sold it to me might have done with it.'

"And of course I've got my wheels working, and I said, 'What do you mean, what he might have done with it?'

" 'Well, he might have killed somebody with it.' I said, 'Oh, now I understand. you were afraid that if they found the gun, and it had killed somebody else, they might put that killing on *you*?'

"He said, 'Yeah.' I said, 'Hey, that makes sense.' Turned to him and said, *'Gayland, this isn't the first time you ever killed anybody!'*

" 'What do you mean, man?'

" 'Gayland, this isn't your first one.'

"I tried another avenue. Started taking him through his past criminal record. Then asked him 'When was the first time you broke the law and didn't get arrested? 'Didn't get caught?' He looked at me like 'You son of a bitch.' Said, 'I quit.' "

And that was it. "Well, he did say one more thing. As we were walking out, I kind of joked. I said to him, 'Hey man, I know more about you than your own mother.' He said, 'Bull____.' I said, 'I know you a whole lot better than your mother, because I know what you have done.' And as I was leaving he pointed his finger at me and said, 'You're slick.' "

"You're slick?"

"Yeah, it was 'Hey man, you're slick.' It's the sociopath's compliment. It's the recognition of the sociopath for somebody who appreciates what he really is."

He's slick, the Doctor, yes. But almost too slick in this case. Because as it turned out, the Doctor's trial appearance the next morning in the Gayland Bradford case was not the expected triumph he'd been brimming over with the night before.

Something happened the next morning on the stand, something I hadn't seen before. The Doctor made a serious misstep, went a little too far in his avidity to nail Gayland Bradford.

What happened could perhaps be attributed to the four martinis over dinner the night before. The Doctor did look a little pale and irritable as he took the stand. It was that irritability, I believe, that caused him to stumble.

Not at first, not during direct testimony. There it was possible to detect an edge, but it came across as aggressiveness. Indeed, he was more aggressive than I had seen him before. Not only did he predict future dangerousness, not only did he attempt to demolish the "I.Q. 75" defense, not only did he inject his uncorroborated suspicion that Gayland Bradford had killed more than once before, he also told the jury, "Gayland Bradford is one of the most dangerous killers I've *ever* examined or come into contact with."

With all that, the Doctor didn't need the haircut remark. But he just couldn't help himself.

Paul Brauchle has a deceptively easygoing manner. Slight, extremely soft-spoken, with a puckish sense of humor, he's cordial to the Doctor, but he has some very strong feelings about the Doctor's practice.

"If you ask me, *he's* the sociopath," Brauchle told me in a courthouse-corridor conversation. "He's the one who, despite reprimands, goes around making pronouncements which have been condemned by his profession. He's the one who does it over and over again with no remorse," Brauchle added. "Just like a sociopath."

Brauchle told me he's learned to be wary of the Doctor on cross, so I wasn't expecting great things; I was surprised when he took the Doctor's haircut comment and blasted it out of the park.

Now, earlier, while discussing the defendant with me, the Doctor had remarked a couple of times upon Gayland Bradford's haircut. It was something of an advanced fashion statement, Gayland Bradford's look. Unlike, say, Aaron Lee Fuller, who tried to craft a whole new, penitent image out of his crew cut, Gayland Bradford was *not* making a fashion statement calculated to ingratiate himself with the all-white jury deciding his fate.

It was a carefully sculpted flattop with shaved sides, common enough in urban areas everywhere by now. But with an added, less common touch: into each stubbly, shaved side of his head Gayland Bradford had had inscribed the unmistakable outline of a lightning bolt.

Despite the fact that his life was hanging by a thread, that thread consisting of the jury's judgment of whether he might be dangerous in the future, Gayland Bradford had chosen a fashion statement that—whatever its private meaning to him—seemed to announce to the jury, *"I am one dangerous dude."*

It was, however, certainly something the jury was already aware of. The Doctor didn't need to point it out to them.

Still, the Doctor couldn't resist taking a shot at it. It happened in the middle of cross-examination. Brauchle was questioning him about whether he'd prejudged the Gayland Bradford case, before he had walked in to examine him.

Perhaps the Doctor knew he was on thin ice on this subject and saw the haircut wisecrack as an escape.

In any case, when Brauchle asked him if he'd formed any *other* opinions about Gayland Bradford before he examined him, the Doctor said, trying for a laugh:

"Well, I thought that was the weirdest haircut I'd ever seen.

There was a bit of nervous laughter in the courtroom which stopped dead when Paul Brauchle shot back:

"Pretty good reason to kill him, right?"

Then there was silence. It was one of those courtroom moments of truth that cut to the heart of the matter.

The Doctor himself was speechless for a moment. Something I'd never seen before.

Then lamely, plaintively he volunteered:

"Well, I'd never *seen* a haircut like that."

At the point the judge, mercifully, decreed a recess.

But for one revealing moment the Doctor's mask had slipped. The image of geniality and nonpartisanship he was so good at projecting to juries was betrayed by what seemed to be hostility. Not just to a haircut, but to Gayland Bradford himself. Not merely to Bradford's crime, but to what he saw as Bradford's cultural alienness. It seemed to call into question the Doctor's ability to get inside Gayland Bradford's head if he couldn't get past his haircut.

Pretty good reason to kill him, right?

Nonetheless, if it bothered the jury, it didn't bother them for too long. The moment of exposure passed rapidly. The Doctor looked shaken during the lunch recess; he knew he'd been roughed up by Brauchle, told me he knew he had to suppress his emotions, cool himself out. When he returned to the stand, he'd adopted a totally Gandhian tactic: soft-spoken, barely audible one-word answers to Brauchle's sallies. No combativeness, total agreeableness. Brauchle gave up and the cross ended with a whimper, not a bang.

As it turned out, this jury did take longer than the Lubbock and Lamesa juries to make up its mind. Not two hours as in Lamesa and Lubbock, but six hours. Still, when they came back they'd followed the Doctor's orders. They'd voted yes unanimously on the Special Issues.

Gayland Bradford was sent down to death row in Huntsville to join Aaron Lee Fuller, Adolfo Hernandez and 322 other condemned murderers waiting out the appeals of their appointments with the Big Needle. * * *

For those who believe the death penalty is a deterrent to murder and who favor more death sentences executed more quickly, the Doctor is something of a hero of productivity. Almost like an Old West Marshall riding into town to swiftly string up evildoers. To those who oppose the death penalty, he's the embodiment of all that's arbitrary and capricious about how we select who gets killed.

But few would disagree with Gayland Bradford's awed assessment of the Doctor: He's *slick*.

Or Justice Blackmun's: He *equates with death itself.*

NOTE

1. *Subsequent developments.*

In 1995, the American Psychiatric Association and the Texas Society of Psychiatric Physicians expelled Dr. Grigson after finding ethical violations arising from his testimony regarding future dangerousness. J. Kirchmeier, *Aggravating and Mitigating Factors: the Paradox of Today's Arbitrary and Mandatory Capital Punishment Scheme*, 6 Wm. & Mary Bill Rts. J. 345, 372 (1998).

PAYNE v. TENNESSEE

501 U.S. 808, 111 S.Ct. 2597, 115 L.Ed.2d 720 (1991).

CHIEF JUSTICE REHNQUIST delivered the opinion of the Court.

In this case we reconsider our holdings in *Booth v. Maryland*, 482 U.S. 496, 107 S.Ct. 2529 (1987), and *South Carolina v. Gathers*, 490 U.S. 805, 109 S.Ct. 2207 (1989), that the Eighth Amendment bars the admission of victim impact evidence during the penalty phase of a capital trial.

Petitioner, Pervis Tyrone Payne, was convicted by a jury on two counts of first-degree murder and one count of assault with intent to commit murder in the first degree. He was sentenced to death for each of the murders and to 30 years in prison for the assault.

The victims of Payne's offenses were 28–year–old Charisse Christopher, her 2–year–old daughter Lacie, and her 3–year–old son Nicholas. The three lived together in an apartment in Millington, Tennessee, across the hall from Payne's girlfriend, Bobbie Thomas. On Saturday, June 27, 1987, Payne visited Thomas' apartment several times in expectation of her return from her mother's house in Arkansas, but found no one at home. On one visit, he left his overnight bag, containing clothes and other items for his weekend stay, in the hallway outside Thomas' apartment. With the bag were three cans of malt liquor.

Payne passed the morning and early afternoon injecting cocaine and drinking beer. Later, he drove around the town with a friend in the friend's car, each of them taking turns reading a pornographic magazine. Sometime around 3 p.m., Payne returned to the apartment complex, entered the Christophers' apartment, and began making sexual advances towards Charisse. Charisse resisted and Payne became violent. A neighbor who resided in the apartment directly beneath the Christophers heard Charisse screaming, " 'Get out, get out,' as if she were telling the children to leave." The noise briefly subsided and then began, " 'horribly loud.' " The neighbor called the police after she heard a "blood curdling scream" from the Christopher's apartment.

When the first police officer arrived at the scene, he immediately encountered Payne, who was leaving the apartment building, so covered with blood that he appeared to be " 'sweating blood.' " The officer confronted Payne, who responded, " 'I'm the complainant.' " When the officer asked, " 'What's going on up there?' " Payne struck the officer with the overnight bag, dropped his tennis shoes, and fled.

Inside the apartment, the police encountered a horrifying scene. Blood covered the walls and floor throughout the unit. Charisse and her children were lying on the floor in the kitchen. Nicholas, despite several wounds inflicted by a butcher knife that completely penetrated through his body from front to back, was still breathing. Miraculously, he survived, but not until after undergoing seven hours of surgery and a transfusion of 1,700 cc's of blood—400 to 500 cc's more than his estimated normal blood volume. Charisse and Lacie were dead.

[Payne's fingerprints were found in the apartment, and, when he was arrested later that day, he had blood on his clothes which matched the victims' blood types.]

At trial, Payne took the stand and, despite the overwhelming and relatively uncontroverted evidence against him, testified that he had not harmed any of the Christophers. Rather, he asserted that another man had raced by him as he was walking up the stairs to the floor where the Christophers lived. He stated that he had gotten blood on himself when, after hearing moans from the Christophers' apartment, he had tried to help the victims. According to his testimony, he panicked and fled when he heard police sirens and noticed the blood on his clothes. The jury returned guilty verdicts against Payne on all counts.

During the sentencing phase of the trial, Payne presented the testimony of four witnesses: his mother and father, Bobbie Thomas, and Dr. John T. Hutson, a clinical psychologist specializing in criminal court evaluation work. Bobbie Thomas testified that she met Payne at church, during a time when she was being abused by her husband. She stated that Payne was a very caring person, and that he devoted much time and attention to her three children, who were being affected by her marital difficulties. She said that the children had come to love him very much and would miss him, and that he "behaved just like a father that loved his kids." She asserted that he did not drink, nor did he use drugs, and that it was generally inconsistent with Payne's character to have committed these crimes.

Dr. Hutson testified that based on Payne's low score on an IQ test, Payne was "mentally handicapped." Hutson also said that Payne was neither psychotic nor schizophrenic, and that Payne was the most polite prisoner he had ever met. Payne's parents testified that their son had no prior criminal record and had never been arrested. They also stated that Payne had no history of alcohol or drug abuse, he worked with his father as a painter, he was good with children, and he was a good son.

The State presented the testimony of Charisse's mother, Mary Zvolanek. When asked how Nicholas had been affected by the murders of his mother and sister, she responded:

"He cries for his mom. He doesn't seem to understand why she doesn't come home. And he cries for his sister Lacie. He comes to me many times during the week and asks me, Grandmama, do you miss my Lacie. And I tell him yes. He says, I'm worried about my Lacie."

In arguing for the death penalty during closing argument, the prosecutor commented on the continuing effects of Nicholas' experience, stating:

"But we do know that Nicholas was alive. And Nicholas was in the same room. Nicholas was still conscious. His eyes were open. He responded to the paramedics. He was able to follow their directions. He was able to hold his intestines in as he was carried to the ambulance. So he knew what happened to his mother and baby sister."

"There is nothing you can do to ease the pain of any of the families involved in this case. There is nothing you can do to ease the pain of Bernice or Carl Payne, and that's a tragedy. There is nothing you can do basically to ease the pain of Mr. and Mrs. Zvolanek, and that's a tragedy. They will have to live with it the rest of their lives.

There is obviously nothing you can do for Charisse and Lacie Jo. But there is something that you can do for Nicholas.

"Somewhere down the road Nicholas is going to grow up, hopefully. He's going to want to know what happened. And he is going to know what happened to his baby sister and his mother. He is going to want to know what type of justice was done. He is going to want to know what happened. With your verdict, you will provide the answer."

In the rebuttal to Payne's closing argument, the prosecutor stated:

"You saw the videotape this morning.[a] You saw what Nicholas Christopher will carry in his mind forever. When you talk about cruel, when you talk about atrocious, and when you talk about heinous, that picture will always come into your mind, probably throughout the rest of your lives. . . .

. . . . .

". . . No one will ever know about Lacie Jo because she never had the chance to grow up. Her life was taken from her at the age of two years old. So, no there won't be a high school principal to talk about Lacie Jo Christopher, and there won't be anybody to take her to her high school prom. And there won't be anybody there—there won't be her mother there or Nicholas' mother there to kiss him at night. His mother will never kiss him good night or pat him as he goes off to bed, or hold him and sing him a lullaby.

. . . . .

"[Petitioner's attorney] wants you to think about a good reputation, people who love the defendant and things about him. He doesn't want you to think about the people who love Charisse Christopher, her mother and daddy who loved her. The people who loved little Lacie Jo, the grandparents who are still here. The brother who mourns for her every single day and wants to know where his best little playmate is. He doesn't have anybody to watch cartoons with him, a little one. These are the things that go into why it is especially cruel, heinous, and atrocious, the burden that that child will carry forever."

The jury sentenced Payne to death on each of the murder counts.

The Supreme Court of Tennessee affirmed the conviction and sentence. * * *

* * *

We granted certiorari to reconsider our holdings in *Booth* and *Gathers* that the Eighth Amendment prohibits a capital sentencing jury from considering "victim impact" evidence relating to the personal characteris-

---

a. The reference is to a videotape of the crime scene, the only substantive evidence other than the testimony Mary Zvolanek introduced by the prosecution at the penalty phase.

tics of the victim and the emotional impact of the crimes on the victim's family.

In *Booth*, the defendant robbed and murdered an elderly couple. As required by a state statute, a victim impact statement was prepared based on interviews with the victims' son, daughter, son-in-law, and grand-daughter. The statement, which described the personal characteristics of the victims, the emotional impact of the crimes on the family, and set forth the family members' opinions and characterizations of the crimes and the defendant, was submitted to the jury at sentencing. The jury imposed the death penalty. The conviction and sentence were affirmed on appeal by the State's highest court.

This Court held by a 5–to–4 vote that the Eighth Amendment prohibits a jury from considering a victim impact statement at the sentencing phase of a capital trial. The Court made clear that the admissibility of victim impact evidence was not to be determined on a case-by-case basis, but that such evidence was *per se* inadmissible in the sentencing phase of a capital case except to the extent that it "relate[d] directly to the circumstances of the crime." In *Gathers*, decided two years later, the Court extended the rule announced in *Booth* to statements made by a prosecutor to the sentencing jury regarding the personal qualities of the victim.

The *Booth* Court began its analysis with the observation that the capital defendant must be treated as a " 'uniquely individual human bein[g],' " (quoting *Woodson v. North Carolina*, 428 U.S. 280, 96 S.Ct. 2978 (1976)), and therefore the Constitution requires the jury to make an individualized determination as to whether the defendant should be executed based on the " 'character of the individual and the circumstances of the crime.' " (quoting *Zant v. Stephens*, 462 U.S. 862, 103 S.Ct. 2733 (1983)). The Court concluded that while no prior decision of this Court had mandated that only the defendant's character and immediate characteristics of the crime may constitutionally be considered, other factors are irrelevant to the capital sentencing decision unless they have "some bearing on the defendant's 'personal responsibility and moral guilt.' " (quoting *Enmund v. Florida*, 458 U.S. 782, 102 S.Ct. 3368 (1982)). To the extent that victim impact evidence presents "factors about which the defendant was unaware, and that were irrelevant to the decision to kill," the Court concluded, it has nothing to do with the "blameworthiness of a particular defendant." Evidence of the victim's character, the Court observed, "could well distract the sentencing jury from its constitutionally required task [of] determining whether the death penalty is appropriate in light of the background and record of the accused and the particular circumstances of the crime." The Court concluded that, except to the extent that victim impact evidence relates "directly to the circumstances of the crime," the prosecution may not introduce such evidence at a capital sentencing hearing because "it creates an impermissible risk that the capital sentencing decision will be made in an arbitrary manner."

Booth and *Gathers* were based on two premises: that evidence relating to a particular victim or to the harm that a capital defendant causes a victim's family do not in general reflect on the defendant's "blameworthiness," and that only evidence relating to "blameworthiness" is relevant to the capital sentencing decision. However, the assessment of harm caused by the defendant as a result of the crime charged has understandably been an important concern of the criminal law, both in determining the elements of the offense and in determining the appropriate punishment. Thus, two equally blameworthy criminal defendants may be guilty of different offenses solely because their acts cause differing amounts of harm. "If a bank robber aims his gun at a guard, pulls the trigger, and kills his target, he may be put to death. If the gun unexpectedly misfires, he may not. His moral guilt in both cases is identical, but his responsibility in the former is greater." *Booth* (SCALIA, J., dissenting). The same is true with respect to two defendants, each of whom participates in a robbery, and each of whom acts with reckless disregard for human life; if the robbery in which the first defendant participated results in the death of a victim, he may be subjected to the death penalty, but if the robbery in which the second defendant participates does not result in the death of a victim, the death penalty may not be imposed. *Tison v. Arizona*, 481 U.S. 137, 107 S.Ct. 1676 (1987).

* * *

We have held that a State cannot preclude the sentencer from considering "any relevant mitigating evidence" that the defendant proffers in support of a sentence less than death. *Eddings v. Oklahoma*, 455 U.S. 104, 102 S.Ct. 869 (1982). Thus we have, as the Court observed in *Booth*, required that the capital defendant be treated as a " 'uniquely individual human bein[g]' " (quoting *Woodson v. North Carolina*). But it was never held or even suggested in any of our cases preceding *Booth* that the defendant, entitled as he was to individualized consideration, was to receive that consideration wholly apart from the crime which he had committed. The language quoted from *Woodson* in the *Booth* opinion was not intended to describe a class of evidence that could not be received, but a class of evidence which must be received. * * * This misreading of precedent in *Booth* has, we think, unfairly weighted the scales in a capital trial; while virtually no limits are placed on the relevant mitigating evidence a capital defendant may introduce concerning his own circumstances, the State is barred from either offering "a quick glimpse of the life" which a defendant "chose to extinguish," *Mills v. Maryland*, 486 U.S. 367, 108 S.Ct. 1860 (1988) (REHNQUIST, C.J., dissenting), or demonstrating the loss to the victim's family and to society which has resulted from the defendant's homicide.

The *Booth* Court reasoned that victim impact evidence must be excluded because it would be difficult, if not impossible, for the defendant to rebut such evidence without shifting the focus of the sentencing hearing away from the defendant, thus creating a " 'mini-trial' on the victim's character." In many cases the evidence relating to the victim is already before the jury at least in part because of its relevance at the guilt phase of the trial. But even as to additional evidence admitted at the sentencing phase, the mere fact that for tactical reasons it might not be prudent for the defense to rebut victim impact evidence makes the case no different than others in which a party is faced with this sort of a dilemma. As we explained in rejecting the contention that expert testimony on future dangerousness should be excluded from capital trials, "the rules of evidence generally extant at the federal and state levels anticipate that relevant, unprivileged evidence should be admitted and its weight left to the factfinder, who would have the benefit of cross-examination and contrary evidence by the opposing party." *Barefoot v. Estelle*, 463 U.S. 880, 103 S.Ct. 3383 (1983).

Payne echoes the concern voiced in *Booth*'s case that the admission of victim impact evidence permits a jury to find that defendants whose victims were assets to their community are more deserving of punishment than those whose victims are perceived to be less worthy. As a general matter, however, victim impact evidence is not offered to encourage comparative judgments of this kind—for instance, that the killer of a hardworking, devoted parent deserves the death penalty, but that the murderer of a reprobate does not. It is designed to show instead each victim's "uniqueness as an individual human being," whatever the jury might think the loss to the community resulting from his death might be. The facts of *Gathers* are an excellent illustration of this: The evidence showed that the victim was an out of work, mentally handicapped individual, perhaps not, in the eyes of most, a significant contributor to society, but nonetheless a murdered human being.

Under our constitutional system, the primary responsibility for defining crimes against state law, fixing punishments for the commission of these crimes, and establishing procedures for criminal trials rests with the States. The state laws respecting crimes, punishments, and criminal procedure are, of course, subject to the overriding provisions of the United States Constitution. Where the State imposes the death penalty for a particular crime, we have held that the Eighth Amendment imposes special limitations upon that process. * * * But, as we noted in *California v. Ramos*, 463 U.S. 992, 103 S.Ct. 3446 (1983), "[b]eyond these limitations ... the Court has deferred to the State's choice of substantive factors relevant to the penalty determination."

"Within the constitutional limitations defined by our cases, the States enjoy their traditional latitude to prescribe the method by which those who commit murder shall be punished." *Blystone v. Pennsylvania*, 494 U.S. 299, 110 S.Ct. 1078 (1990). The States remain free, in capital cases, as well as others, to devise new procedures and new remedies to meet felt needs. Victim impact evidence is simply another form or method of informing the sentencing authority about the specific harm caused by the crime in question, evidence of a general type long considered by sentencing authorities. We think the *Booth* Court was wrong in stating that this kind of evidence leads to the arbitrary imposition of the death penalty. In the majority of cases, and in this case, victim impact evidence serves entirely legitimate purposes. In the event that evidence is introduced that is so unduly prejudicial that it renders the trial fundamentally unfair, the Due Process Clause of the Fourteenth Amendment provides a mechanism for relief. See *Darden v. Wainwright,* 477 U.S. 168, 106 S.Ct. 2464 (1986). Courts have always taken into consideration the harm done by the defendant in imposing sentence, and the evidence adduced in this case was illustrative of the harm caused by Payne's double murder.

We are * * * of the view that a State may properly conclude that for the jury to assess meaningfully the defendant's moral culpability and blameworthiness, it should have before it at the sentencing phase evidence of the specific harm caused by the defendant. "[T]he State has a legitimate interest in counteracting the mitigating evidence which the defendant is entitled to put in, by reminding the sentencer that just as the murderer should be considered as an individual, so too the victim is an individual whose death represents a unique loss to society and in particular to his family." *Booth* (WHITE, J., dissenting). By turning the victim into a "faceless stranger at the penalty phase of a capital trial," *Gathers* (O'CONNOR, J., dissenting), *Booth* deprives the State of the full moral force of its evidence and may prevent the jury from having before it all the information necessary to determine the proper punishment for a first-degree murder.

The present case is an example of the potential for such unfairness. The capital sentencing jury heard testimony from Payne's girlfriend that they met at church; that he was affectionate, caring, and kind to her children; that he was not an abuser of drugs or alcohol; and that it was inconsistent with his character to have committed the murders. Payne's parents testified that he was a good son, and a clinical psychologist testified that Payne was an extremely polite prisoner and suffered from a low IQ. None of this testimony was related to the circumstances of Payne's brutal crimes. In contrast, the only evidence of the impact of Payne's offenses during the sentencing phase was Nicholas' grandmother's description—in response to a single question—that the child misses his mother and baby sister. Payne argues that the Eighth Amendment commands that the jury's death sentence must be set aside because the jury heard this testimony. But the testimony illustrated quite poignantly some of the harm that Payne's killing had caused; there is nothing unfair about allowing the jury to bear in mind that harm at the same time as it considers the mitigating evidence introduced by the defendant. The Supreme Court of Tennessee in this case obviously felt the unfairness of the rule pronounced by *Booth* when it said: "It is an affront to the civilized members of the human race to say that at sentencing in a capital case, a parade of witnesses may praise the background, character and good deeds of Defendant (as was done in this case), without limitation as to relevancy, but nothing may be said that bears upon the character of, or the harm imposed, upon the victims."

In *Gathers*, as indicated above, we extended the holding of *Booth* barring victim impact evidence to the prosecutor's argument to the jury. Human nature being what it is, capable lawyers trying cases to juries try to convey to the jurors that the people involved in the underlying events are, or were, living human beings, with something to be gained or lost from the jury's verdict. Under the aegis of the Eighth Amendment, we have given the broadest latitude to the defendant to introduce relevant mitigating evidence reflecting on his individual personality, and the defendant's attorney may argue that evidence to the jury. Petitioner's attorney in this case did just that. For the reasons discussed above, we now reject the view—expressed in *Gathers*—that a State may not permit the prosecutor to similarly argue to the jury the human cost of the crime of which the defendant stands convicted. We reaffirm the view expressed by Justice Cardozo in *Snyder v. Massachusetts*, 291 U.S. 97, 54 S.Ct. 330 (1934): "[J]ustice, though due to the accused, is due to the accuser also. The concept of fairness must not be strained till it is narrowed to a filament. We are to keep the balance true."

We thus hold that if the State chooses to permit the admission of victim impact evidence and prosecutorial argument on that subject, the Eighth Amendment erects no *per se* bar. A State may legitimately conclude that evidence about the victim and about the impact of the murder on the victim's family is relevant to the jury's decision as to whether or not the death penalty should be imposed. There is no reason to treat such evidence differently than other relevant evidence is treated.

[The Court rejected Payne's argument that the doctrine of *stare decisis* compelled the Court to adhere to *Booth* and *Gathers*, and the Court expressly overruled the two cases. At the same time, the Court limited its holding to the question presented, *i.e.*, whether evidence and argument relating to the victim and the impact of the victim's death on the victim's family are inadmissible at a capital sentencing hearing. "*Booth* also held that the admission of a victim's family members' characterizations and opinions about the crime, the defendant, and the appropriate sentence violates the Eighth Amendment. No evidence of the latter sort was presented at the trial in this case."]

> [Concurring opinion of O'CONNOR, J., joined by WHITE and KENNEDY, JJ., concurring opinion of SCALIA, J., joined in part by O'CONNOR and KENNEDY, JJ., concurring opinion of SOUTER, J., joined by KENNEDY, J. and dissenting opinion of MARSHALL, J., joined by BLACKMUN, J., omitted]

> JUSTICE STEVENS, with whom JUSTICE BLACKMUN joins, dissenting.

The novel rule that the Court announces today represents a dramatic departure from the principles that have governed our capital sentencing jurisprudence for decades. * * * [E]ven if *Booth v. Maryland*, 482 U.S. 496, 107 S.Ct. 2529 (1987), and *South Carolina v. Gathers*, 490 U.S. 805, 109 S.Ct. 2207 (1989), had not been decided, today's decision would represent a sharp break with past decisions. Our cases provide no support whatsoever for the majority's conclusion that the prosecutor may introduce evidence that sheds no light on the defendant's guilt or moral culpability, and thus serves no purpose other than to encourage jurors to decide in favor of death rather than life on the basis of their emotions rather than their reason.

Until today our capital punishment jurisprudence has required that any decision to impose the death penalty be based solely on evidence that tends to inform the jury about the character of the offense and the character of the defendant. Evidence that serves no purpose other than to appeal to the sympathies or emotions of the jurors has never been .considered admissible. Thus, if a defendant, who had murdered a convenience store clerk in cold blood in the course of an armed robbery, offered evidence unknown to him at the time of the crime about the immoral character of his victim, all would recognize immediately that the evidence was irrelevant and inadmissible. Evenhanded justice requires that the same constraint be imposed on the advocate of the death penalty.

* * *

III

Victim impact evidence, as used in this case, has two flaws, both related to the Eighth Amendment's command that the punishment of death may not be meted out arbitrarily or capriciously. First, aspects of the character of the victim unforeseeable to the defendant at the time of his crime are irrelevant to the defendant's "personal responsibility and moral guilt" and therefore cannot justify a death sentence. See *Enmund v. Florida*, 458 U.S. 782, 102 S.Ct. 3368; see also *id.* (O'CONNOR, J., dissenting) ("[P]roportionality requires a nexus between the punishment imposed and the defendant's blameworthiness"); *Tison v. Arizona*, 481 U.S. 137, 107 S.Ct. 1676 (1987) ("The heart of the retribution rationale is that a criminal sentence must be directly related to the personal culpability of the criminal offender").

Second, the quantity and quality of victim impact evidence sufficient to turn a verdict of life in prison into a verdict of death is not defined until after the crime has been committed and therefore cannot possibly be applied consistently in different cases. The sentencer's unguided consideration of victim impact evidence thus conflicts with the principle central to our capital punishment jurisprudence that, "where discretion is afforded a sentencing body on a matter so grave as the determination of whether a human life should be taken or spared, that discretion must be suitably directed and limited so as to minimize the risk of wholly arbitrary and capricious action." *Gregg v. Georgia*, 428 U.S. 153, 96 S.Ct. 2909 (1976) (joint opinion of STEWART, POWELL, and STEVENS, JJ.). Open-ended reliance by a capital sentencer on victim impact evidence simply does not provide a "principled way to distinguish [cases], in which the death penalty [i]s imposed, from the many cases in which it [i]s not." *Godfrey v. Georgia*, 446 U.S. 420, 100 S.Ct. 1759 (1980) (opinion of STEWART, J.).

The majority attempts to justify the admission of victim impact evidence by arguing that "consideration of the harm caused by the crime has been an important factor in the exercise of [sentencing] discretion." This statement is misleading and inaccurate. It is misleading because it is not limited to harm that is foreseeable. It is inaccurate because it fails to differentiate between legislative determinations and judicial sentencing. It is true that an evaluation of the harm caused by different kinds of wrongful conduct is a critical aspect in legislative definitions of offenses and determinations concerning sentencing guidelines. There is a rational correlation between moral culpability and the foreseeable harm caused by criminal conduct. Moreover, in the capital sentencing area, legislative identification of the special aggravating factors that may justify the imposition of the death penalty is entirely appropriate. But the majority cites no authority for the suggestion that unforeseeable and indirect harms to a victim's family are properly considered as aggravating evidence on a case-by-case basis.

The dissents in *Booth* and *Gathers* and the majority today offer only the recent decision in *Tison v. Arizona* and two legislative examples to support their contention that harm to the victim has traditionally influenced sentencing discretion. *Tison* held that the death penalty may be imposed on a felon who acts with reckless disregard for human life if a death occurs in the course of the felony, even though capital punishment cannot be imposed if no one dies as a result of the crime. The first legislative example is that attempted murder and murder are classified as two different offenses subject to different punishments. The second legislative example is that a person who drives while intoxicated is guilty of vehicular homicide if his actions result in a death but is not guilty of this offense if he has the good fortune to make it home without killing anyone. See *Booth* (WHITE, J., dissenting).

These three scenarios, however, are fully consistent with the Eighth Amendment jurisprudence reflected in *Booth* and *Gathers* and do not demonstrate that harm to the victim may be considered by a capital sentencer in the ad hoc and post hoc manner authorized by today's majority. The majority's examples demonstrate only that harm to the victim may justify enhanced punishment if the harm is both foreseeable to the defendant and clearly identified in advance of the crime by the legislature as a class of harm that should in every case result in more severe punishment.

In each scenario, the defendants could reasonably foresee that their acts might result in loss of human life. In addition, in each, the decision that the defendants should be treated differently was made prior to the crime by the legislature, the decision of which is subject to scrutiny for basic rationality. Finally, in each scenario, every defendant who causes the well-defined harm of destroying a human life will be subject to the determination that his conduct should be punished more severely. The majority's scenarios therefore provide no support for its holding, which permits a jury to sentence a defendant to death because of harm to the victim and his family that the defendant could not foresee, which was not even identified until after the crime had been committed, and which may be deemed by the jury, without any rational explanation, to justify a death sentence in one case but not in another. Unlike the rule elucidated by the scenarios on which the majority relies, the majority's holding offends the Eighth Amendment because it permits the sentencer to rely on irrelevant evidence in an arbitrary and capricious manner.

    * * *

IV

The majority thus does far more than validate a State's judgment that "the jury should see 'a quick glimpse of the life petitioner chose to extinguish,' *Mills v. Maryland*, 486 U.S. 367, 108 S.Ct. 1860 (1988) (REHNQUIST, C.J., dissenting)." Instead, it allows a jury to hold a defendant responsible for a whole array of harms that he could not foresee and for which he is therefore not blameworthy. Justice SOUTER argues that these harms are sufficiently foreseeable to hold the defendant accountable because "[e]very defendant knows, if endowed with the mental competence for criminal responsibility, that the life he will take by his homicidal behavior is that of a unique person, like himself, and that the person to be killed probably has close associates, 'survivors,' who will suffer harms and deprivations from the victim's death." (SOUTER, J., concurring). But every juror and trial judge knows this much as well. Evidence about who those survivors are and what harms and deprivations they have suffered is therefore not necessary to apprise the sentencer of any information that was actually foreseeable to the defendant. Its only function can be to "divert the jury's attention away from the defendant's background and record, and the circumstances of the crime." See *Booth*.

Arguing in the alternative, Justice SOUTER correctly points out that victim impact evidence will sometimes come to the attention of the jury during the guilt phase of the trial. He reasons that the ideal of basing sentencing determinations entirely on the moral culpability of the defendant is therefore unattainable unless a different jury is empaneled for the sentencing hearing. Thus, to justify overruling *Booth*, he assumes that the decision must otherwise be extended far beyond its actual holding.

Justice SOUTER's assumption is entirely unwarranted. For as long as the contours of relevance at sentencing hearings have been limited to evidence concerning the character of the offense and the character of the offender, the law has also recognized that evidence that is admissible for a proper purpose may not be excluded because it is inadmissible for other purposes and may indirectly prejudice the jury. In the case before us today, much of what might be characterized as victim impact evidence was properly admitted during the guilt phase of the trial and, given the horrible character of this crime, may have been sufficient to justify the Tennessee Supreme Court's conclusion that the error was harmless because the jury would necessarily have imposed the death sentence even absent the error. The fact that a good deal of such evidence is routinely and properly brought to the attention of the jury merely indicates that the rule of *Booth* may not affect the outcome of many cases.

In reaching our decision today, however, we should not be concerned with the cases in which victim impact evidence will not make a difference. We should be concerned instead with the cases in which it will make a difference. In those cases, defendants will be sentenced arbitrarily to death on the basis of evidence that would not otherwise be admissible because it is irrelevant to the defendants' moral culpability. The Constitution's proscription against the arbitrary imposition of the death penalty must necessarily proscribe the admission of evidence that serves no purpose other than to result in such arbitrary sentences.

V

The notion that the inability to produce an ideal system of justice in which every punishment is precisely married to the defendant's blameworthiness somehow justifies a rule that completely divorces some capital sentencing determinations from moral culpability is incomprehensible to me. Also incomprehensible is the argument that such a rule is required for the jury to take into account that each murder victim is a "unique" human being. The fact that each of us is unique is a proposition so obvious that it surely requires no evidentiary support. What is not obvious, however, is the way in which the character or reputation in one case may differ from that of other possible victims. Evidence offered to prove such differences can only be intended to identify some victims as more worthy of protection than others. Such proof risks decisions based on the same invidious motives as a prosecutor's decision to seek the death penalty if a victim is white but to accept a plea bargain if the victim is black. See *McCleskey v. Kemp*, 481 U.S. 279, 107 S.Ct. 1756 (1987) (STEVENS, J., dissenting).

Given the current popularity of capital punishment in a crime-ridden society, the political appeal of arguments that assume that increasing the severity of sentences is the best cure for the cancer of crime, and the political strength of the "victims' rights" movement, I recognize that today's decision will be greeted with enthusiasm by a large number of concerned and thoughtful citizens. The great tragedy of the decision, however, is the danger that the "hydraulic pressure" of public opinion that Justice Holmes once described[3]—and that properly influences the deliberations of democratic legislatures—has played a role not only in the Court's decision to hear this case, and in its decision to reach the constitutional question without pausing to consider affirming on the basis of the Tennessee Supreme Court's rationale, but even in its resolution of the constitutional issue involved. Today is a sad day for a great institution.

---

   3. *Northern Securities Co. v. United States*, 193 U.S. 197, 24 S.Ct. 436 (1904) (HOLMES, J., dissenting).

NOTES

1. *Response to Payne.*

Payne holds that victim impact evidence and argument does not violate the Eighth Amendment. However, *Payne* does not hold "that victim impact evidence must be admitted, or even that it should be admitted." 501 U.S. at 831, 111 S.Ct. at 2612 (O'Connor, J., concurring). Although constitutional, victim impact evidence is not admissible unless the state or federal capital sentencing law provides for its use. Virtually all death penalty jurisdictions permit the introduction of some form of victim impact evidence at the penalty phase. Some states, such as Georgia, Florida, and, since 1995, Pennsylvania, explicitly provide for victim impact evidence by statute. Ga. Code § 17–10–1.2; Fla. Stat. Ann. 921.141(7); 42 Pa.C.S.A. § 9711(a)(2). In other jurisdictions, the prosecutor may introduce any non-statutory aggravating factor, including victim impact evidence, for which notice has been given. See, *e.g.*, *Jones v. United States*, 527 U.S. 373, 119 S.Ct. 2090 (1999); 18 U.S.C. § 3593(a). In yet other jurisdictions, victim impact evidence is admissible by judicial decision. For example, in Indiana, victim impact evidence is admissible only if it is relevant to the statutory aggravating factors at issue in a given case or to rebut mitigating evidence, *Bivins v. State*, 642 N.E.2d 928 (Ind. 1994), and, in California, victim impact evidence is admissible under the statutory aggravating factor relating to the circumstances of the crime which includes the specific harm caused by the defendant. *People v. Edwards*, 819 P.2d 436 (Cal. 1991).

2. *Limits to Payne.*

Under *Payne* or under state law, what substantive limits, if any, should the lower courts impose on victim impact evidence?

   a. The testimony in *Payne* concerned the emotional impact of the victim's murder. Should victim impact evidence be restricted to emotional impact, or may the financial impact of the victim's death be considered? See *Ledbetter v. State*, 933 P.2d 880 (Okla. 1997) (approving evidence of financial impact on victim's family).

   b. Should victim impact evidence be limited to the effect of the murder on the victim's family or may the impact of the victim's murder on his or her neighbors, co-workers or religious community be considered? See *Walker v. State*, 653 S.E.2d 439 (Ga. 2007) (approving testimony from victim's employee as to impact on her and on the community); *People v. Marks*, 72 P.3d 1222 (Cal. 2003) (approving evidence of impact on "friends, loved ones and the community as a whole"). Should testimony about the community's reaction to the crime be admissible? See *McClain v. State*, 477 S.E.2d 814 (Ga.1996) (testimony about the community's anger about the crime admissible). But see *State v. Burns*, 979 S.W.2d 276 (Tenn. 1998) (testimony about the community's fear engendered by the crime inadmissible).

   c. Should victim impact evidence be permitted with regard to crimes other than the capital murder, *e.g.*, crimes that are introduced in the penalty phase as aggravating factors? See *People v. Mendoza*, 6 P.3d 150 (Cal. 2000) (admitting such evidence); *Sherman v. State*, 965 P.2d 903 (Nev. 1998) (excluding such evidence); *State v. White*, 709 N.E.2d 140 (Ohio 1999) (excluding such evidence).

3. *Victim impact videos*

In addition to, or in lieu of, victim impact testimony, prosecutors in some jurisdictions have introduced victim impact videos at the penalty phase. These videos generally involve a narration of the victim's life with video clips and still photographs of the victim and the victim's family and may include music, interviews with the victim's family and scenes of the family visiting the victim's grave. Most courts to rule on the question have approved the use of such videos. See, *e.g.*, *People v. Zamudio*, 181 P.3d 105, 135–137 (Cal. 2008); *State v. Leon*, 132 P.3d 462, 466–67 (Id. 2006); *State v. Anthony,* 776 So.2d 376, 393–94 (La. 2000), *State v. Allen*, 994 P.2d 728, 751 (N.M. 1999); *State v. Gray*, 887 S.W.2d 369, 389 (Mo. 1994); *Kills On Top v. State*, 15 P.3d 422, 437–38 (Mont. 2000) (all approving admission of victim videos). But see *United States v. Sampson*, 335 F.Supp.2d 166 (D.Mass. 2004); *Salazar v. State*, 90 S.W.3d 330, 335–36 (Tex.Crim.App. 2002) (finding admission of victim videos to be error). The Supreme Court has yet to pass on the constitutionality of admitting such videos. In *Kelly v. California*, __ U.S. __, 129 S.Ct. 564 (2008), three justices dissented from a denial of certiorari in two cases involving victim impact videos. Justice Stevens, one of the dissenters, described the video in the *Kelly* case as follows:

> The prosecution played a 20–minute video consisting of a montage of still photographs and video footage documenting [the 19–year–old victim's] life from her infancy until shortly before she was killed. The video was narrated by the victim's mother with soft music playing in the background, and it showed scenes of her swimming, horseback riding, and attending school and social functions with her family and friends. The video ended with a view of her grave marker and footage of people riding horseback in Alberta, Canada—the " 'kind of heaven' " in which her mother said she belonged.

Justice Stevens argued that the videos' "moving portrayal of the lives of the victims" "added nothing relevant to the jury's deliberations and invited a verdict based on sentiment, rather than reasoned judgment."

4. *Rebuttal to victim impact evidence*

Should the defendant be able to cross-examine the prosecution's victim impact witnesses to dispute the emotional impact of the victim's death? See *Grandison v. State*, 670 A.2d 398 (Md.1995) (denying defendant the right to cross-examine the victim's widow to establish that she remarried 18 months after victim's death and had children with her new husband). Should the defendant, in response to victim impact evidence, be permitted to call witnesses to impugn the character of the victim in order to dispute the impact of the death on the community? See *Clark v. State*, 881 S.W.2d 682 (Tex.Cr.App. 1994) (disapproving of defendant's proffered evidence going to the immoral character of victim).

5. *Problem 9–8.*

Defendant has been convicted of first degree murder, and the prosecution is seeking the death penalty in a state that has not, by statute, placed any limits on the evidence which may be introduced at the penalty hearing. What arguments should be made on the constitutionality of admitting or excluding the following evidence: (a) testimony by a member of the victim's family that Defendant should be sentenced to death; (b) testimony by a member of the victim's family that Defendant should not be sentenced to death; (c) testimony by a member of Defendant's family that Defendant should not be sentenced to death? See, *e.g.*, *Murphy v. State*, 47 P.3d 876 (Okla.Crim.App. 2002) (victim's family in favor of a death sentence); *State v. Smith*, 32 S.W.3d 532 (Mo. 2000) (victim's family in favor of a death sentence); *Kaczmarek v. State*, 91 P.3d 16 (Nev. 2004) (victim's family opposed to a death sentence); *State v. Manning*, 885 So.2d 1044 (La. 2004) (defendant's family opposed to death sentence).

    6.   *Problem 9–9.*

Defendant has been convicted of first degree murder, and the prosecution is seeking the death penalty in a state that has not, by statute, placed any limits on the evidence which may be introduced at the penalty hearing. What arguments should be made on the constitutionality of admitting or excluding the following evidence: (a) testimony by Defendant's family members concerning the pain and loss they will feel after Defendant's execution; (b) testimony by the victim's family that their pain and distress will not end until Defendant is executed. See *People v. Ochoa*, 966 P.2d 442 (Cal. 1998); *State v. Stenson*, 940 P.2d 1239 (Wash. 1997); *Burns v. State*, 699 So.2d 646 (Fla. 1997); *State v. Stevens*, 879 P.2d 162 (Or. 1994).

CAPITAL JURORS' ASSESSMENT OF THE EVIDENCE

The heart of the penalty phase is the prosecutor's presentation of aggravating evidence in support of a death sentence and the defense attorney's presentation of mitigating evidence in support of a life sentence. This chapter and Chapter 4 have looked at some examples of aggravation and mitigation. How do capital jurors assess this evidence, *i.e.*, what kind of evidence is likely to lead to a death verdict, and what type of evidence is likely to encourage a life verdict?

An empirical study of 153 jurors in forty-one South Carolina capital murder trials—twenty-two resulting in sentences of death and nineteen resulting in sentences of life imprisonment—tried to answer that question. See S. Garvey, *Aggravation and Mitigation in Capital Cases: What Do Jurors Think?* 98 Colum. L. Rev. 1538 (1998). Confirming common assumptions about the most aggravated kinds of murders, the study found several factors to be highly aggravating[1]: especially brutal murders involving torture or physical abuse (75.7%); especially bloody or gory murders (59.1%); murders in which the victim suffered before death (72.5%); murders in which the defendant maimed or mutilated the victim after death (72.2%); the murder of a child (62.3%); a defendant with a history of violent crime (52.8%); a defendant who might be a danger to society in the future (57.9%); and a defendant who expressed no remorse (39.8%). The

---

    1.   The numbers given after each factor represent the combined percentage of jurors surveyed who responded that the factor did or would make the juror much more likely or slightly more likely to vote for death.

study further showed that the overall impact of especially bloody or gory murders, murders involving torture or physical abuse, murders in which the victim suffered before death, future dangerousness, and lack of remorse may be even greater than the findings suggest, since a majority of the jurors surveyed believed these factors were present in the cases they had deliberated.

The study also confirmed some common notions about what mitigates a capital murder.[2] The most powerful mitigating factor is residual doubt about the defendant's guilt (77.2%), and the next most powerful mitigating factor is the defendant's mental retardation (73.8%). Circumstances over which the defendant had no control and that diminish his individual responsibility at the time of the crime also are highly mitigating: the defendant having a history of mental illness (56.2%) and the defendant being under the influence of extreme mental or emotional disturbance at the time of the crime (54.6%). Another significant mitigating factor is the defendant being under 18 years old at the time of the crime (41.5%). However, being under the influence of drugs (18.5%) or alcohol (18.3%) or being a drug addict (9.7%) or an alcoholic (13.7%) does not carry much mitigating impact. Circumstances over which the defendant had no control and that may have influenced his character have noticeable but limited mitigating effect: the defendant had been in state institutions but had never received any real help or treatment for his problems (48.2%) and the defendant had been seriously abused as a child (37%).

The study presented some findings that may contradict general assumptions about mitigation. While future dangerousness and a history of violent crime are highly aggravating, the fact that the defendant had no previous criminal record (20%) or would be a well-behaved inmate (26.2%) has only some mitigating potential. According to the study, the fact that the defendant has a loving family (18.8%) or that an accomplice received a lesser sentence in exchange for testimony (17.2%) is roughly as mitigating as the fact that the capital murder was an aberration in the defendant's otherwise crime-free life.

According to another study, a critical factor in the jury's decision-making process is the degree to which the jurors can identify with the victim and empathize with the victim's fate. See S. Sundby, *The Capital Jury and Empathy: the Problem of Worthy and Unworthy Victims*, 88 Cornell L.Rev. 343 (2003). The more the victim is perceived as an innocent or helpless party in the fatal encounter, *e.g.*, a child or an adult chosen at random, the more likely that the jury will bring in a death verdict. By contrast, if the jury believes that the victim had a drug or alcohol problem and was engaging in "high-risk" or "antisocial" behavior, or even that the victim was too careless in getting in harm's way, the jury is more likely to vote for a life sentence. To what extent are the *Payne* dissenters correct that victim impact evidence will cause the jury to consider the victim's

---

2. The numbers given after each factor represent the combined percentage of the jurors surveyed who responded that the factor did or would make the juror much less likely or slightly less likely to vote for death.

"worthiness" apart from the victim's role in the particular situation? A recent study of South Carolina capital jurors suggests that victim impact evidence does not necessarily have that effect. See T. Eisenberg, S. Garvey & M. Wells, *Victim Characteristics and Victim Impact Evidence in South Carolina Capital Cases*, 88 Cornell 306 (2003). The study found that the introduction of victim impact evidence tended to increase the jury's "admiration" of the victim and that the more the jury admired the victim, the more vicious they thought was the murder. However, the study found no significant relationship between victim impact evidence, jurors' views of "victim admirability" and penalty outcomes.

At least two other studies, however, call into question how much attention jurors actually pay to the penalty phase evidence. See U. Bentele & W. Bowers, *How Jurors Decide on Death: Guilt is Overwhelming; Aggravation Requires Death; and Mitigation is no Excuse*, 66 Brook. L.Rev. 1011 (2001); W. Bowers, M. Sandys & B. Steiner, *Foreclosed Impartiality in Capital Sentencing: Jurors' Predispositions, Guilt–Trial Experience, and Premature Decision Making*, 83 Cornell L.Rev. 1476 (1998). The former study of capital jurors in six states found that, in deliberating on their penalty decision, the jurors were preoccupied with discussing the evidence of the defendant's guilt, rather than the evidence introduced at the penalty phase.[3] The latter study of capital jurors in eleven states, found that almost half of the jurors thought they knew what the punishment should be during the guilt phase of the trial.

> Seven out of ten who took a pro-death stand and six of ten who said the punishment should be life were "absolutely convinced." Moreover, nearly all of the remaining jurors who took a stand said they were 'pretty sure.' Only a meager two to five percent of those who said they knew what the punishment should be at the guilt stage characterized themselves as "not too sure."

Id. at 1488–89. The study also revealed that "jurors who take early pro-death and early pro-life stands tend to hold their initial stands for the rest of the decision-making process. Virtually six of ten jurors who thought at the guilt stage of the trial that either death or life was the right punishment held steadfastly to that conviction for the rest of the proceedings." *Id.* at 1491–1492. The study further established that three to four of every ten jurors indicated that the legally irrelevant issue of the defendant's punishment was discussed during guilt deliberations.

Note

1. *Premature decision-making as a constitutional issue.*

Does the fact that, as juror studies have shown, almost half of the jurors make up their minds about penalty during the guilt phase of the trial have constitutional implications? One New Mexico trial court judge thought so and

---

3. This fact is consistent with the finding, noted above, that jurors consider "lingering doubt" as to the defendant's guilt to be the most mitigating factor.

held that the practice of trying guilt and penalty to a single jury was unconstitutional because the jury's premature decision-making would cause a resulting death sentence to be "arbitrary and capricious." S. Sandlin, *Ruling Changes the Face of Trial*, Albuquerque Journal, June 20, 2007, 2007 WLNR 11560567. Other trial court judges came to the opposite conclusion, and the issue was mooted by the New Mexico's abolition of the death penalty in 2009.

Chapter 10

Guiding the Sentencer

■ ■ ■

Once the sentencer's discretion to the impose the death penalty has been limited by a statutory scheme which "genuinely narrows" the death-eligible class [see Chapter 3], what guidance must, or must not, be given to the sentencer in selecting from that class those to receive the death penalty? The five cases in this chapter address the issue. In *Tuilaepa v. California*, the Court explains the difference between the jury's eligibility determination and its selection decision and considers a vagueness challenge to several factors given to the jury for its selection decision. The next two cases concern instructions that the defendant contends were inaccurate and/or had the effect of diminishing the reliability of the jury's verdict. In *California v. Ramos*, the Court addresses the constitutionality of giving an instruction on the governor's power to commute a sentence of life without possibility of parole. In *Caldwell v. Mississippi*, the defendant challenged the prosecutor's argument, approved by the trial court, suggesting that the final responsibility for determining the sentence rested not with the jury, but with the appellate courts. *Simmons v. South Carolina* and *Weeks v. Angelone* are cases where the jury was in fact confused and sought, but did not receive, guidance from the trial court. In *Simmons*, the jury had asked whether the defendant would be eligible for parole if he received a life sentence, and the defendant had requested an instruction that he was parole ineligible. In *Weeks*, the jury had asked whether it was obliged to impose a death sentence if it found an aggravating circumstance, and the defendant had requested an instruction that the jury could bring in a life sentence even after finding an aggravating circumstance. Empirical research on juror understanding of penalty phase instructions is discussed in *What do Jurors Understand?* Finally, the trial of a penalty phase and the process by which the jury reached its decision is described in *In the Face of Death*.

TUILAEPA v. CALIFORNIA
512 U.S. 967, 114 S.Ct. 2630, 129 L.Ed.2d 750 (1994).

JUSTICE KENNEDY delivered the opinion of the Court.

In California, to sentence a defendant to death for first-degree murder the trier of fact must find the defendant guilty and also find one or more of 19 special circumstances listed in Cal. Penal Code Ann. § 190.2. The case then proceeds to the penalty phase, where the trier of fact must consider a number of specified factors in deciding whether to sentence the defendant to death. § 190.3.[1] These two cases present the question whether three of the § 190.3 penalty-phase factors are unconstitutionally vague under decisions of this Court construing the Cruel and Unusual Punishments Clause of the Eighth Amendment, made applicable to the States by the Fourteenth Amendment.

I

Petitioner Tuilaepa's case arises out of a murder he committed [during a robbery] in Long Beach, California, in October 1986. * * * Petitioner Proctor murdered Bonnie Stendal, a 55–year–old school teacher who lived in Burney, a small community in Shasta County, California. [The murder was committed during a burglary and rape and by the infliction of torture.]

     * * *

II

A

Our capital punishment cases under the Eighth Amendment address two different aspects of the capital decisionmaking process: the eligibility decision and the selection decision. To be eligible for the death penalty, the defendant must be convicted of a crime for which the death penalty is a proportionate punishment. *Coker v. Georgia*, 433 U.S. 584, 97 S.Ct. 2861

---

1. Section 190.3 provides in part:

"In determining the penalty, the trier of fact shall take into account any of the following factors if relevant:

"(a) The circumstances of the crime of which the defendant was convicted in the present proceeding and the existence of any special circumstances found to be true pursuant to Section 190.1.

"(b) The presence or absence of criminal activity by the defendant which involved the use or attempted use of force or violence or the express or implied threat to use force or violence.

"(c) The presence or absence of any prior felony conviction.

"(d) Whether or not the offense was committed while the defendant was under the influence of extreme mental or emotional disturbance.

"(e) Whether or not the victim was a participant in the defendant's homicidal conduct or consented to the homicidal act.

"(f) Whether or not the offense was committed under circumstances which the defendant reasonably believed to be a moral justification or extenuation for his conduct.

"(g) Whether or not the defendant acted under extreme duress or under the substantial domination of another person.

"(h) Whether or not at the time of the offense the capacity of the defendant to appreciate the criminality of his conduct or to conform his conduct to the requirements of law was impaired as a result of mental disease or defect, or the [e]ffects of intoxication.

"(i) The age of the defendant at the time of the crime.

"(j) Whether or not the defendant was an accomplice to the offense and his participation in the commission of the offense was relatively minor.

"(k) Any other circumstance which extenuates the gravity of the crime even though it is not a legal excuse for the crime."

(1977). To render a defendant eligible for the death penalty in a homicide case, we have indicated that the trier of fact must convict the defendant of murder and find one "aggravating circumstance" (or its equivalent) at either the guilt or penalty phase. See, *e.g., Lowenfield v. Phelps,* 484 U.S. 231, 108 S.Ct. 546 (1988); *Zant v. Stephens,* 462 U.S. 862, 103 S.Ct. 2733 (1983). The aggravating circumstance may be contained in the definition of the crime or in a separate sentencing factor (or in both). *Lowenfield.* As we have explained, the aggravating circumstance must meet two requirements. First, the circumstance may not apply to every defendant convicted of a murder; it must apply only to a subclass of defendants convicted of murder. See *Arave v. Creech,* 507 U.S. 463, 113 S.Ct. 1534 (1993) ("If the sentencer fairly could conclude that an aggravating circumstance applies to every defendant eligible for the death penalty, the circumstance is constitutionally infirm"). Second, the aggravating circumstance may not be unconstitutionally vague. *Godfrey v. Georgia,* 446 U.S. 420, 100 S.Ct. 1759 (1980); see *Arave, supra* (court " 'must first determine whether the statutory language defining the circumstance is itself too vague to provide any guidance to the sentencer' ") (quoting *Walton v. Arizona,* 497 U.S. 639, 110 S.Ct. 3047 (1990)).

We have imposed a separate requirement for the selection decision, where the sentencer determines whether a defendant eligible for the death penalty should in fact receive that sentence. "What is important at the selection stage is an individualized determination on the basis of the character of the individual and the circumstances of the crime." *Zant, supra.* That requirement is met when the jury can consider relevant mitigating evidence of the character and record of the defendant and the circumstances of the crime. *Blystone v. Pennsylvania,* 494 U.S. 299, 110 S.Ct. 1078 (1990) ("requirement of individualized sentencing in capital cases is satisfied by allowing the jury to consider all relevant mitigating evidence").

The eligibility decision fits the crime within a defined classification. Eligibility factors almost of necessity require an answer to a question with a factual nexus to the crime or the defendant so as to "make rationally reviewable the process for imposing a sentence of death." *Arave, supra.* The selection decision, on the other hand, requires individualized sentencing and must be expansive enough to accommodate relevant mitigating evidence so as to assure an assessment of the defendant's culpability. The objectives of these two inquiries can be in some tension, at least when the inquiries occur at the same time. There is one principle common to both decisions, however: The State must ensure that the process is neutral and principled so as to guard against bias or caprice in the sentencing decision. That is the controlling objective when we examine eligibility and selection factors for vagueness. Indeed, it is the reason that eligibility and selection factors (at least in some sentencing schemes) may not be "too vague." *Walton, supra.*

Because "the proper degree of definition" of eligibility and selection factors often "is not susceptible of mathematical precision," our vagueness review is quite deferential. *Walton, supra.* Relying on the basic principle that a factor is not unconstitutional if it has some "common-sense core of meaning ... that criminal juries should be capable of understanding," *Jurek v. Texas*, 428 U.S. 262, 96 S.Ct. 2950 (1976) (WHITE, J., concurring in judgment), we have found only a few factors vague, and those in fact are quite similar to one another. See *Maynard v. Cartwright*, 486 U.S. 356, 108 S.Ct. 1853 (1988) (question whether murder was "especially heinous, atrocious, or cruel"); *Godfrey, supra* (question whether murder was "outrageously or wantonly vile, horrible or inhuman") * * *

In our decisions holding a death sentence unconstitutional because of a vague sentencing factor, the State had presented a specific proposition that the sentencer had to find true or false (*e.g.*, whether the crime was especially heinous, atrocious, or cruel). We have held, under certain sentencing schemes, that a vague propositional factor used in the sentencing decision creates an unacceptable risk of randomness, the mark of the arbitrary and capricious sentencing process prohibited by *Furman v. Georgia*, 408 U.S. 238, 92 S.Ct. 2726 (1972). Those concerns are mitigated when a factor does not require a yes or a no answer to a specific question, but instead only points the sentencer to a subject matter. See Cal. Penal Code §§ 190.3(a), (k). Both types of factors (and the distinction between the two is not always clear) have their utility. For purposes of vagueness analysis, however, in examining the propositional content of a factor, our concern is that the factor have some "common-sense core of meaning ... that criminal juries should be capable of understanding." *Jurek* (WHITE, J., concurring in judgment).

B

With those principles in mind, we consider petitioners' vagueness challenge to the California scheme. A defendant in California is eligible for the death penalty when the jury finds him guilty of first-degree murder and finds one of the § 190.2 special circumstances true. (Petitioners do not argue that the special circumstances found in their cases were insufficient, so we do not address that part of California's scheme save to describe its relation to the selection phase.) At the penalty phase, the jury is instructed to consider numerous other factors listed in § 190.3 in deciding whether to impose the death penalty on a particular defendant. Petitioners contend that three of those § 190.3 sentencing factors are unconstitutional and that, as a consequence, it was error to instruct their juries to consider them. Both Proctor and Tuilaepa challenge factor (a), which requires the sentencer to consider the "circumstances of the crime of which the defendant was convicted in the present proceeding and the existence of any special circumstances found to be true." Tuilaepa challenges two other factors as well: factor (b), which requires the sentencer to consider "[t]he presence or absence of criminal activity by the defendant which involved the use or attempted use of force or violence or the express or implied threat to use force or violence"; and factor (i), which requires the sentencer to consider "[t]he age of the defendant at the time of the crime." We conclude that none of the three factors is defined in terms that violate the Constitution.

Petitioners' challenge to factor (a) is at some odds with settled principles, for our capital jurisprudence has established that the sentencer should consider the circumstances of the crime in deciding whether to impose the death penalty. See, *e.g., Woodson v. North Carolina*, 428 U.S. 280, 96 S.Ct. 2978 (1976) ("consideration of ... the circumstances of the particular offense [is] a constitutionally indispensable part of the process of inflicting the penalty of death"). We would be hard pressed to invalidate a jury instruction that implements what we have said the law requires. In any event, this California factor instructs the jury to consider a relevant subject matter and does so in understandable terms. The circumstances of the crime are a traditional subject for consideration by the sentencer, and an instruction to consider the circumstances is neither vague nor otherwise improper under our Eighth Amendment jurisprudence.

Tuilaepa also challenges factor (b), which requires the sentencer to consider the defendant's prior criminal activity. The objection fails for many of the same reasons. Factor (b) is phrased in conventional and understandable terms and rests in large part on a determination whether certain events occurred, thus asking the jury to consider matters of historical fact. Under other sentencing schemes, in Texas for example, jurors may be asked to make a predictive judgment, such as "whether there is a probability that the defendant would commit criminal acts of violence that would constitute a continuing threat to society." See *Jurek v. Texas, supra*. Both a backward-looking and a forward-looking inquiry are a permissible part of the sentencing process, however, and the States have considerable latitude in determining how to guide the sentencer's decision in this respect. Here, factor (b) is not vague.

Tuilaepa's third challenge is to factor (i), which requires the sentencer to consider "[t]he age of the defendant at the time of the crime." This again is an unusual challenge in light of our precedents. See *Eddings v. Oklahoma*, 455 U.S. 104, 102 S.Ct. 869 (1982) (age may be relevant factor in sentencing decision). The factual inquiry is of the most rudimentary sort, and there is no suggestion that the term "age" is vague. Petitioner contends, however, that the age factor is equivocal and that in the typical case the prosecution argues in favor of the death penalty based on the defendant's age, no matter how old or young he was at the time of the crime. It is neither surprising nor remarkable that the relevance of the defendant's age can pose a dilemma for the sentencer. But difficulty in application is not equivalent to vagueness. Both the prosecution and the defense may present valid arguments as to the significance of the defendant's age in a particular case. Competing arguments by adversary parties bring perspective to a problem, and thus serve to promote a more reasoned decision, providing guidance as to a factor jurors most likely would discuss in any event. We find no constitutional deficiency in factor (i).

C

Petitioners could not and do not take great issue with the conclusion that factors (a), (b), and (i) provide common and understandable terms to the sentencer. Petitioners argue, however, that selection factors must meet the requirements for eligibility factors and therefore must require an answer to a factual question, as eligibility factors do. According to petitioners, a capital jury may not be instructed simply to consider an open-ended subject matter, such as "the circumstances of the crime" or "the background of the defendant." Apart from the fact that petitioners' argument ignores the obvious utility of these open-ended factors as part of a neutral sentencing process, it contravenes our precedents. Our decisions in *Zant* and *Gregg* reveal that, at the selection stage, the States are not confined to submitting to the jury specific propositional questions. In *Zant*, we found no constitutional difficulty where the jury had been told to consider " 'all facts and circumstances presented in extenuation, mitigation, and aggravation of punishment as well as such arguments as have been presented for the State and for the Defense.' " We also stated that "[n]othing in the United States Constitution prohibits a trial judge from instructing a jury that it would be appropriate to take account of a defendant's prior criminal record in making its sentencing determination." And in *Gregg*, we rejected a vagueness challenge to that same Georgia sentencing scheme in a case in which the "judge ... charged the jury that in determining what sentence was appropriate the jury was free to consider the facts and circumstances, if any, presented by the parties in mitigation or aggravation." In both cases, therefore, the Court found no constitutional problem with a death sentence where the jury instructions directed consideration of the "facts and circumstances" of the case. In these cases as well, we must reject petitioners' suggestion that the Constitution prohibits sentencing instructions that require the trier of fact to consider a relevant subject matter such as the "circumstances of the crime."

Petitioners also suggest that the § 190.3 sentencing factors are flawed because they do not instruct the sentencer how to weigh any of the facts it finds in deciding upon the ultimate sentence. In this regard, petitioners claim that a single list of factors is unconstitutional because it does not guide the jury in evaluating and weighing the evidence and allows the prosecution (as well as the defense) to make wide-ranging arguments about whether the defendant deserves the death penalty. This argument, too, is foreclosed by our cases. A capital sentencer need not be instructed how to weigh any particular fact in the capital sentencing decision. In *California v. Ramos*, 463 U.S. 992, 103 S.Ct. 3446 (1983), for example, we upheld an instruction informing the jury that the Governor had the power to commute life sentences and stated that "the fact that the jury is given no specific guidance on how the commutation factor is to figure into its determination presents no constitutional problem." Likewise, in *Proffitt v. Florida*, 428 U.S. 242, 96 S.Ct. 2960 (1976), we upheld the Florida capital sentencing scheme even though "the various factors to be considered by the sentencing authorities [did] not have numerical weights assigned to them." In *Gregg*, moreover, we "approved Georgia's capital sentencing statute even though it clearly did not channel the jury's discretion by enunciating specific standards to guide the jury's consideration of aggravating and mitigating circumstances." *Zant.* We also rejected an objection "to the wide scope of evidence and argument" allowed at sentencing hearings. In sum, "discretion to evaluate and weigh the circumstances relevant to the particular defendant and the crime he committed" is not impermissible in the capital sentencing process. *McCleskey v. Kemp*, 481 U.S. 279, 107 S.Ct. 1756 (1987). "Once the jury finds that the defendant falls within the legislatively defined category of persons eligible for the death penalty, ... the jury then is free to consider a myriad of factors to determine whether death is the appropriate punishment." *Ramos, supra.* Indeed, the sentencer may be given "unbridled discretion in determining whether the death penalty should be imposed after it has found that the defendant is a member of the class made eligible for that penalty." *Zant, supra.* In contravention of those cases, petitioners' argument would force the States to adopt a kind of mandatory sentencing scheme requiring a jury to sentence a defendant to death if it found, for example, a certain kind or number of facts, or found more statutory aggravating factors than statutory mitigating factors. The States are not required to conduct the capital sentencing process in that fashion.

The instructions to the juries in petitioners' cases directing consideration of factor (a), factor (b), and factor (i) did not violate the Constitution. The judgments of the Supreme Court of California are affirmed.

[Concurring opinions of SCALIA, J. and SOUTER, J. and opinion of STEVENS, J., joined by GINSBURG, J., concurring in the judgment, omitted]

JUSTICE BLACKMUN, dissenting:

* * *

The California capital punishment scheme does more than simply direct the sentencing jurors' attention to certain subject matters. It lists 11 factors and authorizes the jury to treat any of them as aggravating circumstances to be placed on death's side of the scale. Jurors are instructed that they "*shall* impose a death sentence if [they] conclude that the aggravating circumstances outweigh the mitigating circumstances." Cal.Penal Code § 190.3. (emphasis added) Despite the critical—even decisive—role these factors play in the determination of who actually receives the death penalty, jurors are given no guidance in how to consider them. We have stated: "A vague aggravating factor used in the weighing process ... creates the risk that the jury will treat the defendant as more deserving than he might otherwise be by relying upon the existence of an illusory circumstance." *Stringer v. Black*, 503 U.S. 222, 112 S.Ct. 1130 (1992).

The majority introduces a novel distinction between "propositional" and "nonpropositional" aggravating circumstances. The majority acknowledges that the "distinction between the two is not always clear"; I find it largely illusory. The Court suggests, but does not make explicit, that propositional factors are those that "require a yes or a no answer to a specific question," while nonpropositional factors are those that "only poin[t] the sentencer to a subject matter." Presumably, then, asking the jury whether "the murder was especially heinous, atrocious, or cruel," would be a propositional aggravator, while directing the sentencer to "the presence or absence of any especial heinousness, atrocity, or cruelty" would be a nonpropositional factor. I am at a loss to see how the mere rephrasing does anything more to channel or guide jury discretion. Nor does this propositional/nonpropositional distinction appear to play any role in the Court's decision. The Court nowhere discloses specifically where the line is drawn, on which side of it the three challenged factors fall, and what relevance, if any, this distinction should have to the Court's future vagueness analysis.

The more relevant distinction is not how an aggravating factor is presented, but what the sentencer is told to do with it. Where, as in Georgia, "aggravating factors as such have no specific function in the jury's decision whether a defendant who has been found to be eligible for the death penalty should receive it under all the circumstances of the case," *Stringer*, we have not subjected aggravating circumstances to a vagueness analysis. See *Zant v. Stephens*, 462 U.S. 862, 103 S.Ct. 2733 (1983). In California, by contrast, where the sentencer is instructed to weigh the aggravating and mitigating circumstances, a vague aggravator creates the risk of an arbitrary thumb on death's side of the scale, so we analyze aggravators for clarity, objectivity, and principled guidance.

Each of the challenged California factors "leave[s] the sentencer without sufficient guidance for determining the presence or absence of the factor." *Espinosa v. Florida*, 505 U.S. 1079, 112 S.Ct. 2926 (1992). Each of the three—circumstances of the crime, age, and prior criminal activity— has been exploited to convince jurors that just about anything is aggravating.

Prosecutors have argued, and jurors are free to find, that "circumstances of the crime" constitutes an aggravating factor because the defendant killed the victim for some purportedly aggravating motive, such as money, or because the defendant killed the victim for no motive at all; because the defendant killed in cold blood, or in hot blood; because the defendant attempted to conceal his crime, or made no attempt to conceal it; because the defendant made the victim endure the terror of anticipating a violent death, or because the defendant killed without any warning; and because the defendant had a prior relationship with the victim, or because the victim was a complete stranger.[a] Similarly, prosecutors have argued, and juries are free to find, that the age of the victim was an aggravating circumstance because the victim was a child, an adolescent, a

---

a. Justice Blackmun cited a California Supreme Court case for each of the examples, and for each of the subsequent examples.

young adult, in the prime of life, or elderly; or that the method of killing was aggravating, because the victim was strangled, bludgeoned, shot, stabbed, or consumed by fire; or that the location of the killing was an aggravating factor, because the victim was killed in her own home, in a public bar, in a city park, or in a remote location. In short, because neither the California Legislature nor the California courts ever have articulated a limiting construction of this term, prosecutors have been permitted to use the "circumstances of the crime" as an aggravating factor to embrace the entire spectrum of facts present in virtually every homicide—something this Court condemned in *Godfrey v. Georgia*, 446 U.S. 420, 100 S.Ct. 1759 (1980).[15]

The defendant's age as a factor, applied inconsistently and erratically, similarly fails to channel the jurors' discretion. In practice, prosecutors and trial judges have applied this factor to defendants of virtually every age: in their teens, twenties, thirties, forties, and fifties at the time of the crime. Far from applying any narrowing construction, the California Supreme Court has described age as a "metonym for any age-related matter suggested by the evidence or by common experience or morality that might reasonably inform the choice of penalty." *People v. Lucky*, 753 P.2d 1052 (Cal. 1988).

Nor do jurors find meaningful guidance from "the presence or absence of criminal activity by the defendant which involved the use or attempted use of force or violence." Although the California Supreme Court has held that "criminal" is *limited to conduct that violates a penal statute*," *People v. Wright*, 802 P.2d 221 (Cal. 1990) (emphasis in original), and that "force or violence" excludes violence to property, *People v. Boyd*, 700 P.2d 782 (Cal. 1985), that court has not required such an instruction, and petitioner Tuilaepa's jurors were not so instructed. This left the prosecution free to introduce evidence of "trivial incidents of misconduct and ill temper," *People v. Boyd*, and left the jury free to find an aggravator on that basis.

No less a danger is that jurors—or even judges—will treat the mere absence of a mitigator as an aggravator, transforming a neutral or factually irrelevant factor into an illusory aggravator.[18] Although the California Supreme Court has ruled that certain of the factors can serve

---

15. Although we have required that jurors be allowed to consider "*as a mitigating factor*, any aspect of a defendant's character or record and any circumstances of the offense that the defendant proffers as a basis for a sentence less than death," *Lockett v. Ohio*, 438 U.S. 586, 98 S.Ct. 2954 (1978) (emphasis in original), we have never approved such unrestricted consideration of a circumstance in aggravation. Similarly, while we approved the Georgia capital sentencing scheme, which permits jurors to consider all the circumstances of the offense and the offender, we did so in the context of a system in which aggravators performed no function beyond the eligibility decision. See *Zant v. Stephens*.

18. Judges, as well as juries, have fallen into this trap. See, *e.g.*, *People v. Kaurish*, 802 P.2d 278 (Cal. 1990) (trial judge concluded that factor (h), dealing with a defendant's impaired capacity to appreciate the criminality of his actions, was an aggravating factor because defendant did not have diminished capacity or other impairment); *People v. Hamilton*, 774 P.2d 730 (Cal. 1989) (trial court concluded that 10 of 11 factors were aggravating, including factors (d)–(h) and (j)).

only as mitigators,[19] it has not required that the jury be so instructed. Nor has that court restricted jury instructions to those aggravating factors that are factually relevant to the case.[20] Clearly, some of the mitigating circumstances are so unusual that treating their absence as an aggravating circumstance would make them applicable to virtually all murderers. See *People v. Davenport*, 710 P.2d 861 (Cal. 1985) (most murder cases present the absence of the mitigating circumstances of moral justification and victim participation). An aggravating factor that exists in nearly every capital case fails to fulfill its purpose of guiding the jury in distinguishing "those who deserve capital punishment from those who do not." *Arave v. Creech*, 507 U.S. 463, 113 S.Ct. 1534 (1993). Moreover, a process creating the risk that the absence of mitigation will count as aggravation artificially inflates the number of aggravating factors the jury weighs, "creat[ing] the possibility not only of randomness but of bias in favor of death."

In short, open-ended factors and a lack of guidance to regularize the jurors' application of these factors create a system in which, as a practical matter, improper arguments can be made in the courtroom and credited in the jury room. I am at a loss to see how these challenged factors furnish the " 'clear and objective standards' that provide 'specific and detailed guidance,' and that 'make rationally reviewable the process for imposing a sentence of death.' " *Walton v. Arizona*, 497 U.S. 639, 110 S.Ct. 3047 (1990) (SCALIA, J., concurring in part and dissenting in part), quoting *Godfrey v. Georgia*, 446 U.S. 420, 100 S.Ct. 1759 (1980).

* * *

NOTE

1. *Problem 10–1.*

Defendant was found guilty of first-degree murder with the special circumstance that the murder was committed during a rape. At the penalty phase, the trial court instructed the jury to consider and weigh the aggravating and mitigating circumstances, but cautioned that the jury "must not be

---

19. The factors that can serve only as mitigators are:

(d) Whether or not the offense was committed while the defendant was under the influence of extreme mental or emotional disturbance.

(e) Whether or not the victim was a participant in the defendant's homicidal act or consented to the homicidal act.

(f) Whether or not the offense was committed under circumstances which the defendant reasonably believed to be a moral justification or extenuation for his conduct.

(g) Whether or not the defendant acted under extreme duress or under the substantial domination of another person.

(h) Whether or not at the time of the offense the capacity of the defendant to appreciate the criminality of his conduct or to conform his conduct to the requirements of law was impaired as a result of mental disease and defect, or the effects of intoxication.

(j) Whether or not the defendant was an accomplice to the offense and his participation in the commission of the offense was relatively minor.

20. Although the trial judge at petitioner Tuilaepa's trial instructed the jury on only those factors that were factually relevant, the jury at petitioner Proctor's trial was instructed on all of the factors in § 190.3. The prosecutor argued that nine of the 11 factors were aggravating.

swayed by mere sentiment, conjecture, sympathy, passion, prejudice, public opinion or public feeling." Defendant was sentenced to death. On appeal, what arguments should be made as to whether the instruction was constitutional? See *California v. Brown*, 479 U.S. 538, 107 S.Ct. 837, 93 L.Ed.2d 934 (1987).

CALIFORNIA v. RAMOS
463 U.S. 992, 103 S.Ct. 3446, 77 L.Ed.2d 1171 (1983).

JUSTICE O'CONNOR delivered the opinion of the Court.

This case requires us to consider the constitutionality under the Eighth and Fourteenth Amendments of instructing a capital sentencing jury regarding the Governor's power to commute a sentence of life without possibility of parole. Finding no constitutional defect in the instruction, we reverse the decision of the Supreme Court of California and remand for further proceedings.

I

On the night of June 2, 1979, respondent Marcelino Ramos participated in the robbery of a fast food restaurant where he was employed as a janitor. As respondent's codefendant placed a food order, respondent entered the restaurant, went behind the front counter into the work area ostensibly for the purpose of checking his work schedule, and emerged with a gun. Respondent directed the two employees working that night into the restaurant's walk-in refrigerator and ordered them to face the back wall. Respondent entered and emerged from the refrigerator several times, inquiring at one point about the keys to the restaurant safe. When he entered for the last time, he instructed the two employees to kneel on the floor of the refrigerator, to remove their hats, and to pray. Respondent struck both on the head and then shot them, wounding one and killing the other.

Respondent was charged with robbery, attempted murder, and first degree murder. Defense counsel presented no evidence at the guilt phase of respondent's trial, and the jury returned a verdict of guilt on all counts. Under California law, first degree murder is punishable by death or life imprisonment without the possibility of parole where an alleged "special circumstance" is found true by the jury at the guilt phase.[1] At the separate penalty phase, respondent presented extensive evidence in an attempt to mitigate punishment. In addition to requiring jury instructions on aggravating and mitigating circumstances, California law requires that the trial judge inform the jury that a sentence of life imprisonment without the possibility of parole may be commuted by the Governor to a sentence that includes the possibility of parole.[4] At the penalty phase of

---

1. See Cal.Penal Code Ann. § 190.2 (West Supp.1983). The alleged special circumstance found true in respondent's case was commission of the murder during the course of a robbery. § 190.2(a)(17)(i).

4. This instruction, referred to hereinafter as the "Briggs Instruction," was incorporated into the California Penal Code as a result of a 1978 voter initiative popularly known as the Briggs Initiative.

respondent's trial, the judge delivered the following instruction:

> "You are instructed that under the State Constitution a Governor is empowered to grant a reprieve, pardon, or commutation of a sentence following conviction of a crime.

> "Under this power a Governor may in the future commute or modify a sentence of life imprisonment without possibility of parole to a lesser sentence that would include the possibility of parole."

The jury returned a verdict of death.

On appeal the Supreme Court of California affirmed respondent's conviction but reversed the death sentence, concluding that the Briggs Instruction required by Cal. Penal Code Ann. § 190.3 violated the Federal Constitution. The court found two constitutional flaws in the instruction. First, it invites the jury to consider factors that are foreign to its task of deciding whether the defendant should live or die. According to the State Supreme Court, instead of assuring that this decision rests on "consideration of the character and record of the individual offender and the circumstances of the particular offense," *Woodson v. North Carolina*, 428 U.S. 280, 96 S.Ct. 2978 (1976), the instruction focuses the jury's attention on the Governor's power to render the defendant eligible for parole if the jury does not vote to execute him and injects an entirely speculative element into the capital sentencing determination. Second, the court concluded that because the instruction does not also inform the jury that the Governor possesses the power to commute a death sentence, it leaves the jury with the mistaken belief that the only way to keep the defendant off the streets is to condemn him to death. Accordingly, the court remanded for a new penalty phase.

We granted certiorari and now reverse and remand.

II

In challenging the constitutionality of the Briggs Instruction, respondent presses upon us the two central arguments advanced by the Supreme Court of California in its decision. He contends (1) that a capital sentencing jury may not constitutionally consider[8] possible commutation, and (2) that the Briggs Instruction unconstitutionally misleads the jury by selectively informing it of the Governor's power to commute one of its sentencing choices but not the other. Respondent's first argument raises two related, but distinct concerns—*viz.*, that the power of commutation is so speculative a factor that it injects an unacceptable level of unreliability into the capital sentencing determination, and that consideration of this factor deflects the jury from its constitutionally mandated task of basing the penalty decision on the character of the defendant and the nature of

---

8. The Supreme Court of California construed the Briggs Instruction as inviting capital sentencing juries to consider the commutation power in its sentencing determination. We view the statute accordingly.

the offense. We address these points in Parts IIB and C, *infra*, and respondent's second argument in Part III, *infra*. * * *

     * * *

B

Addressing respondent's specific arguments, we find unpersuasive the suggestion that the possible commutation of a life sentence must be held constitutionally irrelevant to the sentencing decision and that it is too speculative an element for the jury's consideration. On this point, we find *Jurek v. Texas*, 428 U.S. 262, 96 S.Ct. 2950 (1976), controlling.

The Texas capital sentencing system upheld in *Jurek* limits capital homicides to intentional and knowing murders committed in five situations. Once the jury finds the defendant guilty of one of these five categories of murder, the jury must answer three statutory questions. If the jury concludes that the State has proved beyond a reasonable doubt that each question is answered in the affirmative, then the death sentence is imposed. In approving this statutory scheme, the joint opinion in *Jurek* rejected the contention that the second statutory question—requiring consideration of the defendant's future dangerousness—was unconstitutionally vague because it involved prediction of human behavior. * * *

By bringing to the jury's attention the possibility that the defendant may be returned to society, the Briggs Instruction invites the jury to assess whether the defendant is someone whose probable future behavior makes it undesireable that he be permitted to return to society. Like the challenged factor in Texas' statutory scheme, then, the Briggs Instruction focuses the jury on the defendant's probable future dangerousness. The approval in *Jurek* of explicit consideration of this factor in the capital sentencing decision defeats respondent's contention that, because of the speculativeness involved, the State of California may not constitutionally permit consideration of commutation.[18]

Nor is there any diminution in the reliability of the sentencing decision of the kind condemned in *Gardner v. Florida*, 430 U.S. 349, 97 S.Ct. 1197 (1977). In *Gardner*, the Court reversed a death sentence that had been imposed in part on the basis of a confidential portion of a presentence investigation report that had not been disclosed to either the defendant or his counsel. Because of the potential that the sentencer might have rested its decision in part on erroneous or inaccurate informa-

---

18. See also ABA Standards for Criminal Justice 18–2.5(c)–(i) (2d ed. 1980) (giving as example of legitimate reason for selecting total confinement fact that "confinement is necessary in order to protect the public from further serious criminal activity by the defendant").

We also observe that, with respect to the relevance of the information conveyed by the Briggs Instruction, the issue of parole or commutation is presented by the language used to describe one of the jury's sentencing choices—*i.e.*, life imprisonment without possibility of parole. The State of California reasonably could have concluded that, while jurors are generally aware of the Governor's power to commute a death sentence, most jurors would not be aware that the Governor also may commute a sentence of life imprisonment without possibility of parole and that they should be so informed to avoid any possible misconception conveyed by the description of the sentencing alternative.

tion that the defendant had no opportunity to explain or deny, the need for reliability in capital sentencing dictated that the death penalty be reversed. *Gardner* provides no support for respondent. The Briggs Instruction gives the jury accurate information of which both the defendant and his counsel are aware, and it does not preclude the defendant from offering any evidence or argument regarding the Governor's power to commute a life sentence.[19]

C

Closely related to, yet distinct from respondent's speculativeness argument is the contention that the Briggs Instruction is constitutionally infirm because it deflects the jury's focus from its central task. Respondent argues that the commutation instruction diverts the jury from undertaking the kind of individualized sentencing determination that, under *Woodson v. North Carolina*, is "a constitutionally indispensable part of the process of inflicting the penalty of death."

As we have already noted, as a functional matter the Briggs Instruction focuses the jury's attention on whether this particular defendant is one whose possible return to society is desirable. In this sense, then, the jury's deliberation is individualized. The instruction invites the jury to predict not so much what some future Governor might do, but more what the defendant himself might do if released into society.

Any contention that injecting this factor into the jury's deliberations constitutes a departure from the kind of individualized focus required in capital sentencing decisions was implicitly rejected by the decision in *Jurek*. Indeed, after noting that consideration of the defendant's future dangerousness was an inquiry common throughout the criminal justice system, the joint opinion of Justices STEWART, POWELL, and STEVENS observed: "What is essential is that the jury have before it all possible relevant information about the individual defendant whose fate it must determine. Texas law clearly assures that all such evidence will be adduced." As with the Texas scheme, the California sentencing system ensures that the jury will have before it information regarding the individual characteristics of the defendant and his offense, including the

---

19. In dissent Justice MARSHALL argues that if a balanced instruction cannot or should not be given, "the solution is not to permit a misleading instruction, but to prohibit altogether any instruction concerning commutation." This observation is incorrect for at least two reasons. First, * * * we do not suggest that there would be any federal constitutional infirmity in giving an instruction concerning the Governor's power to commute the death sentence. We note only that such comment is prohibited under state law. Second, the Briggs Instruction simply is not misleading. On the contrary, the instruction gives the jury accurate information in that it corrects a misleading description of a sentencing choice available to the jury. Although * * * most jurors may have a general awareness of the availability of commutation and parole, the statutory description of one of the sentencing choices as "life imprisonment without possibility of parole" may generate the misleading impression that the Governor could not commute this sentence to one that included the possibility of parole. The Briggs Instruction merely dispels that possible misunderstanding. Further, the defendant may offer evidence or argument regarding the commutation power, and respondent's counsel addressed the possibility of the Governor's commutation of a life sentence in his closing argument. * * *

nature and circumstances of the crime and the defendant's character, background, history, mental condition, and physical condition.

Respondent also relies on *Beck v. Alabama*, 447 U.S. 625, 100 S.Ct. 2382 (1980), as support for his contention that the Briggs Instruction undermines the jury's responsibility to make an individualized sentencing determination. In *Beck* the Court held that the jury in a capital case must be permitted to consider a verdict of guilt of a non-capital offense where the evidence would support such a verdict. In disapproving the Alabama statute that precluded giving a lesser included offense charge in capital cases, the Court concluded that the chief flaw of the statute "is that it interjects irrelevant considerations into the factfinding process, diverting the jury's attention from the central issue of whether the State has satisfied its burden of proving beyond a reasonable doubt that the defendant is guilty of a capital crime." The failure to give a lesser included offense instruction "diverted" the jury in two ways: a jury might convict a defendant of a capital offense because of its belief that he is guilty of some crime, or, given the mandatory nature of the death penalty under Alabama law, the jury might acquit because it does not think that the defendant's crime warrants death. According to the respondent, the Briggs Instruction, like the removal of the lesser included offense option in *Beck*, predisposes the jury to act without regard to whether the death penalty is called for on the facts before it.

We are unconvinced that the Briggs Instruction constrains the jury's sentencing choice in the manner condemned in *Beck*. Restricting the jury in *Beck* to the two sentencing alternatives—conviction of a capital offense or acquittal—in essence placed artificial alternatives before the jury. The unavailability of the "third option" thereby created the risk of an unwarranted conviction. By contrast, the Briggs Instruction does not limit the jury to two sentencing choices, neither of which may be appropriate. Instead, it places before the jury an additional element to be considered, along with many other factors, in determining which sentence is appropriate under the circumstances of the defendant's case.

More to the point, however, is the fundamental difference between the nature of the guilt/innocence determination at issue in *Beck* and the nature of the life/death choice at the penalty phase. As noted above, the Court in *Beck* identified the chief vice of Alabama's failure to provide a lesser included offense option as deflecting the jury's attention from "the *central* issue of whether the State has satisfied its burden of proving beyond a reasonable doubt that the defendant is guilty of a capital crime." (emphasis added). In returning a conviction, the jury must satisfy itself that the necessary elements of the particular crime have been proved beyond a reasonable doubt. In fixing a penalty, however, there is no similar "central issue" from which the jury's attention may be diverted. Once the jury finds that the defendant falls within the legislatively defined category of persons eligible for the death penalty, as did respondent's jury in determining the truth of the alleged special circumstance, the jury then is free to consider a myriad of factors to determine whether death is the appropriate punishment. In this sense, the jury's choice between life and death must be individualized. "But the Constitution does not require the jury to ignore other possible ... factors in the process of selecting ... those defendants who will actually be sentenced to death." *Zant v. Stephens*, 462 U.S. 862, 103 S.Ct. 2733 (1983). As we have noted, the essential effect of the Briggs Instruction is to inject into the sentencing calculus a consideration akin to the aggravating factor of future dangerousness in the Texas scheme. This element "is simply one of the countless considerations weighed by the jury in seeking to judge the punishment appropriate to the individual defendant." Id. (REHNQUIST, J., concurring in the judgment).

* * *

III

Having concluded that a capital sentencing jury's consideration of the Governor's power to commute a life sentence is not prohibited by the Federal Constitution, we now address respondent's contention that the Briggs Instruction must be held unconstitutional because it fails to inform jurors also that a death sentence may be commuted. In essence, respondent complains that the Briggs Instruction creates the misleading impression that the jury can prevent the defendant's return to society only by imposing the death sentence, thus biasing the jury in favor of death. Respondent therefore concludes that "[i]f ... commutation is a factor properly to be considered by the jury, then basic principles of fairness require that full disclosure be made with respect to commutation."

Thus, according to respondent, if the Federal Constitution permits the jury to consider possible commutation of a life sentence, the Federal Constitution requires that the jury also be instructed that a death sentence may be commuted. We find respondent's argument puzzling. If, as we must assume, respondent's principal objection is that the impact of the Briggs Instruction is to skew the jury toward imposing death, we fail to see how an instruction on the Governor's power to commute death sentences as well as life sentences restores the situation to one of "neutrality." Although such an instruction would be "neutral" in the sense of giving the jury complete and factually accurate information about the commutation power, it would not "balance" the impact of the Briggs Instruction, even assuming arguendo that the current instruction has any impermissible skewing effect. Disclosure of the complete nature of the commutation power would not eliminate any skewing in favor of death or increase the reliability of the sentencing choice. A jury concerned about preventing the defendant's potential return to society will not be any less inclined to vote for the death penalty upon learning that even a death sentence may not have such an effect. In fact, advising jurors that a death verdict is theoretically modifiable, and thus not "final," may incline them to approach their sentencing decision with less appreciation for the gravity of their choice and for the moral responsibility reposed in them as sentencers.

In short, an instruction disclosing the Governor's power to commute a death sentence may operate to the defendant's distinct disadvantage. It is precisely this perception that the defendant is prejudiced by an instruction on the possible commutation of a death sentence that led the California Supreme Court in *People v. Morse*, 388 P.2d 33 (Cal. 1964), to prohibit the giving of such an instruction. Thus, state law at the time of respondent Ramos' trial precluded the giving of the "other half" of the commutation instruction that respondent now argues is constitutionally required.[27]

Moreover, we are not convinced by respondent's argument that the Briggs Instruction alone impermissibly impels the jury toward voting for the death sentence. Any aggravating factor presented by the prosecution has this impact. As we concluded in Part II, supra, the State is constitutionally entitled to permit juror consideration of the Governor's power to commute a life sentence. This information is relevant and factually accurate and was properly before the jury. Moreover, the trial judge's instructions "did not place particular emphasis on the role of [this factor] in the jury's ultimate decision." *Zant v. Stephens*.

* * *

IV

In sum, the Briggs Instruction does not violate any of the substantive limitations this Court's precedents have imposed on the capital sentencing process. It does not preclude individualized sentencing determinations or consideration of mitigating factors, nor does it impermissibly inject an element too speculative for the jury's deliberation. Finally, its failure to inform the jury also of the Governor's power to commute a death sentence does not render it constitutionally infirm. Therefore, we defer to the State's identification of the Governor's power to commute a life sentence as a substantive factor to be presented for the sentencing jury's consideration.

Our conclusion is not intended to override the contrary judgment of state legislatures that capital sentencing juries in their States should not be permitted to consider the Governor's power to commute a sentence. It is elementary that States are free to provide greater protections in their criminal justice system than the Federal Constitution requires. We sit as judges, not as legislators, and the wisdom of the decision to permit juror consideration of possible commutation is best left to the States. We hold only that the Eighth and Fourteenth Amendments do not prohibit such an instruction.

The judgment of the Supreme Court of California is reversed, and the case is remanded for further proceedings not inconsistent with this opinion.

---

27. Given our conclusion in Part II, supra, that the State may constitutionally permit consideration of the Governor's power to commute a sentence of life imprisonment without possibility of parole, we do not suggest, of course, that the Federal Constitution prohibits an instruction regarding the Governor's power to commute a death sentence.

[Dissenting opinion of MARSHALL, J., joined by BRENNAN, J. and, in part by BLACKMUN, J., and dissenting opinions of BLACKMUN, J. and STEVENS, J. omitted]

NOTES

1. *Subsequent developments.*

On remand, the California Supreme Court ruled 6–1 that the Briggs instruction violated the state constitution because, as given, it was a "misleading half-truth." The court went on to say that even if the Briggs instruction were modified to add that a death sentence was also subject to the governor's commutation power, the instruction still would be unconstitutional because "its reference to the commutation power invites the jury to consider matters that are both totally speculative and that should not, in any event, influence the jury's determination." The court noted that twenty-five other jurisdictions also barred such an instruction, and only three states permitted it. See *People v. Ramos*, 689 P.2d 430 (Cal. 1984) (*Ramos II*).

In 1990, the California voters passed Proposition 115, the Crime Victims Justice Reform Act, which, *inter alia*, added the following provision to California Constitution, Article I, section 24:

> "In criminal cases the rights of a defendant to equal protection of the laws, to due process of law, to the assistance of counsel, to be personally present with counsel, to a speedy and public trial, to compel the attendance of witnesses, to confront the witnesses against him or her, to be free from unreasonable searches and seizures, to privacy, to not be compelled to be a witness against himself or herself, to not be placed twice in jeopardy for the same offense, and not to suffer the imposition of cruel or unusual punishment, shall be construed by the courts of this state in a manner consistent with the Constitution of the United States. This Constitution shall not be construed by the courts to afford greater rights to criminal defendants than those afforded by the Constitution of the United States, nor shall it be construed to afford greater rights to minors in juvenile proceedings on criminal causes than those afforded by the Constitution of the United States."

How would this provision have affected the holding in *Ramos II*? The California Supreme Court invalidated the provision, finding that the provision was an attempt to revise, rather than amend, the state constitution and that the constitution could be revised only by convening of a constitutional convention followed by popular ratification or by legislative submission of the measure to the voters. See *Raven v. Deukmejian*, 801 P.2d 1077 (Cal. 1990).

2. *Problem 10–2.*

Under the California Constitution, the Governor may not commute the sentence of a prisoner who is a twice-convicted felon without the approval of four judges of the Supreme Court. Defendant was a twice-convicted felon and was convicted of murder with the special circumstances of rape and sodomy. At the penalty phase, the jury was given a Briggs instruction to the effect that the Governor "may in the future commute or modify a sentence of life imprisonment without the possibility of parole to a lesser sentence that would include the possibility of parole." They also were instructed that "the matter of a Governor's commutation power is not to be considered by you in determining the punishment for this defendant" and told not speculate as to if or when a Governor would commute the sentence. Defendant was sentenced to death. What arguments should be made on appeal regarding the validity of the death sentence? See *Calderon v. Coleman*, 525 U.S. 141, 119 S.Ct. 500 (1998).

CALDWELL v. MISSISSIPPI

472 U.S. 320, 105 S.Ct. 2633, 86 L.Ed.2d 231 (1985).

JUSTICE MARSHALL delivered the opinion of the Court, except as to Part IV–A.

This case presents the issue whether a capital sentence is valid when the sentencing jury is led to believe that responsibility for determining the appropriateness of a death sentence rests not with the jury but with the appellate court which later reviews the case. In this case, a prosecutor urged the jury not to view itself as determining whether the defendant would die, because a death sentence would be reviewed for correctness by the State Supreme Court. We granted certiorari to consider petitioner's contention that the prosecutor's argument rendered the capital sentencing proceeding inconsistent with the Eighth Amendment's heightened "need for reliability in the determination that death is the appropriate punishment in a specific case." *Woodson v. North Carolina*, 428 U.S. 280, 96 S.Ct. 2978 (1976) (plurality opinion). Agreeing with the contention, we vacate the sentence.

I

Petitioner shot and killed the owner of a small grocery store in the course of robbing it. In a bifurcated proceeding conducted pursuant to Mississippi's capital punishment statute, petitioner was convicted of capital murder and sentenced to death.

In their case for mitigation, petitioner's lawyers put on evidence of petitioner's youth, family background, and poverty, as well as general character evidence. In their closing arguments they referred to this evidence and then asked the jury to show mercy. The arguments were in large part pleas that the jury confront both the gravity and the responsibility of calling for another's death, even in the context of a capital sentencing proceeding.

> "[E]very life is precious and as long as there's life in the soul of a person, there is hope. There is hope, but life is one thing and death is final. So I implore you to think deeply about this matter. It is his life or death—the decision you're going to have to make, and I implore you to exercise your prerogative to spare the life of Bobby Caldwell.... I'm sure [the prosecutor is] going to say to you that Bobby Caldwell is not a merciful person, but I say unto you he is a human

being. That he has a life that rests in your hands. You can give him life or you can give him death. It's going to be your decision. I don't know what else I can say to you but we live in a society where we are taught that an eye for an eye is not the solution. . . . You are the judges and you will have to decide his fate. It is an awesome responsibility, I know—an awesome responsibility.''

In response, the prosecutor sought to minimize the jury's sense of the importance of its role. Indeed, the prosecutor forcefully argued that the defense had done something wholly illegitimate in trying to force the jury to feel a sense of responsibility for its decision. The prosecutor's argument, defense counsel's objection, and the trial court's ruling were as follows:

"ASSISTANT DISTRICT ATTORNEY: Ladies and gentlemen, I intend to be brief. I'm in complete disagreement with the approach the defense has taken. I don't think it's fair. I think it's unfair. I think the lawyers know better. Now, they would have you believe that you're going to kill this man and they know—they know that your decision is not the final decision. My God, how unfair can you be? Your job is reviewable. They know it. Yet they . . .

"COUNSEL FOR DEFENDANT: Your Honor, I'm going to object to this statement. It's out of order.

"ASSISTANT DISTRICT ATTORNEY: Your Honor, throughout their argument, they said this panel was going to kill this man. I think that's terribly unfair.

"THE COURT: Alright, go on and make the full expression so the Jury will not be confused. I think it proper that the jury realizes that it is reviewable automatically as the death penalty commands. I think that information is now needed by the Jury so they will not be confused.

"ASSISTANT DISTRICT ATTORNEY: Throughout their remarks, they attempted to give you the opposite, sparing the truth. They said 'Thou shalt not kill.' If that applies to him, it applies to you, insinuating that your decision is the final decision and that they're gonna take Bobby Caldwell out in the front of this Courthouse in moments and string him up and that is terribly, terribly unfair. For they know, as I know, and as Judge Baker has told you, that the decision you render is automatically reviewable by the Supreme Court. Automatically, and I think it's unfair and I don't mind telling them so.''

* * *

III

A

On reaching the merits, we conclude that it is constitutionally impermissible to rest a death sentence on a determination made by a sentencer who has been led to believe that the responsibility for determining the appropriateness of the defendant's death rests elsewhere. This Court has repeatedly said that under the Eighth Amendment "the qualitative difference of death from all other punishments requires a correspondingly greater degree of scrutiny of the capital sentencing determination." *California v. Ramos*, 463 U.S. 992, 103 S.Ct. 3446 (1983). Accordingly, many of the limits that this Court has placed on the imposition of capital punishment are rooted in a concern that the sentencing process should facilitate the responsible and reliable exercise of sentencing discretion.

In evaluating the various procedures developed by States to determine the appropriateness of death, this Court's Eighth Amendment jurisprudence has taken as a given that capital sentencers would view their task as the serious one of determining whether a specific human being should die at the hands of the State. Thus, as long ago as the pre-*Furman* case of *McGautha v. California*, 402 U.S. 183, 91 S.Ct. 1454 (1971), Justice Harlan, writing for the Court, upheld a capital sentencing scheme in spite of its reliance on jury discretion. The sentencing scheme's premise, he assumed, was "that jurors confronted with the truly awesome responsibility of decreeing death for a fellow human will act with due regard for the consequences of their decision...." Belief in the truth of the assumption that sentencers treat their power to determine the appropriateness of death as an "awesome responsibility" has allowed this Court to view sentencer discretion as consistent with—and indeed as indispensable to— the Eighth Amendment's "need for reliability in the determination that death is the appropriate punishment in a specific case." *Woodson v. North Carolina* (plurality opinion).

B

In the capital sentencing context there are specific reasons to fear substantial unreliability as well as bias in favor of death sentences when there are state-induced suggestions that the sentencing jury may shift its sense of responsibility to an appellate court.

(1)

Bias against the defendant clearly stems from the institutional limits on what an appellate court can do—limits that jurors often might not understand. The "delegation" of sentencing responsibility that the prosecutor here encouraged would thus not simply postpone the defendant's right to a fair determination of the appropriateness of his death; rather it would deprive him of that right, for an appellate court, unlike a capital sentencing jury, is wholly ill-suited to evaluate the appropriateness of death in the first instance. Whatever intangibles a jury might consider in its sentencing determination, few can be gleaned from an appellate record. This inability to confront and examine the individuality of the defendant would be particularly devastating to any argument for consideration of what this Court has termed "[those] compassionate or mitigating factors stemming from the diverse frailties of humankind." *Woodson, supra.*

When we held that a defendant has a constitutional right to the consideration of such factors, *Eddings v. Oklahoma*, 455 U.S. 104, 102 S.Ct. 869 (1982); *Lockett v. Ohio*, 438 U.S. 586, 98 S.Ct. 2954 (1978), we clearly envisioned that that consideration would occur among sentencers who were present to hear the evidence and arguments and see the witnesses. As the dissenters below noted:

> "The [mercy] plea is made directly to the jury as only they may impose the death sentence. Under our standards of appellate review mercy is irrelevant. There is no appellate mercy. Therefore, the fact that review is mandated is irrelevant to the thought processes required to find that an accused should be denied mercy and sentenced to die."

Given these limits, most appellate courts review sentencing determinations with a presumption of correctness. This is the case in Mississippi, where, as the dissenters below pointed out: "Even a novice attorney knows that appellate courts do not impose a death penalty, they merely review the jury's decision and that review is with a presumption of correctness."

(2)

Writing on this kind of prosecutorial argument in a prior case, Justice STEVENS noted another reason why it presents an intolerable danger of bias toward a death sentence: Even when a sentencing jury is unconvinced that death is the appropriate punishment, it might nevertheless wish to "send a message" of extreme disapproval for the defendant's acts. This desire might make the jury very receptive to the prosecutor's assurance that it can more freely "err because the error may be corrected on appeal." *Maggio v. Williams*, 464 U.S. 46, 104 S.Ct. 311 (1983) (concurring in judgment). A defendant might thus be executed, although no sentencer had ever made a determination that death was the appropriate sentence.

(3)

Bias could similarly stem from the fact that some jurors may correctly assume that a sentence of life in prison could not be increased to a death sentence on appeal. See *Arizona v. Rumsey*, 467 U.S. 203, 104 S.Ct. 2305 (1984). The chance that this will be the assumption of at least some jurors is increased by the fact that, in an argument like the one in this case, appellate review is only raised as an issue with respect to the reviewability of a death sentence. If the jury understands that only a death sentence will be reviewed, it will also understand that any decision to "delegate" responsibility for sentencing can only be effectuated by returning that sentence. But for a sentencer to impose a death sentence out of a desire to avoid responsibility for its decision presents the spectre of the imposition of death based on a factor wholly irrelevant to legitimate sentencing concerns. The death sentence that would emerge from such a sentencing proceeding would simply not represent a decision that the State had demonstrated the appropriateness of the defendant's death. This would thus also create the danger of a defendant's being executed in the absence of any determination that death was the appropriate punishment.

(4)

In evaluating the prejudicial effect of the prosecutor's argument, we must also recognize that the argument offers jurors a view of their role which might frequently be highly attractive. A capital sentencing jury is made up of individuals placed in a very unfamiliar situation and called on to make a very difficult and uncomfortable choice. They are confronted with evidence and argument on the issue of whether another should die, and they are asked to decide that issue on behalf of the community. Moreover, they are given only partial guidance as to how their judgment should be exercised, leaving them with substantial discretion. Given such a situation, the uncorrected suggestion that the responsibility for any ultimate determination of death will rest with others presents an intolerable danger that the jury will in fact choose to minimize the importance of its role. Indeed, one can easily imagine that in a case in which the jury is divided on the proper sentence, the presence of appellate review could effectively be used as an argument for why those jurors who are reluctant to invoke the death sentence should nevertheless give in.

This problem is especially serious when the jury is told that the alternative decision-makers are the justices of the state supreme court. It is certainly plausible to believe that many jurors will be tempted to view these respected legal authorities as having more of a "right" to make such an important decision than has the jury. Given that the sentence will be subject to appellate review only if the jury returns a sentence of death, the chance that an invitation to rely on that review will generate a bias toward returning a death sentence is simply too great.

* * *

IV

The State advances three arguments for why the death sentence should be upheld despite the prosecutor's comments. First, the State argues that under *California v. Ramos*, 463 U.S. 992, 103 S.Ct. 3446 (1983), each State may decide for itself the extent to which a capital sentencing jury should know of postsentencing proceedings. Second, it defends the prosecutor's comments as "invited," in the sense that they were a reasonable response to defense counsel's arguments. Last, the State asserts that an application of this Court's decision in *Donnelly v. DeChristoforo*, 416 U.S. 637, 94 S.Ct. 1868 (1974), precludes a finding of constitutional error based on the sort of impropriety that the state prosecutor's comments are said to contain. None of these arguments is persuasive.

A

Both respondent and the prevailing justices of the Mississippi Supreme Court interpreted *California v. Ramos*, *supra*, as if it had held that

States are free to expose capital sentencing juries to any information and argument concerning postsentencing procedures. This is too broad a view of *Ramos*.

Ramos concerned the constitutionality of California's statutory requirement that capital sentencing juries be informed that the State Governor could commute a sentence of life imprisonment without possibility of parole into a lesser sentence that included the possibility of parole. In upholding this requirement, the Court rested on a determination that this instruction was both accurate and relevant to a legitimate state penological interest—that interest being a concern for the future dangerousness of the defendant should he ever return to society. The Court concluded that this legitimate sentencing concern gave the jury a valid interest in accurate information on the possibility of parole.

In contrast, the argument at issue here cannot be said to be either accurate or relevant to a valid state penological interest. The argument was inaccurate, both because it was misleading as to the nature of the appellate court's review and because it depicted the jury's role in a way fundamentally at odds with the role that a capital sentencer must perform. Similarly, the prosecutor's argument is not linked to any arguably valid sentencing consideration. That appellate review is available to a capital defendant sentenced to death is no valid basis for a jury to return such a sentence if otherwise it might not. It is simply a factor that in itself is wholly irrelevant to the determination of the appropriate sentence. The argument here urged the jurors to view themselves as taking only a preliminary step toward the actual determination of the appropriateness of death—a determination which would eventually be made by others and for which the jury was not responsible. Creating this image in the minds of the capital sentencers is not a valid state goal, and *Ramos* is not to the contrary. Indeed, *Ramos* itself never questioned the indispensability of sentencers who "appreciat[e] . . . the gravity of their choice and . . . the moral responsibility reposed in them as sentencers."

B

Respondent next defends the view of the Mississippi Supreme Court that the prosecutor's argument must be understood as a response to the defense counsel's argument, and that it was not unreasonable in that context. But neither respondent nor the court below explains how the prosecutor's argument was less likely to have distorted the jury's deliberations because of anything defense counsel said.

The Mississippi Supreme Court was less than clear as to the theory of "context" it embraced. The prevailing justices commented on two aspects of the defense's arguments. First, "during defense counsel's argument, . . . he inaccurately sought to convince the jury that if they meted out a life sentence the defendant would remain in prison the remainder of his life. He left them with the impression that there would be no parole or commutation of sentence." Second, the opinion noted that "[defense counsel had] emphasized his pitch for mercy by referring to the Ten Commandments, Jesus and the Heavenly Father.''

The first of these arguments, of course, recalls *Ramos*, in which the Court stated that an instruction describing the alternative to a death sentence as " 'life imprisonment without possibility of parole' may generate the misleading impression that the Governor could not commute this sentence to one that included the possibility of parole.'' But although in *Ramos* the Court concluded that this possible misimpression underscored a valid sentencing need to give more information on the Governor's power to commute life sentences, there is no rational link between the possibility of this specific misimpression and the argument used by the prosecutor in this case. The prosecutor's argument simply had nothing to do with the consequences that would flow from the life sentence mentioned by defense counsel.

The connection between defense counsel's references to religious themes and texts and the prosecutor's arguments regarding appellate review is similarly unclear. As the dissenting justices noted: "Assuming without accepting the majority's position that the defense counsel's argument invited error, it did not invite this error. Asking the jury to show mercy does not invite comment on the system of appellate review. This is true whether the plea for mercy discusses Christian, Judean or Buddhist philosophies, quotes Shakespeare or refers to the heartache suffered by the accused's mother.''

[In addressing the State's third argument, the Court distinguished *Donnelly v. DeChristoforo, supra*, on its facts.]

V

This Court has always premised its capital punishment decisions on the assumption that a capital sentencing jury recognizes the gravity of its task and proceeds with the appropriate awareness of its "truly awesome responsibility.'' In this case, the State sought to minimize the jury's sense of responsibility for determining the appropriateness of death. Because we cannot say that this effort had no effect on the sentencing decision, that decision does not meet the standard of reliability that the Eighth Amendment requires. The sentence of death must therefore be vacated. Accordingly, the judgment is reversed to the extent that it sustains the imposition of the death penalty, and the case is remanded for further proceedings.

It is so ordered.

Justice Powell took no part in the decision of this case.

[Opinion of O'Connor, J., concurring in part and concurring in the judgment, and dissenting opinion of Rehnquist, J., joined by Burger, C.J. and White, J. omitted]

Notes

1. *Problem 10–3.*

Defendant was charged with violating 18 U.S.C. § 1201(a)(2) on allegations that he kidnaped Victim from an air force base, sexually assaulted her and then killed her. The government sought the death penalty under the Federal Death Penalty Act. Defendant was tried and found guilty. Under the Act, in order to find a defendant death-eligible, the jury at the sentencing hearing must first find that the killing was intentional, and then it must find beyond a reasonable doubt the existence of a statutory aggravating factor. If a defendant is found to be death-eligible, the sentencing jury must consider all of the aggravating factors (including nonstatutory aggravating factors for which notice has been given) and mitigating factors and then must determine whether the former outweigh the latter (or, if there are no mitigating factors, whether the aggravating factors alone are sufficient to warrant a death sentence). The Act, however, requires that a jury unanimously agree that the government established the existence of an aggravating factor beyond a reasonable doubt, but the jury may consider a mitigating factor in its weighing process so long as one juror finds that the defendant established its existence by preponderance of the evidence. The penalty for kidnaping resulting in death is either death or imprisonment for life without the possibility of release. In the event the jury is unable to agree on a sentence, the defendant is sentenced to life without the possibility of release.

At his sentencing hearing, Defendant requested that the jury be instructed on the consequences of their inability to agree. The request was denied, and instead the judge instructed, in part:

> If you recommend the imposition of a death sentence, the court is required to impose that sentence. If you recommend a sentence of life without the possibility of release, the court is required to impose that sentence. If you recommend that some other lesser sentence be imposed, the court is required to impose a sentence that is authorized by the law. In deciding what recommendation to make, you are not to be concerned with the question of what sentence the defendant might receive in the event you determine not to recommend a death sentence or a sentence of life without the possibility of release. That is a matter for the court to decide in the event you conclude that a sentence of death or life without the possibility of release should not be recommended.

The judge provided the jury with four decision forms: A, for a finding that the government had not proved intent or an aggravating factor; B, for a death sentence; C, for life imprisonment without possibility of release; and D, for the jury to "recommend some other lesser sentence." The jury found two statutory aggravating factors (death during the commission of another crime and the killing was "especially heinous, cruel and depraved") and two nonstatutory aggravating factors, and there were 11 mitigating factors found by one or more jurors. The jury sentenced Defendant to death. What arguments should be made on Defendant's appeal challenging his death sentence? See *Jones v. United States*, 527 U.S. 373, 119 S.Ct. 2090 (1999).

2. *Problem 10–4.*

Defendant was convicted of capital murder. During the senten
of the trial, the prosecution, over a defense objection, introduced a c
judgment and death sentence Defendant had received in an earlier
case. Although Defendant's prior conviction was relevant to two of th
statutory aggravating circumstances the prosecution had alleged (prior c
tion for a violent felony and future dangerousness), his prior death sent
was irrelevant under state law. The jury was instructed: (1) to determ
whether one or more of the four aggravating circumstances had been prove
beyond a reasonable doubt; and (2) to weigh only such circumstance(s) against
any mitigating circumstances it found in order to reach its penalty decision.
The jury found that all four aggravating circumstances were true and that
they outweighed the mitigating circumstances. Accordingly, the jury imposed
a second death sentence upon Defendant. While the present case was on
appeal, Defendant's prior murder conviction was overturned by the state
supreme court. What arguments should be made in the present case concerning the introduction into evidence of the earlier judgment and death sentence?
See *Romano v. Oklahoma*, 512 U.S. 1, 114 S.Ct. 2004 (1994).

SIMMONS v. SOUTH CAROLINA

512 U.S. 154, 114 S.Ct. 2187, 129 L.Ed.2d 133 (1994).

JUSTICE BLACKMUN announced the judgment of the Court and delivered
an opinion in which JUSTICE STEVENS, JUSTICE SOUTER, and JUSTICE GINSBURG
join.

This case presents the question whether the Due Process Clause of
the Fourteenth Amendment was violated by the refusal of a state trial
court to instruct the jury in the penalty phase of a capital trial that under
state law the defendant was ineligible for parole. We hold that where the
defendant's future dangerousness is at issue, and state law prohibits the
defendant's release on parole, due process requires that the sentencing
jury be informed that the defendant is parole ineligible.

I

A

In July 1990, petitioner beat to death an elderly woman, Josie Lamb,
in her home in Columbia, South Carolina. The week before petitioner's
capital murder trial was scheduled to begin, he pleaded guilty to first
degree burglary and two counts of criminal sexual conduct in connection
with two prior assaults on elderly women. Petitioner's guilty pleas resulted in convictions for violent offenses, and those convictions rendered
petitioner ineligible for parole if convicted for any subsequent violent-
crime offense.

Prior to jury selection, the prosecution advised the trial judge that the
State "[o]bviously [was] going to ask you to exclude any mention of parole
throughout this trial." Over defense counsel's objection, the trial court
granted the prosecution's motion for an order barring the defense from

ring *voir dire* regarding parole. Under the court's
. was forbidden even to mention the subject of
was prohibited from questioning prospective jurors
nderstood the meaning of a "life" sentence under
After a 3–day trial, petitioner was convicted of the

lty phase, the defense brought forward mitigating
show that petitioner's violent behavior reflected
ders that stemmed from years of neglect and extreme
l abuse petitioner endured as an adolescent. While
agreement among witnesses regarding the extent to
mental condition properly could be deemed a "disor-
or both the defense and the prosecution agreed that
sed a continuing danger to elderly women.

its closing argument the prosecution argued that petitioner's
are dangerousness was a factor for the jury to consider when fixing the
appropriate punishment. The question for the jury, said the prosecution,
was "what to do with [petitioner] now that he is in our midst." The
prosecution further urged that a verdict for death would be "a response of
society to someone who is a threat. Your verdict will be an act of self-
defense."

Petitioner sought to rebut the prosecution's generalized argument of
future dangerousness by presenting evidence that, due to his unique
psychological problems, his dangerousness was limited to elderly women,
and that there was no reason to expect further acts of violence once he
was isolated in a prison setting. In support of his argument, petitioner
introduced testimony from a female medical assistant and from two
supervising officers at the Richland County jail where petitioner had been
held prior to trial. All three testified that petitioner had adapted well to
prison life during his pretrial confinement and had not behaved in a
violent manner toward any of the other inmates or staff. Petitioner also
offered expert opinion testimony from Richard L. Boyle, a clinical social
worker and former correctional employee, who had reviewed and observed
petitioner's institutional adjustment. Mr. Boyle expressed the view that,
based on petitioner's background and his current functioning, petitioner
would successfully adapt to prison if he was sentenced to life imprisonment.

Concerned that the jury might not understand that "life imprisonment" did not carry with it the possibility of parole in petitioner's case,
defense counsel asked the trial judge to clarify this point by defining the
term "life imprisonment" for the jury in accordance with S.C.Code § 24–
21–640.[2] To buttress his request, petitioner proffered, outside the presence

---

1. The venire was informed, however, of the meaning of the term "death" under South
Carolina law. The trial judge specifically advised the prospective jurors that "[b]y the death
penalty, we mean death by electrocution." The sentencing jury was also so informed.

2. Section 24–21–640 states: "The board must not grant parole nor is parole authorized to any
prisoner serving a sentence for a second or subsequent conviction, following a separate sentencing

of the jury, evidence conclusively establishing his parole ineligibility. On petitioner's behalf, attorneys for the South Carolina Department of Corrections and the Department of Probation, Parole and Pardons testified that any offender in petitioner's position was in fact ineligible for parole under South Carolina law. The prosecution did not challenge or question petitioner's parole ineligibility. Instead, it sought to elicit admissions from the witnesses that, notwithstanding petitioner's parole ineligibility, petitioner might receive holiday furloughs or other forms of early release. Even this effort was unsuccessful, however, as the cross-examination revealed that Department of Corrections regulations prohibit petitioner's release under early release programs such as work-release or supervised furloughs, and that no convicted murderer serving life without parole ever had been furloughed or otherwise released for any reason.

Petitioner then offered into evidence, without objection, the results of a statewide public-opinion survey conducted by the University of South Carolina's Institute for Public Affairs. The survey had been conducted a few days before petitioner's trial, and showed that only 7.1 percent of all jury-eligible adults who were questioned firmly believed that a inmate sentenced to life imprisonment in South Carolina actually would be required to spend the rest of his life in prison. Almost half of those surveyed believed that a convicted murderer might be paroled within 20 years; nearly three-quarters thought that release certainly would occur in less than 30 years. More than 75 percent of those surveyed indicated that if they were called upon to make a capital-sentencing decision as jurors, the amount of time the convicted murderer actually would have to spend in prison would be an "extremely important" or a "very important" factor in choosing between life and death.

Petitioner argued that, in view of the public's apparent misunderstanding about the meaning of "life imprisonment" in South Carolina, there was a reasonable likelihood that the jurors would vote for death simply because they believed, mistakenly, that petitioner eventually would be released on parole.

The prosecution opposed the proposed instruction, urging the court "not to allow ... any argument by state or defense about parole and not charge the jury on anything concerning parole." * * * [T]he trial court refused petitioner's requested instruction. Petitioner then asked alternatively for the following instruction:

> "I charge you that these sentences mean what they say. That is, if you recommend that the defendant Jonathan Simmons be sentenced to death, he actually will be sentenced to death and executed. If, on the other hand, you recommend that he be sentenced to life imprisonment, he actually will be sentenced to imprisonment in the state penitentiary for the balance of his natural life.

from a prior conviction, for violent crimes as defined in Section 16–1–60." Petitioner's earlier convictions for burglary in the first degree and criminal sexual assault in the first degree are violent offenses under § 16–1–60.

"In your deliberations, you are not to speculate that these sentences mean anything other than what I have just told you, for what I have told you is exactly what will happen to the defendant, depending on what your sentencing decision is."

The trial judge also refused to give this instruction, but indicated that he might give a similar instruction if the jury inquired about parole eligibility.

After deliberating on petitioner's sentence for 90 minutes, the jury sent a note to the judge asking a single question: "Does the imposition of a life sentence carry with it the possibility of parole?" Over petitioner's objection, the trial judge gave the following instruction:

"You are instructed not to consider parole or parole eligibility in reaching your verdict. Do not consider parole or parole eligibility. That is not a proper issue for your consideration. The terms life imprisonment and death sentence are to be understood in their plan [sic] and ordinary meaning."

Twenty-five minutes after receiving this response from the court, the jury returned to the courtroom with a sentence of death.

* * *

II

The Due Process Clause does not allow the execution of a person "on the basis of information which he had no opportunity to deny or explain." *Gardner v. Florida*, 430 U.S. 349, 97 S.Ct. 1197 (1977). In this case, the jury reasonably may have believed that petitioner could be released on parole if he were not executed. To the extent this misunderstanding pervaded the jury's deliberations, it had the effect of creating a false choice between sentencing petitioner to death and sentencing him to a limited period of incarceration. This grievous misperception was encouraged by the trial court's refusal to provide the jury with accurate information regarding petitioner's parole ineligibility, and by the State's repeated suggestion that petitioner would pose a future danger to society if he were not executed. Three times petitioner asked to inform the jury that in fact he was ineligible for parole under state law; three times his request was denied. The State thus succeeded in securing a death sentence on the ground, at least in part, of petitioner's future dangerousness, while at the same time concealing from the sentencing jury the true meaning of its noncapital sentencing alternative, namely, that life imprisonment meant life without parole. We think it is clear that the State denied petitioner due process.[4]

A

This Court has approved the jury's consideration of future dangerousness during the penalty phase of a capital trial, recognizing that a

---

4. We express no opinion on the question whether the result we reach today is also compelled by the Eighth Amendment.

defendant's future dangerousness bears on all sentencing determinations made in our criminal justice system. See *Jurek v. Texas*, 428 U.S. 262, 96 S.Ct. 2950 (1976) (plurality opinion) (noting that "any sentencing authority must predict a convicted person's probable future conduct when it engages in the process of determining what punishment to impose"); *California v. Ramos*, 463 U.S. 992, 103 S.Ct. 3446 (1983) (explaining that it is proper for a sentencing jury in a capital case to consider "the defendant's potential for reform and whether his probable future behavior counsels against the desirability of his release into society").

Although South Carolina statutes do not mandate consideration of the defendant's future dangerousness in capital sentencing, the State's evidence in aggravation is not limited to evidence relating to statutory aggravating circumstances. Thus, prosecutors in South Carolina, like those in other States that impose the death penalty, frequently emphasize a defendant's future dangerousness in their evidence and argument at the sentencing phase; they urge the jury to sentence the defendant to death so that he will not be a danger to the public if released from prison.

* * *

In assessing future dangerousness, the actual duration of the defendant's prison sentence is indisputably relevant. Holding all other factors constant, it is entirely reasonable for a sentencing jury to view a defendant who is eligible for parole as a greater threat to society than a defendant who is not. Indeed, there may be no greater assurance of a defendant's future nondangerousness to the public than the fact that he never will be released on parole. The trial court's refusal to apprise the jury of information so crucial to its sentencing determination, particularly when the prosecution alluded to the defendant's future dangerousness in its argument to the jury, cannot be reconciled with our well-established precedents interpreting the Due Process Clause.

B

In *Skipper v. South Carolina*, 476 U.S. 1, 106 S.Ct. 1669 (1986), this Court held that a defendant was denied due process by the refusal of the state trial court to admit evidence of the defendant's good behavior in prison in the penalty phase of his capital trial. Although the majority opinion stressed that the defendant's good behavior in prison was "relevant evidence in mitigation of punishment," and thus admissible under the Eighth Amendment, the *Skipper* opinion expressly noted that the Court's conclusion also was compelled by the Due Process Clause. The Court explained that where the prosecution relies on a prediction of future dangerousness in requesting the death penalty, elemental due process principles operate to require admission of the defendant's relevant evidence in rebuttal.

The Court reached a similar conclusion in *Gardner v. Florida*, 430 U.S. 349, 97 S.Ct. 1197 (1977). In that case, a defendant was sentenced to death on the basis of a presentence report which was not made available to him and which he therefore could not rebut. A plurality of the Court explained that sending a man to his death "on the basis of information which he had no opportunity to deny or explain" violated fundamental notions of due process. The principle announced in *Gardner* was reaffirmed in *Skipper*, and it compels our decision today.

Like the defendants in *Skipper* and *Gardner*, petitioner was prevented from rebutting information that the sentencing authority considered, and upon which it may have relied, in imposing the sentence of death. The State raised the specter of petitioner's future dangerousness generally, but then thwarted all efforts by petitioner to demonstrate that, contrary to the prosecutor's intimations, he never would be released on parole and thus, in his view, would not pose a future danger to society.[5] The logic and effectiveness of petitioner's argument naturally depended on the fact that he was legally ineligible for parole and thus would remain in prison if afforded a life sentence. Petitioner's efforts to focus the jury's attention on the question whether, in prison, he would be a future danger were futile, as he repeatedly was denied any opportunity to inform the jury that he never would be released on parole. The jury was left to speculate about petitioner's parole eligibility when evaluating petitioner's future dangerousness, and was denied a straight answer about petitioner's parole eligibility even when it was requested.

C

The State and its *amici* contend that petitioner was not entitled to an instruction informing the jury that petitioner is ineligible for parole because such information is inherently misleading. Essentially, they argue that because future exigencies such as legislative reform, commutation, clemency, and escape might allow petitioner to be released into society, petitioner was not entitled to inform the jury that he is parole ineligible. Insofar as this argument is targeted at the specific wording of the instruction petitioner requested, the argument is misplaced. Petitioner's requested instruction ("If ... you recommend that [the defendant] be sentenced to life imprisonment, he actually will be sentenced to imprisonment in the state penitentiary for the balance of his natural life") was proposed only after the trial court ruled that South Carolina law prohibited a plain-language instruction that petitioner was ineligible for parole under state law. To the extent that the State opposes even a simple parole-ineligibility instruction because of hypothetical future developments, the argument has little force. Respondent admits that an instruction informing the jury that petitioner is ineligible for parole is legally accurate. Certainly, such an instruction is more accurate than no instruc-

---

5. Of course, the fact that a defendant is parole ineligible does not prevent the State from arguing that the defendant poses a future danger. The State is free to argue that the defendant will pose a danger to others in prison and that executing him is the only means of eliminating the threat to the safety of other inmates or prison staff. But the State may not mislead the jury by concealing accurate information about the defendant's parole ineligibility. The Due Process Clause will not tolerate placing a capital defendant in a straitjacket by barring him from rebutting the prosecution's arguments of future dangerousness with the fact that he is ineligible for parole under state law.

tion at all, which leaves the jury to speculate whether "life imprisonment" means life without parole or something else.

The State's asserted accuracy concerns are further undermined by the fact that a large majority of States which provide for life imprisonment without parole as an alternative to capital punishment inform the sentencing authority of the defendant's parole ineligibility.[7] The few States that do not provide capital-sentencing juries with any information regarding parole ineligibility seem to rely, as South Carolina does here, on the proposition that *California v. Ramos*, 463 U.S. 992, 103 S.Ct. 3446 (1983), held that such determinations are purely matters of state law.[8]

It is true that *Ramos* stands for the broad proposition that we generally will defer to a State's determination as to what a jury should and should not be told about sentencing. In a State in which parole is available, how the jury's knowledge of parole availability will affect the decision whether or not to impose the death penalty is speculative, and we shall not lightly second-guess a decision whether or not to inform a jury of information regarding parole. States reasonably may conclude that truthful information regarding the availability of commutation, pardon, and the like, should be kept from the jury in order to provide "greater protection in [the States'] criminal justice system than the Federal Constitution requires." Concomitantly, nothing in the Constitution prohibits the prosecution from arguing any truthful information relating to parole or other forms of early release.

But if the State rests its case for imposing the death penalty at least in part on the premise that the defendant will be dangerous in the future, the fact that the alternative sentence to death is life without parole will necessarily undercut the State's argument regarding the threat the defendant poses to society. Because truthful information of parole ineligibility allows the defendant to "deny or explain" the showing of future dangerousness, due process plainly requires that he be allowed to bring it to the

---

7. At present, there are 26 States that both employ juries in capital sentencing and provide for life imprisonment without parole as an alternative to capital punishment. In 17 of these, the jury expressly is informed of the defendant's ineligibility for parole. Nine States [Alabama, Arkansas, California, Connecticut, Delaware, Louisiana, Missouri, New Hampshire, Washington] simply identify the jury's sentencing alternatives as death and life without parole. Eight States [Georgia, Indiana, Maryland, Nevada, Oklahoma, Oregon, Tennessee, Utah] allow the jury to specify whether the defendant should or should not be eligible for parole.

In three States [Colorado, Illinois, Mississippi], statutory or decisional law requires that the sentencing jury be instructed, where accurate, that the defendant will be ineligible for parole.

Three States [Florida, South Dakota, Wyoming] have not considered the question whether jurors should be instructed that the defendant is ineligible for parole under state law. The Florida Supreme Court, however, has approved for publication pattern jury instructions that inform capital sentencing juries of the no-parole feature of Fla.Stat. § 775.0823(1).

Finally, there are four States [Arizona, Idaho, Montana, Nebraska] in which the capital sentencing decision is made by the trial judge alone or by a sentencing panel of judges. Thus, in these States, as well, the sentencing authority is fully aware of the precise parole status of life-sentenced murderers.

8. Only two States other than South Carolina [Pennsylvania, Virginia] have a life-without-parole sentencing alternative to capital punishment for some or all convicted murderers but refuse to inform sentencing juries of this fact. * * *

jury's attention by way of argument by defense counsel or an instruction from the court.

* * *

[Concurring opinion of SOUTER, J., joined by STEVENS, J. and concurring opinion of GINSBURG, J. omitted]

JUSTICE O'CONNOR, with whom THE CHIEF JUSTICE and JUSTICE KENNEDY join, concurring in the judgment.

* * *

When the State seeks to show the defendant's future dangerousness, * * * the fact that he will never be released from prison will often be the only way that a violent criminal can successfully rebut the State's case. I agree with the Court that in such a case the defendant should be allowed to bring his parole ineligibility to the jury's attention—by way of argument by defense counsel or an instruction from the court—as a means of responding to the State's showing of future dangerousness. And despite our general deference to state decisions regarding what the jury should be told about sentencing, I agree that due process requires that the defendant be allowed to do so in cases in which the only available alternative sentence to death is life imprisonment without possibility of parole and the prosecution argues that the defendant will pose a threat to society in the future. Of course, in such cases the prosecution is free to argue that the defendant would be dangerous in prison; the State may also (though it need not) inform the jury of any truthful information regarding the availability of commutation, pardon, and the like.

* * *

[Dissenting opinion of SCALIA, J., joined by THOMAS, J., omitted]

NOTES

1. *Problem 10–5.*

Defendant was convicted of capital murder in South Carolina. At the sentencing phase, Prosecutor introduced evidence that Defendant had made a knife while in prison and had taken part in an escape attempt with plans to hold a female guard hostage. His cross-examination of a defense psychologist brought out evidence of Defendant's sadism and his desires to kill anyone who irritated him. During closing argument, Prosecutor did not argue "future dangerousness" as such but did characterize Defendant as a "dangerous bloody butcher." Defendant's request for a *Simmons* instruction on parole ineligibility was denied. The jury did not ask for a further instruction on parole eligibility and returned a verdict of death. On appeal, what arguments should be made on the constitutionality of the sentence? See *Kelly v. South Carolina*, 534 U.S. 246, 122 S.Ct. 726 (2002).

2. *Problem 10–6.*

Defendant was convicted of capital murder in Virginia. The murder of Victim, a convenience store clerk, occurred during a crime spree, in which

Defendant participated, *inter alia*, in robberies at Pizza Hut and Domino's. At the time of the sentencing phase in the murder case, Defendant had been convicted and sentenced for the Pizza Hut robbery, and he had been found guilty, but not yet sentenced, for the Domino's robbery. At the sentencing phase, the prosecutor submitted the case on the basis of the future dangerousness aggravating circumstance, and he relied almost exclusively on proof of Defendant's extensive criminal history, including the Pizza Hut and Domino's robberies. Under Virginia's "three-strikes law," a defendant convicted and sentenced for a murder and two robberies would be ineligible for parole. While deliberating Defendant's sentence, the jury asked, "[I]f the Defendant is given life, is there a possibility of parole at some time before his natural death?" The court refused to give a *Simmons* instruction and instead instructed that the jury should not concern itself "with what may happen afterwards." The jury sentenced Defendant to death, and, on appeal, State's Supreme Court rejected Defendant's *Simmons* claim on the ground that, at the time of his sentencing hearing, he had not yet been sentenced for the Domino's robbery, so he was not yet parole ineligible. On appeal, what arguments should be made as to the constitutionality of Defendant's sentence? See *Ramdass v. Angelone*, 530 U.S. 156, 120 S.Ct. 2113 (2000).

3. *Should Simmons be applied in all capital cases?*

Should the *Simmons* rule that capital jurors must be accurately informed about the alternative sentence to the death penalty be limited to cases, like *Simmons*, where future dangerousness is an issue and the alternative punishment is life without possibility of parole, or should the rule apply in all capital cases? In a study attempting to provide empirical evidence on that issue, researchers examined what 916 capital jurors from 257 capital trials in 11 states actually believed about the alternative to the death penalty and what effect their beliefs had on their capital sentencing decisions. See W. Bowers & B. Steiner, *Death by Default: An Empirical Demonstration of False and Forced Choices in Capital Sentencing*, 77 Tex.L.Rev. 605 (1999). The study's more salient findings and conclusions include the following:

a. "[J]urors' punishment decisions are markedly influenced by their perceptions of when, as well as if, the defendant would be released from prison. The data demonstrates that the sooner jurors think a defendant will be released from prison, the more likely they are to vote for death and the more likely they are to see the defendant as dangerous."

b. "Jurors underestimate the death penalty alternative in states with parole eligibility in twenty, twenty-five, and thirty or more years, just as they do in states without parole. The data shows that it is these mistaken estimates that dispose jurors toward the death penalty regardless of the true legal provision concerning parole."

c. "The data shows * * * that jurors' release estimates influence the punishments they impose whether or not defendants are alleged or believed to be dangerous. * * * [J]urors often want lengthy imprisonment for reasons of retribution as well as incapacitation. They may be choosing death for retributive reasons when they would have chosen its alternative instead if they had correctly understood its severity."

d. "The false impressions jurors have of the death penalty alternative are not simply random mistakes of the kind pure ignorance or chance would be likely to yield; rather, they are systematic mistakes of the kind bias would produce—they are overwhelming underestimates."

e. "The empirical evidence * * * reveals that the absence (real or imagined) of an LWOP option figured prominently in the decisions of many jurors to impose death. Jurors explained that they voted for the death penalty because the available alternative did not rule out parole; they chose the death penalty not because they thought it was the most appropriate punishment, but because it was preferable to what they believed the alternative would be. The jurors imposed death not as the appropriate, but as the least inappropriate of the available punishment options."

In contrast to the sentencing options of some of the states used in this study, most states with the death penalty now provide life imprisonment without possibility of parole as either the only sentencing alternative or a sentencing option. (See *Simmons v. South Carolina* n.7.) However, this study, like others, suggests that many jurors in such states do not believe that those sentenced to life without the possibility of parole never will be released from prison and cite this concern as a reason for returning a death verdict. See C. Haney, L. Sontag & S. Costanzo, *Deciding to Take a Life: Capital Juries, Sentencing, Instructions, and the Jurisprudence of Death*, Journal of Social Issues, Vol. 50, No. 2 (1994) pp. 170–171.

4. *Extending Simmons.*

In his dissent in *Simmons*, Justice Scalia warned that the holding would permit "the admission of evidence showing that parolable life-sentence murderers are in fact almost never paroled, or are paroled only after age 70; . . . or evidence showing that, though under current law the defendant *will* be parolable in 20 years, the recidivism rate for elderly prisoners released after long incarceration is negligible." 512 U.S. at 184–185, 114 S.Ct. at 2204. Given that empirical studies show that full information on parole likely would have an effect on jurors' decisionmaking (public support for the death penalty drops dramatically when the alternative is life imprisonment with parole ineligibility for 25 years), in a jurisdiction where future dangerousness is an issue at the penalty phase, should the defendant be entitled to present: (1) evidence as to the length of any period of parole ineligibility and the likelihood of parole after that time; and (2) evidence that prisoners become substantially less dangerous over time? See *Brown v. Texas*, 522 U.S. 940, 118 S.Ct. 355 (1997) (opinion of STEVENS, J., joined by SOUTER, GINSBURG and BREYER, JJ., with respect to the denial of cert.).

WEEKS v. ANGELONE

528 U.S. 225, 120 S.Ct. 727, 145 L.Ed.2d 727 (2000).

CHIEF JUSTICE REHNQUIST delivered the opinion of the Court.

This case presents the question whether the Constitution is violated when a trial judge directs a capital jury's attention to a specific paragraph of a constitutionally sufficient instruction in response to a question regarding the proper consideration of mitigating circumstances. We hold that it is not and that habeas relief is barred by 28 U.S.C. § 2254(d).

Petitioner Lonnie Weeks, Jr., was riding from Washington, D.C., to Richmond, Virginia, as a passenger in a car driven by his uncle, Lewis Dukes. Petitioner had stolen the vehicle in a home burglary earlier in the month. The two sped past the marked car of Virginia State Trooper Jose Cavazos, who was monitoring traffic. Trooper Cavazos activated his emergency lights and took chase. After passing other vehicles on the highway shoulder, Dukes stopped on an exit ramp. Trooper Cavazos approached the driver's side of the stolen vehicle on foot. Upon the trooper's request, Dukes alighted and stood near the rear of the car. Trooper Cavazos, still standing near the driver's side, asked petitioner to step out as well. As Weeks stepped out on the passenger's side, he carried a 9–millimeter semiautomatic pistol loaded with hollow-point bullets. Petitioner proceeded to fire six bullets at the trooper, two of which entered his body near the right and left shoulder straps of his protective vest, and four of which entered his forearms and left wrist. Trooper Cavazos died within minutes.

Petitioner was arrested the next morning. During routine questioning about his physical and mental state by classification officers, petitioner confessed, indicating that he was considering suicide because he shot the trooper. Petitioner also voluntarily wrote a letter to a jail officer admitting the killing and expressing remorse.

Petitioner was tried in the Circuit Court for Prince William County, Virginia, in October 1993. After the jury had found him guilty of capital murder, a 2–day penalty phase followed. In this proceeding the prosecution sought to prove two aggravating circumstances: that Weeks "would commit criminal acts of violence that would constitute a continuing serious threat to society" and that his conduct was "outrageously or wantonly vile, horrible or inhuman, in that it involved depravity of mind or aggravated battery." During the penalty phase, the defense presented 10 witnesses, including petitioner, in mitigation.

The jury retired at 10:40 a.m. on the second day to begin deliberations. At around noon, the judge informed counsel that the jury had asked the following question:

> "Does the sentence of life imprisonment in the State of Virginia have the possibility of parole, and if so, under what conditions must be met to receive parole?"

The judge responded to the jury's question as follows:

> "You should impose such punishment as you feel is just under the evidence, and within the instructions of the Court. You are not to concern yourselves with what may happen afterwards."

The prosecution agreed with the judge's response and defense counsel objected. At 12:40 p.m., court reconvened and the judge told the jurors that there would be a one-hour luncheon recess and that they could go to lunch or continue deliberations, as a juror had apparently informed the bailiff that they might be interested in working through lunch. At 12:45 p.m., the jury retired from the courtroom. At 3:15 p.m., the judge informed counsel that he had received the following written question from the jury:

> "If we believe that Lonnie Weeks, Jr. is guilty of at least 1 of the alternatives, then is it our duty as a jury to *issue* the death penalty? Or must we *decide* (even though he is guilty of one of the alternatives) whether or not to issue the death penalty, or one of the life sentences? What is the Rule? Please clarify?" (emphasis in original).

The judge wrote the following response: "See second paragraph of Instruction #2 (Beginning with 'If you find from . . .')." The judge explained to counsel his answer to the jury's question:

> "In instruction number 2 that was given to them, in the second paragraph, it reads, 'If you find from the evidence that the Commonwealth has proved, beyond a reasonable doubt, either of the two alternatives, and as to that alternative, you are unanimous, then you may fix the punishment of the defendant at death, or if you believe from all the evidence that the death penalty is not justified, then you shall fix the punishment of the defendant at imprisonment for life, or imprisonment for life with a fine not to exceed $100,000.' I don't believe I can answer the question any clearer than the instruction, so what I have done is referred them to the second paragraph of instruction number 2, and I told them beginning with, 'if you find from,' et cetera, et cetera, for them to read that paragraph."

The prosecution stated that the judge's solution was appropriate. Defense counsel disagreed, and stated:

> "Your Honor, we would ask that Your Honor instruct the jury that even if they find one or both of the mitigating factors—I'm sorry, the factors that have been proved beyond a reasonable doubt, that they still may impose a life sentence, or a life sentence plus a fine."

Defense counsel asked that his objection be noted.

More than two hours later, the jury returned. The clerk read its verdict:

> "[W]e the jury, on the issue joined, having found the defendant Lonnie Weeks, Jr., guilty of capital murder, and having unanimously found that his conduct in committing the offense is outrageously or wantonly vile, horrible or inhumane, in that it involved depravity of mind and or aggravated battery, and *having considered the evidence in mitigation of the offense*, unanimously fix his punishment at death. . . ." (emphasis added).

The jurors were polled and all responded affirmatively that the foregoing was their verdict in the case.

* * *

Here the trial judge gave no [erroneous] instruction. On the contrary, he gave the instruction that we upheld in *Buchanan v. Angelone*, 522 U.S. 269, 118 S.Ct. 757 (1998), as being sufficient to allow the jury to consider mitigating evidence. And in addition, he gave a specific instruction on mitigating evidence—an instruction that was not given in *Buchanan*—in which he told the jury that "[y]ou must consider a mitigating circumstance if you find there is evidence to support it." Even the dissenters in *Buchanan* said that the ambiguity that they found in the instruction there given would have been cleared up by "some mention of mitigating evidence anywhere in the instructions."

In *Buchanan*, we considered whether the Eighth Amendment required that a capital jury be instructed on particular mitigating factors. Buchanan's jury was given precisely the same Virginia pattern capital instruction that was given to Weeks' jury. We noted that our cases have established that the sentencer may not be precluded from considering, and may not refuse to consider, any constitutionally relevant mitigating evidence, and that the State may structure the jury's consideration of mitigation so long as it does not preclude the jury from giving effect to it. We further noted that the "standard for determining whether jury instructions satisfy these principles was 'whether there is a reasonable likelihood that the jury has applied the challenged instruction in a way that prevents the consideration of constitutionally relevant evidence.'" (quoting *Boyde v. California*, 494 U.S. 370, 110 S.Ct. 1190 (1990)). But, we stated that we have never held that the State must structure in a particular way the manner in which juries consider mitigating evidence. We concluded that the Virginia pattern jury instruction at issue there, and again at issue here, did not violate those principles:

> "The instruction did not foreclose the jury's consideration of any mitigating evidence. By directing the jury to base its decision on 'all the evidence,' the instruction afforded jurors an opportunity to consider mitigating evidence. The instruction informed the jurors that if they found the aggravating factor proved beyond a reasonable doubt then they 'may fix' the penalty at death, but directed that if they believed that all the evidence justified a lesser sentence then they 'shall' impose a life sentence. The jury was thus allowed to impose a life sentence even if it found the aggravating factor proved."

But, as noted above, the jury in this case also received an explicit direction to consider mitigating evidence—an instruction that was not given to the jury in *Buchanan*. Thus, so far as the adequacy of the jury instructions is concerned, their sufficiency here follows *a fortiori* from *Buchanan*.[3]

---

3. Justice STEVENS attempts to distinguish the instruction given here from that given in *Buchanan v. Angelone* on the basis that the first paragraph of "Weeks' instructions contain a longer description" of the aggravating circumstances. The first paragraph is longer here because the prosecution in *Buchanan* sought to prove only one aggravating circumstance. The mere addition of the description of another aggravating circumstance in the first paragraph, however, does not at all affect the second clause of the second paragraph of the instruction—the clause that Justice STEVENS finds "ambiguous."

Given that petitioner's jury was adequately instructed, and given that the trial judge responded to the jury's question by directing its attention to the precise paragraph of the constitutionally adequate instruction that answers its inquiry, the question becomes whether the Constitution requires anything more. We hold that it does not.

A jury is presumed to follow its instructions. *Richardson v. Marsh*, 481 U.S. 200, 107 S.Ct. 1702 (1987). Similarly, a jury is presumed to understand a judge's answer to its question. Weeks' jury did not inform the court that after reading the relevant paragraph of the instruction, it still did not understand its role. To presume otherwise would require reversal every time a jury inquires about a matter of constitutional significance, regardless of the judge's answer.

Here the presumption gains additional support from several empirical factors. First and foremost, each of the jurors affirmed in open court the verdict which included a finding that they had "considered the evidence in mitigation of the offense."[4] It is also significant, we think, that the jurors deliberated for more than two hours after receiving the judge's answer to their question. Over 4 1/2 hours after the jury retired to begin deliberations, the jury asked the question at issue. Again, the question was:

> "If we believe that Lonnie Weeks, Jr. is guilty of at least 1 of the alternatives, then is it our duty as a jury to *issue* the death penalty? Or must we *decide* (even though he is guilty of one of the alternatives) whether or not to issue the death penalty, or one of the life sentences? What is the Rule? Please clarify?" (emphasis in original).

The question indicates that at that time it was asked, the jury had determined that the prosecution had proved one of the two aggravating factors beyond a reasonable doubt. More than two hours passed between the judge directing the jury's attention to the appropriate paragraph of the instruction that answered its question and the jury returning its verdict. We cannot, of course, know for *certain* what transpired during those two hours. But the most likely explanation is that the jury was doing exactly what it was instructed to do: that is, weighing the mitigating circumstances against the aggravating circumstance that it found to be proved beyond a reasonable doubt. If, after the judge's response to its question, the jury thought that it was required to give the death penalty upon

---

More importantly, Justice STEVENS, after stating that his "point is best made by quoting the instruction itself," fails to quote the third paragraph of the instruction. That paragraph expressly applies when the jury finds that the prosecution failed to prove either aggravating circumstance. Specifically, it instructs that if the jury finds no aggravating circumstances, then it must impose a life sentence. The third paragraph stands in contrast to the second paragraph, which expressly applies when the jury finds that the prosecution proved one or both of the aggravating circumstances. The second paragraph offers the jury the option of imposing whichever sentence— death or life imprisonment—it feels is justified in that situation. The existence of the third paragraph makes the function of the second paragraph even clearer.

4. Justice STEVENS' arguments concerning the lack of a jury verdict form stating that the jury finds one or both aggravating circumstances and sentences the petitioner to life imprisonment miss the mark. The life sentence verdict forms do not suggest that a prerequisite for their use is that the jury found no aggravating circumstances. In any event, the claim here is that the trial judge's response to the jury's question was constitutionally insufficient, not that the jury verdict forms were unconstitutionally ambiguous.

finding of an aggravating circumstance, it is unlikely that the jury would have consumed two more hours in deliberation. This particular jury demonstrated that it was not too shy to ask questions, suggesting that it would have asked another if it felt the judge's response unsatisfactory. Finally, defense counsel specifically explained to the jury during closing argument that it could find both aggravating factors proven and still not sentence Weeks to death. Thus, once the jury received the judge's response to its question, it had not only the text of the instruction we approved in *Buchanan*, but also the additional instruction on mitigation, and its own recollection of defense counsel's closing argument for guidance. At best, petitioner has demonstrated only that there exists a slight *possibility* that the jury considered itself precluded from considering mitigating evidence. Such a demonstration is insufficient to prove a constitutional violation under *Boyde*, which requires the showing of a reasonable *likelihood* that the jury felt so restrained.[5]

* * *

The judgment of the Court of Appeals is *Affirmed*.

JUSTICE STEVENS, with whom JUSTICE GINSBURG and JUSTICE BREYER join, and with whom JUSTICE SOUTER joins with respect to all but Part I, dissenting.

Congress has directed us to apply "clearly established Federal law" in the exercise of our habeas corpus jurisdiction. The clearly established rule that should govern the disposition of this case also emphasizes the importance of clarity—clarity in the judge's instructions when there is a reasonable likelihood that the jury may misunderstand the governing rule of law. In this case, as in *Boyde v. California*, 494 U.S. 370, 110 S.Ct. 1190 (1990), we are confronted with a claim that an instruction, though not erroneous, is sufficiently ambiguous to be "subject to an erroneous interpretation." In *Boyde*, we held that "the proper inquiry in such a case is whether there is a reasonable likelihood that the jury has applied the challenged instruction in a way that prevents the consideration of constitutionally relevant evidence."

The record in this case establishes, not just a "reasonable likelihood" of jury confusion, but a virtual certainty that the jury did not realize that

---

5. Justice STEVENS states that the record establishes a "virtual certainty" that the jury did not understand that it could find an aggravating circumstance and still impose a life sentence. In view of the different conclusion reached not only by this Court, but by the Virginia trial judge, seven justices of the Supreme Court of Virginia, a federal habeas district judge, and three judges of the Court of Appeals for the Fourth Circuit, this statement can only be described as extravagant hyperbole.

The dissent also interprets the evidence of the jurors being in tears at the time of the verdict as resulting from having performed what they thought to be their "duty under the law" despite their "strong desire" to impose the life sentence. It is difficult enough to speculate with confidence about the deliberations of jurors in a case such as this, and still more difficult to speculate about their emotions at the time they render a verdict. But if we were to join in this speculation, it is every bit as plausible—if not more so—to think that the reason that jurors were in tears was because they had just been through an exhausting, soul-searching process that led to a conclusion that petitioner, despite the mitigating evidence he presented, still deserved the death sentence.

there were two distinct legal bases for concluding that a death sentence was not "justified." The jurors understood that such a sentence would not be justified unless they found at least one of the two alleged aggravating circumstances. Despite their specific request for enlightenment, however, the judge refused to tell them that *even if* they found one of those circumstances, they did not have a "duty as a jury to issue the death penalty."

* * *

Four different aspects of the record cumulatively provide compelling support for the conclusion that this jury did not understand that the law authorized it "not to issue the death penalty" even though it found petitioner "guilty of at least 1" aggravating circumstance. Each of these points merits separate comment: (1) the text of the instructions; (2) the judge's responses to the jury's inquiries; (3) the verdict forms given to the jury; and (4) the court reporter's transcription of the polling of the jury.

I

Because the prosecutor in this case relied on two separate aggravating circumstances, the critical instruction given in this case differed from that given and upheld by this Court in *Buchanan v. Angelone*, 522 U.S. 269, 118 S.Ct. 757 (1998). The Weeks instructions contain a longer description of the ways in which the jury would be justified in imposing the death penalty; this made it especially unlikely that the jury would understand that it could lawfully impose a life sentence by either (1) refusing to find an aggravator, or (2) concluding that even if it found an aggravator, the mitigating evidence warranted a life sentence. The point is best made by quoting the instruction itself:

> " 'Before the penalty can be fixed at death, the Commonwealth must prove beyond a reasonable doubt, at least one of the following two alternatives: one, that, after consideration of his history and background, there is a probability that he would commit criminal acts of violence that would constitute a continuing serious threat to society, or two, that his conduct in committing the offense was outrageously or wantonly vile, horrible, or inhumane, in that it involved depravity of mind and aggravated battery to the victim, beyond the minimum necessary to accomplish the act of murder.

> " 'If you find from the evidence that the Commonwealth has proved beyond a reasonable doubt, either of the two alternatives, and as to that alternative you are unanimous, then you may fix the punishment of the defendant at death; or, if you believe from all the evidence that the death penalty is not justified, then you shall fix the punishment of the defendant at life imprisonment, or imprisonment for life and a fine of a specific amount, but not more than $100,000.' "

The first paragraph and the first half of the second are perfectly clear. They unambiguously tell the jury: "In order to justify the death penalty, you must find an aggravating circumstance." The second clause in the second paragraph is, however, ambiguous. It could mean either:

　　(1) "even if you find one of the two aggravating alternatives, if you believe from all the evidence that the death penalty is not justified because the mitigating evidence outweighs the aggravating evidence, then you shall fix the punishment [at life];" or

　　(2) "if you believe from all the evidence that the death penalty is not justified because neither of the aggravating circumstances has been proven beyond a reasonable doubt, then you shall fix the punishment [at life]."

It is not necessary to reiterate Justice BREYER's reasons for believing that the latter message is the one a non-lawyer would be most likely to receive. See *Buchanan* (dissenting opinion). Nor is it necessary to disagree with the Court's view in *Buchanan* that trained lawyers and logicians could create a "simple decisional tree" that would enable them to decipher the intended meaning of the instruction, to identify a serious risk that this jury failed to do so.

That risk was magnified by the fact that the instructions did not explain that there were two reasons why mitigating evidence was relevant to its penalty determination. The instructions did make it clear that mitigating evidence concerning the history and background of the defendant should be considered when deciding *whether* either aggravating circumstance had been proved. The instructions did not, however, explain that mitigating evidence could serve another purpose—to provide a lawful justification for a life sentence *even if* the jury found at least one aggravating circumstance. Indeed, given the fact that the first task assigned to the jury was to decide whether "*after consideration of his history and background*, there is a probability that he would commit criminal acts of violence that would constitute a continuing serious threat to society," (emphasis added), it would have been reasonable for the jury to infer that his history and background were only relevant to the threshold question whether an aggravator had been proved. It is of critical importance in understanding the jury's confusion that the instructions failed to inform the jury that mitigating evidence serves this dual purpose.

II

　　The jurors had a written copy of the judge's instructions with them in the jury room during their deliberations. The fact that the jurors submitted the following written inquiry to the trial judge after they had been deliberating for several hours demonstrates both that they were uncertain about the meaning of the ambiguous clause that I have identified, and that their uncertainty had not been dissipated by their recollection of anything said by counsel.

　　"If we believe that Lonnie Weeks, Jr. is guilty of at least 1 of the alternatives, then is it our duty as a jury to *issue* the death penalty? Or must we *decide* (even though he is guilty of one of the alternatives) whether or not to issue the death penalty, or one of the life sentences? What is the Rule? Please clarify.''

The only portion of the written instructions that could possibly have prompted this inquiry is the second half of the second paragraph of the instruction quoted above. The fact that the jurors asked this question about that instruction demonstrates beyond peradventure that the instruction had confused them. There would have been no reason to ask the question if they had understood the instruction to authorize a life sentence even though they found that an aggravator had been proved.

Although it would have been easy to do so, the judge did not give the jurors a straightforward categorical answer to their simple question; he merely told them to re-examine the portion of the instructions that they, in effect, had already said they did not understand. The text of their question indicates that they believed that they had a duty ''to issue the death penalty'' if they believed that ''Weeks is guilty of at least 1 of the alternatives.'' Without a simple, clear-cut statement from the judge that that belief was incorrect, there was surely a reasonable likelihood that they would act on that belief.[3]

Instead of accepting a commonsense interpretation of the colloquy between the jury and the judge, the Court first relies on a presumption that the jury understood the instruction (a presumption surely rebutted by the question itself) and then presumes that the jury must have understood the judge's answer because it did not repeat its question after re-reading the relevant paragraph, and continued to deliberate for another two hours. But if the jurors found it necessary to ask the judge what that paragraph meant in the first place, why should we presume that they would find it any less ambiguous just because the judge told them to read it again? It seems to me far more likely that the reason they did not ask the same question a second time is that the jury believed that it would be disrespectful to repeat a simple, unambiguous question that the judge had already refused to answer directly. The fact that it had previously asked the judge a different question—also related to the effect of a sentencing decision,—that he had also refused to answer would surely have tended to discourage a repetition of the question about the meaning of his instructions.

By the Court's logic, a rather exceptionally assertive jury would have to question the judge at least twice and maybe more on precisely the same topic before one could find it no more than ''reasonably likely'' that the

---

3. The Court suggests this likelihood is impossible in part because, even if the jury were confused by the judge's response, it had not only the text of the instruction but also the benefit of defense counsel's oral argument, in which counsel averred that the jury could award a life sentence even if it found an aggravating factor. But this statement by counsel, coming as it did, of course, before the jury began deliberations, apparently did not prevent the jury from asking the question in the first place. Moreover, as this Court wisely noted in *Boyde*, ''arguments of counsel generally carry less weight with a jury than do instructions from the court. The former are usually billed in advance to the jury as matters of argument, not evidence, and are likely viewed as the statements of advocates; the latter, we have often recognized, are viewed as definitive and binding statements of the law.''

jury was confused. But given the Court's apt recognition that we cannot, of course, actually know what occupied the jury during its final deliberations, and in light of the explanation I have just offered, it is at the very least equally likely that the two hours of deliberation following the judge's answer were devoted to continuing debate about the same instruction, as they were to weighing aggravating and mitigating evidence (having been magically satisfied by the repetition of the instruction that had not theretofore answered its question).

When it comes to the imposition of the death penalty, we have held repeatedly that justice and "the fundamental respect for humanity underlying the Eighth Amendment" require jurors to give full effect to their assessment of the defendant's character, circumstances, and individual worth. *Eddings v. Oklahoma*, 455 U.S. 104, 102 S.Ct. 869 (1982). In this context, even if one finds the explanations of the jury's conduct here in equipoise, a 50–50 chance that the jury has not carried out this mandate seems to me overwhelming grounds for reversal.

Other than the Court's reliance on inapplicable presumptions and speculation, there is no reason to believe that the jury understood the judge's answer to its question. As we squarely held in *Boyde*, the "defendant need not establish that the jury was more likely than not to have been impermissibly inhibited by the instruction," to satisfy the clearly established "reasonable likelihood" standard. The Court's application of that standard in this case effectively drains it of meaning.

III

The judge provided the jury with five verdict forms, three of which provided for the death penalty and two for a life sentence. Three death forms were appropriate because the death penalty might be justified by a finding that the first, the second, or both aggravating circumstances had been proved. One would expect the two life forms to cover the two alternatives, first that no aggravator had been proved, and second that despite proof of at least one aggravator, the mitigating circumstances warranted a life sentence. But that is not why there were two forms; neither referred to the possibility of a life sentence if an aggravator had been proved. Rather, the two life alternatives merely presented the jury with a choice between life plus a fine and a life sentence without a fine.

The first form read as follows:

> "We, the jury, on the issue joined, having found the defendant, LONNIE WEEKS, JR., GUILTY of CAPITAL MURDER and having unanimously found after consideration of his history and background that there is a probability that he would commit criminal acts of violence that would constitute a continuing serious threat to society, and having considered the evidence in mitigation of the offense, unanimously fix his punishment at death."

The jury ultimately refused to select this first form, which would have indicated a finding that there was a probability that petitioner would commit additional crimes that would constitute a serious threat to society. In doing so, it unquestionably gave weight to the unusually persuasive mitigating evidence offered by the defense—evidence that included not only petitioner's personal history but his own testimony describing the relevant events and his extreme remorse. As I explained above, the fact that the jury recognized the relevance of the mitigating "history and background" evidence to the question whether the aggravator had been proved, sheds no light on the question whether it understood that such evidence would also be relevant on the separate question whether a life sentence would be appropriate even if Weeks was "guilty of at least 1 of the alternatives."

The jury's refusal to find that petitioner would constitute a continuing threat to society also explains why it did not use the second form, which covered the option of a death penalty supported by both aggravators. The choice then, was between the third alternative, which included a finding that the second aggravator had been proved, and the fourth or fifth alternatives, neither of which included any such finding. Despite the fact that trial counsel had expressly objected to the verdict forms because they "do not expressly provide for a sentence of life imprisonment, upon finding beyond a reasonable doubt, on one or both of the aggravating factors," the judge failed to use forms that would have answered the question that the jury asked during its deliberations.

The ambiguity of the forms also helps further explain why the Court is wrong in its speculation as to the jury's final hours of deliberation following the judge's response to its question. The Court postulates that before the jury asked whether it had a duty to issue the death penalty "[i]f we believe that Lonnie Weeks, Jr. is guilty of at least 1 of the alternatives," the jury had already so decided. Thus, the remaining hours of deliberation must have been spent weighing the mitigating circumstances against the aggravating circumstance. Of course, the text of the question, which used the word "if" rather than the word "since," does not itself support that speculation. More important, however—inasmuch as we cannot know for certain what transpired during those deliberations—is the fact that after it eliminated the first two verdict options, the remaining forms identified a choice between a death sentence based on a guilty finding on "1 of the alternatives" and a life sentence without any such finding. In my judgment, it is thus far more likely that the conscientious jurors were struggling with the question whether the mitigating evidence not only precluded a finding that petitioner was a continuing threat to society, but also precluded a finding "that his conduct in committing the offense is outrageously or wantonly vile, horrible or inhuman in that it involved depravity of mind and/or aggravated battery." And that question was answered neither by the instruction itself, nor by the judge's reference to the instruction again, nor, we now see, by the text of the jury forms with which the jury was finally faced.

IV

The Court repeatedly emphasizes the facts that the jury was told to consider the mitigating evidence and that the verdict forms expressly recite that the jury had given consideration to such evidence. As its refusal to find the first aggravator indicates, the jury surely did consider that evidence and presumably credited the testimony of petitioner and the other defense witnesses. But, as I have explained, there is a vast difference between considering that evidence as relevant to the question whether either aggravator had been established, and assuming that the jurors were sufficiently sophisticated to understand that it would be lawful for them to rely on that evidence as a basis for a life sentence even if they found the defendant "guilty of at least 1 of the alternatives." For that reason, the Court's reliance on the fact that the jurors affirmed their verdict when polled in open court is misplaced.

The most significant aspect of the polling of the jury is a notation by the court reporter that is unique. (At least I do not recall seeing a comparable notation in any of the transcripts of capital sentencing proceedings that I have reviewed during the past 24–plus years.) The transcript states that, as they were polled, "a majority of the jury members [were] in tears." Given the unusually persuasive character of the mitigating evidence including petitioner's own testimony,[9] it is at least "reasonable" to infer that the conscientious jury members performed what they regarded as their duty under the law, notwithstanding a strong desire to spare the life of Lonnie Weeks. Tragically, there is a "reasonable likelihood" that they acted on the basis of a misunderstanding of that duty.

I respectfully dissent.

NOTES

1. *The question of juror confusion.*

In *Weeks*, the majority and the dissent offer their very different opinions about whether the jurors were confused by their instructions. Could this question have been resolved by holding an evidentiary hearing and asking the jurors themselves? (In fact, Weeks' attorneys had affidavits from two jurors indicating that they had wanted to sentence Weeks to life imprisonment but had misunderstood the instructions.) Under federal law, juror testimony regarding the mental processes of jurors and their conduct during deliberations is inadmissible except insofar as the testimony relates to any extraneous prejudicial information brought to the jury's attention or any outside influence improperly brought to bear upon any juror. See Fed.R.Evid. 606(b); *McDowell v. Calderon*, 107 F.3d 1351, 1367–68 (9th Cir.1997). Should there be

---

9. The evidence showed, among other things, that before this incident Weeks had been a well-behaved student and a star high school athlete, who lived in a poor community, and who was raised by a well-meaning grandmother because of his mother's drug addiction; that Weeks fell in with a bad crowd, missing his chance for college when his girlfriend became pregnant and when he decided to stay and help her raise the child; and, as the jury learned in Weeks' own words, that he was extremely remorseful.

an exception to this rule for capital sentencing? In her dissent in *Jones v. United States*, 527 U.S. 373, 119 S.Ct. 2090 (1999), Justice Ginsburg said:

> While precedent supports the Fifth Circuit's affirmation that statements attesting to the juror's understanding of the instructions are inadmissible, the statements Jones submitted do assert that apprehension of a lesser sentence the judge might impose in fact caused jurors to vote for a death sentence. On a matter so grave, I would not discount those statements altogether.

527 U.S. at 416 n.19, 119 S.Ct. at 2115 n.19.

After the *Weeks* decision, researchers attempted, by means of a mock jury study in Virginia, to test the majority's conclusion that the jurors probably did understand the instructions. See S. Garvey, S. Johnson & P. Marcus, *Correcting Deadly Confusion: Responding to Jury Inquiries in Capital Cases*, 85 Cornell L. Rev. 627 (2000). Using "jurors" obtained through a newspaper ad and "death qualified by interview," the researchers read summaries of the case and arguments to the juries and gave them the actual instructions and verdict forms. The jurors were divided into three groups: the "no-question" group was given no more information; the "actual-reply" group was read the *Weeks* jury's question and the judge's answer; and the "requested-reply" group was read the *Weeks* jury's question and given a version of the answer proposed by Weeks' counsel. The "jurors" were asked to select a verdict and then had to answer questions to test their understanding of the instructions. The results of the study may be summed up as follows: (1) among the no-question group, nearly half misunderstood the pattern instruction and thought they were required to impose a death sentence if they found one of the aggravating circumstances; (2) simply directing the jurors to reread the pattern instruction did nothing to improve their comprehension—a slightly *greater* percentage of the actual-reply group misunderstood and thought they were required to impose the death penalty if they found an aggravating circumstance; (3) in contrast, the requested reply significantly increased comprehension—less than 30% of the requested-reply group misunderstood the instruction; (4) jurors who understood the rule were more likely to vote for life compared to jurors who misunderstood the instruction. If this study had been available prior to the decision in *Weeks*, should it have changed the result?

2. *Problem 10–7.*

Defendant was convicted of capital murder, and, at the penalty phase of the trial, he introduced substantial mitigating evidence to show, *inter alia*, that he would live a constructive life if incarcerated, including his own testimony and testimony from two prison chaplains and his Christian sponsors to the effect that he had embraced Christianity. In closing argument, the prosecution and defense argued the significance of the defendant's evidence, but the prosecutor argued that, in making its penalty decision, the jury was limited to considering the list of eleven sentencing factors set forth in State's statute and that the defendant's religion should not be an influencing factor. The jury was instructed to decide the penalty by weighing the aggravating and mitigating circumstances as set forth in State's statute. Of the eleven factors, only the last—the existence of "[a]ny other circumstance which extenuates the gravity of the crime even though it is not a legal excuse for the crime"—was arguably relevant to defendant's mitigation evidence. During deliberations, several jurors asked questions about how to deal with the aggravating and mitigating circumstances, and the judge instructed them to consider the list of factors read to them and then "balance the sheet." The jury sentenced the defendant to death. What arguments should be made as to whether there was a reasonable likelihood that the jury applied the challenged instruction in a way that prevented them from considering relevant mitigation evidence? See *Ayers v. Belmontes*, 549 U.S. 7, 127 S.Ct. 469 (2006).

WHAT DO JURORS UNDERSTAND?

As noted in *Spaziano v. Florida*, 468 U.S. 447, 104 S.Ct. 3154 (1984) [Chapter 9], the vast majority of death penalty states gives the life-or-death decision at the sentencing hearing to the jury. The jury historically has served as the voice of the community in capital sentencing. See *Witherspoon v. Illinois*, 391 U.S. 510, 88 S.Ct. 1770 (1968) [Chapter 6]. The point of jury instructions is to explain the applicable law to these non-lawyers so they understand the task before them. How well do jurors understand the instructions that are to guide them in deciding whether to sentence a defendant to death or life imprisonment? Researchers have attempted to answer that question.

The meaning of aggravation and mitigation. In *Tuilaepa v. California*, 512 U.S. 967, 114 S.Ct. 2630 (1994), the Supreme Court found that the California sentencing factors, which encompass both aggravating and mitigating factors, were phrased in "understandable terms." However, empirical research suggests that the California capital sentencing instructions do not adequately explain the basic concepts of aggravation and mitigation and that there is confusion over whether a particular sentencing factor is to be considered aggravating or mitigating. In 1994, researchers conducted a study using 491 upper-division undergraduate students to assess whether they "could formulate any meaningful, reasonably accurate definition of these terms that could serve to guide their decision-making process in a consistent, reliable way."[1] They concluded:

> We found that even among these college-educated students there was a widespread inability to comprehend the central terms of capital penalty phase decision making, and that there was far more confusion attached to the concept of mitigation than aggravation. We also found that a very high percentage of our subjects focused their definitions of these terms entirely upon the nature and circumstances of the crime, rather than broadening the definition to include constitutionally required consideration of the background and character of the defendant. In addition, we found that very few subjects were able to provide legally correct definitions of these terms, and that fewer still

---

1. C. Haney & M. Lynch, *Comprehending Life and Death Matters: A Preliminary Study of California's Capital Penalty Instructions*, 18 Law and Hum. Behav. 411, 419 (1994).

were able to provide legally correct definitions of both terms that would guide their decision-making process in the manner supposedly intended by the law....[2]

The study also found juror misunderstanding with regard to the specific sentencing factors. In particular, approximately a quarter of the subjects labeled as aggravating statutory factors that were intended to be mitigating, such as "the offense was committed while the defendant was under the influence of extreme mental or emotional disturbance" and "the defendant acted under extreme duress or under the substantial domination of a person."[3] Over a third of the study subjects believed that California's catch-all mitigating factor—"any other circumstance which extenuates the gravity of the crime even though it is not a legal excuse for the crime," and "any other aspect of the defendant's character or record that the defendant offers as a basis for a sentence less than death"—was an aggravating factor.[4] As the researchers noted, the study may underestimate capital jurors' understanding of the concepts of aggravation and mitigation, since the study did not assess whether juror comprehension would be improved when the instruction was read in the context of the evidence and closing arguments of counsel presented at the penalty trial and through discussion during penalty phase deliberations.[5]

The same researchers conducted a follow-up study in 1997 using 215 upper-division college students and the 1989 revised California sentencing instruction that defined aggravation and mitigation.[6] The study again sought to determine the subjects' understanding of the terms "aggravating" and "mitigating" as well as the notion of "extenuating." The results showed continued misunderstanding despite revision of the instruction:

> Consistent with the data obtained from our original study, most subjects offered substantially incorrect definitions of the central terms of the penalty phase instructions. Further, the inaccuracies were greatest for the two terms related to the lessening of sentencing severity—"mitigating" and "extenuating." Specifically, while 71% of the subjects were able to provide at least a partially correct definition

2. *Id.* at 420. Haney and Lynch found that in defining "aggravation," only 15% of the subjects gave correct answers; 64% of the subjects gave partially correct answers, and 18% gave totally incorrect answers. In defining "mitigation," only 12% of the subjects gave correct answers; 47% of the subjects gave partially correct answers, and 30% gave totally incorrect answers. Only 8% of the subjects were able to correctly define both terms. In addition, 70% of the subjects defined aggravation solely in terms of crime-related factors, and 53% of the subjects defined mitigation in a similar manner.

3. *Id.* at 422.

4. *Id.* at 424 n.12.

5. *Id.* at 425 n.14, 429–430.

6. C. Haney & M. Lynch, *Clarifying Life and Death Matters: An Analysis of Instructional Comprehension and Penalty Phase Closing Arguments*, 21 Law and Hum. Behav. 575, 577–578 (1997). The revised instruction read in part: "An aggravating factor is any fact, condition or event attending the commission of a crime which increases its guilt or enormity, or adds to it injurious consequences which is above and beyond the elements of the crime itself. A mitigating circumstance is any fact, condition or event which as such, does not constitute a justification or excuse for the crime in question, but may be considered as an extenuating circumstance in determining the appropriateness of the death penalty." *Id.* at 594 (CALJIC 8.88 (1989 revision)).

for the term "aggravating," only 52% could do so for "mitigating." Only 41% of our subjects could provide at least a partially correct definition for both aggravation and mitigation. The least understood term, by far, was "extenuating," with just 18% of all subjects providing even a partially correct definition of this word.... A sizeable number of subjects also tended to focus exclusively on the circumstances of the crime in attempting to define aggravating and mitigating. Of those who offered an even partially correct definition of each term, 70% of the aggravating and 60% of the mitigating responses were exclusively crime-focused.[7]

Studies of other states' capital sentencing instructions also indicate juror confusion about the meaning of aggravation and mitigation. Studies of Illinois jurors in 1990 and 1992 explored whether they understood that they could properly consider any possible mitigating factor even if not listed in the Illinois jury instructions. The survey's subjects were death-qualified jurors who had been called to jury service in Cook County, Illinois. In the 1990 survey, 46.9% to 67.7% of the potential jurors gave incorrect answers on the several questions designed to test the principle of non-statutory mitigation under the Illinois pattern instruction. In the 1992 survey, 38.9% to 58.9% of the potential jurors gave incorrect answers under the revised Illinois instruction.[8]

A study conducted under the auspices of the Capital Jury Project in North Carolina found that many jurors who served in capital trials between 1990 and 1994 did not understand the scope of permissible aggravating and mitigating factors.[9] Roughly one-half (48%) of the jurors incorrectly believed that they could consider as an aggravating factor any fact that made the crime worse in their minds, while roughly one-third (36%) of the jurors correctly knew that aggravating factors were limited to those specified by the judge, and the remaining 16% did not know. Jurors had a better, but not total, understanding of mitigation. Well over one-half (59%) of the jurors correctly understood that they could consider any

---

7. *Id.* at 579. A separate study by the same researchers analyzed the arguments of counsel in 20 California capital cases from 16 different counties over a period of 12 years. *Id.* at 583–584. The results showed that the closing arguments by the prosecutor and defense attorney did little to enhance the jurors' understanding of the core concepts underlying the penalty determination. *Id.* at 584.

8. See *Free v. Peters*, 806 F.Supp. 705, 722–726, 766–767 (N.D.Ill. 1992) *rev'd in part* 12 F.3d 700 (7th Cir. 1993) (reporting on the studies by Hans Zeisel); P. Tiersma, *Dictionaries and Death: Do Capital Jurors Understand Mitigation?*, 1995 Utah L. Rev. 1 (hereinafter, "Tiersma") 26–27. The Seventh Circuit rejected the validity of the studies because the test setting, based on a written record of an imaginary case, was not comparable to a real sentencing hearing, in which the jury has spent days or weeks becoming familiar with the case and has had the benefit of oral presentations by witnesses, lawyers, and the judge and group deliberations; and the study lacked a control group. *Free v. Peters*, 12 F.3d at 705–706.

9. J. Luginbuhl & J. Howe, *Discretion in Capital Sentencing Instructions: Guided or Misguided?*, 70 Ind. L.J. 1161 (1995) (hereinafter, "Luginbuhl & Howe"). The Capital Jury Project, established in 1990 with a grant from the Law and Social Sciences Program of the National Science Foundation, is a multidisciplinary study of how capital jurors make their sentencing decisions. Underway in at least 14 states, the research is based on three-to-four hours interviews with 80 to 120 capital jurors in each of the participating states who are selected from both juries that reached life verdicts and juries that returned death sentences. See, W. Bowers, *The Capital Jury Project: Rationale, Design, and Preview of Early Findings*, 70 Ind. L.J. 1043 (1995).

evidence in mitigation, while almost one-fourth (24%) erroneously thought mitigating factors were limited to those mentioned by the judge, and the remaining 17% did not know.[10]

Anecdotal evidence confirms the difficulty encountered by many capital jurors in understanding terms which, according to some courts, are ordinary words with common meaning that do not have to be defined for the jury. In cases from several states jurors have asked the trial court for a definition of "aggravating" or "mitigating."[11] In post-trial interviews, capital jurors have admitted their confusion over these terms:

> The first thing we asked for after the instructions was, could the judge define mitigating and aggravating circumstances.... I said, "I don't know that I exactly understand what it means." And then everybody else said, "No, neither do I," or "I can't give you a definition." So we decided we should ask the judge. Well, the judge wrote back and said, "You have to glean it from the instructions."

> Another juror said: "The mitigating and aggravating [is] where you become—it becomes very, very confusing." A third juror is reported to have remarked during deliberations, "I still don't understand the difference between aggravating and mitigating," and broke down in tears. * * * [Yet another] capital juror is quoted as stating: "The mitigating is against him, right? This is where I'm confused...."[12]

The procedural requirements and statutory formula for the penalty determination. If jurors are to apply correctly a state's capital sentencing law, they must understand not only the concepts of aggravation and mitigation, but the procedural requirements for proving aggravating and mitigating factors as well as the statute's formula for arriving at the appropriate sentence. Empirical studies indicate that a substantial number of jurors also misunderstand these aspects of the sentencing process. The Capital Jury Project study in North Carolina illustrates the problem. The jurors were asked questions about their understanding of the burden of proof for aggravating and mitigating factors and the unanimity requirements for those factors. The study found that a large majority of the jurors correctly understood these principles with regard to aggravating factors: slightly more than two-thirds (68%) of the jurors correctly understood that an aggravating factor had to be proven beyond a reasonable doubt and three-fourths (76%) of the jurors correctly understood that jury unanimity was required to find an aggravating factor.[13] However, their understanding of the procedural rules for mitigating factors was poor. Just under one-half (47%) of the jurors correctly understood that mitigating factors did not require proof beyond a reasonable doubt or a unanimous finding, but almost as many jurors incorrectly believed that proof beyond

---

10. Luginbuhl & Howe at 1165–1166.

11. Tiersma at 9–18.

12. *Id.* at 18–19 (footnotes omitted).

13. Luginbuhl & Howe at 1165–1166.

a reasonable doubt was the standard for mitigating factors (41%) and that unanimity was required (42%).[14]

The North Carolina study also assessed jurors' understanding of when, under the sentencing instruction, a defendant was to be sentenced to life or death. Under North Carolina law, the jury must recommend the death penalty if it finds that the aggravating circumstance or circumstances are sufficiently substantial to call for the imposition of the death penalty and the mitigating circumstance or circumstances are insufficient to outweigh the aggravating circumstance or circumstances.[15] Under this scheme, a jury may find that the mitigating circumstances fail to outweigh the aggravating circumstances, and still may find that the aggravating circumstances are not sufficiently substantial to impose the death penalty.[16] However, if the jury finds that the mitigating circumstances are sufficient to outweigh the aggravating circumstances, then the jury must impose a sentence of life imprisonment.[17] The study found that under the North Carolina capital sentencing instruction "roughly one-fourth of the jurors felt that death was mandatory when it was not and approximately one-half of the jurors failed to appreciate those situations which mandated life."[18] As the researchers acknowledged, an incorrect response rate of one-fourth may not seem extreme.[19] However, responses to other questions further revealed the jurors' inadequate understanding about other aspects of the capital sentencing law such as the effect of certain statutory aggravating factors, non-enumerated aggravating factors, the burden of proof and the unanimity requirement.[20]

Studies in other states have disclosed similar problems with juror understanding. Data gathered as part of the Capital Jury Project demonstrates that South Carolina capital jurors are confused about the different burdens of proof applicable to aggravating factors and mitigating factors and the requirement of unanimity.[21] Almost half the jurors interviewed incorrectly believed that a mitigating factor must be proved beyond a reasonable doubt, and two-thirds of the jurors in the study erroneously thought that there must be jury unanimity before a mitigating factor could be considered.[22]

Potential capital jurors in Illinois also appeared to misunderstand the issue of unanimity and when the statute calls for a life sentence or death

---

14. *Id.* at 1166.

15. N.C.G.S. § 15A–2000(b), (c); *State v. Holden*, 362 S.E.2d 513, 535 (N.C. 1987), *cert. denied*, 486 U.S. 1061, 108 S.Ct. 2835 (1988).

16. See, *McDougall v. Dixon*, 921 F.2d 518, 530–531 (4th Cir. 1990); *People v. Cherry*, 257 S.E.2d 551, 568 (N.C. 1979).

17. N.C.G.S. § 15A–2000(b), (c).

18. Luginbuhl & Howe at 1173.

19. *Ibid.*

20. *Id.* at 1174, 1176–1177.

21. T. Eisenberg and M. Wells, *Deadly Confusion: Juror Instructions in Capital Cases*, 79 Cornell Law Rev. 1 (1993).

22. *Id.* at 11.

sentence. In the 1990 survey, 25% and 36.5% of the subjects gave incorrect answers to two questions testing whether there is a unanimity require-ment for proof of a mitigating factor. In the 1992 survey, jury comprehen-sion improved but still showed misunderstanding with 14.7% and 30.5% giving incorrect answers.[23] The studies also evaluated how well potential jurors understood which party bears the burden of persuasion on the appropriate sentence and the nature of that burden. The potential jurors were asked seven questions about when the jury must vote for or against a death sentence. In the 1990 study, 44.8%–75.0% of the study participants gave incorrect answers, and in the 1992 study, the range of wrong answers decreased to 40.0%–58.9% of the subjects.[24]

Factors Contributing to Jurors' Misunderstanding of Capital Sentenc-ing Instructions. These studies raise an inevitable question: why is juror comprehension of capital sentencing instructions so poor? Researchers have suggested several reasons in relation to the North Carolina instruc-tions that probably apply to other capital sentencing instructions as well. First, the instructions are long and boring. After viewing a videotaped reading of the North Carolina capital sentencing instructions, many jury-eligible citizens admitted difficulty following the instructions because of their length and complexity.[25] Second, the instructions are not clearly and simply written but often use complex syntax, unfamiliar words, and multiple negatives.[26] When jurors ask the trial judge for clarification, they may be told, as was the jury in *Weeks*, simply to reread the instructions they do not understand. Third, the instructions do not highlight concepts that are new or unfamiliar, so jurors are forced to rely on their own prior knowledge or assumptions which may not be accurate.[27]

Capital sentencing instructions should be drafted so that legal terms and unfamiliar concepts are explained in clear, simple and accessible language. The task is not an easy one. The Illinois and California studies suggest that even carefully drafted instructions may not significantly improve juror comprehension of capital sentencing concepts. However, the two studies were limited, and other studies relating to non-capital jury instructions indicate that improved instructions can lead to greater juror understanding of the rules governing their deliberations.[28] The jury is still out on the question.

---

23. *Free v. Peters*, 806 F.Supp. at 720, 766–767; Tiersma at 25.

24. *Free v. Peters*, 806 F.Supp. at 728, 771–774, 781–784; Tiersma at 29.

25. Luginbuhl & Howe at 1169; James Luginbuhl, *Comprehension of Judges' Instruction in the Penalty Phase of a Capital Trial: Focus on Mitigating Circumstances*, 16 Law & Human. Behav. 203, 210 (1992).

26. Luginbuhl & Howe at 1169.

27. *Id.* at 1169–1170.

28. Tiersma at 44 (citing studies).

IN THE FACE OF DEATH

By Alex Kotlowitz.[a]

At 2:40 a.m. on Aug. 26, 1998, along a main drag on the west side of Indianapolis, 18–year–old Jeremy Gross approached a convenience store with a friend. They intended to rob it. At 5–foot–8 and of slender build, Gross was not particularly physically imposing, and he had a distant look about him. He wore his blond hair in a bowl cut and often seemed nervous and fidgety. He knew the store well, since he worked there part time, and he also knew the young man, Christopher Beers, who was the lone clerk that morning. Beers, who was 24, had been raised by his father and had completed one year at Purdue University before running out of money for tuition. He was overweight and, according to his uncle, mild-mannered. He was working to earn money to return to school. An avid reader, he welcomed the graveyard shift; it gave him time with his books.

Gross stood outside the glass doors, behind his accomplice, Joshua Spears. He held a small, black semiautomatic pistol at his side, out of sight. Gross was jumpy, turning his head from side to side to make sure no one was in the parking lot. Beers buzzed them in. Gross took long, hurried strides into the store, raised his right arm and started shooting. It happened so quickly that Beers didn't have a chance to say anything. The first shot hit him in the abdomen. Gross continued to fire. Three shots missed, but a fourth hit Beers in the chest. "Oh, God, please, no," he pleaded. As Beers stumbled into the back office, Gross followed and, to get a better angle, shifted the pistol from his right hand to his left. From close range, Gross shot Beers in the face. With blood now gushing from his eyes, Beers reached out for Gross, as if he were asking for support. Gross pushed him away, and he crumpled to the floor. "Why, Jeremy, why?" Beers asked. Gross told him to shut up.

Gross's partner, Spears, had headed for another room to get the surveillance tape, but he couldn't get the eject to function, so he grabbed the VCR. Meanwhile, Gross emptied the cash register and office safe of $650, then ripped the two telephone cords from the wall. This all happened in less than a minute. The two fled by foot, through a neighborhood of mobile homes to their trailer park not more than half a mile away. Along the way, Gross and Spears threw the gun and the VCR over a wire fence into a retaining pond.

After they left, Beers lifted himself off the floor and shuffled out the door to a pay phone, where he again collapsed. He died under a dangling phone, rivulets of blood running from his head.

A passer-by who was a regular customer at the Convenient Food Mart had seen Gross and Spears enter the store. He gave the police a description, and another employee said that the description sounded like that of Gross. Less than seven hours later, Gross confessed to detectives, steering them to the VCR and gun. They found the VCR lying in shallow water, protruding from the mud; divers recovered the gun.

---

a. © 2003 by Alex Kotlowitz. This article originally appeared in the New York Times Sunday Magazine (July 6, 2003). Reprinted by permission of the author.

F.B.I. experts salvaged the videotape of the murder, and a few weeks later, after viewing the terror of that night, Scott Newman, then the Marion County prosecutor, told a reporter for The Indianapolis Star, "There isn't a jury in this world ... that would not recommend the ultimate penalty in this case, the death penalty."

On the 24–page jury questionnaire, Elizabeth Stone, who is 60 and works as a nurse, wrote that she "strongly favored" the death penalty. "I looked at it as an eye for an eye," she told me when I recently spoke with her. "Someone who takes someone's life deserves death." Another juror, 54–year–old Cheryl Berkowitz (then Cheryl Rader), who works at a drug-treatment center, said during the voir dire that she thought the death penalty was not used often enough. These two, along with nine other women and a man, were chosen to serve on the jury that would decide the case of the State of Indiana v. Jeremy Gross.

Like most juries, this one was composed of a diverse group. There was a manager of a McDonald's, a cook at a child-care center and a machine operator at a foundry. On the questionnaires where it asked, "Whom do you most admire?" one wrote "Ronald Reagan," another "John F. Kennedy," another "Princess Diana" and still another "Montel Williams." But they all shared one thing in common. Each of them told the court that yes, they could vote to end someone's life. This is a requirement to sit on a capital murder case, and it is, in some measure, what attracted me to Jeremy Gross's case. That, and the fact that in what most likely is the only opportunity they would ever get, these 12 jurors, all of whom swore their allegiance to the death penalty, in the end, balked.

The trial took place in the spring of 2000, two years after the shooting * * *

* * *

The murder received a large amount of press locally, including television interviews with Gross shortly after his arrest. Daily coverage of the proceedings was anticipated. A decision was made to sequester the jurors, who were put up at the Indianapolis Athletic Club, an 80–year–old stone structure near the courthouse. They were told to pack enough clothes and books for two weeks. One juror brought an armful of crossword-puzzle books. Another brought a pile of family photographs, planning to make a scrapbook. Still another brought along her Bible as well as a book titled "Tough Questions, Biblical Answers," given to her by her minister shortly before the trial. They could not call family or friends, though they could write letters and receive visitors each Sunday. They were not allowed to visit one another's rooms or watch television. They couldn't venture anywhere—take a walk, visit the exercise room—without being accompanied by a bailiff. It was, many of the jurors told me, one of the most difficult aspects of the trial: having to face alone the weightiest decision of their lives.

Courtroom No. 4 is modest in size. The jurors sat along one wall, slightly elevated, in low-back swivel chairs. The witness stand and the spectators' gallery, which seats 50 and was nearly filled every day, mostly with families and friends of the victim and Gross, were within a few feet of the jury box. A number of the jurors complained of feeling cramped. At one point, a couple of them asked if some of Beers's relatives could be moved to another part of the gallery; they could feel the presence of the men in the first row.

Jeffrey Gill, a 38–year–old deputy prosecutor who had never before tried a death-penalty case, gave the opening statement. He laid out the crime and told the jury about the existence of the videotape. It was a presentation marked by its spareness. The facts in the case were chilling and indisputable.

Then Bob Hill, a 47–year–old defense attorney who had previously represented 14 men facing capital punishment, just flat out conceded to the jury that he had no case. Hill, who has a folksy manner, told the jurors that the prosecution "has plenty of evidence to convict Jeremy Gross. I would be an idiot if I said otherwise." But, he went on, "we have substantial evidence to preserve his life." Hill then played for them the videotape of Gross walking into the Convenient Food Mart and shooting Beers three times. It was a gamble, but he knew the tape would be presented at some point and he thought it best if he did it right up front. "It was the most damning piece of evidence, and we couldn't make it go away," he told me recently. "I made it clear that it was Jeremy who pulled the trigger, and here's the videotape to show that. I told them there's no excuse for what Jeremy did, but I can explain how he gets to that convenience store."

The jurors watched the video on a large television screen. They were, to a person, horrified, though most found it confusing—at least at this first viewing, since four camera angles play out simultaneously, and it all happens in a mere 41 seconds. In the tape, Beers, dressed in a sweatshirt and shorts, seems baffled by Gross's single-minded effort to kill him. Some jurors weren't fully able to make sense of the scene until the very end, when Gross walks into the anteroom and shoots Beers in the head. In the final moments, Beers can be seen reaching out to Gross for support. The jurors were riveted. Gross turned his head. "You're talking about a coldhearted act," Hill told the jurors, "but you're not talking about a cold heart."

In those early days of the trial, the jurors avoided making eye contact with Gross, who at Hill's instructions was cleanshaven and well dressed in a polo shirt, dress slacks and loafers. It was impossible, though, for the jurors not to take notice of him. Some were struck by how young he looked. Indeed, Gross, who had had a buzz cut in jail, had let his hair grow at Hill's request so he'd look more youthful. Gross had also put on nearly 50 pounds since he'd been arrested, so his face appeared pudgy, softening his already boyish features. Others were struck by his lack of affect. One juror thought he looked so disconnected that it was as if he were on trial for shoplifting. In fact, Gross was so nervous that his legs twitched, and he often sat gripping the defense table, looking into space, which he later told me was the one way he could stop his involuntary leg movements.

The jurors were shaken by the video, and during a 20–minute break sat in the jury room in complete silence. "It seemed coldblooded and malicious and premeditated," recalled one juror. "I think everyone was just stunned." In the guilt phase of the trial, which lasted two days, the jurors saw the videotape once again, this time with the audio, as well as photographs from the crime scene, including the snapshot of a bloody Beers lying by the dangling pay phone. They also heard the prosecution make a convincing argument that Gross planned the robbery and went to the Convenient Food Mart intending to kill Beers. And the prosecution played for the jurors Gross's confession to detectives, in which he told them: "He knew it was me.... I just couldn't stop. My fingers just kept going."

Hill did little to counter the evidence but instead began to offer snippets of Gross's childhood. He also suggested that Gross had smoked marijuana before the robbery and murder, which might provide reason to not convict him of intentional murder.

Toward the end of the guilt phase, a juror told the judge about an unnerving incident in the jury room. One juror, playing a game of hangman, drew a gallows on the blackboard and what appeared to be an electric chair. Hill considered asking the judge to excuse the juror but in the end chose not to because he had misgivings about the alternates. But, he said: "That scared me to death. I didn't know if that was a message, or if she was preparing herself for it."

The deliberations took five and a half hours, longer than anyone had anticipated. One juror, Cheryl Berkowitz, who in the voir dire told the lawyers that she believed the death penalty wasn't imposed often enough, had come to believe that Gross must have been high when he committed the murder and so hadn't been in his right mind. But it went deeper than that. Berkowitz had also come to identify with him. She was a recovering cocaine addict and alcoholic. Berkowitz, a soft-featured woman who often looks as if she has a lot on her mind, spent her nights during the trial reading recovery literature. She knew firsthand what drugs could do to one's mental state. "There was a time I thought about robbing a convenience store so I could get thrown in jail and get off of drugs," she told me. She had even once shot at her husband and missed. More than anything, though, Berkowitz was struck by how young Gross looked. "That was everything," she said. "It was hard to put the two together, this young kid sitting there—he looked scared—and this videotape. I have a son, too. He was 23 at the time. I looked at Jeremy and thought, What the hell happened? Why would you be out robbing someone? He was just a kid to me."

Eventually, though, Berkowitz conceded that there was no doubt that Gross was guilty of murder while committing an armed robbery. Most of the other jurors at that point shared none of Berkowitz's reservations.

They thought Gross deserved to die. Kevin Garrison, a 51–year–old father of two who had just retired from his job as an engineer at the phone company, remembers thinking to himself: "This is pretty easy. This won't take long. Guilty. And death." Garrison, a physically fit, white-haired Reagan Republican, was chosen jury foreman, mostly because of his no-nonsense attitude and even-keeled nature. He told me that at that point in the trial, "I thought the death penalty was not only appropriate but was paramount." Another juror, Carrie Tuterow, said, "I had made up my mind: for justice to be imposed, he needed to die."

In fact, many of the jurors figured the trial was over. "I don't think any of us had a clue there was more coming," Garrison told me.

* * *

By the time Bob Hill got Gross's case, he knew it was senseless to spend time trying to gather evidence for an acquittal. So for a year and a half, Hill, along with his co-counsel, Mark Earnest, searched for people who in one manner or another had touched Gross's life. Persuading some of them to testify was tough. This was especially true of Gross's parents, who would essentially have to tell the jury how irresponsible they'd been. It took nearly a dozen visits with Gross's mother before she agreed to lay out her dismal life in court. "I'm a little bit social worker, a little bit psychologist, a little bit friend and a little bit lawyer," Hill said. He might have added storyteller to that list, for in the end that's what makes for the best mitigation: a compelling, believable yarn that, as Hill told me, tries "to make sense out of the nonsensical." It's an art that has little to do with good lawyering. "You don't engage in the in-your-face kind of lawyering you usually do," he said. "I wanted to get the jury to walk in Jeremy's shoes."

To assist them, they hired Cheri Hodson–Guevara, who had worked with recovering alcoholics before becoming a mitigation specialist. Over the course of a year, Hodson–Guevara helped the attorneys find witnesses and worked to gain those witnesses' trust. "You're asking them to tell you things they've never told anyone else before," she told me. "I'm out there to ask the question 'Why?' There's always a 'why.'"

The penalty phase in Gross's trial spanned five days. None of the jurors spoke to me of a single moment of epiphany; rather they described a gradual, cumulative understanding of why Jeremy Gross entered the Convenient Food Mart and murdered Christopher Beers.

Forty-one people testified, including Jeremy's mother. One juror recalls that she never once looked at her son. "It was almost as if she were talking about a complete stranger," another juror told me. But it wasn't only family members who took the stand. The mother of a former girlfriend of Gross's. Friends of Gross's. One of the state's most renowned high-school football coaches. Three psychologists. A former state Supreme Court justice. Three caseworkers for child welfare. And foster parents who had taken Jeremy and his sister in for a year.

Many of the jurors cried during testimony. Many had restless nights. "It's 4:18 a.m.," one juror wrote to her husband. "Can't sleep anymore." One juror recalled that she had one overriding emotion through those days: "I was scared," she said.

Gross's first 18 years were indeed full of misery and suffering. But is that reason to spare someone's life? After all, as the prosecution would point out, not everyone who has a wretched childhood kills. And besides, as the prosecutor Jeffrey Gill pointed out, "Everybody who commits murder comes with a story."

This is what the jury heard the first day. By the time Gross was born, his parents, who were quite young, didn't get along. When his father drank, which was often, he would get violent. One of Jeremy's first memories, from age 6, was of his father slamming his mother's head into the refrigerator. Photographs taken at the time were passed out to the jury. One showed her with a welt on her neck and a blackened and bloodied eye. Another displayed the stitched-up gash on top of her scalp. That same year, Gross's father, Jeff, and his mother, Cindy, both exceedingly drunk after a day spent watching the Indianapolis 500 on television and then bar-hopping, got into another dispute. His father smacked his mother across the face, then a short while later fell asleep on the living-room couch. Cindy doused the sofa with charcoal-lighter fluid, lighted a match and then took her daughter, Jennifer, by the hand, lifted her son, Jeremy, into her arms and walked out the door. Gross's father escaped unscathed, but Cindy, in this same courtroom, was found guilty of arson and placed on probation.

She and her husband separated, and she took Jennifer and Jeremy to live with her at a friend's house, where, among the chaos, a prostitute named Angel had sex with men in the living room. Cindy disappeared for days at a time, frequently consuming vast quantities of alcohol and prescription drugs. Dog feces littered the floors. Jeremy occasionally slept in a closet. He had so few clothes that in two photographs Hill showed the jury, he was wearing the same turquoise-colored shirt. The pictures had been taken more than a year apart. Kids at school would taunt him with the moniker "gross Jeremy," and teachers would send home notes complaining of his dress and hygiene.

Bob Hill unveiled two charts. In mitigation circles, they're called "chaos maps." One listed the 27 addresses where Jeremy had lived by the time he was 16; the other, the 33 schools he had attended. When Jeremy was 8 and his sister was 10, the state child-welfare services took them away from Cindy. "They didn't have a place in this world," a friend of Cindy's testified.

Almost all of the jurors were parents, and they couldn't understand how a mother could be so uncaring for her children. One juror, Sandra Logan, tried to avoid looking at Gross for fear she would weep in the courtroom. When she did catch glimpses of him, his head was often buried in his hands, or his head was lowered as he doodled on a legal pad. (He was writing notes to himself like "be calm" or "it's O.K.")

Jurors began to view what they initially thought was indifference as shame. Logan, whose face is lined with wrinkles from working for 26 years with hot oil as a machine operator, is by her own admission occasionally aloof and gruff, and she didn't interact much with the other jurors. Logan has two sons, one of whom served two years in prison for stealing money from his employer. Looking at Gross, she told me, "I did think, 'Yeah, that could've been my son.'"

Early on in Jeremy's mother's testimony, when she recounted her efforts to set her husband afire, Logan recognized the address. It was down the street from where she lived. She remembered the fire but hadn't known the details. The house is still boarded up. "It upset me more than the murder," she said. "I guess because I couldn't understand how a mother or father could do their child the way they had done him. I felt his parents were more to blame than he was."

A number of the other jurors had begun to feel the same. * * *

* * *

The thinking goes in mitigation circles that it's not enough to present someone as psychically battered and frayed, since if a jury feels he's too far gone, what's left to save? As Hill put it to me, he worried they might just say, "Throw it away; it's broke." But when he found Charles and Gail Garner, who for one year had been foster parents to Jeremy and his sister, Hill began to think he had a chance of persuading the jury that "there's something here worth saving."

The Garners live on the outskirts of Indianapolis in a modest ranch house. Charles, or Buck, as he's usually called, is a big man, with arms and neck thick as an oak. Gail has layered, shoulder-length brown hair and seems as sturdy as her husband. Buck wore blue jeans and his trademark black cowboy boots when he came to court to testify; Gail wore jeans and tennis shoes. "We wasn't no big tycoons," he told me. When Buck took the stand, he glanced over at Jeremy, whom he hadn't seen in a dozen years. "I was still trying to imagine that 8–year–old boy I'd last seen," he said. "That little boy wasn't there anymore." Buck and Gail, who were both in their late 20's in 1988 and had been married seven years, had tried without success to have kids. So they decided to become foster parents. The first and last children they took in were Jeremy and Jennifer.

Buck and Gail testified that they enrolled Jeremy and Jennifer in the Boy Scouts and Girl Scouts, that they gave them chores every day, that they made a point of sitting down as a family every night for dinner to talk about the day. Jeremy did well at school and played Little League baseball. "I was very proud of him," Buck told the jurors, "as if he was my own son."

Buck described how, when their mother was scheduled to come get them for the night, he would dress the children in sweatpants so that if she didn't show—which was usually the case—they could fall asleep on the living-room couch. He recounted the time at a Little League game when Jeremy's mother showed up unannounced. She was falling-down drunk, he said, and she berated the children on the opposing team and then mooned an umpire.

Buck got choked up when he talked about how he and Gail had grown so fond of Jeremy and Jennifer that they considered adopting them. But the child-welfare services, determined to reunite the family, chose to place them back with their mother, though only after she could prove to them she had something to cook on. She purchased a hot plate. Hill asked Buck how it made him feel that for Jeremy that was the best year of his life. "I've been told that by several people," Buck said. "I'm glad to be a part of that young man's life. It was a very good year for me too."

Buck is an understated man, but several of the jurors came to share what they saw as his anger toward the state welfare workers. (He was also angry at Gross, Buck told me.) A number of the jurors noticed that during the Garners' testimony, Gross, for the first time in the trial, made eye contact with a witness. "He latched onto those moments when good things were said about him," Garrison recalled. The Garners attended the remainder of the trial, something the jurors took note of, especially since Gross's mother didn't appear in the courtroom after giving her testimony. (Hill, it turns out, had asked her not to, since he thought she might have to take the stand again.)

In an effort to show that Gross, with some structure, could do well, Hill had a retired state Supreme Court justice testify to having watched Gross participate in a mock trial when he was a youth in a detention facility. The justice had been impressed by Gross's performance. Also, Gross's sixth-grade teacher testified about how he was so talented and such a hard worker that she'd place him in a corner of the classroom out of reach of the class troublemakers. Indeed, Gross, who liked school, received his high-school diploma on time.

Carrie Tuterow, 32, was the youngest juror. She has wavy red hair and an open face, and at the time of the trial, she worked at a day-care center. Her outgoing spirit and assuredness seems the perfect temperament for such work. After convicting Gross, Tuterow had been certain of the appropriate punishment: death. And then the Garners testified. "I made my decision when I heard their testimony," she told me. "I remember writing home that I figured out why I was here."

* * *

As Hill told Jeremy's story, the prosecution pounded away in its cross-examinations at the idea that not everyone who has had a difficult life ends up committing murder. What about his sister, Jennifer Gross? Or his stepbrother, Marion Higgenbotham? Neither had ever committed a crime of any sort.

So Hill had Jennifer and Marion tell their stories. Jennifer, who had been sexually molested by her father and had a child out of wedlock, sought counseling on her own. This is what saved her, she told the jurors. And in Marion's case, Hill brought Richard Dullaghan to testify. Dullaghan is an icon in sports-crazed Indiana. As football coach of Ben Davis High School, he has won five state championships. When Dullaghan, an open-faced, gray-haired man, took the witness stand, Hill asked him about the large ring he was wearing. It's from when he was inducted into the Indiana Football Hall of Fame, Dullaghan told him.

Dullaghan spoke not about Gross, whom he'd never met—Gross's mother had been unable or unwilling to come up with the fees for him to play football—but rather about Marion, who was the punt snapper on the high-school football team. Marion had testified the previous day that Dullaghan had been a kind of father figure for him, and that that helped keep him out of trouble. "I always tell my players, I'm your dad away from home," Dullaghan told the jurors. The implication, of course, was that Gross's mother had denied him every avenue to a better life, including the opportunity to have a stand-in parent like Coach Dullaghan. On his way out out of the courtroom, Dullaghan affectionately patted Marion on the head, a gesture that some jurors noted as a sharp contrast to the detachment of Gross's parents.

When Gross turned 15, his mother remarried. A year later, her new husband gave her an ultimatum: either Jeremy goes or he goes. Gross moved into a one-bedroom apartment with seven friends. A teenage runaway girl testified that Gross made sure none of the guys in the apartment harmed her. She told the jurors that Gross encouraged her to return home and to go back to school. Another girl recounted how Gross had later given to her the one item that meant anything to him: his high-school diploma. He told her he didn't want anything to happen to it.

Three psychologists testified on Gross's behalf. They suggested he had been crying out for attention, and they pointed to a bungled robbery when he was 15, in which Gross, carrying a gun, took a pair of shoes from a store and fled on foot. In the ensuing chase, Gross shot himself in the leg. He was sent to juvenile detention, where he fared rather well. The psychologists testified to his ability to thrive under structure.

The prosecutors asked of one psychologist: "Was he compelled to commit those acts?" At one point, exasperated by the painting of Gross as a victim, one prosecutor suggested that "it almost sounds as if the criminal-justice system would be cruel to punish a person for committing a criminal act."

* * *

During closing arguments, Hill pulled up a chair in front of the jurors and sat down. He'd once seen an attorney he admired do the same, to help defuse a charged moment. But he also fretted that his emotions would get the best of him.

"I think I'm too nervous to move around," he told the jurors. "The law says that we're supposed to sentence people to death that are the worst of the worst.... Jeremy Gross is not the worst of the worst. I think you all sense that in your hearts." He periodically pointed to a chart that one psychologist had put together listing all the risk factors in Gross's life and reminded the jurors how Gross, despite the parental neglect, could be nurturing, both to friends whom he urged to stay in school and to other inmates, whom he read to and tutored. "You kill Jeremy," he told the jurors, "you kill those good things that are existent in his heart, and that's wrong."

Toward the end of his closing, jurors could hear the desperation in Hill's pleas. One juror said Hill spoke of Gross as if he were a son. "I'm begging you," Hill appealed, "to spare his life."

If at this point you're angry that there has been so little about Christopher Beers, the victim, you're not alone. The prosecutors tried, without success, to introduce how much Beers's death had affected those around him. Most states allow some amount of victim impact statements. Some even allow victims' family members to testify about why they think death is the appropriate sentence. But Indiana doesn't permit testimony about the victim. "You come away feeling that the playing field is tilted," Newman, the former prosecutor said. "The only person who becomes humanized is the defendant. The victim becomes a cipher."

It particularly frustrated Gill, the young prosecutor, who knew how strongly Beers's family believed that Gross deserved death. "Mr. Hill has asked you for compassion," Gill began. "The State of Indiana is asking you for justice." Gill told the jury in his closing statement that Jeremy had, indeed, graduated from high school, that he had, indeed, advised others on how to live an honorable life. "Jeremy's childhood is not an excuse for what happened on this videotape," he said. "He can distinguish from right and wrong. He does know how to improve his life. It comes down to the fact that he chose not to." Before stepping down, Gill, one last time, played the 41 seconds of videotape. It was his exclamation point. It underscored the brutality of the crime and Gross's unquestionable guilt. A few of the jurors avoided looking at the television. "I'd seen it enough," one of them told me.

As the jury prepared to leave, one spectator muttered, loud enough for some of the jurors to hear, "He's getting away with murder."

The jurors were escorted to the jury room, a small, unadorned space, where Garrison, the foreman, let everyone collect themselves. The 12 jurors mulled silently for half an hour, helping themselves to cans of pop and orange juice from one of two small refrigerators. They then convened around an oval-shaped, laminated wood table. Since it could accommodate only eight chairs, four of the jurors had to sit against the wall. One juror could be heard mumbling, "I don't want to be doing this." It's how many of them felt. On a blackboard, Carrie Tuterow wrote down the options: death, life without parole and a determinate sentence. Garrison suggested they first take a vote, and so everyone, anonymously, wrote on a piece of paper where he or she stood.

They were surprised by how similar many of them were in their thinking. Nine voted for life without parole, one for a term of years and two for death. Garrison asked each of them to state his or her case, and it soon became evident who was in the minority. Cheryl Berkowitz, the recovering addict, thought Gross deserved another chance, and so said he should have a chance to get out of prison someday. Berkowitz, though, was fairly reticent during deliberations; she chose not to share her own story, as she feared that the other jurors' anger toward Gross's mother would be transferred to her.

A juror named Darlene Sue (she requested that her last name not be used), who had read the Bible every night searching for answers, believed Gross should die. She told her fellow jurors that over the course of the trial she'd come to believe that the Old Testament's notion of an eye for an eye made sense, and she read a short passage from the Bible she had with her. "He wasn't so scarred by his childhood that he didn't know right from wrong," she told me. "I remember his friends who he was living with in the trailer, saying that he talked them into staying in school. That told me he knew what he was doing."

The other juror who initially voted for death also quoted from the Bible, about not sitting in judgment of others. She soon switched her vote.

Garrison wavered. He agreed with Darlene Sue that clearly Gross had a moral compass, but he felt that the abuse that he endured as a child had shattered it. "I began to think not that there's an excuse for what happened, but I had an understanding of his torment," he said. "Sympathetic is too strong a word, but I can't think of a better way to describe how I felt. I struggled with whether he knew the difference between right and wrong." (Garrison said he repeatedly reminded himself of the gruesomeness of the crime, conjuring the one image that haunted most of them, the photograph of Christopher Beers lying face down by the dangling pay phone.)

At one point, one juror said: "Everyone knows a Jeremy. Every neighborhood has a Jeremy." Sandra Logan, who had kept to herself, talked of how the social-service agencies, the courts and his parents had failed Gross, a sentiment echoed by others. Privately, she considered her relationship with her son who'd been to prison. "To me, Gross's parents threw him away," she said. "Even to this day, with my son and all the problems he's had, he's still my son." It became clear that for some of the jurors, they saw some of Gross's frailties echoed in their own lives. Others were struck by how well Gross seemed to do when he was in detention, when he was in a supervised environment. "Maybe," suggested Tuterow, in prison "he'd touch someone else's life."

One juror mentioned the outburst at the end of the trial, that Gross was getting away with murder. She argued that life without parole was, in fact, a pretty severe punishment. In fact, some thought that it was a harsher sentence than death. "He seemed to be a kid with a conscience," Garrison said. "That killing's going to weigh on him every day."

The jurors took several breaks, including one to eat pizza for dinner. On the fourth vote, Darlene Sue gave in, though reluctantly. She worried that if a mistrial was declared, another jury might sentence Gross to a term with the chance of parole. The votes were tallied. It was unanimous. "I said, 'We have a sentence of life,' " Garrison recalled. "And everybody in the room—and I mean everybody—started crying." They waited nearly an hour to gather their composure before buzzing for the bailiff.

Many of the jurors told me that when they returned home, family, friends and colleagues at work chastised them for not putting Gross to death. Some of the jurors tried to convey the details of Gross's life, but it sounded like they were making excuses for him and for themselves. One juror would simply tell friends, "Well, you haven't been where I've been," and leave it at that.

* * *

A number of the jurors said they had considered writing Gross, to urge him to tutor and pursue his own education in prison, to take advantage of the chance they'd given him. They exchanged addresses with one another and talked of a reunion, but it never happened. It was, they each told me separately, probably just as well. The memories of the trial are still painful. Even three years later, some of the jurors I spoke with got teary-eyed when recounting some of the testimony.

The trial also had an unexpected effect on Gill, the young prosecutor. "I was surprised by the feelings of sympathy I had for Jeremy," he told me. "That caught me off guard. You don't learn in law school how to deal with the penalty phase. Nothing prepares you for that." I asked Gill whether he thought Gross deserved to die. He reclined in his chair and pondered the question for a minute or two. "Yes," he said. Then he added, "But I'm not dissatisfied with the jury's decision."

Twelve jurors—each of whom was convinced that some people, given the cruelty of their acts, deserve to die—chose to spare a life. To some, it might seem as if they copped out, that they're hypocritical. To others, their action might appear courageous. What is clear, at least to most of them, is that they no longer feel as certain about the death penalty as they once had.

* * *

PART 4

AFTER THE DEATH JUDGMENT

■ ■ ■

Like other persons incarcerated pursuant to criminal convictions, a person sentenced to death generally may pursue two distinct post-trial procedures for seeking reversal of his or her conviction and/or sentence: direct review by appeal (earlier known as "writ of error") and collateral review (usually by a petition for habeas corpus for state judgments). The scope and rules for direct review are determined by each jurisdiction, but such review generally is limited to claims of error arising from the record of the trial proceedings. Absent specific provisions permitting appellate courts to take evidence, claims on direct review cannot be based on factual information that is not included as evidence in the official transcripts of the trial. The collateral review process also varies from jurisdiction to jurisdiction. It usually involves a civil action or a motion initiated by the prisoner seeking a remedy for an allegedly unlawful incarceration. Collateral review differs from direct review because it is not limited to claims arising from the record in the trial court, so the prisoner may seek review based on non-record evidence. After exhaustion of state post-conviction remedies, a state prisoner may seek federal habeas corpus relief.

The Supreme Court has had little to say about state post-conviction remedies beyond holding that the Constitution requires "some form meaningful appellate review" in death penalty cases (see *Pulley v. Harris* and *Barclay v. Florida* [Chapter 3]) and that the Constitution does not require state collateral remedies and therefore does not require the appointment of counsel for indigent prisoners in any collateral remedies provided (see *Murray v. Giarratano* [Chapter 7]). By contrast, the Court has decided numerous cases brought by death-sentenced prisoners seeking federal habeas corpus. Chapter 11 addresses the principal issues that arise when a prisoner seeks habeas corpus review in federal court. Chapter 12 reviews the constitutional issues that arise after the completion of post-conviction review, issues related to the execution itself.

CHAPTER 11

FEDERAL HABEAS CORPUS REVIEW OF STATE DEATH JUDGMENTS

■ ■ ■

An application for a writ of habeas corpus is a civil action initiated by a person in custody alleging that he or she "is in custody in violation of the Constitution or laws or treaties of the United States." 28 U.S.C. § 2254(a). Although the writ lies to challenge any such custody, its primary use is by prisoners challenging state court judgments.[a] Federal habeas corpus has played a critical role in death penalty litigation. During the period 1973–1995, 40% of the death sentences that survived state direct and post-conviction review were overturned on federal habeas corpus.

The prisoner who fails to obtain relief on direct appeal or collateral review in the state courts initiates an action for a writ of habeas corpus in the federal district court. 28 U.S.C. § 2241, *et seq.* The role of the district court hearing a habeas case is *sui generis.* The district court, of course, has no authority to exercise appellate review over state court decisions. *Rooker v. Fidelity Trust Co.,* 263 U.S. 413, 44 S.Ct. 149 (1923); *District of Columbia Court of Appeals v. Feldman,* 460 U.S. 462, 103 S.Ct. 1303 (1983). However, although styled as an original proceeding to test the constitutionality of the state's custody of the prisoner, habeas review after the state courts' consideration of the prisoner's claim inevitably requires the federal court to second-guess the state courts.

> In this practical sense, postconviction federal habeas has an undeniable appellate flavor. The great intellectual challenge has always been to reconcile the theoretical (original) nature of the federal courts' jurisdiction * * * with the practical (appellate) character of the federal courts' function when the state courts have previously adjudicated prisoners' claims.[b]

This hybrid character of the federal courts' role has raised profound issues of federalism. In conducting habeas corpus review, does the federal court owe any deference to the state court's decision on the merits, to its factual

---

a. A parallel procedure for prisoners challenging federal judgments is established by 28 U.S.C. § 2255.

b. L. Yackle, *A Primer on the New Habeas Corpus Statute,* 44 Buff.L.Rev. 381, 403 (1996).

findings or to its decision not to reach the merits of the prisoner's claims? The federal courts' habeas corpus jurisdiction also has raised questions regarding separation of powers. To what extent must the courts exercise the full extent of the jurisdiction granted by Congress, and, conversely, to what extent may Congress direct the outcome of the courts' review?

Federal habeas corpus is a complex topic and could well be the subject of its own course. For an excellent and thorough discussion of federal habeas corpus, see the two-volume treatise by Professors James S. Liebman and Randy Hertz, *Federal Habeas Corpus Practice and Procedure* (5th Ed. 2005). The present chapter covers a limited number of issues, those which have proved most significant in capital litigation. The chapter begins with an Overview of Federal Habeas Corpus. Section A then addresses the substantive limits on the courts' jurisdiction; Section B addresses procedural limits arising from the petitioner's litigation in the state courts—exhaustion and procedural and factual default; and Section C addresses jurisdictional limits imposed by the Anti–Terrorism and Effective Death Penalty Act of 1996 ("AEDPA").

OVERVIEW OF FEDERAL HABEAS CORPUS

Although the writ of habeas corpus was recognized in the Constitution[1] and provided for in the Judiciary Act of 1789, § 14,[2] for the first eighty years of the country's existence, the federal courts had no general jurisdiction to grant the writ to review the confinement of one convicted of a crime in state court.[3] And, even as to *federal* prisoners, the remedy was an extremely limited one, available only to challenge the jurisdiction of the confining court.[4] This state of affairs was changed by the Civil War.

Expansion of Federal Habeas Corpus: Reconstruction to the 1960s

The triumph of the national government and national interests in the Civil War and the attempted consolidation of that victory during the Reconstruction period led Congress to expand greatly federal authority, and particularly federal judicial authority, into areas formerly subject to state control. In the Judiciary Act of Feb. 5, 1867, ch. 28, § 1, 14 Stat. 385, Congress granted jurisdiction to the federal courts to issue writs of habeas corpus in "all cases where any person may be restrained of his or her liberty in violation of the constitution, or any treaty or law of the United States." Over the course of the next hundred years, three elements

---

1. "The Privilege of the Writ of Habeas Corpus shall not be suspended, unless when in Cases of Rebellion or Invasion the public Safety may require it." U.S. Const. art. I, § 9.

2. 1 Stat. 81–82.

3. The remedy was extended to two very limited classes of state prisoners. In the Force Act of 1833 (4 Stat. 634–635), Congress authorized issuance of the writ for federal officers detained by state courts for acts done "in pursuance of a law of the United States." In the Act of Aug. 29, 1842 (5 Stat. 539–540), Congress authorized issuance of the writ on behalf of subjects or citizens of foreign states.

4. "An imprisonment under a judgment cannot be unlawful, unless that judgment be an absolute nullity; and it is not a nullity if the Court has general jurisdiction of the subject, although it should be erroneous." *Ex parte Watkins*, 28 U.S. (3 Pet.) 193, 203, 7 L.Ed. 650 (1830).

contributed to the dramatic expansion of habeas corpus review of state cases.

First, the Court's view of the scope of the writ changed. In its earlier decisions under the 1867 Act, the Court continued to treat habeas corpus as a remedy challenging the jurisdiction of the state courts, although the Court began to interpret the concept of jurisdictional defect generously, *e.g.*, as including convictions obtained under an unconstitutional statute. See *Yick Wo v. Hopkins*, 118 U.S. 356, 6 S.Ct. 1064 (1886). Later, the Court recognized that habeas corpus was available with regard to all constitutional claims, including claims that were fact-based. See *Frank v. Mangum*, 237 U.S. 309, 35 S.Ct. 582 (1915); *Moore v. Dempsey*, 261 U.S. 86, 43 S.Ct. 265 (1923). Finally, in *Brown v. Allen*, 344 U.S. 443, 73 S.Ct. 397 (1953), the Court held that (unless the Supreme Court had decided the constitutional claim on certiorari review) a prisoner was entitled to *de novo* federal habeas review even when the state court had reviewed and decided the prisoner's claim on the merits.

The second element in the expansion of habeas corpus was the Supreme Court's recognition of new federal constitutional rights in state criminal proceedings. Beginning with *Powell v. Alabama*, 287 U.S. 45, 53 S.Ct. 55 (1932) [Chapter 1], the Court not only expanded the scope of due process protections but, through the due process clause, incorporated, and made applicable to the states, most of the provisions of the Bill of Rights.

The third element in the expansion of habeas corpus was the Court's relaxed application of procedural limits on the exercise of the courts' jurisdiction. In *Ex Parte Royall*, 117 U.S. 241, 6 S.Ct. 734 (1886), the Supreme Court affirmed the denial of a writ to a state prisoner challenging the constitutionality of his prosecution under a state statute. Although acknowledging that it had the power to consider the writ, the Court held that exercise of that power should normally be delayed until the state case became final. In 1948, Congress codified that exhaustion requirement in 28 U.S.C. § 2254(b) and (c). Subsequently, in *Fay v. Noia*, 372 U.S. 391, 434–435, 83 S.Ct. 822, 846–847 (1963), the Court made clear that the exhaustion requirement was not a rule cutting off relief because of procedural default, but only applied to require the petitioner to resort to "remedies still open to the habeas applicant at the time he files his application in federal court."

In *Daniels v. Allen*, a companion case to *Brown v. Allen*, the Court had seemed to enforce a strict rule of procedural default. There, two of the petitioners had been one day late in serving a statement of the case on appeal in the state court, and, as a result, the state supreme court had refused to consider the merits of their appeals. The Supreme Court affirmed the denial of habeas corpus also without reaching the merits. The Court held that the petitioners' procedural default, which barred consideration of their claims in the state supreme court, also barred their consideration in federal court.

> A failure to use a state's available remedy, in the absence of some interference or incapacity * * * bars federal habeas corpus.

344 U.S. at 487, 73 S.Ct. at 422. Ten years later, in *Fay v. Noia*, a case in which the petitioner had failed to appeal his state court conviction (because he apparently believed he might receive the death penalty on retrial), the Court undertook a thorough review of the development of federal habeas corpus in order to determine whether Noia's petition was barred by his state court procedural default. While acknowledging that a defendant's procedural default would create a jurisdictional bar to the Supreme Court's review of the judgment on appeal (because the judgment would be supported by adequate and independent state grounds), there was no such jurisdictional limitation on habeas corpus. The Court held that the federal courts had the *power* to decide even procedurally default-ed claims subject to a limited discretion to deny relief to "an applicant who has deliberately bypassed the orderly procedure of the state courts and in so doing has forfeited his state court remedies." 372 U.S. at 438, 83 S.Ct. at 849.

The adoption, in *Noia*, of a very forgiving rule on procedural defaults was paralleled by the adoption, in *Townsend v. Sain*, 372 U.S. 293, 83 S.Ct. 745 (1963), of a similarly forgiving rule regarding the effect of state factfinding. In *Brown v. Allen*, the Supreme Court had ruled that when the state court had held a trial or hearing on the issues, the federal court need not hold a hearing absent unusual circumstances (344 U.S. at 463, 73 S.Ct. at 410–411) and, even when there was a material conflict of fact, the federal court could "properly depend upon the state's resolution of the issue." (344 U.S. at 458, 73 S.Ct. at 408). *Townsend* superceded *Brown*.

> We hold that a federal court must grant an evidentiary hearing to a habeas applicant under the following circumstances: If (1) the merits of the factual dispute were not resolved in the state hearing; (2) the state factual determination is not fairly supported by the record as a whole; (3) the fact-finding procedure employed by the state court was not adequate to afford a full and fair hearing; (4) there is a substantial allegation of newly discovered evidence; (5) the material facts were not adequately developed at the state-court hearing; or (6) for any reason it appears that the state trier of fact did not afford the habeas applicant a full and fair fact hearing.

372 U.S. at 313, 83 S.Ct. at 757.[5] In its 1966 amendments to the habeas corpus statute, Congress substantially codified the *Townsend* holding, but in an indirect fashion. As amended, 28 U.S.C. § 2254(d) provided that, where the state court had held a hearing and made written findings on the merits of the petitioner's claims, those findings would be presumed to be correct. However, where *Townsend* had listed the circumstances under which a petitioner would be entitled to an evidentiary hearing, § 2254(d)

---

5. In addition to delineating the circumstances under which an evidentiary hearing had to be held, the Court made clear that a district court had the *discretion* to hold an evidentiary hearing where a factual dispute existed, irrespective of whether the case fell within the listed circumstances. 372 U.S. at 318, 83 S.Ct. at 760.

listed eight circumstances, almost identical in substance to the six circumstances of *Townsend*, under which state factfinding would not be entitled to a presumption of correctness. In combination, *Townsend* and § 2254(d) established that, if none of the listed circumstances applied, the petitioner was not entitled to an evidentiary hearing and the presumption of correctness of the state factfinding could only be overcome by "convincing evidence that the factual determination by the State court was erroneous." On the other hand, if the petitioner established that one of the circumstances applied, he or she was entitled to a hearing and there was no presumption of correctness for the state factfinding, in which case the petitioner needed to prove his or her claim only by a preponderance of the evidence.

The rules regarding exhaustion, procedural default and deference to state factfinding were products of a concern about federal-state relations. Congress and the Supreme Court also were concerned about the potential abuse of habeas corpus by repeated filings in federal court. The problem of repeated filings came in two forms: "same-claim" successive petitions (containing claims raised in a previous petition) and "new-claim" successive petitions (containing claims not raised in a previous petition). In the 1948 amendments to the habeas corpus statute, Congress addressed the problem of same-claim successive petitions. Section 2244 provided that a federal judge was authorized to deny claims previously raised and determined, unless the "ends of justice" would be served by consideration of the claims. The statute did not address new-claim successive petitions. In *Sanders v. United States*, 373 U.S. 1, 83 S.Ct. 1068 (1963), the Court relied on the *Noia* and *Townsend* cases as setting forth the guiding principles for the new-claim situation. Such claims would be denied under the "abuse of the writ doctrine" only if the petitioner deliberately withheld or deliberately abandoned the claim in the previous petition and then only if the "ends of justice" would not be served by hearing the claims. In 1966, Congress, in 28 U.S.C. § 2244(b), codified the "abuse of the writ" standard announced in *Sanders*.

Contraction of Federal Habeas Corpus: the Burger and Rehnquist Courts

Beginning with its 1976 decision in *Stone v. Powell*, 428 U.S. 465, 96 S.Ct. 3037 (1976) [see Section A], the Supreme Court under Chief Justices Burger and Rehnquist, acting without the benefit of any changes in the governing statutes, drastically limited the reach of federal habeas corpus. The principal reason expressed by the Court for the contraction of habeas corpus was the concern that broad habeas corpus review evidenced too little respect for, and too little deference to, state processes and decisions. Generally, the Court announced its new restrictions on the availability of the writ in non-capital cases and only later applied them to capital cases.[6]

---

6. The one exception is *McCleskey v. Zant*, 499 U.S. 467, 111 S.Ct. 1454 (1991), a capital case where the Court announced its new restrictions on the filing of successive petitions in federal court.

The Court's decisions limited the scope of the writ in two ways. One group of decisions limited the substantive reach of the writ, redefining what constituted a meritorious claim for purposes of federal habeas corpus. The other group of decisions restricted access to the writ by expanding the scope of various procedural bars to asserting or proving substantively meritorious claims.

Substantive Limits

The first of the substantive limitations was articulated in *Stone v. Powell*. There, the Court held that, although § 2254 granted jurisdiction generally over alleged violations of the Constitution, the federal courts had the discretion not to consider certain classes of constitutional claims. The Court then held that claims based on Fourth Amendment violations, where the petitioner had been accorded "the opportunity for full and fair litigation of his claim in the state courts," would not be addressed on federal habeas corpus.

A far more significant substantive limitation was announced in *Teague v. Lane*, 489 U.S. 288, 109 S.Ct. 1060 (1989). There, the Court announced that, with two narrow exceptions, a habeas corpus petitioner would not be entitled to relief based on a "new rule" of criminal procedure announced after the petitioner's case had become final on direct review. The exceptions were (1) where the new rule places "certain kinds of primary, private individual conduct beyond the power of the criminal law-making authority to proscribe" and (2) where the new rule is a "watershed" rule of criminal procedure. 489 U.S. at 311, 109 S.Ct. at 1075–1076. The effect of the *Teague* non-retroactivity rule is to shift the inquiry from the question whether the petitioner is presently in custody as the result of the violation of his or her constitutional rights to an examination of whether the decision of the state's highest court on direct review was correct *on the law as it then stood*. As Justice O'Connor conceded in her opinion for the plurality, it is not always clear when a claim relies on a "new rule." She set out two definitions:

> In general, * * * a case announces a new rule when it breaks new ground or imposes a new obligation on the States or the Federal Government. To put it differently, as case announces a new rule if the result was not *dictated* by precedent existing at the time the defendant's conviction became final.

489 U.S. at 301, 109 S.Ct. at 1070.[7] Not surprisingly, the *Teague* rule has spawned extensive litigation over what constitutes a new rule and when the exceptions to the rule apply.

---

7. As Liebman and Hertz point out in their treatise, O'Connor's two definitions do not even seem consistent. 2 Federal Habeas Corpus Practice and Procedure, § 25.5, pp. 1179–1180. The problem is that there is no obvious meaning to "new rule."

"One can argue, for example, that there are almost no such things as 'new rules' of judge-made law in a system that distinguishes the legislative function from the judicial function and subjects the latter to the principle of *stare decisis*. On the other hand, one might argue that almost every decision is 'new' inasmuch as almost every decision extends preexisting rules to one degree or another simply by applying them to new facts."

Id. at 1178.

The Court, in *Brecht v. Abrahamson*, 507 U.S. 619, 113 S.Ct. 1710 (1993), developed yet a third substantive limitation on federal habeas corpus when it altered the standard for review of constitutional errors that do not require *per se* reversal. On direct review in the state appellate courts or in the United States Supreme Court, if the court determines that there was constitutional error, reversal is required unless the state establishes that the error was "harmless beyond a reasonable doubt." *Chapman v. California*, 386 U.S. 18, 24, 87 S.Ct. 824, 828 (1967). Prior to *Brecht*, the Supreme Court had applied the *Chapman* test to habeas corpus cases. See *Brecht*, 507 U.S. at 630, 113 S.Ct. at 1718. In *Brecht*, the Court relied on *Powell* and *Teague*, among other cases, for the principle that habeas corpus, an "extraordinary remedy," serves different purposes than direct review and that to apply the *Chapman* harmless error standard on habeas corpus review of "trial error" (after it already was applied on direct review) was unnecessary. Accordingly, the Court held that, on habeas corpus review of trial error, the petitioner has the burden of showing that the error had a "substantial and injurious effect or influence in determining the jury's verdict," *i.e.*, that the petitioner suffered "actual prejudice." 507 U.S. at 637–638, 113 S.Ct. at 1722.

Thus, all three rules had in common the effect of preventing the federal habeas corpus court from considering claimed constitutional errors that would have been sufficient to justify relief on direct review.

Procedural limits

As noted above, meritorious habeas corpus claims might have been defeated under one or another of four doctrines derived from the habeas statutes or set forth in the Supreme Court's decisions: exhaustion of remedies (former § 2254(b)); procedural default (see *Fay v. Noia*); presumption of correctness of state fact-finding (former § 2254(d); see *Townsend v. Sain*); "successive" or "abusive" petition (former § 2244(b), (c); see *United States v. Sanders*). The Burger and Rehnquist Courts, in varying degrees, expanded each of these door-closing doctrines.

The Supreme Court strictly construed the exhaustion requirement. Thus, the Court held that petitioners were required to exhaust state discretionary review procedures even in the absence of any evidence that the state court would consider the petitioners' claims. See *O'Sullivan v. Boerckel*, 526 U.S. 838, 119 S.Ct. 1728 (1999) [see Section B]. The Court has required that the claim raised in federal court be identical with the claim asserted in state court, relying on the same facts, the same constitutional provision, and precisely the same legal theory. See *Gray v. Netherland*, 518 U.S. 152, 116 S.Ct. 2074 (1996). And the Court has held that "mixed" petitions, those with both exhausted and unexhausted claims, must be dismissed on exhaustion grounds. See *Rose v. Lundy*, 455 U.S. 509, 102 S.Ct. 1198 (1982).

The Supreme Court worked its most significant change with its expansion of the doctrine of procedural default. In *Wainwright v. Sykes*, 433 U.S. 72, 97 S.Ct. 2497 (1977), the Court overruled *Fay v. Noia*, and replaced *Noia*'s "deliberate bypass" with a "cause and prejudice" standard. In *Sykes*, the defendant had failed to object to the admission of his confession at trial and, under Florida law, was barred from raising the issue in further proceedings in the state courts. In his federal habeas corpus petition, Sykes sought to challenge the admissibility of the confession. The Supreme Court held that federal review of the challenge was barred by Sykes' procedural default in the state court. The Court analogized the situation to the jurisdictional bar to the Court's consideration on direct review of any judgment which is supported by adequate and independent state grounds. As the Court later explained in *Coleman v. Thompson*, 501 U.S. 722, 729–731, 111 S.Ct. 2546, 2353–2554 (1991) [Section B]:

> This Court will not review a question of federal law decided by a state court if the decision of that court rests on a state law ground that is independent of the federal question and adequate to support the judgment. This rule applies whether the state law ground is substantive or procedural. In the context of direct review of a state court judgment, the independent and adequate state ground doctrine is jurisdictional. * * *

> We have applied the independent and adequate state ground doctrine not only in our own review of state court judgments, but in deciding whether federal district courts should address the claims of state prisoners in habeas corpus actions. The doctrine applies to bar federal habeas when a state court declined to address a prisoner's federal claims because the prisoner had failed to meet a state procedural requirement. In these cases, the state judgment rests on independent and adequate state procedural grounds.

>   * * *

> In the habeas context, the application of the independent and adequate state ground doctrine is grounded in concerns of comity and federalism. Without the rule, a federal district court would be able to do in habeas what this Court could not do on direct review; habeas would offer state prisoners whose custody was supported by independent and adequate state grounds an end run around the limits of this Court's jurisdiction and a means to undermine the State's interest in enforcing its laws.

The Court recognized two exceptions to the rule.

> Under *Sykes* and its progeny, an adequate and independent finding of procedural default will bar federal habeas review of the federal claim, unless the habeas petitioner can show "cause" for the default and 'prejudice attributable thereto' or demonstrate that failure to consider the federal claim will result in a "fundamental miscarriage of justice."

Harris v. Reed, 489 U.S. 255, 262, 109 S.Ct. 1038, 1043 (1989). The Court subsequently applied its procedural default bar to capital cases. See *Smith v. Murray*, 477 U.S. 527, 106 S.Ct. 2661 (1986). Since *Sykes*, the Supreme Court and lower federal courts have struggled with the various elements of the rule: When has a state relied on procedural default? Is the state rule independent of the federal right and adequate to deny relief? What constitutes "cause," "prejudice" or "a fundamental miscarriage of justice"?

In *Keeney v. Tamayo–Reyes*, 504 U.S. 1, 112 S.Ct. 1715 (1992), the Court extended its "cause and prejudice" test to state fact-finding. Tamayo–Reyes sought an evidentiary hearing in federal court on his claim that his state court *nolo contendere* plea was invalid. Relying on *Townsend v. Sain*, he asserted that a hearing was required because the material facts were not adequately developed at the state-court hearing. The Court overruled *Townsend* in part and held that Tamayo–Reyes was not entitled to an evidentiary hearing unless he could show "cause" for his failure to develop facts in the state court hearing and "prejudice" therefrom.

The Court also applied the "cause and prejudice" test to successive petitions in federal court. In *McCleskey v. Zant*, 499 U.S. 467, 111 S.Ct. 1454 (1991), McCleskey filed a second federal habeas petition raising a claim under *Massiah v. United States*, 377 U.S. 201, 84 S.Ct. 1199 (1964) after he had failed to raise the claim in his first federal habeas petition. He claimed that he had not known the basis for the claim until, after judgment on his first habeas petition, the state provided him with a transcript of an interview with the informer who testified against him. The Court rejected the "deliberate abandonment" standard of *United States v. Sanders* and held that McCleskey's claim could not be considered on the merits because he had not shown cause for his failure to assert the claim in the first petition, and failure to consider the claim would not result in a fundamental miscarriage of justice.

Contraction of Federal Habeas Corpus: The Antiterrorism and Effective Death Penalty Act of 1996 (AEDPA)

Calls for statutory reform of federal habeas corpus, which had been heard since the Court's decision in *Brown v. Allen*, finally bore fruit in 1996 when Congress enacted the Antiterrorism and Effective Death Penalty Act of 1996 (AEDPA). The act affected the review of state death judgments in two ways: first, it modified the habeas corpus statute to make more restrictive the rules applicable to all habeas petitions (see 28 U.S.C. §§ 2244, 2253, 2254); and, second, it created a set of special rules applicable, only in death judgment cases, authorizing expedited review of such cases from states meeting certain standards for appointment and compensation of qualified counsel in state collateral review proceedings ("opt-in states"). See 28 U.S.C. §§ 2261–2266.[8]

---

8. Although, prior to AEDPA, death judgments were found to be fatally flawed and were set aside four times as often as non-death judgments (see J. Liebman, J. Fagan & V. West, *A Broken System: Error Rates in Capital Cases, 1973–1995*, http://justice.policy.net/jpreport/liebman2.pdf

With regard to all habeas petitions, AEDPA, for the first time, established a statute of limitations for filing habeas corpus applications (one year from completion of the direct appeal, with tolling during the pendency of properly filed state collateral review proceedings) (§ 2244(d)), and it also limited review of district court judgments by requiring the defendant to obtain a Certificate of Appealability (COA) in order to appeal (§ 2253(c)). The Supreme Court has described the standard governing issuance of a COA as requiring the applicant to "demonstrat[e] that jurists of reason could disagree with the district court's resolution of his constitutional claims or that jurists could conclude the issues presented are adequate to deserve encouragement to proceed further." *Miller–El v. Cockrell*, 537 U.S. 322, 327, 123 S.Ct. 1029, 1034 (2003).

In addition, and more significantly, the act codified and extended the Supreme Court's restrictions on the scope of habeas corpus review in three principal respects. First, the act changed either the standard of review of, or the standard for granting relief from, state court judgments[9] and adopted and extended the "non-retroactivity rule" of *Teague v. Lane*. Section 2254(d) provides that the writ may not be granted as to any claim adjudicated on the merits in the state court, unless the adjudication,

> (1) resulted in a decision that was contrary to, or involved an unreasonable application of clearly established Federal law, as determined by the Supreme Court of the United States; or

> (2) resulted in a decision that was based on an unreasonable determination of the facts in light of the evidence presented in the State court proceeding.

The section requires the federal courts to deny relief from the state courts' erroneous, but reasonable, decisions applying federal law, but the difference between an erroneous decision and an unreasonable decision is not altogether clear. [See *Williams (Terry) v. Taylor*, Section A]. The section also expanded on *Teague* by limiting "clearly established Federal law" to law established in the Supreme Court and virtually eliminating the exceptions to *Teague*.

Second, the act built on *Keeney v. Tamayo–Reyes* to limit review of state factfinding. Section 2254(e)(2) dropped the previous statutory limitation that state court findings be the *written* product of a hearing on the *merits* in order to create a presumption of correctness. More significantly, § 2254(e) drastically limited the circumstances under which an evidentiary hearing will be granted when material facts were not developed in the state court. The section bars the holding of an evidentiary hearing unless:

> (A) the claim relies on—

(2000)), the special provisions for capital cases have the effect of imposing greater restrictions on the review of capital cases than on the review of non-capital cases.

9. How to characterize the section—whether as a limitation on cognizable claims or as a limitation on relief when a constitutional violation is found—has been the subject of debate, but probably has limited practical significance. In its first cases interpreting the section, the Supreme Court did not explicitly address the issue. See *Williams (Terry) v. Taylor*, 529 U.S. 362, 120 S.Ct. 1495 (2000) [Section A].

(i) a new rule of constitutional law, made retroactive to cases on collateral review by the Supreme Court, that was previously unavailable; or

(ii) a factual predicate that could not have been previously discovered through the exercise of due diligence; and

(B) the facts underlying the claim would be sufficient to establish by clear and convincing evidence that but for constitutional error, no reasonable factfinder would have found the applicant guilty of the underlying offense.

Thus, in lieu of the *Tamayo–Reyes* standard, requiring a showing of "cause and prejudice" *or* "fundamental miscarriage of justice," the act appears to require that the petitioner meet a higher standard of "cause" *and* prove a fundamental miscarriage of justice.

Third, the act substantially narrowed the circumstances under which a federal court may hear a successive petition. Preliminarily, the petitioner may not even file a successive petition unless he or she has obtained prior approval from the appropriate Court of Appeals. § 2244(b)(3). As to same-claim petitions, all claims previously presented are barred (apparently without regard to whether the claim was decided). § 2244(b)(1). As to new-claim petitions, in lieu of the *McCleskey v. Zant* standard, § 2244(b)(2) substituted the rule that a claim not presented shall be dismissed unless:

(A) the applicant shows that the claim relies on a new rule of constitutional law, made retroactive to cases on collateral review by the Supreme Court, that was previously unavailable; or

(B) (i) the factual predicate for the claim could not have been discovered previously through the exercise of due diligence; and

(ii) the facts underlying the claim, if proven and viewed in light of the evidence as a whole, would be sufficient to establish by clear and convincing evidence that, but for constitutional error, no reasonable factfinder would have found the applicant guilty of the underlying offense.

The effect of all three of these changes is to limit significantly the substantive scope of habeas corpus review and to deny a remedy for constitutional violations for which relief would be available on direct appeal.

AEDPA's special provisions for capital cases from "opt-in" states accelerate the handling of such cases by creating a short statute of limitations for the filing of a federal habeas petition and by requiring the district court and court of appeals to adjudicate cases quickly. The prisoner must file his or her habeas application within 180 days from the final state court affirmance of the conviction and sentence (subject to tolling during the pendency of a petition for certiorari or state collateral review and a possible 30 day extension). § 2263. The district court must decide the case within 180 days of filing (with a possible 30–day extension). § 2266(b). The court of appeals must decide any appeal within 120 days of the filing of the reply brief (with a possible 30–day extension). § 2266(c). The special provisions also set strict rules regarding the granting of stays of executions. § 2262. Finally, they codify a procedural default rule apparently differing from that established by the Supreme Court in that: (1) there is, in effect, a stricter definition of "cause"; (2) there is no required showing of "prejudice"; (3) and there is no exception for a "manifest miscarriage of justice." § 2264. To take advantage of these provisions, the state must have established a mechanism for the appointment, compensation and payment of expenses of competent counsel for indigent prisoners seeking collateral review in the state courts. §§ 2261, 2265. Prior to the Patriot Act amendments in 2005, changing the method for determining a state's compliance with these standards (see below), no state except Arizona had qualified as an opt-in state. See *e.g.*, *Allen v. Lee*, 366 F.3d 319 (4th Cir. 2004) (North Carolina); *Hall v. Luebbers*, 341 F.3d 706 (8th Cir. 2003) (Missouri); *Tucker v. Catoe*, 221 F.3d 600 (4th Cir. 2000) (South Carolina); *Baker v. Corcoran*, 220 F.3d 276 (4th Cir. 2000) (Maryland); *Ashmus v. Woodford* 202 F.3d 1160 (9th Cir. 2000) (California). Even though Arizona's statutory mechanisms for the appointment of counsel were held to meet the opt-in standards, the state was unable to take advantage of the expedited procedures because it has failed to comply with its own statutes. See *Spears v. Stewart*, 283 F.3d 992 (9th Cir. 2002). The 2005 USA Patriot Improvement and Reauthorization Act (Pub. L. 109–177) amended AEDPA by assigning to the Attorney General, subject to *de novo* review in the D.C. Circuit, the responsibility to certify whether states qualify for "opt-in" treatment. 28 U.S.C. §§ 2261, 2265. As of this writing (2009), implementing regulations have yet to be finalized.

In *Lindh v. Murphy*, 521 U.S. 320, 117 S.Ct. 2059 (1997), the Supreme Court held that AEDPA was applicable to cases filed in the district court after the effective date of the act (April 24, 1996). In *Slack v. McDaniel*, 529 U.S. 473, 120 S.Ct. 1595 (2000), the Court held that AEDPA's provisions governing appeal (§ 2253) were applicable to appeals filed after the effective date of the act. As a result, for a time, there were two bodies of law in effect, determined by the filing date of the case, but, at present, almost all pending habeas cases come under AEDPA.

A.   SUBSTANTIVE LIMITS

This section considers substantive limits on federal habeas corpus review of state death judgments: what claims can be reviewed on habeas corpus? As noted above, in *Stone v. Powell*, the Supreme Court considers whether Fourth Amendment claims are cognizable. In *Herrera v. Collins*, the issue is whether a claim of actual innocence, unsupported by an independent constitutional violation, is cognizable on federal habeas corpus. *Schriro v. Summerlin* considers the application of *Teague v. Lane*, 489 U.S. 288, 109 S.Ct. 1060 (1989), prohibiting habeas relief on the basis of a new rule of law, to the rule announced in *Ring v. Arizona* [Chapter 9].

In the final case, *Williams (Terry) v. Taylor*, the Supreme Court interprets the current § 2254(d)(1), the AEDPA version of the *Teague* rule.

STONE v. POWELL

428 U.S. 465, 96 S.Ct. 3037, 49 L.Ed.2d 1067 (1976).

MR. JUSTICE POWELL delivered the opinion of the Court.

Respondents in these cases were convicted of criminal offenses in state courts, and their convictions were affirmed on appeal. The prosecution in each case relied upon evidence obtained by searches and seizures alleged by respondents to have been unlawful. Each respondent subsequently sought relief in a Federal District Court by filing a petition for a writ of federal habeas corpus under 28 U.S.C. § 2254. The question presented is whether a federal court should consider, in ruling on a petition for habeas corpus relief filed by a state prisoner, a claim that evidence obtained by an unconstitutional search or seizure was introduced at his trial, when he has previously been afforded an opportunity for full and fair litigation of his claim in the state courts. The issue is of considerable importance to the administration of criminal justice.

I

We summarize first the relevant facts and procedural history of these cases.

A

Respondent Lloyd Powell was convicted of murder in June 1968 after trial in a California state court. At about midnight on February 17, 1968, he and three companions entered the Bonanza Liquor Store in San Bernardino, Cal., where Powell became involved in an altercation with Gerald Parsons, the store manager, over the theft of a bottle of wine. In the scuffling that followed Powell shot and killed Parsons' wife. Ten hours later an officer of the Henderson, Nev., Police Department arrested Powell for violation of the Henderson vagrancy ordinance, and in the search incident to the arrest discovered a .38–caliber revolver with six expended cartridges in the cylinder.

[At trial, Parsons's and Powell's two accomplices testified against him. Powell objected to any testimony about the gun, or introduction of the gun, on the ground that it had been discovered through a violation of his Fourth Amendment rights, but the court admitted the evidence. Powell was convicted of second degree murder. The conviction was affirmed, and the state courts denied habeas corpus relief. Powell petitioned for federal habeas corpus, and the District Court denied relief. The Court of Appeals reversed, finding that the evidence should have been excluded and that the error was not harmless.][a]

---

a. The Court's discussion of the facts of the companion case, *Wolff v. Rice*, and of the history of federal habeas corpus are omitted.

III

[Justice POWELL reviewed the Court's development of the Fourth Amendment exclusionary rule. He concluded that, while at one point the Court had justified the exclusion of illegally seized evidence on two grounds—protection of "judicial integrity" and deterrence of unlawful police conduct—the primary justification for the rule was deterrence, and therefore "the application of the rule has been restricted to those areas where its remedial objectives are thought most efficaciously served" (quoting *United States v. Calandra*, 414 U.S. 338, 94 S.Ct. 613 (1974).]

IV

We turn now to the specific question presented by these cases. Respondents allege violations of Fourth Amendment rights guaranteed them through the Fourteenth Amendment. The question is whether state prisoners who have been afforded the opportunity for full and fair consideration of their reliance upon the exclusionary rule with respect to seized evidence by the state courts at trial and on direct review may invoke their claim again on federal habeas corpus review. The answer is to be found by weighing the utility of the exclusionary rule against the costs of extending it to collateral review of Fourth Amendment claims.

The costs of applying the exclusionary rule even at trial and on direct review are well known: the focus of the trial, and the attention of the participants therein, are diverted from the ultimate question of guilt or innocence that should be the central concern in a criminal proceeding. Moreover, the physical evidence sought to be excluded is typically reliable and often the most probative information bearing on the guilt or innocence of the defendant. As Mr. Justice Black emphasized in his dissent in *Kaufman*:

> "A claim of illegal search and seizure under the Fourth Amendment is crucially different from many other constitutional rights; ordinarily the evidence seized can in no way have been rendered untrustworthy by the means of its seizure and indeed often this evidence alone establishes beyond virtually any shadow of a doubt that the defendant is guilty."

Application of the rule thus deflects the truthfinding process and often frees the guilty. The disparity in particular cases between the error committed by the police officer and the windfall afforded a guilty defendant by application of the rule is contrary to the idea of proportionality that is essential to the concept of justice. Thus, although the rule is thought to deter unlawful police activity in part through the nurturing of respect for Fourth Amendment values, if applied indiscriminately it may well have the opposite effect of generating disrespect for the law and administration of justice. These long-recognized costs of the rule persist when a criminal conviction is sought to be overturned on collateral review on the ground that a search-and-seizure claim was erroneously rejected by two or more tiers of state courts.[31]

Evidence obtained by police officers in violation of the Fourth Amendment is excluded at trial in the hope that the frequency of future violations will decrease. Despite the absence of supportive empirical evidence, we have assumed that the immediate effect of exclusion will be to discourage law enforcement officials from violating the Fourth Amendment by removing the incentive to disregard it. More importantly, over the long term, this demonstration that our society attaches serious consequences to violation of constitutional rights is thought to encourage those who formulate law enforcement policies, and the officers who implement them, to incorporate Fourth Amendment ideals into their value system.

We adhere to the view that these considerations support the implementation of the exclusionary rule at trial and its enforcement on direct appeal of state-court convictions. But the additional contribution, if any, of the consideration of search-and-seizure claims of state prisoners on collateral review is small in relation to the costs. To be sure, each case in which such claim is considered may add marginally to an awareness of the values protected by the Fourth Amendment. There is no reason to believe, however, that the overall educative effect of the exclusionary rule would be appreciably diminished if search-and-seizure claims could not be raised in federal habeas corpus review of state convictions. Nor is there reason to assume that any specific disincentive already created by the risk of exclusion of evidence at trial or the reversal of convictions on direct review would be enhanced if there were the further risk that a conviction obtained in state court and affirmed on direct review might be overturned in collateral proceedings often occurring years after the incarceration of the defendant. The view that the deterrence of Fourth Amendment violations would be furthered rests on the dubious assumption that law enforcement authorities would fear that federal habeas review might reveal flaws in a search or seizure that went undetected at trial and on appeal.[35] Even if one rationally could assume that some additional incre-

---

31. Resort to habeas corpus, especially for purposes other than to assure that no innocent person suffers an unconstitutional loss of liberty, results in serious intrusions on values important to our system of government. They include "(i) the most effective utilization of limited judicial resources, (ii) the necessity of finality in criminal trials, (iii) the minimization of friction between our federal and state systems of justice, and (iv) the maintenance of the constitutional balance upon which the doctrine of federalism is founded." *Schneckloth v. Bustamonte*, 412 U.S. 218, 93 S.Ct. 2041 (1973). (POWELL, J., concurring).

We nevertheless afford broad habeas corpus relief, recognizing the need in a free society for an additional safeguard against compelling an innocent man to suffer an unconstitutional loss of liberty. * * * But in the case of a typical Fourth Amendment claim, asserted on collateral attack, a convicted defendant is usually asking society to redetermine an issue that has no bearing on the basic justice of his incarceration.

35. The policy arguments that respondents marshal in support of the view that federal habeas corpus review is necessary to effectuate the Fourth Amendment stem from a basic mistrust of the state courts as fair and competent forums for the adjudication of federal constitutional rights. The argument is that state courts cannot be trusted to effectuate Fourth Amendment values through fair application of the rule, and the oversight jurisdiction of this Court on certiorari is an inadequate safeguard. The principal rationale for this view emphasizes the broad differences in the respective institutional settings within which federal judges and state judges operate. Despite

mental deterrent effect would be presented in isolated cases, the resulting advance of the legitimate goal of furthering Fourth Amendment rights would be outweighed by the acknowledged costs to other values vital to a rational system of criminal justice.

In sum, we conclude that where the State has provided an opportunity for full and fair litigation of a Fourth Amendment claim, a state prisoner may not be granted federal habeas corpus relief on the ground that evidence obtained in an unconstitutional search or seizure was introduced at his trial. In this context the contribution of the exclusionary rule, if any, to the effectuation of the Fourth Amendment is minimal, and the substantial societal costs of application of the rule persist with special force.

Accordingly, the judgments of the Courts of Appeals are *Reversed*.

[Concurring opinion of BURGER, C.J. omitted]

MR. JUSTICE BRENNAN, with whom MR. JUSTICE MARSHALL concurs, dissenting.

The Court today holds "that where the State has provided an opportunity for full and fair litigation of a Fourth Amendment claim, a state prisoner may not be granted federal habeas corpus relief on the ground that evidence obtained in an unconstitutional search or seizure was introduced at his trial." To be sure, my Brethren are hostile to the continued vitality of the exclusionary rule as part and parcel of the Fourth Amendment's prohibition of unreasonable searches and seizures. But these cases, despite the veil of Fourth Amendment terminology employed by the Court, plainly do not involve any question of the right of a defendant to have evidence excluded from use against him in his criminal trial when that evidence was seized in contravention of rights ostensibly secured by the Fourth and Fourteenth Amendments. Rather, they involve the question of the availability of a *federal forum* for vindicating those federally guaranteed rights. Today's holding portends substantial evisceration of federal habeas corpus jurisdiction, and I dissent.

The Court's opinion does not specify the particular basis on which it denies federal habeas jurisdiction over claims of Fourth Amendment violations brought by state prisoners. The Court insists that its holding is based on the Constitution, but in light of the explicit language of 28 U.S.C. § 2254 (significantly not even mentioned by the Court), I can only presume that the Court intends to be understood to hold either that

differences in institutional environment and the unsympathetic attitude to federal constitutional claims of some state judges in years past, we are unwilling to assume that there now exists a general lack of appropriate sensitivity to constitutional rights in the trial and appellate courts of the several States. State courts, like federal courts, have a constitutional obligation to safeguard personal liberties and to uphold federal law. Moreover, the argument that federal judges are more expert in applying federal constitutional law is especially unpersuasive in the context of search-and-seizure claims, since they are dealt with on a daily basis by trial level judges in both systems. In sum, there is "no intrinsic reason why the fact that a man is a federal judge should make him more competent, or conscientious, or learned with respect to the [consideration of Fourth Amendment claims] than his neighbor in the state courthouse." Bator, *Finality in Criminal Law and Federal Habeas Corpus For State Prisoners*, 76 Harv.L.Rev. 441 (1963).

respondents are not, as a matter of statutory construction, "in custody in violation of the Constitution or laws ... of the United States," or that " 'considerations of comity and concern for the orderly administration of criminal justice,' " are sufficient to allow this Court to rewrite jurisdictional statutes enacted by Congress. Neither ground of decision is tenable; the former is simply illogical, and the latter is an arrogation of power committed solely to the Congress.

I

Much of the Court's analysis implies that respondents are not entitled to habeas relief because they are not being unconstitutionally detained. Although purportedly adhering to the principle that the Fourth and Fourteenth Amendments "require exclusion" of evidence seized in violation of their commands, the Court informs us that there has merely been a "view" in our cases that "the effectuation of the Fourth Amendment ... requires the granting of habeas corpus relief when a prisoner has been convicted in state court on the basis of evidence obtained in an illegal search or seizure ..." Applying a "balancing test," the Court then concludes that this "view" is unjustified and that the policies of the Fourth Amendment would not be implemented if claims to the benefits of the exclusionary rule were cognizable in collateral attacks on state-court convictions.

* * *

Under *Mapp v. Ohio*, 367 U.S. 643, 81 S.Ct. 1684 (1961), as a matter of federal constitutional law, a state court *must* exclude evidence from the trial of an individual whose Fourth and Fourteenth Amendment rights were violated by a search or seizure that directly or indirectly resulted in the acquisition of that evidence. As *United States v. Calandra*, 414 U.S. 338, 94 S.Ct. 613 (1974), reaffirmed, "evidence obtained in violation of the Fourth Amendment cannot be used in a criminal proceeding against the victim of the illegal search and seizure." When a state court admits such evidence, it has committed a *constitutional* error, and unless that error is harmless under federal standards, it follows ineluctably that the defendant has been placed "in custody in violation of the Constitution" within the comprehension of 28 U.S.C. § 2254. In short, it escapes me as to what logic can support the assertion that the defendant's unconstitutional confinement obtains during the process of direct review, no matter how long that process takes, but that the unconstitutionality then suddenly dissipates at the moment the claim is asserted in a collateral attack on the conviction.

The only conceivable rationale upon which the Court's "constitutional" thesis might rest is the statement that "the [exclusionary] rule is not a personal constitutional right.... Instead, 'the rule is a judicially created remedy designed to safeguard Fourth Amendment rights generally through its deterrent effect.' " Although my dissent in *Calandra* rejected, in light of contrary decisions establishing the role of the exclusionary rule, the premise that an individual has no constitutional right to have unconstitutionally seized evidence excluded from all use by the government, I need not dispute that point here. For today's holding is not logically defensible even under *Calandra*. However, the Court reinterprets *Mapp*, and whatever the rationale now attributed to *Mapp*'s holding or the purpose ascribed to the exclusionary rule, the prevailing constitutional *rule* is that unconstitutionally seized evidence *cannot be admitted* in the criminal trial of a person whose federal constitutional rights were violated by the search or seizure. The erroneous admission of such evidence is a violation of the Federal Constitution—*Mapp* inexorably means at least this much, or there would be no basis for applying the exclusionary rule in state criminal proceedings—and an accused against whom such evidence is admitted has been convicted in derogation of rights mandated by, and is "in custody in violation," of the Constitution of the United States. Indeed, since state courts violate the strictures of the Federal Constitution by admitting such evidence, then even if federal habeas review did not directly effectuate Fourth Amendment values, a proposition I deny, that review would nevertheless serve to effectuate what is concededly a constitutional principle concerning admissibility of evidence at trial.

     * * *

II

Therefore, the real ground of today's decision—a ground that is particularly troubling in light of its portent for habeas jurisdiction generally—is the Court's novel reinterpretation of the habeas statutes; this would read the statutes as requiring the district courts routinely to deny habeas relief to prisoners "in custody in violation of the Constitution or laws ... of the United States" as a matter of judicial "discretion"—a "discretion" judicially manufactured today contrary to the express statutory language—because such claims are "different in kind" from other constitutional violations in that they "do not 'impugn the integrity of the fact-finding process,'" and because application of such constitutional strictures "often frees the guilty." Much in the Court's opinion suggests that a construction of the habeas statutes to deny relief for non-"guilt-related" constitutional violations, based on this Court's vague notions of comity and federalism is the actual premise for today's decision, and although the Court attempts to bury its underlying premises in footnotes, those premises mark this case as a harbinger of future eviscerations of the habeas statutes that plainly does violence to congressional power to frame the statutory contours of habeas jurisdiction. For we are told that "[r]esort to habeas corpus, especially for purposes other than to assure that no innocent person suffers an unconstitutional loss of liberty, results in serious intrusions on values important to our system of government," including waste of judicial resources, lack of finality of criminal convictions, friction between the federal and state judiciaries, and incursions on "federalism." We are told that federal determination of Fourth Amendment claims merely involves "an issue that has no bearing on the basic justice of [the defendant's] incarceration," and that "the ultimate ques-

tion [in the criminal process should invariably be] guilt or innocence."
* * *

    * * *

I would address the Court's concerns for effective utilization of scarce judicial resources, finality principles, federal-state friction, and notions of "federalism" only long enough to note that such concerns carry no more force with respect to non-"guilt-related" constitutional claims than they do with respect to claims that affect the accuracy of the factfinding process. Congressional conferral of federal habeas jurisdiction for the purpose of entertaining petitions from state prisoners necessarily manifested a conclusion that such concerns could not be controlling, and any argument for discriminating among constitutional rights must therefore depend on the nature of the constitutional right involved.

The Court, focusing on Fourth Amendment rights as it must to justify such discrimination, thus argues that habeas relief for non-"guilt-related" constitutional claims is not mandated because such claims do not affect the "basic justice" of a defendant's detention; this is presumably because the "ultimate goal" of the criminal justice system is "truth and justice."[16] This denigration of constitutional guarantees and *constitutionally mandated procedures*, relegated by the Court to the status of mere utilitarian tools, must appall citizens taught to expect judicial respect and support for their constitutional rights. Even if punishment of the "guilty" were society's highest value—and procedural safeguards denigrated to this end—in a constitution that a majority of the Members of this Court would prefer, that is not the ordering of priorities under the Constitution forged by the Framers, and this Court's sworn duty is to uphold that Constitution and not to frame its own. The procedural safeguards mandated in the Framers' Constitution are not admonitions to be tolerated only to the extent they serve functional purposes that ensure that the "guilty" are punished and the "innocent" freed; rather, every guarantee enshrined in the Constitution, our basic charter and the guarantor of our most precious liberties, is by it endowed with an independent vitality and value, and this Court is not free to curtail those constitutional guarantees even to punish the most obviously guilty. Particular constitutional rights that do not affect the fairness of factfinding procedures cannot for that reason be denied at the trial itself. What possible justification then can there be for denying vindication of such rights on federal habeas when state courts do deny those rights at trial? To sanction disrespect and disregard for the Constitution in the name of protecting society from law-breakers is to make the government itself lawless and to subvert those values upon which our ultimate freedom and liberty depend. * * * Enforcement of Federal constitutional rights that redress constitutional violations directed against the "guilty" is a particular function of *federal* habeas review, lest

---

16. The Court also notes that "attention ... [is] diverted" when trial courts address exclusionary rule issues, and with the result that application of the rule "often frees the guilty." Of course, these "arguments" are true with respect to every constitutional guarantee governing administration of the criminal justice system.

judges trying the "morally unworthy" be tempted not to execute the supreme law of the land. State judges popularly elected may have difficulty resisting popular pressures not experienced by federal judges given lifetime tenure designed to immunize them from such influences, and the federal habeas statutes reflect the congressional judgment that such detached federal review is a salutary safeguard against *any* detention of an individual "in violation of the Constitution or laws ... of the United States."

Federal courts have the duty to carry out the congressionally assigned responsibility to shoulder the ultimate burden of adjudging whether detentions violate federal law, and today's decision substantially abnegates that duty. The Court does not, because it cannot, dispute that institutional constraints totally preclude any possibility that this Court can adequately oversee whether state courts have properly applied federal law, and does not controvert the fact that federal habeas jurisdiction is partially designed to ameliorate that inadequacy. Thus, although I fully agree that state courts "have a constitutional obligation to safeguard personal liberties and to uphold federal law," and that there is no "general lack of appropriate sensitivity to constitutional rights in the trial and appellate courts of the several States," I cannot agree that it follows that, as the Court today holds, federal-court determination of almost all Fourth Amendment claims of state prisoners should be barred and that state-court resolution of those issues should be insulated from the federal review Congress intended. * * *

　　　* * *

[JUSTICE WHITE, dissented but added that he "would join four or more other Justices in substantially limiting the reach of the exclusionary rule as presently administered under the Fourth Amendment in federal and state criminal trials."]

NOTE

1. *Withrow v. Williams.*

In *Withrow v. Williams*, 507 U.S. 680, 113 S.Ct. 1745 (1993), a closely divided Court refused to extend *Powell* to *Miranda* claims raised on federal habeas corpus. The majority distinguished *Powell* on the basis that *Miranda* protects fundamental trial rights and enhances the reliability of the guilt determination and that refusal to consider *Miranda* claims would not significantly lessen the habeas burden on the federal courts since the courts would still have to hear Fifth Amendment "voluntariness" claims based on the same facts supporting the *Miranda* claim. The Court had previously refused to extend *Powell* to claims under the Sixth and Fourteenth Amendments. See *Kimmelman v. Morrison*, 477 U.S. 365, 106 S.Ct. 2574 (1986) (ineffective assistance of counsel for failing to seek suppression of evidence); *Rose v. Mitchell*, 443 U.S. 545, 99 S.Ct. 2993 (1979) (equal protection).

HERRERA v. COLLINS

506 U.S. 390, 113 S.Ct. 853, 122 L.Ed.2d 203 (1993).

CHIEF JUSTICE REHNQUIST delivered the opinion of the Court.

Petitioner Leonel Torres Herrera was convicted of capital murder and sentenced to death in January 1982. He unsuccessfully challenged the conviction on direct appeal and state collateral proceedings in the Texas state courts, and in a federal habeas petition. In February 1992—10 years after his conviction—he urged in a second federal habeas petition that he was "actually innocent" of the murder for which he was sentenced to death, and that the Eighth Amendment's prohibition against cruel and unusual punishment and the Fourteenth Amendment's guarantee of due process of law therefore forbid his execution. He supported this claim with affidavits tending to show that his now-dead brother, rather than he, had been the perpetrator of the crime. Petitioner urges us to hold that this showing of innocence entitles him to relief in this federal habeas proceeding. We hold that it does not.

Shortly before 11 p.m. on an evening in late September 1981, the body of Texas Department of Public Safety Officer David Rucker was found by a passer-by on a stretch of highway about six miles east of Los Fresnos, Texas, a few miles north of Brownsville in the Rio Grande Valley. Rucker's body was lying beside his patrol car. He had been shot in the head.

At about the same time, Los Fresnos Police Officer Enrique Carrisalez observed a speeding vehicle traveling west towards Los Fresnos, away from the place where Rucker's body had been found, along the same road. Carrisalez, who was accompanied in his patrol car by Enrique Hernandez, turned on his flashing red lights and pursued the speeding vehicle. After the car had stopped briefly at a red light, it signaled that it would pull over and did so. The patrol car pulled up behind it. Carrisalez took a flashlight and walked toward the car of the speeder. The driver opened his door and exchanged a few words with Carrisalez before firing at least one shot at Carrisalez' chest. The officer died nine days later.

Petitioner Herrera was arrested a few days after the shootings and charged with the capital murder of both Carrisalez and Rucker. He was tried and found guilty of the capital murder of Carrisalez in January 1982, and sentenced to death. In July 1982, petitioner pleaded guilty to the murder of Rucker.

At petitioner's trial for the murder of Carrisalez, Hernandez, who had witnessed Carrisalez' slaying from the officer's patrol car, identified petitioner as the person who had wielded the gun. A declaration by Officer Carrisalez to the same effect, made while he was in the hospital, was also admitted. Through a license plate check, it was shown that the speeding car involved in Carrisalez' murder was registered to petitioner's "live-in" girlfriend. Petitioner was known to drive this car, and he had a set of keys to the car in his pants pocket when he was arrested. Hernandez identified the car as the vehicle from which the murderer had emerged to fire the fatal shot. He also testified that there had been only one person in the car that night.

The evidence showed that Herrera's Social Security card had been found alongside Rucker's patrol car on the night he was killed. Splatters of blood on the car identified as the vehicle involved in the shootings, and on petitioner's blue jeans and wallet were identified as type A blood—the same type which Rucker had. (Herrera has type O blood.) Similar evidence with respect to strands of hair found in the car indicated that the hair was Rucker's and not Herrera's. A handwritten letter was also found on the person of petitioner when he was arrested, which strongly implied that he had killed Rucker.[1]

Petitioner appealed his conviction and sentence, arguing, among other things, that Hernandez' and Carrisalez' identifications were unreliable and improperly admitted. The Texas Court of Criminal Appeals affirmed, and we denied certiorari. Petitioner's application for state habeas relief was denied. Petitioner then filed a federal habeas petition, again challenging the identifications offered against him at trial. This petition was denied, and we again denied certiorari.

Petitioner next returned to state court and filed a second habeas petition, raising, among other things, a claim of "actual innocence" based on newly discovered evidence. In support of this claim petitioner presented the affidavits of Hector Villarreal, an attorney who had represented petitioner's brother, Raul Herrera, Sr., and of Juan Franco Palacious, one of Raul, Senior's former cellmates. Both individuals claimed that Raul, Senior, who died in 1984, had told them that he—and not petitioner—had killed Officers Rucker and Carrisalez.[2] The State District Court denied

---

1. The letter read:

"To whom it may concern: I am terribly sorry for those I have brought grief to their lives. Who knows why? We cannot change the future's problems with problems from the past. What I did was for a cause and purpose. One law runs others, and in the world we live in, that's the way it is.

"I'm not a tormented person. . . . I believe in the law. What would it be without this [sic] men that risk their lives for others, and that's what they should be doing—protecting life, property, and the pursuit of happiness. Sometimes, the law gets too involved with other things that profit them. The most laws that they make for people to break them, in other words, to encourage crime.

"What happened to Rucker was for a certain reason. I knew him as Mike Tatum. He was in my business, and he violated some of its laws and suffered the penalty, like the one you have for me when the time comes.

"My personal life, which has been a conspiracy since my high school days, has nothing to do with what has happened. The other officer that became part of our lives, me and Rucker's (Tatum), that night had not to do in this [sic]. He was out to do what he had to do, protect, but that's life. There's a lot of us that wear different faces in lives every day, and that is what causes problems for all. [Unintelligible word].

"You have wrote all you want of my life, but think about yours, also. [Signed Leonel Herrera]. * * *"

2. Villarreal's affidavit is dated December 11, 1990. He attested that while he was representing Raul, Senior on a charge of attempted murder in 1984, Raul, Senior had told him that he, petitioner, their father, Officer Rucker, and the Hidalgo County Sheriff were involved in a drug-

this application, finding that "no evidence at trial remotely suggest[ed] that anyone other than [petitioner] committed the offense." The Texas Court of Criminal Appeals affirmed, and we denied certiorari.

In February 1992, petitioner lodged the instant habeas petition—his second—in federal court, alleging, among other things, that he is innocent of the murders of Rucker and Carrisalez, and that his execution would thus violate the Eighth and Fourteenth Amendments. In addition to proffering the above affidavits, petitioner presented the affidavits of Raul Herrera, Jr., Raul Senior's son, and Jose Ybarra, Jr., a schoolmate of the Herrera brothers. Raul, Junior, averred that he had witnessed his father shoot Officers Rucker and Carrisalez and petitioner was not present. Raul, Junior, was nine years old at the time of the killings. Ybarra alleged that Raul, Senior, told him one summer night in 1983 that he had shot the two police officers. Petitioner alleged that law enforcement officials were aware of this evidence, and had withheld it in violation of *Brady v. Maryland*, 373 U.S. 83, 83 S.Ct. 1194 (1963).

The District Court * * * granted petitioner's request for a stay of execution so that he could present his claim of actual innocence, along with the Raul, Junior, and Ybarra affidavits, in state court. Although it initially dismissed petitioner's *Brady* claim on the ground that petitioner had failed to present "any evidence of withholding exculpatory material by the prosecution," the District Court also granted an evidentiary hearing on this claim after reconsideration.

The Court of Appeals vacated the stay of execution. It agreed with the District Court's initial conclusion that there was no evidentiary basis for petitioner's *Brady* claim, and found disingenuous petitioner's attempt to couch his claim of actual innocence in *Brady* terms. Absent an accompanying constitutional violation, the Court of Appeals held that petitioner's claim of actual innocence was not cognizable * * *[4] We granted certiorari, and the Texas Court of Criminal Appeals stayed petitioner's execution. We now affirm.

Petitioner asserts that the Eighth and Fourteenth Amendments to the United States Constitution prohibit the execution of a person who is innocent of the crime for which he was convicted. This proposition has an elemental appeal, as would the similar proposition that the Constitution prohibits the imprisonment of one who is innocent of the crime for which

---

trafficking scheme; that he was the one who had shot Officers Rucker and Carrisalez; that he did not tell anyone about this because he thought petitioner would be acquitted; and that after petitioner was convicted and sentenced to death, he began blackmailing the Hidalgo County Sheriff. According to Villarreal, Raul, Senior, was killed by Jose Lopez, who worked with the sheriff on drug-trafficking matters and was present when Raul, Senior, murdered Rucker and Carrisalez, to silence him.

Palacious' affidavit is dated December 10, 1990. He attested that while he and Raul, Senior, shared a cell together in the Hidalgo County jail in 1984, Raul, Senior, told him that he had shot Rucker and Carrisalez.

4. After the Court of Appeals vacated the stay of execution, petitioner attached a new affidavit by Raul, Junior, to his petition for rehearing, which was denied. The affidavit alleges that during petitioner's trial, various law enforcement officials and the Hidalgo County Sheriff told Raul, Junior, not to say what happened on the night of the shootings and threatened his family.

he was convicted. After all, the central purpose of any system of criminal justice is to convict the guilty and free the innocent. But the evidence upon which petitioner's claim of innocence rests was not produced at his trial, but rather eight years later. In any system of criminal justice, "innocence" or "guilt" must be determined in some sort of a judicial proceeding. Petitioner's showing of innocence, and indeed his constitutional claim for relief based upon that showing, must be evaluated in the light of the previous proceedings in this case, which have stretched over a span of 10 years.

A person when first charged with a crime is entitled to a presumption of innocence, and may insist that his guilt be established beyond a reasonable doubt. *In re Winship*, 397 U.S. 358, 90 S.Ct. 1068 (1970). Other constitutional provisions also have the effect of ensuring against the risk of convicting an innocent person. [The CHIEF JUSTICE cited cases upholding various rights, including: the right to confront adverse witnesses; the right to compulsory process; the right to effective assistance of counsel; the right to jury trial; the right to have the prosecution disclose exculpatory evidence; the right to fair trial in a fair tribunal.] In capital cases, we have required additional protections because of the nature of the penalty at stake. All of these constitutional safeguards, of course, make it more difficult for the State to rebut and finally overturn the presumption of innocence which attaches to every criminal defendant. But we have also observed that "[d]ue process does not require that every conceivable step be taken, at whatever cost, to eliminate the possibility of convicting an innocent person." *Patterson v. New York*, 432 U.S. 197, 97 S.Ct. 2319 (1977). To conclude otherwise would all but paralyze our system for enforcement of the criminal law.

Once a defendant has been afforded a fair trial and convicted of the offense for which he was charged, the presumption of innocence disappears. Here, it is not disputed that the State met its burden of proving at trial that petitioner was guilty of the capital murder of Officer Carrisalez beyond a reasonable doubt. Thus, in the eyes of the law, petitioner does not come before the Court as one who is "innocent," but, on the contrary, as one who has been convicted by due process of law of two brutal murders.

Based on affidavits here filed, petitioner claims that evidence never presented to the trial court proves him innocent notwithstanding the verdict reached at his trial. Such a claim is not cognizable in the state courts of Texas. For to obtain a new trial based on newly discovered evidence, a defendant must file a motion within 30 days after imposition or suspension of sentence. Tex.Rule App.Proc. 31(a)(1) (1992). The Texas courts have construed this 30–day time limit as jurisdictional.

Claims of actual innocence based on newly discovered evidence have never been held to state a ground for federal habeas relief absent an independent constitutional violation occurring in the underlying state criminal proceeding. Chief Justice WARREN made this clear in *Townsend v. Sain*, 372 U.S. 293, 83 S.Ct. 745 (1963) (emphasis added):

> "Where newly discovered evidence is alleged in a habeas application, evidence which could not reasonably have been presented to the state trier of facts, the federal court must grant an evidentiary hearing. Of course, such evidence must bear upon the constitutionality of the applicant's detention; *the existence merely of newly discovered evidence relevant to the guilt of a state prisoner is not a ground for relief on federal habeas corpus.*"

This rule is grounded in the principle that federal habeas courts sit to ensure that individuals are not imprisoned in violation of the Constitution—not to correct errors of fact.

More recent authority construing federal habeas statutes speaks in a similar vein. "Federal courts are not forums in which to relitigate state trials." *Barefoot v. Estelle*, 463 U.S. 880, 103 S.Ct. 3383 (1983). The guilt or innocence determination in state criminal trials is "a decisive and portentous event." *Wainwright v. Sykes*, 433 U.S. 72, 97 S.Ct. 2497 (1977). "Society's resources have been concentrated at that time and place in order to decide, within the limits of human fallibility, the question of guilt or innocence of one of its citizens." Few rulings would be more disruptive of our federal system than to provide for federal habeas review of freestanding claims of actual innocence.

Our decision in *Jackson v. Virginia*, 443 U.S. 307, 99 S.Ct. 2781 (1979), comes as close to authorizing evidentiary review of a state-court conviction on federal habeas as any of our cases. There, we held that a federal habeas court may review a claim that the evidence adduced at a state trial was not sufficient to convict a criminal defendant beyond a reasonable doubt. But in so holding, we emphasized:

> "[T]his inquiry does not require a court to 'ask itself whether *it* believes that the evidence at the trial established guilt beyond a reasonable doubt.' Instead, the relevant question is whether, after viewing the evidence in the light most favorable to the prosecution, *any* rational trier of fact could have found the essential elements of the crime beyond a reasonable doubt. This familiar standard gives full play to the responsibility of the trier of fact fairly to resolve conflicts in the testimony, to weigh the evidence, and to draw reasonable inferences from basic facts to ultimate facts." (emphasis in original).

We specifically noted that "the standard announced ... does not permit a court to make its own subjective determination of guilt or innocence."

The type of federal habeas review sought by petitioner here is different in critical respects than that authorized by *Jackson*. First, the *Jackson* inquiry is aimed at determining whether there has been an independent constitutional violation—*i.e.*, a conviction based on evidence that fails to meet the *Winship* standard. Thus, federal habeas courts act in their historic capacity—to assure that the habeas petitioner is not being held in violation of his or her federal constitutional rights. Second, the sufficiency of the evidence review authorized by *Jackson* is limited to "record evidence." *Jackson* does not extend to nonrecord evidence, including newly discovered evidence. Finally, the *Jackson* inquiry does not focus on whether the trier of fact made the correct guilt or innocence determination, but rather whether it made a rational decision to convict or acquit.

Petitioner is understandably imprecise in describing the sort of federal relief to which a suitable showing of actual innocence would entitle him. In his brief he states that the federal habeas court should have "an important initial opportunity to hear the evidence and resolve the merits of Petitioner's claim." Acceptance of this view would presumably require the habeas court to hear testimony from the witnesses who testified at trial as well as those who made the statements in the affidavits which petitioner has presented, and to determine anew whether or not petitioner is guilty of the murder of Officer Carrisalez. Indeed, the dissent's approach differs little from that hypothesized here.

The dissent would place the burden on petitioner to show that he is "probably" innocent. Although petitioner would not be entitled to discovery "as a matter of right," the District Court would retain its "discretion to order discovery ... when it would help the court make a reliable determination with respect to the prisoner's claim." And although the District Court would not be required to hear testimony from the witnesses who testified at trial or the affiants upon whom petitioner relies, the dissent would allow the District Court to do so "if the petition warrants a hearing." At the end of the day, the dissent would have the District Court "make a case-by-case determination about the reliability of the newly discovered evidence under the circumstances," and then "weigh the evidence in favor of the prisoner against the evidence of his guilt."

The dissent fails to articulate the relief that would be available if petitioner were to meets its "probable innocence" standard. Would it be commutation of petitioner's death sentence, new trial, or unconditional release from imprisonment? The typical relief granted in federal habeas corpus is a conditional order of release unless the State elects to retry the successful habeas petitioner, or in a capital case a similar conditional order vacating the death sentence. Were petitioner to satisfy the dissent's "probable innocence" standard, therefore, the District Court would presumably be required to grant a conditional order of relief, which would in effect require the State to retry petitioner 10 years after his first trial, not because of any constitutional violation which had occurred at the first trial, but simply because of a belief that in light of petitioner's new-found evidence a jury might find him not guilty at a second trial.

Yet there is no guarantee that the guilt or innocence determination would be any more exact. To the contrary, the passage of time only diminishes the reliability of criminal adjudications. * * *

    * * *

Petitioner asserts that this case is different because he has been sentenced to death. But we have "refused to hold that the fact that a death sentence has been imposed requires a different standard of review on federal habeas corpus." *Murray v. Giarratano*, 492 U.S. 1, 109 S.Ct. 2765 (1989) (plurality opinion). We have, of course, held that the Eighth Amendment requires increased reliability of the process by which capital punishment may be imposed. But petitioner's claim does not fit well into the doctrine of these cases, since, as we have pointed out, it is far from clear that a second trial 10 years after the first trial would produce a more reliable result.

Perhaps mindful of this, petitioner urges not that he necessarily receive a new trial, but that his death sentence simply be vacated if a federal habeas court deems that a satisfactory showing of "actual innocence" has been made. But such a result is scarcely logical; petitioner's claim is not that some error was made in imposing a capital sentence upon him, but that a fundamental error was made in finding him guilty of the underlying murder in the first place. It would be a rather strange jurisprudence, in these circumstances, which held that under our Constitution he could not be executed, but that he could spend the rest of his life in prison.

> * * *

Alternatively, petitioner invokes the Fourteenth Amendment's guarantee of due process of law in support of his claim that his showing of actual innocence entitles him to a new trial, or at least to a vacation of his death sentence. "[B]ecause the States have considerable expertise in matters of criminal procedure and the criminal process is grounded in centuries of common-law tradition," we have "exercis[ed] substantial deference to legislative judgments in this area." *Medina v. California*, 505 U.S. 437, 112 S.Ct. 2572 (1992). Thus, we have found criminal process lacking only where it " 'offends some principle of justice so rooted in the traditions and conscience of our people as to be ranked as fundamental.' " (quoting *Patterson v. New York*, 432 U.S. 197, 97 S.Ct. 2319 (1977)). "Historical practice is probative of whether a procedural rule can be characterized as fundamental."

[The CHIEF JUSTICE reviewed the historical practice with regard to new trial motions. New trials in criminal cases were not granted in England until the end of the 17th century. The First Congress provided for new trials for "reasons for which new trials have usually been granted in courts of law," including newly discovered evidence. The early federal cases adhered to the common-law rule that a new trial could be granted only during the term of court in which the final judgment was entered. In 1934, the Court adopted a time limit—60 days after final judgment—for filing new trial motions based on newly discovered evidence, although, four years later, the Court excepted capital cases from the rule. In 1946, the Court, in Rule 33, set a 2–year time limit for filing new trial motions based on newly discovered evidence and abolished the exception for capital cases. A variety of rules developed in the states. Texas is one of 17 States that requires a new trial motion based on newly discovered evidence to be made within 60 days of judgment. One State adheres to the common-law rule and requires that such a motion be filed during the term in which judgment was rendered. Eighteen jurisdictions have time limits ranging between one and three years, with 10 States and the District of Columbia following the 2–year federal time limit. Only 15 States allow a new trial motion based on newly discovered evidence to be filed more than three years after conviction. Of these States, four have waivable time limits of less than 120 days, two have waivable time limits of more than 120 days, and nine States have no time limits.]

In light of the historical availability of new trials, our own amendments to Rule 33, and the contemporary practice in the States, we cannot say that Texas' refusal to entertain petitioner's newly discovered evidence eight years after his conviction transgresses a principle of fundamental fairness "rooted in the traditions and conscience of our people." *Patterson v. New York*. This is not to say, however, that petitioner is left without a forum to raise his actual innocence claim. For under Texas law, petitioner may file a request for executive clemency. Clemency is deeply rooted in our Anglo–American tradition of law, and is the historic remedy for preventing miscarriages of justice where judicial process has been exhausted.

* * *

Of course, although the Constitution vests in the President a pardon power, it does not require the States to enact a clemency mechanism. Yet since the British Colonies were founded, clemency has been available in America. The original States were reluctant to vest the clemency power in the executive. And although this power has gravitated toward the executive over time, several States have split the clemency power between the Governor and an advisory board selected by the legislature. Today, all 36 States that authorize capital punishment have constitutional or statutory provisions for clemency.

Executive clemency has provided the "fail safe" in our criminal justice system. It is an unalterable fact that our judicial system, like the human beings who administer it, is fallible. But history is replete with examples of wrongfully convicted persons who have been pardoned in the wake of after-discovered evidence establishing their innocence. In his classic work, Professor Edwin Borchard compiled 65 cases in which it was later determined that individuals had been wrongfully convicted of crimes. Clemency provided the relief mechanism in 47 of these cases; the remaining cases ended in judgments of acquittals after new trials. Recent authority confirms that over the past century clemency has been exercised frequently in capital cases in which demonstrations of "actual innocence" have been made.

In Texas, the Governor has the power, upon the recommendation of a majority of the Board of Pardons and Paroles, to grant clemency. The board's consideration is triggered upon request of the individual sentenced to death, his or her representative, or the Governor herself. In capital cases, a request may be made for a full pardon, a commutation of death sentence to life imprisonment or appropriate maximum penalty, or a reprieve of execution. The Governor has the sole authority to grant one reprieve in any capital case not exceeding 30 days.

The Texas clemency procedures contain specific guidelines for pardons on the ground of innocence. The board will entertain applications for a recommendation of full pardon because of innocence upon receipt of the following: "(1) a written unanimous recommendation of the current trial officials of the court of conviction; and/or (2) a certified order or judgment of a court having jurisdiction accompanied by certified copy of the findings of fact (if any); and (3) affidavits of witnesses upon which the finding of innocence is based." In this case, petitioner has apparently sought a 30-day reprieve from the Governor, but has yet to apply for a pardon, or even a commutation, on the ground of innocence or otherwise.

* * *

We may assume, for the sake of argument in deciding this case, that in a capital case a truly persuasive demonstration of "actual innocence" made after trial would render the execution of a defendant unconstitutional, and warrant federal habeas relief if there were no state avenue open to process such a claim. But because of the very disruptive effect that entertaining claims of actual innocence would have on the need for finality in capital cases, and the enormous burden that having to retry cases based on often stale evidence would place on the States, the threshold showing for such an assumed right would necessarily be extraordinarily high. The showing made by petitioner in this case falls far short of any such threshold.

Petitioner's newly discovered evidence consists of affidavits. In the new trial context, motions based solely upon affidavits are disfavored because the affiants' statements are obtained without the benefit of cross-examination and an opportunity to make credibility determinations. Petitioner's affidavits are particularly suspect in this regard because, with the exception of Raul Herrera, Jr.'s affidavit, they consist of hearsay. Likewise, in reviewing petitioner's new evidence, we are mindful that defendants often abuse new trial motions "as a method of delaying enforcement of just sentences." *United States v. Johnson,* 327 U.S. 106, 66 S.Ct. 464 (1946). Although we are not presented with a new trial motion *per se,* we believe the likelihood of abuse is as great—or greater—here.

The affidavits filed in this habeas proceeding were given over eight years after petitioner's trial. No satisfactory explanation has been given as to why the affiants waited until the 11th hour—and, indeed, until after the alleged perpetrator of the murders himself was dead—to make their statements. Equally troubling, no explanation has been offered as to why petitioner, by hypothesis an innocent man, pleaded guilty to the murder of Rucker.

Moreover, the affidavits themselves contain inconsistencies, and therefore fail to provide a convincing account of what took place on the night Officers Rucker and Carrisalez were killed. For instance, the affidavit of Raul, Junior, who was nine years old at the time, indicates that there were three people in the speeding car from which the murderer emerged, whereas Hector Villarreal attested that Raul, Senior, told him that there were two people in the car that night. Of course, Hernandez testified at petitioner's trial that the murderer was the only occupant of the car. The affidavits also conflict as to the direction in which the vehicle was heading when the murders took place and petitioner's whereabouts on the night of the killings.

Finally, the affidavits must be considered in light of the proof of petitioner's guilt at trial—proof which included two eyewitness identifications, numerous pieces of circumstantial evidence, and a handwritten letter in which petitioner apologized for killing the officers and offered to turn himself in under certain conditions. That proof, even when considered alongside petitioner's belated affidavits, points strongly to petitioner's guilt.

This is not to say that petitioner's affidavits are without probative value. Had this sort of testimony been offered at trial, it could have been weighed by the jury, along with the evidence offered by the State and petitioner, in deliberating upon its verdict. Since the statements in the affidavits contradict the evidence received at trial, the jury would have had to decide important issues of credibility. But coming 10 years after petitioner's trial, this showing of innocence falls far short of that which would have to be made in order to trigger the sort of constitutional claim which we have assumed, arguendo, to exist.

The judgment of the Court of Appeals is *affirmed*.

JUSTICE O'CONNOR, with whom JUSTICE KENNEDY joins, concurring.

I cannot disagree with the fundamental legal principle that executing the innocent is inconsistent with the Constitution. Regardless of the verbal formula employed—"contrary to contemporary standards of decency," (dissenting opinion), "shocking to the conscience," (dissenting opinion), or offensive to a " ' "principle of justice so rooted in the traditions and conscience of our people as to be ranked as fundamental," ' " (opinion of the Court) (quoting *Medina v. California*, 505 U.S. 437, 112 S.Ct. 2572 (1992), in turn quoting *Patterson v. New York*, 432 U.S. 197, 97 S.Ct. 2319 (1977))—the execution of a legally and factually innocent person would be a constitutionally intolerable event. Dispositive to this case, however, is an equally fundamental fact: Petitioner is not innocent, in any sense of the word.

As the Court explains, petitioner is not innocent in the eyes of the law because, in our system of justice, "the trial is the paramount event for determining the guilt or innocence of the defendant." In petitioner's case, that paramount event occurred 10 years ago. He was tried before a jury of his peers, with the full panoply of protections that our Constitution affords criminal defendants. At the conclusion of that trial, the jury found petitioner guilty beyond a reasonable doubt. Petitioner therefore does not appear before us as an innocent man on the verge of execution. He is instead a legally guilty one who, refusing to accept the jury's verdict, demands a hearing in which to have his culpability determined once again.

Consequently, the issue before us is not whether a State can execute the innocent. It is, as the Court notes, whether a fairly convicted and therefore legally guilty person is constitutionally entitled to yet another judicial proceeding in which to adjudicate his guilt anew, 10 years after conviction, notwithstanding his failure to demonstrate that constitutional error infected his trial. In most circumstances, that question would answer itself in the negative. Our society has a high degree of confidence in its criminal trials, in no small part because the Constitution offers unparalleled protections against convicting the innocent. The question similarly would be answered in the negative today, except for the disturbing nature of the claim before us. Petitioner contends not only that the Constitution's protections "sometimes fail" (dissenting opinion), but that their failure in his case will result in his execution—even though he is factually innocent and has evidence to prove it.

Exercising restraint, the Court and Justice WHITE assume for the sake of argument that, if a prisoner were to make an exceptionally strong showing of actual innocence, the execution could not go forward. Justice BLACKMUN, in contrast, would expressly so hold; he would also announce the precise burden of proof. Resolving the issue is neither necessary nor advisable in this case. The question is a sensitive and, to say the least, troubling one. It implicates not just the life of a single individual, but also the State's powerful and legitimate interest in punishing the guilty, and the nature of state-federal relations. Indeed, as the Court persuasively demonstrates, throughout our history the federal courts have assumed that they should not and could not intervene to prevent an execution so long as the prisoner had been convicted after a constitutionally adequate trial. The prisoner's sole remedy was a pardon or clemency.

Nonetheless, the proper disposition of this case is neither difficult nor troubling. No matter what the Court might say about claims of actual innocence today, petitioner could not obtain relief. The record overwhelmingly demonstrates that petitioner deliberately shot and killed Officers Rucker and Carrisalez the night of September 29, 1981; petitioner's new evidence is bereft of credibility. Indeed, despite its stinging criticism of the Court's decision, not even the dissent expresses a belief that petitioner might possibly be actually innocent. Nor could it: The record makes it abundantly clear that petitioner is not somehow the future victim of "simple murder" (dissenting opinion), but instead himself the established perpetrator of two brutal and tragic ones.

[Justice O'CONNOR reviewed the evidence, in particular, Herrera's note, and concluded there was no likelihood of actual innocence.]

Ultimately, two things about this case are clear. First is what the Court does not hold. Nowhere does the Court state that the Constitution permits the execution of an actually innocent person. Instead, the Court assumes for the sake of argument that a truly persuasive demonstration of actual innocence would render any such execution unconstitutional and that federal habeas relief would be warranted if no state avenue were open to process the claim. Second is what petitioner has not demonstrated. Petitioner has failed to make a persuasive showing of actual innocence. Not one judge—no state court judge, not the District Court Judge, none of the three judges of the Court of Appeals, and none of the Justices of this Court—has expressed doubt about petitioner's guilt. Accordingly, the Court has no reason to pass on, and appropriately reserves, the question whether federal courts may entertain convincing claims of actual innocence. That difficult question remains open. If the Constitution's guarantees of fair procedure and the safeguards of clemency and pardon fulfill their historical mission, it may never require resolution at all.

JUSTICE SCALIA, with whom JUSTICE THOMAS joins, concurring.

We granted certiorari on the question whether it violates due process or constitutes cruel and unusual punishment for a State to execute a person who, having been convicted of murder after a full and fair trial, later alleges that newly discovered evidence shows him to be "actually innocent." I would have preferred to decide that question, particularly since, as the Court's discussion shows, it is perfectly clear what the answer is: There is no basis in text, tradition, or even in contemporary practice (if that were enough) for finding in the Constitution a right to demand judicial consideration of newly discovered evidence of innocence brought forward after conviction. In saying that such a right exists, the dissenters apply nothing but their personal opinions to invalidate the rules of more than two-thirds of the States, and a Federal Rule of Criminal Procedure for which this Court itself is responsible. If the system that has been in place for 200 years (and remains widely approved) "shock[s]" the dissenters' consciences, perhaps they should doubt the calibration of their consciences, or, better still, the usefulness of "conscience shocking" as a legal test.

I nonetheless join the entirety of the Court's opinion, including the final portion—because there is no legal error in deciding a case by assuming, arguendo, that an asserted constitutional right exists, and because I can understand, or at least am accustomed to, the reluctance of the present Court to admit publicly that Our Perfect Constitution* lets stand any injustice, much less the execution of an innocent man who has received, though to no avail, all the process that our society has traditionally deemed adequate. With any luck, we shall avoid ever having to face this embarrassing question again, since it is improbable that evidence of innocence as convincing as today's opinion requires would fail to produce an executive pardon.

---

* See Monaghan, *Our Perfect Constitution*, 56 N.Y.U. L.Rev. 353 (1981).

My concern is that in making life easier for ourselves we not appear to make it harder for the lower federal courts, imposing upon them the burden of regularly analyzing newly-discovered-evidence-of-innocence claims in capital cases (in which event such federal claims, it can confidently be predicted, will become routine and even repetitive). A number of Courts of Appeals have hitherto held, largely in reliance on our unelaborated statement in *Townsend v. Sain*, 372 U.S. 293, 83 S.Ct. 745 (1963), that newly discovered evidence relevant only to a state prisoner's guilt or innocence is not a basis for federal habeas corpus relief. I do not understand it to be the import of today's decision that those holdings are to be replaced with a strange regime that assumes permanently, though only "*arguendo*," that a constitutional right exists, and expends substantial judicial resources on that assumption. The Court's extensive and scholarly discussion of the question presented in the present case does nothing but support our statement in *Townsend* and strengthen the validity of the holdings based upon it.

JUSTICE WHITE, concurring in the judgment.

In voting to affirm, I assume that a persuasive showing of "actual innocence" made after trial, even though made after the expiration of the time provided by law for the presentation of newly discovered evidence, would render unconstitutional the execution of petitioner in this case. To be entitled to relief, however, petitioner would at the very least be required to show that based on proffered newly discovered evidence and the entire record before the jury that convicted him, "no rational trier of fact could [find] proof of guilt beyond a reasonable doubt." *Jackson v. Virginia*, 443 U.S. 307, 99 S.Ct. 2781 (1979). For the reasons stated in the Court's opinion, petitioner's showing falls far short of satisfying even that standard, and I therefore concur in the judgment.

JUSTICE BLACKMUN, with whom JUSTICE STEVENS and JUSTICE SOUTER join with respect to Parts I–IV, dissenting.

Nothing could be more contrary to contemporary standards of decency, see *Ford v. Wainwright*, 477 U.S. 399, 106 S.Ct. 2595 (1986), or more shocking to the conscience, see *Rochin v. California*, 342 U.S. 165, 72 S.Ct. 205 (1952), than to execute a person who is actually innocent.

I therefore must disagree with the long and general discussion that precedes the Court's disposition of this case. That discussion, of course, is dictum because the Court assumes, "for the sake of argument in deciding this case, that in a capital case a truly persuasive demonstration of 'actual innocence' made after trial would render the execution of a defendant unconstitutional." Without articulating the standard it is applying, however, the Court then decides that this petitioner has not made a sufficiently persuasive case. Because I believe that in the first instance the District Court should decide whether petitioner is entitled to a hearing and whether he is entitled to relief on the merits of his claim, I would reverse the order of the Court of Appeals and remand this case for further proceedings in the District Court.

I

The Court's enumeration of the constitutional rights of criminal defendants surely is entirely beside the point. These protections sometimes fail. We really are being asked to decide whether the Constitution forbids the execution of a person who has been validly convicted and sentenced but who, nonetheless, can prove his innocence with newly discovered evidence. Despite the State of Texas' astonishing protestation to the contrary, I do not see how the answer can be anything but "yes."

A

The Eighth Amendment prohibits "cruel and unusual punishments." This proscription is not static but rather reflects evolving standards of decency. I think it is crystal clear that the execution of an innocent person is "at odds with contemporary standards of fairness and decency." *Spaziano v. Florida*, 468 U.S. 447, 104 S.Ct. 3154 (1984). Indeed, it is at odds with any standard of decency that I can imagine.

* * *[2]

Respondent and the United States as *amicus curiae* argue that the Eighth Amendment does not apply to petitioner because he is challenging his guilt, not his punishment. * * * Such reasoning, however, not only contradicts our decision in *Beck v. Alabama*, 447 U.S. 625, 100 S.Ct. 2382 (1980), but also fundamentally misconceives the nature of petitioner's argument. Whether petitioner is viewed as challenging simply his death sentence or also his continued detention, he still is challenging the State's right to punish him. Respondent and the United States would impose a clear line between guilt and punishment, reasoning that every claim that concerns guilt necessarily does not involve punishment. Such a division is far too facile. What respondent and the United States fail to recognize is that the legitimacy of punishment is inextricably intertwined with guilt.

Beck makes this clear. In *Beck*, the petitioner was convicted of the capital crime of robbery-intentional killing. Under Alabama law, however, the trial court was prohibited from giving the jury the option of convicting him of the lesser included offense of felony murder. We held that precluding the instruction injected an impermissible element of uncertainty into the guilt phase of the trial.

> "To insure that the death penalty is indeed imposed on the basis of 'reason rather than caprice or emotion,' we have invalidated procedural rules that tended to diminish the reliability of the sentencing determination. The same reasoning must apply to rules that diminish the reliability of the guilt determination. Thus, if the unavailability of

---

2. [While] [i]t also may violate the Eighth Amendment to imprison someone who is actually innocent * * *, this Court has noted that " 'death is a different kind of punishment from any other which may be imposed in this country.... From the point of view of the defendant, it is different in both its severity and its finality.' " *Beck v. Alabama*, 447 U.S. 625, 100 S.Ct. 2382 (1980), quoting *Gardner v. Florida*, 430 U.S. 349, 97 S.Ct. 1197 (1977) (opinion of STEVENS, J.). We are not asked to decide in this case whether petitioner's continued imprisonment would violate the Constitution if he actually is innocent, and I do not address that question.

a lesser included offense instruction enhances the risk of an unwarranted conviction, [the State] is constitutionally prohibited from withdrawing that option in a capital case."

The decision in *Beck* establishes that, at least in capital cases, the Eighth Amendment requires more than reliability in sentencing. It also mandates a reliable determination of guilt.

The Court also suggests that allowing petitioner to raise his claim of innocence would not serve society's interest in the reliable imposition of the death penalty because it might require a new trial that would be less accurate than the first. This suggestion misses the point entirely. The question is not whether a second trial would be more reliable than the first but whether, in light of new evidence, the result of the first trial is sufficiently reliable for the State to carry out a death sentence. Furthermore, it is far from clear that a State will seek to retry the rare prisoner who prevails on a claim of actual innocence. * * *

I believe it contrary to any standard of decency to execute someone who is actually innocent. Because the Eighth Amendment applies to questions of guilt or innocence, and to persons upon whom a valid sentence of death has been imposed I also believe that petitioner may raise an Eighth Amendment challenge to his punishment on the ground that he is actually innocent.

B

Execution of the innocent is equally offensive to the Due Process Clause of the Fourteenth Amendment. The majority's discussion misinterprets petitioner's Fourteenth Amendment claim as raising a procedural, rather than a substantive, due process challenge.

　　* * *

Petitioner's claim falls within our due process precedents. In *Rochin*, deputy sheriffs investigating narcotics sales broke into Rochin's room and observed him put two capsules in his mouth. The deputies attempted to remove the capsules from his mouth and, having failed, took Rochin to a hospital and had his stomach pumped. The capsules were found to contain morphine. The Court held that the deputies' conduct "shock[ed] the conscience" and violated due process. "Illegally breaking into the privacy of the petitioner, the struggle to open his mouth and remove what was there, the forcible extraction of his stomach's contents—this course of proceeding by agents of government to obtain evidence is bound to offend even hardened sensibilities. They are methods too close to the rack and the screw to permit of constitutional differentiation." The lethal injection that petitioner faces as an allegedly innocent person is certainly closer to the rack and the screw than the stomach pump condemned in *Rochin*. Execution of an innocent person is the ultimate "arbitrary impositio[n]." *Planned Parenthood of Southeastern Pa. v. Casey*, 505 U.S. 833, 112 S.Ct. 2791 (1992). It is an imposition from which one never recovers and for which one can never be compensated. Thus, I also believe that petitioner may raise a substantive due process challenge to his punishment on the ground that he is actually innocent.

[Justice BLACKMUN argued that a defendant who could show, based on all the evidence, that he or she was "probably innocent" should be entitled to relief. "When a defendant seeks to challenge the determination of guilt after he has been validly convicted and sentenced, it is fair to place on him the burden of proving his innocence, not just raising doubt about his guilt." The defendant raising an actual-innocence claim would not be entitled, as a matter of right, to discovery or a hearing with live witnesses, but the District Court would have the discretion to adopt such procedures. Applying this standard, Justice BLACKMUN would have reversed the order of the Court of Appeals and remanded the case to the District Court for a determination on the merits of petitioner's claim.]

I have voiced disappointment over this Court's obvious eagerness to do away with any restriction on the States' power to execute whomever and however they please. See *Coleman v. Thompson*, 501 U.S. 722, 111 S.Ct. 2546 (1991) (dissenting opinion). I have also expressed doubts about whether, in the absence of such restrictions, capital punishment remains constitutional at all. *Sawyer v. Whitley*, 505 U.S. 333, 112 S.Ct. 2514 (1992) (opinion concurring in the judgment). Of one thing, however, I am certain. Just as an execution without adequate safeguards is unacceptable, so too is an execution when the condemned prisoner can prove that he is innocent. The execution of a person who can show that he is innocent comes perilously close to simple murder.

SCHRIRO v. SUMMERLIN

542 U.S. 348, 124 S.Ct. 2519, 159 L.Ed.2d 442 (2004).

JUSTICE SCALIA delivered the opinion of the Court.

In this case, we decide whether *Ring v. Arizona,* 536 U.S. 584, 122 S.Ct. 2428 (2002), applies retroactively to cases already final on direct review.

I

In April 1981, Finance America employee Brenna Bailey disappeared while on a house call to discuss an outstanding debt with respondent Warren Summerlin's wife. That evening, an anonymous woman (later identified as respondent's mother-in-law) called the police and accused respondent of murdering Bailey. Bailey's partially nude body, her skull crushed, was found the next morning in the trunk of her car, wrapped in a bedspread from respondent's home. Police arrested respondent and later overheard him make incriminating remarks to his wife.

Respondent was convicted of first-degree murder and sexual assault. Arizona's capital sentencing provisions in effect at the time authorized the death penalty if one of several enumerated aggravating factors was present. Whether those aggravating factors existed, however, was determined by the trial judge rather than by a jury. In this case the judge, after a hearing, found two aggravating factors: a prior felony conviction involving use or threatened use of violence, and commission of the offense in an especially heinous, cruel, or depraved manner. Finding no mitigating factors, the judge imposed the death sentence. The Arizona Supreme Court affirmed on direct review.

Protracted state and federal habeas proceedings followed. While respondent's case was pending in the Ninth Circuit, we decided *Apprendi v. New Jersey,* 530 U.S. 466, 120 S.Ct. 2348 (2000), and *Ring v. Arizona, supra.* In *Apprendi,* we interpreted the constitutional due-process and jury-trial guarantees to require that, "[o]ther than the fact of a prior conviction, any fact that increases the penalty for a crime beyond the prescribed statutory maximum must be submitted to a jury, and proved beyond a reasonable doubt." In *Ring,* we applied this principle to a death sentence imposed under the Arizona sentencing scheme at issue here. We concluded that, because Arizona law authorized the death penalty only if an aggravating factor was present, *Apprendi* required the existence of such a factor to be proved to a jury rather than to a judge. We specifically overruled our earlier decision in *Walton v. Arizona,* 497 U.S. 639, 110 S.Ct. 3047 (1990), which had upheld an Arizona death sentence against a similar challenge.

The Ninth Circuit, relying on *Ring,* invalidated respondent's death sentence.[2] It rejected the argument that *Ring* did not apply because respondent's conviction and sentence had become final on direct review before *Ring* was decided. We granted certiorari.

II

When a decision of this Court results in a "new rule," that rule applies to all criminal cases still pending on direct review. *Griffith v. Kentucky,* 479 U.S. 314, 107 S.Ct. 708 (1987). As to convictions that are already final, however, the rule applies only in limited circumstances. New *substantive* rules generally apply retroactively. This includes decisions that narrow the scope of a criminal statute by interpreting its terms, see *Bousley v. United States,* 523 U.S. 614, 118 S.Ct. 1604 (1998), as well as constitutional determinations that place particular conduct or persons covered by the statute beyond the State's power to punish, see *Saffle v. Parks,* 494 U.S. 484, 110 S.Ct. 1257 (1990); *Teague v. Lane,* 489 U.S. 288, 109 S.Ct. 1060 (1989) (plurality opinion).[4] Such rules apply retroactively because they "necessarily carry a significant risk that a defendant stands convicted of 'an act that the law does not make criminal'" or faces a punishment that the law cannot impose upon him. *Bousley, supra.*

2. Because respondent filed his habeas petition before the effective date of the Antiterrorism and Effective Death Penalty Act of 1996, the provisions of that Act do not apply.

4. We have sometimes referred to rules of this latter type as falling under an exception to *Teague's* bar on retroactive application of procedural rules, see, *e.g., Horn v. Banks,* 536 U.S. 266, 122 S.Ct. 2147 (2002) *(per curiam);* they are more accurately characterized as substantive rules not subject to the bar.

New rules of procedure, on the other hand, generally do not apply retroactively. They do not produce a class of persons convicted of conduct the law does not make criminal, but merely raise the possibility that someone convicted with use of the invalidated procedure might have been acquitted otherwise. Because of this more speculative connection to innocence, we give retroactive effect to only a small set of " 'watershed rules of criminal procedure' implicating the fundamental fairness and accuracy of the criminal proceeding." *Saffle, supra* (quoting *Teague*). That a new procedural rule is "fundamental" in some abstract sense is not enough; the rule must be one "without which the likelihood of an accurate conviction is *seriously* diminished." *Id.* (emphasis added). This class of rules is extremely narrow, and "it is unlikely that any ... 'ha[s] yet to emerge.' " *Tyler v. Cain,* 533 U.S. 656, 121 S.Ct. 2478 (2001) (quoting *Sawyer v. Smith,* 497 U.S. 227, 110 S.Ct. 2822 (1990)).

The Ninth Circuit agreed with the State that *Ring* announced a new rule. It nevertheless applied the rule retroactively to respondent's case, relying on two alternative theories: first, that it was substantive rather than procedural; and second, that it was a "watershed" procedural rule entitled to retroactive effect. We consider each theory in turn.

A

A rule is substantive rather than procedural if it alters the range of conduct or the class of persons that the law punishes. In contrast, rules that regulate only the *manner of determining* the defendant's culpability are procedural.

Judged by this standard, *Ring's* holding is properly classified as procedural. *Ring* held that "a sentencing judge, sitting without a jury, [may not] find an aggravating circumstance necessary for imposition of the death penalty." Rather, "the Sixth Amendment requires that [those circumstances] be found by a jury." This holding did not alter the range of conduct Arizona law subjected to the death penalty. It could not have; it rested entirely on the Sixth Amendment's jury-trial guarantee, a provision that has nothing to do with the range of conduct a State may criminalize. Instead, *Ring* altered the range of permissible methods for determining whether a defendant's conduct is punishable by death, requiring that a jury rather than a judge find the essential facts bearing on punishment. Rules that allocate decisionmaking authority in this fashion are prototypical procedural rules. * * *

Respondent nevertheless argues that *Ring* is substantive because it modified the elements of the offense for which he was convicted. He relies on our statement in *Ring* that, "[b]ecause Arizona's enumerated aggravating factors operate as 'the functional equivalent of an element of a greater offense,' the Sixth Amendment requires that they be found by a jury." The Ninth Circuit agreed, concluding that *Ring* "reposition[ed] Arizona's aggravating factors as elements of the separate offense of capital murder and reshap[ed] the structure of Arizona murder law."

A decision that modifies the elements of an offense is normally substantive rather than procedural. New elements alter the range of conduct the statute punishes, rendering some formerly unlawful conduct lawful or vice versa. But that is not what *Ring* did; the range of conduct punished by death in Arizona was the same before *Ring* as after. *Ring* held that, *because* Arizona's statutory aggravators restricted (as a matter of state law) the class of death-eligible defendants, those aggravators *effectively were* elements for federal constitutional purposes, and so were subject to the procedural requirements the Constitution attaches to trial of elements. This Court's holding that, *because Arizona* has made a certain fact essential to the death penalty, that fact must be found by a jury, is not the same as *this Court's* making a certain fact essential to the death penalty. The former was a procedural holding; the latter would be substantive. The Ninth Circuit's conclusion that *Ring* nonetheless "reshap[ed] the structure of Arizona murder law" is particularly remarkable in the face of the Arizona Supreme Court's previous conclusion to the contrary.

B

Respondent argues in the alternative that *Ring* falls under the retroactivity exception for " 'watershed rules of criminal procedure' implicating the fundamental fairness and accuracy of the criminal proceeding." *Saffle* (quoting *Teague*). He offers several reasons why juries are more accurate factfinders, including the tendency of group deliberation to suppress individual eccentricities; the jury's protection from exposure to inadmissible evidence; and its better representation of the common sense of the community. The Ninth Circuit majority added others, including the claim that a judge might be too acclimated to capital sentencing and that he might be swayed by political pressure. Respondent further notes that common-law authorities praised the jury's factfinding ability.

The question here is not, however, whether the Framers believed that juries are more accurate factfinders than judges (perhaps so—they certainly thought juries were more independent). Nor is the question whether juries actually *are* more accurate factfinders than judges (again, perhaps so). Rather, the question is whether judicial factfinding so *"seriously* diminishe[s]" accuracy that there is an " 'impermissibly large risk' " of punishing conduct the law does not reach. *Teague, supra* (quoting *Desist v. United States,* 394 U.S. 244, 89 S.Ct. 1030 (1969) (Harlan, J., dissenting)) (emphasis added). The evidence is simply too equivocal to support that conclusion.

First, for every argument why juries are more accurate factfinders, there is another why they are less accurate. The Ninth Circuit dissent noted several, including juries' tendency to become confused over legal standards and to be influenced by emotion or philosophical predisposition. Members of this Court have opined that judicial sentencing may yield more consistent results because of judges' greater experience. See *Proffitt v. Florida,* 428 U.S. 242, 96 S.Ct. 2960 (1976) (joint opinion of STEWART,

POWELL, and STEVENS, JJ.). Finally, the mixed reception that the right to jury trial has been given in other countries, though irrelevant to the meaning and continued existence of that right under our Constitution, surely makes it implausible that judicial factfinding so "*seriously* dimin-ishe[s]" accuracy as to produce an " 'impermissibly large risk' " of injustice. When so many presumably reasonable minds continue to disagree over whether juries are better factfinders *at all,* we cannot confidently say that judicial factfinding *seriously* diminishes accuracy.

* * *

The dissent contends that juries are more accurate because they better reflect community standards in deciding whether, for example, a murder was heinous, cruel, or depraved. But the statute here does not condition death eligibility on whether the offense is heinous, cruel, or depraved *as determined by community standards.* It is easy to find enhanced accuracy in jury determination when one redefines the statute's substantive scope in such manner as to ensure that result. The dissent also advances several variations on the theme that death is different (or rather, "dramatically different"). Much of this analysis is not an application of *Teague,* but a rejection of it, in favor of a broader endeavor to "balance competing considerations." Even were we inclined to revisit *Teague* in this fashion, we would not agree with the dissent's conclusions. * * *

* * *

The right to jury trial is fundamental to our system of criminal procedure, and States are bound to enforce the Sixth Amendment's guarantees as we interpret them. But it does not follow that, when a criminal defendant has had a full trial and one round of appeals in which the State faithfully applied the Constitution as we understood it at the time, he may nevertheless continue to litigate his claims indefinitely in hopes that we will one day have a change of heart. *Ring* announced a new procedural rule that does not apply retroactively to cases already final on direct review. The contrary judgment of the Ninth Circuit is reversed, and the case is remanded for further proceedings consistent with this opinion.

It is so ordered.

JUSTICE BREYER, with whom JUSTICE STEVENS, JUSTICE SOUTER, and JUSTICE GINSBURG join, dissenting.

In *Ring v. Arizona,* 536 U.S. 584, 122 S.Ct. 2428 (2002), this Court held that a jury, not a judge, must make the findings necessary to qualify a person for punishment by death. In my view, that holding amounts to a "watershed" procedural ruling that a federal habeas court must apply when considering a constitutional challenge to a "final" death sentence— *i.e.,* a sentence that was already final on direct review when *Ring* was decided.

Teague v. Lane, 489 U.S. 288, 109 S.Ct. 1060 (1989) (plurality opinion), sets forth the relevant retroactivity criteria. A new procedural rule applies retroactively in habeas proceedings if the new procedure is (1) "implicit in the concept of ordered liberty," implicating "fundamental fairness," and (2) "central to an accurate determination of innocence or guilt," such that its absence "creates an impermissibly large risk that the innocent will be convicted." In the context of a death sentence, where the matter is not one of "innocence or guilt," the second criterion asks whether the new procedure is *"central to an accurate determination" that death is a legally appropriate punishment.* (emphasis added).

The majority does not deny that *Ring* meets the first criterion, that its holding is "implicit in the concept of ordered liberty." Rather, the majority focuses on whether *Ring* meets the second criterion: Is its rule "central to an accurate determination" that death is a legally appropriate punishment?

As I explained in my separate concurrence in *Ring,* I believe the Eighth Amendment demands the use of a jury in capital sentencing because a death sentence must reflect a community-based judgment that the sentence constitutes proper retribution. And a jury is significantly more likely than a judge to "express the conscience of the community on the ultimate question of life or death." *Witherspoon v. Illinois,* 391 U.S. 510, 88 S.Ct. 1770 (1968). As Justice STEVENS has pointed out,

> "Juries—comprised as they are of a fair cross section of the community—are more representative institutions than is the judiciary; they reflect more accurately the composition and experiences of the community as a whole, and inevitably make decisions based on community values more reliably, than can that segment of the community that is selected for service on the bench." *Spaziano v. Florida,* 468 U.S. 447, 104 S.Ct. 3154 (1984) (STEVENS, J., concurring in part and dissenting in part).

On this view of the matter, the right to have jury sentencing in the capital context is both a fundamental aspect of constitutional liberty and also significantly more likely to produce an accurate assessment of whether death is the appropriate punishment.

But my view is not the *Ring* majority's view. The majority held only that the jury must decide whether the special aggravating factors that make the offender *eligible* for death are present. And it rested its decision that a jury, not a judge, must make that determination upon the Court's Sixth Amendment holding in *Apprendi v. New Jersey,* 530 U.S. 466, 120 S.Ct. 2348 (2000) that "any fact that increases the penalty for a crime beyond the prescribed statutory maximum must be submitted to a jury, and proved beyond a reasonable doubt."

In this case, the majority says that *Ring's Apprendi*-related rule cannot satisfy *Teague's* accuracy-enhancing requirement * * * [I]t points out that for "every argument why juries are more accurate factfinders, there is another why they are less accurate." Hence, one cannot say "confidently" that "judicial factfinding *seriously* diminishes accuracy." (emphasis in original)....

The majority, however, overlooks * * * additional considerations that lead me to the opposite conclusion.

First, the factfinder's role in determining the applicability of aggravating factors in a death case is a special role that can involve, not simply the finding of brute facts, but also the making of death-related, community-based value judgments. The leading single aggravator charged in Arizona, for example, requires the factfinder to decide whether the crime was committed in an "especially heinous, cruel, or depraved manner." Three of the other four *Ring*-affected States [Colorado, Idaho and Nebraska] use a similar aggravator. Words like "especially heinous," "cruel," or "depraved"—particularly when asked in the context of a death sentence proceeding—require reference to community-based standards, standards that incorporate values. (Indeed, Nebraska's standard explicitly asks the factfinder to assess the defendant's conduct in light of "ordinary standards of morality and intelligence.") A jury is better equipped than a judge to identify and to apply those standards accurately.

Second, Teague's basic purpose strongly favors retroactive application of *Ring's* rule. *Teague's* retroactivity principles reflect the Court's effort to balance competing considerations. On the one hand, interests related to certain of the Great Writ's basic objectives—protecting the innocent against erroneous conviction or punishment and assuring fundamentally fair procedures—favor applying a new procedural rule retroactively. *Teague, supra.* So too does the legal system's commitment to "equal justice"— *i.e.,* to "assur[ing] a uniformity of ultimate treatment among prisoners." *Id.*

Where death-sentence-related factfinding is at issue, these considerations have unusually strong force. This Court has made clear that in a capital case "the Eighth Amendment requires a greater degree of accuracy ... than would be true in a noncapital case." *Gilmore v. Taylor,* 508 U.S. 333, 113 S.Ct. 2112 (1993). Hence, the risk of error that the law can tolerate is correspondingly diminished. At the same time, the "qualitative difference of death from all other punishments"—namely, its severity and irrevocability—"requires a correspondingly greater degree of scrutiny of the capital sentencing determination" than of other criminal judgments. *California v. Ramos,* 463 U.S. 992, 103 S.Ct. 3446 (1983).

Consider, too, the law's commitment to uniformity. Is treatment "uniform" when two offenders each have been sentenced to death through the use of procedures that we now know violate the Constitution—but one is allowed to go to his death while the other receives a new, constitutionally proper sentencing proceeding? Outside the capital sentencing context, one might understand the nature of the difference that the word "finality" implies: One prisoner is already serving a final sentence, the other's has not yet begun. But a death sentence is different in that it seems to be, and it is, an entirely future event—an event not yet undergone by either prisoner. And in respect to that event, both prisoners are, in every important respect, in the same position. I understand there is a "finality-based" difference. But given the dramatically different nature of death, that difference diminishes in importance.

Certainly the ordinary citizen will not understand the difference. That citizen will simply witness two individuals, both sentenced through the use of unconstitutional procedures, one individual going to his death, the other saved, all through an accident of timing. How can the Court square this spectacle with what it has called the "vital importance to the defendant and to the community that any decision to impose the death sentence be, and appear to be, based on reason"? *Beck v. Alabama,* 447 U.S. 625, 100 S.Ct. 2382 (1980).

Justice SCALIA'S observation, in his concurring opinion in *Ring,* underscores the point. He wrote there that "the repeated spectacle of a man's going to his death because *a judge* found that an aggravating factor existed" would undermine "our people's traditional . . . veneration for the protection of the jury in criminal cases." (emphasis in original). If that is so, it is equally so whether the *judge* found that aggravating factor before or after *Ring.*

On the other hand, *Teague* recognizes that important interests argue against, and indeed generally forbid, retroactive application of new procedural rules. These interests include the "interest in insuring that there will at some point be the certainty that comes with an end to litigation"; the desirability of assuring that "attention will ultimately be focused not on whether a conviction was free from error but rather on whether the prisoner can be restored to a useful place in the community"; and the fact that society does not have endless resources to spend upon retrials, which (where witnesses have become unavailable and other evidence stale) may well produce unreliable results. Comity interests and respect for state autonomy point in the same direction.

Certain of these interests are unusually weak where capital sentencing proceedings are at issue. Retroactivity here, for example, would not require inordinate expenditure of state resources. A decision making *Ring* retroactive would affect approximately 110 individuals on death row. This number, however large in absolute terms, is small compared with the approximately 1.2 million individuals presently confined in state prisons. Consequently, the impact on resources is likely to be much less than if a rule affecting the ordinary criminal process were made retroactive.

Further, where the issue is "life or death," the concern that "attention . . . ultimately" should be focused "on whether the prisoner can be restored to a useful place in the community" is barely relevant. *Mackey v. United States,* 401 U.S. 667, 91 S.Ct. 1160 (1971) (Harlan, J., concuurring in two judgments and dissenting in one). Finally, I believe we should discount ordinary finality interests in a death case, for those interests are comparative in nature and death-related collateral proceedings, in any event, may stretch on for many years regardless.

    * * *

As I have pointed out, the majority does not deny that *Ring's* rule makes *some* contribution to greater accuracy. It simply is unable to say "confidently" that the absence of *Ring's* rule creates an " ' "impermissibly large risk" ' " that the death penalty was improperly imposed. For the reasons stated, I believe that the risk is one that the law need not and should not tolerate. Judged in light of *Teague's* basic purpose, *Ring's* requirement that a jury, and not a judge, must apply the death sentence aggravators announces a watershed rule of criminal procedure that should be applied retroactively in habeas proceedings.

I respectfully dissent.

NOTES

1. *The meaning of "new rule."*

In *Schriro v. Summerlin,* there was no question that the defendant was seeking the benefit of a "new rule" since *Ring v. Arizona,* on which he relied, overruled a contrary precedent directly on point. However, in a number of other cases that have come before the Supreme Court, it has not been clear whether the rule on which the defendant relied was new. As noted in the Overview, *supra,* there is no obvious meaning to "new rule," and the Court has not been consistent in its definition and application of *Teague's* new rule doctrine. In *Teague,* the Court held that a decision announces a new rule "if the result was not dictated by precedent existing at the time the defendant's conviction became final," and if it "breaks new ground" or "imposes a new obligation on the States or the Federal Government." In *Sawyer v. Smith,* 497 U.S. 227, 110 S.Ct. 2822 (1990), the Court also defined a "new rule" as a ruling that decided a question susceptible to "debate among reasonable minds" or to which there were, or could have been, "reasonable, good-faith interpretations of existing precedents" reaching the contrary conclusion. Some justices have explained the "new rule" doctrine as holding that "if a state court has reasonably rejected the legal claim asserted by a habeas petitioner under existing law, then the claim seeks the benefit of a 'new' rule," *Wright v. West,* 505 U.S. 277, 291, 112 S.Ct. 2482, 2490 (1992) (Chief Justice Rehnquist, Justice Scalia and Justice Thomas). Other justices have asserted that "[t]o determine what counts as a new rule, *Teague* requires courts to ask whether the rule a habeas petitioner seeks can be meaningfully distinguished from that established by binding precedent at the time his state court conviction became final." *Wright v. West,* 505 U.S. at 304, 112 S.Ct. at 2497 (Justices Blackmun, Stevens and O'Connor).

2. *Problem 11–1.*

Defendant was convicted of murder, and he was sentenced to death after the prosecutor, in his closing argument, repeatedly assured the jury that they need not take complete responsibility for a death judgment, stating, *inter alia*:

> The law provides that if you find one of those circumstances then what you are doing as a juror, you yourself will not be sentencing Defendant to the electric chair. What you are saying to this Court, to the people of this Parish, to any appellate court, the Supreme Court of this State, the

Supreme Court possibly of the United States, that you the people as a fact finding body from all the facts and evidence you have heard in relationship to this man's conduct are of the opinion that there are aggravating circumstances as defined by the statute, by the State Legislature that this is a type of crime that deserves that penalty. It is merely a recommendation * * *

You are the people that are going to take the initial step and only the initial step and all you are saying to this court, to the people of this Parish, to this man, to all the Judges that are going to review this case after this day, is that you the people do not agree and will not tolerate an individual to commit such a heinous and atrocious crime to degrade such a fellow human being without the authority and the impact, the full authority and impact of the law of Louisiana. All you are saying is that this man from his actions could be prosecuted to the fullest extent of the law. No more and no less.

[I]f you are wrong in your decision believe me, believe me there will be others who will be behind you to either agree with you or to say you are wrong so I ask that you do have the courage of your convictions.

Shortly after Defendant's conviction became final, the Supreme Court decided *Caldwell v. Mississippi*, 472 U.S. 320, 105 S.Ct. 2633 (1985) [Chapter 10]. In *Caldwell*, the Court held that the Eighth Amendment is violated when a jury is led to believe that responsibility for determining the appropriateness of the defendant's penalty rests elsewhere. After exhausting state remedies, Defendant has filed for federal habeas corpus, claiming that the prosecutor's argument violated his Eighth Amendment rights. What arguments should be made as to whether Defendant's claim is barred by *Teague*? See *Sawyer v. Smith*, 497 U.S. 227, 110 S.Ct. 2822 (1990).

WILLIAMS (TERRY) v. TAYLOR

529 U.S. 362, 120 S.Ct. 1495, 146 L.Ed.2d 389 (2000).

JUSTICE STEVENS announced the judgment of the Court and delivered the opinion of the Court with respect to Parts, I, III, and IV, and an opinion with respect to Parts II and V.*

The questions presented are whether Terry Williams' constitutional right to the effective assistance of counsel as defined in *Strickland v. Washington*, 466 U.S. 668, 104 S.Ct. 2052 (1984), was violated, and whether the judgment of the Virginia Supreme Court refusing to set aside his death sentence "was contrary to, or involved an unreasonable application of, clearly established Federal law, as determined by the Supreme Court of the United States," within the meaning of 28 U.S.C. § 2254(d)(1). We answer both questions affirmatively.

I

On November 3, 1985, Harris Stone was found dead in his residence on Henry Street in Danville, Virginia. Finding no indication of a struggle,

---

* Justice SOUTER, Justice GINSBURG, and Justice BREYER join this opinion in its entirety. Justice O'CONNOR and Justice KENNEDY join Parts I, III, and IV of this opinion.

local officials determined that the cause of death was blood alcohol poisoning, and the case was considered closed. Six months after Stone's death, Terry Williams, who was then incarcerated in the "I" unit of the city jail for an unrelated offense, wrote a letter to the police stating that he had killed " 'that man down on Henry Street' " and also stating that he " 'did it' " to that " 'lady down on West Green Street' " and was " 'very sorry.' " The letter was unsigned, but it closed with a reference to "I cell." The police readily identified Williams as its author, and, on April 25, 1986, they obtained several statements from him. In one Williams admitted that, after Stone refused to lend him " 'a couple of dollars,' " he had killed Stone with a mattock and took the money from his wallet. In September 1986, Williams was convicted of robbery and capital murder.

At Williams' sentencing hearing, the prosecution proved that Williams had been convicted of armed robbery in 1976 and burglary and grand larceny in 1982. The prosecution also introduced the written confessions that Williams had made in April. The prosecution described two auto thefts and two separate violent assaults on elderly victims perpetrated after the Stone murder. On December 4, 1985, Williams had started a fire outside one victim's residence before attacking and robbing him. On March 5, 1986, Williams had brutally assaulted an elderly woman on West Green Street—an incident he had mentioned in his letter to the police. That confession was particularly damaging because other evidence established that the woman was in a "vegetative state" and not expected to recover. Williams had also been convicted of arson for setting a fire in the jail while awaiting trial in this case. Two expert witnesses employed by the State testified that there was a "high probability" that Williams would pose a serious continuing threat to society.

The evidence offered by Williams' trial counsel at the sentencing hearing consisted of the testimony of Williams' mother, two neighbors, and a taped excerpt from a statement by a psychiatrist. One of the neighbors had not been previously interviewed by defense counsel, but was noticed by counsel in the audience during the proceedings and asked to testify on the spot. The three witnesses briefly described Williams as a "nice boy" and not a violent person. The recorded psychiatrist's testimony did little more than relate Williams' statement during an examination that in the course of one of his earlier robberies, he had removed the bullets from a gun so as not to injure anyone.

In his cross-examination of the prosecution witnesses, Williams' counsel repeatedly emphasized the fact that Williams had initiated the contact with the police that enabled them to solve the murder and to identify him as the perpetrator of the recent assaults, as well as the car thefts. In closing argument, Williams' counsel characterized Williams' confessional statements as "dumb," but asked the jury to give weight to the fact that he had "turned himself in, not on one crime but on four ... that the [police otherwise] would not have solved." The weight of defense counsel's closing, however, was devoted to explaining that it was difficult to find a reason why the jury should spare Williams' life.

The jury found a probability of future dangerousness and unanimously fixed Williams' punishment at death. The trial judge concluded that such punishment was "proper" and "just" and imposed the death sentence. The Virginia Supreme Court affirmed the conviction and sentence.
* * *

[Williams' petition for collateral relief in the state court was heard by the same judge who had presided over Williams' trial and sentencing. Williams claimed that his trial counsel had been ineffective, and, after two days of hearings, the judge found that Williams' conviction was valid, but that his trial attorneys had been ineffective during sentencing because their failure to discover and present significant mitigating evidence "did not measure up to the standard required under the holding of *Strickland v. Washington*, 466 U.S. 668, 104 S.Ct. 2052 (1984), and [if it had,] there is a reasonable probability that the result of the sentencing phase would have been different." The Virginia Supreme Court did not agree. It found that there was insufficient showing of prejudice and that the trial judge had misapplied the law in two respects. First, relying on *Lockhart v. Fretwell*, 506 U.S. 364, 113 S.Ct. 838 (1993), the court held that it was wrong for the trial judge to rely " 'on mere outcome determination' " when assessing prejudice. Second, it construed the trial judge's opinion as having "adopted a *per se* approach" that would establish prejudice whenever any mitigating evidence was omitted. The court then reviewed the prosecution evidence supporting the "future dangerousness" aggravating circumstance and Williams' criminal history and concluded that there was no reasonable possibility that the omitted evidence would have affected the jury's sentencing recommendation. Having exhausted his state remedies, Williams sought a federal writ of habeas corpus pursuant to 28 U.S.C. § 2254. The district judge granted penalty relief. finding that trial counsel's performance fell below the range of competence and prejudiced Williams' case and that the Virginia Supreme Court's contrary decision "was contrary to, or involved an unreasonable application of, clearly established Federal law" within the meaning of § 2254(d)(1). The Fourth Circuit, relying on its earlier decision in *Green v. French*, 143 F.3d 865 (4th Cir. 1998), reversed. It held that petitioner had failed to establish that the state court had " 'decided the question by interpreting or applying the relevant precedent in a manner that reasonable jurists would all agree is unreasonable.' "]

We granted certiorari and now reverse.

II

* * *

The warden here contends that federal habeas corpus relief is prohibited by the amendment to 28 U.S.C. § 2254, enacted as a part of the Antiterrorism and Effective Death Penalty Act of 1996 (AEDPA). The relevant portion of that amendment provides:

    "(d) An application for a writ of habeas corpus on behalf of a person in custody pursuant to the judgment of a State court shall not be granted with respect to any claim that was adjudicated on the merits in State court proceedings unless the adjudication of the claim—

    "(1) resulted in a decision that was contrary to, or involved an unreasonable application of, clearly established Federal law, as determined by the Supreme Court of the United States; ...."

In this case, the Court of Appeals applied the construction of the amendment that it had adopted in its earlier opinion in *Green v. French*. It read the amendment as prohibiting federal courts from issuing the writ unless:

    "(a) the state court decision is in 'square conflict' with Supreme Court precedent that is controlling as to law and fact or (b) if no such controlling decision exists, 'the state court's resolution of a question of pure law rests upon an objectively unreasonable derivation of legal principles from the relevant [S]upreme [C]ourt precedents, or if its decision rests upon an objectively unreasonable application of established principles to new facts,' " (quoting *Green*).

Accordingly, it held that a federal court may issue habeas relief only if "the state courts have decided the question by interpreting or applying the relevant precedent in a manner that reasonable jurists would all agree is unreasonable."

    We are convinced that that interpretation of the amendment is incorrect. It would impose a test for determining when a legal rule is clearly established that simply cannot be squared with the real practice of decisional law.[9] It would apply a standard for determining the "reasonableness" of state-court decisions that is not contained in the statute itself, and that Congress surely did not intend. And it would wrongly require the federal courts, including this Court, to defer to state judges' interpretations of federal law.

    As the Fourth Circuit would have it, a state-court judgment is "unreasonable" in the face of federal law only if all reasonable jurists would agree that the state court was unreasonable. Thus, in this case, for example, even if the Virginia Supreme Court misread our opinion in *Lockhart*, we could not grant relief unless we believed that none of the judges who agreed with the state court's interpretation of that case was a "reasonable jurist." But the statute says nothing about "reasonable judges," presumably because all, or virtually all, such judges occasionally commit error; they make decisions that in retrospect may be characterized

---

    9. * * * [W]e note that the Fourth Circuit's construction of the amendment's inquiry in this respect is especially problematic. It separates cases into those for which a "controlling decision" exists and those for which no such decision exists. The former category includes very few cases, since a rule is "controlling" only if it matches the case before the court both "as to law and fact," and most cases are factually distinguishable in some respect. A literal application of the Fourth Circuit test would yield a particularly perverse outcome in cases involving the *Strickland* rule for establishing ineffective assistance of counsel, since that case, which established the "controlling" rule of law on the issue, contained facts insufficient to show ineffectiveness.

as "unreasonable." Indeed, it is most unlikely that Congress would deliberately impose such a requirement of unanimity on federal judges. As Congress is acutely aware, reasonable lawyers and lawgivers regularly disagree with one another. Congress surely did not intend that the views of one such judge who might think that relief is not warranted in a particular case should always have greater weight than the contrary, considered judgment of several other reasonable judges.

The inquiry mandated by the amendment relates to the way in which a federal habeas court exercises its duty to decide constitutional questions; the amendment does not alter the underlying grant of jurisdiction in § 2254(a).[10] When federal judges exercise their federal-question jurisdiction under the "judicial Power" of Article III of the Constitution, it is "emphatically the province and duty" of those judges to "say what the law is." *Marbury v. Madison*, 1 Cranch 137 (1803). At the core of this power is the federal courts' independent responsibility—independent from its co-equal branches in the Federal Government, and independent from the separate authority of the several States—to interpret federal law. A construction of AEDPA that would require the federal courts to cede this authority to the courts of the States would be inconsistent with the practice that federal judges have traditionally followed in discharging their duties under Article III of the Constitution. If Congress had intended to require such an important change in the exercise of our jurisdiction, we believe it would have spoken with much greater clarity than is found in the text of AEDPA.

This basic premise informs our interpretation of both parts of § 2254(d)(1): first, the requirement that the determinations of state courts be tested only against "clearly established Federal law, as determined by the Supreme Court of the United States," and second, the prohibition on the issuance of the writ unless the state court's decision is "contrary to, or involved an unreasonable application of," that clearly established law. We address each part in turn.

The "clearly established law" requirement

In *Teague v. Lane*, 489 U.S. 288, 109 S.Ct. 1060 (1989), we held that the petitioner was not entitled to federal habeas relief because he was relying on a rule of federal law that had not been announced until after his state conviction became final. The antiretroactivity rule recognized in

---

10. Indeed, Congress roundly rejected an amendment to the bill eventually adopted that directly invoked the text of the jurisdictional grant, 28 U.S.C. § 2254(a) (providing that the federal courts "*shall entertain* an application for a writ of habeas corpus" (emphasis added)). The amendment read: "Notwithstanding any other provision of law, an application for a writ of habeas corpus in behalf of a person in custody pursuant to a judgment or order of a State court *shall not be entertained* by a court of the United States unless the remedies in the courts of the State are inadequate or ineffective to test the legality of the person's detention." (amendment of Sen. Kyl) (emphasis added). In speaking against the Kyl amendment, Senator Specter (a key proponent of the eventual habeas reform) explained that when "dealing with the question of jurisdiction of the Federal courts to entertain questions on Federal issues, on constitutional issues, I believe it is necessary that the Federal courts retain that jurisdiction as a constitutional matter."

Teague, which prohibits reliance on "new rules," is the functional equivalent of a statutory provision commanding exclusive reliance on "clearly established law." Because there is no reason to believe that Congress intended to require federal courts to ask both whether a rule sought on habeas is "new" under *Teague*—which remains the law—and also whether it is "clearly established" under AEDPA, it seems safe to assume that Congress had congruent concepts in mind. It is perfectly clear that AEDPA codifies *Teague* to the extent that *Teague* requires federal habeas courts to deny relief that is contingent upon a rule of law not clearly established at the time the state conviction became final.

* * *

To this, AEDPA has added, immediately following the "clearly established law" requirement, a clause limiting the area of relevant law to that "determined by the Supreme Court of the United States." 28 U.S.C. § 2254(d)(1). If this Court has not broken sufficient legal ground to establish an asked-for constitutional principle, the lower federal courts cannot themselves establish such a principle with clarity sufficient to satisfy the AEDPA bar. * * *

In the context of this case, we also note that, as our precedent interpreting *Teague* has demonstrated, rules of law may be sufficiently clear for habeas purposes even when they are expressed in terms of a generalized standard rather than as a bright-line rule. As Justice KENNEDY has explained:

> "If the rule in question is one which of necessity requires a case-by-case examination of the evidence, then we can tolerate a number of specific applications without saying that those applications themselves create a new rule ... Where the beginning point is a rule of this general application, a rule designed for the specific purpose of evaluating a myriad of factual contexts, it will be the infrequent case that yields a result so novel that it forges a new rule, one not dictated by precedent." *Wright v. West*, 505 U.S. 277, 112 S.Ct. 2482 (1992) (opinion concurring in judgment).

Moreover, the determination whether or not a rule is clearly established at the time a state court renders its final judgment of conviction is a question as to which the "federal courts must make an independent evaluation." *Wright* (O'Connor, J., concurring in judgment).

* * *

We are convinced that in the phrase, "clearly established law," Congress did not intend to modify that independent obligation.

The "contrary to, or an unreasonable application of," requirement

The message that Congress intended to convey by using the phrases, "contrary to" and "unreasonable application of" is not entirely clear. The prevailing view in the Circuits is that the former phrase requires de novo review of "pure" questions of law and the latter requires some sort of "reasonability" review of so-called mixed questions of law and fact.

We are not persuaded that the phrases define two mutually exclusive categories of questions. Most constitutional questions that arise in habeas corpus proceedings—and therefore most "decisions" to be made—require the federal judge to apply a rule of law to a set of facts, some of which may be disputed and some undisputed. For example, an erroneous conclusion that particular circumstances established the voluntariness of a confession, or that there exists a conflict of interest when one attorney represents multiple defendants, may well be described either as "contrary to" or as an "unreasonable application of" the governing rule of law.

* * *

The statutory text * * * does not obviously prescribe a specific, recognizable standard of review for dealing with either phrase. Significantly, it does not use any term, such as *"de novo"* or "plain error," that would easily identify a familiar standard of review. Rather, the text is fairly read simply as a command that a federal court not issue the habeas writ unless the state court was wrong as a matter of law or unreasonable in its application of law in a given case. The suggestion that a wrong state-court "decision"—a legal judgment rendered "after consideration of *facts, and . . . law,*" Black's Law Dictionary (emphasis added)—may no longer be redressed through habeas (because it is unreachable under the "unreasonable application" phrase) is based on a mistaken insistence that the § 2254(d)(1) phrases have not only independent, but mutually exclusive, meanings. Whether or not a federal court can issue the writ "under [the] 'unreasonable application' clause," the statute is clear that habeas may issue under § 2254(d)(1) if a state court "decision" is "contrary to . . . clearly established Federal law." We thus anticipate that there will be a variety of cases, like this one, in which both phrases may be implicated.

Even though we cannot conclude that the phrases establish "a body of rigid rules," they do express a "mood" that the federal judiciary must respect. In this respect, it seems clear that Congress intended federal judges to attend with the utmost care to state-court decisions, including all of the reasons supporting their decisions, before concluding that those proceedings were infected by constitutional error sufficiently serious to warrant the issuance of the writ. Likewise, the statute in a separate provision provides for the habeas remedy when a state-court decision "was based on an unreasonable determination of the facts *in light of the evidence presented in the State court proceeding.*" 28 U.S.C. § 2254(d)(2) (emphasis added). While this provision is not before us in this case, it provides relevant context for our interpretation of § 2254(d)(1); in this respect, it bolsters our conviction that federal habeas courts must make as the starting point of their analysis the state courts' determinations of fact, including that aspect of a "mixed question" that rests on a finding of fact. AEDPA plainly sought to ensure a level of "deference to the determinations of state courts," provided those determinations did not conflict with federal law or apply federal law in an unreasonable way. Congress wished to curb delays, to prevent "retrials" on federal habeas, and to give effect to state convictions to the extent possible under law. When federal courts are able to fulfill these goals within the bounds of the law, AEDPA instructs them to do so.

On the other hand, it is significant that the word "deference" does not appear in the text of the statute itself. Neither the legislative history, nor the statutory text, suggests any difference in the so-called "deference" depending on which of the two phrases is implicated. Whatever "deference" Congress had in mind with respect to both phrases, it surely is not a requirement that federal courts actually defer to a state-court application of the federal law that is, in the independent judgment of the federal court, in error. * * *

Our disagreement with Justice O'CONNOR about the precise meaning of the phrase "contrary to," and the word "unreasonable," is, of course, important, but should affect only a narrow category of cases. The simplest and first definition of "contrary to" as a phrase is "in conflict with." Webster's Ninth New Collegiate Dictionary. In this sense, we think the phrase surely capacious enough to include a finding that the state-court "decision" is simply "erroneous" or wrong. (We hasten to add that even "diametrically different" from, or "opposite" to, an established federal law would seem to include "decisions" that are wrong in light of that law.) And there is nothing in the phrase "contrary to"—as Justice O'CONNOR appears to agree—that implies anything less than independent review by the federal courts. Moreover, state-court decisions that do not "conflict" with federal law will rarely be "unreasonable" under either her reading of the statute or ours. We all agree that state-court judgments must be upheld unless, after the closest examination of the state-court judgment, a federal court is firmly convinced that a federal constitutional right has been violated. Our difference is as to the cases in which, at first-blush, a state-court judgment seems entirely reasonable, but thorough analysis by a federal court produces a firm conviction that that judgment is infected by constitutional error. In our view, such an erroneous judgment is "unreasonable" within the meaning of the act even though that conclusion was not immediately apparent.

In sum, the statute directs federal courts to attend to every state-court judgment with utmost care, but it does not require them to defer to the opinion of every reasonable state-court judge on the content of federal law. If, after carefully weighing all the reasons for accepting a state court's judgment, a federal court is convinced that a prisoner's custody—or, as in this case, his sentence of death—violates the Constitution, that independent judgment should prevail. Otherwise the federal "law as determined by the Supreme Court of the United States" might be applied by the federal courts one way in Virginia and another way in California. In light of the well-recognized interest in ensuring that federal courts interpret federal law in a uniform way, we are convinced that Congress did not intend the statute to produce such a result.

III

In this case, Williams contends that he was denied his constitutionally guaranteed right to the effective assistance of counsel when his trial lawyers failed to investigate and to present substantial mitigating evidence to the sentencing jury. The threshold question under AEDPA is whether Williams seeks to apply a rule of law that was clearly established at the time his state-court conviction became final. That question is easily answered because the merits of his claim are squarely governed by our holding in *Strickland v. Washington*, 466 U.S. 668, 104 S.Ct. 2052 (1984).

* * *

It is past question that the rule set forth in *Strickland* qualifies as "clearly established Federal law, as determined by the Supreme Court of the United States." That the *Strickland* test "of necessity requires a case-by-case examination of the evidence," obviates neither the clarity of the rule nor the extent to which the rule must be seen as "established" by this Court. This Court's precedent "dictated" that the Virginia Supreme Court apply the *Strickland* test at the time that court entertained Williams' ineffective-assistance claim. And it can hardly be said that recognizing the right to effective counsel "breaks new ground or imposes a new obligation on the States." Williams is therefore entitled to relief if the Virginia Supreme Court's decision rejecting his ineffective-assistance claim was either "contrary to, or involved an unreasonable application of," that established law. It was both.

IV

The Virginia Supreme Court erred in holding that our decision in *Lockhart v. Fretwell*, 506 U.S. 364, 113 S.Ct. 838 (1993), modified or in some way supplanted the rule set down in *Strickland*. * * *

* * *

The trial judge analyzed the ineffective-assistance claim under the correct standard; the Virginia Supreme Court did not.

We are likewise persuaded that the Virginia trial judge correctly applied both components of that standard to Williams' ineffectiveness claim. Although he concluded that counsel competently handled the guilt phase of the trial, he found that their representation during the sentencing phase fell short of professional standards—a judgment barely disputed by the State in its brief to this Court. The record establishes that counsel did not begin to prepare for that phase of the proceeding until a week before the trial. They failed to conduct an investigation that would have uncovered extensive records graphically describing Williams' nightmarish childhood, not because of any strategic calculation but because they incorrectly thought that state law barred access to such records. Had they done so, the jury would have learned that Williams' parents had been imprisoned for the criminal neglect of Williams and his siblings, that Williams had been severely and repeatedly beaten by his father, that he had been committed to the custody of the social services bureau for two years during his parents' incarceration (including one stint in an abusive foster home), and then, after his parents were released from prison, had been returned to his parents' custody.

Counsel failed to introduce available evidence that Williams was "borderline mentally retarded" and did not advance beyond sixth grade in school. They failed to seek prison records recording Williams' commendations for helping to crack a prison drug ring and for returning a guard's missing wallet, or the testimony of prison officials who described Williams as among the inmates "least likely to act in a violent, dangerous or provocative way." Counsel failed even to return the phone call of a certified public accountant who had offered to testify that he had visited Williams frequently when Williams was incarcerated as part of a prison ministry program, that Williams "seemed to thrive in a more regimented and structured environment," and that Williams was proud of the carpentry degree he earned while in prison.

Of course, not all of the additional evidence was favorable to Williams. The juvenile records revealed that he had been thrice committed to the juvenile system—for aiding and abetting larceny when he was 11 years old, for pulling a false fire alarm when he was 12, and for breaking and entering when he was 15. But as the Federal District Court correctly observed, the failure to introduce the comparatively voluminous amount of evidence that did speak in Williams' favor was not justified by a tactical decision to focus on Williams' voluntary confession. Whether or not those omissions were sufficiently prejudicial to have affected the outcome of sentencing, they clearly demonstrate that trial counsel did not fulfill their obligation to conduct a thorough investigation of the defendant's background.

We are also persuaded, unlike the Virginia Supreme Court, that counsel's unprofessional service prejudiced Williams within the meaning of *Strickland*. After hearing the additional evidence developed in the postconviction proceedings, the very judge who presided at Williams' trial and who once determined that the death penalty was "just" and "appropriate," concluded that there existed "a reasonable probability that the result of the sentencing phase would have been different" if the jury had heard that evidence. We do not agree with the Virginia Supreme Court that Judge Ingram's conclusion should be discounted because he apparently adopted "a *per se* approach to the prejudice element" that placed undue "emphasis on mere outcome determination." Judge Ingram did stress the importance of mitigation evidence in making his "outcome determination," but it is clear that his predictive judgment rested on his assessment of the totality of the omitted evidence rather than on the notion that a single item of omitted evidence, no matter how trivial, would require a new hearing.

The Virginia Supreme Court's own analysis of prejudice reaching the contrary conclusion was thus unreasonable in at least two respects. First, as we have already explained, the State Supreme Court mischaracterized at best the appropriate rule, made clear by this Court in *Strickland*, for determining whether counsel's assistance was effective within the meaning of the Constitution. While it may also have conducted an "outcome determinative" analysis of its own, it is evident to us that the court's decision turned on its erroneous view that a "mere" difference in outcome is not sufficient to establish constitutionally ineffective assistance of counsel. Its analysis in this respect was thus not only "contrary to," but also, inasmuch as the Virginia Supreme Court relied on the inapplicable exception recognized in *Lockhart*, an "unreasonable application of" the clear law as established by this Court.

Second, the State Supreme Court's prejudice determination was unreasonable insofar as it failed to evaluate the totality of the available mitigation evidence—both that adduced at trial, and the evidence adduced in the habeas proceeding—in reweighing it against the evidence in aggravation. This error is apparent in its consideration of the additional mitigation evidence developed in the postconviction proceedings. The court correctly found that as to "the factual part of the mixed question," there was "really ... n[o] ... dispute" that available mitigation evidence was not presented at trial. As to the prejudice determination comprising the "legal part" of its analysis, it correctly emphasized the strength of the prosecution evidence supporting the future dangerousness aggravating circumstance.

But the state court failed even to mention the sole argument in mitigation that trial counsel did advance—Williams turned himself in, alerting police to a crime they otherwise would never have discovered, expressing remorse for his actions, and cooperating with the police after that. While this, coupled with the prison records and guard testimony, may not have overcome a finding of future dangerousness, the graphic description of Williams' childhood, filled with abuse and privation, or the reality that he was "borderline mentally retarded," might well have influenced the jury's appraisal of his moral culpability. The circumstances recited in his several confessions are consistent with the view that in each case his violent behavior was a compulsive reaction rather than the product of cold-blooded premeditation. Mitigating evidence unrelated to dangerousness may alter the jury's selection of penalty, even if it does not undermine or rebut the prosecution's death-eligibility case. The Virginia Supreme Court did not entertain that possibility. It thus failed to accord appropriate weight to the body of mitigation evidence available to trial counsel.

V

In our judgment, the state trial judge was correct both in his recognition of the established legal standard for determining counsel's effectiveness, and in his conclusion that the entire postconviction record, viewed as a whole and cumulative of mitigation evidence presented originally, raised "a reasonable probability that the result of the sentencing proceeding would have been different" if competent counsel had presented and explained the significance of all the available evidence. It follows that the Virginia Supreme Court rendered a "decision that was contrary to, or involved an unreasonable application of, clearly established Federal law." Williams' constitutional right to the effective assistance of counsel as defined in *Strickland v. Washington* was violated.

Accordingly, the judgment of the Court of Appeals is reversed, and the case is remanded for further proceedings consistent with this opinion.

It is so ordered.

JUSTICE O'CONNOR delivered the opinion of the Court with respect to Part II (except as to the footnote), concurred in part, and concurred in the judgment.*

* * *

II

A

* * *

Justice STEVENS' opinion in Part II essentially contends that § 2254(d)(1) does not alter the previously settled rule of independent review. Indeed, the opinion concludes its statutory inquiry with the somewhat empty finding that § 2254(d)(1) does no more than express a " 'mood' that the federal judiciary must respect." For Justice STEVENS, the congressionally enacted "mood" has two important qualities. First, "federal courts [must] attend to every state-court judgment with utmost care" by "carefully weighing all the reasons for accepting a state court's judgment." Second, if a federal court undertakes that careful review and yet remains convinced that a prisoner's custody violates the Constitution, "that independent judgment should prevail."

One need look no further than our decision in *Miller v. Fenton*, 474 U.S. 104, 106 S.Ct. 445 (1985) to see that Justice STEVENS' interpretation of § 2254(d)(1) gives the 1996 amendment no effect whatsoever. The command that federal courts should now use the "utmost care" by "carefully weighing" the reasons supporting a state court's judgment echoes our pre-AEDPA statement in *Miller* that federal habeas courts "should, of course, give great weight to the considered conclusions of a coequal state judiciary." Similarly, the requirement that the independent judgment of a federal court must in the end prevail essentially repeats the conclusion we reached in the very next sentence in *Miller* with respect to the specific issue presented there: "But, as we now reaffirm, the ultimate question whether, under the totality of the circumstances, the challenged confession was obtained in a manner compatible with the requirements of the Constitution *is a matter for independent federal determination*."

* * *

---

* Justice KENNEDY joins this opinion in its entirety. THE CHIEF JUSTICE and Justice THOMAS join this opinion with respect to Part II. Justice SCALIA joins this opinion with respect to Part II, except as to the footnote [which cited to the legislative history of the act—Ed.].

The Court of Appeals for the Fourth Circuit properly accorded both the "contrary to" and "unreasonable application" clauses independent meaning. The Fourth Circuit's interpretation of § 2254(d)(1) in Williams' case relied, in turn, on that court's previous decision in *Green v. French*, 143 F.3d 865 (1998). ("[T]he standard of review enunciated in *Green v. French* continues to be the binding law of this Circuit"). With respect to the first of the two statutory clauses, the Fourth Circuit held in *Green* that a state-court decision can be "contrary to" this Court's clearly established precedent in two ways. First, a state-court decision is contrary to this Court's precedent if the state court arrives at a conclusion opposite to that reached by this Court on a question of law. Second, a state-court decision is also contrary to this Court's precedent if the state court confronts facts that are materially indistinguishable from a relevant Supreme Court precedent and arrives at a result opposite to ours.

The word "contrary" is commonly understood to mean "diametrically different," "opposite in character or nature," or "mutually opposed." Webster's Third New International Dictionary 495 (1976). The text of § 2254(d)(1) therefore suggests that the state court's decision must be substantially different from the relevant precedent of this Court. The Fourth Circuit's interpretation of the "contrary to" clause accurately reflects this textual meaning. A state-court decision will certainly be contrary to our clearly established precedent if the state court applies a rule that contradicts the governing law set forth in our cases. Take, for example, our decision in *Strickland v. Washington*, 466 U.S. 668, 104 S.Ct. 2052 (1984). If a state court were to reject a prisoner's claim of ineffective assistance of counsel on the grounds that the prisoner had not established by a preponderance of the evidence that the result of his criminal proceeding would have been different, that decision would be "diametrically different," "opposite in character or nature," and "mutually opposed" to our clearly established precedent because we held in *Strickland* that the prisoner need only demonstrate a "reasonable probability that . . . the result of the proceeding would have been different." A state-court decision will also be contrary to this Court's clearly established precedent if the state court confronts a set of facts that are materially indistinguishable from a decision of this Court and nevertheless arrives at a result different from our precedent. Accordingly, in either of these two scenarios, a federal court will be unconstrained by § 2254(d)(1) because the state-court decision falls within that provision's "contrary to" clause.

* * *

The Fourth Circuit's interpretation of the "unreasonable application" clause of § 2254(d)(1) is generally correct. That court held in *Green* that a state-court decision can involve an "unreasonable application" of this Court's clearly established precedent in two ways. First, a state-court decision involves an unreasonable application of this Court's precedent if the state court identifies the correct governing legal rule from this Court's cases but unreasonably applies it to the facts of the particular state prisoner's case. Second, a state-court decision also involves an unreasonable application of this Court's precedent if the state court either unreasonably extends a legal principle from our precedent to a new context where it should not apply or unreasonably refuses to extend that principle to a new context where it should apply.

A state-court decision that correctly identifies the governing legal rule but applies it unreasonably to the facts of a particular prisoner's case certainly would qualify as a decision "involv[ing] an unreasonable application of . . . clearly established Federal law." * * *

The Fourth Circuit also held in *Green* that state-court decisions that unreasonably extend a legal principle from our precedent to a new context where it should not apply (or unreasonably refuse to extend a legal principle to a new context where it should apply) should be analyzed under § 2254(d)(1)'s "unreasonable application" clause. * * * Today's case does not require us to decide how such "extension of legal principle" cases should be treated under § 2254(d)(1). For now it is sufficient to hold that when a state-court decision unreasonably applies the law of this Court to the facts of a prisoner's case, a federal court applying § 2254(d)(1) may conclude that the state-court decision falls within that provision's "unreasonable application" clause.

B

There remains the task of defining what exactly qualifies as an "unreasonable application" of law under § 2254(d)(1). The Fourth Circuit held in *Green* that a state-court decision involves an "unreasonable application of . . . clearly established Federal law" only if the state court has applied federal law "in a manner that reasonable jurists would all agree is unreasonable." * * *

Defining an "unreasonable application" by reference to a "reasonable jurist," however, is of little assistance to the courts that must apply § 2254(d)(1) and, in fact, may be misleading. Stated simply, a federal habeas court making the "unreasonable application" inquiry should ask whether the state court's application of clearly established federal law was objectively unreasonable. * * * As I explained in *Wright v. West*, 505 U.S 277, 112 S.Ct. 2482 (1992), with respect to the "reasonable jurist" standard in the *Teague* context, "[e]ven though we have characterized the new rule inquiry as whether 'reasonable jurists' could disagree as to whether a result is dictated by precedent, the standard for determining when a case establishes a new rule is 'objective,' and the mere existence of conflicting authority does not necessarily mean a rule is new."

The term "unreasonable" is no doubt difficult to define. That said, it is a common term in the legal world and, accordingly, federal judges are familiar with its meaning. For purposes of today's opinion, the most important point is that an *unreasonable* application of federal law is different from an *incorrect* application of federal law. * * * In § 2254(d)(1), Congress specifically used the word "unreasonable," and not a term like "erroneous" or "incorrect." Under § 2254(d)(1)'s "unreasonable application" clause, then, a federal habeas court may not issue the writ simply because that court concludes in its independent judgment that the relevant state-court decision applied clearly established federal law erroneously or incorrectly. Rather, that application must also be unreasonable.

* * *

Throughout this discussion the meaning of the phrase "clearly established Federal law, as determined by the Supreme Court of the United States" has been put to the side. That statutory phrase refers to the holdings, as opposed to the dicta, of this Court's decisions as of the time of the relevant state-court decision. In this respect, the "clearly established Federal law" phrase bears only a slight connection to our *Teague* jurisprudence. With one caveat, whatever would qualify as an old rule under our *Teague* jurisprudence will constitute "clearly established Federal law, as determined by the Supreme Court of the United States" under § 2254(d)(1). The one caveat, as the statutory language makes clear, is that § 2254(d)(1) restricts the source of clearly established law to this Court's jurisprudence.

In sum, § 2254(d)(1) places a new constraint on the power of a federal habeas court to grant a state prisoner's application for a writ of habeas corpus with respect to claims adjudicated on the merits in state court. Under § 2254(d)(1), the writ may issue only if one of the following two conditions is satisfied—the state-court adjudication resulted in a decision that (1) "was contrary to ... clearly established Federal law, as determined by the Supreme Court of the United States," or (2) "involved an unreasonable application of ... clearly established Federal law, as determined by the Supreme Court of the United States." Under the "contrary to" clause, a federal habeas court may grant the writ if the state court arrives at a conclusion opposite to that reached by this Court on a question of law or if the state court decides a case differently than this Court has on a set of materially indistinguishable facts. Under the "unreasonable application" clause, a federal habeas court may grant the writ if the state court identifies the correct governing legal principle from this Court's decisions but unreasonably applies that principle to the facts of the prisoner's case.

III

Although I disagree with Justice STEVENS concerning the standard we must apply under § 2254(d)(1) in evaluating Terry Williams' claims on habeas, I agree with the Court that the Virginia Supreme Court's adjudication of Williams' claim of ineffective assistance of counsel resulted in a decision that was both contrary to and involved an unreasonable application of this Court's clearly established precedent. Specifically, I believe that the Court's discussion in Parts III and IV is correct and that it demonstrates the reasons that the Virginia Supreme Court's decision in Williams' case, even under the interpretation of § 2254(d)(1) I have set forth above, was both contrary to and involved an unreasonable application of our precedent.

* * *

[Opinion of REHNQUIST, C.J., concurring in part and dissenting in part, joined by SCALIA and THOMAS, JJ. omitted]

NOTE

1.   *The relationship of § 2254(d) and Teague.*

In *Horn v. Banks*, 536 U.S. 266, 122 S.Ct. 2147 (2002), the Supreme Court addressed the relationship of § 2254(d) to *Teague* and held that they are separate limitations on the claims a district court may consider, *i.e.*, that even if a defendant makes a sufficient showing on a claim to justify relief under § 2254(d), the claim may still fail under *Teague*. In *Banks*, after defendant's case became final on direct appeal, the Supreme Court decided *Mills v. Maryland*, 486 U.S. 367, 108 S.Ct. 1860 (1988). In state postconviction proceedings, Banks raised a *Mills* challenge to the instructions and jury verdict forms in his case. The state supreme court analyzed the case under *Mills* and rejected Banks' claim on the merits. On federal habeas corpus, the District Court rejected Banks' claim, but the Court of Appeals reversed, finding that the state court decision was an unreasonable application of *Mills* under § 2254(d). The Supreme Court, in turn, reversed, holding that, because the state had raised the *Teague* issue and because *Teague* was a "threshold question in every habeas case," the lower courts should have considered whether Banks' claim was *Teague*-barred before analyzing the claim under AEDPA.

B.   PROCEDURAL LIMITS: EXHAUSTION AND PROCEDURAL AND FACTUAL DEFAULT

This section looks at procedural limits on federal habeas corpus review arising from the petitioner's state court litigation of the claims now presented to the federal court. *Coleman v. Thompson* addresses application of the procedural default bar in capital cases. The case concerns two issues: whether a default occurred and whether there was "cause" for the default. In *House v. Bell*, the Court explains and applies the "actual innocence" exception to the procedural default rule. *O'Sullivan v. Boerckel* concerns the exhaustion requirement of § 2254(b) and the relationship between exhaustion and procedural default. The last case, *Williams (Michael) v. Taylor*, considers the issue of "factual default" under AEDPA, *i.e.*, the failure of the petitioner to develop the facts in support of a claim in state court.

COLEMAN v. THOMPSON

501 U.S. 722, 111 S.Ct. 2546, 115 L.Ed.2d 640 (1991).

JUSTICE O'CONNOR delivered the opinion of the Court.

This is a case about federalism. It concerns the respect that federal courts owe the States and the States' procedural rules when reviewing the claims of state prisoners in federal habeas corpus.

I

A Buchanan County, Virginia, jury convicted Roger Keith Coleman of rape and capital murder and fixed the sentence at death for the murder. The trial court imposed the death sentence, and the Virginia Supreme Court affirmed both the convictions and the sentence. This Court denied certiorari.

Coleman then filed a petition for a writ of habeas corpus in the Circuit Court for Buchanan County, raising numerous federal constitutional claims that he had not raised on direct appeal. After a 2–day evidentiary hearing, the Circuit Court ruled against Coleman on all claims. The court entered its final judgment on September 4, 1986.

Coleman filed his notice of appeal with the Circuit Court on October 7, 1986, 33 days after the entry of final judgment. Coleman subsequently filed a petition for appeal in the Virginia Supreme Court. The Commonwealth of Virginia, as appellee, filed a motion to dismiss the appeal. The sole ground for dismissal urged in the motion was that Coleman's notice of appeal had been filed late. Virginia Supreme Court Rule 5:9(a) provides that no appeal shall be allowed unless a notice of appeal is filed with the trial court within 30 days of final judgment.

The Virginia Supreme Court did not act immediately on the Commonwealth's motion, and both parties filed several briefs on the subject of the motion to dismiss and on the merits of the claims in Coleman's petition. On May 19, 1987, the Virginia Supreme Court issued the following order, dismissing Coleman's appeal:

> "On December 4, 1986 came the appellant, by counsel, and filed a petition for appeal in the above-styled case.
>
> "Thereupon came the appellee, by the Attorney General of Virginia, and filed a motion to dismiss the petition for appeal; on December 19, 1986 the appellant filed a memorandum in opposition to the motion to dismiss; on December 19, 1986 the appellee filed a reply to the appellant's memorandum; on December 23, 1986 the appellee filed a brief in opposition to the petition for appeal; on December 23, 1986 the appellant filed a surreply in opposition to the appellee's motion to dismiss; and on January 6, 1987 the appellant filed a reply brief.
>
> "Upon consideration whereof, the motion to dismiss is granted and the petition for appeal is dismissed."

This Court again denied certiorari.

Coleman next filed a petition for writ of habeas corpus in the United States District Court for the Western District of Virginia. In his petition, Coleman presented four federal constitutional claims he had raised on direct appeal in the Virginia Supreme Court and seven claims he had raised for the first time in state habeas. The District Court concluded that, by virtue of the dismissal of his appeal by the Virginia Supreme Court in state habeas, Coleman had procedurally defaulted the seven claims. The District Court nonetheless went on to address the merits of all 11 of Coleman's claims. The court ruled against Coleman on all of the claims and denied the petition.

The United States Court of Appeals for the Fourth Circuit affirmed. The court held that Coleman had defaulted all of the claims that he had presented for the first time in state habeas. Coleman argued that the Virginia Supreme Court had not "clearly and expressly" stated that its decision in state habeas was based on a procedural default, and therefore the federal courts could not treat it as such under the rule of *Harris v. Reed*, 489 U.S. 255, 109 S.Ct. 1038 (1989). The Fourth Circuit disagreed. It concluded that the Virginia Supreme Court had met the "plain statement" requirement of *Harris* by granting a motion to dismiss that was based solely on procedural grounds. The Fourth Circuit held that the Virginia Supreme Court's decision rested on independent and adequate state grounds and that Coleman had not shown cause to excuse the default. As a consequence, federal review of the claims Coleman presented only in the state habeas proceeding was barred. We granted certiorari to resolve several issues concerning the relationship between state procedural defaults and federal habeas review, and now affirm.

* * *

[The Court reviewed its decisions in *Michigan v. Long*, 463 U.S. 1032, 103 S.Ct. 3469 (1983), *Caldwell v. Mississippi*, 472 U.S. 320, 105 S.Ct. 2633 (1985) and *Harris v. Reed*, 489 U.S. 255, 109 S.Ct. 1038 (1989), cases concerning when to treat a state court decision as based on state law, rather than federal law. In *Long*, a direct appeal case, the Court established a conclusive presumption of jurisdiction (*i.e.*, that the state decision did not rest on adequate and independent state grounds) to be applied in ambiguous cases:

> "[W]hen * * * a state court decision fairly appears to rest primarily on federal law, or to be interwoven with the federal law, and when the adequacy and independence of any possible state law ground is not clear from the face of the opinion, we will accept as the most reasonable explanation that the state court decided the case the way it did because it believed that federal law required it to do so."

In *Caldwell*, another direct appeal case, the Court applied the presumption because the state decision fairly appeared "to rest primarily on federal law," and did not contain a clear and express statement that the state court "was relying on procedural default as an independent ground."

In *Harris*, the Court applied the rule from *Long* and *Caldwell* to a habeas case. Because the state court did not "clearly and expressly" rely on state procedural grounds in rejecting Harris' claim, federal habeas relief was not barred.]

III

A

Coleman contends that the presumption of *Long* and *Harris* applies in this case and precludes a bar to habeas because the Virginia Supreme Court's order dismissing Coleman's appeal did not "clearly and expressly" state that it was based on state procedural grounds. Coleman reads *Harris* too broadly. A predicate to the application of the *Harris* presumption is that the decision of the last state court to which the petitioner presented his federal claims must fairly appear to rest primarily on federal law or to be interwoven with federal law.

* * *

B

The *Harris* presumption does not apply here. Coleman does not argue, nor could he, that it "fairly appears" that the Virginia Supreme Court's decision rested primarily on federal law or was interwoven with such law. The Virginia Supreme Court stated plainly that it was granting the Commonwealth's motion to dismiss the petition for appeal. That motion was based solely on Coleman's failure to meet the Supreme Court's time requirements. There is no mention of federal law in the Virginia Supreme Court's three-sentence dismissal order. It "fairly appears" to rest primarily on state law.

Coleman concedes that the Virginia Supreme Court dismissed his state habeas appeal as untimely, applying a state procedural rule. He argues instead that the court's application of this procedural rule was not independent of federal law.

Virginia Supreme Court Rule 5:5(a) declares that the 30–day requirement for filing a notice of appeal is "mandatory." The Virginia Supreme Court has reiterated the unwaivable nature of this requirement. Despite these forthright pronouncements, Coleman contends that in this case the Virginia Supreme Court did not automatically apply its time requirement. Rather, Coleman asserts, the court first considered the merits of his federal claims and applied the procedural bar only after determining that doing so would not abridge one of Coleman's constitutional rights. In *Ake v. Oklahoma*, 470 U.S. 68, 105 S.Ct. 1087 (1985), this Court held that a similar Oklahoma rule, excusing procedural default in cases of "fundamental trial error," was not independent of federal law so as to bar direct review because "the State ha[d] made application of the procedural bar depend on an antecedent ruling on federal law." For the same reason, Coleman argues, the Virginia Supreme Court's time requirement is not independent of federal law.

Ake was a direct review case. We have never applied its rule regarding independent state grounds in federal habeas. But even if *Ake* applies here, it does Coleman no good because the Virginia Supreme Court relied on an independent state procedural rule.

Coleman cites *Tharp v. Commonwealth*, 175 S.E.2d 277 (Va. 1970). In that case, the Virginia Supreme Court announced that it was ending its practice of allowing extensions of time for petitions of writs of error in criminal and state habeas cases:

> "Henceforth we will extend the time for filing a petition for a writ of error only if it is found that to deny the extension would abridge a constitutional right."

Coleman contends that the Virginia Supreme Court's exception for constitutional claims demonstrates that the court will conduct at least a cursory review of a petitioner's constitutional claims on the merits before dismissing an appeal.

We are not convinced that *Tharp* stands for the rule that Coleman believes it does. Coleman reads that case as establishing a practice in the Virginia Supreme Court of examining the merits of all underlying constitutional claims before denying a petition for appeal or writ of error as time barred. A more natural reading is that the Virginia Supreme Court will only grant an extension of time if the denial itself would abridge a constitutional right. That is, the Virginia Supreme Court will extend its time requirement only in those cases in which the petitioner has a constitutional right to have the appeal heard.

    * * *

Finally, Coleman argues that the Virginia Supreme Court's dismissal order in this case is at least ambiguous because it was issued "[u]pon consideration" of all the filed papers, including Coleman's petition for appeal and the Commonwealth's brief in opposition, both of which discussed the merits of Coleman's federal claims. There is no doubt that the Virginia Supreme Court's "consideration" of all filed papers adds some ambiguity, but we simply cannot read it as overriding the court's explicit grant of a dismissal motion based solely on procedural grounds. Those grounds are independent of federal law.

[Accordingly, the Court found that Coleman's seven defaulted claims were barred unless he could demonstrate "cause" and "prejudice."]

V

A

Coleman maintains that there was cause for his default. The late filing was, he contends, the result of attorney error of sufficient magnitude to excuse the default in federal habeas.

Murray v. Carrier, 477 U.S. 478, 106 S.Ct. 2639 (1986), considered the circumstances under which attorney error constitutes cause. Carrier argued that his attorney's inadvertence in failing to raise certain claims in his state appeal constituted cause for the default sufficient to allow federal habeas review. We rejected this claim, explaining that the costs associated with an ignorant or inadvertent procedural default are no less than where the failure to raise a claim is a deliberate strategy: It deprives the state courts of the opportunity to review trial errors. When a federal habeas court hears such a claim, it undercuts the State's ability to enforce its procedural rules just as surely as when the default was deliberate. We concluded: "So long as a defendant is represented by counsel whose performance is not constitutionally ineffective under the standard established in *Strickland v. Washington*, [466 U.S. 668, 104 S.Ct. 2052 (1984)], we discern no inequity in requiring him to bear the risk of attorney error that results in a procedural default."

Applying the *Carrier* rule as stated, this case is at an end. There is no constitutional right to an attorney in state post-conviction proceedings. *Pennsylvania v. Finley*, 481 U.S. 551, 107 S.Ct. 1990 (1987); *Murray v. Giarratano*, 492 U.S. 1, 109 S.Ct. 2765 (1989) (applying the rule to capital cases). Consequently, a petitioner cannot claim constitutionally ineffective assistance of counsel in such proceedings. See *Wainwright v. Torna*, 455 U.S. 586, 102 S.Ct. 1300 (1982) (where there is no constitutional right to counsel there can be no deprivation of effective assistance). Coleman contends that it was his attorney's error that led to the late filing of his state habeas appeal. This error cannot be constitutionally ineffective; therefore Coleman must "bear the risk of attorney error that results in a procedural default."

Coleman attempts to avoid this reasoning by arguing that *Carrier* does not stand for such a broad proposition. He contends that *Carrier* applies by its terms only in those situations where it is possible to state a claim for ineffective assistance of counsel. Where there is no constitutional right to counsel, Coleman argues, it is enough that a petitioner demonstrate that his attorney's conduct would meet the *Strickland* standard, even though no independent Sixth Amendment claim is possible.

This argument is inconsistent not only with the language of *Carrier*, but with the logic of that opinion as well. We explained clearly that "cause" under the cause and prejudice test must be something external to the petitioner, something that cannot fairly be attributed to him: "[W]e think that the existence of cause for a procedural default must ordinarily turn on whether the prisoner can show that some objective factor external to the defense impeded counsel's efforts to comply with the State's procedural rule." For example, "a showing that the factual or legal basis for a claim was not reasonably available to counsel, . . . or that 'some interference by officials' . . . made compliance impracticable, would constitute cause under this standard."

Attorney ignorance or inadvertence is not "cause" because the attorney is the petitioner's agent when acting, or failing to act, in furtherance of the litigation, and the petitioner must "bear the risk of attorney error." Attorney error that constitutes ineffective assistance of counsel is cause, however. This is not because, as Coleman contends, the error is so bad that "the lawyer ceases to be an agent of the petitioner." In a case such as this, where the alleged attorney error is inadvertence in failing to file a timely notice, such a rule would be contrary to well-settled principles of agency law. Rather, as *Carrier* explains, "if the procedural default is the result of ineffective assistance of counsel, the Sixth Amendment itself requires that responsibility for the default be imputed to the State." In other words, it is not the gravity of the attorney's error that matters, but that it constitutes a violation of petitioner's right to counsel, so that the error must be seen as an external factor, *i.e.*, "imputed to the State."

Where a petitioner defaults a claim as a result of the denial of the right to effective assistance of counsel, the State, which is responsible for the denial as a constitutional matter, must bear the cost of any resulting default and the harm to state interests that federal habeas review entails. A different allocation of costs is appropriate in those circumstances where the State has no responsibility to ensure that the petitioner was represented by competent counsel. As between the State and the petitioner, it is the petitioner who must bear the burden of a failure to follow state procedural rules. In the absence of a constitutional violation, the petitioner bears the risk in federal habeas for all attorney errors made in the course of the representation, as *Carrier* says explicitly.

B

Among the claims Coleman brought in state habeas, and then again in federal habeas, is ineffective assistance of counsel during trial, sentencing, and appeal. Coleman contends that, at least as to these claims, attorney error in state habeas must constitute cause. This is because, under Virginia law at the time of Coleman's trial and direct appeal, ineffective assistance of counsel claims related to counsel's conduct during trial or appeal could be brought only in state habeas. Coleman argues that attorney error in failing to file timely in the first forum in which a federal claim can be raised is cause.

We reiterate that counsel's ineffectiveness will constitute cause only if it is an independent constitutional violation. *Finley* and *Giarratano* established that there is no right to counsel in state collateral proceedings. For Coleman to prevail, therefore, there must be an exception to the rule of *Finley* and *Giarratano* in those cases where state collateral review is the first place a prisoner can present a challenge to his conviction. We need not answer this question broadly, however, for one state court has addressed Coleman's claims: the state habeas trial court. The effectiveness of Coleman's counsel before that court is not at issue here. Coleman contends that it was the ineffectiveness of his counsel during the appeal from that determination that constitutes cause to excuse his default. We thus need to decide only whether Coleman had a constitutional right to counsel on appeal from the state habeas trial court judgment. We conclude that he did not.

* * *

Because Coleman had no right to counsel to pursue his appeal in state habeas, any attorney error that led to the default of Coleman's claims in state court cannot constitute cause to excuse the default in federal habeas. As Coleman does not argue in this Court that federal review of his claims is necessary to prevent a fundamental miscarriage of justice, he is barred from bringing these claims in federal habeas. Accordingly, the judgment of the Court of Appeals is

Affirmed.

[Concurring opinion of WHITE, J. omitted]

JUSTICE BLACKMUN, with whom JUSTICE MARSHALL and JUSTICE STEVENS join, dissenting.

Federalism; comity; state sovereignty; preservation of state resources; certainty: The majority methodically inventories these multifarious state interests before concluding that the plain-statement rule of *Michigan v. Long*, 463 U.S. 1032, 103 S.Ct. 3469 (1983), does not apply to a summary order. One searches the majority's opinion in vain, however, for any mention of petitioner Coleman's right to a criminal proceeding free from constitutional defect or his interest in finding a forum for his constitutional challenge to his conviction and sentence of death. Nor does the majority even allude to the "important need for uniformity in federal law," which justified this Court's adoption of the plain-statement rule in the first place. Rather, displaying obvious exasperation with the breadth of substantive federal habeas doctrine and the expansive protection afforded by the Fourteenth Amendment's guarantee of fundamental fairness in state criminal proceedings, the Court today continues its crusade to erect petty procedural barriers in the path of any state prisoner seeking review of his federal constitutional claims. Because I believe that the Court is creating a Byzantine morass of arbitrary, unnecessary, and unjustifiable impediments to the vindication of federal rights, I dissent.

I

The Court cavalierly claims that "[t]his is a case about federalism" and proceeds without explanation to assume that the purposes of federalism are advanced whenever a federal court refrains from reviewing an ambiguous state-court judgment. Federalism, however, has no inherent normative value: It does not, as the majority appears to assume, blindly protect the interests of States from any incursion by the federal courts. Rather, federalism secures to citizens the liberties that derive from the diffusion of sovereign power. "Federalism is a device for realizing the concepts of decency and fairness which are among the fundamental principles of liberty and justice lying at the base of all our civil and political institutions." Brennan, *Federal Habeas Corpus and State Prisoners: An Exercise in Federalism*, 7 Utah L.Rev. 423 (1961). In this context, it cannot lightly be assumed that the interests of federalism are fostered by a rule that impedes federal review of federal constitutional claims.

Moreover, the form of federalism embraced by today's majority bears little resemblance to that adopted by the Framers of the Constitution and ratified by the original States. The majority proceeds as if the sovereign interests of the States and the Federal Government were coequal. Ours, however, is a federal republic, conceived on the principle of a supreme federal power and constituted first and foremost of citizens, not of sovereign States. The citizens expressly declared: "This Constitution, and the Laws of the United States which shall be made in Pursuance thereof ... shall be the supreme Law of the Land." U.S. Const., Art. VI, cl. 2. James Madison felt that a constitution without this Clause "would have been evidently and radically defective." The Federalist No. 44, p. 286 (C. Rossiter ed. 1961). The ratification of the Fourteenth Amendment by the citizens of the several States expanded federal powers even further, with a corresponding diminution of state sovereignty. Thus, "the sovereignty of the States is limited by the Constitution itself." *Garcia v. San Antonio Metropolitan Transit Authority*, 469 U.S. 528, 105 S.Ct. 1005 (1985).

Federal habeas review of state-court judgments, respectfully employed to safeguard federal rights, is no invasion of state sovereignty. Since 1867, Congress has acted within its constitutional authority to " 'interpose the federal courts between the States and the people, as guardians of the people's federal rights—to protect the people from unconstitutional action.' " *Reed v. Ross*, 468 U.S. 1, 104 S.Ct. 2901 (1984), quoting *Mitchum v. Foster*, 407 U.S. 225, 92 S.Ct. 2151 (1972). See 28 U.S.C. § 2254. Justice Frankfurter, in his separate opinion in *Brown v. Allen*, 344 U.S. 443, 73 S.Ct. 397 (1953), recognized this:

> "Insofar as [federal habeas] jurisdiction enables federal district courts to entertain claims that State Supreme Courts have denied rights guaranteed by the United States Constitution, it is not a case of a lower court sitting in judgment on a higher court. It is merely one aspect of respecting the Supremacy Clause of the Constitution whereby federal law is higher than State law."

Thus, the considered exercise by federal courts—in vindication of fundamental constitutional rights—of the habeas jurisdiction conferred on them by Congress exemplifies the full expression of this Nation's federalism.

That the majority has lost sight of the animating principles of federalism is well illustrated by its discussion of the duty of a federal court to determine whether a state-court judgment rests on an adequate and independent state ground. According to the majority's formulation, establishing this duty in the federal court serves to diminish the risk that a federal habeas court will review the federal claims of a prisoner in custody pursuant to a judgment that rests upon an adequate and independent state ground. In reality, however, this duty of a federal court to determine its jurisdiction originally was articulated to ensure that federal rights were not improperly denied a federal forum. Thus, the quote artfully reconstituted by the majority originally read: "[I]t is incumbent upon this Court, when it is urged that the decision of the state court rests upon a non-federal ground, to ascertain for itself, *in order that constitutional guarantees may appropriately be enforced*, whether the asserted non-federal ground independently and adequately supports the judgment." *Abie State Bank v. Bryan*, 282 U.S. 765, 51 S.Ct. 252 (1931) (emphasis added). Similarly, the Court has stated that the duty "cannot be disregarded without neglecting or renouncing a jurisdiction conferred by the law and designed to protect and maintain the supremacy of the Constitution and the laws made in pursuance thereof." *Ward v. Board of Comm'rs of Love County*, 253 U.S. 17, 40 S.Ct. 419 (1920). Indeed, the duty arose out of a distinct distrust of state courts, which this Court perceived as attempting to evade federal review. See *Broad River Power Co. v. South Carolina ex rel. Daniel*, 281 U.S. 537, 50 S.Ct. 401 (1930) ("Even though the constitutional protection invoked be denied on non-federal grounds, it is the province of this Court to inquire whether the decision of the state court rests upon a fair and substantial basis. If unsubstantial, constitutional obligations may not thus be evaded").

From these noble beginnings, the Court has managed to transform the duty to protect federal rights into a self-fashioned abdication. Defying the constitutional allocation of sovereign authority, the Court now requires a federal court to scrutinize the state-court judgment with an eye to denying a litigant review of his federal claims rather than enforcing those provisions of the Federal Bill of Rights that secure individual autonomy.

II

Even if one acquiesced in the majority's unjustifiable elevation of abstract federalism over fundamental precepts of liberty and fairness, the Court's conclusion that the plain-statement rule of *Michigan v. Long* does not apply to a summary order defies both settled understandings and compassionate reason.

A

[Justice BLACKMUN argued that *Harris* had made clear that the *Long* plain-statement rule was not limited to cases where the state court had addressed federal law questions, citing the following language: "a procedural default does not bar consideration of a federal claim on either direct or habeas review unless the last state court rendering a judgment in the case ' "clearly and expressly" ' states that its judgment rests on a state procedural bar." *Harris* quoting *Caldwell v. Mississippi*, 472 U.S. 320, 105 S.Ct. 2633 (1985), in turn quoting *Long*.]

B

Notwithstanding the clarity of the Court's holding in *Harris*, the majority asserts that Coleman has read the rule announced therein "out of context." I submit, however, that it is the majority that has wrested *Harris* out of the context of a preference for the vindication of fundamental constitutional rights and that has set it down in a vacuum of rhetoric about federalism. In its attempt to justify a blind abdication of responsibility by the federal courts, the majority's opinion marks the nadir of the Court's recent habeas jurisprudence, where the discourse of rights is routinely replaced with the functional dialect of interests. The Court's habeas jurisprudence now routinely, and without evident reflection, subordinates fundamental constitutional rights to mere utilitarian interests. * * *

It is well settled that the existence of a state procedural default does not divest a federal court of jurisdiction on collateral review. See *Wainwright v. Sykes*, 433 U.S. 72, 97 S.Ct. 2497 (1977). Rather, the important office of the federal courts in vindicating federal rights gives way to the States' enforcement of their procedural rules to protect the States' interest in being an equal partner in safeguarding federal rights. This accommodation furthers the values underlying federalism in two ways. First, encouraging a defendant to assert his federal rights in the appropriate state forum makes it possible for transgressions to be arrested sooner and before they influence an erroneous deprivation of liberty. Second, thorough examination of a prisoner's federal claims in state court permits more effective review of those claims in federal court, honing the accuracy of the writ as an implement to eradicate unlawful detention. See *Rose v. Lundy*, 455 U.S. 509, 102 S.Ct. 1198 (1982); *Brown v. Allen* (opinion of FRANKFURTER, J.). The majority ignores these purposes in concluding that a State need not bear the burden of making clear its intent to rely on such a rule. When it is uncertain whether a state-court judgment denying relief from federal claims rests on a procedural bar, it is inconsistent with federalism principles for a federal court to exercise discretion to decline to review those federal claims.

* * *

III

Having abandoned the plain-statement rule with respect to a summary order, the majority must consider Coleman's argument that the untimely filing of his notice of appeal was the result of attorney error of sufficient magnitude as to constitute cause for his procedural default. In a sleight of logic that would be ironic if not for its tragic consequences, the majority concludes that a state prisoner pursuing state collateral relief must bear the risk of his attorney's grave errors—even if the result of those errors is that the prisoner will be executed without having presented his federal claims to a federal court—because this attribution of risk represents the appropriate "allocation of costs." Whether unprofessional attorney conduct in a state postconviction proceeding should bar federal habeas review of a state prisoner's conviction and sentence of death is not a question of costs to be allocated most efficiently. It is, rather, another circumstance where this Court must determine whether federal rights should yield to state interests. In my view, the obligation of a federal habeas court to correct fundamental constitutional violations, particularly in capital cases, should not accede to the State's "discretion to develop and implement programs to aid prisoners seeking to secure postconviction review." *Pennsylvania v. Finley*, 481 U.S. 551, 107 S.Ct. 1990 (1987).

The majority first contends that this Court's decision in *Murray v. Carrier*, 477 U.S. 478, 106 S.Ct. 2639 (1986), expressly resolves this issue. Of course, that cannot be so, as the procedural default at issue in *Murray* occurred on direct review, not collateral attack, and this Court has no authority to resolve issues not before it. Moreover, notwithstanding the majority's protestations to the contrary, the language of *Murray* strongly suggests that the Court's resolution of the issue would have been the same regardless of when the procedural default occurred. The Court in *Murray* explained: "A State's procedural rules serve vital purposes at trial, on appeal, and *on state collateral attack*." (emphasis added). Rejecting Carrier's argument that, with respect to the standard for cause, procedural defaults on appeal should be treated differently from those that occur during the trial, the Court stated that "the standard for cause should not vary depending on the timing of a procedural default or on the strength of an uncertain and difficult assessment of the relative magnitude of the benefits attributable to the state procedural rules that attach at *each successive stage of the judicial process*." (emphasis added).

The rule foreshadowed by this language, which the majority today evades, most faithfully adheres to a principled view of the role of federal habeas jurisdiction. As noted above, federal courts forgo the exercise of their habeas jurisprudence over claims that are procedurally barred out of respect for the state interests served by those rules. Recognition of state procedural forfeitures discourages petitioners from attempting to avoid state proceedings and accommodates the State's interest in finality. No rule, however, can deter gross incompetence. To permit a procedural default caused by attorney error egregious enough to constitute ineffective assistance of counsel to preclude federal habeas review of a state prisoner's federal claims in no way serves the State's interest in preserving the integrity of its rules and proceedings. The interest in finality, standing alone, cannot provide a sufficient reason for a federal habeas court to compromise its protection of constitutional rights.

The majority's conclusion that Coleman's allegations of ineffective assistance of counsel, if true, would not excuse a procedural default that occurred in the state postconviction proceeding is particularly disturbing because, at the time of Coleman's appeal, state law precluded defendants from raising certain claims on direct appeal. As the majority acknowledges, under state law as it existed at the time of Coleman's trial and appeal, Coleman could raise his ineffective-assistance-of-counsel claim with respect to counsel's conduct during trial and appeal only in state habeas. This Court has made clear that the Fourteenth Amendment obligates a State " 'to assure the indigent defendant an adequate opportunity to present his claims fairly in the context of the State's appellate process,' " *Pennsylvania v. Finley*, quoting *Ross v. Moffitt*, 417 U.S. 600, 94 S.Ct. 2437 (1974), and "require[s] that the state appellate system be 'free from unreasoned distinctions.' " While the State may have wide latitude to structure its appellate process as it deems most effective, it cannot, consistent with the Fourteenth Amendment, structure it in such a way as to deny indigent defendants meaningful access. Accordingly, if a State desires to remove from the process of direct appellate review a claim or category of claims, the Fourteenth Amendment binds the State to ensure that the defendant has effective assistance of counsel for the entirety of the procedure where the removed claims may be raised. Similarly, fundamental fairness dictates that the State, having removed certain claims from the process of direct review, bear the burden of ineffective assistance of counsel in the proceeding to which the claim has been removed.

Ultimately, the Court's determination that ineffective assistance of counsel cannot constitute cause of a procedural default in a state postconviction proceeding is patently unfair. In concluding that it was not inequitable to apply the cause and prejudice standard to procedural defaults that occur on appeal, the *Murray* Court took comfort in the "additional safeguard against miscarriages of justice in criminal cases": the right to effective assistance of counsel. The Court reasoned: "The presence of such a safeguard may properly inform this Court's judgment in determining '[w]hat standards should govern the exercise of the habeas court's equitable discretion' with respect to procedurally defaulted claims." "[F]undamental fairness is the central concern of the writ of habeas corpus." *Strickland v. Washington* 466 U.S. 668, 104 S.Ct. 2052 (1984). It is the quintessence of inequity that the Court today abandons that safeguard while continuing to embrace the cause and prejudice standard.

I dissent.

Note

1.　*The adequacy of the state procedural rule.*

In *Coleman v. Thompson*, the Court addresses how a federal court is to determine when a state court has dismissed a habeas petitioner's claim in reliance on a state procedural rule. Another much-litigated issue is when a state procedural rule relied on by the state court is to be deemed "adequate," *i.e.*, firmly established and regularly followed.

Ford v. Georgia, 498 U.S. 411, 111 S.Ct. 850 (1991) is an example of the Supreme Court's treatment of the adequacy of a procedural rule. In *Ford*, the trial was held prior to the Supreme Court's decision in *Batson v. Kentucky*, 476 U.S. 79, 106 S.Ct. 1712 (1986) [discussed in Chapter 6] holding unconstitutional the use of race-based peremptory challenges. Prior to trial, the defense counsel filed a "Motion to Restrict Racial Use of Peremptory Challenges" alleging that the prosecutor for Coweta County had "over a long period of time" excluded black persons from juries "where the issues to be tried involved members of the opposite race." The motion stated that Ford "anticipated" the prosecutor would continue the pattern of racial exclusion in this case because of the different races of the accused and the victim. The attorney requested an order forbidding the State to use "its peremptory challenges in a racially biased manner that would exclude members of the black race from serving on the Jury." The motion was denied. The prosecutor then used 9 of his 10 peremptory challenges to strike black prospective jurors. Subsequently, on the second day of trial, there was further discussion of the issue. The prosecutor asked whether he needed to make any showing of his reasons for his peremptory challenges, and the judge said he was not asking for any. The defendant was convicted and raised his *"Batson"* claim on appeal. The Georgia Supreme Court affirmed.

While Ford's petition for certiorari was pending, *Batson* was decided, and the Supreme Court vacated and remanded Ford's case for further consideration. The Georgia Supreme Court held that Ford's equal protection claim was procedurally barred. The court applied the state procedural rule announced in *State v. Sparks*, 355 S.E.2d 658 (Ga. 1987), that a *Batson* claim must "be raised prior to the time the jurors selected to try the case are sworn." Reading *Sparks* as requiring a contemporaneous objection to a defendant's jury "after it was selected and before the trial commenced," the court concluded that petitioner had failed to make such an objection, with the result that any *Batson* claim was barred by a valid state procedural rule.

The Supreme Court reversed and explained:

> * * * In *James v. Kentucky*, 466 U.S. 341, 104 S.Ct. 1830 (1984), we held that only a 'firmly established and regularly followed state practice' may be interposed by a State to prevent subsequent review by this Court of a federal constitutional claim.
>
> The Supreme Court of Georgia's application of its decision in *Sparks* to the case before us does not even remotely satisfy the requirement of *James* that an adequate and independent state procedural bar to the entertainment of constitutional claims must have been 'firmly established and regularly followed' by the time as of which it is to be applied. At the time of petitioner's trial, Georgia's procedural law was just what it was when the *Sparks* defendant was tried, for *Sparks* was decided more than two years after petitioner in this case filed his motion on the prosecution's use of peremptory challenges and long after petitioner's trial was over. When petitioner filed his pretrial motion, he was subject to the same law that had allowed the defendant in *Sparks* to object even after the jury had been sworn. The very holding in *Sparks* was that the defendant was not procedurally barred from raising a *Batson* claim after the jury had been sworn and given preliminary instructions, and after the trial court had held a lengthy hearing on an unrelated matter. The court entertained the claim as having been raised 'relatively promptly' because no prior decision of the Supreme Court of Georgia had required an earlier objection.
>
> To apply *Sparks* retroactively to bar consideration of a claim not raised between the jurors' selection and oath would therefore apply a rule unannounced at the time of petitioner's trial and consequently inadequate to serve as an independent state ground within the meaning of *James*. Indeed, the Georgia court itself in *Sparks* disclaimed any such effect for that decision. It was only as to cases tried *"hereafter* [that] any

claim under *Batson* should be raised prior to the time the jurors selected to try the case are sworn." (emphasis added). This case was not tried "hereafter," and the rule announced prospectively in *Sparks* would not, even by its own terms, apply to petitioner's case. Since the rule was not firmly established at the time in question, there is no need to dwell on the further point that the state court's inconsistent application of the rule in petitioner's case and *Sparks* would also fail the second *James* requirement that the state practice have been regularly followed.

498 U.S, at 423–425, 111 S.Ct. at 857–858.

In *Lee v. Kemna*, 534 U.S. 362, 122 S.Ct. 877 (2002) (a non-capital case), the Supreme Court held that, in some cases, even a "firmly established and regularly followed" procedural rule might not be adequate to bar federal review. On the third day of trial, Lee's three alibi witnesses, who were under subpoena, left the courtroom before the beginning of the defense case and could not be located. Lee's counsel orally requested a continuance to the following day to find the witnesses and enforce the subpoena, but the motion was denied because the judge was not available the following day. The judge made no mention of court rules requiring that continuance motions be made in writing with certain factual allegations. Lee then presented no defense and was convicted. On appeal, and in state post-conviction, Lee claimed that the denial of his motion was a denial of due process, but the state appellate court held that the claim was procedurally defaulted by Lee's failure to comply with the court rules. The Supreme Court held (6–3) that the case was one of the "exceptional cases in which exorbitant application of a generally sound rule renders the state ground inadequate to stop consideration of a federal question." The Court found the application exorbitant because: (1) the judge's reason for the denial could not have been countered by a motion complying with the rules, and the failure to comply with the rules was never brought up so Lee could correct the record; (2) no state court decision directed flawless compliance with the rules; and (3) Lee's motion served the all the purposes of the rules.

HOUSE v. BELL

547 U.S. 518, 126 S.Ct. 2064, 165 L.Ed.2d 1 (2006).

JUSTICE KENNEDY delivered the opinion of the Court.

Some 20 years ago in rural Tennessee, Carolyn Muncey was murdered. A jury convicted petitioner Paul Gregory House of the crime and sentenced him to death, but new revelations cast doubt on the jury's verdict. House, protesting his innocence, seeks access to federal court to pursue habeas corpus relief based on constitutional claims that are procedurally barred under state law. Out of respect for the finality of state-court judgments federal habeas courts, as a general rule, are closed to claims that state courts would consider defaulted. In certain exceptional cases involving a compelling claim of actual innocence, however, the state procedural default rule is not a bar to a federal habeas corpus petition. See *Schlup v. Delo*, 513 U.S. 298, 115 S.Ct. 851 (1995). After careful review of the full record, we conclude that House has made the stringent showing required by this exception; and we hold that his federal habeas action may proceed.

[At trial, the prosecution's evidence against House was as follows. Mrs. Muncey was last seen by any of the witnesses on Saturday evening. That night her 10–year old daughter, Lora, was awakened by the sound of a man or men talking with her mother. The man's voice sounded like Lora's grandfather and said that her father, Mr. Muncey, "had a wreck down the road." Lora heard her mother crying. Some time later, Lora and her brother realized their mother was not in the house and went to look for her. She was still not at home when Mr. Muncey later returned. The following afternoon, Ray Hensley, Mrs. Muncey's cousin, was driving to the Muncey house when he saw House, an acquaintance of the Munceys appear next to an embankment about 100 yards from the Munceys' driveway. He also saw a white Plymouth parked near a sawmill. Hensley drove on to the house, but seeing no car in the driveway, retraced his route. He encountered House in the Plymouth and flagged him down. House said he had heard of Mrs. Muncey's disappearance and that Mr. Muncey, who was an alcoholic, was elsewhere "getting drunk." The conversation aroused Hensley's suspicions, and he and a friend returned to the embankment and discovered Mrs. Muncey's body concealed in brush and tree branches near where House's car had been parked. Later that day the county sheriff questioned House about his whereabouts the previous evening, and House claimed falsely that he had spent the entire evening with his girlfriend, Donna Turner, and, when asked, House falsely stated that the pants he was wearing were the same ones he wore the night before. The sheriff observed that House had scratches on his arms and hands, and a knuckle on a finger was bruised. Turner testified that House left her trailer at 10:30 or 10:45 to go for a walk, and when he returned, he was hot and panting and missing his shirt and his shoes. House told her that he had been harassed by some people in a vehicle and had swung around and hit something, after which he took off running and heard two shots. The pants House was wearing on Saturday night were seized and tested by the FBI. Agent Bigbee identified small bloodstains consistent with Mrs. Muncey's blood, but not House's, on the pants, and he determined that semen consistent with House's was present on Mrs. Muncey's nightgown and panties.

[The jury found House guilty of first degree murder. At the sentencing phase, the prosecution presented evidence that House was on parole after a sexual assault and asked the jury to find three aggravating factors to support a death sentence: (1) that House had previously been convicted of a felony involving the use or threat of violence; (2) that the homicide was especially heinous, atrocious, or cruel in that it involved torture or depravity of mind; and (3) that the murder was committed while House was committing, attempting to commit, or fleeing from the commission of, rape or kidnaping. As mitigation, the defense offered testimony by House's father and mother. The jury found all three aggravating factors and sentenced House to death.

[The Tennessee Supreme Court affirmed House's conviction and sentence, describing the evidence against House as "circumstantial" but "quite strong." House's subsequent petition for postconviction relief, raising several claims, including ineffective assistance of counsel, was dismissed by the trial court. On appeal, House's attorney raised only a jury instruction claim, which was rejected by the Tennessee Court of Criminal Appeals, and the Tennessee Supreme Court denied review. House filed a second postconviction petition, again raising an ineffectiveness of counsel claim in state court, but, after extensive litigation, the petition was dismissed as a successor petition. House sought federal habeas relief on the grounds of ineffective assistance of counsel and prosecutorial misconduct. The district court deemed House's claims procedurally defaulted, but held an evidentiary hearing to determine whether House fell within the "actual innocence" exception to procedural default. The court denied relief, and a divided panel of the Sixth Circuit affirmed, but the case was taken en banc. The en banc court in turn affirmed (8–7), and the Supreme Court granted certiorari.]

IV

As a general rule, claims forfeited under state law may support federal habeas relief only if the prisoner demonstrates cause for the default and prejudice from the asserted error. See *Murray v. Carrier,* 477 U.S. 478, 106 S.Ct. 2639 (1986); *Engle v. Isaac,* 456 U.S. 107, 102 S.Ct. 1558 (1982); *Wainwright v. Sykes,* 433 U.S. 72, 97 S.Ct. 2497 (1977). The rule is based on the comity and respect that must be accorded to state-court judgments. The bar is not, however, unqualified. In an effort to "balance the societal interests in finality, comity, and conservation of scarce judicial resources with the individual interest in justice that arises in the extraordinary case," *Schlup,* the Court has recognized a miscarriage-of-justice exception. " '[I]n appropriate cases,' " the Court has said, "the principles of comity and finality that inform the concepts of cause and prejudice 'must yield to the imperative of correcting a fundamentally unjust incarceration,' " *Carrier, supra* (quoting *Engle, supra*).

In *Schlup,* the Court adopted a specific rule to implement this general principle. It held that prisoners asserting innocence as a gateway to defaulted claims must establish that, in light of new evidence, "it is more likely than not that no reasonable juror would have found petitioner guilty beyond a reasonable doubt." This formulation, *Schlup* explains, "ensures that petitioner's case is truly 'extraordinary,' while still providing petitioner a meaningful avenue by which to avoid a manifest injustice." *Ibid.* (quoting *McCleskey v. Zant,* 499 U.S. 467, 111 S.Ct. 1454 (1991)). In the usual case the presumed guilt of a prisoner convicted in state court counsels against federal review of defaulted claims. Yet a petition supported by a convincing *Schlup* gateway showing "raise[s] sufficient doubt about [the petitioner's] guilt to undermine confidence in the result of the trial without the assurance that that trial was untainted by constitutional

AFTER THE DEATH JUDGMENT

error"; hence, "a review of the merits of the constitutional claims" is justified.

For purposes of this case several features of the *Schlup* standard bear emphasis. First, although "[t]o be credible" a gateway claim requires "new reliable evidence—whether it be exculpatory scientific evidence, trustworthy eyewitness accounts, or critical physical evidence—that was not presented at trial," the habeas court's analysis is not limited to such evidence. There is no dispute in this case that House has presented some new reliable evidence; the State has conceded as much. In addition, because the District Court held an evidentiary hearing in this case, and because the State does not challenge the court's decision to do so, we have no occasion to elaborate on *Schlup's* observation that when considering an actual-innocence claim in the context of a request for an evidentiary hearing, the District Court need not "test the new evidence by a standard appropriate for deciding a motion for summary judgment," but rather may "consider how the timing of the submission and the likely credibility of the affiants bear on the probable reliability of that evidence." Our review in this case addresses the merits of the *Schlup* inquiry, based on a fully developed record, and with respect to that inquiry *Schlup* makes plain that the habeas court must consider "all the evidence," old and new, incriminating and exculpatory, without regard to whether it would necessarily be admitted under "rules of admissibility that would govern at trial." Based on this total record, the court must make "a probabilistic determination about what reasonable, properly instructed jurors would do." The court's function is not to make an independent factual determination about what likely occurred, but rather to assess the likely impact of the evidence on reasonable jurors.

Second, it bears repeating that the *Schlup* standard is demanding and permits review only in the "extraordinary" case. At the same time, though, the *Schlup* standard does not require absolute certainty about the petitioner's guilt or innocence. A petitioner's burden at the gateway stage is to demonstrate that more likely than not, in light of the new evidence, no reasonable juror would find him guilty beyond a reasonable doubt—or, to remove the double negative, that more likely than not any reasonable juror would have reasonable doubt.

Finally, as the *Schlup* decision explains, the gateway actual-innocence standard is "by no means equivalent to the standard of *Jackson v. Virginia,* 443 U.S. 307, 99 S.Ct. 2781 (1979)," which governs claims of insufficient evidence. When confronted with a challenge based on trial evidence, courts presume the jury resolved evidentiary disputes reasonably so long as sufficient evidence supports the verdict. Because a *Schlup* claim involves evidence the trial jury did not have before it, the inquiry requires the federal court to assess how reasonable jurors would react to the overall, newly supplemented record. If new evidence so requires, this may include consideration of "the credibility of the witnesses presented at trial."

[The Court rejected the State's argument that AEDPA had replaced the *Schlup* standard with a more stringent standard requiring a petitioner to "show[ ] by clear and convincing evidence that, but for a constitutional error, no reasonable juror would have found the petitioner eligible for the death penalty under the applicable state law." The Court also rejected the State's argument that the Court was bound by the findings of the District Court absent a showing of clear error, instead reasoning that the *Schlup* inquiry requires a "holistic judgment" and does not turn on "discrete findings regarding disputed points of fact." The Court added that the District Court "did not clearly apply *Schlup*'s predictive standard" and the basis for some of its conclusions was unclear.]

With this background in mind we turn to the evidence developed in House's federal habeas proceedings.

DNA Evidence

First, in direct contradiction of evidence presented at trial, DNA testing has established that the semen on Mrs. Muncey's nightgown and panties came from her husband, Mr. Muncey, not from House. The State, though conceding this point, insists this new evidence is immaterial. At the guilt phase at least, neither sexual contact nor motive were elements of the offense, so in the State's view the evidence, or lack of evidence, of sexual assault or sexual advance is of no consequence. We disagree. In fact we consider the new disclosure of central importance.

From beginning to end the case is about who committed the crime. When identity is in question, motive is key. The point, indeed, was not lost on the prosecution, for it introduced the evidence and relied on it in the final guilt-phase closing argument. Referring to "evidence at the scene," the prosecutor suggested that House committed, or attempted to commit, some "indignity" on Mrs. Muncey that neither she "nor any mother on that road would want to do with Mr. House." Particularly in a case like this where the proof was, as the State Supreme Court observed, circumstantial, we think a jury would have given this evidence great weight. Quite apart from providing proof of motive, it was the only forensic evidence at the scene that would link House to the murder.

Law and society, as they ought to do, demand accountability when a sexual offense has been committed, so not only did this evidence link House to the crime; it likely was a factor in persuading the jury not to let him go free. At sentencing, moreover, the jury came to the unanimous conclusion, beyond a reasonable doubt, that the murder was committed in the course of a rape or kidnaping. The alleged sexual motivation relates to both those determinations. This is particularly so given that, at the sentencing phase, the jury was advised that House had a previous conviction for sexual assault.

A jury informed that fluids on Mrs. Muncey's garments could have come from House might have found that House trekked the nearly two miles to the victim's home and lured her away in order to commit a sexual offense. By contrast a jury acting without the assumption that the semen could have come from House would have found it necessary to establish some different motive, or, if the same motive, an intent far more speculative. When the only direct evidence of sexual assault drops out of the case, so, too, does a central theme in the State's narrative linking House to the crime. In that light, furthermore, House's odd evening walk and his false statements to authorities, while still potentially incriminating, might appear less suspicious.

Bloodstains

The other relevant forensic evidence is the blood on House's pants, which appears in small, even minute, stains in scattered places. As the prosecutor told the jury, they were stains that, due to their small size, "you or I might not detect[,] [m]ight not see, but which the FBI lab was able to find on [House's] jeans." The stains appear inside the right pocket, outside that pocket, near the inside button, on the left thigh and outside leg, on the seat of the pants, and on the right bottom cuff, including inside the pants. Due to testing by the FBI, cuttings now appear on the pants in several places where stains evidently were found. (The cuttings were destroyed in the testing process, and defense experts were unable to replicate the tests.) At trial, the government argued "nothing that the defense has introduced in this case explains what blood is doing on his jeans, all over [House's] jeans, that is scientifically, completely different from his blood." House, though not disputing at this point that the blood is Mrs. Muncey's, now presents an alternative explanation that, if credited, would undermine the probative value of the blood evidence.

During House's habeas proceedings, Dr. Cleland Blake, an Assistant Chief Medical Examiner for the State of Tennessee and a consultant in forensic pathology to the TBI for 22 years, testified that the blood on House's pants was chemically too degraded, and too similar to blood collected during the autopsy, to have come from Mrs. Muncey's body on the night of the crime. The blood samples collected during the autopsy were placed in test tubes without preservative. Under such conditions, according to Dr. Blake, "you will have enzyme degradation. You will have different blood group degradation, blood marker degradation." The problem of decay, moreover, would have been compounded by the body's long exposure to the elements, sitting outside for the better part of a summer day. In contrast, if blood is preserved on cloth, "it will stay there for years"; indeed, Dr. Blake said he deliberately places blood drops on gauze during autopsies to preserve it for later testing. The blood on House's pants, judging by Agent Bigbee's tests, showed "similar deterioration, breakdown of certain of the named numbered enzymes" as in the autopsy samples. "[I]f the victim's blood had spilled on the jeans while the victim was alive and this blood had dried," Dr. Blake stated, "the deterioration would not have occurred," and "you would expect [the blood on the jeans] to be different than what was in the tube." Dr. Blake thus concluded the blood on the jeans came from the autopsy samples, not from Mrs. Muncey's live (or recently killed) body.

Other evidence confirms that blood did in fact spill from the vials. It appears the vials passed from Dr. Carabia, who performed the autopsy, into the hands of two local law enforcement officers, who transported it to the FBI, where Agent Bigbee performed the enzyme tests. The blood was contained in four vials, evidently with neither preservative nor a proper seal. The vials, in turn, were stored in a styrofoam box, but nothing indicates the box was kept cool. Rather, in what an evidence protocol expert at the habeas hearing described as a violation of proper procedure, the styrofoam box was packed in the same cardboard box as other evidence including House's pants (apparently in a paper bag) and other clothing (in separate bags). The cardboard box was then carried in the officers' car while they made the 10–hour journey from Tennessee to the FBI lab. Dr. Blake stated that blood vials in hot conditions (such as a car trunk in the summer) could blow open; and in fact, by the time the blood reached the FBI it had hemolyzed, or spoiled, due to heat exposure. By the time the blood passed from the FBI to a defense expert, roughly a vial and a half were empty, though Agent Bigbee testified he used at most a quarter of one vial. Blood, moreover, had seeped onto one corner of the styrofoam box and onto packing gauze inside the box below the vials.

In addition, although the pants apparently were packaged initially in a paper bag and FBI records suggest they arrived at the FBI in one, the record does not contain the paper bag but does contain a plastic bag with a label listing the pants and Agent Scott's name—and the plastic bag has blood on it. The blood appears in a forked streak roughly five inches long and two inches wide running down the bag's outside front. Though testing by House's expert confirmed the stain was blood, the expert could not determine the blood's source. Speculations about when and how the blood got there add to the confusion regarding the origins of the stains on House's pants.

[The State responded with Agent Bigbee's testimony that he did not observe any blood spillage in the styrofoam box when he received it and the testimony of a blood spatter expert tending to show that all the blood spillage occurred after the pants were examined. The State also challenged Dr. Blake's scientific conclusions. In turn, House established that Bigbee did not handle the evidence according FBI procedures, and he challenged the scientific conclusions of the blood spatter expert as to the timing of the blood spill.]

In sum, considering "all the evidence," *Schlup*, on this issue, we think the evidentiary disarray surrounding the blood, taken together with Dr. Blake's testimony and the limited rebuttal of it in the present record, would prevent reasonable jurors from placing significant reliance on the blood evidence. We now know, though the trial jury did not, that an Assistant Chief Medical Examiner believes the blood on House's jeans must have come from autopsy samples; that a vial and a quarter of autopsy blood is unaccounted for; that the blood was transported to the FBI together with the pants in conditions that could have caused vials to spill; that the blood did indeed spill at least once during its journey from Tennessee authorities through FBI hands to a defense expert; that the pants were stored in a plastic bag bearing both a large blood stain and a label with TBI Agent Scott's name; and that the styrofoam box containing the blood samples may well have been opened before it arrived at the FBI lab. Thus, whereas the bloodstains, emphasized by the prosecution, seemed strong evidence of House's guilt at trial, the record now raises substantial questions about the blood's origin.

A Different Suspect

Were House's challenge to the State's case limited to the questions he has raised about the blood and semen, the other evidence favoring the prosecution might well suffice to bar relief. There is, however, more; for in the post-trial proceedings House presented troubling evidence that Mr. Muncey, the victim's husband, himself could have been the murderer.

At trial, as has been noted, the jury heard that roughly two weeks before the murder Mrs. Muncey's brother received a frightened phone call from his sister indicating that she and Mr. Muncey had been fighting, that she was scared, and that she wanted to leave him. The jury also learned that the brother once saw Mr. Muncey "smac[k]" the victim. House now has produced evidence from multiple sources suggesting that Mr. Muncey regularly abused his wife. For example, one witness—Kathy Parker, a lifelong area resident who denied any animosity towards Mr. Muncey— recalled that Mrs. Muncey "was constantly with black eyes and busted mouth." In addition Hazel Miller, who is Kathy Parker's mother and a lifelong acquaintance of Mr. Muncey, testified at the habeas hearing that two or three months before the victim's death Mr. Muncey came to Miller's home and "tried to get my daughter [Parker] to go out with him." (Parker had dated Mr. Muncey at age 14.) According to Miller, Muncey said "[h]e was upset with his wife, that they had had an argument and he said he was going to get rid of that woman one way or the other."

Another witness—Mary Atkins, also an area native who "grew up" with Mr. Muncey and professed no hard feelings claims she saw Mr. Muncey "backhan[d]" Mrs. Muncey on the very night of the murder. Atkins recalled that during a break in the recreation center dance, she saw Mr. Muncey and his wife arguing in the parking lot. Mr. Muncey "grabbed her and he just backhanded her." After that, Mrs. Muncey "left walking." There was also testimony from Atkins' mother, named Artie Lawson. A self-described "good friend" of Mr. Muncey, Lawson said Mr. Muncey visited her the morning after the murder, before the body was found. According to Lawson, Mr. Muncey asked her to tell anyone who inquired not only that she had been at the dance the evening before and had seen him, but also that he had breakfasted at her home at 6 o'clock that morning. Lawson had not in fact been at the dance, nor had Mr. Muncey been with her so early.

Of most importance is the testimony of Kathy Parker and her sister Penny Letner. They testified at the habeas hearing that, around the time of House's trial, Mr. Muncey had confessed to the crime. Parker recalled that she and "some family members and some friends [were] sitting around drinking" at Parker's trailer when Mr. Muncey "just walked in and sit down." Muncey, who had evidently been drinking heavily, began "rambling off ... [t]alking about what happened to his wife and how it happened and he didn't mean to do it." According to Parker, Mr. Muncey "said they had been into [an] argument and he slapped her and she fell and hit her head and it killed her and he didn't mean for it to happen." Parker said she "freaked out and run him off."

Letner similarly recalled that at some point either "during [House's] trial or just before," Mr. Muncey intruded on a gathering at Parker's home. Appearing "pretty well blistered," Muncey "went to crying and was talking about his wife and her death and he was saying that he didn't mean to do it." "[D]idn't mean to do what[?]," Letner asked, at which point Mr. Muncey explained:

> "[S]he was 'bitching him out' because he didn't take her fishing that night, that he went to the dance instead. He said when he come home that she was still on him pretty heavily 'bitching him out' again and that he smacked her and that she fell and hit her head. He said I didn't mean to do it, but I had to get rid of her, because I didn't want to be charged with murder."

Letner, who was then 19 years old with a small child, said Mr. Muncey's statement "scared [her] quite badly," so she "got out of there immediately." Asked whether she reported the incident to the authorities, Letner stated, "I was frightened, you know.... I figured me being 19 year old they wouldn't listen to anything I had to say." Parker, on the other hand, claimed she (Parker) in fact went to the Sherriff's Department, but no one would listen:

> "I tried to speak to the Sheriff but he was real busy. He sent me to a deputy. The deputy told me to go upstairs to the courtroom and talk to this guy, I can't remember his name. I never did really get to talk to anybody."

Parker said she did not discuss the matter further because "[t]hey had it all signed, sealed and delivered. We didn't know anything to do until we heard that they reopened [House's] trial." Parker's mother, Hazel Miller, confirmed she had driven Parker to the courthouse, where Parker "went to talk to some of the people about this case."

Other testimony suggests Mr. Muncey had the opportunity to commit the crime. According to Dennis Wallace, a local law enforcement official who provided security at the dance on the night of the murder, Mr. Muncey left the dance "around 10:00, 10:30, 9:30 to 10:30." Although Mr. Muncey told law enforcement officials just after the murder that he left the dance only briefly and returned, Wallace could not recall seeing him back there again. Later that evening, Wallace responded to Mr. Muncey's report that his wife was missing. Muncey denied he and his wife had been "a fussing or a fighting"; he claimed his wife had been "kidnapped." Wallace did not recall seeing any blood, disarray, or knocked-over furniture, although he admitted he "didn't pay too much attention" to whether the floor appeared especially clean. According to Wallace, Mr. Muncey said "let's search for her" and then led Wallace out to search "in the weeds" around the home and the driveway (not out on the road where the body was found).

In the habeas proceedings, then, two different witnesses (Parker and Letner) described a confession by Mr. Muncey; two more (Atkins and Lawson) described suspicious behavior (a fight and an attempt to construct a false alibi) around the time of the crime; and still other witnesses described a history of abuse.

As to Parker and Letner, the District Court noted that it was "not impressed with the allegations of individuals who wait over ten years to come forward with their evidence," especially considering that "there was no physical evidence in the Munceys' kitchen to corroborate [Mr. Muncey's] alleged confession that he killed [his wife] there." Parker and Letner, however, did attempt to explain their delay coming forward, and the record indicates no reason why these two women, both lifelong acquaintances of Mr. Muncey, would have wanted either to frame him or to help House. Furthermore, the record includes at least some independent support for the statements Parker and Letner attributed to Mr. Muncey. The supposed explanation for the fatal fight—that his wife was complaining about going fishing—fits with Mrs. Muncey's statement to [a neighbor] earlier that evening that her husband's absence was "all right, because she was going to make him take her fishing the next day." And Dr. Blake testified, in only partial contradiction of Dr. Carabia [the State's pathologist], that Mrs. Muncey's head injury resulted from "a surface with an edge" or "a hard surface with a corner," not from a fist. (Dr. Carabia had said either a fist or some other object could have been the cause.)

Mr. Muncey testified at the habeas hearing, and the District Court did not question his credibility. Though Mr. Muncey said he seemed to remember visiting Lawson the day after the murder, he denied either killing his wife or confessing to doing so. Yet Mr. Muncey also claimed, contrary to Constable Wallace's testimony and to his own prior statement, that he left the dance on the night of the crime only when it ended at midnight. Mr. Muncey, moreover, denied ever hitting Mrs. Muncey; the State itself had to impeach him with a prior statement on this point.

It bears emphasis, finally, that Parker's and Letner's testimony is not comparable to the sort of eleventh-hour affidavit vouching for a defendant and incriminating a conveniently absent suspect that Justice O'Connor described in her concurring opinion in *Herrera v. Collins*, 506 U.S. 390, 113 S.Ct. 853 (1993), as "unfortunate" and "not uncommon" in capital cases; nor was the confession Parker and Letner described induced under pressure of interrogation. The confession evidence here involves an alleged spontaneous statement recounted by two eyewitnesses with no evident motive to lie. For this reason it has more probative value than, for example, incriminating testimony from inmates, suspects, or friends or relations of the accused.

The evidence pointing to Mr. Muncey is by no means conclusive. If considered in isolation, a reasonable jury might well disregard it. In combination, however, with the challenges to the blood evidence and the lack of motive with respect to House, the evidence pointing to Mr. Muncey likely would reinforce other doubts as to House's guilt.

Other Evidence

Certain other details were presented at the habeas hearing. First, Dr. Blake, in addition to testifying about the blood evidence and the victim's head injury, examined photographs of House's bruises and scratches and concluded, based on 35 years' experience monitoring the development and healing of bruises, that they were too old to have resulted from the crime. In addition Dr. Blake claimed that the injury on House's right knuckle was indicative of "[g]etting mashed"; it was not consistent with striking someone. (That of course would also eliminate the explanation that the injury came from the blow House supposedly told Turner he gave to his unidentified assailant.)

The victim's daughter, Lora Muncey (now Lora Tharp), also testified at the habeas hearing. She repeated her recollection of hearing a man with a deep voice like her grandfather's and a statement that her father had had a wreck down by the creek. She also denied seeing any signs of struggle or hearing a fight between her parents, though she also said she could not recall her parents ever fighting physically. The District Court found her credible, and this testimony certainly cuts in favor of the State.

Finally, House himself testified at the habeas proceedings. He essentially repeated the story he allegedly told Turner about getting attacked on the road. The District Court found, however, based on House's demeanor, that he "was not a credible witness."

Conclusion

This is not a case of conclusive exoneration. Some aspects of the State's evidence—Lora Muncey's memory of a deep voice, House's bizarre evening walk, his lie to law enforcement, his appearance near the body, and the blood on his pants—still support an inference of guilt. Yet the central forensic proof connecting House to the crime—the blood and the semen—has been called into question, and House has put forward substantial evidence pointing to a different suspect. Accordingly, and although the issue is close, we conclude that this is the rare case where—had the jury heard all the conflicting testimony—it is more likely than not that no reasonable juror viewing the record as a whole would lack reasonable doubt.

V

In addition to his gateway claim under *Schlup*, House argues that he has shown freestanding innocence and that as a result his imprisonment and planned execution are unconstitutional. In *Herrera*, decided three years before *Schlup*, the Court assumed without deciding that "in a capital case a truly persuasive demonstration of 'actual innocence' made after trial would render the execution of a defendant unconstitutional, and warrant federal habeas relief if there were no state avenue open to process such a claim." "[T]he threshold showing for such an assumed right would necessarily be extraordinarily high," the Court explained, and petitioner's evidence there fell "far short of that which would have to be made in order to trigger the sort of constitutional claim which we have assumed, *arguendo*, to exist." House urges the Court to answer the question left open in *Herrera* and hold not only that freestanding innocence claims are possible but also that he has established one.

We decline to resolve this issue. We conclude here, much as in *Herrera*, that whatever burden a hypothetical freestanding innocence claim would require, this petitioner has not satisfied it. To be sure, House has cast considerable doubt on his guilt—doubt sufficient to satisfy *Schlup's* gateway standard for obtaining federal review despite a state procedural default. In *Herrera*, however, the Court described the threshold for any hypothetical freestanding innocence claim as "extraordinarily high." The sequence of the Court's decisions in *Herrera* and *Schlup*—first leaving unresolved the status of freestanding claims and then establishing the gateway standard—implies at the least that *Herrera* requires more convincing proof of innocence than *Schlup*. It follows, given the closeness of the *Schlup* question here, that House's showing falls short of the threshold implied in *Herrera*.

* * *

House has satisfied the gateway standard set forth in *Schlup* and may proceed on remand with procedurally defaulted constitutional claims. The judgment of the Court of Appeals is reversed, and the case is remanded for further proceedings consistent with this opinion.

JUSTICE ALITO took no part in the consideration or decision of this case.

CHIEF JUSTICE ROBERTS, with whom JUSTICE SCALIA and JUSTICE THOMAS join, concurring in the judgment in part and dissenting in part.

To overcome the procedural hurdle that Paul House created by failing to properly present his constitutional claims to a Tennessee court, he must demonstrate that the constitutional violations he alleges "ha[ve] probably resulted in the conviction of one who is actually innocent," such that a federal court's refusal to hear the defaulted claims would be a "miscarriage of justice." *Schlup v. Delo*, 513 U.S. 298, 115 S.Ct. 851 (1995) (internal quotation marks omitted). To make the requisite showing of actual innocence, House must produce "new *reliable* evidence" and "must show that it is more likely than not that no reasonable juror would have convicted him in the light of the new evidence." *Id.* (emphasis added). The question is not whether House was prejudiced at his trial because the jurors were not aware of the new evidence, but whether all the evidence, considered together, proves that House was actually innocent, so that no reasonable juror would vote to convict him. Considering all the evidence, and giving due regard to the District Court's findings on whether House's new evidence was reliable, I do not find it probable that no reasonable juror would vote to convict him, and accordingly I dissent.

Because I do not think that House has satisfied the actual innocence standard set forth in *Schlup,* I do not believe that he has met the higher threshold for a freestanding innocence claim, assuming such a claim exists. See *Herrera v. Collins,* 506 U.S. 390, 113 S.Ct. 853 (1993). I therefore concur in the judgment with respect to the Court's disposition of that separate claim.

I

In *Schlup,* we stated that a habeas petitioner attempting to present a defaulted claim to a federal court must present "new *reliable* evidence— whether it be exculpatory scientific evidence, trustworthy eyewitness accounts, or critical physical evidence—that was not presented at trial." (emphasis added). Implicit in the requirement that a habeas petitioner present reliable evidence is the expectation that a factfinder will assess reliability. The new evidence at issue in *Schlup* had not been subjected to such an assessment—the claim in *Schlup* was for an evidentiary hearing— and this Court specifically recognized that the "new statements may, of course, be unreliable." The Court stated that the District Court, as the "reviewing tribunal," was tasked with assessing the "probative force" of the petitioner's new evidence of innocence, and "may have to make some credibility assessments." Indeed, the Supreme Court took the unusual step of remanding the case to the Court of Appeals "with instructions to remand to the District Court," so that the District Court could consider how the "likely credibility of the affiants" bears upon the "probable reliability" of the new evidence. In short, the new evidence is not simply taken at face value; its reliability has to be tested.

Critical to the Court's conclusion here that House has sufficiently demonstrated his innocence are three pieces of new evidence presented to the District Court: DNA evidence showing that the semen on Carolyn Muncey's clothing was from her husband, Hubert Muncey, not from House; testimony from new witnesses implicating Mr. Muncey in the murder; and evidence indicating that Mrs. Muncey's blood spilled from test tubes containing autopsy samples in an evidence container. To determine whether it should open its door to House's defaulted constitutional claims, the District Court considered this evidence in a comprehensive evidentiary hearing. As House presented his new evidence, and as the State rebutted it, the District Court observed the witnesses' demeanor, examined physical evidence, and made findings about whether House's new evidence was in fact reliable. This factfinding role is familiar to a district court. "The trial judge's major role is the determination of fact, and with experience in fulfilling that role comes expertise." *Anderson v. Bessemer City,* 470 U.S. 564, 105 S.Ct. 1504 (1985).

The State did not contest House's new DNA evidence excluding him as the source of the semen on Mrs. Muncey's clothing, but it strongly contested the new testimony implicating Mr. Muncey, and it insisted that the blood spillage occurred *after* the FBI tested House's jeans and determined that they were stained with Mrs. Muncey's blood.

At the evidentiary hearing, sisters Kathy Parker and Penny Letner testified that 14 years earlier, either during or around the time of House's trial, they heard Mr. Muncey drunkenly confess to having accidentally killed his wife when he struck her in their home during an argument, causing her to fall and hit her head. *Schlup* provided guidance on how a district court should assess this type of new evidence: The court "may consider how the timing of the submission and the likely credibility of the affiants bear on the probable reliability of that evidence," and it "must assess the probative force of the newly presented evidence in connection with the evidence of guilt adduced at trial." Consistent with this guidance, the District Court concluded that the sisters' testimony was not credible. The court noted that it was "not impressed with the allegations of individuals who wait over ten years to come forward." It also considered how the new testimony fit within the larger web of evidence, observing that Mr. Muncey's alleged confession contradicted the testimony of the Munceys' "very credible" daughter, Lora Tharp, who consistently testified that she did not hear a fight in the house that night, but instead heard a man with a deep voice who lured her mother from the house by saying that Mr. Muncey had been in a wreck near the creek.

The District Court engaged in a similar reliability inquiry with regard to House's new evidence of blood spillage. At the evidentiary hearing, House conceded that FBI testing showed that his jeans were stained with Mrs. Muncey's blood, but he set out to prove that the blood spilled from test tubes containing autopsy samples, and that it did so before the jeans were tested by the FBI. The District Court summarized the testimony of the various witnesses who handled the evidence and their recollections about bloodstains and spillage; it acknowledged that House's expert, Dr. Cleland Blake, disagreed with FBI Agent Paul Bigbee about how to interpret the results of Agent Bigbee's genetic marker analysis summary; and it summarized the testimony of the State's blood spatter expert, Paulette Sutton. After reviewing all the evidence, the District Court stated: "Based upon the evidence introduced during the evidentiary hearing ... the court concludes that the spillage occurred *after* the FBI crime laboratory received and tested the evidence." (emphasis added).

Normally, an appellate court reviews a district court's factual findings only for clear error. The Sixth Circuit deferred to the District Court's factual findings, and *Schlup* did not purport to alter—but instead reaffirmed and highlighted—the district court's critical role as factfinder. Yet the majority asserts that the clear error standard "overstates the effect of the District Court's ruling," and then dismisses the District Court's reliability findings because it is "uncertain about" them, while stopping short of identifying clear error. This is a sharp departure from the guidance in *Schlup*.

In *Schlup,* we contrasted a district court's role in assessing the reliability of new evidence of innocence with a district court's role in deciding a summary judgment motion. We explained that, in the latter situation, the district court does not assess credibility or weigh the evidence, but simply determines whether there is a genuine factual issue for trial. Assessing the reliability of new evidence, on the other hand, is a typical factfinding role, requiring credibility determinations and a weighing of the "probative force" of the new evidence in light of "the evidence of guilt adduced at trial." We found it "obviou[s]" that a habeas court conducting an actual innocence inquiry must do more than simply check whether there are genuine factual issues for trial. The point of the actual innocence inquiry is for the federal habeas court to satisfy itself that it should suspend the normal procedural default rule, disregard the important judicial interests of finality and comity, and allow a state prisoner to present his defaulted constitutional claims to a federal court.

The majority surprisingly states that this guidance is inapplicable here because this case involves a "fully developed record," while the district court in *Schlup* had declined to conduct an evidentiary hearing. But the guidance is clearly applicable: The point in *Schlup* was not simply that a hearing was required, but why—because the district court had to assess the probative force of the petitioner's newly presented evidence, by engaging in factfinding rather than performing a summary judgment-type inquiry. That is precisely what the District Court did here. In addition to a "fully developed record," we have the District Court's factual findings about the reliability of the new evidence in that record, factual findings which the majority disregards without finding clear error.

* * *

I have found no clear error in the District Court's reliability findings. Not having observed Ms. Parker and Ms. Letner testify, I would defer to the District Court's determination that they are not credible, and the evidence in the record undermining the tale of an accidental killing during a fight in the Muncey home convinces me that this credibility finding is not clearly erroneous. Dr. Alex Carabia, who performed the autopsy, testified to injuries far more severe than a bump on the head: Mrs. Muncey had bruises on the front and back of her neck, on both thighs, on her lower right leg and left knee, and her hands were bloodstained up to the wrists; her injuries were consistent with a struggle and traumatic strangulation. And, of course, Lora Tharp has consistently recalled a deep-voiced visitor arriving late at night to tell Mrs. Muncey that her husband was in a wreck near the creek.

I also find abundant evidence in the record to support the District Court's finding that blood spilled within the evidence container after the FBI received and tested House's jeans. Agent Bigbee testified that there was no leakage in the items submitted to him for testing. The majority's entire analysis on this point assumes the agent flatly lied, though there was no attack on his credibility below. Moreover, Ms. Sutton determined, in her expert opinion, that the wide distribution of stains "front and back, top to bottom," the fact that some bloodstains were mixed with mud, and the presence of bloodstains inside the pocket and inside the fly, showed that the blood was spattered and wiped—not spilled—on House's jeans.

It is also worth noting that the blood evidently spilled inside the evidence container when the jeans were protected inside a plastic zip lock bag, as shown by the presence of a bloodstain on the outside of that bag. House's expert tested the exterior and interior of that plastic bag for bloodstains using an "extremely sensitive" test, and only the exterior of the bag tested positive for blood. The evidence in the record indicates that the jeans were placed in the plastic bag *after* they arrived at the FBI: FBI records show that the jeans arrived there in a *paper* bag, and the plastic bag has FBI markings on it. The bloodstain on the outside of the *plastic* bag therefore further supports the District Court's conclusion that the blood spilled *after* the evidence was received and tested by the FBI, and not en route when the jeans were in a paper bag. I suppose it is theoretically possible that the jeans were contaminated by spillage before arriving at the FBI, that Agent Bigbee either failed to note or lied about such spillage, and that the FBI then transferred the jeans into a plastic bag and put them back inside the evidence container with the spilled blood still sloshing around sufficiently to contaminate the outside of the plastic bag as extensively as it did. This sort of unbridled speculation can theoretically defeat any inconvenient fact, but does not suffice to convince me that the District Court's factual finding—that the blood spilled *after* FBI testing—was clearly erroneous.

* * *

The District Court attentively presided over a complex evidentiary hearing, often questioning witnesses extensively during the presentation of critical evidence. The court concisely summarized the evidence presented, then dutifully made findings about the reliability of the testimony it heard and the evidence it observed. We are poorly equipped to second-guess the District Court's reliability findings and should defer to them, consistent with the guidance we provided in *Schlup*.

II

With due regard to the District Court's reliability findings, this case invites a straightforward application of the legal standard adopted in *Schlup*. A petitioner does not pass through the *Schlup* gateway if it is "more likely than not that there is *any* juror who, acting reasonably, would have found the petitioner guilty beyond a reasonable doubt." (O'Connor, J., concurring) (emphasis added).

The majority states that if House had presented just one of his three key pieces of evidence—or even two of the three—he would not pass through the *Schlup* gateway. ("* * * In combination, * * * with the challenges to the blood evidence and the lack of motive with respect to House, the evidence pointing to Mr. Muncey likely would reinforce other doubts as to House's guilt"). According to the majority, House has picked the trifecta of evidence that places conviction outside the realm of choices *any* juror, acting reasonably, would make. Because the case against House remains substantially unaltered from the case presented to the jury, I disagree.

[The Chief Justice reviewed the evidence against House: the Munceys' daughter's testimony regarding perpetrator arriving at the house and telling Mrs. Muncey about her husband being in a wreck; House's lies to the police about his whereabouts at the time of the murder and about what pants he had been wearing at the time; his bruises and scratches; Ms. Turner's testimony about House's actions that night and his reported fight with assailants; and the blood on House's pants.]

Noticeably absent from the State's story about what happened to Mrs. Muncey on the night of her death was much mention of the semen found on Mrs. Muncey's clothing. House's single victory at the evidentiary hearing was new DNA evidence proving that the semen was deposited by Mr. Muncey. The majority identifies the semen evidence as "[c]entral to the State's case" against House, but House's jury would probably be quite surprised by this characterization. At trial, Agent Bigbee testified that from the semen stains on Mrs. Muncey's clothing, he could determine that the man who deposited the semen had type A blood, and was a secretor. Agent Bigbee also testified that House and Mr. Muncey both have type A blood, that House is a secretor, and that "[t]here is an *eighty (80%) percent* chance that [Mr. Muncey] is a secretor." (emphasis added). Moreover, Agent Bigbee informed the jury that because 40 percent of people have type A blood, and 80 percent of those people are secretors, the semen on Mrs. Muncey's clothing could have been deposited by roughly one out of every three males. The jury was also informed several times by the defense that Mrs. Muncey's body was found fully clothed.

The majority describes House's sexual motive as "a central theme in the State's narrative linking House to the crime," and states that without the semen evidence, "a jury . . . would have found it necessary to establish some different motive, or, if the same motive, an intent far more speculative." The State, however, consistently directed the jury's attention *away* from motive, and sexual motive was far from a "central theme" of the State's case—presumably because of the highly ambiguous nature of the semen evidence recounted above. The Tennessee Supreme Court did not mention that evidence in cataloging the "[p]articularly incriminating" or "[d]amaging" evidence against House. The State did not mention the semen evidence in its opening statement to the jury, instead focusing on premeditation. The defense used its opening statement to expose lack of motive as a weakness in the State's case. After the State's equivocal presentation of the semen evidence through Agent Bigbee's testimony at trial, the State again made no reference to the semen evidence or to a motive in its closing argument, prompting the defense to again highlight this omission. ("[W]hy was Carolyn Muncey killed? We don't know. Is it important to have some motive? In your minds? What motive did Paul Gregory House have to go over and kill a woman that he barely knew? Who was still dressed, still clad in her clothes").

In rebuttal, the State disclaimed any responsibility to prove motive, again shifting the jury's focus to premeditation:

> "The law says that if you take another person's life, you beat them, you strangle them, and then you don't succeed, and then you kill them by giving them multiple blows to the head, and one massive blow to the head, and that that causes their brains to crash against the other side of their skull, and caused such severe bleeding inside the skull itself, that you die—that it does not make any difference under God's heaven, what the motive was. That is what the law is. The law is that if motive is shown, it can be considered by the jury as evidence of guilt. But the law is that if you prove that a killing was done, beyond a reasonable doubt, by a person, and that he premeditated it, he planned it, it is not necessary for the jury to conclude why he did it."

As a follow-up to this explanation, when the trial was almost over and only in response to the defense's consistent prodding, the State made its first and only reference to a possible motive, followed immediately by another disclaimer:

> "Now, you may have an idea why he did it. The evidence at the scene which seemed to suggest that he was subjecting this lady to some kind of indignity, why would you get a lady out of her house, late at night, in her night clothes, under the trick that her husband has had a wreck down by the creek? . . . Why is it that you choke her? Why is it that you repeatedly beat her? Why is it that she has scrapes all over her body? Well, it is because either you don't want her to tell what indignities you have subjected her to, or she is unwilling and fights against you, against being subjected to those indignities. . . . That is what the evidence at the scene suggests about motive. But motive is not an element of the crime. It is something that you can consider, or ignore. Whatever you prefer. The issue is not motive. The issue is premeditation."

It is on this "obliqu[e]" reference to the semen evidence during the State's closing argument that the majority bases its assertion that House's sexual motive was a "central theme in the State's narrative." Although it is possible that one or even some jurors might have entertained doubt about House's guilt absent the clearest evidence of motive, I do not find it more likely than not that *every* juror would have done so, and that is the legal standard under *Schlup*. The majority aphoristically states that "[w]hen identity is in question, motive is key." Not at all. Sometimes, when identity is in question, alibi is key. Here, House came up with one—and it fell apart, later admitted to be fabricated when his girlfriend would not lie to protect him. Scratches from a cat, indeed. Surely a reasonable juror would give the fact that an alibi had been made up and discredited significant weight. People facing a murder charge, who are innocent, do not make up a story out of concern that the truth might somehow disturb their parole officer. And people do not lie to the police about which jeans they were wearing the night of a murder, if they have no reason to believe the jeans would be stained with the blood shed by the victim in her last desperate struggle to live.

In *Schlup,* we made clear that the standard we adopted requires a "stronger showing than that needed to establish prejudice." In other words, House must show more than just a "reasonable probability that ... the factfinder would have had a reasonable doubt respecting guilt." *Strickland v. Washington,* 466 U.S. 668, 104 S.Ct. 2052 (1984). House must present such compelling evidence of innocence that it becomes more likely than not that no single juror, acting reasonably, would vote to convict him. The majority's conclusion is that given the sisters' testimony (if believed), and Dr. Blake's rebutted testimony about how to interpret Agent Bigbee's enzyme marker analysis summary (if accepted), combined with the revelation that the semen on Mrs. Muncey's clothing was deposited by her husband (which the jurors knew was just as likely as the semen having been deposited by House), no reasonable juror would vote to convict House. Given the District Court's reliability findings about the first two pieces of evidence, the evidence before us now is not substantially different from that considered by House's jury. I therefore find it more likely than not that in light of this new evidence, at least one juror, acting reasonably, would vote to convict House. The evidence as a whole certainly does not establish that House is actually innocent of the crime of murdering Carolyn Muncey, and accordingly I dissent.

NOTES

1. *Sawyer v. Whitley.*

In *Sawyer v. Whitley,* 505 U.S. 333, 112 S.Ct. 2514 (1992) (cited in *House*), the Court had addressed how the "actual innocence" exception to procedural default applied to claimed constitutional violations affecting only the death sentence. The Court held that where the barred constitutional claim relates only to the determination of the penalty, the petitioner must show by clear and convincing evidence that, but for constitutional error, no reasonable juror would have found him death eligible. The Court refused to extend the "actual innocence" exception to the penalty selection decision, finding that it is relatively easy to evaluate a showing of actual innocence of the crime or aggravating circumstances, but far more difficult "to assess how jurors would have reacted to additional showings of mitigating factors."

2. *Schlup v. Delo.*

In *Schlup v. Delo,* 513 U.S. 298, 115 S.Ct. 851 (1995), discussed in *House,* the Supreme Court held that the *Sawyer v. Whitley* standard does not govern the miscarriage of justice inquiry when a death-sentenced petitioner alleges that he is innocent of the crime in order to avoid procedural bar to the consideration of his constitutional claims. Instead, the proper, and less stringent, standard is found in *Murray v. Carrier*, 477 U.S. 478, 106 S.Ct. 2639 (1986) which requires that a habeas petitioner show that "a constitutional violation has probably resulted in the conviction of one who is actually innocent."

Schlup was convicted of participating in a prison murder and sentenced to death. No physical evidence connected Schlup to the crime, and the case against him rested primarily on the testimony of the two other inmates who were linked to the crime by physical evidence and who also were charged with the murder. Schlup at all times maintained his innocence. Since a prison videotape showed that Schlup entered the dining room for lunch a minute before guards responded to a distress call about the murder, a key question at trial was how soon after the murder the distress call went out. Schlup's first federal habeas petition, filed *pro se*, alleged ineffective assistance of counsel and was denied without an evidentiary hearing. Schlup, represented by counsel, then filed a second habeas petition alleging actual innocence, ineffective assistance of counsel and withholding of material evidence by the prosecution. Schlup's claim of actual innocence was supported by a statement in the prosecution's possession indicating that the distress call had gone out immediately after the murder, statements from other inmates that Schlup had not participated in the murder and an affidavit from a former prison officer stating that he had talked with Schlup for a period of time while Schlup was on his way to lunch and had noticed nothing out of the ordinary. Schlup's petition was dismissed as a successor petition in the lower courts.

The Supreme Court, in a 5–4 decision, reversed. First, the Court explained that Schlup did not have to meet the high standard suggested by *Herrera v. Collins* [Section A] for actual innocence claims, since Schlup's innocence claim was made to overcome the procedural bar to reaching his other constitutional claims and not, as in *Herrera*, to challenge the execution of an innocent person after a error-free trial. Second, the Court held that the *Sawyer* standard, which addressed a claim that the petitioner was "innocent of the death penalty," was insufficient to protect against the greater miscarriage of justice of executing a petitioner who has presented substantial evidence that he was actually innocent of the crime. Finally, the Court held that to satisfy *Carrier*'s "actual innocence" standard, a petitioner must show that, in light of the new evidence, it is more likely than not that no reasonable juror would have found him guilty beyond a reasonable doubt. The Court held Schlup had made a sufficient showing to permit consideration of his second petition.

O'SULLIVAN v. BOERCKEL

526 U.S. 838, 119 S.Ct. 1728, 144 L.Ed.2d 1 (1999).

JUSTICE O'CONNOR delivered the opinion of the Court.

Federal habeas relief is available to state prisoners only after they have exhausted their claims in state court. 28 U.S.C. §§ 2254(b)(1), (c). In this case, we are asked to decide whether a state prisoner must present his claims to a state supreme court in a petition for discretionary review in order to satisfy the exhaustion requirement. We conclude that he must.

I

In 1977, respondent Darren Boerckel was tried in the Circuit Court of Montgomery County, Illinois, for the rape, burglary, and aggravated battery of an 87–year–old woman. The central evidence against him at trial was his written confession to the crimes, a confession admitted over Boerckel's objection. The jury convicted Boerckel on all three charges, and he was sentenced to serve 20 to 60 years' imprisonment on the rape charge, and shorter terms on the other two charges, with all sentences to be served concurrently.

Boerckel appealed his convictions to the Appellate Court of Illinois, raising several issues. He argued, among other things, that his confession should have been suppressed because the confession was the fruit of an illegal arrest, because the confession was coerced, and because he had not knowingly and intelligently waived his rights under *Miranda v. Arizona*, 384 U.S. 436, 86 S.Ct. 1602 (1966). Boerckel also claimed that prosecutorial misconduct denied him a fair trial, that he had been denied discovery of exculpatory material held by the police, and that the evidence was insufficient to support his conviction. The Illinois Appellate Court, with one justice dissenting, rejected Boerckel's claims and affirmed his convictions and sentences.

Boerckel next filed a petition for leave to appeal to the Illinois Supreme Court. In this petition, he raised only three issues. Boerckel claimed first that his confession was the fruit of an unlawful arrest because, contrary to the Appellate Court's ruling, he was under arrest when he gave his confession. Boerckel also contended that he was denied a fair trial by prosecutorial misconduct and that he had been erroneously denied discovery of exculpatory material in the possession of the police. The Illinois Supreme Court denied the petition for leave to appeal, and this Court denied Boerckel's subsequent petition for a writ of certiorari.

In 1994, Boerckel filed a *pro se* petition for a writ of habeas corpus under 28 U.S.C. § 2254 in the United States District Court for the Central District of Illinois. The District Court appointed counsel for Boerckel, and Boerckel's counsel filed an amended petition in March 1995. The amended petition asked for relief on six grounds: (1) that Boerckel had not knowingly and intelligently waived his Miranda rights; (2) that his confession was not voluntary; (3) that the evidence against him was insufficient to sustain the conviction; (4) that his confession was the fruit of an illegal arrest; (5) that he received ineffective assistance of counsel at trial and on appeal; and (6) that his right to discovery of exculpatory material under *Brady v. Maryland*, 373 U.S. 83, 83 S.Ct. 1194 (1963), was violated.

[The District Court held that the first three claims were procedurally defaulted by Boerckel's failure to include them in his petition for leave to appeal to the Illinois Supreme Court and that Boerckel had failed to show he fell within the "fundamental miscarriage of justice" exception to the procedural default rule. The Court of Appeals reversed on this issue, concluding that Boerckel was not required to present his claims in a petition for discretionary review to the Illinois Supreme Court to satisfy the exhaustion requirement. The Supreme Court granted certiorari to resolve a conflict in the Circuits.]

II

Before a federal court may grant habeas relief to a state prisoner, the prisoner must exhaust his remedies in state court. In other words, the state prisoner must give the state courts an opportunity to act on his claims before he presents those claims to a federal court in a habeas petition. The exhaustion doctrine, first announced in *Ex parte Royall*, 117 U.S. 241, 6 S.Ct. 734 (1886), is now codified at 28 U.S.C. § 2254(b)(1). This doctrine, however, raises a recurring question: What state remedies must a habeas petitioner invoke to satisfy the federal exhaustion requirement? The particular question posed by this case is whether a prisoner must seek review in a state court of last resort when that court has discretionary control over its docket.

Illinois law provides for a two-tiered appellate review process. Criminal defendants are tried in the local circuit courts, and although some criminal appeals (*e.g.*, those in which the death penalty is imposed) are heard directly by the Supreme Court of Illinois, most criminal appeals are heard first by an intermediate appellate court, the Appellate Court of Illinois. A party may petition for leave to appeal a decision by the Appellate Court to the Illinois Supreme Court (with exceptions that are irrelevant here), but whether "such a petition will be granted is a matter of sound judicial discretion." Rule 315(a). Rule 315 elaborates on the exercise of this discretion as follows:

> "The following, while neither controlling nor fully measuring the court's discretion, indicate the character of reasons which will be considered: the general importance of the question presented; the existence of a conflict between the decision sought to be reviewed and a decision of the Supreme Court, or of another division of the Appellate Court; the need for the exercise of the Supreme Court's supervisory authority; and the final or interlocutory character of the judgment sought to be reviewed."

Boerckel's amended federal habeas petition raised three claims that he had not included in his petition for leave to appeal to the Illinois Supreme Court. To determine whether Boerckel was required to present those claims to the Illinois Supreme Court in order to exhaust his state remedies, we turn first to the language of the federal habeas statute. Section 2254(c) provides that a habeas petitioner "shall not be deemed to have exhausted the remedies available in the courts of the State ... if he has the right under the law of the State to raise, by any available procedure, the question presented." Although this language could be read to effectively foreclose habeas review by requiring a state prisoner to invoke *any possible* avenue of state court review, we have never interpreted the exhaustion requirement in such a restrictive fashion. Thus, we have not interpreted the exhaustion doctrine to require prisoners to file repetitive petitions. See *Brown v. Allen*, 344 U.S. 443, 73 S.Ct. 397 (1953) (holding that a prisoner does not have "to ask the state for collateral relief, based on the same evidence and issues already decided by direct review"). We have also held that state prisoners do not have to invoke extraordinary remedies when those remedies are alternatives to the standard review process and where the state courts have not provided relief through those remedies in the past. See *Wilwording v. Swenson*, 404 U.S. 249, 92 S.Ct. 407 (1971) (*per curiam*) (rejecting suggestion that state prisoner should have invoked "any of a number of possible alternatives to state habeas including 'a suit for injunction, a writ of prohibition, or mandamus or a declaratory judgment in the state courts,' or perhaps other relief under the State Administrative Procedure Act").

Section 2254(c) requires only that state prisoners give state courts a fair opportunity to act on their claims. State courts, like federal courts, are obliged to enforce federal law. Comity thus dictates that when a prisoner alleges that his continued confinement for a state court conviction violates federal law, the state courts should have the first opportunity to review this claim and provide any necessary relief. *Rose v. Lundy*, 455 U.S. 509, 102 S.Ct. 1198 (1982); *Darr v. Burford*, 339 U.S. 200, 70 S.Ct. 587 (1950). This rule of comity reduces friction between the state and federal court systems by avoiding the "unseem[liness]" of a federal district court's overturning a state court conviction without the state courts having had an opportunity to correct the constitutional violation in the first instance.

Because the exhaustion doctrine is designed to give the state courts a full and fair opportunity to resolve federal constitutional claims before those claims are presented to the federal courts, we conclude that state prisoners must give the state courts one full opportunity to resolve any constitutional issues by invoking one complete round of the State's established appellate review process. Here, Illinois's established, normal appellate review procedure is a two-tiered system. Comity, in these circumstances, dictates that Boerckel use the State's established appellate review procedures before he presents his claims to a federal court. Unlike the extraordinary procedures that we found unnecessary in *Brown v. Allen* and *Wilwording v. Swenson*, a petition for discretionary review in Illinois's Supreme Court is a normal, simple, and established part of the State's appellate review process. In the words of the statute, state prisoners have "the right . . . to raise" their claims through a petition for discretionary review in the state's highest court. § 2254(c). Granted, as Boerckel contends, he has no right to review in the Illinois Supreme Court, but he does have a "right . . . to raise" his claims before that court. That is all § 2254(c) requires.

Boerckel contests this conclusion with two related arguments. His first argument is grounded in a stylized portrait of the Illinois appellate review process. According to Boerckel, Illinois's appellate review procedures make the intermediate appellate courts the primary focus of the system; all routine claims of error are directed to those courts. The Illinois Supreme Court, by contrast, serves only to answer "questions of broad significance." Boerckel's view of Illinois's appellate review process derives from Ill. Sup.Ct. Rule 315(a) (1998). He reads this Rule to discourage the filing of petitions raising routine allegations of error and to direct litigants to present only those claims that meet the criteria defined by the Rule. Rule 315(a), by its own terms, however, does not "contro[l]" or "measur[e]" the Illinois Supreme Court's discretion. The Illinois Supreme Court is free to take cases that do not fall easily within the descriptions listed in the Rule. Moreover, even if we were to assume that the Rule discourages the filing of certain petitions, it is difficult to discern which cases fall into the "discouraged" category. In this case, for example, the parties disagree about whether, under the terms of Rule 315(a), Boerckel's claims should have been presented to the Illinois Supreme Court.

The better reading of Rule 315(a) is that the Illinois Supreme Court has the opportunity to decide which cases it will consider on the merits. The fact that Illinois has adopted a discretionary review system may reflect little more than that there are resource constraints on the Illinois Supreme Court's ability to hear every case that is presented to it. It may be that, given the necessity of a discretionary review system, the Rule allows the Illinois Supreme Court to expend its limited resources on "questions of broad significance." We cannot conclude from this Rule, however, that review in the Illinois Supreme Court is unavailable. By requiring state prisoners to give the Illinois Supreme Court the opportunity to resolve constitutional errors in the first instance, the rule we announce today serves the comity interests that drive the exhaustion doctrine.

Boerckel's second argument is related to his first. According to Boerckel, because the Illinois Supreme Court has announced (through Rule 315(a)) that it does not want to hear routine allegations of error, a rule requiring state prisoners to file petitions for review with that court offends comity by inundating the Illinois Supreme Court with countless unwanted petitions. This point, of course, turns on Boerckel's interpretation of Rule 315(a), an interpretation that, as discussed above, we do not find persuasive. Nor is it clear that the rule we announce today will have the effect that Boerckel predicts. We do not know, for example, what percentage of Illinois state prisoners who eventually seek federal habeas relief decline, in the first instance, to seek review in the Illinois Supreme Court.

We acknowledge that the rule we announce today—requiring state prisoners to file petitions for discretionary review when that review is part of the ordinary appellate review procedure in the State—has the *potential* to increase the number of filings in state supreme courts. We also recognize that this increased burden may be unwelcome in some state courts because the courts do not wish to have the opportunity to review constitutional claims before those claims are presented to a federal habeas court. See, *e.g.*, *In re Exhaustion of State Remedies in Criminal and Post–Conviction Relief Cases*, 471 S.E.2d 454 (S.C. 1990); see also *State v. Sandon*, 777 P.2d 220 (Ariz. 1989). Under these circumstances, Boerckel may be correct that the increased, unwelcome burden on state supreme courts disserves the comity interests underlying the exhaustion doctrine. In this regard, we note that nothing in our decision today requires the exhaustion of any specific state remedy when a State has provided that that remedy is unavailable. Section 2254(c), in fact, directs federal courts to consider whether a habeas petitioner has "the right *under the law of the State to raise, by any available procedure*, the question presented" (emphasis added). The exhaustion doctrine, in other words, turns on an inquiry into what procedures are "available" under state law. In sum, there is nothing in the exhaustion doctrine requiring federal courts to ignore a state law or rule providing that a given procedure is not available. We hold today only that the creation of a discretionary review system does not, without more, make review in the Illinois Supreme Court unavailable.

Boerckel's amended federal habeas petition raised three claims that he had pressed before the Appellate Court of Illinois, but that he had not included in his petition for leave to appeal to the Illinois Supreme Court. There is no dispute that this state court remedy—a petition for leave to appeal to the Illinois Supreme Court—is no longer available to Boerckel; the time for filing such a petition has long past. Thus, Boerckel's failure to present three of his federal habeas claims to the Illinois Supreme Court in a timely fashion has resulted in a procedural default of those claims.

We do not disagree with Justice STEVENS' general description of the law of exhaustion and procedural default. Specifically, we do not disagree with his description of the interplay of these two doctrines. As Justice STEVENS notes, a prisoner could evade the exhaustion requirement—and thereby undercut the values that it serves—by "letting the time run" on state remedies. To avoid this result, and thus "protect the integrity" of the federal exhaustion rule, we ask not only whether a prisoner has exhausted his state remedies, but also whether he has properly exhausted those remedies, i.e., whether he has fairly presented his claims to the state courts. Our disagreement with Justice STEVENS in this case turns on our differing answers to this last question: Whether a prisoner who fails to present his claims in a petition for discretionary review to a state court of last resort has properly presented his claims to the state courts. Because we answer this question "no," we conclude that Boerckel has procedurally defaulted his claims. Accordingly, the judgment of the Court of Appeals for the Seventh Circuit is reversed.

It is so ordered.

[Concurring opinion of SOUTER, J. omitted]

JUSTICE STEVENS, with whom JUSTICE GINSBURG and JUSTICE BREYER join, dissenting.

The Court's opinion confuses two analytically distinct judge-made rules: (1) the timing rule, first announced in *Ex parte Royall*, 117 U.S. 241, 6 S.Ct. 734 (1886), and later codified at 28 U.S.C. § 2254(b)(1), that requires a state prisoner to exhaust his state remedies before seeking a federal writ of habeas corpus; and (2) the waiver, or so-called procedural default, rule, applied in cases like *Francis v. Henderson*, 425 U.S. 536, 96 S.Ct. 1708 (1976), that forecloses relief even when the petitioner has exhausted his remedies.

Properly phrased, the question presented by this case is not whether respondent's claims were exhausted; they clearly were because no state remedy was available to him when he applied for the federal writ. The question is whether we should hold that his claims are procedurally defaulted and thereby place still another procedural hurdle in the path of applicants for federal relief who have given at least two state courts a fair opportunity to consider the merits of their constitutional claims. Before addressing that question, I shall briefly trace the history of the two separate doctrines that the Court has improperly commingled.

I

"[T]he problem of waiver is separate from the question whether a state prisoner has exhausted state remedies." *Engle v. Isaac*, 456 U.S. 107, 102 S.Ct. 1558 (1982). The question of exhaustion "refers only to remedies still available at the time of the federal petition"; it requires federal courts to ask whether an applicant for federal relief could still get the relief he seeks in the state system. If the applicant currently has a state avenue available for raising his claims, a federal court, in the interest of comity, must generally abstain from intervening. This time-honored rule has developed over several decades of cases, always with the goal of respecting the States' interest in passing first on their prisoners' constitutional claims in order to act as the primary guarantor of those prisoners' federal rights, and always separate and apart from rules of waiver.

[Justice STEVENS reviewed the Court's development of the exhaustion rule prior to its incorporation into the habeas statute.]

The 1948 statute changed neither that rule nor its exclusive emphasis on timing. * * *The statute as enacted provided that an application for a writ by a state prisoner "shall not be granted" unless the applicant has exhausted his state remedies and, as the amended statute still does today, further provided that the applicant shall not be deemed to have done so "if he has the right under the law of the State to raise, by any available procedure, the question presented." We interpreted this statute in *Rose v. Lundy*, 455 U.S. 509, 102 S.Ct. 1198 (1982) as requiring "total exhaustion"—that is, as requiring federal courts to dismiss habeas petitions when any of the claims could still be brought in state court. Conversely, of course, if no state procedure is available for raising any claims at the time a state prisoner applies for federal relief, the exhaustion requirement is satisfied.

To be sure, the fact that a prisoner has failed to invoke an available state procedure may provide the basis for a conclusion that he has waived a claim. But the exhaustion inquiry focuses entirely on the availability of state procedures at the time when the federal court is asked to entertain a habeas petition. * * *

Neither party argues that respondent currently has any state remedies available to him. The Court recognizes this circumstance, but still purports to analyze whether respondent has "exhausted [his] claims in state court." Since I do not believe that this case raises an exhaustion issue, I turn to the subject of waiver.

II

In order to protect the integrity of our exhaustion rule, we have also crafted a separate waiver rule, or—as it is now commonly known—the procedural default doctrine. The purpose of this doctrine is to ensure that state prisoners not only become ineligible for state relief before raising their claims in federal court, but also that they give state courts a sufficient opportunity to decide those claims before doing so. If we allowed state prisoners to obtain federal review simply by letting the time run on adequate and accessible state remedies and then rushing into the federal system, the comity interests that animate the exhaustion rule could easily be thwarted. We therefore ask in federal habeas cases not only whether an applicant has exhausted his state remedies; we also ask how he has done so. This second inquiry forms the basis for our procedural default doctrine: A habeas petitioner who has concededly exhausted his state remedies must also have properly done so by giving the State a fair "opportunity to pass upon [his claims]." *Darr v. Burford*, 339 U.S. 200, 70 S.Ct. 587 (1950). When a prisoner has deprived the state courts of such an opportunity, he has procedurally defaulted his claims and is ineligible for federal habeas relief save a showing of "cause and prejudice," *Murray v. Carrier*, 477 U.S. 478, 106 S.Ct. 2639 (1986), or "a fundamental miscarriage of justice."

* * *

In *Coleman v. Thompson*, 501 U.S. 722, 111 S.Ct. 2546 (1991), the Court extended our procedural default doctrine to state collateral appellate proceedings. The Court held that an inmate's constitutional claims that he had advanced in a state habeas proceeding could not be entertained by a federal court because his appeal from the state trial court's denial of collateral relief had been filed three days late. The Court, as I noted above, expressly stated that the exhaustion requirement had been satisfied because "there [were] no state remedies any longer 'available' to him." But because the State had consistently and strictly applied its timing deadlines for filing such appellate briefs in this and other cases, we concluded that Coleman had effectively deprived the State of a fair opportunity to pass on his claims and thus had procedurally defaulted them.

On the other hand, we have continually recognized, as the Court essentially does again today, that a state prisoner need not have invoked every conceivably "available" state remedy in order to avoid procedural default. As far back as *Brown v. Allen*, 344 U.S. 443, 73 S.Ct. 397 (1953), we held that even when a State offers post-conviction procedures, a prisoner does not have "to ask the state for collateral relief, based on the same evidence and issues already decided by direct review." We later held that prisoners who have exhausted state habeas procedures need not have requested in state courts an injunction, a writ of prohibition, mandamus relief, a declaratory judgment, or relief under the State Administrative Procedure Act, even if those procedures were technically available. *Wilwording v. Swenson*, 404 U.S. 249, 92 S.Ct. 407 (1971) (*per curiam*). Federal courts also routinely and correctly hold that prisoners have exhausted their state remedies, and have not procedurally defaulted their claims, when those prisoners had the right under state law to file a petition for rehearing from the last adverse state-court decision and failed to do so.

* * *

III

I come now to the real issue presented by this case: whether respondent's failure to include all six of his current claims in his petition for leave to appeal to the Illinois Supreme Court should result in his procedurally defaulting the three claims he did not raise.

The Court barely answers this question. Even though no one contends that respondent currently has any state remedy available to him, the Court concentrates instead on exhaustion. It states that respondent has not exhausted his claims because he had " 'the right ... to raise' [his] claims through a petition for discretionary review in the [Illinois Supreme Court]." The Court adds to this that "the creation of a discretionary review system does not, without more, make review in the Illinois Supreme Court unavailable." But, as the Court acknowledges almost immediately thereafter, the fact that "the time for filing [a petition to that court] has long past" most assuredly makes such review unavailable in this case. The Court then resolves this case's core issue in a single sentence and two citations: "Thus, Boerckel's failure to present three of his federal habeas claims to the Illinois Supreme Court in a timely fashion has resulted in a procedural default of those claims. *Coleman v. Thompson*; *Engle v. Isaac*, 456 U.S. 107, 102 S.Ct. 1558 (1982)."

I disagree that respondent has procedurally defaulted these three claims, and neither *Engle* nor *Coleman* suggests otherwise. The question we must ask is whether respondent has given the State a fair opportunity to pass on these claims. This Court has explained that the best way to determine the answer to this question is to "respect ... state procedural rules" and to inquire whether the State has denied (or would deny) relief to the prisoner based on his failure to abide by any such rule. *Coleman*. Thus, we held in *Engle* that a prisoner defaults a claim by failing to follow a state rule requiring that it be raised at trial or on direct appeal. The Court in *Coleman* felt so strongly about "the important interests served by state procedural rules at every stage of the judicial process and the harm to the States that results when federal courts ignore these rules," that it imposed procedural default on a death-row inmate for filing his appellate brief in state postconviction review just three days after the State's deadline.

Surely the Illinois Supreme Court's discretionary review rule, and respondent's attempt to follow it, are entitled to at least as much respect. It is reasonable to assume that the Illinois Supreme Court, like this Court, has established a discretionary review system in order to reserve its resources for issues of broad significance. Claims of violations of well-established constitutional rules, important as they may be to individual litigants, do not ordinarily present such issues.

Discretionary review rules not only provide an effective tool for apportioning limited resources, but they also foster more useful and effective advocacy. We have recognized on numerous occasions that the "process of 'winnowing out weaker arguments on appeal and focusing on' those more likely to prevail ... is the hallmark of effective appellate advocacy.'" *Smith v. Murray*, 477 U.S. 527, 106 S.Ct. 2661 (1986) (quoting *Jones v. Barnes*, 463 U.S. 745, 103 S.Ct. 3308 (1983)). This maxim is even more germane regarding petitions for certiorari. The most helpful and persuasive petitions for certiorari to this Court usually present only one or two issues, and spend a considerable amount of time explaining why those questions of law have sweeping importance and have divided or confused other courts. Given the page limitations that we impose, a litigant cannot write such a petition if he decides, or is required, to raise every claim that might possibly warrant reversal in his particular case.

The Court of Appeals for the Seventh Circuit found that these same factors animate the Illinois Supreme Court's discretionary review rule. It also pointed out that Illinois courts in state habeas proceedings dismiss claims like respondent's on res judicata—not waiver—grounds once they have been pressed at trial and on direct appeal; it makes no difference whether the prisoner has raised the claim in a petition for review to the Illinois Supreme Court. The Illinois courts, in other words, are prepared to stand behind the merits of their decisions regarding constitutional criminal procedure once a trial court and an appellate court have passed on them. No state procedural ground independently supports such decisions, so federal courts do not undercut Illinois's procedural rules by reaching the merits of the constitutional claims resolved therein.

We ordinarily defer to a federal court of appeals' interpretation of state-law questions. The Court today nevertheless refuses to conclude that the Illinois rule "discourages the filing of certain petitions" (or even certain claims in petitions), and surmises instead that the rule does nothing more than announce the State Supreme Court's desire to decide for itself which cases it will consider on the merits. This analysis strikes me as unsatisfactory. I would, consistent with the Seventh Circuit's view, read the Illinois rule as dissuading the filing of fact-intensive claims of error that fail to present any issue of broad significance. I would also deduce from the rule that Illinois prisoners need not present their claims in discretionary review petitions before raising them in federal court.

The Court's decision to the contrary is unwise. It will impose unnecessary burdens on habeas petitioners; it will delay the completion of litigation that is already more protracted than it should be; and, most ironically, it will undermine federalism by thwarting the interests of those state supreme courts that administer discretionary dockets. If, as the Court has repeatedly held, the purpose of our waiver doctrine is to cultivate comity by respecting state procedural rules, then I agree with the Court of Appeals that we should not create procedural obstacles when state prisoners follow those rules. * * *

      * * *

The Court of Appeals, in effect, held that federal courts should respect state procedural rules regardless of whether applying them impedes access to federal habeas review or signals the availability of such relief. The Court today, on the other hand, admits that its decision may "disserv[e] ... comity" and may cause an "unwelcome" influx of filings in state supreme courts. It takes no issue with the Court of Appeals' finding that Illinois would not invoke an independent state procedural ground as an alternative basis for denying relief to prisoners in respondent's situation. The Court today nevertheless requires defendants in every criminal case in States like Illinois to present to the state supreme court every federal issue that the defendants think might possibly warrant some relief if brought in a future federal habeas petition.

Thankfully, the Court leaves open the possibility that state supreme courts with discretionary dockets may avoid a deluge of undesirable claims by making a plain statement—as Arizona and South Carolina have done—that they do not wish the opportunity to review such claims before they pass into the federal system. * * *

I see no compelling reason to require States that already have discretionary docket rules to take this additional step of expressly disavowing any desire to be presented with every such claim. In my view, it should be enough to avoid waiving a claim that a state prisoner in a State like Illinois raised that claim at trial and in his appeal as of right.

I respectfully dissent.

[Dissenting opinion of BREYER, J., joined by STEVENS and GINSBURG, JJ. omitted]

NOTE

1. *State court response.*

In his concurring opinion in *Boerckel*, Justice Souter elaborated on the Court's statement that "nothing in the exhaustion doctrine requir[es] federal courts to ignore a state law or rule providing that a given procedure is not available": "I understand that we leave open the possibility that a state prisoner is * * * free to skip a procedure even when a state court has occasionally employed it to provide relief, so long as the State has identified the procedure as outside the standard review process and has plainly said that it need not be sought for the purpose of exhaustion." 526 U.S. at 849–850; 119 S.Ct. at 1735. Several state supreme courts have made such statements, and the statements have been recognized as sufficient to circumvent the *Boerckel* holding. See, *e.g.*, *Lambert v. Blackwell*, 387 F.3d 210, 233 (3rd Cir. 2004) (Pennsylvania); *Adams v. Holland,* 330 F.3d 398, 401–02 (6th Cir. 2003) (Tennessee); *Randolph v. Kemna,* 276 F.3d 401, 404 (8th Cir. 2002) (Missouri).

WILLIAMS (MICHAEL) v. TAYLOR

529 U.S. 420, 120 S.Ct. 1479, 146 L.Ed.2d 435 (2000).

JUSTICE KENNEDY delivered the opinion of the Court.

Petitioner Michael Wayne Williams received a capital sentence for the murders of Morris Keller, Jr., and Keller's wife, Mary Elizabeth. Petitioner later sought a writ of habeas corpus in federal court. Accompanying his petition was a request for an evidentiary hearing on constitutional claims which, he alleged, he had been unable to develop in state-court proceedings. The question in this case is whether 28 U.S.C. § 2254(e)(2), as amended by the Antiterrorism and Effective Death Penalty Act of 1996 (AEDPA), 110 Stat. 1214, bars the evidentiary hearing petitioner seeks. If petitioner "has failed to develop the factual basis of [his] claim[s] in State court proceedings," his case is subject to § 2254(e)(2), and he may not receive a hearing because he concedes his inability to satisfy the statute's further stringent conditions for excusing the deficiency.

I

On the evening of February 27, 1993, Verena Lozano James dropped off petitioner and his friend Jeffrey Alan Cruse near a local store in a rural area of Cumberland County, Virginia. The pair planned to rob the store's employees and customers using a .357 revolver petitioner had stolen in the course of a quadruple murder and robbery he had committed two months earlier. Finding the store closed, petitioner and Cruse walked to the Kellers' home. Petitioner was familiar with the couple, having grown up down the road from where they lived. He told Cruse they would have "a couple thousand dollars." Cruse, who had been holding the .357, handed the gun to petitioner and knocked on the door. When Mr. Keller opened the door, petitioner pointed the gun at him as the two intruders forced their way inside. Petitioner and Cruse forced Mr. Keller to the kitchen, where they discovered Mrs. Keller. Petitioner ordered the captives to remove their clothing. While petitioner kept guard on the Kellers, Cruse searched the house for money and other valuables. He found a .38–caliber handgun and bullets. Upon Cruse's return to the kitchen, petitioner had Cruse tie their captives with telephone cords. The Kellers were confined to separate closets while the intruders continued ransacking the house.

When they gathered all they wanted, petitioner and Cruse decided to rape Mrs. Keller. With Mrs. Keller pleading with them not to hurt her or her husband, petitioner raped her. Cruse did the same. Petitioner then ordered the Kellers to shower and dress and "take a walk" with him and Cruse. As they were leaving, petitioner told Mrs. Keller he and Cruse were going to burn down the house. Mrs. Keller begged to be allowed to retrieve her marriage license, which she did, guarded by petitioner.

As the prosecution later presented the case, details of the murders were as follows. Petitioner, now carrying the .38, and Cruse, carrying the .357, took the Kellers to a thicket down a dirt road from the house. With petitioner standing behind Mr. Keller and Cruse behind Mrs. Keller, petitioner told Cruse, "We'll shoot at the count of three." At the third count, petitioner shot Mr. Keller in the head, and Mr. Keller collapsed to the ground. Cruse did not shoot Mrs. Keller at the same moment. Saying "he didn't want to leave no witnesses," petitioner urged Cruse to shoot Mrs. Keller. Cruse fired one shot into her head. Despite his wound, Mr. Keller stood up, but petitioner shot him a second time. To ensure the Kellers were dead, petitioner shot each of them two or three more times.

After returning to the house and loading the stolen property into the Kellers' jeep, petitioner and Cruse set fire to the house and drove the jeep to Fredericksburg, Virginia, where they sold some of the property. They threw the remaining property and the .357 revolver into the Rappahannock River and set fire to the jeep.

Pursuing a lead from Verena James, the police interviewed Cruse about the fire at the Kellers' home. Petitioner had fled to Florida. Cruse provided no useful information until the police discovered the bodies of the victims, at which point Cruse consulted counsel. In a plea bargain Cruse agreed to disclose the details of the crimes in exchange for the Commonwealth's promise not to seek the death penalty against him. Cruse described the murders but made no mention of his own act of rape. When the Commonwealth discovered the omission, it revoked the plea agreement and charged Cruse with capital murder.

Petitioner was arrested and charged with robbery, abduction, rape, and the capital murders of the Kellers. At trial in January 1994, Cruse was the Commonwealth's main witness. He recounted the murders as we have just described. Cruse testified petitioner raped Mrs. Keller, shot Mr. Keller at least twice, and shot Mrs. Keller several times after she had been felled by Cruse's bullet. He also described petitioner as the mastermind of the murders. The circumstances of the first plea agreement between the Commonwealth and Cruse and its revocation were disclosed to the jury. Testifying on his own behalf, petitioner admitted he was the first to shoot Mr. Keller and it was his idea to rob the store and set fire to the house. He denied, however, raping or shooting Mrs. Keller, and claimed to have shot

Mr. Keller only once. Petitioner blamed Cruse for the remaining shots and disputed some other parts of Cruse's testimony.

The jury convicted petitioner on all counts. After considering the aggravating and mitigating evidence presented during the sentencing phase, the jury found the aggravating circumstances of future dangerousness and vileness of the crimes and recommended a death sentence. The trial court imposed the recommended sentence. The Supreme Court of Virginia affirmed petitioner's convictions and sentence, and we denied certiorari. In a separate proceeding, Cruse pleaded guilty to the capital murder of Mrs. Keller and the first-degree murder of Mr. Keller. After the prosecution asked the sentencing court to spare his life because of his testimony against petitioner, Cruse was sentenced to life imprisonment.

[Williams' petition for state habeas corpus relief, alleging that the prosecution had failed to disclose a second agreement with Cruse regarding his testimony, was denied. In his federal habeas corpus petition, Williams realleged his claim regarding a second agreement and raised three new claims: (1) that the prosecution had failed to disclose the report of a confidential pre-trial psychiatric examination of Cruse; (2) that one of the jurors, at *voir dire*, had failed to reveal possible sources of bias; and (3) that one of the prosecutors failed to reveal his knowledge of the juror's possible bias. The District Court initially granted a hearing on the second and third additional claims. However, after review and remand by the Court of Appeals, the District Court vacated its order and dismissed the petition. The Court of Appeals affirmed, and the Supreme Court granted certiorari.]

II

A

Petitioner filed his federal habeas petition after AEDPA's effective date, so the statute applies to his case. The Commonwealth argues AEDPA bars petitioner from receiving an evidentiary hearing on any claim whose factual basis was not developed in state court, absent narrow circumstances not applicable here. Petitioner did not develop, or raise, his claims of juror bias, prosecutorial misconduct, or the prosecution's alleged *Brady* violation regarding Cruse's psychiatric report until he filed his federal habeas petition. Petitioner explains he could not have developed the claims earlier because he was unaware, through no fault of his own, of the underlying facts. As a consequence, petitioner contends, AEDPA erects no barrier to an evidentiary hearing in federal court.

Section 2254(e)(2), the provision which controls whether petitioner may receive an evidentiary hearing in federal district court on the claims that were not developed in the Virginia courts, becomes the central point of our analysis. It provides as follows:

"If the applicant has failed to develop the factual basis of a claim in State court proceedings, the court shall not hold an evidentiary hearing on the claim unless the applicant shows that—

"(A) the claim relies on—

"(i) a new rule of constitutional law, made retroactive to cases on collateral review by the Supreme Court, that was previously unavailable; or

"(ii) a factual predicate that could not have been previously discovered through the exercise of due diligence; and

"(B) the facts underlying the claim would be sufficient to establish by clear and convincing evidence that but for constitutional error, no reasonable factfinder would have found the applicant guilty of the underlying offense."

* * *

B

We start, as always, with the language of the statute. Section 2254(e)(2) begins with a conditional clause, "[i]f the applicant has failed to develop the factual basis of a claim in State court proceedings," which directs attention to the prisoner's efforts in state court. We ask first whether the factual basis was indeed developed in state court, a question susceptible, in the normal course, of a simple yes or no answer. Here the answer is no.

The Commonwealth would have the analysis begin and end there. Under its no-fault reading of the statute, if there is no factual development in the state court, the federal habeas court may not inquire into the reasons for the default when determining whether the opening clause of § 2254(e)(2) applies. We do not agree with the Commonwealth's interpretation of the word "failed."

We do not deny "fail" is sometimes used in a neutral way, not importing fault or want of diligence. So the phrase "We fail to understand his argument" can mean simply "We cannot understand his argument." This is not the sense in which the word "failed" is used here, however.

We give the words of a statute their " 'ordinary, contemporary, common meaning,' " absent an indication Congress intended them to bear some different import. *Walters v. Metropolitan Educational Enterprises, Inc.*, 519 U.S. 202, 117 S.Ct. 660 (1997) (quoting *Pioneer Investment Services Co. v. Brunswick Associates Ltd. Partnership*, 507 U.S. 380, 113 S.Ct. 1489 (1993)). In its customary and preferred sense, "fail" connotes some omission, fault, or negligence on the part of the person who has failed to do something. See, *e.g.*, Webster's New International Dictionary 910 (2d ed. 1939) (defining "fail" as "to be wanting; to fall short; to be or become deficient in any measure or degree," and "failure" as "a falling short," "a deficiency or lack," and an "[o]mission to perform"); Webster's New International Dictionary 814 (3d ed. 1993) ("to leave some possible or expected action unperformed or some condition unachieved"). To say a person has failed in a duty implies he did not take the necessary steps to fulfill it. He is, as a consequence, at fault and bears responsibility for the failure. In this sense, a person is not at fault when his diligent efforts to perform an act are thwarted, for example, by the conduct of another or by happenstance. Fault lies, in those circumstances, either with the person who interfered with the accomplishment of the act or with no one at all. We conclude Congress used the word "failed" in the sense just described. Had Congress intended a no-fault standard, it would have had no difficulty in making its intent plain. It would have had to do no more than use, in lieu of the phrase "has failed to," the phrase "did not."

Under the opening clause of § 2254(e)(2), a failure to develop the factual basis of a claim is not established unless there is lack of diligence, or some greater fault, attributable to the prisoner or the prisoner's counsel. In this we agree with the Court of Appeals and with all other courts of appeals which have addressed the issue.

Our interpretation of § 2254(e)(2)'s opening clause has support in *Keeney v. Tamayo–Reyes*, 504 U.S. 1, 112 S.Ct. 1715 (1992), a case decided four years before AEDPA's enactment. In *Keeney* a prisoner with little knowledge of English sought an evidentiary hearing in federal court, alleging his nolo contendere plea to a manslaughter charge was not knowing and voluntary because of inaccuracies in the translation of the plea proceedings. The prisoner had not developed the facts of his claim in state collateral proceedings, an omission caused by the negligence of his state postconviction counsel. The Court characterized this as the "prisoner's failure to develop material facts in state court." We required the prisoner to demonstrate cause and prejudice excusing the default before he could receive a hearing on his claim unless the prisoner could "show that a fundamental miscarriage of justice would result from failure to hold a federal evidentiary hearing."

Section 2254(e)(2)'s initial inquiry into whether "the applicant has failed to develop the factual basis of a claim in State court proceedings" echoes *Keeney*'s language regarding "the state prisoner's failure to develop material facts in state court." * * * As is evident from the similarity between the Court's phrasing in *Keeney* and the opening clause of § 2254(e)(2), Congress intended to preserve at least one aspect of *Keeney*'s holding: prisoners who are at fault for the deficiency in the state-court record must satisfy a heightened standard to obtain an evidentiary hearing. To be sure, in requiring that prisoners who have not been diligent satisfy § 2254(e)(2)'s provisions rather than show cause and prejudice, and in eliminating a freestanding "miscarriage of justice" exception, Congress raised the bar *Keeney* imposed on prisoners who were not diligent in state-court proceedings. Contrary to the Commonwealth's position, however, there is no basis in the text of § 2254(e)(2) to believe Congress used "fail" in a different sense than the Court did in *Keeney* or otherwise intended the statute's further, more stringent requirements to control the availability of an evidentiary hearing in a broader class of cases than were covered by *Keeney*'s cause and prejudice standard.

In sum, the opening clause of § 2254(e)(2) codifies *Keeney*'s threshold standard of diligence, so that prisoners who would have had to satisfy *Keeney*'s test for excusing the deficiency in the state-court record prior to AEDPA are now controlled by § 2254(e)(2). When the words of the Court are used in a later statute governing the same subject matter, it is respectful of Congress and of the Court's own processes to give the words the same meaning in the absence of specific direction to the contrary.

* * *

The Commonwealth argues a reading of "failed to develop" premised on fault empties § 2254(e)(2)(A)(ii) of its meaning. To treat the prisoner's lack of diligence in state court as a prerequisite for application of § 2254(e)(2), the Commonwealth contends, renders a nullity of the statute's own diligence provision requiring the prisoner to show "a factual predicate [of his claim] could not have been previously discovered through the exercise of due diligence." § 2254(e)(2)(A)(ii). We disagree.

The Commonwealth misconceives the inquiry mandated by the opening clause of § 2254(e)(2). The question is not whether the facts could have been discovered but instead whether the prisoner was diligent in his efforts. The purpose of the fault component of "failed" is to ensure the prisoner undertakes his own diligent search for evidence. Diligence for purposes of the opening clause depends upon whether the prisoner made a reasonable attempt, in light of the information available at the time, to investigate and pursue claims in state court; it does not depend, as the Commonwealth would have it, upon whether those efforts could have been successful. Though lack of diligence will not bar an evidentiary hearing if efforts to discover the facts would have been in vain, see § 2254(e)(2)(A)(ii), and there is a convincing claim of innocence, see § 2254(e)(2)(B), only a prisoner who has neglected his rights in state court need satisfy these conditions. The statute's later reference to diligence pertains to cases in which the facts could not have been discovered, whether there was diligence or not. In this important respect § 2254(e)(2)(A)(ii) bears a close resemblance to (e)(2)(A)(i), which applies to a new rule that was not available at the time of the earlier proceedings. In these two parallel provisions Congress has given prisoners who fall within § 2254(e)(2)'s opening clause an opportunity to obtain an evidentiary hearing where the legal or factual basis of the claims did not exist at the time of state-court proceedings.

We are not persuaded by the Commonwealth's further argument that anything less than a no-fault understanding of the opening clause is contrary to AEDPA's purpose to further the principles of comity, finality, and federalism. There is no doubt Congress intended AEDPA to advance these doctrines. Federal habeas corpus principles must inform and shape the historic and still vital relation of mutual respect and common purpose existing between the States and the federal courts. In keeping this delicate balance we have been careful to limit the scope of federal intrusion into state criminal adjudications and to safeguard the States' interest in the integrity of their criminal and collateral proceedings.

It is consistent with these principles to give effect to Congress' intent to avoid unneeded evidentiary hearings in federal habeas corpus, while recognizing the statute does not equate prisoners who exercise diligence in pursuing their claims with those who do not. Principles of exhaustion are premised upon recognition by Congress and the Court that state judiciaries have the duty and competence to vindicate rights secured by the Constitution in state criminal proceedings. Diligence will require in the usual case that the prisoner, at a minimum, seek an evidentiary hearing in state court in the manner prescribed by state law. * * * For state courts to have their rightful opportunity to adjudicate federal rights, the prisoner must be diligent in developing the record and presenting, if possible, all claims of constitutional error. If the prisoner fails to do so, himself or herself contributing to the absence of a full and fair adjudication in state court, § 2254(e)(2) prohibits an evidentiary hearing to develop the relevant claims in federal court, unless the statute's other stringent requirements are met. Federal courts sitting in habeas are not an alternative forum for trying facts and issues which a prisoner made insufficient effort to pursue in state proceedings. Yet comity is not served by saying a prisoner "has failed to develop the factual basis of a claim" where he was unable to develop his claim in state court despite diligent effort. In that circumstance, an evidentiary hearing is not barred by § 2254(e)(2).

III

Now we apply the statutory test. If there has been no lack of diligence at the relevant stages in the state proceedings, the prisoner has not "failed to develop" the facts under § 2254(e)(2)'s opening clause, and he will be excused from showing compliance with the balance of the subsection's requirements. We find lack of diligence as to one of the three claims but not as to the other two.

A

Petitioner did not exercise the diligence required to preserve the claim that nondisclosure of Cruse's psychiatric report was in contravention of *Brady v. Maryland*, 373 U.S. 83, 83 S.Ct. 1194 (1963). The report concluded Cruse "ha[d] little recollection of the [murders of the Kellers], other than vague memories, as he was intoxicated with alcohol and marijuana at the time." The report had been prepared in September 1993, before petitioner was tried; yet it was not mentioned by petitioner until he filed his federal habeas petition and attached a copy of the report. Petitioner explained that an investigator for his federal habeas counsel discovered the report in Cruse's court file but state habeas counsel had not seen it when he had reviewed the same file. State habeas counsel averred as follows:

> "Prior to filing [petitioner's] habeas corpus petition with the Virginia Supreme Court, I reviewed the Cumberland County court

files of [petitioner] and of his co-defendant, Jeffrey Cruse.... I have reviewed the attached psychiatric evaluation of Jeffrey Cruse.... I have no recollection of seeing this report in Mr. Cruse's court file when I examined the file. Given the contents of the report, I am confident that I would remember it."

The trial court was not satisfied with this explanation for the late discovery. Nor are we.

There are repeated references to a "psychiatric" or "mental health" report in a transcript of Cruse's sentencing proceeding, a copy of which petitioner's own state habeas counsel attached to the state habeas petition he filed with the Virginia Supreme Court. The transcript reveals that Cruse's attorney described the report with details that should have alerted counsel to a possible *Brady* claim. * * *

The transcript put petitioner's state habeas counsel on notice of the report's existence and possible materiality. The sole indication that counsel made some effort to investigate the report is an October 30, 1995, letter to the prosecutor in which counsel requested "[a]ll reports of physical and mental examinations, scientific tests, or experiments conducted in connection with the investigation of the offense, including but not limited to: ... [a]ll psychological test or polygraph examinations performed upon any prosecution witness and all documents referring or relating to such tests...." After the prosecution declined the requests absent a court order, it appears counsel made no further efforts to find the specific report mentioned by Cruse's attorney. Given knowledge of the report's existence and potential importance, a diligent attorney would have done more. Counsel's failure to investigate these references in anything but a cursory manner triggers the opening clause of § 2254(e)(2).

As we hold there was a failure to develop the factual basis of this *Brady* claim in state court, we must determine if the requirements in the balance of § 2254(e)(2) are satisfied so that petitioner's failure is excused. Subparagraph (B) of § 2254(e)(2) conditions a hearing upon a showing, by clear and convincing evidence, that no reasonable factfinder would have found petitioner guilty of capital murder but for the alleged constitutional error. Petitioner concedes he cannot make this showing, and the case has been presented to us on that premise. For these reasons, we affirm the Court of Appeals' judgment barring an evidentiary hearing on this claim.

B

We conclude petitioner has met the burden of showing he was diligent in efforts to develop the facts supporting his juror bias and prosecutorial misconduct claims in collateral proceedings before the Virginia Supreme Court.

Petitioner's claims are based on two of the questions posed to the jurors by the trial judge at *voir dire*. First, the judge asked prospective jurors, "Are any of you related to the following people who may be called as witnesses?" Then he read the jurors a list of names, one of which was "Deputy Sheriff Claude Meinhard." Bonnie Stinnett, who would later become the jury foreperson, had divorced Meinhard in 1979, after a 17–year marriage with four children. Stinnett remained silent, indicating the answer was "no." Meinhard, as the officer who investigated the crime scene and interrogated Cruse, would later become the prosecution's lead-off witness at trial.

After reading the names of the attorneys involved in the case, including one of the prosecutors, Robert Woodson, Jr., the judge asked, "Have you or any member of your immediate family ever been represented by any of the aforementioned attorneys?" Stinnett again said nothing, despite the fact Woodson had represented her during her divorce from Meinhard.

In an affidavit she provided in the federal habeas proceedings, Stinnett claimed "[she] did not respond to the judge's [first] question because [she] did not consider [herself] 'related' to Claude Meinhard in 1994 [at voir dire].... Once our marriage ended in 1979, I was no longer related to him." As for Woodson's earlier representation of her, Stinnett explained as follows:

> "When Claude and I divorced in 1979, the divorce was uncontested and Mr. Woodson drew up the papers so that the divorce could be completed. Since neither Claude nor I was contesting anything, I didn't think Mr. Woodson 'represented' either one of us."

Woodson provided an affidavit in which he admitted "[he] was aware that Juror Bonnie Stinnett was the ex-wife of then Deputy Sheriff Claude Meinhard and [he] was aware that they had been divorced for some time." Woodson stated, however, "[t]o [his] mind, people who are related only by marriage are no longer 'related' once the marriage ends in divorce." Woodson also "had no recollection of having been involved as a private attorney in the divorce proceedings between Claude Meinhard and Bonnie Stinnett." He explained that "[w]hatever [his] involvement was in the 1979 divorce, by the time of trial in 1994 [he] had completely forgotten about it."

Even if Stinnett had been correct in her technical or literal interpretation of the question relating to Meinhard, her silence after the first question was asked could suggest to the finder of fact an unwillingness to be forthcoming; this in turn could bear on the veracity of her explanation for not disclosing that Woodson had been her attorney. Stinnett's failure to divulge material information in response to the second question was misleading as a matter of fact because, under any interpretation, Woodson had acted as counsel to her and Meinhard in their divorce. Coupled with Woodson's own reticence, these omissions as a whole disclose the need for an evidentiary hearing. It may be that petitioner could establish that Stinnett was not impartial or that Woodson's silence so infected the trial as to deny due process.

In ordering an evidentiary hearing on the juror bias and prosecutorial misconduct claims, the District Court concluded the factual basis of the claims was not reasonably available to petitioner's counsel during state habeas proceedings. After the Court of Appeals vacated this judgment, the District Court dismissed the petition and the Court of Appeals affirmed under the theory that state habeas counsel should have discovered Stinnett's relationship to Meinhard and Woodson.

We disagree with the Court of Appeals on this point. The trial record contains no evidence which would have put a reasonable attorney on notice that Stinnett's non-response was a deliberate omission of material information. State habeas counsel did attempt to investigate petitioner's jury, though prompted by concerns about a different juror. Counsel filed a motion for expert services with the Virginia Supreme Court, alleging "irregularities, improprieties and omissions exist[ed] with respect to the empaneling [sic] of the jury." Based on these suspicions, counsel requested funding for an investigator "to examine all circumstances relating to the empanelment of the jury and the jury's consideration of the case." The Commonwealth opposed the motion, and the Virginia Supreme Court denied it and dismissed the habeas petition, depriving petitioner of a further opportunity to investigate. The Virginia Supreme Court's denial of the motion is understandable in light of petitioner's vague allegations, but the vagueness was not the fault of petitioner. Counsel had no reason to believe Stinnett had been married to Meinhard or been represented by Woodson. The underdevelopment of these matters was attributable to Stinnett and Woodson, if anyone. We do not suggest the State has an obligation to pay for investigation of as yet undeveloped claims; but if the prisoner has made a reasonable effort to discover the claims to commence or continue state proceedings, § 2254(e)(2) will not bar him from developing them in federal court.

The Court of Appeals held state habeas counsel was not diligent because petitioner's investigator on federal habeas discovered the relationships upon interviewing two jurors who referred in passing to Stinnett as "Bonnie Meinhard." The investigator later confirmed Stinnett's prior marriage to Meinhard by checking Cumberland County's public records. ("The documents supporting [petitioner's] Sixth Amendment claims have been a matter of public record since Stinnett's divorce became final in 1979. Indeed, because [petitioner's] federal habeas counsel located those documents, there is little reason to think that his state habeas counsel could not have done so as well"). We should be surprised, to say the least, if a district court familiar with the standards of trial practice were to hold that in all cases diligent counsel must check public records containing personal information pertaining to each and every juror. Because of Stinnett and Woodson's silence, there was no basis for an investigation into Stinnett's marriage history. Section 2254(e)(2) does not apply to petitioner's related claims of juror bias and prosecutorial misconduct.

We further note the Commonwealth has not argued that petitioner could have sought relief in state court once he discovered the factual bases of these claims some time between appointment of federal habeas counsel on July 2, 1996, and the filing of his federal habeas petition on November 20, 1996. As an indigent, petitioner had 120 days following appointment of state habeas counsel to file a petition with the Virginia Supreme Court. State habeas counsel was appointed on August 10, 1995, about a year before petitioner's investigator on federal habeas uncovered the information regarding Stinnett and Woodson. As state postconviction relief was no longer available at the time the facts came to light, it would have been futile for petitioner to return to the Virginia courts. In these circumstances, though the state courts did not have an opportunity to consider the new claims, petitioner cannot be said to have failed to develop them in state court by reason of having neglected to pursue remedies available under Virginia law.

Our analysis should suffice to establish cause for any procedural default petitioner may have committed in not presenting these claims to the Virginia courts in the first instance. Questions regarding the standard for determining the prejudice that petitioner must establish to obtain relief on these claims can be addressed by the Court of Appeals or the District Court in the course of further proceedings. These courts * * * will take due account of the District Court's earlier decision to grant an evidentiary hearing based in part on its belief that "Juror Stinnett deliberately failed to tell the truth on voir dire."

* * *

C. AEDPA'S ADDITIONAL PROCEDURAL BARS

This section considers some additional procedural bars to habeas relief imposed by AEDPA. One such bar is the one-year statute of limitations. In *Lawrence v. Florida*, the issue is how to interpret the provision of AEDPA tolling the statute while the petitioner pursues remedies in the state courts. *Rhines v. Weber* concerns the interplay between the statute and the rule of *Rose v. Lundy*, 455 U.S. 509, 102 S.Ct. 1198 (1982) requiring federal district courts to dismiss "mixed" habeas corpus petitions—those containing both unexhausted and exhausted claims. The last case, *Panetti v. Quarterman (Part I)*, construes AEDPA's bar against successive habeas petitions in federal court.

LAWRENCE v. FLORIDA

549 U.S. 327, 127 S.Ct. 1079, 166 L.Ed.2d 924 (2007).

JUSTICE THOMAS delivered the opinion of the Court.

Congress established a 1–year statute of limitations for seeking federal habeas corpus relief from a state-court judgment, 28 U.S.C. § 2244 (d), and further provided that the limitations period is tolled while an "application for State post-conviction or other collateral review" "is pending,"

§ 2244(d)(2). We must decide whether a state application is still "pending" when the state courts have entered a final judgment on the matter but a petition for certiorari has been filed in this Court. We hold that it is not.

I

Petitioner Gary Lawrence and his wife used a pipe and baseball bat to kill Michael Finken. A Florida jury convicted Lawrence of first-degree murder, conspiracy to commit murder, auto theft, and petty theft. The trial court sentenced Lawrence to death. The Florida Supreme Court affirmed Lawrence's conviction and sentence on appeal, and this Court denied certiorari on January 20, 1998.

On January 19, 1999, 364 days later, Lawrence filed an application for state postconviction relief in a Florida trial court.[1] The court denied relief, and the Florida Supreme Court affirmed, issuing its mandate on November 18, 2002. Lawrence sought review of the denial of state postconviction relief in this Court. We denied certiorari on March 24, 2003.

While Lawrence's petition for certiorari was pending, he filed the present federal habeas application. The Federal District Court dismissed it as untimely under § 2244(d)'s 1–year limitations period. All but one day of the limitations period had lapsed during the 364 days between the time Lawrence's conviction became final and when he filed for state postconviction relief. The limitations period was then tolled while the Florida courts entertained his state application. After the Florida Supreme Court issued its mandate, Lawrence waited another 113 days—well beyond the one day that remained in the limitations period—to file his federal habeas application. As a consequence, his federal application could be considered timely only if the limitations period continued to be tolled during this Court's consideration of his petition for certiorari. * * * [T]he District Court concluded that Lawrence had only one day to file a federal habeas application after the Florida Supreme Court issued its mandate. The Eleventh Circuit affirmed. We granted certiorari and now affirm.

II

The Antiterrorism and Effective Death Penalty Act of 1996 (AEDPA), sets a one-year statute of limitations for seeking federal habeas corpus relief from a state-court judgment. This limitations period is tolled while a state prisoner seeks postconviction relief in state court:

"The time during which a properly filed application for State postconviction or other collateral review with respect to the pertinent

---

1. Lawrence contends that delays in Florida's program for appointing postconviction counsel and other issues outside of his control caused 298 days to pass before Florida appointed an attorney who took an active role in his postconviction case. These facts have little relevance to our analysis. Lawrence did not seek certiorari on the question whether these facts entitle him to equitable tolling. Indeed, Lawrence was able to file his state postconviction petition on time in spite of these delays. And before this Court, he argues that his attorney mistakenly missed the federal habeas deadline, not that he lacked adequate time to file a federal habeas application.

judgment or claim is pending shall not be counted toward any period of limitation under this subsection." § 2244(d)(2).

Based on this provision, the parties agree that AEDPA's limitations period was tolled from the filing of Lawrence's petition for state postconviction relief until the Florida Supreme Court issued its mandate affirming the denial of that petition. At issue here is whether the limitations period was also tolled during the pendency of Lawrence's petition for certiorari to this Court seeking review of the denial of state postconviction relief. If it was tolled, Lawrence's federal habeas application was timely. So we must decide whether, according to § 2244(d)(2), an "application for State postconviction or other collateral review" "is pending" while this Court considers a certiorari petition.

Read naturally, the text of the statute must mean that the statute of limitations is tolled only while state courts review the application. As we stated in *Carey v. Saffold,* 536 U.S. 214, 122 S.Ct. 2134 (2002), a state postconviction application "remains pending" "until the application has achieved final resolution through the State's postconviction procedures." This Court is not a part of a "State's post-conviction procedures." State review ends when the state courts have finally resolved an application for state postconviction relief. After the State's highest court has issued its mandate or denied review, no other state avenues for relief remain open. And an application for state postconviction review no longer exists. All that remains is a separate certiorari petition pending before a *federal* court. The application for state postconviction review is therefore not "pending" after the state court's postconviction review is complete, and § 2244(d)(2) does not toll the 1–year limitations period during the pendency of a petition for certiorari.

If an application for state postconviction review were "pending" during the pendency of a certiorari petition in this Court, it is difficult to understand how a state prisoner could exhaust state postconviction remedies without filing a petition for certiorari. Indeed, AEDPA's exhaustion provision and tolling provision work together:

"The tolling provision of § 2244(d)(2) balances the interests served by the exhaustion requirement and the limitation period.... Section 2244(d)(1)'s limitation period and § 2244(d)(2)'s tolling provision, together with § 2254(b)'s exhaustion requirement, encourage litigants *first* to exhaust all state remedies and *then* to file their federal habeas petitions *as soon as possible." Duncan v. Walker,* 533 U.S. 167, 121 S.Ct. 2120 (2001)

Yet we have said that state prisoners need not petition for certiorari to exhaust state remedies. *Fay v. Noia,* 372 U.S. 391, 83 S.Ct. 822 (1963) State remedies are exhausted at the end of state-court review.

Lawrence argues that § 2244(d)(2) should be construed to have the same meaning as § 2244(d)(1)(A), the trigger provision that determines when AEDPA's statute of limitations begins to run. But § 2244(d)(1)(A) uses much different language from § 2244(d)(2), referring to "the date on which the judgment became final by *the conclusion of direct review* or the expiration of the time for seeking such review." § 2244(d)(1)(A). When interpreting similar language in § 2255, we explained that "direct review" has long included review by this Court. *Clay v. United States,* 537 U.S. 522, 123 S.Ct. 1072 (2003). Indeed, we noted that "[t]he Courts of Appeals have uniformly interpreted 'direct review in § 2244(d)(1)(A) to encompass review of a state conviction by this Court." By contrast, § 2244(d)(2) refers exclusively to "*State* post-conviction or other collateral review," language not easily interpreted to include participation by a federal court.

Furthermore, § 2244(d)(1)(A) refers to the "time for seeking" direct review, which includes review by this Court under *Clay.* By parity of reasoning, the "time for seeking" review of a state postconviction judgment arguably would include the period for filing a certiorari petition before this Court. However, § 2244(d)(2) makes no reference to the "time for seeking" review of a state postconviction court's judgment. Instead, it seeks to know when an application for "State ... review" is pending. The linguistic difference is not insignificant: When the state courts have issued a final judgment on a state application, it is no longer pending even if a prisoner has additional time for seeking review of that judgment through a petition for certiorari.

A more analogous statutory provision is § 2263(b)(2), which is part of AEDPA's "opt-in" provisions for States that comply with specific requirements relating to the provision of postconviction counsel. Under § 2263, the limitations period is tolled "from the date on which the first petition for post-conviction review or other collateral relief is filed until the final State court disposition of such petition." Lawrence concedes that under this language there would be no tolling for certiorari petitions seeking review of state postconviction applications. And although he correctly notes that the language in § 2263 differs from the language of § 2244(d)(2), it is clear that the language used in both sections provides that tolling hinges on the pendency of state review. Given Congress' clear intent in § 2263 to provide tolling for certiorari petitions on direct review but not for certiorari petitions following state postconviction review, it is not surprising that Congress would make the same distinction in § 2244.

Lawrence also argues that our interpretation would result in awkward situations in which state prisoners have to file federal habeas applications while they have certiorari petitions from state postconviction proceedings pending before this Court. But these situations will also arise under the express terms of § 2263, and Lawrence admits that Congress intended that provision to preclude tolling for certiorari petitions. Because Congress was not concerned by this potential for awkwardness in § 2263, there is no reason for us to construe the statute to avoid it in § 2244(d)(2).

Contrary to Lawrence's suggestion, our interpretation of § 2244(d)(2) results in few practical problems. As Justice STEVENS has noted, "this Court rarely grants review at this stage of the litigation even when the application for state collateral relief is supported by arguably meritorious federal constitutional claims," choosing instead to wait for "federal habeas proceedings." *Kyles v. Whitley,* 498 U.S. 931, 111 S.Ct. 333 (1990) (opinion concurring in denial of stay of execution). Thus, the likelihood that the District Court will duplicate work or analysis that might be done by this Court if we granted certiorari to review the state postconviction proceeding is quite small. And in any event, a district court concerned about duplicative work can stay the habeas application until this Court resolves the case or, more likely, denies the petition for certiorari.

Lawrence argues that even greater anomalies result from our interpretation when the state court grants relief to a prisoner and the state petitions for certiorari. In that hypothetical, Lawrence maintains that the prisoner would arguably lack standing to file a federal habeas application immediately after the state court's judgment (because the state court granted him relief) but would later be time barred from filing a federal habeas application if we granted certiorari and the State prevailed. Again, this particular procedural posture is extremely rare. Even so, equitable tolling may be available, in light of the arguably extraordinary circumstances and the prisoner's diligence.[3] We cannot base our interpretation of the statute on an exceedingly rare inequity that Congress almost certainly was not contemplating and that may well be cured by equitable tolling.

In contrast to the hypothetical problems identified by Lawrence, allowing the statute of limitations to be tolled by certiorari petitions would provide incentives for state prisoners to file certiorari petitions as a delay tactic. By filing a petition for certiorari, the prisoner would push back § 2254's deadline while we resolved the petition for certiorari. This tolling rule would provide an incentive for prisoners to file certiorari petitions— regardless of the merit of the claims asserted—so that they receive additional time to file their habeas applications.

III

Lawrence also argues that equitable tolling applies to his otherwise untimely claims. We have not decided whether § 2244(d) allows for equitable tolling. Because the parties agree that equitable tolling is available, we assume without deciding that it is. To be entitled to equitable tolling, Lawrence must show "(1) that he has been pursuing his rights diligently, and (2) that some extraordinary circumstance stood in his way" and prevented timely filing.

Lawrence makes several arguments in support of his contention that equitable tolling applies to his case. First, he argues that legal confusion about whether AEDPA's limitations period is tolled by certiorari petitions justifies equitable tolling. But at the time the limitations period expired in Lawrence's case, the Eleventh Circuit and every other Circuit to address the issue agreed that the limitations period was not tolled by certiorari

---

3. As discussed below, we assume, as the parties do, the availability of equitable tolling under § 2244.

petitions. The settled state of the law at the relevant time belies any claim to legal confusion.

Second, Lawrence argues that his counsel's mistake in miscalculating the limitations period entitles him to equitable tolling. If credited, this argument would essentially equitably toll limitations periods for every person whose attorney missed a deadline. Attorney miscalculation is simply not sufficient to warrant equitable tolling, particularly in the postconviction context where prisoners have no constitutional right to counsel.

Third, Lawrence argues that his case presents special circumstances because the state courts appointed and supervised his counsel. But a State's effort to assist prisoners in postconviction proceedings does not make the State accountable for a prisoner's delay. Lawrence has not alleged that the State prevented him from hiring his own attorney or from representing himself. It would be perverse indeed if providing prisoners with postconviction counsel deprived States of the benefit of the AEDPA statute of limitations.

Fourth, Lawrence argues that his mental incapacity justifies his reliance upon counsel and entitles him to equitable tolling. Even assuming this argument could be legally credited, Lawrence has made no factual showing of mental incapacity. In sum, Lawrence has fallen far short of showing "extraordinary circumstances" necessary to support equitable tolling.

IV

The Court of Appeals correctly determined that the filing of a petition for certiorari before this Court does not toll the statute of limitations under § 2244(d)(2). It also correctly declined to equitably toll the limitations period in the factual circumstances of Lawrence's case. For these reasons, the judgment of the Court of Appeals is affirmed.

[Dissenting opinion by GINSBURG, J., joined by STEVENS, SOUTER and BREYER, JJ. omitted]

NOTES

1. *The statute of limitations and statutory tolling.*

The one-year statute of limitations begins to run when the defendant's state conviction becomes final, *i.e.*, when the United States Supreme Court has ruled on the defendant's petition for certiorari or the time to seek certiorari has passed. In *Woodford v. Garceau*, 538 U.S. 202, 123 S.Ct. 1398 (2003), the Court held that a federal habeas suit begins "with the filing of an application for habeas corpus relief," and not with a request for appointment of counsel or for a stay of execution. The Court had previously decided in *Duncan v. Walker*, 533 U.S. 167, 121 S.Ct. 2120 (2001) that the statute of limitations is not tolled during the time a case is pending in federal court. On the other hand, in *Carey v. Saffold*, 536 U.S. 214, 122 S.Ct. 2134 (2002), a case cited in *Lawrence*, the Court held that the statute of limitations is tolled, *i.e.*, state collateral review is "pending," during the time between a lower state court's decision and the filing of a timely appeal or original writ in a reviewing court. Other conditions must be met to qualify for statutory tolling under AEDPA. In three cases, the Court has addressed the statutory requirement that the state petition be "properly filed." In *Artuz v. Bennett*, 531 U.S. 4, 121 S.Ct. 361 (2000), the Court held that state time limits on postconviction petitions are conditions to filing, such that an untimely petition is not "properly filed." In *Pace v. DiGuglielmo*, 544 U.S. 408, 125 S.Ct. 1807 (2005), the Court applied the same rule to a state statute of limitations that contained exceptions to the time bar. And in *Allen v. Siebert*, 552 U.S. 3, 128 S.Ct. 2 (2007), the Court applied the same rule to a time limit that did not create a jurisdictional bar under state law.

2.　*The statute of limitations and equitable tolling.*

As the Court noted in *Lawrence*, the Court has not decided whether § 2244(d) allows for equitable tolling. In *Pliler v. Ford*, 542 U.S. 225, 124 S.Ct. 2441 (2004), a 7–2 decision, three of justices in the majority suggested that equitable tolling was an issue to be considered on remand. The lower courts have assumed that equitable tolling would apply where extraordinary circumstances beyond a petitioner's control made it impossible for the petitioner to file within the one-year period. For example, the courts have recognized that equitable tolling would apply if: (1) the petitioner was deceived by his attorney as to the status of the state case and the attorney's intent to file a federal petition (see *Vineyard v. Dretke*, 125 Fed.Appx. 551 (5th Cir. 2005)); (2) a correctional officer confiscated the petitioner's legal materials while he was writing his petition (see *Valverde v. Stinson*, 224 F.3d 129 (2nd Cir. 2000)); (3) the petitioner was mentally incompetent during the statutory period (see *Laws v. Lamarque*, 351 F.3d 919 (9th Cir. 2003)); or (4) the petitioner was actually innocent of the crime (see *Gibson v. Klinger*, 232 F.3d 799 (10th Cir. 2000)).

3.　*Roper v. Weaver*

In *Roper v. Weaver*, 550 U.S. 598, 127 S.Ct. 2022 (2007), the Court relied on *Lawrence* to hold that the District Court's dismissal of Weaver's pre-AEDPA petition on exhaustion grounds as premature because Weaver was seeking certiorari from the denial of state post-conviction relief was error. Consequently, the District Court was required to treat his subsequently filed post-AEDPA petition as governed by pre-AEDPA standards.

RHINES v. WEBER

544 U.S. 269, 125 S.Ct. 1528, 161 L.Ed.2d 440 (2005).

JUSTICE O'CONNOR delivered the opinion of the Court.

We confront here the problem of a "mixed" petition for habeas corpus relief in which a state prisoner presents a federal court with a single petition containing some claims that have been exhausted in the state courts and some that have not. More precisely, we consider whether a federal district court has discretion to stay the mixed petition to allow the petitioner to present his unexhausted claims to the state court in the first instance, and then to return to federal court for review of his perfected petition.

I

Petitioner Charles Russell Rhines was convicted in South Dakota state court of first-degree murder and third-degree burglary and sentenced to death. His conviction became final on December 2, 1996, when we denied his initial petition for certiorari. On December 5, 1996, Rhines filed a petition for state habeas corpus. The state court denied his petition, and the Supreme Court of South Dakota affirmed on February 9, 2000. Rhines filed his *pro se* petition for federal habeas corpus pursuant to 28 U.S.C. § 2254 in the United States District Court for the District of South Dakota on February 22, 2000. Because the 1–year statute of limitations imposed by the Antiterrorism and Effective Death Penalty Act of 1996 (AEDPA) was tolled while Rhines' state habeas corpus petition was pending, he still had more than 11 months left before the expiration of the limitations period.

With the assistance of court-appointed counsel, Rhines filed an amended petition for writ of habeas corpus and statement of exhaustion on November 20, 2000, asserting 35 claims of constitutional defects in his conviction and sentence. The State challenged 12 of those claims as unexhausted. On July 3, 2002, approximately 18 months after Rhines had filed his amended federal habeas corpus petition, the District Court held that 8 of the 35 claims had not been exhausted. At this time, the AEDPA 1–year statute of limitations had run. See *Duncan v. Walker,* 533 U.S. 167, 121 S.Ct. 2120 (2001) (holding that the statute of limitations is not tolled during the pendency of a federal petition). As a result, if the District Court had dismissed Rhines' mixed petition at that point, he would have been unable to refile in federal court after exhausting the unexhausted claims. Rhines therefore moved the District Court to hold his pending habeas petition in abeyance while he presented his unexhausted claims to the South Dakota courts. On July 3, 2002, the District Court granted the motion and issued a stay "conditioned upon petitioner commencing state court exhaustion proceedings within sixty days of this order and returning to this court within sixty days of completing such exhaustion." In compliance with that order, Rhines filed his second state habeas corpus petition on August 22, 2002.

[The Eighth Circuit reversed, holding that there was no authority for employing a "stay-and-abeyance" procedure absent "truly exceptional circumstances."]

II

Fourteen years before Congress enacted AEDPA, we held in *Rose v. Lundy,* 455 U.S. 509, 102 S.Ct. 1198 (1982), that federal district courts may not adjudicate mixed petitions for habeas corpus, that is, petitions containing both exhausted and unexhausted claims. We reasoned that the interests of comity and federalism dictate that state courts must have the first opportunity to decide a petitioner's claims. We noted that "[b]ecause 'it would be unseemly in our dual system of government for a federal district court to upset a state court conviction without an opportunity to the state courts to correct a constitutional violation,' federal courts apply the doctrine of comity." (quoting *Darr v. Burford,* 339 U.S. 200, 70 S.Ct. 587 (1950)). That doctrine " 'teaches that one court should defer action on causes properly within its jurisdiction until the courts of another sovereignty with concurrent powers, and already cognizant of the litigation, have had an opportunity to pass upon the matter.' "

Accordingly, we imposed a requirement of "total exhaustion" and directed federal courts to effectuate that requirement by dismissing mixed petitions without prejudice and allowing petitioners to return to state court to present the unexhausted claims to that court in the first instance. When we decided *Lundy,* there was no statute of limitations on the filing of federal habeas corpus petitions. As a result, petitioners who returned to state court to exhaust their previously unexhausted claims could come back to federal court to present their perfected petitions with relative ease. See *Slack v. McDaniel,* 529 U.S. 473, 120 S.Ct. 1595 (2000) (dismissal without prejudice under *Lundy* "contemplated that the prisoner could return to federal court after the requisite exhaustion").

The enactment of AEDPA in 1996 dramatically altered the landscape for federal habeas corpus petitions. AEDPA preserved *Lundy's* total exhaustion requirement, but it also imposed a 1-year statute of limitations on the filing of federal petitions. Although the limitations period is tolled during the pendency of a "properly filed application for State postconviction or other collateral review," the filing of a petition for habeas corpus in federal court does not toll the statute of limitations, *Duncan, supra.*

As a result of the interplay between AEDPA's 1-year statute of limitations and *Lundy's* dismissal requirement, petitioners who come to federal court with "mixed" petitions run the risk of forever losing their opportunity for any federal review of their unexhausted claims. If a petitioner files a timely but mixed petition in federal district court, and the district court dismisses it under *Lundy* after the limitations period has expired, this will likely mean the termination of any federal review. For example, if the District Court in this case had dismissed the petition because it contained unexhausted claims, AEDPA's 1-year statute of limitations would have barred Rhines from returning to federal court after exhausting the previously unexhausted claims in state court. Similarly, if a district court dismisses a mixed petition close to the end of the 1-year period, the petitioner's chances of exhausting his claims in state court and refiling his petition in federal court before the limitations period runs are slim. The problem is not limited to petitioners who file close to the AEDPA deadline. Even a petitioner who files early will have no way of controlling when the district court will resolve the question of exhaustion.

Thus, whether a petitioner ever receives federal review of his claims may turn on which district court happens to hear his case.

We recognize the gravity of this problem and the difficulty it has posed for petitioners and federal district courts alike. In an attempt to solve the problem, some district courts have adopted a version of the "stay-and-abeyance" procedure employed by the District Court below. Under this procedure, rather than dismiss the mixed petition pursuant to *Lundy,* a district court might stay the petition and hold it in abeyance while the petitioner returns to state court to exhaust his previously unexhausted claims. Once the petitioner exhausts his state remedies, the district court will lift the stay and allow the petitioner to proceed in federal court.

District courts do ordinarily have authority to issue stays where such a stay would be a proper exercise of discretion. AEDPA does not deprive district courts of that authority, but it does circumscribe their discretion. Any solution to this problem must therefore be compatible with AEDPA's purposes.

One of the statute's purposes is to "reduce delays in the execution of state and federal criminal sentences, particularly in capital cases." *Woodford v. Garceau,* 538 U.S. 202, 123 S.Ct. 1398 (2003). AEDPA's 1–year limitations period "quite plainly serves the well-recognized interest in the finality of state court judgments." *Duncan, supra.* It "reduces the potential for delay on the road to finality by restricting the time that a prospective federal habeas petitioner has in which to seek federal habeas review." *Id.*

Moreover, Congress enacted AEDPA against the backdrop of *Lundy's* total exhaustion requirement. The tolling provision in § 2244(d)(2) "balances the interests served by the exhaustion requirement and the limitation period," "by protecting a state prisoner's ability later to apply for federal habeas relief while state remedies are being pursued." *Duncan, supra.* AEDPA thus encourages petitioners to seek relief from state courts in the first instance by tolling the 1–year limitations period while a "properly filed application for State post-conviction or other collateral review" is pending. This scheme reinforces the importance of *Lundy's* "simple and clear instruction to potential litigants: before you bring any claims to federal court, be sure that you first have taken each one to state court."

Stay and abeyance, if employed too frequently, has the potential to undermine these twin purposes. Staying a federal habeas petition frustrates AEDPA's objective of encouraging finality by allowing a petitioner to delay the resolution of the federal proceedings. It also undermines AEDPA's goal of streamlining federal habeas proceedings by decreasing a petitioner's incentive to exhaust all his claims in state court prior to filing his federal petition.

For these reasons, stay and abeyance should be available only in limited circumstances. Because granting a stay effectively excuses a petitioner's failure to present his claims first to the state courts, stay and abeyance is only appropriate when the district court determines there was good cause for the petitioner's failure to exhaust his claims first in state court. Moreover, even if a petitioner had good cause for that failure, the district court would abuse its discretion if it were to grant him a stay when his unexhausted claims are plainly meritless. Cf. 28 U.S.C. § 2254(b)(2) ("An application for a writ of habeas corpus may be denied on the merits, notwithstanding the failure of the applicant to exhaust the remedies available in the courts of the State").

Even where stay and abeyance is appropriate, the district court's discretion in structuring the stay is limited by the timeliness concerns reflected in AEDPA. A mixed petition should not be stayed indefinitely. Though, generally, a prisoner's "principal interest ... is in obtaining speedy federal relief on his claims," *Lundy, supra* (plurality opinion), not all petitioners have an incentive to obtain federal relief as quickly as possible. In particular, capital petitioners might deliberately engage in dilatory tactics to prolong their incarceration and avoid execution of the sentence of death. Without time limits, petitioners could frustrate AEDPA's goal of finality by dragging out indefinitely their federal habeas review. Thus, district courts should place reasonable time limits on a petitioner's trip to state court and back. And if a petitioner engages in abusive litigation tactics or intentional delay, the district court should not grant him a stay at all.

On the other hand, it likely would be an abuse of discretion for a district court to deny a stay and to dismiss a mixed petition if the petitioner had good cause for his failure to exhaust, his unexhausted claims are potentially meritorious, and there is no indication that the petitioner engaged in intentionally dilatory litigation tactics. In such circumstances, the district court should stay, rather than dismiss, the mixed petition. In such a case, the petitioner's interest in obtaining federal review of his claims outweighs the competing interests in finality and speedy resolution of federal petitions. For the same reason, if a petitioner presents a district court with a mixed petition and the court determines that stay and abeyance is inappropriate, the court should allow the petitioner to delete the unexhausted claims and to proceed with the exhausted claims if dismissal of the entire petition would unreasonably impair the petitioner's right to obtain federal relief. See *Lundy, supra* (plurality opinion) ("[A petitioner] can always amend the petition to delete the unexhausted claims, rather than returning to state court to exhaust all of his claims").

The Court of Appeals erred to the extent it concluded that stay and abeyance is always impermissible. We therefore vacate the judgment of the Court of Appeals and remand the case for that court to determine, consistent with this opinion, whether the District Court's grant of a stay in this case constituted an abuse of discretion.

[Concurring statement of STEVENS, J., joined by GINSBURG and BREYER, JJ. omitted]

JUSTICE SOUTER, with whom JUSTICE GINSBURG and JUSTICE BREYER join, concurring in part and concurring in the judgment.

I join the Court's opinion with one reservation, not doctrinal but practical. Instead of conditioning stay-and-abeyance on "good cause" for delay, I would simply hold the order unavailable on a demonstration of "intentionally dilatory litigation tactics." The trickiness of some exhaustion determinations promises to infect issues of good cause when a court finds a failure to exhaust; *pro se* petitioners (as most habeas petitioners are) do not come well trained to address such matters. I fear that threshold enquiries into good cause will give the district courts too much trouble to be worth the time; far better to wait for the alarm to sound when there is some indication that a petitioner is gaming the system.

NOTE

1. *Problem 11–2.*

A petition for a writ of habeas corpus may be amended or supplemented as provided by the Federal Rules of Civil Procedure. 28 U.S.C. § 2242. Under Rule 15(c)(2), an amendment made after the statute of limitations has run relates back to the date of the original pleading if the claim asserted in the amended pleading "arose out of the conduct, transaction, or occurrence set forth or attempted to be set forth in the original pleading."

Defendant was convicted of murder and robbery in a state court. After exhausting his remedies in state court, Defendant filed a timely petition for habeas corpus in federal court alleging that his rights under the Confrontation Clause of the Sixth Amendment were violated by the admission at trial of videotaped prosecution witness testimony. Eight months later, and after the expiration of the 1–year statute of limitations period under AEDPA, Defendant has moved to amend his petition to allege that his Fifth Amendment rights were violated by the admission at trial of his pretrial statements allegedly coerced by the police. What are the arguments as to whether the amendment is time-barred? See *Mayle v. Felix*, 545 U.S. 644, 125 S.Ct. 2562 (2005)

PANETTI v. QUARTERMAN (Part 1)
551 U.S. 930, 127 S.Ct. 2842, 168 L.Ed.2d 662 (2007).

JUSTICE KENNEDY delivered the opinion of the Court.

[Scott Panetti was found guilty of a double murder and sentenced to death in a Texas state court. After unsuccessfully pursuing various post-trial remedies, including a petition for federal habeas corpus, seeking to overturn his conviction and sentence, Panetti eventually filed a second petition for federal habeas corpus alleging that he was incompetent to be executed under *Ford v. Wainwright*, 477 U.S. 399, 106 S.Ct. 2595 (1986). The facts of the case and description of the trial and subsequent proceedings are set out in Part 2 of the opinion, addressing the merits of Panetti's *Ford* claim (Chapter 12).]

II

We first consider our jurisdiction. The habeas corpus application on review is the second one petitioner has filed in federal court. Under the gatekeeping provisions of 28 U.S.C. § 2244(b)(2), "[a] claim presented in a second or successive habeas corpus application under section 2254 that was not presented in a prior application shall be dismissed" except under certain, narrow circumstances.

The State maintains that, by direction of § 2244, the District Court lacked jurisdiction to adjudicate petitioner's § 2254 application. Its argument is straightforward: "[Petitioner's] first federal habeas application, which was fully and finally adjudicated on the merits, failed to raise a *Ford* claim," and, as a result, "[his] subsequent habeas application, which did raise a *Ford* claim, was a 'second or successive' application" under the terms of § 2244(b)(2). The State contends, moreover, that any *Ford* claim brought in an application governed by § 2244's gatekeeping provisions must be dismissed.

The State acknowledges that *Ford*-based incompetency claims, as a general matter, are not ripe until after the time has run to file a first federal habeas petition. The State nevertheless maintains that its rule would not foreclose prisoners from raising *Ford* claims. Under *Stewart v. Martinez–Villareal,* 523 U.S. 637, 118 S.Ct. 1618 (1998), the State explains, a federal court is permitted to review a prisoner's *Ford* claim once it becomes ripe if the prisoner preserved the claim by filing it in his first federal habeas application. Under the State's approach a prisoner contemplating a future *Ford* claim could preserve it by this means.

The State's argument has some force. The results it would produce, however, show its flaws. As in *Martinez–Villareal,* if the State's "interpretation of 'second or successive' were correct, the implications for habeas practice would be far reaching and seemingly perverse." A prisoner would be faced with two options: forgo the opportunity to raise a *Ford* claim in federal court; or raise the claim in a first federal habeas application (which generally must be filed within one year of the relevant state-court ruling), even though it is premature. The dilemma would apply not only to prisoners with mental conditions indicative of incompetency but also to those with no early sign of mental illness. All prisoners are at risk of deteriorations in their mental state. As a result, conscientious defense attorneys would be obliged to file unripe (and, in many cases, meritless) *Ford* claims in each and every § 2254 application. This counterintuitive approach would add to the burden imposed on courts, applicants, and the States, with no clear advantage to any.

We conclude there is another reasonable interpretation of § 2244, one that does not produce these distortions and inefficiencies.

The phrase "second or successive" is not self-defining. It takes its full meaning from our case law, including decisions predating the enactment of the Antiterrorism and Effective Death Penalty Act of 1996 (AEDPA). The Court has declined to interpret "second or successive" as referring to all § 2254 applications filed second or successively in time, even when the later filings address a state-court judgment already challenged in a prior § 2254 application. See, *e.g.*, *Slack v. McDaniel,* 529 U.S. 473, 120 S.Ct. 1595 (2000) (concluding that a second § 2254 application was not "second or successive" after the petitioner's first application, which had challenged the same state-court judgment, had been dismissed for failure to exhaust state remedies).

Our interpretation of § 2244 in *Martinez–Villareal* is illustrative. There the prisoner filed his first habeas application before his execution date was set. In the first application he asserted, *inter alia,* that he was incompetent to be executed, citing *Ford.* The District Court, among other holdings, dismissed the claim as premature; and the Court of Appeals affirmed the ruling. When the State obtained a warrant for the execution, the prisoner filed, for the second time, a habeas application raising the same incompetency claim. The State argued that because the prisoner "already had one 'fully-litigated habeas petition, the plain meaning of § 2244(b) ... requires his new petition to be treated as successive.'"

We rejected this contention. While the later filing "may have been the second time that [the prisoner] had asked the federal courts to provide relief on his *Ford* claim," the Court declined to accept that there were, as a result, "two separate applications, [with] the second ... necessarily subject to § 2244(b)." The Court instead held that, in light of the particular circumstances presented by a *Ford* claim, it would treat the two filings as a single application. The petitioner "was entitled to an adjudication of all the claims presented in his earlier, undoubtedly reviewable, application for federal habeas relief."

Our earlier holding does not resolve the jurisdictional question in the instant case. *Martinez–Villareal* did not address the applicability of § 2244(b) "where a prisoner raises a *Ford* claim for the first time in a petition filed after the federal courts have already rejected the prisoner's initial habeas application." Yet the Court's willingness to look to the "implications for habeas practice" when interpreting § 2244 informs the analysis here. We conclude, in accord with this precedent, that Congress did not intend the provisions of AEDPA addressing "second or successive" petitions to govern a filing in the unusual posture presented here: a § 2254 application raising a *Ford*-based incompetency claim filed as soon as that claim is ripe.

Our conclusion is confirmed when we consider AEDPA's purposes. The statute's design is to "further the principles of comity, finality, and federalism." *Miller–El v. Cockrell,* 537 U.S. 322, 123 S.Ct. 1029 (2003) (internal quotation marks omitted).

These purposes, and the practical effects of our holdings, should be considered when interpreting AEDPA. This is particularly so when petitioners "run the risk" under the proposed interpretation of "forever losing their opportunity for any federal review of their unexhausted claims." *Rhines v. Weber,* 544 U.S. 269, 125 S.Ct. 1528 (2005). * * *

     * * *

In the usual case, a petition filed second in time and not otherwise permitted by the terms of § 2244 will not survive AEDPA's "second or successive" bar. There are, however, exceptions. We are hesitant to construe a statute, implemented to further the principles of comity, finality, and federalism, in a manner that would require unripe (and, often, factually unsupported) claims to be raised as a mere formality, to the benefit of no party.

The statutory bar on "second or successive" applications does not apply to a *Ford* claim brought in an application filed when the claim is first ripe. Petitioner's habeas application was properly filed, and the District Court had jurisdiction to adjudicate his claim.

     * * *

JUSTICE THOMAS, with whom THE CHIEF JUSTICE, JUSTICE SCALIA, and JUSTICE ALITO join, dissenting.

Scott Panetti's mental problems date from at least 1981. While Panetti's mental illness may make him a sympathetic figure, state and federal courts have repeatedly held that he is competent to face the consequences of the two murders he committed. In a competency hearing prior to his trial in 1995, a jury determined that Panetti was competent to stand trial. A judge then determined that Panetti was competent to represent himself. At his trial, the jury rejected Panetti's insanity defense, which was supported by the testimony of two psychiatrists. Since the trial, both state and federal habeas courts have rejected Panetti's claims that he was incompetent to stand trial and incompetent to waive his right to counsel.

This case should be simple. Panetti brings a claim under *Ford v. Wainwright,* 477 U.S. 399, 106 S.Ct. 2595 (1986), that he is incompetent to be executed. Presented for the first time in Panetti's second federal habeas application, this claim undisputedly does not meet the statutory requirements for filing a "second or successive" habeas application. As such, Panetti's habeas application must be dismissed. * * *

I

The Antiterrorism and Effective Death Penalty Act of 1996 (AEDPA) requires applicants to receive permission from the court of appeals prior to filing second or successive federal habeas applications. 28 U.S.C. § 2244(b)(3). Even if permission is sought, AEDPA requires courts to decline such requests in all but two narrow circumstances. Panetti raised his *Ford* claim for the first time in his second federal habeas application, but he admits that he did not seek authorization from the Court of Appeals and that his claim does not satisfy either of the statutory exceptions. Accordingly, § 2244(b) requires dismissal of Panetti's "second ... habeas corpus application."

The Court reaches a contrary conclusion by reasoning that AEDPA's phrase "second or successive" "takes its full meaning from our case law, including decisions predating the enactment of [AEDPA]." (citing *Slack v. McDaniel,* 529 U.S. 473, 120 S.Ct. 1595 (2000)). But the Court fails to identify any pre-AEDPA case that defines, explains, or modifies the phrase "second or successive." Nor does the Court identify any pre-AEDPA case in which a subsequent habeas application challenging the same state-court judgment was considered anything but "second or successive." To my knowledge, there are no such cases.

Before AEDPA's enactment, the phrase "second or successive" meant the same thing it does today—any subsequent federal habeas application challenging a state-court judgment that had been previously challenged in a federal habeas application. Prior to AEDPA, however, second or successive habeas applications were not always dismissed. Rather, the pre-AEDPA abuse of the writ doctrine allowed courts to entertain second or successive applications in certain circumstances. See 28 U.S.C. § 2254(b) Rule 9(b) ("A second or successive petition may be dismissed [when] new and different grounds are alleged [if] the judge finds that the failure of the petitioner to assert those grounds in a prior petition constituted an abuse of the writ") Consistent with this practice, prior to AEDPA, federal courts treated *Ford* claims raised in subsequent habeas applications as "second or successive" but usually allowed such claims to proceed under the abuse of the writ doctrine. Still, though, at least one court found a *Ford* claim raised in a subsequent application to be an abuse of the writ.

* * *

When it enacted AEDPA, Congress "further restrict[ed] the availability of relief to habeas petitioners" and placed new "limits on successive petitions." *Felker v. Turpin,* 518 U.S. 651, 116 S.Ct. 2333 (1996). Instead of the judicial discretion that governed second or successive habeas applications prior to AEDPA, Congress required dismissal of all second and successive applications except in two specified circumstances. § 2244(b)(2). AEDPA thus eliminated much of the discretion that previously saved second or successive habeas petitions from dismissal.

Stating that we "ha[ve] declined to interpret 'second or successive' as referring to all § 2254 applications filed second or successively in time," the Court relies upon *Stewart v. Martinez–Villareal,* 523 U.S. 637, 640, 118 S.Ct. 1618 (1998), in which we held that a subsequent application raising a *Ford* claim could go forward. In that case, however, the applicant had raised a *Ford* claim in his initial habeas application, and the District Court had dismissed it as unripe. Refusing to treat the applicant's subsequent application as second or successive, the Court simply held that the second application renewed the *Ford* claim originally presented in the prior application * * *

In other words, *Martinez–Villareal* held that where an applicant raises a *Ford* claim in an initial habeas application, § 2244 does not bar a second application once the claim ripens because the second application is a continuation of the first application. *Martinez–Villareal* does not apply here because Panetti did not bring his *Ford* claim in his initial habeas application.

The Court does not and cannot argue that any time a claim would not be ripe in the first habeas petition, it may be raised in a later habeas petition. We unanimously rejected such an argument in *Burton v. Stewart,* 549 U.S. 147, 127 S.Ct. 793 (2007). In *Burton,* the petitioner filed a federal habeas petition challenging his convictions but not challenging his sentence, which was at that time still on review in the state courts. After the state courts rejected his sentencing claims, the petitioner filed a second federal habeas petition, this time challenging his sentence. The Ninth Circuit held that Burton's second petition was not "second or successive" under AEDPA, "reason[ing] that because Burton had not exhausted his sentencing claims in state court when he filed the [first] petition, they were not ripe for federal habeas review at that time." The Ninth Circuit found that the second petition was not foreclosed by AEDPA since the claim would not have been ripe if raised in the first petition. We rejected the Ninth Circuit's view and held that AEDPA barred Burton's second petition. In light of *Burton,* it simply cannot be maintained that Panetti is excused from § 2244's requirements solely because his *Ford* claim would have been unripe had he included it in his first habeas application. Today's decision thus stands only for the proposition that *Ford* claims somehow deserve a special (and unjustified) exemption from the statute's plain import.

Because neither AEDPA's text, pre-AEDPA precedent, nor our AEDPA jurisprudence supports the Court's understanding of "second or successive," the Court falls back on judicial economy considerations. The Court suggests that my interpretation of the statute would create an incentive for every prisoner, regardless of his mental state, to raise and preserve a *Ford* claim in the event the prisoner later becomes insane. Even if this comes to pass, it would not be the catastrophe the Court suggests. District courts could simply dismiss unripe *Ford* claims outright, and habeas applicants could then raise them in subsequent petitions under the safe harbor established by *Martinez–Villareal.* Requiring that *Ford* claims be included in an initial habeas application would have the added benefit of putting a State on notice that a prisoner intends to challenge his or her competency to be executed. In any event, regardless of whether the Court's concern is justified, judicial economy considerations cannot override AEDPA's plain meaning. Remaining faithful to AEDPA's mandate, I would dismiss Panetti's application as second or successive.

* * *

NOTES

1. *The exception for new rules "made retroactive to cases on collateral review."*

In *Tyler v. Cain*, 533 U.S. 656, 121 S.Ct. 2478 (2001), a non-capital case, the Supreme Court interpreted the exception in § 2244(b)(2)(A) permitting the filing of a successive federal habeas corpus application if the defendant "shows that the claim relies on a new rule of constitutional law, made retroactive to cases on collateral review by the Supreme Court, that was previously unavailable." After Tyler was convicted of second-degree murder, had exhausted his state appeals and been denied habeas corpus relief in the state and federal courts, the Supreme Court decided *Cage v. Louisiana*, 498 U.S. 39, 111 S.Ct. 328 (1990) (*per curiam*), holding unconstitutional a Louisiana jury instruction, which reasonably could have been interpreted to allow conviction without proof beyond a reasonable doubt. After obtaining permission from the Court of Appeals, Tyler filed a second federal habeas petition, seeking relief under *Cage*. The Supreme Court decided (5–4) that Tyler did not come within § 2244(b)(2)(A). The majority held that the Court only "makes" a rule retroactive when it "holds" that a rule is retroactive. The Court, in *Cage*, did not purport to, and could not, hold that the *Cage* rule was retroactive, and the Court, in *Tyler*, could not so hold because the Court would only be able to consider Tyler's petition if he could show that the Court had already made the *Cage* rule retroactive. What was needed was an intervening case applying the *Cage* rule retroactively or some other case making clear that a class of cases (of which *Cage* was a member) would be applied retroactively, and there was none. Justice O'Connor, who concurred, and whose vote was necessary for the judgment, emphasized that, "[t]he relationship between the conclusion that a new rule is retroactive and the holdings that 'ma[k]e' this rule retroactive, however, must be strictly logical— *i.e.*, the holdings *dictate* the conclusion and not merely provide principles from which one *may* conclude that the rule applies retroactively." In light of the Court's decision will there be any cases that actually fall within this exception?

2. *Limits on Supreme Court review.*

As the Court noted in *Panetti*, the decision of the Court of Appeals whether to permit a successive petition is not reviewable by appeal or certiorari. (See § 2244(b)(3)(E).) The constitutionality of this limitation was challenged in *Felker v. Turpin*, 518 U.S. 651, 116 S.Ct. 2333 (1996). Petitioner, whose application to file a successive federal habeas corpus petition was denied by the Court of Appeals, sought an original writ of habeas corpus in the Supreme Court and a writ of certiorari to review the lower court's decision. He contended that AEDPA was unconstitutional under Article III, § 2 because it eliminated the Supreme Court's original and appellate jurisdiction and under Art. I, § 9, cl. 2 because it amounted to a suspension of the writ of habeas corpus. The Court held there was no violation of Art. III, § 2 because AEDPA did not eliminate the Supreme Court's original jurisdiction, and AEDPA's new restrictions did not amount to a "suspension of the writ."

CHAPTER 12

EXECUTION

■ ■ ■

The material in this chapter encompasses legal issues arising after all judicial remedies to challenge a conviction and death sentence have been exhausted, issues concerning the execution itself. In his memorandum respecting the denial of certiorari in *Lackey v. Texas*, Justice Stevens argues that the long delays in carrying out executions raise constitutional problems. In *Ford v. Wainwright*, the Supreme Court is called upon to decide whether the Constitution bars the execution of a prisoner who has become insane and, if so, whether the Florida procedure for making that determination satisfied due process. In *Panetti v. Quarterman* (Part II), the Court addresses both aspects of the *Ford* holding—the definition of insanity and the constitutional adequacy of the procedures employed to determine sanity—in a Texas case. The condemned defendant's last hope to avoid execution is executive clemency. In *Ohio Adult Parole Authority v. Woodward*, the Supreme Court addresses the question whether the defendant has any constitutional rights at stake in clemency proceedings. In *Baze v. Rees*, the Court is called upon to decide whether execution by lethal injection, the primary execution method employed by the federal government and all of the states, comports with the Eighth Amendment.

LACKEY v. TEXAS

514 U.S. 1045, 115 S.Ct. 1421, 131 L.Ed.2d 304 (1995).

Memorandum of JUSTICE STEVENS, respecting the denial of certiorari.

Petitioner raises the question whether executing a prisoner who has already spent some 17 years on death row violates the Eighth Amendment's prohibition against cruel and unusual punishment. Though the importance and novelty of the question presented by this certiorari petition are sufficient to warrant review by this Court, those factors also provide a principled basis for postponing consideration of the issue until after it has been addressed by other courts.

Though novel, petitioner's claim is not without foundation. In *Gregg v. Georgia*, 428 U.S. 153, 96 S.Ct. 2909 (1976), this Court held that the Eighth Amendment does not prohibit capital punishment. Our decision rested in large part on the grounds that (1) the death penalty was considered permissible by the Framers (opinion of STEWART, POWELL, and STEVENS, JJ.), and (2) the death penalty might serve "two principal social purposes: retribution and deterrence."

It is arguable that neither ground retains any force for prisoners who have spent some 17 years under a sentence of death. Such a delay, if it ever occurred, certainly would have been rare in 1789, and thus the practice of the Framers would not justify a denial of petitioner's claim. Moreover, after such an extended time, the acceptable state interest in retribution has arguably been satisfied by the severe punishment already inflicted. Over a century ago, this Court recognized that "when a prisoner sentenced by a court to death is confined in the penitentiary awaiting the execution of the sentence, one of the most horrible feelings to which he can be subjected during that time is the uncertainty during the whole of it." *In re Medley*, 134 U.S. 160, 10 S.Ct. 384 (1890). If the Court accurately described the effect of uncertainty in *Medley*, which involved a period of four weeks, that description should apply with even greater force in the case of delays that last for many years.* Finally, the additional deterrent effect from an actual execution now, on the one hand, as compared to 17 years on death row followed by the prisoner's continued incarceration for life, on the other, seems minimal. As Justice White noted, when the death penalty "ceases realistically to further these purposes, ... its imposition would then be the pointless and needless extinction of life with only marginal contributions to any discernible social or public purposes. A penalty with such negligible returns to the State would be patently excessive and cruel and unusual punishment violative of the Eighth Amendment." *Furman v. Georgia*, 408 U.S. 238, 92 S.Ct. 2726 (1972) (opinion concurring in judgment).

Petitioner's argument draws further strength from conclusions by English jurists that "execution after inordinate delay would have infringed the prohibition against cruel and unusual punishments to be found in section 10 of the Bill of Rights 1689." *Riley v. Attorney General of Jamaica*, 3 All E.R. 469 (P.C. 1983) (Lord Scarman, dissenting, joined by Lord Brightman). As we have previously recognized, that section is undoubtedly the precursor of our own Eighth Amendment.

Finally, as petitioner notes, the highest courts in other countries have found arguments such as petitioner's to be persuasive. See *Pratt v. Attorney General of Jamaica*, 4 All E.R. 769 (P.C. 1993) (en banc).

---

* See also *People v. Anderson*, 493 P.2d 880 (Cal.1972) ("The cruelty of capital punishment lies not only in the execution itself and the pain incident thereto, but also in the dehumanizing effects of the lengthy imprisonment prior to execution during which the judicial and administrative procedures essential to due process of law are carried out. Penologists and medical experts agree that the process of carrying out a verdict of death is often so degrading and brutalizing to the human spirit as to constitute psychological torture"); *Furman v. Georgia*, 408 U.S. 238, 92 S.Ct. 2726 (1972) (Brennan, J., concurring) ("[T]he prospect of pending execution exacts a frightful toll during the inevitable long wait between the imposition of sentence and the actual infliction of death"); *Solesbee v. Balkcom*, 339 U.S. 9, 70 S.Ct. 457 (1950) (Frankfurter, J., dissenting) ("In the history of murder, the onset of insanity while awaiting execution of a death sentence is not a rare phenomenon"); *Suffolk County District Attorney v. Watson*, 411 N.E.2d 1274 (Mass. 1980) (Braucher, J., concurring) (death penalty is unconstitutional under State Constitution in part because "[i]t will be carried out only after agonizing months and years of uncertainty").

Closely related to the basic question presented by the petition is a question concerning the portion of the 17–year delay that should be considered in the analysis. There may well be constitutional significance to the reasons for the various delays that have occurred in petitioner's case. It may be appropriate to distinguish, for example, among delays resulting from (a) a petitioner's abuse of the judicial system by escape or repetitive, frivolous filings; (b) a petitioner's legitimate exercise of his right to review; and (c) negligence or deliberate action by the State. Thus, though English cases indicate that the prisoner should not be held responsible for delays occurring in the latter two categories, it is at least arguable that some portion of the time that has elapsed since this petitioner was first sentenced to death in 1978 should be excluded from the calculus.

As I have pointed out on past occasions, the Court's denial of certiorari does not constitute a ruling on the merits. Often, a denial of certiorari on a novel issue will permit the state and federal courts to "serve as laboratories in which the issue receives further study before it is addressed by this Court." *McCray v. New York*, 461 U.S. 961, 103 S.Ct. 2438 (1983). Petitioner's claim, with its legal complexity and its potential for far-reaching consequences, seems an ideal example of one which would benefit from such further study.

JUSTICE BREYER agrees with JUSTICE STEVENS that the issue is an important undecided one.

NOTES

1. *"Lackey" claims.*

Citing Justice Stevens' memorandum, defendants have raised *"Lackey"* claims in a number of cases. The lower courts have uniformly rejected the claims, and the Supreme Court, over dissents by Justice Breyer and, in some cases, Justice Stevens, has refused to consider such claims. See *Thompson v. McNeil*, ___ U.S. ___, 129 S.Ct. 1299 (2009) (petitioner on death row for 32 years); *Smith v. Arizona*, ___ U.S. ___, 128 S.Ct. 2997 (2007) (petitioner on death row for 30 years); *Foster v. Florida*, 537 U.S. 990, 123 S.Ct. 470 (2002) (petitioner on death row for 27 years); *Knight v. Florida* and *Moore v. Nebraska*, 528 U.S. 990, 120 S.Ct. 459 (1999) (petitioners on death row for 24 and 19 years, respectively); *Elledge v. Florida*, 525 U.S. 944, 119 S.Ct. 366 (1998) (petitioner on death row for 23 years). Justice Thomas used the occasion of the denial of certiorari in *Knight* to respond to Justice Stevens' *Lackey* memorandum:

> I write only to point out that I am unaware of any support in the American constitutional tradition or in this Court's precedent for the proposition that a defendant can avail himself of the panoply of appellate and collateral procedures and then complain when his execution is delayed. Indeed, were there any such support in our own jurisprudence, it would be unnecessary for proponents of the claim to rely on the European

Court of Human Rights, the Supreme Court of Zimbabwe, the Supreme Court of India, or the Privy Council.

528 U.S. at 990, 120 S.Ct. at 459. He concluded:

> Five years ago, Justice STEVENS issued an invitation to state and lower courts to serve as 'laboratories' in which the viability of this claim could receive further study. These courts have resoundingly rejected the claim as meritless.

528 U.S. at 992, 120 S.Ct. at 461.

2. *The impact of delay.*

As of 2008, the average time between imposition of a sentence of death sentence and execution was almost 13 years.[a] An inmate living on death row is subjected to harsh physical conditions.[b] And, as some judges have recognized, prolonged incarceration of death row has significant psychological impacts on the inmate.[c] The suicide rate for death row inmates is estimated to be more than ten times the rate for society at large and approximately two and a half times that in the general prison population.[d] The number of prisoners counted as suicides does not include prisoners who "volunteer" for execution by waiving their appeals.[e] That number is estimated to constitute more than 10% of the inmates executed since *Furman.* Are the numbers of suicides and volunteers evidence that prolonged incarceration on death row is cruel and unusual punishment?

FORD v. WAINWRIGHT

477 U.S. 399, 106 S.Ct. 2595, 91 L.Ed.2d 335 (1986).

JUSTICE MARSHALL announced the judgment of the Court and delivered the opinion of the Court with respect to Parts I and II and an opinion with respect to Parts III, IV, and V, in which JUSTICE BRENNAN, JUSTICE BLACKMUN, and JUSTICE STEVENS join.

For centuries no jurisdiction has countenanced the execution of the insane, yet this Court has never decided whether the Constitution forbids the practice. Today we keep faith with our common-law heritage in holding that it does.

---

a. *Thompson v. McNeil,* ___ U.S. ___, 129 S.Ct. 1299, 1300 (2009) (Stevens, J. statement respecting denial of cert.).

b. In virtually every state, death-row inmates are "locked down" in their cell for most of the day, have little or no access to educational or other prison programs, and experience great isolation and loss of relationships. J. Blume, *Killing the Willing: "Volunteers," Suicide and Competency,* 103 Mich. L. Rev. 939, 966 (2005).

c. See, *e.g., Furman v. Georgia,* 408 U.S. 238, 288, 92 S.Ct. 2726 (1972) (Brennan, J., concurring) ("[T]he prospect of pending execution exacts a frightful toll during the inevitable long wait between the imposition of sentence and the actual infliction of death"); *People v. Anderson,* 493 P.2d 880, 894 (Cal. 1972) ("[T]he process of carrying out a verdict of death is often so degrading and brutalizing to the human spirit as to constitute psychological torture."

d. A. Smith, *Not "Waiving" but Drowning: The Anatomy of Death Row Syndrome and Volunteering for Execution,* 17 B.U. Pub. Int. L.J. 237, 238 (2008).

e. See J. Blume, *supra* n. b at 939–940.

I

Alvin Bernard Ford was convicted of murder in 1974 and sentenced to death. There is no suggestion that he was incompetent at the time of his offense, at trial, or at sentencing. In early 1982, however, Ford began to manifest gradual changes in behavior. They began as an occasional peculiar idea or confused perception, but became more serious over time. After reading in the newspaper that the Ku Klux Klan had held a rally in nearby Jacksonville, Florida, Ford developed an obsession focused upon the Klan. His letters to various people reveal endless brooding about his "Klan work," and an increasingly pervasive delusion that he had become the target of a complex conspiracy, involving the Klan and assorted others, designed to force him to commit suicide. He believed that the prison guards, part of the conspiracy, had been killing people and putting the bodies in the concrete enclosures used for beds. Later, he began to believe that his women relatives were being tortured and sexually abused somewhere in the prison. This notion developed into a delusion that the people who were tormenting him at the prison had taken members of Ford's family hostage. The hostage delusion took firm hold and expanded, until Ford was reporting that 135 of his friends and family were being held hostage in the prison, and that only he could help them. By "day 287" of the "hostage crisis," the list of hostages had expanded to include "senators, Senator Kennedy, and many other leaders." In a letter to the Attorney General of Florida, written in 1983, Ford appeared to assume authority for ending the "crisis," claiming to have fired a number of prison officials. He began to refer to himself as "Pope John Paul, III," and reported having appointed nine new justices to the Florida Supreme Court.

Counsel for Ford asked a psychiatrist who had examined Ford earlier, Dr. Jamal Amin, to continue seeing him and to recommend appropriate treatment. On the basis of roughly 14 months of evaluation, taped conversations between Ford and his attorneys, letters written by Ford, interviews with Ford's acquaintances, and various medical records, Dr. Amin concluded in 1983 that Ford suffered from "a severe, uncontrollable, mental disease which closely resembles 'Paranoid Schizophrenia With Suicide Potential' "—a "major mental disorder ... severe enough to substantially affect Mr. Ford's present ability to assist in the defense of his life."

Ford subsequently refused to see Dr. Amin again, believing him to have joined the conspiracy against him, and Ford's counsel sought assistance from Dr. Harold Kaufman, who interviewed Ford in November 1983. Ford told Dr. Kaufman that "I know there is some sort of death penalty, but I'm free to go whenever I want because it would be illegal and the executioner would be executed." When asked if he would be executed, Ford replied: "I can't be executed because of the landmark case. I won. Ford v. State will prevent executions all over." These statements appeared amidst long streams of seemingly unrelated thoughts in rapid succession. Dr. Kaufman concluded that Ford had no understanding of why he was being executed, made no connection between the homicide of which he had been convicted and the death penalty, and indeed sincerely believed that he would not be executed because he owned the prisons and could control the Governor through mind waves. Dr. Kaufman found that there was "no reasonable possibility that Mr. Ford was dissembling, malingering or otherwise putting on a performance. ..." The following month, in an interview with his attorneys, Ford regressed further into nearly complete incomprehensibility, speaking only in a code characterized by intermittent use of the word "one," making statements such as "Hands one, face one. Mafia one. God one, father one, Pope one. Pope one. Leader one."

Counsel for Ford invoked the procedures of Florida law governing the determination of competency of a condemned inmate, Fla.Stat. § 922.07 (1985). Following the procedures set forth in the statute, the Governor of Florida appointed a panel of three psychiatrists to evaluate whether, under § 922.07(2), Ford had "the mental capacity to understand the nature of the death penalty and the reasons why it was imposed upon him." At a single meeting, the three psychiatrists together interviewed Ford for approximately 30 minutes. Each doctor then filed a separate two- or three-page report with the Governor, to whom the statute delegates the final decision. One doctor concluded that Ford suffered from "psychosis with paranoia" but had "enough cognitive functioning to understand the nature and the effects of the death penalty, and why it is to be imposed on him." Another found that, although Ford was "psychotic," he did "know fully what can happen to him." The third concluded that Ford had a "severe adaptational disorder," but did "comprehend his total situation including being sentenced to death, and all of the implications of that penalty." He believed that Ford's disorder, "although severe, seem[ed] contrived and recently learned." Thus, the interview produced three different diagnoses, but accord on the question of sanity as defined by state law.

The Governor's decision was announced on April 30, 1984, when, without explanation or statement, he signed a death warrant for Ford's execution. Ford's attorneys unsuccessfully sought a hearing in state court to determine anew Ford's competency to suffer execution. Counsel then filed a petition for habeas corpus in the United States District Court for the Southern District of Florida, seeking an evidentiary hearing on the question of Ford's sanity, proffering the conflicting findings of the Governor-appointed commission and subsequent challenges to their methods by other psychiatrists. The District Court denied the petition without a hearing. The Court of Appeals granted a certificate of probable cause and stayed Ford's execution * * * The Court of Appeals then addressed the merits of Ford's claim and a divided panel affirmed the District Court's denial of the writ. This Court granted Ford's petition for certiorari in order to resolve the important issue whether the Eighth Amendment prohibits the execution of the insane and, if so, whether the District Court should have held a hearing on petitioner's claim.

II

Since this Court last had occasion to consider the infliction of the death penalty upon the insane, our interpretations of the Due Process Clause and the Eighth Amendment have evolved substantially. In *Solesbee v. Balkcom*, 339 U.S. 9, 70 S.Ct. 457 (1950), a condemned prisoner claimed a due process right to a judicial determination of his sanity, yet the Court did not consider the possible existence of a right under the Eighth Amendment, which had not yet been applied to the States. The sole question the Court addressed was whether Georgia's procedure for ascertaining sanity adequately effectuated that State's own policy of sparing the insane from execution. Now that the Eighth Amendment has been recognized to affect significantly both the procedural and the substantive aspects of the death penalty, the question of executing the insane takes on a wholly different complexion. The adequacy of the procedures chosen by a State to determine sanity, therefore, will depend upon an issue that this Court has never addressed: whether the Constitution places a substantive restriction on the State's power to take the life of an insane prisoner.

      * * *

A

We begin, then, with the common law. The bar against executing a prisoner who has lost his sanity bears impressive historical credentials; the practice consistently has been branded "savage and inhuman." 4 W. Blackstone, *Commentaries* (hereinafter Blackstone). Blackstone explained:

> "[I]diots and lunatics are not chargeable for their own acts, if committed when under these incapacities: no, not even for treason itself. Also, if a man in his sound memory commits a capital offence, and before arraignment for it, he becomes mad, he ought not to be arraigned for it: because he is not able to plead to it with that advice and caution that he ought. And if, after he has pleaded, the prisoner becomes mad, he shall not be tried: for how can he make his defence? If, after he be tried and found guilty, he loses his senses before judgment, judgment shall not be pronounced; and if, after judgment, he becomes of nonsane memory, execution shall be stayed: for peradventure, says the humanity of the English law, had the prisoner been of sound memory, he might have alleged something in stay of judgment or execution."

Sir Edward Coke had earlier expressed the same view of the common law of England: "[B]y intendment of Law the execution of the offender is for example, ... but so it is not when a mad man is executed, but should be a miserable spectacle, both against Law, and of extream inhumanity and cruelty, and can be no example to others." E. Coke, *Institutes* (6th ed. 1680) (hereinafter Coke). Other recorders of the common law concurred.

As is often true of common-law principles, the reasons for the rule are less sure and less uniform than the rule itself. One explanation is that the execution of an insane person simply offends humanity; another, that it provides no example to others and thus contributes nothing to whatever deterrence value is intended to be served by capital punishment. Other commentators postulate religious underpinnings: that it is uncharitable to dispatch an offender "into another world, when he is not of a capacity to fit himself for it." It is also said that execution serves no purpose in these cases because madness is its own punishment: *furiosus solo furore punitur*. More recent commentators opine that the community's quest for "retribution"—the need to offset a criminal act by a punishment of equivalent "moral quality"—is not served by execution of an insane person, which has a "lesser value" than that of the crime for which he is to be punished. Hazard & Louisell, *Death, the State, and the Insane: Stay of Execution*, 9 UCLA L.Rev. 381 (1962). * * * We know of virtually no authority condoning the execution of the insane at English common law.

Further indications suggest that this solid proscription was carried to America, where it was early observed that "the judge is bound" to stay the execution upon insanity of the prisoner. 1 J. Chitty, *A Practical Treatise on the Criminal Law*.

B

This ancestral legacy has not outlived its time. Today, no State in the Union permits the execution of the insane. It is clear that the ancient and humane limitation upon the State's ability to execute its sentences has as firm a hold upon the jurisprudence of today as it had centuries ago in England. The various reasons put forth in support of the common-law restriction have no less logical, moral, and practical force than they did when first voiced. For today, no less than before, we may seriously question the retributive value of executing a person who has no comprehension of why he has been singled out and stripped of his fundamental right to life. Similarly, the natural abhorrence civilized societies feel at killing one who has no capacity to come to grips with his own conscience or deity is still vivid today. And the intuition that such an execution simply offends humanity is evidently shared across this Nation. Faced with such widespread evidence of a restriction upon sovereign power, this Court is compelled to conclude that the Eighth Amendment prohibits a State from carrying out a sentence of death upon a prisoner who is insane. Whether its aim be to protect the condemned from fear and pain without comfort of understanding, or to protect the dignity of society itself from the barbarity of exacting mindless vengeance, the restriction finds enforcement in the Eighth Amendment.

III

The Eighth Amendment prohibits the State from inflicting the penalty of death upon a prisoner who is insane. Petitioner's allegation of insanity in his habeas corpus petition, if proved, therefore, would bar his execution. The question before us is whether the District Court was under an obligation to hold an evidentiary hearing on the question of Ford's sanity. In answering that question, we bear in mind that, while the underlying social values encompassed by the Eighth Amendment are rooted in historical traditions, the manner in which our judicial system protects those values is purely a matter of contemporary law. Once a substantive right or restriction is recognized in the Constitution, therefore, its enforcement is in no way confined to the rudimentary process deemed adequate in ages past.

A

In a habeas corpus proceeding, "a federal evidentiary hearing is required unless the state-court trier of fact has after a full hearing reliably found the relevant facts." *Townsend v. Sain*, 372 U.S. 293, 83 S.Ct. 745 (1963). The habeas corpus statute, following this Court's decision in *Townsend*, provides that, in general, "a determination after a hearing on the merits of a factual issue, made by a State court of competent jurisdiction ..., shall be presumed to be correct," and an evidentiary hearing not required. 28 U.S.C. § 2254(d). In this case, it is clear that no state court has issued any determination to which that presumption of correctness could be said to attach; indeed, no court played any role in the rejection of petitioner's claim of insanity. Thus, quite simply, *Townsend* and § 2254 require the District Court to grant a hearing *de novo* on that question.

* * *

C

Florida law directs the Governor, when informed that a person under sentence of death may be insane, to stay the execution and appoint a commission of three psychiatrists to examine the prisoner. "The examination of the convicted person shall take place with all three psychiatrists present at the same time." After receiving the report of the commission, the Governor must determine whether "the convicted person has the mental capacity to understand the nature of the death penalty and the reasons why it was imposed on him." If the Governor finds that the prisoner has that capacity, then a death warrant is issued; if not, then the prisoner is committed to a mental health facility. The procedure is conducted wholly within the executive branch, *ex parte*, and provides the exclusive means for determining sanity.

Petitioner received the statutory process. The Governor selected three psychiatrists, who together interviewed Ford for a total of 30 minutes, in the presence of eight other people, including Ford's counsel, the State's attorneys, and correctional officials. The Governor's order specifically directed that the attorneys should not participate in the examination in any adversarial manner. This order was consistent with the present Governor's "publicly announced policy of excluding all advocacy on the part of the condemned from the process of determining whether a person under a sentence of death is insane."

After submission of the reports of the three examining psychiatrists, reaching conflicting diagnoses but agreeing on the ultimate issue of competency, Ford's counsel attempted to submit to the Governor some other written materials, including the reports of the two other psychiatrists who had examined Ford at greater length, one of whom had concluded that the prisoner was not competent to suffer execution. The Governor's office refused to inform counsel whether the submission would be considered. The Governor subsequently issued his decision in the form of a death warrant. That this most cursory form of procedural review fails to achieve even the minimal degree of reliability required for the protection of any constitutional interest, and thus falls short of adequacy under Townsend, is self-evident.

IV

A

The first deficiency in Florida's procedure lies in its failure to include the prisoner in the truth-seeking process. Notwithstanding this Court's longstanding pronouncement that "[t]he fundamental requisite of due process of law is the opportunity to be heard," *Grannis v. Ordean*, 234 U.S. 385, 34 S.Ct. 779 (1914), state practice does not permit any material relevant to the ultimate decision to be submitted on behalf of the prisoner facing execution. In all other proceedings leading to the execution of an accused, we have said that the factfinder must "have before it all possible relevant information about the individual defendant whose fate it must determine." *Jurek v. Texas*, 428 U.S. 262, 96 S.Ct. 2950 (1976) (plurality opinion). And we have forbidden States to limit the capital defendant's submission of relevant evidence in mitigation of the sentence. *Skipper v. South Carolina*, 476 U.S. 1, 106 S.Ct. 1669 (1986); *Lockett v. Ohio*, 438 U.S. 586, 98 S.Ct. 2954 (1978) (joint opinion). It would be odd were we now to abandon our insistence upon unfettered presentation of relevant information, before the final fact antecedent to execution has been found.

Rather, consistent with the heightened concern for fairness and accuracy that has characterized our review of the process requisite to the taking of a human life, we believe that any procedure that precludes the prisoner or his counsel from presenting material relevant to his sanity or bars consideration of that material by the factfinder is necessarily inadequate. "[T]he minimum assurance that the life-and-death guess will be a truly informed guess requires respect for the basic ingredient of due process, namely, an opportunity to be allowed to substantiate a claim before it is rejected." *Solesbee v. Balkcom, supra* (Frankfurter, J., dissenting).

We recently had occasion to underscore the value to be derived from a factfinder's consideration of differing psychiatric opinions when resolving contested issues of mental state. In *Ake v. Oklahoma*, 470 U.S. 68, 105 S.Ct. 1087 (1985), we recognized that, because "psychiatrists disagree widely and frequently on what constitutes mental illness [and] on the appropriate diagnosis to be attached to given behavior and symptoms," the factfinder must resolve differences in opinion within the psychiatric profession "on the basis of the evidence offered by each party" when a defendant's sanity is at issue in a criminal trial. The same holds true after conviction; without any adversarial assistance from the prisoner's representative—especially when the psychiatric opinion he proffers is based on much more extensive evaluation than that of the state-appointed commission—the factfinder loses the substantial benefit of potentially probative information. The result is a much greater likelihood of an erroneous decision.

B

A related flaw in the Florida procedure is the denial of any opportunity to challenge or impeach the state-appointed psychiatrists' opinions. "[C]ross-examination ... is beyond any doubt the greatest legal engine ever invented for the discovery of truth." 5 J. Wigmore, *Evidence* § 1367 (J. Chadbourn rev. 1974). Cross-examination of the psychiatrists, or perhaps a less formal equivalent, would contribute markedly to the process of seeking truth in sanity disputes by bringing to light the bases for each expert's beliefs, the precise factors underlying those beliefs, any history of error or caprice of the examiner, any personal bias with respect to the issue of capital punishment, the expert's degree of certainty about his or her own conclusions, and the precise meaning of ambiguous words used in the report. Without some questioning of the experts concerning their technical conclusions, a factfinder simply cannot be expected to evaluate the various opinions, particularly when they are themselves inconsistent. The failure of the Florida procedure to afford the prisoner's representative any opportunity to clarify or challenge the state experts' opinions or methods creates a significant possibility that the ultimate decision made in reliance on those experts will be distorted.

C

Perhaps the most striking defect in the procedures of Fla.Stat. § 922.07, as noted earlier, is the State's placement of the decision wholly within the executive branch. Under this procedure, the person who appoints the experts and ultimately decides whether the State will be able to carry out the sentence that it has long sought is the Governor, whose subordinates have been responsible for initiating every stage of the prosecution of the condemned from arrest through sentencing. The commander of the State's corps of prosecutors cannot be said to have the neutrality that is necessary for reliability in the factfinding proceeding.

Historically, delay of execution on account of insanity was not a matter of executive clemency (*ex mandato regis*) or judicial discretion (*ex arbitrio judicias*); rather, it was required by law (*ex necessitate legis*). Thus, history affords no better basis than does logic for placing the final determination of a fact, critical to the trigger of a constitutional limitation upon the State's power, in the hands of the State's own chief executive. In no other circumstance of which we are aware is the vindication of a constitutional right entrusted to the unreviewable discretion of an administrative tribunal.

V

A

Having identified various failings of the Florida scheme, we must conclude that the State's procedures for determining sanity are inadequate to preclude federal redetermination of the constitutional issue. We do not here suggest that only a full trial on the issue of sanity will suffice to protect the federal interests; we leave to the State the task of developing appropriate ways to enforce the constitutional restriction upon its execution of sentences. It may be that some high threshold showing on behalf of the prisoner will be found a necessary means to control the number of nonmeritorious or repetitive claims of insanity. Other legitimate pragmatic considerations may also supply the boundaries of the procedural safeguards that feasibly can be provided.

Yet the lodestar of any effort to devise a procedure must be the overriding dual imperative of providing redress for those with substantial claims and of encouraging accuracy in the factfinding determination. The stakes are high, and the "evidence" will always be imprecise. It is all the more important that the adversary presentation of relevant information be as unrestricted as possible. Also essential is that the manner of selecting and using the experts responsible for producing that "evidence" be conducive to the formation of neutral, sound, and professional judgments as to the prisoner's ability to comprehend the nature of the penalty. Fidelity to these principles is the solemn obligation of a civilized society.

B

Today we have explicitly recognized in our law a principle that has long resided there. It is no less abhorrent today than it has been for centuries to exact in penance the life of one whose mental illness prevents him from comprehending the reasons for the penalty or its implications. In light of the clear need for trustworthiness in any factual finding that will prevent or permit the carrying out of an execution, we hold that Fla.Stat. § 922.07 provides inadequate assurances of accuracy to satisfy the requirements of *Townsend v. Sain*, 372 U.S. 293, 83 S.Ct. 745 (1963). Having been denied a factfinding procedure "adequate to afford a full and fair hearing" on the critical issue, 28 U.S.C. § 2254(d)(2), petitioner is entitled to an evidentiary hearing in the District Court, *de novo*, on the question of his competence to be executed.

The judgment of the Court of Appeals is reversed, and the case is remanded for further proceedings consistent with this opinion.

It is so ordered.

JUSTICE POWELL, concurring in part and concurring in the judgment.

I join Parts I and II of the Court's opinion. As Justice MARSHALL ably demonstrates, execution of the insane was barred at common law precisely because it was considered cruel and unusual. In *Solem v. Helm*, 463 U.S. 277, 103 S.Ct. 3001 (1983), we explained that while the Framers "may have intended the Eighth Amendment to go beyond the scope of its English counterpart, their use of the language of the English Bill of Rights is convincing proof that they intended to provide at least the same protection." It follows that the practice of executing the insane is barred by our own Constitution.

* * *

II

Petitioner concedes that the Governor of Florida has determined that he is not insane under the standard prescribed by Florida's statute, which is the same as the standard just described. Petitioner further concedes that there is expert evidence that supports the Governor's finding. * * *

* * *

* * * [T]he question in this case is whether Florida's procedures for determining petitioner's sanity comport with the requirements of due process.

Together with Justice MARSHALL and Justice O'CONNOR, I would hold that they do not. As Justice O'CONNOR states, "[i]f there is one 'fundamental requisite' of due process, it is that an individual is entitled to an 'opportunity to be heard.' " (quoting *Grannis v. Ordean*, 234 U.S. 385, 34 S.Ct. 779 (1914)). In this case, petitioner was deprived of that opportunity. The Florida statute does not require the Governor to consider materials submitted by the prisoner, and the present Governor has a "publicly announced policy of excluding" such materials from his consideration. Thus, the determination of petitioner's sanity appears to have been made solely on the basis of the examinations performed by state-appointed psychiatrists. Such a procedure invites arbitrariness and error by preventing the affected parties from offering contrary medical evidence or even from explaining the inadequacies of the State's examinations. It does not, therefore, comport with due process. It follows that the State's procedure was not "fair," and that the District Court on remand must consider the question of petitioner's competency to be executed.

III

While the procedures followed by Florida in this case do not comport with basic fairness, I would not require the kind of full-scale "sanity trial" that Justice MARSHALL appears to find necessary. Due process is a flexible concept, requiring only "such procedural protections as the particular situation demands." *Mathews v. Eldridge*, 424 U.S. 319, 96 S.Ct. 893 (1976); *Morrissey v. Brewer*, 408 U.S. 471, 92 S.Ct. 2593 (1972). In this instance, a number of considerations support the conclusion that the requirements of due process are not as elaborate as Justice MARSHALL suggests.

First, the Eighth Amendment claim at issue can arise only after the prisoner has been validly convicted of a capital crime and sentenced to death. Thus, in this case the State has a substantial and legitimate interest in taking petitioner's life as punishment for his crime. That interest is not called into question by petitioner's claim. Rather, the only question raised is not *whether*, but *when*, his execution may take place.[5] This question is important, but it is not comparable to the antecedent question whether petitioner should be executed at all. It follows that this Court's decisions imposing heightened procedural requirements on capital trials and sentencing proceedings do not apply in this context.

Second, petitioner does not make his claim of insanity against a neutral background. On the contrary, in order to have been convicted and sentenced, petitioner must have been judged competent to stand trial, or his competency must have been sufficiently clear as not to raise a serious question for the trial court. The State therefore may properly presume that petitioner remains sane at the time sentence is to be carried out, and may require a substantial threshold showing of insanity merely to trigger the hearing process.

Finally, the sanity issue in this type of case does not resemble the basic issues at trial or sentencing. Unlike issues of historical fact, the question of petitioner's sanity calls for a basically subjective judgment. And unlike the determination of whether the death penalty is appropriate in a particular case, the competency determination depends substantially on expert analysis in a discipline fraught with "subtleties and nuances." This combination of factors means that ordinary adversarial procedures— complete with live testimony, cross-examination, and oral argument by counsel—are not necessarily the best means of arriving at sound, consistent judgments as to a defendant's sanity.

We need not determine the precise limits that due process imposes in this area. In general, however, my view is that a constitutionally acceptable procedure may be far less formal than a trial. The State should provide an impartial officer or board that can receive evidence and argument from the prisoner's counsel, including expert psychiatric evidence that may differ from the State's own psychiatric examination. Beyond these basic requirements, the States should have substantial leeway to determine what process best balances the various interests at stake. As long as basic fairness is observed, I would find due process satisfied, and would apply the presumption of correctness of § 2254(d) on federal habeas corpus.

* * *

---

5. It is of course true that some defendants may lose their mental faculties and never regain them, and thus avoid execution altogether. My point is only that if petitioner is cured of his disease, the State is free to execute him.

JUSTICE O'CONNOR, with whom JUSTICE WHITE joins, concurring in the result in part and dissenting in part.

I am in full agreement with Justice REHNQUIST's conclusion that the Eighth Amendment does not create a substantive right not to be executed while insane. Accordingly, I do not join the Court's reasoning or opinion. Because, however, the conclusion is for me inescapable that Florida positive law has created a protected liberty interest in avoiding execution while incompetent, and because Florida does not provide even those minimal procedural protections required by due process in this area, I would vacate the judgment and remand to the Court of Appeals with directions that the case be returned to the Florida system so that a hearing can be held in a manner consistent with the requirements of the Due Process Clause. I cannot agree, however, that the federal courts should have any role whatever in the substantive determination of a defendant's competency to be executed.

As we explained in *Hewitt v. Helms*, 459 U.S. 460, 103 S.Ct. 864 (1983), "[l]iberty interests protected by the Fourteenth Amendment may arise from two sources—the Due Process Clause itself and the laws of the States." With Justice REHNQUIST, I agree that the Due Process Clause does not independently create a protected interest in avoiding the execution of a death sentence during incompetency. The relevant provision of the Florida statute, however, provides that the Governor "shall" have the prisoner committed to a "Department of Corrections mental health treatment facility" if the prisoner "does not have the mental capacity to understand the nature of the death penalty and why it was imposed on him." Fla.Stat. § 922.07(3). Our cases leave no doubt that where a statute indicates with "language of an unmistakable mandatory character," that state conduct injurious to an individual will not occur "absent specified substantive predicates," the statute creates an expectation protected by the Due Process Clause. That test is easily met here. Nor is it relevant that the statute creating the interest also specifies the procedures to be followed when the State seeks to deprive the individual of that interest. As we reaffirmed last Term, "[t]he categories of substance and procedure are distinct." *Cleveland Board of Education v. Loudermill*, 470 U.S. 532, 105 S.Ct. 1487 (1985). Thus, regardless of the procedures the State deems adequate for determining the preconditions to adverse official action, federal law defines the kind of process a State must afford prior to depriving an individual of a protected liberty or property interest.

* * *

JUSTICE REHNQUIST, with whom THE CHIEF JUSTICE joins, dissenting.

The Court today holds that the Eighth Amendment prohibits a State from carrying out a lawfully imposed sentence of death upon a person who is currently insane. This holding is based almost entirely on two unremarkable observations. First, the Court states that it "know[s] of virtually no authority condoning the execution of the insane at English common law." Second, it notes that "[t]oday, no State in the Union permits the execution of the insane." Armed with these facts, and shielded by the claim that it is simply "keep[ing] faith with our common-law heritage," the Court proceeds to cast aside settled precedent and to significantly alter both the common-law and current practice of not executing the insane. It manages this feat by carefully ignoring the fact that the Florida scheme it finds unconstitutional, in which the Governor is assigned the ultimate responsibility of deciding whether a condemned prisoner is currently insane, is fully consistent with the "common-law heritage" and current practice on which the Court purports to rely.

The Court places great weight on the "impressive historical credentials" of the common-law bar against executing a prisoner who has lost his sanity. What it fails to mention, however, is the equally important and unchallenged fact that at common law it was the executive who passed upon the sanity of the condemned. See 1 N. Walker, *Crime and Insanity in England* (1968). So when the Court today creates a constitutional right to a determination of sanity outside of the executive branch, it does so not in keeping with but at the expense of "our common-law heritage."

In *Solesbee v. Balkcom*, 339 U.S. 9, 70 S.Ct. 457 (1950), a condemned prisoner claimed that he had a constitutional right to a judicial determination of his sanity. There, as here, the State did not approve the execution of insane persons and vested in the Governor the responsibility for determining, with the aid of experts, the sanity *vel non* of persons sentenced to death. In rejecting the prisoner's claim, this Court stated:

> "Postponement of execution because of insanity bears a close affinity not to trial for a crime but rather to reprieves of sentences in general. The power to reprieve has usually sprung from the same source as the power to pardon. Power of executive clemency in this country undoubtedly derived from the practice as it had existed in England. Such power has traditionally rested in governors or the President, although some of that power is often delegated to agencies such as pardon or parole boards. Seldom, if ever, has this power of executive clemency been subjected to review by the courts."

Despite references to "evolving standards of decency," and "the jurisprudence of today," the Court points to no change since *Solesbee* in the States' approach to determining the sanity of a condemned prisoner. Current statutes quite often provide that initiation of inquiry into and/or final determination of postsentencing insanity is a matter for the executive or the prisoner's custodian. The Court's profession of "faith to our common-law heritage" and "evolving standards of decency" is thus at best a half-truth. It is Florida's scheme—which combines a prohibition against execution of the insane with executive-branch procedures for evaluating claims of insanity—that is more faithful to both traditional and modern practice. And no matter how longstanding and universal, laws providing that the State should not execute persons the Executive finds insane are not themselves sufficient to create an Eighth Amendment right that sweeps away as inadequate the procedures for determining sanity crafted by those very laws.

Petitioner makes the alternative argument, not reached by the Court, that even if the Eighth Amendment does not prohibit execution of the insane, Florida's decision to bar such executions creates a right in condemned persons to trial-type procedures to determine sanity. Here, too, *Solesbee* is instructive:

> "Recently we have pointed out the necessary and inherent differences between trial procedures and post-conviction procedures such as sentencing. *Williams v. New York*, 337 U.S. 241, 69 S.Ct. 1079 (1949). In that case we emphasized that certain trial procedure safeguards are not applicable to the process of sentencing. This principle applies even more forcefully to an effort to transplant every trial safeguard to a determination of sanity after conviction. * * * [T]o require judicial review every time a convicted defendant suggested insanity would make the possibility of carrying out a sentence depend upon 'fecundity in making suggestion after suggestion of insanity.' *Nobles v. Georgia*, 168 U.S. 398, 18 S.Ct. 87 (1897). To protect itself society must have power to try, convict, and execute sentences. Our legal system demands that this governmental duty be performed with scrupulous fairness to the accused. We cannot say that it offends due process to leave the question of a convicted person's sanity to the solemn responsibility of a state's highest executive with authority to invoke the aid of the most skillful class of experts on the crucial questions involved."

Even the sole dissenter in *Solesbee*, Justice Frankfurter, agreed that if the Constitution afforded condemned prisoners no substantive right not to be executed when insane, then the State would be free to place on the Governor the responsibility for determining sanity.

Petitioner argues that *Solesbee* is no longer controlling because it was decided "at a time when due process analysis still turned on the right-privilege distinction." But as petitioner concedes, his due process claim turns on a showing that the Florida statute at issue here created an individual right not to be executed while insane. Even a cursory reading of the statute reveals that the only right it creates in a condemned prisoner is to inform the Governor that the prisoner may be insane. Fla.Stat. § 922.07(1). The only legitimate expectation it creates is that "*[i]f the Governor decides* that the convicted person does not have the mental capacity to understand the nature of the death penalty and why it was imposed on him, he shall have him committed to a Department of Corrections mental health treatment facility." § 922.07(3) (emphasis added). * * * I do not think this state of the law requires the conclusion that Florida has granted petitioner the sort of entitlement that gives rise to the procedural protections for which he contends.

In any event, I see no reason to reject the *Solesbee* Court's conclusion that wholly executive procedures can satisfy due process in the context of a post-trial, postappeal, postcollateral-attack challenge to a State's effort to carry out a lawfully imposed sentence. Creating a constitutional right to a judicial determination of sanity before that sentence may be carried out, whether through the Eighth Amendment or the Due Process Clause, needlessly complicates and postpones still further any finality in this area of the law. The defendant has already had a full trial on the issue of guilt, and a trial on the issue of penalty; the requirement of still a third adjudication offers an invitation to those who have nothing to lose by accepting it to advance entirely spurious claims of insanity. A claim of insanity may be made at any time before sentence and, once rejected, may be raised again; a prisoner found sane two days before execution might claim to have lost his sanity the next day, thus necessitating another judicial determination of his sanity and presumably another stay of his execution.

Since no State sanctions execution of the insane, the real battle being fought in this case is over what procedures must accompany the inquiry into sanity. The Court reaches the result it does by examining the common law, creating a constitutional right that no State seeks to violate, and then concluding that the common-law procedures are inadequate to protect the newly created but common-law based right. I find it unnecessary to "constitutionalize" the already uniform view that the insane should not be executed, and inappropriate to "selectively incorporate" the common-law practice. I therefore dissent.

PANETTI v. QUARTERMAN (Part 2)

551 U.S. 930, 127 S.Ct. 2842, 168 L.Ed.2d 662 (2007).

JUSTICE KENNEDY delivered the opinion of the Court.

"[T]he Eighth Amendment prohibits a State from carrying out a sentence of death upon a prisoner who is insane." *Ford v. Wainwright,* 477 U.S. 399, 106 S.Ct. 2595 (1986). The prohibition applies despite a prisoner's earlier competency to be held responsible for committing a crime and to be tried for it. Prior findings of competency do not foreclose a prisoner from proving he is incompetent to be executed because of his present mental condition. Under *Ford,* once a prisoner makes the requisite preliminary showing that his current mental state would bar his execution, the Eighth Amendment, applicable to the States under the Due Process Clause of the Fourteenth Amendment, entitles him to an adjudication to determine his condition. These determinations are governed by the substantive federal baseline for competency set down in *Ford.*

[Scott Panetti was found guilty of a double murder and sentenced to death in a Texas state court. After unsuccessfully pursuing various post-trial remedies, including federal habeas corpus, seeking to overturn his conviction and sentence, Panetti eventually filed a second petition for federal habeas corpus relief alleging that he was incompetent to be executed under *Ford v. Wainwright*, 477 U.S. 399, 106 S.Ct. 2595 (1986). The Court's discussion regarding the jurisdiction of the federal courts to hear Panetti's second habeas petition is set forth in Part 1 of the opinion. (Chapter 11)]

I

On a morning in 1992 petitioner awoke before dawn, dressed in camouflage, and drove to the home of his estranged wife's parents. Breaking the front-door lock, he entered the house and, in front of his wife and daughter, shot and killed his wife's mother and father. He took his wife and daughter hostage for the night before surrendering to police.

Tried for capital murder in 1995, petitioner sought to represent himself. The court ordered a psychiatric evaluation, which indicated that petitioner suffered from a fragmented personality, delusions, and hallucinations. The evaluation noted that petitioner had been hospitalized numerous times for these disorders. Evidence later revealed that doctors had prescribed medication for petitioner's mental disorders that, in the opinion of one expert, would be difficult for a person not suffering from extreme psychosis even to tolerate. ("I can't imagine anybody getting that dose waking up for two to three days. You cannot take that kind of medication if you are close to normal without absolutely being put out"). Petitioner's wife described one psychotic episode in a petition she filed in 1986 seeking extraordinary relief from the Texas state courts. She explained that petitioner had become convinced the devil had possessed their home and that, in an effort to cleanse their surroundings, petitioner had buried a number of valuables next to the house and engaged in other rituals. Petitioner nevertheless was found competent to be tried and to waive counsel. At trial he claimed he was not guilty by reason of insanity.

During his trial petitioner engaged in behavior later described by his standby counsel as "bizarre," "scary," and "trance-like." According to the attorney, petitioner's behavior both in private and in front of the jury made it evident that he was suffering from "mental incompetence," and the net effect of this dynamic was to render the trial "truly a judicial farce, and a mockery of self-representation." There was evidence on the record, moreover, to indicate that petitioner had stopped taking his antipsychotic medication a few months before trial, a rejection of medical advice that, it appears, petitioner has continued to this day with one brief exception. According to expert testimony, failing to take this medication tends to exacerbate the underlying mental dysfunction. And it is uncontested that, less than two months after petitioner was sentenced to death, the state trial court found him incompetent to waive the appointment of state habeas counsel. It appears, therefore, that petitioner's condition has only worsened since the start of trial.

* * *

* * * On February 4, 2004, the District Court stayed petitioner's execution to "allow the state court a reasonable period of time to consider the evidence of [petitioner's] current mental state."

The state court had before it, at that time, petitioner's Renewed Motion To Determine Competency To Be Executed (hereinafter Renewed Motion To Determine Competency). Attached to the motion were a letter and a declaration from two individuals, a psychologist and a law professor, who had interviewed petitioner while on death row on February 3, 2004. The new evidence, according to counsel, demonstrated that petitioner did not understand the reasons he was about to be executed.

Due to the absence of a transcript, the state-court proceedings after this point are not altogether clear. The claims raised before this Court nevertheless make it necessary to recount the procedural history in some detail. Based on the docket entries and the parties' filings it appears the following occurred.

The state trial court ordered the parties to participate in a telephone conference on February 9, 2004, to discuss the status of the case. There followed a court directive instructing counsel to submit, by February 20, the names of mental health experts the court should consider appointing pursuant to Art. 46.05(f). ("If the trial court determines that the defendant has made a substantial showing of incompetency, the court shall order at least two mental health experts to examine the defendant"). The court also gave the parties until February 20 to submit any motions concerning the competency procedures and advised it would hold another status conference on that same date.

On February 19, 2004, petitioner filed 10 motions related to the Art. 46.05 proceedings. They included requests for transcription of the proceedings, a competency hearing comporting with the procedural due process requirements set forth in *Ford,* and funds to hire a mental health expert.

On February 20 the court failed to hold its scheduled status conference. Petitioner's counsel called the courthouse and was advised Judge Ables was out of the office for the day. Counsel then called the Gillespie County District Attorney, who explained that the judge had informed state attorneys earlier that week that he was cancelling the conference he had set and would appoint the mental health experts without input from the parties.

On February 23, 2004, counsel for petitioner received an order, dated February 20, advising that the court was appointing two mental health experts pursuant to Art. § 46.05(f). On February 25, at an informal status conference, the court denied two of petitioner's motions, indicating it would consider the others when the court-appointed mental health experts completed their evaluations. On March 4, petitioner filed a motion explaining that a delayed ruling would render a number of the motions moot. There is no indication the court responded to this motion.

The court-appointed experts returned with their evaluation on April 28, 2004. Concluding that petitioner "knows that he is to be executed, and that his execution will result in his death," and, moreover, that he "has the ability to understand the reason he is to be executed," the experts alleged that petitioner's uncooperative and bizarre behavior was due to calculated design: "Mr. Panetti deliberately and persistently chose to control and manipulate our interview situation," they claimed. They maintained that petitioner "could answer questions about relevant legal issues ... if he were willing to do so."

The judge sent a letter to counsel, including petitioner's attorney, Michael C. Gross, dated May 14, 2004. It said:

"Dear Counsel:

"It appears from the evaluations performed by [the court-appointed experts] that they are of the opinion that [petitioner] is competent to be executed in accordance with the standards set out in Art. 46.05 of the Code of Criminal Procedure.

"Mr. Gross, if you have any other matters you wish to have considered, please file them in the case papers and get me copies by 5:00 p.m. on May 21, 2004."

Petitioner responded with a filing entitled "Objections to Experts' Report, Renewed Motion for Funds To Hire Mental Health Expert and Investigator, Renewed Motion for Appointment of Counsel, and Motion for Competency Hearing" in Cause No. 3310 (May 24, 2004) (hereinafter Objections to Experts' Report). In this filing petitioner criticized the methodology and conclusions of the court-appointed experts; asserted his continued need for a mental health expert as his own criticisms of the report were "by necessity limited"; again asked the court to rule on his outstanding motions for funds and appointment of counsel; and requested a competency hearing. Petitioner also argued, as a more general matter, that the process he had received thus far failed to comply with Art. 46.05 and the procedural mandates set by *Ford*.

The court, in response, closed the case. On May 26, it released a short order identifying the report submitted by the court-appointed experts and explaining that "[b]ased on the aforesaid doctors' reports, the Court finds that [petitioner] has failed to show, by a preponderance of the evidence, that he is incompetent to be executed." Order Regarding Competency To Be Executed in Cause No. 3310, 1 App. 99. The order made no mention of petitioner's motions or other filings. Petitioner did not appeal the ruling to the Court of Criminal Appeals, and he did not petition this Court for certiorari.

This background leads to the matter now before us. Petitioner returned to federal court, seeking resolution of the § 2254 petition he had filed on January 26. The District Court granted petitioner's motions to reconsider, to stay his execution, to appoint counsel, and to provide funds. The court, in addition, set the case for an evidentiary hearing, which included testimony by a psychiatrist, a professor, and two psychologists, all called by petitioner, as well as two psychologists and three correctional officers, called by respondent. We describe the substance of the experts' testimony in more detail later in our opinion.

On September 29, 2004, the District Court denied petitioner's habeas application on the merits. It concluded that the state trial court had failed to comply with Art. 46.05; found the state proceedings "constitutionally inadequate" in light of *Ford;* and reviewed petitioner's Eighth Amendment claim without deferring to the state court's finding of competency. The court nevertheless denied relief. It found petitioner had not shown incompetency as defined by Circuit precedent. "Ultimately," the court explained, "the Fifth Circuit test for competency to be executed requires the petitioner know no more than the fact of his impending execution and the factual predicate for the execution." The Court of Appeals affirmed, and we granted certiorari.

* * *

III

A

Petitioner claims that the Eighth and Fourteenth Amendments of the Constitution, as elaborated by *Ford,* entitled him to certain procedures not provided in the state court; that the failure to provide these procedures constituted an unreasonable application of clearly established Supreme Court law; and that under § 2254(d) this misapplication of *Ford* allows federal-court review of his incompetency claim without deference to the state court's decision.

We agree with petitioner that no deference is due. The state court's failure to provide the procedures mandated by *Ford* constituted an unreasonable application of clearly established law as determined by this Court. It is uncontested that petitioner made a substantial showing of incompetency. This showing entitled him to, among other things, an adequate means by which to submit expert psychiatric evidence in response to the evidence that had been solicited by the state court. And it is clear from the record that the state court reached its competency determination after failing to provide petitioner with this process, notwithstanding counsel's sustained effort, diligence, and compliance with court orders. As a result of this error, our review of petitioner's underlying incompetency claim is unencumbered by the deference AEDPA normally requires.

Ford identifies the measures a State must provide when a prisoner alleges incompetency to be executed. The four-Justice plurality in *Ford* concluded as follows:

> "Although the condemned prisoner does not enjoy the same presumptions accorded a defendant who has yet to be convicted or sentenced, he has not lost the protection of the Constitution altogether; if the Constitution renders the fact or timing of his execution contingent upon establishment of a further fact, then that fact must be determined with the high regard for truth that befits a decision affecting the life or death of a human being. Thus, the ascertainment of a prisoner's sanity as a predicate to lawful execution calls for no less

stringent standards than those demanded in any other aspect of a capital proceeding."

Justice Powell's concurrence, which also addressed the question of procedure, offered a more limited holding. When there is no majority opinion, the narrower holding controls. Under this rule Justice Powell's opinion constitutes "clearly established" law for purposes of § 2254 and sets the minimum procedures a State must provide to a prisoner raising a *Ford*-based competency claim.

Justice Powell's opinion states the relevant standard as follows. Once a prisoner seeking a stay of execution has made "a substantial threshold showing of insanity," the protection afforded by procedural due process includes a "fair hearing" in accord with fundamental fairness. This protection means a prisoner must be accorded an "opportunity to be heard," though "a constitutionally acceptable procedure may be far less formal than a trial." As an example of why the state procedures on review in *Ford* were deficient, Justice Powell explained, the determination of sanity "appear[ed] to have been made *solely* on the basis of the examinations performed by state-appointed psychiatrists." "Such a procedure invites arbitrariness and error by preventing the affected parties from offering contrary medical evidence or even from explaining the inadequacies of the State's examinations."

Justice Powell did not set forth "the precise limits that due process imposes in this area." He observed that a State "should have substantial leeway to determine what process best balances the various interests at stake" once it has met the "basic requirements" required by due process. These basic requirements include an opportunity to submit "evidence and argument from the prisoner's counsel, including expert psychiatric evidence that may differ from the State's own psychiatric examination."

Petitioner was entitled to these protections once he had made a "substantial threshold showing of insanity." He made this showing when he filed his Renewed Motion To Determine Competency—a fact disputed by no party, confirmed by the trial court's appointment of mental health experts pursuant to Article 46.05(f), and verified by our independent review of the record. The Renewed Motion included pointed observations made by two experts the day before petitioner's scheduled execution; and it incorporated, through petitioner's first Motion To Determine Competency, references to the extensive evidence of mental dysfunction considered in earlier legal proceedings.

In light of this showing, the state court failed to provide petitioner with the minimum process required by *Ford*.

The state court refused to transcribe its proceedings, notwithstanding the multiple motions petitioner filed requesting this process. To the extent a more complete record may have put some of the court's actions in a more favorable light, this only constitutes further evidence of the inadequacy of the proceedings. Based on the materials available to this Court, it appears the state court on repeated occasions conveyed information to petitioner's counsel that turned out not to be true; provided at least one significant update to the State without providing the same notice to petitioner; and failed in general to keep petitioner informed as to the opportunity, if any, he would have to present his case. There is also a strong argument the court violated state law by failing to provide a competency hearing. If this did, in fact, constitute a violation of the procedural framework Texas has mandated for the adjudication of incompetency claims, the violation undermines any reliance the State might now place on Justice Powell's assertion that "the States should have substantial leeway to determine what process best balances the various interests at stake." What is more, the order issued by the state court implied that its determination of petitioner's competency was made solely on the basis of the examinations performed by the psychiatrists it had appointed—precisely the sort of adjudication Justice Powell warned would "invit[e] arbitrariness and error."

The state court made an additional error, one that *Ford* makes clear is impermissible under the Constitution: It failed to provide petitioner with an adequate opportunity to submit expert evidence in response to the report filed by the court-appointed experts. The court mailed the experts' report to both parties in the first week of May. The report, which rejected the factual basis for petitioner's claim, set forth new allegations suggesting that petitioner's bizarre behavior was due, at least in part, to deliberate design rather than mental illness. Petitioner's counsel reached the reasonable conclusion that these allegations warranted a response. On May 14 the court told petitioner's counsel, by letter, to file "any other matters you wish to have considered" within a week. Petitioner, in response, renewed his motions for an evidentiary hearing, funds to hire a mental health expert, and other relief. He did not submit at that time expert psychiatric evidence to challenge the court-appointed experts' report, a decision that in context made sense: The court had said it would rule on his outstanding motions, which included a request for funds to hire a mental-health expert and a request for an evidentiary hearing, once the court-appointed experts had completed their evaluation. Counsel was justified in relying on this representation by the court.

Texas law, moreover, provides that a court's finding of incompetency will be made on the basis of, *inter alia,* a "final competency hearing." Had the court advised counsel it would resolve the case without first ruling on petitioner's motions and without holding a competency hearing, petitioner's counsel might have managed to procure the assistance of experts, as he had been able to do on a *pro bono* basis the day before petitioner's previously scheduled execution. It was, in any event, reasonable for counsel to refrain from procuring and submitting expert psychiatric evidence while waiting for the court to rule on the timely filed motions, all in reliance on the court's assurances.

But at this point the court simply ended the matter.

The state court failed to provide petitioner with a constitutionally adequate opportunity to be heard. After a prisoner has made the requisite threshold showing, *Ford* requires, at a minimum, that a court allow a prisoner's counsel the opportunity to make an adequate response to evidence solicited by the state court. In petitioner's case this meant an opportunity to submit psychiatric evidence as a counterweight to the report filed by the court-appointed experts. Yet petitioner failed to receive even this rudimentary process.

In light of this error we need not address whether other procedures, such as the opportunity for discovery or for the cross-examination of witnesses, would in some cases be required under the Due Process Clause. As *Ford* makes clear, the procedural deficiencies already identified constituted a violation of petitioner's federal rights.

       * * *

IV

A

This brings us to the question petitioner asks the Court to resolve: whether the Eighth Amendment permits the execution of a prisoner whose mental illness deprives him of "the mental capacity to understand that [he] is being executed as a punishment for a crime."

A review of the expert testimony helps frame the issue. Four expert witnesses testified on petitioner's behalf in the District Court proceedings. One explained that petitioner's mental problems are indicative of "schizoaffective disorder," resulting in a "genuine delusion" involving his understanding of the reason for his execution. According to the expert, this delusion has recast petitioner's execution as "part of spiritual warfare ... between the demons and the forces of the darkness and God and the angels and the forces of light." As a result, the expert explained, although petitioner claims to understand "that the state is saying that [it wishes] to execute him for [his] murder[s]," he believes in earnest that the stated reason is a "sham" and the State in truth wants to execute him "to stop him from preaching." Petitioner's other expert witnesses reached similar conclusions concerning the strength and sincerity of this "fixed delusion."

While the State's expert witnesses resisted the conclusion that petitioner's stated beliefs were necessarily indicative of incompetency, particularly in light of his perceived ability to understand certain concepts and, at times, to be "clear and lucid," they acknowledged evidence of mental problems. Petitioner's rebuttal witness attempted to reconcile the experts' testimony:

> "Well, first, you have to understand that when somebody is schizophrenic, it doesn't diminish their cognitive ability.... Instead, you have a situation where—and why we call schizophrenia thought disorder[—]the logical integration and reality connection of their thoughts are disrupted, so the stimulus comes in, and instead of being analyzed and processed in a rational, logical, linear sort of way, it gets

scrambled up and it comes out in a tangential, circumstantial, symbol-ic ... not really relevant kind of way. That's the essence of somebody being schizophrenic.... Now, it may be that if they're dealing with someone who's more familiar ... [in] what may feel like a safer, more enclosed environment ... those sorts of interactions may be reason-ably lucid whereas a more extended conversation about more loaded material would reflect the severity of his mental illness."

The legal inquiry concerns whether these delusions can be said to render him incompetent. The Court of Appeals held that they could not. That holding, we conclude, rests on a flawed interpretation of *Ford*.

The Court of Appeals stated that competency is determined by wheth-er a prisoner is aware " 'that he [is] going to be executed and why he [is] going to be executed,' " To this end, the Court of Appeals identified the relevant District Court findings as follows: first, petitioner is aware that he committed the murders; second, he is aware that he will be executed; and, third, he is aware that the reason the State has given for the execution is his commission of the crimes in question. Under Circuit precedent this ends the analysis as a matter of law; for the Court of Appeals regards these three factual findings as necessarily demonstrating that a prisoner is aware of the reason for his execution.

The Court of Appeals concluded that its standard foreclosed petitioner from establishing incompetency by the means he now seeks to employ: a showing that his mental illness obstructs a rational understanding of the State's reason for his execution. As the court explained, "[b]ecause we hold that 'awareness,' as that term is used in *Ford*, is not necessarily synonymous with 'rational understanding,' as argued by [petitioner,] we conclude that the district court's findings are sufficient to establish that [petitioner] is competent to be executed."

In our view the Court of Appeals' standard is too restrictive to afford a prisoner the protections granted by the Eighth Amendment. The opin-ions in *Ford*, it must be acknowledged, did not set forth a precise standard for competency. The four-Justice plurality discussed the substantive stan-dard at a high level of generality; and Justice Powell wrote only for himself when he articulated more specific criteria. Yet in the portion of Justice Marshall's discussion constituting the opinion of the Court (the portion Justice Powell joined) the majority did reach the express conclu-sion that the Constitution "places a substantive restriction on the State's power to take the life of an insane prisoner." * * *

Writing for four Justices, Justice Marshall concluded by indicating that the Eighth Amendment prohibits execution of "one whose mental illness prevents him from comprehending the reasons for the penalty or its implications." Justice Powell, in his separate opinion, asserted that the Eighth Amendment "forbids the execution only of those who are unaware of the punishment they are about to suffer and why they are to suffer it."

The Court of Appeals' standard treats a prisoner's delusional belief system as irrelevant if the prisoner knows that the State has identified his crimes as the reason for his execution. Yet the *Ford* opinions nowhere indicate that delusions are irrelevant to "comprehen[sion]" or "aware [ness]" if they so impair the prisoner's concept of reality that he cannot reach a rational understanding of the reason for the execution. If anything, the *Ford* majority suggests the opposite.

Explaining the prohibition against executing a prisoner who has lost his sanity, Justice Marshall in the controlling portion of his opinion set forth various rationales, including recognition that "the execution of an insane person simply offends humanity"; that it "provides no example to others"; that "it is uncharitable to dispatch an offender into another world, when he is not of a capacity to fit himself for it"; that "madness is its own punishment"; and that executing an insane person serves no retributive purpose.

Considering the last—whether retribution is served—it might be said that capital punishment is imposed because it has the potential to make the offender recognize at last the gravity of his crime and to allow the community as a whole, including the surviving family and friends of the victim, to affirm its own judgment that the culpability of the prisoner is so serious that the ultimate penalty must be sought and imposed. The potential for a prisoner's recognition of the severity of the offense and the objective of community vindication are called in question, however, if the prisoner's mental state is so distorted by a mental illness that his awareness of the crime and punishment has little or no relation to the understanding of those concepts shared by the community as a whole. This problem is not necessarily overcome once the test set forth by the Court of Appeals is met. And under a similar logic the other rationales set forth by *Ford* fail to align with the distinctions drawn by the Court of Appeals.

Whether *Ford's* inquiry into competency is formulated as a question of the prisoner's ability to "comprehen[d] the reasons" for his punishment or as a determination into whether he is "unaware of . . . why [he is] to suffer it," then, the approach taken by the Court of Appeals is inconsistent with *Ford*. The principles set forth in *Ford* are put at risk by a rule that deems delusions relevant only with respect to the State's announced reason for a punishment or the fact of an imminent execution, as opposed to the real interests the State seeks to vindicate. We likewise find no support elsewhere in *Ford*, including in its discussions of the common law and the state standards, for the proposition that a prisoner is automatically foreclosed from demonstrating incompetency once a court has found he can identify the stated reason for his execution. A prisoner's awareness of the State's rationale for an execution is not the same as a rational understanding of it. *Ford* does not foreclose inquiry into the latter.

This is not to deny the fact that a concept like rational understanding is difficult to define. And we must not ignore the concern that some prisoners, whose cases are not implicated by this decision, will fail to understand why they are to be punished on account of reasons other than those stemming from a severe mental illness. The mental state requisite for competence to suffer capital punishment neither presumes nor requires a person who would be considered "normal," or even "rational," in a layperson's understanding of those terms. Someone who is condemned to death for an atrocious murder may be so callous as to be unrepentant; so self-centered and devoid of compassion as to lack all sense of guilt; so adept in transferring blame to others as to be considered, at least in the colloquial sense, to be out of touch with reality. Those states of mind, even if extreme compared to the criminal population at large, are not what petitioner contends lie at the threshold of a competence inquiry. The beginning of doubt about competence in a case like petitioner's is not a misanthropic personality or an amoral character. It is a psychotic disorder.

Petitioner's submission is that he suffers from a severe, documented mental illness that is the source of gross delusions preventing him from comprehending the meaning and purpose of the punishment to which he has been sentenced. This argument, we hold, should have been considered.

The flaws of the Court of Appeals' test are pronounced in petitioner's case. Circuit precedent required the District Court to disregard evidence of psychological dysfunction that, in the words of the judge, may have resulted in petitioner's "fundamental failure to appreciate the connection between the petitioner's crime and his execution." To refuse to consider evidence of this nature is to mistake *Ford's* holding and its logic. Gross delusions stemming from a severe mental disorder may put an awareness of a link between a crime and its punishment in a context so far removed from reality that the punishment can serve no proper purpose. It is therefore error to derive from *Ford,* and the substantive standard for incompetency its opinions broadly identify, a strict test for competency that treats delusional beliefs as irrelevant once the prisoner is aware the State has identified the link between his crime and the punishment to be inflicted.

B

Although we reject the standard followed by the Court of Appeals, we do not attempt to set down a rule governing all competency determinations. The record is not as informative as it might be, even on the narrower issue of how a mental illness of the sort alleged by petitioner might affect this analysis. In overseeing the development of the record and in making its factual findings, the District Court found itself bound to analyze the question of competency in the terms set by Circuit precedent. It acknowledged, for example, the "difficult issue" posed by the delusions allegedly interfering with petitioner's understanding of the reason behind his execution, but it refrained from making definitive findings of fact with respect to these matters. See [opinion] (identifying testimony by Dr. Mark Cunningham indicating that petitioner "believes the State is in league with the forces of evil that have conspired against him" and, as a result, "does not even understand that the State of Texas is a lawfully constituted authority," but refraining from setting forth definitive findings of fact concerning whether this was an accurate characterization of petitioner's mindset).

The District Court declined to consider the significance those findings might have on the ultimate question of competency under the Eighth Amendment. And notwithstanding the numerous questions the District Court asked of the witnesses, it did not press the experts on the difficult issue it identified in its opinion. The District Court, of course, was bound by Circuit precedent, and the record was developed pursuant to a standard we have found to be improper. As a result, we find it difficult to amplify our conclusions or to make them more precise. We are also hesitant to decide a question of this complexity before the District Court and the Court of Appeals have addressed, in a more definitive manner and in light of the expert evidence found to be probative, the nature and severity of petitioner's alleged mental problems.

The underpinnings of petitioner's claims should be explained and evaluated in further detail on remand. The conclusions of physicians, psychiatrists, and other experts in the field will bear upon the proper analysis. Expert evidence may clarify the extent to which severe delusions may render a subject's perception of reality so distorted that he should be deemed incompetent. And there is precedent to guide a court conducting Eighth Amendment analysis. See, *e.g.*, *Roper v. Simmons,* 543 U.S. 551, 125 S.Ct. 1183 (2005); *Atkins v. Virginia,* 536 U.S. 304, 122 S.Ct. 2242 (2002); *Ford, supra.*

It is proper to allow the court charged with overseeing the development of the evidentiary record in this case the initial opportunity to resolve petitioner's constitutional claim. These issues may be resolved in the first instance by the District Court.

    * * *

The judgment of the Court of Appeals is reversed, and the case is remanded for further proceedings consistent with this opinion.

[In his dissenting opinion, Justice Thomas, joined by The Chief Justice, Justice Scalia and Justice Alito, argued that, even if Justice Powell's opinion constituted clearly established federal law, the state-court proceedings did not result in a "decision that was contrary to, or involved an unreasonable application of clearly established Federal law" as required by 28 U.S.C. § 2254(d)(1). In the dissenters' view, petitioner's motion did not meet the "substantial threshold showing of insanity" necessary to trigger the *Ford* procedures, and, in any case, *Ford* was satisfied because the petitioner had the opportunity to present his claim and supporting evidence before a neutral decision-maker.]

Note

1. *"Curing" the defendant for execution.*

As Justice Powell points out in his opinion in *Ford*, although the prisoner may not be executed while he or she is insane, the execution may take place as soon as the prisoner recovers his or her sanity. What steps may the state take to "cure" the prisoner for execution? In *Singleton v. Norris*, 319 F.3d 1018 (8th Cir. 2003) (*en banc*), the Eighth Circuit held, over a strong dissent, that the state could, without violating the due process clause, forcibly medicate a defendant to render him competent to be executed. Applying standards similar to those later articulated by the Supreme Court in the context of forcibly medicating a defendant to restore competence to stand trial (*Sell v. United States*, 539 U.S. 166, 123 S.Ct. 2174 (2003)) the majority found: that the state had a particularly great interest in carrying out a capital sentence; that the defendant preferred the antipsychotic medication to being in an unmedicated state and suffered no side effects; that there was no less intrusive method of rendering the defendant competent; and that the antipsychotic medication was "medically appropriate" even though administering it would lead to the defendant's execution. The court went on to reject the defendant's argument that the Eighth Amendment forbids the execution of a prisoner who is "artificially competent," finding that *Ford* prohibited only the execution of a prisoner who is unaware of the punishment he is about to receive and why he is to receive it. The dissenters argued that, for purposes of *Ford*, the defendant was still insane even if "powerful, mind-altering drugs" caused him to "sometimes appears lucid and rational." The defendant's petition for certiorari was denied, and he was executed. The decision contrasts with earlier decisions in the state courts interpreting state constitutions. See *Singleton v. South Carolina*, 437 S.E.2d 53 (S.C. 1993); *State v. Perry*, 610 So.2d 746 (La. 1992).

A related issue is whether psychiatrists may even participate in "curing" a prisoner for execution. The American Medical Association has taken the position that it is unethical for a physician to do so:

> When a condemned prisoner has been declared incompetent to be executed, physicians should not treat the prisoner for the purpose of restoring competence unless a commutation order is issued before treatment begins. * * * If the incompetent prisoner is undergoing extreme suffering as a result of psychosis or any other illness, medical intervention intended to mitigate the level of suffering is ethically permissible.

Code of Medical Ethics, Current Opinions E–2.06.[a] The American Psychiatric Association takes the same position. See Annotation No. 4 to Code of Medical Ethics, Section 1. These ethical rules can stymie executions, as occurred in the Arizona case of Claude Maturana. See USA Today, Nov. 9, 1999, p. 4A. After being convicted of murder and sentenced to death, Maturana was determined

---

a. In fact, the opinion states that it is a violation of medical ethics for a physician to participate in an execution in any way.

Physician participation in an execution includes, but is not limited to, the following actions: prescribing or administering tranquilizers and other psychotropic agents and medications that are part of the execution procedure; monitoring vital signs on site or remotely (including monitoring electrocardiograms); attending or observing an execution as a physician; and rendering of technical advice regarding execution.

In the case where the method of execution is lethal injection, the following actions by the physician would also constitute physician participation in execution: selecting injection sites; starting intravenous lines as a port for a lethal injection device; prescribing, preparing, administering, or supervising injection drugs or their doses or types; inspecting, testing, or maintaining lethal injection devices; and consulting with or supervising lethal injection personnel.

to be insane, suffering from chronic paranoid schizophrenia. He was convinced he was an agent of the "world police" and spoke frequently in numbers and initials whose meaning was known only to him. Maturana was under the care of Dr. Jerry Dennis, the Arizona State Hospital's chief medical officer, who visited him periodically to monitor his condition and treated him with a regimen of tranquilizers which maintained his equilibrium but did not improve his mental state. Dennis could have treated Maturana more aggressively and restored him to the point where he would understand that he was going to be executed for committing a crime, but Dennis refused, citing his ethical obligations. Dennis was threatened with contempt, and hospital administrators attempted to find a replacement for Dennis, through a mailing to all 1,400 Arizona psychiatrists and nurse practitioners and by classified ads and calls to professionals in other death penalty states. None of the Arizona psychiatrists responded, and, even though a Georgia psychiatrist came forward, examined Maturana and found him competent (see G. Dell'Orto, *Mentally Ill Man Awaits Execution*, AP May 8, 2001, 2001 WL 21142939), when the decision in *Ring v. Arizona* [Chapter 9] called into question all Arizona death sentences, Maturana's execution was stayed, and he died of natural causes in 2002.

OHIO ADULT PAROLE AUTHORITY v. WOODARD

523 U.S. 272, 118 S.Ct. 1244, 140 L.Ed.2d 387 (1998).

CHIEF JUSTICE REHNQUIST announced the judgment of the Court and delivered the opinion of the Court with respect to Parts I and III, and an opinion with respect to Part II in which JUSTICE SCALIA, JUSTICE KENNEDY, and JUSTICE THOMAS join.

This case requires us to resolve two inquiries as to constitutional limitations on state clemency proceedings. The first is whether an inmate has a protected life or liberty interest in clemency proceedings, under either *Connecticut Bd. of Pardons v. Dumschat*, 452 U.S. 458, 101 S.Ct. 2460 (1981), or *Evitts v. Lucey*, 469 U.S. 387, 105 S.Ct. 830 (1985). The second is whether giving inmates the option of voluntarily participating in an interview as part of the clemency process violates an inmate's Fifth Amendment rights.

We reaffirm our holding in *Dumschat, supra*, that "pardon and commutation decisions have not traditionally been the business of courts; as such, they are rarely, if ever, appropriate subjects for judicial review." The Due Process Clause is not violated where, as here, the procedures in question do no more than confirm that the clemency and pardon power is committed, as is our tradition, to the authority of the executive.[1] We further hold that a voluntary inmate interview does not violate the Fifth Amendment.

---

1. Justice Stevens in dissent says that a defendant would be entitled to raise an equal protection claim in connection with a clemency decision. But respondent has raised no such claim here, and therefore we have no occasion to decide that question.

I

The Ohio Constitution gives the Governor the power to grant clemency upon such conditions as he thinks proper. The Ohio General Assembly cannot curtail this discretionary decision-making power, but it may regulate the application and investigation process. The General Assembly has delegated in large part the conduct of clemency review to petitioner Ohio Adult Parole Authority.

In the case of an inmate under death sentence, the Authority must conduct a clemency hearing within 45 days of the scheduled date of execution. Prior to the hearing, the inmate may request an interview with one or more parole board members. Counsel is not allowed at that interview. The Authority must hold the hearing, complete its clemency review, and make a recommendation to the Governor, even if the inmate subsequently obtains a stay of execution. If additional information later becomes available, the Authority may in its discretion hold another hearing or alter its recommendation.

Respondent Eugene Woodard was sentenced to death for aggravated murder committed in the course of a carjacking. His conviction and sentence were affirmed on appeal, and this Court denied certiorari. When respondent failed to obtain a stay of execution more than 45 days before his scheduled execution date, the Authority commenced its clemency investigation. It informed respondent that he could have a clemency interview on September 9, 1994, if he wished, and that his clemency hearing would be on September 16, 1994.

Respondent did not request an interview. Instead, he objected to the short notice of the interview and requested assurances that counsel could attend and participate in the interview and hearing. When the Authority failed to respond to these requests, respondent filed suit in United States District Court on September 14, alleging * * * that Ohio's clemency process violated his Fourteenth Amendment right to due process and his Fifth Amendment right to remain silent.

The District Court granted the State's motion for judgment on the pleadings. The Court of Appeals for the Sixth Circuit affirmed in part and reversed in part. That court determined that under a "first strand" of due process analysis, arising out of the clemency proceeding itself, respondent had failed to establish a protected life or liberty interest. It noted that our decision in *Dumschat* "decisively rejected the argument that federal law can create a liberty interest in clemency."

The Court of Appeals further concluded that there was no state-created life or liberty interest in clemency. Since the Governor retains complete discretion to make the final decision, and the Authority's recommendation is purely advisory, the State has not created a protected interest. * * *

The Court of Appeals went on to consider, however, a "second strand" of due process analysis centered on "the role of clemency in the entire punitive scheme." The court relied on our statement in *Evitts* that "if a State has created appellate courts as 'an integral part of the ... system for finally adjudicating the guilt or innocence of a defendant,' the procedures used in deciding appeals must comport with the demands of" due process. (quoting *Griffin v. Illinois*, 351 U.S. 12, 76 S.Ct. 585 (1956)). The court thought this reasoning logically applied to subsequent proceedings, including discretionary appeals, post-conviction proceedings, and clemency.

Due process thus protected respondent's "original" life and liberty interests that he possessed before trial at each proceeding. But the amount of process due was in proportion to the degree to which the stage was an "integral part" of the trial process. Clemency, while not required by the Due Process Clause, was a significant, traditionally available remedy for preventing miscarriages of justice when judicial process was exhausted. It therefore came within the *Evitts* framework as an "integral part" of the adjudicatory system. However, since clemency was far removed from trial, the process due could be minimal. The Court did not itself decide what that process should be, but remanded to the District Court for that purpose.

Finally, the Court of Appeals also agreed with respondent that the voluntary interview procedure presented him with a "Hobson's choice" between asserting his Fifth Amendment rights and participating in the clemency review process, raising the specter of an unconstitutional condition. There was no compelling state interest that would justify forcing such a choice on the inmate. On the other hand, the inmate had a measurable interest in avoiding incrimination in ongoing postconviction proceedings, as well as with respect to possible charges for other crimes that could be revealed during the interview. While noting some uncertainties surrounding application of the unconstitutional conditions doctrine, the Court of Appeals concluded the doctrine could be applied in this case.

The dissenting judge would have affirmed the District Court's judgment. He agreed with the majority's determination that there was no protected interest under *Dumschat*. But he thought that the majority's finding of a due process interest under *Evitts* was necessarily inconsistent with the holding and rationale of *Dumschat*. *Evitts* did not purport to overrule *Dumschat*. He also concluded that respondent's Fifth Amendment claim was too speculative, given the voluntary nature of the clemency interview.

II

Respondent argues first, in disagreement with the Court of Appeals, that there is a life interest in clemency broader in scope than the "original" life interest adjudicated at trial and sentencing. *Ford v. Wainwright*, 477 U.S. 399, 106 S.Ct. 2595 (1986). This continuing life interest, it is argued, requires due process protection until respondent is executed.[2]

---

2. Respondent alternatively tries to characterize his claim as a challenge only to the application process conducted by the Authority, and not to the final discretionary decision by the

Relying on Eighth Amendment decisions holding that additional procedural protections are required in capital cases, respondent asserts that *Dumschat* does not control the outcome in this case because it involved only a liberty interest. Justice Stevens' dissent agrees on both counts.

In *Dumschat*, an inmate claimed Connecticut's clemency procedure violated due process because the Connecticut Board of Pardons failed to provide an explanation for its denial of his commutation application. The Court held that "an inmate has 'no constitutional or inherent right' to commutation of his sentence." It noted that, unlike probation decisions, "pardon and commutation decisions have not traditionally been the business of courts; as such, they are rarely, if ever, appropriate subjects for judicial review." The Court relied on its prior decision in *Greenholtz v. Inmates of Neb. Penal and Correctional Complex*, 442 U.S. 1, 99 S.Ct. 2100 (1979), where it rejected the claim "that a constitutional entitlement to release [on parole] exists independently of a right explicitly conferred by the State." The individual's interest in release or commutation " 'is indistinguishable from the initial resistance to being confined,' " and that interest has already been extinguished by the conviction and sentence. (quoting *Greenholtz*). The Court therefore concluded that a petition for commutation, like an appeal for clemency, "is simply a unilateral hope."

Respondent's claim of a broader due process interest in Ohio's clemency proceedings is barred by *Dumschat*. The process respondent seeks would be inconsistent with the heart of executive clemency, which is to grant clemency as a matter of grace, thus allowing the executive to consider a wide range of factors not comprehended by earlier judicial proceedings and sentencing determinations. The dissent agrees with respondent that because "a living person" has a constitutionally protected life interest, it is incorrect to assert that respondent's life interest has been "extinguished." We agree that respondent maintains a residual life interest, *e.g.*, in not being summarily executed by prison guards. However, as *Greenholtz* helps to make clear, respondent cannot use his interest in not being executed in accord with his sentence to challenge the clemency determination by requiring the procedural protections he seeks.[3]

The reasoning of *Dumschat* did not depend on the fact that it was not a capital case. The distinctions accorded a life interest to which respondent and the dissent point are primarily relevant to trial. And this Court has generally rejected attempts to expand any distinctions further. See, *e.g.*, *Murray v. Giarratano*, 492 U.S. 1, 109 S.Ct. 2765 (1989) (opinion of

---

Governor. But, respondent still must have a protected life or liberty interest in the application process. Otherwise, as the Court of Appeals correctly noted, he is asserting merely a protected interest in process itself, which is not a cognizable claim.

3. For the same reason, respondent's reliance on *Ford v. Wainwright*, 477 U.S. 399, 106 S.Ct. 2595 (1986), is misplaced. In *Ford*, the Court held that the Eighth Amendment prevents the execution of a person who has become insane since the time of trial. This substantive constitutional prohibition implicated due process protections. This protected interest, however, arose subsequent to trial, and was separate from the life interest already adjudicated in the inmate's conviction and sentence. This interest therefore had not been afforded due process protection. The Court's recognition of a protected interest thus did not rely on the notion of a continuing "original" life interest.

REHNQUIST, C.J.) (there is no constitutional right to counsel in collateral proceedings for death row inmates; cases recognizing special constraints on capital proceedings have dealt with the trial stage); *Satterwhite v. Texas*, 486 U.S. 249, 108 S.Ct. 1792 (1988) (applying traditional standard of appellate review to a Sixth Amendment claim in a capital case); *Smith v. Murray*, 477 U.S. 527, 106 S.Ct. 2661 (1986) (applying same standard of review on federal habeas in capital and noncapital cases). The Court's analysis in *Dumschat*, moreover, turned, not on the fact that it was a non-capital case, but on the nature of the benefit sought: "In terms of the Due Process Clause, a Connecticut felon's expectation that a lawfully imposed sentence will be commuted or that he will be pardoned is no more substantial than an inmate's expectation, for example, that he will not be transferred to another prison; it is simply a unilateral hope." A death row inmate's petition for clemency is also a "unilateral hope." The defendant in effect accepts the finality of the death sentence for purposes of adjudication, and appeals for clemency as a matter of grace.

Respondent also asserts that as in *Greenholtz*, Ohio has created protected interests by establishing mandatory clemency application and review procedures. In *Greenholtz*, the Court held that the expectancy of release on parole created by the mandatory language of the Nebraska statute was entitled to some measure of constitutional protection.

Ohio's clemency procedures do not violate due process. Despite the Authority's mandatory procedures, the ultimate decisionmaker, the Governor, retains broad discretion. Under any analysis, the Governor's executive discretion need not be fettered by the types of procedural protections sought by respondent. See *Greenholtz* (recognizing the Nebraska parole statute created a protected liberty interest, yet rejecting a claim that due process necessitated a formal parole hearing and a statement of evidence relied upon by the parole board). There is thus no substantive expectation of clemency. * * *

Respondent also relies on the "second strand" of due process analysis adopted by the Court of Appeals. He claims that under the rationale of *Evitts v. Lucey*, 469 U.S. 387, 105 S.Ct. 830 (1985), clemency is an integral part of Ohio's system of adjudicating the guilt or innocence of the defendant and is therefore entitled to due process protection. Clemency, he says, is an integral part of the judicial system because it has historically been available as a significant remedy, its availability impacts earlier stages of the criminal justice system, and it enhances the reliability of convictions and sentences. Respondent further suggests, as did the Sixth Circuit, that *Evitts* established a due process continuum across all phases of the judicial process.

In *Evitts*, the Court held that there is a constitutional right to effective assistance of counsel on a first appeal as of right. This holding, however, was expressly based on the combination of two lines of prior decisions. One line of cases held that the Fourteenth Amendment guarantees a criminal defendant pursuing a first appeal as of right certain minimum safeguards necessary to make that appeal adequate and effective, including the right to counsel. See *Griffin v. Illinois*, 351 U.S. 12, 76 S.Ct. 585 (1956); *Douglas v. California*, 372 U.S. 353, 83 S.Ct. 814 (1963). The second line of cases held that the Sixth Amendment right to counsel at trial comprehended the right to effective assistance of counsel. See *Gideon v. Wainwright*, 372 U.S. 335, 83 S.Ct. 792 (1963); *Cuyler v. Sullivan*, 446 U.S. 335, 100 S.Ct. 1708 (1980). These two lines of cases justified the Court's conclusion that a criminal defendant has a right to effective assistance of counsel on a first appeal as of right. *Evitts*.

The Court did not thereby purport to create a new "strand" of due process analysis. And it did not rely on the notion of a continuum of due process rights. Instead, the Court evaluated the function and significance of a first appeal as of right, in light of prior cases. Related decisions similarly make clear that there is no continuum requiring varying levels of process at every conceivable phase of the criminal system. See, *e.g.*, *Giarratano* (no due process right to counsel for capital inmates in state postconviction proceedings).

An examination of the function and significance of the discretionary clemency decision at issue here readily shows it is far different from the first appeal of right at issue in *Evitts*. Clemency proceedings are not part of the trial—or even of the adjudicatory process. They do not determine the guilt or innocence of the defendant, and are not intended primarily to enhance the reliability of the trial process. They are conducted by the Executive Branch, independent of direct appeal and collateral relief proceedings. *Greenholtz*. And they are usually discretionary, unlike the more structured and limited scope of judicial proceedings. While traditionally available to capital defendants as a final and alternative avenue of relief, clemency has not traditionally "been the business of courts." *Dumschat*. Cf. *Herrera v. Collins*, 506 U.S. 390, 113 S.Ct. 853 (1993) (recognizing the traditional availability and significance of clemency as part of executive authority, without suggesting that clemency proceedings are subject to judicial review); *Ex parte Grossman*, 267 U.S. 87, 45 S.Ct. 332 (1925) (executive clemency exists to provide relief from harshness or mistake in the judicial system, and is therefore vested in an authority other than the courts).

Thus, clemency proceedings are not "an integral part of the ... system for finally adjudicating the guilt or innocence of a defendant." *Evitts*. Procedures mandated under the Due Process Clause should be consistent with the nature of the governmental power being invoked. Here, the executive's clemency authority would cease to be a matter of grace committed to the executive authority if it were constrained by the sort of procedural requirements that respondent urges. Respondent is already under a sentence of death, determined to have been lawfully imposed. If clemency is granted, he obtains a benefit; if it is denied, he is no worse off than he was before.

III

[The CHIEF JUSTICE rejected respondent's claim that the provision of a voluntary inmate interview, without the benefit of counsel or a grant of immunity violated his Fifth Amendment rights. He reasoned:

"It is difficult to see how a voluntary interview could 'compel' respondent to speak. He merely faces a choice quite similar to the sorts of choices that a criminal defendant must make in the course of criminal proceedings, none of which has ever been held to violate the Fifth Amendment."]

IV

We hold that neither the Due Process Clause nor the Fifth Amendment privilege against self-incrimination are violated by Ohio's clemency proceedings. The judgment of the Court of Appeals is therefore *Reversed*.

JUSTICE O'CONNOR, with whom JUSTICE SOUTER, JUSTICE GINSBURG, and JUSTICE BREYER join, concurring in part and concurring in the judgment.

A prisoner under a death sentence remains a living person and consequently has an interest in his life. The question this case raises is the issue of what process is constitutionally necessary to protect that interest in the context of Ohio's clemency procedures. It is clear that "once society has validly convicted an individual of a crime and therefore established its right to punish, the demands of due process are reduced accordingly." *Ford v. Wainwright*, 477 U.S. 399, 106 S.Ct. 2595 (1986) (O'CONNOR, J., concurring in result in part and dissenting in part). I do not, however, agree with the suggestion in the principal opinion that, because clemency is committed to the discretion of the executive, the Due Process Clause provides no constitutional safeguards. THE CHIEF JUSTICE's reasoning rests on our decisions in *Connecticut Bd. of Pardons v. Dumschat*, 452 U.S. 458, 101 S.Ct. 2460 (1981), and *Greenholtz v. Inmates of Neb. Penal and Correctional Complex*, 442 U.S. 1, 99 S.Ct. 2100 (1979). In those cases, the Court found that an inmate seeking commutation of a life sentence or discretionary parole had no protected liberty interest in release from lawful confinement. When a person has been fairly convicted and sentenced, his liberty interest, in being free from such confinement, has been extinguished. But it is incorrect, as Justice STEVENS' dissent notes, to say that a prisoner has been deprived of all interest in his life before his execution. Thus, although it is true that "pardon and commutation decisions have not traditionally been the business of courts," *Dumschat, supra*, and that the decision whether to grant clemency is entrusted to the Governor under Ohio law, I believe that the Court of Appeals correctly concluded that some minimal procedural safeguards apply to clemency proceedings. Judicial intervention might, for example, be warranted in the face of a scheme whereby a state official flipped a coin to determine whether to grant clemency, or in a case where the State arbitrarily denied a prisoner any access to its clemency process.

In my view, however, a remand to permit the District Court to address respondent's specific allegations of due process violations is not required. The Ohio Death Penalty Clemency Procedure provides that, if a stay has not yet issued, the parole board must schedule a clemency hearing 45 days before an execution for a date approximately 21 days in advance of the execution. The board must also advise the prisoner that he is entitled to a pre-hearing interview with one or more parole board members. Although the Parole Authority complied with those instructions here, respondent raises several objections to the process afforded him. He contends that 3 days' notice of his interview and 10 days' notice of the hearing were inadequate; that he did not have a meaningful opportunity to prepare his clemency application because postconviction proceedings were pending; that his counsel was improperly excluded from the interview and permitted to participate in the hearing only at the discretion of the parole board chair; and that he was precluded from testifying or submitting documentary evidence at the hearing. I do not believe that any of these allegations amounts to a due process violation. The process respondent received, including notice of the hearing and an opportunity to participate in an interview, comports with Ohio's regulations and observes whatever limitations the Due Process Clause may impose on clemency proceedings. Moreover, I agree that the voluntary inmate interview that forms part of Ohio's process did not violate respondent's Fifth and Fourteenth Amendment privilege against self-incrimination.

Accordingly, I join Parts I and III of the Court's opinion and concur in the judgment.

> [JUSTICE STEVENS concurred in part and dissented in part. He agreed with JUSTICE O'CONNOR that the due process clause must apply to clemency proceedings, otherwise "procedures infected by bribery, personal or political animosity, or the deliberate fabrication of false evidence would be constitutional," but he would have remanded the case to the District Court for a determination whether Ohio's procedures met the minimum requirements of due process.]

NOTES

1. *The clemency process.*

The process for granting clemency varies from state to state. The governor of a state, or a clemency board, generally has authority to grant three types of relief: a reprieve of the execution for a set period of time, a commutation of the death sentence to a lesser sentence, or a pardon which exonerates the inmate. In some states, the governor has sole authority to grant or deny clemency just as the President has sole authority over clemency decisions in federal cases. In some states, the governor is empowered to grant clemency only upon a recommendation from a clemency or pardon board; in others, the governor decides after receiving a non-binding recommendation from a clemency or pardon board. In a few states, the clemency or pardon board makes the decision without the governor, and in a few states, the governor is a member of the clemency or pardon board which makes the decision.

It has been estimated that, prior to *Furman v. Georgia*, clemency was granted to approximately 25% of defendants sentenced to death.[a] Since the reinstatement of capital punishment following *Gregg v. Georgia,* clemency in capital cases has been granted more rarely. From 1976 through 2008, 1,136 condemned defendants were executed, and 56 condemned defendants were granted clemency on an individual basis.[b] Death Penalty Information Center, http://www.deathpenaltyinfo.org/clemency. In addition, there were four broad clemency grants covering 188 condemned defendants: New Mexico (1986)–5; Ohio (1991)–8; Illinois (2003)–167; New Jersey (2007)–8. Three main reasons given for these clemency decisions have been lingering doubt about the condemned person's guilt, mental problems that reduced the condemned person's blameworthiness, and disproportionate punishments among equally culpable codefendants. Can the more sparing use of clemency in the post-*Furman* era be seen as a product of the more careful appellate and post-conviction review of death penalty cases by the courts?

2. *The Illinois commutations.*

On January 11, 2003, shortly before leaving office, Illinois governor George Ryan, commuted the sentences of all 167 prisoners on Illinois's death row. Governor Ryan, who, a day earlier, had pardoned four death row prisoners on the ground that they were probably innocent, cited the numerous exonerations of death row prisoners in Illinois as evidence that the state's criminal justice system was "haunted by the demon of error. He also said that the criminal justice system was "arbitrary and capricious and therefore immoral" because who received the death penalty turned on geography, race, the defendant's income, the philosophy of the prosecutor and the ability of the defense attorney. As a result of Governor Ryan's action, more prisoners were removed from death row than had been removed at one time since the Supreme Court's decision in *Furman v. Georgia*. The action sparked substantial controversy. Was the "blanket commutation" a misuse of the governor's clemency powers?

BAZE v. REES
___ U.S. ___, 128 S.Ct. 1520, 170 L.Ed.2d 420 (2008).

Chief Justice Roberts announced the judgment of the Court and delivered an opinion, in which Justice Kennedy and Justice Alito join.

Like 35 other States and the Federal Government, Kentucky has chosen to impose capital punishment for certain crimes. As is true with respect to each of these States and the Federal Government, Kentucky has altered its method of execution over time to more humane means of carrying out the sentence. That progress has led to the use of lethal injection by every jurisdiction that imposes the death penalty.

---

a. D. Kobil, *Chance and the Constitution in Capital Clemency*, 28 Cap. U. L.Rev. 567, 572 (2000).

b. This number does not include the over 40 grants of clemency in Texas and Virginia on grounds of "judicial expediency," *i.e.*, a commutation based on a decision not to retry a defendant following a court reversal of a conviction or death sentence.

Petitioners in this case—each convicted of double homicide—acknowledge that the lethal injection procedure, if applied as intended, will result in a humane death. They nevertheless contend that the lethal injection protocol is unconstitutional under the Eighth Amendment's ban on "cruel and unusual punishments," because of the risk that the protocol's terms might not be properly followed, resulting in significant pain. They propose an alternative protocol, one that they concede has not been adopted by any State and has never been tried.

The trial court held extensive hearings and entered detailed Findings of Fact and Conclusions of Law. It recognized that "[t]here are no methods of legal execution that are satisfactory to those who oppose the death penalty on moral, religious, or societal grounds," but concluded that Kentucky's procedure "complies with the constitutional requirements against cruel and unusual punishment." The State Supreme Court affirmed. We too agree that petitioners have not carried their burden of showing that the risk of pain from maladministration of a concededly humane lethal injection protocol, and the failure to adopt untried and untested alternatives, constitute cruel and unusual punishment. The judgment below is affirmed.

I

A

By the middle of the 19th century, "hanging was the 'nearly universal form of execution' in the United States." *Campbell* v. *Wood*, 511 U.S. 1119, 114 S.Ct. 2125 (1994) (Blackmun, J., dissenting from denial of certiorari) (quoting *State* v. *Frampton*, 627 P. 2d 922 (Wash. 1981)); Denno, Getting to Death: Are Executions Constitutional? 82 Iowa L. Rev. 319, 364 (1997) (counting 48 States and Territories that employed hanging as a method of execution). In 1888, following the recommendation of a commission empaneled by the Governor to find "the most humane and practical method known to modern science of carrying into effect the sentence of death," New York became the first State to authorize electrocution as a form of capital punishment. By 1915, 11 other States had followed suit, motivated by the "well-grounded belief that electrocution is less painful and more humane than hanging." *Malloy* v. *South Carolina*, 237 U.S. 180, 35 S.Ct. 507 (1915).

Electrocution remained the predominant mode of execution for nearly a century, although several methods, including hanging, firing squad, and lethal gas were in use at one time. Following the 9–year hiatus in executions that ended with our decision in *Gregg* v. *Georgia*, 428 U.S. 153, 96 S.Ct. 2909 (1976), however, state legislatures began responding to public calls to reexamine electrocution as a means of assuring a humane death. In 1977, legislators in Oklahoma, after consulting with the head of the anesthesiology department at the University of Oklahoma College of Medicine, introduced the first bill proposing lethal injection as the State's method of execution. A total of 36 States have now adopted lethal injection as the exclusive or primary means of implementing the death penalty, making it by far the most prevalent method of execution in the United States.[1] It is also the method used by the Federal Government.

Of these 36 States, at least 30 (including Kentucky) use the same combination of three drugs in their lethal injection protocols. The first drug, sodium thiopental (also known as Pentathol), is a fast-acting barbiturate sedative that induces a deep, comalike unconsciousness when given in the amounts used for lethal injection. The second drug, pancuronium bromide (also known as Pavulon), is a paralytic agent that inhibits all muscular-skeletal movements and, by paralyzing the diaphragm, stops respiration. Potassium chloride, the third drug, interferes with the electrical signals that stimulate the contractions of the heart, inducing cardiac arrest. The proper administration of the first drug ensures that the prisoner does not experience any pain associated with the paralysis and cardiac arrest caused by the second and third drugs.

B

Kentucky replaced electrocution with lethal injection in 1998. The Kentucky statute does not specify the drugs or categories of drugs to be used during an execution, instead mandating that "every death sentence shall be executed by continuous intravenous injection of a substance or combination of substances sufficient to cause death." Prisoners sentenced before 1998 have the option of electing either electrocution or lethal injection, but lethal injection is the default if—as is the case with petitioners—the prisoner refuses to make a choice at least 20 days before the scheduled execution. If a court invalidates Kentucky's lethal injection method, Kentucky law provides that the method of execution will revert to electrocution.

Shortly after the adoption of lethal injection, officials working for the Kentucky Department of Corrections set about developing a written protocol to comply with the requirements of [the statute]. Kentucky's protocol called for the injection of 2 grams of sodium thiopental, 50 milligrams of pancuronium bromide, and 240 milliequivalents of potassium chloride. In 2004, as a result of this litigation, the department chose to increase the amount of sodium thiopental from 2 grams to 3 grams. Between injections, members of the execution team flush the intravenous (IV) lines with 25 milligrams of saline to prevent clogging of the lines by precipitates that may form when residual sodium thiopental comes into contact with pancuronium bromide. The protocol reserves responsibility for inserting the IV catheters to qualified personnel having at least one year of professional experience. Currently, Kentucky uses a certified

---

1. Twenty-seven of the 36 States that currently provide for capital punishment require execution by lethal injection as the sole method. Nine States allow for lethal injection in addition to an alternative method, such as electrocution [Alabama, Florida, South Carolina, Virginia], hanging [New Hampshire, Washington], lethal gas [California, Missouri], or firing squad [Idaho]. Nebraska is the only State whose statutes specify electrocution as the sole method of execution, but the Nebraska Supreme Court recently struck down that method under the Nebraska Constitution, see *State* v. *Mata*, 745 N.W.2d 229 (2008). [Nebraska has since enacted legislation to provide for execution by lethal injection.—Eds]

phlebotomist and an emergency medical technician (EMT) to perform the venipunctures necessary for the catheters. They have up to one hour to establish both primary and secondary peripheral intravenous sites in the arm, hand, leg, or foot of the inmate. Other personnel are responsible for mixing the solutions containing the three drugs and loading them into syringes.

Kentucky's execution facilities consist of the execution chamber, a control room separated by a one-way window, and a witness room. The warden and deputy warden remain in the execution chamber with the prisoner, who is strapped to a gurney. The execution team administers the drugs remotely from the control room through five feet of IV tubing. If, as determined by the warden and deputy warden through visual inspection, the prisoner is not unconscious within 60 seconds following the delivery of the sodium thiopental to the primary IV site, a new 3–gram dose of thiopental is administered to the secondary site before injecting the pancuronium and potassium chloride. In addition to assuring that the first dose of thiopental is successfully administered, the warden and deputy warden also watch for any problems with the IV catheters and tubing.

A physician is present to assist in any effort to revive the prisoner in the event of a last-minute stay of execution. By statute, however, the physician is prohibited from participating in the "conduct of an execution," except to certify the cause of death. An electrocardiogram (EKG) verifies the death of the prisoner. Only one Kentucky prisoner, Eddie Lee Harper, has been executed since the Commonwealth adopted lethal injection. There were no reported problems at Harper's execution.

        * * *

                              II

The Eighth Amendment to the Constitution, applicable to the States through the Due Process Clause of the Fourteenth Amendment, provides that "[e]xcessive bail shall not be required, nor excessive fines imposed, nor cruel and unusual punishments inflicted." We begin with the principle, settled by *Gregg*, that capital punishment is constitutional. It necessarily follows that there must be a means of carrying it out. Some risk of pain is inherent in any method of execution—no matter how humane—if only from the prospect of error in following the required procedure. It is clear, then, that the Constitution does not demand the avoidance of all risk of pain in carrying out executions.

Petitioners do not claim that it does. Rather, they contend that the Eighth Amendment prohibits procedures that create an "unnecessary risk" of pain. Specifically, they argue that courts must evaluate "(a) the severity of pain risked, (b) the likelihood of that pain occurring, and (c) the extent to which alternative means are feasible, either by modifying existing execution procedures or adopting alternative procedures." Petitioners envision that the quantum of risk necessary to make out an Eighth Amendment claim will vary according to the severity of the pain and the availability of alternatives, but that the risk must be "significant" to trigger Eighth Amendment scrutiny.

Kentucky responds that this "unnecessary risk" standard is tantamount to a requirement that States adopt the "least risk" alternative in carrying out an execution, a standard the Commonwealth contends will cast recurring constitutional doubt on any procedure adopted by the States. Instead, Kentucky urges the Court to approve the "substantial risk" test used by the courts below.

A

This Court has never invalidated a State's chosen procedure for carrying out a sentence of death as the infliction of cruel and unusual punishment. In *Wilkerson v. Utah*, 99 U.S. 130 (1879), we upheld a sentence to death by firing squad imposed by a territorial court, rejecting the argument that such a sentence constituted cruel and unusual punishment. We noted there the difficulty of "defin[ing] with exactness the extent of the constitutional provision which provides that cruel and unusual punishments shall not be inflicted." Rather than undertake such an effort, the *Wilkerson* Court simply noted that "it is safe to affirm that punishments of torture, . . . and all others in the same line of unnecessary cruelty, are forbidden" by the Eighth Amendment. By way of example, the Court cited cases from England in which "terror, pain, or disgrace were sometimes superadded" to the sentence, such as where the condemned was "embowelled alive, beheaded, and quartered," or instances of "public dissection in murder, and burning alive." In contrast, we observed that the firing squad was routinely used as a method of execution for military officers. What each of the forbidden punishments had in common was the deliberate infliction of pain for the sake of pain—"superadd[ing]" pain to the death sentence through torture and the like.

We carried these principles further in *In re Kemmler*, 136 U.S. 436, 10 S.Ct. 930 (1890). There we rejected an opportunity to incorporate the Eighth Amendment against the States in a challenge to the first execution by electrocution, to be carried out by the State of New York. In passing over that question, however, we observed that "[p]unishments are cruel when they involve torture or a lingering death; but the punishment of death is not cruel within the meaning of that word as used in the Constitution. It implies there something inhuman and barbarous, something more than the mere extinguishment of life." We noted that the New York statute adopting electrocution as a method of execution "was passed in the effort to devise a more humane method of reaching the result."

B

Petitioners do not claim that lethal injection or the proper administration of the particular protocol adopted by Kentucky by themselves constitute the cruel or wanton infliction of pain. Quite the contrary, they concede that "if performed properly," an execution carried out under Kentucky's procedures would be "humane and constitutional." That is because, as counsel for petitioners admitted at oral argument, proper administration of the first drug, sodium thiopental, eliminates any meaningful risk that a prisoner would experience pain from the subsequent injections of pancuronium and potassium chloride.

Instead, petitioners claim that there is a significant risk that the procedures will *not* be properly followed—in particular, that the sodium thiopental will not be properly administered to achieve its intended effect—resulting in severe pain when the other chemicals are administered. Our cases recognize that subjecting individuals to a risk of future harm—not simply actually inflicting pain—can qualify as cruel and unusual punishment. To establish that such exposure violates the Eighth Amendment, however, the conditions presenting the risk must be *"sure or very likely* to cause serious illness and needless suffering," and give rise to "sufficiently *imminent* dangers." *Helling* v. *McKinney*, 509 U.S. 25, 113 S.Ct. 2475 (1993) (emphasis added). We have explained that to prevail on such a claim there must be a "substantial risk of serious harm," an "objectively intolerable risk of harm" that prevents prison officials from pleading that they were "subjectively blameless for purposes of the Eighth Amendment." *Farmer* v. *Brennan*, 511 U.S. 825, 114 S.Ct. 1970 (1994).

Simply because an execution method may result in pain, either by accident or as an inescapable consequence of death, does not establish the sort of "objectively intolerable risk of harm" that qualifies as cruel and unusual. In *Louisiana ex rel. Francis* v. *Resweber*, 329 U.S. 459, 67 S.Ct. 374 (1947), a plurality of the Court upheld a second attempt at executing a prisoner by electrocution after a mechanical malfunction had interfered with the first attempt. The principal opinion noted that "[a]ccidents happen for which no man is to blame" and concluded that such "an accident, with no suggestion of malevolence" did not give rise to an Eighth Amendment violation.

As Justice Frankfurter noted in a separate opinion based on the Due Process Clause, however, "a hypothetical situation" involving "a series of abortive attempts at electrocution" would present a different case (concurring opinion). In terms of our present Eighth Amendment analysis, such a situation—unlike an "innocent misadventure"—would demonstrate an "objectively intolerable risk of harm" that officials may not ignore. In other words, an isolated mishap alone does not give rise to an Eighth Amendment violation, precisely because such an event, while regrettable, does not suggest cruelty, or that the procedure at issue gives rise to a "substantial risk of serious harm."

C

Much of petitioners' case rests on the contention that they have identified a significant risk of harm that can be eliminated by adopting alternative procedures, such as a one-drug protocol that dispenses with the use of pancuronium and potassium chloride, and additional monitoring by trained personnel to ensure that the first dose of sodium thiopental has been adequately delivered. Given what our cases have said about the nature of the risk of harm that is actionable under the Eighth Amendment, a condemned prisoner cannot successfully challenge a State's method of execution merely by showing a slightly or marginally safer alternative.

Permitting an Eighth Amendment violation to be established on such a showing would threaten to transform courts into boards of inquiry charged with determining "best practices" for executions, with each ruling supplanted by another round of litigation touting a new and improved methodology. Such an approach finds no support in our cases, would embroil the courts in ongoing scientific controversies beyond their expertise, and would substantially intrude on the role of state legislatures in implementing their execution procedures-a role that by all accounts the States have fulfilled with an earnest desire to provide for a progressively more humane manner of death. Accordingly, we reject petitioners' proposed "unnecessary risk" standard, as well as the dissent's "untoward" risk variation. (opinion of GINSBURG, J.).

Instead, the proffered alternatives must effectively address a "substantial risk of serious harm." *Farmer, supra.* To qualify, the alternative procedure must be feasible, readily implemented, and in fact significantly reduce a substantial risk of severe pain. If a State refuses to adopt such an alternative in the face of these documented advantages, without a legitimate penological justification for adhering to its current method of execution, then a State's refusal to change its method can be viewed as "cruel and unusual" under the Eighth Amendment.

III

In applying these standards to the facts of this case, we note at the outset that it is difficult to regard a practice as "objectively intolerable" when it is in fact widely tolerated. Thirty-six States that sanction capital punishment have adopted lethal injection as the preferred method of execution. The Federal Government uses lethal injection as well. This broad consensus goes not just to the method of execution, but also to the specific three-drug combination used by Kentucky. Thirty States, as well as the Federal Government, use a series of sodium thiopental, pancuronium bromide, and potassium chloride, in varying amounts. No State uses or has ever used the alternative one-drug protocol belatedly urged by petitioners. This consensus is probative but not conclusive with respect to that aspect of the alternatives proposed by petitioners.

In order to meet their "heavy burden" of showing that Kentucky's procedure is "cruelly inhumane," *Gregg*, petitioners point to numerous aspects of the protocol that they contend create opportunities for error. Their claim hinges on the improper administration of the first drug, sodium thiopental. It is uncontested that, failing a proper dose of sodium thiopental that would render the prisoner unconscious, there is a substantial, constitutionally unacceptable risk of suffocation from the administration of pancuronium bromide and pain from the injection of potassium chloride. We agree with the state trial court and State Supreme Court, however, that petitioners have not shown that the risk of an inadequate dose of the first drug is substantial. And we reject the argument that the Eighth Amendment requires Kentucky to adopt the untested alternative procedures petitioners have identified.

A

Petitioners contend that there is a risk of improper administration of thiopental because the doses are difficult to mix into solution form and load into syringes; because the protocol fails to establish a rate of injection, which could lead to a failure of the IV; because it is possible that the IV catheters will infiltrate into surrounding tissue, causing an inadequate dose to be delivered to the vein; because of inadequate facilities and training; and because Kentucky has no reliable means of monitoring the anesthetic depth of the prisoner after the sodium thiopental has been administered.

As for the risk that the sodium thiopental would be improperly prepared, petitioners contend that Kentucky employs untrained personnel who are unqualified to calculate and mix an adequate dose, especially in light of the omission of volume and concentration amounts from the written protocol. The state trial court, however, specifically found that "[i]f the manufacturers" instructions for reconstitution of Sodium Thiopental are followed, . . . there would be minimal risk of improper mixing, despite converse testimony that a layperson would have difficulty performing this task." We cannot say that this finding is clearly erroneous, particularly when that finding is substantiated by expert testimony describing the task of reconstituting powder sodium thiopental into solution form as "[n]ot difficult at all. . . . You take a liquid, you inject it into a vial with the powder, then you shake it up until the powder dissolves and, you're done. The instructions are on the package insert."

Likewise, the asserted problems related to the IV lines do not establish a sufficiently substantial risk of harm to meet the requirements of the Eighth Amendment. Kentucky has put in place several important safeguards to ensure that an adequate dose of sodium thiopental is delivered to the condemned prisoner. The most significant of these is the written protocol's requirement that members of the IV team must have at least one year of professional experience as a certified medical assistant, phlebotomist, EMT, paramedic, or military corpsman. Kentucky currently uses a phlebotomist and an EMT, personnel who have daily experience establishing IV catheters for inmates in Kentucky's prison population. Moreover, these IV team members, along with the rest of the execution team, participate in at least 10 practice sessions per year. These sessions, required by the written protocol, encompass a complete walk-through of the execution procedures, including the siting of IV catheters into volunteers. In addition, the protocol calls for the IV team to establish both primary and backup lines and to prepare two sets of the lethal injection drugs before the execution commences. These redundant measures ensure that if an insufficient dose of sodium thiopental is initially administered through the primary line, an additional dose can be given through the backup line before the last two drugs are injected.

The IV team has one hour to establish both the primary and backup IVs, a length of time the trial court found to be "not excessive but rather necessary," contrary to petitioners' claim that using an IV inserted after any "more than ten or fifteen minutes of unsuccessful attempts is dangerous because the IV is almost certain to be unreliable." And, in any event, merely because the protocol gives the IV team one hour to establish intravenous access does not mean that team members are required to spend the entire hour in a futile attempt to do so. The qualifications of the IV team also substantially reduce the risk of IV infiltration.

In addition, the presence of the warden and deputy warden in the execution chamber with the prisoner allows them to watch for signs of IV problems, including infiltration. Three of the Commonwealth's medical experts testified that identifying signs of infiltration would be "very obvious," even to the average person, because of the swelling that would result. Kentucky's protocol specifically requires the warden to redirect the flow of chemicals to the backup IV site if the prisoner does not lose consciousness within 60 seconds. In light of these safeguards, we cannot say that the risks identified by petitioners are so substantial or imminent as to amount to an Eighth Amendment violation.

B

Nor does Kentucky's failure to adopt petitioners' proposed alternatives demonstrate that the Commonwealth's execution procedure is cruel and unusual.

First, petitioners contend that Kentucky could switch from a three-drug protocol to a one-drug protocol by using a single dose of sodium thiopental or other barbiturate. That alternative was not proposed to the state courts below. As a result, we are left without any findings on the effectiveness of petitioners' barbiturate-only protocol, despite scattered references in the trial testimony to the sole use of sodium thiopental or pentobarbital as a preferred method of execution.

In any event, the Commonwealth's continued use of the three-drug protocol cannot be viewed as posing an "objectively intolerable risk" when no other State has adopted the one-drug method and petitioners proffered no study showing that it is an equally effective manner of imposing a death sentence. Indeed, the State of Tennessee, after reviewing its execution procedures, rejected a proposal to adopt a one-drug protocol using sodium thiopental. The State concluded that the one-drug alternative would take longer than the three-drug method and that the "required dosage of sodium thiopental would be less predictable and more variable when it is used as the sole mechanism for producing death. . . ." We need not endorse the accuracy of those conclusions to note simply that the comparative efficacy of a one-drug method of execution is not so well established that Kentucky's failure to adopt it constitutes a violation of the Eighth Amendment.

Petitioners also contend that Kentucky should omit the second drug, pancuronium bromide, because it serves no therapeutic purpose while suppressing muscle movements that could reveal an inadequate administration of the first drug. The state trial court, however, specifically found that pancuronium serves two purposes. First, it prevents involuntary physical movements during unconsciousness that may accompany the injection of potassium chloride. The Commonwealth has an interest in preserving the dignity of the procedure, especially where convulsions or seizures could be misperceived as signs of consciousness or distress. Second, pancuronium stops respiration, hastening death. Kentucky's decision to include the drug does not offend the Eighth Amendment.

Petitioners' barbiturate-only protocol, they contend, is not untested; it is used routinely by veterinarians in putting animals to sleep. Moreover, 23 States, including Kentucky, bar veterinarians from using a neuromuscular paralytic agent like pancuronium bromide, either expressly or, like Kentucky, by specifically directing the use of a drug like sodium pentobarbital. If pancuronium is too cruel for animals, the argument goes, then it must be too cruel for the condemned inmate. Whatever rhetorical force the argument carries, it overlooks the States' legitimate interest in providing for a quick, certain death. In the Netherlands, for example, where physician-assisted euthanasia is permitted, the Royal Dutch Society for the Advancement of Pharmacy recommends the use of a muscle relaxant (such as pancuronium dibromide) in addition to thiopental in order to prevent a prolonged, undignified death. That concern may be less compelling in the veterinary context, and in any event other methods approved by veterinarians—such as stunning the animal or severing its spinal cord—make clear that veterinary practice for animals is not an appropriate guide to humane practices for humans.

Petitioners also fault the Kentucky protocol for lacking a systematic mechanism for monitoring the "anesthetic depth" of the prisoner. Under petitioners' scheme, qualified personnel would employ monitoring equipment, such as a Bispectral Index (BIS) monitor, blood pressure cuff, or EKG to verify that a prisoner has achieved sufficient unconsciousness before injecting the final two drugs. The visual inspection performed by the warden and deputy warden, they maintain, is an inadequate substitute for the more sophisticated procedures they envision.

At the outset, it is important to reemphasize that a proper dose of thiopental obviates the concern that a prisoner will not be sufficiently sedated. All the experts who testified at trial agreed on this point. The risks of failing to adopt additional monitoring procedures are thus even more "remote" and attenuated than the risks posed by the alleged inadequacies of Kentucky's procedures designed to ensure the delivery of thiopental.

But more than this, Kentucky's expert testified that a blood pressure cuff would have no utility in assessing the level of the prisoner's unconsciousness following the introduction of sodium thiopental, which depresses circulation. Furthermore, the medical community has yet to endorse the use of a BIS monitor, which measures brain function, as an indication of anesthetic awareness. The asserted need for a professional anesthesiologist to interpret the BIS monitor readings is nothing more than an argument against the entire procedure, given that both Kentucky law and the American Society of Anesthesiologists' own ethical guidelines prohibit anesthesiologists from participating in capital punishment. Nor is it pertinent that the use of a blood pressure cuff and EKG is "the standard of care in surgery requiring anesthesia," as the dissent points out. Petitioners have not shown that these supplementary procedures, drawn from a different context, are necessary to avoid a substantial risk of suffering.

The dissent believes that rough-and-ready tests for checking consciousness—calling the inmate's name, brushing his eyelashes, or presenting him with strong, noxious odors—could materially decrease the risk of administering the second and third drugs before the sodium thiopental has taken effect. Again, the risk at issue is already attenuated, given the steps Kentucky has taken to ensure the proper administration of the first drug. Moreover, the scenario the dissent posits involves a level of unconsciousness allegedly sufficient to avoid detection of improper administration of the anesthesia under Kentucky's procedure, but not sufficient to prevent pain. There is no indication that the basic tests the dissent advocates can make such fine distinctions. If these tests are effective only in determining whether the sodium thiopental has entered the inmate's bloodstream, the record confirms that the visual inspection of the IV site under Kentucky's procedure achieves that objective.

The dissent would continue the stay of these executions (and presumably the many others held in abeyance pending decision in this case) and send the case back to the lower courts to determine whether such added measures redress an "untoward" risk of pain. But an inmate cannot succeed on an Eighth Amendment claim simply by showing one more step the State could take as a failsafe for other, independently adequate measures. This approach would serve no meaningful purpose and would frustrate the State's legitimate interest in carrying out a sentence of death in a timely manner.

Justice Stevens suggests that our opinion leaves the disposition of other cases uncertain, but the standard we set forth here resolves more challenges than he acknowledges. A stay of execution may not be granted on grounds such as those asserted here unless the condemned prisoner establishes that the State's lethal injection protocol creates a demonstrated risk of severe pain. He must show that the risk is substantial when compared to the known and available alternatives. A State with a lethal injection protocol substantially similar to the protocol we uphold today would not create a risk that meets this standard.

* * *

Reasonable people of good faith disagree on the morality and efficacy of capital punishment, and for many who oppose it, no method of execution would ever be acceptable. But as Justice Frankfurter stressed in *Resweber*, "[o]ne must be on guard against finding in personal disapproval a reflection of more or less prevailing condemnation." (concurring opinion). This Court has ruled that capital punishment is not prohibited under our Constitution, and that the States may enact laws specifying that sanction. "[T]he power of a State to pass laws means little if the State cannot enforce them." *McCleskey* v. *Zant*, 499 U.S. 467, 111 S.Ct. 1454 (1991). State efforts to implement capital punishment must certainly comply with the Eighth Amendment, but what that Amendment prohibits is wanton exposure to "objectively intolerable risk," *Farmer*, not simply the possibility of pain.

Kentucky has adopted a method of execution believed to be the most humane available, one it shares with 35 other States. Petitioners agree that, if administered as intended, that procedure will result in a painless death. The risks of maladministration they have suggested—such as improper mixing of chemicals and improper setting of IVs by trained and experienced personnel—cannot remotely be characterized as "objectively intolerable." Kentucky's decision to adhere to its protocol despite these asserted risks, while adopting safeguards to protect against them, cannot be viewed as probative of the wanton infliction of pain under the Eighth Amendment. Finally, the alternative that petitioners belatedly propose has problems of its own, and has never been tried by a single State.

Throughout our history, whenever a method of execution has been challenged in this Court as cruel and unusual, the Court has rejected the challenge. Our society has nonetheless steadily moved to more humane methods of carrying out capital punishment. The firing squad, hanging, the electric chair, and the gas chamber have each in turn given way to more humane methods, culminating in today's consensus on lethal injection. The broad framework of the Eighth Amendment has accommodated this progress toward more humane methods of execution, and our approval of a particular method in the past has not precluded legislatures from taking the steps they deem appropriate, in light of new developments, to ensure humane capital punishment. There is no reason to suppose that today's decision will be any different.

The judgment below concluding that Kentucky's procedure is consistent with the Eighth Amendment is, accordingly, affirmed.

It is so ordered.

JUSTICE ALITO, concurring.

I join the plurality opinion but write separately to explain my view of how the holding should be implemented. * * *

I

As the plurality opinion notes, the constitutionality of capital punishment is not before us in this case, and therefore we proceed on the assumption that the death penalty is constitutional. From that assumption, it follows that there must be a constitutional means of carrying out a death sentence.

We also proceed in this case on the assumption that lethal injection is a constitutional means of execution. Lethal injection was adopted by the Federal Government and 36 States because it was thought to be the most humane method of execution, and petitioners here do not contend that lethal injection should be abandoned in favor of any of the methods that it replaced—execution by electric chair, the gas chamber, hanging, or a firing squad. Since we assume for present purposes that lethal injection is constitutional, the use of that method by the Federal Government and the States must not be blocked by procedural requirements that cannot practicably be satisfied.

Prominent among the practical constraints that must be taken into account in considering the feasibility and availability of any suggested modification of a lethal injection protocol are the ethical restrictions applicable to medical professionals. The first step in the lethal injection protocols currently in use is the anesthetization of the prisoner. If this step is carried out properly, it is agreed, the prisoner will not experience pain during the remainder of the procedure. Every day, general anesthetics are administered to surgical patients in this country, and if the medical professionals who participate in these surgeries also participated in the anesthetization of prisoners facing execution by lethal injection, the risk of pain would be minimized. But the ethics rules of medical professionals—for reasons that I certainly do not question here—prohibit their participation in executions.

[Justice ALITO cited to the guidelines of the American Medical Association, the American Nurses Association and the National Association of Emergency Medical Technicians.]

Recent litigation in California has demonstrated the effect of such ethics rules. Michael Morales, who was convicted and sentenced to death for a 1981 murder, filed a federal civil rights action challenging California's lethal injection protocol, which, like Kentucky's, calls for the sequential administration of three drugs: sodium pentothal, pancuronium bromide, and potassium chloride. The District Court enjoined the State from proceeding with the execution unless it either (1) used only sodium pentothal or another barbiturate or (2) ensured that an anesthesiologist was present to ensure that Morales remained unconscious throughout the process. The Ninth Circuit affirmed the District Court's order, and the State arranged for two anesthesiologists to be present for the execution. However, they subsequently concluded that "they could not proceed for reasons of medical ethics," and neither Morales nor any other prisoner in California has since been executed.

Objections to features of a lethal injection protocol must be considered against the backdrop of the ethics rules of medical professionals and related practical constraints. Assuming, as previously discussed, that lethal injection is not unconstitutional *per se*, it follows that a suggested modification of a lethal injection protocol cannot be regarded as "feasible" or "readily" available if the modification would require participation— either in carrying out the execution or in training those who carry out the execution—by persons whose professional ethics rules or traditions impede their participation.

* * *

JUSTICE STEVENS, concurring in the judgment.

When we granted certiorari in this case, I assumed that our decision would bring the debate about lethal injection as a method of execution to a close. It now seems clear that it will not. The question whether a similar three-drug protocol may be used in other States remains open, and may well be answered differently in a future case on the basis of a more complete record. Instead of ending the controversy, I am now convinced that this case will generate debate not only about the constitutionality of the three-drug protocol, and specifically about the justification for the use of the paralytic agent, pancuronium bromide, but also about the justification for the death penalty itself.

I

Because it masks any outward sign of distress, pancuronium bromide creates a risk that the inmate will suffer excruciating pain before death occurs. There is a general understanding among veterinarians that the risk of pain is sufficiently serious that the use of the drug should be proscribed when an animal's life is being terminated. As a result of this understanding among knowledgeable professionals, several States—including Kentucky—have enacted legislation prohibiting use of the drug in animal euthanasia. It is unseemly—to say the least—that Kentucky may well kill petitioners using a drug that it would not permit to be used on their pets.

Use of pancuronium bromide is particularly disturbing because—as the trial court specifically found in this case—it serves "no therapeutic purpose." The drug's primary use is to prevent involuntary muscle movements, and its secondary use is to stop respiration. In my view, neither of these purposes is sufficient to justify the risk inherent in the use of the drug.

The plurality believes that preventing involuntary movement is a legitimate justification for using pancuronium bromide because "[t]he Commonwealth has an interest in preserving the dignity of the procedure, especially where convulsions or seizures could be misperceived as signs of consciousness or distress." This is a woefully inadequate justification. Whatever minimal interest there may be in ensuring that a condemned inmate dies a dignified death, and that witnesses to the execution are not made uncomfortable by an incorrect belief (which could easily be corrected) that the inmate is in pain, is vastly outweighed by the risk that the inmate is actually experiencing excruciating pain that no one can detect.

Nor is there any necessity for pancuronium bromide to be included in the cocktail to inhibit respiration when it is immediately followed by potassium chloride, which causes death quickly by stopping the inmate's heart.

Moreover, there is no nationwide endorsement of the use of pancuronium bromide that merits any special presumption of respect. While state legislatures have approved lethal injection as a humane method of execution, the majority have not enacted legislation specifically approving the use of pancuronium bromide, or any given combination of drugs.[4] And when the Colorado Legislature focused on the issue, it specified a one-drug protocol consisting solely of sodium thiopental.[5] In the majority of States that use the three-drug protocol, the drugs were selected by unelected Department of Correction officials with no specialized medical knowledge and without the benefit of expert assistance or guidance. As such, their drug selections are not entitled to the kind of deference afforded legislative decisions.

Nor should the failure of other state legislatures, or of Congress, to outlaw the use of the drug on condemned prisoners be viewed as a nationwide endorsement of an unnecessarily dangerous practice. Even in those States where the legislature specifically approved the use of a paralytic agent, review of the decisions that led to the adoption of the three-drug protocol has persuaded me that they are the product of "administrative convenience" and a "stereotyped reaction" to an issue, rather than a careful analysis of relevant considerations favoring or disfavoring a conclusion. See *Mathews* v. *Lucas,* 427 U.S. 495, 96 S.Ct. 2755 (1976) (STEVENS, J., dissenting). Indeed, the trial court found that "the various States simply fell in line" behind Oklahoma, adopting the protocol without any critical analysis of whether it was the best available alternative.[6]

* * *

In my view, therefore, States wishing to decrease the risk that future litigation will delay executions or invalidate their protocols would do well to reconsider their continued use of pancuronium bromide.

[Justice STEVENS went on to question whether the death penalty itself was cruel and unusual punishment since, in his view, it serves no penological purpose and procedures to protect against its arbitrary, discriminatory and erroneous imposition have proved inadequate. However, out of respect for precedents, he put aside those concerns and concurred in

---

4. Of the 35 state statutes providing for execution by lethal injection, only approximately one-third specifically approve the use of a chemical paralytic agent. Twenty of the remaining States do not specify any particular drugs.

5. Colorado's statute provides for "a continuous intravenous injection of a lethal quantity of sodium thiopental or other equally or more effective substance sufficient to cause death." Despite the fact that the statute specifies only sodium thiopental, it appears that Colorado uses the same three drugs as other States.

6. Notably, the Oklahoma medical examiner who devised the protocol has disavowed the use of pancuronium bromide. When asked in a recent interview why he included it in his formula, he responded: "It's a good question. If I were doing it now, I would probably eliminate it."

the finding that Kentucky's protocol did not violate the Eighth Amendment.]

[Opinion of SCALIA, J., joined by THOMAS, J., responding to JUSTICE STEVENS' concerns about the constitutionality of the death penalty omitted]

JUSTICE THOMAS, with whom JUSTICE SCALIA joins, concurring in the judgment.

Although I agree that petitioners have failed to establish that Kentucky's lethal injection protocol violates the Eighth Amendment, I write separately because I cannot subscribe to the plurality opinion's formulation of the governing standard. As I understand it, that opinion would hold that a method of execution violates the Eighth Amendment if it poses a substantial risk of severe pain that could be significantly reduced by adopting readily available alternative procedures. This standard—along with petitioners' proposed "unnecessary risk" standard and the dissent's "untoward risk" standard—finds no support in the original understanding of the Cruel and Unusual Punishments Clause or in our previous method-of-execution cases; casts constitutional doubt on long-accepted methods of execution; and injects the Court into matters it has no institutional capacity to resolve. Because, in my view, a method of execution violates the Eighth Amendment only if it is deliberately designed to inflict pain, I concur only in the judgment.

I

The Eighth Amendment's prohibition on the "inflict[ion]" of "cruel and unusual punishments" must be understood in light of the historical practices that led the Framers to include it in the Bill of Rights. JUSTICE STEVENS' ruminations notwithstanding, it is clear that the Eighth Amendment does not prohibit the death penalty. That is evident both from the ubiquity of the death penalty in the founding era and from the Constitution's express provision for capital punishment, see, *e.g.*, Amdt. 5 (requiring an indictment or presentment of a grand jury to hold a person for "a capital, or otherwise infamous crime," and prohibiting deprivation of "life" without due process of law).

That the Constitution permits capital punishment in principle does not, of course, mean that all methods of execution are constitutional. In English and early colonial practice, the death penalty was not a uniform punishment, but rather a range of punishments, some of which the Framers likely regarded as cruel and unusual. Death by hanging was the most common mode of execution both before and after 1791, and there is no doubt that it remained a permissible punishment after enactment of the Eighth Amendment. "An ordinary death by hanging was not, however, the harshest penalty at the disposal of the seventeenth-and eighteenth-century state." S. Banner, *The Death Penalty: An American History* (2002). In addition to hanging, which was intended to, and often did, result in a quick and painless death, "[o]fficials also wielded a set of tools capable of *intensifying* a death sentence," that is, "ways of producing a punishment worse than death."

[Justice THOMAS listed and described "burning at the stake," "gibbeting" "embowelling alive, beheading, and quartering."]

The principal object of these aggravated forms of capital punishment was to terrorize the criminal, and thereby more effectively deter the crime. Their defining characteristic was that they were purposely designed to inflict pain and suffering beyond that necessary to cause death. As Blackstone put it, "in very atrocious crimes, other circumstances of terror, pain, or disgrace [were] superadded." These "superadded" circumstances "were carefully handed out to apply terror where it was thought to be most needed," and were designed "to ensure that death would be slow and painful, and thus all the more frightening to contemplate." Banner.

Although the Eighth Amendment was not the subject of extensive discussion during the debates on the Bill of Rights, there is good reason to believe that the Framers viewed such enhancements to the death penalty as falling within the prohibition of the Cruel and Unusual Punishments Clause. By the late 18th century, the more violent modes of execution had "dwindled away," and would for that reason have been "unusual" in the sense that they were no longer "regularly or customarily employed," *Harmelin* v. *Michigan*, 501 U.S. 957, 111 S.Ct. 2680 (1991) (opinion of SCALIA, J.) Embellishments upon the death penalty designed to inflict pain for pain's sake also would have fallen comfortably within the ordinary meaning of the word "cruel."

[Justice THOMAS cited examples from the debates on the Constitution and the early commentators referring to the Eighth Amendment as barring "tortuous" and "barbarous" punishments.]

II

Consistent with the original understanding of the Cruel and Unusual Punishments Clause, this Court's cases have repeatedly taken the view that the Framers intended to prohibit torturous modes of punishment akin to those that formed the historical backdrop of the Eighth Amendment. See, *e.g.*, *Estelle* v. *Gamble*, 429 U.S. 97, 97 S.Ct. 285 (1976) ("[T]he primary concern of the drafters was to proscribe 'torture[s]' and other 'barbar[ous]' methods of punishment"); *Weems* v. *United States*, 217 U.S. 349, 30 S.Ct. 544 (White, J., dissenting) ("[I]t may not be doubted, and indeed is not questioned by any one, that the cruel punishments against which the bill of rights provided were the atrocious, sanguinary and inhuman punishments which had been inflicted in the past upon the persons of criminals"). That view has permeated our method-of-execution cases. Thrice the Court has considered a challenge to a modern method of execution, and thrice it has rejected the challenge, each time emphasizing that the Eighth Amendment is aimed at methods of execution purposely designed to inflict pain.

[Justice THOMAS reviewed the holdings in *Wilkerson* v. *Utah*, 99 U.S. 130, 25 L.Ed. 345 (1879) (firing squad), *In re Kemmler*, 136 U.S. 436, 10 S.Ct. 930 (1890) (electrocution), *Louisiana ex rel. Francis* v. *Resweber*, 329 U.S. 459, 67 S.Ct. 374 (1947) (second attempt at electrocution) and concluded that the Court had not, in those cases, engaged in a comparative risk analysis, but rather had looked to whether the execution method evinced a *purpose* to inflict unnecessary pain.]

IV

Aside from lacking support in history or precedent, the various risk-based standards proposed in this case suffer from other flaws, not the least of which is that they cast substantial doubt on every method of execution other than lethal injection. It may well be that other methods of execution such as hanging, the firing squad, electrocution, and lethal gas involve risks of pain that could be eliminated by switching to lethal injection. Indeed, they have been attacked as unconstitutional for that very reason. But the notion that the Eighth Amendment permits only one mode of execution, or that it requires an anesthetized death, cannot be squared with the history of the Constitution.

It is not a little ironic—and telling—that lethal injection, hailed just a few years ago as *the* humane alternative in light of which every other method of execution was deemed an unconstitutional relic of the past, is the subject of today's challenge. It appears the Constitution is "evolving" even faster than I suspected. And it is obvious that, for some who oppose capital punishment on policy grounds, the only acceptable end point of the evolution is for this Court, in an exercise of raw judicial power unsupported by the text or history of the Constitution, or even by a contemporary moral consensus, to strike down the death penalty as cruel and unusual in all circumstances. In the meantime, though, the next best option for those seeking to abolish the death penalty is to embroil the States in never-ending litigation concerning the adequacy of their execution procedures. But far from putting an end to abusive litigation in this area, and thereby vindicating in some small measure the States' "significant interest in meting out a sentence of death in a timely fashion," *Nelson* v. *Campbell*, 541 U.S. 637, 124 S.Ct. 2117 (2004), today's decision is sure to engender more litigation. At what point does a risk become "substantial"? Which alternative procedures are "feasible" and "readily implemented"? When is a reduction in risk "significant"? What penological justifications are "legitimate"? Such are the questions the lower courts will have to grapple with in the wake of today's decision. Needless to say, we have left the States with nothing resembling a bright-line rule.

Which brings me to yet a further problem with comparative-risk standards: They require courts to resolve medical and scientific controversies that are largely beyond judicial ken. Little need be said here, other than to refer to the various opinions filed by my colleagues today. Under the competing risk standards advanced by the plurality opinion and the dissent, for example, the difference between a lethal injection procedure that satisfies the Eighth Amendment and one that does not may well come down to one's judgment with respect to something as hairsplitting as whether an eyelash stroke is necessary to ensure that the inmate is unconscious, or whether instead other measures have already provided sufficient assurance of unconsciousness. We have neither the authority nor the expertise to micromanage the States' administration of the death penalty in this manner. There is simply no reason to believe that "unelected" judges without scientific, medical, or penological training are any better suited to resolve the delicate issues surrounding the administration of the death penalty than are state administrative personnel specifically charged with the task.

In short, I reject as both unprecedented and unworkable any standard that would require the courts to weigh the relative advantages and disadvantages of different methods of execution or of different procedures for implementing a given method of execution. To the extent that there is any comparative element to the inquiry, it should be limited to whether the challenged method inherently inflicts significantly more pain than traditional modes of execution such as hanging and the firing squad.

V

Judged under the proper standard, this is an easy case. It is undisputed that Kentucky adopted its lethal injection protocol in an effort to make capital punishment more humane, not to add elements of terror, pain, or disgrace to the death penalty. And it is undisputed that, if administered properly, Kentucky's lethal injection protocol will result in a swift and painless death. As the Sixth Circuit observed in rejecting a similar challenge to Tennessee's lethal injection protocol, we "do not have a situation where the State has any intent (or anything approaching intent) to inflict unnecessary pain; the complaint is that the State's *pain-avoidance procedure* may fail because the executioners may make a mistake in implementing it." *Workman* v. *Bredesen*, 486 F. 3d 896 (2007). But "[t]he risk of negligence in implementing a death-penalty procedure ... does not establish a cognizable Eighth Amendment claim." *Id.* Because Kentucky's lethal injection protocol is designed to eliminate pain rather than to inflict it, petitioners' challenge must fail. I accordingly concur in the Court's judgment affirming the decision below.

> [Justice BREYER, agreeing with the dissenters as to the standard to be applied, nevertheless found the evidence in the record was insufficient to meet that standard and therefore concurred in the judgment.]

JUSTICE GINSBURG, with whom JUSTICE SOUTER joins, dissenting.

It is undisputed that the second and third drugs used in Kentucky's three-drug lethal injection protocol, pancuronium bromide and potassium chloride, would cause a conscious inmate to suffer excruciating pain. Pancuronium bromide paralyzes the lung muscles and results in slow asphyxiation. Potassium chloride causes burning and intense pain as it circulates throughout the body. Use of pancuronium bromide and potassium chloride on a conscious inmate, the plurality recognizes, would be "constitutionally unacceptable."

The constitutionality of Kentucky's protocol therefore turns on whether inmates are adequately anesthetized by the first drug in the protocol, sodium thiopental. Kentucky's system is constitutional, the plurality states, because "petitioners have not shown that the risk of an inadequate dose of the first drug is substantial." I would not dispose of the case so swiftly given the character of the risk at stake. Kentucky's protocol lacks basic safeguards used by other States to confirm that an inmate is unconscious before injection of the second and third drugs. I would vacate and remand with instructions to consider whether Kentucky's omission of those safeguards poses an untoward, readily avoidable risk of inflicting severe and unnecessary pain.

I

The Court has considered the constitutionality of a specific method of execution on only three prior occasions. Those cases, and other decisions cited by the parties and *amici*, provide little guidance on the standard that should govern petitioners' challenge to Kentucky's lethal injection protocol.

[Justice Ginsburg concluded that *Wilkerson v. Utah*, 99 U.S. 130, 25 L.Ed. 345 (1879), *In re Kemmler*, 136 U.S. 436, 10 S.Ct. 930 (1890) and *Louisiana ex rel. Francis v. Resweber*, 329 U.S. 459, 67 S.Ct. 374 (1947) established no clear standard and that, in any event, "the age of the opinions limits their utility."]

Relying on *Gregg v. Georgia*, 428 U.S. 153, 96 S.Ct. 2909 (1976) and our earlier decisions, the Kentucky Supreme Court stated that an execution procedure violates the Eighth Amendment if it "creates a substantial risk of wanton and unnecessary infliction of pain, torture or lingering death." Petitioners respond that courts should consider "(a) the severity of pain risked, (b) the likelihood of that pain occurring, *and* (c) the extent to which alternative means are feasible." (emphasis added). The plurality settles somewhere in between, requiring a "substantial risk of serious harm" and considering whether a "feasible, readily implemented" alternative can "significantly reduce" that risk.

I agree with petitioners and the plurality that the degree of risk, magnitude of pain, and availability of alternatives must be considered. I part ways with the plurality, however, to the extent its "substantial risk" test sets a fixed threshold for the first factor. The three factors are interrelated; a strong showing on one reduces the importance of the others.

Lethal injection as a mode of execution can be expected, in most instances, to result in painless death. Rare though errors may be, the consequences of a mistake about the condemned inmate's consciousness are horrendous and effectively undetectable after injection of the second drug. Given the opposing tugs of the degree of risk and magnitude of pain, the critical question here, as I see it, is whether a feasible alternative exists. Proof of "a slightly or marginally safer alternative" is, as the plurality notes, insufficient. But if readily available measures can materially increase the likelihood that the protocol will cause no pain, a State fails to adhere to contemporary standards of decency if it declines to employ those measures.

II

Kentucky's Legislature adopted lethal injection as a method of execution in 1998. Lawmakers left the development of the lethal injection protocol to officials in the Department of Corrections. Those officials, the trial court found, were "given the task without the benefit of scientific aid or policy oversight." "Kentucky's protocol," that court observed, "was copied from other states and accepted without challenge." Kentucky "did not conduct any independent scientific or medical studies or consult any medical professionals concerning the drugs and dosage amounts to be injected into the condemned." Instead, the trial court noted, Kentucky followed the path taken in other States that "simply fell in line" behind the three-drug protocol first developed by Oklahoma in 1977.

Kentucky's protocol begins with a careful measure: Only medical professionals may perform the venipunctures and establish intravenous (IV) access. Members of the IV team must have at least one year's experience as a certified medical assistant, phlebotomist, emergency medical technician (EMT), paramedic, or military corpsman. Kentucky's IV team currently has two members: a phlebotomist with 8 years' experience and an EMT with 20 years' experience. Both members practice siting catheters at ten lethal injection training sessions held annually.

Other than using qualified and trained personnel to establish IV access, however, Kentucky does little to ensure that the inmate receives an effective dose of sodium thiopental. After siting the catheters, the IV team leaves the execution chamber. From that point forward, only the warden and deputy warden remain with the inmate. Neither the warden nor the deputy warden has any medical training.

The warden relies on visual observation to determine whether the inmate "appears" unconscious. In Kentucky's only previous execution by lethal injection, the warden's position allowed him to see the inmate best from the waist down, with only a peripheral view of the inmate's face. No other check for consciousness occurs before injection of pancuronium bromide. Kentucky's protocol does not include an automatic pause in the "rapid flow" of the drugs or any of the most basic tests to determine whether the sodium thiopental has worked. No one calls the inmate's name, shakes him, brushes his eyelashes to test for a reflex, or applies a noxious stimulus to gauge his response.

Nor does Kentucky monitor the effectiveness of the sodium thiopental using readily available equipment, even though the inmate is already connected to an electrocardiogram (EKG). A drop in blood pressure or heart rate after injection of sodium thiopental would not prove that the inmate is unconscious, but would signal that the drug has entered the inmate's bloodstream. Kentucky's own expert testified that the sodium thiopental should "cause the inmate's blood pressure to become very, very low" and that a precipitous drop in blood pressure would "confir[m]" that the drug was having its expected effect. Use of a blood pressure cuff and EKG, the record shows, is the standard of care in surgery requiring anesthesia.

A consciousness check supplementing the warden's visual observation before injection of the second drug is easily implemented and can reduce a risk of dreadful pain. Pancuronium bromide is a powerful paralytic that prevents all voluntary muscle movement. Once it is injected, further monitoring of the inmate's consciousness becomes impractical without sophisticated equipment and training. Even if the inmate were conscious and in excruciating pain, there would be no visible indication.

Recognizing the importance of a window between the first and second drugs, other States have adopted safeguards not contained in Kentucky's protocol. [Justice Ginsburg cited to the Florida, Missouri, California, Alabama and Indiana execution procedures, all of which require the performance of some tests to determine whether the inmate is unconscious before the administration of the second and third chemicals.]

These checks provide a degree of assurance—missing from Kentucky's protocol—that the first drug has been properly administered. They are simple and essentially costless to employ, yet work to lower the risk that the inmate will be subjected to the agony of conscious suffocation caused by pancuronium bromide and the searing pain caused by potassium chloride. The record contains no explanation why Kentucky does not take any of these elementary measures.

The risk that an error administering sodium thiopental would go undetected is minimal, Kentucky urges, because if the drug was mistakenly injected into the inmate's tissue, not a vein, he "would be awake and screaming." That argument ignores aspects of Kentucky's protocol that render passive reliance on obvious signs of consciousness, such as screaming, inadequate to determine whether the inmate is experiencing pain.

First, Kentucky's use of pancuronium bromide to paralyze the inmate means he will not be able to scream after the second drug is injected, no matter how much pain he is experiencing. Kentucky's argument, therefore, appears to rest on the assertion that sodium thiopental is itself painful when injected into tissue rather than a vein. The trial court made no finding on that point, and Kentucky cites no supporting evidence from executions in which it is known that sodium thiopental was injected into the inmate's soft tissue.

Second, the inmate may receive enough sodium thiopental to mask the most obvious signs of consciousness without receiving a dose sufficient to achieve a surgical plane of anesthesia. If the drug is injected too quickly, the increase in blood pressure can cause the inmate's veins to burst after a small amount of sodium thiopental has been administered. Kentucky's protocol does not specify the rate at which sodium thiopental should be injected. The executioner, who does not have any medical training, pushes the drug "by feel" through five feet of tubing. In practice sessions, unlike in an actual execution, there is no resistance on the catheter; thus the executioner's training may lead him to push the drugs too fast.

"The easiest and most obvious way to ensure that an inmate is unconscious during an execution," petitioners argued to the Kentucky Supreme Court, "is to check for consciousness prior to injecting pancuronium [bromide]." The court did not address petitioners' argument. I would therefore remand with instructions to consider whether the failure to include readily available safeguards to confirm that the inmate is unconscious after injection of sodium thiopental, in combination with the other elements of Kentucky's protocol, creates an untoward, readily avoidable risk of inflicting severe and unnecessary pain.

NOTES

1. *Doctor participation in executions.*

The American Medical Association (AMA) and other medical professional organizations, including the American Society of Anesthesiologists (ASA), the American Nurses Association (ANA) and the National Association of Emergency Medical Technicians (NAEMT), have determined that it is unethical for medical professionals to participate in executions. In *Baze*, the justices appeared to assume that, therefore, doctors could not, or would not, participate in executions and the constitutionality of execution procedures had to be determined with that fact in mind.[a] That assumption may have been correct with regard to Kentucky because a state statute subjects Kentucky doctors to sanctions for violation of the AMA's principles of medical ethics. Ky.Rev.Stat. Ann. § 311.597(4). However, that assumption may not be correct for the majority of death penalty states, and, according to one researcher, doctors may participate, are willing to participate and do participate in executions. See, T. Alper, *The Truth About Physician Participation in Lethal Injection Executions*, 88 N.C. L. Rev. ___ (2009). In judging the constitutionality of lethal injection protocols should the possibility of doctor participation be a factor?

2. *Continuing lethal injection challenges.*

In his dissent in *Baze*, Justice Stevens predicted that the decision would not put an end to challenges to the various lethal injection protocols. One year after the *Baze* decision, numerous lethal injection challenges are pending, and executions are on hold in a half dozen states while such challenges are being resolved.

---

a. See 128 S.Ct. at 1536 (plurality opinion) (citing the ethical guidelines of the ASA); *id.* at 1539 (Alito, J., concurring) (citing to the ethical guidelines of the AMA, ANA and NAEMT); *id.* at 1566 (Breyer, J., concurring) (citing to the ethical guidelines of the AMA and ANA).

3. *Public viewing of executions.*

Once dramatic public rituals, executions now are carried out behind prison walls before a limited number of invited witnesses. The question of public and media access to executions raises two issues: (1) how much of the execution process are the witnesses entitled to see, and (2) is there a right to film or televise executions? Over a century ago, the Supreme Court upheld a state law limiting the number of witnesses to an execution and banning all newspaper reporters as witnesses. *Holden v. Minnesota*, 137 U.S. 483, 11 S.Ct. 143 (1890). More recently, the Court applied the principle that " 'the First Amendment does not guarantee the press a constitutional right of special access to information not available to the public generally.' " *Pell v. Procunier*, 417 U.S. 817, 833, 94 S.Ct. 2800, 2810 (1974). Nevertheless the public and the press do have at least a limited First Amendment right to view executions. See *California First Amendment Coalition v. Woodford*, 299 F.3d 868 (9th Cir. 2002) (upholding a permanent injunction prohibiting prison officials "from preventing uninterrupted viewing of executions from the moment the condemned enters the execution chamber through, to and including, the time the condemned is declared dead"); *Oregon Newspaper Publishers Association v. Oregon Department of Corrections*, 988 P.2d 359 (Ore. 1999) (holding that prison rules limiting observation to point when lethal injection is administered and causes death violate statutory right of witnesses to view the execution). Although scholars and commentators have articulated a constitutional right of access by the media to televise or videotape executions (see, *e.g.*, J. Bessler, *Televised Executions and the Constitution: Recognizing a First Amendment Right of Access to State Executions*, 45 Fed. Comm. L. J. 355 (1993)), no court has yet agreed. See *Garrett v. Estelle*, 556 F.2d 1274 (5th Cir. 1977) (holding there is no First Amendment right of news cameraman to film executions for television); *Halquist v. Department of Corrections*, 783 P.2d 1065 (Wash. 1989) (holding ban on videotaping executions did not violate state constitutional prohibition on prior restraints on dissemination of information); *KQED, Inc. v. Vasquez,* 1995 WL 489485 (N.D.Cal. 1991) (striking down the warden's ban on all news reporters at an execution but upholding the ban on cameras and video equipment). Setting aside the First Amendment question and considering the purposes of capital punishment, should executions be televised or otherwise made more public? What weight should be given to the condemned inmates' privacy interests?

PART 5

THE DEATH PENALTY RECONSIDERED

∎ ∎ ∎

The cases and other materials in this Part revisit the questions raised in Part 1 concerning the proper role, if any, of the death penalty in the United States. In light of the law developed by the Supreme Court, as set forth in the intervening chapters, should the United States continue to employ the death penalty, and, if so, how should it be administered? The two chapters offer different perspectives on current United States death penalty law. Chapter 13 considers the death penalty from the vantage point of international law and norms. From the point of view of the international community, the administration of the death penalty in the United States has become an international human rights issue. Chapter 14 contains the views of Justice Blackmun (disputed by Justice Scalia) and a major empirical study suggesting, for different reasons, that the system is broken.

CHAPTER 13

THE DEATH PENALTY IN THE
INTERNATIONAL
CONTEXT

■ ■ ■

For a number of years, support for the death penalty on the international level has been declining. On December 18, 2007, the United Nations General Assembly, for the first time, passed a resolution calling on all states still maintaining the death penalty to "[e]stablish a moratorium on executions with a view to abolishing the death penalty."[a] The United States voted against the resolution and is one of a minority of countries in the world that employs the death penalty for ordinary crimes. According to Amnesty International, as of 2008, 59 countries retained and employed the death penalty for ordinary crimes, while 138 had abolished the death penalty for ordinary crimes, by abolishing the death penalty altogether (92 countries), by abolishing it for ordinary crimes and reserving it for such crimes as treason or crimes against humanity (10 countries), or by abolishing it in practice by establishing a policy against using the death penalty and having no execution for at least 10 years (36 countries).[b] The distribution of "abolitionist" and "retentionist" countries creates striking patterns. All of the countries of Europe, except Belarus, have abolished the death penalty. The same is true of all the countries of Latin America, except Cuba and Guatemala. By contrast, in the Middle East and North Africa, only Israel and Turkey are abolitionist, and virtually all the countries of Asia, including the world's two largest countries, China and India, retain and employ the death penalty. The countries of sub-Saharan Africa are fairly evenly divided between abolitionist (*e.g.*, Angola, Congo (Republic), Mozambique, Senegal, South Africa) and retentionist (*e.g.*, Congo (Democratic Republic), Sierra Leone, Nigeria, Uganda, Zimbabwe). Australia, Canada and New Zealand, the other principal countries with English legal systems, have abolished the death penalty. What accounts for this distribution?

---

a. A/RES/62/149. The vote on the resolution was 104 to 54 with 29 abstentions. See P. Steinfels, *Milestone in Death Penalty Fight, but Still a Way to Go*, N.Y. Times, Dec. 22, 2007 at B6.

b. See Amnesty International, *Death Sentences and Executions in 2008*, http://www.amnesty.org.au/images/uploads/adp/DP_report_2008.pdf.

The United States has been criticized for its administration of the death penalty by international bodies, including the International Association of Jurists,[c] the Special Rapporteur of the United Nations Commission on Human Rights[d] and the United Nations Committee on the Elimination of Racial Discrimination.[e] The opposition of the European countries and most of the Western Hemisphere countries to the death penalty has affected the United States in concrete terms when the United States has attempted to extradite from those countries persons charged with murder in the United States. *Minister of Justice v. Burns* is a unanimous decision of the Supreme Court of Canada holding that extradition of two Canadians to face murder charges in the State of Washington would violate the Canadian Charter of Rights and Freedoms unless Canada first obtained assurances that the death penalty would not be imposed. In the course of the decision, the court reviews both the state of international law with regard to the death penalty and the then-recent developments in the death penalty debate in the United States. The United States has ratified several international treaties that arguably apply to the country's administration of the death penalty. The treaties and their possible applications are outlined in *International Treaties and the Death Penalty*. Should the views of the international community and/or the United States' treaty obligations affect the administration of the death penalty?

MINISTER OF JUSTICE v. BURNS

1 S.C.R. 283, 2001 SCC 7 (2001).

THE SUPREME COURT OF CANADA—

[In July, 1994, the father, mother and sister of Atif Ahmad Rafay were found bludgeoned to death in their home in Bellevue, Washington. Police suspected Rafay and a friend, Glen Sebastian Burns, but they did not have enough evidence to bring charges. The suspects were 18 years-old at the time and were citizens of Canada. When Rafay and Burns returned to British Columbia, the Bellevue police sought the cooperation of the Royal Canadian Mounted Police, and the RCMP initiated an elaborate undercover operation in an effort to develop information about the murders. During the course of conversations with an undercover officer, the suspects admitted that Burns had done the killings (while Rafay watched), and Rafay allegedly said that the killings were "a necessary sacrifice in order that he could get what he wanted in life," presumably because he would inherit his parents' estate. Following the suspects' arrest, the Minister of Justice signed an order for their extradition to the State of Washington to stand trial pursuant to the *Extradition Treaty between Canada and the United States of America*, Can. T.S. 1976 No. 3. The

c. *Administration of the Death Penalty in the United States* (1996).

d. *Report of the Special Rapporteur on Extrajudicial, Summary or Arbitrary Executions* (1998).

e. *Concluding Observations of the Committee on the Elimination of Racial Discrimination*, CERD/C/USA/CO/6 (2008).

treaty permitted Canada to refuse extradition of fugitives unless provided with assurances that if extradited and convicted they will not suffer the death penalty, but the Minister declined to seek such assurances. The suspects had argued to the Minister that, under §§ 6(1), 7 and 12 of the *Canadian Charter of Rights and Freedoms*, he was required to seek assurances, and they had sought to distinguish *Kindler v. Canada (Minister of Justice)*, [1991] 2 S.C.R. 779, and *Reference Re Ng Extradition (Can.)*, [1991] 2 S.C.R. 858, cases where the Supreme Court had permitted extradition to the United States in potential death penalty cases without assurances. A divided British Columbia Court of Appeal set aside the Minister's decision and directed the Minister to seek the assurances described in Article 6 of the extradition treaty as a condition of surrender, finding that, if the suspects were put to death in the State of Washington, they would no longer be able to exercise a right of return to Canada under § 6(1) of the *Charter*.]

* * *

VII.   Analysis

28.   The evidence amply justifies the extradition of the respondents to Washington State to stand trial on charges of aggravated first degree murder. Under the law of that state, a conviction would carry a minimum sentence of imprisonment for life without the possibility of release or parole. If the prosecutors were to seek the death penalty, they would have the burden of persuading the jury that "there are not sufficient mitigating circumstances" in favour of the respondents. If the jury is so satisfied, the death penalty would be administered by lethal injection or (at the option of the convicted individual), by hanging. If the jury is not so satisfied, the convicted murderer is locked up for life without any possibility of release or parole. * * *

29.   The respondents' position is that the death penalty is so horrific, the chances of error are so high, the death row phenomenon is so repugnant, and the impossibility of correction is so draconian, that it is simply unacceptable that Canada should participate, however indirectly, in its imposition. While the government of Canada would not itself administer the lethal injection or erect the gallows, no executions can or will occur without the act of extradition by the Canadian government. The Minister's decision is a prior and essential step in a process that may lead to death by execution.

[The Court acknowledged that the *Extradition Act* conferred a broad statutory discretion on the Minister but found that the rights embodied in the *Charter* were necessarily a limit on that discretion. The Court then rejected the respondents' argument that § 6(1) ("the right to enter, remain in and leave Canada") invalidated extradition without assurances. The Court also rejected the respondents' § 12 ("cruel and unusual treatment or punishment") argument, finding that the rights in question were not implicated by Canada's decision to hand fugitives over to law enforcement authorities in another country.]

5. *The Outcome of this Appeal is Governed by Section 7 of the Charter ("Fundamental Justice").*

58. Section 7 of the *Charter* provides that:

7. Everyone has the right to life, liberty and security of the person and the right not to be deprived thereof except in accordance with the principles of fundamental justice.

59. It is evident that the respondents are deprived of their liberty and security of the person by the extradition order. Their lives are potentially at risk. The issue is whether the threatened deprivation is in accordance with the principles of fundamental justice.

60. This Court has recognized from the outset that the punishment or treatment reasonably anticipated in the requesting country is clearly relevant. Section 7 is concerned not only with the act of extraditing, but also the *potential* consequences of the act of extradition. * * *

[The Court explained that whether extradition without assurances in death penalty cases would violate Section 7 was to be determined by balancing the factors for and against extradition. The Court concluded that "in the absence of exceptional circumstances, which we refrain from trying to anticipate, assurances in death penalty cases are always constitutionally required."]

8. *Factors that Arguably Favour Extradition Without Assurances*

72. Within this overall approach, a number of the "basic tenets of our legal system" relevant to this appeal may be found in previous extradition cases:

— that individuals accused of a crime should be brought to trial to determine the truth of the charges, the concern in this case being that if assurances are sought and refused, the Canadian government could face the possibility that the respondents might avoid a trial altogether;

— that justice is best served by a trial in the jurisdiction where the crime was allegedly committed and the harmful impact felt;

— that individuals who choose to leave Canada leave behind Canadian law and procedures and must generally accept the local law, procedure and punishments which the foreign state applies to its own residents. * * *

— that extradition is based on the principles of comity and fairness to other cooperating states in rendering mutual assistance in bringing fugitives to justice; subject to the principle that the fugitive must be able to receive a fair trial in the requesting state.

* * *

9. *Countervailing Factors that Arguably Favour Extradition Only with Assurances*

75.   We now turn to the factors that appear to weigh against extradition without assurances that the death penalty will not be imposed.

(a) *Principles of Criminal Justice as Applied in Canada*

76.   The death penalty has been rejected as an acceptable element of criminal justice by the Canadian people, speaking through their elected federal representatives, after years of protracted debate. Canada has not executed anyone since 1962. Parliament abolished the last legal vestiges of the death penalty in 1998 * * * In his letter to the respondents, the Minister of Justice emphasized that "in Canada, Parliament has decided that capital punishment is not an appropriate penalty for crimes committed here, and I am firmly committed to that position."

77.   While government policy at any particular moment may or may not be consistent with principles of fundamental justice, the fact that successive governments and Parliaments over a period of almost 40 years have refused to inflict the death penalty reflects, we believe, a fundamental Canadian principle about the appropriate limits of the criminal justice system.

* * *

(b) *The Abolition of the Death Penalty Has Emerged as a Major Canadian Initiative at the International Level, and Reflects a Concern Increasingly Shared by Most of the World's Democracies.*

79.   In *Re B.C. Motor Vehicle Act*, [1985] 2 S.C.R. 486, Lamer J. expressly recognized that international law and opinion is of use to the courts in elucidating the scope of fundamental justice:

> [Principles of fundamental justice] represent principles which have been recognized by the common law, the international conventions and by the very fact of entrenchment in the *Charter*, as essential elements of a system for the administration of justice which is founded upon the belief in the dignity and worth of the human person and the rule of law.

* * *

[The Court found:

(1) That Canada has supported international initiatives opposing extradition without assurances. These included Article 4(d) of the *Model Treaty on Extradition*, which states that extradition may be refused:

> if the offence for which extradition is requested carries the death penalty under the law of the requesting State, unless that State gives such assurance as the requested State considers sufficient that the death penalty will not be imposed or, if imposed, will not be carried out.

(2) That Canada has supported initiatives to abolish the death penalty on an international level, including reports and resolution in the United Nations Commission on Human Rights.

(3) That state practice increasingly favours abolition of the death penalty (85 percent of the world's executions in 1999 were accounted for by only five countries: the United States, China, the Congo, Saudi Arabia and Iran) and that abolitionist states include all of the major democracies except some of the United States, India and Japan.]

92.   The existence of an international trend against the death penalty is useful in testing our values against those of comparable jurisdictions. This trend against the death penalty supports some relevant conclusions. First, criminal justice, according to international standards, is moving in the direction of abolition of the death penalty. Second, the trend is more pronounced among democratic states with systems of criminal justice comparable to our own. The United States (or those parts of it that have retained the death penalty) is the exception, although of course it is an important exception. Third, the trend to abolition in the democracies, particularly the Western democracies, mirrors and perhaps corroborates the principles of fundamental justice that led to the rejection of the death penalty in Canada.

* * *

(d) *Other Factors*

94.   Other factors that weigh against extradition without assurances include the growing awareness of the rate of wrongful convictions in murder cases, and concerns about the "death row phenomenon", aptly described by Lord Griffiths in *Pratt v. Attorney General for Jamaica*, [1993] 4 All E.R. 769 (J.P.C.):

> There is an instinctive revulsion against the prospect of hanging a man after he has been held under sentence of death for many years. What gives rise to this instinctive revulsion? The answer can only be our humanity: we regard it as an inhuman act to keep a man facing the agony of execution over a long extended period of time.

As these factors call for extended treatment, they will be dealt with separately under the headings which follow.

10.   An Accelerating Concern about Potential Wrongful Convictions is a Factor of Increased Weight

* * *

[The Court described the Canadian experience with wrongful convictions of murder.]

(b) *The U.S. Experience*

105.   Concerns in the United States have been raised by such authoritative bodies as the American Bar Association which in 1997 recommended a moratorium on the death penalty throughout the United States
* * *

106. The ABA takes no position on the death penalty as such (except to oppose it in the case of juveniles and the mentally retarded). Its call for a moratorium has been echoed by local or state bars in California, Connecticut, Ohio, Virginia, Illinois, Louisiana, Massachusetts, New Jersey and Pennsylvania. The ABA reports that state or local bars in Florida, Kentucky, Missouri, Nebraska, North Carolina and Tennessee are also examining aspects of the death penalty controversy.

107. On August 4, 2000, the Board of Governors of the Washington State Bar Association, being the state seeking the extradition of the respondents, unanimously adopted a resolution to review the death penalty process. The Governor was urged to obtain a comprehensive report addressing the concerns of the American Bar Association as they apply to the imposition of the death penalty in the State of Washington. In particular, the Governor was asked to determine "[w]hether the reversal of capital cases from our state by the federal courts indicates any systemic problems regarding how the death penalty is being implemented in Washington State".

108. Other retentionist jurisdictions in the United States have also expressed recent disquiet about the conduct of capital cases, and the imposition and the carrying out of the death penalty.

[The Court cited to the following: (1) the moratorium on executions imposed by Governor George Ryan of Illinois; (2) the *Chicago Tribune* newspaper study of Illinois death penalty cases that found a system "plagued by unprofessionalism, imprecision and bias"; (3) the exoneration of Anthony Porter in Illinois 48 hours prior to his scheduled execution; (4) the passage of legislation in New Hampshire to abolish the death penalty; (5) the approval, by the Nebraska legislature, of a two-year moratorium on executions; (6) Senator Russ Feingold's bill calling for a national moratorium; (7) the release of a Justice Department study suggesting the existence of racial and geographical disparities in the administration of the federal death penalty.]

110. Finally, we should note the recent Columbia University study by Professor James Liebman and others which concludes that 2 out of 3 death penalty sentences in the United States were reversed on appeal: *A Broken System: Error Rates in Capital Cases, 1973–1995* (June 12, 2000). The authors gathered and analyzed all of the available cases from the period of 1973 to 1995, the former being the year that states began to enact new death penalty statutes following the United States Supreme Court's decision in *Furman*, *supra*, invalidating the existing regimes. Collection of the data for the study began in 1991, the year *Kindler* and *Ng* were decided. In their executive summary, the authors report that "the overall rate of prejudicial error in the American capital punishment system was 68%." These errors were detected at one of three stages of appeal in the American legal system. The authors say that with "so many mistakes that it takes three judicial inspections to catch them" there must be "grave doubt about whether we *do* catch them all" (emphasis in

original). The authors point out in footnote 81 that "[b]etween 1972 and the beginning of 1998, 68 people were released from death row on the grounds that their convictions were faulty, and there was too little evidence to retry the prisoner" and as of May 2000 "the number of inmates released from death row as factually or legally innocent apparently has risen to 87, including nine released in 1999 alone."

* * *

[The Court described the experience with wrongful murder convictions in the United Kingdom.]

(d) *Conclusion*

The recent and continuing disclosures of wrongful convictions for murder in Canada, the United States and the United Kingdom provide tragic testimony to the fallibility of the legal system, despite its elaborate safeguards for the protection of the innocent. When fugitives are sought to be tried for murder by a retentionist state, however similar in other respects to our own legal system, this history weighs powerfully in the balance against extradition without assurances.

11. *The "Death Row Phenomenon" is of Increasing Concern Even to Retentionists.*

118.   The evidence filed on this appeal includes a report by Chief Justice Richard P. Guy, Chief Justice of the State of Washington, dated March 2000 entitled "Status Report on the Death Penalty in Washington State". In the report the Chief Justice notes the following statistics relevant to the present discussion:

— Since 1981, 25 men have been convicted and sentenced to death. Four have had their judgments reversed by the federal courts, 2 have had their sentences reversed by the Washington State Supreme Court, and 3 have been executed.

— The case of one defendant who was sentenced to be executed 18 years ago is still pending.

— Two of the three executed defendants chose not to pursue appeals to the federal courts.

— For cases completed in the federal courts, state and federal review has taken an average of 11.2 years.

— State review after conviction has averaged 5.5 years.

In his introduction to the Status Report, the Chief Justice made the following observations:

Because a death sentence is irreversible, opportunities for proving innocence in addition to those furnished in other felony cases are offered to the defendant in order to avoid erroneous executions. The importance of the review system is illustrated by the current situation in Illinois, a state in which 12 men have been executed since the 1980s but another 13 men sentenced to death have been exonerated. Appellate review of their cases resulted in reversal of their judgments after they were able to prove their innocence through the use of newly discovered DNA techniques or for other reasons.

119. These statistics are comparable to the degree of delay on "death row" that concerned the European Court of Human Rights in Eur. Court H.R., *Soering* case, judgment of 7 July 1989, Series A No. 161. The evidence was that if Soering were to be sentenced to death under Virginia law he would face an average of six to eight years on death row. The European Court commented on the serious human rights consequences of holding a convict under the threat of death for a prolonged length of time:

> However well-intentioned and even potentially beneficial is the provision of the complex of post-sentence procedures in Virginia, the consequence is that the condemned prisoner has to endure for many years the conditions on death row and the anguish and mounting tension in the ever-present shadow of death.

* * *

122. There is now, however, as is shown in the report of Chief Justice Guy of Washington State, *supra*, a widening acceptance amongst those closely associated with the administration of justice in retentionist states that the finality of the death penalty, combined with the determination of the criminal justice system to satisfy itself fully that the conviction is not wrongful, seems inevitably to provide lengthy delays, and the associated psychological trauma. It is apposite to recall in this connection the observation of Frankfurter J. of the United States Supreme Court, dissenting, in *Solesbee v. Balkcom*, 339 U.S. 9, 70 S.Ct. 457 (1950), that the "onset of insanity while awaiting execution of a death sentence is not a rare phenomenon". Related concerns have been expressed by Breyer J., dissenting from decisions not to issue writs of *certiorari* in *Elledge v. Florida*, 525 U.S. 944, 119 S. Ct. 366 (1998), and *Knight v. Florida*, 528 U.S. 990, 120 S. Ct. 459 (1999). In the latter case, Breyer J. cited a Florida study of inmates which showed that 35 percent of those committed to death row attempted suicide.

123. The death row phenomenon is not a controlling factor in the § 7 balance, but even many of those who regard its horrors as self-inflicted concede that it is a relevant consideration. To that extent, it is a factor that weighs in the balance against extradition without assurances.

12. *The Balance of Factors in This Case Renders Extradition of the Respondents Without Assurances a Prima Facie Infringement of their Section 7 Rights.*

124. Reviewing the factors for and against unconditional extradition, we conclude that to order extradition of the respondents without obtaining assurances that the death penalty will not be imposed would violate the principles of fundamental justice.

* * *

INTERNATIONAL TREATIES AND
THE DEATH PENALTY

Under the Constitution, Art. VI, cl. 2, all treaties of the United States are, along with the Constitution and laws, the supreme law of the land. In recent years, defendants in death penalty cases and prisoners under death sentences have claimed rights under international treaties in an effort to prevent application of the death penalty. The United States is party to international treaties which arguably bear on at least three aspects of death penalty administration: (1) extended incarceration on death row; (2) race discrimination; and (3) execution of foreign nationals. Perhaps because three of the treaties relied on were not ratified until the 1990s, the Supreme Court has yet to address the merits of any of the treaty claims, so what follows is only an outline of the claims and possible responses to the claims.

Extended Incarceration on Death Row

In 1992, the United States ratified the International Covenant on Civil and Political Rights ("ICCPR"). In 1994, the United States ratified the Convention Against Torture and Other Cruel, Inhuman or Degrading Treatment or Punishment ("Torture Convention"). Both treaties forbid the use of torture or "cruel, inhuman or degrading treatment or punishment." ICCPR, Article 7; Torture Convention, Articles 1, 16. In light of the *Soering* case [discussed in *Burns*] and other foreign cases, in particular, *Pratt v. Attorney General of Jamaica* [1994] 2 A.C.U.K. 1, 29 (delay of 14 years in execution was " 'inhuman or degrading punishment or other treatment' " forbidden by Jamaican Constitution unless "due entirely to the fault of the accused") and *Catholic Commission for Justice and Peace in Zimbabwe v. Attorney–General*, [1993] 1 Zimb. L.R. 239, 240 (delays in execution of five and six years are "inordinate" and constitute "torture or * * * inhuman or degrading punishment or other such treatment"), it has been argued that extended incarceration on death row is cruel, inhuman or degrading punishment under international law and, therefore, a violation of the ICCPR and the Torture Convention.

Even if extended incarceration on death row does violate a prisoner's rights under the two conventions, there are two problems with enforcing those rights in United States courts. First, in ratifying the ICCPR and the Torture Convention, the Senate made certain reservations. As to the ICCPR provision on torture, the reservation stated:

> The United States considers itself bound by Article 7 to the extent that "cruel, inhuman or degrading treatment or punishment" means the cruel and unusual treatment or punishment prohibited by the Fifth, Eighth or Fourteenth Amendments to the Constitution of the United States.

The Senate made a similar reservation to the Torture Convention and then went on to state the following "understanding":

[T]he United States understands that international law does not prohibit the death penalty, and does not consider this convention to restrict or prohibit the United States from applying the death penalty consistent with the Fifth, Eighth and/or Fourteenth Amendments to the Constitution of the United States, including any constitutional period of confinement prior to the imposition of the death penalty.

Whether the Senate's reservations and "understanding" have any force is open to question. The United Nations Human Rights Committee found the reservation to the ICCPR to be invalid because it was "incompatible with the object and purpose of the Covenant."[1]

Second, the Senate declared the treaties not to be "self-executing," thereby suggesting that legislation would be required to make the treaties enforceable. As is the case with the Senate's reservations, it is questionable whether the declaration is valid under international law. It also is questionable whether the declaration has any effect in domestic law since it may violate the doctrine of separation of powers both as an attempt to limit the president's treaty-making power and as an invasion of the province of the judiciary to "say what the law is." *Marbury v. Madison*, 5 U.S. (1 Cranch) 137, 177 (1803). Further, even if the treaty provisions are not self-executing, that fact would not necessarily bar the use of the treaties *defensively* by a criminal defendant. See C. Vasquez, *Treaty–Based Rights and Remedies of Individuals*, 92 Colum. L. Rev. 1082, 1143–1146 (1992). Nor, one might argue, would a death row prisoner be barred from relying on treaty rights in a federal habeas corpus proceeding since relief may be granted when the prisoner is "in custody in violation of the Constitution or laws or *treaties* of the United States." 28 U.S.C. § 2254(a). (emphasis added).

In *White v. Johnson*, 79 F.3d 432 (5th Cir. 1996), the Court of Appeals squarely rejected the petitioner's claim based on a violation of the ICCPR on the ground that, the defendant's conviction having become final before the United States ratified the treaties, defendant was seeking application of a "new rule" [see Chapter 11] and on the ground that the Senate reservations meant that the treaties had no broader coverage than the Eighth Amendment, which was not violated by delay in execution [see Chapter 12].

Race Discrimination

In 1994, the Senate ratified the International Convention on the Elimination of All Forms of Racial Discrimination (ICERD), which defines racial discrimination as: "any distinction, exclusion, restriction or preference based on race, color, descent, or national or ethnic origin which has the purpose or effect of nullifying or impairing the recognition, enjoyment or exercise, on an equal footing, of human rights and fundamental

---

1. *Consideration of reports submitted by states parties under article 40 of the Covenant, Comments of the Human Rights committee, United States*—Initial Report, UN Doc. CCPR/C/79/Add.50 (1995)

freedoms in the political, economic, social, cultural or any other field of public life" (Art. 1) and further provides:

Article 2

1. States Parties condemn racial discrimination and undertake to pursue by all appropriate means and without delay a policy of eliminating racial discrimination in all its forms and promoting understanding among all races, and, to this end:

(*a*) Each State Party undertakes to engage in no act or practice of racial discrimination against persons, groups of persons or institutions and to ensure that all public authorities and public institutions, national and local, shall act in conformity with this obligation;

(*b*) Each State Party undertakes not to sponsor, defend or support racial discrimination by any persons or organizations;

(*c*) Each State Party shall take effective measures to review governmental, national and local policies, and to amend, rescind or nullify any laws and regulations which have the effect of creating or perpetuating racial discrimination wherever it exists;

(*d*) Each State Party shall prohibit and bring to an end, by all appropriate means, including legislation as required by circumstances, racial discrimination by any persons, group or organization;

* * *

Because ICERD defines racial discrimination in terms of "effect" as well as "purpose" and commits the signatories to eliminating laws which have the "effect" of continuing racial discrimination, the treaty arguably overturns *McCleskey v. Kemp*, 481 U.S. 279, 107 S.Ct. 1756 (1987) [Chapter 3] and requires the courts to find invalid death penalty schemes which produce discriminatory effects. See International Commission of Jurists, Administration of the Death Penalty in the United States (1996) 58–60. The argument that the provisions are not self-executing may be stronger with regard to ICERD than with regard to the other treaties because the provisions of Article 2 are framed as directives to the state rather than as guaranties to the individual.

Execution of Foreign Nationals

While the other three treaties under discussion were only recently ratified by the United States, the United States has been a party to the Vienna Convention on Consular Relations, April 24, 1963, 21 U.S.T. 77, T.I.A.S. No. 6820, since 1969. The Convention provides that officials arresting a foreign national must inform the arrestee of his or her right to consult with the embassy of the arrestee's home country. 21 U.S.T. at 100–101. It appears that state officers routinely ignore this requirement. In recent years, defendants have attempted to assert the state's violation of the Convention as a basis for obtaining relief from a conviction and death sentence, but, in a series of cases, the Supreme Court has avoided ruling on the merits of their claims. In *Breard v. Greene*, 523 U.S. 371, 118

S.Ct. 1352 (1998), Angel Breard, a Paraguayan citizen who had been sentenced to death in Virginia, sought federal habeas corpus relief on the ground that his Vienna Convention rights had been violated. The Republic of Paraguay and Paraguayan officials also sued Virginia officials for the violation. In addition, Paraguay instituted proceedings in the International Court of Justice ("ICJ"), which noted jurisdiction and ordered the United States to "take all measures at its disposal to ensure that Angel Francisco Breard is not executed pending the final decision in these proceedings...." The District Court denied relief, and the Fourth Circuit affirmed. The Supreme Court held that Breard was not entitled to a stay and consideration of his petition because he had procedurally defaulted his claim by not raising it in state court. In addition, he would not be able to prove his claim because he had failed to develop the facts in state court, so, under AEDPA, he would not be entitled to an evidentiary hearing. The Court affirmed the dismissal of Paraguay's suit on several grounds, including that the Convention did not provide for a private right of action and that the suit was barred by the Eleventh Amendment. Following the decision, Breard was executed. A year later, the Federal Republic of Germany also sued the United States in the ICJ for violation, by Arizona, of the Vienna Convention and obtained an interim order directing the United States to take all measures to prevent the execution of two German citizens, Karl and Walter LaGrand. Germany then sought leave to bring an original action in the Supreme Court and sought a stay of execution. See *Federal Republic of Germany v. United States*, 526 U.S. 111, 119 S.Ct. 1016 (1999). The Court again denied relief, finding, *inter alia*, that the United States had not waived its immunity from suit and suit against Arizona was barred by the Eleventh Amendment, and the LaGrands were executed.

In 2003, Mexico sued the United States in the ICJ on behalf Mexican nationals on death rows in nine different states, alleging that those defendants had been deprived of their rights under the Vienna Convention, and, in its response, the United States conceded that its authorities had violated the Convention. See *Case Concerning Avena and other Mexican Nationals (Mexico v. United States of America)*, I.C.J. No. 128 (2004). On March 31, 2004, the court issued its judgment, finding that the rights of Mexican nationals on death rows had been violated, and ordering the United States to have its courts review and reconsider the convictions and sentences of the 51 Mexican nationals then on death rows. Shortly thereafter, Governor Brad Henry of Oklahoma, citing the court's decision, commuted the sentence Osbaldo Torres Aguilera, one of the defendants covered by the judgment. A. Liptak, *Execution of Mexican is Halted*, New York Times, May 14, 2004 at A23. By contrast, Texas Governor Rick Perry took the position that the international court did not have jurisdiction in his state and he would follow only Texas and U.S. law. L. Post, *Ruling in the Hague Undercuts Death Case*, 26 National Law Journal 31 at 1. On February 28, 2005, President George Bush issued a memorandum requiring state courts to give effect to the *Avena* decision, and, a week later, the

United States withdrew from the optional protocol giving the ICJ jurisdiction over the United States in disputes arising under the Vienna Convention. A. Liptak, *U.S. Says It Has Withdrawn From World Judicial Body*, New York Times, March 10, 2005 at A16. Meanwhile, the Supreme Court had granted certiorari in a case brought by Jose Medellin, one of the defendants covered by the *Avena* decision who was seeking enforcement of the ICJ judgement, but the Court ultimately dismissed the writ as improvidently granted. *Medellin v. Dretke*, 544 U.S. 660, 125 S.Ct. 2088 (2005). The majority based its decision on the fact that, relying on President Bush's order, Medellin had filed an application for a writ of habeas corpus in the Texas Court of Criminal Appeals and that he might obtain relief in that action, rendering federal court consideration unnecessary. The majority also noted the numerous difficult threshold questions the Court would have had to address—whether Medellin's claim was cognizable on habeas corpus; whether the state courts' ruling was "contrary to, or an unreasonable application of clearly established federal law" under AEDPA; whether Medellin sought the benefit of a "new rule"; and whether Medellin was entitled to a certificate of appealability under AEDPA—even to reach the merits of Medellin's claim.

Medellin's application for a writ of habeas corpus based on his Vienna Convention claim was dismissed by the Texas Court of Criminal Appeals as an abuse of the writ because he had failed to raise the claim in a timely manner. The Supreme Court granted certiorari and affirmed, holding: (1) the *Avena* decision is not directly enforceable as domestic law because the treaty sources concerning judgments of the IJC are not "self-executing" and Congress has enacted no legislation to enforce the Convention; and (2) President Bush's memorandum requiring the states to give effect to the *Avena* decision has no effect because the President cannot unilaterally make a non-self-executing treaty binding on domestic courts. *Medellin v. Texas*, ___ U.S. ___, 128 S.Ct. 1346 (2008).

CHAPTER 14

A BROKEN SYSTEM?

■ ■ ■

This chapter sets out Justice Blackmun's critique of the Supreme Court's death penalty jurisprudence in *Callins v. Collins* followed by Justice Scalia's response and then reports on the most extensive empirical study of the death penalty in operation in *The Frequency of Error in Capital Sentencing*.

CALLINS v. COLLINS

510 U.S. 1141, 114 S.Ct. 1127, 127 L.Ed.2d 435 (1994).

JUSTICE BLACKMUN, dissenting [from the denial of certiorari].

On February 23, 1994, at approximately 1:00 a.m., Bruce Edwin Callins will be executed by the State of Texas. Intravenous tubes attached to his arms will carry the instrument of death, a toxic fluid designed specifically for the purpose of killing human beings. The witnesses, standing a few feet away, will behold Callins, no longer a defendant, an appellant, or a petitioner, but a man, strapped to a gurney, and seconds away from extinction.

Within days, or perhaps hours, the memory of Callins will begin to fade. The wheels of justice will churn again, and somewhere, another jury or another judge will have the unenviable task of determining whether some human being is to live or die. We hope, of course, that the defendant whose life is at risk will be represented by competent counsel—someone who is inspired by the awareness that a less than vigorous defense truly could have fatal consequences for the defendant. We hope that the attorney will investigate all aspects of the case, follow all evidentiary and procedural rules, and appear before a judge who is still committed to the protection of defendants' rights—even now, as the prospect of meaningful judicial oversight has diminished. In the same vein, we hope that the prosecution, in urging the penalty of death, will have exercised its discretion wisely, free from bias, prejudice, or political motive, and will be humbled, rather than emboldened, by the awesome authority conferred by the State.

But even if we can feel confident that these actors will fulfill their roles to the best of their human ability, our collective conscience will remain uneasy. Twenty years have passed since this Court declared that the death penalty must be imposed fairly, and with reasonable consistency, or not at all, see *Furman v. Georgia*, 408 U.S. 238, 92 S.Ct. 2726 (1972), and, despite the effort of the States and courts to devise legal formulas and procedural rules to meet this daunting challenge, the death penalty remains fraught with arbitrariness, discrimination, caprice, and mistake. This is not to say that the problems with the death penalty today are identical to those that were present 20 years ago. Rather, the problems that were pursued down one hole with procedural rules and verbal formulas have come to the surface somewhere else, just as virulent and pernicious as they were in their original form. Experience has taught us that the constitutional goal of eliminating arbitrariness and discrimination from the administration of death, can never be achieved without compromising an equally essential component of fundamental fairness—individualized sentencing. See *Lockett v. Ohio*, 438 U.S. 586, 98 S.Ct. 2954 (1978).

It is tempting, when faced with conflicting constitutional commands, to sacrifice one for the other or to assume that an acceptable balance between them already has been struck. In the context of the death penalty, however, such jurisprudential maneuvers are wholly inappropriate. The death penalty must be imposed "fairly, and with reasonable consistency, or not at all." *Eddings v. Oklahoma*, 455 U.S. 104, 102 S.Ct. 869 (1982).

To be fair, a capital sentencing scheme must treat each person convicted of a capital offense with that "degree of respect due the uniqueness of the individual." *Lockett v. Ohio* (plurality opinion). That means affording the sentencer the power and discretion to grant mercy in a particular case, and providing avenues for the consideration of any and all relevant mitigating evidence that would justify a sentence less than death. Reasonable consistency, on the other hand, requires that the death penalty be inflicted evenhandedly, in accordance with reason and objective standards, rather than by whim, caprice, or prejudice. Finally, because human error is inevitable, and because our criminal justice system is less than perfect, searching appellate review of death sentences and their underlying convictions is a prerequisite to a constitutional death penalty scheme.

On their face, these goals of individual fairness, reasonable consistency, and absence of error appear to be attainable: Courts are in the very business of erecting procedural devices from which fair, equitable, and reliable outcomes are presumed to flow. Yet, in the death penalty area, this Court, in my view, has engaged in a futile effort to balance these constitutional demands, and now is retreating not only from the *Furman* promise of consistency and rationality, but from the requirement of individualized sentencing as well. Having virtually conceded that both fairness and rationality cannot be achieved in the administration of the death penalty, see *McCleskey v. Kemp*, 481 U.S. 279, 107 S.Ct. 1756 (1987), the Court has chosen to deregulate the entire enterprise, replacing, it would seem, substantive constitutional requirements with mere esthetics, and abdicating its statutorily and constitutionally imposed duty to provide meaningful judicial oversight to the administration of death by the States.

From this day forward, I no longer shall tinker with the machinery of death. For more than 20 years I have endeavored—indeed, I have struggled—along with a majority of this Court, to develop procedural and substantive rules that would lend more than the mere appearance of fairness to the death penalty endeavor. Rather than continue to coddle the Court's delusion that the desired level of fairness has been achieved and the need for regulation eviscerated, I feel morally and intellectually obligated simply to concede that the death penalty experiment has failed. It is virtually self-evident to me now that no combination of procedural rules or substantive regulations ever can save the death penalty from its inherent constitutional deficiencies. The basic question—does the system accurately and consistently determine which defendants "deserve" to die?—cannot be answered in the affirmative. It is not simply that this Court has allowed vague aggravating circumstances to be employed, see, *e.g., Arave v. Creech,* 507 U.S. 463, 113 S.Ct. 1534 (1993), relevant mitigating evidence to be disregarded, see, *e.g., Johnson v. Texas,* 509 U.S. 350, 113 S.Ct. 2658 (1993), and vital judicial review to be blocked, see, *e.g., Coleman v. Thompson,* 501 U.S. 722, 111 S.Ct. 2546 (1991). The problem is that the inevitability of factual, legal, and moral error gives us a system that we know must wrongly kill some defendants, a system that fails to deliver the fair, consistent, and reliable sentences of death required by the Constitution.

I

In 1971, in an opinion which has proved partly prophetic, the second Justice Harlan, writing for the Court, observed:

> "Those who have come to grips with the hard task of actually attempting to draft means of channeling capital sentencing discretion have confirmed the lesson taught by the history recounted above. To identify before the fact those characteristics of criminal homicides and their perpetrators which call for the death penalty, and to express these characteristics in language which can be fairly understood and applied by the sentencing authority, appear to be tasks which are beyond present human ability.... For a court to attempt to catalog the appropriate factors in this elusive area could inhibit rather than expand the scope of consideration, for no list of circumstances would ever be really complete." *McGautha v. California,* 402 U.S. 183, 91 S.Ct. 1454 (1971)

In *McGautha,* the petitioner argued that a statute which left the penalty of death entirely in the jury's discretion, without any standards to govern its imposition, violated the Fourteenth Amendment. Although the Court did not deny that serious risks were associated with a sentencer's unbounded discretion, the Court found no remedy in the Constitution for the inevitable failings of human judgment.

A year later, the Court reversed its course completely in *Furman v. Georgia*, 408 U.S. 238, 92 S.Ct. 2726 (1972) (per curiam, with each of the nine Justices writing separately). The concurring Justices argued that the glaring inequities in the administration of death, the standardless discretion wielded by judges and juries, and the pervasive racial and economic discrimination rendered the death penalty, at least as administered, "cruel and unusual" within the meaning of the Eighth Amendment. * * *

I dissented in *Furman*. Despite my intellectual, moral, and personal objections to the death penalty, I refrained from joining the majority because I found objectionable the Court's abrupt change of position in the single year that had passed since *McGautha*. While I agreed that the Eighth Amendment's prohibition against cruel and unusual punishments " 'may acquire meaning as public opinion becomes enlightened by a humane justice,' " quoting *Weems v. United States*, 217 U.S. 349, 30 S.Ct. 544 (1910), I objected to the "suddenness of the Court's perception of progress in the human attitude since decisions of only a short while ago." Four years after *Furman* was decided, I concurred in the judgment in *Gregg v. Georgia*, 428 U.S. 153, 96 S.Ct. 2909 (1976), and its companion cases which upheld death sentences rendered under statutes passed after *Furman* was decided.

A

There is little doubt now that *Furman*'s essential holding was correct. Although most of the public seems to desire, and the Constitution appears to permit, the penalty of death, it surely is beyond dispute that if the death penalty cannot be administered consistently and rationally, it may not be administered at all. *Eddings v. Oklahoma*. I never have quarreled with this principle; in my mind, the real meaning of *Furman*'s diverse concurring opinions did not emerge until some years after *Furman* was decided. See *Gregg v. Georgia*, (opinion of STEWART, POWELL, and STEVENS, JJ.) ("*Furman* mandates that where discretion is afforded a sentencing body on a matter so grave as the determination of whether a human life should be taken or spared, that discretion must be suitably directed and limited so as to minimize the risk of wholly arbitrary and capricious action"). Since *Gregg*, I faithfully have adhered to the *Furman* holding and have come to believe that it is indispensable to the Court's Eighth Amendment jurisprudence.

Delivering on the *Furman* promise, however, has proved to be another matter. *Furman* aspired to eliminate the vestiges of racism and the effects of poverty in capital sentencing; it deplored the "wanton" and "random" infliction of death by a government with constitutionally limited power. *Furman* demanded that the sentencer's discretion be directed and limited by procedural rules and objective standards in order to minimize the risk of arbitrary and capricious sentences of death.

In the years following *Furman*, serious efforts were made to comply with its mandate. State legislatures and appellate courts struggled to provide judges and juries with sensible and objective guidelines for determining who should live and who should die. Some States attempted to define who is "deserving" of the death penalty through the use of carefully chosen adjectives, reserving the death penalty for those who commit crimes that are "especially heinous, atrocious, or cruel" [Florida], or "wantonly vile, horrible or inhuman" [Georgia]. Other States enacted mandatory death penalty statutes, reading *Furman* as an invitation to eliminate sentencer discretion altogether [North Carolina]. Still other States specified aggravating and mitigating factors that were to be considered by the sentencer and weighed against one another in a calculated and rational manner [Georgia, Texas].

Unfortunately, all this experimentation and ingenuity yielded little of what *Furman* demanded. It soon became apparent that discretion could not be eliminated from capital sentencing without threatening the fundamental fairness due a defendant when life is at stake. Just as contemporary society was no longer tolerant of the random or discriminatory infliction of the penalty of death, see *Furman, supra,* evolving standards of decency required due consideration of the uniqueness of each individual defendant when imposing society's ultimate penalty.

This development in the American conscience would have presented no constitutional dilemma if fairness to the individual could be achieved without sacrificing the consistency and rationality promised in *Furman*. But over the past two decades, efforts to balance these competing constitutional commands have been to no avail. Experience has shown that the consistency and rationality promised in *Furman* are inversely related to the fairness owed the individual when considering a sentence of death. A step toward consistency is a step away from fairness.

B

There is a heightened need for fairness in the administration of death. This unique level of fairness is born of the appreciation that death truly is different from all other punishments a society inflicts upon its citizens. "Death, in its finality, differs more from life imprisonment than a 100–year prison term differs from one of only a year or two." *Woodson v. North Carolina,* 428 U.S. 280, 96 S.Ct. 2978 (1976) (opinion of STEWART, POWELL, and STEVENS, JJ.). Because of the qualitative difference of the death penalty, "there is a corresponding difference in the need for reliability in the determination that death is the appropriate punishment in a specific case." In *Woodson,* a decision striking down mandatory death penalty statutes as unconstitutional, a plurality of the Court explained: "A process that accords no significance to relevant facets of the character and record of the individual offender or the circumstances of the particular offense excludes from consideration in fixing the ultimate punishment of death the possibility of compassionate or mitigating factors stemming from the diverse frailties of humankind."

* * *

The Court elaborated on the principle of individualized sentencing in *Lockett v. Ohio*, 438 U.S. 586, 98 S.Ct. 2954 (1978). In that case, a plurality acknowledged that strict restraints on sentencer discretion are necessary to achieve the consistency and rationality promised in *Furman*, but held that, in the end, the sentencer must retain unbridled discretion to afford mercy. Any process or procedure that prevents the sentencer from considering *"as a mitigating factor*, any aspect of a defendant's character or record and any of the circumstances of the offense that the defendant proffers as a basis for a sentence less than death" creates the constitutionally intolerable risk that "the death penalty will be imposed in spite of factors which may call for a less severe penalty." (emphasis in original). The Court's duty under the Constitution therefore is to "develop a system of capital punishment at once consistent and principled but also humane and sensible to the uniqueness of the individual." *Eddings v. Oklahoma.*

C

I believe the *Woodson–Lockett* line of cases to be fundamentally sound and rooted in American standards of decency that have evolved over time. The notion of prohibiting a sentencer from exercising its discretion "to dispense mercy on the basis of factors too intangible to write into a statute," is offensive to our sense of fundamental fairness and respect for the uniqueness of the individual. * * *

Yet, as several Members of the Court have recognized, there is real "tension" between the need for fairness to the individual and the consistency promised in *Furman*. On the one hand, discretion in capital sentencing must be " 'controlled by clear and objective standards so as to produce non-discriminatory [and reasoned] application.' " *Gregg* (opinion of STEWART, POWELL, and STEVENS, JJ.), quoting *Coley v. State*, 204 S.E.2d 612 (Ga. 1974). On the other hand, the Constitution also requires that the sentencer be able to consider "any relevant mitigating evidence regarding the defendant's character or background, and the circumstances of the particular offense." *California v. Brown*, 479 U.S. 538, 107 S.Ct. 837 (1987) (O'CONNOR, J., concurring). The power to consider mitigating evidence that would warrant a sentence less than death is meaningless unless the sentencer has the discretion and authority to dispense mercy based on that evidence. Thus, the Constitution, by requiring a heightened degree of fairness to the individual, and also a greater degree of equality and rationality in the administration of death, demands sentencer discretion that is at once generously expanded and severely restricted.

This dilemma was laid bare in *Penry v. Lynaugh*, 492 U.S. 302, 109 S.Ct. 2934 (1989). The defendant in *Penry* challenged the Texas death penalty statute, arguing that it failed to allow the sentencing jury to give full mitigating effect to his evidence of mental retardation and history of child abuse. The Texas statute required the jury, during the penalty phase, to answer three "special issues"; if the jury unanimously answered "yes" to each issue, the trial court was obligated to sentence the defendant to death. Only one of the three issues—whether the defendant posed a "continuing threat to society"—was related to the evidence Penry offered in mitigation. But Penry's evidence of mental retardation and child abuse was a two-edged sword as it related to that special issue: "[I]t diminish[ed] his blameworthiness for his crime even as it indicate[d] that there [was] a probability that he [would] be dangerous in the future." The Court therefore reversed Penry's death sentence, explaining that a reasonable juror could have believed that the statute prohibited a sentence less than death based upon his mitigating evidence.

After *Penry*, the paradox underlying the Court's post-*Furman* jurisprudence was undeniable. Texas had complied with *Furman* by severely limiting the sentencer's discretion, but those very limitations rendered Penry's death sentence unconstitutional.

D

The theory underlying *Penry* and *Lockett* is that an appropriate balance can be struck between the *Furman* promise of consistency and the *Lockett* requirement of individualized sentencing if the death penalty is conceptualized as consisting of two distinct stages. In the first stage of capital sentencing, the demands of *Furman* are met by "narrowing" the class of death-eligible offenders according to objective, fact-bound characteristics of the defendant or the circumstances of the offense. Once the pool of death-eligible defendants has been reduced, the sentencer retains the discretion to consider whatever relevant mitigating evidence the defendant chooses to offer.

Over time, I have come to conclude that even this approach is unacceptable: It simply reduces, rather than eliminates, the number of people subject to arbitrary sentencing.[4] It is the decision to sentence a defendant to death—not merely the decision to make a defendant eligible for death—that may not be arbitrary. While one might hope that providing the sentencer with as much relevant mitigating evidence as possible will lead to more rational and consistent sentences, experience has taught otherwise. It seems that the decision whether a human being should live or die is so inherently subjective—rife with all of life's understandings, experiences, prejudices, and passions—that it inevitably defies the rationality and consistency required by the Constitution.

E

The arbitrariness inherent in the sentencer's discretion to afford mercy is exacerbated by the problem of race. Even under the most sophisticated death penalty statutes, race continues to play a major role in determining who shall live and who shall die. Perhaps it should not be surprising that the biases and prejudices that infect society generally would influence the determination of who is sentenced to death, even

---

4. The narrowing of death-eligible defendants into a smaller subgroup coupled with the unbridled discretion to pick among them arguably emphasizes rather than ameliorates the inherent arbitrariness of the death penalty.

within the narrower pool of death-eligible defendants selected according to objective standards. No matter how narrowly the pool of death-eligible defendants is drawn according to objective standards, *Furman*'s promise still will go unfulfilled so long as the sentencer is free to exercise unbridled discretion within the smaller group and thereby to discriminate. " '[T]he power to be lenient [also] is the power to discriminate.' " *McCleskey v. Kemp*, quoting K. Davis, *Discretionary Justice* (1973).

A renowned example of racism infecting a capital sentencing scheme is documented in *McCleskey v. Kemp*. Warren McCleskey, an African–American, argued that the Georgia capital sentencing scheme was administered in a racially discriminatory manner, in violation of the Eighth and Fourteenth Amendments. In support of his claim, he proffered a highly reliable statistical study (the Baldus study) which indicated that, "after taking into account some 230 nonracial factors that might legitimately influence a sentencer, the jury *more likely than not* would have spared McCleskey's life had his victim been black." (emphasis in original) (Brennan, J., dissenting). The Baldus study further demonstrated that blacks who kill whites are sentenced to death "at nearly *22 times* the rate of blacks who kill blacks, and more than *7 times* the rate of whites who kill blacks." (emphasis in original).

Despite this staggering evidence of racial prejudice infecting Georgia's capital sentencing scheme, the majority turned its back on McCleskey's claims, apparently troubled by the fact that Georgia had instituted more procedural and substantive safeguards than most other States since *Furman*, but was still unable to stamp out the virus of racism. Faced with the apparent failure of traditional legal devices to cure the evils identified in *Furman*, the majority wondered aloud whether the consistency and rationality demanded by the dissent could ever be achieved without sacrificing the discretion which is essential to fair treatment of individual defendants:

> "[I]t is difficult to imagine guidelines that would produce the predictability sought by the dissent without sacrificing the discretion essential to a humane and fair system of criminal justice.... The dissent repeatedly emphasizes the need for 'a uniquely high degree of rationality in imposing the death penalty'.... Again, no suggestion is made as to how greater 'rationality' could be achieved under any type of statute that authorizes capital punishment.... Given these safeguards already inherent in the imposition and review of capital sentences, the dissent's call for greater rationality is no less than a claim that a capital punishment system cannot be administered in accord with the Constitution."

I joined most of Justice Brennan's significant dissent which expounded McCleskey's Eighth Amendment claim, and I wrote separately to explain that McCleskey also had a solid equal protection argument under the Fourteenth Amendment. I still adhere to the views set forth in both dissents, and, as far as I know, there has been no serious effort to impeach the Baldus study. Nor, for that matter, have proponents of capital punishment provided any reason to believe that the findings of that study are unique to Georgia.

The fact that we may not be capable of devising procedural or substantive rules to prevent the more subtle and often unconscious forms of racism from creeping into the system does not justify the wholesale abandonment of the *Furman* promise. To the contrary, where a morally irrelevant—indeed, a repugnant—consideration plays a major role in the determination of who shall live and who shall die, it suggests that the continued enforcement of the death penalty in light of its clear and admitted defects is deserving of a "sober second thought." * * *

F

In the years since *McCleskey*, I have come to wonder whether there was truth in the majority's suggestion that discrimination and arbitrariness could not be purged from the administration of capital punishment without sacrificing the equally essential component of fairness—individualized sentencing. Viewed in this way, the consistency promised in *Furman* and the fairness to the individual demanded in *Lockett* are not only inversely related, but irreconcilable in the context of capital punishment. Any statute or procedure that could effectively eliminate arbitrariness from the administration of death would also restrict the sentencer's discretion to such an extent that the sentencer would be unable to give full consideration to the unique characteristics of each defendant and the circumstances of the offense. By the same token, any statute or procedure that would provide the sentencer with sufficient discretion to consider fully and act upon the unique circumstances of each defendant would "thro[w] open the back door to arbitrary and irrational sentencing." *Graham v. Collins*, 506 U.S. 461, 113 S.Ct. 892 (1993) (THOMAS, J., concurring). All efforts to strike an appropriate balance between these conflicting constitutional commands are futile because there is a heightened need for both in the administration of death.

But even if the constitutional requirements of consistency and fairness are theoretically reconcilable in the context of capital punishment, it is clear that this Court is not prepared to meet the challenge. In apparent frustration over its inability to strike an appropriate balance between the *Furman* promise of consistency and the *Lockett* requirement of individualized sentencing, the Court has retreated from the field, allowing relevant mitigating evidence to be discarded,[6] vague aggravating circumstances to

---

6. See *Johnson v. Texas*, 509 U.S. 350, 113 S.Ct. 2658 (1993) (affirming death sentence even though the jurors were not allowed to give full mitigating effect to the defendant's youth under the Texas death penalty statute); *Graham v. Collins*, 506 U.S. 461, 113 S.Ct. 892 (1993). See also *Saffle v. Parks*, 494 U.S. 484, 110 S.Ct. 1257 (1990) (upholding death sentence where jurors were instructed to avoid "any influence of sympathy," because the claim was raised on federal habeas and a ruling for the petitioner would constitute a "new rule" of constitutional law); *Boyde v. California*, 494 U.S. 370, 110 S.Ct. 1190 (1990) (upholding death sentence where jurors reasonably may have believed that they could not consider the defendant's mitigating evidence regarding his character and background); *Walton v. Arizona*, 497 U.S. 639, 110 S.Ct. 3047 (1990) (affirming placement upon the defendant of the burden to establish mitigating circumstances sufficient to call for leniency).

be employed,[7] and providing no indication that the problem of race in the administration of death will ever be addressed. In fact some Members of the Court openly have acknowledged a willingness simply to pick one of the competing constitutional commands and sacrifice the other. See *Graham* (THOMAS, J., concurring) (calling for the reversal of *Penry*); *Walton v. Arizona*, 497 U.S. 639, 110 S.Ct. 3047 (1990) (SCALIA, J., concurring in part and concurring in judgment) (announcing that he will no longer enforce the requirement of individualized sentencing, and reasoning that either *Furman* or *Lockett* is wrong and a choice must be made between the two). These developments are troubling, as they ensure that death will continue to be meted out in this country arbitrarily and discriminatorily, and without that "degree of respect due the uniqueness of the individual." *Lockett*. In my view, the proper course when faced with irreconcilable constitutional commands is not to ignore one or the other, nor to pretend that the dilemma does not exist, but to admit the futility of the effort to harmonize them. This means accepting the fact that the death penalty cannot be administered in accord with our Constitution.

II

My belief that this Court would not enforce the death penalty (even if it could) in accordance with the Constitution is buttressed by the Court's "obvious eagerness to do away with any restriction on the States' power to execute whomever and however they please." *Herrera v. Collins*, 506 U.S. 390, 113 S.Ct. 853 (1993) (BLACKMUN, J., dissenting). I have explained at length on numerous occasions that my willingness to enforce the capital punishment statutes enacted by the States and the Federal Government, "notwithstanding my own deep moral reservations ... has always rested on an understanding that certain procedural safeguards, chief among them the Federal Judiciary's power to reach and correct claims of constitutional error on federal habeas review, would ensure that death sentences are fairly imposed." *Sawyer v. Whitley*, 505 U.S. 333, 112 S.Ct. 2514 (1992) (BLACKMUN, J., concurring in judgment). In recent years, I have grown increasingly skeptical that "the death penalty really can be imposed fairly and in accordance with the requirements of the Eighth Amendment," given the now limited ability of the federal courts to remedy constitutional errors. *Sawyer* (BLACKMUN, J., concurring in judgment).

* * *

The Court has also refused to hold the death penalty unconstitutional *per se* for juveniles, see *Stanford v. Kentucky*, 492 U.S. 361, 109 S.Ct. 2969 (1989), and the mentally retarded, see *Penry v. Lynaugh*, 492 U.S. 302, 109 S.Ct. 2934 (1989).

7. See *Arave v. Creech*, 507 U.S. 463, 113 S.Ct. 1534 (1993) (holding that an Idaho statute, as interpreted by the Idaho Supreme Court, which authorizes the death penalty for those murderers who have displayed "utter disregard for human life," genuinely narrows the class of death-eligible defendants); *Lewis v. Jeffers*, 497 U.S. 764, 110 S.Ct. 3092 (1990) (affirming lenient standard for the review of the constitutional adequacy of aggravating circumstances).

III

Perhaps one day this Court will develop procedural rules or verbal formulas that actually will provide consistency, fairness, and reliability in a capital sentencing scheme. I am not optimistic that such a day will come. I am more optimistic, though, that this Court eventually will conclude that the effort to eliminate arbitrariness while preserving fairness "in the infliction of [death] is so plainly doomed to failure that it—and the death penalty—must be abandoned altogether." *Godfrey v. Georgia*, 446 U.S. 420, 100 S.Ct. 1759 (1980) (MARSHALL, J., concurring in judgment). I may not live to see that day, but I have faith that eventually it will arrive. The path the Court has chosen lessens us all. I dissent.

JUSTICE SCALIA, concurring.

Justice BLACKMUN dissents from the denial of certiorari in this case with a statement explaining why the death penalty "as currently administered" is contrary to the Constitution of the United States. That explanation often refers to "intellectual, moral and personal" perceptions, but never to the text and tradition of the Constitution. It is the latter rather than the former that ought to control. The Fifth Amendment provides that "[n]o person shall be held to answer for a capital . . . crime, unless on a presentment or indictment of a Grand Jury, . . . nor be deprived of life, . . . without due process of law." This clearly permits the death penalty to be imposed, and establishes beyond doubt that the death penalty is not one of the "cruel and unusual punishments" prohibited by the Eighth Amendment.

As Justice BLACKMUN describes, however, over the years since 1972 this Court has attached to the imposition of the death penalty two quite incompatible sets of commands: The sentencer's discretion to impose death must be closely confined, see *Furman v. Georgia,* 408 U.S. 238, 92 S.Ct. 2726 (1972) (*per curiam*), but the sentencer's discretion *not* to impose death (to extend mercy) must be unlimited, see *Eddings v. Oklahoma,* 455 U.S. 104, 102 S.Ct. 869 (1982); *Lockett v. Ohio,* 438 U.S. 586, 98 S.Ct. 2954 (1978) (plurality opinion). These commands were invented without benefit of any textual or historical support; they are the product of just such "intellectual, moral, and personal" perceptions as Justice BLACKMUN expresses today, some of which (viz., those that have been "perceived" simultaneously by five Members of the Court) have been made part of what is called "the Court's Eighth Amendment jurisprudence."

Though Justice BLACKMUN joins those of us who have acknowledged the incompatibility of the Court's *Furman* and *Lockett–Eddings* lines of jurisprudence, he unfortunately draws the wrong conclusion from the acknowledgment. He says:

"[T]he proper course when faced with irreconcilable constitutional commands is not to ignore one or the other, nor to pretend that the dilemma does not exist, but to admit the futility of the effort to harmonize them. This means accepting the fact that the death penalty cannot be administered in accord with our Constitution."

Surely a different conclusion commends itself—to wit, that at least one of these judicially announced irreconcilable commands which cause the Constitution to prohibit what its text explicitly permits must be wrong.

Convictions in opposition to the death penalty are often passionate and deeply held. That would be no excuse for reading them into a Constitution that does not contain them, even if they represented the convictions of a majority of Americans. Much less is there any excuse for using that course to thrust a minority's views upon the people. Justice BLACKMUN begins his statement by describing with poignancy the death of a convicted murderer by lethal injection. He chooses, as the case in which to make that statement, one of the less brutal of the murders that regularly come before us—the murder of a man ripped by a bullet suddenly and unexpectedly, with no opportunity to prepare himself and his affairs, and left to bleed to death on the floor of a tavern. The death-by-injection which Justice BLACKMUN describes looks pretty desirable next to that. It looks even better next to some of the other cases currently before us which Justice BLACKMUN did not select as the vehicle for his announcement that the death penalty is always unconstitutional—for example, the case of the 11–year–old girl raped by four men and then killed by stuffing her panties down her throat. How enviable a quiet death by lethal injection compared with that! If the people conclude that such more brutal deaths may be deterred by capital punishment; indeed, if they merely conclude that justice requires such brutal deaths to be avenged by capital punishment; the creation of false, untextual, and unhistorical contradictions within "the Court's Eighth Amendment jurisprudence" should not prevent them.

THE FREQUENCY OF ERROR IN CAPITAL SENTENCING

Even the death penalty's strongest supporters concede that innocent people have been sentenced to death in the United States and that innocent people probably have been executed. Although there is no agreement as to how many such wrongful executions have occurred,[1] in the period 1972–2009, 135 death row inmates were exonerated.[2] Since there were 1160 executions during the same period,[3] approximately 10% of the cases that were finally concluded were wrongly decided on the facts. The frequency of exonerations varies dramatically among death penalty juris-

---

1. See, *e.g.*, M. Radelet, H. Bedau & C. Putnam, In Spite of Innocence (1992); but see S. Markman & P. Cassell, *Protecting the Innocent: A Response to the Bedeau–Radelet Study*, 41 Stan. L. Rev. 121 (1988).

2. Death Penalty Information Center, http://www.deathpenaltyinfo.org/documents/FactSheet. pdf.

3. *Id.*

dictions. Florida and Illinois between them account for more than 30% of the total number of exonerations.[4]

Another measure of capital sentencing error is how often, when a capital sentence is set aside, there is a different result upon reconsideration in the trial court. In 2000, researchers at Columbia University reported on their study of all death penalty cases completed during the 23–year period 1973–1995.[5] They determined that state reviewing courts found prejudicial error and set aside death judgments in 47% of the cases during the period, and in 82% of the cases where a death judgment was set aside, the defendant was not sentenced to death on remand. In sum, the state courts themselves ultimately determined that in almost 40% of the cases where a defendant was sentenced to death, capital punishment was not appropriate.

The researchers also found:

- Nationally, during the 23–year study period, federal courts set aside death judgments in 40% of the cases that had survived state court review, so that, combining the results of state court and federal court review, 68% of the death judgments were set aside.

- The most common errors requiring reversal were: (1) ineffective representation by defense lawyers and (2) suppression of material evidence by the police or prosecutors.

- By the end of the study period, the average time from death sentence to execution was 10.6 years.

The researchers concluded that the system was broken, that operating an extensive system of judicial review, warehousing the prisoners on death row in the meantime and having to try two out of three cases again was irrational: "This much error, and the time needed to cure it, impose terrible costs on taxpayers, victims' families, the judicial system, and the wrongly condemned. And it renders unattainable the finality, retribution and deterrence that are the reasons usually given for having a death penalty."

Why is there so much error? The Columbia researchers suggested some answers to that question in Part II of their study.[6] The researchers' principal findings were:

- The higher the rate at which a state or county imposes death verdicts, the greater the probability that *each* death verdict will have to be reversed because of serious error.

- In particular, the more often states impose death sentences in cases that are not highly aggravated, the higher the risk of serious error.

---

4. *Id.*

5. J. Liebman, J. Fagan & V. West, *A Broken System: Error Rates in Capital Cases, 1973–1995*, http://justice.policy.net/jpreport/liebman2.pdf (2000).

6. J. Liebman, J. Fagan, A. Gelman, V. West, G. Davies & A. Kiss, *A Broken System, Part II: Why There Is So Much Error in Capital Cases, and What Can Be Done About It*, http://www.law.columbia.edu/brokensystem2/ (2002).

- Comparisons of particular counties' and states' capital-sentencing and capital-error rates illustrate the strong relationship between frequent death sentencing and error.

- The higher the proportion of African–Americans in a state—and in one analysis, the more welfare recipients in a state—the higher the rate of serious capital error.

- The lower the rate at which states apprehend, convict and imprison serious criminals, the higher their capital error rates.

- The more often and directly state trial judges are subject to popular election, and the more partisan those elections are, the higher the state's rate of serious capital error.

They summarized their findings as follows:

> The lower the rate at which a state imposes death sentences—and the more it confines those verdicts to the worst of the worst—the less likely it is that serious error will be found. The fewer death verdicts a state imposes, the less overburdened its capital appeal system is, and the more likely it is to carry out the verdicts it imposes. The more often states succumb to pressures to inflict capital sentences in marginal cases, the higher is the risk of error and delay, the lower is the chance verdicts will be carried out, and the greater is the temptation to approve flawed verdicts on appeal. Among the disturbing sources of pressure to overuse the death penalty are political pressures on elected judges, well-founded doubts about the state's ability to convict serious criminals, and the race of the state's residents and homicide victims.

NOTES

1. *Constitutional implications of exonerations.*

Does the number of exonerations call into question the constitutionality of the death penalty? In *Kansas v. Marsh* [Chapter 4], Justice Souter, writing for the four dissenters, cited the "repeated exonerations of convicts under death sentences, in numbers never imagined before the development of DNA tests" in support of his argument that the risk of error was too great to permit the state to mandate death when the evidence for and against death was in equipoise. 543 U.S. at 207–211; 126 S.Ct. at 2544–2546. Justice Scalia responded: (1) that the dissent had failed to cite a single case of the execution of an innocent person and that studies purporting to identify such cases have been criticized and, in any event, largely discuss cases from an earlier era; (2) that the number of "exonerations" cited by the dissenters is inflated; and (3) that, with regard to the punishment of death, the possibility of mistake "has been reduced to an insignificant minimum." 543 U.S. at 188–199; 126 S.Ct. at 2533–2539 (concurring opinion).

One district court relied on the number of exonerations to hold the Federal Death Penalty Act unconstitutional. In *United States v. Quinones*, 196 F.Supp.2d 416 (S.D.N.Y. 2002) and 205 F.Supp.2d 256 (S.D.N.Y. 2002), the court held the Act was unconstitutional on substantive and procedural due process grounds because of the frequency with which innocent people are sentenced to death:

> In brief, the Court [finds] that the best available evidence indicates that, on the one hand, innocent people are sentenced to death with materially greater frequency than was previously supposed and that, on the other hand, convincing proof of their innocence often does not emerge until long after their convictions. It is therefore fully foreseeable that in enforcing the death penalty a meaningful number of innocent people will be executed who otherwise would eventually be able to prove their innocence. It follows that implementation of the Federal Death Penalty Act not only deprives innocent people of a significant opportunity to prove their innocence, and thereby violates procedural due process, but also creates an undue risk of executing innocent people, and thereby violates substantive due process.

205 F.Supp.2d at 257. The decision was reversed on appeal on the ground that the Supreme Court has long been aware of the argument that innocents were being executed and had never found the death penalty unconstitutional for that reason. *United States v. Quinones*, 313 F.3d 49 (2nd Cir. 2002). Would the challenge be more persuasive against a death penalty scheme in a state, *e.g.*, Illinois or Florida, with an unusually high percentage of exonerations?

   2.   *Reexamination and recommendations for reform.*

   In recent years, a number of state-appointed and non-governmental commissions have reexamined the death penalty. In two states—New Jersey and Maryland—the state-appointed commissions recommended abolition of the death penalty, a recommendation followed in New Jersey.[a] Other state-appointed commissions have recommended substantial reforms.[b] During the period 2004–2007, the American Bar Association Death Penalty Implementation Project conducted assessments in eight states and recommended various reforms after concluding that "serious problems were found in every state death penalty system."[c] Recommendations for reform have come from other sources as well.[d] In general, such recommendations have focused on narrowing the category of death-eligible crimes, providing competent and adequately compensated defense counsel, limiting prosecutorial discretion to seek the death penalty and providing for more searching review of death judgments.

---

   a.   See *New Jersey Death Penalty Study Commission Report* (2007), http://www.njleg.state.nj.us/committees/dpsc_final.pdf; *Maryland Commission on Capital Punishment Final Report to the General Assembly* (2008), http://www.goccp.maryland.gov/capital-punishment/documents/death-penalty-commission-final-report.pdf.

   b.   See, *e.g., Report of the Governor's Commission on Capital Punishment (Illinois)* (2002), available at http://www.idoc.state.il.us/ccp/ccp/reports/commission_report/; *California Commission on the Fair Administration of Justice Report and Recommendations on the Administration of the Death Penalty in California* (2008), http://www.ccfaj.org/documents/reports/dp/official/FINAL%20REPORT%20DEATH%20PENALTY.pdf.

   c.   *State Death Penalty Assessments: Key Findings* (2008), http://www.abanet.org/moratorium/assessmentproject/keyfindings.doc.

   d.   See, *e.g.*, The Constitution Project, *Mandatory Justice–Eighteen Reforms to the Death Penalty* (2001).

3. A "model" death penalty scheme.

Perhaps the most ambitious set of reform recommendations is contained in the report of Massachusetts' Council on Capital Punishment, issued as a result of Governor Mitt Romney's call to reintroduce the death penalty in Massachusetts.[e] The report sets out ten recommendations to create a death penalty scheme "as narrow, and as foolproof, as possible." The recommendations may be summarized as follows:

(1) a narrow definition of capital murder: premeditated murder with one of the following additional elements:

(a) the murder was committed as an act of political terrorism; (b) the murder was committed to interfere with the criminal justice system (*e.g.*, killing of an officer, official or witness); (c) the defendant intentionally tortured the victim; (d) the defendant committed multiple murders; (e) the defendant had a previous conviction of first degree murder; (f) the defendant committed the murder while under a sentence of life without possibility of parole;

(2) controls over prosecutorial discretion: (a) requiring the District Attorneys' Association to develop a uniform set of protocols for charging capital cases; and (b) requiring the Attorney General to review all capital charges under a set of protocols developed for that review;

(3) rigorous standards developed by the Supreme Judicial Court for capital defense attorneys; requiring: each attorney to have had substantial experience and training; two attorneys for the defense at trial; and appointed counsel for all post-conviction proceedings;

(4) a defendant's right, after conviction of murder, to elect to have a new jury for the sentencing hearing;

(5) special jury instructions, at both phases of the trial, concerning the use of human evidence to establish the defendant's guilt, warning the jury of the possible unreliability of: (a) eyewitness identification; (b) cross-racial identifications; (c) statements made by a defendant in police custody, particularly if the statement is not recorded; (d) statements made by co-defendants and informants;

(6) a requirement, at the penalty phase, that there be conclusive scientific evidence that corroborates the defendant's guilt;

(7) a heightened burden of proof as to guilt for imposition of the death penalty: "beyond all doubt";

(8) independent scientific review of all scientific evidence;

(9) broad authority for the trial court or Supreme Judicial Court to set aside a death sentence for errors of law or fact or "for any other reason that justice may require";

(10) the creation of an executive branch death-penalty review commission to review a defendant's claims of substantive error and to study the causes of such error.

Would adopting these recommendations solve the present problems with the death penalty in the United States?

---

e. *Report of the Governor's Council on Capital Punishment*, 80 Ind. L.J. 1 (2005).

APPENDIX

A. SELECTED STATE DEATH PENALTY SCHEMES

■ ■ ■

This section presents excerpts from the current statutes of four states illustrating the variation among death penalty schemes in the United States. California broadly defines death eligibility through special circumstances and has a sentencing formula directing the jury to impose death if "the aggravating circumstances outweigh the mitigating circumstances." Florida divides the sentencing responsibility between the jury and judge, requiring the jury to determine whether aggravating circumstances exist and to render an advisory verdict, but leaving the ultimate decision on sentence to the judge. Georgia is a "non-weighing" state and provides no statutory mitigating circumstances and no sentencing formula; however, it requires comparative proportionality review. Texas, with eight enumerated categories of capital murder, defines death eligibility more narrowly than many other states and, since revision of its capital sentencing statute in 1991, employs two statutory questions, along with an assessment of whether the mitigating circumstances warrant a life sentence rather than a death sentence, to guide the jury's sentencing decision.

CALIFORNIA

California Penal Code § 189. Murder; degrees

All murder which is perpetrated by means of a destructive device or explosive, a weapon of mass destruction, knowing use of ammunition designed primarily to penetrate metal or armor, poison, lying in wait, torture, or by any other kind of willful, deliberate, and premeditated killing, or which is committed in the perpetration of, or attempt to perpetrate, arson, rape, carjacking, robbery, burglary, mayhem, kidnapping, train wrecking, or any act punishable under Section 206 [torture], 286 [sodomy], 288 [lewd and lascivious act on child under 14], 288a [oral copulation], or 289 [rape by instrument], or any murder which is perpetrated by means of discharging a firearm from a motor vehicle, intentionally at another person outside of the vehicle with the intent to inflict death, is murder of the first degree. All other kinds of murders are of the second degree.

* * *

896

California Penal Code § 190.1. Death penalty cases; procedures

A case in which the death penalty may be imposed pursuant to this chapter shall be tried in separate phases as follows:

(a) The question of the defendant's guilt shall be first determined. If the trier of fact finds the defendant guilty of first degree murder, it shall at the same time determine the truth of all special circumstances charged as enumerated in Section 190.2 except for a special circumstance charged pursuant to paragraph (2) of subdivision (a) of Section 190.2 where it is alleged that the defendant had been convicted in a prior proceeding of the offense of murder in the first or second degree.

(b) If the defendant is found guilty of first degree murder and one of the special circumstances is charged pursuant to paragraph (2) of subdivision (a) of Section 190.2 which charges that the defendant had been convicted in a prior proceeding of the offense of murder of the first or second degree, there shall thereupon be further proceedings on the question of the truth of such special circumstance.

(c) If the defendant is found guilty of first degree murder and one or more special circumstances as enumerated in Section 190.2 has been charged and found to be true, his sanity on any plea of not guilty by reason of insanity under Section 1026 shall be determined as provided in Section 190.4. If he is found to be sane, there shall thereupon be further proceedings on the question of the penalty to be imposed. Such proceedings shall be conducted in accordance with the provisions of Section 190.3 and 190.4.

California Penal Code § 190.2. Death penalty or life imprisonment without parole; special circumstances

(a) The penalty for a defendant who is found guilty of murder in the first degree is death or imprisonment in the state prison for life without the possibility of parole if one or more of the following special circumstances has been found under Section 190.4 to be true:

(1) The murder was intentional and carried out for financial gain.

(2) The defendant was convicted previously of murder in the first or second degree. For the purpose of this paragraph, an offense committed in another jurisdiction, which if committed in California would be punishable as first or second degree murder, shall be deemed murder in the first or second degree.

(3) The defendant, in this proceeding, has been convicted of more than one offense of murder in the first or second degree.

(4) The murder was committed by means of a destructive device, bomb, or explosive planted, hidden, or concealed in any place, area, dwelling, building, or structure, and the defendant knew, or reasonably should have known, that his or her act or acts would create a great risk of death to one or more human beings.

(5) The murder was committed for the purpose of avoiding or preventing a lawful arrest, or perfecting or attempting to perfect, an escape from lawful custody.

(6) The murder was committed by means of a destructive device, bomb, or explosive that the defendant mailed or delivered, attempted to mail or deliver, or caused to be mailed or delivered, and the defendant knew, or reasonably should have known, that his or her act or acts would create a great risk of death to one or more human beings.

(7) The victim was a peace officer * * * who, while engaged in the course of the performance of his or her duties, was intentionally killed, and the defendant knew, or reasonably should have known, that the victim was a peace officer engaged in the performance of his or her duties; or the victim was a peace officer * * * or a former peace officer * * *, and was intentionally killed in retaliation for the performance of his or her official duties.

(8) The victim was a federal law enforcement officer or agent who, while engaged in the course of the performance of his or her duties, was intentionally killed, and the defendant knew, or reasonably should have known, that the victim was a federal law enforcement officer or agent engaged in the performance of his or her duties; or the victim was a federal law enforcement officer or agent, and was intentionally killed in retaliation for the performance of his or her official duties.

(9) The victim was a firefighter * * * who, while engaged in the course of the performance of his or her duties, was intentionally killed, and the defendant knew, or reasonably should have known, that the victim was a firefighter engaged in the performance of his or her duties.

(10) The victim was a witness to a crime who was intentionally killed for the purpose of preventing his or her testimony in any criminal or juvenile proceeding, and the killing was not committed during the commission or attempted commission, of the crime to which he or she was a witness; or the victim was a witness to a crime and was intentionally killed in retaliation for his or her testimony in any criminal or juvenile proceeding. * * *

(11) The victim was a prosecutor or assistant prosecutor or a former prosecutor or assistant prosecutor of any local or state prosecutor's office in this or any other state, or of a federal prosecutor's office, and the murder was intentionally carried out in retaliation for, or to prevent the performance of, the victim's official duties.

(12) The victim was a judge or former judge of any court of record in the local, state, or federal system in this or any other state, and the murder was intentionally carried out in retaliation for, or to prevent the performance of, the victim's official duties.

(13) The victim was an elected or appointed official or former official of the federal government, or of any local or state government of this or

any other state, and the killing was intentionally carried out in retaliation for, or to prevent the performance of, the victim's official duties.

(14) The murder was especially heinous, atrocious, or cruel, manifesting exceptional depravity. As used in this section, the phrase "especially heinous, atrocious, or cruel, manifesting exceptional depravity" means a conscienceless or pitiless crime that is unnecessarily torturous to the victim.

(15) The defendant intentionally killed the victim by means of lying in wait.

(16) The victim was intentionally killed because of his or her race, color, religion, nationality, or country of origin.

(17) The murder was committed while the defendant was engaged in, or was an accomplice in, the commission of, attempted commission of, or the immediate flight after committing, or attempting to commit, the following felonies:

(A) Robbery * * *.

(B) Kidnapping * * *.

(C) Rape * * *.

(D) Sodomy * * *.

(E) The performance of a lewd or lascivious act upon the person of a child under the age of 14 years * * *.

(F) Oral copulation * * *.

(G) Burglary * * *.

(H) Arson * * *.

(I) Train wrecking * * *.

(J) Mayhem * * *.

(K) Rape by instrument * * *.

(L) Carjacking * * *.

(M) To prove the special circumstances of kidnapping in subparagraph (B), or arson in subparagraph (H), if there is specific intent to kill, it is only required that there be proof of the elements of those felonies. If so established, those two special circumstances are proven even if the felony of kidnapping or arson is committed primarily or solely for the purpose of facilitating the murder.

(18) The murder was intentional and involved the infliction of torture.

(19) The defendant intentionally killed the victim by the administration of poison.

(20) The victim was a juror in any court of record in the local, state, or federal system in this or any other state, and the murder was intention-

ally carried out in retaliation for, or to prevent the performance of, the victim's official duties.

(21) The murder was intentional and perpetrated by means of discharging a firearm from a motor vehicle, intentionally at another person or persons outside the vehicle with the intent to inflict death. * * *

(22) The defendant intentionally killed the victim while the defendant was an active participant in a criminal street gang * * *, and the murder was carried out to further the activities of the criminal street gang.

(b) Unless an intent to kill is specifically required under subdivision (a) for a special circumstance enumerated therein, an actual killer, as to whom the special circumstance has been found to be true under Section 190.4, need not have had any intent to kill at the time of the commission of the offense which is the basis of the special circumstance in order to suffer death or confinement in the state prison for life without the possibility of parole.

(c) Every person, not the actual killer, who, with the intent to kill, aids, abets, counsels, commands, induces, solicits, requests, or assists any actor in the commission of murder in the first degree shall be punished by death or imprisonment in the state prison for life without the possibility of parole if one or more of the special circumstances enumerated in subdivision (a) has been found to be true under Section 190.4.

(d) Notwithstanding subdivision (c), every person, not the actual killer, who, with reckless indifference to human life and as a major participant, aids, abets, counsels, commands, induces, solicits, requests, or assists in the commission of a felony enumerated in paragraph (17) of subdivision (a) which results in the death of some person or persons, and who is found guilty of murder in the first degree therefor, shall be punished by death or imprisonment in the state prison for life without the possibility of parole if a special circumstance enumerated in paragraph (17) of subdivision (a) has been found to be true under Section 190.4.

    * * *

California Penal Code § 190.3. Determination of death penalty or life imprisonment; evidence of aggravating and mitigating circumstances; considerations

If the defendant has been found guilty of murder in the first degree, and a special circumstance has been charged and found to be true, or if the defendant may be subject to the death penalty after having been found guilty of * * * [hindering preparation for defense or war, or making defects or omitting to note defects in articles intended for war or defense, which cause death; treason; willful perjury or subornation of perjury that results in the execution of an innocent person; trainwrecking resulting in death; and assault with a deadly weapon or by means of force likely to produce great bodily injury by a person serving a life sentence], the trier of fact shall determine whether the penalty shall be death or confinement in state prison for a term of life without the possibility of parole. In the proceedings on the question of penalty, evidence may be presented by both the people and the defendant as to any matter relevant to aggravation, mitigation, and sentence including, but not limited to, the nature and circumstances of the present offense, any prior felony conviction or convictions whether or not such conviction or convictions involved a crime of violence, the presence or absence of other criminal activity by the defendant which involved the use or attempted use of force or violence or which involved the express or implied threat to use force or violence, and the defendant's character, background, history, mental condition and physical condition.

However, no evidence shall be admitted regarding other criminal activity by the defendant which did not involve the use or attempted use of force or violence or which did not involve the express or implied threat to use force or violence. As used in this section, criminal activity does not require a conviction.

However, in no event shall evidence of prior criminal activity be admitted for an offense for which the defendant was prosecuted and acquitted. The restriction on the use of this evidence is intended to apply only to proceedings pursuant to this section and is not intended to affect statutory or decisional law allowing such evidence to be used in any other proceedings.

Except for evidence in proof of the offense or special circumstances which subject a defendant to the death penalty, no evidence may be presented by the prosecution in aggravation unless notice of the evidence to be introduced has been given to the defendant within a reasonable period of time as determined by the court, prior to trial. Evidence may be introduced without such notice in rebuttal to evidence introduced by the defendant in mitigation.

The trier of fact shall be instructed that a sentence of confinement to state prison for a term of life without the possibility of parole may in future after sentence is imposed, be commuted or modified to a sentence that includes the possibility of parole by the Governor of the State of California.

In determining the penalty, the trier of fact shall take into account any of the following factors if relevant:

(a) The circumstances of the crime of which the defendant was convicted in the present proceeding and the existence of any special circumstances found to be true pursuant to Section 190.1.

(b) The presence or absence of criminal activity by the defendant which involved the use or attempted use of force or violence or the express or implied threat to use force or violence.

(c) The presence or absence of any prior felony conviction.

(d) Whether or not the offense was committed while the defendant was under the influence of extreme mental or emotional disturbance.

(e) Whether or not the victim was a participant in the defendant's homicidal conduct or consented to the homicidal act.

(f) Whether or not the offense was committed under circumstances which the defendant reasonably believed to be a moral justification or extenuation for his conduct.

(g) Whether or not defendant acted under extreme duress or under the substantial domination of another person.

(h) Whether or not at the time of the offense the capacity of the defendant to appreciate the criminality of his conduct or to conform his conduct to the requirements of law was impaired as a result of mental disease or defect, or the affects of intoxication.

(i) The age of the defendant at the time of the crime.

(j) Whether or not the defendant was an accomplice to the offense and his participation in the commission of the offense was relatively minor.

(k) Any other circumstance which extenuates the gravity of the crime even though it is not a legal excuse for the crime.[a]

After having heard and received all of the evidence, and after having heard and considered the arguments of counsel, the trier of fact shall consider, take into account and be guided by the aggravating and mitigating circumstances referred to in this section, and shall impose a sentence of death if the trier of fact concludes that the aggravating circumstances outweigh the mitigating circumstances. If the trier of fact determines that the mitigating circumstances outweigh the aggravating circumstances the trier of fact shall impose a sentence of confinement in state prison for a term of life without the possibility of parole.[b]

California Penal Code § 190.4. Special findings on truth of each alleged special circumstance; penalty hearing; application for modification

(a) Whenever special circumstances as enumerated in Section 190.2 are alleged and the trier of fact finds the defendant guilty of first degree

---

a. A capital sentencing jury is to be instructed that under this provision it may also consider as a mitigating factor "any other 'aspect of [the] defendant's character or record ... that the defendant proffers as a basis for a sentence less than death.'" *People v. Easley*, 671 P.2d 813, 826 n. 10 (Cal. 1983).

b. Juries are to be instructed that this weighing provision has the following meaning:

The weighing of aggravating and mitigating circumstances does not mean a mere mechanical counting of factors on each side of an imaginary scale, or the arbitrary assignment of weights to any of them. You are free to assign whatever moral or sympathetic value you deem appropriate to each and all of the various factors you are permitted to consider. In weighing the various circumstances you determine under the relevant evidence which penalty is justified and appropriate by considering the totality of the aggravating circumstances with the totality of the mitigating circumstances. To return a judgment of death, each of you must be persuaded that the aggravating circumstances are so substantial in comparison with the mitigating circumstances that it warrants death instead of life without parole.

CALJIC 8.88 (2000 Revision) Penalty Trial—Concluding Instruction; *People v. Brown*, 726 P.2d 516, 532 (Cal.1985).

murder, the trier of fact shall also make a special finding on the truth of each alleged special circumstance. The determination of the truth of any or all of the special circumstances shall be made by the trier of fact on the evidence presented at the trial or at the hearing held pursuant to Subdivision (b) of Section 190.1.

In case of a reasonable doubt as to whether a special circumstance is true, the defendant is entitled to a finding that it is not true. The trier of fact shall make a special finding that each special circumstance charged is either true or not true. Whenever a special circumstance requires proof of the commission or attempted commission of a crime, such crime shall be charged and proved pursuant to the general law applying to the trial and conviction of the crime.

If the defendant was convicted by the court sitting without a jury, the trier of fact shall be a jury unless a jury is waived by the defendant and by the people, in which case the trier of fact shall be the court. If the defendant was convicted by a plea of guilty, the trier of fact shall be a jury unless a jury is waived by the defendant and by the people.

If the trier of fact finds that any one or more of the special circumstances enumerated in Section 190.2 as charged is true, there shall be a separate penalty hearing, and neither the finding that any of the remaining special circumstances charged is not true, nor if the trier of fact is a jury, the inability of the jury to agree on the issue of the truth or untruth of any of the remaining special circumstances charged, shall prevent the holding of a separate penalty hearing.

In any case in which the defendant has been found guilty by a jury, and the jury has been unable to reach an unanimous verdict that one or more of the special circumstances charged are true, and does not reach a unanimous verdict that all the special circumstances charged are not true, the court shall dismiss the jury and shall order a new jury impaneled to try the issues, but the issue of guilt shall not be tried by such jury, nor shall such jury retry the issue of the truth of any of the special circumstances which were found by an unanimous verdict of the previous jury to be untrue. If such new jury is unable to reach the unanimous verdict that one or more of the special circumstances it is trying are true, the court shall dismiss the jury and in the court's discretion shall either order a new jury impaneled to try the issues the previous jury was unable to reach the unanimous verdict on, or impose a punishment of confinement in state prison for a term of 25 years.

(b) If defendant was convicted by the court sitting without a jury the trier of fact at the penalty hearing shall be a jury unless a jury is waived by the defendant and the people, in which case the trier of fact shall be the court. If the defendant was convicted by a plea of guilty, the trier of fact shall be a jury unless a jury is waived by the defendant and the people.

If the trier of fact is a jury and has been unable to reach a unanimous verdict as to what the penalty shall be, the court shall dismiss the jury and shall order a new jury impaneled to try the issue as to what the penalty shall be. If such new jury is unable to reach a unanimous verdict as to what the penalty shall be, the court in its discretion shall either order a new jury or impose a punishment of confinement in state prison for a term of life without the possibility of parole.

(c) If the trier of fact which convicted the defendant of a crime for which he may be subject to the death penalty was a jury, the same jury shall consider any plea of not guilty by reason of insanity * * *, the truth of any special circumstances which may be alleged, and the penalty to be applied, unless for good cause shown the court discharges that jury in which case a new jury shall be drawn. The court shall state facts in support of the finding of good cause upon the record and cause them to be entered into the minutes.

(d) In any case in which the defendant may be subject to the death penalty, evidence presented at any prior phase of the trial, including any proceeding under a plea of not guilty by reason of insanity * * * shall be considered an any subsequent phase of the trial, if the trier of fact of the prior phase is the same trier of fact at the subsequent phase.

(e) In every case in which the trier of fact has returned a verdict or finding imposing the death penalty, the defendant shall be deemed to have made an application for modification of such verdict or finding * * *. In ruling on the application, the judge shall review the evidence, consider, take into account, and be guided by the aggravating and mitigating circumstances referred to in Section 190.3, and shall make a determination as to whether the jury's findings and verdicts that the aggravating circumstances outweigh the mitigating circumstances are contrary to law or the evidence presented. The judge shall state on the record the reasons for his findings.

The judge shall set forth the reasons for his ruling on the application and direct that they be entered on the Clerk's minutes. The denial of the modification of the death penalty verdict * * * shall be reviewed on the defendant's automatic appeal pursuant to subdivision (b) of Section 1239. The granting of the application shall be reviewed on the People's appeal pursuant to paragraph (6).

California Penal Code § 1239. Automatic appeal from death judgment

     * * *

(b) When upon any plea a judgment of death is rendered, an appeal is automatically taken by the defendant without any action by him or her or his or her counsel. * * *

FLORIDA

Florida Statutes Annotated § 775.082.

(1) A person who has been convicted of a capital felony shall be punished by death if the proceeding held to determine sentence according

to the procedure set forth in § 921.141 results in findings by the court that such person shall be punished by death, otherwise such person shall be punished by life imprisonment and shall be ineligible for parole.

     * * *

Florida Statutes Annotated § 782.04.

(1)(a) The unlawful killing of a human being:

1. When perpetrated from a premeditated design to effect the death of the person killed or any human being;

2. When committed by a person engaged in the perpetration of, or in the attempt to perpetrate, any:

    a. Trafficking offense prohibited by § 893.135(1),

    b. Arson,

    c. Sexual battery,

    d. Robbery,

    e. Burglary,

    f. Kidnapping,

    g. Escape,

    h. Aggravated child abuse,

    i. Aggravated abuse of an elderly person or disabled adult,

    j. Aircraft piracy,

    k. Unlawful throwing, placing, or discharging of a destructive device or bomb,

    l. Carjacking,

    m. Home-invasion robbery,

    n. Aggravated stalking,

    o. Murder of another human being,

    p. Resisting an officer with violence to his or her person,

    q. Felony that is an act of terrorism or is in furtherance of an act of terrorism; or

3. Which resulted from the unlawful distribution of any substance controlled under § 893.03(1), cocaine as described in § 893.03(2)(a)4., or opium or any synthetic or natural salt, compound, derivative, or preparation of opium by a person 18 years of age or older, when such drug is proven to be the proximate cause of the death of the user,

is murder in the first degree and constitutes a capital felony, punishable as provided in § 775.082.

(b) In all cases under this section, the procedure set forth in
§ 921.141 shall be followed in order to determine sentence of death or life
imprisonment.

* * *

Florida Statutes Annotated § 893.135

* * *

(b)

* * *

2. Any person who knowingly sells, purchases, manufactures, deliv-
ers, or brings into this state, or who is knowingly in actual or constructive
possession of, 150 kilograms or more of cocaine * * * commits the first
degree felony of trafficking in cocaine. A person who has been convicted of
the first degree felony of trafficking in cocaine under this subparagraph
shall be punished by life imprisonment and is ineligible for any form of
discretionary early release except pardon or executive clemency or conditional medical release under § 947.149. However, if the court determines
that, in addition to committing any act specified in this paragraph:

a. The person intentionally killed an individual or counseled, commanded, induced, procured, or caused the intentional killing of an
individual and such killing was the result; or

b. The person's conduct in committing that act led to a natural,
though not inevitable, lethal result,

such person commits the capital felony of trafficking in cocaine, punishable as provided in §§ 775.082 and 921.142. * * *

3. Any person who knowingly brings into this state 300 kilograms or
more of cocaine * * * and who knows that the probable result of such
importation would be the death of any person, commits capital importation of cocaine, a capital felony punishable as provided in §§ 775.082 and
921.142.

[Capital murder provisions parallel to para. 2 above also apply to
trafficking in: 30 kilograms of morphine, opium, etc. (§ 893.135(c)); and
30 kilograms or more of flunitrazepam or any mixture containing flunitrazepam (§ 893.135(g)). The capital murder provisions of para. 3 above also
apply to trafficking in: 800 grams or more of phencyclidine or of any
mixture containing phencyclidine (§ 893.135(d)); 50 kilograms or more of
methaqualone or of any mixture containing methaqualone (§ 893.135(e));
400 grams or more of amphetamine, or methamphetamine, or of any
mixture containing amphetamine or methamphetamine, or phenylacetone,
phenylacetic acid, pseudoephedrine, or ephedrine in conjunction with
other chemicals and equipment used in the manufacture of amphetamine
or methamphetamine (§ 893.135(f)); 150 kilograms or more of gamma-
hydroxybutyric acid (GHB) or any mixture containing gamma-hydroxybu-
tyric acid (GHB) (§ 893.135(h)); 150 kilograms or more of gamma-butyrolactone (GBL) or any mixture containing gamma-butyrolactone (GBL)

(§ 893.135(i)); 150 kilograms or more of 1,4–Butanediol or any mixture containing 1,4–Butanediol (§ 893.135(j)); 30 kilograms or more of any of a list of 15 amphetamine compounds (§ 893.135(k)); 7 grams or more of lysergic acid diethylamide (LSD) or any mixture containing lysergic acid diethylamide (LSD) (§ 893.135(*l*)).]

Florida Statutes Annotated § 921.141

(1) Separate proceedings on issue of penalty.—Upon conviction or adjudication of guilt of a defendant of a capital felony, the court shall conduct a separate sentencing proceeding to determine whether the defendant should be sentenced to death or life imprisonment as authorized by § 775.082. The proceeding shall be conducted by the trial judge before the trial jury as soon as practicable. If, through impossibility or inability, the trial jury is unable to reconvene for a hearing on the issue of penalty, having determined the guilt of the accused, the trial judge may summon a special juror or jurors * * * to determine the issue of the imposition of the penalty. If the trial jury has been waived, or if the defendant pleaded guilty, the sentencing proceeding shall be conducted before a jury impaneled for that purpose, unless waived by the defendant. In the proceeding, evidence may be presented as to any matter that the court deems relevant to the nature of the crime and the character of the defendant and shall include matters relating to any of the aggravating or mitigating circumstances enumerated in subsections (5) and (6). Any such evidence which the court deems to have probative value may be received, regardless of its admissibility under the exclusionary rules of evidence, provided the defendant is accorded a fair opportunity to rebut any hearsay statements. However, this subsection shall not be construed to authorize the introduction of any evidence secured in violation of the Constitution of the United States or the Constitution of the State of Florida. The state and the defendant or the defendant's counsel shall be permitted to present argument for or against sentence of death.

(2) Advisory sentence by the jury.—After hearing all the evidence, the jury shall deliberate and render an advisory sentence to the court, based upon the following matters:

(a) Whether sufficient aggravating circumstances exist as enumerated in subsection (5);

(b) Whether sufficient mitigating circumstances exist which outweigh the aggravating circumstances found to exist; and

(c) Based on these considerations, whether the defendant should be sentenced to life imprisonment or death.

(3) Findings in support of sentence of death.—Notwithstanding the recommendation of a majority of the jury, the court, after weighing the aggravating and mitigating circumstances, shall enter a sentence of life imprisonment or death, but if the court imposes a sentence of death, it shall set forth in writing its findings upon which the sentence of death is based as to the facts:

(a) That sufficient aggravating circumstances exist as enumerated in subsection (5), and

(b) That there are insufficient mitigating circumstances to outweigh the aggravating circumstances.

In each case in which the court imposes the death sentence, the determination of the court shall be supported by specific written findings of fact based upon the circumstances in subsections (5) and (6) and upon the records of the trial and the sentencing proceedings. If the court does not make the findings requiring the death sentence within 30 days after the rendition of the judgment and sentence, the court shall impose sentence of life imprisonment in accordance with § 775.082.

(4) Review of judgment and sentence.—The judgment of conviction and sentence of death shall be subject to automatic review by the Supreme Court of Florida and disposition rendered within 2 years after the filing of a notice of appeal. Such review by the Supreme Court shall have priority over all other cases and shall be heard in accordance with rules promulgated by the Supreme Court.

(5) Aggravating circumstances.—Aggravating circumstances shall be limited to the following:

(a) The capital felony was committed by a person previously convicted of a felony and under sentence of imprisonment or placed on community control or on felony probation.

(b) The defendant was previously convicted of another capital felony or of a felony involving the use or threat of violence to the person.

(c) The defendant knowingly created a great risk of death to many persons.

(d) The capital felony was committed while the defendant was engaged, or was an accomplice, in the commission of, or an attempt to commit, or flight after committing or attempting to commit, any: robbery; sexual battery; aggravated child abuse; abuse of an elderly person or disabled adult resulting in great bodily harm, permanent disability, or permanent disfigurement; arson; burglary; kidnapping; aircraft piracy; or unlawful throwing, placing, or discharging of a destructive device or bomb.

(e) The capital felony was committed for the purpose of avoiding or preventing a lawful arrest or effecting an escape from custody.

(f) The capital felony was committed for pecuniary gain.

(g) The capital felony was committed to disrupt or hinder the lawful exercise of any governmental function or the enforcement of laws.

(h) The capital felony was especially heinous, atrocious, or cruel.

(i) The capital felony was a homicide and was committed in a cold, calculated, and premeditated manner without any pretense of moral or legal justification.

(j) The victim of the capital felony was a law enforcement officer engaged in the performance of his or her official duties.

(k) The victim of the capital felony was an elected or appointed public official engaged in the performance of his or her official duties if the motive for the capital felony was related, in whole or in part, to the victim's official capacity.

(l) The victim of the capital felony was a person less than 12 years of age.

(m) The victim of the capital felony was particularly vulnerable due to advanced age or disability, or because the defendant stood in a position of familial or custodial authority over the victim.

(n) The capital felony was committed by a criminal gang member, as defined in § 874.03.

(o) The capital felony was committed by a person designated as a sexual predator * * *

(6) Mitigating circumstances.—Mitigating circumstances shall be the following:

(a) The defendant has no significant history of prior criminal activity.

(b) The capital felony was committed while the defendant was under the influence of extreme mental or emotional disturbance.

(c) The victim was a participant in the defendant's conduct or consented to the act.

(d) The defendant was an accomplice in the capital felony committed by another person and his or her participation was relatively minor.

(e) The defendant acted under extreme duress or under the substantial domination of another person.

(f) The capacity of the defendant to appreciate the criminality of his or her conduct or to conform his or her conduct to the requirements of law was substantially impaired.

(g) The age of the defendant at the time of the crime.

(h) The existence of any other factors in the defendant's background that would mitigate against imposition of the death penalty.

(7) Victim impact evidence.—Once the prosecution has provided evidence of the existence of one or more aggravating circumstances as described in subsection (5), the prosecution may introduce, and subsequently argue, victim impact evidence. Such evidence shall be designed to demonstrate the victim's uniqueness as an individual human being and the resultant loss to the community's members by the victim's death. Characterizations and opinions about the crime, the defendant, and the appropriate sentence shall not be permitted as a part of victim impact evidence.

(8) Applicability.—This section does not apply to a person convicted or adjudicated guilty of a capital drug trafficking felony under § 893.135.

Florida Statutes Annotated § 921.142.

(1) Findings.—The Legislature finds that trafficking in cocaine or opiates carries a grave risk of death or danger to the public; that a reckless disregard for human life is implicit in knowingly trafficking in cocaine or opiates; and that persons who traffic in cocaine or opiates may be determined by the trier of fact to have a culpable mental state of reckless indifference or disregard for human life.

(2) Separate proceedings on issue of penalty.—Upon conviction or adjudication of guilt of a defendant of a capital felony under § 893.135, the court shall conduct a separate sentencing proceeding to determine whether the defendant should be sentenced to death or life imprisonment as authorized by § 775.082. The proceeding shall be conducted by the trial judge before the trial jury as soon as practicable. If, through impossibility or inability, the trial jury is unable to reconvene for a hearing on the issue of penalty, having determined the guilt of the accused, the trial judge may summon a special juror or jurors * * * to determine the issue of the imposition of the penalty. If the trial jury has been waived, or if the defendant pleaded guilty, the sentencing proceeding shall be conducted before a jury impaneled for that purpose, unless waived by the defendant. In the proceeding, evidence may be presented as to any matter that the court deems relevant to the nature of the crime and the character of the defendant and shall include matters relating to any of the aggravating or mitigating circumstances enumerated in subsections (6) and (7). Any such evidence which the court deems to have probative value may be received, regardless of its admissibility under the exclusionary rules of evidence, provided the defendant is accorded a fair opportunity to rebut any hearsay statements. However, this subsection shall not be construed to authorize the introduction of any evidence secured in violation of the Constitution of the United States or the Constitution of the State of Florida. The state and the defendant or the defendant's counsel shall be permitted to present argument for or against sentence of death.

(3) Advisory sentence by the jury.—After hearing all the evidence, the jury shall deliberate and render an advisory sentence to the court, based upon the following matters:

(a) Whether sufficient aggravating circumstances exist as enumerated in subsection (6);

(b) Whether sufficient mitigating circumstances exist which outweigh the aggravating circumstances found to exist; and

(c) Based on these considerations, whether the defendant should be sentenced to life imprisonment or death.

(4) Findings in support of sentence of death.—Notwithstanding the recommendation of a majority of the jury, the court, after weighing the aggravating and mitigating circumstances, shall enter a sentence of life imprisonment or death, but if the court imposes a sentence of death, it shall set forth in writing its findings upon which the sentence of death is based as to the facts:

(a) That sufficient aggravating circumstances exist as enumerated in subsection (6), and

(b) That there are insufficient mitigating circumstances to outweigh the aggravating circumstances.

In each case in which the court imposes the death sentence, the determination of the court shall be supported by specific written findings of fact based upon the circumstances in subsections (6) and (7) and upon the records of the trial and the sentencing proceedings. If the court does not make the findings requiring the death sentence within 30 days after the rendition of the judgment and sentence, the court shall impose sentence of life imprisonment in accordance with § 775.082, and that person shall be ineligible for parole.

(5) Review of judgment and sentence.—The judgment of conviction and sentence of death shall be subject to automatic review and disposition rendered by the Supreme Court of Florida within 2 years after the filing of a notice of appeal. Such review by the Supreme Court shall have priority over all other cases and shall be heard in accordance with rules promulgated by the Supreme Court.

(6) Aggravating circumstances.—Aggravating circumstances shall be limited to the following:

(a) The capital felony was committed by a person under a sentence of imprisonment.

(b) The defendant was previously convicted of another capital felony or of a state or federal offense involving the distribution of a controlled substance that is punishable by a sentence of at least 1 year of imprisonment.

(c) The defendant knowingly created grave risk of death to one or more persons such that participation in the offense constituted reckless indifference or disregard for human life.

(d) The defendant used a firearm or knowingly directed, advised, authorized, or assisted another to use a firearm to threaten, intimidate, assault, or injure a person in committing the offense or in furtherance of the offense.

(e) The offense involved the distribution of controlled substances to persons under the age of 18 years, the distribution of controlled substances within school zones, or the use or employment of persons under the age of 18 years in aid of distribution of controlled substances.

(f) The offense involved distribution of controlled substances known to contain a potentially lethal adulterant.

(g) The defendant:

　　1.　Intentionally killed the victim;

2.   Intentionally inflicted serious bodily injury which resulted in the death of the victim; or

3.   Intentionally engaged in conduct intending that the victim be killed or that lethal force be employed against the victim, which resulted in the death of the victim.

(h) The defendant committed the offense as consideration for the receipt, or in the expectation of the receipt, of anything of pecuniary value.

(i) The defendant committed the offense after planning and premeditation.

(j) The defendant committed the offense in a heinous, cruel, or depraved manner in that the offense involved torture or serious physical abuse to the victim.

(7) Mitigating circumstances.—Mitigating circumstances shall include the following:

(a) The defendant has no significant history of prior criminal activity.

(b) The capital felony was committed while the defendant was under the influence of extreme mental or emotional disturbance.

(c) The defendant was an accomplice in the capital felony committed by another person, and the defendant's participation was relatively minor.

(d) The defendant was under extreme duress or under the substantial domination of another person.

(e) The capacity of the defendant to appreciate the criminality of her or his conduct or to conform her or his conduct to the requirements of law was substantially impaired.

(f) The age of the defendant at the time of the offense.

(g) The defendant could not have reasonably foreseen that her or his conduct in the course of the commission of the offense would cause or would create a grave risk of death to one or more persons.

(h) The existence of any other factors in the defendant's background that would mitigate against imposition of the death penalty.

(8) Victim impact evidence.—Once the prosecution has provided evidence of the existence of one or more aggravating circumstances as described in subsection (6), the prosecution may introduce, and subsequently argue, victim impact evidence. Such evidence shall be designed to demonstrate the victim's uniqueness as an individual human being and the resultant loss to the community's members by the victim's death. Characterizations and opinions about the crime, the defendant, and the appropriate sentence shall not be permitted as a part of victim impact evidence.

GEORGIA

Code of Georgia § 16–5–1 Murder; felony murder.

(a) A person commits the offense of murder when he unlawfully and with malice aforethought, either express or implied, causes the death of another human being.

(b) Express malice is that deliberate intention unlawfully to take the life of another human being which is manifested by external circumstances capable of proof. Malice shall be implied where no considerable provocation appears and where all the circumstances of the killing show an abandoned and malignant heart.

(c) A person also commits the offense of murder when, in the commission of a felony, he causes the death of another human being irrespective of malice.

(d) A person convicted of the offense of murder shall be punished by death, by imprisonment for life without parole, or by imprisonment for life.

Code of Georgia § 17–10–30 Mitigating and aggravating circumstances; death penalty.

(a) The death penalty may be imposed for the offenses of aircraft hijacking or treason in any case.

(b) In all cases of other offenses for which the death penalty may be authorized, the judge shall consider, or he shall include in his instructions to the jury for it to consider, any mitigating circumstances or aggravating circumstances otherwise authorized by law and any of the following statutory aggravating circumstances which may be supported by the evidence:

(1) The offense of murder, rape, armed robbery, or kidnapping was committed by a person with a prior record of conviction for a capital felony;

(2) The offense of murder, rape, armed robbery, or kidnapping was committed while the offender was engaged in the commission of another capital felony or aggravated battery, or the offense of murder was committed while the offender was engaged in the commission of burglary or arson in the first degree;

(3) The offender, by his act of murder, armed robbery, or kidnapping, knowingly created a great risk of death to more than one person in a public place by means of a weapon or device which would normally be hazardous to the lives of more than one person;

(4) The offender committed the offense of murder for himself or another, for the purpose of receiving money or any other thing of monetary value;

(5) The murder of a judicial officer, former judicial officer, district attorney or solicitor-general, or former district attorney, solicitor, or

solicitor-general was committed during or because of the exercise of his or her official duties;

(6) The offender caused or directed another to commit murder or committed murder as an agent or employee of another person;

(7) The offense of murder, rape, armed robbery, or kidnapping was outrageously or wantonly vile, horrible, or inhuman in that it involved torture, depravity of mind, or an aggravated battery to the victim;

(8) The offense of murder was committed against any peace officer, corrections employee, or fireman while engaged in the performance of his official duties;

(9) The offense of murder was committed by a person in, or who has escaped from, the lawful custody of a peace officer or place of lawful confinement;

(10) The murder was committed for the purpose of avoiding, interfering with, or preventing a lawful arrest or custody in a place of lawful confinement, of himself or another; or

(11) The offense of murder, rape, or kidnapping was committed by a person previously convicted of rape, aggravated sodomy, aggravated child molestation, or aggravated sexual battery.

* * *

Code of Georgia § 17–10–31 Capital felonies; jury verdict and sentence.

(a) Where, upon a trial by jury, a person is convicted of an offense which may be punishable by death, a sentence of death shall not be imposed unless the jury verdict includes a finding of at least one statutory aggravating circumstance and a recommendation that such sentence be imposed. Where a statutory aggravating circumstance is found and a recommendation of death is made, the court shall sentence the accused to death. Where a statutory aggravating circumstance is not found or where a statutory circumstance is found but a recommendation of death is not made, the jury shall decide whether to recommend a sentence of life imprisonment without parole or life imprisonment with the possibility of parole. Unless the jury trying the case makes a finding of at least one statutory aggravating circumstance and recommends the death sentence in its verdict, the court shall not sentence the defendant to death, provided that no such finding of statutory aggravating circumstance shall be necessary in offenses of treason or aircraft hijacking. This Code section shall not affect a sentence when the case is tried without a jury or when the judge accepts a plea of guilty.

(b) During the sentencing phase before a jury, counsel for the state and the accused may present argument and the trial judge may instruct the jury:

(1) That "life without parole" means that the defendant shall be incarcerated for the remainder of his or her natural life and shall not be

eligible for parole unless such person is subsequently adjudicated to be innocent of the offense for which he or she was sentenced; and

(2) That "life imprisonment" means that the defendant will be incarcerated for the remainder of his or her natural life but will be eligible for parole during the term of such sentence.

(c) If the jury is unable to reach a unanimous verdict as to sentence, the judge shall dismiss the jury and shall impose a sentence of either life imprisonment or imprisonment for life without parole.

Code of Georgia § 17–10–35 Review of death sentences.

(a) Whenever the death penalty is imposed, upon the judgment becoming final in the trial court, the sentence shall be reviewed on the record by the Supreme Court of Georgia. * * *

(b) The Supreme Court shall consider the punishment as well as any errors enumerated by way of appeal.

(c) With regard to the sentence, the court shall determine:

(1) Whether the sentence of death was imposed under the influence of passion, prejudice, or any other arbitrary factor;

(2) Whether, in cases other than treason or aircraft hijacking, the evidence supports the jury's or judge's finding of a statutory aggravating circumstance as enumerated in subsection (b) of Code Section 17–10–30; and

(3) Whether the sentence of death is excessive or disproportionate to the penalty imposed in similar cases, considering both the crime and the defendant.

(d) Both the defendant and the state shall have the right to submit briefs within the time provided by the court and to present oral argument to the court.

(e) The court shall include in its decision a reference to those similar cases which it took into consideration. In addition to its authority regarding correction of errors, the court, with regard to review of death sentences, shall be authorized to:

(1) Affirm the sentence of death; or

(2) Set the sentence aside and remand the case for resentencing by the trial judge based on the record and argument of counsel. The records of those similar cases referred to by the Supreme Court in its decision and the extracts prepared * * * shall be provided to the resentencing judge for his consideration.

(f) The sentence review shall be in addition to direct appeal, if taken, and the review and appeal shall be consolidated for consideration. The court shall render its decision on legal errors enumerated, the factual substantiation of the verdict, and the validity of the sentence.

TEXAS

Texas Penal Code § 19.02. Murder

(a) In this section:

(1) "Adequate cause" means cause that would commonly produce a degree of anger, rage, resentment, or terror in a person of ordinary temper, sufficient to render the mind incapable of cool reflection.

(2) "Sudden passion" means passion directly caused by and arising out of provocation by the individual killed or another acting with the person killed which passion arises at the time of the offense and is not solely the result of former provocation.

(b) A person commits an offense if he:

(1) intentionally or knowingly causes the death of an individual;

(2) intends to cause serious bodily injury and commits an act clearly dangerous to human life that causes the death of an individual; or

(3) commits or attempts to commit a felony, other than manslaughter, and in the course of and in furtherance of the commission or attempt, or in immediate flight from the commission or attempt, he commits or attempts to commit an act clearly dangerous to human life that causes the death of an individual.

(c) Except as provided by Subsection (d), an offense under this section is a felony of the first degree.

(d) At the punishment stage of a trial, the defendant may raise the issue as to whether he caused the death under the immediate influence of sudden passion arising from an adequate cause. If the defendant proves the issue in the affirmative by a preponderance of the evidence, the offense is a felony of the second degree.

Texas Penal Code § 19.03. Capital Murder

(a) A person commits an offense if he commits murder as defined under Section 19.02(b)(1) and:

(1) the person murders a peace officer or fireman who is acting in the lawful discharge of an official duty and who the person knows is a peace officer or fireman;

(2) the person intentionally commits the murder in the course of committing or attempting to commit kidnapping, burglary, robbery, aggravated sexual assault, arson, or obstruction or retaliation;

(3) the person commits the murder for remuneration or the promise of remuneration or employs another to commit the murder for remuneration or the promise of remuneration;

(4) the person commits the murder while escaping or attempting to escape from a penal institution;

(5) the person, while incarcerated in a penal institution, murders another:

(A) who is employed in the operation of the penal institution; or

(B) with the intent to establish, maintain, or participate in a combination or in the profits of a combination;

(6) the person:

(A) while incarcerated for an offense under this section or Section 19.02, murders another; or

(B) while serving a sentence of life imprisonment or a term of 99 years for an offense * * * [of aggravated kidnapping, aggravated sexual assault, or aggravated robbery], murders another;

(7) the person murders more than one person:

(A) during the same criminal transaction; or

(B) during different criminal transactions but the murders are committed pursuant to the same scheme or course of conduct; or

(8) the person murders an individual under six years of age; or

(9) the person murders another person in retaliation for or on account of the service or status of the other person as a judge or justice of the supreme court, the court of criminal appeals, a district court, a criminal district court, a constitutional county court, a statutory county court, a justice court, or a municipal court.

(b) An offense under this section is a capital felony.

(c) If the jury or, when authorized by law, the judge does not find beyond a reasonable doubt that the defendant is guilty of an offense under this section, he may be convicted of murder or of any other lesser included offense.

Texas Code of Criminal Procedure Article 37.071. Procedure in capital case

Sec. 1. If a defendant is found guilty in a capital felony case in which the state does not seek the death penalty, the judge shall sentence the defendant to life imprisonment without parole.

Sec. 2. (a)(1) If a defendant is tried for a capital offense in which the state seeks the death penalty, on a finding that the defendant is guilty of a capital offense, the court shall conduct a separate sentencing proceeding to determine whether the defendant shall be sentenced to death or life imprisonment. The proceeding shall be conducted in the trial court and * * * before the trial jury as soon as practicable. In the proceeding, evidence may be presented by the state and the defendant or the defendant's counsel as to any matter that the court deems relevant to sentence, including evidence of the defendant's background or character or the circumstances of the offense that mitigates against the imposition of the death penalty. This subdivision shall not be construed to authorize the introduction of any evidence secured in violation of the Constitution of the United States or of the State of Texas. The state and the defendant or the defendant's counsel shall be permitted to present argument for or against sentence of death. * * * The court, the attorney representing the state, the defendant, or the defendant's counsel may not inform a juror or a prospective juror of the effect of a failure of a jury to agree on issues submitted under Subsection (c) or (e) of this article.

(2) Notwithstanding Subdivision (1), evidence may not be offered by the state to establish that the race or ethnicity of the defendant makes it likely that the defendant will engage in future criminal conduct.

(b) On conclusion of the presentation of the evidence, the court shall submit the following issues to the jury:

(1) whether there is a probability that the defendant would commit criminal acts of violence that would constitute a continuing threat to society; and

(2) in cases in which the jury charge at the guilt or innocence stage permitted the jury to find the defendant guilty as a party under [provisions setting out criminal responsibility for the conduct of another] whether the defendant actually caused the death of the deceased or did not actually cause the death of the deceased but intended to kill the deceased or another or anticipated that a human life would be taken.

(c) The state must prove each issue submitted under Subsection (b) of this article beyond a reasonable doubt, and the jury shall return a special verdict of "yes" or "no" on each issue submitted under Subsection (b) of this Article.

(d) The court shall charge the jury that:

(1) in deliberating on the issues submitted under Subsection (b) of this article, it shall consider all evidence admitted at the guilt or innocence stage and the punishment stage, including evidence of the defendant's background or character or the circumstances of the offense that militates for or mitigates against the imposition of the death penalty;

(2) it may not answer any issue submitted under Subsection (b) of this article "yes" unless it agrees unanimously and it may not answer any issue "no" unless 10 or more jurors agree; and

(3) members of the jury need not agree on what particular evidence supports a negative answer to any issue submitted under Subsection (b) of this article.

(e)(1) The court shall instruct the jury that if the jury returns an affirmative finding to each issue submitted under Subsection (b) of this article, it shall answer the following issue:

Whether, taking into consideration all of the evidence, including the circumstances of the offense, the defendant's character and background, and the personal moral culpability of the defendant, there is a sufficient mitigating circumstance or circumstances to warrant that a sentence of life imprisonment rather than a death sentence be imposed.

(2) The court shall::

(A) instruct the jury that if the jury answers that a circumstance or circumstances warrant that a sentence of life imprisonment without parole rather than a death sentence be imposed, the court will sentence the defendant to imprisonment in the institutional division of the Texas Department of Criminal Justice for life without parole; and

(B) charge the jury that a defendant sentenced to confinement for life without parole under this article is ineligible for release from the department on parole.

(f) The court shall charge the jury that in answering the issue submitted under Subsection (e) of this article, the jury:

(1) shall answer the issue "yes" or "no";

(2) may not answer the issue "no" unless it agrees unanimously and may not answer the issue "yes" unless 10 or more jurors agree;

(3) need not agree on what particular evidence supports an affirmative finding on the issue; and

(4) shall consider mitigating evidence to be evidence that a juror might regard as reducing the defendant's moral blameworthiness.

(g) If the jury returns an affirmative finding on each issue submitted under Subsection (b) of this article and a negative finding on an issue submitted under Subsection (e) of this article, the court shall sentence the defendant to death. If the jury returns a negative finding on any issue submitted under Subsection (b) of this article or an affirmative finding on an issue submitted under Subsection (e) or is unable to answer any issue submitted under Subsection (b) or (e) of this article, the court shall sentence the defendant to confinement in the institutional division of the Texas Department of Criminal Justice for life without parole.

(h) The judgment of conviction and sentence of death shall be subject to automatic review by the Court of Criminal Appeals.

* * *

B. FEDERAL DEATH PENALTY STATUTES

In 1988, Congress enacted the first post-*Furman* death penalty statute, the Anti–Drug Abuse Act of 1988, codified at 21 U.S.C. § 848 (e)–(r). This statute encompassed only so-called "drug king-pin" murders and drug-related murders of law enforcement officials. Six years later, Congress enacted the Federal Death Penalty Act of 1994 as a part of the Violent Crime Control and Law Enforcement Act of 1994, codified at 18 U.S.C. § 3591 *et seq.*[a] This statute greatly expanded the federal death penalty by creating new capital offenses. There are more than 40 federal

---

a. Excerpts from the Federal Death Penalty Act of 1994 are set forth below.

capital crimes, including both homicidal and non-homicidal offenses, which may be divided into four categories: (1) genocide,[b] (2) murder[c] and other offenses resulting in death,[d] (3) espionage and treason,[e] and (4) non-homicidal continuing criminal enterprise drug offenses involving large quantities of drugs or money or the attempted murder of any public officer, juror, witness, or member of such person's family or household.[f] In addition, the federal death penalty statutes contain provisions designed to ensure against discrimination on the basis of the race, color, religious beliefs, national origin or sex of the defendant or the victim[g] and forbid making participation in a capital prosecution or execution a condition of employment.[h]

The trial and sentencing procedure is similar under the two federal death penalty statutes, 21 U.S.C. § 848 and 18 U.S.C. § 3591 *et seq.* The United States Attorney General personally must authorize the local United-ed States Attorney to seek the death penalty for a capital offense before a capital prosecution may be brought. Under the Federal Death Penalty Act of 1994, each separate offense has its own list of statutory aggravating circumstances. Under both death penalty statutes, the trial is bifurcated between the guilt-innocence phase and the sentencing phase. The same jury tries both questions. The government must prove aggravating circumstances beyond a reasonable doubt. Although aggravating circumstances are enumerated in the statutes, the statutory list is not exclusive, and, with notice to the defendant, the government may assert non-statutory aggravating circumstances. The defense must prove mitigating circumstances by a preponderance of the evidence. Like aggravating circumstances, mitigating circumstances are enumerated in the statute, but the statutory list is not exclusive. At the penalty phase, the jury weighs and balances the aggravating and mitigating circumstances.

THE FEDERAL DEATH PENALTY ACT OF 1994.

18 U.S.C. § 3591. Sentence of death

(a) A defendant who has been found guilty of—

(1) an offense described in section 794 [espionage] or section 2381 [treason]; or

---

b. 18 U.S.C. § 1091.

c. See, *e.g.*, first-degree murder (18 U.S.C. § 1111); murder by a federal prisoner (18 U.S.C. § 1118); murder of a court officer or juror (18 U.S.C. § 1503); murder committed in a federal government facility (18 U.S.C. § 930); murder involving torture (18 U.S.C. §§ 2340, 2340A); murder related to a carjacking (18 U.S.C. § 2119).

d. See, *e.g.*, death resulting from various forms of sexual abuse (18 U.S.C. §§ 2241–2245); death resulting from air piracy (18 U.S.C. § 46502); use of chemical weapons resulting in death (18 U.S.C. § 2332c); willful train-wrecking resulting in death (18 U.S.C. § 1992).

e. 18 U.S.C. § 794, 18 U.S.C. § 2381.

f. 18 U.S.C. §§ 3591(a)(1), 3591(b)(1)–(2).

g. 21 U.S.C. § 848(*o*); 18 U.S.C. § 3593(f).

h. 18 U.S.C. § 848(r) and 18 U.S.C. § 3597.

(2) any other offense for which a sentence of death is provided, if the defendant, as determined beyond a reasonable doubt at the hearing under section 3593—

(A) intentionally killed the victim;

(B) intentionally inflicted serious bodily injury that resulted in the death of the victim;

(C) intentionally participated in an act, contemplating that the life of a person would be taken or intending that lethal force would be used in connection with a person, other than one of the participants in the offense, and the victim died as a direct result of the act; or

(D) intentionally and specifically engaged in an act of violence, knowing that the act created a grave risk of death to a person, other than one of the participants in the offense, such that participation in the act constituted a reckless disregard for human life and the victim died as a direct result of the act, shall be sentenced to death if, after consideration of the factors set forth in section 3592 in the course of a hearing held pursuant to section 3593, it is determined that imposition of a sentence of death is justified, except that no person may be sentenced to death who was less than 18 years of age at the time of the offense.

(b) A defendant who has been found guilty of—

(1) an offense * * * committed as part of a continuing criminal enterprise offense [which involved a specified quantity of controlled substance] or [specified gross receipts from drug trafficking]; or

(2) an offense * * * committed as part of a continuing criminal enterprise * * * where the defendant is a principal administrator, organizer, or leader of such an enterprise, and the defendant, in order to obstruct the investigation or prosecution of the enterprise or an offense involved in the enterprise, attempts to kill or knowingly directs, advises, authorizes, or assists another to attempt to kill any public officer, juror, witness, or members of the family or household of such a person, shall be sentenced to death if, after consideration of the factors set forth in section 3592 in the course of a hearing held pursuant to section 3593, it is determined that imposition of a sentence of death is justified, except that no person may be sentenced to death who was less than 18 years of age at the time of the offense.

18 U.S.C. § 3592. Mitigating and aggravating factors to be considered in determining whether a sentence of death is justified

(a) **Mitigating factors**.—In determining whether a sentence of death is to be imposed on a defendant, the finder of fact shall consider any mitigating factor, including the following:

(1) Impaired capacity.—The defendant's capacity to appreciate the wrongfulness of the defendant's conduct or to conform conduct to the requirements of law was significantly impaired, regardless of whether the capacity was so impaired as to constitute a defense to the charge.

(2) Duress.—The defendant was under unusual and substantial duress, regardless of whether the duress was of such a degree as to constitute a defense to the charge.

(3) Minor participation.—The defendant is punishable as a principal in the offense, which was committed by another, but the defendant's participation was relatively minor, regardless of whether the participation was so minor as to constitute a defense to the charge.

(4) Equally culpable defendants.—Another defendant or defendants, equally culpable in the crime, will not be punished by death.

(5) No prior criminal record.—The defendant did not have a significant prior history of other criminal conduct.

(6) Disturbance.—The defendant committed the offense under severe mental or emotional disturbance.

(7) Victim's consent.—The victim consented to the criminal conduct that resulted in the victim's death.

(8) Other factors.—Other factors in the defendant's background, record, or character or any other circumstance of the offense that mitigate against imposition of the death sentence.

(b) Aggravating factors for espionage and treason.—In determining whether a sentence of death is justified for an offense described in section 3591(a)(1), the jury, or if there is no jury, the court, shall consider each of the following aggravating factors for which notice has been given and determine which, if any, exist:

(1) Prior espionage or treason offense.—The defendant has previously been convicted of another offense involving espionage or treason for which a sentence of either life imprisonment or death was authorized by law.

(2) Grave risk to national security.—In the commission of the offense the defendant knowingly created a grave risk of substantial danger to the national security.

(3) Grave risk of death.—In the commission of the offense the defendant knowingly created a grave risk of death to another person.

The jury, or if there is no jury, the court, may consider whether any other aggravating factor for which notice has been given exists.

(c) Aggravating factors for homicide.—In determining whether a sentence of death is justified for an offense described in section 3591(a)(2), the jury, or if there is no jury, the court, shall consider each of the following aggravating factors for which notice has been given and determine which, if any, exist:

(1) Death during commission of another crime.—The death, or injury resulting in death, occurred during the commission or attempted commission of, or during the immediate flight from the commission of, an offense [of destruction of aircraft or aircraft facilities, destruction of motor vehicles or motor vehicle facilities, violence at international airports, violence against Members of Congress, Cabinet officers, or Supreme Court Justices,

escape or attempted escape by prisoners, gathering or delivering defense information to aid a foreign government, transportation of explosives in interstate commerce for certain purposes, destruction of Government property by explosives, murder by federal prisoner serving life term, kidnapping, destruction of property affecting interstate commerce by explosives, killing or attempted killing of diplomats, hostage taking, wrecking trains, sexual exploitation and other abuse of children, maritime violence, maritime platform violence, terrorist acts abroad against United States nationals, use of weapons of mass destruction, treason or aircraft piracy].

(2) Previous conviction of violent felony involving firearm.—For any offense, other than an offense for which a sentence of death is sought on the basis of section 924(c), the defendant has previously been convicted of a Federal or State offense punishable by a term of imprisonment of more than 1 year, involving the use or attempted or threatened use of a firearm * * * against another person.

(3) Previous conviction of offense for which a sentence of death or life imprisonment was authorized.—The defendant has previously been convicted of another Federal or State offense resulting in the death of a person, for which a sentence of life imprisonment or a sentence of death was authorized by statute.

(4) Previous conviction of other serious offenses.—The defendant has previously been convicted of 2 or more Federal or State offenses, punishable by a term of imprisonment of more than 1 year, committed on different occasions, involving the infliction of, or attempted infliction of, serious bodily injury or death upon another person.

(5) Grave risk of death to additional persons.—The defendant, in the commission of the offense, or in escaping apprehension for the violation of the offense, knowingly created a grave risk of death to 1 or more persons in addition to the victim of the offense.

(6) Heinous, cruel, or depraved manner of committing offense.—The defendant committed the offense in an especially heinous, cruel, or depraved manner in that it involved torture or serious physical abuse to the victim.

(7) Procurement of offense by payment.—The defendant procured the commission of the offense by payment, or promise of payment, of anything of pecuniary value.

(8) Pecuniary gain.—The defendant committed the offense as consideration for the receipt, or in the expectation of the receipt, of anything of pecuniary value.

(9) Substantial planning and premeditation.—The defendant committed the offense after substantial planning and premeditation to cause the death of a person or commit an act of terrorism.

(10) Conviction for two felony drug offenses.—The defendant has previously been convicted of 2 or more State or Federal offenses punisha-

ble by a term of imprisonment of more than one year, committed on different occasions, involving the distribution of a controlled substance.

(11) Vulnerability of victim.—The victim was particularly vulnerable due to old age, youth, or infirmity.

(12) Conviction for serious Federal drug offenses.—The defendant had previously been convicted of violating title II or III of the Comprehensive Drug Abuse Prevention and Control Act of 1970 for which a sentence of 5 or more years may be imposed or had previously been convicted of engaging in a continuing criminal enterprise.

(13) Continuing criminal enterprise involving drug sales to minors.— The defendant committed the offense in the course of engaging in a continuing criminal enterprise in violation of section 408(c) of the Controlled Substances Act (21 U.S.C. 848(c)), and that violation involved the distribution of drugs to persons under the age of 21 * * *.

(14) High public officials.—The defendant committed the offense against—

(A) the President of the United States, the President-elect, the Vice President, the Vice President-elect, the Vice President-designate, or, if there is no Vice President, the officer next in order of succession to the office of the President of the United States, or any person who is acting as President under the Constitution and laws of the United States;

(B) a chief of state, head of government, or the political equivalent, of a foreign nation;

(C) a foreign official listed in section 1116(b)(3)(A), if the official is in the United States on official business; or

(D) a Federal public servant who is a judge, a law enforcement officer, or an employee of a United States penal or correctional institution—

(i) while he or she is engaged in the performance of his or her official duties;

(ii) because of the performance of his or her official duties; or

(iii) because of his or her status as a public servant.

For purposes of this subparagraph, a "law enforcement officer" is a public servant authorized by law or by a Government agency or Congress to conduct or engage in the prevention, investigation, or prosecution or adjudication of an offense, and includes those engaged in corrections, parole, or probation functions.

(15) Prior conviction of sexual assault or child molestation.—In the case of an offense of * * * (sexual abuse) or * * * (sexual abuse of children), the defendant has previously been convicted of a crime of sexual assault or crime of child molestation.

(16) Multiple killings or attempted killings.—The defendant intentionally killed or attempted to kill more than one person in a single criminal episode.

The jury, or if there is no jury, the court, may consider whether any other aggravating factor for which notice has been given exists.

(d) Aggravating factors for drug offense death penalty.—In determining whether a sentence of death is justified for an offense described in section 3591(b), the jury, or if there is no jury, the court, shall consider each of the following aggravating factors for which notice has been given and determine which, if any, exist:

(1) Previous conviction of offense for which a sentence of death or life imprisonment was authorized.—The defendant has previously been convicted of another Federal or State offense resulting in the death of a person, for which a sentence of life imprisonment or death was authorized by statute.

(2) Previous conviction of other serious offenses.—The defendant has previously been convicted of two or more Federal or State offenses, each punishable by a term of imprisonment of more than one year, committed on different occasions, involving the importation, manufacture, or distribution of a controlled substance * * * or the infliction of, or attempted infliction of, serious bodily injury or death upon another person.

(3) Previous serious drug felony conviction.—The defendant has previously been convicted of another Federal or State offense involving the manufacture, distribution, importation, or possession of a controlled substance * * * for which a sentence of five or more years of imprisonment was authorized by statute.

(4) Use of firearm.—In committing the offense, or in furtherance of a continuing criminal enterprise of which the offense was a part, the defendant used a firearm or knowingly directed, advised, authorized, or assisted another to use a firearm to threaten, intimidate, assault, or injure a person.

(5) Distribution to persons under 21.—The offense, or a continuing criminal enterprise of which the offense was a part, involved [distribution of controlled substance to a person under 21 years of age] which was committed directly by the defendant.

(6) Distribution near schools.—The offense, or a continuing criminal enterprise of which the offense was a part, involved [distribution or possession with intent to distribute a controlled substance near a school, playground, or other specified facility] which was committed directly by the defendant.

(7) Using minors in trafficking.—The offense, or a continuing criminal enterprise of which the offense was a part, involved [employment, use, or coercion of a person under eighteen years of age in an illegal drug offense] which was committed directly by the defendant.

(8) Lethal adulterant.—The offense involved the importation, manufacture, or distribution of a controlled substance * * * mixed with a potentially lethal adulterant, and the defendant was aware of the presence of the adulterant.

The jury, or if there is no jury, the court, may consider whether any other aggravating factor for which notice has been given exists.

18 U.S.C. § 3593. Special hearing to determine whether a sentence of death is justified

(a) Notice by the government.—If, in a case involving an offense described in section 3591, the attorney for the government believes that the circumstances of the offense are such that a sentence of death is justified under this chapter, the attorney shall, a reasonable time before the trial or before acceptance by the court of a plea of guilty, sign and file with the court, and serve on the defendant, a notice—

(1) stating that the government believes that the circumstances of the offense are such that, if the defendant is convicted, a sentence of death is justified under this chapter and that the government will seek the sentence of death; and

(2) setting forth the aggravating factor or factors that the government, if the defendant is convicted, proposes to prove as justifying a sentence of death.

The factors for which notice is provided under this subsection may include factors concerning the effect of the offense on the victim and the victim's family, and may include oral testimony, a victim impact statement that identifies the victim of the offense and the extent and scope of the injury and loss suffered by the victim and the victim's family, and any other relevant information. The court may permit the attorney for the government to amend the notice upon a showing of good cause.

(b) Hearing before a court or jury.—If the attorney for the government has filed a notice as required under subsection (a) and the defendant is found guilty of or pleads guilty to an offense described in section 3591, the judge who presided at the trial or before whom the guilty plea was entered, or another judge if that judge is unavailable, shall conduct a separate sentencing hearing to determine the punishment to be imposed. The hearing shall be conducted—

(1) before the jury that determined the defendant's guilt;

(2) before a jury impaneled for the purpose of the hearing if—

(A) the defendant was convicted upon a plea of guilty;

(B) the defendant was convicted after a trial before the court sitting without a jury;

(C) the jury that determined the defendant's guilt was discharged for good cause; or

(D) after initial imposition of a sentence under this section, reconsideration of the sentence under this section is necessary; or

(3) before the court alone, upon the motion of the defendant and with the approval of the attorney for the government.

A jury impaneled pursuant to paragraph (2) shall consist of 12 members, unless, at any time before the conclusion of the hearing, the parties stipulate, with the approval of the court, that it shall consist of a lesser number.

(c) **Proof of mitigating and aggravating factors.**—Notwithstanding rule 32 of the Federal Rules of Criminal Procedure, when a defendant is found guilty or pleads guilty to an offense under section 3591, no presentence report shall be prepared. At the sentencing hearing, information may be presented as to any matter relevant to the sentence, including any mitigating or aggravating factor permitted or required to be considered under section 3592. Information presented may include the trial transcript and exhibits if the hearing is held before a jury or judge not present during the trial, or at the trial judge's discretion. The defendant may present any information relevant to a mitigating factor. The government may present any information relevant to an aggravating factor for which notice has been provided under subsection (a). Information is admissible regardless of its admissibility under the rules governing admission of evidence at criminal trials except that information may be excluded if its probative value is outweighed by the danger of creating unfair prejudice, confusing the issues, or misleading the jury. For the purposes of the preceding sentence, the fact that a victim * * * attended or observed the trial shall not be construed to pose a danger of creating unfair prejudice, confusing the issues, or misleading the jury. The government and the defendant shall be permitted to rebut any information received at the hearing, and shall be given fair opportunity to present argument as to the adequacy of the information to establish the existence of any aggravating or mitigating factor, and as to the appropriateness in the case of imposing a sentence of death. The government shall open the argument. The defendant shall be permitted to reply. The government shall then be permitted to reply in rebuttal. The burden of establishing the existence of any aggravating factor is on the government, and is not satisfied unless the existence of such a factor is established beyond a reasonable doubt. The burden of establishing the existence of any mitigating factor is on the defendant, and is not satisfied unless the existence of such a factor is established by a preponderance of the information.

(d) **Return of special findings**.—The jury, or if there is no jury, the court, shall consider all the information received during the hearing. It shall return special findings identifying any aggravating factor or factors set forth in section 3592 found to exist and any other aggravating factor for which notice has been provided under subsection (a) found to exist. A finding with respect to a mitigating factor may be made by 1 or more members of the jury, and any member of the jury who finds the existence of a mitigating factor may consider such factor established for purposes of this section regardless of the number of jurors who concur that the factor has been established. A finding with respect to any aggravating factor must be unanimous. If no aggravating factor set forth in section 3592 is found to exist, the court shall impose a sentence other than death authorized by law.

(e) Return of a finding concerning a sentence of death.—If, in the case of—

(1) an offense described in section 3591(a)(1), an aggravating factor required to be considered under section 3592(b) is found to exist;

(2) an offense described in section 3591(a)(2), an aggravating factor required to be considered under section 3592(c) is found to exist; or

(3) an offense described in section 3591(b), an aggravating factor required to be considered under section 3592(d) is found to exist,

The jury, or if there is no jury, the court, shall consider whether all the aggravating factor or factors found to exist sufficiently outweigh all the mitigating factor or factors found to exist to justify a sentence of death, or, in the absence of a mitigating factor, whether the aggravating factor or factors alone are sufficient to justify a sentence of death. Based upon this consideration, the jury by unanimous vote, or if there is no jury, the court, shall recommend whether the defendant should be sentenced to death, to life imprisonment without possibility of release or some other lesser sentence.

(f) Special precaution to ensure against discrimination.—In a hearing held before a jury, the court, prior to the return of a finding under subsection (e), shall instruct the jury that, in considering whether a sentence of death is justified, it shall not consider the race, color, religious beliefs, national origin, or sex of the defendant or of any victim and that the jury is not to recommend a sentence of death unless it has concluded that it would recommend a sentence of death for the crime in question no matter what the race, color, religious beliefs, national origin, or sex of the defendant or of any victim may be. The jury, upon return of a finding under subsection (e), shall also return to the court a certificate, signed by each juror, that consideration of the race, color, religious beliefs, national origin, or sex of the defendant or any victim was not involved in reaching his or her individual decision and that the individual juror would have made the same recommendation regarding a sentence for the crime in question no matter what the race, color, religious beliefs, national origin, or sex of the defendant or any victim may be.

18 U.S.C. § 3594. Imposition of a sentence of death

Upon a recommendation under section 3593(e) that the defendant should be sentenced to death or life imprisonment without possibility of release, the court shall sentence the defendant accordingly. Otherwise, the court shall impose any lesser sentence that is authorized by law. Notwithstanding any other law, if the maximum term of imprisonment for the offense is life imprisonment, the court may impose a sentence of life imprisonment without possibility of release.

18 U.S.C. § 3595. Review of a sentence of death

(a) Appeal.—In a case in which a sentence of death is imposed, the sentence shall be subject to review by the court of appeals upon appeal by the defendant. Notice of appeal must be filed within the time specified for the filing of a notice of appeal. An appeal under this section may be consolidated with an appeal of the judgment of conviction and shall have priority over all other cases.

(b) Review.—The court of appeals shall review the entire record in the case, including—

(1) the evidence submitted during the trial;

(2) the information submitted during the sentencing hearing;

(3) the procedures employed in the sentencing hearing; and

(4) the special findings returned under section 3593(d).

(c) Decision and disposition.—

(1) The court of appeals shall address all substantive and procedural issues raised on the appeal of a sentence of death, and shall consider whether the sentence of death was imposed under the influence of passion, prejudice, or any other arbitrary factor and whether the evidence supports the special finding of the existence of an aggravating factor required to be considered under section 3592.

(2) Whenever the court of appeals finds that—

(A) the sentence of death was imposed under the influence of passion, prejudice, or any other arbitrary factor;

(B) the admissible evidence and information adduced does not support the special finding of the existence of the required aggravating factor; or

(C) the proceedings involved any other legal error requiring reversal of the sentence that was properly preserved for appeal under the rules of criminal procedure,

The court shall remand the case for reconsideration under section 3593 or imposition of a sentence other than death. The court of appeals shall not reverse or vacate a sentence of death on account of any error which can be harmless, including any erroneous special finding of an aggravating factor, where the Government establishes beyond a reasonable doubt that the error was harmless.

(3) The court of appeals shall state in writing the reasons for its disposition of an appeal of a sentence of death under this section.

18 U.S.C. § 3596. Implementation of a sentence of death

(a) In general.—A person who has been sentenced to death pursuant to this chapter shall be committed to the custody of the Attorney General until exhaustion of the procedures for appeal of the judgment of conviction and for review of the sentence. When the sentence is to be implemented, the Attorney General shall release the person sentenced to death to the custody of a United States marshal, who shall supervise implementation of the sentence in the manner prescribed by the law of the State in which the sentence is imposed. If the law of the State does not provide for implementation of a sentence of death, the court shall designate another State, the law of which does provide for the implementation of a sentence of death, and the sentence shall be implemented in the latter State in the manner prescribed by such law.

(b) Pregnant woman.—A sentence of death shall not be carried out upon a woman while she is pregnant.

(c) Mental capacity.—A sentence of death shall not be carried out upon a person who is mentally retarded. A sentence of death shall not be carried out upon a person who, as a result of mental disability, lacks the mental capacity to understand the death penalty and why it was imposed on that person.

18 U.S.C. § 3597. Use of State facilities

(a) In general.—A United States marshal charged with supervising the implementation of a sentence of death may use appropriate State or local facilities for the purpose, may use the services of an appropriate State or local official or of a person such an official employs for the purpose, and shall pay the costs thereof in an amount approved by the Attorney General.

(b) Excuse of an employee on moral or religious grounds.—No employee of any State department of corrections, the United States Department of Justice, the Federal Bureau of Prisons, or the United States Marshals Service, and no employee providing services to that department, bureau, or service under contract shall be required, as a condition of that employment or contractual obligation, to be in attendance at or to participate in any prosecution or execution under this section if such participation is contrary to the moral or religious convictions of the employee. In this subsection, "participation in executions" includes personal preparation of the condemned individual and the apparatus used for execution and supervision of the activities of other personnel in carrying out such activities.

18 U.S.C. § 3598. Special provisions for Indian country

Notwithstanding sections 1152 and 1153, no person subject to the criminal jurisdiction of an Indian tribal government shall be subject to a capital sentence under this chapter for any offense the Federal jurisdiction for which is predicated solely on Indian country * * * and which has occurred within the boundaries of Indian country, unless the governing body of the tribe has elected that this chapter have effect over land and persons subject to its criminal jurisdiction.

C. EXCERPTS FROM THE FEDERAL HABEAS CORPUS STATUTE[a]

28 U.S.C. § 2241. Power to grant writ

(a) Writs of habeas corpus may be granted by the Supreme Court, any justice thereof, the district courts and any circuit judge within their respective jurisdictions. The order of a circuit judge shall be entered in the records of the district court of the district wherein the restraint complained of is had.

(b) The Supreme Court, any justice thereof, and any circuit judge may decline to entertain an application for a writ of habeas corpus and may transfer the application for hearing and determination to the district court having jurisdiction to entertain it.

(c) The writ of habeas corpus shall not extend to a prisoner unless—

(1) He is in custody under or by color of the authority of the United States or is committed for trial before some court thereof; or

(2) He is in custody for an act done or omitted in pursuance of an Act of Congress, or an order, process, judgment or decree of a court or judge of the United States; or

(3) He is in custody in violation of the Constitution or laws or treaties of the United States; or

(4) He, being a citizen of a foreign state and domiciled therein is in custody for an act done or omitted under any alleged right, title, authority, privilege, protection, or exemption claimed under the commission, order or sanction of any foreign state, or under color thereof, the validity and effect of which depend upon the law of nations; or

(5) It is necessary to bring him into court to testify or for trial.

(d) Where an application for a writ of habeas corpus is made by a person in custody under the judgment and sentence of a State court of a State which contains two or more Federal judicial districts, the application may be filed in the district court for the district wherein such person is in custody or in the district court for the district within which the State court was held which convicted and sentenced him and each of such district courts shall have concurrent jurisdiction to entertain the application. The district court for the district wherein such an application is filed in the exercise of its discretion and in furtherance of justice may transfer the application to the other district court for hearing and determination.

* * *

28 U.S.C. § 2242. Application

Application for a writ of habeas corpus shall be in writing signed and verified by the person for whose relief it is intended or by someone acting in his behalf.

---

a. The provisions contained in 28 U.S.C. §§ 2243, 2245–2250 and 2252 which address habeas corpus pleadings and procedures, evidence, and notice are not included in this appendix.

It shall allege the facts concerning the applicant's commitment or detention, the name of the person who has custody over him and by virtue of what claim or authority, if known.

It may be amended or supplemented as provided in the rules of procedure applicable to civil actions.

If addressed to the Supreme Court, a justice thereof or a circuit judge it shall state the reasons for not making application to the district court of the district in which the applicant is held.

28 U.S.C. § 2244. Finality of determination

(a) No circuit or district judge shall be required to entertain an application for a writ of habeas corpus to inquire into the detention of a person pursuant to a judgment of a court of the United States if it appears that the legality of such detention has been determined by a judge or court of the United States on a prior application for a writ of habeas corpus, except as provided in section 2255.

(b)(1) A claim presented in a second or successive habeas corpus application under section 2254 that was presented in a prior application shall be dismissed.

(2) A claim presented in a second or successive habeas corpus application under section 2254 that was not presented in a prior application shall be dismissed unless—

(A) the applicant shows that the claim relies on a new rule of constitutional law, made retroactive to cases on collateral review by the Supreme Court, that was previously unavailable; or

(B)(i) the factual predicate for the claim could not have been discovered previously through the exercise of due diligence; and

(ii) the facts underlying the claim, if proven and viewed in light of the evidence as a whole, would be sufficient to establish by clear and convincing evidence that, but for constitutional error, no reasonable factfinder would have found the applicant guilty of the underlying offense.

(3)(A) Before a second or successive application permitted by this section is filed in the district court, the applicant shall move in the appropriate court of appeals for an order authorizing the district court to consider the application.

(B) A motion in the court of appeals for an order authorizing the district court to consider a second or successive application shall be determined by a three-judge panel of the court of appeals.

(C) The court of appeals may authorize the filing of a second or successive application only if it determines that the application makes a prima facie showing that the application satisfies the requirements of this subsection.

(D) The court of appeals shall grant or deny the authorization to file a second or successive application not later than 30 days after the filing of the motion.

(E) The grant or denial of an authorization by a court of appeals to file a second or successive application shall not be appealable and shall not be the subject of a petition for rehearing or for a writ of certiorari.

(4) A district court shall dismiss any claim presented in a second or successive application that the court of appeals has authorized to be filed unless the applicant shows that the claim satisfies the requirements of this section.

(c) In a habeas corpus proceeding brought in behalf of a person in custody pursuant to the judgment of a State court, a prior judgment of the Supreme Court of the United States on an appeal or review by a writ of certiorari at the instance of the prisoner of the decision of such State court, shall be conclusive as to all issues of fact or law with respect to an asserted denial of a Federal right which constitutes ground for discharge in a habeas corpus proceeding, actually adjudicated by the Supreme Court therein, unless the applicant for the writ of habeas corpus shall plead and the court shall find the existence of a material and controlling fact which did not appear in the record of the proceeding in the Supreme Court and the court shall further find that the applicant for the writ of habeas corpus could not have caused such fact to appear in such record by the exercise of reasonable diligence.

(d)(1) A 1–year period of limitation shall apply to an application for a writ of habeas corpus by a person in custody pursuant to the judgment of a State court. The limitation period shall run from the latest of—

(A) the date on which the judgment became final by the conclusion of direct review or the expiration of the time for seeking such review;

(B) the date on which the impediment to filing an application created by State action in violation of the Constitution or laws of the United States is removed, if the applicant was prevented from filing by such State action;

(C) the date on which the constitutional right asserted was initially recognized by the Supreme Court, if the right has been newly recognized by the Supreme Court and made retroactively applicable to cases on collateral review; or

(D) the date on which the factual predicate of the claim or claims presented could have been discovered through the exercise of due diligence.

(2) The time during which a properly filed application for State post-conviction or other collateral review with respect to the pertinent judgment or claim is pending shall not be counted toward any period of limitation under this subsection.

28 U.S.C. § 2251. Stay of State court proceedings

(a) In General.—

(1) Pending matters.—A justice or judge of the United States before whom a habeas corpus proceeding is pending, may, before final judgment or after final judgment of discharge, or pending appeal, stay any proceeding against the person detained in any State court or by or under the authority of any State for any matter involved in the habeas corpus proceeding.

(2) Matter not pending.—For purposes of this section, a habeas corpus proceeding is not pending until the application is filed.

(3) Application for appointment of counsel.—If a State prisoner sentenced to death applies for appointment of counsel * * * in a court that would have jurisdiction to entertain a habeas corpus application regarding that sentence, that court may stay execution of the sentence of death, but such stay shall terminate not later than 90 days after counsel is appointed or the application for appointment of counsel is withdrawn or denied.

(b) No Further Proceedings.—After the granting of such a stay, any such proceeding in any State court or by or under the authority of any State shall be void. If no stay is granted, any such proceeding shall be as valid as if no habeas corpus proceedings or appeal were pending.

28 U.S.C. § 2253. Appeal

(a) In a habeas corpus proceeding or a proceeding under section 2255 before a district judge, the final order shall be subject to review, on appeal, by the court of appeals for the circuit in which the proceeding is held.

(b) There shall be no right of appeal from a final order in a proceeding to test the validity of a warrant to remove to another district or place for commitment or trial a person charged with a criminal offense against the United States, or to test the validity of such person's detention pending removal proceedings.

(c)(1) Unless a circuit justice or judge issues a certificate of appealability, an appeal may not be taken to the court of appeals from—

(A) the final order in a habeas corpus proceeding in which the detention complained of arises out of process issued by a State court; or

(B) the final order in a proceeding under section 2255.

(2) A certificate of appealability may issue under paragraph (1) only if the applicant has made a substantial showing of the denial of a constitutional right.

(3) The certificate of appealability under paragraph (1) shall indicate which specific issue or issues satisfy the showing required by paragraph (2).

28 U.S.C. § 2254. State custody; remedies in Federal courts

(a) The Supreme Court, a Justice thereof, a circuit judge, or a district court shall entertain an application for a writ of habeas corpus in behalf of a person in custody pursuant to the judgment of a State court only on the ground that he is in custody in violation of the Constitution or laws or treaties of the United States.

(b)(1) An application for a writ of habeas corpus on behalf of a person in custody pursuant to the judgment of a State court shall not be granted unless it appears that—

(A) the applicant has exhausted the remedies available in the courts of the State; or

(B)(i) there is an absence of available State corrective process; or

(ii) circumstances exist that render such process ineffective to protect the rights of the applicant.

(2) An application for a writ of habeas corpus may be denied on the merits, notwithstanding the failure of the applicant to exhaust the remedies available in the courts of the State.

(3) A State shall not be deemed to have waived the exhaustion requirement or be estopped from reliance upon the requirement unless the State, through counsel, expressly waives the requirement.

(c) An applicant shall not be deemed to have exhausted the remedies available in the courts of the State, within the meaning of this section, if he has the right under the law of the State to raise, by any available procedure, the question presented.

(d) An application for a writ of habeas corpus on behalf of a person in custody pursuant to the judgment of a State court shall not be granted with respect to any claim that was adjudicated on the merits in State court proceedings unless the adjudication of the claim—

(1) resulted in a decision that was contrary to, or involved an unreasonable application of, clearly established Federal law, as determined by the Supreme Court of the United States; or

(2) resulted in a decision that was based on an unreasonable determination of the facts in light of the evidence presented in the State court proceeding.

(e)(1) In a proceeding instituted by an application for a writ of habeas corpus by a person in custody pursuant to the judgment of a State court, a determination of a factual issue made by a State court shall be presumed to be correct. The applicant shall have the burden of rebutting the presumption of correctness by clear and convincing evidence.

(2) If the applicant has failed to develop the factual basis of a claim in State court proceedings, the court shall not hold an evidentiary hearing on the claim unless the applicant shows that—

(A) the claim relies on—

(i) a new rule of constitutional law, made retroactive to cases on collateral review by the Supreme Court, that was previously unavailable; or

(ii) a factual predicate that could not have been previously discovered through the exercise of due diligence; and

(B) the facts underlying the claim would be sufficient to establish by clear and convincing evidence that but for constitutional error, no reasonable factfinder would have found the applicant guilty of the underlying offense.

(f) If the applicant challenges the sufficiency of the evidence adduced in such State court proceeding to support the State court's determination of a factual issue made therein, the applicant, if able, shall produce that part of the record pertinent to a determination of the sufficiency of the evidence to support such determination. If the applicant, because of indigency or other reason is unable to produce such part of the record, then the State shall produce such part of the record and the Federal court shall direct the State to do so by order directed to an appropriate State official. If the State cannot provide such pertinent part of the record, then the court shall determine under the existing facts and circumstances what weight shall be given to the State court's factual determination.

(g) A copy of the official records of the State court, duly certified by the clerk of such court to be a true and correct copy of a finding, judicial opinion, or other reliable written indicia showing such a factual determination by the State court shall be admissible in the Federal court proceeding.

(h) Except as provided in section 408 of the Controlled Substances Act, in all proceedings brought under this section, and any subsequent proceedings on review, the court may appoint counsel for an applicant who is or becomes financially unable to afford counsel, except as provided by a rule promulgated by the Supreme Court pursuant to statutory authority.
* * *

(i) The ineffectiveness or incompetence of counsel during Federal or State collateral post-conviction proceedings shall not be a ground for relief in a proceeding arising under section 2254.

28 U.S.C. § 2255. Federal custody; remedies on motion attacking sentence

(a) A prisoner in custody under sentence of a court established by Act of Congress claiming the right to be released upon the ground that the sentence was imposed in violation of the Constitution or laws of the United States, or that the court was without jurisdiction to impose such sentence, or that the sentence was in excess of the maximum authorized by law, or is otherwise subject to collateral attack, may move the court which imposed the sentence to vacate, set aside or correct the sentence.

(b) Unless the motion and the files and records of the case conclusively show that the prisoner is entitled to no relief, the court shall cause notice thereof to be served upon the United States attorney, grant a prompt hearing thereon, determine the issues and make findings of fact and conclusions of law with respect thereto. If the court finds that the judgment was rendered without jurisdiction, or that the sentence imposed was not authorized by law or otherwise open to collateral attack, or that there has been such a denial or infringement of the constitutional rights of the prisoner as to render the judgment vulnerable to collateral attack, the court shall vacate and set the judgment aside and shall discharge the prisoner or resentence him or grant a new trial or correct the sentence as may appear appropriate.

(c) A court may entertain and determine such motion without requiring the production of the prisoner at the hearing.

(d) An appeal may be taken to the court of appeals from the order entered on the motion as from a final judgment on application for a writ of habeas corpus.

(e) An application for a writ of habeas corpus in behalf of a prisoner who is authorized to apply for relief by motion pursuant to this section, shall not be entertained if it appears that the applicant has failed to apply for relief, by motion, to the court which sentenced him, or that such court has denied him relief, unless it also appears that the remedy by motion is inadequate or ineffective to test the legality of his detention.

(f) A 1–year period of limitation shall apply to a motion under this section. The limitation period shall run from the latest of—

(1) the date on which the judgment of conviction becomes final;

(2) the date on which the impediment to making a motion created by governmental action in violation of the Constitution or laws of the United States is removed, if the movant was prevented from making a motion by such governmental action;

(3) the date on which the right asserted was initially recognized by the Supreme Court, if that right has been newly recognized by the Supreme Court and made retroactively applicable to cases on collateral review; or

(4) the date on which the facts supporting the claim or claims presented could have been discovered through the exercise of due diligence.

(g) Except as provided in section 408 of the Controlled Substances Act, in all proceedings brought under this section, and any subsequent proceedings on review, the court may appoint counsel, except as provided by a rule promulgated by the Supreme Court pursuant to statutory authority. * * *

(h) A second or successive motion must be certified as provided in section 2244 by a panel of the appropriate court of appeals to contain—

(1) newly discovered evidence that, if proven and viewed in light of the evidence as a whole, would be sufficient to establish by clear and convincing evidence that no reasonable factfinder would have found the movant guilty of the offense; or

(2) a new rule of constitutional law, made retroactive to cases on collateral review by the Supreme Court, that was previously unavailable.

28 U.S.C. § 2261. Prisoners in State custody subject to capital sentence; appointment of counsel; requirement of rule of court or statute; procedures for appointment

(a) This chapter shall apply to cases arising under section 2254 brought by prisoners in State custody who are subject to a capital sentence. It shall apply only if the provisions of subsections (b) and (c) are satisfied.

(b) Counsel—This chapter is applicable if—

(1) the Attorney General of the United States certifies that a State has established a mechanism for providing counsel in postconviction proceedings as provided in section 2265; and

(2) counsel was provided pursuant to that mechanism, petitioner validly waived counsel, petitioner retained counsel, or petitioner was found not to be indigent.

(c) Any mechanism for the appointment, compensation, and reimbursement of counsel as provided in subsection (b) must offer counsel to all State prisoners under capital sentence and must provide for the entry of an order by a court of record—

(1) appointing one or more counsels to represent the prisoner upon a finding that the prisoner is indigent and accepted the offer or is unable competently to decide whether to accept or reject the offer;

(2) finding, after a hearing if necessary, that the prisoner rejected the offer of counsel and made the decision with an understanding of its legal consequences; or

(3) denying the appointment of counsel upon a finding that the prisoner is not indigent.

(d) No counsel appointed pursuant to subsections (b) and (c) to represent a State prisoner under capital sentence shall have previously represented the prisoner at trial in the case for which the appointment is made unless the prisoner and counsel expressly request continued representation.

(e) The ineffectiveness or incompetence of counsel during State or Federal post-conviction proceedings in a capital case shall not be a ground for relief in a proceeding arising under section 2254. This limitation shall not preclude the appointment of different counsel, on the court's own motion or at the request of the prisoner, at any phase of State or Federal post-conviction proceedings on the basis of the ineffectiveness or incompetence of counsel in such proceedings.

28 U.S.C. § 2262. Mandatory stay of execution; duration; limits on stays of execution; successive petitions

(a) Upon the entry in the appropriate State court of record of an order under section 2261(c), a warrant or order setting an execution date for a State prisoner shall be stayed upon application to any court that would have jurisdiction over any proceedings filed under section 2254. The application shall recite that the State has invoked the post-conviction review procedures of this chapter and that the scheduled execution is subject to stay.

(b) A stay of execution granted pursuant to subsection (a) shall expire if—

(1) a State prisoner fails to file a habeas corpus application under section 2254 within the time required in section 2263;

(2) before a court of competent jurisdiction, in the presence of counsel, unless the prisoner has competently and knowingly waived such counsel, and after having been advised of the consequences, a State prisoner under capital sentence waives the right to pursue habeas corpus review under section 2254; or

(3) a State prisoner files a habeas corpus petition under section 2254 within the time required by section 2263 and fails to make a substantial showing of the denial of a Federal right or is denied relief in the district court or at any subsequent stage of review.

(c) If one of the conditions in subsection (b) has occurred, no Federal court thereafter shall have the authority to enter a stay of execution in the case, unless the court of appeals approves the filing of a second or successive application under section 2244(b).

28 U.S.C. § 2263. Filing of habeas corpus application; time requirements; tolling rules

(a) Any application under this chapter for habeas corpus relief under section 2254 must be filed in the appropriate district court not later than 180 days after final State court affirmance of the conviction and sentence on direct review or the expiration of the time for seeking such review.

(b) The time requirements established by subsection (a) shall be tolled—

(1) from the date that a petition for certiorari is filed in the Supreme Court until the date of final disposition of the petition if a State prisoner files the petition to secure review by the Supreme Court of the affirmance of a capital sentence on direct review by the court of last resort of the State or other final State court decision on direct review;

(2) from the date on which the first petition for post-conviction review or other collateral relief is filed until the final State court disposition of such petition; and

(3) during an additional period not to exceed 30 days, if—

(A) a motion for an extension of time is filed in the Federal district court that would have jurisdiction over the case upon the filing of a habeas corpus application under section 2254; and

(B) a showing of good cause is made for the failure to file the habeas corpus application within the time period established by this section.

28 U.S.C. § 2264. Scope of Federal review; district court adjudications

(a) Whenever a State prisoner under capital sentence files a petition for habeas corpus relief to which this chapter applies, the district court shall only consider a claim or claims that have been raised and decided on the merits in the State courts, unless the failure to raise the claim properly is—

(1) the result of State action in violation of the Constitution or laws of the United States;

(2) the result of the Supreme Court's recognition of a new Federal right that is made retroactively applicable; or

(3) based on a factual predicate that could not have been discovered through the exercise of due diligence in time to present the claim for State or Federal post-conviction review.

(b) Following review subject to subsections (a), (d), and (e) of section 2254, the court shall rule on the claims properly before it.

28 U.S.C. § 2265. Certification and judicial review

(a) Certification.—

(1) In general.—If requested by an appropriate State official, the Attorney General of the United States shall determine—

(A) whether the State has established a mechanism for the appointment, compensation, and payment of reasonable litigation expenses of competent counsel in State postconviction proceedings brought by indigent prisoners who have been sentenced to death;

(B) the date on which the mechanism described in subparagraph(A) was established; and

(C) whether the State provides standards of competency for the appointment of counsel in proceedings described in subparagraph (A).

(2) Effective date.—The date the mechanism described in paragraph (1)(A) was established shall be the effective date of the certification under this subsection.

(3) Only express requirements.—There are no requirements for certification or for application of this chapter other than those expressly stated in this chapter.

(b) Regulations.—The Attorney General shall promulgate regulations to implement the certification procedure under subsection (a).

(c) Review of Certification.—

(1) In general.—The determination by the Attorney General regarding whether to certify a State under this section is subject to review exclusively as provided under chapter 158 of this title.

(2) Venue.—The Court of Appeals for the District of Columbia Circuit shall have exclusive jurisdiction over matters under paragraph (1), subject to review by the Supreme Court under section 2350 of this title.

(3) Standard of review.—The determination by the Attorney General regarding whether to certify a State under this section shall be subject to de novo review.

28 U.S.C. § 2266. Limitation periods for determining applications and motions

(a) The adjudication of any application under section 2254 that is subject to this chapter, and the adjudication of any motion under section 2255 by a person under sentence of death, shall be given priority by the district court and by the court of appeals over all noncapital matters.

(b)(1)(A) A district court shall render a final determination and enter a final judgment on any application for a writ of habeas corpus brought under this chapter in a capital case not later than 450 days after the date on which the application is filed, or 60 days after the date on which the case is submitted for decision, whichever is earlier.

(B) A district court shall afford the parties at least 120 days in which to complete all actions, including the preparation of all pleadings and briefs, and if necessary, a hearing, prior to the submission of the case for decision.

(C)(i) A district court may delay for not more than one additional 30–day period beyond the period specified in subparagraph (A), the rendering of a determination of an application for a writ of habeas corpus if the court issues a written order making a finding, and stating the reasons for the finding, that the ends of justice that would be served by allowing the delay outweigh the best interests of the public and the applicant in a speedy disposition of the application.

(ii) The factors, among others, that a court shall consider in determining whether a delay in the disposition of an application is warranted are as follows:

(I) Whether the failure to allow the delay would be likely to result in a miscarriage of justice.

(II) Whether the case is so unusual or so complex, due to the number of defendants, the nature of the prosecution, or the existence of novel questions of fact or law, that it is unreasonable to expect adequate briefing within the time limitations established by subparagraph (A).

(III) Whether the failure to allow a delay in a case that, taken as a whole, is not so unusual or so complex as described in subclause (II), but would otherwise deny the applicant reasonable time to obtain counsel, would unreasonably deny the applicant or the government continuity of counsel, or would deny counsel for the applicant or the government the reasonable time necessary for effective preparation, taking into account the exercise of due diligence.

(iii) No delay in disposition shall be permissible because of general congestion of the court's calendar.

(iv) The court shall transmit a copy of any order issued under clause (i) to the Director of the Administrative Office of the United States Courts for inclusion in the report under paragraph (5).

(2) The time limitations under paragraph (1) shall apply to—

(A) an initial application for a writ of habeas corpus;

(B) any second or successive application for a writ of habeas corpus; and

(C) any redetermination of an application for a writ of habeas corpus following a remand by the court of appeals or the Supreme Court for further proceedings, in which case the limitation period shall run from the date the remand is ordered.

(3)(A) The time limitations under this section shall not be construed to entitle an applicant to a stay of execution, to which the applicant would otherwise not be entitled, for the purpose of litigating any application or appeal.

(B) No amendment to an application for a writ of habeas corpus under this chapter shall be permitted after the filing of the answer to the application, except on the grounds specified in section 2244(b).

(4)(A) The failure of a court to meet or comply with a time limitation under this section shall not be a ground for granting relief from a judgment of conviction or sentence.

(B) The State may enforce a time limitation under this section by petitioning for a writ of mandamus to the court of appeals. The court of appeals shall act on the petition for a writ of mandamus not later than 30 days after the filing of the petition.

(5)(A) The Administrative Office of the United States Courts shall submit to Congress an annual report on the compliance by the district courts with the time limitations under this section.

(B) The report described in subparagraph (A) shall include copies of the orders submitted by the district courts under paragraph (1)(B)(iv).

(c)(1)(A) A court of appeals shall hear and render a final determination of any appeal of an order granting or denying, in whole or in part, an application brought under this chapter in a capital case not later than 120 days after the date on which the reply brief is filed, or if no reply brief is filed, not later than 120 days after the date on which the answering brief is filed.

(B)(i) A court of appeals shall decide whether to grant a petition for rehearing or other request for rehearing en banc not later than 30 days after the date on which the petition for rehearing is filed unless a responsive pleading is required, in which case the court shall decide whether to grant the petition not later than 30 days after the date on which the responsive pleading is filed.

(ii) If a petition for rehearing or rehearing en banc is granted, the court of appeals shall hear and render a final determination of the appeal not later than 120 days after the date on which the order granting rehearing or rehearing en banc is entered.

(2) The time limitations under paragraph (1) shall apply to—

(A) an initial application for a writ of habeas corpus;

(B) any second or successive application for a writ of habeas corpus; and

(C) any redetermination of an application for a writ of habeas corpus or related appeal following a remand by the court of appeals en banc or the Supreme Court for further proceedings, in which case the limitation period shall run from the date the remand is ordered.

(3) The time limitations under this section shall not be construed to entitle an applicant to a stay of execution, to which the applicant would otherwise not be entitled, for the purpose of litigating any application or appeal.

(4)(A) The failure of a court to meet or comply with a time limitation under this section shall not be a ground for granting relief from a judgment of conviction or sentence.

(B) The State may enforce a time limitation under this section by applying for a writ of mandamus to the Supreme Court.

(5) The Administrative Office of the United States Courts shall submit to Congress an annual report on the compliance by the courts of appeals with the time limitations under this section.

*

INDEX

References are to Pages

**ELIGIBILITY AND SELECTION DETER-
MINATIONS**
Generally, 239
Bifurcation of, 315
Broad death-eligibility states, 163
Distinctions, 239
Eighth Amendment requirements, 605
Guilt phase eligibility states, 315
Individualized determination at selection stage, 607
Jury instructions, 605
Legislative eligibility standards, 19
Nonexclusive eligibility factors, 137
Penalty phase eligibility states, 315
Selection decision distinguished, 239
Vague eligibility standards, 605
Weighing and nonweighing states, 137

EMPIRICAL STUDIES
See also Policy Considerations, this index
Character Studies, this index
Declining rates of execution, 50
Deterrence value of capital punishment, 12, 13
Gender disparities, 26
Innocents, executions of, 16
Juror understanding of instructions, 605, 653
National consensus. See Eighth Amendment, this index
Racial disparities
Generally, 26, 122
ABA study, 196
Sentencing study, 182
Sociopathic disorders, 40
Statistical studies methodology, 182

EQUAL PROTECTION
Arbitrariness, this index
Eighth Amendment protections compared, 47
Fairness Considerations, this index
Fourteenth Amendment incorporation doctrine, 75
Right to counsel, 28
State laws, state court applications of, 175
Uniformity of treatment and guided discretion, 231

EXECUTIONS
Generally, 803 et seq.
Chessman execution, 25
Clemency proceedings, 833
Death row incarceration conditions, 806
Death row incarceration costs, 15
Declining rates of, 50
Delay and retribution purpose, 11
Delay and victims' rights, 11
Delay as cruel and unusual, 803
Deterrence purposes, effect of delay on, 804
Eleventh hour appeals, 109
Family of prisoner, 115
Humane methods, 51
Humanity denial, execution as, 49
Illinois commutations, 841
Insane persons
Generally, 262, 287, 806
Curing for execution, 831
Post-conviction insanity, 820

EXECUTIONS—Cont'd
Juveniles
Generally, 276
See also Juvenile Executions, this index
Lackey claims, 805
Lethal injection, challenges as cruel and unusual, 841, 858
Mentally retarded persons
Generally, 258
See also Mentally Retarded Persons, Executions of
Narrative, execution day, 109
Physicians' ethical concerns, 863
Public executions, 23
Public viewings, 863
Rarity of, 50
Retribution purposes, effect of delay on, 804
Suicides on death row, 806

EXPERT WITNESSES
Aggravating factors opinions, 562
Appointment costs, 15
Character study of penalty-phase prosecution expert, 564
Competency to stand trial, 390
Cross-examination of experts, value of, 559
Deterrence effect of capital punishment, 12
Empirical Studies, this index
Future dangerousness opinions
Aggravating factors determinations, 562
American Psychiatric Association view, 576, 586
Penalty hearings, 545, 547
Race-based, 563
Insanity opinions, cross-examination rights, 813
Mentally retarded defendants, 259
Penalty hearings
Generally, 545
Future dangerousness opinions, 547
Reliability challenges, 561
Self-incrimination privileges, 561
Race-based dangerousness opinions, 563
Social histories of defendants, 410
Sociopathic disorders, 40
Statistical studies methodology, 182

FACTUAL INNOCENCE
See Innocence Questions, this index

FAIRNESS CONSIDERATIONS
See also Equal Protection, this index
Appointed counsel for indigents, 17
Arbitrariness
Generally, 17
See also Arbitrariness, this index
Arguments for and against death penalty, 8, 15
Empirical studies, 15
Innocents, executions of, 16
Moral weighing of justice vs equality, 17
Prosecutorial discretion and risk of arbitrariness, 17
Racial bias
Generally, 16
See also Racial Disparities, this index
Reversal rates of death sentences, 15

RELIGION—Cont'd
Colonial era, religion and capital punishment in, 21
Conscientious objectors, disqualification of from juries, 330
Policy considerations based on, 8

RESIDUAL DOUBT
See also Lingering Doubt, this index; Innocence Questions, this index
Mitigator, jury treatment as, 602
Penalty hearings, residual doubt evidence at, 422
Unitary vs bifurcated proceedings, 352

RETARDATION, MENTAL
See Mentally Retarded Persons, Executions of, this index

RETRIBUTION PURPOSES
See also Deterrence Purposes, this index
Arguments for and against death penalty, 7
Culpability weighing, 250
Delay, effect of, 804
Delay between crime and execution, 11
Justifications for punishment, 59
Juvenile executions, 281
Kantian ethics, 9
Mentally retarded defendants, 263
Proportionality of retribution, 10, 250, 256
Society's interest in, weighing, 53
Validity of, 84
Victim impact evidence at penalty hearings, 545, 586

RIGHT TO COUNSEL
See Assistance of Counsel, this index

ROBBERY PUNISHMENT
Armed robbery
Proportionality, 250
Proportionality
Armed robbery, 250

RULES
New Rules of Supreme Court Jurisprudence, this index
Supreme Court Jurisprudence, this index

SELECTION
See Eligibility and Selection Determinations, this index

SENTENCING HEARINGS
See Penalty Hearings, this index

SIXTH AMENDMENT
Generally, 328
Habeas corpus, assistance of counsel on the writ, 457
Jury vs court sentencing, 514, 518, 526

SLAVERY
Black Codes of slave states, 23
Historical background of death penalty practice in southern states, 22

SOCIOLOGY
Empirical Studies, this index

SOCIOLOGY—Cont'd
Expert Witnesses, this index

STANDARD OF PROOF
Penalty determinations, 92

STATE LAWS
Generally, 896 et seq.
Abolition proposals at state law level, 894
Aggravating and mitigating factors in weighing and non-weighing states, 136
Arbitrariness risk, limiting at legislative stage, 137
Assistance of counsel on habeas corpus applications, 466
Broad death-eligibility states, 163
California statutes, 896
Catchall statutory aggravators, 145, 149
Child rape, 295, 306
Commutation powers of governors, 615, 622
Comparative states homicide rate study, 12
Eligibility standards, 19
Excessiveness of statutory aggravators, 144
Federal habeas corpus authority
Generally, 672 et seq.
See also Habeas Corpus, this index
Federal Laws, this index
Federalism, this index
Florida statutes, 905
Furman decision
Invalidations of state regimes, 75
Referenda after, 82
Responsive legislation, 26, 177
Georgia statutes, 913
Habeas corpus proceedings, assistance of counsel, 466
Juvenile executions, 278
Mentally retarded defendants, 261, 274
Mitigating circumstances, statutory, 207
Model death penalty scheme, 894
Model Penal Code, this index
Narrowing of aggravating factors, statutory, 138, 144
Nullification instructions, elimination of, 218
Overbroad statutory aggravators
Generally, 145, 163
Narrowing constructions, 152
Pyramidal aggravating and mitigating factors schemes, 125, 135
Recidivism rate studies, 14
Referenda after Furman decision, 82
Reform proposals at state law level, 894
Special circumstances regimes, 176, 179, 317, 606, 896
Texas statutes, 916
Vague statutory aggravators, 145, 162
Victim impact evidence, 599
Weighing and non-weighing states, 136

STATISTICAL STUDIES
Empirical Studies, this index
Methodology, 182

TORTURE CONVENTION
US ratification, 875

†